PENGUIN REFERENCE

The New Penguin Dictionary of Modern Quotations

Robert Andrews is an experienced quotations sleuth. Among other works, he has edited the *Routledge Dictionary of Quotations* and the *Cassell Dictionary of Contemporary Quotations* as well as the monumental *Columbia Dictionary of Quotations*. He has also written travel guides on Britain and Southern Italy. He lives in Bristol.

From early *I-Spy* days Kate Hughes has indulged her researcher tendencies, first in Victorian Studies at Leicester University and later for travel guides and dictionaries of quotations.

The New Penguin Dictionary of **Modern Quotations**

Robert Andrews

With the assistance of Kate Hughes

PENGUIN BOOKS

PENGUIN BOOKS

Published by the Penguin Group
Penguin Books Ltd, 80 Strand, London WC2R ORL, England
Penguin Putnam Inc., 375 Hudson Street, New York, New York 10014, USA
Penguin Books Australia Ltd, 250 Camberwell Road, Camberwell, Victoria 3124, Australia
Penguin Books Canada Ltd, 10 Alcorn Avenue, Toronto, Ontario, Canada M4V 3B2
Penguin Books India (P) Ltd, 11 Community Centre, Panchsheel Park, New Delhi – 110 017, India
Penguin Books (NZ) Ltd, Cnr Rosedale and Airborne Roads, Albany, Auckland, New Zealand
Penguin Books (South Africa) (Pty) Ltd, 24 Sturdee Avenue, Rosebank 2196, South Africa

Penguin Books Ltd, Registered Offices: 80 Strand, London WC2R ORL, England

www.penguin.com

First published by Allen Lane The Penguin Press 2000
Published in Penguin Books 2001
This new edition published 2003
1

Copyright © Robert Andrews, 2001, 2003
All rights reserved

The moral right of the editor has been asserted

Set in Minion and ITC Officina
Designed by Richard Marston
Typeset by Rowland Phototypesetting Ltd, Bury St Edmunds, Suffolk
Printed in Great Britain by Clays Ltd, St Ives plc

To the gallant Uharts: Ju, Paul, Clelia,
Thomas, James and Beatrice

Contents

Along the tried-and-tested route of the 'who said what' quotation, with a spotlight on by the likes of George Orwell, Winston Churchill, John F. Kennedy, W. H. Auden, Dorothy Parker, Germaine Greer and Sigmund Freud, the book also includes numerous less famous extracts that encapsulate the various

Preface

'It's better to be quotable than honest' – Tom Stoppard

The quotations collected here offer a broad survey of the whole of the 'modern era', that rather shapeless span of recent history which for the purposes of this book we have defined as dating from 1914. As running commentaries go, however, it's an unruly, rambunctious overview, lacking any common vision or voice. Indeed, what characterizes the writings and sayings of the various artists, thinkers, politicians and media stars represented here is their sheer heterogeneity, for few other periods in history of a similar short length can have contributed such a cacophony of dissent and disputation. Not so much a commentary, then, as a long, rambling debate, involving innumerable voices and viewpoints, often funny, occasionally heated and violent, and each illustrating a different facet of these 'interesting' times. The keynote, if there is one, is of multiplicity, contrast, uncertainty. 'The trouble with our age', wrote the critic Louis Kronenberger, 'is that it is all signpost and no destination.' For Jonathan Sacks, 'Modernity is the transition from fate to choice', while for Tony Blair, 'The defining characteristic of the modern world is insecurity.' In an epoch of singularity, perversity and eccentricity, mavericks and rebels have become our models, and style is the new morality. Small surprise, then, that the quotations of our times have such a chaotic, contentious character. You don't need to delve deep into this collection to encounter remarks and observations which infuriate and repel, while others eloquently chime with one's own deepest beliefs. The book provides a tour of some of the most far-reaching notions mooted and refuted over the last ninety-odd years, evoking the high and low points of the era, its particular illusions and obsessions, its humour and shame.

Alongside the best-known remarks of the time, the 'classic' quotations written and spoken by the likes of George Orwell, Winston Churchill, John F. Kennedy, W. H. Auden, Dorothy Parker, Germaine Greer and Sigmund Freud, the book also includes numerous less famous extracts that encapsulate the various contributions to our world-view by the most significant personalities of the age, for example Iris Murdoch, Susan Sontag, Noam Chomsky, Sartre, Borges and Picasso. Entries are taken from a wide range of sources, including film, television, radio, popular music and websites – the various strands of the mass communications network that further distinguishes the period. Nowadays, you are as likely to hear quoted the lines 'R-E-S-P-E-C-T/Find out what it means to me' (sung by Aretha Franklin) as anything of a weightier nature by, say, T. S. Eliot or Virginia Woolf – although these writers, each with an enduring presence on school curricula, still chalk up some fifty quotes each, to Aretha Franklin's single entry. The book also includes those catch-phrases, advertising slogans, newspaper headlines and graffiti which have become established in common currency, however fleetingly. A dictionary of modern quotations must embrace ephemera, and, when necessary, must drop superannuated entries from future editions. In the second edition of this collection, many quotes have been jettisoned, and others have been added which themselves may not long endure. Such a work can only be a snapshot of a period, but one which, I hope, encompasses its idiosyncrasies and kaleidoscopic complexity.

Although the authors are arranged alphabetically, the quotations under each name are listed chronologically, according to their original utterance, composition, performance or publication, whichever is known to be earlier. Quotes have generally been ascribed to the person with whom they are most commonly associated, a system which produces occasional anomalies, usually in the fields of music and film, but which on the whole reflects our familiarity with the lines in question. For example, 'I did it my way', 'Hasta la vista, baby' and 'States like these . . . constitute an axis of evil' are respectively entered under Frank Sinatra, Arnold Schwarzenegger and George W. Bush, rather than the names of the songwriter, screenwriter and speechwriter who first penned the words – although the names of these (where known) are specified in the citation. In some cases, however, where the author is known for a body of work – for example Woody Allen or Irving Berlin – the words are credited to their originator. Brief biographies are appended under each name, except where material was not readily available, and any contextual information that may enhance the reader's understanding of a quotation is given in the citation, in the firm belief that quotations out of context can be meaningless, especially where the person quoted is not already well known. Dates of translations are given when these were made significantly later than the original composition, or when they are specific versions among many, and translators are named when they are well known. In letters, addressees are mentioned when they are members of the writer's family, or otherwise well known.

Most of the research for this second edition was undertaken by Kate Hughes, the engine without whom the project would have stalled on the first lap. Gratitude is also due to Richard Davoll, whose meticulous eye and memory guided us through many a pitfall, and, at Penguin, to Martin Toseland for his patience and willingness to incorporate all the many revisions. On the home front, acknowledgement is once again due to Fiona and Verity, for aural massage, and to Jo, Quin and Evvy for non-technical interventions and a few jokes.

Diane Abbott (b. 1953)

BRITISH POLITICIAN

She became the first black woman MP when she
was elected to the seat of Hackney North and Stoke
Newington for Labour in 1987.

1 The honest truth is that if this Government were to propose a massacre of the
first-born, it would still have no difficulty
in getting it through the Commons.

Quoted in the *Independent on Sunday* 12 July
1998

Mumia Abu-Jamal (b. 1954)

US JOURNALIST AND ENVIRONMENTALIST

America's most celebrated prisoner on Death
Row was convicted of the murder of a police
officer in Philadelphia in 1981. His case has been
championed by NORMAN MAILER, WHOOPI
GOLDBERG *and Paul Newman, among others.*

1 Prison is a second-by-second assault on
the soul, a day-to-day degradation of the
self, an oppressive steel and brick umbrella
that transforms seconds into hours and
hours into days.

Live from Death Row, pt 1, 'Nightraiders Meet
Rage' (1995)

Chinua Achebe (b. 1930)

NIGERIAN NOVELIST

Originally Albert Chinualumogo. His books deal
with the impact of European colonialism on
Africa, and with post-colonial African politics.
Among the most notable are his first, Things Fall
Apart *(1958), one of the first African novels to*
make an international impact, and Anthills of the
Savanna *(1987).*

1 For I do honestly believe that in the fat-
dripping, gummy, eat-and-let-eat régime
just ended – a régime which inspired the
common saying that a man could only be
sure of what he had put away safely in his
gut or, in language ever more suited to the
times; 'you chop, me self I chop, palaver
finish'; a régime in which you see a fellow
cursed in the morning for stealing a blind
man's stick and later in the evening saw
him again mounting the altar of the new
shrine in the presence of all the people to
whisper into the ear of the chief celebrant
– in such a régime, I say, you died a good
death if your life had inspired someone to
come forward and shoot your murderer in
the chest – without asking to be paid.

A Man of the People, ch. 13 (1966). In this closing sentence of the book, the narrator (Odili
Samalu) refers to the end of the repressive
régime of Chief Nanga.

Dean Acheson (1893–1971)

US POLITICIAN

Adviser to four presidents and Secretary of State to President TRUMAN *(1949–53), he was instrumental in implementing the Marshall Aid Plan to Europe and the Truman Doctrine (1947), and in the formation of NATO (1949).*

1 Great Britain has lost an Empire and has not yet found a role.

Speech at US Military Academy, West Point, 5 December 1962, publ. in *Vital Speeches* (1963)

2 The first requirement of a statesman is that he be dull. This is not always easy to achieve.

Quoted in the *Observer* 21 June 1970

3 A memorandum is written not to inform the reader but to protect the writer.

Quoted in the *Wall Street Journal* 8 September 1977

Gilbert Adair (b. 1944)

BRITISH AUTHOR AND CRITIC

He is principally known as a cultural critic, his essays collected in Myths & Memories *(1986) and* Hollywood's Vietnam *(1989). He has also published novels and translations.*

1 The earth is mankind's ultimate haven, our blessed *terra firma*. When it trembles and gives way beneath our feet, it's as though one of God's cheques has bounced.

Quoted in the *Sunday Correspondent* 24 December 1989

2 Postmodernism is, almost by definition, a transitional cusp of social, cultural, economic and ideological history when modernism's high-minded principles and preoccupations have ceased to function, but before they have been replaced with a totally new system of values. It represents a moment of suspension before the batteries are recharged for the new millennium, an acknowledgment that preceding the future is a strange and hybrid interregnum that might be called the last gasp of the past.

Sunday Times 21 April 1991

3 The arts in this country exist primarily to fuel the culture industry.

The Post-Modernist Always Rings Twice, title essay (1992)

Douglas Adams (1952–2001)

BRITISH AUTHOR

The Hitch Hiker's Guide to the Galaxy, *a satirical science-fiction series originally broadcast on radio in 1978, became a huge success, subsequently becoming a book and adapted for television, stage and a computer game.*

1 Don't panic.

The Hitch Hiker's Guide to the Galaxy, Preface and *passim* (1979). The words are inscribed in 'large friendly letters' on the cover of the (fictional) book, 'The Hitch Hiker's Guide to the Galaxy'. The same words were also a catchphrase of the excitable Corporal Jones (played by Clive Dunn) in the TV series *Dad's Army* (1968–77).

2 I think you ought to know I'm feeling very depressed.

Marvin the robot, ibid., ch. 11. The first words in the book spoken by this prototype for a new generation of robots with 'Genuine People Personalities'. Adams claims he based Marvin's character on Andrew Marshall, the comedy writer, though he also acknowledges the influence of Eeyore in A. A. MILNE's *Winnie-the-Pooh*.

3 Life . . . don't talk to me about Life.

Marvin, ibid.

4 I've been ordered to take you down to the bridge. Here I am, brain the size of a planet and they ask me to take you down to the bridge. Call that *job satisfaction*? 'Cos I don't.

Marvin, ibid. Marvin makes a similar complaint in *The Restaurant at the End of the Universe*, ch. 17 (1980)

5 The Answer to the Great Question . . . Of Life, the Universe and Everything . . . Is . . . Forty-two.

The computer Deep Thought, ibid., ch. 27

6 So long, and thanks for all the fish.

The dolphins' farewell message to humanity, in *So Long, and Thanks for All the Fish*, ch. 31 (fourth book in the *Hitch Hiker's Guide to the Galaxy* series, 1984)

Franklin Pierce Adams (1881–1960)

US JOURNALIST AND HUMORIST

A byword from the 1930s for wit and erudition, he set a precedent for the contemporary newspaper column with 'The Conning Tower', which appeared in the Herald Tribune *1913–37.*

1 Years ago we discovered the exact point, the dead center of middle age. It occurs when you are too young to take up golf and too old to rush up to the net.

Nods and Becks, 'Valentine' (1944)

2 *Too much Truth*
Is uncouth.

Ibid., 'From the New England Primer'

3 The trouble with this country is that there are too many politicians who believe, with a conviction based on experience, that you can fool all of the people all of the time.

Ibid., 'Baseball Note'. The allusion is to the famous saying credited to both Abraham Lincoln and Phineas Barnum, 'You may fool all the people some of the time; you can even fool some of the people all the time; but you can't fool all of the people all the time.'

Gerry Adams (b. 1948)
IRISH POLITICIAN

President of Sinn Féin, he was elected to the Northern Ireland Assembly in 1982 and became MP for Belfast West in 1983, though refusing to take his seat at Westminster. He was a principal negotiator in the IRA ceasefire (1994–6) and the Good Friday peace agreement (1999).

1 The IRA aren't the cause of violence in Ireland. They are a symptom of it. If this was a normal society, we wouldn't have the violence we are now having to endure.

Column as 'Brownie' in the *Belfast Republican News*, 1976, repr. in *Man of War, Man of Peace* (1997) by David Sharrock and Mark Devenport. Adams, then in prison in Long Kesh, maintained that the 'Brownie' articles were not written solely by him, but were the work of a number of prisoners.

2 Hunger strike is unlike any other form of struggle. An IRA volunteer does not go out to get killed; if he or she gets killed it is because he or she makes a mistake or some circumstance arises. But a hunger striker embarks on a process which, from day one, is designed to end in his or her death.

Selected Writings, 'Political Status' (1994)

3 He [David Trimble] is a man I can do business with; he is a man I have to do business with; and he is a man who I will do business with. This is more important than the personalities involved.

Quoted in the *Guardian* 11 September 1998. Referring to his meeting with the Ulster Unionist leader, the first time Unionist and Sinn Féin leaders had met since 1922.

Harold Adamson (1906–80)
US SONGWRITER

He provided Broadway and Hollywood musicals with a number of successful songs, working with celebrated jazz composers to produce such standards as 'Manhattan Serenade' (1948). He also wrote lyrics for films including Gentlemen Prefer Blondes (1953).

1 Comin' in on a wing and a pray'r.

'Comin' in on a Wing and a Pray'r' (song, 1943). The phrase is said to have originated from a pilot's radioed words while attempting a landing with a damaged plane.

Fleur Adcock (b. 1934)
NEW ZEALAND POET AND EDITOR

Based in England since 1963, she is known for the unsentimental, often ironic style of her verse, collected in The Eye of the Hurricane (1964), In Focus (1977) and Time Zones (1991), among other

volumes. *She has also edited anthologies and worked as a translator.*

1 I write in praise of the solitary act:
of not feeling a trespassing tongue
forced into one's mouth, one's breath
smothered, nipples crushed against the
ribcage, and that metallic tingling
in the chin set off by a certain odd nerve:
unpleasure.

'Against Coupling', publ. in *High Tide in the Garden* (1971)

Alfred Adler (1870–1937)
AUSTRIAN PSYCHIATRIST

A founder member of the Vienna Psychoanalytic Society, he developed his own school of Individual Psychology from 1911. The Neurotic Character (1912) was his first and most significant book.

1 The truth is often a terrible weapon of aggression. It is possible to lie, and even to murder, for the truth.

The Problems of Neurosis, ch. 2 (1929)

2 It is always easier to fight for one's principles than to live up to them.

Quoted in *Alfred Adler: Apostle of Freedom*, ch. 5 (1939) by Phyllis Bottome. The words were quoted by ADLAI STEVENSON in a speech in New York, 27 August 1952.

Polly Adler (1900–62)
US BROTHEL-KEEPER AND AUTHOR

A New York 'madam' in the 1920s and '30s, she retired in 1945. Her memoirs were filmed in 1964.

1 A House is Not a Home.

A House is Not a Home (memoirs, 1954)

2 What it comes down to is this: the grocer, the butcher, the baker, the merchant, the landlord, the druggist, the liquor dealer, the policeman, the doctor, the city father and the politician – these are the people who make money out of prostitution, these are the real reapers of the wages of sin.

Ibid., ch. 9

Theodor W. Adorno (1903–69)
GERMAN PHILOSOPHER, SOCIOLOGIST AND MUSICOLOGIST

A member of the Frankfurt School of philosophy, he fled the Nazis to the USA, returning to assume the post of Director of the Frankfurt Institute for Social Research (1958–69). His publications include The Dialectic of Enlightenment *(1947).*

1 Technology is making gestures precise and brutal, and with them men. It expels from movements all hesitation, deliberation, civility.

Minima Moralia, pt 1 (dated 1944), 'Do Not Knock' (1951, transl. G. F. N. Jephcott, 1978)

2 True thoughts are those alone which do not understand themselves.
Ibid., pt 3 (dated 1946–7), 'Monograms'

3 Culture is only true when implicitly critical, and the mind which forgets this revenges itself in the critics it breeds. Criticism is an indispensable element of culture.
Prisms, 'Cultural Criticism and Society' (1967)

Advertising slogans See also NEWS OF THE WORLD, SAATCHI AND SAATCHI

1 Access – your flexible friend.
Access credit card, 1980s

2 American Express? . . . That'll do nicely, sir.
American Express credit card, 1970s

3 And all because the lady loves Milk Tray.
Cadbury's Milk Tray chocolates, 1960s

4 Can you tell Stork from butter?
Stork margarine, 1950s

5 Cool as a mountain stream.
Consulate menthol cigarettes, 1960s

6 Even your closest friends won't tell you.
Listerine mouthwash (US), 1920s. The campaign, which focused on halitosis, ran from 1922 mainly in women's magazines. It hugely boosted sales of the product, and was an early demonstration of the power of advertising, also giving birth to the technique of playing on people's neuroses by inventing unheard-of complaints. It was subsequently widely copied, and the 'halitosis influence' became part of standard advertising jargon (discussed in *The Mirror Makers: A History of American Advertising*, 1984, by Stephen Fox).

7 Full of Eastern promise.
Fry's Turkish Delight, from 1950s

8 Go to work on an egg.
British Egg Marketing Board, from 1957. Claimed to have been written by FAY WELDON.

9 Guinness Is Good for You.
Guinness beer, credited to Oswald Greene in 1929 in *The Book of Guinness Advertising*, ch. 4 (1985) by Brian Sibley. Other slogans famously associated with Guinness include 'Guinness Gives You Strength' (also from 1929), which first appeared as 'Guinness Is So Strengthening' and was accompanied by an image of a workman carrying a girder on his fingertips, and 'My Goodness, My Guinness', which was devised by DOROTHY L. SAYERS, then an advertising copywriter.

10 Heineken refreshes the parts other beers cannot reach.
Heineken lager, from 1970s

11 I'm Mandy, fly me.
TWA, 1975. The words, spoken by an air hostess, were a target of feminists and the title of a hit song by 10cc in 1976.

12 I'm only here for the beer.
Double Diamond beer, from 1971, credited to Ros Levenstein

13 It could be you.
British National Lottery, from 1994

14 It's finger lickin' good.
Kentucky Fried Chicken, from 1950s

15 It's good to talk.
British Telecom, from 1994, later changed to 'It's good to listen'

16 Just when you thought it was safe to go back in the water.
Publicity for *Jaws 2* (film, 1978)

17 Let the train take the strain.
British Rail, from 1970s

18 Let your fingers do the walking.
Yellow Pages telephone book, from 1960s in USA and Britain

19 A Mars a day helps you work, rest and play.
Mars bar, from 1960s

20 *A million housewives every day Pick up a tin of beans and say Beanz Meanz Heinz!*
Heinz Baked Beans, from 1967, credited to Maurice Drake

21 The mint with the hole.
Polo mints, from 1940s, also used in the US for Life-Savers, 1920s

22 Nice one, Cyril.
Wonderloaf bread, 1972. The phrase was adopted by supporters of Tottenham Hotspur football club referring to Cyril Knowles, and was the title of a song recorded by the 'Cockerel Chorus' in 1973.

23 Put a tiger in your tank.
Esso petrol, 1960s

24 Sssch . . . you know who.
Schweppes drinks, 1960s

25 Snap! Crackle! Pop!
Kellogg's Rice Krispies, from 1920s

26 Tell Sid.
British Gas, 1986, advertising shares at privatization

27 Things go better with Coke.
Coca Cola, from 1960s

28 Top people take *The Times*.
The Times, from 1959

29 *Vorsprung durch Technik.* (Progress through technology.)
Audi cars, from 1980s

30 *We are the Ovaltineys, Happy girls and boys.*
'We are the Ovaltineys' (song), promoting the drink Ovaltine from 1930s

31 Wouldn't it be nice if all cities were like
Milton Keynes?
For the town of Milton Keynes, 1990s

32 You're never alone with a Strand.
Strand cigarettes, 1960. The music was later
released as a record called 'The Lonely Man
Theme'.

Æ (1867–1935)
IRISH POET AND ESSAYIST
*Pseudonym of George William Russell. He was
prominent in the Irish literary revival and edited
the Irish Homestead (1905–23) and the Irish
Statesman (1923–30). His poems and plays,
among them The Divine Vision (1902), were
inspired by mysticism and magic.*

1 *In ancient shadows and twilights*
Where childhood had strayed,
The world's great sorrows were born
And its heroes were made.
In the lost boyhood of Judas
Christ was betrayed.
'Germinal' (1931), repr. in *Selected Poems by Æ*
(1935)

James Agate (1877–1947)
BRITISH DRAMA CRITIC
*An exacting drama critic of the Sunday Times
from 1923 until his death, he was also an assiduous
diary-writer. His journals were published in the
nine-part Ego (1935–49).*

1 The Englishman can get along with sex
quite perfectly so long as he can pretend
that it isn't sex but something else.
Journal entry, 14 October 1932, publ. in *Ego*
(1935)

2 Shaw's plays are the price we pay for
Shaw's prefaces.
Journal entry, 10 March 1933, publ. ibid.

3 *Don't pity me now,*
Don't pity me never;
I'm going to do nothing
For ever and ever.
A 'charwoman's epitaph', in journal entry,
14 March 1933, publ. ibid. The subject of Agate's
verse was a 'self-deceiver', he claimed. 'At least
I will lay odds that anybody meeting her in
Heaven will find her scrubbing marble and dust-
ing porphyry with a new-born gleam in her old
eye.'

4 I was asked to-night why I refuse to have
truck with intellectuals after business
hours. But of course I won't. 1. I am not an
intellectual. Two minutes' talk with Aldous
Huxley, William Glock, or any of the *New
Statesman* crowd would expose me utterly.
2. I am too tired after my day's work to
man the intellectual palisade. 3. When my
work is finished I want to eat, drink,
smoke, and relax. 4. I don't know very

much, but what I do know I know better
than anybody, and I don't want to argue
about it. I know what I think about an
actor or an actress, and am not interested
in what anybody else thinks. My mind is
not a bed to be made and re-made.
Journal entry, 9 June 1943, publ. in *Ego 6* (1946)

Spiro T. Agnew (1918–96)
US POLITICIAN, VICE-PRESIDENT
*Spiro Theodore Agnew. Elected Republican Gov-
ernor of Maryland as a liberal and anti-racist in
1966, he later adopted a more conservative position
and was vice-president under RICHARD NIXON
1969–73. He resigned after charges of tax evasion
were brought against him.*

1 I didn't say I wouldn't go into ghetto
areas. I've been in many of them and to
some extent I would have to say this: If
you've seen one city slum you've seen
them all.
Speech in Detroit, 18 October 1968, quoted in
the *Detroit Free Press* 19 October 1968

2 A spirit of national masochism prevails,
encouraged by an effete corps of impudent
snobs who characterize themselves as intellectuals.
Speech in New Orleans, 19 October 1969, publ.
in *Collected Speeches of Spiro Agnew* (1971)

3 Ultraliberalism today translates into a
whimpering isolationism in foreign policy,
a mulish obstructionism in domestic
policy, and a pusillanimous pussyfooting
on the critical issue of law and order.
Speech at Springfield, Illinois, 10 September
1970, publ. ibid.

Ama Ata Aidoo (b. 1942)
GHANAIAN SCHOLAR AND AUTHOR
*Her work describes the dilemmas in reconciling
Western influence with traditional African culture,
as in the semi-autobiographical Our Sister Killjoy
(1966). She has written plays, including The
Dilemma of a Ghost (1965), as well as novels,
short stories and poems.*

1 *From all around the Third World,*
You hear the same story;
Rulers
Asleep to all things at
All times –
Conscious only of
Riches, which they gather in a
Coma –
Intravenously.
'The Plum', publ. in *Our Sister Killjoy: Reflec-
tions from a Blackeyed Squint* (1966)

2 It's a sad moment, really, when parents
first become a bit frightened of their
children.
'The Message', publ. in *Fragment from a Lost*

Diary and Other Stories (ed. Naomi Katz and Nancy Milton, 1973)

Jonathan Aitken (b. 1942)

BRITISH BUSINESSMAN AND POLITICIAN

Formerly a journalist, he was elected a Conservative MP in 1974 and rose to be Chief Secretary to the Treasury (1994–5). Allegations about his business dealings led to a court case in 1998 and a conviction for perjury and perverting the course of justice, for which he served a prison sentence.

1 If it falls to me to start a fight to cut out the cancer of bent and twisted journalism in our country with the simple sword of truth and and the trusty shield of British fair play, so be it, I am ready for the fight.
   Remark 10 April 1995, quoted in the *Guardian* 11 April 1995. Referring to libel writs issued against the *Guardian* and the *World in Action* television programme over allegations of fraudulent business dealings with the Saudi royal family.

2 As far as the physical miseries go, I am sure I will cope. I lived at Eton in the 1950s and I know all about life in uncomfortable quarters.
   Quoted in the *Daily Express* 19 January 1999. On his probable imprisonment.

3 It's a fairly unique position: to have been in charge of prison funding and then to have been an inmate. I wish I'd been more generous.
   Quoted in *The Times* 3 June 2000

Anna Akhmatova (1889–1966)

RUSSIAN POET

Originally Anna Andreyevna Gorenko. A member of the Acmeist group, she was suppressed for the predominantly Christian tone of Anno Domini (1922), but rehabilitated in 1956. Later works include Requiem *(1940) and* Poem without a Hero *(1940–62).*

1 *It was a time when only the dead smiled, happy in their peace.*
   Requiem, Introduction (written 1935–40, transl. Richard McKane, 1985). Akhmatova's long poem about the Stalinist purges – during which her only son was arrested – was not published until 1963 in West Germany, and not in its entirety in the Soviet Union until 1987.

2 *Stars of Death stood over us, and innocent Russia squirmed under the bloody boots, under the wheels of black Marias.*
   Ibid. Final words of introduction.

3 The triumphs of a mysterious non-meeting are desolate ones; unspoken phrases, silent words.
   Two Poems, no. 2 (1956, transl. Dimitri Obolensky, 1965)

Zoë Akins (1886–1958)

US PLAYWRIGHT

Although she also wrote screenplays, she is best known for her work for the theatre, for example the comedies Daddy's Gone A-Hunting *(1921) and* The Greeks Had a Word for It *(1930), and a dramatization of* The Old Maid *by Edith Wharton (1935).*

1 The Greeks Had a Word for It.
   Title of play (1930). The word in question is said to have been *hetaera* ('strumpet'). In a passage deleted from the play's final script, one of the characters states, 'Even the Anglo-Saxons have a word for her sort, and it's usually spelt with a dash.' Neither do the words of the play's title appear in the final version.

Alain (1868–1951)

FRENCH PHILOSOPHER

Émile-Auguste Chartier. Taking his pen-name from a medieval French poet, he wrote over 5,000 essays, or Propos, *written in a lucid, terse style with a strong anti-idealist theme. Other works include* History of My Thoughts *(1936).*

1 It is the human condition to question one god after another, one appearance after another, or better, one apparition after another, always pursuing the truth of the imagination, which is not the same as the truth of appearance.
   The Gods, Introduction (1934, transl. 1988)

2 Nothing is more dangerous than an idea, when you have only one idea.
   Propos sur la religion, no. 74 (1938)

Damon Albarn (b. 1967)

BRITISH ROCK MUSICIAN

Singer and co-writer with the band Blur, he has a laddish, photogenic appeal which smoothed the band's transition from Indie obscurity to spearheading the Britpop scene.

1 Whenever I don't know what to write about, I just close my eyes and think of Essex.
   Interview in *Blah Blah Blah* April 1996

Edward Albee (b. 1928)

US PLAYWRIGHT

Though such early plays as The Zoo Story *(1959) labelled him as an exponent of the Theatre of the Absurd, he is chiefly known for the naturalistic* Who's Afraid of Virginia Woolf? *(1962, filmed 1966), a harsh portrayal of married life. Later works such as* Seascape *(1975) were more abstract.*

1 What I wanted to get at is the value difference between pornographic playing-cards when you're a kid, and pornographic playing-cards when you're older. It's that when you're a kid you use the cards as a substitute for a real experience, and when

you're older you use real experience as a substitute for the fantasy.

Jerry, in *The Zoo Story* (1959)

2 Who's Afraid of Virginia Woolf?

Title of play (1962). The words are sung by Martha to the tune of 'Who's Afraid of the Big Bad Wolf?' (see FRANK E. CHURCHILL 1).

3 I have a fine sense of the ridiculous, but no sense of humor.

Martha, in *Who's Afraid of Virginia Woolf?*, act 1 (1962)

4 Martha, won't you show her where we keep the . . . euphemism?

George, ibid., after a guest, Honey, states: 'I want to put some powder on my nose.'

Richard Aldington (1892–1962)

BRITISH AUTHOR

A leading Imagist poet, translator, critic and editor, he established his name with Death of a Hero (1929), a novel which drew on his experiences in the First World War. He also produced controversial biographies of D. H. LAWRENCE *(1950) and* T. E. LAWRENCE *(1955).*

1 Patriotism is a lively sense of collective responsibility. Nationalism is a silly cock crowing on its own dunghill and calling for larger spurs and brighter beaks. I fear that nationalism is one of England's many spurious gifts to the world.

Purfleet, in *The Colonel's Daughter*, pt 1, ch. 6 (1931)

2 Pure scholarship, like pure science and art, is entirely useless. That is why it is admirable, a demonstration that civilised man is neither an animal nor a savage nor a peasant, for whom nothing exists but what is immediately useful.

Life for Life's Sake, ch. 5 (1941)

3 Certainly, truth prevails in the long run, but only when it is too late to have any real influence on affairs.

Ibid., ch. 10

Brian Aldiss (b. 1925)

BRITISH SCIENCE FICTION WRITER

He is a prolific writer of classic as well as experimental science fiction, notably The Helliconia Trilogy *(1982–5).* Billion-Year Spree *(1973, rev. 1986 as* Trillion-Year Spree*) is a history of the genre.*

1 Science fiction is no more written for scientists than ghost stories are written for ghosts.

Penguin Science Fiction, Introduction (1962)

2 *The bombs were only
In his head
On his memorial tree
A joker wrote*

*KEEP VIOLENCE IN THE MIND
WHERE IT BELONGS*

Barefoot in the Head, 'Charteris' (1969). Closing lines of book, in which Colin Charteris is the main character.

Nelson Algren (1909–81)

US NOVELIST

He was the 'poet of the Chicago slums' for such uncompromising works as The Man with the Golden Arm *(1949) and* A Walk on the Wild Side *(1956), both of which were filmed. His affair with* SIMONE DE BEAUVOIR *inspired her novel* The Mandarins *(1956).*

1 A Walk on the Wild Side.

Title of novel (1956, filmed 1962). 'Take a Walk on the Wild Side' was the title of one of the biggest-selling records of LOU REED in 1973.

2 Never play cards with a man called Doc. Never eat at a place called Mom's. Never sleep with a woman whose troubles are worse than your own. Never let nobody talk you into shaking another man's jolt. And never you cop another man's plea. I've tried 'em all and I know. They don't work.

Cross-Country Kline advising Dove Linkhorn, in *A Walk on the Wild Side*, pt 3 (1956)

3 The avocation of assessing the failures of better men can be turned into a comfortable livelihood, providing you back it up with a Ph.D.

Interview in *Writers at Work* (first series, ed. Malcolm Cowley, 1958)

4 I went out there [Hollywood] for a thousand a week, and I worked Monday, and I got fired Wednesday. The guy that hired me was out of town Tuesday.

Ibid.

5 The hard necessity of bringing the judge on the bench down into the dock has been the peculiar responsibility of the writer in all ages of man.

Preface added to his prose-poem *Chicago: City on the Make* (1961, original work publ. 1951)

Muhammad Ali (b. 1942)

US BOXER

Originally Cassius Clay, he changed his name in 1964 when he joined the Nation of Islam. He won the World Heavyweight title in 1964, 1974 and 1978 (the only boxer to be world champion three times), but was stripped of his title in 1967 for refusing to be drafted to the Vietnam War.

1 I am the greatest.

Slogan used from 1961, quoted in *The Greatest*, ch. 4 (autobiography, 1975). He describes the origin of his famous brag in Las Vegas in June 1961: 'Before the fight, for the first time I'd talk openly about beating my opponent . . . I kept calling out "I'm the Greatest! I can't be beat!"'

I'd seen good fighters carry on bloody brawls with hardly anybody caring which one won or lost. At least now they were interested in my fight, even if they wanted me to lose.'

2 At home I am a nice guy: but I don't want the world to know. Humble people, I've found, don't get very far.
   Sunday Express 13 January 1963

3 Float like a butterfly, sting like a bee.
   Quoted in *The Story of Cassius Clay*, ch. 8 (1964) by George Edward Sullivan. Ali's catchphrase is said to have originated with his aide Drew 'Bundini' Brown.

4 It's just a job. Grass grows, birds fly, waves pound the sand. I beat people up.
   The New York Times 6 April 1977

Tariq Ali (b. 1943)
PAKISTANI-BORN BRITISH ACTIVIST AND AUTHOR
A left-wing journalist, he became a leading member of Fourth International. He published The Coming British Revolution *in 1972 and collaborated on theatre scripts in the 1980s and '90s.*

1 The logic of war dictated that the Americans *should* win, but this logic had been superseded by one superior and infinitely more powerful: the logic of revolution. It remains a logic which can never be properly understood: its richness and diversity always excludes the minds of its opponents.
   1968 and After: Inside the Revolution, ch. 1 (1978). Referring to the Vietnam War.

2 The idea that a revolution in the West could be based on a small minority, however active and militant, is totally absurd. It is a view of revolution advanced only by those who fear the masses. Or by those products of 1968 who, despairing of the mass parties and their domination of working-class politics, have abandoned politics and picked up sub machine-guns and bombs.
   Ibid., ch. 7

Saul Alinsky (1909–72)
US RADICAL ACTIVIST
Believing that the solution for social ills lay in organization, not charity, he devoted much of his life to setting up community groups, the prototype of which was the Back of the Yards Council (1938) in his home town of Chicago.

1 History is a relay of revolutions.
   Rules for Radicals, 'Of Means and Ends' (1971)

2 Life is a corrupting process from the time a child learns to play his mother off against his father in the politics of when to go to bed; he who fears corruption fears life.
   Ibid.

Fred Allen (1894–1957)
US RADIO COMIC
Originally John Florence Sullivan. Influencing a generation of radio and television performers with his dry wit and laconic style, he is most remembered for The Fred Allen Show *(1939–49), for which he wrote almost all of the episodes.*

1 California is a fine place to live – if you happen to be an orange.
   American Magazine December 1945

2 Hollywood is a place where people from Iowa mistake each other for stars.
   Quoted in *No People Like Show People*, ch. 8 (1951) by Maurice Zolotow

3 The American arrives in Paris with a few French phrases he has culled from a conversational guide or picked up from a friend who owns a beret.
   Quoted in *Paris After Dark*, Introduction (1954) by Art Buchwald

4 An advertising agency is 85 per cent confusion and 15 per cent commission.
   Treadmill to Oblivion, pt 2 (1954)

5 We are living in the machine age. For the first time in history the comedian has been compelled to supply himself with jokes and comedy material to compete with the machine. Whether he knows it or not, the comedian is on a treadmill to oblivion.
   Ibid., pt 4

6 I have just returned from Boston, it is the only sane thing to do if you find yourself up there.
   Quoted in *The Groucho Letters*, 'Touching on Television' (1967) by GROUCHO MARX

7 Committee – a group of men who individually can do nothing but as a group decide that nothing can be done.
   Attributed

Hervey Allen (1889–1949)
US AUTHOR
He won critical acclaim with his first novel, Anthony Adverse *(1933), set in the Napoleonic era. He also wrote poetry and biography.*

1 The only time you really live fully is from thirty to sixty . . . The young are slaves to dreams; the old servants of regrets. Only the middle-aged have all their five senses in the keeping of their wits.
   Anthony Adverse, ch. 31 (1933, filmed 1936)

Woody Allen (b. 1935)
US FILM-MAKER AND ACTOR
Originally Allen Stewart Konigsberg. Stand-up comic and TV scriptwriter turned film-maker, he stars in most of his own films, which developed from wacky farces such as Sleeper *(1973) to convoluted tales of sexual neurosis set in New York,*

including Annie Hall *(1977) and* Hannah and Her Sisters *(1986). See also* DIANE KEATON 1.

1 **Some guy hit my fender the other day, and I said unto him, 'Be fruitful, and multiply.' But not in those words.**

Comedy routine at Chicago night-club, March 1964, recorded on *Woody Allen*, 'Private Life' (album, 1964). Woody Allen's first live recorded monologue describes an acting class rehearsing a play where Allen takes the part of God, and, as he recounts, 'it was method acting, so two weeks beforehand I started to live the part offstage'.

2 **I had a rough marriage. . . . It was partially my fault that we got a divorce. I had a lousy attitude toward her. For the first year of our marriage, I tended to place my wife underneath a pedestal all the time. We used to argue and fight and finally we decided we should either take a vacation or get a divorce. We discussed it very maturely and we decided on the divorce because we felt we had a limited amount of money to spend. A vacation in Bermuda is over in two weeks but a divorce is something that you always have.**

Ibid., 'My Marriage'. Allen's accounts of the break-up of his first marriage to Harlene Rosen in 1962 and the repeated jokes at her expense in his comedy acts eventually led her to sue him for a million dollars in 1967; they settled out of court and did not meet again, according to *The Woody Allen Companion*, ch. 4 (1993) by Stephen Spignesi.

3 **Is sex dirty? Only if it's done right.**

'Chapter' title, in *Everything You Always Wanted to Know About Sex (But Were Afraid to Ask)* (film, 1972, written and directed by Woody Allen). See also DAVID REUBEN 1.

4 **I'm not the heroic type. I was beaten up by Quakers.**

Miles Monroe (Woody Allen), in *Sleeper* (film, 1973, screenplay by Woody Allen and Marshall Brickman, directed by Woody Allen)

5 **[My brain . . .] it's my second favorite organ.**

Ibid.

6 **I don't want to achieve immortality through my work . . . I want to achieve it through not dying.**

Quoted in *Woody Allen and his Comedy*, ch. 12 (1975) by Eric Lax

7 **The important thing, I think, is not to be bitter. If it turns out that there is a God, I don't think that he's evil. But the worst thing you can say about him is that he's basically an underachiever. After all, you know, there are worse things in life than death.**

Boris Grushenko (Woody Allen), in *Love and Death* (film, 1975, written and directed by Woody Allen)

8 **Some men are heterosexual, and some men are homosexual, and some men don't think about sex at all. They become lawyers.**

Ibid.

9 **To me nature is . . . spiders and bugs, and big fish eating little fish, and plants eating plants, and animals eating . . . It's like an enormous restaurant, that's the way I see it.**

Ibid.

10 **I want to tell you a terrific story about oral contraception. I asked this girl to sleep with me and she said 'no'.**

Quoted in *Woody Allen: Clown Prince of American Humor*, ch. 2 (1975) by B. Adler and J. Feinman

11 **It [bisexuality] immediately doubles your chances for a date on Saturday night.**

The New York Times 1 December 1975

12 **It's not that I'm afraid to die, I just don't want to be there when it happens.**

Kleinman, in 'Death (A Play)', publ. in *Without Feathers* (1976)

13 **The chief problem about death, incidentally, is the fear that there may be no after-life – a depressing thought, particularly for those who have bothered to shave. Also, there is the fear that there is an afterlife but no one will know where it's being held.**

'The Early Essays', publ. ibid. In the film *Love and Death*, there is the line, 'I don't believe in an afterlife although I'm bringing a change of underwear.'

14 **Money is better than poverty, if only for financial reasons.**

Ibid.

15 **If only God would give me some clear sign! Like making a large deposit in my name at a Swiss bank.**

'Selections from the Allen Notebooks', publ. ibid.

16 **Hey, don't knock masturbation! It's sex with someone I love.**

Alvy Singer (Woody Allen), in *Annie Hall* (film, 1977, screenplay by Woody Allen and Marshall Brickman, directed by Woody Allen)

17 **I don't wanna live in a city where the only cultural advantage is that you can make a right turn on a red light.**

Ibid. Comparing Los Angeles unfavourably to Manhattan.

18 **I was depressed . . . I was suicidal; as a matter of fact, I would have killed myself but I was in analysis with a strict Freudian and if you kill yourself they make you pay for the sessions you miss.**

Ibid. The gag can also be heard on *The Nightclub Years*, 'Second Marriage' (1968), a live recording of a stand-up routine in San Francisco, August 1968.

19 I was thrown out of NYU my freshman year . . . for cheating on my metaphysics final. You know, I looked within the soul of the boy sitting next to me.
Ibid. Alvy is performing in front of a college audience.

20 In Beverly Hills . . . they don't throw their garbage away. They make it into television shows.
Ibid.

21 Life is divided up into the horrible and the miserable.
Ibid.

22 A relationship, I think, is like a shark, you know? It has to constantly move forward or it dies. And I think what we got on our hands is a dead shark.
Ibid. On the end of his affair with Annie Hall (played by Diane Keaton).

23 That [sex] was the most fun I've ever had without laughing.
Ibid.

24 I finally had an orgasm and my doctor told me it was the wrong kind.
Polly (Tisa Farrow), in *Manhattan* (film, 1979, screenplay by Woody Allen and Marshall Brickman, directed by Woody Allen)

25 Why is life worth living? That's a very good question. Ummm . . . Well there are certain things, I guess, that make it worthwhile. Uh, like what? Okay. Um, for me . . . oh, I would say . . . what, Groucho Marx, to name one thing, and . . . Willie Mays, and . . . the second movement of the Jupiter Symphony, and . . . Louis Armstrong's recording of 'Potatohead Blues' . . . Swedish movies, naturally . . . *Sentimental Education* by Flaubert . . . and Marlon Brando, Frank Sinatra . . . those incredible apples and pears by Cézanne.
Isaac Davis (Woody Allen), ibid.

26 More than any other time in history, mankind faces a crossroads. One path leads to despair and utter hopelessness. The other, to total extinction. Let us pray we have the wisdom to choose correctly.
Side Effects, 'My Speech to the Graduates' (1980)

27 You can't control life. It doesn't wind up perfectly. Only . . . only art you can control. Art and masturbation. Two areas in which I am an absolute expert.
Sandy Bates (Woody Allen), in *Stardust Memories* (film, 1980, written and directed by Woody Allen)

28 Child molestation is a touchy subject. . . . Read the papers! Half the country's doing it!
Mickey Sachs (Woody Allen), in *Hannah and*

Her Sisters (film, 1986, written and directed by Woody Allen). Allen caused controversy in 1993 when a relationship with Soon-Yi Previn, the adopted daughter of Mia Farrow, led to accusations of child abuse and a court case over custody of their children. He married Soon-Yi in 1997.

29 Life doesn't imitate art, it imitates bad television.
Rain (Juliette Lewis), in *Husbands and Wives* (film, 1992, written and directed by Woody Allen)

Isabel Allende (b. 1942)
CHILEAN NOVELIST
A writer associated with the 'magic realist' school, she wrote her first and best-selling novel, The House of the Spirits *(1982, filmed 1993), in exile from Chile following the overthrow of her uncle* SALVADOR ALLENDE. *Other books include* Of Love and Shadows *(1984) and* Eva Luna *(1987).*

1 Misfortune had spiritualized her.
The House of the Spirits, ch. 5 (1982). Referring to Clara Trueba.

2 Charity, like Socialism, is an invention of the weak to exploit the strong and bring them to their knees.
Esteban Trueba, ibid., ch. 10

3 Photographs deceive time, freezing it on a piece of cardboard where the soul is silent.
Irene Beltran, in *Of Love and Shadows*, pt 1 (1987)

Salvador Allende (1908–73)
CHILEAN STATESMAN AND PRESIDENT
A founder of the Chilean Socialist Party, he became President in 1970. His nationalization of US-owned copper mines was the prelude to CIA involvement in the 1973 coup in which he died.

1 Our Vietnam is neither in Moscow, nor in Peking, Havana or Belgrade. It is in Chile.
Quoted in the *Observer* 1 November 1970

Svetlana Alliluyeva (b. 1925)
RUSSIAN AUTHOR
Stalin's only daughter, she defected to the USA in 1967. Her writings include Twenty Letters to a Friend *(1967),* Only One Year *(1969) and* The Faraway Music *(1984), which records her disenchantment with the West.*

1 Moscow, breathing fire like a human volcano with its smouldering lava of passion, ambition and politics, its hurly-burly of meetings and entertainment. . . . Moscow seethes and bubbles and gasps for air. It's always thirsting for something new, the newest events, the latest sensation. Every-

one wants to be the first to know. It's the rhythm of life today.

Twenty Letters to a Friend, Introduction (written 1963, publ. 1967)

2 He [Stalin] is gone, but his shadow still stands over all of us. It still dictates to us and we, very often, obey.

Ibid., ch. 2

3 As a result of half a century of Soviet rule people have been weaned from a belief in human kindness.

Only One Year, 'The Journey's End' (1969)

Lisa Alther (b. 1944)

US NOVELIST

Her ribald feminist tales include Kinflicks *(1976),* Original Sins *(1981) and* Bedrock *(1990).*

1 I happen to feel that the degree of a person's intelligence is directly reflected by the number of conflicting attitudes she can bring to bear on the same topic.

Ginny Babcock, in *Kinflicks,* ch. 7 (1976)

Robert Altman (b. 1925)

US FILM-MAKER

He made his name with the antiwar comedy M*A*S*H *(1970) and went on to direct* McCabe and Mrs Miller *(1971) and* Nashville *(1976) among other films. Neglected in the 1980s, he re-established his reputation with* The Player *(1992).*

1 What's a cult? It just means not enough people to make a minority.

Interview in the *Guardian* 11 April 1981

A. Alvarez (b. 1929)

BRITISH CRITIC, POET AND NOVELIST

Alfred Alvarez. He is chiefly noted for his criticism, including The Shaping Spirit *(1958) and* The School of Donne *(1961). Later, he focused on poetry and fiction, for example* Day of Atonement *(1991).*

1 Despair, in short, seeks its own environment as surely as water finds its own level.

The Savage God, pt 3, 'Theories' (1971)

2 There is something . . . not quite right about night life, something shadowy in every sense. However efficiently artificial light annihilates the difference between night and day, it never wholly eliminates the primitive suspicion that night people are up to no good.

Night, Preface (1995)

Leo Amery (1873–1955)

BRITISH POLITICIAN

A Conservative MP from 1911, he was a fierce critic of the Munich Agreement and was instrumental in

bringing down the government of NEVILLE CHAM- BERLAIN *in 1940. He served as Secretary of State for India and Burma 1940–45.*

1 Speak for England.

Said in House of Commons, 2 September 1939, quoted in *My Political Life,* vol. 3 (1955). The exhortation was addressed to MP Arthur Green- wood, Deputy Leader of the Labour Party, who was about to speak on the situation in Europe, a day after the Nazi invasion of Poland and on the eve of the declaration of war on Germany by Britain and France. The MP Robert Boothby is also credited with the words.

2 I will quote certain other words. I do it with great reluctance, because I am speak- ing of those who are old friends and associ- ates of mine, but they are words which, I think, are applicable to the present situa- tion. This is what Cromwell said to the Long Parliament when he thought it was no longer fit to conduct the affairs of the nation: 'You have sat too long here for any good you have been doing. Depart, I say, and let us have done with you. In the name of God, go.'

Speech to House of Commons, in *Hansard* 7 May 1940. Amery was addressing NEVILLE CHAMBERLAIN's government, blamed for the failed policy of appeasement to Germany and now faced with the German invasion of Norway. Chamberlain resigned 10 May, to be replaced by WINSTON CHURCHILL. Cromwell's words were uttered 20 April 1653, shortly before becoming Lord Protector of England.

(Sir) Kingsley Amis (1922–95)

BRITISH NOVELIST AND POET

He won great success with his first novel Lucky Jim *(1954, filmed 1957), a satire on provincial academic life. Later novels include* The Old Devils *(1986), and he also published short stories and poetry. He once commented: 'If you can't annoy somebody, there's little point in writing.' He was the father of* MARTIN AMIS.

1 *We men have got love well weighed up; our stuff*
   Can get by without it.
   Women don't seem to think that's good enough;
   They will write about it.

'A Bookshop Idyll', publ. in *A Case of Samples* (1956)

2 Women are really much nicer than men: No wonder we like them.

Ibid.

3 More will mean worse.

Encounter July 1960. On the expansion of higher education in the UK, attacking the notion that 'there are thousands of young people about who are capable of benefiting from university train- ing, but have somehow failed to find their way there'.

4 Outside every fat man there was an even
    fatter man trying to close in.
    Roger Micheldene, in *One Fat Englishman*, ch. 3
    (1963). Micheldene, the book's protagonist, is 'a
    shortish fat Englishman of forty', here musing
    over a particularly heavy lunch. Earlier versions
    of the remark exist: see CYRIL CONNOLLY 18
    and GEORGE ORWELL 7.

5 He was of the faith chiefly in the sense that
    the church he currently did not attend was
    Catholic.
    Ibid., ch. 8. Referring to Roger Micheldene.

6 Growing older, I have lost the need to be
    political, which means, in this country, the
    need to be left. I am driven into grudging
    toleration of the Conservative Party
    because it is the party of non-politics, of
    resistance to politics.
    Sunday Telegraph 2 July 1967

7 *Death has got something to be said for it:*
    There's no need to get out of bed for it;
    Wherever you may be,
    They bring it to you, free.
    'Delivery Guaranteed' (1979), publ. in *Collected
    Poems (1944–79)*. In his novel *Money* (1984),
    Kingsley's son MARTIN AMIS wrote: 'Addictions
    do come in handy sometimes: at least you have
    to get out of bed for them.'

8 If there's one word that sums up every-
    thing that's gone wrong since the War, it's
    Workshop.
    Jake, in *Jake's Thing*, ch. 14 (1979). '. . . After
    Youth, that is,' Jake added.

9 Alun's life was coming to consist more and
    more exclusively of being told at dictation
    speed what he knew.
    The Old Devils, ch. 7, sect. 1 (1986). Of author
    and 'professional Welshman' Alun Weaver.

10 The fact that it is not a sensual or sexy
    beauty does not make it a less sexual
    beauty, and that sexuality is still, I believe,
    an underrated factor in her appeal (or
    repellence). Envy of it among women, con-
    sciousness of its unavailability among
    men, retains power even when advancing
    age should have disposed of it.
    Of MARGARET THATCHER in *Memoirs*, 'Mar-
    garet Thatcher' (1991). Amis referred to her as
    his 'dream-girl . . . who, more than any other,
    tends to recur in my dreams'.

11 It is not extraordinary that the extraterres-
    trial origin of women was a recurrent
    theme of science fiction, though I have
    never seen their imperfect grasp of their
    native language put forward as one more
    piece of evidence.
    *The King's English: A Guide to Modern English
    Usage*, 'Womanese' (1997)

Martin Amis (b. 1949)
BRITISH AUTHOR
*He writes novels in which, in his words, 'everyone
has a bad time'. His scabrous wit and American literary influences are evident in such works as* The
Rachel Papers *(1973, filmed 1989)*, Money *(1984)
and* The Information *(1995)*.

1 Only one writer has ever written convinc-
    ingly about happiness and that's Tolstoy.
    Nobody else seems to make it swing on the
    page.
    Interview in *Time Out* 27 March 1981

2 Making lots of money – it's not that hard,
    you know. It's overestimated. Making lots
    of money is a breeze. You watch.
    Money (1984)

3 And being rich is about acting too, isn't it?
    A style, a pose, an interpretation that you
    force upon the world? Whether or not
    you've made the stuff yourself, you have to
    set about pretending that you merit it, that
    money chose right in choosing you, and
    that you'll do right by money in your turn.
    Moneymad or just moneysmug, you have
    to pretend it's the natural thing.
    Ibid.

4 Weapons are like money; no one knows
    the meaning of *enough*.
    Einstein's Monsters, Introduction (1987)

5 For myself and my loved ones, I want the
    heat, which comes at the speed of light. I
    don't want to have to hang about for the
    blast, which idles along at the speed of sound.
    Ibid.

6 The literary interview won't tell you what a
    writer is *like*. Far more compellingly, to
    some, it will tell you what a writer is *like to
    interview*.
    Observer 30 August 1987, repr. in *Visiting Mrs
    Nabokov*, 'John Updike' (1993)

7 And meanwhile time goes about its
    immemorial work of making everyone
    look and feel like shit.
    London Fields, ch. 2 (1989)

8 Class! Yes, it's still here. Terrific staying
    power, and against the historical odds.
    What *is* it with that old, *old* crap? The class
    system just doesn't know when to call it a
    day. Even a nuclear holocaust, I think,
    would fail to make that much of a dent in it.
    Ibid.

9 You can't be consumed by another person
    if you're a writer because your relationship
    is basically with yourself. You're being inti-
    mate with your abilities, with your talent.
    This means in some very viable sense that
    for a lot of the time you're just having a
    wank.
    Interview in the *Guardian* 18 March 1995

10 Why do the men cry? Because of fights and feats and marathon preferment, because they want their mothers, because they are blind in time, because of all the hard-ons they have to whistle up out of the thin blue yonder, because of all that men have done. Because they can't be happy or sad any more – only smashed or nuts. And because they don't know how to do it when they're awake.

The Information, pt 1 (1995)

11 These days he smoked and drank largely to solace himself for what drinking and smoking had done to him – but smoking and drinking had done a lot to him, so he drank and smoked a lot.

Of Richard Tull, ibid.

12 Never trust a poet who can drive. Never trust a poet at the wheel. If he *can* drive, distrust the poems.

Ibid.

13 Sunday morning, and everyone was staggering around with their personal burden of prolixity, of fantastic garrulity, of uncontainable communicativeness: the *Sunday Times*.

Heavy Water, 'The Coincidence of the Arts' (1998)

14 The [football] crowd . . . is asking something of you; the surrender of your identity. And it will not be opposed. It cannot be opposed. The crowd is a wraparound millipede of rage and yearning, with the body heat of 180,000 torched armpits, with its ear-hurting roars, and that incensed whistling like a billion babies joined in one desperate scream.

Quoted in the *Observer* 30 May 1999

15 We live in the age of mass loquacity. We are all writing it or at any rate talking it: the memoir, the apologia, the c.v., the *cri de coeur*. Nothing, for now, can compete with experience – so unanswerably authentic, and so liberally and democratically dispensed.

Experience, pt 1, 'Introductory: My Missing' (2000)

16 It's not the case that in the future everyone will be famous for fifteen minutes. In the future everyone will be famous all the time – but only in their own minds. It is lookalike fame, karaoke fame.

Ibid. (footnote). See ANDY WARHOL 6.

Cleveland Amory (b. 1917)
US AUTHOR
He wrote social histories and animal stories, and was founder (1967) and President of the animal welfare organization Fund for Animals.

1 The New England conscience . . . does not stop you from doing what you shouldn't – it just stops you from enjoying it.

New York 5 May 1980

Kofi Annan (b. 1938)
GHANAIAN OFFICIAL AT UN
Having joined the United Nations in 1962, he became the first Secretary-General to be elected from its ranks (1997).

1 Today, Aids has a woman's face.

Quoted in the *Independent* 3 January 2003

Brett Anderson (b. 1947)
BRITISH ROCK MUSICIAN
He is the androgynous vocalist of the band Suede, which he formed in 1990 and which released its eponymous debut album amid much media attention in 1993.

1 I see myself as a bisexual man who has never had a homosexual experience.

Quoted in *Arena* May/June 1993. Anderson's comments provoked accusations of hijacking gay imagery. He defended himself: 'If you are asking am I insincere to pose as a sodomite when I've never had someone's cock up my arse, then no, I'm not. The sexuality you express is not limited to the things you've experienced. I mean, if you're a virgin, does that make you asexual?'

2 I've never had any time for classical music. . . . It just bores me because it's too easy. Anyone can be that complicated. Three notes is far cleverer than three hundred if they're arranged in the right way, and that's what pop music is all about.

Interview in *i-D* October 1994

Gerry Anderson (b. 1929)
BRITISH PROGRAMME-MAKER FOR CHILDREN'S TV
Together with his wife Silvia Anderson, he created some of the classic puppet programmes for children's TV of the 1960s, including Supercar *(1960),* Thunderbirds *(1965–6) and* Captain Scarlet *(1967).*

1 Thunderbirds are go!

Thunderbirds (TV puppet series, 1965–6, created by Gerry and Silvia Anderson, written by the Andersons et al.)

Ian Anderson (b. 1947)
BRITISH ROCK MUSICIAN
He was singer and leader of the blues-rock band Jethro Tull, whose albums Aqualung *(1971) and* Thick as a Brick *(1972) gained them a huge following.*

1 A lot of pop music is about stealing pocket money from children.

Rolling Stone 30 November 1989

Maxwell Anderson (1888–1959)
US PLAYWRIGHT
His writings include the verse-play Elizabeth the
Queen *(1930), the screenplay for* All Quiet on the
Western Front *(1930) and the prose satire* Both
Your Houses *(1933).*

> 1 But it's a long, long while
>   From May to December;
>   And the days grow short
>   When you reach September.

'September Song' (song, written with Kurt
Weill) from the stage musical *Knickerbocker Holi-
day* (1938). Among the singers associated with
the number are BING CROSBY, FRANK SINA-
TRA, and, most famously, MAURICE
CHEVALIER, in the musical *Pepe* (1960).

Maxwell Anderson (1888–1959) and Laurence Stallings (1894–1968)
US PLAYWRIGHTS
*Stallings worked on numerous film screenplays
from 1925 to 1954, but achieved greatest success for
his collaboration with Anderson in the play* What
Price Glory? *(1924).*

> 1 What Price Glory?

Title of anti-First World War play (1924, filmed
1926 and 1952)

Robert Anderson (b. 1917)
US PLAYWRIGHT
His first and most successful play, Tea and Sym-
pathy *(1953, filmed 1956), was followed by lesser
Broadway hits such as* You Know I Can't Hear
You When the Water's Running *(1967).*

> 1 All you're supposed to do is every once in
>   a while give the boys a little tea and
>   sympathy.

Bill, in *Tea and Sympathy*, act 1 (1953). Giving
advice about not getting too involved with
schoolchildren

(Sir) James Anderton (b. 1932)
BRITISH SENIOR POLICE OFFICER
*Chief Constable of Greater Manchester Police
1976–91, he has been involved in a range of Christian and philanthropic causes, though has often
attracted criticism for his outspoken comments.*

> 1 Everywhere I go I see increasing evidence
>   of people swirling about in a human cess-
>   pit of their own making.

On AIDS, quoted in the *Guardian* 12 December
1986

> 2 God works in mysterious ways. Given my
>   love of God and my belief in God and in
>   Jesus Christ, I have to accept that I may
>   well be used by God in this way.

Radio interview, 18 January 1987, quoted in the
Daily Telegraph 19 January 1987. Referring to the
possibility that he may have prophetic powers.

Giulio Andreotti (b. 1919)
ITALIAN POLITICIAN
*A leading member of the Christian Democrat
party throughout the post-war period, he was several times Prime Minister between 1972 and 1992,
and was convicted on charges of complicity in the
murder of a journalist in 2002.*

> 1 At times, we who live in a world of active
>   politics make the mistake of believing that
>   political facts are the only ones with a true
>   meaning and a resonance.

*The USA up Close: From the Atlantic Pact to
Bush*, ch. 24 (1992)

> 2 Power tires only those who do not have it.

Quoted in the *Independent on Sunday* 5 April
1992. Reply when asked how his party had
endured in government for so long.

(Dame) Julie Andrews (b. 1935)
BRITISH ACTRESS AND SINGER
*Having made an impact in Broadway musicals
including* My Fair Lady *(1956) and* Camelot
(1960), she went on to star in the films Mary
Poppins *(1964) and* The Sound of Music
(1965).

> 1 Just a spoonful of sugar helps the medicine
>   go down.

'A Spoonful of Sugar' (song written by Richard
and Robert Sherman), in *Mary Poppins* (film
musical, 1964, screenplay by Bill Walsh and
Don Da Gradi based on the Mary Poppins
books by P. L. Travers, directed by Robert
Stevenson). Julie Andrews played the title role
in the film.

> 2 Supercalifragilisticexpialidocious!
>   Even though the sound of it is something
>   quite atrocious!
>   If you say it loud enough you'll always
>   sound precocious.
>   Supercalifragilisticexpialidocious!

'Supercalifragilisticexpialidocious!' ibid.

Maya Angelou (b. 1928)
US AUTHOR AND POET
*Active in the Black civil rights movement of the
1950s and '60s, she chronicled her 'roller coaster
of a life' in several volumes of autobiography, the
first of which,* I Know Why the Caged Bird Sings
*(1969), was an instant success. She is also a prolific
poet.*

> 1 I Know Why the Caged Bird Sings.

Title of book (1969). The line is taken from the
poem 'Sympathy' by US poet H. Lawrence
Dunbar (1872–1906). 'Caged Bird', a poem from
Angelou's 1983 collection *Shaker, Why Don't You
Sing?*, contains the lines: 'The caged bird sings/
with a fearful trill/of things unknown/but longed
for still/and his tune is heard/on the distant hill/
for the caged bird/sings of freedom.'

2 Children's talent to endure stems from their ignorance of alternatives.
I Know Why the Caged Bird Sings, ch. 17 (1969)

3 The quality of strength lined with tenderness is an unbeatable combination, as are intelligence and necessity when unblunted by formal education.
Ibid., ch. 29

4 At fifteen life had taught me undeniably that surrender, in its place, was as honorable as resistance, especially if one had no choice.
Ibid., ch. 31

5 The fact that the adult American Negro female emerges a formidable character is often met with amazement, distaste and even belligerence. It is seldom accepted as an inevitable outcome of the struggle won by survivors, and deserves respect if not enthusiastic acceptance.
Ibid., ch. 34

6 *My life has been one great big joke,*
A dance that's walked
A song that's spoke,
I laugh so hard I almost choke
When I think about myself.
'When I Think About Myself', publ. in *Just Give Me a Cool Drink of Water 'fore I Diiie* (1971)

7 For Africa to me . . . is more than a glamorous fact. It is a historical truth. No man can know where he is going unless he knows exactly where he has been and exactly how he arrived at his present place.
Quoted in *The New York Times* 16 April 1972. Angelou lived and worked in Ghana and Egypt 1962–6.

8 Life loves the liver of it.
Interview in *Black Scholar* January/February 1977, repr. in *Conversations with Maya Angelou* (ed. Jeffrey M. Elliot, 1989)

9 *You may write me down in history*
With your bitter, twisted lies,
You may trod me in the very dirt
But still, like dust, I'll rise.
'Still I Rise', publ. in *And Still I Rise* (1978)

10 I love to see a young girl go out and grab the world by the lapels. Life's a bitch. You've got to go out and kick ass.
Interview in *Girl About Town* 13 October 1986, repr. in *Conversations with Maya Angelou* (ed. Jeffrey M. Elliot, 1989)

11 We allow our ignorance to prevail upon us and make us think we can survive alone, alone in patches, alone in groups, alone in races, even alone in genders.
Address at Centenary College of Louisiana, March 1990, publ. in *The New York Times* 11 March 1990

12 A rose by any other name may smell as sweet, but a woman called by a devaluing name will only be weakened by the misnomer.
Wouldn't Take Nothing for my Journey Now, 'In All Ways a Woman' (1993)

Paul Anka See FRANK SINATRA 4.

Anne, Princess Royal of Great Britain and Northern Ireland
(b. 1950)
Only daughter of ELIZABETH II, *she is patron of over eighty charities, and is also a skilled horsewoman, representing Britain in the 1976 Olympics.*

1 It could be said that the AIDS pandemic is a classic own-goal scored by the human race against itself.
Quoted in the *Daily Telegraph* 27 January 1988

2 The very idea that all children want to be cuddled by a complete stranger I find utterly amazing.
Quoted in the *Observer* 27 December 1998. Referring to her public duties visiting children.

Anonymous

1 *Arbeit macht frei.*
(Work liberates.)
Inscribed on the gates of Dachau concentration camp, 1933

2 Careless talk costs lives.
Ministry of Information slogan, July 1940, quoted in *Keep Smiling Through: The Home Front 1939–1945*, 'Don't Fence Me In' (1976) by Susan Briggs. The government's poster campaign to persuade people not to betray the war effort through gossip was illustrated with memorable cartoons by Fougasse. Other slogans included 'Tittle-tattle lost the battle' and 'Walls have ears'. According to Jonathon Green in *Says Who?* (1988), the campaign was toned down 'when the over patriotic began denouncing their more verbose but innocent acquaintances to the authorities'. The equivalent slogan in the USA was 'Loose talk costs lives'.

3 The difficult we do immediately; the impossible takes a little longer.
US Armed Forces' slogan. The words are said to be an interpretation of a remark ascribed to Charles Alexandre de Calonne (1734–1802) during the French Revolution: *Madame, si c'est possible, c'est fait; impossible? cela se fera* ('Madam, if it is possible, consider it done; the impossible? that will be done').

4 *I don't like the family Stein!*
There is Gert, there is Ep, there is Ein.
Gert's writings are punk,
Ep's statues are junk,
Nor can anyone understand Ein.
A 'low-brow American limerick current in the 20s', according to *The Long Weekend: A Social History of Great Britain 1918–1939*, ch. 12 (1940) by ROBERT GRAVES and Alan Hodge. Another

version, noted in *Einstein*, ch. 18 (1973) by R.W. Clark, runs, 'Three wonderful people called Stein;/There's Gert and there's Ep and there's Ein./Gert writes in blank verse,/Ep's sculptures are worse,/And nobody understands Ein.' Clark is unable to find a source for this, though suggests it may have been inspired by 'Precious Steins', a piece of verse which appeared in *Punch* 11 September 1929. The sculptor Jacob Epstein obtained three sittings for a bust of ALBERT EINSTEIN at Roughton Heath, near Cromer, Norfolk, where Einstein stayed for a month in September 1933 prior to leaving for the US. Neither, as far as is known, had any dealings with GERTRUDE STEIN.

5 **If you can remember the 1960s you can't have been there.**

Origin untraced

6 **In the great department store of life, baseball is the toy department.**

Quoted in the *Independent* 28 September 1991. George F. Will, in the conclusion to his book *Men at Work: The Craft of Baseball* (1990), quotes 'Sport is the toy department of life.'

7 **It became necessary to destroy the town to save it.**

Unnamed US army major, quoted in *The New York Times* 8 February 1968. The report concerned the battle for Ben Tre during the Tet offensive, South Vietnam.

8 **It's not the bullet with my name on it that worries me. It's the one that says 'To whom it may concern'.**

Belfast resident, quoted in the *Guardian* 16 October 1991

9 **A liberal is a socialist with a wife and two children.**

Thought to have been coined in the 1930s, quoted by ALISTAIR COOKE in *Letter From America*, BBC Radio 4, 8 April 1990

10 **Nil carborundum illegitimi. (Don't let the bastards grind you down.)**

British army motto 1939–45, in *A Dictionary of Catchphrases* (second edn, 1983) by Eric Partridge. The expression was current among army intelligence, gradually becoming more widespread in the army, chiefly among officers.

11 **Not So Much a Programme, More a Way of Life.**

Comedy series title (BBC, 1964–5). The programme was a successor to the satirical series *That Was the Week That Was* (1962–3), using a similar format and with DAVID FROST as anchorman. It consisted of interviews and discussion around topical subjects.

12 *O Death, where is thy sting-a-ling-a-ling, O Grave, thy victor-ee? The bells of hell go ting-a-ling-a-ling, For you but not for me.*

'The Bells of Hell' (song, 1914–18). Sung to the tune of 'She Only Answered "Ting-a-ling-a-ling" ', which itself is believed to be founded on an old Salvation Army song, discussed in *The Long Trail: What the British Soldier Sang and Said 1914–1918*, pt 1, ch. 2 (fourth edn, 1965) by John Brophy and Eric Partridge. The words are taken from 1 Corinthians 15:55, 'O death, where is thy sting? O grave, where is thy victory.'

13 **Once again we silence the mighty roar of London's traffic . . .**

Introduction to *In Town Tonight* (BBC radio series, 1933–60), quoted in *The Golden Age of Radio* (1985) by Denis Gifford. The words opened each episode of this live outside-broadcast in which Lionel Gamlin gave spot interviews to passers-by in central London on a Saturday night.

14 **The only reason I might go to the funeral is to make absolutely sure that he's dead.**

An 'eminent editor', of press baron Lord Beaverbrook, quoted in *Anatomy of Britain Today*, ch. 9 (1965) by ANTHONY SAMPSON

15 **The opera ain't over till the fat lady sings.**

There is no agreed origin for this modern proverb, used similarly to 'don't count your chickens before they're hatched'. Both *The Concise Oxford Dictionary of Proverbs* (ed. John Simpson, 1982) and *Bartlett's Familiar Quotations* (sixteenth edn, 1992) cite sports commentator Dan Cook in the *Washington Post* 13 June 1978, but it was probably already current then. *Bartlett's* notes another version in *Southern Words and Sayings* (ed. Fabia Rue Smith and Charles Rayford Smith, 1976): 'Church ain't out till the fat lady sings.'

16 **Rest in peace. The mistake shall not be repeated.**

Inscription on the cenotaph at Hiroshima, Japan

17 *She was poor, but she was honest, Victim of the squire's whim: For he wooed and he seduced her, And she had a child by him.*

'She Was Poor, But She Was Honest', soldiers' song in the First World War, sung to a pre-1914 melody, publ. in *The Long Trail: What the British Soldier Sang and Said 1914–1918*, pt 1, ch. 3 (fourth edn, 1965) by John Brophy and Eric Partridge

18 **There is no such thing as a free lunch.**

Popularized in the 1960s, the words have no known source, though have been ascribed to an Italian immigrant outside New York's Grand Central Station in ALISTAIR COOKE's *America* (epilogue, 1973). 'Free lunches' appeared in the US in the 1840s with the advent of the new saloons which sold lager beer when it first became widely available, chiefly in Milwaukee. The expression appears in *The Moon is a Harsh Mistress*, ch. 11 (1966) by Robert A. Heinlein, but has become most closely associated with economist MILTON FRIEDMAN, who made it the title of a book in 1975.

19 Today he plays jazz; tomorrow he betrays
his country.

Stalinist propaganda slogan in the Soviet Union,
1920s

20 *We're here*
Because
We're here
Because
We're here
Because we're here.

'We're Here Because', First World War soldiers'
marching song, sung to the tune of 'Auld Lang
Syne', publ. in *The Long Trail: What the British
Soldier Sang and Said 1914–1918*, pt 1, ch. 1
(fourth edn, 1965) by John Brophy and Eric
Partridge

21 What we've got is passion. All they've got
is four quid an hour.

Anonymous anti-roads protester, referring to
the hired security at the Newbury roads protest,
quoted in the *Guardian* 6 April 1996

22 Who Dares Wins.

Motto of the Special Air Services from 1941. In
The S.A.S. at War: 1941–1945, ch. 1 (1991) by
Anthony Kemp, the motto is ascribed to David
Sterling (b. 1915) who created the SAS in 1941.

Jean Anouilh (1910–87)

FRENCH PLAYWRIGHT
*His plays which, as he declared, present a 'great
thirst for purity', include the fantasy* Thieves' Carnival *(1938), the historical drama* Becket *(1959)
and his re-workings of Greek myths,* Antigone
(1944) and Medea *(1946).*

1 However tight I shut my eyes, there will
always be a stray dog somewhere in the
world who'll stop me being happy.

Thérèse Tard, in *Restless Heart (La Sauvage)*,
act 3 (1938). Thérèse's last speech in the play.

2 It is restful, tragedy, because one knows
that there is no more lousy hope left. You
know you're caught, caught at last like a
rat with all the world on its back. And the
only thing left to do is shout – not moan,
or complain, but yell out at the top of your
voice.

The Chorus, in *Antigone* (1944)

3 To say yes, you have to sweat and roll up
your sleeves and plunge both hands into
life up to the elbows. It's easy to say no,
even if it means dying.

Creon, ibid.

4 It takes a certain courage and a certain
greatness to be truly base.

Le Général, in *Ardèle*, act 1 (1947)

5 There is love of course. And then there's
life, its enemy.

Ibid.

6 Poor little men, poor little cocks! As soon
as they're old enough, they swell their plu-
mage to be conquerors . . . If they only
knew that it's enough to be just a little bit
wounded and sad in order to obtain everything without fighting for it.

Araminthe, in *Cécile* (1951)

7 Everything ends this way in France. Weddings, christenings, duels, burials, swin-
dlings, affairs of state – everything is a
pretext for a good dinner.

Monsieur Orlas, ibid.

8 Every man thinks God is on his side. The
rich and powerful know he is.

Charles, in *The Lark* (1953, adapted by LILLIAN
HELLMAN, 1955). The words echo those of soldier and writer Comte de Bussy-Rabutin (1618–
93), in a letter of 1677: 'As you know, God is generally on the side of the big squadrons against
the small ones.'

9 Saintliness is also a temptation.

Thomas à Becket, in *Becket*, act 3 (1959)

Bryan Appleyard (b. 1951)

BRITISH JOURNALIST AND AUTHOR
He has written widely on society and the arts as in
The Pleasures of Peace *(1989) and* Understand-
ing the Present *(1992).*

1 Modernism may be seen as an attempt to
reconstruct the world in the absence of
God.

The Culture Club: Crisis in the Arts, ch. 6 (1984)

Yasser Arafat (b. 1929)

PALESTINIAN LEADER
*He helped found the resistance group Al Fatah in
the late 1950s and won control of the Palestine Liberation Organization in 1969. Having gained
limited autonomy in the West Bank and Gaza
Strip in 1993, he was elected President of the Palestinian National Council in 1996.*

1 Palestine is the cement that holds the Arab
world together, or it is the explosive that
blows it apart.

Time 11 November 1974

Louis Aragon (1897–1982)

FRENCH POET, AUTHOR AND JOURNALIST
Originally Louis Andrieux. With ANDRÉ BRETON
he founded the Surrealist review Littérature *(1919)
to promote the same 'passionate and unruly use of
stupefying images' that characterized his poetry.
He became a Communist after visiting Russia in
1930.*

1 No more painters, no more scribblers, no
more musicians, no more sculptors, no
more religions, no more royalists, no more
radicals, no more imperialists, no more
anarchists, no more socialists, no more
communists, no more proletariat, no more
democrats, no more republicans, no more
bourgeois, no more aristocrats, no more

arms, no more police, no more nations, an end at last to all this stupidity, nothing left, nothing at all, nothing, nothing.

'Manifesto of the Dada Movement', read out at the second Dada event, 5 February 1920, Salon des Indépendents, Paris, publ. in *Littérature* May 1920, repr. in *The History of Surrealism*, ch. 3 (1964) by Maurice Nadeau

2 There are strange flowers of reason to match each error of the senses.

Paris Peasant, 'Preface to a Modern Mythology' (1926)

3 We know that the nature of genius is to provide idiots with ideas twenty years later.

Treatise on Style, pt 1, 'The Pen' (1928)

4 *O months of blossoming, months of trans-*
figurations,
May without cloud and June stabbed to the
heart,
I shall not ever forget the lilacs or the roses
Nor those the spring has kept folded away
apart.

'Les Lilas et les roses', publ. in *Le Crève-Coeur* (1940)

Diane Arbus (1923–71)

US PHOTOGRAPHER
She is best remembered for her monochrome images of strange or unusual subjects from the streets of New York and other US cities in the 1960s, for example transvestites and midgets. In the view of NORMAN MAILER, *'Giving a camera to Diane Arbus is like putting a live grenade in the hands of a child.'*

1 There's a quality of legend about freaks. Like a person in a fairy tale who stops you and demands that you answer a riddle. Most people go through life dreading they'll have a traumatic experience. Freaks were born with their trauma. They've already passed their test in life. They're aristocrats.

From classes given in 1971, publ. in *Diane Arbus: An Aperture Monograph* (1972)

2 A photograph is a secret about a secret. The more it tells you the less you know.

Quoted in *Diane Arbus: A Biography*, Preface (1985) by Patricia Bosworth

Jeffrey Archer (b. 1940)

BRITISH AUTHOR, BUSINESSMAN AND POLITICIAN
Baron Archer of Weston-super-Mare. He was a Conservative MP (1969–74) and Deputy Chairman of the Conservative Party (1985), and has written bestselling novels including First Among Equals *(1984). In 2000 he was given a four-year sentence for perjury. The writer and politician Gyles Brandreth called him 'a modern day Toad of Toad Hall . . . historic, but disaster-prone'.*

1 I was unemployed with debts of £400,000. I know what unemployment is like and a lot of it is getting off your backside and finding a job.

Quoted in the *Observer* 13 October 1985

2 I was allowed to ring the bell for five minutes until everyone was in assembly. It was the beginning of power.

On his schooldays, in the *Daily Telegraph* 16 March 1988

3 If I am given the privilege of becoming the first democratically elected Lord Mayor I'll never write another book.

Independent 21 March 1998. Although a front-runner to be Conservative candidate for Mayor of London, Archer was forced to withdraw in 1999 in the wake of revelations of perjury.

4 I'm down to my last hundred million.

Quoted in the *Guardian* 28 September 1998. On selling his Andy Warhol collection.

The Archers

BRITISH RADIO SOAP OPERA
The world's longest-running radio serial started in 1951, its tales of village life continuing to draw a strong audience today. Episodes were written first by Edward J. Mason and Geoffrey Webb; John Keir Cross took over Webb's place on the latter's death in 1962, and different writers were later used.

1 An everyday story of country folk.

Introduction to each episode. After a trial week's broadcast on the BBC's Midland Home Service in 1950, the series began transmitting nationally on the Light Programme 1 January 1951 with this preamble. It continued: 'The Archers are country folk – farmers . . . children of the soil, and like most work-a-day folk they have their joys and troubles, their ups and downs . . .' (quoted in *The Archers: The First Thirty Years* (ed. William Smethurst, 1980).

Hannah Arendt (1906–75)

GERMAN-BORN US POLITICAL PHILOSOPHER
A refugee from the Nazis, she was active in Jewish organizations in New York from the 1940s, and in 1951 published The Origins of Totalitarianism, *which related the development of totalitarianism to the anti-Semitism, nationalism and imperialism of the nineteenth century.*

1 Totalitarianism is never content to rule by external means, namely, through the state and a machinery of violence; thanks to its peculiar ideology and the role assigned to it in this apparatus of coercion, totalitarianism has discovered a means of dominating and terrorizing human beings from within.

The Origins of Totalitarianism, ch. 10, sect. 1 (1951)

2 The human condition is such that pain and effort are not just symptoms which

can be removed without changing life itself; they are the modes in which life itself, together with the necessity to which it is bound, makes itself felt. For mortals, the 'easy life of the gods' would be a lifeless life.

The Human Condition, 'Labor', ch. 16 (1958)

3 The fearsome, word-and-thought-defying banality of evil.

Eichmann in Jerusalem, ch. 15 (1963)

4 What makes it so plausible to assume that hypocrisy is the vice of vices is that integrity can indeed exist under the cover of all other vices except this one. Only crime and the criminal, it is true, confront us with the perplexity of radical evil; but only the hypocrite is really rotten to the core.

On Revolution, ch. 2, sect. 5 (1963)

5 It is well known that the most radical revolutionary will become a conservative the day after the revolution.

New Yorker 12 September 1970

6 Under conditions of tyranny it is far easier to act than to think.

Quoted in *A Certain World*, 'Tyranny' (1970) by W.H. AUDEN

7 The Third World is not a reality but an ideology.

Crises of the Republic, 'On Violence', sect. 1 (1972)

Giorgio Armani (b. 1934)

ITALIAN FASHION DESIGNER

Presenting collections from the mid-1970s, he is known for his elegant, minimalist style. In his own words, 'I was the first to soften the image of men, and harden the image of women.'

1 I would like to be remembered as the person who created a modern elegance.

Interview in the *Guardian* 4 February 1995

Simon Armitage (b. 1963)

BRITISH POET

A public poet with a colloquial style, he has published Zoom (1989), Kid (1992), The Dead Sea Poems (1995) *and the novel* Little Green Man (2001), *among other works.*

1 The North, where England tucks its shirt in its underpants.

All Points North, 'Where You're At' (1998)

2 *Drugs is
your own tattoos coming alive on your skin,
opening a door and letting a light in
is what drugs is.*

Ibid., 'Saturday Night'

3 *And a well shod president walks to the
    camera to say why
we should put in the boot,*

*and when that happens, a well-dressed
    prime minister
usually follows suit.*

'Killing Time' (1999)

4 *Then the Chinese whisper of a countdown
    spreads across the crowd,
first to be lit by a century's morning,
mad to say they were there and then when
    the moment came,
wild for the starlight that passes for
    meaning.*

Ibid.

Louis Armstrong (1900–71)

US JAZZ MUSICIAN

Nicknamed Satchmo ('Satchel Mouth'), he was famous for his gravelly voice, big smile and improvisatory trumpet solos with his Hot Five and Hot Seven ensembles (1925–8). He is said to have invented the 'scat' style of singing.

1 *Hello, Dolly, well, hello Dolly
It's so nice to have you back where you
    belong.*

'Hello, Dolly' (song, written by Jerry Herman) in *Hello, Dolly* (stage musical 1964, filmed 1969). In the original stage production, the number was sung by Carol Channing, though it is most associated with Armstrong, who won a Grammy award for Song of the Year in 1964 and later performed it in the film version.

2 *And I think to myself
What a wonderful world.*

'What a Wonderful World' (song, written by George David Weiss and George Douglas) on the album *What a Wonderful World* (1967)

3 If you still have to ask . . . shame on you.

On being asked what jazz is, quoted in *Louis*, 'Ambassadors of Jazz' (1971, rev. 1975) by Max Jones and John Chilton. Many versions of the riposte exist, along the lines of 'If you have to ask what jazz is, you'll never know', and variously attributed.

4 All music is folk music, I ain't never heard no horse sing a song.

Quoted in *The New York Times* 7 July 1971. The words have also been attributed to blues guitarist Big Bill Broonzy

Neil Armstrong (b. 1930)

US ASTRONAUT

Commander of the Apollo 11 moon mission in 1969, he was the first person to set foot on the moon.

1 Houston, Tranquility Base here. The Eagle has landed.

Radio message to earth announcing the first manned moon landing, 20 July 1969, quoted in the *Washington Post* 21 July 1969. The message was transmitted as the lunar module 'Eagle' touched down in the Sea of Tranquillity. The words have also been attributed to 'Buzz' Aldrin

(Edwin Eugene Aldrin Jnr), a fellow crew-
member and the second man on the moon.

2 **That's one small step for a man, one giant
leap for mankind.**

Quoted in *The New York Times* 21 July 1969. On
his first steps on the moon's surface, 10.56 p.m.
(EDT), 20 July 1969. Armstrong's actual message
– possibly garbled or obscured by static – was
originally reported 'one small step for man, one
giant leap for mankind'.

Robert Armstrong (1890–1973)
US SCREEN ACTOR

*Originally Donald Robert Smith. A character actor
associated with action roles, he is mostly
remembered in the part of the film producer who
brought the ape to New York in* King Kong (1933).

1 **Oh no, it wasn't the aviators, it was beauty
that killed the beast.**

Carl Denham (Robert Armstrong), in *King Kong*
(film, 1933, screenplay by James Creelman and
Ruth Rose based on a story by Merian Cooper
and Edgar Wallace, directed by Merian Cooper
and Ernest Schoedsack). Last lines of the movie,
which are often misquoted with 'airplanes'
instead of 'aviators'.

(Sir) Robert Armstrong (b. 1927)
BRITISH CIVIL SERVANT

*Baron Armstrong of Ilminster. Secretary of the
Cabinet (1979–87) and Head of the Civil Service
(1981–7) in the Thatcher government, he played a
prominent role during the 'Spycatcher' affair in
1987.*

1 **It contains a misleading impression, not a
lie. It was being economical with the truth.**

Remark to Supreme Court, New South Wales,
18 November 1986, quoted in the *Daily Telegraph*
19 November 1986. Referring to a letter written
by Armstrong when the British government was
attempting to suppress publication of the book
Spycatcher by ex-secret service agent Peter
Wright. As Armstrong made clear, he was quoting Edmund Burke in *Two Letters on Proposals
for Peace* (1796): 'Falsehood and delusion are
allowed in no case whatsoever: But, as in the
exercise of all the virtues, there is an economy of
truth.' Mark Twain harked back to this notion
in *Following the Equator* (1897): 'Truth is the
most valuable thing we have. Let us economize
it', while Tory minister ALAN CLARK also
echoed the words when he admitted he had been
'economical with the actualités' when discussing
his role in the Matrix Churchill arms-to-Iraq
affair in 1990.

Peter Arno (1904–68)
US CARTOONIST

*Originally Curtis Arnoux Peters. From the 1920s
until his death he was associated with the* New
Yorker *magazine, where his quirky cartoons gently
satirized New York's café society.*

1 **Well, back to the old drawing board.**

Caption to cartoon in the *New Yorker*, repr. in
Peter Arno's Cartoon Revue (1942). The words
are spoken by the designer of a plane just
crashed.

Jean Arp (1887–1966)
FRENCH-GERMAN ARTIST AND POET

*Also known as Hans Arp. One of the founders of
the Dada movement (1916) and associated with the
Surrealists during the 1920s, he produced organic
abstract sculpture, and after the Second World
War also wrote poems and essays.*

1 **Soon silence will have passed into legend.
Man has turned his back on silence. Day
after day he invents machines and devices
that increase noise and distract humanity
from the essence of life, contemplation,
meditation. . . . Tooting, howling, screeching, booming, crashing, whistling, grind-
ing, and trilling bolster his ego. His anxiety
subsides. His inhuman void spreads mon-
strously like a grey vegetation.**

On My Way, 'Sacred Silence' (ed. Robert Motherwell, 1948)

Antonin Artaud (1896–1948)
FRENCH THEATRE PRODUCER, ACTOR AND
THEORIST

*The anarchistic principles of his Theatre of
Cruelty, which aimed to attack the complacency of
the audience, were expounded in his Manifesto of
the Theatre of Cruelty (1932 and 1933) and* The
Theatre and Its Double *(1938). His best known acting role was as Marat in Abel Gance's film* Napo-
léon *(1927).*

1 **If I commit suicide, it will not be to
destroy myself but to put myself back
together again. Suicide will be for me only
one means of violently reconquering
myself, of brutally invading my being, of
anticipating the unpredictable approaches
of God. By suicide, I reintroduce my
design in nature, I shall for the first time
give things the shape of my will.**

'On Suicide', first publ. in *Le Disque vert* no. 1
(1925), repr. in *Artaud Anthology* (ed. Jack
Hirschman, 1965)

2 *Theatre of cruelty* **means a theatre difficult
and cruel for myself first of all. And, on the
level of performance, it is not the cruelty
we can exercise upon each other by hack-
ing at each other's bodies, carving up our
personal anatomies, or, like Assyrian
emperors, sending parcels of human ears,
noses, or neatly detached nostrils through
the mail, but the much more terrible and
necessary cruelty which things can exercise
against us. We are not free. And the sky
can still fall on our heads. And the theatre**

has been created to teach us that first of all.

The Theatre and Its Double, ch. 1 (1938, transl. 1958)

3 *All true language*
is incomprehensible,
Like the chatter
of a beggar's teeth.
'Ci-Gît' (1947), repr. in *Selected Writings*, pt 36 (ed. Susan Sontag, 1976)

4 *Where there is a stink of shit*
there is a smell of being.
To Have Done with the Judgment of God, 'The Pursuit of Fecality' (1947)

5 No one has ever written, painted, sculpted, modeled, built, or invented except literally to get out of hell.
Van Gogh, the Man Suicided by Society (1947)

6 Tragedy on the stage is no longer enough for me, I shall bring it into my own life.
Quoted in the memoirs of Jean-Louis Barrault, *Memories for Tomorrow*, pt 2, 'The Grenier des Grands-Augustins' (1972)

George Asaf (1880–1951)
BRITISH SONGWRITER

1 *What's the use of worrying?*
It never was worth while,
So, pack up your troubles in your old
kit-bag,
And smile, smile, smile.
'Pack up Your Troubles' (song, 1915, with music by Felix Powell)

Herbert Asbury (1889–1963)
US AUTHOR
Mostly written in documentary style, his books, such as Gangs of New York *(1928) and* Barbary Coast *(1933), focused on the seamier side of New York life.*

1 The basic creed of the gangster, and for that matter of any other type of criminal, is that whatever a man has is his only so long as he can keep it, and that the one who takes it away from him has not done anything wrong, but has merely demonstrated his smartness.
Gangs of New York, Introduction (1928, filmed 2002)

Neal Ascherson (b. 1932)
BRITISH JOURNALIST
Formerly a foreign correspondent and a regular contributor of political columns for the Observer *and the* Independent on Sunday, *he has also published books on central and eastern Europe, for example* Black Sea *(1995).*

1 The use of the word 'heritage' as a term of obligation, binding people not only to

respect relics of the past but also to understand them in one prescribed way as 'national symbols', is not spontaneous. It is a form of manipulation, devised by politicians and quangocrats to make the tatty, dishevelled building-site of the present look more imposing.
Independent on Sunday 19 February 1995

2 War is also the day after the war, when the noise stops. It's the day when what looks like a bald old beggar is helped down from the train returning from the prison camps and the small boy asks his mother: 'Is that my dad? Does he live with us?'
Observer 6 September 1998

3 Childhood, long worshipped as a separate secret garden of innocence, has become inconvenient and embarrassing, and is now rapidly collapsing into Youth. Wired-up children as defined by advertisers and journalists haranguing working mums, are now little more than young people under five feet high.
Observer 15 November 1998

(Sir) Paddy Ashdown (b. 1941)
BRITISH POLITICIAN
Jeremy John Durham Ashdown. Having served with the Royal Marines and in the diplomatic service, he was elected a Liberal MP in 1983 and was leader of the amalgamated Liberal and Social Democrat (later Liberal Democrat) Party 1988–99.

1 Politics is about putting yourself in a state of grace.
Daily Telegraph 16 September 1992

2 Lord, make my words sweet and reasonable. For some day I may have to eat them.
Speech at Liberal Party Conference, Brighton, broadcast on *Radio 5 Live* 24 September 1998

Isaac Asimov (1920–92)
RUSSIAN-BORN US AUTHOR
A pioneering figure in science fiction and also a distinguished biochemist, he is principally known for his collection of short stories I, Robot *(1950) and* The Foundation Trilogy *(1951–3).*

1 Let's start with the three fundamental Rules of Robotics. . . . We have: one, a robot may not injure a human being, or, through inaction, allow a human being to come to harm. Two, a robot must obey the orders given it by human beings except where such orders would conflict with the First Law. And three, a robot must protect its own existence as long as such protection does not conflict with the First or Second Laws.
Powell, in 'Runaround', a story first publ. in *Astounding Science Fiction* March 1942, repr. in *I, Robot* (1950). According to Asimov, who called

the formulation his most important contribution to science fiction, these three laws have been generally adopted by writers on robots. Asimov also claimed that this passage contains the first recorded use of the term 'Robotics' (discussed in his essay 'My Robots' in *Robot Visions*, 1993).

2 **Science fiction writers foresee the inevitable, and although problems and catastrophes may be inevitable, solutions are not.**

'How Easy to See the Future', first publ. in *Natural History* April 1975, repr. in *Asimov on Science Fiction* (1981)

3 **It is change, continuing change, inevitable change, that is the dominant factor in society today. No sensible decision can be made any longer without taking into account not only the world as it is, but the world as it will be. . . . This, in turn, means that our statesmen, our businessmen, our everyman must take on a science fictional way of thinking.**

'My Own View', publ. in *The Encyclopedia of Science Fiction* (ed. Robert Holdstock, 1978)

Elizabeth Asquith (1897–1945)

The daughter of HERBERT ASQUITH, *she married Prince Antoine Bibesco, a Romanian diplomat, in 1919, and subsequently wrote novels, plays and poetry.*

1 **Kitchener is a great poster.**

Quoted by Herbert Asquith, in *More Memories*, ch. 6 (1933) by Margot Asquith. The quote is often misattributed to MARGOT ASQUITH, as in *Kitchener: Portrait of an Imperialist*, ch. 14 (1980) by Sir Philip Magnus, where the quote appears in the form, 'If Kitchener was not a great man, he was, at least, a great poster.'

Herbert Asquith (1852–1928)

BRITISH STATESMAN

Soon after entering parliament as a Liberal MP in 1886, he served as Home Secretary and then Chancellor of the Exchequer. He was prime minister 1908–16 but was ousted as leader of the wartime coalition by LLOYD GEORGE's *wing of the party.*

1 **Youth would be an ideal state if it came a little later in life.**

Quoted in the *Observer* 15 April 1923

2 **It is fitting that we should have buried the Unknown Prime Minister by the side of the Unknown Soldier.**

Quoted in *The Unknown Prime Minister*, ch. 32, sect. 2 (1955) by Robert Blake. Referring to Andrew Bonar Law, Prime Minister 1922–3. Bonar Law (died 30 October 1923) was the first prime minister to be buried in Westminster Abbey since Gladstone in 1898, though it was contrary to his own wishes. Blake comments,

'Asquith certainly intended no compliment by this remark, but Bonar Law would not have resented it. He cared little enough for fame in his own lifetime, still less for the verdict of posterity.'

Margot Asquith (1864–1945)

BRITISH SOCIALITE

Second wife of HERBERT ASQUITH, *she was a renowned society hostess who published three volumes of revelatory autobiography (1920–43) and an autobiographical novel* Octavia *(1928). As* DOROTHY PARKER *quipped, 'The affair between Margot Asquith and Margot Asquith will live as one of the prettiest love stories in all literature.'*

1 **From the happy expression on their faces you might have supposed that they welcomed the war. I have met with men who loved stamps, and stones, and snakes, but I could not imagine any man loving war.**

On the crowds outside Downing Street 3 August 1914, the eve of the declaration of the First World War, in *The Autobiography of Margot Asquith* vol. 2, ch. 7 (1922)

2 **He could not see a belt without hitting below it.**

Of former Prime Minister DAVID LLOYD GEORGE, quoted by Mark Bonham Carter in the Introduction to Margot Asquith's *Autobiography* (1962 edn, first publ. 1920)

3 **No, no, Jean. The *t* is *silent*, as in *Harlow*.**

Quoted in *Great Tom: Notes Towards a Definition of T. S. Eliot*, ch. 7 (1973) by T. S. Matthews. Said to the actress Jean Harlow, who had been mispronouncing her name. The anecdote is remembered by Emily Hale, a friend of T.S. ELIOT.

Nancy Astor (1879–1964)

US-BORN BRITISH POLITICIAN

In 1919 she was the first woman to take her seat in the House of Commons, succeeding her husband as Conservative MP for Plymouth. Generally considered a wit, she was portrayed as a 'sort of V-2 rocket' by her husband.

1 **I married beneath me – all women do.**

Attributed, speech at Oldham, 1951, also quoted in *Dictionary of National Biography*

2 **The penalty of success is to be bored by people who snub you.**

Quoted in the *Sunday Express* 12 January 1956

Brooks Atkinson (1894–1984)

US CRITIC AND ESSAYIST

Drama critic of The New York Times *(1925–42 and 1946–60), he published collections of essays and articles, as well as histories of the theatre.*

1 **After each war there is a little less democracy to save.**

Once Around the Sun, '7 January' (1951)

2 The virtue of the camera is not the power it has to transform the photographer into an artist, but the impulse it gives him to keep on looking.

Ibid. '28 August'

Charles Atlas (1893–1972)

ITALIAN-BORN US BODYBUILDER

Originally Angelo Siciliano. With his partner, Charles P. Roman, he devised and ran a highly successful mail-order bodybuilding programme which during the 1920s caused him to be dubbed 'America's Most Perfectly Developed Man'.

1 You too can have a body like mine.

Quoted in *The Life and Times of Charles Atlas*, pt 1 (1942) by Charles Gaines. The slogan was coined by Atlas's partner, Charles Roman c. 1929.

(Sir) David Attenborough (b. 1926)

BRITISH NATURALIST AND BROADCASTER

Inspired by the 'splendour and fecundity of the natural world', he began filming wildlife in exotic locations for the BBC series Zoo Quest *(1954–64). His documentary series include* Life on Earth *(1979) and* The Life of Mammals *(2002).*

1 It is more than likely that if men were to disappear from the face of the earth, for whatever reason, there is a modest, unobtrusive creature somewhere that would develop into a new form and take our place.

Life on Earth, 'The Compulsive Communicators' (1979)

2 We can now manipulate images to such an extraordinary degree that there is no lie you can't tell.

Quoted in the *Observer* 18 October 1998

3 One cannot get bored by a bluebell.

Quoted in *The Times* 22 April 2000

Clement Attlee (1883–1967)

BRITISH POLITICIAN AND PRIME MINISTER

He was the first Labour prime minister to hold an absolute majority in the House of Commons. His premiership (1945–51) saw the initiation of the welfare state and the nationalization of major industries. ANEURIN BEVAN *remarked: 'He brings to the fierce struggle of politics the tepid enthusiasm of a lazy summer afternoon at a cricket match.' See also* ANEURIN BEVAN 5, WINSTON CHURCHILL 46, 55 *and* 56.

1 Few thought he was even a starter
There were many who thought themselves smarter
But he ended PM
CH and OM
An earl and a knight of the garter.

Quoted in *Attlee*, ch. 29 (1982) by Kenneth Harris. Describing himself in a letter to his brother Tom Attlee, 8 April 1956, shortly before being enrolled as a Knight of the Garter.

2 [Russian Communism is] the illegitimate child of Karl Marx and Catherine the Great.

Speech at Aarhus University, Denmark, 11 April 1956, quoted in *The Times* 12 April 1956

3 Democracy means government by discussion, but it is only effective if you can stop people talking.

Speech at Oxford, 14 June 1957, quoted in *The Times* 15 June 1957

Margaret Atwood (b. 1939)

CANADIAN NOVELIST, POET AND CRITIC

Described by MICHAEL ONDAATJE *as 'the quiet Mata Hari, the mysterious violent figure . . . who pits herself against the ordered, too-clean world like an arsonist', she has been influenced by feminism and science fiction in her novels, which include* The Handmaid's Tale *(1986, filmed 1990) and* The Blind Assassin *(2001).*

1 Everyone thinks writers must know more about the inside of the human head, but that is wrong. They know less, that's why they write. Trying to find out what everyone else takes for granted.

Dancing Girls, 'Lives of the Poets' (1977)

2 The beginning of Canadian cultural nationalism was not 'Am I really that oppressed?' but 'Am I really that boring?'

Interview with JOYCE CAROL OATES in the *Ontario Review* fall/winter 1978, repr. in *Conversations*, 'Dancing on the Edge of the Precipice' (ed. Earl G. Ingersoll, 1990)

3 Gardening is not a rational act. What matters is the immersion of the hands in the earth, that ancient ceremony of which the Pope kissing the tarmac is merely a pallid vestigial remnant. In the spring, at the end of the day, you should smell like dirt.

Bluebeard's Egg, 'Unearthing Suite' (1983)

4 We yearned for the future. How did we learn it, that talent for insatiability?

The Handmaid's Tale, ch. 1 (1986)

5 As all historians know, the past is a great darkness, and filled with echoes. Voices may reach us from it; but what they say to us is imbued with the obscurity of the matrix out of which they come; and try as we may, we cannot always decipher them precisely in the clearer light of our day.

Ibid., 'Historical Note'

6 All fathers . . . are invisible in daytime; daytime is ruled by mothers. But fathers come out at night. Darkness brings home the fathers, with their real, unspeakable power. There is more to them than meets the eye.

Cat's Eye, ch. 31 (1989)

W. H. Auden (1907–73)

ANGLO-AMERICAN POET AND CRITIC

One of the wave of left-wing literati of the 1930s, he was, according to PERCY WYNDHAM LEWIS, *'all ice and woodenfaced acrobatics'. He established his reputation with* Look, Stranger! *(1936) and* Spain *(1937) before emigrating to the USA in 1939. He also wrote plays, libretti and literary criticism.*

1 *Let us honour if we can*
The vertical man,
Though we value none
But the horizontal one.
Epigraph to *Poems* (1930), repr. in *Collected Shorter Poems 1927–1957*, 'Shorts' (1966)

2 *Harrow the house of the dead; look shining at*
New styles of architecture, a change of heart.
'Sir, No Man's Enemy', publ. in *Poems* (1930)

3 *Private faces in public places*
Are wiser and nicer
Than public faces in private places.
The Orators, epigraph (1932)

4 *This is the Night Mail crossing the border,*
Bringing the cheque and the postal order,
Letters for the rich, letters for the poor,
The shop at the corner, the girl next door.
Pulling up Beattock, a steady climb:
The gradient's against her, but she's on time.
Past cotton-grass and moorland border,
Shovelling white steam over her shoulder.
'Night Mail', sect. 1 (1936), repr. in *Collected Shorter Poems 1927–1957* (1966). Opening lines of poem written as a commentary for a Post Office documentary film.

5 *And none will hear the postman's knock*
Without a quickening of the heart.
For who can bear to feel himself forgotten?
Ibid. Concluding lines.

6 *And make us as Newton was, who in his garden watching*
The apple falling towards England, became aware
Between himself and her of an eternal tie.
'O Love, the Interest Itself', publ. in *Look, Stranger!* (1936). The words 'falling towards England' provided CLIVE JAMES with the title for his second volume of 'unreliable memoirs' in 1985.

7 *A shilling life will give you all the facts.*
Title and first line of poem, publ. ibid.

8 *The desires of the heart are as crooked as corkscrews*
Not to be born is the best for man.
'Death's Echo', publ. in *Spain* (1937). The second line quoted echoes lines by W.B. YEATS in 'From "Oedipus at Colonus"' (1928) – 'Never to have lived is best, ancient writers say/Never to have drawn the breath of life, never to have looked into the eye of day' – which in turn recall a line from Sophocles.

9 *To-morrow for the young the poets exploding like bombs,*
The walks by the lake, the weeks of perfect communion;
To-morrow the bicycle races
Through the suburbs on summer evenings.
But to-day the struggle.
'Spain', st. 23, publ. ibid.

10 *To-day the deliberate increase in the chances of death,*
The conscious acceptance of guilt in the necessary murder.
Ibid., st. 24

11 *The stars are dead. The animals will not look.*
We are left alone with our day, and the time is short, and
History to the defeated
May say Alas but cannot help nor pardon.
Ibid., st. 26

12 *'I'll love you, dear, I'll love you*
Till China and Africa meet
And the river jumps over the mountain
And the salmon sing in the street,

'I'll love you till the ocean
Is folded and hung up to dry
And the seven stars go squawking
Like geese about the sky.'
'As I Walked Out One Evening', publ. in *Another Time* (1940)

13 *'O plunge your hands in water,*
Plunge them in up to the wrist;
Stare, stare in the basin
And wonder what you've missed.

'The glacier knocks in the cupboard,
The desert sighs in the bed,
And the crack in the tea-cup opens
A lane to the land of the dead.'
Ibid.

14 *When he laughed, respectable senators burst with laughter,*
And when he cried the little children died in the streets.
'Epitaph on a Tyrant', publ. ibid. The lines may have been inspired by a description of William of Orange in *The Rise of the Dutch Republic* (1856) by John Lothrop Motley: 'As long as he lived, he was the guiding-star of a whole brave nation, and when he died the little children cried in the streets.'

15 *He was my North, my South, my East and West,*
My working week and my Sunday rest,
My noon, my midnight, my talk, my song;
I thought that love would last for ever: I was wrong.
'Funeral Blues', publ. ibid. The poem was recited

during the funeral scene in the film *Four Wed-dings and a Funeral* (1994)

16 *For one who lived among enemies so long:*
If often he was wrong and at times absurd,
To us he is no more a person
Now but a whole climate of opinion.
'In Memory of Sigmund Freud', st. 17, publ. ibid.

17 *Mad Ireland hurt you into poetry.*
Now Ireland has her madness and her
weather still.
'In Memory of W. B. Yeats', pt 2, written February 1939, publ. ibid.

18 *For poetry makes nothing happen: it survives*
In the valley of its saying where executives
Would never want to tamper.
Ibid.

19 *Earth, receive an honoured guest:*
William Yeats is laid to rest.
Let the Irish vessel lie
Emptied of its poetry.
Ibid., pt 3

20 *In the nightmare of the dark*
All the dogs of Europe bark,
And the living nations wait,
Each sequestered in its hate.
Ibid.

21 *Intellectual disgrace*
Stares from every human face.
Ibid.

22 *Lay your sleeping head, my love,*
Human on my faithless arm.
'Lay your sleeping head, my love', publ. ibid. Opening lines.

23 *But in my arms till break of day*
Let the living creature lie,
Mortal, guilty, but to me
The entirely beautiful.
Ibid.

24 *About suffering they were never wrong,*
The Old Masters: how well they understood
Its human position; how it takes place
While someone else is eating or opening a
window or just walking dully along.
'Musée des Beaux Arts', publ. ibid. Opening lines.

25 *I and the public know*
What all schoolchildren learn,
Those to whom evil is done
Do evil in return.
'September 1, 1939', st. 2, publ. ibid.

26 *We must love one another or die.*
Ibid., st. 8. Auden later repudiated the line, insisting that it be altered for a 1955 anthology to 'We must love one another and die'. He referred to the poem as 'the most dishonest poem I have ever written'.

27 *Blessed Cecilia, appear in visions*
To all musicians, appear and inspire:

Translated Daughter, come down and
startle
Composing mortals with immortal fire.
'Anthem for St Cecilia's Day', pt 1, publ. in *New Year Letter*, in USA *The Double Man* (1941)

28 *At Dirty Dick's and Sloppy Joe's*
We drank our liquor straight,
Some went upstairs with Margery,
And some, alas, with Kate.
The Sea and the Mirror, pt 2, 'Master and Boatswain', publ. in *For the Time Being* (1944)

29 *Thou shalt not sit*
With statisticians nor commit
A social science.
'Under Which Lyre', st. 27, written 1946, publ. in *Nones* (1951)

30 Criticism should be a casual conversation.
The Table Talk of W.H. Auden, 'November 16, 1946' (comp. Alan Ansen, ed. Nicholas Jenkins, 1990)

31 *Sob, heavy world,*
Sob as you spin
Mantled in mist, remote from the happy.
'The Dirge', publ. in *The Age of Anxiety* (1947)

32 The detective must be either the official representative of the ethical or the exceptional individual who is in a state of grace.
'The Guilty Vicarage', first publ. in *Harper's* May 1948, repr. in *The Dyer's Hand*, pt 3 (1962)

33 Routine, in an intelligent man, is a sign of ambition.
'The Life of That-There Poet' (1958), publ. in the *New Yorker* 26 April 1958

34 *What reverence is rightly paid*
To a Divinity so odd
He lets the Adam whom he made
Perform the Acts of God?
'Friday's Child', publ. in *Homage to Clio* (1960)

35 *To the man-in-the-street, who, I'm sorry to*
say,
Is a keen observer of life,
The word 'Intellectual' suggests straight
away
A man who's untrue to his wife.
'New Year Letter' (1961), publ. in *Collected Poems* (1976)

36 It is a sad fact about our culture that a poet can earn much more money writing or talking about his art than he can by practising it.
The Dyer's Hand, Foreword (1962). Opening words.

37 Some books are undeservedly forgotten; none are undeservedly remembered.
Ibid., pt 1, 'Reading'

38 No poet or novelist wishes he were the only one who ever lived, but most of them wish they were the only one alive, and

quite a number fondly believe their wish has been granted.
Ibid.

39 It takes little talent to see clearly what lies under one's nose, a good deal of it to know in which direction to point that organ.
Ibid., 'Writing'

40 Fame often makes a writer vain, but seldom makes him proud.
Ibid.

41 When I find myself in the company of scientists, I feel like a shabby curate who has strayed by mistake into a drawing room full of dukes.
Ibid., pt 2, 'The Poet & the City'. Auden had specialized in science studies before switching to English at Oxford.

42 A man has his distinctive personal scent which his wife, his children and his dog can recognize. A crowd has a generalized stink. The public is odourless.
Ibid.

43 Between friends differences in taste or opinion are irritating in direct proportion to their triviality.
Ibid., pt 3, 'Hic et Ille', sect. D

44 Among those whom I like or admire, I can find no common denominator, but among those whom I love, I can: all of them make me laugh.
Ibid., pt 7, 'Notes on the Comic'

45 A verbal art like poetry is reflective; it stops to think. Music is immediate, it goes on to become.
Ibid., pt 8, 'Notes on Music and Opera'

46 *God bless the USA, so large,*
So friendly, and so rich.
'On the Circuit', written 1963, publ. in *Collected Poems* (1976)

47 *Some thirty inches from my nose*
The frontier of my Person goes,
And all the untilled air between
Is private pagus or demesne.
Stranger, unless with bedroom eyes
I beckon you to fraternize,
Beware of rudely crossing it:
I have no gun, but I can spit.
'Prologue: The Birth of Architecture: Postscript', publ. in *About the House* (1965)

48 *Healing,*
Papa would tell me,
'is not a science,
but the intuitive art
of wooing Nature.'
'The Art of Healing', written 1969, publ. in *Collected Poems* (1976)

49 Of course, Behaviourism 'works.' So does torture. Give me a no-nonsense, down-to-earth behaviourist, a few drugs, and simple

electrical appliances, and in six months I will have him reciting the Athanasian Creed in public.
A Certain World, 'Behaviourism' (1970)

50 All sin tends to be addictive, and the terminal point of addiction is what is called damnation.
Ibid., 'Hell'

51 Proper names are poetry in the raw. Like all poetry they are untranslatable.
Ibid., 'Names, Proper'

52 As a poet there is only one political duty, and that is to defend one's language against corruption. When it is corrupted, people lose faith in what they hear and this leads to violence.
Quoted in the *Observer* 31 October 1971

53 You will be a poet because you will always be humiliated.
Quoted by Stephen Spender in his *Journals 1939–1983* (1985), entry for 11 April 1979. Spender was reminiscing on his first meeting with Auden at Oxford.

54 My face looks like a wedding-cake left out in the rain.
Quoted in *W.H. Auden*, pt 2, ch. 6 (1981) by Humphrey Carpenter. On the subject of faces, Auden wrote (in *The Dyer's Hand*, 1962): 'Every European visitor to the United States is struck by the comparative rarity of what he would call a face. . . . To have a face, in the European sense of the word, it would seem that one must not only enjoy and suffer but also desire to preserve the memory of even the most humiliating and unpleasant experiences of the past.'

Daw Aung San Suu Kyi (b. 1945)
BURMESE OPPOSITION LEADER
The daughter of General Aung San, the architect of Burmese independence, she co-founded in 1988 the National League for Democracy. Although her party won the 1990 elections, she was placed under house arrest by the military junta on several occasions.

1 It may take time and it won't be easy. But what's ten years?
Sunday Telegraph 4 April 1999. Referring to her persecution by the Burmese government, and her hopes to re-establish democracy in Burma.

Paul Auster (b. 1947)
US AUTHOR
The New York Trilogy (1987) established him as an experimental writer on the themes of modern city life. Other works include Leviathan *(1992) and* Timbuktu *(1999).*

1 We construct a narrative for ourselves, and that's the thread that we follow from one day to the next. People who disintegrate as

personalities are the ones who lose that thread.

Interview in the *Sunday Times* 16 April 1989

2 Our lives don't really belong to us, you see – they belong to the world, and in spite of our efforts to make sense of it, the world is a place beyond our understanding.

Interview 1989/90, publ. in *The Red Notebook* (1995)

Tex Avery (1907–80)

US ANIMATOR

Originally Frederick Bean. He was famous for creating such cartoon characters as Bugs Bunny and Daffy Duck, which appeared on television and in the films King Size Canary *(1947) and* Bad Luck Blackie *(1949), among other classics.*

1 Th-th-th-th-that's all, folks!

Porky Pig, in *Looney Tunes/Merrie Melodies* (Warner Brothers cartoons, 1935–65). The sign-off line (created and voiced by Mel Blanc from 1938) was also used to close various other Warner Brothers' cartoons, and was affectionately reprised at the end of the 1972 film *What's Up Doc?* (see below). Porky Pig first appeared in the *Looney Tunes* cartoon *I Haven't Got a Hat* (1935).

2 Eh, what's up Doc?

Bugs Bunny's running gag, ibid. The rabbit made his first appearance in a Warner Brothers *Looney Tunes* cartoon in 1937, voiced by Mel Blanc. In 1940 Tex Avery gave him his name (after West Coast mobster Bugsy Siegel) and his famous catchphrase, and directed the first official Bugs Bugs Bunny cartoon, *A Wild Hare* (1940). *What's up Doc?* was also the title of Peter Bogdanovich's screwball comedy with Barbra Streisand and Ryan O'Neal (1972).

Reverend W. Awdry (1911–97)

BRITISH WRITER OF CHILDREN'S BOOKS

Wilbert Vere Awdry. A country clergyman, he wrote the Thomas the Tank Engine *series of stories for children, the first of which appeared in 1945, and which have since gathered a huge following.*

1 You've a lot to learn about trucks, little Thomas. They are silly things and must be kept in their place. After pushing them about here for a few weeks you'll know almost as much about them as Edward. Then you'll be a Really Useful Engine.

The Fat Director, in *Thomas the Tank Engine,* 'Thomas and the Trucks' (1946)

Hoyt Axton (b. 1938)

US SONGWRITER AND ROCK MUSICIAN

A composer of songs for Glen Campbell, RINGO STARR *and the group Steppenwolf, among many others, he also recorded his own material in the 1970s. His mother co-wrote 'Heartbreak Hotel' (1955), a hit for* ELVIS PRESLEY.

1 God damn the pusher man.

'The Pusher' (song) on the album *Steppenwolf* (1968) by Steppenwolf. The anti-drug anthem featured in DENNIS HOPPER's film *Easy Rider* (1969), though was banned on the radio.

(Sir) Alan Ayckbourn (b. 1939)

BRITISH PLAYWRIGHT

Prolific and master farceur of what he terms 'inspired nonsense', he depicts middle-class suburban life with acid wit in such plays as The Norman Conquests *(1975).*

1 The only thing for old age is a brave face, a good tailor and comfortable shoes.

Reg, in *Table Manners,* act 2, sc. 1, first of the trilogy *The Norman Conquests* (1975)

2 Where's the romance gone? Destroyed by cynics and liberationalists. . . . Forget the flowers, the chocolates, the soft word – rather woo her with a self-defence manual in one hand and a family planning leaflet in the other.

Norman, in *Round and Round the Garden,* act 1, sc. 1, third of the trilogy *The Norman Conquests* (1975)

3 This place, you tell them you're interested in the arts, you get messages of sympathy.

Dafydd, in *A Chorus of Disapproval,* act 2 (1986)

(Sir) A. J. Ayer (1910–89)

BRITISH PHILOSOPHER

Alfred Jules Ayer. His first book Language, Truth and Logic *(1936), which expounded the theory of logical positivism as associated with the Vienna Circle, was iconoclastic and influential. He was Wykeham Professor of Logic at Oxford (1959–78).*

1 The traditional disputes of philosophers are, for the most part, as unwarranted as they are unfruitful.

Language, Truth and Logic, ch. 1 (1936). Opening sentence of book.

2 No moral system can rest solely on authority.

Humanist Outlook, Introduction (1968). In a later essay, Ayer wrote, 'To say that authority, whether secular or religious, supplies no ground for morality is not to deny the obvious fact that it supplies a sanction.' ('The Meaning of Life', 1990)

3 There never comes a point where a theory can be said to be true. The most that one can claim for any theory is that it has shared the successes of all its rivals and that it has passed at least one test which they have failed.

Philosophy in the Twentieth Century, ch. 4 (1982)

Dan Aykroyd (b. 1950)

CANADIAN ACTOR, DIRECTOR AND WRITER

Born Daniel Agraluscarsacra. He developed his writing and performing skills on the TV show Saturday Night Live *before co-starring in* The Blues Brothers *(1980) and the* Ghostbusters *films (1984, 1989 and 1998).*

1 They're not going to catch us. We're on a mission from God.

Elwood (Dan Aykroyd), in *The Blues Brothers* (film, 1980, screenplay by John Landis and Dan Aykroyd, directed by John Landis)

Pam Ayres (b. 1947)

BRITISH WRITER OF HUMOROUS VERSE

Composer of comic verse since the 1970s, she also writes books for children and performs a one-woman show.

1 *I'm glad tomorrow's Thursday,*
'Cause with a bit of luck,
As far as I remember,
That's the day they pass the buck.

'The Bunny Poem', publ. in *Some of Me Poetry* (1976)

2 *Oh, I wish I'd looked after me teeth,*
And spotted the perils beneath,
All the toffees I chewed,
And the sweet sticky food,
Oh, I wish I'd looked after me teeth.

'Oh, I wish I'd looked after me teeth', publ. ibid.

3 *I see the Time and Motion clock,*
Is sayin' nearly noon,
I 'spec me squirt of water,
Will come flyin' at me soon,
And then me spray of pellets,
Will nearly break me leg,
And I'll bite the wire nettin'
And lay one more bloody egg.

'The Battery Hen', publ. ibid.

4 *Medicinal discovery,*
It moves in mighty leaps,
It leapt straight past the common cold
And gave it us for keeps.

'Oh no, I got a cold', publ. ibid.

Lauren Bacall (b. 1924)

US ACTRESS

Billed as 'slinky, sultry and sensational', she co-starred with her husband HUMPHREY BOGART *in a succession of hit films including* To Have and Have Not *(1944)*, The Big Sleep *(1946) and* Key Largo *(1948)*.

1 **Anybody got a match?**

Marie Browning (Lauren Bacall), in *To Have and Have Not* (film, 1944, screenplay by Jules Furthman and William Faulkner, based on Ernest Hemingway's 1937 novel of the same name, produced and directed by Howard Hawks). Lauren Bacall's screen-debut line, in a film best remembered for the on- and offscreen romance between Bogart and Bacall which resulted in marriage the following year.

2 **You know you don't have to act with me, Steve. You don't have to say anything, and you don't have to do anything. Not a thing. Oh, maybe just whistle. You know how to whistle, don't you, Steve? You just put your lips together, and blow.**

Ibid. Spoken to Harry Morgan (Humphrey Bogart).

3 **I think your whole life shows in your face and you should be proud of that.**

Daily Telegraph 2 March 1988

Gaston Bachelard (1884–1962)

FRENCH SCIENTIST, PHILOSOPHER AND LITERARY THEORIST

He belonged to the 'criticism of science' school, believing that reverie and imagination were as important as observation and analysis for the understanding of reality. Major works include The Psychoanalysis of Fire *(1938) and* The Right to Dream *(1970)*.

1 **Man is a creation of desire, not a creation of need.**

The Psychoanalysis of Fire, ch. 2, 'Fire and Reverie' (1938)

2 **Reverie is not a mind vacuum. It is rather the gift of an hour which knows the plenitude of the soul.**

The Poetics of Reverie, ch. 2, sect. 3 (1960)

3 **The words of the world want to make sentences.**

Ibid., ch. 5, sect. 4

Joan Baez (b. 1941)

US SINGER

Prominent in the American folk revival of the early 1960s, she was also associated with the protest movement, performing frequently at rallies and festivals. Her albums include Any Day Now *(1968) and* Diamonds and Rust *(1975)*.

1 **To sing is to love and to affirm, to fly and soar, to coast into the hearts of the people who listen, to tell them that life is to live,**

that love is there, that nothing is a promise, but that beauty exists, and must be hunted for and found.
Daybreak, 'Singing' (1970)

2 The only thing that's been a worse flop than the organization of nonviolence has been the organization of violence.
Ibid., 'What Would You Do If?'

3 Instead of getting hard on ourselves and trying to compete, women should try and give their best qualities to men – bring them softness, teach them how to cry.
Quoted in the *Los Angeles Times* 26 May 1974

4 I've never had a humble opinion in my life. If you're going to have one, why bother to be humble about it?
International Herald Tribune 2 December 1992

Enid Bagnold (1889–1981)
BRITISH NOVELIST AND PLAYWRIGHT
She adapted several of her own novels as plays, the best-known of which, the horse-racing tale National Velvet *(1935), was also filmed in 1944. Her last play,* The Chalk Garden *(1953), was her most successful on both sides of the Atlantic.*

1 Judges don't age. Time decorates them.
Judge, in *The Chalk Garden*, act 2 (1953)

2 The theatre is a gross art, built in sweeps and over-emphasis. Compromise is its second name.
Autobiography, ch. 3 (1969)

3 Sex – the great inequality, the great miscalculator, the great Irritator.
Ibid., ch. 6

David Bailey (b. 1938)
BRITISH PHOTOGRAPHER
The 'personification of the photographer as pop hero', in the words of GEORGE MELLY, *he specialized in fashion pictures, making the model Jean Shrimpton an icon of the time. His collection* Goodbye Baby and Amen *(1969) was a bittersweet farewell to the 1960s.*

1 All that Swinging Sixties nonsense, we all thought it was passé at the time.
Interview in *The Face* December 1984

2 It takes a lot of imagination to be a good photographer. You need less imagination to be a painter, because you can invent things. But in photography everything is so ordinary; it takes a lot of looking before you learn to see the ordinary.
Ibid.

3 I never cared for fashion much, amusing little seams and witty little pleats: it was the girls I liked.
Independent 5 November 1990

(Dame) Beryl Bainbridge (b. 1934)
BRITISH AUTHOR
She has reproduced the milieu of her childhood in post-war Liverpool in her richly ironic comedies, which she calls 'horror stories told like everyday gossip', for example The Dressmaker *(1973, filmed 1979) and* An Awfully Big Adventure *(1989, filmed 1995). She is the author most often shortlisted for the Booker Prize without having won it.*

1 And life was war in a more subtle form, that lasted for ever, and only discipline and careful entrenchment would see you through until your own great Armistice Day.
Lionel, in *Another Part of the Wood*, ch. 5 (1968)

2 Emotions weren't like washing. There was no call to peg them out for all the world to view.
Uncle Vernon, in *An Awfully Big Adventure*, ch. 1 (1989)

3 It never ceases to puzzle me that, while men and women's bodies fit jigsaw tight in an altogether miraculous way their minds remain wretchedly unaligned.
Evans, in *The Birthday Boys*, 'Petty Officer (Taff) Evans, June 1910' (1991)

4 There is nothing more guaranteed to reduce a man to the essentials than to live beneath the sky.
Master Georgie, plate 3, 'August 1854: Tug-of-war Beside the Sweet Waters of Europe' (1998)

5 When passion is mutual, there is always the danger of the fire burning to ashes.
Ibid., plate 4, 'August 1854: Concert Party at Varna'

6 Women are programmed to love completely, and men are programmed to spread it around. We are fools to think it's any different.
Sunday Times 1 November 1998

7 The older one becomes the quicker the present fades into sepia and the past looms up in glorious technicolour.
Quoted in the *Observer* 27 December 1998

8 You've got to learn to speak properly. You don't take people seriously who speak badly.
Quoted in the *Sunday Times* 7 March 1999. Bainbridge renounced her own Liverpool accent.

James Baker (b. 1930)
US POLITICIAN
A shrewd political manager for the Republican Party, he was REAGAN's *Chief of Staff (1981–5) and successfully oversaw* GEORGE BUSH's *presidential campaign. He was appointed Secretary of State in 1989 and in 1992 again served as White House Chief of Staff.*

1 Who could not be moved by the sight of

that poor, demoralized rabble, outwitted, outflanked, outmanoeuvred by the US military? Yet, given time, I think the press will bounce back.

Quoted in the *Guardian* 26 March 1991. Referring to the media pack during the Gulf War.

Kenneth Baker (b. 1934)

BRITISH POLITICIAN

Elected Conservative MP in 1968, he rose to become Secretary of State for the Environment (1985–6) and Education (1986–9) during the THATCHER *government. He was Chairman of the Conservative Party (1989–90) and, under* JOHN MAJOR, *Home Secretary (1990–92).*

1 Socialists make the mistake of confusing individual worth with success. They believe you cannot allow people to succeed in case those who fail feel worthless.

Quoted in the *Observer* 13 July 1986

2 He has conferred on the practice of vacillation the aura of statesmanship.

Of SDP leader Dr David Owen, in the *Daily Telegraph* 11 October 1989

Nicholson Baker (b. 1957)

US AUTHOR

He said of his books, 'I got rid of the plot', and his off-beat fiction, notably The Mezzanine *(1988) and* Room Temperature *(1990), typically eschews action, dialogue and character in favour of detailed observation.*

1 Shoes are the first adult machines we are given to master.

The Mezzanine, ch. 2 (1988)

2 In my case, adulthood itself was not an advance, although it was a useful waymark.

Ibid., ch. 3

3 Footnotes are the finer-suckered surfaces that allow tentacular paragraphs to hold fast to the wider reality of the library.

Ibid., ch. 14, footnote

4 When the excessively shy force themselves to be forward, they are frequently surprisingly unsubtle and overdirect and even rude: they have entered an extreme region beyond their normal personality, an area of social crime where gradations don't count. Unavailable to them are the instincts and taboos that booming extroverts, who know the territory of self-advancement far better, can rely on.

U and I: A True Story, ch. 9 (1991)

Russell Baker (b. 1925)

US JOURNALIST

Known for his 'Observer' column in The New York Times, *he has satirized politicians, bureaucrats and the excesses of America. Time summar-*

ized him as 'funny, but full of the pain and absurdity of the age'.

1 Inanimate objects are classified scientifically into three major categories – those that don't work, those that break down and those that get lost.

The New York Times 18 June 1968

2 So there he is at last. Man on the moon. The poor magnificent bungler! He can't even get to the office without undergoing the agonies of the damned, but give him a little metal, a few chemicals, some wire and twenty or thirty billion dollars and, vroom! there he is, up on a rock a quarter of a million miles up in the sky.

The New York Times 21 July 1969. On the first manned moon landing.

Jim Bakker (b. 1940)

US EVANGELIST

One-time president of the Inspirational and Praise the Lord television networks, he resigned in 1987 due to sexual scandal and in 1989 was sentenced to five years' imprisonment for fraud.

1 I started out by believing God for a newer car than the one I was driving. I started out believing God for a nicer apartment than I had. Then I moved up.

Quoted in the *New Yorker* 23 April 1990. Bakker was explaining the large sums of money needed to finance his luxury religious centre, Heritage USA. As he said, 'Why should I apologize because God throws in crystal chandeliers, mahogany floors, and the best construction in the world?'

James Baldwin (1924–87)

US AUTHOR

Brought up in poverty in Harlem where most of his works are set, he later lived in Paris. His autobiographical first novel, Go Tell It on the Mountain *(1953), and others such as* Giovanni's Room *(1956) and* Another Country *(1962) were bleak depictions of sexual and racial relationships.*

1 The American ideal, after all, is that everyone should be as much alike as possible.

'The Harlem Ghetto', first publ. in *Commentary* February 1948, repr. in *Notes of a Native Son*, pt 2 (1955)

2 It is only in his music, which Americans are able to admire because a protective sentimentality limits their understanding of it, that the Negro in America has been able to tell his story.

'Many Thousands Gone', first publ. in *Partisan Review* November/December 1951, repr. ibid., pt 1

3 Any writer, I suppose, feels that the world into which he was born is nothing less

than a conspiracy against the cultivation of his talent.

Notes of a Native Son, 'Autobiographical Notes' (1955)

4 Children have never been very good at listening to their elders, but they have never failed to imitate them. They must, they have no other models.

'Fifth Avenue, Uptown: A Letter from Harlem', first publ. in *Esquire* July 1960, repr. in *Nobody Knows My Name* (1961)

5 American history is longer, larger, more various, more beautiful, and more terrible than anything anyone has ever said about it.

'A Talk to Teachers', 16 October 1963, publ. in *The Price of the Ticket* (1985)

6 It comes as a great shock around the age of five, six or seven to discover that the flag to which you have pledged allegiance, along with everybody else, has not pledged allegiance to you. It comes as a great shock to see Gary Cooper killing off the Indians and, although you are rooting for Gary Cooper, that the Indians are you.

Speech to Cambridge Union, Cambridge University, 17 February 1965, quoted in *The New York Times* 7 March 1965

7 If they take you in the morning, they will be coming for us that night.

'Open Letter to my Sister, Angela Davis', publ. in the *New York Review of Books* 7 January 1971

8 You know, it's not the world that was my oppressor, because what the world does to you, if the world does it to you long enough and effectively enough, you begin to do to yourself.

In conversation with NIKKI GIOVANNI, London, 4 November 1971, publ. in *A Dialogue* (1973)

9 He may be a very nice man. But I haven't got the time to figure that out. All I know is, he's got a uniform and a gun and I have to relate to him that way. That's the only way to relate to him because one of us may have to die.

Of the police, ibid.

10 Whereas England may have been doomed to civilize the world, no power under heaven can civilize England.

The Devil Finds Work, ch. 2 (1976)

11 The condition that is now called gay was then called queer. The operative word was *faggot* and, later, *pussy*, but those epithets really had nothing to do with the question of sexual preference: You were being told simply that you had no balls.

'Freaks and the American Ideal of Manhood', first publ. in *Playboy* January 1985, repr. in *The Price of the Ticket*, 'Here Be Dragons' (1985)

Stanley Baldwin (1867–1947)

BRITISH POLITICIAN AND PRIME MINISTER
First Earl of Bewdley. Serving three times as Conservative Prime Minister (1923–4, 1924–9 and 1935–7), he opposed the rearmament of Britain against the rise of HITLER, *which precipitated his resignation. Lord Beaverbrook called him a 'well-meaning man of indifferent judgement'. See also* WINSTON CHURCHILL 42 *and* RUDYARD KIPLING 1.

1 A platitude is simply a truth repeated until people get tired of hearing it.

Speech to House of Commons, 29 May 1924, quoted in the *Observer* 1 June 1924

2 I hate elections, but you have got to have them; they are medicine.

Quoted in the *Observer* 11 October 1931

3 I think it is well also for the man in the street to realize that there is no power on earth that can protect him from being bombed. Whatever people may tell him, the bomber will always get through. The only defence is in offence, which means that you have to kill more women and children more quickly than the enemy if you want to save yourselves.

Speech to House of Commons, 10 November 1932, publ. in *The Penguin Book of Twentieth-Century Speeches* (ed. Brian MacArthur, 1999). Baldwin's ambiguous speech strengthened the public mood against rearmament.

4 Let us never forget this – since the day of the air the old frontiers are gone. When you think of the defence of England you no longer think of the chalk cliffs of Dover; you think of the Rhine. That is where our frontier lies.

Speech to House of Commons, 30 July 1934, publ. in *Hansard*

5 Do not run up your nose dead against the Pope or the NUM!

Quoted in *The Art of Memory*, 'Iain Macleod' (1982) by Lord [R.A.B.] Butler

A. J. Balfour (1848–1930)

BRITISH POLITICIAN AND PRIME MINISTER
Arthur James Balfour, first Earl of Balfour. He entered parliament as a Conservative MP in 1874. While Prime Minister (1902–5) he established the Committee of Imperial Defence and initiated the entente cordiale with France. As Foreign Secretary (1916–19) he was responsible for the Balfour Declaration (see below).

1 His Majesty's Government view with favour the establishment in Palestine of a national home for the Jewish people, and will use their best endeavours to facilitate the achievement of this object, it being clearly understood that nothing shall be done which may prejudice the civil and religious rights of existing non-Jewish

communities in Palestine, or the rights and political status enjoyed by Jews in any other country.

Letter to Lord Rothschild, 2 November 1917, publ. in *The Middle East Conflict: Notes and Documents (1915–1967)*. The document, which became known as the 'Balfour Declaration', represented a commitment of British support for a Jewish national home in Palestine, though the original wording suggested by Chaim Weizmann, on behalf of the Political Committee of the Zionist Organization (which Rothschild represented), was that the government should recognize Palestine as 'the national home of the Jewish people'.

2 The General Strike has taught the working classes more in four days than years of talking could have done.

Speech 7 May 1926, quoted in the *Observer* 14 November 1926. Five days after the speech, the Trades Unions Congress was forced to call off the General Strike, which, though bringing the country to a virtual standstill, was unable to prevent volunteers from manning essential services.

3 Biography should be written by an acute enemy.

Quoted in the *Observer* 30 January 1927

Hugo Ball (1886–1927)
GERMAN POET

With RICHARD HUELSENBECK *he was in 1916 the co-founder of Dada in Zurich, where he performed the first 'sound poem' dressed in cardboard tubes and a cape. He later turned to political journalism and gnostic Catholicism.*

1 We should burn all libraries and allow to remain only that which everyone knows by heart. A beautiful age of the legend would then begin.

Journal entry, 9 January 1917, in *Flight out of Time: A Dada Diary* (1927)

2 The symbolic view of things is a consequence of long absorption in images. Is sign language the real language of Paradise?

Journal entry, 8 April 1917, ibid.

J. G. Ballard (b. 1930)
BRITISH AUTHOR

James Graham Ballard. His science fiction typically portrays apocalyptic visions, as in The Drowned World *(1962). Experimental and controversial novels such as* Crash *(1973, filmed 1996) contrast with his more mainstream autobiographical works, notably* Empire of the Sun *(1984, filmed 1988).*

1 A car crash harnesses elements of eroticism, aggression, desire, speed, drama, kinaesthetic factors, the stylizing of motion, consumer goods, status – all these in one

event. I myself see the car crash as a tremendous sexual event really: a liberation of human and machine libido (if there is such a thing).

Interview in *Penthouse* September 1970

2 Everything is becoming science fiction. From the margins of an almost invisible literature has sprung the intact reality of the 20th century.

'Fictions of Every Kind', publ. in *Books and Bookmen* February 1971. Ballard continued: 'Even the worst science fiction is better . . . than the best conventional fiction. The future is a better key to the present than the past.'

3 The car as we know it is on the way out. To a large extent, I deplore its passing, for as a basically old-fashioned machine, it enshrines a basically old-fashioned idea: freedom. In terms of pollution, noise and human life, the price of that freedom may be high, but perhaps the car, by the very muddle and confusion it causes, may be holding back the remorseless spread of the regimented, electronic society.

'The Car, The Future', publ. in *Drive* autumn 1971

4 Science and technology multiply around us. To an increasing extent they dictate the languages in which we speak and think. Either we use those languages, or we remain mute.

Crash, Introduction to French edn (1974)

5 A widespread taste for pornography means that nature is alerting us to some threat of extinction.

Myths of the Near Future, 'News from the Sun' (1982)

6 I would sum up my fear about the future in one word: *boring*. And that's my one fear: that everything has happened; nothing exciting or new or interesting is ever going to happen again . . . the future is just going to be a vast, conforming *suburb of the soul*.

Interview, 30 October 1982, publ. in *Re/Search* no. 8/9 1984

7 'Responsible' TV is far more dangerous than the most mindless entertainment. At its worst, American TV merely trivializes the already trivial, while British TV consistently trivializes the serious.

The Atrocity Exhibition: With Author's Annotations, 'Love and Napalm: Export USA', annotation (1993, original text publ. 1970, rev. 1990)

Whitney Balliet (b. 1926)
US AUTHOR

He was a long-serving jazz critic for the New Yorker *and published collections of pieces on jazz musicians.*

1 The Sound of Surprise.
Title of book on jazz (1959)

2 A critic is a bundle of biases held loosely together by a sense of taste.
Dinosaurs in the Morning, Introductory note (1962)

Lester Bangs (1948–82)
US ROCK JOURNALIST
A gentle yet acerbic critic of the 1970s, he was the first to popularize the term 'heavy metal' and his magazine Creem *became the model for punk-rock and heavy-metal fanzines. From 1976 he contributed to* Village Voice.

1 The ultimate sin of any performer is contempt for the audience.
Village Voice 29 August 1977

2 At its best New Wave/punk represents a fundamental and age-old Utopian dream: that if you give people the license to be as outrageous as they want in absolutely any fashion they can dream up, *they'll be creative about it*, and do something good besides.
New Musical Express 24 December 1977

3 I think that if most guys in America could somehow get their fave-rave poster girl in bed and have total license to do whatever they wanted with this legendary body for one afternoon, at least 75 percent of the guys in the country would elect to beat her up.
Quoted in *Sound Effects: Youth, Leisure and the Politics of Rock*, ch. 10 (1979) by Simon Frith

Tallulah Bankhead (1903–68)
US ACTRESS
Notorious for her extravagant personality, 'more of an act than an actress' in the words of one critic, she appeared in plays, on radio and in films, most famously in HITCHCOCK'*s* Lifeboat, *1944. See* LILLIAN HELLMAN 7.

1 There is less in this than meets the eye.
Quoted in *Shouts and Murmurs*, ch. 4 (1922) by ALEXANDER WOOLLCOTT. Remark to Woollcott, referring to a revival of Maeterlinck's play *Aglavaine and Selysette*.

2 I'm as pure as the driven slush.
Quoted in the *Saturday Evening Post* 12 April 1947

3 Let's not quibble! I'm the foe of moderation, the champion of excess. If I may lift a line from a die-hard whose identity is lost in the shuffle, 'I'd rather be strongly wrong than weakly right.'
Tallulah, ch. 4 (1952)

4 Cocaine habit-forming? Of course not. I ought to know. I've been using it for years.
Ibid. This was, she said, the riposte she used to shock people when taking throat-lozenges: apart from on one occasion, she claimed never to have used cocaine 'except medicinally'. However, LILLIAN HELLMAN, writer of *The Little Foxes* in which Bankhead starred, witnessed her habit – eliciting the actress's stock rejoinder – as described in her *Pentimento* (1973).

5 I've tried several varieties of sex. The conventional position makes me claustrophobic and the others give me a stiff neck or lockjaw.
Quoted in *Miss Tallulah Bankhead* (1972) by Lee Israel

Tony Banks (b. 1945)
BRITISH POLITICIAN
Elected a Labour MP in 1983, he established a reputation as a forthright and lippy left-winger and supporter of animal rights. He was Sports Minister 1997–9.

1 They have elected a foetus as party leader. I bet there's a lot of Tory MPs who wish they hadn't voted against abortion now.
Of WILLIAM HAGUE, at speech at Labour Party Conference, Brighton, 30 September 1997, quoted in the *Daily Telegraph* 2 October 1997

Nancy Banks-Smith
BRITISH COLUMNIST
She is a TV reviewer for the Guardian *of many years standing, known for her quirky critiques and wry digressions.*

1 In my experience, if you have to keep the lavatory door shut by extending your left leg, it's modern architecture.
Guardian 20 February 1979

[Imamu] Amiri Baraka (b. 1934)
US POET AND PLAYWRIGHT
Known as LeRoi Jones until 1967, when he converted to Islam. A confrontational writer of verse collections including The Dead Lecturer (1964) *and plays such as* The Dutchman (1964), *he has been active in black arts and community organizations from the late 1960s.*

1 *Lately, I've become accustomed to the way*
The ground opens up and envelops me
Each time I go out to walk the dog.
'Preface to a Twenty Volume Suicide Note', publ. in *Preface to a Twenty Volume Suicide Note* (1961). Opening lines.

2 A man is either free or he is not. There cannot be any apprenticeship for freedom.
'Tokenism', publ. in *Kulchur* spring 1962

3 You can't steal nothing from a white man, he's already stole it, he owes you anything you want, even his life. All the stores will open if you will say the magic words. The

magic words are: Up against the wall
motherfucker this is a stick-up!

'Black People!', publ. in *Evergreen Review* sum-
mer 1967, repr. in *Black Magic* (1969). The
poem/manifesto was read out by the judge at
Baraka's trial for illegal arms possesion in
Newark, July 1967, with the obscenities omitted.
Baraka was involved with the anarchist group
Up Against the Wall Motherfucker.

4 When I die, the consciousness I carry I will
to black people. May they pick me apart
and take the useful parts, the sweet meat of
my feelings. And leave the bitter bullshit
rotten white parts alone.

'leroy', publ. in *Black Magic* (1969)

5 James Brown and Frank Sinatra are two
different quantities in the universe. They
represent two different experiences of the
world.

Interview in *The Americans*, 'Is Democracy a
White Man's Word?' (1970) by David Frost

Lynn Barber (b. 1944)
BRITISH JOURNALIST
*A feature writer and celebrity interviewer for maga-
zines and the Sunday press, she has also published
handbooks on sex.*

1 The best interviews – like the best biographies – should sing the strangeness and
variety of the human race.

Independent on Sunday 24 February 1991

Brigitte Bardot (b. 1934)
FRENCH ACTRESS
*Originally Camille Javal. The archetypal 'sex kit-
ten', she was already a movie starlet when, aged
eighteen, she married ROGER VADIM who directed
her in And God Created Woman (1956). As the
publicity of the time declared, 'God Created
Woman, but the devil made Bardot.' She subsequently starred in a succession of light sex comedies in the 1960s. See ROGER VADIM 1.*

1 I leave before being left. I decide.

Quoted in *Newsweek* 5 March 1973

2 I really am a cat transformed into a
woman.

Quoted in *Bebe: The Films of Brigitte Bardot*,
'The BBeginning' (1975) by Tony Crawley

3 If I could do anything about the way
people behave towards each other, I would,
but since I can't I'll stick to the animals.

Quoted in *Bardot*, ch. 15 (1984) by Glenys
Roberts

4 I am leaving the town to the invaders:
increasingly numerous, mediocre, dirty,
badly behaved, shameless tourists.

Quoted in the *International Herald Tribune*
10 August 1989. On moving out of her long-time
home in Saint Tropez.

Daniel Barenboim (b. 1942)
ARGENTINIAN-BORN ISRAELI PIANIST AND
CONDUCTOR
*He gained his reputation with the English
Chamber Orchestra from 1964, going on to be Con-
ductor of the New York Philharmonic Orchestra in
1970 and Director of the Chicago Symphony
Orchestra in 1991 and of the Berlin Staatsoper in
1992. He was married to the cellist Jacqueline du
Pré.*

1 Every great work of art has two faces, one
toward its own time and one toward the
future, toward eternity.

International Herald Tribune 20 January 1989

Pat Barker (b. 1943)
BRITISH NOVELIST
*She gained her reputation with spare and unsenti-
mental novels of working-class women in industrial England, such as Blow Your House Down
(1984), but achieved greater success with the First
World War trilogy Regeneration (1991), The Eye
in the Door (1993) and The Ghost Road (1995).*

1 Poor Siegfried's rebellion hadn't counted
for much, though he reminded himself
that he couldn't know that. It had been a
completely honest action, and such actions
are seeds carried on the wind. Nobody can
tell where, or in what circumstances, they
will bear fruit.

W. H. R. Rivers, in *Regeneration*, ch. 23 (1991).
The army psychologist reflects on SIEGFRIED
SASSOON, having discharged him from Craig-
lockhart War Hospital from which he was to
return to the front in the First World War.

2 Even the living were only ghosts in the
making.

Lieutenant Billy Prior, in *The Ghost Road*, pt 1,
ch. 3 (1995)

3 First-person narrators can't die, so long as
we keep telling the story of our own lives
we're safe. Ha bloody fucking Ha.

Lieutenant Billy Prior, ibid., pt 2, ch. 7

Ronnie Barker (b. 1929)
BRITISH COMIC ACTOR
*A hugely popular but intensely private figure in
British comedy, he is chiefly known for his TV
appearances in The Two Ronnies (1971–86), with
Ronnie Corbett, and Porridge (1974–7).*

1 The marvellous thing about a joke with a
double meaning is that it can only mean
one thing.

Sauce, 'Daddie's Sauce' (1977)

Djuna Barnes (1892–1982)
US AUTHOR, POET AND COLUMNIST
*An established figure of literary Paris in the 1920s
and '30s, she published influential works of modernist fiction including Ladies Almanack (1928), a*

satire of literary lesbians, and her masterpiece,
Nightwood *(1936). She was admired by* T.S.
ELIOT, *who jibed, 'She's always pissing on the
parade.'*

1 After all, it is not where one washes one's
neck that counts but where one moistens
one's throat.
'Greenwich Village as It Is', publ. in *Pearson's
Magazine* October 1916, repr. in *Djuna Barnes's
New York* (1989)

2 The heart of the jealous knows the best
and most satisfying love, that of the other's
bed, where the rival perfects the lover's
imperfections.
Doctor, in *Nightwood*, ch. 5 (1936)

Julian Barnes (b. 1946)

BRITISH NOVELIST
*He worked as a journalist and lexicographer before
winning acclaim for Metroland (1981), his first
novel, and Flaubert's Parrot (1984), a tribute to
his acknowledged influence, Flaubert. Later works
include A History of the World in 10½ Chapters
(1989) and Cross Channel (1996), a collection of
short stories.*

1 Why does the writing make us chase the
writer? Why can't we leave well alone?
Why aren't the books enough?
The narrator (Geoffrey Braithwaite), in *Flaubert's Parrot*, ch. 1 (1984)

2 I don't care much for coincidences. There's
something spooky about them: you sense
momentarily what it must be like to live in
an ordered, God-run universe, with Himself looking over your shoulder and helpfully dragging coarse hints about a cosmic
plan.
Ibid., ch. 5. The narrator adds, 'One way of legitimising coincidences, of course, is to call them
ironies. That's what smart people do.'

3 Do not imagine that Art is something
which is designed to give gentle uplift and
self-confidence. Art is not a *brassière*. At
least not in the English sense. But do not
forget that *brassière* is the French for lifejacket.
Ibid., ch. 10

4 The greatest patriotism is to tell your
country when it is behaving dishonourably, foolishly, viciously.
Ibid.

5 The writer must be universal in sympathy
and an outcast by nature: only then can he
see clearly.
Ibid.

6 Books are where things are explained to
you; life is where things aren't. I'm not surprised some people prefer books. Books
make sense of life. The only problem is
that the lives they make sense of are other
people's lives, never your own.
Ibid., ch. 13

7 We must still believe that objective truth is
obtainable; or we must believe that it is 99
per cent obtainable; or if we can't believe
this we must believe that 43 per cent objective truth is better that 41 per cent. We
must do so because if we don't we're lost,
we fall into beguiling relativity, we value
one liar's version as much as another liar's.
A History of the World in 10½ Chapters, 'Parenthesis' (1989)

8 Imagine the organ of recollection as a leftluggage clerk at some thrumming terminus
who looks after your picayune possessions
until you next need them. Now consider
what you're asking him to take care of.
And for so little money! And for so little
thanks! It's no wonder the counter isn't
manned half the time.
Oliver, in *Talking It Over*, ch. 1 (1991)

9 It's a sort of primitive law of survival –
find someone worse off than yourself and
beside them you will blossom.
Stuart, ibid., ch. 2

10 As you go on living with someone, you
slowly lose the power to make them happy,
while your capacity to hurt them remains
undiminished. And vice versa, of course.
Mme Wyatt, ibid., ch. 15

11 Love is only what people agree exists, what
they agree to put a notional value on. Nowadays it's prized as a commodity by almost
everyone. Only not by me. If you ask me, I
think love is trading artificially high. One
of these days the bottom is going to fall
out of love.
Stuart, ibid., ch. 16

12 We have moved into an era when 'character' is a misleading concept. Character has
been replaced by ego, and the exercise of
authority as a reflection of character has
been replaced by the psychopathic retention of power by all possible means and in
mockery of all implausibilities.
Solinsky, in *Porcupine* (1992)

13 If you're an old geezer in his rocker on the
porch, you don't play basketball with kids.
Old geezers don't jump. You sit and make
a virtue of what you have. And what you
also do is this; you make the kids think
that anyone, *anyone* can jump, but it takes
a wise old buzzard to know how to sit
there and rock.
Jerry, in *England, England*, pt 1, 'Dream a Little'
(1998)

14 Women have traditionally accommodated
themselves to men's needs. Men's needs

being, of course, double. You put us on a pedestal in order to look up our skirts.
Martha, ibid., 'Others May Like'

15 I only said the English weren't famous for sex, that's all. Like the Boat Race, in out, in out, then everyone collapsed over their oars.
Martha, ibid., 'Do You Think?'

Ann Barr (b. 1929) and
Peter York (b. 1950)
BRITISH JOURNALISTS
Ann Barr was features editor on Harper's & Queen *and women's editor of the* Observer. *She co-authored the 1980s best-seller* The Official Sloane Ranger Handbook *(1982) with* PETER YORK.

1 Sloane minds are undeveloped but intuitive, wild places where they go out to bag an idea or see how things are going. They do *not* like theory, unless it produces a joke.
The Official Sloane Ranger Handbook, 'Sloane Language' (1982). See also PETER YORK 1.

Roseanne Barr (b. 1952)
US STAND-UP COMEDIENNE AND ACTRESS
Originally an actress, she is famous for her outspoken personality and appearance in the ABC television series Roseanne *(1988–97) and* The Roseanne Talk Show *(1998–2000).*

1 I hate the word housewife; I don't like the word home-maker either. I want to be called – domestic goddess.
Roseanne (TV sitcom), quoted in *Funny Business*, 'Roseanne Barr' (1992) by David Housham and John Frank-Keyes

2 You may marry the man of your dreams, ladies, but 14 years later you're married to a couch that burps.
Ibid.

(Sir) J. M. Barrie (1860–1937)
BRITISH PLAYWRIGHT AND NOVELIST
James Matthew Barrie. Described by MRS PATRICK CAMPBELL *as 'a little child whom the Gods have whispered to', he frequently returned to the themes of childhood and disenchantment with the adult world. He achieved success with his plays* Quality Street *(1901) and* The Admirable Crighton *(1902), but is most associated with* Peter Pan *(1904).*

1 Some one said that God gave us memory so that we might have roses in December.
Rectorial address at St Andrew's University, 3 May 1922, publ. in *Courage* (1922)

2 Never ascribe to an opponent motives meaner than your own.
Ibid.

3 We are all failures – at least, all the best of us are.
Ibid.

4 You must have been warned against letting the golden hours slip by. Yes, but some of them are golden only because we let them slip.
Ibid.

Ethel Barrymore (1897–1959)
US ACTRESS
As the sister of actors John and Lionel Barrymore she was one of the 'Fabulous Barrymores'. Her stage roles in The Second Mrs Tanqueray *(1924) and* The Corn is Green *(1942) helped to establish her as 'the first lady of the American theater'.*

1 For an actress to be a success, she must have the face of Venus, the brains of a Minerva, the grace of Terpsichore, the memory of a Macaulay, the figure of Juno, and the hide of a rhinoceros.
Quoted in *The Theatre in the Fifties* (1953) by GEORGE JEAN NATHAN

2 I never let them [audiences] cough. They wouldn't dare.
New York Post 7 June 1956

Don Barthelme (1931–89)
US AUTHOR
He called cutting up and pasting together pictures his 'secret vice', and this collage effect is evident in his minimalist short stories, such as Come Back, Dr Caligari *(1964) and* City Life *(1970), and his novels, for example* Snow White *(1967).*

1 The distinction between children and adults, while probably useful for some purposes, is at bottom a specious one, I feel. There are only individual egos, crazy for love.
The narrator (Joseph), in 'Me And Miss Mandible', first publ. in *Come Back, Dr Caligari* (1964)

Roland Barthes (1915–80)
FRENCH SEMIOLOGIST
He was one of France's leading post-war critics whose writings on literature and semiotics demystified the language of mass culture and helped to establish structuralism and the New Criticism. Mythologies *(1957),* Death of the Author *(1968) and* S/Z *(1970) number among his most influential publications.*

1 What I claim is to live to the full the contradiction of my time, which may well make sarcasm the condition of truth.
Mythologies, Preface (1957, transl. 1972)

2 What the public wants is the image of passion, not passion itself.
Ibid., 'The World of Wrestling'

3 The face of Garbo is an Idea, that of Hepburn an Event.
Ibid., 'The Face of Garbo'

4 Through the mythology of Einstein, the world blissfully regained the image of knowledge reduced to a formula.
Ibid., 'The Brain of Einstein'

5 I think that cars today are almost the exact equivalent of the great Gothic cathedrals: I mean the supreme creation of an era, conceived with passion by unknown artists, and consumed in image if not in usage by a whole population which appropriates them as a purely magical object.
Ibid., 'The New Citroën'

6 Myth is neither a lie nor a confession: it is an inflexion.
Ibid., 'Myth Today: Reading and Deciphering Myth'

7 Once the Author is removed, the claim to decipher a text becomes quite futile. To give a text an Author is to impose a limit on that text, to furnish it with a final signifier, to close the writing.
Image–Music–Text, 'The Death of the Author' (1966, transl. 1978)

8 There is only one way left to escape the alienation of present day society: to retreat ahead of it.
The Pleasure of the Text, 'Modern' (1975)

9 The bastard form of mass culture is humiliated repetition . . . always new books, new programmes, new films, news items, but always the same meaning.
Ibid.

10 Language is legislation, speech is its code. We do not see the power which is in speech because we forget that all speech is a classification, and that all classifications are oppressive.
Inaugural lecture, Collège de France, 7 January 1977, publ. in Leçon (1978), repr. in Barthes: Selected Writings (ed. Susan Sontag, 1982)

11 Literature is without proofs. By which it must be understood that it cannot prove, not only what it says, but even that it is worth the trouble of saying it.
'Deliberation', first publ. in Tel Quel winter 1979, repr. ibid.

Bernard Baruch (1870–1965)
US FINANCIER
He was instrumental in drafting the economic sections of the Treaty of Versailles (1919) and was an adviser to FRANKLIN D. ROOSEVELT and WINSTON CHURCHILL during the Second World War. He later served on the UN Atomic Energy Commission (1946–51).

1 Let us not be deceived – we are today in the midst of a cold war. Our enemies are to be found abroad and at home.
Speech to South Carolina Legislature, 16 April 1947, quoted in The New York Times 17 April 1947. A year later Baruch told the Senate War Investigating Committee, 'We are in the midst of a cold war which is getting warmer.' Baruch claimed the expression had been suggested to him by his speechwriter, the former editor of the New York World, Herbert Bayard Swope.

2 To me, old age is always fifteen years older than I am.
Quoted in the Observer 21 August 1955

3 A political leader must keep looking over his shoulder all the time to see if the boys are still there. If they aren't still there, he's no longer a political leader.
Quoted in obituary, The New York Times 21 June 1965

Jacques Barzun (b. 1907)
US ACADEMIC AND AUTHOR
Influential in the development of higher education in America, he advocated a broad approach rather than specialization. His publications include Pleasures of Music (1951), The House of the Intellect (1959), and The Use and Abuse of Art (1974).

1 Whoever wants to know the heart and mind of America had better learn baseball, the rules and realities of the game.
God's Country and Mine, ch. 8 (1954)

2 Teaching is not a lost art, but the regard for it is a lost tradition.
Newsweek 5 December 1955

Augusto Roa Bastos (b. 1917)
PARAGUAYAN NOVELIST
From 1947–70 he lived in exile in Buenos Aires. His works, including the novel Son of Man (1960) and his masterpiece I the Supreme (1974), deal largely with Paraguayan history.

1 The things that have come into being change continually. The man with a good memory remembers nothing because he forgets nothing.
I the Supreme (1974, transl. 1986)

2 Anyone who attempts to relate his life loses himself in the immediate. One can only speak of another.
Ibid.

Georges Bataille (1897–1962)
FRENCH NOVELIST AND CRITIC
He founded the influential journal Critique in 1946 and remained its editor until his death. His themes are atheism, mysticism, and freedom through excess rather than self-denial. Publications include The Birth of Art (1955) and Eroticism (1957). He wrote in English under the name of Lord Auch.

1 Intellectual despair results in neither weakness nor dreams, but in violence. . . . It is only a matter of knowing how to give vent to one's rage; whether one only wants to wander like madmen around prisons, or whether one wants to overturn them.

'The "Lugubrious Game" ', first publ. in *Documents* December 1929, repr. in *Visions of Excess: Selected Writings 1927–1939* (ed. Allan Stoekl, 1985)

2 Eroticism is assenting to life even in death.

Eroticism, Introduction (1957)

3 Beauty is desired in order that it may be befouled; not for its own sake, but for the joy brought by the certainty of profaning it.

Ibid., ch. 13

4 I believe that truth has only one face: that of a violent contradiction.

The Deadman, Preface (1967)

H. E. Bates (1905–74)

BRITISH AUTHOR

Herbert Ernest Bates. A master of the short story and a prolific novelist, he wrote of rural England, as in The Darling Buds of May *(1958, televised 1980s).*

1 Perfick!

Pop Larkin, in *A Breath of French Air*, ch. 1 (1959)

Kathy Bates (b. 1948)

US ACTRESS

On the stage she made an impact with Frankie and Johnny in the Clair de Lune *(1987), while her films have included* Misery *(1990) and* Diabolique *(1996).*

1 I'm your number-one fan.

Annie Wilkes (Kathy Bates), in *Misery* (film, 1990, screenplay by William Goldman based on 1987 short story by Stephen King, directed and co-produced by Rob Reiner)

Jean Baudrillard (b. 1929)

FRENCH SEMIOLOGIST

His postmodernist theories on the consumer society, media, art and metaphysics are laid out in In the Shadow of Silent Majorities *(1978) and* Simulations and Simulacra *(1981) among other titles. The* New York Times *called him 'the sharp-shooting Lone Ranger of the post-Marxist left'.*

1 Driving is a spectacular form of amnesia. Everything is to be discovered, everything to be obliterated.

America, 'Vanishing Point' (1986)

2 What you have to do is enter the fiction of America, enter America as fiction. It is, indeed, on this fictive basis that it dominates the world.

Ibid., 'Astral America'

3 It is always the same: once you are liberated, you are forced to ask who you are.

Ibid.

4 The skylines lit up at dead of night, the air-conditioning systems cooling empty hotels in the desert and artificial light in the middle of the day all have something both demented and admirable about them. The mindless luxury of a rich civilization, and yet of a civilization perhaps as scared to see the lights go out as was the hunter in his primitive night.

Ibid. Referring to the US, which Baudrillard called 'deep down . . . the *only remaining primitive society*'.

5 The Yuppies are not defectors from revolt, they are a new race, assured, amnestied, exculpated, moving with ease in the world of performance, mentally indifferent to any objective other than that of change and advertising.

Ibid., 'The End of US Power?'

6 With the truth, you need to get rid of it as soon as possible and pass it on to someone else. As with illness, this is the only way to be cured of it. The person who keeps truth in his hands has lost.

Cool Memories, ch. 1 (1987)

7 The sad thing about artificial intelligence is that it lacks artifice and therefore intelligence.

Ibid., ch. 4

8 Information can tell us everything. It has all the answers. But they are answers to questions we have not asked, and which doubtless don't even arise.

Ibid., ch. 5

Vicki Baum (1888–1960)

AUSTRIAN-BORN US NOVELIST

Originally Vicki Hedvig. Her principal achievement was the novel Grand Hotel *(1930), whose success as a play in New York (1931) allowed her to emigrate to America. It was later filmed with* GRETA GARBO *in the main role.*

1 The events that happen to people in a big hotel do not constitute entire human destinies, complete and rounded off. They are fragments merely, scraps, pieces. The people behind its doors may signify much or little. They may be rising or falling in the scale of life. Prosperity and disaster may be parted by no more than the thickness of a wall. The revolving door twirls around, and what passes between arrival and departure is nothing complete in itself.

Grand Hotel (1930)

2 Marriage always demands the greatest

understanding of the art of insincerity possible between two human beings.
Results of an Accident (1932)

Stephen Bayley (b. 1951)
BRITISH DESIGN CRITIC
*Founder and Chief Executive (1981–90) of the
Design Museum, he quit as Creative Director of
the Millennium Dome in 1999 after political dis-
agreements. He is author of* Sex, Drink and Fast
Cars *(1986), among other titles.*

1 Where *do* architects and designers get their
ideas? The answer, of course, is mainly
from other architects and designers, so is it
mere casuistry to distinguish between tradition and plagiarism?
Commerce and Culture, ch. 3 (1989)

2 Everyone has taste, yet it is more of a
taboo subject than sex or money. The
reason for this is simple: claims about your
attitudes to or achievements in the carnal
and financial arenas can be disputed only
by your lover and your financial advisers,
whereas by making statements about your
taste you expose body and soul to terrible
scrutiny. Taste is a merciless betrayer of
social and cultural attitudes. Thus, while
anybody will tell you as much (and perhaps more than) you want to know about
their triumphs in bed and at the bank, it is
taste that gets people's nerves tingling.
Taste, pt 1, 'Taste: The Story of an Idea' (1991)

3 Viewed holistically, interior design is a trav-
esty of the architectural process and a
frightening condemnation of the credulity,
helplessness and gullibility of the most formidable consumers – the rich.
Ibid., pt 2, 'Interiors: Vacuums of Taste'

4 Alas, in a culture that encourages feeble-
minded political correctness, great monuments and great works of art are not to be
expected.
Independent 17 January 1998. Referring to the
influence of focus groups on the Millennium
Dome project. Two years after resigning as Creative Director of the Dome, he referred to it in
an interview as 'an ocean of vulgarity and
mediocrity . . . a perfect advertisement for New
Labour – philosophically vapid and cack-handed
in execution'.

5 Design is the great adventure of the twentieth century; it's led . . . to the aestheticis-
ation of the everyday object, to the
democratisation of luxury. Today, you, me
and even young Peter Mandelson can buy
a disposable Bic razor for next to nothing
and get a better shave than ever Augustus
Caesar or the Sun King could.
Quoted in the *Guardian* 21 November 1998

André Bazin (1918–58)
FRENCH FILM CRITIC
As a proponent of the auteur *theory of film-
making and co-founder in 1951 of Europe's most
influential film periodical,* Les Cahiers du
Cinéma, *he was called the 'spiritual father of the
New Wave'. His writings were condensed into one
volume in English,* What is Cinema? *(1967).*

1 The cinema gives us a substitute world
which fits our desires.
Quoted in *The New Wave*, ch. 7 (1976) by James
Monaco. The words appear in the closing credits
of JEAN-LUC GODARD's film *Le Mépris* (1963).

BBC (British Broadcasting Corporation)

1 Nation shall speak peace unto nation.
Motto from 1927. Devised by Montague John
Rendall (1862–1950), a schoolmaster and
member of the first BBC Board of Governors, it
was probably inspired by Isaiah 2:4, 'They shall
beat their swords into ploughshares, and their
spears into pruninghooks: nation shall not lift
up sword against nation, neither shall they learn
war any more' (also Micah 4:3, Joel 3:10).

Warren Beatty (b. 1937)
US SCREEN ACTOR AND FILM-MAKER
*Originally Henry Warren Beaty. He had his great-
est successes with* Bonnie and Clyde *(1967) and*
Reds *(1981), both of which he produced and
starred in.*

1 I don't think there's anything to be
admired in lying, cheating or philandering.
But there might be something to be
admired in not burning people at the stake
because they have those weaknesses.
Observer 7 February 1999. Referring to 'Monica-
gate', the revelations about President CLINTON's
adultery.

Ernest Becker (1924–74)
US PSYCHOLOGIST AND CULTURAL
ANTHROPOLOGIST
*His premise was that mortality, not sexuality as
propounded by* FREUD, *was the basis of man's
primary repression. His publications include* The
Denial of Death *(1973).*

1 When we understand that man is the only
animal who must *create* meaning, who
must open a wedge into neutral nature, we
already understand the essence of love.
Love is the problem of an animal who
must *find* life, *create* a dialogue with
nature in order to experience his own
being.
The Structure of Evil, pt 2, ch. 9, 'A Brief Ontol-
ogy of Love' (1968)

Samuel Beckett (1906–89)

IRISH PLAYWRIGHT AND NOVELIST

A major influence on absurdist and postmodern literature, he presents a simultaneously comic and bleakly pessimistic portrayal of the human condition, as in the plays Waiting for Godot *(1952)* and Endgame *(1957). From 1932 he lived mainly in Paris, and composed most of his later works both in French and English. See* JAMES FENTON 4.

1 I shall state silences more competently than ever a better man spangled the butter-flies of vertigo.

Belacqua, in *Dream of Fair to Middling Women* (written 1932, publ. 1992)

2 Nothing to be done.

Estragon, in *Waiting for Godot*, act 1 (1952). The opening words are repeated in the play.

3 There's man all over for you, blaming on his boots the fault of his feet.

Vladimir, ibid.

4 Estragon: Let's go.
Vladimir: We can't.
Estragon: Why not?
Vladimir: We're waiting for Godot.

Ibid. The exchange is repeated several times during the play.

5 The tears of the world are a constant quality. For each one who begins to weep, somewhere else another stops. The same is true of the laugh.

Pozzo, ibid.

6 Let us not then speak ill of our generation, it is not any unhappier than its predecessors. Let us not speak well of it either. Let us not speak of it at all.

Ibid.

7 Nothing happens, nobody comes, nobody goes, it's awful!

Estragon, ibid.

8 Don't touch me! Don't question me! Don't speak to me! Stay with me!

Ibid., act 2

9 We always find something, eh Didi, to give us the impression we exist?

Ibid.

10 We all are born mad. Some remain so.

Ibid.

11 But we breathe, we change! We lose our hair, our teeth! Our bloom! Our ideals!

Hamm, in *Endgame* (1957)

12 Nothing is funnier than unhappiness, I grant you that.... Yes, yes, it's the most comical thing in the world. And we laugh, we laugh, with a will, in the beginning. But it's always the same thing. Yes, it's like the funny story we have heard too often, we still find it funny, but we don't laugh any more.

Nell, ibid.

13 The bastard! He doesn't exist!

Hamm, after attempting to pray, ibid. Clov replies, 'Not yet'.

14 Let me go to hell, that's all I ask, and go on cursing them there, and them look down and hear me, that might take some of the shine off their bliss.

The narrator speaking of his parents, in *From an Abandoned Work* (1958), repr. in *Six Residua* (1978)

15 Just under the surface I shall be, all together at first, then separate and drift, through all the earth and perhaps in the end through a cliff into the sea, something of me. A ton of worms in an acre, that is a wonderful thought, a ton of worms, I believe it.

Ibid.

16 To find a form that accommodates the mess, that is the task of the artist now.

Conversation with Tom Driver in 1961, quoted in *Samuel Beckett, a Biography*, ch. 21 (1978) by Deirdre Bair

17 What do I know of man's destiny? I could tell you more about radishes.

'Enough', first publ. in *No's Knife* (1967), repr. in *Six Residua* (1978)

18 Personally I have no bone to pick with graveyards, I take the air there willingly, perhaps more willingly than elsewhere, when take the air I must.

First Love (1970)

19 I couldn't have done it otherwise. Gone on, I mean. I could not have gone through the awful wretched mess of life without having left a stain upon the silence.

Quoted in *Samuel Beckett, a Biography*, ch. 26 (1978) by Deirdre Bair. Variations of this remark were made on different occasions.

20 Birth was the death of him.

'A Piece of Monologue', publ. in *Three Occasional Pieces* (1982)

21 Ever tried. Ever failed. No matter. Try again. Fail again. Fail better.

Worstward Ho (1983)

22 Make sense who may. I switch off.

Bam, in *What Where* (1984)

Sybille Bedford (b. 1911)

BRITISH AUTHOR

Born into the German aristocracy, she drew on her detailed observation of the upper classes to produce autobiographical novels such as A Legacy *(1956), and books on travel and legal trials.*

1 A part, a large part, of travelling is an engagement of the ego v. the world....

The world is hydra headed, as old as the rocks and as changing as the sea, enmeshed inextricably in its ways. The ego wants to arrive at places safely and on time.

'The Quality of Travel', first publ. in *Esquire* November 1961, repr. in *As It Was* (1990)

(Sir) Thomas Beecham (1879–1961)

BRITISH CONDUCTOR
He introduced Diaghilev's Ballets Russes to London (1911) and founded the Royal Philharmonic Orchestra (1947). He was famous for his 'Lollipop' encores and for his forthright pronouncements. Sir John Barbirolli remarked that he 'conducted like a dancing dervish'.

1 All the arts in America are a gigantic racket run by unscrupulous men for unhealthy women.

Quoted in the *Observer* 5 May 1946

2 Great music is that which penetrates the ear with facility and leaves the memory with difficulty. Magical music never leaves the memory.

Speech, c. 1950, quoted in the *Sunday Times* 16 September 1962

3 Composers should write tunes the chauffeurs and errand boys can whistle.

Quoted in *The New York Times* 9 March 1961

4 The English may not like music, but they absolutely love the noise it makes.

Quoted in the *New York Herald Tribune* 9 March 1961

5 Like two skeletons copulating on a corrugated tin roof.

Quoted in *Beecham Stories* (1978) by Harold Atkins and Archie Newman and referring to the sound of the harpsichord. Another version likens it to 'a bird-cage played with toasting forks'.

6 Madam, you have between your legs an instrument capable of giving pleasure to thousands – and all you can do is scratch it.

Attributed remark to a cellist. Also quoted as '. . . the most sensitive instrument known to man . . .'

Max Beerbohm (1872–1956)

BRITISH ESSAYIST AND CARICATURIST
He was a drama critic, and the author of numerous witty collections of essays and caricatures and one novel, Zuleika Dobson *(1911), a parody of Oxford life.* SHAW *called him 'the incomparable Max', but* VITA SACKVILLE-WEST *remembered him as a 'shallow, affected, self-conscious fribble'.*

1 One might well say that mankind is divisible into two great classes: hosts and guests.

'Hosts and Guests', essay written 1918, repr. in *And Even Now* (1920)

2 To say that a man is vain means merely that he is pleased with the effect he produces on other people. A conceited man is satisfied with the effect he produces on himself.

'Quia Imperfectum', ibid.

3 It seems to be a law of nature that no man, unless he has some obvious physical deformity, ever is loth to sit for his portrait.

Ibid.

Brendan Behan (1923–64)

IRISH PLAYWRIGHT
A supporter of Irish nationalism from an early age, he began writing while in prison, an experience incorporated in his first play, The Quare Fellow *(1954, filmed 1962). His heavy drinking limited his creative output, though his play* The Hostage *(1958) and autobiographical novel* Borstal Boy *(1958) were acclaimed.*

1 He was born an Englishman and remained one for years.

Pat, in *The Hostage*, act 1 (1958). Referring to Monsewer, who later 'found out he was an Irishman'.

2 Pat: He was an Anglo-Irishman.
Meg: In the blessed name of God, what's that?
Pat: A Protestant with a horse.

Ibid. Referring to Monsewer.

3 When I came back to Dublin, I was court-martialled in my absence, and sentenced to death in my absence, so I said they could shoot me in my absence.

Pat, on his experiences in the IRA, ibid.

4 All publicity is good, except an obituary notice.

Quoted in the *Sunday Express* 5 January 1964

5 I am a daylight atheist.

Quoted by Rae Jeffs, publicist and assistant to Behan, in *Sacred Monsters*, 'Rousting in Dublin' (1988) by Daniel Farson

6 One drink is too many for me and a thousand not enough.

Ibid. See also BILLY WILDER 1.

Harry Belafonte (b. 1927)

US SINGER AND CIVIL RIGHTS ACTIVIST
Known as the 'King of Calypso' in the late 1950s, he had hits with 'Banana Boat Song' (1956) and 'Mary's Boy Child' (1957), and later became committed to the advancement of black culture.

1 You can cage the singer but not the song.

International Herald Tribune 3 October 1988. Referring to the suppression of the arts in South Africa.

Gertrude Bell (1868–1926)

BRITISH ARCHAEOLOGIST AND DIPLOMAT
Her explorations in the Middle East on the eve of the First World War led to her appointment to the Mesopotamia Expeditionary Force in Basra and Baghdad. There, she continued her archaeological research and contributed to the inception of the modern state of Iraq.

1 When you have drunk the milk of the naga [mother camel] over the camp fire of Abu Tayyi you are baptised of the desert and there is no other salvation for you.

Letter to her father, Hugh Bell, 4 February 1914, publ. in *The Letters of Gertrude Bell*, vol. 1 (ed. Lady Florence Bell, 1927)

2 When people talk of our muddling through it throws me into a passion. Muddle through! why yes so we do – wading through blood and tears that need never have been shed.

Letter to her stepmother, Florence Bell, 27 April 1916, publ. ibid. Referring to 'the co-ordinating of Arab politics and the creation of an Arabian policy', which Bell believed had been poorly managed by the War Office.

3 The real difficulty under which we labour here is that we don't know, and I suppose can't know till the end of the war, exactly what we intend to do in this country. You are continually confronted with that uncertainty. Can you persuade people to take your side when you are not sure in the end whether you'll be there to take theirs?

Letter to Hugh and Florence Bell, 15 July 1916, publ. ibid. Speaking of Iraq, from which British forces had expelled the Ottoman administration during the First World War. In 1920 the country was placed under a League of Nations mandate to be administered by the British, which continued until 1932.

4 It is almost impossible to believe that a few years ago the human race was more or less governed by reason and considered consequences, before it did things. . . . At the back of my mind I have a feeling that we people of the war can never return to complete sanity. The shock has been too great: we're unbalanced.

Letter to her father, 16 January 1923, publ. ibid. vol. 2. Speaking of the excavation at Niffar (ancient Nippur): 'You see in section age after age of civilization extending over a period of three or four thousand years. It's amazing and rather horrible to be brought face to face with millenniums of human effort and then to consider what a mess we've made of it.'

Martin Bell (b. 1938)

BRITISH JOURNALIST AND POLITICIAN
Before his election as Independent MP for Tatton (1997–2001), he was a foreign correspondent for the BBC, reporting from the Gulf War and Bosnia among other assignments.

1 I am not a saint. I never claimed to be a saint. My suits are not white, they're off-white.

Independent 24 May 1997. Said after his election; during and after the campaign Bell continued to don the white suits he had previously worn while reporting for television as a foreign correspondent.

(Sir) Tim Bell (b. 1941)

BRITISH ADVERTISING EXECUTIVE
As a specialist in public relations, he was the original 'spin doctor' and midwife of the general election victory by MARGARET THATCHER *in 1979, when he was the Managing Director at* SAATCHI & SAATCHI, *the Conservative Party's publicity agency.*

1 I'd rather be called a spin doctor than a hidden persuader. Actually I rather like the term. After all, doctors are qualified professionals, and putting the right spin on things is exactly what we do.

PR Week 13 October 1995. *The Hidden Persuaders* (1973) was a book by Vance Packard about the manipulative methods of the advertising industry.

2 Don't write a press release when a good leak will do.

Remark at Marketing Society lunch, 8 December 1995, quoted in *Campaign* 5 January 1996. Bell added, 'The truth is that a strong story placed in the newspaper, picked up by everybody else will actually have more impact than an advertising campaign.'

Hilaire Belloc (1870–1953)

BRITISH AUTHOR
A devout Roman Catholic, he was the author of travel books, historical studies and satirical novels, though is probably best known for his children's nonsense verse Cautionary Tales *(1907). He was a lifelong friend of* G.K. CHESTERTON *who illustrated his books, the pair said to be 'two buttocks of one bum'.*

1 It is sometimes necessary to lie damnably in the interests of the nation.

Letter to G.K. CHESTERTON, 12 December 1917, quoted in *Life of Hilaire Belloc*, ch. 16 (1957) by Robert Speaight. Belloc was a zealous propagandist during the First World War.

2 *When I am dead, I hope it may be said: 'His sins were scarlet, but his books were read.'*

'On His Books', publ. in *Sonnets and Verse* (1923). The reference is to Isaiah 1:18, 'Though your sins be as scarlet, they shall be as white as snow.'

3 *The Devil, having nothing else to do,*
Went off to tempt My Lady Poltagrue.
My Lady, tempted by a private whim,
To his extreme annoyance, tempted him.
'On Lady Poltagrue', publ. ibid.

4 *I'm tired of Love; I'm still more tired of*
Rhyme.
But Money gives me pleasure all the time.
'Fatigue', publ. ibid.

5 *Do you remember an Inn,*
Miranda?
Do you remember an Inn?
And the tedding and the spreading
Of the straw for a bedding,
And the fleas that tease in the High
Pyrenees
And the wine that tasted of the tar?
'Tarantella', publ. in *Sonnets and Verse* (1923). Opening lines.

6 *Strong brother in God and last companion,*
Wine.
'Heroic Poem upon Wine', publ. in *Short Talks with the Dead* (1926)

7 *Like many of the Upper Class*
He liked the Sound of Broken Glass.
'About John', publ. in *New Cautionary Tales* (1930)

8 *Pale Ebenezer thought it wrong to fight,*
But Roaring Bill (who killed him) thought
it right.
'The Pacifist', publ. in *Sonnets and Verse* (second edn, 1938)

9 *Believing Truth is staring at the sun*
Which but destroys the power that could
perceive.
So naught of our poor selves can be at one
With burning Truth, nor utterly believe.
'De Fide: To Lady Diana Cooper', no. 2, publ. ibid.

Saul Bellow (b. 1915)
CANADIAN-BORN US NOVELIST
A leading figure in post-war American fiction, he typically set his novels and short stories in Chicago with Jewish intellectuals as protagonists. Notable works include Herzog (1964) and Humboldt's Gift (1975).

1 Everybody knows there is no fineness or accuracy of suppression; if you hold down one thing, you hold down the adjoining.
The Adventures of Augie March, ch. 1 (1953)

2 As for types like my own, obscurely motivated by the conviction that our existence was worthless if we didn't make a turning point of it, we were assigned to the humanities, to poetry, philosophy, painting – the nursery games of humankind, which had to be left behind when the age of science

began. The humanities would be called upon to choose a wallpaper for the crypt, as the end drew near.
Ibid., ch. 6 (1949)

3 I think that New York is not the cultural centre of America, but the business and administrative centre of American culture.
BBC radio interview, publ. in the *Listener* 22 May 1969

4 There are evils . . . that have the ability to survive identification and go on for ever . . . money, for instance, or war.
Albert Corde, in *The Dean's December*, ch. 13 (1982)

5 Psycho-analysis pretends to investigate the Unconscious. The Unconscious by definition is what you are not conscious of. But the Analysts already know what's in it – they should, because they put it all in beforehand.
Ibid., ch. 18

6 In the greatest confusion there is still an open channel to the soul. It may be difficult to find because by midlife it is overgrown, and some of the wildest thickets that surround it grow out of what we describe as our education. But the channel is always there, and it is our business to keep it open, to have access to the deepest part of ourselves.
Foreword to *The Closing of the American Mind* (1987) by ALLAN BLOOM

7 There were two varieties of truth, one symbolized by the Tree of Knowledge, the other by the Tree of Life, one the truth of striving and the other the truth of receptivity. Knowledge divorced from life equals sickness.
More Die of Heartbreak, ch. 1 (1987)

8 If you think that historical forces are sending everybody straight to hell you can either go resignedly with the procession or hold out, and hold out not from pride or other personal motives, but from admiration and love for human abilities and powers to which, without exaggeration, the words 'miracle' and 'sublimity' can be applied.
Ibid., ch. 2

9 Everything has to be tried out. Funnily enough, the same mind that takes in 'Dallas' or rap music is also accessible to Homer and Shakespeare.
It All Adds Up, 'Mozart: an Overture' (1994)

10 Wedding invitations now are apt to bring to mind divorce statistics, sexual instability, reflections on the sexual revolution and on venereal disease, on the effects of herpes and AIDS on marital infidelity. . . . Your contemporary wedding guest has

been transported by modern forces of malign magic into a sphere of distraction where instead of hearing village musicians he is blasted by a great noise – the modern noise.

Ibid., 'The Distracted Public'

11 Human character is smaller now, people don't have durable passions; they've replaced passions with excitement. But this won't give you love as strong as death.

Quoted in the *Guardian* 10 September 1997

John Belushi (1949–82)

US COMEDIAN, SINGER AND ACTOR

An anti-Establishment comic who rose to fame with NBC's Saturday Night Live, *he attained cult status with the films* National Lampoon's Animal House *(1978) and* The Blues Brothers *(1980). He died from a drugs overdose.*

1 It's all false pressure; you put the heat on yourself, you get it from the networks and record companies and movie studios, and then you put more pressure on yourself to make everything that much harder because work is no longer challenging. You say, 'Well, I'll get all screwed up and then it'll be a real challenge again.' So stupid – I've often wondered why people do these things. You're so much happier if you don't, but I guess happiness is not a state you want to be in all the time.

Interview in *Cosmopolitan* December 1981

2 In your 20s, you feel like you're indestructible, that nothing can kill you and you laugh at death. You go on and stay up for days and do as many things as you can and then, in your 30s, you think, well, maybe I'll be around here a little longer, so I'm going to maybe take better care of myself.

Interview in *Rolling Stone* 21 January 1982. Belushi died of an overdose of cocaine and heroin two months later.

3 I give so much pleasure to so many people. Why can I not get some pleasure for myself? Why do I have to stop?

Quoted in *Wired: The Short Life and Fast Times of John Belushi*, pt 1, ch. 7 (1984) by Bob Woodward. Referring to his drug addiction.

Robert Benchley (1889–1945)

US HUMOROUS WRITER

A drama critic, sketchwriter and editor for Vanity Fair *and the* New Yorker *among other publications, he was a founder member of the New York dinner-club of literati and wits, the Algonquin Round Table.*

1 One square foot less and it would be adulterous.

Quoted in the *New Yorker* 5 January 1946. On the office he shared with DOROTHY PARKER,

who echoed this remark in an interview in 1956: 'He [Robert Benchley] and I had an office so tiny that an inch smaller and it would have been adultery.'

2 It took me fifteen years to discover that I had no talent for writing, but I couldn't give it up because by that time I was too famous.

Quoted in *Robert Benchley*, ch. 1 (1955) by Nathaniel Benchley

3 A dog teaches a boy fidelity, perseverance, and to turn around three times before lying down.

Quoted in *Artemus Ward, His Book*, Introduction (1964 edn)

4 In America there are two classes of travel – first class and with childen.

Quoted in *The Algonquin Wits* (ed. Robert E. Drennan, 1968)

5 I do most of my work sitting down. That's where I shine.

Ibid.

6 Anyone can do any amount of work, provided it isn't the work he is supposed to be doing.

Ibid.

7 Streets flooded. Please advise.

Ibid. Telegram on arrival at Venice.

Ruth Benedict (1887–1948)

US ANTHROPOLOGIST

Her studies of primitive societies led her to argue for cultural relativity and against the imposition of cultural values. Patterns of Culture *(1934) is regarded as her most important work.*

1 No man ever looks at the world with pristine eyes. He sees it edited by a definite set of customs and institutions and ways of thinking.

Patterns of Culture, ch. 1 (1934)

2 Racism is an *ism* to which everyone in the world today is exposed; for or against, we must take sides. And the history of the future will differ according to the decision which we make.

Race: Science and Politics, ch. 1 (1940)

Stephen Vincent Benét (1898–1943)

US POET AND AUTHOR

He published numerous novels and short stories on themes of American history, but is chiefly known for his long poem on the Civil War, John Brown's Body *(1928), which was dramatized by Charles Laughton in 1953.*

1 *I have fallen in love with American names, The sharp, gaunt names that never get fat, The snakeskin titles of mining claims,*

The plumed war-bonnet of Medicine Hat,
Tucson and Deadwood and Lost Mule Flat.

'American Names', st. 1, first publ. in *Yale Review*, vol. 17 (1927), repr. in *America in Poetry* (ed. Charles Sullivan, 1988)

2 *I shall not rest quiet in Montparnasse.*
I shall not lie easy at Winchelsea.
You may bury my body in Sussex grass,
You may bury my tongue at Champmédy.
I shall not be there, I shall rise and pass.
Bury my heart at Wounded Knee.

Ibid., st. 7. Wounded Knee, a creek in South Dakota, was site of the last major battle of the Indian Wars, 1890. *Bury My Heart at Wounded Knee* was the title of a history of the Indian wars by Dee Brown (1970).

David Ben-Gurion (1886–1973)
ISRAELI STATESMAN

Born in Poland, he became an active Zionist and emigrated to Palestine in 1906. In 1930 he was elected leader of the Mapai (Labour) party, and in 1948 became the first Israeli prime minister, serving two terms 1948–63. He was honoured during his lifetime as 'Father of the Nation'.

1 In Israel, in order to be a realist you must believe in miracles.

Interview on CBS-TV, 5 October 1956

Walter Benjamin (1892–1940)
GERMAN CRITIC AND PHILOSOPHER

Considered one of Germany's most original critics, he incorporated Marxism and Jewish mysticism in his essays and aphorisms, which are collected in One-Way Street (1928) and Illuminations (1961). He moved to Paris in 1933, where he committed suicide after a failed attempt to escape the Nazi occupation.

1 Work on good prose has three steps: a musical stage when it is composed, an architectonic one when it is built, and a textile one when it is woven.

One-Way Street, 'Caution: Steps' (1928)

2 Genuine polemics approach a book as lovingly as a cannibal spices a baby.

Ibid. 'Post No Bills: The Critic's Technique in Thirteen Theses'

3 The art of the critic in a nutshell: to coin slogans without betraying ideas. The slogans of an inadequate criticism peddle ideas to fashion.

Ibid.

4 Books and harlots have their quarrels in public.

Ibid., 'No. 13'

5 Truth wants to be startled abruptly, at one stroke, from her self-immersion, whether by uproar, music or cries for help.

Ibid., 'Technical Aid'

6 Quotations in my work are like wayside robbers who leap out armed and relieve the stroller of his conviction.

Ibid., 'Hardware'

7 Of all the ways of acquiring books, writing them oneself is regarded as the most praiseworthy method. . . . Writers are really people who write books not because they are poor, but because they are dissatisfied with the books which they could buy but do not like.

'Unpacking my Library' (1931), repr. in *Illuminations* (1961; ed. Hannah Arendt, 1968)

8 The destructive character lives from the feeling, not that life is worth living, but that suicide is not worth the trouble.

'The Destructive Character', first publ. in *Frankfurter Zeitung* 20 November 1931, repr. in *One-Way Street and Other Writings* (1978)

9 Opinions are a private matter. The public has an interest only in judgments.

'Karl Kraus', first publ. in *Frankfurter Zeitung* no. 76, 1931, repr. in *Illuminations* (1961; ed. Hannah Arendt, 1968)

10 Boredom is the dream bird that hatches the egg of experience. A rustling in the leaves drives him away.

'The Storyteller', sect. 9 (1936), repr. ibid.

11 Death is the sanction of everything the story-teller can tell. He has borrowed his authority from death.

Ibid., sect. 11

Tony Benn (b. 1925)
BRITISH POLITICIAN

Originally Anthony Wedgwood Benn. A committed parliamentary radical who is also a staunch traditionalist, he was a Labour MP 1950–2001, apart from the period 1960–63, when he inherited his father's title and subsequently renounced it. He held various government posts under HAROLD WILSON *and* JAMES CALLAGHAN. *According to* HAROLD MACMILLAN, *he 'immatures with age'.*

1 The House of Lords is the British Outer Mongolia for retired politicians.

Quoted in the *Observer* 4 February 1962. Comment made during his campaign to disclaim his hereditary peerage. In his *Diaries 1963–67*, Benn states that the words came from a speech made in San Francisco in 1961, and were also used by the Russian former foreign minister Molotov. Benn was relieved to have escaped the Lords, though he was, he said, 'not a reluctant peer but a persistent commoner'.

2 Britain today is suffering from galloping obsolescence.

Speech 31 January 1963, quoted in the *Observer* 2 February 1963

3 We thought we could put the economy

right in five years. We were wrong. It will probably take ten.

Speech at Bristol, 18 April 1968, quoted in *The Times* 19 April 1968. Benn was then Minister of Technology.

4 The Marxist analysis has got nothing to do with what happened in Stalin's Russia: it's like blaming Jesus Christ for the Inquisition in Spain.

Quoted in the *Observer* 27 April 1980

5 A holy war with atom bombs could end the human family for ever. I say this as a socialist whose political commitment owes much more to the teachings of Jesus – without the mysteries within which they are presented – than to the writings of Marx whose analysis seems to lack an understanding of the deeper needs of humanity.

Arguments for Democracy, ch. 7 (1981)

6 For those without personal wealth or political authority a trade union card and a ballot paper are the only two routes to political power.

Ibid., ch. 9

7 I did not enter the Labour Party forty-seven years ago to have our manifesto written by Dr Mori, Dr Gallup and Mr Harris.

Guardian 13 June 1988

8 A faith is something you die for, a doctrine is something you kill for. There is all the difference in the world.

BBC television broadcast, 11 April 1989

9 It's the same each time with progress. First they ignore you, then they say you're mad, then dangerous, then there's a pause and then you can't find anyone who disagrees with you.

Quoted in the *Observer* 6 October 1991

10 Mr Tony Benn welcomes compulsory homework for pensioners.

Sunday Telegraph 8 November 1998. Illustrating the kind of New Labour press briefing to which he takes exception.

Alan Bennett (b. 1934)
BRITISH PLAYWRIGHT
At the heart of the satire boom of the 1960s, he was a contributor to the revue Beyond the Fringe *(1960–61) and had further success with his first stage play* Forty Years On *(1969). Later plays include* The Madness of George III *(1991, filmed 1995).*

1 Life, you know, is rather like opening a tin of sardines. We are all of us looking for the key.

'Sermon', in *Beyond the Fringe* (revue, 1960–61), publ. in *From Fringe to Flying Circus*, ch. 1 (1980) by Roger Wilmut. Bennett first wrote the sketch in 1956 for a concert organized with Russell Harty at Oxford University. 'It took about half

an hour to write, and was, I suppose, the most profitable half-hour's work I've ever done. Once I had hit on the form I used to be able to run up sermons for all sorts of occasions.'

2 Never read the Bible as if it means something. Or at any rate don't *try* and mean it. Nor prayers. The liturgy is best treated and read as if it's someone announcing the departure of trains.

Journal entry, 30 June 1984, publ. in *Writing Home*, 'Diaries 1980–1990' (1994)

3 The majority of people perform well in a crisis and when the spotlight is on them; it's on the Sunday afternoons of this life, when nobody is looking, that the spirit falters.

Journal entry, 13 Oct 1984, ibid.

4 It's a good job Mrs T. isn't Archbishop of Canterbury, or we would just be left with the cathedrals and a few other 'viable places of worship'.

Journal entry, 20 May 1985, ibid.

5 When people are on their best behaviour they aren't always at their best.

'Dinner at Noon', broadcast April 1988 in BBC TV series *Byline*, publ. ibid.

6 Biography is all about cutting people down to size. Getting an unruly quart into a pint pot.

Quoted in *Beyond the Fringe . . . and Beyond*, pt 4 (1989) by Ronald Bergan

7 Definition of a classic: a book everyone is assumed to have read and often thinks they have.

Independent on Sunday 27 January 1991

8 I generally assume that childhoods more or less ended with the First World War. . . . Anyone born after 1940 got the Utility version, childhood according to the Authorized Economy Standard.

Writing Home, 'Bad John' (1994)

9 Language is balls coming at you from every angle.

Miss Fozzard quoting Mr Clarkson-Hall in *Talking Heads* 2, 'Miss Fozzard Finds Her Feet' (1998)

Arnold Bennett (1867–1931)
BRITISH NOVELIST, PLAYWRIGHT AND CRITIC
He set much of his best work in the Potteries region of his boyhood, notably Anna of the Five Towns *(1902) and* The Old Wives' Tale *(1908). He also wrote for the theatre and was an influential reviewer.* WYNDHAM LEWIS *called him the 'Hitler of the book-racket'.*

1 A cause may be inconvenient, but it's

magnificent. It's like champagne or high heels, and one must be prepared to suffer for it.

Hildegarde Culver, in *The Title*, act 1 (1918)

2 Examine the Honours List and you can instantly tell how the Government feels in its inside. When the Honours List is full of rascals, millionaires, and – er – chumps, you may be quite sure that the Government is dangerously ill.

Arthur Culver, ibid.

3 Being a husband is a whole-time job. That is why so many husbands fail. They can't give their entire attention to it.

Ibid.

4 Journalists say a thing that they know isn't true, in the hope that if they keep on saying it long enough it *will* be true.

Ibid., act 2

5 Literature's always a good card to play for Honours. It makes people think that Cabinet ministers are educated.

Hildegarde Culver, ibid. act 3

6 A test of a first-rate work, and a test of your sincerity in calling it a first-rate work, is that you finish it.

Things That Have Interested Me, 'Finishing Books' (first series, 1921)

7 The price of justice is eternal publicity.

Ibid., 'Secret Trials' (second series, 1923)

8 Good taste is better than bad taste, but bad taste is better than no taste, and men without individuality have no taste – at any rate no taste that they can impose on their publics.

Evening Standard 21 August 1930

Jill Bennett (1931–90)

BRITISH ACTRESS

Having gained her first success in ANOUILH*'s* Dinner With the Family (1957), *she performed in many plays by her husband* JOHN OSBORNE, *such as* West of Suez (1971) *and* Watch It Come Down (1976).

1 Never marry a man who hates his mother, because he'll end up hating you.

Quoted in the *Observer* 12 September 1982. See JOHN OSBORNE 14.

Connie Bensley (b. 1929)

BRITISH POET

In her sharp and often satirical poems she focuses on the preoccupations of everyday life and social pretension. Her collections include Moving In (1984) *and* Choosing To Be a Swan (1994).

1 *I sing the love homeopathic:*
it cures you before very long.
You just take a speck

of that pain-in-the-neck
and let it dissolve on your tongue.

'A Cure for Love', publ. in *Choosing To Be a Swan* (1994). The first line is a parody of Walt Whitman's poem, 'I Sing the Body Electric' (1885).

Stella Benson (1892–1933)

BRITISH AUTHOR

Themes of loneliness and alienation in her novels and short stories reflect her own isolation after her marriage and move to China in 1922. Her most successful work was Tobit Transplanted (1930).

1 Family jokes, though rightly cursed by strangers, are the bond that keeps most families alive.

Pipers and a Dancer, ch. 9 (1924)

Lloyd Bentsen (b. 1921)

US POLITICIAN

A member of the House of Representatives (1948–55) and the Senate (1971–93), he was the Democratic vice-presidential candidate in 1988 and Secretary of the Treasury (1993–94) under President CLINTON.

1 Senator, I served with Jack Kennedy. I knew Jack Kennedy. Jack Kennedy was a friend of mine. Senator, you're no Jack Kennedy.

TV vice-presidential debate, 6 October 1988, publ. in *Lend Me Your Ears*, pt 4 (ed. WILLIAM SAFIRE, 1992). Bentsen was responding to the assertion by DAN QUAYLE that the latter possessed 'as much experience in the Congress as Jack Kennedy had when he sought the presidency'. Safire calls the riposte, 'the most effective single punch in the history of televised presidential debates'.

Nikolai A. Berdyaev (1874–1948)

RUSSIAN PHILOSOPHER

He founded the Academy of Philosophy and Religion in Berlin in 1922 (transferred in 1924 to Paris). As a leader of the Christian existentialist school, he was a consistent critic of Russian Communism. His books include The Meaning of History (1923) *and* The Destiny of Man (1931).

1 In sex we have the source of man's true connection with the cosmos and of his servile dependence. The categories of sex, male and female, are cosmic categories, not merely anthropological categories.

The Meaning of the Creative Act (1916)

2 We find the most terrible form of atheism, not in the militant and passionate struggle against the idea of God himself, but in the practical atheism of everyday living, in indifference and torpor. We often encounter these forms of atheism among those who are formally Christians.

Truth and Revelation (1953)

Candice Bergen (b. 1946)

US SCREEN ACTRESS

Known for her film roles in Carnal Knowledge *(1971) and* Starting Over *(1979), she has also appeared in the late-1980s TV comedy series* Murphy Brown.

1 I may not be a great actress but I've become the greatest at screen orgasms. Ten seconds of heavy breathing, roll your head from side to side, simulate a slight asthma attack and die a little.

From the *Daily Mirror*, 1971, quoted in *Halliwell's Filmgoer's Companion* (1984)

John Berger (b. 1926)

BRITISH AUTHOR AND CRITIC

An uncompromising Marxist-influenced critic, he has written extensively on culture and society, as in Ways of Seeing *(1972) and his novels, which include the late-modernist* G *(1972) and the trilogy* Into Their Labours *(1991), which charts peasant life in France.*

1 Nothing fortuitous happens in a child's world. There are no accidents. Everything is connected with everything else and everything can be explained by everything else . . . For a young child everything that happens is a necessity.

A Fortunate Man (1967)

2 Is boredom anything less than the sense of one's faculties slowly dying?

Ibid.

3 Nakedness reveals itself. Nudity is placed on display. . . . The nude is condemned to never being naked. Nudity is a form of dress.

Ways of Seeing, ch. 3 (1972)

4 The envied are like bureaucrats; the more impersonal they are, the greater the illusion (for themselves and for others) of their power.

Ibid., ch. 7

5 A peasant becomes fond of his pig and is glad to salt away its pork. What is significant, and is so difficult for the urban stranger to understand, is that the two statements are connected by an *and* and not by a *but*.

About Looking, 'Why Look at Animals?' (1980)

6 The zoo cannot but disappoint. The public purpose of zoos is to offer visitors the opportunity of looking at animals. Yet nowhere in a zoo can a stranger encounter the look of an animal. At the most, the animal's gaze flickers and passes on. They look sideways. They look blindly beyond.

Ibid.

7 The camera relieves us of the burden of memory. It surveys us like God, and it surveys for us. Yet no other god has been so cynical, for the camera records in order to forget.

Ibid., 'Uses of Photography'

8 One can say of language that it is potentially the only human home, the only dwelling place that cannot be hostile to man.

And Our Faces, My Heart, Brief as Photos, pt 2 (1984)

9 Emigration, forced or chosen, across national frontiers or from village to metropolis, is the quintessential experience of our time.

Ibid.

10 Autobiography begins with a sense of being alone. It is an orphan form.

'Mother', first publ. in *Threepenny Review* summer 1986, repr. in *Keeping a Rendezvous* (1992)

11 Every city has a sex and an age which have nothing to do with demography. Rome is feminine. So is Odessa. London is a teenager, an urchin, and, in this, hasn't changed since the time of Dickens. Paris, I believe, is a man in his twenties in love with an older woman.

'Imagine Paris', first publ. in *Harper's* January 1987, repr. in *Keeping a Rendezvous* (1992)

12 What makes shit such a universal joke is that it's an unmistakeable reminder of our duality, of our soiled nature and of our will to glory. It is the ultimate *lèse-majesté*.

'Muck and Its Entanglements', first publ. in *Harper's* May 1989, repr. ibid. as 'A Load of Shit'

13 Compassion has no place in the natural order of the world which operates on the basis of necessity. Compassion opposes this order and is therefore best thought of as being in some way supernatural.

Guardian 19 December 1991

14 The first step towards building an alternative world has to be a refusal of the world-picture implanted in our minds and all the false promises used everywhere to justify and idealise the delinquent and insatiable need to sell. Another space is vitally necessary.

'Against the Great Defeat of the World', publ. in *Race and Class* October 1998–March 1999

Ingmar Bergman (b. 1918)

SWEDISH STAGE DIRECTOR AND FILM-MAKER

Often bleak in outlook and preoccupied with guilt, repression and loneliness, his films include The Seventh Seal *(1956),* The Virgin Spring *(1959) and the more optimistic and autobiographical* Fanny and Alexander *(1982).*

1 Today the individual has become the highest form and the greatest bane of artistic creation. The smallest wound or pain of the ego is examined under the microscope

as if it were of eternal importance. The artist considers his isolation, his subjectivity, his individualism almost holy. Thus we finally gather in one large pen, where we stand and bleat about our loneliness without listening to each other and without realizing that we are smothering each other to death.

Spoken introduction to *The Seventh Seal* (film, 1956, written and directed by Ingmar Bergman)

2 My basic view of things is – not to have any basic view of things.

Interview in *Bergman on Bergman*, 'Solna, 25 June 1968' (1970)

3 Professionally, morals aren't too much of a problem. Over the years one has learned certain things by experience. They mount up. And gradually they crystallize into a pattern of behaviour which afterwards – to use a superior expression – one calls one's professional ethics.

Interview ibid. 'Rasunda, 3 July 1968'

4 I hope I never get so old I get religious.

International Herald Tribune 8 September 1989

Ingrid Bergman (1915–82)
SWEDISH-BORN SCREEN ACTRESS
A hugely popular romantic star from 1939 when she was brought to the US by DAVID SELZNICK, *she won an Oscar for* Gaslight *(1944) but was ostracized from Hollywood after her affair with the director Roberto Rossellini in 1949.*

1 Play it Sam. Play 'As Time Goes By'.

Ilsa Lund (Ingrid Bergman), in *Casablanca* (film, 1942, screenplay by Julius Epstein, Philip Epstein and Howard Koch, from the unproduced play *Everybody Goes to Rick's* by Murray Burnett and Joan Alison, directed by Michael Curtiz). Ilsa makes the request to the piano player Sam (Dooley Wilson); later in the film, Rick Blaine (Humphrey Bogart) repeats the request: 'You played it for her, you can play it for me. If she can stand it, I can. Play it!' (usually misquoted 'Play it again Sam', the title of WOODY ALLEN's 1972 movie). For the song, see HERMAN HUPFELD 1.

Steven Berkoff (b. 1937)
BRITISH PLAYWRIGHT, ACTOR AND DIRECTOR
Having formed the London Theatre Group in 1968, he embarked on a series of adaptations of classic dramas. His own radical, often brutal plays, in which he often acts, include East *(1975) and* Greek *(1979).*

1 So demure on the outside
such a whore within
fashion is so divine it makes dressing up a
sin

Helen, in *Decadence*, sc. 10 (1981)

2 Wake up, you git, we need a war . . .
Establish once again our might and strength
Shake our old mane, out fly the moths
Oh God, I start to feel myself again
Now where is this damn Falkland Isle?

Maggot Scratcher, in *Sink the Belgrano!* (1987)

3 That just ain't cricket, is it dear?
Or they may say, and it will be true,
Britain does not rule the waves
She simply waives the bloody rules!

Command, ibid.

Irving Berlin (1888–1989)
RUSSIAN-BORN US SONGWRITER
Originally Israel Baline. He was a pivotal figure in US popular music, already established as a composer when 'Alexander's Ragtime Band' was a hit in 1911. He received a presidential citation as composer of patriotic songs in 1954. 'Irving Berlin has no place in American music', Jerome Kern asserted, 'Irving Berlin is American music.'

1 From the mountains to the prairies,
To the oceans white with foam,
God bless America,
My home sweet home!

'God Bless America' (song, written 1917, recorded 1938). This unofficial national anthem originally written for (though not appearing in) the Broadway show *Yip Yip Yaphank* (1918) is said to have provoked Woody Guthrie to compose 'This Land Is Your Land' (see WOODY GUTHRIE 2).

2 The song is ended (but the melody lingers on).

'The Song Is Ended (But the Melody Lingers On)' (song) in *Will O' the Whispers* (stage musical, 1927). Sung by Jack 'Whispering' Smith in the show, the song was popularized by Ruth Etting, and re-released in 1948 by Nellie Lutcher.

3 I'm puttin' on my top hat,
Tyin' up my white tie,
Brushin' off my tails.

'Top Hat, White Tie and Tails' (song) in *Top Hat* (film, 1935). The song was performed by Fred Astaire.

4 Heaven – I'm in Heaven –
And my heart beats so that I can hardly speak;
And I seem to find the happiness I seek
When we're out together dancing cheek to cheek.

'Cheek to Cheek' (song) ibid. Written for GINGER ROGERS and Fred Astaire.

5 There may be trouble ahead,
But while there's moonlight and music and love and romance,
Let's face the music and dance.

'Let's Face the Music and Dance' in *Follow the Fleet* (film, 1936). The song was a hit for Fred Astaire.

6 *I'm dreaming of a white Christmas,*
Just like the ones I used to know.
'White Christmas' (song) in *Holiday Inn* (film,
1942). First recorded by BING CROSBY, the song
was featured again in the film *White Christmas*
(Michael Curtiz, 1954), and recorded by artists as
diverse as FRANK SINATRA (1944), Mantovani
(1952) and the Drifters (1954). Crosby's sales
alone exceeded 25 million.

7 *There's no business like show business.*
'There's No Business Like Show Business' (song)
in *Annie Get Your Gun* (musical show 1946,
filmed 1949). Sung by Ethel Merman on Broadway and by Betty Hutton in the movie version,
the title was borrowed for the 1954 movie in
which MARILYN MONROE sang Berlin's 'Heat
Wave'.

8 *Anything you can do, I can do better,*
I can do anything better than you.
'Anything You Can Do' (song), in *Annie Get*
Your Gun

9 The toughest thing about success is that
you've got to keep on being a success.
Talent is only a starting point in this
business. You've got to keep on working
that talent. Someday I'll reach for it and it
won't be there.
Theatre Arts February 1958

10 Everybody ought to have a lower East Side
in their life.
Vogue 1 November 1962

(Sir) Isaiah Berlin (1909–97)

LATVIAN-BORN BRITISH PHILOSOPHER
Regarded as one of the leading liberal thinkers
of his generation, he was Professor of Social and
Political Theory at Oxford (1957–67). Among his
major works on political philosophy are Karl Marx
(1939), Historical Inevitability *(1954) and* The
Age of Enlightenment *(1956).*

1 Injustice, poverty, slavery, ignorance –
these may be cured by reform or revolution. But men do not live only by fighting
evils. They live by positive goals, individual and collective, a vast variety of
them, seldom predictable, at times incompatible.
'Political Ideas in the Twentieth Century' (1950),
repr. in *Four Essays on Liberty* (1969)

2 A great man need not be morally good, or
upright, or kind, or sensitive, or delightful,
or possess artistic or scientific talent. To
call someone a great man is to claim that
he has intentionally taken (or perhaps
could have taken) a large step, one far
beyond the normal capacities of men, in
satisfying, or materially affecting, central
human interests.
'Chaim Weizmann' (1958), repr. in *Personal*
Impressions (1981)

3 It is only a very vulgar historical materialism that denies the power of ideas, and
says that ideals are mere material interests
in disguise. It may be that, without the
pressure of social forces, political ideas
are stillborn: what is certain is that these
forces, unless they clothe themselves in
ideas, remain blind and undirected.
'Two Concepts of Liberty' (1958), repr. in *Four*
Essays on Liberty (1969)

4 One belief, more than any other, is responsible for the slaughter of individuals on the
altars of the great historical ideals . . . the
belief that somewhere, in the past or in the
future, in divine revelation or in the mind
of an individual thinker, in the pronouncements of history or science, or in the
simple heart of an uncorrupted good man,
there is a final solution.
Ibid.

5 Scepticism, driven to extremes, defeats
itself by becoming self-refuting.
Four Essays on Liberty, Introduction (1969)

Georges Bernanos (1888–1948)

FRENCH AUTHOR
A Roman Catholic polemicist, he wrote in support
of royalism and, in A Diary of My Times *(1938),*
against Franco. His preoccupation with the con-
flicting forces of good and evil is a theme of his
novels The Star of Satan *(1926) and* The Diary of
a Country Priest *(1936, filmed 1951).*

1 The wish to pray is a prayer in itself . . .
God can ask no more than that of us.
The Diary of a Country Priest, ch. 4 (1936)

2 Faith is not a thing which one 'loses', we
merely cease to shape our lives by it.
Ibid.

3 Hell is not to love any more, madame. Not
to love any more!
The priest, ibid. ch. 5

4 No one ever discovers the depths of his
own loneliness.
Ibid., ch. 7

5 Civilization exists precisely so that there
may be no masses but rather men alert
enough never to constitute masses.
The Last Essays of Georges Bernanos, 'Why Freedom?' (1955)

Carl Bernstein (b. 1944)

US JOURNALIST
Together with Bob Woodward he unmasked the
Watergate cover-up which led to the downfall of
RICHARD NIXON, *as described in* All the Presi-
dent's Men *(1974, filmed 1976). He was married to*
NORA EPHRON.

1 We are in the process of creating what
deserves to be called the idiot culture. Not
an idiot sub-culture, which every society has

bubbling beneath the surface and which can provide harmless fun; but the culture itself. For the first time, the weird and the stupid and the coarse are becoming our cultural norm, even our cultural ideal.

Guardian 3 June 1992

2 The failures of the press have contributed immensely to the emergence of a talk-show nation, in which public discourse is reduced to ranting and raving and posturing. We now have a mainstream press whose news agenda is increasingly influenced by this netherworld.

Ibid.

Leonard Bernstein (1918–90)

US COMPOSER AND CONDUCTOR

An accomplished composer in both the classical and modern idiom, he was also a popular and flamboyant conductor. His compositions include symphonies and the musical West Side Story *(1957).*

1 Technique is communication: the two words are synonymous in conductors.

The Times 27 June 1989

Yogi Berra (b. 1925)

US BASEBALL PLAYER

Lawrence Peter Berra. He held many world championship titles during his career as catcher with the New York Yankees and Mets (1946–65), and was famous for his malapropisms.

1 It ain't over till it's over.

Attributed

Chuck Berry (b. 1926)

US ROCK MUSICIAN

One of the first rock and roll stars to attract a large teenage following, he was a major influence on British and US rock bands of the 1960s. According to JOHN LENNON, *'if you tried to give rock 'n' roll another name, you might call it Chuck Berry'.*

1 Roll over, Beethoven,
And tell Tchaikovsky the news.

'Roll over, Beethoven' (song, 1956) on the album *Greatest Hits* (1965)

2 Hail, hail rock 'n' roll,
Deliver me from the days of old.

'School Days' (song, 1957) on ibid.

3 Go Johnny go!

'Johnny B. Goode' (song, 1958) on ibid. *Go Johnny Go* was the title of a rock and roll film in 1959, in which Berry appeared.

John Berryman (1914–72)

US POET

He established his reputation with Homage to Mistress Bradstreet *(1956) but is remembered chiefly for his* Dream Songs, *the 1964 volume of which*

won the Pulitzer Prize. An alcoholic, he committed suicide by jumping into the Mississippi River.

1 We must travel in the direction of our fear.

'A Point of Age', publ. in *Poems* (1942)

2 Life, friends, is boring. We must not say so.
After all, the sky flashes, the great sea
yearns,
we ourselves flash and yearn,
and moreover my mother told me as a boy
(repeatedly) 'Ever to confess you're bored
means you have no
Inner Resources.' I conclude now I have no
inner resources, because I am heavy bored.

77 Dream Songs, no. 14 (1964)

3 The world is gradually becoming a place
Where I do not care to be any more.

His Toy, His Dream, His Rest, no. 149 (1968). The lines were incorporated into the final version of *The Dream Songs* (1969).

4 The artist is extremely lucky who is presented with the worst possible ordeal which will not actually kill him. At that point, he's in business.

Interview in *Paris Review*, winter 1972, repr. in *Writers at Work* (fourth series, ed. George Plimpton, 1976)

Bernardo Bertolucci (b. 1940)

ITALIAN FILM-MAKER

Having directed his first film aged 22, he went on to achieve success with The Spider's Stratagem *(1970),* Last Tango in Paris *(1972),* 1900 *(1976) and* The Last Emperor *(1987).*

1 If New York is the Big Apple, tonight Hollywood is the Big Nipple.

Said at Oscar presentation ceremony, quoted in the *Guardian* 13 April 1988. Bertolucci's film *The Last Emperor* notched up nine awards.

2 Socialism is finished. That's why I got into Buddhism . . . In fact I thought that, being a little orphan of Marx, here at least was another space where I could feel comfortable.

Quoted in the *Independent on Sunday* 1 May 1994. On his reasons for making the film, *Little Buddha*.

George Best (b. 1946)

NORTHERN IRISH FOOTBALLER

Arguably the finest post-war British player, excelling in all positions, he played for Manchester United. Alcohol and fast-living meant that his footballing career was over by the time he was twenty-five, however. 'If I'd been born ugly, you'd never have heard of Pele', he once said.

1 You just can't explain what it's like to score a great goal to someone who's never done it. I said years ago that if you'd given me the choice of going out and beating four men and smashing a goal in from

thirty yards against Liverpool or going to bed with Miss World, it would have been a difficult choice. Luckily, I had both. It's just that you do one of those things in front of fifty thousand people.

Quoted in 'The Afterlife' by Paul Morley, first publ. 1991, repr. in *The Esquire Book of Sports Writing* (ed. Greg Williams (1995)

Mary McLeod Bethune (1875–1955)

US ACADEMIC

She was founder and President of the National Council of Negro Women (1935–49) and advised the New Deal administration of FRANKLIN D. ROOSEVELT *on minority issues.*

1 The true worth of a race must be measured by the character of its womanhood.

Address to Chicago Women's Federation, 3 June 1933, publ. in *Black Women in White America*, 'A Century of Progress of Negro Women' (ed. Gerda Lerner, 1972)

(Sir) John Betjeman (1906–84)

BRITISH POET

Quintessentially English and a champion of tradition, he mingled satire with humour and nostalgia in his poems. His verse autobiography Summoned by Bells *(1960) was an instant success, and he was appointed Poet Laureate in 1972. His future mother-in-law Lady Chetwoode said of him: 'We invite people like that to tea, but we don't marry them.'*

1 *Oh! Chintzy, chintzy cheeriness,*
   Half dead and half alive!
   'Death in Leamington', publ. in *Mount Zion* (1931)

2 *Broad of Church and broad of mind,*
   Broad before and broad behind,
   A keen ecclesiologist,
   A rather dirty Wykehamist.
   'The Wykehamist', publ. ibid. Opening lines.

3 *Ghastly Good Taste, or A Depressing Story of the Rise and Fall of English Architecture.*
   Title of book (1933)

4 *He rose, and he put down* The Yellow Book.
   He staggered – and, terrible-eyed,
   He brushed past the palms on the staircase
   And was helped to a hansom outside.
   'The Arrest of Oscar Wilde at the Cadogan Hotel', st. 9, publ. in *Continual Dew* (1937). Closing lines of poem.

5 *Come, friendly bombs, and fall on Slough!*
   It isn't fit for humans now,
   There isn't grass to graze a cow.
   Swarm over, Death!
   'Slough', st. 1, publ. in *Continual Dew* (1937). Betjeman's renowned antipathy towards modern architecture and town planning was directed par-

ticularly at the 'new towns' of the home counties.

6 *Gracious Lord, oh bomb the Germans.*
   Spare their women for Thy Sake,
   And if that is not too easy
   We will pardon Thy Mistake.
   But gracious Lord, whate'er shall be,
   Don't let anyone bomb me.
   'In Westminster Abbey', st. 2, publ. in *Old Lights for New Chancels* (1940)

7 *Keep our Empire undismembered*
   Guide our Forces by Thy Hand,
   Gallant blacks from far Jamaica,
   Honduras and Togoland;
   Protect them Lord in all their fights,
   And, even more, protect the whites.
   Ibid., st. 3

8 *Think of what our Nation stands for,*
   Books from Boots' and country lanes,
   Free speech, free passes, class distinction,
   Democracy and proper drains.
   Ibid., st. 4

9 *For we, at any rate, England stands for the Church of England, eccentric incumbents, oil-lit churches, Women's Institutes, modest village inns, arguments about cow parsley on the altar, the noise of mowing machines on Saturday afternoons, local newspapers, local auctions, the poetry of Tennyson, Crabbe, Hardy and Matthew Arnold, local talent, local concerts, a visit to the cinema, branch-line trains, light railways, leaning on gates and looking across fields.*
   BBC broadcast 25 February 1943, first publ. in the *Listener* 11 March 1943 as 'Oh to be in England . . .', publ. in *Coming Home* as 'Coming Home' (1997)

10 *Miss J. Hunter Dunn, Miss J. Hunter Dunn,*
   Furnish'd and burnish'd by Aldershot sun,
   What strenuous singles we played after tea,
   We in the tournament – you against me!
   'A Subaltern's Love-song', st. 1, publ. in *New Bats in Old Belfries* (1945)

11 *I have a Vision of the Future, chum.*
   The workers' flats in fields of soya beans
   Tower up like silver pencils, score on score.
   'The Planster's Vision', publ. ibid.

12 *And is it true? And is it true,*
   This most tremendous tale of all,
   Seen in a stained-glass window's hue,
   A Baby in an ox's stall?
   The Maker of the stars and sea
   Become a Child on earth for me?
   'Christmas', st. 6, publ. in *A Few Late Chrysanthemums* (1954)

13 *Phone for the fish-knives, Norman*
   As Cook is a little unnerved;

You kiddies have crumpled the serviettes
And I must have things daintily served.
'How to Get on in Society' (1954), publ. ibid.
Opening lines of poem.

14 Still they stand, the churches of England,
their towers grey above billowy globes of
elm trees, the red cross of St George flying
over their battlements, the Duplex Envelope System employed for collections,
schoolmistresses at the organ, incumbent
in the chancel, scattered worshippers in the
nave, Tortoise stove slowly consuming its
ration as the familiar seventeenth-century
phrases come echoing down arcades of
ancient stone.
English Parish Churches, Introduction (1958)

15 *The dread of beatings! Dread of being late!*
And, greatest dread of all, the dread of
games!
Summoned by Bells, ch. 7 (1960)

16 *We spray the fields and scatter*
The poison on the ground
So that no wicked wild flowers
Upon our farm be found.
'Harvest Hymn', publ. in *High and Low* (1966)

17 *All concrete sheds around us*
And Jaguars in the yard,
The telly lounge and deep-freeze
Are ours from working hard.
Ibid.

18 People's backyards are much more interesting than their front gardens, and houses
that back on to railways are public bene-
factors.
Quoted in the *Observer* 20 March 1983

Aneurin Bevan (1897–1960)

BRITISH POLITICIAN
Known as Nye Bevan. He served as Labour MP for
Ebbw Vale 1929–60, and as Minister of Health
(1945–51) established the National Health Service
(1948), later resigning in protest against proposed
charges. A brilliant orator, though also called a
'merchant of discourtesy' by WINSTON CHUR-
CHILL, *he inspired a 'Bevanite' faction of the party*
which opposed the reformist policies of CLEMENT
ATTLEE.

1 Freedom is the by-product of economic
surplus.
Quoted in *Aneurin Bevan*, vol. 1, ch. 3 (1962) by
MICHAEL FOOT. The remark was often reiterated by Bevan from the 1920s onwards.

2 The worst thing I can say about democracy
is that it has tolerated the Right Honourable Gentleman for four and a half years.
Referring to NEVILLE CHAMBERLAIN, in speech
to House of Commons 23 July 1929, publ. in
Hansard. Bevan did not attempt to hide his poor
opinion of Chamberlain. 'He has the lucidity
which is the by-product of a fundamentally

sterile mind,' he declared on another occasion.
'He does not have to struggle . . . with the
crowded pulsations of a fecund imagination. On
the contrary he is almost devoid of imagination.'

3 Fascism is not in itself a new order of
society. It is the future refusing to be born.
Remark, July 1940, quoted in *Aneurin Bevan*,
vol. 1, ch. 10 (1962) by Michael Foot

4 His ear is so sensitively attuned to the bugle
note of history that he is often deaf to the
more raucous clamour of contemporary
life. The seven-league tempo of his imagination hastens him on to the 'sunny uplands'
of the future, but he is apt to forget that the
slow steps of humanity must travel every
inch of the weary road that leads there.
Of WINSTON CHURCHILL, in remark made in
late 1940, ibid.

5 He seems determined to make a trumpet
sound like a tin whistle.
Of CLEMENT ATTLEE, in remark in 1945, quoted
ibid., ch. 14. Referring to Attlee's playing subordi-
nate role to ANTHONY EDEN when the two were
delegated to represent Britain at a UN conference in San Francisco. Attlee, according to
Bevan, had 'consistently underplayed his position and opportunities. . . . He brings to the
fierce struggle of politics the tepid enthusiasm of
a lazy summer afternoon at a cricket match.'

6 This island is made mainly of coal and surrounded by fish. Only an organizing
genius could produce a shortage of coal
and fish at the same time.
Speech at Blackpool, 24 May 1945, quoted in the
Daily Herald 25 May 1945. Bevan's speech was
made on the day that WINSTON CHURCHILL
announced the formation of a Conservative
'caretaker' government in the wake of VE Day
and the dissolution of the wartime coalition.
The Conservatives were to be ejected from office
in the general election two months later, when
Labour won a landslide victory.

7 No amount of cajolery, and no attempts at
ethical or social seduction, can eradicate
from my heart a deep burning hatred for
the Tory Party. . . . So far as I am concerned they are lower than vermin.
Speech at Manchester, 4 July 1948, quoted in *The*
Times 5 July 1948. Bevan was referring to the
social policies of the Conservative Party, which
'condemned millions of first-class people to
semi-starvation'. His invective, which formed
part of a speech to inaugurate the National
Health Service, provoked outrage in the press
and embarrassment within his own party.

8 He is a man suffering from petrified ado-
lescence.
Of WINSTON CHURCHILL, quoted in *Aneurin*
Bevan, ch. 11 (1953) by Vincent Brome

9 We know what happens to people who stay
in the middle of the road. They get run over.
Quoted in the *Observer* 6 December 1953

10 **I know that the right kind of leader for the Labour Party is a kind of desiccated calculating machine.**

Speech to Tribune Group at Labour Party Conference, 29 September 1954, quoted in *Aneurin Bevan*, vol. 2, ch. 11 (1973) by Michael Foot. The remark was taken to refer to HUGH GAITSKELL, though Bevan later denied this.

11 **If we complain about the tune, there is no reason to attack the monkey when the organ grinder is present.**

Speech to House of Commons, 16 May 1957, publ. in *Hansard*. Bevan was referring to Foreign Minister Selwyn Lloyd and Prime Minister HAROLD MACMILLAN, holding the latter accountable for the Suez fiasco the previous autumn. Although Macmillan, as Chancellor of the Exchequer, had no direct involvement in foreign affairs during the crisis, he had urged a tough response to Nasser's nationalization of the canal.

12 **If you carry this resolution you will send Britain's Foreign Secretary naked into the conference chamber.**

Speech at Labour Party Conference, Brighton, 3 October 1957, quoted in the *Daily Herald* 4 October 1957. As Shadow Foreign Secretary under Gaitskell's leadership of the party, Bevan spoke in opposition to a motion in favour of unilateral nuclear disarmament.

13 **The Prime Minister has an absolute genius for putting flamboyant labels on empty luggage.**

Referring to HAROLD MACMILLAN, in Queen's Speech debate in House of Commons, 3 November 1959, quoted in *Aneurin Bevan*, vol. 2, ch. 16 (1973) by Michael Foot

14 **I read the newspapers avidly. It is my one form of continuous fiction.**

The Times 29 March 1960

15 **He is a man walking backwards with his face to the future.**

Quoted in *The Fine Art of Political Wit*, ch. 9 (1964) by Leon Harris. Referring to Sir Walter Elliot, the Conservative Minister of Agriculture.

16 **The purpose of getting power is to be able to give it away.**

Quoted in *Aneurin Bevan*, vol. 2, ch. 1 (1973) by Michael Foot

17 **You're not an MP, you're a gastronomic pimp.**

Quoted ibid., ch. 6. Said to a colleague who complained of a heavy week of Rotarian lunches and Chamber of Commerce dinners.

William Beveridge (1879–1963)

BRITISH ECONOMIST

Baron Beveridge. He was Director of the London School of Economics (1919–37) and Master of University College, Oxford (1937–45). In 1942 he produced the Beveridge Report, a scheme of comprehensive social insurance that was the blueprint for the British welfare state.

1 **The object of government in peace and in war is not the glory of rulers or of races, but the happiness of the common man.**

Social Insurance and Allied Services, pt 7 (1942)

2 **The adventure of full employment in a free society is not like the directed flight of an aircraft on a beam. It is a voyage among shifting and dangerous currents. All that can be done is to see that the craft is well found, and that the pilot has all the necessary controls, and the instruments to guide his use of them.**

Full Employment in a Free Society, pt 4 (1944)

3 **Ignorance is an evil weed, which dictators may cultivate among their dupes, but which no democracy can afford among its citizens.**

Ibid., pt 7

Ernest Bevin (1881–1951)

BRITISH POLITICIAN

A veteran trades union campaigner, he was General Secretary of the Transport and General Workers Union 1921–40, and as a Labour MP served in Churchill's War Cabinet and was Foreign Secretary (1945–51). A.J.P. TAYLOR commented, 'He objected to ideas only when others had them.'

1 **The most conservative man in the world is the British Trade Unionist when you want to change him.**

Speech to Trades Union Congress, Edinburgh, 8 September 1927, publ. in *Report of Proceedings of the Trades Union Congress* (1927)

2 **My [foreign] policy is to be able to take a ticket at Victoria Station and go anywhere I damn well please.**

Quoted in the *Spectator* 20 April 1951

Georges Bidault (1899–1983)

FRENCH RESISTANCE LEADER AND STATESMAN

He headed the National Council of Resistance in 1943 and was Prime Minister in 1946, 1949–50 and 1958. Opposed to the Algerian policy pursued by DE GAULLE, *he was charged with treason and went into exile 1962–8.*

1 **Freedom is when one hears the bell at 7 o'clock in the morning and knows it is the milkman and not the Gestapo.**

Quoted in the *Observer* 23 April 1950

2 **The weak have one weapon: the errors of those who think they are strong.**

Quoted in the *Observer* 15 July 1962

Kathryn Bigelow (b. 1951)

US FILM-MAKER

She won acclaim as director of the horror film Near Dark (1987) and the thrillers Blue Steel *(1990) and* Strange Days *(1995).*

1 Films don't cause violence, people do. Violence defines our existence. To shield oneself is more dangerous than trying to reflect it.

Interview in the *Guardian* 23 December 1995

Steve Biko (1946–77)

SOUTH AFRICAN ANTI-APARTHEID ACTIVIST

He was founder and leader of the Black Consciousness Movement in South Africa and became President of the Black People's Convention in 1972. Banned from political activity in 1973, he died in police custody.

1 The claim by whites of monopoly on comfort and security has always been so exclusive that blacks see whites as the major obstacle in their progress towards peace, prosperity and a sane society. . . . At best therefore blacks see whiteness as a concept that warrants being despised, hated, destroyed and replaced by an aspiration with more human content in it. At worst blacks envy white society for the comfort it has usurped and at the centre of this envy is the wish – nay, the secret determination – in the innermost minds of most blacks who think like this, to kick whites off those comfortable garden chairs that one sees as he rides in a bus, out of town, and to claim them for themselves.

'Fear – an Important Determinant in South African Politics', first publ. in 1971 in SASO newsletter, one of a series of articles entitled 'I Write What I Like' under the pseudonym of Frank Talk, repr. in *I Write What I Like* (ed. Aelred Stubbs, 1978). The words were repeated by the judge at Biko's trial in 1976.

2 Powerlessness breeds a race of beggars who smile at the enemy and swear at him in the sanctity of their toilets; who shout 'Baas' willingly during the day and call the white man a dog in their buses as they go home. Once again the concept of fear is at the heart of this two-faced behaviour on the part of the conquered blacks.

Ibid.

3 The philosophy of Black Consciousness therefore expresses group pride and the determination of the black to rise and attain the envisaged self. . . . At the heart of this kind of thinking is the realization by blacks that the most potent weapon in the hands of the oppressor is the mind of the oppressed.

'Black Consciousness and the Quest for a True Humanity', first publ. in *Black Theology: The South African Voice* (ed. Basil Moore, 1973), repr. ibid.

4 The power of a movement lies in the fact that it can indeed change the habits of people. This change is not the result of force but of dedication, of moral persuasion.

Interview in July 1976, quoted in *Biko*, ch. 2 (1978) by Donald Woods

5 Whites must be made to realize that they are only human, not superior. Same with blacks. They must be made to realize that they are also human, not inferior.

Quoted in the *Boston Globe* 26 October 1977

6 You are either alive and proud or you are dead, and when you are dead, you can't care anyway. And your method of death can itself be a politicizing thing. So you die in the riots. For a hell of a lot of them, in fact, there's really nothing to lose – almost literally, given the kind of situations they come from. So if you can overcome the personal fear of death, which is a highly irrational thing, you know, then you're on the way.

Interview first publ. in the *New Republic* 7 January 1978, repr. in *I Write What I Like*, 'On Death' (ed. Aelred Stubbs, 1978)

7 Listen, if you guys want to do this your way, you have got to handcuff me and bind my feet together, so that I can't respond. If you allow me to respond, I'm certainly going to respond. And I'm afraid you may have to kill me in the process even if it's not your intention.

To his gaolers, quoted ibid. With these words Biko forecast the manner of his death at the hands of the South African police at Port Elizabeth Jail, 12 September 1977.

8 If you want to say something radical, you should dress conservative.

Advice given to the young BARBARA FOLLETT, quoted by her in the *Observer* 25 February 1996

Laurence Binyon (1869–1943)

BRITISH POET

His collections include Lyric Poems *(1894) and* Odes *(1901), though he is best remembered for his poem 'For the Fallen' (1914). He was Professor of Poetry at Harvard (1933–4).*

1 *They shall grow not old, as we that are left
      grow old:
   Age shall not weary them, nor the years
      condemn.
   At the going down of the sun and in the
      morning
   We will remember them.*

'For the Fallen', first publ. in *The Times* 21 September 1914, repr. in *Collected Poems*

(1931). The lines which were set to music by Elgar are inscribed on war memorials throughout Britain and the Commonwealth.

William Norman Birkett (1883–1962)
BRITISH LAWYER
Baron Birkett of Ulveston. A Liberal MP (1923–4 and 1929–31), he established a reputation as counsel in murder trials and was prominent in the summing up of the Nuremberg Trials (1945–6). He was Lord Justice of Appeal 1950–57.

1 I do not object to people looking at their watches when I am speaking. But I strongly object when they start shaking them to make certain they are still going.
Quoted in the *Observer* 30 Oct 1960

(Sir) John Birt (b. 1944)
BRITISH TELEVISION EXECUTIVE
He joined Granada television in 1968 and worked on World in Action. *He was later Deputy Director of the BBC (1987) and Director-General (1993–9), during which time he instituted controversial reforms.*

1 The BBC is the most successful cultural institution in the world, one of the great inventions of the twentieth century. Let it flower; let it blossom; let it flourish; let it pioneer; let it grow. It is not difficult to see why it became easier to bash the BBC than to revere it. But do not take the BBC for granted.
James MacTaggart Memorial Lecture, Edinburgh, 23 August 1996, publ. in the *Guardian* 24 August 1996

(Sir) Harrison Birtwistle (b. 1934)
BRITISH COMPOSER
An avant-garde composer, he co-founded The Fires of London (1967) with Peter Maxwell Davies. His works include the orchestral Tragoedia *(1965) and the opera* Punch and Judy *(1967).*

1 People basically only want very little from music, and I want a lot from it. It's capable of amazing journeys and meanings. And if you understand that, the problem with the kind of music I write is no problem at all.
Interview in the *Independent on Sunday* 7 April 1996

Elizabeth Bishop (1911–79)
US POET
Having grown up in New England and Nova Scotia, she lived for sixteen years in Brazil, the subject of much of her poetry. She received the Pulitzer Prize in 1956 for her first two collections North and South *(1946) and* Cold Spring *(1955).*

1 *The armored cars of dreams, contrived to let us do
so many a dangerous thing.*
'Sleeping Standing Up', st. 2, publ. in *Poems: North and South* (1946)

2 *Topography displays no favorites; North's as near as West.
More delicate than the historians' are the map-makers' colors.*
'The Map', publ. ibid.

3 *Should we have stayed at home and thought of here?
Where should we be today?
Is it right to be watching strangers in a play in this strangest of theatres?*
'Questions of Travel', st. 2, publ. in *Questions of Travel* (1965)

4 *What childishness is it that while there's breath of life
in our bodies, we are determined to rush to see the sun the other way around?*
Ibid.

5 *The art of losing isn't hard to master;
so many things seem filled with the intent to be lost that their loss is no disaster.*
'One Art', publ. in *Geography III* (1976)

Björk (b. 1965)
ICELANDIC SINGER
Renowned for her gymnastic vocal technique and breath control, she released her first solo album Debut *after leaving the Sugarcubes in 1992. Other albums include* Post *(1995).*

1 I tell women, 'Go and masturbate! Get loads of kinky books and masturbate every day! *They* do it from the age of nine!'
Remark in 1993, quoted in *New Musical Express* 4 February 1995

Conrad Black (b. 1944)
CANADIAN-BORN BRITISH NEWSPAPER PROPRIETOR
Baron Black of Crossharbour. He has spent thirty years building up the Hollinger media empire, acquiring the Telegraph *newspaper group in 1986. In 2000 he took British citizenship, renouncing his Canadian citizenship the following year.*

1 My experience with journalists authorises me to record that a very large number of them are ignorant, lazy, opinionated, intellectually dishonest and inadequately supervised.
Testimony to a Canadian Senate Committee, quoted in the *Observer* 28 January 1996

Cherie Blair (b. 1954)
BRITISH LAWYER
The wife of TONY BLAIR, *she is a specialist in employment law and a judge.*

1 I'm not Superwoman. . . . The reality of my daily life is that I am juggling a lot of balls in the air . . . and sometimes some of the balls get dropped. There just aren't enough hours in the day.

Speech 10 December 2002, publ. in the *Daily Telegraph* 11 December 2002. Explaining her error of judgement in enlisting the help of Peter Foster, the boyfriend of her personal adviser Carol Caplin and a convicted fraudster, as an agent to buy property in Bristol.

Tony Blair (b. 1953)

BRITISH POLITICIAN AND PRIME MINISTER
Elected leader of the Labour Party in 1994, he achieved a landslide victory in the 1997 general election, becoming the youngest prime minister since 1812. He was re-elected in 2001. See MICHAEL FOOT 3, SUN 9.

1 The art of leadership is saying no, not saying yes. It is very easy to say yes.

Quoted in the *Mail on Sunday* 2 October 1994

2 Any parent wants the best for their children. I am not going to make a choice for my child on the basis of what is the politically correct thing to do.

Quoted in the *Independent on Sunday* 1 January 1995. Blair provoked controversy by sending his children to a school outside the comprehensive system.

3 Ask me my three main priorities for Government, and I tell you: education, education and education.

Speech at Labour Party Conference, 1 October 1996, quoted in *The Times* 2 October 1996

4 People everywhere . . . kept faith with Princess Diana. They liked her, they loved her, they regarded her as one of the people. She was the People's Princess, and that is how she will stay, how she will remain in our hearts and our memories for ever.

Speech at Sedgefield, 31 August 1997, quoted in *The Times* 1 September 1997. Blair had been informed of DIANA's death a few hours before.

5 This is not a time for soundbites. We've left them at home. I feel the hand of history upon our shoulders.

Press conference in Belfast, Radio 5 Live, 7 April 1998. The Prime Minister had arrived in Northern Ireland as the peace discussions appeared to be on the brink of collapse. Blair also used the phrase 'hand of history' on the occasion of the opening of the Northern Ireland Assembly at Stormont Castle, 2 December 1999, the day when the Republic of Ireland dropped its constitutional claim over Northern Ireland.

6 In these past few days, the irresistible force, the political will, has met the immovable object, the legacy of the past, and we have moved in.

Speech at Stormont, 10 April 1998, quoted in *The Times* 11 April 1998. Blair was celebrating Senator George Mitchell's announcement of the signing of the Good Friday Agreement after twenty-two months of negotiation.

7 My friends! The class war is over.

Speech to Labour Party Conference, Bournemouth, quoted in *The Times* 2 October 1999

8 This is not a battle between the United States of America and terrorism but between the free and democratic world and terrorism. We therefore here in Britain stand shoulder to shoulder with our American friends in this hour of tragedy and we, like them, will not rest until this evil is driven from our world.

Quoted in *The Times* 12 September 2001

9 The starving, the wretched, the dispossessed, the ignorant, those living in want and squalor from the deserts of Northern Africa to the slums of Gaza, to the mountain ranges of Afghanistan: they too are our cause.

Speech to Labour Party conference, Brighton, 2 October 2001, quoted in the *Guardian* 3 October 2001

10 The defining characteristic of the modern world is insecurity.

Quoted in the *Scotsman* 1 January 2003

11 Let us say one thing: If we are wrong, we will have destroyed a threat that at its least is responsible for inhuman carnage and suffering. That is something I am confident history will forgive. But if our critics are wrong, if we are right, as I believe with every fibre of instinct and conviction I have that we are, and we do not act, then we will have hesitated in the face of this menace when we should have given leadership. That is something history will not forgive.

Speech to US Congress 17 July 2003, quoted in the *Washington Post* 18 July 2003. On the war against Iraq.

Raymond Blanc (b. 1949)

FRENCH CHEF AND RESTAURATEUR
In England since 1972, he opened the prestigious Le Manoir aux Quat' Saisons in 1984, quickly established as one of the top gastronomic destinations outside London.

1 To me, when a mother puts food in a microwave for her children, it is an act of hate.

Quoted in the *Daily Telegraph* 21 October 1995

Maurice Blanchot (1907–2003)

FRENCH LITERARY THEORIST AND AUTHOR
After wartime renunciation of Fascism, he became a man of letters. His critical works include The Space of Literature *(1955) and his fiction* Death Sentence *(1948) and* The Last Man *(1957).*

1 To write is to make oneself the echo of
what cannot cease speaking.
The Space of Literature, ch. 1, 'The Essential Solitude' (1955, transl. 1982)

Alan Bleasdale (b. 1946)

BRITISH PLAYWRIGHT AND NOVELIST
He won a large audience for the TV series The
Boys from the Blackstuff *(1982) and* GBH *(1991),
both set in his native Liverpool, and for his adapta-
tion of* Oliver Twist *(1999). Stage works include*
Are You Lonesome Tonight? *(1985).*

1 Gizza job, go on, gizzit!
Yosser Hughes, in *The Boys from the Blackstuff*
(TV series, 1982). The catchphrase is usually
quoted, 'gissa job!'

Edward Blishen (1920–96)

BRITISH AUTHOR
*For many years a teacher, he was the editor of
anthologies and the author of reference works for
children as well as of biography and novels, for
example* Roaring Boys *(1955).*

1 Life is amazing: and the teacher had better
prepare himself to be a medium for that
amazement.
Donkey Work, pt 2, ch. 5 (autobiography, 1983).
Blishen rejected the idea that teaching is a discipline, but considered it to be 'half vocational,
half an emptiness dressed up in garments
borrowed from philosophy, psychology,
literature'.

Alexander Blok (1880–1921)

RUSSIAN POET
*Considered the leading Russian Symbolist, he took
the 1917 Revolution as inspiration for his masterpiece* The Twelve *(1918), though later became disillusioned with the Bolshevik régime. As Trotsky
commented, 'Certainly Blok was not one of us, but
he came towards us. And that is what broke him.'*

1 Ah, a bitter bitterness,
A sweet life we've won,
With a tattered overcoat
And an Austrian gun.
The Twelve, sect. 3 (1918), repr. in *A Second Book
of Russian Verse* (ed. C. M. Bowra, 1948). The
poem describes the experiences of twelve guards
during the October Revolution.

2 Like the dog, stands the bourgeois, hungry,
A silent question to the sky;
The old world, like a homeless mongrel,
With tail between its legs stands by.
Ibid., sect. 9

3 On they march with sovereign tread,
With a starving dog behind,
With a blood-red flag ahead –
In the storm where none can see,
From the rifle bullets free,
Gently walking on the snow,
Where like pearls the snowflakes glow,

Marches rose-crowned in the van
Jesus Christ, the Son of Man.
Ibid., sect. 12. Last lines of poem.

Allan Bloom (1930–92)

US ACADEMIC AND AUTHOR
*A Professor of Philosophy and Political Science
whose writings have stoked debate about the state
of America, he called himself 'the corrosive force
that appeals to liberals'. His most controversial
book,* The Closing of the American Mind *(1987),
is a critique of the education system.*

1 Only Socrates knew, after a lifetime of
unceasing labor, that he was ignorant.
Now every high-school student knows
that. How did it become so easy?
The Closing of the American Mind, Introduction
(1987)

2 The spirit is at home, if not entirely satis-
fied, in America.
Ibid., pt 2, 'Two Revolutions and Two States of
Nature'

3 We are like ignorant shepherds living on a
site where great civilizations once
flourished. The shepherds play with the
fragments that pop up to the surface, having no notion of the beautiful structures of
which they were once a part.
Ibid., 'Our Ignorance'

4 The most important function of the university in an age of reason is to protect reason
from itself.
Ibid., pt 3, 'From Socrates' *Apology* to Heidegger's *Rektoratsrede*'

Harold Bloom (b. 1930)

US LITERARY CRITIC
*He has taught continuously at Yale University
since 1955, while retaining his independence of the
academic world, which he sees as dominated 'by
fools, knaves, charlatans and bureaucrats'.*

1 The Anxiety of Influence.
Book title (1973). Bloom's most influential work
used Freudian concepts to postulate an unconscious literary battle between generations of
poets and authors.

2 People cannot stand the saddest truth I
know about the very nature of reading and
writing imaginative literature, which is
that poetry does not teach us how to talk
to other people: it teaches us how to talk to
ourselves. What I'm desperately trying to
do is to get students to talk to themselves
as though they are indeed themselves, and
not someone else.
Interview in the *Guardian* 6 March 1999

David Blunkett (b. 1947)

BRITISH POLITICIAN
*Elected Labour MP for Sheffield, Brightside, in
1987, he became Secretary of State for Education*

and Employment in 1997 and Home Secretary in 2001. He has been blind since birth.

1 Old Labour is the idea that you did things *to* people, New Labour is about enabling people to do things for themselves.

Quoted in the *Guardian* 18 July 1998

Robert Bly (b. 1926)

US POET AND AUTHOR

His magazine The Fifties *(later* The Sixties *and* The Seventies*) published lesser-known European and South American poets. The first book of his own poetry,* Silence in the Snowy Fields, *appeared in 1962,* Morning Poems *in 1997.*

1 Every modern male has, lying at the bottom of his psyche, a large, primitive being covered with hair down to his feet. Making contact with this Wild Man is the step the Eighties male or the Nineties male has yet to take. That bucketing-out process has yet to begin in our contemporary culture.

Iron John, ch. 1, 'Finding Iron John' (1990)

Enid Blyton (1897–1968)

BRITISH CHILDREN'S WRITER

She achieved enormous popularity with over 600 books featuring Noddy and Big Ears, the Famous Five and the Secret Seven.

1 Golliwogs are merely lovable black toys, not Negroes. Teddy bears are also toys, but if there happens to be a naughty one in my books for younger children, this does not mean that I hate bears.

Quoted in *The Enid Blyton Story*, ch. 5 (1987) by Bob Mullan. Blyton's books were criticized from the 1960s for their stereotyping.

Ivan F. Boesky (b. 1937)

US FINANCIER

The best known of Wall Street arbitrageurs, he was fined $100 million for insider dealing in 1986 and served a prison sentence.

1 Greed is all right, by the way . . . I think greed is healthy. You can be greedy and still feel good about yourself.

Commencement Address, School of Business Administration, University of California, Berkeley, 18 May 1986. Boesky's words were later picked up in OLIVER STONE's film, *Wall Street* (1987), spoken by Gordon Gekko (played by Michael Douglas): 'Greed is good. Greed is right. Greed clarifies, cuts through, and captures. Greed has marked the upward surge of mankind.' Boesky himself was later convicted of conspiring to file false documents with the federal government, involving insider trading violations.

Louise Bogan (1897–1970)

US POET AND CRITIC

Poetry editor for the New Yorker *(1931–69), she published six volumes of her own verse, from* Body

of this Death *(1923) to* The Blue Estuaries *(1968), as well as the highly regarded* Achievement in American Poetry 1900–1950 *(1951).*

1 *Women have no wilderness in them,*
   They are provident instead,
   Content in the tight hot cell of their hearts
   To eat dusty bread.

'Women', st. 1, publ. in *Body of this Death* (1923)

2 But childhood prolonged cannot remain a fairyland. It becomes a hell.

'Childhood's False Eden' (1940), repr. in *Selected Criticism: Poetry and Prose* (1955). Referring to KATHERINE MANSFIELD.

3 The intellectual is a middle-class product; if he is not born into the class he must soon insert himself into it, in order to exist. He is the fine nervous flower of the bourgeoisie.

'Some Notes on Popular and Unpopular Art' (1943), repr. ibid.

Humphrey Bogart (1899–1957)

US SCREEN ACTOR

After an uneven stage career and myriad B-parts in movies, he gave birth to the 'Bogie' cult with the films High Sierra *and* The Maltese Falcon *(both 1941). He co-starred with his fourth wife* LAUREN BACALL *in* To Have and Have Not *(1944) and* The Big Sleep *(1946). See also* INGRID BERGMAN 1, RAYMOND CHANDLER 1, DASHIELL HAMMETT 1.

1 Of all the gin joints in all the towns in all the world, she walks into mine.

Rick Blaine (Humphrey Bogart), in *Casablanca* (film, 1942, screenplay by Julius Epstein, Philip Epstein and Howard Koch, from the play *Everybody Goes to Rick's* by Murray Burnett and Joan Alison, directed by Michael Curtiz)

2 Here's looking at you, kid.

Ibid. Toast spoken to Ilsa Lund (Ingrid Bergman)

3 I stick my neck out for nobody. I'm the only cause I'm interested in.

Ibid. Bogart's words are echoed in another speech by him in JOHN HUSTON's film *Key Largo* (1948), where he says: 'I fight nobody's battles but my own', and also recall a similar statement by CLARK GABLE as Rhett Butler in *Gone with the Wind* (1939).

4 I'm no good at being noble, but it doesn't take much to see that the problems of three little people don't amount to a hill of beans in this crazy world. Someday you'll understand that.

Ibid. Spoken in the final scenes of the film to Ilsa Lund (Ingrid Bergman), escaping from Casablanca with her husband.

5 Louis, I think this is the beginning of a beautiful friendship.

Ibid. Spoken to Cpt. Louis Renault (Claude

Rains) in the film's last words. In her 1980 autobiography, INGRID BERGMAN recounted the uncertainty over how the film was going to end, and even whether or not she was to get on the plane, until this closing scene was shot.

6 **My, my. Such a lot of guns around town and so few brains.**

Philip Marlowe (Humphrey Bogart), in *The Big Sleep* (film, 1946, screenplay by WILLIAM FAULK-NER, Leigh Brackett and Jules Furthman adapted from Raymond Chandler's novel, directed by Howard Hawks)

7 **You're not a star until they can spell your name in Karachi.**

Quoted in *Star Billing* (1985) by David Brown. The showbiz saying has also been attributed to ROGER MOORE.

8 **Tennis, anyone?**

Attributed sole line in first speaking part, but denied by Bogart. In contrast to his later cynical film roles, his early parts on stage were as romantic leads: as critic DAVID THOMSON commented, 'He was from the upper classes, and he usually played young men who asked girls for tennis.'

Niels Bohr (1885–1962)

DANISH PHYSICIST
He founded and directed the Institute of Theoretical Physics in Copenhagen (1920–62), produced a new model of atomic structure, and contributed to the development of quantum physics.

1 **An expert is a man who has made all the mistakes which can be made in a very narrow field.**

Quoted in *The Harvest of a Quiet Eye* (1977) by Alan L. Mackay

William Bolitho (1890–1930)

BRITISH AUTHOR
William Bolitho Ryall. He is principally known for his offbeat biographical studies such as Murder for Profit *(1926), a study of five mass murderers, and* Twelve Against the Gods *(1929).*

1 **The shortest way out of Manchester is notoriously a bottle of Gordon's gin.**

Twelve Against the Gods, 'Cagliostro (and Seraphina)' (1929)

Robert Bolt (1924–95)

BRITISH PLAYWRIGHT
He achieved major success with his play A Man for All Seasons *(1960), and wrote the screenplay for the film (1967). He also wrote the screenplays of* Lawrence of Arabia *(1962),* Dr Zhivago *(1965) and* The Mission *(1986).*

1 **Morality's *not* practical. Morality's a gesture. A complicated gesture learned from books.**

Sir Thomas More, in *A Man for All Seasons*, act 2 (1960)

2 **The nobility of England, my lord, would have snored through the Sermon on the Mount.**

Ibid.

3 **The law is not a 'light' for you or any man to see by; the law is not an instrument of any kind. The law is a causeway upon which so long as he keeps to it a citizen may walk safely.**

Ibid.

Edward Bond (b. 1934)

BRITISH PLAYWRIGHT
The brutal imagery of his early plays Saved *(1965) and* Early Morning *(1968) caused them to be banned, and the resulting public outcry helped to bring about the end of censorship on the English stage.*

1 **I write about violence as naturally as Jane Austen wrote about manners. Violence shapes and obsesses our society, and if we do not stop being violent we have no future.**

Lear, Preface (1972)

Violet Bonham-Carter (1887–1969)

BRITISH POLITICIAN
Lady Asquith. The daughter of HERBERT ASQUITH, *she was President of the Liberal Party 1944–5.*

1 **[He] has a brilliant mind until it is made up.**

Quoted in *The Fine Art of Political Wit*, ch. 12 (1964) by Leon Harris. Referring to Labour politician Sir Stafford Cripps.

Bono (b. 1960)

IRISH ROCK MUSICIAN
Originally Paul Hewson. He is lead singer of U2, which in the 1980s became the world's biggest rock band based on the sales of such albums as War *(1983) and* The Joshua Tree *(1987). He has campaigned to cancel Third World debt and on environmental issues.*

1 **What a city, what a night, what a crowd, what a bomb, what a mistake, what a wanker you have for a president**

Acceptance speech at MTV Europe Music Awards in Paris, quoted in *Mojo* January 1996. Referring to French nuclear testing in the Pacific.

2 **These days, everyone wants John Lennon's sunglasses, accent and swagger, but no one is prepared to take their clothes off and stand naked like he did in his songs. Putting your head over the parapet means**

something completely different these days, but it's still a big part of what rock is all about for me. You have to use your celebrity, negotiate your position and be aware that celebrity can diminish a cause as much as illuminate it.

Interview in the *Guardian* 4 March 2000

Murray Bookchin (b. 1921)

US ECOLOGIST

His books Our Synthetic Environment *(1962) and* Crisis in Our Cities *(1965) were among the earliest warnings of the dangers to the environment, arguing that 'formless urban agglomerations' should be replaced by 'human-scaled ecotechnologies'.*

1 Humanity has passed through a long history of one-sidedness and of a social condition that has always contained the potential of destruction, despite its creative achievements in technology. The great project of our time must be to open the other eye: to see all-sidedly and wholly, to heal and transcend the cleavage between humanity and nature that came with early wisdom.

   The Ecology of Freedom, ch. 1 (1982)

John Boorman (b. 1933)

BRITISH FILM-MAKER

His greatest successes over an uneven career include Point Blank *(1967),* Deliverance *(1972),* Excalibur *(1981) and* Hope and Glory *(1987).*

1 What is passion? It is surely the becoming of a person. Are we not, for most of our lives, marking time? Most of our being is at rest, unlived. In passion, the body and the spirit seek expression outside of self. Passion is all that is other from self. Sex is only interesting when it releases passion. The more extreme and the more expressed that passion is, the more unbearable does life seem without it. It reminds us that if passion dies or is denied, we are partly dead and that soon, come what may, we will be wholly so.

   Journal entry, 16 May 1991, publ. in *Projections* (ed. John Boorman and Walter Donohue, 1992)

Daniel J. Boorstin (b. 1914)

US HISTORIAN

Daniel Joseph Boorstin. Professor of American History at Chicago University 1944–69, he is the author of A History of the United States *(1980) and* The Americans *trilogy (1965–73), among other works. He was Librarian of Congress 1975–87.*

1 We need not be theologians to see that we have shifted responsibility for making the world interesting from God to the newspaperman.

   The Image, ch. 1 (1961)

2 The celebrity is a person who is known for his well-knownness.

   Ibid., ch. 2

3 We read advertisements . . . to discover and enlarge our desires. We are always ready – even eager – to discover, from the announcement of a new product, what we have all along wanted without really knowing it.

   Ibid., ch. 5

4 The world of crime . . . is a last refuge of the authentic, uncorrupted, spontaneous event.

   Ibid., ch. 6

5 The most important American addition to the World Experience was the simple surprising fact of America. We have helped prepare mankind for all its later surprises.

   Reith Lecture, October 1975, publ. in *The Exploring Spirit: America and the World Experience*, lecture 6 (1976)

Clare Boothe See CLARE BOOTHE LUCE.

Jorge Luis Borges (1899–1986)

ARGENTINIAN AUTHOR

One of the foremost Latin American writers of modern times, he is considered the progenitor of the 'magic realist' school. From 1923 he published poems and essays, and from 1941 collections of stories, notably The Aleph *(1949) and* El Hacedor *(1960).*

1 One concept corrupts and confuses the others. I am not speaking of the Evil whose limited sphere is ethics; I am speaking of the infinite.

   Avatars of the Tortoise (1939), repr. in *Other Inquisitions* (1960)

2 I thought that a man can be the enemy of other men, of the moments of other men, but not of a country: not of fireflies, words, gardens, streams of water, sunsets.

   Ficciones, 'The Garden of Forking Paths' (1944, transl. 1962)

3 The truth is that we live out our lives putting off all that can be put off; perhaps we all know deep down that we are immortal and that sooner or later all men will do and know all things.

   Ibid., 'Funes the Memorious'

4 Like all writers, he [Jaromir Hladik] measured the achievements of others by what they had accomplished, asking of

them that they measure him by what he envisaged or planned.

Ibid., 'The Secret Miracle'

5 Universal history is the history of a few metaphors.

Other Inquisitions, 'Pascal's Sphere' (1952)

6 Every writer 'creates' his own precursors. His work modifies our conception of the past, as it will modify the future.

Ibid., 'Kafka and his Precursors'

7 Literature is not exhaustible, for the sufficient and simple reason that a single book is not. A book is not an isolated entity: it is a narration, an axis of innumerable narrations. One literature differs from another, either before or after it, not so much because of the text as for the manner in which it is read.

Ibid., 'For Bernard Shaw'

8 To fall in love is to create a religion that has a fallible god.

Ibid., 'The Meeting in a Dream'

9 I cannot walk through the suburbs in the solitude of the night without thinking that the night pleases us because it suppresses idle details, just as our memory does.

Ibid., 'A New Refutation of Time'

10 Time is the substance from which I am made. Time is a river which carries me along, but I am the river; it is a tiger that devours me, but I am the tiger; it is a fire that consumes me, but I am the fire.

Ibid.

11 The flattery of posterity is not worth much more than contemporary flattery, which is worth nothing.

El Hacedor (transl. as *Dreamtigers*), 'Dead Men's Dialogue' (1960)

12 Each man is given, in dreams, a little personal eternity which allows him to see the recent past and the near future.

'Nightmares', lecture in Buenos Aires 1976, publ. in *Seven Nights* (1980, transl. 1984)

13 The Falklands thing was a fight between two bald men over a comb.

Time 14 February 1983

14 Life itself is a quotation.

Quoted in *Cool Memories*, ch. 5 (1987) by JEAN BAUDRILLARD

P. W. Botha (b. 1916)

SOUTH AFRICAN POLITICIAN AND PRIME MINISTER

Pieter Willelm Botha. He was Prime Minister 1978–84, and first State President (1984–9). Although committed to white supremacy, he initiated limited constitutional reforms and concessions to non-whites.

1 There is only one element that can break

the Afrikaner, and that is the Afrikaner himself. It is when the Afrikaner, like a baboon shot in the stomach, pulls out his own intestines. We must guard against that.

Speech 26 April 1984, quoted in the *Independent on Sunday* 15 March 1992

2 I'm not here to apologize.

Statement in court, quoted in the *Daily Telegraph* 24 January 1998. Botha was answering charges of refusing to appear before the Truth and Reconciliation Commission.

Ian Botham (b. 1955)

BRITISH CRICKETER

One of the great cricketing all-rounders, he played for Somerset, Worcester and Durham, was Captain of England (1980–81), and was England's leading wicket taker by the end of his 102 tests.

1 When you're on the way up there are plenty of people climbing over each other to buy you drinks, but when things start going wrong, more often than not, you drink alone.

Botham: My Autobiography, ch. 7 (1994)

2 To be No. 1 in sport you have to have a narrow tunnel vision. Dedication. You want to call it selfishness, arrogance, whatever. It's dog eat dog. There are no prisoners taken; there's none expected.

Interview in the *Guardian* 10 September 1994

Pierre Boulez (b. 1925)

FRENCH COMPOSER AND CONDUCTOR

An advocate of the twentieth-century repertoire, he was Conductor of the New York Philharmonic Orchestra (1971–8) and of the BBC Symphony Orchestra (1971–5). His reputation as a composer was established with Le Marteau sans Maître (1954).

1 Revolutions are celebrated when they are no longer dangerous.

Guardian 13 January 1989. Referring to the bicentenary celebrations of the French Revolution.

2 Composing is a constant urge – it never stops. But it's organic, like a seed growing inside. Sometimes it has to wait, you must water it, trim it.

Quoted in the *Daily Telegraph* 29 January 2000

Paul Bourget (1852–1935)

FRENCH NOVELIST AND CRITIC

Although such novels as Le Disciple (1889) are distinguished by their psychological insights, he was better known for his works of criticism.

1 One must live the way one thinks or end up thinking the way one has lived.

Le Démon de midi, 'Conclusion' (1914)

Boutros Boutros-Galli (b. 1922)

EGYPTIAN POLITICIAN AND DIPLOMAT

*While Foreign Minister (1977–91), he was a
member of the diplomatic mission that resulted in
the Camp David Agreement (1978). He was
Secretary-General of the United Nations 1992–6,
the first Arab and first African to hold the post.*

1 When I have tense relations with my
wife, we speak Arabic. When we talk
business, then we speak English. And when
our relationship is better, then we talk
French.

Quoted in the *Mail on Sunday* 15 November
1998

Elizabeth Bowen (1899–1973)

ANGLO-IRISH AUTHOR

*She set her novels and short stories in the milieu
she knew best, the country houses of the Anglo-
Irish and the homes of London's upper classes. Her
works include* The Death of the Heart *(1938) and*
The Heat of the Day *(1949).*

1 There is no end to the violations committed by children on children, quietly talking
alone.

The House in Paris, pt 1, ch. 2 (1935)

2 Intimacies between women go backwards,
beginning with revelations and ending up
in small talk without loss of esteem.

The Death of the Heart, pt 2, ch. 1 (1938)

3 Only in a house where one has learnt to be
lonely does one have this solicitude for
things. One's relation to them, the daily seeing or touching, begins to become love,
and to lay one open to pain.

Ibid., pt 2, ch. 2

4 The heart may think it knows better: the
senses know that absence blots people out.
We really have no absent friends. The
friend becomes a traitor by breaking, however unwillingly or sadly, out of our own
zone: a hard judgment is passed on him,
for all the pleas of the heart.

Ibid.

5 Pity the selfishness of lovers: it is brief, a
forlorn hope; it is impossible.

Ibid., ch. 4

6 Nobody can be kinder than the narcissist
while you react to life in his own terms.

Ibid., pt 3, ch. 3

7 The charm, one might say the genius of
memory, is that it is choosy, chancy, and
temperamental: it rejects the edifying
cathedral and indelibly photographs the
small boy outside, chewing a hunk of
melon in the dust.

Vogue 15 September 1955

David Bowie (b. 1947)

BRITISH ROCK MUSICIAN

*Originally David Jones. At the height of his success
during the glam-rock era of the 1970s, he was
known for his theatrical stage performances and
space-age lyrics. His biggest-selling albums include*
Ziggy Stardust *(1972),* Heroes *(1977) and* Let's
Dance *(1983), and he has also acted in films and
on stage.*

1 *Ground control to Major Tom.*

'Space Oddity' (song) on the album *Man of
Words, Man of Music* (1969)

2 *Oh you pretty things
Don't you know you're driving your
Mamas and papas insane?
Let me make it plain
You gotta make way for Homo Superior.*

'Oh! You Pretty Things' (song) on the album
Hunky Dory (1971)

3 I think that we have created a new kind of
person in a way. We have created a child
who will be so exposed to the media that
he will be lost to his parents by the time he
is twelve.

Quoted in *Melody Maker* 22 January 1972

4 Yes, I believe very strongly in fascism. . . .
People have always responded with greater
efficiency under a regimental leadership. A
liberal wastes time saying, 'Well, now,
what ideas have you got?' Show them what
to do, for God's sake. If you don't, nothing
will get done. I can't stand people just
hanging about.

Interview, February 1976, repr. in *Bowie in His
Own Words*, 'Politics' (ed. Miles, 1980). Bowie
had earlier voiced similar opinions in an interview in August 1975, though he later dismissed
his remarks as 'glib, theatrical observations', calling himself 'apolitical'.

5 *I
I will be king
and you
you will be queen,
though nothing will drive them away
We can be heroes
Just for one day.*

'Heroes' (song) on the album *Heroes* (1977)

6 *Fashion – turn to the left
Fashion – turn to the right.*

'Fashion' (song) on the album *Scary Monsters
and Super Creeps* (1980)

(Sir) Maurice Bowra (1898–1971)

BRITISH SCHOLAR

*Professor of Poetry (1946–51) and Vice Chancellor
(1951–4) at Oxford, he wrote widely on classical
literature and ancient and modern poetry, as in*
Greek Lyric Poetry *(1936) and* Poetry and Politics, 1900–1960 *(1966).*

1 **I'm a man more dined against than dining.**
Quoted in *Summoned by Bells*, ch. 9 (1960) by
JOHN BETJEMAN. Alluding to Lear's words in
King Lear: 'I am a man/More sinned against
than sinning.'

Boy George (b. 1961)
BRITISH SINGER
*Originally George O'Dowd. With his glamorous
looks, cross-dressing and openly gay image, he led
his band Culture Club to a string of chart successes
in the 1980s.*

1 **Sex has never been an obsession with me.
It's just like eating a bag of crisps. Quite
nice, but nothing marvellous.**
Quoted in the *Sun* 21 October 1982

2 **In England, glamour's in the gutter, it's
everywhere, anywhere you want to find it.**
Interview in *Smash Hits* 23 December 1982

3 **If you have to be in a soap opera try not to
get the worst role.**
Interview in *The Face* December 1984

William Boyd (b. 1952)
BRITISH NOVELIST
*Having spent his early years in Ghana, he often
used an African setting for his novels, among
which are* A Good Man in Africa *(1981, filmed
1994) and* Brazzaville Beach *(1990).*

1 **We all want to be happy, and we're all
going to die. . . . You might say those are
the only two unchallengeably true facts
that apply to every human being on this
planet.**
Loomis Gage, in *Stars and Bars*, pt 2, ch. 6 (1984)

Charles Boyer (1899–1978)
FRENCH ACTOR
*After moving to Hollywood in 1929, he became
known as the screen's 'great lover' playing romantic roles in* Mayerling *(1937) and* Algiers *(1938).*

1 **Come with me to the Casbah.**
Attributed. The words have been ascribed to
Boyer in the film *Algiers* (1938), but do not
appear in it.

Malcolm Bradbury (1932–2000)
BRITISH AUTHOR
*Closely involved from 1970 with the creative writ-
ing programme at the University of East Anglia, he
was one of the principal exponents of the satirical
'campus novel', as in* Eating People is Wrong
(1959) and The History Man *(1975).*

1 **I like the English. They have the most rigid
code of immorality in the world.**
Herr Schumann, in *Eating People is Wrong*, ch. 5
(1959)

2 **Reading someone else's newspaper is like
sleeping with someone else's wife. Nothing**

seems to be precisely in the right place,
and when you find what you are looking
for, it is not clear then how to respond to
it.
Dr Jochum, in *Stepping Westward*, bk 1, ch. 1
(1965)

3 **The English are polite by telling lies. The
Americans are polite by telling the truth.**
Dr Bernard Froelich, ibid., bk 2, ch. 5

4 **A conventional good read is usually a bad
read, a relaxing bath in what we know
already. A true good read is surely an act
of innovative creation in which we, the
readers, become conspirators.**
Sunday Times 29 November 1987

Ray Bradbury (b. 1920)
US SCIENCE FICTION AUTHOR
*His imaginative novels and short stories intro-
duced the genre of science fiction to a wider audience. Many have been filmed, including*
Fahrenheit 451 *(1953, filmed 1966) and* The Martian Chronicles *(1950, filmed 1966, televised 1980).*

1 **I don't try to describe the future. I try to
prevent it.**
Quoted by ARTHUR C. CLARKE in the *Independent* 16 July 1992

Omar Bradley (1893–1981)
US GENERAL
*He commanded the US First Army in the Nor-
mandy invasion (1944) and was first Permanent
Chairman of US Joint Chiefs of Staff 1949–53.*

1 **We have grasped the mystery of the atom
and rejected the Sermon on the Mount. . . .
The world has achieved brilliance without
wisdom, power without conscience. Ours
is a world of nuclear giants and ethical
infants.**
Armistice Day speech, 1948, publ. in *Collected
Writings*, vol. 1 (1967)

2 **The wrong war, at the wrong place, at the
wrong time, and with the wrong enemy.**
Speech to Senate Committees on Armed Services
and Foreign Relations, 15 May 1951, publ. in *The
Military Situation in the Far East*, 'Senate Hearings' (1951). Bradley was giving testimony before
a Senate inquiry into General MACARTHUR's
proposal to carry the Korean conflict into China;
Bradley opposed the scheme, arguing that 'Red
China is not the powerful nation seeking to
dominate the world.'

3 **I am convinced that the best service a
retired general can perform is to turn in
his tongue along with his suit, and to moth-
ball his opinions.**
Armed Forces Day address, quoted in *The New
York Times* 17 May 1959

Melvyn Bragg (b. 1939)
BRITISH BROADCASTER AND AUTHOR
Lord Bragg of Wigton. A television and radio presenter, he has written numerous novels, many set in his native Cumbria. He has also worked with Ken Russell on screenplays and documentaries.

1 There's nothing the British like better than a bloke who comes from nowhere, makes it, and then gets clobbered.
Guardian 23 September 1988. Referring to RICHARD BURTON, whose biography by Bragg, *Rich*, was published that year.

Marlon Brando (b. 1924)
US SCREEN ACTOR
A 'method' actor, he caused a sensation with his steamy performance in A Streetcar Named Desire *(1951), and won Oscars for* On the Waterfront *(1954) and* The Godfather *(1972) – though he refused the latter award in protest against Hollywood's portrayal of Native Americans.* BERTOLUCCI *called him 'an angel as a man, a monster as an actor'. See also* GEORGE GLASS 1.

1 What've ya got?
Johnny (Marlon Brando), on being asked what he is rebelling against, in *The Wild One* (film, 1953, screenplay by John Paxton from a story by Micky Rooney, directed by Laslo Benedek)

2 What do I get – a couple of bucks and a one-way ticket to Palookaville. It was you, Charley. You was my brother. You should've looked out for me. Instead of making me take them dives for the short-end money. . . . You don't understand! I could've been a contender. I could've had class and been somebody. Real class. Instead of a bum, which is what I am. It was you, Charley.
Terry Mallon (Marlon Brando), in *On The Waterfront* (film, 1954, screenplay by Budd Schulberg, directed by Elia Kazan). The lines are addressed to Mallon's brother (Rod Steiger) whom he blamed for his failed boxing career. The screenplay was based on a series of Pulitzer Prize-winning articles called 'Crime on the Waterfront' by Malcolm Johnson, publ. in the *New York Sun* November–December 1948.

3 To grasp the full significance of life is the actor's duty, to interpret it is his problem, and to express it his dedication.
Said in 1960, quoted in *Marlon Brando*, ch. 1 (1974, rev. 1989) by David Shipman

4 Privacy is not something that I'm merely entitled to, it's an absolute prerequisite.
Quoted ibid., ch. 11

5 Acting is the expression of a neurotic impulse. It's a bum's life. . . . The principal benefit acting has afforded me is the money to pay for my psychoanalysis.
Quoted in *Marlon Brando: The Only Contender*, ch. 13 (1985) by Gary Carey

6 It is a simple fact that all of us use the techniques of acting to achieve whatever ends we seek. . . . Acting serves as the quintessential social lubricant and a device for protecting our interests and gaining advantage in every aspect of life.
The Technique of Acting, Introduction (1988) by Stella Adler

7 Mr Dean appears to be wearing my last year's wardrobe and using my last year's talent . . .
Quoted in *James Dean in his Own Words*, 'The Things They Said . . . About Jimmy' (ed. Mick St Michael, 1989). Referring to James Dean; an intense rivalry is said to have existed between the two actors.

8 I don't mind that I'm fat. You still get the same money.
International Herald Tribune 9 October 1989

9 I have the eyes of a dead pig.
Screen International 18 January 1991

Wernher von Braun (1912–77)
GERMAN-BORN US ROCKET ENGINEER
After developing V-2 rockets for Germany in the Second World War, he moved to the US to work on the first American satellite Explorer 1, *launched in 1958, and to develop the Saturn rocket used in the Apollo 8 moon landing in 1969.*

1 Don't tell me that man doesn't belong out there [space]. Man belongs wherever he wants to go – and he'll do plenty well when he gets there.
Time 17 February 1958

Richard Brautigan (1935–84)
US NOVELIST AND POET
Lacking conventional plot and character development, his novels A Confederate General from Big Sur *(1965) and* Trout Fishing in America *(1967) established him as a cult figure of the late 1960s.*

1 If you get hung up on everybody else's hang-ups, then the whole world's going to be nothing more than one huge gallows.
The Abortion: An Historical Romance 1966 (1970)

Berke Breathed (b. 1957)
US CARTOONIST AND AUTHOR
Guy Berkeley Breathed. He is regarded as one of America's most popular cartoonists with his long-running, nation-wide strip 'Bloom County' (from 1980s).

1 I could draw *Bloom County* with my nose and pay my cleaning lady to write it, and I'd bet I wouldn't lose 10% of my papers over the next twenty years. Such is the nature of comic-strips. Once established,

their half-life is usually more than nuclear waste.

Time 25 December 1989

Bertolt Brecht (1898–1956)
GERMAN DRAMATIST AND POET

One of Germany's foremost dramatists and a committed Marxist, he collaborated with Kurt Weill to produce The Threepenny Opera *in 1928. Most of his best work was composed during exile from Hitler's Germany (1933–48), including* Mother Courage *(1941) and* The Caucasian Chalk Circle *(1948).*

1 *Oh, the shark has pretty teeth, dear –*
  And he shows them pearly white –
  Just a jackknife has Macheath, dear –
  And he keeps it out of sight.
  'The Ballad of Mack the Knife', in *The Threepenny Opera*, Prologue (1928)

2 A man who sees another man on the street corner with only a stump for an arm will be so shocked the first time he'll give him sixpence. But the second time it'll only be a threepenny bit. And if he sees him a third time, he'll have him cold-bloodedly handed over to the police.
  Peachum, ibid., act 1, sc. 1

3 Food first, then morality.
  Ibid., act 2, sc. 6, 'What Keeps Mankind Alive?'

4 *For once you must try not to shirk the facts:*
  Mankind is kept alive by bestial acts.
  Ibid.

5 The law was made for one thing alone, for the exploitation of those who don't understand it, or are prevented by naked misery from obeying it.
  Peachum, ibid., act 3, sc. 7

6 What's breaking into a bank compared with founding a bank?
  Mac, ibid., sc. 9

7 You don't need to pray to God any more when there are storms in the sky, but you do have to be insured.
  Pelagea Vlasova, in *The Mother*, sc. 10 (1932)

8 Don't be afraid of death so much as an inadequate life.
  Ibid.

9 *Let nothing be called natural*
  In an age of bloody confusion,
  Ordered disorder, planned caprice,
  And dehumanized humanity, lest all things
  Be held unalterable!
  The Exception and the Rule, Prologue (1937)

10 Literary works cannot be taken over like factories, or literary forms of expression like industrial methods. Realist writing, of which history offers many widely varying examples, is likewise conditioned by the question of how, when and for what class it is made use of.
  'The Popular and the Realistic', written 1938, first publ. 1958, repr. in *Brecht on Theatre* (ed. and transl. John Willett, 1964)

11 *The world of knowledge takes a crazy turn*
   When teachers themselves are taught to learn.
   The Life of Galileo, sc. 6 (1939, transl. Howard Brenton, 1980)

12 Unhappy the land that is in need of heroes.
   Galileo, ibid., sc. 13. Responding to Andrea's remark, 'Unhappy the land that has no heroes.'

13 Science knows only one commandment – contribute to science.
   Andrea, ibid., sc. 14

14 What they could do with round here is a good war. What else can you expect with peace running wild all over the place? You know what the trouble with peace is? No organization.
   The Sergeant, in *Mother Courage and Her Children*, sc. 1 (1939, transl. Eric Bentley, 1941)

15 War is like love, it always finds a way.
   The Chaplain, ibid., sc. 6

16 No one can be good for long if goodness is not in demand.
   First God, in *The Good Woman of Setzuan*, sc. 1a (1941)

17 Mixing one's wines may be a mistake, but old and new wisdom mix admirably.
   The Singer, in *The Caucasian Chalk Circle*, Prologue (1944)

18 Berlin, an etching by Churchill, after an idea by Hitler.
   Journal entry, 27 October 1948, publ. in *Arbeitsjournal*, vol. 2 (1973)

19 We need a type of theatre which not only releases the feelings, insights and impulses possible within the particular historical field of human relations in which the action takes place, but employs and encourages those thoughts and feelings which help transform the field itself.
   'A Short Organum for the Theatre', para. 35 (1949), repr. in *Brecht on Theatre* (ed. and transl. John Willett, 1964)

Rory Bremner (b. 1961)
BRITISH COMIC

An accomplished mimic, he has starred in various satirical television shows since 1986, including The Rory Bremner Show *(1989–1992) and* Bremner, Bird and Fortune *(1999–2002).*

1 In the country of the bland, the one idea is king.
  Independent 6 May 1990. On Britain under Thatcherism.

Howard Brenton (b. 1942) and
David Hare (b. 1947)
BRITISH PLAYWRIGHTS
*Brenton is known for his provocative politicized
plays such as* The Churchill Play *(1974) and* The
Romans in Britain *(1980). He has collaborated
with David Hare on* Pravda *(1985) and with*
TARIQ ALI *on* Moscow Gold *(1990). See also*
DAVID HARE.

1 The press and politicians. A delicate
   relationship. Too close, and danger ensues.
   Too far apart and democracy itself cannot
   function without the essential exchange of
   information. Creative leaks, a discreet
   lunch, interchange in the Lobby, the art of
   the unattributable telephone call, late at
   night.
   Quince, in Pravda, *act 1, sc. 4 (1985)*

Jimmy Breslin (b. 1929)
US JOURNALIST AND AUTHOR
*The voice of New York's Irish-American working
class, he was prominent in the New Journalism of
the 1970s. Best known for his newspaper columns,
he has also written fiction and biographies.*

1 Rage is the only quality which has kept me,
   or anybody I have ever studied, writing columns for newspapers.
   The Times 9 May 1990

Robert Bresson (1907–99)
FRENCH FILM-MAKER
*He won international acclaim with the austere and
introspective films* The Ladies of the Bois de Boul-
ogne *(1945),* Diary of a Country Priest *(1951) and*
A Man Escaped *(1956). Before turning to film he
studied painting which, he said, 'taught me to
make not beautiful images but necessary ones'.*

1 In the NUDE, all that is not beautiful is
   obscene.
   *Notes on the Cinematographer, 'Further Notes
   1960–1974' (1975)*

2 Model. Two mobile eyes in a mobile head,
   itself on a mobile body.
   Ibid., 'On Automatism'

3 The true is inimitable, the false untrans-
   formable.
   Ibid., 'The Real'

4 When you do not know what you are
   doing and what you are doing is the best –
   that is inspiration.
   Ibid.

5 Films can only be made by by-passing the
   will of those who appear in them, using
   not what they do, but what they are.
   The Times 1 November 1990

André Breton (1896–1966)
FRENCH SURREALIST WRITER
*Having been a leader of the Dadaists in 1916, he
became one of the founders of the Surrealist movement, publishing the* Surrealist Manifesto *in 1924.
His novel* Nadja *was published in 1928 and his collected poems in 1948.*

1 Surrealism, n. Pure psychic automatism,
   by which it is intended to express, whether
   verbally or in writing, or in any other way,
   the real process of thought. Thought's dic-
   tation, free from any control by the reason,
   independent of any aesthetic or moral preoccupation.
   Manifesto of Surrealism (1924)

2 It is living and ceasing to live that are
   imaginary solutions. Existence is
   elsewhere.
   *Ibid. A reference to Rimbaud's famous line 'La
   vraie vie est absente' (from his poem 'Délires'),
   usually translated 'Life is elsewhere'. See also*
   V.S. PRITCHETT 5.

3 It is impossible for me to envisage a picture as being other than a window, and . . .
   my first concern is then to know what it
   looks out on.
   Surrealism and Painting (1928)

4 If surrealism ever comes to adopt a particular line of moral conduct, it has only to
   accept the discipline that Picasso has
   accepted and will continue to accept.
   Ibid.

5 To speak of God, to think of God, is in
   every respect to show what one is made of
   . . . *I have always wagered against God* and
   I regard the little that *I have won* in this
   world as simply the outcome of this bet.
   However paltry may have been the stake
   (my life) I am conscious of having won to
   the full. Everything that is doddering,
   squint-eyed, vile, polluted and grotesque is
   summoned up for me in that one word:
   God!
   Footnote, ibid.

6 The approval of the public is to be avoided
   like the plague. It is absolutely essential to
   keep the public from *entering* if one wishes
   to avoid confusion. I must add that the
   public must be kept panting in expectation
   at the gate by a system of challenges and
   provocations.
   Second Manifesto of Surrealism (1930)

Fanny Brice (1891–1951)
US ENTERTAINER
*Originally Fanny Borach. A singing comedienne,
she was a star of the Ziegfeld Follies, famous for
her satiric sketches, the song 'My Man', and for her
'Baby Snooks' character which transferred to radio
in 1938.*

1 Men always fall for frigid women because
they put on the best show.

Quoted in *A Child of the Century*, bk 5, 'Don
Juan in Hollywood' (1954) by Ben Hecht

British Board of Film Censors

1 This film is so cryptic as to be almost meaningless. If there is a meaning, it is doubtless objectionable.

Statement refusing a certificate to the Surrealist
film *The Seashell and the Clergyman* (*La Coquille
et l'ecclésiastique*, film, screenplay by ANTONIN
ARTAUD, directed by Germaine Dulac, 1928).
This was the only one of Artaud's scenarios ever
to be produced, and was ridiculed by him and
other Surrealists at the premiere, possibly
because he didn't feature in it or because it was
introduced as his 'personal dream'.

Vera Brittain (1896–1970)

BRITISH AUTHOR AND PACIFIST

*Her experiences as a nurse in the First World War,
recounted in* Testament of Youth *(1933), helped to
shape her life-long commitment to pacifism, which
she interpreted from a feminist perspective. She
was the mother of* SHIRLEY WILLIAMS.

1 All that a pacifist can undertake – but it is
a very great deal – is to refuse to kill, injure
or otherwise cause suffering to another
human creature, and untiringly to order
his life by the rule of love though others
may be captured by hate.

'What Can We Do in Wartime?', first publ. in
Forward 9 September 1939, repr. in *Wartime
Chronicle: Vera Brittain's Diary 1939–1945* (1989)

2 Politics are usually the executive
expression of human immaturity.

The Rebel Passion, ch. 1 (1964)

3 I know one husband and wife who, what
ever the official reasons given to the court
for the break up of their marriage, were
really divorced because the husband
believed that nobody ought to read while
he was talking and the wife that nobody
ought to talk while she was reading.

Quoted in *Violets and Vinegar*, 'The Battle Done'
(1980) by Jilly Cooper and Tom Hartman

Benjamin Britten (1913–76)

BRITISH COMPOSER

*Baron Britten of Aldeburgh. He wrote mainly for
the voice, notably for Peter Pears as in* Peter
Grimes *(1945). Other works include the orchestral*
The Young Person's Guide to the Orchestra
(1946) and the opera Billy Budd *(1951).*

1 It is cruel, you know, that music should be
so beautiful. It has the beauty of loneliness
& of pain: of strength & freedom. The
beauty of disappointment & never-satisfied

love. The cruel beauty of nature, and everlasting beauty of monotony.

Letter, 29 June 1937, publ. in *Letters from a Life:
Letters and Diaries of Benjamin Britten*, vol. 1, 'A
Working Life' (1991). Britten wrote this while
listening to the 'Abschied', the finale of Mahler's
song cycle *Das Lied von der Erde.*

Hermann Broch (1886–1951)

AUSTRIAN NOVELIST

*He is known for his innovative and multidimen-
sional novels, for example* The Sleepwalkers *(trilogy 1931–2), which charts the disintegration of
nineteenth-century European society. Imprisoned
by the Nazis, he emigrated to America in 1940.*

1 Those who live by the sea can hardly form
a single thought of which the sea would
not be part.

The Spell, Foreword (1976, transl. 1987)

2 No one's death comes to pass without
making some impression, and those close
to the deceased inherit part of the liberated
soul and become richer in their
humaneness.

Ibid., ch. 2

3 While love ceaselessly strives toward that
which lies at the hiddenmost centre, hatred
only perceives the topmost surface and perceives it so exclusively that the devil of
hatred, despite all his terror-inspiring
cruelty, never is entirely free of ridicule
and of a somewhat dilettantish aspect. One
who hates is a man holding a magnifying-
glass, and when he hates someone, he
knows precisely that person's surface, from
the soles of his feet all the way up to each
hair on the hated head. Were one merely
to seek information, one should inquire of
the man who hates, but if one wishes to
know what truly is, one better ask the one
who loves.

Ibid., ch. 9

4 The world has always gone through
periods of madness so as to advance a bit
on the road to reason.

The doctor, ibid., ch. 11

Fawn M. Brodie (1915–81)

US BIOGRAPHER

*Her psychobiographies occasionally aroused contro-
versy, as in the case of* No Man Knows My History *(1945), a biography of Joseph Smith, which
caused her to be excommunicated from the Mor-
mon church.*

1 A man's memory is bound to be a distortion of his past in accordance with his present interests, and the most faithful
autobiography is likely to mirror less what
a man was than what he has become.

No Man Knows My History, ch. 19 (1945)

Harold Brodkey (1930–96)

US AUTHOR

Originally Aaron Roy Weintraub. While staff writer on the New Yorker *magazine for thirty years he worked on the autobiographical novel* The Runaway Soul, *finally published in 1991.*

1 Athletes have studied how to leap and how to survive the leap some of the time and return to the ground. They don't always do it well. But they are our philosophers of actual moments and the body and soul in them, and of our manoeuvres in our emergencies and longings.

'Meditations on an Athlete', publ. in *Cape* July 1992

2 One may be tired of the world – tired of the prayer-makers, the poem-makers, whose rituals are distracting and human and pleasant but worse than irritating because they have no reality – while reality itself remains very dear. One wants glimpses of the real. God is an immensity, while this disease, this death, which is in me, this small tightly defined pedestrian event, is merely and perfectly real, without miracle – or instruction.

'Passage into Non-Existence', publ. in the *Independent on Sunday* 11 February 1996. The article was Brodkey's last piece of published writing before his death from AIDS.

Joseph Brodsky (1940–96)

RUSSIAN-BORN US POET AND CRITIC

Composed in both Russian and English, his poetry deals with loss and exile, influenced by his imprisonment and then banishment from the Soviet Union in 1972. His collections include The End of a Beautiful Era *(1977) and* To Urania *(1984).*

1 The real history of consciousness starts with one's first lie.

'Less Than One', sect. 1, first publ. 1976, repr. in *Less Than One: Selected Essays* (1986)

2 Every individual ought to know at least one poet from cover to cover: if not as a guide through the world, then as a yardstick for the language.

'To Please a Shadow', sect. 5, first publ. 1983, repr. ibid. Brodsky recommended W.H. AUDEN as qualified on both counts.

3 The delirium and horror of the East. The dusty catastrophe of Asia. Green only on the banner of the Prophet. Nothing grows here except mustaches.

Less Than One: Selected Essays (1986), 'Flight from Byzantium', sect. 9

4 Racism? But isn't it only a form of misanthropy? . . . Snobbery? But it's only a form of despair.

Ibid.

5 For aesthetics is the mother of ethics. . . . Were we to choose our leaders on the basis of their reading experience and not their political programs, there would be much less grief on earth. I believe – not empirically, alas, but only theoretically – that for someone who has read a lot of Dickens to shoot his like in the name of an idea is harder than for someone who has read no Dickens.

'Uncommon Visage', Nobel Prize acceptance speech, 1987, publ. in *On Grief and Reason* (1996)

6 After all, it is hard to master both life and work equally well. So if you are bound to fake one of them, it had better be life.

Interview in *Writers at Work* (eighth series, ed. George Plimpton, 1988)

7 There are worse crimes than burning books. One of them is not reading them.

Said at press conference on acceptance of US poet laureateship, Washington DC, quoted in the *Independent on Sunday* 19 May 1991

Jacob Bronowski (1908–74)

BRITISH SCIENTIST AND AUTHOR

A popularizer of science and the history of thought, he published The Common Sense of Science *(1951) and* The Western Intellectual Tradition *(1960), and presented the TV series* The Ascent of Man *in 1973.*

1 Man masters nature not by force but by understanding. This is why science has succeeded where magic failed: because it has looked for no spell to cast over nature.

'The Creative Mind', lecture, 26 February 1953, given at the Massachusetts Institute of Technology, publ. in *Science and Human Values*, sect. 4 (1961)

2 Has there ever been a society which has died of dissent? Several have died of conformity in our lifetime.

'The Sense of Human Dignity', sect. 5, lecture given at the Massachusetts Institute of Technology, 19 March 1953, publ. in *Science and Human Values* (1961)

3 Science has nothing to be ashamed of even in the ruins of Nagasaki. The shame is theirs who appeal to other values than the human imaginative values which science has evolved.

Ibid., sect. 11

4 No science is immune to the infection of politics and the corruption of power.

Encounter, July 1971

5 That is the essence of science: ask an impertinent question, and you are on the way to a pertinent answer.

The Ascent of Man, ch. 4 (1973)

6 One aim of the physical sciences has been to give an exact picture of the material world. One achievement of physics in the twentieth century has been to prove that that aim is unattainable.
Ibid., ch. 11

7 The University is a Mecca to which students come with something less than perfect faith. It is important that students bring a certain ragamuffin, barefoot irreverence to their studies; they are not here to worship what is known, but to question it.
Ibid.

Rupert Brooke (1887–1915)
BRITISH POET

The most dashing of the Georgian poets, he came to symbolize the golden youth sacrificed in the First World War after his death from blood poisoning en route to the Dardanelles. 'The Old Vicarage, Grantchester' and his 'war sonnets' are his best known works. F.R. LEAVIS *summarized his verse as 'rather like Keats's vulgarity with a Public School accent'.*

1 *One may not doubt that, somehow, good Shall come of water and of mud; And sure, the reverent eye must see A purpose in liquidity.*
'Heaven', publ. in *1914 and Other Poems* (1915)

2 *But somewhere, beyond Space and Time, Is wetter water, slimier slime! And there (they trust) there swimmeth One Who swam ere rivers were begun, Immense, of fishy form and mind, Squamous, omnipotent, and kind.*
Ibid.

3 *The cool kindliness of sheets, that soon Smooth away trouble; and the rough male kiss Of blankets.*
'The Great Lover', ibid.

4 *If I should die, think only this of me: That there's some corner of a foreign field That is for ever England.*
'The Soldier', first publ. in *New Numbers*, no. 4 (1914), ibid. Brooke is buried on the island of Skyros, Greece.

5 *Now, God be thanked Who has matched us with His hour, And caught our youth, and wakened us from sleeping, With hand made sure, clear eye, and sharpened power, To turn, as swimmers into cleanness leaping.*
'Peace', ibid.

6 *And all the little emptiness of love!*
Ibid.

Anita Brookner (b. 1938)
BRITISH NOVELIST AND ART HISTORIAN

An expert on eighteenth-century painting, she is more widely known for her melancholy novels in which the main characters are women, including Hôtel du Lac *(1984),* A Friend from England *(1987) and* Visitors *(1997).*

1 She was a handsome woman of forty-five and would remain so for many years.
Hôtel du Lac, ch. 4 (1984)

2 You have no idea how promising the world begins to look once you have decided to have it all for yourself. And how much healthier your decisions are once they become entirely selfish.
Mr Neville, ibid., ch. 7

3 Good women always think it is their fault when someone else is being offensive. Bad women never take the blame for anything.
Ibid.

4 Writing novels preserves you in a state of innocence – a lot passes you by – simply because your attention is otherwise diverted.
Novelists in Interview (ed. John Haffenden, 1985)

5 Time misspent in youth is sometimes all the freedom one ever has.
Blanche Vernon, in *The Misalliance*, ch. 10 (1986)

6 It will be a pity if women in the more conventional mould are to be phased out, for there will never be anyone to go home to.
Rachel, in *A Friend from England*, ch. 10 (1987)

7 What is interesting about self-analysis is that it leads nowhere – it is an art form in itself.
Interview in *Writers at Work* (eighth series, ed. George Plimpton, 1988)

8 A complete woman is probably not a very admirable creature. She is manipulative, uses other people to get her own way, and works within whatever system she is in.
Ibid.

Gwendolyn Brooks (b. 1917)
US POET

In 1950 she was the first black author to be awarded the Pulitzer Prize, for her collection of poems, Annie Allen *(1949). As with her first collection,* A Street in Bronzeville *(1945), this dealt principally with the lives of the urban black poor.*

1 *Abortions will not let you forget. You remember the children you got that you did not get.*
'The Mother', publ. in *A Street in Bronzeville* (1945)

Mel Brooks (b. 1926)
US FILM-MAKER AND ACTOR

An irreverent gag-writer and script-doctor turned director of his own screenplays, he excelled in brash bad taste. The Producers (1968) was followed by the spoofs Blazing Saddles *(1974) and* Silent Movie *(1976), among others.*

1 *Springtime for Hitler and Germany, Winter for France and Poland.*

'Springtime for Hitler', in *The Producers* (film, 1968, written and directed by Mel Brooks). The song was the centrepiece of the musical of the same name staged by 'the producers' to guarantee a loss.

2 How could this happen? I was so careful. I picked the wrong play, the wrong director, the wrong cast. Where did I go right?

Max Bialystock (Zero Mostel), ibid.

3 Let's face it, sweetheart, without Jews, fags, and Gypsies, there is no theatre.

Frederick Bronski (Mel Brooks), in *To Be or Not To Be* (film, 1983, screenplay by Thomas Meehan and Ronny Graham, directed by Alan Johnson)

Pierce Brosnan (b. 1953)
IRISH ACTOR

After playing the investigator Remington Steele on TV (1982–7) and appearing in the film Mrs Doubtfire *(1993), he took on the role of James Bond in a series of films, starting with* Goldeneye *(1995).*

1 Fame is like a big piece of meringue – it's beautiful and you keep eating it, but it doesn't really fill you up.

Quoted in *The Times* 19 January 2002

Heywood Broun (1888–1939)
US JOURNALIST AND NOVELIST

He is chiefly remembered for his columns 'It Seems to Me' in the Tribune *and* World *in the 1920s, and 'Shoot the Works' in the* New Republic *from 1935 until his death.*

1 The tragedy of life is not that man loses, but that he almost wins.

Pieces of Hate, and Other Enthusiasms, 'Sport for Art's Sake' (1922)

2 Just as every conviction begins as a whim so does every emancipator serve his apprenticeship as a crank. A fanatic is a great leader who is just entering the room.

New York World 6 February 1928

3 A technical objection is the first refuge of a scoundrel.

New Republic 15 December 1937

Craig Brown (b. 1957)
BRITISH JOURNALIST

A specialist in parody and satire, he writes for Private Eye, *the* Daily Telegraph *and the* Independent, *sometimes in the guise of Bel Littlejohn or Wallace Arnold.*

1 Journalism could be described as turning one's enemies into money.

Daily Telegraph 28 September 1990

2 The most common form of parody is, of course, self-parody. It is a disease to which every columnist is prone, for it is always easier to reassemble the usual range of columnar emotions – outrage, pity, etc. – than to feel them afresh.

Spectator 22 November 1999

3 A satirist is a humorist who wants to be a politician. Deep down, he believes that the Kingdom of Sense is at hand, and that a dig in the ribs might make it come to pass.

Guardian 25 January 2003

H. Rap Brown (b. 1943)
US RADICAL AND AUTHOR

Originally Hubert Gerold. A black activist, he was chairman of the Student Nonviolent Coordinating Committee (SNCC) in Alabama and expressed his inflammatory views in Die Nigger Die *(1969). While imprisoned for robbery (1971–6), he converted to Islam, changing his name to Jamil Abdullah al-Amin.*

1 Violence is as American as cherry pie.

Press conference at SNCC, Washington DC, 27 July 1967, quoted in the *Evening Star* 27 July 1967

James Brown (b. 1928)
US SOUL SINGER

The 'Godfather of Soul' grew up in rural poverty on a diet of gospel. His charismatic stage act was captured on the album Live at the Apollo *(1962), which sold a million copies, unprecedented for an album by a black artist.*

1 *It's a man's world, but it wouldn't be nothing without a woman or a girl.*

'It's a Man's Man's Man's World' (song), on the album *It's a Man's Man's Man's World* (1966)

2 *We're tired of beating our head against the wall*
And working for someone else
We're people, we're like the birds and the bees
But we'd rather die on our feet than keep living on our knees.

. . .

Say it loud! I'm black and I'm proud!

'Say it Loud! I'm Black and I'm Proud!' (song, 1968, written with Alfred Ellis) on the album *Say it Loud! I'm Black and I'm Proud!* (1969)

Lew Brown See BUDDY DE SYLVA and LEW BROWN.

Lenny Bruce (1925–66)
US SATIRICAL COMEDIAN
Originally Leonard Alfred Schneider. One of the first comics to 'disturb rather than amuse', he built up a cult following with his darkly satirical routines, which were often considered offensive. He was imprisoned for obscenity in 1961 and banned from entering Britain in 1963.

1 A lot of people say to me, 'Why did you kill Christ?' 'I dunno . . . it was one of those parties, got out of hand, you know.' We killed him because he didn't want to become a doctor, that's why we killed him.
The Essential Lenny Bruce, 'The Jews' (ed. John Cohen, 1967)

2 The reason I'm in this business, I assume all performers are – it's 'Look at me, Ma!' It's acceptance, you know – 'Look at me, Ma, look at me, Ma, look at me, Ma.' And if your mother watches, you'll show off till you're exhausted; but if your mother goes, *Ptshew!*
Ibid., 'Performing and the Art of Comedy'

3 The only honest art form is laughter, comedy. You can't fake it . . . try to fake three laughs in an hour – ha ha ha ha ha – they'll take you away, man. You can't.
Ibid.

4 All my humor is based upon destruction and despair. If the whole world were tranquil, without disease and violence, I'd be standing on the breadline right in back of J. Edgar Hoover.
Ibid. The words also appear as the book's epigraph.

5 Satire is tragedy plus time. You give it enough time, the public, the reviewers will allow you to satirize it. Which is rather ridiculous, when you think about it.
Ibid.

6 The liberals can understand everything but people who don't understand them.
Ibid., 'Politics'

7 I'll die young but it's like kissing God.
Quoted in *Playpower*, ch. 4 (1970) by RICHARD NEVILLE. On his drug addiction; Bruce died from a drugs overdose.

Frank Bruno (b. 1961)
BRITISH BOXER
He became WBC world heavyweight champion in 1995 but was defeated by MIKE TYSON the following year, since when he has become a popular media figure.

1 Boxing is just show business with blood.
Guardian 19 November 1991

2 Know what I mean, 'Arry?
Often repeated remark to the sports commentator Harry Carpenter on TV interviews, from 1980s

Robert Brustein (b. 1927)
US STAGE DIRECTOR, AUTHOR AND CRITIC
During his period as Director of Yale Repertory Theater Company (1966–79), he was also Dean of Yale's school of drama, transforming it into a pre-eminent theatre school. He was author of The Third Theater *(1969) and* Revolution as Theater *(1971).*

1 Theatregoing is a communal act, moviegoing a solitary one.
Who Needs Theatre?, Introduction (1987)

2 The primary function of a theater is not to please itself, or even to please its audience. It is to serve talent.
Ibid., pt 3, 'The Humanist and the Artist'

Bill Bryson (b. 1951)
US AUTHOR AND JOURNALIST
As well as his best-selling books on his world travels, including Notes from a Small Island *(1995) and* Down Under *(2000), he has published works on the English language, for example* Mother Tongue *(1990).*

1 There are things you just can't do in life. You can't beat the phone company, you can't make a waiter see you until he's ready to see you, and you can't go home again.
The Lost Continent: Travels in Small Town America, ch. 2 (1989)

2 The average Southerner has the speech patterns of someone slipping in and out of consciousness. I can change my shoes and socks faster than most people in Mississippi can speak a sentence.
Ibid., ch. 7

3 It is an interesting experience to become acquainted with a country through the eyes of the insane, and, if I may say so, a particularly useful grounding for life in Britain.
Notes from a Small Island, ch. 5 (1995)

4 Here are instructions for being a pigeon: 1. Walk around aimlessly for a while, pecking at cigarette butts and other inappropriate items. 2. Take fright at someone walking along the platform and fly off to a girder. 3. Have a shit. 4. Repeat.
Ibid., ch. 10

5 Here is a country that fought and won a noble war, dismantled a mighty empire in a generally benign and enlightened way, created a far-seeing welfare state – in short, did nearly everything right – and then

spent the rest of the century looking on itself as a chronic failure.

Ibid., ch. 29

John Buchan (1875–1940)

BRITISH AUTHOR AND STATESMAN

Baron Tweedsmuir. MP for the Scottish Universities (1927–35) and Governor General of Canada (1935–40), he was also a prolific writer of thrillers, of which The Thirty-Nine Steps *(1915, filmed 1935) is considered his best.*

1 Every man at the bottom of his heart believes that he is a born detective.

Leithen, in *The Power-House*, ch. 2 (1916)

2 An atheist is a man who has no invisible means of support.

Quoted in *On Being a Real Person*, ch. 10 (1943) by H. E. Fosdick

Patrick Buchanan (b. 1938)

US JOURNALIST AND POLITICIAN

Host of the radio show Buchanan & Co, *he was speechwriter and senior adviser to* RICHARD NIXON *(1969–74) and an unsuccessful candidate for the Republican nomination for president in 1992 and 1996. Representing the Reform Party, he made another bid for president in 2000.*

1 Anti-Catholicism is the anti-semitism of the intellectual.

Observer 15 December 1991. Peter Viereck, in *Shame and Glory of the Intellectuals*, ch. 3 (1953), had earlier written: 'Catholic-baiting is the anti-Semitism of the liberals.'

2 If America does not wish to end her days in the same nursing home as Britannia she had best end this geo-babble about new world orders. Our war, the Cold War, is over. It is time for America to come home.

Ibid.

3 Listen, my friend, I've just come back from Mississippi and over there when you talk about the West Bank they think you mean Arkansas.

Spectator 13 March 1992

Frank Buchman (1878–1961)

US EVANGELIST

He is principally known as the founder of the non-denominational Moral Rearmament Movement at Oxford in 1921, which after the Second World War became more politically oriented and opposed to Communism.

1 I thank heaven for a man like Adolf Hitler, who built a front line of defense against the anti-Christ of Communism.

Interview in the *New York World-Telegram* 25 August 1936

2 There is enough in the world for everyone's need, but not enough for everyone's greed.

Remaking the World (1947)

Art Buchwald (b. 1925)

US HUMORIST

Arthur Buchwald. Known for his 'Art Buchwald' column, syndicated worldwide, he was hailed by DEAN ACHESON *'the greatest satirist since Pope and Swift' and was celebrated for over twenty-five years as the 'court jester of Washington society'.*

1 If you attack the establishment long enough and hard enough, they will make you a member of it.

International Herald Tribune 24 May 1989

Pearl S. Buck (1892–1973)

US AUTHOR

Pearl Sydenstricker Buck. She spent her early life in China, the setting for The Good Earth *(1931), the first novel of a trilogy. She also produced biographies, short stories and translations, and in 1938 she became the first American woman to win the Nobel Prize for Literature.*

1 None who have always been free can understand the terrible fascinating power of the hope of freedom to those who are not free.

What America Means to Me, ch. 4 (1943)

Gesualdo Bufalino (1920–96)

SICILIAN AUTHOR

'Discovered' by his fellow Sicilian author Leonardo Sciascia, he published his first book, The Plague Sower *(1981), late in life. Other titles followed in quick succession, and he won the Strega Prize for* Night's Lies *in 1988.*

1 Don't forget that even our most obscene vices nearly always bear the seal of sullen greatness.

Guardian 21 May 1992. Speaking of the Sicilian character.

Bill Buford (b. 1954)

US EDITOR AND AUTHOR

He was editor of Granta *(1979–95) and subsequently literary and fiction editor of the* New Yorker.

1 Violence is one of the most intensely lived experiences and, for those capable of giving themselves over to it, is one of the most intense pleasures.

Among the Thugs, pt 2, 'Dawes Road, Fulham' (1991)

2 This bored, empty, decadent generation consists of nothing more than what it appears to be. It is a lad culture without

mystery, so deadened that it uses violence to wake itself up. It pricks itself so that it has feeling, burns its flesh so that it has smell.

Ibid., pt 3, 'Düsseldorf'

Charles Bukowski (1920–94)

GERMAN-BORN US AUTHOR AND POET

He gained a cult following for his poetry, short stories and novels, sardonic tales of survival in a down-and-out society. Works include Flower, Fist and Bestial Wail *(1959) and* Tales of Ordinary Madness *(1967, filmed 1972).*

1 A man does not get old because he nears death; a man gets old because he can no longer see the false from the good.

Letter written early 1962, publ. in *Screams from the Balcony: Selected Letters* (1993)

2 Show me a man who lives alone and has a perpetually clean kitchen, and 8 times out of 9 I'll show you a man with detestable spiritual qualities.

Tales of Ordinary Madness, 'Too Sensitive' (1967)

3 You begin saving the world by saving one man at a time; all else is grandiose romanticism or politics.

Ibid.

4 Almost everybody is born a genius and buried an idiot.

Notes of a Dirty Old Man (1969)

5 If you want to know who your friends are, get yourself a jail sentence.

Ibid.

6 Sexual intercourse is kicking death in the ass while singing.

Ibid.

7 An intellectual is a man who says a simple thing in a difficult way; an artist is a man who says a difficult thing in a simple way.

Ibid.

8 There's always somebody about to ruin your day, if not your life.

The narrator (Nicky Belane), in *Pulp*, ch. 28 (1994)

Basil Bunting (1900–1985)

BRITISH POET

Influenced by EZRA POUND *and the Imagists, he established his reputation with the lyrical* Briggflatts *(1966), a semi-autobiographical poem which portrays his native Northumbria.*

1 *To appreciate present conditions collate them with those of antiquity.*

'Chomei at Toyama' (1932), publ. in *Collected Poems* (1968)

2 The mystic purchases a moment of exhilaration with a lifetime of confusion; and the exhilaration is incommunicable but the confusion is infectious and destructive. It is confusing and destructive to try and explain anything in terms of anything else, poetry in terms of psychology.

Letter to poet Louis Zukofsky, September 1932, quoted in *The Poetry of Basil Bunting*, ch. 2 (1991) by Victoria Forde

3 *Can a moment of madness make up for an age of consent?*

'The Well of Lycopolis', written 1935, publ. in *Poems* (1950)

4 I hate Science. It denies a man's responsibility for his own deeds, abolishes the brotherhood that springs from God's fatherhood. It is a hectoring, dictating expertise, which makes the least lovable of the Church Fathers seem liberal by contrast. It is far easier for a Hitler or a Stalin to find a mock-scientific excuse for persecution than it was for Dominic to find a mock-Christian one.

Letter to the poet Louis Zukofsky, 1 January 1947, quoted in *The Poetry of Basil Bunting*, ch. 6 (1991) by Victoria Forde

5 *Man's life so little worth, do we fear to take or lose it? No ill companion on a journey, Death lays his purse on the table and opens the wine.*

'The Spoils', first publ. in *Poetry* (1951), repr. in *Loquitur* (1965). Opening lines of poem.

6 *But their determination to banish fools foundered ultimately in the installation of absolute idiots.*

Ibid. On the decline of government under the Turkish Seljuk dynasty.

7 Sooner or later we must absorb Islam if our own culture is not to die of anemia.

Preface to *Arabic and Persian Poems* (1970) by Omar Pound

Luis Buñuel (1900–1983)

SPANISH FILM-MAKER

He collaborated with SALVADOR DALÍ *on his first films* Un Chien andalou *(1928) and* L'Age d'or *(1930), both of which caused a sensation. Later films include* Los Olvidados *(1950),* Belle de jour *(1967) and* The Discreet Charm of the Bourgeoisie *(1972).*

1 Work's a curse, Saturno. I say to hell with the work you have to do to earn a living! That kind of work does us no honour; all it does is fill up the bellies of the pigs who exploit us. But the work you do because you like to do it, because you've heard the call, you've got a vocation – that's ennobling! We should all be able to work like that. Look at me, Saturno – I don't

work. And I don't care if they hang me, I *won't* work! Yet I'm alive! I may live badly, but at least I don't have to work to do it!

Don Lope (Fernando Rey), in *Tristana* (film, 1970, written and directed by Luis Buñuel). Buñuel's screenplay was derived from the novel of the same name by Benito Pérez Galdós, but where Galdós criticized his character for laziness, Buñuel praised him.

2 You have to begin to lose your memory, if only in bits and pieces, to realize that memory is what makes our lives. Life without memory is no life at all, just as an intelligence without the possibility of expression is not really an intelligence. Our memory is our coherence, our reason, our feeling, even our action. Without it, we are nothing.

My Last Breath, ch. 1 (1983). 'I can only wait for the final amnesia', Buñuel wrote, 'the one that can erase an entire life.'

3 The bar . . . is an exercise in solitude. Above all else, it must be quiet, dark, very comfortable – and, contrary to modern mores, no music of any kind, no matter how faint. In sum, there should be no more than a dozen tables, and a clientele that doesn't like to talk.

Ibid., ch. 6

4 Tobacco and alcohol, delicious fathers of abiding friendships and fertile reveries.

Ibid.

5 God and Country are an unbeatable team; they break all records for oppression and bloodshed.

Ibid., ch. 14

6 A paranoiac . . . like a poet, is born, not made.

Ibid., ch. 18

7 In the name of Hippocrates, doctors have invented the most exquisite form of torture ever known to man: survival.

Ibid., ch. 21

Julie Burchill (b. 1960)
BRITISH JOURNALIST AND AUTHOR
Starting in journalism with the New Musical Express, *she went on to co-found the* Modern Review, *and has subsequently worked as a contentious columnist for the* Mail on Sunday, *the* Observer *and the* Guardian. *She has also published novels.*

1 A woman who looks like a girl and thinks like a man is the best sort, the most enjoyable to be and the most pleasurable to have and to hold.

Damaged Gods, 'Born again Cows' (1986)

2 Feminism seeks to turn the biggest, bloodiest carnivore in the world – passion – into

a right-on cud-chewing vegan. It can never work. Sex was never meant to be that way. Sex, on the whole, was meant to be short, nasty and brutish. If what you want is cuddling, you should buy a puppy.

'The Dead Zone', first publ. in 1988, repr. in *Sex and Sensibility* (1992)

3 It has been said that a pretty face is a passport. But it's not, it's a visa, and it runs out fast.

'Kiss and Sell', ibid.

4 A good part – and definitely the most fun part – of being a feminist is about frightening men.

Time Out 16 November 1989

5 Punk, far from being a peasants' revolt, was just another English spectacle, like the Royal Wedding: a chance for us to congratulate ourselves on our talent for tableaux.

Modern Review autumn 1991

6 She [Princess DIANA] showed the House of Windsor up for what it was: a dumb, numb dinosaur, lumbering along in a world of its own, gorged sick on arrogance and ignorance.

Guardian 2 September 1997

7 The Age of Diana has not ended but has rather just begun. Frozen forever at the height of her beauty, compassion and power by death, she will be the mourner at every royal wedding and the blushing bride at every Coronation.

Diana, Foreword (1998)

8 A wedding is a funeral which masquerades as a feast. And the greater the pageantry, the deeper the savagery.

Ibid., ch. 1

9 A cynic should never marry an idealist. For the cynic, marriage represents the welcome end of romantic life, with all its agony and ecstasy. But for the idealist, it is only the beginning.

Ibid., ch. 4

Anthony Burgess (1917–93)
BRITISH AUTHOR AND CRITIC
John Anthony Burgess Wilson. With an inexhaustible intellect, he wrote novels, memoirs, biographies, reviews and libretti, but had greatest success with A Clockwork Orange *(1962, filmed 1971), a disturbing vision of the future.*

1 Bath twice a day to be really clean, once a day to be passably clean, once a week to avoid being a public menace.

Inside Mr Enderby, ch. 2, sect. 1 (1963). A 'grim apothegm' in a women's magazine.

2 Do they merit vitriol, even a drop of it?

Yes, because they corrupt the young, persuading them that the mature world, which produced Beethoven and Schweitzer, sets an even higher value on the transient anodynes of youth than does youth itself . . . They are the Hollow Men. They are electronic lice.

Of disc jockeys, in *Punch* 20 September 1967

3 If you write fiction you are, in a sense, corrupted. There's a tremendous corruptibility for the fiction writer because you're dealing mainly with sex and violence. These remain the basic themes, they're the basic themes of Shakespeare whether you like it or not.

Interview in *The Face* December 1984

4 All human life is here, but the Holy Ghost seems to be somewhere else.

Of the Vatican, in book review in the *Observer* 25 May 1986

5 I've always felt that English women had to be approached in a sisterly manner, rather than an erotic manner.

The Times 27 July 1988

6 The trouble began with Forster. After him it was considered ungentlemanly to write more than five or six novels.

Guardian 24 February 1989. Burgess himself wrote more than twenty novels.

7 We are supposed to be the children of Seth; but Seth is too much of an effete nonentity to deserve ancestral regard. No, we are the sons of Cain, and with violence can be associated the attacks on sound, stone, wood and metal that produced civilisation.

Book review in the *Observer* 26 November 1989

8 In Europe we tend to see marital love as an eternity which encompasses hate and also indifference: when we promise to love we really mean that we promise to honour a contract. Americans, seeming to take marriage with not enough seriousness, are really taking love and sex with too much.

You've Had Your Time, ch. 2 (1990)

9 Novelists are perhaps the last people in the world to be entrusted with opinions. The nature of a novel is that it has no opinions, only the dialectic of contrary views, some of which, all of which, may be untenable and even silly. A novelist should not be too intelligent either, although . . . he may be permitted to be an intellectual.

Ibid.

10 Violence among young people . . . is an aspect of their desire to create. They don't know how to use their energy creatively so they do the opposite and destroy.

Independent 31 January 1990

Gelett Burgess (1866–1951)
US HUMORIST AND ILLUSTRATOR
His works include books on Goops (bad-mannered children), Why Men Hate Women (1927), and Look Eleven Years Younger (1937). He is credited with enlarging the English language with words such as 'blurb'.

1 *Ah, yes, I wrote the 'Purple Cow' –*
I'm sorry, now, I wrote it!
But I can tell you, anyhow,
I'll kill you if you quote it.

'Cinq Ans Après', publ. in *The Burgess Nonsense Book* (1914). Burgess penned the popular verse 'The Purple Cow' in 1895.

2 To appreciate nonsense requires a serious interest in life.

The Romance of the Commonplace, 'The Sense of Humor' (1916)

Johnny Burke (1908–64)
US SONGWRITER
In the late 1930s and '40s, he wrote a number of hit songs in collaboration with the composer Jimmy Van Heusen, many of them for films starring BING CROSBY.

1 *Every time it rains, it rains*
Pennies from heaven.
Don't you know each cloud contains
Pennies from heaven?

'Pennies from Heaven' (1936 song; music by Arthur Johnston)

George Burns (1896–1996)
US COMEDIAN
Originally Nathan Birnbaum. With his wife Gracie Allen he formed a highly successful comedy double act, performing from the 1920s to the 1950s in vaudeville and films, and on radio and television. He turned to acting in later life and won an Oscar for his role in The Sunshine Boys *(1975).*

1 Too bad that all the people who know how to run the country are busy driving taxicabs and cutting hair.

Life December 1979

2 If it's a good script I'll do it. And if it's a bad script, and they pay me enough, I'll do it.

International Herald Tribune 9 November 1988

Edgar Rice Burroughs (1875–1950)
US AUTHOR
His series of Tarzan books, the first of which appeared in 1914, led to films, radio programmes and comic strips. He was also the author of science fiction and other adventure stories.

1 Me Tarzan, you Jane.

Attributed to Tarzan. In Burroughs' book *Tarzan of the Apes* (1914), Tarzan's words are: 'I am Tarzan of the Apes. I want you. I am yours. You are mine' (ch. 18). In the movie, *Tarzan the Ape Man* (1932), Johnny Weissmuller, as Tarzan, never utters the words, 'Me Tarzan, you Jane'.

William Burroughs (1914–97)

US AUTHOR

Associated with the Beats in the 1950s, he frankly depicted a heroin addict's life in Junkie *(1953) and* The Naked Lunch *(1959, filmed 1991). Other works such as* The Soft Machine *(1961) helped to establish his cult status.*

1 A junky runs on junk time. When his junk is cut off, the clock runs down and stops. All he can do is hang on and wait for non-junk time to start.

Junkie, ch. 10 (1953)

2 *1. Never give anything away for nothing.*
2. Never give more than you have to give (always catch the buyer hungry and always make him wait).
3. Always take everything back if you possibly can.

The Naked Lunch, Introduction (1959). The basic principles of dealing heroin.

3 Junk is the ideal product . . . the ultimate merchandise. No sales talk necessary. The client will crawl through a sewer and beg to buy.

Ibid.

4 America is not a young land: it is old and dirty and evil before the settlers, before the Indians. The evil is there waiting.

Ibid., opening chapter (untitled)

5 A *functioning* police state needs no police.

Dr Benway, ibid. 'Benway'

6 The exact objectives of Islam Inc. are obscure. Needless to say everyone involved has a different angle, and they all intend to cross each other up somewhere along the line.

Ibid., 'Islam Inc. and the Parties of Interzone'

7 The face of 'evil' is always the face of total need.

'Deposition: Testimony Concerning a Sickness', publ. in the *Evergreen Review* January/February 1960, repr. as Introduction to *The Naked Lunch* (1962 edn)

8 I feel that any form of so called psycho-therapy is strongly contraindicated for addicts. . . . The question 'Why did you start using narcotics in the first place?' should never be asked. It is quite as irrelevant to treatment as it would be to ask a malarial patient why he went to a malarial area.

The Soft Machine, Appendix (1961, rev. 1966)

9 In my writing I am acting as a map maker, an explorer of psychic areas . . . a cosmonaut of inner space, and I see no point in exploring areas that have already been thoroughly surveyed.

Remark in 1964, quoted in *William Burroughs: The Algebra of Need*, pt 1, ch. 1 (1977) by Eric Mottram

10 I think there are innumerable gods. What we on earth call God is a little tribal God who has made an awful mess. Certainly forces operating through human consciousness control events.

Interview in *Paris Review*, fall 1965, repr. in *Writers at Work* (third series, ed. George Plimpton, 1967)

11 The people in power will not disappear voluntarily, giving flowers to the cops just isn't going to work. This thinking is fostered by the establishment; they like nothing better than love and nonviolence. The only way I like to see cops given flowers is in a flower pot from a high window.

The Job: Interviews with Daniel Odier, 'Prisoners of the Earth Come Out' (1969)

12 England has the most sordid literary scene I've ever seen. They all meet in the same pub. This guy's writing a foreword for this person. They all have to give radio programs, they *have* to do all this just in order to scrape by. They're all scratching each other's backs.

Taped conversation in New York, 1980, publ. in *With William Burroughs: A Report from the Bunker*, 'Burroughs in London' (1981) by Victor Bockris

13 I think that what we call love is a fraud perpetrated by the female sex, and that the point of sexual relations between men is nothing that we could call love, but rather what we might call *recognition*.

Quoted by EDMUND WHITE in 'This is Not a Mammal', first publ. in *Soho News* 18 February 1981, repr. in *The Burning Library* (1994)

14 Man is an artifact designed for space travel. He is not designed to remain in his present biologic state any more than a tadpole is designed to remain a tadpole.

The Adding Machine, 'Civilian Defense' (1985)

15 Kerouac opened a million coffee bars and sold a million pairs of Levis to both sexes. Woodstock rises from his pages.

Ibid., 'Remembering Jack Kerouac'

16 In deep sadness there is no place for sentimentality.

Queer, ch. 8 (1985)

17 So cheat your landlord if you can and must, but do not try to shortchange the Muse. It cannot be done. You can't fake

quality any more than you can fake a good meal.

The Western Lands, ch. 2 (1987)

18 Black magic operates most effectively in preconscious, marginal areas. Casual curses are the most effective.

Ibid., ch. 3

Richard Burton (1925–84)

BRITISH ACTOR

Originally Richard Walter Jenkins. Equally adept in Shakespearian roles and in Hollywood films, he was twice married to Elizabeth Taylor, with whom he co-starred in Who's Afraid of Virginia Woolf? *(1966) and* The Taming of the Shrew *(1967).*

1 Richard Burton is now my epitaph, my cross, my title, my image. I have achieved a kind of diabolical fame. It has nothing to do with my talents as an actor. That counts for little now. I am the diabolically famous Richard Burton.

Interview in 1963, quoted in *Elizabeth Taylor*, ch. 21 (1964) by Ruth Waterbury

2 When I played drunks I had to remain sober because I didn't know how to play them when I was drunk.

Quoted in *Halliwell's Who's Who in the Movies* (ed. John Walker, 1999)

George Bush (b. 1924)

US POLITICIAN AND PRESIDENT

Director of the CIA 1976–7, he served as Republican Vice-President under RONALD REAGAN *1981–8, whom he succeeded as President 1989–93. His administration coincided with the fall of the Berlin Wall and the Gulf conflict in 1990–91. See* MICHAEL KINSLEY 1.

1 The vision thing.

Time 26 January 1987. Speaking of his long-term policies.

2 What's wrong with being a boring kind of guy?

Quoted in the *Daily Telegraph* 28 April 1988

3 I'm proud to be his partner. We've had triumphs, we've made mistakes, we've had sex.

Speech at College of Southern Idaho, 6 May 1988, quoted in the *International Herald Tribune* 13 May 1988. Bush's gaffe occurred in a speech extolling the Reagan/Bush partnership. He corrected himself: '. . . setbacks, we've had setbacks . . .' Moments later he joked, 'I feel like the javelin competitor who won the toss and elected to receive.'

4 Let the others have the charisma. I've got the class.

Comment in California during presidential campaign, quoted in the *Guardian* 3 December 1988

5 The Congress will push me to raise taxes and I'll say no, and they'll push, and I'll say no, and they'll push me again. And I'll say to them: 'Read my lips: no new taxes.'

Acceptance speech for presidential nomination, Republican National Convention, New Orleans, 18 August 1988, quoted in *The New York Times* 19 August 1988. PEGGY NOONAN was mainly responsible for the speech, though the expression 'Read my lips' had been in general usage since the 1970s or earlier. Bush eventually raised taxes.

6 I want a kinder, gentler nation.

Ibid. Similar words were spoken by CHARLIE CHAPLIN at the end of *The Great Dictator* (1940), when he urged: 'More than cleverness, we need kindness and gentleness.'

7 I will keep America moving forward, always forward – for a better America, for an endless enduring dream and a thousand points of light.

Ibid. The phrase 'a thousand points of light', written for Bush by speechwriter PEGGY NOONAN, was used on various occasions during the 1988 presidential campaign. The words are not original, echoing similar phrases by Charles Dickens and THOMAS WOLFE, among others. As president, Bush initiated a 'Points of Light' reform programme in June 1989.

8 We can see a new world coming into view. A world in which there is the very real prospect of a new world order.

Speech quoted in *The New York Times* 7 March 1991

George W. Bush (b. 1946)

US POLITICIAN AND PRESIDENT

George Walker Bush. The son of the former President GEORGE BUSH, *he was elected Republican Governor of Texas in 1994 and, after two weeks of protracted recounts, became US President in 2000.*

1 We'll let our friends be the peacemakers and the great country called America will be the pacemakers.

Speech at Houston, Texas, 6 September 2000, quoted in *George W. Bushisms* (ed. Jacob Weisberg, 2001)

2 Freedom itself was attacked this morning by a faceless coward and freedom will be defended. Make no mistake, the United States will hunt down and punish those responsible for these cowardly acts.

On the terrorist attacks of '9/11', in speech, 11 September 2001, quoted in the *Daily Telegraph* 12 September 2001

3 This crusade, this war on terrorism is going to take a while. And the American people must be patient. I'm going to be patient. But I can assure the American people I am determined, I'm not going to

be distracted, I will keep my focus to make sure that not only are these brought to justice, but anybody who's been associated will be brought to justice. Those who harbor terrorists will be brought to justice. It is time for us to win the first war of the 21st century decisively, so that our children and our grandchildren can live peacefully into the 21st century.

Press conference, Washington DC, 16 September 2001, on www.whitehouse.gov

4 I have opinions of my own – strong opinions – but I don't always agree with them.

Quoted in *The Times* 19 January 2002

5 States like these, and their terrorist allies, constitute an axis of evil, arming to threaten the peace of the world. By seeking weapons of mass destruction, these regimes pose a grave and growing danger.

State of the Union address, 31 January 2002, published in the *Washington Times* 1 February 2002. Referring to Iran, Iraq and North Korea.

6 In cells and camps, terrorists are plotting further destruction, and building new bases for their war against civilization. And our greatest fear is that terrorists will find a shortcut to their mad ambitions when an outlaw regime supplies them with the technologies to kill on a massive scale. In one place – in one regime – we find all these dangers, in their most lethal and aggressive forms.

Address to United Nations, New York, 12 September 2002, published in the *Guardian* 13 September 2002. Referring to SADDAM HUSSEIN's regime in Iraq. 'The first time we may be completely certain he has nuclear weapons is when, God forbids, he uses one,' Bush declared.

Vannevar Bush (1890–1974)

US ELECTRICAL ENGINEER AND PHYSICIST
Having built several of the earliest electronic analog computers during the 1920s and '30s, he became Director of the Office of Scientific Research and Development in 1941, and was a champion of the 'missionary' function of science.

1 Science has a simple faith, which transcends utility. Nearly all men of science, all men of learning for that matter, and men of simple ways too, have it in some form and in some degree. It is the faith that it is the privilege of man to learn to understand, and that this is his mission. If we abandon that mission under stress we shall abandon it forever, for stress will not cease. Knowledge for the sake of understanding, not merely to prevail, that is the

essence of our being. None can define its limits, or set its ultimate boundaries.

Science Is Not Enough, 'The Search for Understanding' (1967).

Marilyn Butler (b. 1937)

BRITISH ACADEMIC AND AUTHOR
A professor of literature at Oxford and Exeter, she has written extensively on the Romantic period, including Jane Austen and the War of Ideas *(1975) and* Romantics, Rebels and Reactionaries *(1981).*

1 English literature is a kind of training in social ethics. . . . English trains you to handle a body of information in a way that is conducive to action.

Guardian 3 March 1989

A. S. Byatt (b. 1936)

BRITISH AUTHOR
Antonia Susan Byatt. Art, literary and social history, and philosophy are woven into her novels, such as The Virgin in the Garden *(1978) and* Possession *(1990). She is the sister of* MARGARET DRABBLE.

1 Pain hardens, and great pain hardens greatly, whatever the comforters say, and suffering does not ennoble, though it may occasionally lend a certain rigid dignity of manner to the suffering frame.

Quoted in the *Daily Telegraph* 21 July 1986

Stephen Byers (b. 1953)

BRITISH POLITICIAN
Elected Labour MP in 1992, he rose to become Secretary of State for Transport, Local Government and the Regions (2001–2002). According to Andrew Rawnsley he is 'proof that New Labour has perfected the science of human cloning'.

1 Reformers versus wreckers; that is the battle for this parliament and it's one we must win.

Speech at the Labour Party Conference, Cardiff, 2 February 2002, quoted in the *Daily Mail* 4 February 2002. Referring to the use of private investment for the modernization of schools and hospitals.

David Byrne (b. 1952)

US ROCK MUSICIAN
Singer and main force behind Talking Heads, one of the most influential bands of the 1970s and '80s, he has also composed film music and directed the film True Stories *(1986).*

1 *Facts all come with points of view*
Facts don't do what I want them to.

'Crosseyed and Painless' (song, written by David Byrne and BRIAN ENO) on the album *Remain in Light* (1980) by Talking Heads. The words were incorporated into 'Wordy Rappinghood' by

Tom Tom Club (see TINA WEYMOUTH AND CHRIS FRANTZ).

2 *And you may find yourself behind the wheel of a large automobile*
And you may find yourself in a beautiful house
With a beautiful wife

And you may ask yourself
Well, how did I get here?
'Once in a Lifetime' (song), on ibid.

3 **To shake your rump is to be environmentally aware.**
Sleeve notes on Byrne's compilation of Brazilian Samba music, *O Samba: Brazil Classics 2* (1989)

James Branch Cabell (1879–1958)

US NOVELIST AND ESSAYIST

He was highly regarded in his day for his romantic and satirical novels, set in the fantasy medieval world of Poictesme (pronounced Pwahtem). The most popular, Jurgen (1919), was considered by some pornographic.

1 **The optimist proclaims that we live in the best of all possible worlds; and the pessimist fears this is true.**

Coth of the Rocks, in *The Silver Stallion*, bk 4, ch. 26 (1926). The words recall those of Voltaire, 'All is for the best in the best of all possible worlds', from *Candide* (1759).

Irving Caesar (1895–1996)

US SONGWRITER

He was a Tin Pan Alley composer of more than 1,000 published songs, most famously 'Tea for Two' (1924), 'Crazy Rhythm' (1928) and 'Swanee' (1936). 'Sometimes I write lousy, but always fast,' he said.

1 *Picture you upon my knee,*
Just tea for two and two for tea.

'Tea for Two' (song, 1925). Caesar claimed that he composed the song in less than five minutes (though also admitted it might have taken him as long as fifteen).

John Cage (1912–92)

US COMPOSER

A pupil of Schoenberg (for whom he was 'not a composer, but an inventor – of genius'), he used new methods of notation, invented the 'prepared' piano and was a pioneer of aleatory (chance) music.

1 *I have nothing to say*
and I am saying   and that is
poetry.

'Lecture on Nothing', publ. in *Silence* (1961)

2 **There is no such thing as silence.**

'Everything We Do Is Music', interview in the *Saturday Evening Post* 19 October 1968, repr. in *Conversing with Cage*, 'His Own Music (to 1970)' (ed. Richard Kostelanetz, 1988). Cage claimed his silent piece, 4′33″, to be his personal favourite: 'It has three movements and in all of these movements there are no sounds. I wanted my work to be free of my own likes and dislikes, because I think music should be free of the feelings of the composer.' (Interview in the *Soho Weekly News* 12 September 1974)

James Cagney (1899–1986)

US SCREEN ACTOR

Shooting to fame as the feisty gangster in the seminal film The Public Enemy (1931), he was in demand for the next thirty years, showing his versatility as Bottom in A Midsummer Night's Dream (1935) and drawing on his song-and-dance background for Yankee Doodle Dandy (1942).

1 **You dirty, double-crossing rat.**
Blonde Crazy (film, 1931). The words were popularized and shortened to 'You dirty rat' which
Cagney, in his autobiography *Cagney by Cagney*
(1976), stridently denied ever having said.

Sammy Cahn (1913–93)
US SONGWRITER
*Originally Samuel Cohen. He collaborated with
Jule Styne on films and Broadway musicals, includ-
ing* Three Coins in the Fountain *(1954), and later
with Jimmy Van Heusen, with whom he wrote 'All
the Way' (1957), 'High Hopes' (1959), and 'Call
Me Irresponsible' (1963) – all hits for* FRANK
SINATRA.

1 *Give me five minutes more,
Only five minutes more,
Let me stay,
Let me stay in your arms.*
'Five Minutes More' (song, 1946, with music by
Jule Styne). The song was recorded by FRANK
SINATRA.

2 *Love and marriage, love and marriage
Go together like a horse and carriage
Dad was told by mother
You can't have one without the other.*
'Love and Marriage' (song, with music by Jimmy
Van Heusen) from the TV musical *Our Town*
(1955). The song was first aired by SINATRA, for
whom it was a million-seller.

James M. Cain (1892–1977)
US NOVELIST
*Subscribing to the 'hard-boiled' school of Ameri-
can fiction, he is noted for such works as* The Post-
man Always Rings Twice *(1934) and* Mildred
Pierce *(1941), both of which became movie classics.*

1 **The Postman Always Rings Twice.**
The Postman Always Rings Twice (novel, 1934,
filmed 1946 and 1981)

(Sir) Michael Caine (b. 1933)
BRITISH ACTOR
*Originally Maurice Micklewhite. A prolific per-
former on stage and screen, he is famous for his
roles in the films* The Ipcress File *(1965),* Alfie
(1966) and Cider House Rules *(2000). He is, he
says, 'every bourgeois's nightmare – a Cockney
with intelligence and a million dollars'.*

1 **Not many people know that.**
Catch-phrase and book title (1984). Caine's
catch-phrase, which found its way into his films
and was made the title of an 'Almanac of Amazing Information' compiled by him, is said to
have been his comment when habitually offering
information garnered from *The Guinness Book of
Records*.

2 **Be like a duck, my mother used to tell me.
Remain calm on the surface and paddle
like hell underneath.**
Interview in *Time Out* 16 September 1992

3 **My name is Michael Caine.**
Attributed. Much mimicked, notably in the song
by Madness, 'Michael Caine' (1984), the line was
said to have originated with PETER SELLERS.
As Caine explained: 'Peter always had the new
gadgets. So he was the first one to have an
answerphone. I called him one day and he
wasn't in, and there was me saying "My name is
Michael Caine and I just want to tell you that
Peter Sellers isn't in. And not many people know
that." '

Roberto Calasso (b. 1941)
ITALIAN AUTHOR
*He writes complex novels of ideas, specializing in
turning ancient myths into modern literature, as
in* The Marriage of Cadmus and Harmony
(1988), and Ka *(1996).*

1 **To invite the gods ruins our relationship
with them but sets history in motion. A life
in which the gods are not invited is not
worth living. It will be quieter, but there
won't be any stories. And you could suppose that these dangerous invitations were
in fact contrived by the gods themselves,
because the gods get bored with men with
no stories.**
The Marriage of Cadmus and Harmony, ch. 12
(1988)

Charles Calhoun See BILL HALEY 2 and 3.

James Callaghan (b. 1912)
BRITISH POLITICIAN
*Leonard James Callaghan, Baron Callaghan of
Cardiff. Elected Labour MP in 1945, he held posts
as Home and Foreign Secretary before becoming
Prime Minister (1976–9). His government fell after
a series of strikes had paralysed essential services.
See* ROY JENKINS 1.

1 **I don't think other people in the world
would share the view there is mounting
chaos.**
Interview at London Airport, 10 January 1979, in
the *Sun* 11 January 1979. Callaghan was returning
from the Guadeloupe Summit conference after
the Labour Party's policy of cooperation with
the unions had been torn apart by a wave of
strikes – the so-called 'winter of discontent' (see
below). See SUN 1 for its famous headline paraphrase.

2 **I had known it was going to be a 'winter of
discontent'.**
Quoted in the *Daily Telegraph* 9 February 1979.
The New Year had seen a succession of labour
disputes, with hospitals picketed and refuse piled
in the streets. Callaghan's failure to control the
unions led directly to MARGARET THATCHER'S
election victory later that year and to a subsequent raft of legislation designed to limit their
power. The phrase is from the opening line of
Shakespeare's *Richard III*, spoken by Gloucester.

Italo Calvino (1923–85)

ITALIAN AUTHOR AND CRITIC

Early novels, including his first, A Path to the Nest of Spiders *(1947), are naturalistic, while later books, such as* If on a Winter's Night a Traveller *(1979) are 'magic realist' in style. 'He is far too intelligent to become really cerebral,'* URSULA LE GUIN *commented.*

1 You only have to start saying of something: 'Ah, how beautiful! We must photograph it!' and you are already close to the view of the person who thinks that everything that is not photographed is lost, as if it had never existed, and that therefore in order really to live you must photograph as much as you can, and to photograph as much as you can you must either live in the most photographic way possible, or else consider photographable every moment of your life. The first course leads to stupidity; the second, to madness.

Difficult Loves, 'The Adventure of a Photographer' (1970, transl. 1984)

2 It is not the voice that commands the story: it is the ear.

Marco Polo, in *Invisible Cities* (1972)

3 The catalogue of forms is endless: until every shape has found its city, new cities will continue to be born. When the forms exhaust their variety and come apart, the end of cities begins.

Invisible Cities (1972)

4 The universe will express itself as long as somebody will be able to say 'I read, therefore it writes.'

If on a Winter's Night a Traveller, pt 8, 'From the Diary of Silas Flannery' (1979)

5 Everything can change, but not the language that we carry inside us, like a world more exclusive and final than one's mother's womb.

'By Way of an Autobiography', first publ. in *Grand Bazaar* September/October 1980, repr. in *The Literature Machine* (1987)

6 A classic is a book that has never finished saying what it has to say.

'Why Read the Classics?', first publ. in *L'Espresso* 28 June 1981, repr. ibid. One of a series of definitions of a 'classic'.

James Cameron (1911–85)

BRITISH JOURNALIST

He made his name as a freelance journalist, addressing issues of war and social justice with integrity and wit. He also wrote and presented TV shows such as Men of Our Time *(1963).*

1 Now, standing up unsteadily from the sea, was the famous Mushroom. . . . It climbed like a fungus; it looked like a towering mound of firm cream shot with veins and rivers of wandering red; it mounted tirelessly through the clouds as though it were made of denser, solider stuff, as no doubt it was. The only similes that came to mind were banal: a sundae, red ink in a pot of distemper. From behind me I heard a frenetic ticking of typewriters; very soon I found I was fumbling with my own. The reportage had begun. Many of us will never live it down.

Point of Departure, ch. 3 (1967). On the first atomic-bomb test on the Bikini atoll, summer 1946.

2 The *New York Times* is the best and the worst newspaper on earth, a daily monument to the sloppy and extravagant simplification of the overdone; the *Daily Mirror* is the worst and the best newspaper, a gymnastic in the dedicated technical expertise of the persuasive non-think. I have worked for them both, but I cannot yet determine which I like least.

Ibid., ch. 4

3 Objectivity in some circumstances is both meaningless and impossible. I still do not see how a reporter attempting to define a situation involving some sort of ethical conflict can do it with sufficient demonstrable neutrality to fulfil some arbitrary concept of 'objectivity'. It never occurred to me, in such a situation, to be other than subjective, and as obviously so as I could manage to be. I may not always have been satisfactorily balanced; I always tended to argue that objectivity was of less importance than the truth, and that the reporter whose technique was informed by no opinion lacked a very serious dimension.

Ibid.

4 The test of a good classical moralization is that it seems to have been written for oneself alone.

Ibid. Discussing the saying, *Video meliora proboque; deteriora sequor* ('I see and approve of the better things; I follow the worse').

5 Islam is the youngest of the major religions and it has the arrogance of youth.

Quoted by Moni Cameron (James Cameron's wife) in letter to the *Guardian* 15 March 1989

6 Is not Christmas the only occasion when one gets drunk *for the children's sake*?

Quoted in the *Independent on Sunday* 20 December 1991

James Cameron (b. 1954)

CANADIAN FILM DIRECTOR AND SCREENWRITER

Described as 'the high priest of Hollywood Bloat' and 'the movies' mad toymaker', he achieved his first major success with The Terminator *(1984), fol-*

lowed by Aliens (1986) and the multi-award-winning Titanic (1997).

1 **The social battles of the video age are fought with images, not guns.**
Commentary in *Strange Days* (film, 1995, screenplay by James Cameron and Jay Cocks, directed by KATHRYN BIGELOW)

2 **Every paradigm on Earth is falling apart at the same time . . . every system, vision, constitution, revelation . . . is breaking down. Being toppled or abandoned . . . all at the same time! And you know what really scares me? There's no new ideas. Everything's been done. Rock music, punk music, rap music, techno, techno-Mex . . . long hair, short hair . . . no hair. Doesn't it feel like everything's been tried? Whaddya do that's new? Something new in art? Forget it. Somebody somewhere has done it.**
Max Peltier, ibid.

Beatrix Campbell (b. 1947)
BRITISH JOURNALIST
A commentator on women's and social issues and columnist for periodicals including the New Statesman *and* Feminist Review, *she is the author of* Wigan Pier Revisited *(1984) among other works.*

1 **Children's bodies aren't like automobiles with the assailant's fingerprints lingering on the wheel. The world of sexual abuse is quintessentially secret. It is the perfect crime.**
Unofficial Secrets, ch. 2 (1988). In the book's Introduction, Campbell quotes a police source on the subject: 'Sexual abuse is like a corpse on a slab, saying nothing. You've got nothing to go on. It's a police officer's nightmare. You just want it to go away.'

2 **These people like excitement. They have their ways of doing things – they've spent generations practising; and they have their ways of *having* things – called gratification. These people have got 'love' and 'hate' tattooed on their tiaras.**
Of the Royal Family, in *Diana Princess of Wales*, pt 2, ch. 7 (1998)

3 **The politics of seeing and being seen, are about power as well as pleasure, voyeurism and exhibitionism, censorship and surveillance, knowledge and ignorance, celebrity and harassment, espionage and jealousy.**
Ibid., pt 3, ch. 13

Joseph Campbell (1904–87)
US WRITER ON MYTHOLOGY
Mythological archetypes were his principal interest. His major work was a study of world mythology in four volumes, The Masks of God *(1959–67).*

1 **Religions, philosophies, arts, the social forms of primitive and historic man, prime discoveries in science and technology, the very dreams that blister sleep, boil up from the basic, magic ring of myth.**
The Hero With a Thousand Faces, Prologue, sect. 1 (1949)

2 **The myths of failure touch us with the tragedy of life, but those of success only with their own incredibility.**
Ibid., pt 1, ch. 3, sect. 2

Mrs Patrick Campbell (1865–1940)
BRITISH ACTRESS
Originally Beatrice Stella Tanner. Described by YEATS *as possessing 'an ego like a raging tooth', she came to notice with her performance in* The Second Mrs Tanqueray *(1893).* SHAW, *with whom she formed a lasting friendship, created the part of Eliza Doolittle for her in* Pygmalion *(1914).*

1 **To be made to hold his tongue is the greatest insult you can offer him – though he might be ready with a poker to make you hold yours.**
Of GEORGE BERNARD SHAW, in *My Life and Some Letters*, ch. 16 (1922)

2 **The deep, deep peace of the double-bed after the hurly-burly of the chaise-longue.**
Quoted in *While Rome Burns*, 'The First Mrs Tanqueray' (1934) by ALEXANDER WOOLLCOTT. Discussing the benefits of her recent marriage. Woollcott remarked of Mrs Campbell: 'Her failure to be polite took on the proportions of a magnificent gesture.'

3 **Does it *really* matter what these affectionate people do – so long as they don't do it in the streets *and frighten the horses!***
Quoted in *Mrs Patrick Campbell*, ch. 15 (1961) by Alan Dent. Referring to rumours of a homosexual liaison between two actors. The words are quoted in various forms, commonly 'I don't mind where people make love', and 'My dear, I don't care what they do . . .'

Albert Camus (1913–60)
FRENCH-ALGERIAN PHILOSOPHER AND AUTHOR
His works principally deal with l'homme révolté *(the misfit), as in the essay* The Myth of Sisyphus *(1942) and his first novel* The Outsider *(1942), both of which explore the absurdity of the human situation. Later novels include* The Plague *(1947) and* The Fall *(1956)*

1 **An intellectual is someone whose mind watches itself. I like this, because I am happy to be both halves, the watcher and the watched. 'Can they be brought together?' This is a practical question. We must get down to it. 'I despise intelligence' really means: 'I cannot bear my doubts.'**
Journal entry, May 1936, publ. in *Carnets 1935–1942* (1962, transl. and ed. Philip Thody, 1963)

2 Culture: the cry of men in face of their
destiny.
Journal entry, June 1937, ibid.

3 There is but one truly serious philosophical problem and that is suicide. Judging
whether life is or is not worth living
amounts to answering the fundamental
question of philosophy. All the rest –
whether or not the world has three dimensions, whether the mind has nine or twelve
categories – comes afterwards. These are
games.
The Myth of Sisyphus, 'Absurdity and Suicide'
(1942, transl. 1955). Opening sentences.

4 At any street corner the feeling of absurdity can strike any man in the face.
Ibid., 'Absurd Walls'

5 The struggle itself towards the heights is
enough to fill a man's heart. One must
imagine Sisyphus happy.
Ibid., 'The Myth of Sisyphus'. Closing words of
book.

6 Mother died today. Or, maybe, yesterday;
I can't be sure.
Meursault, in *The Outsider*, pt 1, ch. 1 (1942).
Opening words of book.

7 If Christianity is pessimistic as to man, it
is optimistic as to human destiny. Well, I
can say that, pessimistic as to human destiny, I am optimistic as to man.
Address to monks of Latour-Maubourg, 1948,
publ. in *Resistance, Rebellion and Death*, 'The
Unbeliever and Christians' (1961)

8 Man is the only creature who refuses to be
what he is.
The Rebel, Introduction (1951)

9 What is a rebel? A man who says no.
Ibid., ch. 1. Opening sentence.

10 All modern revolutions have ended in a
reinforcement of the power of the state.
Ibid., ch. 3, 'State Terrorism and Irrational
Terror'

11 Every revolutionary ends by becoming
either an oppressor or a heretic.
Ibid., 'Rebellion and Revolution'

12 In the midst of winter, I finally learned
that there was in me an invincible summer.
L'Été, 'Return to Tipasa' (1954)

13 I sometimes think of what future historians will say of us. A single sentence will
suffice for modern man: he fornicated and
read the papers.
Narrator (Jean-Baptiste Clamence), in *The Fall*
(1956)

14 You know what charm is: a way of getting
the answer yes without having asked any
clear question.
Ibid.

15 Men are never convinced of your reasons,
of your sincerity, of the seriousness of your
sufferings, except by your death. So long as
you are alive, your case is doubtful; you
have a right only to their scepticism.
Ibid.

16 Martyrs, *cher ami*, must choose between
being forgotten, mocked, or made use of.
As for being understood – never!
Ibid.

17 I'll tell you a great big secret, *mon cher*.
Don't wait for the Last Judgment. It takes
place every day.
Ibid.

18 Ah, *mon cher*, for anyone who is alone,
without God and without a master, the
weight of days is dreadful.
Ibid.

19 I have always denounced terrorism. I must
also denounce a terrorism which is exercised blindly, in the streets of Algiers for
example, and which some day could strike
my mother or my family. I believe in justice, but I shall defend my mother above
justice.
Debate at University of Stockholm, 1957, quoted
in *Camus: A Biography*, ch. 45 (1979) by Herbert
R. Lottman. Camus provoked much criticism
with his remarks, taken as a betrayal of the
struggle for Algerian independence.

20 We come into the world laden with the
weight of an infinite necessity.
Resistance, Rebellion and Death, 'Reflections on
the Guillotine' (1961)

21 The more I produce the less I am certain.
On the road along which the artist walks,
night falls ever more densely. Finally he
dies blind.
Undated letter, quoted in *Camus: A Biography*,
ch. 43 (1979) by Herbert R. Lottman

Elias Canetti (1905–94)
BULGARIAN AUTHOR AND PHILOSOPHER
His only novel Die Blendung *(1936, translated as
both* Auto da Fé *and* The Tower of Babel*) charts
the destruction of a reclusive sinologist, while his
greatest work* Crowds and Power *(1960) reflects
his central concern, the psychology of crowds.*

1 Justice begins with the recognition of the
necessity of sharing. The oldest law is that
which regulates it, and this is still the most
important law today and, as such, has
remained the basic concern of all movements which have at heart the community
of human activities and of human existence in general.
Crowds and Power, 'Distribution and Increase'
(1960)

2 Whether or not God is dead: it is imposs-

ible to keep silent about him who was
there for so long.
*The Secret Heart of the Clock: Notes, Aphorisms,
Fragments 1973–1985*, '1973' (1991)

3 There is no doubt: the study of man is just
beginning, at the same time that his end is
in sight.
Ibid., '1980'

Eric Cantona (b. 1966)
FRENCH FOOTBALLER
*A skilful forward and an idol for a generation of
fans, he played for Manchester United 1993–7, and
has since embarked on an acting career.*

1 When the seagulls follow the trawler, it is
because they think sardines will be thrown
into the sea.
Quoted in the *Independent* 1 April 1995, after he
had won his appeal against a prison sentence for
his conviction of assault on a hostile fan. He was
made to perform community service instead.
'Seagulls Follow the Trawler' was adopted as the
name of a sports discussion programme on BBC
Radio 4 in 1999.

Cao Yu (1910–96)
CHINESE DRAMATIST
*Originally Wan Jiabao. China's foremost
twentieth-century playwright, he took as his theme
the corruption of society, producing his best known
work* Thunderstorm *in 1935.*

1 Art for art's sake is a philosophy of the
well-fed.
Observer 13 April 1980

Karel Čapek (1890–1938)
CZECH WRITER
*He is best remembered for the play R.U.R. (Ros-
sum's Universal Robots) (1920), in which he
coined the word 'robot' (derived from the Czech
word for forced labour). With his brother Josef, he
wrote the comic satire* The Insect Play *(1921).*

1 Man will never be enslaved by machinery
if the man tending the machine be paid
enough.
Quoted in obituary in the *News Chronicle*
27 December 1938

Al Capone (1899–1947)
US GANGSTER
*'Neapolitan by birth and Neanderthal by instinct',
Alphonse ('Scarface') Capone was America's most
famous gangster, allegedly earning $30 million a
year during the Prohibition years. He was eventually gaoled in 1931 for tax evasion.*

1 My rackets are run on strictly American
lines and they're going to stay that way.
Interview *c.* 1930, publ. in *Cockburn Sums Up*,
'Mr Capone, Philosopher' (1981) by Claud
Cockburn

2 Virgin territory for whorehouses.
Quoted in *The Bootleggers*, ch. 16 (1961) by Kenneth Allsop. Referring to suburban Chicago.

Truman Capote (1924–84)
US AUTHOR
*Originally Truman Streckfus Persons. A versatile
writer, he is remembered for his first novel* Other
Voices, Other Rooms *(1948), the novella* Breakfast at Tiffany's *(1958, filmed 1961), and* In Cold
Blood *(1966, filmed 1967) which he termed a non-
fiction novel.* GORE VIDAL *remarked: 'He has
made lying an art. A minor art.'*

1 That isn't writing at all – it's typing.
Quoted in the *New Republic* 9 February 1959.
Remark in TV discussion, referring to the Beat
novelists.

2 Venice is like eating an entire box of chocolate liqueurs at one go.
Quoted in the *Observer* 26 November 1961

3 Even an attorney of moderate talent can
postpone doomsday year after year, for the
system of appeals that pervades American
jurisprudence amounts to a legalistic wheel
of fortune, a game of chance, somewhat
fixed in the favor of the criminal, that the
participants play interminably.
In Cold Blood, ch. 4 (1966)

4 Failure is the condiment that gives success
its flavor.
'Self-Portrait' (1972), repr. in *A Capote Reader*
(1987)

5 Anyone who is consistently consistent has
a head made of biscuit.
Ibid.

6 When God hands you a gift, he also hands
you a whip; and the whip is intended solely
for self-flagellation.
Music for Chameleons, Preface (1980)

7 It's like a jumble of huts in a jungle somewhere. I don't understand how you can
live there. It's really, completely dead.
Walk along the street, there's nothing
moving. I've lived in small Spanish fishing
villages which were literally sunny all day
long everyday of the week, but they
weren't as boring as Los Angeles.
Of Los Angeles, in *Conversations With Truman
Capote*, ch. 7, 'Hollywood' (ed. Lawrence Gro-
bel, 1985)

Al Capp (1909–79)
US CARTOONIST
*Originally Alfred Caplin. He introduced the comic
strip, featuring the hillbilly character Li'l Abner
and friends, to the* New York Mirror *in 1934. Its
popularity ensured that it ran for more than forty
years.*

1 A product of the untalented, sold by the unprincipled to the utterly bewildered.

Of abstract art, quoted in the *National Observer* 1 July 1963

Philip Caputo (b. 1941)

US AUTHOR AND JOURNALIST

He worked as a foreign correspondent for the Chicago Tribune *(1969–72) and drew on his experiences as a soldier in Vietnam for his memoir* A Rumor of War *(1977).*

1 Our mission was not to win terrain, or seize positions, but simply to kill: to kill Communists and to kill as many of them as possible. Stack 'em like cordwood. Victory was a high body-count, defeat a low-kill ratio, war a matter of arithmetic.

A Rumor of War, Prologue (1977)

(Sir) Neville Cardus (1889–1975)

BRITISH JOURNALIST AND CRITIC

He wrote mainly for the Manchester Guardian *which he joined in 1916 as music critic, and he later also became responsible for the paper's cricket coverage.*

1 It is far more than a game, this cricket. It somehow holds the mirror up to English nature. We are not hypocrites, but we try to make the best of things of contrary appeal.

English Cricket (1945)

2 It is because cricket does not always hurry along, a constant hurly burly, every player propelled here and there by the pace of continuous action, that there is time for character to reveal itself. We remember not the scores and the results in after years; it is the men who remain in our minds, in our imagination.

Ibid.

3 Such reproductions may not interest the reader; but after all, this is my autobiography, not his; he is under no obligation to read further in it; he was under none to begin. . . . A modest or inhibited autobiography is written without entertainment to the writer and read with distrust by the reader.

Autobiography, pt 1 (1947)

George Carey (b. 1935)

BRITISH ECCLESIASTIC, ARCHBISHOP OF CANTERBURY

Formerly a theology lecturer, he was Primate of the Church of England (1991–2002), during which time he drew some criticism for his liberal and modernizing tendencies.

1 People have described me as a 'management bishop' but I say to my critics 'Jesus was a management expert too.'

Daily Telegraph 26 February 1991

2 I believe with all my heart that the Church of Jesus Christ should be a Church of blurred edges.

Independent 15 July 1992

John Carey (b. 1934)

BRITISH AUTHOR AND CRITIC

Professor of English at Oxford 1976–2001 and principal book reviewer for the Sunday Times *since 1977, he has written works on Milton, Thackeray, Donne and* WILLIAM GOLDING.

1 A blank helpless sort of face, rather like a rose just before you drench it with DDT.

Sunday Times 20 September 1981, repr. in *Original Copy*, pt 2, 'Keeping Up With the Coopers' (1987). Referring to photographs of society figure Lady DIANA COOPER.

2 It follows that, if society wants to be civilized, it must establish conditions favourable to the preservation of the gifted few.

The Intellectuals and the Masses, ch. 4 (1992)

Peter Carey (b. 1943)

AUSTRALIAN AUTHOR

His novels, which include Bliss *(1981, filmed 1985), set in the world of advertising in which he formerly worked, and* Oscar and Lucinda *(1988, filmed 1997), combine fantasy, comedy and history.*

1 We're built, as a nation, on the grounds of a concentration camp. It's like saying 'OK, here's Auschwitz. Here's where we'll start our country.'

Interview in *City Limits* 7 April 1988

Robert Carlyle (b. 1956)

SCOTTISH ACTOR

First known for his TV role as the policeman Hamish Macbeth, he achieved box-office success in the films Trainspotting *(1996),* The Full Monty *(1996) and* Angela's Ashes *(2000).*

1 Do you use the telephone, do you watch television, do you drive on the road with tyres? There's four things that have come out of this tiny, wee country. But it is also a country whose people are either capable of great or terrible things. A psychotic nation.

Of Scotland, in interview in *The Times* 17 January 1998

Stokely Carmichael (1941–99)

TRINIDAD-BORN US POLITICAL ACTIVIST

He was at the forefront of civil rights movements throughout the 1960s, though publicly broke with the Black Panthers in 1968. He later changed his name to Kwame Touré.

1 This is the 27th time I have been arrested – I ain't going to jail no more. I ain't going to jail no more. Every courthouse in Mississippi ought to be burned down to get rid of the dirt. We want Black Power!

Speech from steps of courthouse in Greenwood, Mississippi, June 1966, quoted in *The New York Times* 17 June 1966. The slogan 'Black Power' (uttered five times by Carmichael) was taken up by the gathered crowd, who were participating in the James Meredith March from Memphis to Jackson to promote black voting. MARTIN LUTHER KING, also on the march, expressed his unease at the slogan and encouraged instead 'Freedom Now', though by the end of the march this had been eclipsed by Carmichael's more inflammatory call. Carmichael was responsible for popularizing the slogan and published a book with that title in 1967 (see below).

2 Those of us who advocate Black Power are quite clear in our own minds that a 'non-violent' approach to civil rights is an approach black people cannot afford and a luxury white people do not deserve.

Black Power, ch. 2 (written with Charles Vernon Hamilton, 1967)

Dale Carnegie (1888–1955)
US WRITER AND LECTURER
A pioneer in the field of public speaking, he is best remembered for his book How to Win Friends and Influence People *(1936). He went on to found numerous branches of the Dale Carnegie Institute for Effective Speaking and Human Relations.*

1 How to Win Friends and Influence People.
Title of book (1936)

E. H. Carr (1892–1982)
BRITISH AUTHOR AND ACADEMIC
Edward Hallett Carr. He worked in the Foreign Office before becoming assistant editor of The Times *(1941–6). His magnum opus was* A History of Soviet Russia 1917–29 *(14 vols. 1950–78).*

1 History begins when men begin to think of the passage of time in terms not of natural processes – the cycle of the seasons, the human life-span – but of a series of specific events in which men are consciously involved and which they can consciously influence.
What Is History?, Lecture 6 (1961)

J. L. Carr (1912–94)
BRITISH NOVELIST
James Lloyd Carr. For many years a teacher, he encapsulated English provincial life in such novels as The Harpole Report *(1972) and* A Month in the Country *(1980), while his* Dictionary of Extraordinary Cricketers *(1977) has also become a minor classic.*

1 A school is not a factory. Its raison d'être is to provide opportunity for experience.
The Harpole Report, ch. 6 (1972)

2 You have not had thirty years' experience . . . You have had one year's experience 30 times.
Ibid., ch. 21

Jim Carroll (b. 1951)
US AUTHOR
A heroin addict, he wrote autobiographically, notably in The Basketball Diaries *(1980, filmed 1995), written between the ages of twelve and fifteen, in which he explored the 'dark underbelly of the Sixties' counterculture'.*

1 Junk is just another nine to five gig in the end, only the hours are a bit more inclined towards shadows.
The Basketball Diaries, 'Summer 66' (1980)

Johnny Carson (b. 1925)
US CHAT-SHOW HOST AND COMEDIAN
After presenting his own shows on television and hosting the game show Who Do You Trust? *(1957–62), he took over* The Tonight Show, *hosting it for the next thirty years.*

1 Heeeeere's Johnny!
Spoken by Ed McMahon introducing *The Tonight Show Starring Johnny Carson* (US TV variety show, 1962–92). The intro was often copied, and was famously – and manically – mimicked by JACK NICHOLSON's character (Jack Torrance) in *The Shining* (film, 1980).

Rachel Carson (1907–64)
US MARINE BIOLOGIST AND AUTHOR
Through her books, notably The Sea Around Us *(1951) and* Silent Spring *(1962), she increased public awareness of the dangers of environmental pollution, which in turn led to US legislation on the use of pesticides.*

1 The sea lies all about us. . . . In its mysterious past it encompasses all the dim origins of life and receives in the end, after, it may be, many transmutations, the dead husks of that same life. For all at last returns to the sea – to Oceanus, the ocean river, like the ever-flowing stream of time, the beginning and the end.
The Sea Around Us, pt 3, ch. 14 (1951)

2 Under the philosophy that now seems to guide our destinies, nothing must get in the way of the man with the spray gun.
Silent Spring, ch. 7 (1962)

3 Over increasingly large areas of the United States, spring now comes unheralded by the return of the birds, and the early morn-

ings are strangely silent where once they were filled with the beauty of bird song.

Ibid., ch. 8

4 The 'control of nature' is a phrase conceived in arrogance, born of the Neanderthal age of biology and the convenience of man.

Ibid., ch. 17

Angela Carter (1940–92)
BRITISH AUTHOR

Her fiction combined eroticism, feminism and fantasy, for example the stories 'The Magic Toyshop' (1967, filmed 1986) and 'The Company of Wolves' (1977, filmed 1984), for which she also wrote the screenplays, and the novels Nights at the Circus (1984) and Wise Children (1991).

1 Midnight, and the clock strikes. It is Christmas Day, the werewolves' birthday, the door of the solstice still wide enough open to let them all slink through.

'The Company of Wolves', first publ. in *Bananas* (ed. Emma Tennant, 1977)

2 Never stray from the path, never eat a windfall apple and never trust a man whose eyebrows meet in the middle.

Ibid.

3 The victim style of the 1970s has a behavioural style to match. They never smile, these infants of the recession: they sneer. Defiant untouchables, tattooed at the extremities and accessoried with offensive weapons, lips and fingernails stained black and blue and the skin round their eyes painted up like rococo window-frames.

'Ups and Downs for the Babes in Bondage', publ. in *New Society* 22 December 1977

4 We do not go to bed in single pairs; even if we choose not to refer to them, we still drag there with us the cultural impedimenta of our social class, our parents' lives, our bank balances, our sexual and emotional expectations, our whole biographies – all the bits and pieces of our unique existences.

The Sadeian Woman, 'Polemical Preface' (1979)

5 Pornographers are the enemies of women only because our contemporary ideology of pornography does not encompass the possibility of change, as if we were the slaves of history and not its makers. . . . Pornography is a satire on human pretensions.

Ibid.

6 The bed is now as public as the dinner table and governed by the same rules of formal confrontation.

Ibid., 'Speculative Finale'

7 If *Miss* means respectably unmarried, and *Mrs.* respectably married, then *Ms.* means nudge, nudge, wink, wink.

'The Language of Sisterhood', publ. in *The State of the Language* (ed. Christopher Ricks, 1980)

8 If the Christ were content with humble toilers for disciples, that wasn't good enough for our Bert. He wanted dukes' half sisters and belted earls wiping his feet with their hair; grand apotheosis of the snob, to humiliate the objects of his own awe by making them venerate him.

New Society 3 June 1982. Referring to D. H. Lawrence.

9 I think it's one of the scars in our culture that we have too high an opinion of ourselves. We align ourselves with the angels instead of the higher primates.

Marxism Today January 1985

10 I think the adjective 'post-modernist' really means 'mannerist'. Books about books is fun but frivolous.

Novelists in Interview (ed. John Haffenden, 1985)

11 Morality as regards woman has nothing to do with ethics; it means sexual morality and nothing but sexual morality. To be a wayward girl usually has something to do with pre-marital sex; to be a wicked woman has something to do with adultery. This means it is far easier for a woman to lead a blameless life than it is for a man; all she has to do is to avoid sexual intercourse like the plague.

Wayward Girls and Wicked Women, Introduction (ed. Angela Carter, 1986)

12 Just because we're sisters under the skin doesn't mean we've got much in common.

Guardian 25 October 1990

13 Comedy is tragedy that happens to *other* people.

Wise Children, ch. 4 (1991)

Jimmy Carter (b. 1924)
US POLITICIAN AND PRESIDENT

From a farming background, he rose to become Democratic Governor of Georgia (1970–74) and US President (1977–81). His subsequent work in conflict resolution earned him the accolade 'the best ex-president America has ever had' by the head of the Nobel prize committee when he was awarded the Peace Prize in 2002.

1 I've looked on a lot of women with lust. I've committed adultery in my heart many times. This is something God recognizes I will do – and I have done it – and God forgives me for it.

Interview in *Playboy* November 1976. The remark caused widespread surprise when it was published at the height of the presidential campaign in which he stood against GERALD FORD.

Carter's wife Rosalynn remarked simply, 'Jimmy talks too much . . .'

2 **I thought a lot about our nation and what I should do as president. And Sunday night before last, I made a speech about two problems of our country – energy and malaise.**
Speech at Bardstown, Kentucky, 31 July 1979, publ. in *Public Papers of the Presidents of the United States* (1979). The speech to which Carter referred, broadcast 15 July from the White House, did not include the word 'malaise', though Carter's identification of these two issues provoked much discussion.

3 **I never really had any affinity for politics. I've always looked on politics as a means to an end. . . . It has never been a natural part of my life.**
Interview in the *Guardian* 7 February 1998. In an interview with Carter's biographer, his vice-president WALTER MONDALE charged his former boss with having 'the coldest political nose of any politician'.

Stephen Carter (b. 1954)
US LAWYER AND AUTHOR
An advocate of affirmative action for African Americans, he has written widely on matters of race and on the role of religion in politics.

1 **The new grammar of race is constructed in a way that George Orwell would have appreciated, because its rules make some ideas impossible to express – unless, of course, one wants to be called a racist.**
Reflections of an Affirmative Action Baby, ch. 8 (1992)

Sydney Carter (b. 1915)
BRITISH SONGWRITER
A teacher, he has written folk songs as well as popular hymns.

1 *Dance then wherever you may be,*
I am the Lord of the Dance, said he,
And I'll lead you all, wherever you may be
And I'll lead you all in the dance, said he.
'Lord of the Dance' (song), publ. in *Nine Carols or Ballads* (1967)

2 *One more step along the world I go,*
One more step along the world I go,
From the old things to the new
Keep me travelling along with You.
'One More Step Along the World I Go' (hymn, 1971)

(Dame) Barbara Cartland
(1901–2000)
BRITISH NOVELIST
Hailed 'the queen of romantic fiction', she sold over 650 million copies of her 623 books, whose sheer number enabled her to claim the longest entry in Who's Who. *She was famous for her pink chiffon, extravagant false eyelashes and traditional views on romance.*

1 **The great majority of people in England and America are modest, decent and pure-minded and the amount of virgins in the world today is stupendous.**
Interview in *Speaking Frankly* (1978) by Wendy Leigh. But on another occasion, Cartland was reported as saying: 'Only the English and the Americans are improper. East of Suez everyone wants a virgin.'

2 **The right diet directs sexual energy into the parts that matter.**
Quoted in the *Observer* 11 January 1981

3 **France is the only place where you can make love in the afternoon without people hammering on your door.**
Quoted in the *Guardian* 24 December 1984

Raymond Carver (1939–88)
US SHORT-STORY WRITER AND POET
Identified with 'dirty realism', he established his reputation with Will You Please Be Quiet, Please? *(1976), followed by* Cathedral *(1984) and* Where I'm Calling From *(1988).* JAY MCINERNEY *commented: 'The trout in Carver's streams were apt to be pollution-deformed mutants, the romance of drinking replaced by the dull grind of full-time alcoholism.'*

1 **Writers don't need tricks or gimmicks or even necessarily need to be the smartest fellows on the block. At the risk of appearing foolish, a writer sometimes needs to be able to just stand and gape at this or that thing – a sunset or an old shoe – in absolute and simple amazement.**
'A Storyteller's Notebook', first publ. in *The New York Times Book Review* 15 February 1981, repr. as 'On Writing' in *Fires* (1985)

Joyce Cary (1888–1957)
BRITISH AUTHOR
He is best remembered for his trilogies dealing with art and politics, and especially for The Horse's Mouth *(1944), a picaresque portrait of a disreputable artist.* V.S. PRITCHETT *called him 'the chameleon among contemporary novelists'.*

1 **Sara could commit adultery at one end and weep for her sins at the other, and enjoy both operations at once.**
Narrator (Gulley Jimson), in *The Horse's Mouth*, ch. 8 (1944)

2 **God is a character, a real and consistent being, or He is nothing. If God did a miracle He would deny His own nature and the universe would simply blow up, vanish, become nothing.**
Interview in *Writers at Work* (first series, ed. Malcolm Cowley, 1958)

Pablo Casals (1876–1973)
SPANISH CELLIST, CONDUCTOR AND
COMPOSER

Called by Rostropovich 'the greatest name in cello history', he is famous for his interpretations of Bach, especially the cello suites. He founded the Barcelona Orchestra in 1919 and conducted it until 1936 when, in protest against the Franco regime, he moved to France.

1 I go back to Bach as a sick dog instinctively grubs at the roots and herbs that are its right medicine.

Quoted in the *Observer* 27 November 1921

2 It [the cello] is like a beautiful woman who has not grown older, but younger with time, more slender, more supple, more graceful.

Quoted in *Time* 29 April 1957

(Sir) Roger Casement (1864–1916)
COLONIAL ADMINISTRATOR AND IRISH
NATIONALIST

An Ulster Protestant, he gained his knighthood after denouncing cruelty and exploitation while consul in the Congo and Brazil. In Ireland, his efforts to enlist German support for the Easter Rising in 1916 resulted in his execution for high treason.

1 As I stand face to face with death, I feel just as if they were going to kill a boy. For I feel like a boy – and my hands are so free from blood and my heart always so compassionate and pitiful that I cannot comprehend that anyone wants to hang me.

Note found in Casement's condemned cell, Pentonville, London, August 1916, quoted in *The Lives of Roger Casement*, ch. 30 (1976) by B. L. Reid.

William Casey (1913–87)
US LAWYER AND INTELLIGENCE CHIEF

As REAGAN'*s Director of the CIA (1981–7), he intensified the agency's anti-communist activities. Investigations into his role in the Iran–Contra affair were interrupted by his death.*

1 I pass the test that says a man who isn't a socialist at 20 has no heart, and a man who is a socialist at 40 has no head.

Quoted in obituary, *Washington Post* 7 May 1987. The saying has been attributed to French socialist politician and premier Aristide Briand.

Johnny Cash (b. 1932)
US COUNTRY SINGER

Nicknamed 'The Man in Black' after one of his songs, he became a top Country and Western recording artist in the late 1950s. He has penned more than 1,500 songs including 'I Walk the Line' (1956) and 'A Boy Named Sue' (1969).

1 I shot a man in Reno
Just to watch him die.
'Folsom Prison Blues' (song, 1956)

2 I thank God for all the freedom we have in this country, I cherish it – even the right to burn the flag. But we also have the right to bear arms and if you burn my flag – *I'll shoot you!*

Quoted by TONY PARSONS in the *Daily Telegraph* 10 April 1992. The speech is a routine preamble to Cash's hymn to the Stars and Stripes, 'Ragged Old Flag', usually to a standing ovation.

Neal Cassady (1926–68)
US WRITER

An outlaw hero of the Beat generation, he was mythologized as Dean Moriarty ('the holy con man with the shining mind') in KEROUAC'*s* On the Road. *Fragments of autobiography and his correspondence have been published in* The First Third *(1971) and* Grace Beats Karma *(1993).*

1 Art is good when it springs from necessity. This kind of origin is the guarantee of its value; there is no other.

Letter to Jack Kerouac, 7–8 January 1948, quoted in *Memory Babe*, ch. 5, sect. 5 (1983) by Gerald Nicosia

2 Billboards, billboards, drink this, eat that, use all manner of things, EVERYONE, the best, the cheapest, the purest and most satisfying of all their available counterparts. Red lights flicker on every horizon, airplanes beware; cars flash by, more lights. Workers repair the gas main. Signs, signs, lights, lights, streets, streets.

'Leaving LA by Train at Night, High . . .', written *c.* 1950, publ. in *The First Third and Other Writings* (1971)

(Sir) Hugh Casson (1910–99)
BRITISH ARCHITECT

After directing the architecture at the Festival of Britain (1948–51), he was Professor of Interior Design at the Royal College of Art (1953–75) and President of the Royal Academy (1976–84).

1 The British love permanence more than they love beauty.

Quoted in the *Observer* 14 June 1964

Ted Castle (1907–79)
BRITISH JOURNALIST

Baron Castle of Islington. The husband of Labour politician Barbara Castle, he was Editor of Picture Post *(1944–52) and an alderman of the Greater London Council (1964–70).*

1 In Place of Strife.

White Paper on industrial relations, 17 January 1969. The title was suggested to Employment Secretary Barbara Castle by her husband, as recalled in *The Barbara Castle Diaries*, 15 January

1969 (1984). It was probably inspired by ANEURIN BEVAN's book setting out his political credo, *In Place of Fear* (1952).

Fidel Castro (b. 1926)
CUBAN REVOLUTIONARY AND PRESIDENT
He established a Communist regime in Cuba after ousting President Batista in 1959. Surviving the US-backed Bay of Pigs invasion in 1961 and the Cuban Missile Crisis of 1962, he became President in 1976.

1 History will absolve me.
   Last words of speech during trial, 16 October 1953, publ. in *The Penguin Book of Twentieth-Century Speeches* (ed. Brian MacArthur, 1999). Castro had led an unsuccessful assault on the Moncada barracks in July 1953. Sentenced to fifteen years' imprisonment, he was released within a year under an amnesty, returning from exile in 1956 and assuming power soon after. The words *La historia me absolverá* were the title of a revolutionary pamphlet published during the struggle.

2 I feel my belief in sacrifice and struggle getting stronger. I despise the kind of existence that clings to the miserly trifles of comfort and self-interest. I think that a man should not live beyond the age when he begins to deteriorate, when the flame that lighted the brightest moment of his life has weakened.
   Letter written from a prison cell on the island of Pines, 19 December 1953, publ. in *Diary of the Cuban Revolution* (1980) by Carlos Franqui

3 I began revolution with 82 men. If I had [to] do it again, I do it with 10 or 15 and absolute faith. It does not matter how small you are if you have faith and plan of action.
   The New York Times 22 April 1959

Willa Cather (1876–1947)
US AUTHOR
She portrayed the frontier life in Nebraska as she had known it in her childhood in her novels and stories, of which O Pioneers! *(1913) and* My Antonia *(1918) are judged her finest achievements.*

1 Artistic growth is, more than it is anything else, a refining of the sense of truthfulness. The stupid believe that to be truthful is easy; only the artist, the great artist, knows how difficult it is.
   The Song of the Lark, pt 6, ch. 11 (1915)

2 Winter lies too long in country towns; hangs on until it is stale and shabby, old and sullen.
   My Antonia, bk 2, ch. 7 (1918)

3 Art, it seems to me, should simplify ... finding what conventions of form and what detail one can do without and yet preserve the spirit of the whole – so that all

that one has suppressed and cut away is there to the reader's consciousness as much as if it were in type on the page.
   'On the Art of Fiction' (written 1920), publ. in *On Writing* (1949)

4 When kindness has left people, even for a few moments, we become afraid of them as if their reason had left them. When it has left a place where we have always found it, it is like shipwreck; we drop from security into something malevolent and bottomless.
   My Mortal Enemy (1926)

5 Oh, the Germans classify, but the French arrange!
   Death Comes for the Archbishop, Prologue (1927)

6 Only solitary men know the full joys of friendship. Others have their family; but to a solitary and an exile his friends are everything.
   Father Hector Saint-Cyr, in *Shadows on the Rock*, bk 3, ch. 5 (1931)

7 The world has a habit of being in a bad way from time to time, and art has never contributed anything to help matters – except escape.
   'Four Letters: Escapism', first publ. in *Commonweal* 17 April 1936, repr. in *On Writing* (1949)

8 Give the people a new word and they think they have a new fact.
   Ibid.

9 Religion and art spring from the same root and are close kin. Economics and art are strangers.
   Ibid.

(Sir) Bernard Caulfield (1914–94)
BRITISH LAWYER
He held the position of Judge of the High Court of Justice 1968–81.

1 Is Jeffrey Archer in need of cold, unloving, rubber-insulated sex? ... Remember Mary Archer in the witness box. Your vision of her will probably never disappear. Has she elegance? Has she fragrance? Would she have – without the strain of this trial – a radiance?
   Quoted in *The Times* 24 July 1987. Summary at libel case between JEFFREY ARCHER and the *News of the World* 23 July 1987. Archer, who had been implicated in a scandal involving a call girl, won the case and £500,000 damages, though in 1999 it emerged that he had asked a friend to commit perjury at the trial to protect his cover.

Charles Causley (b. 1917)
BRITISH POET
His poetry, written for both children and adults, evokes Cornwall, where he has lived and worked for much of his life, and often deals with contemporary concerns in traditional form.

1 *Timothy Winters comes to school*
With eyes as wide as a football-pool,
Ears like bombs and teeth like splinters:
A blitz of a boy is Timothy Winters.
'Timothy Winters', publ. in *Union Street* (1957)

2 *They are waiting for me somewhere beyond*
Eden Rock.
'Eden Rock', publ. in *Field of Vision* (1988)

Edith Cavell (1865–1915)
BRITISH NURSE
A heroine of the First World War, she was
executed for assisting Allied soldiers to escape to
the Netherlands from German-occupied Belgium.

1 Standing, as I do, in view of God and eternity, I realise that patriotism is not
enough. I must have no hatred or bitterness towards anyone.
Quoted in *The Times* 23 October 1915. The
words, often erroneously claimed to be Cavell's
last, were spoken in conversation with her chaplain 11 October 1915, the eve of her execution in
Brussels.

Paul Celan (1920–70)
GERMAN POET
Pseudonym of Paul Antschel. Though he lived in
France from 1948, he was one of the foremost poets
of post-war German literature. His work is allus-
ive, surrealistic, and informed by his experience as
a Jew in a forced labour camp. He committed
suicide.

1 *Black milk of daybreak we drink you at*
night
we drink you at noon death is a master
from Germany
we drink you at sundown and in the morn-
ing we drink and we drink you
death is a master from Germany his eyes
are blue
he strikes you with leaden bullets his aim is
true.
'Death Fugue', publ. in *Mohn und Gedächtnis*
(1952, transl. Michael Hamburger as *Poppy and*
Memory, 1988)

Louis-Ferdinand Céline (1894–1961)
FRENCH AUTHOR
Originally Louis-Ferdinand Destouches. Trained
and practising as a doctor, he was recognized as a
literary innovator but criticized for his misan-
thropy and obscenity, and for his vitriolic anti-
Semitic pamphlets. His best-known novel is the
autobiographical Journey to the End of Night
(1932).

1 Love, Arthur, is a poodle's chance of
attaining the infinite, and personally I have
my pride.
Narrator (Ferdinand Bardamu), in *Journey to the*
End of the Night (1932)

2 The North will at least preserve your flesh
for you; Northerners are pale for good and
all. There's very little difference between a
dead Swede and a young man who's had a
bad night. But the Colonial is full of mag-
gots the day after he gets off the boat.
Ibid.

3 To philosophize is only another way of
being afraid and leads hardly anywhere but
to cowardly make-believe.
Ibid.

4 The whole business of your life over-
whelms you when you live alone. One's stu-
pefied by it. To get rid of it you try to daub
some of it off on to people who come to
see you, and they hate that. To be alone
trains one for death.
Ibid.

5 To hell with reality! I want to die in music,
not in reason or in prose.
Letter, 30 June 1947, publ. in *Critical Essays on*
Louis-Ferdinand Céline (ed. William K. Buckley,
1989)

6 Life is filigree work. . . . What is written
clearly is not worth much, it's the transparency that counts.
Féerie pour une autre fois (1952), quoted in
Céline, ch. 8 (1975) by Patrick McCarthy

7 Experience is a dim lamp, which only
lights the one who bears it.
Interview in *Writers at Work* (third series, ed.
George Plimpton, 1967)

Henry Chadwick (b. 1920)
BRITISH EDUCATOR AND HISTORIAN
A professor of divinity at Cambridge, he has pub-
lished books on Christian thought and the early
Christian Church.

1 A Church which has lost its memory is in a
sad state of senility.
Daily Telegraph 10 February 1988

Marc Chagall (1889–1985)
FRENCH ARTIST
His rich colours and dream-like images, often
inspired from folklore, placed him in the avant-
garde of twentieth-century art. Born in Belorussia,
he lived in Russia, France and the USA.

1 When I am finishing a picture I hold some
God-made object up to it – a rock, a
flower, the branch of a tree or my hand –
as a kind of final test. If the painting stands
up beside a thing man cannot make, the
painting is authentic. If there's a clash
between the two, it is bad art.
Saturday Evening Post 2 December 1962

Neville Chamberlain (1869–1940)

BRITISH POLITICIAN AND PRIME MINISTER
Prime Minister of a coalition government 1937–40,
he was party to the Munich Agreement (1938) but
reversed his policy of appeasement on HITLER*'s*
invasion of Czechoslovakia in 1939. LLOYD
GEORGE *claimed that he viewed foreign policy*
'through the wrong end of a municipal drainpipe'.
See also ANEURIN BEVAN 2 *and* HUGH
MACDIARMID 1.

1 How horrible, fantastic, incredible it is that
  we should be digging trenches and trying
  on gas masks here because of a quarrel in a
  faraway country between people of whom
  we know nothing.
  BBC radio broadcast, 27 September 1938, quoted
  in *The Times* 28 September 1938. On Germany's
  annexation of the Sudetenland, Czechoslovakia,
  shortly before Chamberlain left for Munich to
  confer with HITLER, MUSSOLINI and Daladier.

2 My good friends, this is the second time in
  our history that there has come back from
  Germany to Downing Street peace with
  honour. I believe it is peace for our time.
  We thank you from the bottom of our
  hearts. And now I recommend you to go
  home and sleep quietly in your beds.
  Speech at Downing Street, 30 September 1938,
  publ. in *The Penguin Book of Twentieth-Century*
  Speeches (ed. Brian MacArthur, 1999). Chamberlain had returned the previous day from
  Munich, where it was agreed that Sudetenland
  should be transferred to Germany while guaran-
  teeing Czechoslovakia's remaining frontiers.
  Chamberlain's words are often misquoted 'peace
  in our time'.

3 This morning the British Ambassador in
  Berlin handed the German Government a
  final Note stating that, unless we heard
  from them by 11 o'clock that they were prepared at once to withdraw their troops
  from Poland, a state of war would exist
  between us. I have to tell you now that no
  such undertaking has been received, and
  that consequently this country is at war
  with Germany.
  BBC radio broadcast 3 September 1939 on the
  declaration of war, publ. ibid.

4 Whatever may be the reason, whether it
  was that Hitler thought he might get away
  with what he had got without fighting for
  it, or whether it was that after all the preparations were not sufficiently complete –
  however, one thing is certain: he missed
  the bus.
  Speech to Conservative and Unionist Associations, Central Hall, London, 4 April 1940,
  quoted in *The Times* 5 April 1940. Chamberlain
  referred to the postponement of Hitler's attack
  on the Western Front, the anxious period
  known as the 'Phoney War'. Five days later, German troops invaded Denmark and Norway, followed shortly after by the invasion of the
  Netherlands, Belgium, Luxembourg and France,
  and the start of the Battle of Britain.

Raymond Chandler (1888–1959)

US CRIMEWRITER
Regarded as the 'pick of the hard-boiled mystery
scribblers', he was largely responsible for elevating
the pulp detective novel into a successful literary
genre. Many of his books have been filmed, includ-
ing The Big Sleep *(1939),* Farewell, My Movely
(1940) and The Long Goodbye *(1953), all featur-*
ing the detective Philip Marlowe.

1 I don't mind if you don't like my manners.
  They're pretty bad. I grieve over them on
  the long winter evenings.
  Philip Marlowe, in *The Big Sleep*, ch. 3 (1939). In
  the film version (1946), Marlowe, played by
  HUMPHREY BOGART, says, 'I don't mind if you
  don't like my manners. I don't like 'em
  myself . . .'

2 What did it matter where you lay once you
  were dead? In a dirty sump or in a marble
  tower on top of a high hill? You were dead,
  you were sleeping the big sleep, you were
  not bothered by things like that. Oil and
  water were the same as wind and air to
  you.
  Ibid., ch. 32

3 He looked about as inconspicuous as a tar-
  antula on a slice of angel food.
  Philip Marlowe describing Moose Malloy, in
  Farewell, My Lovely, ch. 1 (1940)

4 It was a blonde. A blonde to make a bishop
  kick a hole in a stained-glass window.
  Philip Marlowe describing Helen Grayle, ibid.,
  ch. 13

5 She [Helen Grayle] gave me a smile I could
  feel in my hip pocket.
  Ibid., ch. 18

6 I needed a drink, I needed a lot of life
  insurance, I needed a vacation, I needed a
  home in the country. What I had was a
  coat, a hat and a gun.
  Philip Marlowe, ibid., ch. 34. The words have
  been parodied many times, memorably by
  CHARLES BUKOWSKI in *Pulp*, ch. 8 (1994), when
  the narrator, Nicky Belane, laments 'I needed a
  vacation. I needed 5 women. I needed to get the
  wax out of my ears. My car needed an oil
  change. I'd failed to file my damned income tax.
  . . . I hadn't laughed in six years. I tended to
  worry when there was nothing to worry about.
  And when there was something to worry about,
  I got drunk.'

7 Down these mean streets a man must go
  who is not himself mean, who is neither
  tarnished nor afraid. . . . He is the hero, he is
  everything. He must be a complete man and
  a common man and yet an unusual man. He
  must be, to use a rather weathered phrase, a

man of honor, by instinct, by inevitability, without thought of it, and certainly without saying it. He must be the best man in his world and a good enough man for any world.

'The Simple Art of Murder', first publ. in *Atlantic Monthly* December 1944, repr. in *Pearls Are a Nuisance* (1950). The opening words of this article – which defended detective fiction as a genre requiring 'writers with tough minds and a cool spirit of detachment' – inspired plenty of pastiches, and the title of a collection of Chandler's writings, *Down These Mean Streets a Man Must Go* (1963) by Philip Durham. The phrase 'mean streets', however, had been in use since the nineteenth century to describe tough life in the city, and was borrowed by MARTIN SCORSESE as the title of his 1973 film about petty criminality in the Bronx.

8 **The English may not always be the best writers in the world, but they are incomparably the best dull writers.**
Ibid.

9 **If my books had been any worse, I should not have been invited to Hollywood, and . . . if they had been any better, I should not have come.**
Letter to *Atlantic Monthly*, 12 December 1945, repr. in *Raymond Chandler Speaking* (ed. Dorothy Gardiner and Kathrine S. Walker, 1962). Chandler's letter was responding to criticism of his article, 'Writers in Hollywood'.

10 **Would you convey my compliments to the purist who reads your proofs and tell him or her that I write in a sort of broken-down patois which is something like the way a Swiss waiter talks, and that when I split an infinitive, God damn it, I split it so it will stay split, and when I interrupt the velvety smoothness of my more or less literate syntax with a few sudden words of bar-room vernacular, that is done with the eyes wide open and the mind relaxed but attentive. The method may not be perfect, but it is all I have.**
Letter to *Atlantic Monthly* editor Edward Weeks, 18 January 1948, publ. ibid. The letter produced a comic sequel in which Chandler composed a poem to the proof-reader, a certain Margaret Mutch, titled 'Lines to a Lady with an Un-split Infinitive', in which she was made to reproach him: 'Though you went to Yale, your grammar is frail/She snarled as she jabbed his eye./Though you went to Princeton I never winced on/Such a horrible relative clause!'

11 **I used to like this town. . . . Los Angeles was just a big dry sunny place with ugly homes and no style, but good-hearted and peaceful. . . . Now . . . we've got the big money, the sharpshooters, the percentage workers, the fast dollar boys, the hoodlums out of New York and Chicago and Detroit – and Cleveland. We've got the flash restaurants and night clubs they run, and the hotels and apartment houses they own, and the grifters and con men and female bandits that live in them. The luxury trades, the pansy decorators, the Lesbian dress designers, the riff-raff of a big hard-boiled city with no more personality than a paper cup.**
Philip Marlowe, in *The Little Sister*, ch. 26 (1949)

12 **I guess God made Boston on a wet Sunday.**
Letter, 21 March 1949, publ. in *The Selected Letters of Raymond Chandler* (ed. Frank MacShane, 1981). Chandler was referring to a novel by J. P. Marquand, *Point of No Return*, which he had just finished reading, in which the portrait of Boston reminded him of 'a steel engraving with no color at all'.

13 **Alcohol is like love. The first kiss is magic, the second is intimate, the third is routine. After that you take the girl's clothes off.**
Terry Lennox, in *The Long Goodbye*, ch. 4 (1953)

14 **The kind of lawyer you hope the other fellow has.**
Ibid., ch. 17

15 **You can always tell a detective on TV. He never takes his hat off.**
Philip Marlowe, in *Playback*, ch. 14 (1958)

Coco Chanel (1883–1971)
FRENCH COUTURIÈRE
Originally Gabrielle Bonheur Chanel. Extolled by PICASSO *as 'the woman with the most sense in Europe', she introduced designs which combined comfort with elegance. Her domination of Parisian haute couture extended to a highly successful range of perfumes.*

1 **Fashion is made to become unfashionable.**
Life 19 August 1957

2 **Elegance does not consist in putting on a new dress.**
Quoted in *Coco Chanel: Her Life, Her Secrets*, ch. 21 (1971) by Marcel Haedrich

3 **Why am I so determined to put the shoulder where it belongs? Women have very round shoulders that push forward slightly; this touches me and I say: 'One must not hide that!' Then someone tells you: 'The shoulder is on the back.' I've never seen women with shoulders on their backs.**
Ibid.

4 **Fashion is architecture: it is a matter of proportions.**
Ibid.

5 **Innovation! One cannot be forever innovating. I want to create classics.**
Ibid.

(Sir) Charlie Chaplin (1889–1977)

BRITISH COMIC ACTOR AND FILM-MAKER

The greatest of the silent film stars, he combined pathos with clowning in the role of the self-styled 'little fellow'. From 1919, he directed all his films, including The Goldrush *(1925) and* Modern Times *(1936). 'Charlie Chaplin's genius was in comedy,' his second wife Lita Chaplin declared. 'He has no sense of humour, particularly about himself.'*

1 All I need to make a comedy is a park, a policeman and a pretty girl.
   My Autobiography, ch. 10 (1964)

2 The basic essential of a great actor is that he loves himself in acting.
   Ibid., ch. 16

3 The saddest thing I can imagine is to get used to luxury.
   Ibid., ch. 22

4 I remain just one thing, and one thing only – and that is a clown. It places me on a far higher plane than any politician.
   Quoted in the *Observer* 17 June 1960

5 Life is a tragedy when seen in close-up, but a comedy in long-shot.
   Quoted in obituary, *Guardian* 28 December 1977

6 I have no further use for America. I wouldn't go back there if Jesus Christ was President.
   Quoted in *Halliwell's Who's Who in the Movies* (ed. John Walker, 1999). Accused of subversion and pressed for back taxes, Chaplin left the USA in 1952, renouncing his re-entry permit and only returning in 1972 to accept an Academy Award.

Arthur Chapman (1873–1935)

US JOURNALIST

He worked on a number of newspapers in Chicago, Denver and New York as editor and staff writer.

1 *Out where the handclasp's a little stronger, Out where the smile dwells a little longer, That's where the West begins.*
   'Out Where the West Begins', st. 1, publ. in *Out Where the West Begins* (1917)

Charles, Prince of Wales (b. 1948)

Invested Prince of Wales in 1969, he was founder of the Prince's Trust charity and has particular interests in architecture and organic farming. He was married to Princess DIANA *1981–96. According to* PAUL MCCARTNEY, *'His heart is in the right place, but he is born into the wrong family.'*

1 It looks as if we may be presented with a kind of vast municipal fire station. . . . I would understand better this type of high-tech approach if you demolished the whole

of Trafalgar Square, but what is proposed is like a monstrous carbuncle on the face of a much loved and elegant friend.
   Speech to Royal Institute of British Architects, Hampton Court, 30 May 1984, quoted in *The Times* 31 May 1984. Charles was referring to a proposed extension to London's National Gallery – a design which, in the ensuing furore, was rejected in favour of a more classical structure. Charles's words may have been inspired by a passage recently written by Princess Diana's stepmother, Raine Spencer, in *The Spencers on Spas* (1983): 'Alas, for our towns and cities. Monstrous carbuncles of concrete have erupted in gentle Georgian squares.' In January 2000, Charles called the Millennium Dome at Greenwich a 'monstrous blancmange'.

2 I rather feel that deep in the soul of mankind there is a reflection as on the surface of a mirror, of a mirror-calm lake, of the beauty and harmony of the universe. . . . So much depends, I think, on how each one of us is introduced to and made aware of that reflection within us.
   Speech in Prince George, British Columbia, 4 May 1986, quoted in *The Prince of Wales: A Biography,* ch. 20 (1994) by Jonathan Dimbleby

3 I just come and talk to the plants, really – very important to talk to them, they respond I find.
   Television interview 21 September 1986, quoted in the *Daily Telegraph* 22 December 1986. Charles's half-joking remark helped to establish his reputation as a new-age eccentric. Responding humorously to this, he was later quoted as saying, 'Only the other day I was inquiring of an entire bed of old-fashioned roses, forced to listen to my ramblings on the meaning of the universe as I sat cross-legged in the lotus position in front of them' (*Daily Telegraph* 15 November 1988).

4 You have to give this much to the Luftwaffe: when it knocked down our buildings it did not replace them with anything more offensive than rubble. We did that.
   Speech at Mansion House, London, 1 December 1987, quoted in *The Times* 2 December 1987

5 All the people I have in my office, they can't speak English properly. All the letters sent from my office I have to correct myself. And that is because English is taught so bloody badly.
   Off-the-cuff remark to business executives, 29 June 1989, quoted in *The Prince of Wales: A Biography,* ch. 23 (1994) by Jonathan Dimbleby

6 Conservation must come before recreation.
   The Times 5 July 1989

7 If English is spoken in heaven . . . God undoubtedly employs Cranmer as his

speechwriter. The angels of the lesser ministries probably use the language of the New English Bible and the Alternative Service Book for internal memos.

Remark when judging a reading competition, quoted in *The Times* 20 December 1989

8 Perhaps we just have to accept it as God's will that the unorthodox individual is doomed to years of frustration, ridicule and failure in order to act his role in the scheme of things.

Quoted in the *Independent* 8 November 1998. Referring to an earlier speech made to the British Medical Association in 1984.

9 We should show greater respect for the genius of nature's designs, rigorously tested and refined over millions of years. This means being careful to use science to understand how nature works, not to change what nature is, as we do when genetic manipulation seeks to transform a process of biological evolution into something altogether different.

Reith Lecture, broadcast 17 May 2000, BBC Radio 4. See RICHARD DAWKINS 9.

Bruce Chatwin (1940–89)
BRITISH AUTHOR
An expert in modern art, he wrote books which combine fiction, history, travel and philosophy. All show an interest in nomads and the dispossessed, including In Patagonia *(1977) and* The Songlines *(1987).*

1 Music is a memory bank for finding one's way about the world.

Arkady, in *The Songlines*, ch. 21 (1987). Songlines are the invisible pathways that cover Australia, believed by Aborigines to mark ancestral and personal territory.

2 An object in a museum case must suffer the de-natured existence of an animal in the zoo. In any museum the object dies – of suffocation and the public gaze – whereas private ownership confers on the owner the right and the need to touch. As a young child will reach out to handle the thing it names, so the passionate collector, his eye in harmony with his hand, restores to the object the life-giving touch of its maker.

Kaspar Utz, in *Utz* (1988)

3 Wars, pogroms and revolutions offer excellent opportunities for the collector.

Ibid.

John Cheever (1912–82)
US AUTHOR
Called 'the Chekhov of the suburbs' for his portrayals of middle-class life in New England, he was a regular contributor to the New Yorker *from the age of twenty-two. His best known novels are* The Wapshot Chronicle *(1957) and* The Wapshot Scandal *(1964).*

1 When the beginnings of self-destruction enter the heart it seems no bigger than a grain of sand.

Journal entry, 1952, publ. in *John Cheever: The Journals*, 'The Late Forties and the Fifties' (ed. Robert Gottlieb, 1991)

2 I do not understand the capricious lewdness of the sleeping mind.

Journal entry, 1955, ibid.

3 People named John and Mary never divorce. For better or for worser, in madness and in saneness, they seem bound together for eternity by their rudimentary nomenclature. They may loathe and despise one another, quarrel, weep, and commit mayhem, but they are not free to divorce. Tom, Dick, and Harry can go to Reno on a whim, but nothing short of death can separate John and Mary.

Journal entry, 1966, ibid., 'The Sixties'. Cheever's wife was named Mary.

4 Then it is dark; it is a night where kings in golden suits ride elephants over the mountains.

'The Country Husband', publ. in *The Stories of John Cheever* (1978)

5 My veins are filled, once a week with a Neapolitan carpet cleaner distilled from the Adriatic and I am as bald as an egg. However I still get around and am mean to cats.

Letter to PHILIP ROTH discussing his treatment for cancer, 10 May 1982, publ. in *The Letters of John Cheever* (1989)

Victor Mikhailovich Chernov
(1873–1972)
RUSSIAN SOCIALIST REVOLUTIONARY AND WRITER
Founder of the Russian Social Revolutionary Party in 1902 and Minister of Agriculture in the provisional government of 1917, he opposed the Bolsheviks and lived the last part of his life in exile, in Paris and the USA.

1 The savages set up gods to which they pray, and which they punish if one of their prayers is not answered. . . . That is what is happening at this moment. . . . Yesterday Kerensky; today Lenin and Trotsky; another tomorrow . . .

Speech at Peasants' Congress, Petrograd, 28 November 1917, quoted in *Ten Days that Shook the World*, ch. 12 (1926) by JOHN REED

G. K. Chesterton (1874–1936)

BRITISH AUTHOR

An exuberant personality, he wrote poetry both in ballad and comic form, as well as social and literary criticism, much of it published in his own G.K.'s Weekly. His most popular works of fiction are the tales of the priest-sleuth Father Brown (1911–35). SHAW *described Chesterton's 'resolute conviviality' as 'about as genial as an* auto da fé *of teetotallers'.*

1 *And Noah he often said to his wife when he sat down to dine,*
'I don't care where the water goes if it doesn't get into the wine.'
'Wine and Water', publ. in *The Flying Inn*, ch. 5 (1914)

2 *They haven't got no noses*
The fallen sons of Eve;
Even the smell of roses
Is not what they supposes;
But more than mind discloses
And more than men believe.
'The Song of Quoodle', publ. ibid., ch. 15

3 *And goodness only knowses*
The Noselessness of Man.
Ibid.

4 *Tea, although an Oriental,*
Is a gentleman at least;
Cocoa is a cad and coward,
Cocoa is a vulgar beast.
'Song of Right and Wrong', publ. ibid., ch. 18

5 *The rolling English drunkard made the rolling English road.*
A reeling road, a rolling road, that rambles round the shire.
'The Rolling English Road', publ. ibid., ch. 21

6 *But there is good news yet to hear and fine things to be seen*
Before we go to Paradise by way of Kensal Green.
Ibid., closing lines of poem. London's Kensal Green Cemetery holds many of Britain's illustrious dead.

7 To be clever enough to get all that money, one must be stupid enough to want it.
Muscari, in *The Wisdom of Father Brown*, 'Paradise of Thieves' (1914)

8 Journalism largely consists in saying 'Lord Jones Dead' to people who never knew that Lord Jones was alive.
Mr Finn, ibid., 'The Purple Wig'

9 *Are they clinging to their crosses, F. E. Smith?*
'Antichrist', publ. in *Poems* (1915). Referring to F. E. Smith (Lord Birkenhead) pontificating on the Welsh Disestablishment Bill.

10 *Strong gongs groaning as the guns boom far,*
Don John of Austria is going to the war.
'Lepanto', publ. ibid. Don John, brother of Philip II of Spain, commanded the combined Spanish, Venetian and Papal fleets which defeated the Turks at Lepanto in 1571.

11 *They have given us into the hand of new unhappy lords,*
Lords without anger and honour, who dare not carry their swords.
They fight by shuffling papers; they have bright dead alien eyes;
They look at our labour and laughter as a tired man looks at flies.
'The Secret People', publ. ibid.

12 *But we are the people of England; and we have not spoken yet.*
Smile at us, pay us, pass us. But do not quite forget.
Ibid. Closing lines of poem

13 Your next-door neighbour . . . is not a man; he is an environment. He is the barking of a dog; he is the noise of a pianola; he is a dispute about a party wall; he is drains that are worse than yours, or roses that are better than yours.
The Uses of Diversity, 'The Irishman' (1920)

14 They died to save their country and they only saved the world.
'English Graves', publ. in *The Ballad of St Barbara* (1922)

15 It is as healthy to enjoy sentiment as to enjoy jam.
Generally Speaking, 'On Sentiment' (1928)

16 A puritan is a person who pours righteous indignation into the wrong things.
The New York Times 21 November 1930

17 Democracy means government by the uneducated, while aristocracy means government by the badly educated.
The New York Times 1 February 1931

18 There is nothing the matter with Americans except their ideals. The real American is all right; it is the ideal American who is all wrong.
Ibid.

19 The disadvantage of men not knowing the past is that they do not know the present. History is a hill or high point of vantage, from which alone men see the town in which they live or the age in which they are living.
All I Survey, 'On St George Revivified' (1933)

20 It isn't that they can't see the solution. It is that they can't see the problem.
Scandal of Father Brown, 'Point of a Pin' (1935)

21 Boyhood is a most complex and incomprehensible thing. Even when one has been through it, one does not understand what

it was. A man can never quite understand a
boy, even when he has been the boy.
Autobiography, ch. 3 (1936)

22 There is no better test of a man's ultimate
chivalry and integrity than how he behaves
when he is wrong. . . . A stiff apology is a
second insult.
The Common Man, 'The Real Dr Johnson' (1950)

23 Ten thousand women marched through
the streets of London saying: 'We will not
be dictated to,' and then went off to
become stenographers.
Quoted in *G. K. Chesterton*, ch. 1 (1986) by M.
Ffinch. Referring to early feminists.

24 Am in Market Harborough. Where ought I
to be?
Attributed telegram to wife in London. In his
Autobiography, ch. 16 (1936), Chesterton wrote:
'I cannot remember whether this story is true;
but it is not unlikely, or, I think, unreasonable.'

Maurice Chevalier (1888–1972)

FRENCH SINGER AND ACTOR
*Having first appeared in the Folies Bergères (1909–
13), he enjoyed a film career spanning three
decades. 'Paris has two monuments,' JEAN COC-
TEAU declared, 'the Eiffel tower and Maurice
Chevalier.'*

1 *Thank heaven for little girls!*
For little girls get bigger every day.
'Thank Heaven for Little Girls' (song, written by
ALAN JAY LERNER with music by Frederick
Loewe) in *Gigi* (film, 1958)

2 Old age isn't so bad when you consider the
alternative.
The New York Times 9 October 1960. Remark on
his seventy-second birthday.

Chiang Kai-shek (1887–1975)

CHINESE STATESMAN AND PRESIDENT
*He became commander-in-chief of the army of the
Chinese Revolutionary National Party (Kuomin-
tang) in 1925 and established himself as president
(1928–38 and 1943–9). After the Communist
takeover in 1949 he fled to Taiwan where he
remained as president until his death.*

1 If one does not act, one cannot
understand.
China's Destiny, ch. 6 (1943)

Madame Chiang Kai-shek (b. 1897)

CHINESE SOCIOLOGIST AND REFORMER
*Soong Mei Ling. The wife of the former leader of
China (see above), she was involved throughout
her life in children's aid, war relief and education
organizations.*

1 There is no shadow of protection to be had
by sheltering behind the slender stockades
of visionary speculation, or by hiding

behind the wagon-wheels of pacific
theories.
Quoted in the *New York Herald Tribune*
21 March 1938

2 Every clique is a refuge for incompetence.
It fosters corruption and disloyalty, it
begets cowardice, and consequently is a
burden upon and a drawback to the progress of the country. Its instincts and
actions are those of the pack.
China Shall Rise Again, pt 1, ch. 8 (1941)

Erskine Childers (1870–1922)

BRITISH-BORN IRISH NATIONALIST AND
AUTHOR
*Robert Erskine Childers. Already famous for his
spy yarn The Riddle of the Sands (1903), he was
elected to the Irish Assembly as a Sinn Féin deputy
in 1921. After the establishment of the Irish Free
State, he fought in the Civil War but was captured
and executed.*

1 Come closer, boys. It will be easier for you.
To the firing squad at his execution, quoted in
The Zeal of the Convert, ch. 26 (1976) by Burke
Wilkinson. Childers was granted an hour's postponement to see the sun rise and shook hands
with each member of the firing squad before his
execution 24 November 1922. The charge was
'outstandingly wicked activity'.

Jacques Chirac (b. 1932)

FRENCH POLITICIAN AND PRESIDENT
*Twice Prime Minister (1974–6 and 1986–8), he re-
established the Gaullist Party (RPR) and was
elected President in 1995 and 2002.*

1 I am not prepared to accept the economics
of a housewife.
Quoted in the *Sunday Times* 27 December 1987.
Referring to MARGARET THATCHER. On a later
occasion, Chirac extolled the virtues of 'the
woman of the old days, who works hard, serves
the men at their meals, never sits at table with
them, and does not talk' (*Daily Telegraph*
7 February 1998).

Noam Chomsky (b. 1928)

US LINGUIST AND POLITICAL ANALYST
*From the mid-1950s he developed a revolutionary
and influential theory of linguistics known as
transformational-generative grammar, which he
described in Syntactic Structures (1957). He has
been a strong critic of US foreign policy in numerous books and essays.*

1 Colorless green ideas sleep furiously.
Syntactic Structures, ch. 2 (1957). Example of a
sentence which is 'grammatical' without being
'meaningful'. Chomsky gave the following
example of a sentence lacking both meaning and
correct grammatical structure: 'Furiously sleep
ideas green colorless.'

2 The war is simply an obscenity, a depraved act by weak and miserable men, including all of us who have allowed it to go on and on with endless fury and destruction – all of us who would have remained silent had stability and order been secured. It is not pleasant to use such words, but candor permits no less.

Of the war in Vietnam, in *American Power and the New Mandarins*, Introduction (1969)

3 Language is a process of free creation; its laws and principles are fixed, but the manner in which the principles of generation are used is free and infinitely varied. Even the interpretation and use of words involves a process of free creation.

'Language and Freedom', lecture at Loyola University Chicago, January 1970, first publ. 1970, repr. in *For Reasons of State* (1973)

4 Unlimited economic growth has the marvelous quality of stilling discontent while maintaining privilege, a fact that has not gone unnoticed among liberal economists.

For Reasons of State, Introduction (1973)

5 The intellectual tradition is one of servility to power, and if I didn't betray it I'd be ashamed of myself.

Interview on *The Late Show*, BBC2, 25 November 1992. Responding to an accusation of betrayal by ARTHUR SCHLESINGER JR.

6 If we don't believe in freedom of expression for people we despise, we don't believe in it at all.

Ibid.

(Dame) Agatha Christie (1890–1976)

BRITISH MYSTERY WRITER

Her whodunnits, many of which have been filmed, have sold more than 100 million copies, while her play The Mousetrap *(1952) holds a world record for the longest continuous run at one theatre. She described herself as 'a sausage machine, a perfect sausage machine'.*

1 These little grey cells. It is 'up to them' – as you say over here.

Hercule Poirot, in *The Mysterious Affair at Styles*, ch. 10 (1920). Christie's first detective novel introduced both Belgian sleuth Hercule Poirot and Poirot's famous reference to the efficacy of brain-power – the 'little grey cells' – to solve mysteries, a faith he drew attention to in almost every subsequent appearance.

2 Every murderer is probably somebody's old friend. You cannot mix up sentiment and reason.

Poirot, ibid., ch. 11

3 Crime is terribly revealing. Try and vary your methods as you will, your tastes, your habits, your attitude of mind, and your soul is revealed by your actions.

Poirot, in *The ABC Murders*, ch. 17 (1936)

4 There is nothing so dangerous for anyone who has something to hide as conversation! . . . A human being, Hastings, cannot resist the opportunity to reveal himself and express his personality which conversation gives him. Every time he will give himself away.

Poirot, ibid., ch. 31

5 An archaeologist is the best husband any woman can have: the older she gets, the more interested he is in her.

Attributed remark referring to her own second husband Sir Max Mallowan, quoted in news report 9 March 1954 but later denied by her.

Ivan Chtcheglov (b. 1934)

FRENCH POLITICAL THEORIST

His reputation rests largely on his essay 'Formulary for a New Urbanism' (written under his pseudonym Gilles Ivain), a seminal work on architecture and urban life for the Situationist group Lettriste Internationale (1952–7).

1 A mental disease has swept the planet: banalization. . . . Presented with the alternative of love or a garbage disposal unit, young people of all countries have chosen the garbage disposal unit.

'Formulary for a New Urbanism', publ. in *Internationale Situationiste* no. 1, June 1958, repr. in *Situationist International Anthology* (ed. Ken Knabb, 1981)

Caryl Churchill (b. 1938)

BRITISH PLAYWRIGHT

To date, her greatest success is a satire on high finance, Serious Money *(1987), written in rhyming couplets. Other plays include* Top Girls *(1982) and* The Skriker *(1994).*

1 Zac:
The IMF is not a charity.
It has to insist on absolute austerity.
Nigel:
Absolutely. It can't be namby pamby.
These countries must accept restricted diets.
The governments must explain, if there are food riots,
That paying the western banks is the priority.

Serious Money, act 2 (1987)

2 There's ugly greedy and sexy greedy, you dope.
At the moment you're ugly which is no hope.
If you stay ugly, god knows what your fate is.
But sexy greedy is the late eighties.

Starr, ibid.

Frank E. Churchill (1901–42)

US COMPOSER

*He joined Walt Disney studios in 1930 and
composed for the Silly Symphonies in the 1930s,*
Snow White and the Seven Dwarfs *(1937),*
Dumbo *(1941) and* Bambi *(1942).*

1 *Who's afraid of the big bad wolf?*
'Who's Afraid of the Big Bad Wolf?' (song, 1933,
probably written in collaboration with Ann
Ronell). See also EDWARD ALBEE 2

Jennie Jerome Churchill (1854–1921)

ANGLO-AMERICAN SOCIETY FIGURE

*A noted beauty and society hostess and the mother
of* WINSTON CHURCHILL, *she was responsible for
introducing women for the first time into the Conservative Party's Primrose League.*

1 Treat your friends as you do your pictures,
and place them in their best light.
Small Talk on Big Subjects, 'Friendship' (1916)

(Sir) Winston Churchill (1874–1965)

BRITISH STATESMAN AND AUTHOR

*Hailed by Henry 'Chips' Channon as the 'saviour
of the civilized world' and credited with a
'hundred-horse-power mind' by* STANLEY BALD-
WIN, *he led the wartime coalition government as
Prime Minister 1940–45, and regained the premiership in 1951. His writings include* The Second
World War *(1948–54) and* A History of the English-Speaking Peoples *(1956–8). See* ED
MURROW 2.

1 Business carried on as usual during alter-
ations on the map of Europe.
On the self-adopted 'motto' of the British people
at the start of the First World War, in speech at
Guildhall, London, 9 November 1914, publ. in
*Winston S. Churchill: His Complete Speeches,
1897–1963,* vol. 3 (ed. Robert Rhodes James,
1974)

2 Remember, we are confronted with a foe
who would without the slightest scruple
extirpate us, man, woman and child, by
any method open to him if he had the
opportunity. We are fighting a foe who
would not hesitate one moment to obliter-
ate every single soul in this great country
this afternoon if it could be done by
pressing a button. We are fighting a foe
who would think as little of that as a gardener would think of smoking out a wasps'
nest.
Speech in Dundee, 5 June 1915, publ. in *The
Speeches of Winston Churchill* (ed. David Cannadine, 1990). The speech was made shortly before
Churchill's resignation from the Admiralty for
his failed Dardanelles policy.

3 Anyone can rat, but it takes a certain
amount of ingenuity to re-rat.
Remark in 1923, quoted in *Irrepressible Churchill*
(1966) by Kay Halle. Churchill was referring to

his own rejoining of the Conservative Party, having earlier left it to join the Liberals.

4 I decline utterly to be impartial as between
the fire brigade and the fire.
Speech to House of Commons, 7 July 1926, publ.
in *Hansard.* Churchill was replying to
complaints of bias while editing the *British Gazette*
during the General Strike, when he referred to
the strikers as 'the enemy'.

5 It is a good thing for an uneducated man
to read books of quotations. . . . The quotations, when engraved upon the memory,
give you good thoughts. They also make
you anxious to read the authors and look
for more.
My Early Life, ch. 9 (1930)

6 The War was decided in the first twenty
days of fighting, and all that happened
afterwards consisted in battles which, however formidable and devastating, were but
desperate and vain appeals against the
decision of Fate.
Of the First World War, in Preface to *Liaison
1914* (1930) by E. L. Spears

7 I remember, when I was a child, being
taken to the celebrated Barnum's circus,
which contained an exhibition of freaks
and monstrosities, but the exhibit on the
programme which I most desired to see
was the one described as 'The Boneless
Wonder'. My parents judged that that spectacle would be too revolting and demoraliz-
ing for my youthful eyes, and I have waited
50 years to see the boneless wonder sitting
on the Treasury Bench.
Of Labour Prime Minister Ramsay MacDonald,
in speech to House of Commons, 28 January
1931, publ. in *Hansard*

8 It is alarming and also nauseating to see
Mr Gandhi, a seditious Middle Temple
lawyer, now posing as a fakir of a type
well-known in the East, striding half-naked
up the steps of the Viceregal Palace, while
he is still organising and conducting a
defiant campaign of civil disobedience, to
parley on equal terms with the representative of the King Emperor.
Speech at Winchester House, Epping,
23 February 1931, publ. in *The Speeches of Winston Churchill* (ed. David Cannadine, 1990).
Referring to GANDHI's release from prison in
India to discuss political devolution with the
Viceroy.

9 India is an abstraction. . . . India is no
more a political personality than Europe.
India is a geographical term. It is no more
a united nation than the Equator.
Speech at Royal Albert Hall, 18 March 1931,
quoted in *Maxims and Reflections* (ed. Colin
Coote, 1947)

10 So they go on in strange paradox, decided

only to be undecided, resolved to be irresol-
ute, adamant for drift, solid for fluidity,
all-powerful to be impotent.

Of Baldwin's government in speech to House of
Commons, 12 November 1936, publ. in *The
Speeches of Winston Churchill* (ed. David Cannad-
ine, 1990)

11 Dictators ride to and fro upon tigers which
they dare not dismount. And the tigers are
getting hungry.

Letter, 11 November 1937, publ. in *Step by Step*
(1937). Churchill was quoting a 'Hindustani'
proverb, though it is cited as Chinese in the *Concise Oxford Dictionary of Proverbs* (ed. John Simpson, 1982).

12 All is over. Silent, mournful, abandoned,
broken, Czechoslovakia recedes into darkness. . . . We have sustained a defeat without a war.

Speech to House of Commons, 5 October 1938,
publ. in *The Speeches of Winston Churchill* (ed.
David Cannadine, 1990). On the German annexation of the Sudetenland, in Czechoslovakia.

13 I cannot forecast to you the action of
Russia. It is a riddle wrapped in a mystery
inside an enigma.

Radio broadcast, 1 October 1939, publ. in *Winston S. Churchill: His Complete Speeches, 1897–
1963*, vol. 6 (ed. Robert Rhodes James, 1974).
Churchill added: 'But perhaps there is a key . . .
Russian national interest.'

14 I have nothing to offer but blood, toil,
tears and sweat.

Churchill's maiden speech to House of Commons as Prime Minister, 13 May 1940, publ.
ibid.

15 You ask, What is our policy? I will say: It is
to wage war, by sea, land, and air, with all
our might and with all the strength that
God can give us: to wage war against a
monstrous tyranny, never surpassed in the
dark, lamentable catalogue of human
crime. That is our policy. You ask, What is
our aim? I can answer in one word: Victory
– victory at all costs, victory in spite of all
terror; victory, however long and hard the
road may be; for without victory there is
no survival.

Ibid.

16 We shall go on to the end, we shall fight in
France, we shall fight on the seas and
oceans, we shall fight with growing confidence and growing strength in the air, we
shall defend our island, whatever the cost
may be, we shall fight on the beaches, we
shall fight on the landing grounds, we shall
fight in the fields and in the streets, we
shall fight in the hills; we shall never surrender.

Speech to House of Commons, 4 June 1940, following the retreat from Dunkirk, publ. ibid.

Churchill continued, in what may have been a
coded appeal to the US: 'And even if, which I do
not for a moment believe, this island or a large
part of it were subjugated and starving, then our
Empire beyond the seas, armed and guarded by
the British Fleet, would carry on the struggle,
until in God's good time the new world, with all
its power and might, steps forth to the rescue
and the liberation of the old.'

17 Let us therefore brace ourselves to our
duties, and so bear ourselves that if the
British Empire and its Commonwealth last
for a thousand years, men will still say,
'This was their finest hour.'

Speech to House of Commons, 18 June 1940,
announcing the fall of France and the start of
the 'Battle of Britain', publ. ibid. Two days
later, a week after German troops had entered
Paris, France concluded an armistice with
Germany.

18 Never in the field of human conflict was so
much owed by so many to so few.

Speech to House of Commons, 20 August 1940,
publ. ibid. Referring to the pilots who repulsed
the German Luftwaffe during the Battle of
Britain.

19 *Nous attendons l'invasion promise de
longue date. Les poissons aussi.* (We are
waiting for the long-promised invasion. So
are the fishes.)

Radio broadcast to the French people,
21 October 1940, publ. in *Into Battle* (1941)

20 Here is the answer which I will give to
President Roosevelt . . . Give us the tools
and we will finish the job.

Radio broadcast, 9 February 1941, publ. ibid. The
Lend Lease Bill, which allowed the president to
sell, lend or lease material to countries whose
defence was important to the USA, was then
being debated by Congress; it was signed a
month later.

21 The British nation is unique in this
respect. They are the only people who like
to be told how bad things are, who like to
be told the worst.

Speech to House of Commons, 10 June 1941,
publ. in *Hansard*

22 If Hitler invaded hell I would make at least
a favourable reference to the devil in the
House of Commons.

Comment to Churchill's private secretary, John
Colville, 21 June 1941, regarding British support
for Communist Russia, as recounted in *The
Second World War*, vol. 3, 'The Grand Alliance',
ch. 20 (1950)

23 All his usual formalities of perfidy were
observed with scrupulous technique.

Of Hitler's invasion of Russia, in radio broadcast
21 June 1941

24 Do not let us speak of darker days; let us
rather speak of sterner days. These are not

dark days: these are great days – the greatest days our country has ever lived.

Speech at Harrow School, 29 October 1941, publ.
in *Winston S. Churchill: His Complete Speeches,
1897–1963*, vol. 6 (ed. Robert Rhodes James,
1974)

25 When we consider the resources of the
United States and the British Empire compared to those of Japan, when we remember those of China, which has so long and
valiantly withstood invasion and when also
we observe the Russian menace which
hangs over Japan, it becomes still more
difficult to reconcile Japanese action with
prudence or even with sanity. What kind
of a people do they think we are?

Speech to Joint Session of US Congress,
26 December 1941, publ. ibid. Britain and the
USA had declared war on Japan 8 December
1941, following the surprise attack on Pearl
Harbor, Hawaii. Japanese forces rapidly
advanced into US and British possessions in the
Pacific and Asian mainland; Hong Kong surrendered on Christmas Day, 1941.

26 When I warned them [the French Govern-
ment] that Britain would fight on alone
whatever they did, their generals told their
Prime Minister and his divided Cabinet,
'In three weeks England will have her neck
wrung like a chicken.' Some chicken! Some
neck!

Speech to Canadian Parliament, Ottawa,
30 December 1941, publ. ibid.

27 Now this is not the end. It is not even the
beginning of the end. But it is, perhaps, the
end of the beginning.

Speech at Lord Mayor's Day Luncheon, Mansion House, 10 November 1942, publ. in *The End
of the Beginning* (1943). Churchill was referring
to the Eighth Army's victory against Rommel at
El Alamein. See CHURCHILL 43.

28 We mean to hold our own. I have not
become the King's First Minister in order
to preside over the liquidation of the
British Empire.

Ibid.

29 The problems of victory are more agreeable than the problems of defeat, but they
are no less difficult.

Speech to House of Commons, 11 November
1942, publ. in *Hansard*

30 We make this wide encircling movement
in the Mediterranean, having for its
primary object the recovery of the command of that vital sea, but also having for
its object the exposure of the under-belly
of the Axis, especially Italy, to heavy
attack.

Ibid. The words are the origin of the phrase 'the
soft under-belly of the Axis'.

31 National compulsory insurance for all

classes for all purposes from the cradle to
the grave.

Radio broadcast, 21 March 1943, publ. in *Winston S. Churchill: His Complete Speeches, 1897–
1963*, vol. 7 (ed. Robert Rhodes James, 1974)

32 There is no finer investment for any community than putting milk into babies.

Ibid.

33 The empires of the future are the empires
of the mind.

Speech at Harvard, 6 September 1943, publ. in
Onwards to Victory (1944)

34 We shape our buildings: thereafter they
shape us.

Speech in London, 28 October 1943, on the
rebuilding of the House of Commons after
bomb damage, quoted in *Time* 12 September
1960

35 Neither the sure prevention of war, nor
the continuous rise of world organization
will be gained without what I have
called the fraternal association of the
English-speaking peoples. This means a
special relationship between the British
Commonwealth and Empire and the
United States.

Speech at Westminster College, Fulton, Missouri, 5 March 1946, publ. in *Complete Speeches*,
vol. 7 (ed. Robert Rhodes James, 1974).

36 A shadow has fallen upon the scenes so
lately lighted by the Allied victory. . . .
From Stettin in the Baltic to Trieste in the
Adriatic, an iron curtain has descended
across the Continent.

Ibid. The phrase 'iron curtain' was not original:
Churchill had also used the phrase in early 1946
in a telegram to President TRUMAN, and the
words had earlier been used by JOSEPH GOEB-
BELS in the Nazi propaganda weekly *Das Reich*
23 February 1945: 'Should the German people lay
down their arms, the Soviets . . . would occupy
all eastern and south-eastern Europe together
with the greater part of the Reich. Over all this
territory, which with the Soviet Union included,
would be of enormous extent, an iron curtain
[*ein eiserner Vorhang*] would at once descend.'
In fact 'iron curtain' had been used with reference to Communism from 1920 or earlier, while
the geographical area from Stettin to Trieste had
already been defined by Friedrich Engels in an
article for the *New York Daily Tribune* in 1853:
'It would appear that the natural frontier of
Russia runs from Dantzic or perhaps Stettin to
Trieste.'

37 No one pretends that democracy is perfect
or all-wise. Indeed, it has been said that
democracy is the worst form of Government except all those other forms that
have been tried from time to time.

Speech to House of Commons, 11 November
1947, publ. in *Hansard*

38 **The English never draw a line without blur-ring it.**
Speech to House of Commons, 16 November 1948

39 **Moral of the Work. In war: resolution. In defeat: defiance. In victory: magnanimity. In peace: goodwill.**
Epigraph in each volume of *The Second World War* (1948–54). Churchill had first conceived his 'moral' shortly after the end of the First World War.

40 **I felt as if I were walking with destiny, and that all my past life had been but a prep-aration for this hour and this trial. Eleven years in the political wilderness had freed me from ordinary Party antagonisms. My warnings over the last six years had been so numerous, so detailed, and were now so terribly vindicated, that no one could gain-say me. I could not be reproached either for making the war or with want of prep-aration for it. I thought I knew a good deal about it all, and I was sure I should not fail. Therefore, although impatient for the morning, I slept soundly and had no need for cheering dreams. Facts are better than dreams.**
On assuming the office of prime minister in 1940, in *The Second World War*, vol. 1, 'The Gath-ering Storm', bk 2, ch. 17 (1948)

41 **Thus, then, on the night of the tenth of May, at the outset of this mighty battle, I acquired the chief power in the State, which henceforth I wielded in ever-growing measure for five years and three months of world war, at the end of which time, all our enemies having surrendered unconditionally or being about to do so, I was immediately dismissed by the British electorate from all further conduct of their affairs.**
Ibid. Though re-elected prime minister in 1951, Churchill never forgot what he considered a slight by the electorate.

42 **The candle in that great turnip has gone out.**
Of STANLEY BALDWIN, as related by Patrick Leigh Fermor, quoted in journal entry, 17 August 1950, publ. in *Diaries and Letters 1945–62* (1968) by HAROLD NICOLSON

43 **It may almost be said, 'Before Alamein we never had a victory. After Alamein we never had a defeat.'**
The Second World War, vol. 4, 'The Hinge of Fate', ch. 33 (1951)

44 **Without tradition, art is a flock of sheep without a shepherd. Without innovation, it is a corpse.**
Address to Royal Academy of Arts, quoted in *Time* 11 May 1954

45 **Better to jaw-jaw than to war-war.**
Remark at the White House, 26 June 1954,

quoted in *The New York Times* 27 June 1954. The words were reported with slight variations in different newspapers, and also within the same edition of *The New York Times*.

46 **He is a modest little man who has a good deal to be modest about.**
Of CLEMENT ATTLEE, quoted in the *Chicago Sunday Tribune Magazine of Books* 27 June 1954

47 **A fanatic is one who can't change his mind and won't change the subject.**
Quoted in *The New York Times* 5 July 1954

48 **I am prepared to meet my Maker. Whether my Maker is prepared for the great ordeal of meeting me is another matter.**
Remark on his seventy-fifth birthday, 30 November 1951, quoted in *Winston Churchill: His Wit and Wisdom*

49 **I have never accepted what many people have kindly said – namely, that I inspired the nation . . . It was the nation and the race dwelling all round the globe that had the lion's heart. I had the luck to be called upon to give the roar. I also hope that I sometimes suggested to the lion the right place to use his claws.**
Speech at Westminster Hall, 30 November 1954, quoted in *The Times* 1 December 1954

50 **This is the sort of English up with which I will not put.**
Quoted in *The Complete Plain Words*, 'The Handling of Words' by Ernest Gowers (1954). Said to be a marginal comment by Churchill against a sentence that clumsily avoided ending with a preposition.

51 **Dead birds don't fall out of nests.**
Response to a colleague who told him his flies were open, quoted in *Letters*, vol. 2 (1957) by Lyttleton Hart-Davis

52 **In defeat unbeatable: in victory unbearable.**
On VISCOUNT MONTGOMERY, quoted in *Ambrosia and Small Beer*, ch. 5 (1964) by Edward Marsh

53 **I have taken more out of alcohol than alco-hol has taken out of me.**
Quoted in *By Quentin Reynolds*, ch. 11 (1964) by Quentin Reynolds

54 **The ability to foretell what is going to hap-pen tomorrow, next week, next month, and next year. And to have the ability after-wards to explain why it didn't happen.**
Quoted in *The Churchill Wit* (1965) by Bill Adler. Describing the qualifications desirable in a prospective politician.

55 **A sheep in sheep's clothing.**
Said to refer to CLEMENT ATTLEE, in *The Way the Wind Blows*, ch. 6 (1976) by Lord Home, though Churchill is later said to have claimed he had used the words to describe Labour Prime Minister Ramsay MacDonald. The phrase had also been used by the critic and essayist Sir

Edmund Gosse of the 'woolly-bearded poet'
Sturge Moore, quoted in *Under the Bridge* (1943)
by F. Greenslet.

56 **An empty taxi arrived at 10 Downing
Street, and when the door was opened
Attlee got out.**

Attributed. Kenneth Harris writes (in *Attlee*,
ch. 16, sect. 2, 1982) that Churchill's private secretary John Colville repeated this remark to Churchill, who, clearly discomfited and 'after an
awful pause', replied: 'Mr Attlee is an honourable and gallant gentleman, and a faithful colleague who served his country well at the time of
her greatest need. I should be obliged if you
would make it clear whenever an occasion arises
that I would never make such a remark about
him, and that I strongly disapprove of anybody
who does.' However, when Colville suggested
that Attlee be invited to join Churchill's dining
club, Churchill replied, 'I think not. He is an
admirable character, but not a man with whom
it is agreeable to dine.'

Galeazzo Ciano (1903–44)

ITALIAN POLITICIAN

The Conte di Cortelazzo was son-in-law of MUSSO-
LINI *and a leading Fascist. Minister of Foreign
Affairs from 1936, he openly opposed Italy's alliance with Germany, and was later tried for treason
by the pro-Mussolini faction and executed.*

1 **Victory has a hundred fathers but defeat is
an orphan.**

Journal entry, 9 September 1942, publ. in *Diario
1939–1943* (1946). President KENNEDY is quoted
as having made the same remark in the wake of
the Bay of Pigs invasion in April 1961. The original Italian (*nessuno vuole riconoscere l'insuccesso*)
is more accurately translated 'no one wants to
recognize failure'.

E. M. Cioran (1911–95)

ROMANIAN-BORN WRITER AND
PHILOSOPHER

*Emil Mihai Cioran. The 'last of the moralists'
lived in Paris from 1937 onwards, where he found a
congenial home for his ideas, which he regarded as
both a continuation and negation of Nietzsche's
philosophy.*

1 **No human beings more dangerous than
those who have suffered for a belief: the
great persecutors are recruited from the
martyrs not quite beheaded. Far from dim-
inishing the appetite for power, suffering
exasperates it.**

A Short History of Decay, ch. 1, 'Genealogy of
Fanaticism' (1949)

2 **Reason is a whore, surviving by simulation, versatility, and shamelessness.**

The Temptation to Exist, 'Rages and Resignations: Luther' (1956)

3 **Much more than our other needs and
endeavours, it is sexuality that puts us on
an even footing with our kind: the more
we practise it, the more we become like
everyone else: it is in the performance of a
reputedly bestial function that we prove
our status as citizens: nothing is more
public than the sexual act.**

Ibid., 'Rages and Resignations: Gogol'

4 **We derive our vitality from our store of
madness.**

Ibid., 'The Temptation to Exist'

5 **A civilization is destroyed only when its
gods are destroyed.**

The New Gods (Le Mauvais démiurge), 'The New
Gods' (1969)

6 **There is no means of *proving* it is preferable to be than not to be.**

Ibid., 'Strangled Thoughts', sect. 1

7 **Alone, even doing nothing, you do not
waste your time. You do, almost always, in
company. No encounter with yourself can
be altogether sterile: Something necessarily
emerges, even if only the hope of some day
meeting yourself again.**

Ibid., sect. 2

8 **What we want is not freedom but its
appearances. It is for these simulacra that
man has always striven. And since freedom, as has been said, is no more than a
sensation, what difference is there between
being free and believing ourselves free?**

Ibid., sect. 3

9 **We would not be interested in human
beings if we did not have the hope of someday meeting someone worse off than ourselves.**

Ibid.

10 **It is not worth the bother of killing yourself, since you always kill yourself *too late*.**

The Trouble with Being Born, ch. 2 (1973)

11 **Consciousness is much more than the
thorn, it is the *dagger* in the flesh.**

Ibid., ch. 3

12 **Progress is the injustice each generation
commits with regard to its predecessors.**

Ibid., ch. 8

13 **God: a disease we imagine we are cured of
because no one dies of it nowadays.**

Ibid., ch. 10

14 **One does not inhabit a country; one
inhabits a language. That is our country,
our fatherland – and no other.**

Anathemas and Admirations, 'On the Verge of
Existence' (1986). This recalls a remark made by
ALBERT CAMUS in his *Notebooks*: 'Yes, I have a
fatherland: the French language.'

15 The fact that life has no meaning is a
reason to live – moreover, the only one.
Ibid., 'Fractures'

Bob Clampett (1913–84)
US ANIMATOR
He began animating for the Warner Brothers'
Looney Tunes *series in the early 1930s and went
on to direct cartoons such as the surreal* Porky in
Wackyland *(1938) and the slapstick* Big Snooze
(1946).

1 I tawt I taw a puddy tat a-cweepin' up on
me.
Tweety, in *Looney Tunes/Merrie Melodies*
(Warner Brothers cartoon, 1944–60s). Created
by Bob Clampett, voiced by Mel Blanc, the little
yellow canary first appeared in the Warners' *Mer-
rie Melodies* cartoon *Birdy and the Beast* (1944),
soon to be chased by the lisping cat Sylvester,
whose own favourite line was 'Suffering Suc-
cotash!'

Anthony Clare (b. 1942)
IRISH-BORN BRITISH PSYCHIATRIST
*Based in Dublin and London, he has established a
high media profile as a result of his radio programmes, particularly* In the Psychiatrist's Chair,
*a series of in-depth interviews with figures from
public life, on BBC Radio 4 from 1982.*

1 Whatever is true about the nature of the
unconscious itself, it might be said that
since the time of Freud it has been shrink-
ing. Less is buried there.
In the Psychiatrist's Chair, Introduction (1984)

Alan Clark (1928–99)
BRITISH POLITICIAN AND HISTORIAN
*Notorious for his rakish womanizing, he was the
son of* KENNETH CLARK, *and Conservative MP
for Plymouth (1974–92) and Kensington and Chelsea (1997–9), and Minister of State for Defence
(1989–92). He was also noted as a military historian* (Donkeys, 1961, *and* Aces High, 1973) *and
diarist.*

1 Most of them are buffers, or demi-buffers,
of *buffers-aspirant.* They amount to
nothing.
Journal entry, 18 November 1986, publ. in
Diaries (1993). Referring to backbenchers in the
House of Commons.

2 There are no true friends in politics. We
are all sharks circling, and waiting, for
traces of blood to appear in the water.
Journal entry, 30 November 1990, publ. ibid.
Clark was musing on the 'descending parabola'
of his political career.

3 We all know the principal preoccupation
of politicians is how they can do down
their colleagues so that they can advance
their own careers.
Interview with John Humphrys in *On the Ropes*,

BBC Radio 4, 16 May 1995. Clark was explaining
how the main regret of his political career was
not destabilising his boss at the Ministry of
Defence, Tom King.

4 There is practically no figure whom the
press would rather vilify than the wise
virgin.
Quoted in the *Observer* 27 September 1998. On a
newspaper claim that MARGARET THATCHER
used to hoard food.

5 Dear boy, I can hardly close the door.
Quoted in the *Observer* 27 December 1998. On
being asked if he had any skeletons in his
cupboard.

Eugenie Clark (b. 1922)
US MARINE BIOLOGIST AND AUTHOR
*A pioneer in the artificial insemination of fish, she
researched sea life chiefly in the South Seas.
Among her books are* Lady with a Spear *(1953)
and* The Lady and the Shark *(1969).*

1 It seems as though women keep growing.
Eventually they can have little or nothing
in common with the men they chose long
ago.
Quoted in *Ms.* August 1979

Kenneth (Lord) Clark (1903–83)
BRITISH ART HISTORIAN
*He was director of the National Gallery (1934–45)
and first chairman of the Independent Television
Authority (1954–7). An expert on the Italian
Renaissance, he wrote popular works on art and
presented the TV series based on his book* Civilis-
ation *(1969).*

1 People sometimes tell me that they prefer
barbarism to civilization. I doubt if they
have given it a long enough trial. Like the
people of Alexandria, they are bored by
civilisation; but then all the evidence suggests that the boredom of barbarism is
infinitely greater.
Civilisation, ch. 1 (1969)

2 Opera, next to Gothic architecture, is one
of the strangest inventions of Western
man. It could not have been foreseen by
any logical process.
Ibid., ch. 9

3 It is lack of confidence, more than anything else, that kills a civilisation. We can
destroy ourselves by cynicism and disillusion, just as effectively as by bombs. . . .
The moral and intellectual failure of Marxism has left us with no alternative to heroic
materialism, and that isn't enough. One
may be optimistic, but one can't exactly be
joyful at the prospect before us.
Ibid., ch. 13. Last words of book.

Ramsey Clark (b. 1927)

US LAWYER

As Attorney-General (1967–9) he prosecuted anti-Vietnam War protesters, but later became a critic of US foreign policy, and was criticized for his support of SADDAM HUSSEIN.

1 A right is not what someone gives you; it's what no one can take from you.

The New York Times 2 October 1977

2 The measure of your quality as a public person, as a citizen, is the gap between what you do and what you say.

International Herald Tribune 18 June 1991

3 Oil and democracy don't mix. Oil has never enhanced democratic institutions or economic justice where it has been found.

The Fire This Time, ch. 6, 'The War and Human Rights' (1992)

John Cooper Clarke (b. 1950)

BRITISH PUNK POET

After he began mixing his poems with musical backing in the 1970s, live appearances with the Buzzcocks and other groups helped to establish his popularity among punk audiences, inspiring a new wave of poets and 'ranters'.

1 *On a BSA with two bald tyres,*
you drove a million miles.
You cut your hair with rusty pliers
and you suffer with the pillion piles.
You've got built-in obsolescence,
oh, you've got guts,
but you won't reach adolescence,
slow down psycle sluts!

'Psycle Sluts: pt 1' on the album *Disguise in Love* (1978), publ. in *Ten Years in an Open Necked Shirt* (1983)

2 *In a cybernetic fit of rage*
She pissed off to another age
She lives in 1999
With her new boyfriend, a blob of slime.
Each time I see a translucent face
I remember the monster from outer space.
'i married a monster from outer space', ibid.

3 *beans greens tangerines*
and low cholesterol margarines
his limbs are loose his teeth are clean
he's a high-octane fresh-air fiend
you've got to admit he's keen
what can you do but be impressed
he's a health fanatic give it a rest.
'Health Fanatic', ibid.

4 *people turn to poison quick*
as lager turns to piss
sweethearts are physically sick
every time they kiss
it's a sociologist's paradise
each day repeats

uneasy cheesy greasy queasy beastly beezley
*   street.*
'Beezley Street' on the album *Snap Crackle and Bop* (1978), publ. ibid.

5 *roman catholic marxist leninist*
happily married to an eloquent feminist.
'euro communist/gucci socialist', publ. ibid.

Jeremy Clarkson (b. 1960)

BRITISH JOURNALIST AND TV PRESENTER

A motoring guru known for his provocative banter, he contributes regularly to newspapers and magazines including Top Gear, *which he founded in 1993.*

1 The British motor industry is really owned by Nazis.

Quoted in the *Daily Telegraph* 26 October 1998. The comment was made during an informal quiz show at the *Top Gear* stand at the National Motor Show. He also offended staff on the Hyundai stand by stating that South Koreans were 'too busy eating dogs to design a decent car'.

2 To argue that a car is simply a means of conveyance is like arguing that Blenheim Palace is simply a house.

Quoted in the *Guardian* 23 January 1999

Julian Clary (b. 1959)

BRITISH COMEDIAN AND ENTERTAINER

A maestro of sexual innuendo and camp, he appeared with Fanny the Wonderdog in his stand-up comedy routine The Joan Collins Fan Club *(1988) and in game shows such as* Sticky Moments *(1989–90).*

1 The English like eccentrics. They just don't like them living next door.

Daily Telegraph 2 September 1992

Eldridge Cleaver (1935–98)

US BLACK LEADER AND WRITER

After becoming a follower of MALCOLM X, *he was Minister of Information for the Black Panthers and subsequently ran the Party's headquarters in Algiers, where he had fled after a shoot-out in 1968. He returned to New York in 1975, a born-again Christian.*

1 I, for one, do not think homosexuality is the latest advance over heterosexuality in the scale of human evolution. Homosexuality is a sickness, just as are baby-rape or wanting to become head of General Motors.

Soul on Ice, pt 2, 'Notes on a Native Son' (1968)

2 Americans think of themselves collectively as a huge rescue squad on twenty-four-hour call to any spot on the globe where dispute and conflict may erupt.

Ibid. 'Rallying Round the Flag'

3 Every time I embrace a black woman I'm

embracing slavery, and when I put my
arms around a white woman, well, I'm hugging freedom. The white man forbade me
to have the white woman on pain of death.
. . . I will not be free until the day I can
have a white woman in my bed.

Lazarus, ibid. 'The Allegory of the Black
Eunuchs'

4 It's been said that today, you're part of the
solution or you're part of the problem.
There is no more middle ground.

'Stanford Speech', San Francisco, 1 October 1968,
publ. in *Post Prison Writings and Speeches* (ed.
Robert Scheer, 1969)

John Cleese (b. 1939)
BRITISH COMIC ACTOR AND AUTHOR
He made his name in Monty Python's Flying
Circus *(1969–74) and subsequently co-wrote and
starred in* Fawlty Towers *(1975, 1979) and the film*
A Fish Called Wanda *(1988). See also* MONTY
PYTHON'S FLYING CIRCUS.

1 Don't mention the war.

Basil Fawlty, on the pending arrival of German
guests, in *Fawlty Towers*, 'The Germans' (TV
series co-written with Connie Booth, 1975), publ.
in *The Complete Fawlty Towers* (1988)

2 So Harry says, 'You don't like me any
more. Why not?' And he says, 'Because
you've got so terribly pretentious.' And
Harry says, 'Pretentious? *Moi?*'

Mr Johnson, chatting to Sybil, ibid. 'The Psychiatrist' (1979)

3 He's from Barcelona.

Basil or Sybil apologizing for Manuel, ibid. (various episodes). Manuel's most quoted remark is
'Qué?'

Georges Clemenceau (1841–1929)
FRENCH STATESMAN
*Known as 'The Tiger', he held two terms as
premier (1906–9, 1917–20), and presided at the
peace talks in Versailles (1919). He founded several
journals including* L'Aurore *(1897).*

1 My home policy: I wage war; my foreign
policy: I wage war. All the time I wage war!
The Russians betray us, I continue to wage
war. Rumania is forced to capitulate: I continue to wage war, and I will continue to
the very end.

Speech to Chamber of Deputies, 8 March 1918,
publ. in *Discours de guerre* (1968). Clemenceau
was about to confront the Ludendorff offensive
of March–July 1918, which pushed deep into the
Allied lines and was only halted when Foch's
counter-offensive eventually drove the German
army back behind its own border and led to the
armistice.

2 Yes, we have won the war, and not without

difficulty. But now we must win the peace,
and perhaps that will be harder.

Remark to General J. H. H. Mordacq,
11 November 1918 (Armistice Day), quoted in
The Tiger, ch. 16 (1976). Clemenceau expressed
the idea on different occasions, and it has also
been quoted in a simplified form from a speech
at Verdun, 20 July 1919: 'It is easier to make war
than to make peace.'

3 America is the only nation in history
which miraculously has gone directly from
barbarism to degeneration without the
usual interval of civilization.

Attributed, in the *Saturday Review of Literature*
1 December 1945

Harlan Cleveland (b. 1918)
US GOVERNMENT OFFICIAL AND
DIPLOMAT
*He was Assistant Secretary for International
Organization Affairs under* JOHN F. KENNEDY
(1961–5) and Ambassador to NATO *(1965–9).*

1 The revolution of rising expectations.

'Reflections on the Revolution of Rising Expectations', speech at Colgate University, 1949,
quoted in *The New Language of Politics* (1972) by
William Safire. The phrase was echoed in the
title of a later speech that Cleveland delivered to
the UN in 1954: 'The Evolution of Rising Responsibilities'.

Jimmy Cliff (b. 1948)
JAMAICAN REGGAE SINGER
*Originally James Chambers. The first reggae super-
star, he had worldwide success with the song
'Wonderful World, Beautiful People' (1969) and in
the film* The Harder They Come *(1972).*

1 *So as sure as the sun will shine
I'm going to get my share now, what's
    mine
And then the harder they come, the harder
    they fall
One and all.*

'The Harder They Come' (song, 1970) written
and performed by Cliff in *The Harder They
Come* (film, 1972), in which he starred as Ivan,
a small-time hood. The song was a hit for Desmond Dekker in 1970.

2 *Many rivers to cross
But I can't seem to find my way over.*

'Many Rivers to Cross' (song, 1970), ibid. The
song was covered by Cher and UB40, among
others.

Max Clifford (b. 1943)
BRITISH PUBLIC RELATIONS AGENT
*He was press officer for EMI records and went on
to found Max Clifford Associates in 1968, the best
known of celebrity PR companies.*

1 Most of what you read in the papers is lies. And I should know, because a lot of the lies you see in the papers are mine.

Quoted in the *Observer* 17 February 2002

Bill Clinton (b. 1946)

US POLITICIAN AND PRESIDENT

Democratic Governor of Arkansas 1979–81 and 1983–92, he was President 1993–2001. Though he played a significant role in the 1995 Bosnian settlement, his reputation was damaged by the 'Zippergate' sex scandal, and he narrowly escaped impeachment in 1998. See JOAN COLLINS 2, HENRY KISSINGER 17.

1 When I was in England I experimented with marijuana a time or two, and I didn't like it. I didn't inhale.

Remark during TV debate with Jerry Brown, a rival candidate for the Democratic Party nomination, quoted in *The New York Times* 30 March 1992. Under close questioning to ascertain whether the two men had ever broken state, federal or international laws, Clinton admitted his misdemeanour while a Rhodes Scholar at Oxford University.

2 Indeed I did have a relationship with Ms Lewinsky that was not appropriate. In fact it was wrong. It constituted a critical lapse in judgment and a personal failure on my part for which I am solely and completely responsible. . . . Even presidents have private lives.

Broadcast to the nation, 17 August 1998, publ. in the *Daily Telegraph* 19 August 1998. See also MONICA LEWINSKY 1

3 It depends upon what the meaning of the word 'is' means. If 'is' means is, and never has been, that's one thing. If it means, there is none, that was a completely true statement.

Answer to grand jury, broadcast on CNN 21 September 1998. Clinton was attempting to justify his earlier statement, 'There is no sex of any kind, in any manner, shape or form, with Ms Lewinsky.'

4 The most difficult job in the world is not being President. It's being a parent.

Quoted in the *Observer* 25 October 1998

5 The people have spoken but it's going to take a little while to determine what they said.

Quoted in *The Times* 9 November 2000. Referring to the inconclusive results of the US presidential election. The final decision in favour of GEORGE W. BUSH was declared five weeks later.

6 Peace is not a spectator sport. . . . The enemies of peace don't need your approval. All they need is your apathy.

Speech in Northern Ireland, quoted in *The Times* 16 December 2000

Hillary Clinton (b. 1947)

US LAWYER AND FIRST LADY

Wife of BILL CLINTON, she became in 2000 the first First Lady to be elected to the Senate.

1 It takes a village to raise a child.

Speech at Democratic National Convention, Chicago, 26 August 1996. The African proverb was adopted by Hillary Clinton as the motto for her drive to encourage community awareness. Her book, *It Takes a Village: And Other Lessons Children Teach Us* (1996), which discusses family issues and social policies, topped the *New York Times* non-fiction best-seller list in its first week of publication.

2 The great story here . . . is this vast right-wing conspiracy that has been conspiring against my husband since the day he announced for president.

NBC Today, 27 January 1998. On 'Zippergate' and the accusations of adultery and perjury made against BILL CLINTON.

Brian Clough (b. 1935)

BRITISH FOOTBALLER AND MANAGER

He scored more goals per game than any other post-war footballer and was a successful and controversial manager of Nottingham Forest (1964–75).

1 I couldn't motivate a bee to sting you if it didn't have the equipment. I couldn't motivate a snake to bite you if it didn't have the teeth. You can only bring out of people what they are capable of giving. Two of the great myths circulating now are that Heinz's beans are the best and that I can get more out of men than they have inside them.

Quoted by Hugh McIlvanney in the *Observer* 15 November 1975, repr. in *McIlvanney on Football*, 'The Big Man and Other Giants' (1994). Clough was famous as 'the master motivator'.

Harold Clurman (1901–80)

US STAGE DIRECTOR AND CRITIC

He co-founded and was Director of the experimental Group Theater (1931–40), and directed plays in Hollywood and on Broadway. He contributed drama reviews to the Nation *from 1953 until his death.*

1 Unlike other people, our reviewers are powerful because they believe in nothing.

Quoted in *Who Needs Theatre?*, pt 1, 'The Vitality of Harold Clurman' (1987) by Robert Brustein

Kurt Cobain (1967–94)

US ROCK MUSICIAN

He was lead singer, guitarist and writer with Nirvana, the leading 'grunge' band of the 1990s. Beset with drugs problems, he shot himself at his home in Seattle. See WENDY O'CONNOR 1.

1 *I found it hard, it was hard to find,*
  Oh well, whatever, never mind.

  'Smells Like Teen Spirit' (song) on the Nirvana
  album *Nevermind* (1991)

2 *Teenage angst has paid off well,*
  Now I'm bored and old.

  'Serve the Servants' (song) on the Nirvana
  album *In Utero* (1993)

3 Thank you all from the pit of my burning,
  nauseous stomach for your letters and concerns during the last years. I'm too much
  of an erratic, moody person, and I don't
  have the passion anymore.

  Suicide note, publ. in *The Kurt Cobain Story*,
  ch. 1 (1994) by Dave Thompson. Parts of the
  note were read out by his wife Courtney Love at
  a memorial ceremony for the singer in Seattle,
  10 April 1994. Cobain suffered intense pain and
  discomfort from habitual stomach cramps
  which resulted in fits of vomiting for which he'd
  been on regular medication. 'For five years during the time I had my stomach [pain],' he once
  said, 'I wanted to kill myself every day.'

Eddie Cochran (1938–60)

US ROCK MUSICIAN

*One of the giants of rock 'n' roll, he recorded the
classics 'C'mon Everybody' (1959) and 'Three Steps
to Heaven' (1960). He was killed in a car accident
while on a British tour.*

1 *There ain't no cure for the summertime
  blues.*

  'Summertime Blues' (song, 1958, co-written with
  Cochran's manager, Jerry Capeheart) on the
  album *Swinging to My Baby* (1960)

Alexander Cockburn (b. 1941)

ANGLO-IRISH JOURNALIST

*Son of CLAUD COCKBURN and known as an acer-
bic political commentator, he has written widely
for the US press, and published on diverse topics.*

1 Be careful about Burma. Most people cannot remember whether it was Siam and has
  become Thailand, or whether it is now part
  of Malaysia and should be called Sri Lanka.

  'How to be a Foreign Correspondent', first publ.
  in *More*, May 1976, repr. in *Corruptions of
  Empire*, pt 1 (1988)

2 A childish soul not inoculated with compulsory prayer is a soul open to any religious
  infection.

  'Heatherdown', first publ. 1985, repr. ibid.

3 A 'just war' is hospitable to every self-
  deception on the part of those waging it,
  none more than the certainty of virtue,
  under whose shelter every abomination
  can be committed with a clear conscience.

  New Statesman and Society 8 February 1991

Claud Cockburn (1904–81)

BRITISH AUTHOR AND JOURNALIST

As a journalist he was called by MALCOLM MUG-
GERIDGE *'the most perfect specimen of the genus
ever to exist'. He was correspondent for the* Daily
Worker *and founded the left-wing newsletter* The
Week *(1933).*

1 Small earthquake in Chile. Not many dead.

  Suggestion for a headline in *The Times* c. 1929,
  quoted in *In Time of Trouble*, ch. 10 (1956). As
  Cockburn (then working as a subeditor on the
  paper) explained: 'For further entertainment in
  the long evenings, someone had invented a game
  – a competition with a small prize for the winner – to see who could write the dullest headline. It had to be a genuine headline, that is to
  say one which was actually printed in the next
  morning's newspaper. I won it only once with a
  headline which announced: "Small earthquake
  in Chile. Not many dead." ' There is no trace of
  this headline ever being printed.

2 Nothing sets a person up more than having something turn out just the way it's
  supposed to be, like falling into a Swiss
  snowdrift and seeing a big dog come up
  with a little cask of brandy round its neck.

  I, Claud, 'Printing House Square' (1967)

3 Evidently there are plenty of people in
  journalism who have neither got what they
  liked nor quite grown to like what they get.
  They write pieces they do not much enjoy
  writing, for papers they totally despise, and
  the sad process ends by ruining their style
  and disintegrating their personality, two
  developments which in a writer cannot be
  separate, since his personality and style
  must progress or deteriorate together, like
  a married couple in a country where death
  is the only permissible divorce.

  Ibid., 'Mr Capone, Philosopher'

4 What arouses the indignation of the
  honest satirist is not, unless the man is a
  prig, the fact that people in positions of
  power or influence behave idiotically, or
  even that they behave wickedly. It is that
  they conspire successfully to impose upon
  the public a picture of themselves as so
  very sagacious, honest and well-
  intentioned.

  Ibid., 'The Worst Possible Taste'

Jarvis Cocker (b. 1963)

BRITISH ROCK MUSICIAN

*Dubbed by Ben Thompson the 'tower-block mes-
siah' who 'dares to claim the middle ground
between Alan Bennett and Barry White', he led his
band Pulp to success in the 1990s with the albums
His 'N' Hers (1994) and Different Class (1995).*

1 *You'll never live like common people,
  you'll never do what common people do,
  you'll never fail like common people,*

*you'll never watch your life slide out of view
and dance and drink and screw
because there's nothing else to do.*

'Common People' (song) on the album *Different Class* (1995) by Pulp

2 *Is this the way they say the future's meant
      to feel?
   Or just 20,000 people standing in a field.
   And I don't quite understand just what this
      feeling is.
   But that's okay 'cos we're all sorted out for
      E's & wizz.*

'Sorted for E's & Wizz', ibid.

3 *The hangover is over
   Men are over
   Women are over
   Cholesterol is over
   Tapers are over
   Irony is over
   Bye bye bye bye.*

'The Day After the Revolution' (song) on the album *This Is Hardcore* (1998) by Pulp

4 Life is like the car, and your art, or whatever you produce, is the caravan. As long as the car's in front of the caravan you can go places. The other way round, you're not going anywhere.

Mojo November 2001

Jean Cocteau (1889–1963)

FRENCH AUTHOR AND FILM-MAKER
Inspired by Diaghilev's phrase 'Étonne-moi', he was in the forefront of most of the avant-garde movements of the first half of the twentieth century, working as a poet, librettist, novelist, actor, film director, critic and painter.

1 Art is science made clear.

'Le Coq et l'Arlequin' (1918), later publ. in *Le Rappel à l'ordre* (1926), repr. in *Collected Works*, vol. 9 (1950)

2 Tact in audacity consists in knowing how far we may go too far.

Ibid.

3 The worst tragedy for a poet is to be admired through being misunderstood.

Ibid.

4 What the public criticizes in you, cultivate. It is you.

Ibid.

5 If it has to choose who is to be crucified, the crowd will always save Barabbas.

Ibid. Barabbas was the thief and insurrectionist leader reprieved at Christ's crucifixion, following the custom at Passover (Matthew 27).

6 The Louvre is like the morgue; one goes there to identify one's friends.

'Le Secret professionnel' (1922), later publ. in *Le Rappel à l'ordre* (1926), repr. ibid.

7 I am a lie who always speaks the truth.

Opéra, 'Le Paquet rouge' (1925). Similarly, in his *Journals* (1956), Cocteau wrote, 'The matters I relate/Are true lies.'

8 Living is a horizontal fall.

Opium (1930)

9 Everything one does in life, even love, occurs in an express train racing toward death. To smoke opium is to get out of the train while it is still moving. It is to concern oneself with something other than life or death.

Ibid. Cocteau experimented with opium in the 1920s. 'It is not I who become addicted,' he wrote, 'it is my body.'

10 Victor Hugo was a madman who believed himself to be Victor Hugo.

Ibid. Quoting himself from a previous occasion.

11 Poetry is indispensable – if I only knew what for.

Quoted in *The Necessity of Art*, ch. 1 (1959) by ERNST FISCHER

12 A film is a petrified fountain of thought.

Esquire February 1961

Dr F. D. Coggan (1909–2000)

BRITISH ECCLESIASTIC, ARCHBISHOP OF CANTERBURY
Frederick Donald Coggan, Baron Coggan of Canterbury. He was Archbishop of York (1961–74) and Archbishop of Canterbury (1974–80).

1 [The Church] can always be a gadfly in the conscience of those who make the economic order, and I think that is its main function.

Interview on ITV, 11 June 1961

George M. Cohan (1878–1942)

US SONGWRITER, PLAYWRIGHT AND PRODUCER
Steeped in vaudeville and theatre from an early age, he is credited with creating the first American musical, Little Johnny Jones, *in 1903. The musical* Yankee Doodle Dandy *(1942), titled after one of his songs, was the story of his life, with* JAMES CAGNEY *in the lead role.*

1 *Over there, over there,
   Send the word, send the word over there
   That the Yanks are coming, the Yanks are
      coming,
   The drums rum-tumming everywhere.
   So prepare, say a prayer,
   Send the word, send the word to beware.
   We'll be over, we're coming over
   And we won't come back till it's over, over
      there.*

'Over There' (song, 1917). The song quickly became established as an upbeat patriotic classic, called by WOODROW WILSON 'a genuine inspiration to all American manhood'.

Leonard Cohen (b. 1934)

CANADIAN SINGER, POET AND NOVELIST
The 'Bard of the Bedsits' has published volumes of poetry since 1956, releasing the first of his many melancholic albums, Songs of Leonard Cohen, in 1967. His two most successful novels are The Favourite Game (1963) and Beautiful Losers (1966).

1 Let judges secretly despair of justice: their verdicts will be more acute. Let generals secretly despair of triumph; killing will be defamed. Let priests secretly despair of faith: their compassion will be true.
The Spice-Box of Earth, 'Lines from My Grandfather's Journal' (1961)

2 Some say that no one ever leaves Montreal, for that city, like Canada itself, is designed to preserve the past, a past that happened somewhere else.
The Favourite Game, bk 2, ch. 19 (1963)

3 A woman watches her body uneasily, as though it were an unreliable ally in the battle for love.
Ibid., bk 3, ch. 8

4 History is a needle
for putting men asleep
anointed with the poison
of all they want to keep.
'On Hearing a Name Long Unspoken', st. 3, publ. in Flowers for Hitler (1964)

5 I am an old scholar, better-looking now than when I was young. That's what sitting on your ass does to your face.
Beautiful Losers, bk 1, 'The History of Them All' (1966)

6 To every people the land is given on condition. Perceived or not, there is a Covenant, beyond the constitution, beyond sovereign guarantee, beyond the nation's sweetest dreams of itself.
Book of Mercy, sect. 27 (1984)

7 The term clinical depression finds its way into too many conversations these days. One has a sense that a catastrophe has occurred in the psychic landscape.
International Herald Tribune 4 November 1988

8 I don't consider myself a pessimist at all. I think of a pessimist as someone who is waiting for it to rain. And I feel completely soaked to the skin.
Quoted in the Independent on Sunday 2 May 1993

9 I've always held the song in high regard because songs have got me through so many sinks of dishes and so many humiliating courting events.
Quoted in the Observer 27 September 1998

Frank Moore Colby (1865–1925)

US EDITOR AND ESSAYIST
He wrote for encyclopedias throughout his life and edited the New International Year Book from 1898 until his death. He also contributed widely and wittily to diverse magazines.

1 Men will confess to treason, murder, arson, false teeth, or a wig. How many of them will own up to a lack of humor?
The Colby Essays, vol. 1, 'Satire and Teeth' (1926)

2 Persecution was at least a sign of personal interest. Tolerance is composed of nine parts of apathy to one of brotherly love.
Ibid., 'Trials of an Encyclopedist'

Colette (1873–1954)

FRENCH AUTHOR
Born Sidonie Gabrielle Colette. Her series of Claudine novels (1900–1903) was written in collaboration with her first husband Gauthier-Villars under his pen name, Willy. She later established a reputation in her own right with Chéri (1920), Gigi (1944) and La Chatte (The Cat, 1953). In her old age, Cecil Beaton likened her to 'an old chinchilla marmoset sitting deep in a sofa'.

1 Among all the modernized aspects of the most luxurious of industries, the model, a vestige of voluptuous barbarianism, is like some plunder-laden prey. She is the object of unbridled regard, a living bait, the passive realization of an ideal. . . . No other female occupation contains such potent impulses to moral disintegration as this one, applying as it does the outward signs of riches to a poor and beautiful girl.
'Models', first publ. in Vogue (1925–7), repr. in Journey for Myself (1971)

2 Is suffering so very serious? I have come to doubt it. It may be quite childish, a sort of undignified pastime – I'm referring to the kind of suffering a man inflicts on a woman or a woman on a man. It's extremely painful. I agree that it's hardly bearable. But I very much fear that this sort of pain deserves no consideration at all. It's no more worthy of respect than old age or illness.
'Break of Day' (1928), repr. in Earthly Paradise, pt 4, 'The South of France' (ed. Robert Phelps, 1966)

3 It is wise to apply the oil of refined politeness to the mechanism of friendship.
The Pure and the Impure, ch. 9 (1933, transl. 1966)

4 But just as delicate fare does not stop you from craving for saveloys, so tried and exquisite friendship does not take away your taste for something new and dubious.
Chambre d'hôtel, 'The Rainy Moon' (1940)

5 Don't ever wear artistic jewellery; it wrecks a woman's reputation.

Aunt Alicia, in *Gigi* (1944, transl. 1953). When asked (by Gilberte) 'What is an artistic jewel?' Aunt Alicia replies, 'It all depends. A mermaid in gold, with eyes of chrysoprase. An Egyptian scarab. A large engraved amethyst. A not very heavy bracelet said to have been chased by a master-hand. A lyre or star, mounted as a brooch. A studded tortoise. In a word, all of them frightful. Never wear baroque pearls, not even as hat-pins. Beware, above all things, of family jewels!'

6 A pretty little collection of weaknesses and a terror of spiders are our indispensable stock-in-trade with the men.

Ibid.

R. G. Collingwood (1889–1943)

BRITISH PHILOSOPHER
Robin George Collingwood. Professor of Philosophy at Oxford (1934–41), he argued that philosophy can only be understood within a historical framework. He was also an authority on Roman Britain.

1 Like other revolutionaries I can thank God for the reactionaries. They clarify the issue.

An Autobiography, ch. 6 (1939)

2 A man ceases to be a beginner in any given science and becomes a master in that science when he has learned that . . . he is going to be a beginner all his life.

The New Leviathan, pt 1, ch. 1, aph. 46 (1942)

Joan Collins (b. 1933)

BRITISH ACTRESS
She starred in The Stud *(1979) and* The Bitch *(1980), based on novels written by her sister Jackie Collins, but found greatest success in the US TV soap opera* Dynasty *(1981–9). Her career, according to* ERICA JONG, *was 'a testimony to menopausal chic'.*

1 I've never yet met a man who could look after me. I don't need a husband. What I need is a wife.

Quoted in the *Sunday Times* 27 December 1987

2 America should let Bill Clinton get back to doing his job, even if he will always be remembered among presidents for one with a penchant for bonking trailer-park trash.

Quoted in the *Observer* 13 September 1998

Pauline Collins (b. 1940)

BRITISH ACTRESS
She is best known as a stage actress and for her roles in the TV series Upstairs, Downstairs *(1971–3) and the film* Shirley Valentine *(1989).*

1 You can't bring logic into this. We're talking about marriage. Marriage is like the Middle East. There's no solution.

Shirley (Pauline Collins), in *Shirley Valentine* (film, 1989, screenplay by Willy Russell based on his 1986 play, directed by Lewis Gilbert)

John Coltrane (1926–67)

US JAZZ MUSICIAN
An influential saxophonist, intense and emotional in style, he experimented with 'changing the notes of a chord around to see how many ways I can play it'. Classic albums include My Favorite Things *(1960) and* A Love Supreme *(1964).*

1 All a musician can do is to get closer to the sources of nature, and so feel that he is in communion with the natural laws. Then he can feel he is interpreting them to the best of his ability.

Interview in *Jazz Journal* January 1962, repr. in *The John Coltrane Companion* (ed. Carl Woideck, 1998)

2 I think the main thing a musician would like to do is to give a picture to the listener of the many wonderful things he knows of and senses in the universe. That's what music is to me – it's just another way of saying this is a big, beautiful universe we live in, that's been given to us, and here's an example of just how magnificent and encompassing it is.

Down Beat 12 April 1962, repr. ibid.

3 If the music doesn't say it, how can the words say it for the music?

Quoted in *Jazz Is*, ch. 5 (1976) by Nat Hentoff

Betty Comden (b. 1915) and Adolph Green (1915–2002)

US LIBRETTISTS, LYRICISTS AND SCREENWRITERS
During a fifty-year career the duo was associated with a string of Broadway hits. Their collaborators included LEONARD BERNSTEIN, *Jule Styne and Gene Kelly; with the latter they made the films* On the Town *(1949),* Singin' in the Rain *(1952) and* It's Always Fair Weather *(1955). See also* JEAN HAGEN 1.

1 *New York, New York – a helluva town,*
The Bronx is up but the Battery's down,
And people ride in a hole in the ground:
New York, New York – it's a helluva town.

'New York, New York' (song from the stage musical *On the Town*, 1944, filmed 1949). The song opens the story, which follows the adventures of a group of sailors on shore leave in New York.

2 *A million faces pass before your eye,*
Still it's a lonely town.
Unless there's love,
A love that's shining like a harbor light –

You're lost in the night
Unless there's love.
'Lonely Town' (song, ibid.)

3 *The party's over, it's time to call it a day.*
'The Party's Over' (song, with music by Jule Styne), in *The Bells are Ringing* (stage musical 1956, filmed 1960)

Alex Comfort (1920–2000)

BRITISH SEXOLOGIST, AUTHOR AND POET
He was the author of Sex and Society *(1963),* The Anxiety Makers *(1967) and* The Joy of Sex *(1972), his most famous work, dubbed the 'Kamasutra for the coffee table'.*

1 The Joy of Sex.
Book title (1972)

2 There are two modes of sex, the duet and the solo, and a good concert alternates between them.
The Joy of Sex, Preface (1972, rev. 1991)

Ivy Compton-Burnett (1884–1969)

BRITISH NOVELIST
Her stylized novels rely heavily on dialogue to portray the internal wranglings of upper-class Victorian or Edwardian families. Titles include Pastors and Masters *(1925) and* Mother and Son *(1955).*

1 Well, of course, people are only human. But it really does not seem much for them to be.
Dudley Gaveston, in *A Family and a Fortune*, ch. 2 (1939)

2 We must use words as they are used or stand aside from life.
Julius Hume, in *Mother and Son*, ch. 9 (1955)

3 There is danger in courage. Cowardice is a power for good. We hardly know what it prevents.
Angus, in *The Last and First*, ch. 6 (1971)

Richard Condon (1915–96)

US NOVELIST, SCREENWRITER AND JOURNALIST
A Hollywood scriptwriter until the late 1950s, he devised a successful recipe of political thrillers and pulp prose mixed with conspiracy paranoia, as in The Manchurian Candidate *(1959, filmed 1962).*

1 Television – the key to all minds and hearts because it permits the people to be entertained by their government, without ever having to participate in it.
International Herald Tribune 7 June 1990

Billy Connolly (b. 1942)

SCOTTISH COMEDIAN
Originally a welder on the Clyde shipyards, the 'Big Yin' moved from music into comedy, setting

out, as he put it, 'to be a cross between Lenny Bruce and Robert the Bruce'. He has also appeared in films, notably as Queen Victoria's gamekeeper in Mrs Brown (1997).

1 I would hate to have been born, lived and died and nobody noticed. It's proof you exist, that all the practising with your banjo in your bedroom paid off.
On fame, in interview in 1984, quoted in *The Big Yin: The Life and Times of Billy Connolly*, ch. 10 (1994) by Jonathan Margolis

2 You're 'Connolly' all your life until you become famous, then you're 'that bastard Connolly'.
Quoted in the *Observer* 9 June 1991. Referring to fellow Glaswegians.

3 I totally refuse to be part of it [political correctness] . . . those new comedy people who say no racism, no sexism, no that-ism, no this-ism. How dare you? Comedy's been here for thousands of years. How dare you start rewriting the rule book? There is no rule book. Funny is funny is funny.
South Bank Show, ITV, 4 October 1992, quoted in *The Big Yin: The Life and Times of Billy Connolly*, ch. 10 (1994) by Jonathan Margolis

Cyril Connolly (1903–74)

BRITISH CRITIC
A fastidious wit, he founded and edited the literary magazine Horizon *(1939–50) and was a regular contributor to the* Sunday Times *(1951–74). His essays, reflections and aphorisms were published in* Enemies of Promise *(1938) and* The Unquiet Grave *(written as 'Palinurus', 1944).*

1 Green leaves on a dead tree is our epitaph – green leaves, dear reader, on a dead tree.
'The Journal of Cyril Connolly 1928–1937', publ. in *Journal and Memoir* by David Pryce-Jones (1983). Pryce-Jones chose these words for his book's epigraph.

2 A best-seller is the golden touch of mediocre talent.
Ibid.

3 Idleness [is] only a coarse name for my infinite capacity for living in the present.
Ibid.

4 Destroy him as you will, the bourgeois always bounces up – execute him, expropriate him, starve him out *en masse*, and he reappears in your children.
Quoted in the *Observer* 7 March 1937

5 I shall christen this style the Mandarin, since it is beloved by literary pundits, by those who would make the written word as unlike as possible to the spoken one. It is

the style of all those writers whose tendency is to make their language convey more than they mean or more than they feel, it is the style of most artists and all humbugs and one which is always menaced by a puritan opposition.

Enemies of Promise, pt 1, ch. 2 (1938, rev. 1948). Connolly referred to a style of English prose popularized by authors such as Addison – who was 'responsible for many of the evils from which English prose has since suffered. He made prose artful and whimsical, he made it sonorous when sonority was not needed, affected when it did not require affectation . . .'

6 Literature is the art of writing something that will be read twice; journalism what will be grasped at once.

Ibid., ch. 3

7 As repressed sadists are supposed to become policemen or butchers so those with an irrational fear of life become publishers.

Ibid., pt 2, ch. 10

8 Whom the gods wish to destroy they first call promising.

Ibid., ch. 13

9 There is no more sombre enemy of good art than the pram in the hall.

Ibid., ch. 14

10 All charming people have something to conceal, usually their total dependence on the appreciation of others.

Ibid., ch. 16

11 Were I to deduce any system from my feelings on leaving Eton, it might be called *The Theory of Permanent Adolescence*. It is the theory that the experiences undergone by boys at the great public schools, their glories and disappointments, are so intense as to dominate their lives and to arrest their development. From these it results that the greater part of the ruling class remains adolescent, school-minded, self-conscious, cowardly, sentimental, and in the last analysis homosexual.

Ibid., pt 3, ch. 24

12 Perfect fear casteth out love.

Quoted in obituary notice in the *Observer* 1 December 1974, by Philip Toynbee, to whom Connolly made this remark during the Blitz. The reference is to the Bible, 1 John 4:18: 'Perfect love casteth out fear.'

13 The more books we read, the clearer it becomes that the true function of a writer is to produce a masterpiece and that no other task is of any consequence.

The Unquiet Grave, pt 1 (1944, rev. 1951). Opening words of book.

14 Slums may well be breeding-grounds of

crime, but middle-class suburbs are incubators of apathy and delirium.

Ibid.

15 No city should be too large for a man to walk out of in a morning.

Ibid.

16 Civilization is an active deposit which is formed by the combustion of the Present with the Past. Neither in countries without a Present nor in those without a Past is it to be encountered.

Ibid., pt 2. Connolly continued: 'Proust in Venice, Matisse's birdcages overlooking the flower market at Nice, Gide on the seventeenth-century quais of Toulon, Lorca in Granada, Picasso by Saint-Germain-des-Prés: there lies civilization and for me it can exist only under those liberal regimes in which the Present is alive and therefore capable of assimilating the Past.'

17 The goal of every culture is to decay through over-civilization; the factors of decadence – luxury, scepticism, weariness and superstition – are constant. The civilization of one epoch becomes the manure of the next.

Ibid.

18 Imprisoned in every fat man a thin one is wildly signalling to be let out.

Ibid. The remark had been used earlier by GEORGE ORWELL (see 7); for a later variant see KINGSLEY AMIS 4.

19 The true index of a man's character is the health of his wife.

Ibid.

20 We are all serving a life-sentence in the dungeon of self.

Ibid.

21 Our memories are card indexes consulted and then returned in disorder by authorities whom we do not control.

Ibid., pt 3

22 The boredom of Sunday afternoon, which drove de Quincey to drink laudanum, also gave birth to surrealism: hours propitious for making bombs.

Ibid.

23 It is closing time in the gardens of the West and from now on an artist will be judged only by the resonance of his solitude or the quality of his despair.

Horizon December 1949

James Connolly (1870–1916)

IRISH SYNDICALIST AND REPUBLICAN LEADER

Having helped found the Irish Socialist Republican Party (1896) and, in New York (1902–10), the Industrial Workers of the World ('Wobblies'), he established the Irish Labour Party with James

Larkin in 1912. He was shot for his part in the Easter Rising of 1916.

1 Without the power of the Industrial Union behind it, Democracy can only enter the State as the victim enters the gullet of the Serpent.
The Re-Conquest of Ireland, ch. 9 (1915)

2 Ireland, as distinct from her people, is nothing to me; and the man who is bubbling over with love and enthusiasm for 'Ireland', and can yet pass unmoved through our streets and witness all the wrong and the suffering, the shame and the degradation wrought upon the people of Ireland – yea, wrought by Irishmen upon Irish men and women, without burning to end it, is, in my opinion, a fraud and a liar in his heart, no matter how he loves that combination of chemical elements he is pleased to call Ireland.
Labour in Ireland, epigraph (1916)

Jimmy Connors (b. 1952)
US TENNIS PLAYER
One of the first players to use a two-handed backhand, he dominated international tournaments during the 1970s and '80s, winning the US Open five times.

1 New Yorkers love it when you spill your guts out there [Flushing Meadow]. Spill your guts at Wimbledon and they make you stop and clean it up.
Quoted in the *Guardian* 24 December 1984

Peter Conrad (b. 1948)
AUSTRALIAN AUTHOR AND CRITIC
He has written fiction, literary criticism and on opera, and is also a reviewer and features writer for the Observer.

1 New York is more now than the sum of its people and buildings. It makes sense only as a mechanical intelligence, a transporter system for the daily absorbing and nightly redeploying of the human multitudes whose services it requires.
The Art of the City, ch. 13 (1984)

2 Losing faith in your own singularity is the start of wisdom, I suppose; also the first announcement of death.
Down Under: Revisiting Tasmania, pt 6, 'In the Family' (1988)

Shirley Conran (b. 1932)
BRITISH DESIGNER AND JOURNALIST
The first woman editor of the Observer Colour Magazine *(1964–9), she became a bestseller with her* Superwoman *series (1974–7, 1990), and her novels, including* Lace *(1982) and* Tiger Eyes *(1984).*

1 Life is too short to stuff a mushroom.
Superwoman, epigraph (1975)

2 I make no secret of the fact that I would rather lie on a sofa than sweep beneath it. But you have to be efficient if you're going to be lazy.
Ibid., 'The Reason Why'

3 First things first, second things never.
Family motto, ibid. 'How to be a Working Wife and Mother'

4 Women want men to change, but they don't. Men want women to stay the same, but they can't.
Quoted in *The Times* 23 December 2000

(Sir) Terence Conran (b. 1931)
BRITISH BUSINESSMAN AND DESIGNER
A furniture designer by profession, he has written widely on interior design and championed modern, affordable design through his Habitat stores (1971–88).

1 Perhaps believing in good design is like believing in God, it makes you an optimist.
Daily Telegraph 12 June 1989

Conservative Party manifesto

1 The Conservative Party by long tradition and settled belief is the party of Empire. We are proud of its past. We see it as the surest hope in our own day. We proclaim our abiding faith in its destiny.
'Britain Strong and Free' (1950), quoted by John Barnes in 'Ideology and Factions' publ. in *Conservative Century*, pt 2 (ed. Anthony Seldon and Stuart Ball, 1994)

Peter Cook (1937–95)
BRITISH COMEDIAN
After the success of Beyond the Fringe *(1959–64), he collaborated with Dudley Moore in the TV series* Not Only . . . But Also *(1965–71), creating the forlorn figure E. L. Wisty. He was co-founder of the satirical magazine* Private Eye.

1 I go to the theatre to be entertained. I don't want to see plays about rape, sodomy and drug addiction – I can get all that at home.
Cartoon caption in the *Observer* 8 July 1962. The joke also appeared in the revue *Beyond the Fringe*, and has been credited to ALAN BENNETT.

2 There's terrific merit in having no sense of humour, no sense of irony, practically no sense of anything at all. If you're born with these so-called defects you have a very good chance of getting to the top.
Quoted in *Beyond the Fringe . . . and Beyond*, pt 4 (1989) by Ronald Bergan

Robin Cook (b. 1946)

BRITISH POLITICIAN

Originally Robert Cook. He became a Labour MP in 1974, Foreign Secretary in 1997 and Leader of the House of Commons in 2001, resigning from that post in 2003 over the government's policy on Iraq.

1 Our foreign policy must have an ethical dimension and must support the demands of other peoples for the democratic rights on which we insist for ourselves.

Statement on assuming post of Foreign Secretary, 12 May 1997, quoted in *The Times* 13 May 1997

2 It's better to send middle-aged men abroad to bore each other than send young men abroad to kill each other.

Independent 14 February 1998. Referring to UN negotiations with Saddam Hussein.

3 Chicken Tikka Massala is now a true British national dish, not only because it is the most popular, but because it is a perfect illustration of the way Britain absorbs and adapts external influences.

Speech to the Social Market Foundation, London, quoted in the *Guardian* 19 April 2001. Other reports quote the words '. . . Britain's true national dish'.

4 I have already had my fill of this bloody and unnecessary war. I want our troops home and I want them home before more of them are killed.

Sunday Mirror 30 March 2003. On the war in Iraq. Cook softened his stance when he was interviewed on BBC radio on the same day, claiming he did not favour abandoning the war or 'letting Saddam off the hook'.

Alistair Cooke (b. 1908)

BRITISH-BORN US BROADCASTER AND JOURNALIST

An urbane observer on current affairs in America, he has published several books on his subject and broadcast the weekly Letter from America *on BBC radio since 1946.*

1 If the fads of the young follow their usual practice and pass over into the settled habits of middle age, attributable to no country but to the period they were learned in, then in another quarter-century England indeed will be the fifty-first state. For the most compelling social characteristic of the British people today is not the wide gamut of native qualities and habits, but the greater range of American habits, customs, and conventions they seem to have incorporated, without complaint, since the war.

'New Ways in English Life', publ. in the *Manchester Guardian* 16 July 1959, repr. in *America Observed* (1988, selected by Ronald A. Wells)

2 Cocktail music he accepts as audible wallpaper.

'The Innocent American', publ. in *Holiday* July 1962. The words are usually misquoted as 'Canned music is like audible wallpaper.'

3 All Presidents start out to run a crusade but after a couple of years they find they are running something less heroic and much more intractable: namely the presidency.

Radio broadcast, 1963, publ. in *Talk About America*, ch. 31 (1968)

4 Was Vietnam indeed a crusade or a vast miscalculation? Was it the wrong war in the wrong place, or the right war in the wrong place? What matters, or will come to matter to most people, I think, is not any new balance we can strike in the old argument; but the realisation that America, which has never lost a war, is not invincible; and the very late discovery that an elephant can trumpet and shake the earth but not the self-possession of the ants who hold it.

Letter from America, BBC radio broadcast, 24 March 1968

Sam Cooke (1931–64)

US SOUL MUSICIAN

His gospel-influenced vocal style and strong commercial appeal made him a major figure in soul music, inspiring numerous covers of such songs as 'You Send Me' (1957), 'Only Sixteen' (1959) *and* 'Bring it on Home to Me' (1963).

1 Don't know much about history
Don't know much about biology.

'Wonderful World' (song, 1960). In *A Change is Gonna Come: Music, Race & the Soul of America* (1998) by Craig Werner, the author makes this comment on the lines: 'The cliché's worth a second thought. Because, if there are two things that a black man in pop music needed to encourage the white audience to forget, they were history and biology, at least the parts involving skin color and sexuality.'

2 It's been a long time coming
But I know a change is gonna come.

'A Change is Gonna Come' (song) on the album *Ain't That Good News* (1964). The song was partly modelled on BOB DYLAN's 'Blowin' in the Wind' and assumed almost anthemic importance during the rise of the Black Consciousness movement. Among the artists who recorded it were Prince Buster and, most famously, Otis Redding, who dedicated the song to Cooke in concert.

Calvin Coolidge (1872–1933)

US POLITICIAN AND PRESIDENT

As Republican president (1923–9) with the slogan 'Keep Cool with Coolidge', he was noted for non-interference in business, industry and foreign

*affairs. Modest and frugal throughout his life,
he was equally known for his dullness.* H.L.
MENCKEN *concluded: 'He had no ideas, but was
not a nuisance.' See also* DOROTHY PARKER 11.

1 There is no right to strike against the
public safety by anybody, anywhere, any
time.

Telegram to Samuel Gompers, President of
American Federation of Labor, 14 September
1919, quoted in *Have Faith in Massachusetts*
(1919). Coolidge, then Governor of Massachusetts, was referring to a strike by the Boston
police.

2 Civilization and profits go hand in hand.

Speech in New York, 27 November 1920, quoted
in *The New York Times* 28 November 1920

3 After all, the chief business of the American people is business.

Speech to the Society of American Newspaper
Editors, Washington DC, 17 January 1925, publ.
in *Foundations of the Republic* (1926)

4 Well, they hired the money, didn't they?

Attributed comment in 1925 to US ambassador
to France on a proposal to restructure European
war debts, quoted in *The Wit and Wisdom of
Calvin Coolidge* (ed. John H. McKee, 1933). Coolidge's biographer, Claud M. Fuess, failed to find
any evidence that Coolidge spoke these words,
though his wife observed, 'I don't know whether
he said it, but it is just what he might have said.'

5 I do not choose to run for President in
nineteen twenty-eight.

Statement to reporters, Rapid City, South
Dakota, 2 August 1927, quoted in *The New York
Times* 3 August 1927. The words were said to
have been written out and handed to the
assembled journalists, in what was taken to be a
perfect illustration of Coolidge's legendary taci-
turnity. Regarding this, one Washington hostess
is supposed to have commented: 'Every time he
opens his mouth, a moth flies out.'

Diana Cooper (1892–1986)

BRITISH ACTRESS, AUTHOR AND SOCIETY
FIGURE

*Married to the diplomat Duff Cooper, she made
her name in the role of the Madonna in the play*
The Miracle *(1923) by Max Reinhardt. For Cecil
Beaton, she was 'a card – a flamboyant eccentric –
and a real professional extrovert'. See also* JOHN
CAREY 1.

1 *Age wins and one must learn to grow old
. . . I must learn to walk this long unlovely
wintry way, looking for spectacles, shun-
ning the cruel looking-glass, laughing at
my clumsiness before others mistakenly
condole, not expecting gallantry yet disappointed to receive none, apprehending
every ache or shaft of pain, alive to blinding flashes of mortality, unarmed, totally
vulnerable.*

Trumpets from the Steep, ch. 8 (memoir, 1960)

Gary Cooper (1901–61)

US SCREEN ACTOR

*The archetypal strong, silent loner, he remained
a Hollywood star for more than thirty years, best
remembered for his role in* High Noon *(1952).*

1 In Westerns you were permitted to kiss
your horse but never your girl.

'Well, It Was This Way', publ. in the *Saturday
Evening Post* 17 March 1958

Jilly Cooper (b. 1937)

BRITISH JOURNALIST AND AUTHOR

A regular columnist for the Sunday Times *(1969–
82) and the* Daily Mail *(1982–7), she has published a succession of steamy bestsellers including*
Riders *(1978) and* Polo *(1991).*

1 Nostalgia excuses everything, enabling
people to click their tongues over the outdated inequalities, yet guiltily enjoy the
sense of hierarchy.

Class, Introduction (1980)

2 I've always felt reading romantic novels
was a bit like eating a whole box of chocolates or going to bed with a rotter. You
can't stop because it's so nice, but afterwards you wish you hadn't.

Quoted in the *Sunday Correspondent*
24 December 1989

Tommy Cooper (1922–84)

BRITISH COMEDIAN

*With his trademark red fez, he was the comedian's
comedian, enjoying success in variety and his own
TV series from the 1950s. He died on stage during
a live TV transmission.*

1 Just like that!

Catch-phrase and title of autobiography (1975)

Wendy Cope (b. 1945)

BRITISH POET

*She published her first volume of wry and parodic
verse,* Making Cocoa for Kingsley Amis, *in 1986,
followed by* Serious Concerns *in 1992.*

1 *I used to think all poets were Byronic.
They're mostly wicked as a ginless tonic
And wild as pension plans.*

'Triolet', publ. in *Making Cocoa for Kingsley
Amis* (1986)

2 *The Thames runs, bones rattle, rats creep;
Tiresias fancies a peep –
A typist is laid,
A record is played –
Wei la la. After that it gets deep.*

'Waste Land Limericks', publ. ibid.

3 *Bloody men are like bloody buses –
You wait for about a year
And as soon as one approaches your stop
Two or three others appear.*

'Bloody Men', publ. in *Serious Concerns* (1992).

The men/buses analogy had been current for some time: newspaper editor Wendy Henry was quoted in the *Observer* 30 January 1983: 'Men are like buses. If you miss one, there's always another round the corner. But don't get caught at the wrong stop.'

4 *They say that men suffer,*
As badly, as long.
I worry, I worry,
In case they are wrong.
'I Worry', publ. ibid.

5 I think it's a question which particularly arises over women writers: whether it's better to have a happy life or a good supply of tragic plots.
Independent 9 March 1992

6 *Hope is a long leash,*
drawn in slowly.
'After Prague', publ. in *If I Don't Know* (2001)

Aaron Copland (1900–90)
US COMPOSER
Originally Aaron Kaplan. Early pieces influenced by STRAVINSKY *were a fusion of classical and jazz styles. Later works such as the ballet* Billy the Kid *(1938) and* Appalachian Spring *(1944) drew on the American folk tradition.*

1 The whole problem can be stated quite simply by asking, 'Is there a meaning to music?' My answer to that would be, 'Yes.' And 'Can you state in so many words what the meaning is?' My answer to that would be, 'No.'
What to Listen for in Music, ch. 2 (1939)

2 At no point can you seize the musical experience and hold it. Unlike that moment in a film when a still shot suddenly immobilizes a complete scene, a single musical moment immobilized makes audible only one chord, which in itself is comparatively meaningless. This never-ending flow of music *forces* us to use our imaginations, for music is in a continual state of becoming.
Music and Imagination: The Charles Eliot Norton Lectures 1951/2, Introduction (1952)

3 Listening implies an inborn talent of some degree, which, again like any other talent, can be trained and developed. This talent has a certain 'purity' about it. We exercise it, so to speak, for ourselves alone; there is nothing to be gained from it in a material sense. Listening is its own reward; there are no prizes to be won, no contests of creative listening. But I hold that person fortunate who has the gift, for there are few pleasures in art greater than the secure sense that one can recognise beauty when one comes upon it.
Ibid., pt 1, ch. 1

4 The greatest moments of the human spirit may be deduced from the greatest moments in music.
'Music as an Aspect of the Human Spirit', radio broadcast, 1954, publ. in *Musical Courier* 1 February 1955 and *Man's Right to Knowledge* (second series, 1955)

Francis Ford Coppola (b. 1939)
US FILM-MAKER
He won universal acclaim for the epic Mafia drama The Godfather *(1972), which he co-wrote and directed, and its two sequels. Other films include* Apocalypse Now *(1979) and* The Cotton Club *(1984).*

1 If anything in this life is certain, if history has taught us anything, it's that everyone can be killed.
Michael Corleone (Al Pacino), in *The Godfather Part II* (film, 1974, screenplay by Francis Ford Coppola and Mario Puzo, directed by Francis Ford Coppola)

2 Nothing else in the world smells like that . . . I love the smell of napalm in the morning . . . It smells like victory.
Colonel Kilgore (Robert Duvall), in *Apocalypse Now* (film, 1979, screenplay by John Milius and Francis Ford Coppola, produced and directed by Francis Ford Coppola). The film's title, credited to John Milius, was derived from a badge popular with hippies in the 1960s, 'Nirvana Now'.

3 Charlie don't surf.
Colonel Kilgore (Robert Duvall), ibid. Referring to the Viet Cong.

4 I don't believe that talented people today have less gifts than their artistic ancestors. The *times* are exhausted – stories come from the structure of ideas, ethics, beliefs, actualities of the times. Our *times* are exhausted – not our artists.
Quoted in *Coppola*, ch. 8 (1989) by Peter Cowie

Alan Coren (b. 1938)
BRITISH EDITOR AND HUMORIST
A professional wit, he was Editor of Punch *(1978–87), has authored numerous books and contributes regularly to newspapers, periodicals and radio programmes.*

1 Apart from cheese and tulips, the main product of the country is advocaat, a drink made from lawyers.
The Sanity Inspector, 'All You Need to Know about Europe' (1974)

2 The Act of God designation on all insurance policies: which means, roughly, that you cannot be insured for the accidents that are most likely to happen to you. If your ox kicks a hole in your neigh-

bour's Maserati, however, indemnity is instantaneous.

The Lady from Stalingrad Mansions, 'A Short History of Insurance' (1977)

3 Having a high-profile magazine that loses lots of money, being a vanity publisher if you like, is rather like having a trophy wife. It's nice to have her on your arm, but you can't do anything with her because you are too old and clapped out – and it's as expensive as running an Ivana Trump, I can tell you. Rich men do it because it gets them invited to the right dinner parties and to meet politicians, that sort of thing. It also means that when they are asked what they do they can say, 'I own the *Spectator*' rather than, 'I export pipe linings.'

Quoted in the *Observer* 11 February 1996

F. M. Cornford (1874–1943)

BRITISH AUTHOR AND ACADEMIC

Francis Macdonald Cornford. Professor of Ancient Philosophy at Cambridge University (1931–9), he was a leading Platonic scholar, and published mainly on the ancient Greeks.

1 Propaganda is that branch of the art of lying which consists in nearly deceiving your friends without quite deceiving your enemies.

Quoted in the *New Statesman* 15 September 1978

Gregory Corso (b. 1930)

US POET

One of the Beat poets, he first came to attention in the late 1950s for his anarchic verse. His numerous collections include Gasoline (1958) and Earth Egg (1974).

1 *I HATE OLD POETMEN!*
   Especially old poetmen who retract
   who consult other old poetmen
   who speak their youth in whispers,
   saying: – I did those then
   but that was then
   that was then –
   'I am 25', publ. in *Gasoline* (1958)

2 *Must one keep home to keep Rome Rome?*
   Surely then this England visit
   will spoil whatever dream I have of it.
   'How One Looks at It', publ. in *Long Live Man* (1962)

Bill Cosby (b. 1937)

US COMEDIAN AND ACTOR

His role in the TV series I Spy (1965–8) was a landmark in the screen portrayal of African-Americans. He later scored consistently high ratings for The Cosby Show (1984–92) and Cosby (1996).

1 No matter how calmly you try to referee, parenting will eventually produce bizarre behavior, and I'm not talking about the kids. *Their* behavior is always normal.

Fatherhood, ch. 4 (1986)

Elvis Costello (b. 1954)

BRITISH ROCK MUSICIAN

Originally Declan Patrick McManus. His intelligent, impassioned lyrics on his debut album My Aim is True (1977) marked him out in the punk era. He later collaborated with PAUL MCCARTNEY and with the classical Brodsky Quartet.

1 *Somebody said that someone got filled in*
   For saying that people get killed in
   The result of their shipbuilding
   With all the will in the world
   Diving for dear life
   When we could be diving for pearls.
   'Shipbuilding' (song) on the album *Punch the Clock* (1983). The track, which was inspired by the Falklands War, was first recorded by Robert Wyatt in 1982.

2 To me, getting it wrong is just another original idea. Ninety per cent of pop music is trying to copy something and getting it wrong.

Quoted in the *Guardian* 19 September 1998

Kevin Costner (b. 1955)

US ACTOR AND FILM-MAKER

He was acclaimed for his performances in Field of Dreams (1989) and Dances with Wolves (1990), which he also directed.

1 Well, I believe in the soul, the cock, the pussy, the small of a woman's back, the hangin' curved ball, high fiber, good Scotch, that the novels of Susan Sontag are self-indulgent overrated crap. I believe Lee Harvey Oswald acted alone, I believe there ought to be a constitutional amendment outlawing astro-turf . . . I believe in the sweet spot, soft-core pornography, opening your presents Christmas morning rather than Christmas Eve, and I believe in long slow deep soft wet kisses that last three days.

Crash Davis (Kevin Costner), in *Bull Durham* (film, 1988, written and directed by Ron Shelton)

Billy Cotton (1899–1969)

BRITISH BANDLEADER

He formed his own band in 1924 which toured from the 1930s. His Billy Cotton Bandshow, broadcast on radio and television (1949–68), became a national institution.

1 Wakey wakey!

Standard show opener, from 1940s. The catchphrase originated in a Sunday morning live radio show. In Cotton's words: 'The boys had been sitting up all night in third-class railway carriages. When we broke before the actual performance they just slumped where they were. I came into the studio only a few minutes before the red light was due to go on, and they were slouched around like a lot of tired giraffes. "Oi, come on," I said. "*Wakey Wakey!*" It worked, and everybody got so cheerful that the producer said that we could well start the actual show with it. And that was the beginning of Wakey Wakey.' (*I Did it My Way*, ch. 10, 1970)

Douglas Coupland (b. 1961)
CANADIAN AUTHOR

His novel Generation X *(1991) lent its name to the subculture of disaffected twenty-somethings whose lives it chronicled. Other works, such as* Microserfs *(1995) and* Polaroids from the Dead *(1996), describe the 'accelerated culture' of our times.*

1 **McJob: A low-pay, low-prestige, low-dignity, low-benefit, no-future job in the service sector.**
Marginal note in *Generation X*, 'The Sun is Your Enemy' (1991)

2 **Consensus Terrorism: The process that decides in-office attitudes and behavior.**
Marginal note ibid., 'I Am Not a Target Market'

3 **Yuppies never gamble, they calculate. They have no aura: ever been to a yuppie party? It's like being in an empty room: empty hologram people walking around peeking at themselves in mirrors and surreptitiously misting their tonsils with Bianca spray, just in case they have to kiss another ghost like themselves. There's just nothing there.**
Dag, ibid.

4 **You really have to wonder why we even bother to get *up* in the morning. I mean, really: *Why work?* Simply to buy more *stuff?***
Dag, ibid., 'Quit Your Job'

5 **My friends are all either married, boring, and depressed; single, bored, and depressed; or moved out of town to avoid boredom and depression.**
Narrator (Andy), ibid., 'MTV Not Bullets'

6 **You've had most of your important memories by the time you're thirty. After that, memory becomes water overflowing into an already full cup.**
Life After God, 'My Hotel Year' (1994)

7 **Sometimes I think the people to feel the saddest for are people who once knew what profoundness was, but who lost or became numb to the sensation of wonder – people who closed the door that leads us into the secret world – or who had the doors closed for them by time and neglect and decisions made in time of weakness.**
Ibid.

8 **When you're young, you always feel that**

life hasn't yet begun – that 'life' is always scheduled to begin next week, next month, next year, after the holidays – whenever. But then suddenly you're old and the scheduled life didn't arrive. You find yourself asking 'well then, exactly what was it I was having – that interlude – the scrambly madness – all that time I had before?'
Ibid., 'Gettysburg'

9 **There is something about a monolithic tech culture like Microsoft that makes humans seriously rethink fundamental aspects of the relationship between their brains and their bodies – their souls and their ambitions; things and thoughts.**
Microserfs, 'Oop: Thursday–Later That Week' (1995)

10 **I've never met anyone who has entered the technological realm and not come out of it happier, enhanced and more fulfilled.**
Without Walls: J'Accuse – Technonerds, television broadcast, Channel 4, 19 March 1996

11 **The New World isn't new anymore. The New World – the Americas – it's over. People don't have dominion over Nature. It's gone beyond that. Human beings and the world are now the same thing.**
Jared, in *Girlfriend in a Coma*, ch. 34 (1998)

(Sir) Noël Coward (1899–1973)
BRITISH ACTOR, PLAYWRIGHT AND COMPOSER

Blessed, in his own words, with 'a talent to amuse', he was a sophisticated and versatile performer, and the writer of the classic comedy plays Hay Fever *(1925),* Private Lives *(1930, filmed 1931) and* Blithe Spirit *(1941, filmed 1945), as well as numerous musicals and revues. He also appeared in films, and wrote and produced the patriotic* In Which We Serve *(1942) and* Brief Encounter *(1946).*

1 *Poor little rich girl,*
  You're a bewitched girl,
  Better beware!
'Poor Little Rich Girl' (song) in *On with the Dance* (musical revue), 1925

2 **Very flat, Norfolk.**
Amanda, in *Private Lives*, act 1 (1930)

3 **Extraordinary how potent cheap music is.**
Amanda, ibid. Often quoted 'Strange how potent cheap music is', after the version used in the 1930 recording of the play (spoken by Gertrude Lawrence).

4 **Elyot: It doesn't suit women to be promiscuous.**
  Amanda: It doesn't suit men for women to be promiscuous.
Ibid., act 2

5 **Certain women should be struck regularly like gongs.**
Elyot, ibid., act 3

6 *In Bengal to move at all*
   Is seldom, if ever, done,
   But mad dogs and Englishmen
   Go out in the midday sun.
   'Mad Dogs and Englishmen' (song, 1930)

7 *We give lovely parties that last through the*
      night,
   I dress as a woman and scream with
      delight,
   We wake up at lunch time and find we're
      still tight.
   What could be duller than that?
   'Bright Young People' (song, 1930)

8 Let's drink to our sons who made part of
   the pattern and to our hearts that died
   with them. Let's drink to the spirit of gallantry and courage that made a strange
   Heaven out of unbelievable Hell, and let's
   drink to the hope that one day this country
   of ours, which we love so much, will find
   dignity and greatness and peace again.
   Jane, toasting New Year's Eve with Robert, in
   Cavalcade, pt 3, sc. 1 (1932). Last speech of play.

9 *Blues, nothing to win or to lose.*
   It's getting me down.
   Blues, I've got those weary Twentieth Cen-
      tury Blues.
   'Twentieth Century Blues' (song), ibid., pt 3,
   sc. 2

10 *Mad about the boy,*
    I know it's stupid to be mad about the boy,
    I'm so ashamed of it
    But must admit
    The sleepless nights I've had about the boy.
    On the Silver Screen
    He melts my foolish heart in every single
       scene.
    'Mad About the Boy' (song) in *Words and Music*
    (musical revue, 1932)

11 *Don't put your daughter on the stage,*
       Mrs Worthington,
    Don't put your daughter on the stage.
    'Mrs Worthington' (song, 1935, with music by
    COLE PORTER). Noël Coward sang the song in
    the original recording.

12 *The Stately Homes of England,*
    How beautiful they stand,
    To prove the upper classes
    Have still the upper hand.
    'The Stately Homes of England' (song) in *Oper-
    ette* (musical show, 1938). Parody of opening
    lines of Felicia Hemans's 1849 poem, 'The
    Homes of England': 'The stately homes of Eng-
    land,/How beautiful they stand!/Amidst their tall
    ancestral trees,/O'er all the pleasant land.' See
    also QUENTIN CRISP 9.

13 The good old imperialism was a bloody
    sight wiser and healthier than all this
    woolly-headed, muddled, 'all men are
    equal' humanitarianism which has lost us
    so much pride and dignity and prestige in

the modern world. The British Empire was
a great and wonderful social, economic
and even spiritual experiment, and all the
parlour pinks and eager, ill-informed intellectuals cannot convince me to the
contrary.
Journal entry, 3 February 1957, publ. in *The Noël
Coward Diaries* (ed. Graham Payn and Sheridan
Morley, 1982)

14 *Please do not think that I criticize or cavil*
    At a genuine urge to roam,
    But why oh why do the wrong people travel
    When the right people stay back home?
    'Why Do the Wrong People Travel?' (song) in
    Sail Away (musical show, 1962)

Jim Crace (b. 1946)
BRITISH AUTHOR
He had success with his first novel, Continent
(1986), which was followed by The Gift of Stones
(1988) and Quarantine *(1997).*

1 Fame is something different from popularity. It is less demanding for a start and
   has more to do with talent than virtue. But
   not even much to do with talent.
   Continent, 'Cross Country' (1986)

2 'The secret of the story-teller,' father said,
   'is Never Smile. A straight mouth and a
   pair of honest eyes is all it takes to turn a
   stone to leaf.'
   The Gift of Stones, ch. 14 (1988)

Hart Crane (1899–1932)
US POET
Influenced by Rimbaud and T. S. ELIOT, *he is
remembered for his main work, the epic* The
Bridge *(1930), a wide-ranging portrait of Ameri-
can culture. He committed suicide.*

1 *Cowslip and shad-blow, flaked like tethered*
      foam
   Around bared teeth of stallions, bloomed
      that spring
   When first I read thy lines, rife as the loam
   Of prairies, yet like breakers cliffward
      leaping!
   'Cape Hatteras', publ. in *The Bridge*, sect. 4
   (1930)

2 *yes, Walt,*
   Afoot again, and onward without halt, –
   Not soon, nor suddenly, – no, never to let go
   My hand
   in yours,
   Walt Whitman –
   so –
   Ibid. Final lines of poem.

3 *And through that cordage, threading with*
      its call
   One arc synoptic of all tides below –
   Their labyrinthine mouths of history
   Pouring reply as though all ships at sea

*Complighted in one vibrant breath made
    cry, –*
'*Make thy love sure – to weave whose song
    we ply!*'
'Atlantis', publ. in *The Bridge*, sect. 8 (1930)

4 *We left the haven hanging in the night –
    Sheened harbor lanterns backward fled the
    keel.
    Pacific here at time's end, bearing corn. –
    Eyes stammer through the pangs of dust
    and steel.*
    Ibid.

Edith Cresson (b. 1934)

FRENCH POLITICIAN AND PRIME MINISTER
*Called the 'fiery socialist equivalent of Margaret
Thatcher', she was appointed France's first woman
prime minister under the presidency of François
Mitterand in 1991, though she resigned within a
year and became a European Commissioner.*

1 Life here is hellish for a woman in politics
   unless she is elderly and ugly.
   Quoted in the *Guardian* 16 May 1991. On becoming Prime Minister.

2 Men are not in any sense irreplaceable,
   except in one's private life.
   Quoted in the *International Herald Tribune*
   20 May 1991

Harry Crews (b. 1935)

US AUTHOR
*A writer of unconventional tales of ostensibly con-
ventional people, he published his first novel* The
Gospel Singers *in 1968, and an acclaimed autobiography* A Childhood *in 1995.*

1 If you give someone a white shirt and a tie
   and a ring of keys you'll find out what kind
   of a son of a bitch he is. Give them to him
   in the morning and you'll know before
   noon.
   Interview in *Dazed and Confused* April 1995

Quentin Crisp (1908–99)

BRITISH AUTHOR AND RACONTEUR
*Originally Dennis Pratt. Following the success of
his autobiography* The Naked Civil Servant
*(1968), he moved permanently to New York. In
1993 he fulfilled his dream to be crowned Queen of
England in the role of Elizabeth I in the film*
Orlando. *'Had surgery existed in my youth,' he
declared, 'I would have had the op and opened a
knitting shop in Carlisle.'*

1 In an expanding universe, time is on the
   side of the outcast. Those who once
   inhabited the suburbs of human contempt
   find that without changing their address
   they eventually live in the metropolis.
   The Naked Civil Servant, ch. 1 (1968)

2 Keeping up with the Joneses was a full-
   time job with my mother and father. It was

not until many years later when I lived
alone that I realized how much cheaper it
was to drag the Joneses down to my level.
Ibid.

3 Masturbation is not only an expression of
   self-regard: it is also the natural emotional
   outlet of those who . . . have already
   accepted as inevitable the wide gulf
   between their real futures and the expectations of their fantasies.
   Ibid., ch. 2

4 Vice is its own reward. It is virtue which, if
   it is to be marketed with consumer appeal,
   must carry Green Shield stamps.
   Ibid., ch. 2

5 The poverty from which I have suffered
   could be diagnosed as 'Soho' poverty. It
   comes from having the airs and graces of a
   genius and no talent.
   Ibid., ch. 7

6 To know all is not to forgive all. It is to
   despise everybody.
   Ibid., ch. 11

7 There was no need to do any housework at
   all. After the first four years the dirt
   doesn't get any worse.
   Ibid., ch. 15

8 Life was a funny thing that happened to
   me on the way to the grave.
   Ibid., ch. 18

9 I became one of the stately homos of
   England.
   Ibid., ch. 24. Alluding to Noël Coward's song
   and Felicia Hemans's poem. See also NOËL
   COWARD 12.

10 An autobiography is an obituary in serial
    form with the last instalment missing.
    Ibid., ch. 29

11 The very purpose of existence is to rec-
    oncile the glowing opinion we have of our-
    selves with the appalling things that other
    people think about us.
    How to Become a Virgin, ch. 2 (1981)

12 It is explained that all relationships require
    a little give and take. This is untrue. Any
    partnership demands that we give and give
    and give and at the last, as we flop into our
    graves exhausted, we are told that we
    didn't give enough.
    Ibid., ch. 4

13 Wherever I am on this earth, I am and
    shall always be only a resident alien.
    People are never with me, they are always
    in my presence. I am never involved in con-
    versation, I am always being interviewed.
    Ibid., 'The End'

14 Living *en famille* provides the strongest

motives for rudeness combined with the maximum opportunity for displaying it.

Manners from Heaven, ch. 2 (1984)

15 Manners are love in a cool climate.

Ibid., ch. 2

16 Euphemisms are not, as many young people think, useless verbiage for that which can and should be said bluntly; they are like secret agents on a delicate mission, they must airily pass by a stinking mess with barely so much as a nod of the head, make their point of constructive criticism and continue on in calm forbearance. Euphemisms are unpleasant truths wearing diplomatic cologne.

Ibid., ch. 5

17 A gentleman doesn't pounce . . . he glides.

Ibid., ch. 6

18 The formula for achieving a successful relationship is simple: you should treat all disasters as if they were trivialities but never treat a triviality as if it were a disaster.

Ibid. ch. 7

19 Love is the extra effort we make in our dealings with those whom we do not like and once you understand that, you understand all. This idea that love overtakes you is nonsense. This is but a polite manifestation of sex. To love another you have to undertake some fragment of their destiny.

'Love Lies Bleeding', TV broadcast on Channel 4, 6 August 1991, publ. in the *New Statesman and Society* 9 August 1991

20 The time comes for everyone to do deliberately what he used to do by mistake. . . . If you are effeminate by nature, you have to find some way of telling the world that you know you are, otherwise they keep telling you.

Quoted in obituary, *The Times* 22 November 1999

Julian Critchley (b. 1930)

BRITISH POLITICIAN

His sceptical and often maverick political views expressed while Conservative MP for Aldershot (1970–97) ensured that he remained an outsider at Westminster, though his newspaper columns and books have kept him in the public eye.

1 The only safe pleasure for a parliamentarian is a bag of boiled sweets.

Listener 10 June 1982. *A Bag of Boiled Sweets* was the title of Critchley's memoirs (1994).

2 She has been beastly to the Bank of England, has demanded that the BBC 'set its house in order' and tends to believe the worst of the Foreign and Commonwealth Office. She cannot see an institution without hitting it with her handbag.

Of MARGARET THATCHER, in *The Times* 21 June 1982

3 In order to succeed in our party the backbencher must be as wise as a dove and as innocent as a serpent. He will, of course, have already recognised that what the party is presently suffering from is an addiction to an *idée en marche*, and he should promptly join the back of the column. Not to be a monetarist in today's party is to suffer from a severe handicap, it is the political equivalent of being young, black and unemployed.

Westminster Blues, ch. 12 (1985)

Richmal Crompton (1890–1969)

BRITISH AUTHOR

Originally Richmal Crompton Lamburn. She made her name with the schoolboy character William Brown, who appeared in magazines from 1919 and in thirty-eight books, starting with Just William *(1922).*

1 I'll thcream and thcream and thcream till I'm thick.

Violet Elizabeth Bott, in *Still William*, ch. 8 (1925). Violet, who demands that William 'play houth' with her, is renowned for her scream: in *William in Trouble* it would 'have put a factory siren to shame' and was 'guaranteed to reduce anyone within ten yards of it to quite an expensive nervous breakdown'.

2 I like you better than *any* insect, Joan.

William, ibid., ch. 14. William explains his intention to marry Joan, the girl next door, as long as he wasn't expected 'to talk a lot of soppy stuff'.

3 There's Conservatives an' they want to make things better by keepin' 'em jus' like what they are now. An' there's Lib'rals an' they want to make things better by alterin' them jus' a bit, but not so's anyone'd notice, an' there's communists an' they want to make things better by killin' everyone but themselves.

Henry, in *William the Bad*, ch. 3 (1930)

David Cronenberg (b. 1943)

CANADIAN FILM-MAKER

Specializing in outlandish and experimental horror films, he has acquired cult status with such films as The Dead Zone *(1983),* The Fly *(1986) and the controversial* Crash *(1996). 'I don't have a moral plan,' he once said, 'I'm a Canadian.'*

1 Everybody's a mad scientist, and life is their lab. We're all trying to experiment to find a way to live, to solve problems, to fend off madness and chaos.

Cronenberg on Cronenberg, ch. 1 (ed. Chris Rodley, 1992)

2 I think of horror films as art, as films of confrontation. Films that make you confront aspects of your own life that are difficult to face. Just because you're making a horror film doesn't mean you can't make an artful film.

Ibid., ch. 4

3 Censors tend to do what only psychotics do: they confuse reality with illusion.

Ibid., ch. 5

Bing Crosby (1903–77)

US SINGER AND ACTOR

Hugely popular throughout a career spanning fifty years, he was known for his rich, crooning voice and roles in light comedy. His version of the song 'White Christmas' (1942) sold more than 25 million copies (see IRVING BERLIN 6*). He co-starred in the* Road to . . . *comedy series,* Going My Way *(1944) and* High Society *(1956).*

1 He was an average guy who could carry a tune.

Suggested epitaph for himself, in *Newsweek* 24 October 1977

Tony Crosland (1918–77)

BRITISH POLITICIAN

Considered Labour's leading intellectual in his time, he became an MP in 1950 and was author of the influential analysis of his party's role, The Future of Socialism *(1956). He held five ministerial positions before his sudden death ten months after becoming Foreign Secretary.*

1 If it's the last thing I do, I'm going to destroy every fucking grammar school in England. And Wales. And Northern Ireland.

Quoted in *Tony Crosland*, ch. 16 (1982). Said to his wife c. 1965, when Crosland was Secretary for Education and Science. 'The school system in Britain remains the most divisive, unjust, and wasteful of all aspects of social equality,' he wrote in *The Future of Socialism.*

Amanda Cross See CAROLYN HEILBRUN.

Richard Crossman (1907–74)

BRITISH POLITICIAN

Elected Labour MP for Coventry East in 1945, he held cabinet posts in the government of HAROLD WILSON. *He is chiefly remembered for the detailed political diary which he kept from 1952, published posthumously. Bessie Braddock described him as 'a man of many opinions, most of them of short duration'.*

1 My Minister's room is like a padded cell, and in certain ways I am like a person who is suddenly certified a lunatic and put safely into this great, vast room, cut off from real life and surrounded by male and female trained nurses and attendants. When I am in a good mood they occasionally allow an ordinary human being to come and visit me; but they make sure that I behave right, and that the other person behaves right; and they know how to handle me. Of course, they don't behave *quite* like nurses because the Civil Service is profoundly deferential – 'Yes, Minister! No, Minister! If you wish it, Minister!'

Journal entry, 22 October 1964, after his first week in the Cabinet as Minister of Housing, publ. in *The Crossman Diaries* (1979). The passage may have been the inspiration for the title of the TV series by ANTONY JAY and JONATHAN LYNN, *Yes, Minister* (1980–85), depicting a minister's relationship with the Civil Service.

Kieran Crowley

US JOURNALIST

A New York Post *reporter since 1978, he has specialized in the coverage of murders, and has written the 'true crime' books,* Sleep Little Dead *(1997) and* Burned Alive *(1999) as well as short fiction.*

1 I realize that to many ageing flower children it is heresy to say it, but the Woodstock festival was a catastrophe mitigated only by the camaraderie often seen at floods or train crashes.

Quoted in the *Daily Telegraph* 18 August 1989

Dan Cruickshank (b. 1949)

BRITISH ARCHITECTURAL CRITIC

A specialist in Georgian architecture. he has worked as features editor of the Architects' *Journal and published books including* Rape of Britain *(1975) and* Life in the Georgian City *(1989).*

1 In short, the building becomes a theatrical demonstration of its functional ideal. In this romanticism, High-Tech architecture is, of course, no different in spirit – if totally different in form – from all the romantic architecture of the past.

Commerce and Culture, ch. 4, 'Tradition' (ed. Stephen Bayley, 1989)

Robert Crumb (b. 1943)

US CARTOONIST

One of America's most influential comic-book artists in the 1960s, he depicted a hippie subculture of political emancipation and sexual freedom. His Zap *(from 1967) is regarded as the first underground comic book.*

1 Keep on truckin' . . . truckin' on down the line . . . hey, hey, hey
I said keep on truckin' . . . truckin' my blues away.

Caption to cartoon, first publ. in *Zap Comix* no. 1 (1967), repr. in *R. Crumb's Head Comix* (1968, rev. 1988). The cartoon showed various large-booted characters walking through the city. 'Keep on truckin'' became one of the key hippie slogans of the 1960s and '70s, and was the subject of litigation proceedings over copyright ownership.

2 **When people are forced to deny their natural urges they get weird, twisted and mean.**

Interview in *The Apex Treasury of Underground Comics* (ed. Susan Goodrick and Don Donahue, 1974)

Billy Crystal (b. 1947)

US ACTOR

Originally a stand-up comedian, he came to public attention in Soap (1977–81), playing the first openly gay role on a US sitcom. He later starred in the films When Harry Met Sally *(1989) and* City Slickers *(1991). See also* NORA EPHRON 3.

1 **Women need a reason to have sex. Men just need a place.**

Mitch Robbins (Billy Crystal), in *City Slickers* (film, 1991, screenplay by Lowell Ganz and Babaloo Mandel, directed by Ron Underwood)

Macaulay Culkin (b. 1980)

US ACTOR

The epitome of blond-headed cuteness, he made his stage debut at the age of four, and was the star of Home Alone *(1990), becoming for a time one of the highest paid stars in Hollywood.*

1 **Families suck! I wish they would all disappear.**

Kevin (Macaulay Culkin), in *Home Alone* (film, 1990, screenplay by John Hughes, directed by Chris Columbus)

E. E. Cummings (1894–1962)

US POET

Edward Estlin Cummings. He won international acclaim with The Enormous Room *(1922), an account of his wartime internment in France, but is now chiefly remembered for his poetry, either satirical or lyrical and set out in unorthodox typography.*

1 *Humanity i love you because*
when you're hard up you pawn your
intelligence to buy a drink

'La Guerre no. 2', publ in *XLI Poems* (1925)

2 **It is with roses and locomotives (not to mention acrobats Spring electricity Coney Island the 4th of July the eyes of mice and Niagara Falls) that my 'poems' are competing.**

is 5, Foreword (1926)

3 *'next to of course god america i*
love you land of the pilgrims' and so forth
oh

say can you see by the dawn's early my
country 'tis of centuries come and go
and are no more what of it we should
worry
in every language even deafanddumb
thy sons acclaim your glorious name by
gorry
by jingo by gee by gosh by gum

'next to of course god america i', ibid. (1926)

4 **The tabloid newspaper actually means to the typical American of the era what the Bible is popularly supposed to have meant to the typical Pilgrim Father:** *viz.* **a very present help in times of trouble, plus a means of keeping out of trouble via harmless, since vicarious, indulgence in the pomps and vanities of this wicked world.**

'The Tabloid Newspaper', publ. in *Vanity Fair* December 1926, repr. in *A Miscellany* (ed. George J. Firmage, 1958)

5 **America makes prodigious mistakes, America has colossal faults, but one thing cannot be denied: America is always on the move. She may be going to Hell, of course, but at least she isn't standing still.**

'Why I Like America', publ. in *Vanity Fair* May 1927, repr. ibid.

6 *a politician is an arse upon*
which everyone has sat except a man.

1 x 1, 'No. 10' (1944)

7 *pity this busy monster, manunkind,*
not. Progress is a comfortable disease.

Ibid., 'No. 14'

8 *We doctors know*
a hopeless case if – listen: there's a hell
of a good universe next door; let's go.

Ibid.

9 *when man determined to destroy*
himself he picked the was
of shall and finding only why
smashed it into because

Ibid., 'No. 26'

10 *anyone lived in a pretty how town*
(with up so floating many bells down)
spring summer autumn winter
he sang his didn't he danced his did.

50 Poems, 'No. 29' (1949)

11 **It takes three to make a child.**

'Jottings', first publ. in *Wake* no. 10 (1951), repr. in *A Miscellany* (ed. George J. Firmage, 1958)

12 **Knowledge is a polite word for dead but not buried imagination.**

Ibid.

13 *for whatever we lose (like a you or a me)*
it's always ourselves we find in the sea

'maggie and milly and molly and may', publ. in *95 Poems* (1958)

14 The sensual mysticism of entire vertical
being.
Of New York City, quoted in the *Architectural
Digest* September 1986

William Thomas Cummings
(1903–45)
US PRIEST

1 There are no atheists in the foxholes.
Sermon, Bataan (1942), quoted in *I Saw the Fall
of the Philippines*, ch. 1 (1943) by Carlos P.
Romulo. The peninsula saw ferocious fighting
when it was heroically defended for three
months by US and Filipino forces. Its capture by
the Japanese in April 1942 was followed by the
notorious 'Bataan death march', in which thousands died.

Mario Cuomo (b. 1932)
US POLITICIAN
*A Democrat, he held office as Governor of New
York (1983–94) and was regarded as a potential
presidential nominee in 1984, 1988 and 1992.*

1 You campaign in poetry. You govern in
prose.
New Republic 8 April 1985

Edwina Currie (b. 1946)
BRITISH POLITICIAN AND AUTHOR
*She became Conservative MP for Derbyshire
South in 1983, and was Minister for Women's
Health (1986–8). Since losing her seat in 1997, she
has established herself as a novelist and radio pre-
senter on Radio 5 Live.*

1 Good Christian people who wouldn't
dream of misbehaving will not catch Aids.
My message to the businessmen of this
country when they go abroad on business
is that there is one thing above all they can
take with them to stop them catching Aids
– and that is the wife.
Speech at Runcorn, Cheshire, 12 February 1987,
quoted in the *Guardian* 13 February 1987

2 Most of the egg production in this
country sadly is now infected with sal-
monella.
TV interview, 3 March 1988. Currie's statement
led to a national outcry and her resignation a
fortnight later.

Richard Curtis (b. 1956)
BRITISH SCREENWRITER
*An accomplished comedy writer, he describes him-
self as a 'great campaigner for light-hearted
cinema'. For TV he co-wrote the* Blackadder
(1984–9) and Mr Bean *(1989–95) series for
Rowan Atkinson, and for the cinema the
screenplays of* Four Weddings and a Funeral
(1994) and Notting Hill *(1999).*

1 So basically you're saying marriage is just
a way of getting out of an embarrassing
pause in conversation.
Charles (Hugh Grant), in *Four Weddings and a
Funeral* (film, 1994, screenplay by Richard
Curtis, directed by Mike Newell). Gareth
answers, 'Yup. The definitive ice-breaker.'

2 It's pretty easy. Just say 'I do' whenever
anyone asks you a question.
Carrie (Andie MacDowell), ibid.

Lord Curzon (1859–1925)
BRITISH POLITICIAN
Described by LLOYD GEORGE *as 'a supreme civil
servant' and by* MAX BEERBOHM *as 'Britannia's
butler', he was Viceroy of India 1898–1905, and
Foreign Secretary in the Conservative government
(1919–24). A verse composed about him while he
was at Oxford encapsulated one image of him: 'My
name is George Nathaniel Curzon,/I am a most
superior person,/My cheek is pink, my hair is
sleek,/I dine at Blenheim twice a week.'*

1 Dear me, I never knew that the lower
classes had such white skins.
Attributed in *Superior Person*, ch. 12 (1969) by
Kenneth Rose. The words were supposedly said
by Curzon when touring the lines as a member
of the War Cabinet during the First World War,
when he saw troops bathing in beer kegs.

2 Not even a public figure. A man of no
experience. And of the utmost insignificance.
Of STANLEY BALDWIN, quoted in *Curzon: the
Last Phase*, ch. 12 (1934) by Harold Nicolson.
Curzon is supposed to have made the remark on
hearing that Baldwin had become Prime Minister in 1923, a post Curzon himself had long
aspired to. His rancour was suggested in a
remark attributed to Baldwin when PM: 'I met
Curzon in Downing Street, from whom I got the
sort of greeting a corpse would give to an
undertaker.'

D:Ream
British pop group

1 **Things Can Only Get Better.**
Song title (written by Jame Petrie and Peter Cunnah, 1993). The song reached the top thirty in early 1993 and was number one when re-mixed in 1994. Chosen as New Labour's election anthem in 1997, it was re-issued and peaked at number nineteen.

Edward Dahlberg (1900–1977)
US AUTHOR AND CRITIC
His travels as a hobo formed the basis for his first novels. In later life, he became something of a 'literary Jeremiah', attacking American materialism.

1 **The earnings of a poet could be reckoned by a metaphysician rather than a bookkeeper.**
Alms for Oblivion, 'For Sale' (1964)

2 **To write is a humiliation.**
The Carnal Myth, Introduction (1968)

Daily Express

1 **It's that man again . . . !**
Headline in the *Daily Express* 2 May 1939, referring to HITLER. The acronym ITMA was the title of a weekly satire on BBC radio (1939–49) starring Tommy Handley

Daily Mirror

1 **Whose finger do you want on the trigger?**
Headline in the *Daily Mirror* 21 September 1951. Warning against electing the Conservative Party into power in the coming general election.

Dalai Lama (Tenzin Gyatso)
(b. 1935)
SPIRITUAL AND TEMPORAL HEAD OF TIBET
He assumed his role as Dalai Lama in 1940, but he and his followers were forced to flee Tibet after the unsuccessful uprising against the occupying Chinese forces. He set up a government-in-exile in Dharamsala, India.

1 **I have done nothing, really nothing for world peace. The only thing I do for peace is talk about it a great deal.**
Interview in the *Sunday Telegraph* 9 August 1998

Richard J. Daley (1902–76)
US POLITICIAN
Richard Joseph Daley. One of the last of the big city bosses, he was Democratic Mayor of Chicago from 1955 until his death, ruling through an efficient 'Daley Machine'. His influence in Illinois is thought to have ensured the return of JOHN KENNEDY in the presidential election of 1960.

1 **The policeman isn't there to create disorder; the policeman is there to preserve disorder.**
To the press, on the riots during the Democratic Convention in 1968, quoted in *Don't Make No Waves: Don't Back No Losers* (1975) by Milton N. Rakove. Daley was well known for his malapropisms. Others include: 'Ladies and gentlemen of the League of Women Voters' and 'It is amazing what they will be able to do once they get the atom harassed.'

Salvador Dalí (1904–89)
SPANISH ARTIST
He became the most high-profile member of the Paris Surrealists which he joined in 1928, though they later spurned him. 'The Persistence of Memory' (better known as 'Limp Watches', 1931) is probably the best known example of his dream-like juxtapositions. For ANDRÉ BRETON *'Dalí is like a man who hesitates between talent and genius, or, as one might once have said, between vice and virtue.'*

1 **Picasso is Spanish, I am too. Picasso is a genius. I am too. Picasso will be seventy-two and I about forty-eight. Picasso is known in every country of the world; so am I. Picasso is a Communist; I am not.**
Lecture in Madrid, 12 October 1951, quoted in *Dalí*, ch. 12 (1992) by Meredith Etherington-Smith. Dalí's lecture contained an apology to the Spanish Left who had branded him a coward and renegade during the Spanish Civil War, and a condemnation of PICASSO's espousal of Communism and his absence from Spain.

2 **There is only one difference between a madman and me. I am not mad.**
Journal entry, May 1952, in *Diary of a Genius* (1966)

3 **Don't bother about being modern. Unfortunately it is the one thing that, whatever you do, you cannot avoid.**
Journal entry, 15 July 1952, ibid.

4 **I seated ugliness on my knee, and almost immediately grew tired of it.**
Journal entry, 1 August 1953, ibid. Dalí's words echo those of Rimbaud: 'One evening I sat Beauty on my knees – And I found her bitter – And I reviled her.' (*Une Saison en enfer*, 1874)

5 **This grandiose tragedy that we call modern art.**
Dalí by Dalí, 'The Futuristic Dalí' (1970)

Daniel Daly (1874–1937)
GUNNERY SERGEANT, US MARINES

1 **Come on you sons of bitches! Do you want to live for ever?**
Attributed, at Belleau Wood, 4 June 1918. A similar exhortation was said to have been made by

Frederick the Great, 18 June 1757, when rallying his troops at Kolin, Bohemia.

Mary Daly (b. 1928)
US THEOLOGIAN AND AUTHOR
Her books, for example The Church and the Second Sex *(1968) and* Beyond God the Father *(1973), address the male bias in the Roman Catholic church from a feminist viewpoint.*

1 **If God is male, then male is God. The divine patriarch castrates women as long as he is allowed to live on in the human imagination.**
Beyond God the Father, ch. 1 (1973)

Serge Daney (1944–92)
FRENCH FILM CRITIC
Regarded as one of France's greatest film critics, he was Editor of Cahiers du Cinéma *(1973–81), and contributed film columns to* Libération *during the 1980s.*

1 **In an age of synthetic images and synthetic emotions, the chances of an accidental encounter with reality are remote indeed.**
'Falling out of Love', publ. in *Sight and Sound* July 1992

Joe Darion (1917–2001)
US SONGWRITER
He was the lyricist for a number of Broadway musical shows in the 1960s, most successful of which was Man of La Mancha *(1965, filmed 1972).*

1 *To dream the impossible dream,*
   To reach the unreachable star!
'The Impossible Dream' (song, 1965, music by Mitch Leigh). The song (sung by Simon Gilbert) was dubbed onto the film *Man of La Mancha* (1972, adapted from the 1965 musical play by Darion and Mitch Leigh) for PETER O'TOOLE, in the role of Don Quixote, to mime to.

Linda Darnell (1921–65)
US SCREEN ACTRESS
Originally Monetta Eloisa Darnell. She was one of Hollywood's most popular leading ladies of the 1940s, in such films as It Happened Tomorrow *(1944).* JOAN COLLINS *commented: 'She was a firm believer in moving her facial muscles as little as possible.'*

1 **I used to live in a sewer. Now I live in a swamp. I've come up in the world.**
Edie Johnson (Linda Darnell), in *No Way Out* (film, 1950, screenplay by Lesser Samuels and Joseph L. Mankiewicz, directed by Joseph L. Mankiewicz)

James Darren (b. 1936)
US SCREEN ACTOR AND SINGER
Originally James William Ercolani. He was a teen idol in the 1950s, most famously in the film Gidget

(1956). His hit songs include 'Goodbye Cruel World' (1961).

1 **Maybe I'm gonna die. You've got even bigger problems – you're gonna live.**

Johnny Rico (James Darren) to his brother, in *The Brothers Rico* (film, 1957, screenplay by Lewis Meltzer and Ben Perry adapted from GEORGES SIMENON's novella, directed by Phil Karlson)

Charles Brace Darrow (1889–1967)
US INVENTOR

When Parker Bros rejected his game Monopoly, he produced and marketed it himself. Parker Bros subsequently took up the option in 1935, since when over 200 million sets in twenty-six languages have been sold.

1 **Go to jail. Go directly to jail. Do not pass go. Do not collect $200.**

Instruction in *Monopoly* (1933). *Monopoly* was devised by Darrow *c.* 1931, adapted from *The Landlord's Game* invented by Joanna Pitman in 1904.

Clarence Darrow (1857–1938)
US LAWYER AND WRITER

As a leading defence counsel he opposed capital punishment, Prohibition and segregation. His most famous cases were those of EUGENE DEBS, who called the Pullman Strike (1894), and the so-called 'monkey trial' of John T. Scopes (1925).

1 **I do not pretend to know where many ignorant men are sure – that is all that agnosticism means.**

Speech at Dayton, Tennessee, 13 July 1925, quoted in *The World's Most Famous Court Trial* ch. 4 (1925). Darrow was defending John Thomas Scopes on trial for teaching Darwinism. Scopes was found guilty, though the decision was later overturned by the State Supreme Court.

2 **When I was a boy I was told that anybody could become President. I'm beginning to believe it.**

Quoted in *Clarence Darrow for the Defence*, ch. 6 (1941) by Irving Stone

(Sir) Francis Darwin (1848–1925)
BRITISH BOTANIST

He is known for his publications relating to his father, Charles Darwin, as well as for his work on vegetable physiology.

1 **In science the credit goes to the man who convinces the world, not to the man to whom the idea first occurs.**

'Francis Galton', First Galton Lecture before the Eugenics Society, publ. in *Eugenics Review* April 1914

René Daumal (1908–44)
FRENCH POET AND CRITIC

He was co-founder in 1928 of Le Grand Jeu, *both a review and a quasi-mystical group. His posthumous fame rests principally on his novels,* A Night of Serious Drinking *(1938) and* Mount Analogue *(1952).*

1 **Each time dawn appears, the mystery is there in its entirety.**

'Poetry Black, Poetry White', first publ. in *Fontaine* March/April 1942, repr. in *The Powers of the Word* (ed./transl. Mark Polizzotti, 1991). *Chaque fois que l'aube paraît* was the title given to a posthumous anthology of Daumal's writings.

Andrew Davies (b. 1936)
BRITISH SCREENWRITER

He has made skilful TV adaptations of classic novels, including Pride and Prejudice *(1995),* Wives and Daughters *(1999) and* Daniel Deronda *(2002).*

1 **You might say that, my dear: I couldn't possibly comment.**

Francis Urquhart (Ian Richardson) to the journalist Mattie Storin (Susannah Harker), in *House of Cards* (TV series, 1992, written by Andrew Davies, based on the original novel by Michael Dobbs)

Jack Davies (1913–94) and
Ken Annakin (b. 1914)
BRITISH SCREENWRITER AND BRITISH DIRECTOR

Davies was a comedy scriptwriter for Will Hay, Norman Wisdom and the 'Doctor' series of films. Annakin is better known as the director of such films as Swiss Family Robinson *(1960) and* The Fast Lady *(1963).*

1 **Those Magnificent Men in Their Flying Machines, or How I Flew from London to Paris in 25 Hours and 11 Minutes.**

Title of film (1965, screenplay by Jack Davies and Ken Annakin, directed by Ken Annakin). The film, from which an eponymous song was penned, was a comic account of the first London–Paris air race at the beginning of the twentieth century.

Robertson Davies (1913–95)
CANADIAN NOVELIST AND JOURNALIST

Described as 'Jane Austen reworking Rabelais', he is known for his articles written under the pseudonym Samuel Marchbanks, and for his tales of provincial life the Deptford Trilogy (1970–5) and the Cornish Trilogy (1981–8).

1 **Nothing is so easy to fake as the inner vision.**

Saraceni, in *What's Bred in the Bone*, pt 4, 'What Would Not out of the Flesh?' (1985)

2 Canada is not really a place where you are encouraged to have large spiritual adventures.

The Enthusiasms of Robertson Davies, 'The Table Talk of Robertson Davies' (1990)

3 The world is burdened with young fogies. Old men with ossified minds are easily dealt with. But men who look young, act young and everlastingly harp on the fact that they are young, but who nevertheless think and act with a degree of caution that would be excessive in their grandfathers, are the curse of the world. Their very conservatism is secondhand, and they don't know what they are conserving.

Ibid.

W. H. Davies (1871–1940)

BRITISH POET AND AUTHOR

William Henry Davies. He published numerous collections of verse, but his most successful work was an account of his itinerant life, Autobiography of a Super-tramp *(1906).*

1 And hear the pleasant cuckoo, loud and long –
The simple bird that thinks two notes a song.

'April's Charms', publ. in *Child Lovers* (1916)

2 Girls scream,
Boys shout;
Dogs bark,
School's out.

'School's Out', publ. in *The Poems of W. H. Davies* (1934)

Angela Davis (b. 1944)

US PHILOSOPHER AND POLITICAL ACTIVIST

Combining an academic career with a commitment to black rights, she gained international publicity in 1970 when she was acquitted of charges of supplying guns for the murder of a judge. In 1980 she was the Communist vice-presidential candidate.

1 No potential victim of the fascist terror should be without the knowledge that the greatest menace to racism and fascism is unity!

If They Come in the Morning . . . , pt 2, 'Political Prisoners, Prisons and Black Liberation' (1971)

Bette Davis (1908–89)

US SCREEN ACTRESS

Originally Ruth Elizabeth Davis. She played strong, independent roles for more than five decades, memorably opposite Joan Crawford in Whatever Happened to Baby Jane? *(1962).* JACK L. WARNER *remembered her as 'an explosive little broad with a straight left'.*

1 Oh, Jerry, don't let's ask for the moon – we have the stars.

Charlotte Vale (Bette Davis), in *Now, Voyager* (film, 1942, screenplay by Casey Robinson based on the 1941 novel by Olive Higgins Prouty, directed by Irving Rapper). The movie's title is taken from Walt Whitman's *Leaves of Grass*.

2 What a dump!

Rosa Moline (Bette Davis) in *Beyond the Forest* (film, 1949, screenplay by Leonore Coffee based on a novel by Stuart Engstrand, directed by King Vidor). The line, which is spoken by Bette Davis about her small-town Wisconsin home which she dreams of escaping, was famously used in EDWARD ALBEE's *Who's Afraid of Virginia Woolf?* (1962). In the film version of this (1966), Martha (Elizabeth Taylor) mimics Bette Davis' voice. According to Davis, 'this is the only claim to fame that the film [*Beyond the Forest*] had or ever will have.'

3 Fasten your seat belts. It's going to be a bumpy night.

Margo Channing (Bette Davis), bracing for an inauspicious party, in *All About Eve* (film, 1950, written and directed by Joseph L. Mankiewicz)

4 To look back is to relax one's vigil.

The Lonely Life, ch. 1 (autobiography, 1962)

5 I see – she's the original good time that was had by all.

Attributed in *Parade* 15 February 1981, referring to a starlet

Geena Davis (b. 1957)

US SCREEN ACTRESS

Called 'a feminist spirit in the body of a goddess', she won acclaim for her roles in The Accidental Tourist *(1988) and the women's road movie* Thelma and Louise *(1991).*

1 I finally understand what all the fuss is about now. It's just like a whole other ball game.

Thelma (Geena Davis) on the subject of sex, in *Thelma and Louise* (film, 1991, screenplay by Callie Khouri, directed and co-produced by Ridley Scott)

Miles Davis (1926–91)

US JAZZ MUSICIAN

Arguably the most influential post-war jazz stylist and trumpet player, he pioneered 'cool' jazz (with the album Birth of the Cool, *1949), modal improvisation (*Kind of Blue, *1959), and jazz–rock fusion (*Bitches' Brew, *1970).*

1 I've come close to matching the feeling of that night in 1944 in music, when I first heard Diz and Bird, but I've never got there . . . I'm always looking for it, listening and feeling for it, though, trying to always feel it in and through the music I play everyday.

Miles: The Autobiography, Prologue (1989).

Referring to Dizzy Gillespie and Charlie 'Bird' Parker.

2 A legend is an old man with a cane known for what he used to do. I'm still doing it.

International Herald Tribune 17 July 1991

Sammy Davis Jr (1925–90)

US ENTERTAINER

In his own words a 'one-eyed Jewish Negro', he was an accomplished singer, tap dancer, musician, mime and comedian. He starred in Broadway musicals such as Mr Wonderful *(1956), and also appeared in films.*

1 Being a star has made it possible for me to get insulted in places where the average Negro could never hope to go and get insulted.

Yes I Can, pt 3, ch. 23 (1965)

Richard Dawkins (b. 1941)

BRITISH BIOLOGIST AND AUTHOR

The Selfish Gene *(1976) was the first of a series of books which helped to explain and popularize sociobiology from a Darwinian perspective. In 1995 he became the first Professor of Public Understanding of Science at Oxford.*

1 Much as we might wish to believe otherwise, universal love and the welfare of the species as a whole are concepts which simply do not make evolutionary sense.

The Selfish Gene, ch. 1 (1976)

2 They are in you and in me; they created us, body and mind; and their preservation is the ultimate rationale for our existence – they go by the name of genes, and we are their survival machines.

Ibid., ch. 2

3 Natural selection, the blind, unconscious, automatic process which Darwin discovered, and which we now know is the explanation for the existence and apparently purposeful form of all life, has no purpose in mind. It has no mind and no mind's eye. It does not plan for the future. It has no vision, no foresight, no sight at all. If it can be said to play the role of the watchmaker in nature, it is the *blind* watchmaker.

The Blind Watchmaker, ch. 1 (1986)

4 However many ways there may be of being alive, it is certain that there are vastly more ways of being dead.

Ibid.

5 The essence of life is statistical improbability on a colossal scale.

Ibid., ch. 11

6 The universe we observe has precisely the properties we should expect if there is, at bottom, no design, no purpose, no evil and no good, nothing but blind, pitiless indifference. . . . DNA neither cares nor knows. DNA just is. And we dance to its music.

River out of Eden, ch. 4 (1995)

7 We are going to die, and that makes us the lucky ones. Most people are never going to die because they are never going to be born.

Unweaving the Rainbow, ch. 1 (1998). Opening lines of book.

8 The spirit of wonder which led Blake to Christian mysticism, Keats to Arcadian myth and Yeats to Fenians and fairies, is the very same spirit that moves great scientists; a spirit which, if fed back to poets in scientific guise, might inspire still greater poetry.

Ibid., ch. 2

9 If we want to sustain the planet into the future, the first thing we must do is stop taking advice from nature. Nature is a short-term Darwinian profiteer.

Observer 21 May 2000. Open letter to Prince Charles in response to his Reith Lecture. See CHARLES, PRINCE OF WALES 9.

Christopher Dawson (1889–1970)

BRITISH HISTORIAN

An esteemed Catholic scholar, he published works on European history, culture and religion, including The Age of the Gods *(1928) and* Religion and Culture *(1948).*

1 As soon as men decide that all means are permitted to fight an evil, then their good becomes indistinguishable from the evil that they set out to destroy.

The Judgement of the Nations (1942)

Lord Dawson of Penn (1864–1945)

BRITISH PHYSICIAN

Bertrand Edward Dawson, Viscount Dawson of Penn. Physician to several members of the British royal family, he helped to draw up a white paper for the inception of the National Health Service in 1944.

1 The King's life is moving peacefully towards its close.

Bulletin on the eve of the king's death, 20 January 1936, in *King George V*, ch. 1 (1983) by Kenneth Rose. The wording was supposedly drafted on a menu card at Buckingham Palace.

Dorothy Day (1897–1980)

US REFORMER AND AUTHOR

A socialist, pacifist and Catholic convert, she co-founded the Catholic Worker *in 1933 and established the Catholic Worker movement, which aided victims of the Depression.*

1 Tradition! We scarcely know the word anymore. We are afraid to be either proud of

our ancestors or ashamed of them. We scorn nobility in name and in fact. We cling to a bourgeois mediocrity which would make it appear we are all Americans, made in the image and likeness of George Washington.

The Long Loneliness, pt 1 (1952)

2 The best thing to do with the best things in life is to give them up.

Quoted in *Time* 29 December 1975

(Sir) Robin Day (1915–2000)

BRITISH JOURNALIST AND BROADCASTER

Known for his formidable interviewing techniques, he presented on BBC television Panorama *(1967–72) and* Question Time *(1979–89), and on radio* The World at One *(1979–87).*

1 Television thrives on unreason, and unreason thrives on television. It strikes at the emotions rather than the intellect.

Financial Times 8 November 1989

2 I am in the departure lounge of life; my only hope is that my plane will be delayed.

Speech at Oxford Union, quoted in the *Daily Telegraph* 21 February 1998

Cecil Day Lewis (1904–72)

BRITISH POET

Initially influenced by W. H. AUDEN *and his circle, he later became more of an Establishment figure, Professor of Poetry at Oxford (1951–6) and appointed Poet Laureate in 1968.*

1 *Desire is a witch*
And runs against the clock.
It can unstitch
The decent hem
Where space tacks on to time;
It can unlock
Pandora's privacies.

Transitional Poem, pt 2 (1929)

2 *With me, my lover makes*
The clock assert its chime:
But when she goes, she takes
The mainspring out of time.

Ibid., pt 3, sect. 27

3 *Tempt me no more; for I*
Have known the lightning's hour,
The poet's inward pride,
The certainty of power.

The Magnetic Mountain, sect. 24 (1933)

4 *You that love England, who have an ear for*
her music,
The slow movement of clouds in ben-
ediction,
Clear arias of light thrilling over her
uplands,
Over the chords of summer sustained
peacefully.

Ibid., sect. 32

5 *We'd like to fight but we fear defeat,*
We'd like to work but we're feeling too
weak,
We'd like to be sick but we'd get the sack,
We'd like to behave, we'd like to believe,
We'd like to love, but we've lost the knack.

Ibid., sect. 33

6 *It is the logic of our times,*
No subject for immortal verse –
That we who lived by honest dreams
Defend the bad against the worse.

'Where are the War Poets?', publ. in *Word Over All* (1943)

7 *Hurry! We burn*
For Rome so near us, for the Phoenix
moment
When we have thrown off this traveller's
trance,
And mother-naked and ageless-ancient
Wake in her warm nest of renaissance.

An Italian Visit, pt 2, 'Flight to Italy' (written 1948–9, publ. 1953)

8 *I went to school with a glee of dolphins*
Bowling their hoops round the brine
tongued isles.

Ibid., pt 5, 'Florence: Works of Art'

Daniel Day Lewis (b. 1957)

BRITISH ACTOR

The son of CECIL DAY LEWIS, *he gained critical acclaim for his roles in* My Beautiful Laundrette *(1985) and* Gangs of New York *(2002).*

1 Being at the centre of a film is a burden one takes on with innocence – the first time. Thereafter, you take it on with trepidation.

Interview in *City Limits* 7 April 1988

2 The thing about performance, even if it's only an illusion, is that it is a celebration of the fact that we do contain within ourselves infinite possibilities.

Interview in *Rolling Stone* 8 February 1990

Simone de Beauvoir (1908–86)

FRENCH PHILOSOPHER AND AUTHOR

A celebrated feminist and existentialist, she had a lifelong association with JEAN-PAUL SARTRE, *with whom she founded the review* Les Temps modernes *(1945). Her book* The Second Sex *(1949) became a classic feminist text.*

1 It is not in giving life but in risking life that man is raised above the animal; that is why superiority has been accorded in humanity not to the sex that brings forth but to that which kills.

The Second Sex, bk 1, pt 2, ch. 1 (1949)

2 One is not born, but rather becomes, a woman.

Ibid., bk 2, pt 4, ch. 1. Feminist critic ANDREA

DWORKIN was perhaps alluding to de Beauvoir's famous statement when she wrote: 'Woman is not born: she is made. In the making, her humanity is destroyed. She becomes symbol of this, symbol of that: mother of the earth, slut of the universe; but she never becomes herself because it is forbidden for her to do so.' (*Pornography*, ch. 4, 1981)

3 To *make* oneself an object, to *make* oneself passive, is a very different thing from *being* a passive object.
Ibid., bk 2, pt 4, ch. 3

4 Sex pleasure in woman . . . is a kind of magic spell; it demands complete abandon; if words or movements oppose the magic of caresses, the spell is broken.
Ibid.

5 Between women love is contemplative; caresses are intended less to gain possession of the other than gradually to recreate the self through her; separateness is abolished, there is no struggle, no victory, no defeat; in exact reciprocity each is at once subject and object, sovereign and slave; duality become mutuality.
Ibid., bk 2, pt 4, ch. 4

6 The curse which lies upon marriage is that too often the individuals are joined in their weakness rather than in their strength – each asking from the other instead of finding pleasure in giving. It is even more deceptive to dream of gaining through the child a plenitude, a warmth, a value, which one is unable to create for oneself; the child brings joy only to the woman who is capable of disinterestedly desiring the happiness of another, to one who without being wrapped up in self seeks to transcend her own existence.
Ibid., bk 2, pt 5, ch. 2

7 Since it is the Other within us who is old, it is natural that the revelation of our age should come to us from outside – from others. We do not accept it willingly.
The Coming of Age, pt 2, ch. 5 (1970)

8 It is old age, rather than death, that is to be contrasted with life. Old age is life's parody, whereas death transforms life into a destiny: in a way it preserves it by giving it the absolute dimension. . . . Death does away with time.
Ibid. Conclusion

Louis de Bernières (b. 1951)
BRITISH NOVELIST
His stories are concerned with issues of freedom, power and ideology, as in Captain Corelli's Mandolin (1994, filmed 2001). *Among his other books are* Señor Vivo and the Coca Lord (1992) *and* Red Dog (2001).

1 A guilty man wishes only to be understood, because to be understood is to appear to be forgiven.
Carlo, in *Captain Corelli's Mandolin*, ch. 10 (1994)

2 It's a fact of life that the honour of a family derives from the conduct of its women. I don't know why this is, and possibly matters are different elsewhere. But we live here, and I note the fact scientifically in the same way that I observe that there is snow on Mt Aenos in January and that we have no rivers.
Dr Iannis, ibid., ch. 47

3 Italians always act without thinking, it's the glory and the downfall of your civilisation. A German plans a month in advance what his bowel movements will be at Easter, and the British plan everything in retrospect, so it always looks as though everything occurred as they intended. The French plan everything whilst appearing to be having a party, and the Spanish . . . well, God knows.
Dr Iannis to Captain Corelli, ibid., ch. 49

4 Every Greek, man, woman, and child, has two Greeks inside. We even have technical terms for them. They are a part of us, as inevitable as the fact that we all write poetry and the fact that every one of us thinks that he knows everything that there is to know.
Ibid. The two types, Iannis explained, correspond to the 'Hellene' and the 'Romoi'.

5 God is an oppressor, He is incapable of human sympathy; behind a smiling face He hides an evil heart.
The Book of Job, Introduction (1998)

6 The real index of civilisation is when people are kinder than they need be.
Robert, in 'The Turks are So Wonderful with Children', publ. in the *Guardian* 1 January 2000

Joost de Blank (1908–68)
SOUTH AFRICAN CHURCHMAN
Archbishop of Cape Town 1957–63.

1 Christ in this country would quite likely have been arrested under the Suppression of Communism Act.
Quoted in the *Observer* 27 October 1963

Edward De Bono (b. 1933)
BRITISH PSYCHOLOGIST
His concept of 'lateral thinking' as a creative approach to problem solving was first propounded in The Use of Lateral Thinking (1967) *and has since been widely used in business and management studies.*

1 Some people are aware of another sort of thinking which . . . leads to those simple ideas that are obvious only after they have been thought of . . . the term 'lateral thinking' has been coined to describe this other sort of thinking; 'vertical thinking' is used to denote the conventional logical process.
The Use of Lateral Thinking, Foreword (1967)

2 Unhappiness is best defined as the difference between our talents and our expectations.
Quoted in the *Observer* 12 June 1977

3 Humour is by far the most significant activity of the human brain.
Daily Mail 29 January 1990

Michel de Certeau (1925–86)
FRENCH AUTHOR AND CRITIC
Formerly a Jesuit priest, he was a psychoanalytic theorist, an erudite historian and ethnologist, and an influential postmodern cultural critic, whose publications include The Practice of Everyday Life *(1974) and* La Fable mystique *(1982).*

1 The only freedom supposed to be left to the masses is that of grazing on the ration of simulacra the system distributes to each individual.
The Practice of Everyday Life, ch. 12 (1974)

Malcolm de Chazal (1902–81)
FRENCH AUTHOR
From semi-isolation on Mauritius he wrote his major work Sens plastique *(1946), which described the sexual act as a mediator between birth and death and caused a sensation when published in Paris.*

1 The idealist walks on tiptoe, the materialist on his heels.
Sens plastique, vol. 2 (1946)

Luciano de Crescenzo (b. 1928)
ITALIAN AUTHOR
His wide-ranging interests are reflected in his various publications, which include Thus Spake Bellavista *(1977), an account of Naples, and* History of Greek Philosophy: The Pre-Socratics *(1983).*

1 A Neapolitan will tell you that he has never paid to watch a football match with as much pride as if he were telling you, for instance, that his ancestors fought in the Crusades. If, on the other hand, anyone in Naples finds himself having to pay for a ticket, it means he's a failure, he knows nobody and counts for nothing.
Antonio Caramanna, in *Thus Spake Bellavista*, ch. 6 (1977, transl. 1988)

Lee De Forest (1873–1961)
US PHYSICIST AND INVENTOR
Following his invention of the Audion vacuum tube in 1906, he made significant contributions to the development of radio and telephone, as well as radar, television and computers.

1 You have debased [my] child. . . . You have made him a laughing-stock of intelligence . . . a stench in the nostrils of the gods of the ionosphere.
Speech to National Association of Broadcasters, quoted in obituary in *Time* 7 July 1961

Charles de Gaulle (1890–1970)
FRENCH GENERAL AND PRESIDENT
Having directed the Free French movement from Britain during the Second World War, he led the provisional French government (1944–6) and was architect and first president of the Fifth Republic (1959–69). He bequeathed to France 'Gaullism' as a political philosophy and a Gaullist party.

1 Nothing strengthens authority so much as silence.
Quoted in *The Art of Living*, 'The Art of Leadership' (1940) by André Maurois

2 France has lost a battle. But France has not lost the war!
Speech in London, broadcast 18 June 1940, publ. in *Speeches of General de Gaulle* (1941). De Gaulle's famous words were not part of the official typescript for this speech, and not issued in written form until the following month.

3 Since they whose duty it was to wield the sword of France have let it fall shattered to the ground, I have taken up the broken blade.
Speech, 13 July 1940, publ. in *Discours et messages* (1942)

4 Now she is like everybody else.
(*Maintenant elle est comme les autres.*)
Remark at the funeral of his handicapped daughter, Anne, 1948, quoted in *De Gaulle*, ch. 8 (1965) by Jean Lacouture. De Gaulle was devoted to his daughter, who had Down's Syndrome. 'Without Anne,' he explained, 'perhaps I should not have done all that I have done. She made me understand so many things. She gave me so much heart and spirit.'

5 The French will only be united under the threat of danger. How else can one govern a country that produces 246 different kinds of cheese?
Speech, 1951, quoted in *Les Mots du Général* (ed. Ernest Mignon, 1962)

6 I have understood you.
(*Je vous ai compris.*)
Speech at Algiers, 4 June 1958, publ. in *Discours et messages*, vol. 3 (1970). De Gaulle was addressing French settlers, whose interests were threatened by Algerian nationalists. De Gaulle was granted emergency powers to resolve the crisis.

7 Old France, weighed down with history,
prostrated by wars and revolutions, endlessly vacillating from greatness to decline,
but revived, century after century, by the
genius of renewal!
War Memoirs, vol. 3, ch. 7 (1959)

8 In the tumult of men and events, solitude
was my temptation; now it is my friend.
What other satisfaction can be sought once
you have confronted History?
Ibid.

9 Politics are too serious a matter to be left
to the politicians.
Quoted in Attlee: A Prime Minister Remembers,
ch. 4 (1961). De Gaulle was responding to CLE-
MENT ATTLEE's remark that 'De Gaulle is a very
good soldier and a very bad politician.'

10 I respect only those who resist me; but I
cannot tolerate them.
Quoted in The New York Times Magazine
12 May 1966

11 Vive le Québec Libre!
(Long live Free Quebec!)
Speech at Montreal, 24 July 1967, publ. in
Speeches of General de Gaulle (1970). His rallying
call aroused controversy for appearing to advo-
cate the cause of Quebec separatists.

12 No country without an atom bomb could
properly consider itself independent.
Quoted in The New York Times 12 May 1968

13 One does not arrest Voltaire.
Quoted in Encounter June 1975. Referring to the
inflammatory Communist activities of JEAN-
PAUL SARTRE during the 1960s.

14 We are not here to laugh.
(On n'est pas là pour rigoler.)
Attributed on frequent occasions

F. W. de Klerk (b. 1936)
SOUTH AFRICAN POLITICIAN AND
PRESIDENT
Frederik Willem de Klerk. As President (1989–94),
he began the process of dismantling apartheid, lifting the ban on the African National Congress and
releasing NELSON MANDELA in 1990. He served
as Vice-President in the Mandela administration
(1994–6).

1 Today we have closed the book on
apartheid.
Quoted in the Independent 19 March 1992. Referring to the results of the referendum endorsing
his proposals for constitutional and political
reform.

2 We have gone on our knees before God
Almighty to pray for His forgiveness.
Apologizing for apartheid, quoted in the
Observer 25 August 1996. De Klerk's attitude con-
trasted starkly with Botha's (see P. W.
BOTHA 2).

Willem De Kooning (1904–97)
DUTCH-BORN US ARTIST
By the 1950s he was a key figure of the Abstract
Expressionist movement in New York. A superb
draughtsman, he alternated between the abstract
and figurative, as in the Woman series (1950–53).

1 Whatever an artist's personal feelings are,
as soon as an artist fills a certain area on
the canvas or circumscribes it, he becomes
historical. He acts from or upon other
artists.
'A Desperate View', paper delivered to friends in
New York 18 February 1949, first publ. in Willem
De Kooning (1968) by Thomas B. Hess

2 The attitude that nature is chaotic and that
the artist puts order into it is a very absurd
point of view, I think. All that we can hope
for is to put some order into ourselves.
'The Renaissance and Order', lecture in New
York, 1950, publ. in Collected Writings (ed.
George Scrivani, 1988)

3 If you pick up some paint with your brush
and make somebody's nose with it, this is
rather ridiculous when you think of it,
theoretically or philosophically. It's really
absurd to make an image, like a human
image, with paint, today.
'Painting as Self Discovery', interview
30 December 1960, first publ. in Location, spring
1963 as 'Content is a Glimpse . . .', quoted in Willem De Kooning (1988) by Diane Waldman

Walter de la Mare (1873–1956)
BRITISH POET AND NOVELIST
He was placed by DYLAN THOMAS in a compart-
ment marked 'Subtlety and Sensitivity. Perishable
With Care', but admired by AUDEN for the 'graceful architecture of his stanzas'. His lyrical writing
reflects his preoccupation with fantasy and the
imaginative world of childhood.

1 A face peered. All the grey night
In chaos of vacancy shone;
Nought but vast Sorrow was there –
The sweet cheat gone.
'The Ghost', publ. in Motley and Other Poems
(1918)

2 Look thy last on all things lovely,
Every hour. Let no night
Seal thy sense in deadly slumber
Till to delight
Thou have paid thy utmost blessing;
Since that all things thou wouldst praise
Beauty took from those who loved them
In other days.
'Fare Well', publ. ibid.

3 How shall I know that the end of things is
coming?
The drummers will be drumming; the
fiddlers at their thrumming;

Nuns at their beads; the mummers at their
   mumming;
Heaven's solemn Seraph stoopt weary o'er
   his summing;
The palsied fingers plucking, the way-worn
   feet numbing –
And the end of things coming.
'A Sign', publ. in *The Veil and Other Poems*
(1921)

4 Hi! handsome hunting man
Fire your little gun.
Bang! Now the animal
Is dead and dumb and done.
'Hi!', publ. in *Poems for Children* (1930)

5 In the long drouth of life,
Its transient wilderness,
The mindless euthanasia of a kiss
Reveals that in
An instant's beat
Two souls in flesh confined
May yet in an immortal freedom meet.
'The Kiss', first publ. in *The Saturday Book*
(1947), repr. in *Inward Companion: Poems* (1950)

Lothar de Maizière (b. 1940)
GERMAN LAWYER AND POLITICIAN
Leader of the Christian Democratic Union (1989–
90), he became the first democratically elected
premier of East Germany in 1990 and as such nego-
tiated the country's unification with West
Germany.

1 The era of long parades past an official
podium filled with cold faces is gone. Celebrating is now a right, not a duty.
Speech 1 May 1990, quoted in the *Independent*
5 May 1990. Said while East German prime minister, referring to the fall of Communism.

Paul de Man (1919–83)
BELGIAN-BORN US LITERARY CRITIC
He taught at various universities including Yale,
where he became a leading advocate of deconstruc-
tion. His essays were published in Blindness and
Insight *(1971) and* Allegories of Reading *(1979).*

1 Curiously enough, it seems to be only in
describing a mode of language which does
not mean what it says that one can actually
say what one means.
'The Rhetoric of Temporality', sect. 2, first publ.
in *Interpretation* (ed. Charles Singleton, 1969),
repr. in *Blindness and Insight* (1971, rev. 1983)

2 The critical method which denies literary
modernity would appear – and even, in certain respects, would be – the most modern
of critical movements.
'Literary History and Literary Modernity', lecture September 1969, repr. ibid.

3 Literature . . . is condemned (or privileged)
to be forever the most rigorous and, conse-

quently, the most reliable of terms in
which man names and transforms himself.
Allegories of Reading, pt 1, ch. 1, 'Semiology and
Rhetoric' (1979)

4 Death is a displaced name for a linguistic
predicament.
Quoted in *Signs of the Times*, ch. 4 (1991) by
David Lehman. LEHMAN called this 'the ultimate statement of the deconstructive credo'.

Agnes De Mille (1908–93)
US CHOREOGRAPHER AND DANCER
The niece of CECIL B. DE MILLE, *she danced with*
the Ballet Rambert, and later choreographed musi-
cals such as Oklahoma! *(1943) and* Carousel
(1945).

1 Theater people are always pining and agonizing because they're afraid that they'll be
forgotten. And in America they're quite
right. They will be.
Quoted in *Life* 15 November 1963

Cecil B. De Mille (1881–1959)
US FILM-MAKER
Cecil Blount De Mille. Called 'the director to end
all directors', he became known for spectacular
epics, for example The Ten Commandments
(1923, remade 1956) and The Greatest Show on
Earth *(1952).*

1 The really important question to ask about
a motion picture is not 'What did it cost?',
but 'What is it worth?'. . . Many, in all
walks of life, testified that to them this film
[*The Ten Commandments*] had been not a
moving picture, but an experience that
moved their souls. That is what a picture
can be worth and that is why some pictures are worth making, whatever they
cost.
The Autobiography of Cecil B. DeMille, ch. 11,
sect. 6 (ed. Donald Hayne, 1959). Commenting
on the then astronomical cost of the film *The
Ten Commandments* (1923 version) at $1.5 mil-
lion. It eventually grossed over $4 million. The
cost of the 1956 re-make of De Mille's epic,
which employed 25,000 extras, was $13.5
million.

2 What I have crossed out I didn't like.
What I haven't crossed out I am dissatis-
fied with.
Note attached to rejected script, quoted in *Halli-
well's Who's Who in the Movies* (ed. John
Walker, 1999)

Robert De Niro (b. 1943)
US ACTOR
Favouring tough, working-class roles, and closely
associated with the films of MARTIN SCORSESE,
he has starred in Mean Streets *(1973),* The Deer-
hunter *(1978) and* Raging Bull *(1980).*

1 They're all animals anyway. All the criminals come out at night. Whores, skunk pussies, buggers, queens, fairies, dopers, junkies, sick, venal. Someday a *real* rain will come and wash all this scum off the streets.

Voiceover by Travis Bickle (Robert De Niro), in *Taxi Driver* (film, 1976, screenplay by Paul Schrader, directed by Martin Scorsese)

2 You talkin' to me?

Travis Bickle, ibid.

3 Better to be a king for a night than a schmuck for a lifetime.

Rupert Pupkin (Robert De Niro), in *The King of Comedy* (film, 1983, screenplay by Paul Zimmerman, directed by Martin Scorsese)

Guy de Rothschild See ROTHSCHILD.

Buddy De Sylva (1895–1950) and Lew Brown (1893–1958)
US SONGWRITERS
De Sylva (originally George Gard De Sylva) and Brown caught the spirit of the jazz age with such songs as 'Black Bottom' and 'The Birth of the Blues' (1926). De Sylva later became a film producer and was co-founder of Capitol records.

1 *The moon belongs to everyone,*
The best things in life are free.

'The Best Things in Life are Free' (song, 1927, music by Ray Henderson)

Peter De Vries (1910–93)
US AUTHOR
Underpinned by his Dutch Calvinist upbringing, his humour is displayed in such novels as The Tunnel of Love *(1954) and* Slouching Towards Kalamazoo *(1983), depictions of the affluent American middle classes.*

1 Gluttony is an emotional escape, a sign something is eating us.

Crystal, in *Comfort Me with Apples*, ch. 15 (1956)

2 You can make a sordid thing sound like a brilliant drawing-room comedy. Probably a fear we have of facing up to the real issues. Could you say we were guilty of Noel Cowardice?

Narrator, ibid.

3 It is the final proof of God's omnipotence that he need not exist in order to save us.

The Reverend Andrew Mackerel, in *The Mackerel Plaza*, ch. 1 (1958). This aphorism 'seemed to his hearers so much better than anything Voltaire had said on the subject that he was given an immediate hike in pay and invited out to more dinners than he could possibly eat'.

4 Everybody hates me because I'm so universally liked.

Narrator (Joe Sandwich), in *The Vale of Laughter*, pt 1, ch. 1 (1967)

Guy Debord (1931–94)
FRENCH PHILOSOPHER
A leading figure of the Situationist movement, he dealt with the interplay of modernity, capitalism and everyday life. His main work is The Society of the Spectacle *(1967). See also* MARSHALL MCLUHAN.

1 Boredom is always counter-revolutionary. Always.

'The Bad Old Days Will End', first publ. November 1963, repr. in *The Incomplete Works of the Situationist International* (ed. Christopher Gray, 1974)

2 In societies where modern conditions of production prevail, all of life presents itself as an immense accumulation of *spectacles*. Everything that was directly lived has moved away into a representation.

The Society of the Spectacle, ch. 1, sect. 1 (1967)

3 Young people everywhere have been allowed to choose between love and a garbage disposal unit. Everywhere they have chosen the garbage disposal unit.

The Incomplete Works of the Situationist International, 'Formula for a New City' (ed. Christopher Gray, 1974)

4 Quotations are useful in periods of ignorance or obscurantist beliefs.

Panegyric, pt 1 (first volume of autobiography, 1989)

Eugene Debs (1855–1926)
US TRADE UNIONIST AND POLITICAL LEADER
President of the American Railway Union from 1893, he stood as Socialist candidate for the US presidency five times 1900–1920. Hearing him speak, said Art Young, was 'to listen to a hammer riveting a chamber in Hell for the oppressors of the poor'.

1 When great changes occur in history, when great principles are involved, as a rule the majority are wrong.

Speech in Cleveland, Ohio, 11 September 1918, publ. in *Eugene V. Debs Speaks* (ed. Jean Y. Tussey, 1970). Debs was defending himself against charges of violating the 1917 Espionage Act, for which he was found guilty and sentenced to ten years in jail. He was pardoned by the incoming President Harding in 1921.

2 While there is a lower class, I am in it, while there is a criminal element, I am of it, and while there is a soul in prison, I am not free.

Speech from the dock at Cleveland, Ohio, 14 September 1918, publ. in *The Penguin Book of*

Twentieth-Century Speeches (ed. Brian Mac-Arthur, 1999)

Midge Decter (b. 1927)

US AUTHOR, EDITOR AND CRITIC

She was Editor of Harper's *magazine (1968–71) and is author of, among other books,* The New Chastity *(1972), which takes issue with some of the core arguments of feminism.*

1 Women's Liberation calls it enslavement but the real truth about the sexual revolution is that it has made of sex an almost chaotically limitless and therefore unmanageable realm in the life of women.

The New Chastity and Other Arguments Against Women's Liberation, ch. 2 (1972)

Shelagh Delaney (b. 1939)

BRITISH PLAYWRIGHT

She is principally known for A Taste of Honey, *(1958, filmed 1961), which earned her the title of 'Angry Young Woman'. She has also written screenplays.*

1 Women never have young minds. They are born three thousand years old.

Jo's boyfriend, in *A Taste of Honey*, act 1, sc. 2 (1958)

Don DeLillo (b. 1936)

US AUTHOR

A leading exponent of the 'postmodern novel', he writes oblique analyses of contemporary US society which focus on subcultures such as American football in End Zone *(1972) and baseball in* Underworld *(1997).*

1 People stress the violence. That's the smallest part of it. Football is brutal only from a distance. In the middle of it there's a calm, a tranquility. The players accept pain. There's a sense of order even at the end of a running play with bodies strewn everywhere. When the systems interlock, there's a satisfaction to the game that can't be duplicated. There's a harmony.

Emmett Creed, in *End Zone*, ch. 28 (1972)

2 I've come to think of Europe as a hardcover book, America as the paperback version.

Owen Brademas, in *The Names*, ch. 1 (1982)

3 Don't you realize that as long as you have to sit down to pee, you'll never be a dominant force in the world? You'll never be a convincing technocrat or middle manager. Because people will know. She's in there *sitting down*.

James Axton to his wife Kathryn, ibid., ch. 5

4 Men with secrets tend to be drawn to each other, not because they want to share what they know but because they need the company of the like-minded, the fellow afflicted.

Walter Everett Jr, in *Libra*, pt 1, '17 April' (1988)

5 There's never a dearth of reasons to shoot at the President.

Larry Parmenter, ibid., '26 April'

6 If we are on the outside, we assume a conspiracy is the perfect working of a scheme. Silent nameless men with unadorned hearts. A conspiracy is everything that ordinary life is not. It's the inside game, cold, sure, undistracted, forever closed off to us. We are the flawed ones, the innocents, trying to make some rough sense of the daily jostle. Conspirators have a logic and a daring beyond our reach. All conspiracies are the same taut story of men who find coherence in some criminal act.

Ibid., pt 2, 'In Dallas'

7 That's the thing about baseball . . . You do what they did before you. That's the connection you make. There's a whole long line. A man takes his kid to a game and thirty years later this is what they talk about when the poor old mutt's wasting away in the hospital.

Bill Waterson, in *Underworld*, 'Prologue, The Triumph of Death' (1997)

8 Prayer is a practical strategy, the gaining of temporal advantage in the capital markets of Sin and Remission.

Narrator, ibid., pt 2, 'Elegy for Left Hand Alone, Mid-1980s–Early 1990s', ch. 8

9 If you know you're worth nothing, only a gamble with death can gratify your vanity.

Ibid.

10 Corporations are great and appalling things. They take you and shape you in nearly nothing flat, twist and swivel you. And they do it without overt persuasion, they do it with smiles and nods, a collective inflection of the voice.

Ibid., pt 3, 'The Cloud of Unknowing: Spring 1978', ch. 1

11 Sex is what you can get. For some people, most people, it's the most important thing they can get without being born rich or smart or stealing. This is what life can give you that's equal to others or better, even, that you don't have to go to college six years to get. And it's not religion and it's not science but you can explore it and learn things about yourself.

Donna, ibid.

Jack Dempsey (1895–1983)

US BOXER

Born William Harrison Dempsey. Nicknamed 'the Manassa Mauler', he was world heavyweight champion *(1919–26)*. *His 1921 title fight was the first to amass a million dollars from the gate.*

1 **Honey, I just forgot to duck.**

Quoted in *Dempsey*, ch. 24 *(1977)* by Jack and Barbara P. Dempsey. This celebrated remark made to his wife after losing a title fight in 1926 was famously repeated by RONALD REAGAN to NANCY REAGAN after John Hinckley III's assassination attempt on the president, 30 March 1981.

Catherine Deneuve (b. 1943)

FRENCH ACTRESS

Born Cathérine Dorléac. Once called 'the most beautiful woman in the world', she is a powerful dramatic presence in such films as The Umbrellas of Cherbourg *(1964)*, Repulsion *(1965) and* Belle de jour *(1967)*.

1 **Sexuality is such a part of life, but sexuality in movies – I have a hard time finding it.**

Interview in *Première* April 1993

Gérard Depardieu (b. 1948)

FRENCH ACTOR

He has appeared in over seventy films, including Jean de Florette *(1986)*, Cyrano de Bergerac *(1990), and* Le Tartuffe *(1984), in which he directed himself.*

1 **I learnt to be in the light. The stage is like a cage of light. People are no longer afraid of you – they are the ones out there in the dark, watching.**

Quoted in *Depardieu*, ch. 3 (1991) by Marianne Gray. Describing how acting saved him from a life of crime.

2 **At twenty you have many desires which hide the truth, but beyond forty there are only real and fragile truths – your abilities and your failings.**

Daily Mail 4 March 1991

John Derek (1926–98)

US ACTOR AND DIRECTOR

Born Derek Harris. A leading man in the 1940s and '50s, he later turned to photography and directing films.

1 **Live fast, die young and have a good-looking corpse.**

Nick Romano (John Derek), in *Knock on Any Door* (film, 1949, screenplay by Daniel Taradash and John Monks Jr, based on Willard Motley's novel, directed by Nicholas Ray)

Jacques Derrida (b. 1930)

ALGERIAN-BORN FRENCH LITERARY THEORIST

In the 1960s he introduced the theory of deconstruc-

tion into literary criticism, in the paper 'Structure, Sign, and Play' *(1966) and such books as* Speech and Writing *(1967)*.

1 **Writing in the common sense is the dead letter, it is the carrier of death. It exhausts life.**

Of Grammatology, pt 1, ch. 1 (1967, rev. 1998)

2 **There is nothing outside of the text.**

Ibid., pt 2, ch. 2

3 **Were I not so frequently associated with this adventure of deconstruction, I would risk, with a smile, the following hypothesis: America *is* deconstruction. . . . [The United States] is that historical space which today, in all its dimensions and through all its power plays, reveals itself as being undeniably the most sensitive, receptive, or responsive space of all to the themes and effects of deconstruction.**

Mémoirs: For Paul de Man (1989). Written shortly after the death of the critic PAUL DE MAN in 1983.

Helene Deutsch (1884–1982)

POLISH-BORN US PSYCHIATRIST

A pupil of FREUD, *she broke new ground with her work on the female libido. Her publications include* The Psychology of Women *(1944–5)*.

1 **All observations point to the fact that the intellectual woman is masculinized; in her, warm, intuitive knowledge has yielded to cold unproductive thinking.**

The Psychology of Women, vol. 1, ch. 8 (1944)

2 **The embattled gates to equal rights indeed opened up for modern women, but I sometimes think to myself: 'That is not what I meant by freedom – it is only "social progress".'**

Confrontations with Myself, ch. 1 (1973)

Bernard DeVoto (1897–1955)

US HISTORIAN AND CRITIC

Winning acclaim for Mark Twain's America *(1932), he published a trilogy on the American West and wrote the 'Easy Chair' column in* Harper's *magazine 1935–55.*

1 **You can no more keep a martini in the refrigerator than you can keep a kiss there. The proper union of gin and vermouth is a great and sudden glory; it is one of the happiest marriages on earth, and one of the shortest-lived.**

Harper's December 1949

2 **Sure the people are stupid: the human race is stupid. Sure Congress is an inefficient instrument of government. But the people are not stupid enough to abandon representative government for any other kind,**

including government by the guy who knows.

The Easy Chair, 'Sometimes They Vote Right Too' (1955)

Lord Dewar (1864–1930)

BRITISH INDUSTRIALIST

Thomas, Lord Dewar of Homestall. He was Managing Director of Scotch Whisky Brands and published books of his epigrammatic humour.

1 [There are] only two classes of pedestrians in these days of reckless motor traffic – the quick, and the dead.

Quoted in *Looking Back on Life*, ch. 28 (1933) by George Robey

Diana, Princess of Wales (1961–97)

Originally Lady Diana Frances Spencer. She was married to CHARLES, PRINCE OF WALES *1981–96. As Honorary President of numerous charities she focused world attention on the issues of AIDS and landmines. Her death in a car accident gave rise to unprecedented national mourning.*

1 Everyone said I was the Marilyn Monroe of the 1980s and I was adoring every minute of it. Actually I've never sat down and said: 'Hooray how wonderful.' Never. The day I do we're in trouble.

Quoted in *Diana: Her True Story*, ch. 9 (1992) by Andrew Morton

2 I have it on very good authority that the quest for perfection our society demands can leave the individual gasping for breath at every turn. From early childhood, many have felt they were expected to be perfect but did not feel they had the right to express their true feelings to those around them – feelings of guilt, of self-revulsion and low personal esteem, creating in them a compulsion to *dissolve* like a *Disprin* and disappear.

Speech at International Eating Disorders conference in London, 27 April 1993, quoted in the *Guardian* 28 April 1993. Princess Diana suffered from bulimia.

3 I don't even know how to use a parking meter, let alone a phone box.

Quoted in the *Guardian* 22 August 1994. Said to Richard Kay, royal correspondent for the *Daily Mail*, on allegations that she had pestered art dealer Oliver Hoare with telephone calls.

4 When I see them around all the time, it is like being raped.

Quoted in the *Guardian* 6 April 1995. Referring to press photographers.

5 I'd like to be a queen of people's hearts, in people's hearts, but I don't see myself being Queen of this country.

Interview on *Panorama*, BBC1, 20 November 1995, publ. in *The Times* 21 November 1995

6 She won't go quietly, that's the problem. I'll fight to the end.

Ibid. Speaking of herself.

7 There were three of us in this marriage.

Ibid. On Prince Charles's relationship with Camilla Parker-Bowles.

8 You are going to get a big surprise with the next thing I do.

Quoted in the *Observer* 20 July 1997. Remark to reporters while holidaying on AL-FAYED's yacht at St Tropez.

9 I touch people. I think everyone needs that. Placing a hand on a friend's face means making contact.

Interview in *Le Monde* 27 August 1997

Leonardo DiCaprio (b. 1974)

US SCREEN ACTOR

After winning praise for roles in What's Eating Gilbert Grape? *(1993) and* Romeo and Juliet *(1996), he became a global superstar for his part in* Titanic *(1997).*

1 I would not want to become an adult in every sense of the word. Who the hell does?

Quoted in the *Sunday Times* 16 January 2000

Philip K. Dick (1928–82)

US SCIENCE FICTION WRITER

His novels and short stories such as Do Androids Dream of Electric Sheep? *(1968, filmed as* Blade Runner, *1982) explore standard science fiction ideas with a bizarre humour. He generated a cult following in the 1960s.*

1 Reality is that which, when you stop believing in it, doesn't go away.

Definition given in 1972, quoted by Dick in *I Hope I Shall Arrive Soon*, 'How to Build a Universe That Doesn't Fall Apart Two Days Later' (1986)

2 One of the most effective forms of industrial or military sabotage limits itself to damage that can never be thoroughly proven – or even proven at all – to be anything deliberate.

A Scanner Darkly, ch. 3 (1977)

3 Drug misuse is not a disease, it is a decision, like the decision to step out in front of a moving car. You would call that not a disease but an error of judgment.

Ibid., Author's Note

4 We are not individuals. We are stations in a single Mind.

Valis, ch. 7 (1981)

5 Science fiction writers, I am sorry to say, really do not know anything. We can't talk about science, because our knowledge of it

is limited and unofficial, and usually our fiction is dreadful.

I Hope I Shall Arrive Soon, 'How to Build a Universe That Doesn't Fall Apart Two Days Later' (1986)

6 The basic tool for the manipulation of reality is the manipulation of words. If you can control the meaning of words, you can control the people who must use the words.

Ibid.

Joan Didion (b. 1934)

US ESSAYIST

Her essay collections Slouching Towards Bethlehem *(1968) and* The White Album *(1979) chronicled the transformation of American life in the 1960s and '70s.*

1 Most of our platitudes notwithstanding, self-deception remains the most difficult deception. The tricks that work on others count for nothing in that very well-lit back alley where one keeps assignations with oneself: no winning smiles will do here, no prettily drawn lists of good intentions.

'On Self-Respect', first publ. 1961, repr. in *Slouching Towards Bethlehem* (1968)

2 California is a place in which a boom mentality and a sense of Chekhovian loss meet in uneasy suspension; in which the mind is troubled by some buried but ineradicable suspicion that things had better work here, because here, beneath that immense bleached sky, is where we run out of continent.

'Notes from a Native Daughter', first publ. 1965, repr. ibid.

3 When we start deceiving ourselves into thinking not that we want something or need something, not that it is a pragmatic necessity for us to have it, but that it is a *moral imperative* that we have it, then is when we join the fashionable madmen, and then is when the thin whine of hysteria is heard in the land, and then is when we are in bad trouble.

'On Morality', first publ. 1965, repr. ibid.

4 We are well advised to keep on nodding terms with the people we used to be, whether we find them attractive company or not. Otherwise they turn up unannounced and surprise us, come hammering on the mind's door at 4am of a bad night and demand to know who deserted them, who betrayed them, who is going to make amends. We forget all too soon the things we thought we could never forget.

'On Keeping a Notebook', first publ. 1966, repr. ibid.

5 Writers are always selling somebody out.

Slouching Towards Bethlehem, Preface (1968)

6 Many people I know in Los Angeles believe that the Sixties ended abruptly on August 9, 1969, ended at the exact moment when word of the murders on Cielo Drive traveled like brushfire through the community, and in a sense this is true. The tension broke that day. The paranoia was fulfilled.

'The White Album: A Chronicle of Survival in the Sixties', first publ. in *New West* 4 June 1979, repr. in *The White Album* (1979). Referring to the Charles Manson murders.

Marlene Dietrich (1901–92)

GERMAN-BORN US ACTRESS AND ENTERTAINER

Originally Maria Magdalene von Losch. One of the most glamorous and sensual of film icons, she starred in the German film The Blue Angel *(1930) and in Hollywood films such as* Blonde Venus *(1932), and later became a cabaret star.*

1 *Falling in love again,*
I never wanted to
What am I to do?
I can't help it.

'Falling in Love Again' (song, written by Fredrich Hollander and Sammy Lerner from German lyrics by Robert Liebmann) in the film *The Blue Angel* (1930)

2 In Europe it doesn't matter if you're a man or a woman. We make love with anyone we find attractive.

Remark, 1930, quoted in *Dietrich*, ch. 5 (1992) by Donald Spoto. Addressed to a woman fellow passenger who had declined Marlene's advances. The actress was on a ship making her first voyage to America.

3 It took more than one man to change my name to Shanghai Lily.

Shanghai Lily (Marlene Dietrich), in *Shanghai Express* (film, 1932, screenplay by Jules Furthman based on a story by Harry Hervey, directed by Josef von Sternberg)

4 A country without bordels is like a house without bathrooms.

Marlene Dietrich's ABC, 'Bordel' (1962)

5 There comes a time when suddenly you realize that laughter is something you remember and that *you* were the one laughing.

Ibid., 'Laughter'

6 He is gentle, as all real men are gentle; without tenderness, a man is uninteresting.

Of ERNEST HEMINGWAY, quoted in *Papa Hemingway*, pt 1, ch. 1 (1955) by A. E. Hotchner. Hemingway, one of Dietrich's lovers, called her 'that damn Kraut', but also said she was 'the best who ever entered the ring'.

7 Most people who make movies are in real

life a bitter disappointment. I, on the other hand, am so much better in real life.

Said to critic Sheridan Morley, quoted by him in the *Sunday Times* 24 May 1992

Howard Dietz (1896–1983)

US SONGWRITER AND PUBLICIST

Director of advertising and publicity for Metro-Goldwyn-Mayer film studios (1919–57), he was responsible for devising its 'roaring lion' trademark and accompanying motto. He later wrote Broadway musicals and revues.

1 *Ars gratia artis.* (Art for art's sake.)

Motto of MGM studios, adopted in the 1930s. The phrase 'Art for art's sake' was not new: the French politician and philosopher Benjamin Constant (1767–1834) wrote, in his *Journal intime*: 'Art for art's sake, with no purpose, for any purpose perverts art. But art achieves a purpose which is not its own.'

Annie Dillard (b. 1945)

US AUTHOR AND POET

She was Editor of Harper's magazine (1973–85) and published Pilgrim at Tinker Creek *(1974), which was compared to Thoreau's* Walden *and enjoyed an immediate success.*

1 I don't know what it is about fecundity that so appalls. I suppose it is the teeming evidence that birth and growth, which we value, are ubiquitous and blind, that life itself is as astonishingly cheap, that nature is as careless as it is bountiful, and that with extravagance goes a crushing waste that will one day include our own cheap lives.

Narrator, in *Pilgrim at Tinker Creek*, ch. 10 (1974)

Joe DiMaggio (1914–99)

US BASEBALL PLAYER

Nicknamed 'Joltin' Joe' and 'The Yankee Clipper', he was the star player of the New York Yankees (1936–51). He was briefly married to MARILYN MONROE *in 1954.*

1 A ball player's got to be kept hungry to become a big leaguer. That's why no boy from a rich family ever made the big leagues.

The New York Times 30 April 1961

Isak Dinesen (1885–1962)

DANISH AUTHOR

Pen name of Baroness Karen Blixen, born Karen Christence Dinesen. She lived in Kenya following her marriage to her cousin (1914). Returning to Denmark in 1931, she published Seven Gothic Tales *(1934) and her autobiography* Out of Africa *(1937, filmed 1985).*

1 What is life, when you come to think upon it, but a most excellent, accurately set, infinitely complicated machine for turning fat playful puppies into old mangy blind dogs, and proud war horses into skinny nags, and succulent young boys, to whom the world holds great delight and terrors, into old weak men, with running eyes, who drink ground rhino-horn? What is man, when you come to think upon him, but a minutely set, ingenious machine for turning, with infinite artfulness, the red wine of Shiraz into urine?

Mira, in *Seven Gothic Tales*, 'The Dreamers' (1934)

2 If I know a song of Africa – I thought – of the giraffe, and the African new moon lying on her back, of the ploughs in the fields, and the sweaty faces of the coffee-pickers, does Africa know a song of me?

Out of Africa, pt 1, ch. 4 (1937)

3 The true aristocracy and the true proletariat of the world are both in understanding with tragedy. To them it is the fundamental principle of God, and the key – the minor key – to existence. They differ in this way from the bourgeoisie of all classes, who deny tragedy, who will not tolerate it, and to whom the word tragedy means in itself unpleasantness.

Ibid., pt 3, ch. 5

Christian Dior (1905–57)

FRENCH COUTURIER

He founded his own Paris house in 1945 and shocked the public with the extravagant designs of his New Look in 1947. He later devised the 'H' and 'A' line, and 'discovered' YVES SAINT LAURENT.

1 Women are most fascinating between the ages of thirty-five and forty, after they have won a few races and know how to pace themselves. Since few women ever pass forty, maximum fascination can continue indefinitely.

Collier's Magazine 10 June 1955

2 The maintenance of the tradition of fashion is in the nature of an act of faith. In a century which attempts to tear the heart out of every mystery, fashion guards its secret well, and is the best possible proof that there is still magic abroad.

Dior by Dior, pt 4, ch. 19 (1957)

Thomas M. Disch (b. 1940)

US AUTHOR

He established the New Wave genre of science fiction, and has also written other forms of fiction as well as opera libretti and poetry.

1 A predilection for genre fiction is symptomatic of a kind of arrested development.
Quoted in *The Face* March 1986

Walt Disney (1901–66)

US ANIMATOR AND FILM-MAKER

Having created Mickey Mouse (for whom he provided the original voice) in 1927 and Donald Duck in 1936, he produced the first full-length colour cartoon film, Snow White and the Seven Dwarfs *in 1937. 'Disney has the best casting,' ALFRED HITCHCOCK once remarked. 'If he doesn't like an actor, he just tears him up.'*

1 Dream, diversify – and never miss an angle.
Quoted in *The Disney Studio Story*, Introduction (1988) by Richard Holliss and Brian Sibley

2 I love Mickey Mouse more than any woman I've ever known.
Quoted in *Halliwell's Who's Who in the Movies* (ed. John Walker, 1999)

Mort Dixon (1892–1956)

US SONGWRITER

A leading lyricist of popular songs of the 1920s and '30s, he collaborated with Ray Henderson, Harry Woods and ALLIE WRUBEL, *among others, on such hits as 'Bye Bye Blackbird' (1926) and 'You're My Everything' (1931).*

1 *Bye Bye Blackbird.*
'Bye Bye Blackbird' (song, 1926, music by Ray Henderson)

2 *I'm looking over a four leaf clover That I overlooked before.*
'I'm Looking over a Four Leaf Clover' (song, 1927, music by Harry Woods)

Milovan Djilas (1911–95)

YUGOSLAV POLITICAL LEADER AND AUTHOR

A leading partisan in the Second World War and subsequently a minister in Tito's cabinet, he was made President of the Federal People's Assembly in 1953, but his outspoken criticism of the Communist Party caused him to lose his posts and leave the Party.

1 The Party line is that there is no Party line.
Comment on reforms of Yugoslavian Communist Party, November 1951, quoted in *Disputed Barricade*, ch. 15 (1957) by Fitzroy Maclean

2 The terrible thing is that one cannot be a Communist and not let oneself in for the shameful act of recantation. One cannot be a Communist and preserve an iota of one's personal integrity.
Encounter December 1979

3 Normal life cannot sustain revolutionary attitudes for long.
Guardian 9 April 1990

J. Frank Dobie (1888–1964)

US AUTHOR

James Frank Dobie. Nicknamed Professor Pancho, he described himself as a 'historian of the long-horns, the mustangs, the coyote and other characters of the West' in such books as Apache Gold *(1939) and* The Longhorns *(1941).*

1 The average PhD thesis is nothing but a transference of bones from one graveyard to another.
A Texan in England, ch. 1 (1945)

E. L. Doctorow (b. 1931)

US NOVELIST

Edgar Lawrence Doctorow. His books, taking the form of historical novels, westerns or science fiction, blend fact with invention. They include Ragtime *(1975, filmed 1981) and* Billy Bathgate *(1989, filmed 1991).*

1 Tracks! Tracks! It seemed to the visionaries who wrote for the popular magazines that the future lay at the end of parallel rails. There were long-distance locomotive railroads and interurban electric railroads and street railways and elevated railroads, all laying their steel stripes on the land, criss-crossing like the texture of an indefatigable civilization.
Ragtime, pt 1, ch. 13 (1975)

2 There is no longer any such thing as fiction or nonfiction; there's only narrative.
The New York Times Book Review 27 January 1988

3 It's like driving a car at night. You never see further than your headlights, but you can make the whole trip that way.
Interview in *Writers at Work* (eighth series, ed. George Plimpton, 1988). Discussing his writing technique.

4 Murders are exciting and lift people into a heart-beating awe as religion is supposed to do, after seeing one in the street young couples will go back to bed and make love, people will cross themselves and thank God for the gift of their stuporous lives, old folks will talk to each other over cups of hot water with lemon because murders are enlivened sermons to be analyzed and considered and relished, they speak to the timid of the dangers of rebellion, murders are perceived as momentary descents of God and so provide joy and hope and righteous satisfaction to parishioners, who will talk about them for years afterward to anyone who will listen.
Billy Bathgate, ch. 19 (1989)

5 Like art and politics, gangsterism is a very important avenue of assimilation into society.
International Herald Tribune 1 October 1990

6 Lullabies, school songs, anthems, battle hymns, work songs, chanteys, love songs, bawdy songs, laments, requiems. They're there in every age of life, for every occasion, in the sepulchral voices of the choir, in the stomp and shout of the whorehouse piano player. But all songs are songs of justification.

'Standards: How Great Songs Name Us', publ. in *Harper's* November 1991

7 The radical's role is to propose intolerable ideas, and to be sacrificed for them, so that subsequent generations can absorb them as privileges.

Interview in the *Guardian* 4 June 1994

Ken Dodd (b. 1931)

BRITISH COMIC

Primarily a stand-up comedian, he has appeared in variety and pantomime and on television and radio since his debut in 1954. His hit songs include 'Happiness' (1964) and 'Tears' (1965).

1 The trouble with Freud is that he never played the Glasgow Empire Saturday night.

The Laughter Makers, TV interview, quoted in *The Times* 7 August 1965

2 If I get a hard audience they are not going to get away until they laugh. Those seven laughs a minute – I've got to have them.

Daily Telegraph 20 September 1990

Robert Doisneau (1912–94)

FRENCH PHOTOGRAPHER

He immortalized post-war Paris through his black-and-white photographs, capturing everyday life in order to 'show the world as I would like it to be at all times'.

1 A hundredth of a second here, a hundredth of a second there – even if you put them end to end, they still only add up to one, two, perhaps three seconds, snatched from eternity.

Guardian 4 April 1992

J. P. Donleavy (b. 1926)

IRISH-AMERICAN AUTHOR

James Patrick Donleavy. The Ginger Man (1955) was the first of a series of bawdy picaresque novels, mostly set in Ireland.

1 To marry the Irish is to look for poverty.

The Ginger Man, ch. 2 (1955)

2 But Jesus, when you don't have any money, the problem is food. When you have money, it's sex. When you have both, it's health, you worry about getting ruptured or something. If everything is simply jake then you're frightened of death.

O'Keefe, ibid., ch. 5

3 When I die I want to decompose in a barrel of porter and have it served in all the pubs in Dublin.

Sebastian Dangerfield, ibid., ch. 31

4 Writing is turning one's worst moments into money.

Playboy May 1979. He has expressed the aphorism on various occasions.

Terence Donovan (1936–96)

BRITISH PHOTOGRAPHER

He became a freelance photographer in 1959 and recorded the London of the Swinging Sixties through his black-and-white documentary-style images.

1 The magic of photography is metaphysical. What you see in the photograph isn't what you saw at the time. The real skill of photography is organised visual lying.

Guardian 19 November 1983

Ariel Dorfman (b. 1942)

CHILEAN AUTHOR

Forced into exile by the 1973 military coup in Chile, he expressed his revulsion of political oppression in his novels, for example My House is on Fire *(1990), and plays, notably* Death and the Maiden *(1991, filmed 1995).*

1 *Reader's Digest* is a tourist guidebook for the geography of ignorance.

The Empire's Old Clothes, ch. 4 (1983)

2 The enemy is inside, and we find it hard to distinguish him from some of our innermost thoughts and nurturings.

Ibid., 'Conclusion'

3 Compromise, an agreement, a negotiation. Everything in this country is done by consensus isn't it. Isn't that what this transition is all about? They let us have democracy, but they keep control of the economy and of the armed forces? The Commission can investigate the crimes but nobody is punished for them? There's freedom to say anything you want as long as you don't say everything you want?

Paulina, in *Death and the Maiden*, act 2, sc. 1 (1991)

(Sir) Reginald Dorman-Smith (1899–1977)

BRITISH POLITICIAN

Conservative MP for Petersfield, Hampshire (1935–46), he served as Minister for Agriculture and Fisheries (1939–40) and Governor of Burma (1941–6).

1 Let 'Dig for Victory' be the motto of every one with a garden and of every able-bodied

Douglas 147

man and woman capable of digging an
allotment in their spare time.
Radio broadcast, 3 October 1939, quoted in *The
Times* 4 October 1939

John Dos Passos (1896–1970)
US NOVELIST
Praised by EDMUND WILSON *as 'perhaps the first
really important writer to have succeeded in using
colloquial American', he described the disillusionment of war and the decline of a materialist society
in his novels, which include* Three Soldiers *(1921)
and the trilogy* USA *(1930–6).*

1 The only man that gets anything out of
capitalism is a crook, an' he gets to be a
millionaire in short order . . .
Tim O'Hara, in *42nd Parallel*, 'Mac' (first title in
the *USA* trilogy, 1930)

2 A revolutionist ought to be careful about
the girls he went with, women took a class-
conscious workingman's mind off his aims,
they were the main seduction of capitalist
society.
Nick Gigli, in *1919*, 'Ben Compton' (second title
in the *USA* trilogy, 1932)

3 People don't choose their careers; they are
engulfed by them.
The New York Times 25 October 1959

Keith Douglas (1920–44)
BRITISH POET
*One of the few British poets associated with the
Second World War, he served as a tank com-
mander in North Africa, and died in action in Nor-
mandy.* Selected Poems *appeared in 1943, and*
Alamein to Zem Zem, *his account of the desert
campaign, in 1946.*

1 *Remember me when I am dead
And simplify me when I'm dead.*
'Simplify me when I'm Dead', written 1941, publ.
in *Collected Poems* (1966)

2 *Under the parabola of a ball,
a child turning into a man,
I looked into the air too long.
The ball fell in my hand, it sang
In the closed fist: Open Open
Behold a gift designed to kill.*
'How to Kill', written in North Africa, 1943,
publ. ibid.

3 *The weightless mosquito touches
her tiny shadow on the stone,
and with how like, how infinite
a lightness, man and shadow meet.
They fuse. A shadow is a man
when the mosquito death approaches.*
Ibid.

4 *For here the lover and killer are mingled
who had one body and one heart.*

*And death, who had the soldier singled
has done the lover mortal hurt.*
'Vergissmeinnicht', written at Homs hospital
June/July 1943, publ. ibid.

5 *If at times my eyes are lenses
through which the brain explores
constellations of feeling
my ears yielding like swinging doors
admit princes to the corridors
into the mind, do not envy me.
I have a beast on my back*
'Bête Noire', written early 1944 in England, publ.
ibid.

Michael Douglas (b. 1944)
US SCREEN ACTOR
Son of Kirk Douglas, he co-produced One Flew
Over the Cuckoo's Nest *(1975) and produced and
starred in* Romancing the Stone *(1984). He also
had starring roles in* Wall Street *and* Fatal Attraction *(both 1987).*

1 Lunch is for wimps.
Gordon Gekko (Michael Douglas), in *Wall Street*
(film, 1987, screenplay by Oliver Stone and Stanley Weiser, directed by Oliver Stone)

2 Money isn't lost or made. It's simply transformed from one perception to another.
Ibid.

Norman Douglas (1868–1952)
BRITISH AUTHOR
His best-known novel, the symposium-like South
Wind *(1917), reflects his diverse interests – art,
ethics, food and religion – which are also aired in
his travel books* Siren Land *(1911) and* Old Cal-
abria *(1915).*

1 You can tell the ideals of a nation by its
advertisements.
Don Francesco, in *South Wind*, ch. 7 (1917)

2 Shall I give you my recipe for happiness? I
find everything useful and nothing indispensable. I find everything wonderful and
nothing miraculous. I reverence the body.
I avoid first causes like the plague.
Mr Keith, ibid., ch. 18

3 Many a man who thinks to found a home
discovers that he has merely opened a
tavern for his friends.
Mr Keith, ibid., ch. 24

4 I wish the English still possessed a shred of
the old sense of humour which Puritanism,
and dyspepsia, and newspaper reading,
and tea-drinking have nearly extinguished.
Ibid., ch. 32

5 To find a friend one must close one eye.
To keep him – two.
An Almanac (1941)

Coleman Dowell (1925–85)

US NOVELIST, PLAYWRIGHT AND LYRICIST

His novels dealing with sexual obsession and homosexuality include One of the Children is Crying *(1968) and* White on Black on White *(1983). Plays include* Eve of the Green Grass *(1963).*

1 Being is a fiction invented by those who suffer from becoming.

Entry in Mrs October's journals, in *Mrs October Was Here*, pt 3, 'Tasmania, Now' (1973)

(Sir) Arthur Conan Doyle
(1859–1930)

BRITISH AUTHOR

He established the genre of detective fiction with his Sherlock Holmes stories. His other adventure tales include The White Company *(1891) and* The Lost Valley *(1912), and he also published books on spiritualism.*

1 The vocabulary of 'Bradshaw' is nervous and terse, but limited. The selection of words would hardly lend itself to the sending of general messages.

Sherlock Holmes, in *The Valley of Fear*, pt 1, ch. 1 (1915). Watson had suggested that Bradshaw, the railway timetable, might contain the key to decipher a code; Holmes opted instead for *Whitaker's Almanack*.

2 Mediocrity knows nothing higher than itself, but talent instantly recognizes genius.

Ibid.

3 But here, unless I am mistaken, is our client.

Sherlock Holmes, in *His Last Bow*, 'Wisteria Lodge', ch. 1 (1917)

4 All other men are specialists, but his specialism is omniscience.

Sherlock Holmes referring to his brother, Mycroft, ibid., 'The Bruce-Partington Plans'

5 Of all ruins that of a noble mind is the most deplorable.

Ibid., 'The Dying Detective'. The words recall those of Scrope Davies (c. 1783–1852), who wrote: 'Babylon in all its desolation is a sight not so awful as that of the human mind in ruins' (letter, May 1835).

6 Holmes: I followed you.
Watson: I saw no one.
Holmes: That is what you may expect to see when I follow you.

Ibid., 'Devil's Foot'

7 Good old Watson! You are the one fixed point in a changing age.

Sherlock Holmes, ibid., 'His Last Bow'

8 Matilda Briggs . . . was a ship which is associated with the giant rat of Sumatra, a

story for which the world is not yet prepared.

Sherlock Holmes, in *The Case-Book of Sherlock Holmes*, 'The Sussex Vampire' (1927)

Roddy Doyle (b. 1958)

IRISH NOVELIST

A teacher who turned to writing plays and novels about the inner life of Dublin, he won praise for The Commitments *(1987, filmed 1991), first of the Barrytown trilogy, and* Paddy Clarke Ha Ha Ha *(1993).*

1 The Irish are the niggers of Europe, lads. An' Dubliners are the niggers of Ireland. . . . An' the northside Dubliners are the niggers o' Dublin. – Say it loud, I'm black an' I'm proud.

Jimmy Rabbitte, in *The Commitments* (1987). See also JAMES BROWN 2.

2 Soul is the politics o' the people. Our people. – Soul is the rhythm o' sex. . . . Soul is dynamic. It can't be caught. It can't be chained. They could chain the nigger slaves but they couldn't chain their soul.

Ibid.

3 Being out of a job makes you passive. You spend a lot of time in bed, and you can't be angry while you're asleep.

Interview in the *Independent on Sunday* 14 April 1996. Referring to Jimmy in Doyle's 1990 novel, *The Snapper*.

Margaret Drabble (b. 1939)

BRITISH NOVELIST

Her novels, including The Radiant Way *(1987) and* The Gates of Ivory *(1991), explore the everyday experience and ideas of educated middle-class women. She is wife of biographer* MICHAEL HOLROYD *and sister of* A. S. BYATT.

1 Human contact seemed to her [Jane] so frail a thing that the hope that two people might want each other in the same way, at the same time and with the possibility of doing something about it, seemed infinitely remote.

The Waterfall (1969)

2 Perhaps I could take a religion that denied free will, that placed God in his true place, arbitrary, carelessly kind, idly malicious, intermittently attentive, and himself subject as Zeus was, to necessity. Necessity is my God.

Jane, ibid.

3 Faces, they have, those suburban people, faces and identity, despite their mortgages and their alarms: and there are few emotions more ignoble, more contemptible, than the terror that seizes such as myself

when we drive, quickly, past their net cur-
tained windows.

Ibid. The protagonist, Jane, is visiting her
parents-in-law in suburbia. which she does
'through social masochism, knowing that only
by sinking could I avoid the deadly, human,
incriminating impulse to rise'.

4 Affluence was, quite simply, a question of
texture . . . The threadbare carpets of
infancy, the coconut matting, the ill-laid
linoleum, the utility furniture . . . had all
spoken of a life too near the bones of subsistence, too little padded, too severely
worn.

The Needle's Eye, pt 1 (1972)

5 England's not a bad country. It's just a
mean, cold, ugly, divided, tired, clapped-
out, post-imperial, post-industrial slag-
heap covered in polystyrene hamburger
cartons.

Alix, in *A Natural Curiosity* (1989)

6 You learn to put your emotional luggage
where it will do some good, instead of
using it to shit on other people, or blow up
aeroplanes.

Quoted in the *Observer* 6 October 1991

Nick Drake (1948–74)

BRITISH SINGER AND SONGWRITER
*His music was characterized by his wistful voice,
nimble guitar and bleak lyrics. His premature
death was due to a drugs overdose, probably accidental.*

1 *Fame is but a fruit tree*
So very unsound
It can never flourish
Till its stalk is in the ground.
'Fruit Tree' (song) on the album *Five Leaves Left*
(1969)

Marie Dressler (1869–1934)

CANADIAN-BORN US ACTRESS
*Born Leila Marie Koerber, she started her stage
career aged fourteen and became a star of vaudeville. In her first film,* Tillie's Punctured Romance
(1914), she co-starred with CHARLIE CHAPLIN.

1 By the time we hit fifty, we have learned
our hardest lessons. We have found out
that only a few things are really important.
We have learned to take life seriously, but
never ourselves.

My Own Story, ch. 17 (1934)

Elizabeth Drew (1887–1965)

ANGLO-AMERICAN AUTHOR AND CRITIC
She wrote widely on literature including The
Modern Novel *(1926),* Discovering Drama *(1937)
and* The Literature of Gossip *(1964).*

1 The test of literature is, I suppose, whether

we ourselves live more intensely for the
reading of it.

The Modern Novel, 'Is There a "Feminine" Fiction?' (1926)

W. E. B. Du Bois (1868–1963)

US HISTORIAN AND CIVIL RIGHTS LEADER
*William Edward Burghardt Du Bois. His writings
concerned the history of African Americans. He
was a founder of the National Association for the
Advancement of Colored People, joined the Communist Party aged ninety-three, and died a citizen
of Ghana.*

1 Is a civilization naturally backward
because it is different? Outside of cannibal-
ism, which can be matched in this country,
at least, by lynching, there is no vice and
no degradation in native African customs
which can begin to touch the horrors
thrust upon them by white masters. Drunkenness, terrible diseases, immorality, all
these things have been gifts of European
civilization.

'Reconstruction and Africa', first publ. 1919,
repr. in *The Seventh Son*, vol. 2 (1971)

2 If there is anybody in this land who
thoroughly believes that the meek shall
inherit the earth they have not often let
their presence be known.

The Gift of Black Folk, ch. 9 (1924)

3 One thing alone I charge you. As you live,
believe in life! Always human beings will
live and progress to greater, broader and
fuller life. The only possible death is to
lose belief in this truth simply because the
great end comes slowly, because time is
long.

Last message, written 26 June 1957 and read at
his funeral, publ. in *Journal of Negro History*
April 1964

Alexander Dubček (1921–92)

CZECHOSLOVAKIAN POLITICIAN
*His promotion of political liberalization while First
Secretary of the Communist Party led to the 1968
invasion of Czechoslovakia by Warsaw Pact forces
and his replacement. After the fall of Communism
in 1989 he was elected Chairman of the new Federal Assembly.*

1 Socialism with a human face.
Dubček's words, repeated in various forms on
different occasions, became a slogan of the
'Prague Spring' of 1968.

Al Dubin (1891–1945)

US SONGWRITER
*Collaborating with the composer Harry Warren
during the 1930s, he wrote songs for twenty musicals, including the film* 42nd Street *(1933).*

1 *Tiptoe through the tulips.*
'Tiptoe through the Tulips' (song, 1929, with music by Joseph Burke)

Jean Dubuffet (1901–85)
FRENCH SCULPTOR AND PAINTER
Regarded as the forerunner of late-twentieth-century art styles, he pioneered the concept of Art Brut (raw art), the antidote to museum art, derived from his studies of children and the mentally ill.

1 Art is the most passionate orgy within man's grasp.
'Notes for the Well-Read' (1946), repr. in *Jean Dubuffet: Towards an Alternative Reality* (ed. Marc Glimcher, 1987)

2 Art should always make people laugh a little and frighten them a little. Anything but bore them. Art has no right to be boring.
Rough draft for 'Popular Lecture in Painting' (1946), repr. ibid.

3 It is not men who are great. It is man who is great. It is not wonderful to be exceptional. It is wonderful to be a man.
'Notes for the Well-Lettered', first publ. in *Prospectus* (1946), repr. in *Art in Theory* (ed. Charles Harrison and Paul Wood, 1992)

4 Caprice, independence and rebellion, which are opposed to the social order, are essential to the good health of an ethnic group. We shall measure the good health of this group by the number of its delinquents. Nothing is more immobilizing than the spirit of *deference.*
'Asphyxiating Culture' (1968), repr. in *Asphyxiating Culture and Other Writings* (1986)

Marcel Duchamp (1887–1968)
FRENCH ARTIST
A precursor of conceptual art and leader of the Dadaists, he was famous for his 'ready-mades', everyday objects that became works of art. The urinal he entered in an exhibition (1917) and his moustachioed Mona Lisa (1919) provoked scandal.

1 I have forced myself to contradict myself in order to avoid conforming to my own taste.
Quoted in 'Marcel Duchamp: Anti-Artist' by Harriet and Sidney Janis, first publ. in *View* 21 March 1945, repr. in *Dada Painters and Poets* (1951) by Robert Motherwell

2 I am still a victim of chess. It has all the beauty of art – and much more. It cannot be commercialized. Chess is much purer than art in its social position.
Time 10 March 1952. Duchamp had given up painting in favour of chess in the 1920s. In an address to the New York State Chess Association 30 August 1952, he said: 'I have come to the personal conclusion that while all artists are not chess players, all chess players are artists.'

Carol Ann Duffy (b. 1955)
BRITISH POET
Tackling a range of subjects in a humorous, often passionate style, she makes use of monologue to articulate character types and moral dilemmas. She has also written plays.

1 Some nights, although we are faithless, the truth
enters our hearts, that small familiar pain;
then a man will stand stock-still, hearing his youth
in the distant Latin chanting of a train.
'Prayer', publ. in *Mean Time* (1993)

2 Whatever 'in love' means,
true love is talented.
'September 1997', publ. in the *Guardian* 6 September 1997. Referring to the reply made by Prince CHARLES when asked, on his engagement to Princess DIANA, if he was in love: 'Yes, whatever that means.'

3 The dead are so talented.
The living walk by the edge of a vast lake
near the wise, drowned silence of the dead.
'Eurydice', publ. in *The World's Wife* (1999)

Olympia Dukakis (b. 1931)
US ACTRESS
Principally a stage actress, she has also appeared in films including Moonstruck *(1987) and in the TV series* Tales from the City *(1993).*

1 The only thing that separates us from the animals is our ability to accessorize.
Clairee Belcher (Olympia Dukakis), in *Steel Magnolias* (film, 1989, screenplay by Robert Harling based on his own play, directed by Herbert Ross)

John Foster Dulles (1888–1959)
US POLITICIAN AND LAWYER
As a Republican and ardent anti-Communist, he did much to strengthen the position of America and NATO during the Cold War, serving as Secretary of State (1953–9) under EISENHOWER.

1 The ability to get to the verge without getting into the war is the necessary art. . . . If you try to run away from it, if you are scared to go to the brink, you are lost.
Quoted in *Life* 16 January 1956. The Democrat ADLAI STEVENSON characterized the Dulles–Eisenhower foreign policy as 'the power of positive brinking'.

(Dame) Daphne Du Maurier (1907–89)
BRITISH NOVELIST
She specialized in melodramatic romances in a Cornish setting such as Jamaica Inn *(1936) and*

Rebecca *(1938, filmed 1940)*. *'I don't know another author who* imagines *so hard all the time,' commented a reader at Gollancz after perusing the manuscript of* Rebecca.

1 Last night I dreamt I went to Manderley again.
Rebecca, ch. 1 (1938). Opening words.

2 It's people like me who have careers who really have bitched up the old relationship between men and women. Women ought to be soft and gentle and dependent. Disembodied spirits like myself are all *wrong*.
Letter to Ellen Doubleday, 2 September 1948, publ. in *Daphne Du Maurier*, ch. 14 (1993) by Margaret Forster

3 I think one has to choose, you know. Either to create after one's fashion, or be a woman and breed. The two don't go together and never will.
Letter to Ellen Doubleday, 22 February 1950, publ. ibid., ch. 15

4 What makes people get the craving? . . . There never seems an answer. You might say loneliness. But to my mind, drinking and making love are the two most lonely pastimes on earth.
Letter to Ellen Doubleday, 8 August 1952, publ. ibid., ch. 16. Reflecting on desire and lust.

Isadora Duncan (1878–1927)
US DANCER
Born Dora Angela Duncan. A 'glorious bounding Minerva in the midst of a cautious corseted decade', she was a pioneer of modern dance, taking her inspiration from the flowing forms of classical Greek art to produce free, barefoot expression.

1 The only dance masters I could have were Jean-Jacques Rousseau, Walt Whitman and Nietzsche.
My Life, ch. 8 (1927)

2 Perhaps he was a bit different from other people, but what really sympathetic person is not a little mad?
Of the Grand Duke Ferdinand of Hungary, ibid., ch. 11

3 Any intelligent woman who reads the marriage contract and then goes into it, deserves all the consequences.
Ibid., ch. 19. Duncan herself was married (for one year) to the Russian poet Sergei Yesenin

4 The real American type can never be a ballet dancer. The legs are too long, the body too supple and the spirit too free for this school of affected grace and toe walking.
Ibid., ch. 30

5 Farewell, my friends. I go to glory.
Quoted in *Isadora Duncan's End*, ch. 25 (1929) by Mary Desti. Duncan was accidentally strangled when her long scarf caught in the wheel of her car moments after uttering these words (*je vais à la gloire*), which have also been rendered as 'I see glory' (*je vois la gloire*).

Ian Dunlop (b. 1940)
BRITISH ART CRITIC

1 The Shock of the New.
Book title (1972). The full title is *The Shock of the New: Seven Historic Exhibitions of Modern Art*.

Douglas Dunn (b. 1942)
SCOTTISH POET
He fell under the influence of PHILIP LARKIN, *especially in his early work which explores urban working-class culture. Later collections such as* Elegies *(1985) and* Northlight *(1988) reflect wider concerns.*

1 *Heavy rain everywhere washes up the bones of British.*
Where did all that power come from, the wish
To be inert, but rich and strong, to have too much?
'A Poem in Praise of the British', publ. in *Terry Street* (1969)

2 *Film is just a reflection*
Of the matchless despair of the century.
There have been twenty centuries since charity began.
Indignation is day-to-day stuff;
It keeps us off the streets, it keeps us watching.
'I am a Cameraman', publ. in *Love or Nothing* (1974)

3 *Politics soften everything.*
Truth is known only to its victims.
All else is photographs – a documentary
The starving and the playboys perish in.
Life disguises itself with professionalism.
Ibid.

4 *God so loved the world*
He puked every time he looked at it,
With a few miraculous exceptions. He's gone now.
'The White Poet (Homage to Jules Laforgue)', publ. ibid.

5 *And I must mourn*
Until Equator crawls to Capricorn
Or murder in the sun melts down
The Arctic and Antarctica.
'Reincarnations', publ. in *Elegies* (1985)

6 *Snow is its own country, and it beckons*
With its white finger crooked, and is calling
From the hush of its chilled bulk, its tons
And territories, its white ground falling.
'Snow Days', ibid.

7 *Day by nomadic day*
Our anniversaries go by,

Dates anchored in an inner sky,
To utmost ground, interior clay.
'Anniversaries', publ. ibid.

Finley Peter Dunne (1867–1936)

US JOURNALIST AND HUMORIST
As 'Mr Dooley', he presented a common-sense
Irish-American slant on current events in news-
paper sketches from 1892.

1 A man's idea in a card game is war – cruel, devastating and pitiless. A lady's idea of it is a combination of larceny, embezzlement and burglary.
   Mr Dooley on Making a Will, 'On the Game of Cards' (1919)

2 The mission of a modern newspaper is to comfort the afflicted and afflict the comfortable.
   Attributed

J. W. Dunne (1875–1949)

BRITISH INVENTOR AND PHILOSOPHER
John William Dunne. The designer of the first
British military aeroplane (1906–7), he expounded
his theory of the serial nature of time in An Experiment with Time *(1927), an influence on the 'time*
plays' of J. B. PRIESTLEY.

1 We have now arrived within introductory range of that very meek-spirited creature known to modern science as the '*Observer*'. It is a permanent obstacle in the path of our search for external reality that we can never entirely get rid of this individual.
   An Experiment with Time, ch. 3 (1927, rev. 1939)

2 It is never entirely safe to laugh at the metaphysics of the 'man-in-the-street'. Basic ideas which have become enshrined in popular language cannot be wholly foolish or unwarranted.
   Ibid., ch. 17

Will Durant (1885–1981)

US HISTORIAN
Following the international success of The Story of
Philosophy *(1926), he collaborated with his wife*
Ariel on The Story of Civilization *(11 vols. 1935–*
75).

1 Civilization is a stream with banks. The stream is sometimes filled with blood from people killing, stealing, shouting and doing the things historians usually record, while on the banks, unnoticed, people build homes, make love, raise children, sing songs, write poetry and even whittle statues. The story of civilization is the story of what happened on the banks. Historians are pessimists because they ignore the banks for the river.
   Life 18 October 1963

Marguerite Duras (1914–96)

FRENCH AUTHOR AND FILM-MAKER
Pseudonym of Marguerite Donnadieu. Successful
as a novelist from 1950, she gained wider recog-
nition for her screenplays, notably Hiroshima,
mon amour *(1959). She adapted her autobio-*
graphical novel The Lover *(1984) as a film in 1992.*

1 Nowhere is one more alone than in Paris . . . and yet surrounded by crowds. Nowhere is one more likely to incur greater ridicule. And no visit is more essential.
   'Tourists in Paris', first publ. in *France-Observateur* (1957), repr. in *Outside: Selected Writings* (1984)

2 Journalism without a moral position is impossible. Every journalist is a moralist. It's absolutely unavoidable. A journalist is someone who looks at the world and the way it works, someone who takes a close look at things every day and reports what she sees, someone who represents the world, the event, for others. She cannot do her work without judging what she sees.
   Outside: Selected Writings, Foreword (1984)

3 No other human being, no woman, no poem or music, book or painting can replace alcohol in its power to give man the illusion of real creation.
   Practicalities, 'Alcohol' (1987)

4 I believe that always, or almost always, in all childhoods and in all the lives that follow them, the mother represents madness. Our mothers always remain the strangest, craziest people we've ever met.
   Ibid., 'House and Home'

5 You have to be very fond of men! Very, very fond. You have to be very fond of them to love them. Otherwise they're simply unbearable.
   Ibid., 'Men'

Paul Durcan (b. 1944)

IRISH POET
Inventive and lyrical, his poetry portrays with com-
passion and surreal humour characters who are
ostracized or victims of their circumstances. Collec-
tions include O Westport in the Light of Asia
Minor *(1975) and* Jesus, Break His Fall *(1980).*

1 *I have my troubles and I shall always have*
   them
   But I should rather live with you for ever
   Than exchange my troubles for a changeless
   kingdom.
   'The Difficulty that is Marriage', publ. in *Teresa's Bar* (1976)

2 *At a ritual ceremony in a fairy ring fort*
   Near Bodenstown Graveyard, Co. Kildare
   (Burial place of Theobald Wolfe Tone)

Margaret Thatcher joined the IRA
And the IRA joined Margaret Thatcher.
'Margaret Thatcher Joins IRA', publ. in *Sam's Cross* (1978)

3 *Bring me back to the dark school – to the dark school of childhood:*
To where tiny is tiny, and massive is massive.
'En Famille, 1979', publ. in *Jesus, Break His Fall* (1980)

4 *There – but for the clutch of luck – go I.*
'The Death by Heroin of Sid Vicious', first publ. in 1980, repr. in *A Snail in My Prime* (1993). Opening line.

Leo Durocher (1906–91)
US BASEBALL COACH
Nicknamed Leo the Lip, he combined a brilliant baseball career with high living and gambling, though was also criticized for his aggressive approach to the game.

1 Take a look at them. All nice guys. They'll finish last. Nice guys. Finish last.
Remark about the New York Giants, 6 July 1946, quoted in *Nice Guys Finish Last*, pt 1 (1975)

Lawrence Durrell (1914–91)
BRITISH AUTHOR
Brother of the zoologist Gerald Durrell, he was an expatriate for most of his life, using primarily Mediterranean settings for his fiction and poetry. He won acclaim for The Alexandria Quartet *(1957–60) and* Bitter Lemons *(1957).*

1 Everyone loathes his own country and countrymen if he is any sort of artist.
Letter to HENRY MILLER, March 1948, publ. in *The Durrell–Miller Letters 1935–80* (1988)

2 Journeys, like artists, are born and not made. A thousand differing circumstances contribute to them, few of them willed or determined by the will – whatever we may think.
Bitter Lemons, 'Towards an Eastern Landfall' (1957). Opening words.

3 There are only three things to be done with a woman. You can love her, suffer for her, or turn her into literature.
Clea, in *Justine*, pt 1 (1957)

4 No one can go on being a rebel too long without turning into an autocrat.
Pursewarden writing to D. H. Lawrence, in *Balthazar*, pt 2, ch. 6 (1958)

5 Perhaps our only sickness is to desire a truth which we cannot bear rather than to rest content with the fictions we manufacture out of each other.
Justine, in *Clea*, ch. 1, sect. 3 (1960)

6 Music was invented to confirm human loneliness.
Clea, ibid., ch. 1, sect. 4

7 Old age is an insult. It's like being smacked.
Interview in the *Sunday Times* 20 November 1988

8 The appalling thing is the degree of charity women are capable of. You see it all the time . . . love lavished on absolute fools. Love's a charity ward, you know.
Interview in the *Observer* 11 November 1990

Ian Dury (1942–2000)
BRITISH ROCK MUSICIAN
Disabled by polio, he had numerous hits with his band the Blockheads, starting with the album New Boots and Panties *(1977). He later pursued an acting and writing career*

1 *Sex and drugs and rock and roll.*
Is all my brain and body need
Sex and drugs and rock and roll
Is very good indeed.
'Sex and Drugs and Rock and Roll' (song, written with Chaz Jankel) on the album *Sex and Drugs and Rock and Roll* (1976). The song also appeared on a compilation of the same name in 1987.

2 *I'm from Essex, in case you couldn't tell*
My given name Is Dickie
I come from Billericay
And I'm doing . . . very well.
Intro to 'Billericay Dickie' (song, written with Nugent) on the album *New Boots and Panties* (1977) by Ian Dury and the Blockheads

3 *I could be the catalyst that sparks the revolution*
I could be an inmate in a long term institution
I could dream to wide extremes, I could do or die
I could yawn and be withdrawn and watch the world go by
What a waste.
'What a Waste' (song, 1978, written by the band) on the album *Sex and Drugs and Rock and Roll* (1987)

4 *Hit me with your rhythm stick. Hit me! Hit me!*
'Hit Me with Your Rhythm Stick' (song, 1978, written with Chaz Jankel), ibid.

5 *There ain't half been some clever bastards.*
'There Ain't Half Been Some Clever Bastards', ibid.

6 *Reasons to be cheerful.*
'Reasons to be Cheerful (pt 3)' (song, written with Chaz Jankel) on the album *Do It Yourself* (1979) by Ian Dury and the Blockheads

7 *I want to be straight, I want to be straight*
I'm sick and tired of taking drugs and staying up late.

I want to confirm I want to conform
I want to be be safe and I want to be snug
and I want to be warm.

'I Want to be Straight' (song, written with Mickey Gallagher) on the album *Laughter* (1980)

8 Groups are an ecological miracle. In any group of six people you'll always find five bad apples.

Quoted in the *Daily Telegraph* 21 November 1998

Eleonora Duse (1858–1924)

ITALIAN ACTRESS

Rivalling SARAH BERNHARDT, *she toured extensively and was mistress of the poet Gabriele D'Annunzio who wrote parts for her*

1 I did not use paint. I made myself up morally.

Quoted in *Le Gaulois* 27 July 1922. Duse claimed not to 'act' her parts, but 'lived' them.

Andrea Dworkin (b. 1946)

US FEMINIST CRITIC

She has called for pornography to be outlawed in Pornography: Men Possessing Women *(1981), among other works.* Scapegoat: Jews, Israel and Women's Liberation *(2000) examined the role of women in Judaism.*

1 Men who want to support women in our struggle for freedom and justice should understand that it is not terrifically important to us that they learn to cry; it is important to us that they stop the crimes of violence against us.

'The Rape Atrocity and the Boy Next Door', speech at State University of New York, 1 March 1975, publ. in *Our Blood*, ch. 4 (1976)

2 Only when manhood is dead – and it will perish when ravaged femininity no longer sustains it – only then will we know what it is to be free.

'The Root Cause', speech, 26 September 1975, Massachusetts Institute of Technology, publ. in *Our Blood*, ch. 9 (1976). Last words of book.

3 Seduction is often difficult to distinguish from rape. In seduction, the rapist bothers to buy a bottle of wine.

'Sexual Economics: The Terrible Truth', speech, 1976, publ. in *Letters from a War-Zone* (1987)

4 No woman needs intercourse; few women escape it.

Right-Wing Women, ch. 3 (1978)

5 Marriage as an institution developed from rape as a practice. Rape, originally defined as abduction, became marriage by capture. Marriage meant the taking was to extend in time, to be not only use of but possession of, or ownership.

Pornography, ch. 1 (1981)

6 Money speaks, but it speaks with a male voice.

Ibid.

7 Women, for centuries not having access to pornography and now unable to bear looking at the muck on the supermarket shelves, are astonished. Women do not believe that men believe what pornography says about women. But they do. From the worst to the best of them, they do.

Ibid., ch. 5

Bob Dylan (b. 1941)

US SINGER AND SONGWRITER

Originally Robert Zimmerman. One of the seminal influences on popular song in the 1960s, he started as a folk singer, writing songs that became anthems of the protest movement. His lyrics became more abstruse and later reflected his religious convictions. For BRUCE SPRINGSTEEN, *'Bob freed your mind the way Elvis freed your body. . . . He had the vision and the talent to make a pop record that contained the whole world.'*

1 *The answer, my friend, is blowin' in the wind,*
The answer is blowin' in the wind.

'Blowin' in the Wind' (song) on the album *The Freewheelin' Bob Dylan* (1963). On the sleeve notes to the record, Dylan wrote: 'The first way to answer the questions in the song is by asking them. But lots of people have to first find the wind.' One of Dylan's biographers, Bob Spitz, believed this might be the only one of his songs to be remembered a hundred years later. By the end of 1964, it had already been recorded by some sixty artists, and the lyric was quoted by Pope JOHN PAUL II during the Second Eucharist Congress in 1997.

2 *I saw ten thousand talkers whose tongues were all broken,*
I saw guns and sharp swords in the hands of young children,
And it's a hard, it's a hard, it's a hard, it's a hard,
It's a hard rain's a-gonna fall.

'A Hard Rain's A-Gonna Fall' (song) on ibid.

3 *Come mothers and fathers*
Throughout the land
And don't criticize
What you can't understand
Your sons and your daughters
Are beyond your command
Your old road is rapidly agin'.

'The Times They Are A-Changin'' (song) on ibid.

4 *The line it is drawn*
The curse it is cast
The slow one now
Will later be fast
As the present now
Will later be past

The order is
Rapidly fadin'.
And the first one now
Will later be last
For the times they are a-changin'.
Ibid.

5 *Flashing for the warriors whose strength is*
not to fight
Flashing for the refugees on the unarmed
road of flight
An' for each an' ev'ry underdog soldier in
the night
An' we gazed upon the chimes of freedom
flashing.
'Chimes of Freedom' (song) on the album
Another Side of Bob Dylan (1964)

6 *Ah, but I was so much older then,*
I'm younger than that now.
'My Back Pages' (song) on ibid.

7 *You don't need a weather man*
To know which way the wind blows.
'Subterranean Homesick Blues' (song) on the
album *Bringing it All Back Home* (1965)

8 *Don't follow leaders*
And watch the parkin' meters.
Ibid.

9 *I ain't gonna work on Maggie's farm no*
more.
'Maggie's Farm' on ibid. 'Maggie's Farm' was
the name of a strip cartoon created by Steve Bell
during MARGARET THATCHER's government.

10 *In the dime stores and bus stations,*
People talk of situations,
Read books, repeat quotations,
Draw conclusions on the wall.
'Love Minus Zero/No Limit' (song) on ibid.

11 *She knows there's no success like failure*
And that failure's no success at all.
Ibid.

12 *In ceremonies of the horsemen,*
Even the pawn must hold a grudge.
Ibid.

13 *Hey! Mr Tambourine Man, play a song for*
me.
I'm not sleepy and there is no place I'm
going to.
Hey! Mr Tambourine Man, play a song for
me.
In the jingle jangle morning I'll come follow-
ing you.
'Mr Tambourine Man' (song) on ibid.

14 *At times I think there are no words*
But these to tell what's true
And there are no truths outside the Gates of
Eden.
'Gates of Eden' (song) on ibid.

15 *He not busy being born*
Is busy dying.
'It's Alright Ma (I'm Only Bleeding)' (song) on

ibid. In a 'Communiqué' dated 1 May 1971, the
anarchist Angry Brigade wrote: 'If you're not
busy being born you're busy buying.' (*The Angry
Brigade 1967–84: Documents and Chronology* ed.
Jean Weir, 1985)

16 *Everything from toy guns that spark*
To flesh-colored Christs that glow in the
dark
It's easy to see without looking too far
That not much is really sacred.
Ibid.

17 *But even the President of the United States*
Sometimes must have
To stand naked.
Ibid.

18 *Although the masters make the rules*
For the wise men and the fools
I got nothing, Ma, to live up to.
Ibid.

19 *Money doesn't talk, it swears.*
Ibid.

20 *The vagabond who's rapping at your door*
Is standing in the clothes that you once
wore.
Strike another match, go start anew
And it's all over now, Baby Blue.
'It's All Over Now, Baby Blue' (song) on ibid.

21 **A song is anything that can walk by itself.**
Sleeve notes on ibid.

22 *You got a lotta nerve*
To say you are my friend
When I was down
You just stood there grinning.
'Positively 4th Street' (song, 1965) on the album
Bob Dylan's Greatest Hits (1967)

23 *How does it feel*
To be without a home
Like a complete unknown
Like a rolling stone?
'Like a Rolling Stone' (song) on the album *High-
way 61 Revisited* (1965)

24 *Something is happening here*
But you don't know what it is
Do you, Mister Jones?
'Ballad of a Thin Man' (song) on ibid.

25 *You know it balances on your head*
Just like a mattress balances
On a bottle of wine
Your brand new leopard-skin pill-box hat.
'Leopard-Skin Pill-Box Hat' (song) on the
album *Blonde on Blonde* (1966)

26 *They'll stone you when you're riding in*
your car.
They'll stone you when you're playing your
guitar.
Yes, but I would not feel so all alone,
Everybody must get stoned.
'Rainy Day Women 12 & 35' (song) on ibid.

27 *To live outside the law, you must be honest.*
'Absolutely Sweet Marie' (song) on ibid. A similar line is spoken in Don Siegel's film *The Line-Up* (1958).

28 *She takes just like a woman, yes she does*
She makes love just like a woman, yes she does
And she aches just like a woman
But she breaks just like a little girl.
'Just Like a Woman' (song) on ibid.

29 *I see my light come shining*
From the west unto the east
Any day now, any day now,
I shall be released.
'I Shall Be Released' (song, recorded 1967) on the album *The Basement Tapes* (Bob Dylan and the Band, 1975)

30 **You learn from a conglomeration of the incredible past – whatever experience gotten in any way whatsoever.**
Tarantula, 'Subterranean Homesick Blues & the Blond Waltz' (1970)

31 *If I had wings and I could fly,*
I know where I would go.
But right now I'll just sit here so contentedly
And watch the river flow.
'Watching the River Flow' (song, 1971) on the album *More Greatest Hits* (1972)

32 **I like America, just as everybody else does. I love America, I gotta say that. But America will be judged.**
On stage at Tempe, Arizona, 26 November 1979, quoted in *Wanted Man*, 'Saved: Bob Dylan's Conversion to Christianity' (ed. John Bauldie, 1990)

33 *Democracy don't rule the world,*
You'd better get that in your head;
This world is ruled by violence
But I guess that's better left unsaid.
'Union Sundown' (song) on the album *Infidels* (1983)

34 **In writing songs I've learned as much from Cézanne as I have from Woody Guthrie.**
Quoted in *Dylan: Behind the Shades*, ch. 25 (1991) by Clinton Heylin

35 **People today are still living off the table scraps of the sixties. They are still being passed around – the music and the ideas.**
Guardian 13 February 1992

Freeman Dyson (b. 1923)

BRITISH-BORN US PHYSICIST AND AUTHOR
Professor of Physics at the Institute of Advanced Study, Princeton (1953–94), he is known for his research into quantum electrodynamics, and for his work on the nuclear test ban treaty.

1 **If we had a reliable way to label our toys good and bad, it would be easy to regulate technology wisely. But we can rarely see far enough ahead to know which road leads to damnation. Whoever concerns himself with big technology, either to push it forward or to stop it, is gambling in human lives.**
Disturbing the Universe, pt 1, ch. 1 (1979)

2 **A good scientist is a person with original ideas. A good engineer is a person who makes a design that works with as few original ideas as possible. There are no prima donnas in engineering.**
Ibid., pt 1, ch. 10

Terry Eagleton (b. 1943)
BRITISH CRITIC

He has written numerous books of literary criticism within a Marxist framework, including Literary Theory: An Introduction *(1983) and* The Ideology of the Aesthetic *(1990).*

1 Postmodernism is among other things a sick joke at the expense of . . . revolutionary avant-gardism.

'Capitalism, Modernism and Postmodernism', first publ. 1985, repr. in *Against The Grain*, ch. 9 (1986)

2 *Chaucer was a class traitor*
Shakespeare hated the mob
Donne sold out a bit later
Sidney was a nob.

'The Ballad of English Literature' (to the tune of 'Land of Hope and Glory'), publ. ibid., ch. 14

3 Post-structuralism is among other things a kind of theoretical hangover from the failed uprising of '68 – a way of keeping the revolution warm at the level of language, blending the euphoric libertarianism of that moment with the stoical melancholia of its aftermath.

Guardian 27 October 1992

Amelia Earhart (1897–1937)
US AVIATOR AND AUTHOR

In 1932 she was the first woman to fly solo across the Atlantic. She lost her life in an attempt to fly around the world when her plane went down over the Pacific.

1 *Courage is the price that Life exacts for*
granting peace,
The soul that knows it not, knows no
release
From little things;
Knows not the livid loneliness of fear,
Nor mountain heights where bitter joy can
hear
The sound of wings.

'Courage' (1927), publ. in *The Sound of Wings*, ch. 1 (biography, 1989) by Mary S. Lovell

Gerald Early (b. 1952)
US AUTHOR AND ACADEMIC

He has written on themes of race, culture and identity in his essays, collected in Tuxedo Junction *(1989) and* The Culture of Bruising *(1993).*

1 Everyone in our culture wants to win a prize. Perhaps that is the grand lesson we have taken with us from kindergarten in the age of perversions of Dewey-style education: everyone gets a ribbon, and praise becomes a meaningless narcotic to soothe egoistic distemper.

'Life with Daughters: Watching the Miss America Pageant', publ. in *Kenyon Review* autumn 1990, repr. in *The Culture of Bruising* (1993)

Stephen T. Early (1889–1951)

US JOURNALIST AND GOVERNMENT OFFICIAL
One of America's top reporters, he became, in the words of HARRY S. TRUMAN, *'Roosevelt's secretary, friend and sagacious adviser', and was involved in publicity for the New Deal.*

1 I received a card the other day from Steve Early which said, 'Don't Worry Me – I am an 8 Ulcer Man on 4 Ulcer Pay.'

Quoted by Harry S. Truman in letter in 1949, publ. in *Mr President: Personal Diaries, Private Letters, Papers and Revealing Interviews of Harry S. Truman*, pt 5 (1952) by William Hillman

Daniel Easterman (b. 1949)

IRISH AUTHOR
With a special interest in the Middle East, he has published academic books including New Jerusalems: Reflections on Islam, Fundamentalism and the Rushdie Affair *(1993), and novels, such as* The Final Judgement *(1996).*

1 We ignore thriller writers at our peril. Their genre is the political condition. They massage our dreams and magnify our nightmares. If it is true that we always need enemies, then we will always need writers of fiction to encode our fears and fantasies.

Million Magazine September/October 1991

Clint Eastwood (b. 1930)

US ACTOR AND FILM-MAKER
Having established himself as the lean loner in spaghetti westerns such as The Good, the Bad and the Ugly *(1966) and crime thrillers such as* Dirty Harry *(1971), he turned to directing, receiving an Oscar for* Unforgiven *(1992).*

1 I know what you're thinking. Did he fire six shots or only five? Well, to tell you the truth, in all this excitement I've kinda lost track myself. But being this is a .44 Magnum, the most powerful handgun in the world, and would blow your head clean off – you've got to ask yourself one question: Do I feel lucky? Well, do ya, punk?

Harry Callahan (Clint Eastwood), in *Dirty Harry* (film, 1971, screenplay by Harry and Rita Fink and Dean Riesner, directed by Don Siegel). The words are addressed to a bank-robber, at whose head Harry has his gun aimed, following a foiled heist.

2 Everybody knows nobody ever stood in the street and let the heavy draw first. That's where I disagree with the [John] Wayne concept. I do all the stuff Wayne would never do. I play bigger-than-life characters

but I'll shoot a guy in the back. I go by the expediency of the moment.

Variety 14 September 1976

3 Go ahead. Make my day.

Harry Callahan (Clint Eastwood), in *Sudden Impact* (film, 1983, screenplay by Joseph Stinson, produced and directed by Clint Eastwood). RONALD REAGAN, a self-confessed Eastwood fan, borrowed the words in 1985: 'I have only one thing to say to the tax increasers: "Go ahead and make my day." '

Eazy-E (1963–95)

US RAPPER
Originally Eric Wright. A founding member of the controversial Californian group NWA (Niggaz With Attitude), he was one of the earliest exponents of 'gangsta rap' in the 1980s.

1 **Fuck tha police coming straight out the underground**
A young nigger got it bad cause I'm brown
And not the other color.

'Fuck tha Police' (song) on the album *Straight Outta Compton* (1989) by NWA. The inflammatory lyrics provoked outrage in the US, and calls for the recording to be withdrawn.

Abba Eban (1915–2002)

ISRAELI POLITICIAN AND DIPLOMAT
Originally Aubrey Solomon. He was ambassador to the United States in Washington (1950–59), won a seat in the Knesset in 1959 and was Foreign Minister 1966–74.

1 History teaches us that men and nations behave wisely once they have exhausted all other alternatives.

Speech in London, 16 December 1970, quoted in *The Times* 17 December 1970

2 It is our experience that political leaders do not always mean the opposite of what they say.

Quoted in the *Observer* 5 December 1971

Umberto Eco (b. 1932)

ITALIAN SEMIOLOGIST AND NOVELIST
A high-profile European intellectual and a pioneer in the science of signs, he is the author of A Theory of Semiotics *(1976) and the best-selling novels* The Name of the Rose *(1980), a postmodern medieval murder mystery, and* Foucault's Pendulum *(1988).*

1 There is a constant in the average American imagination and taste, for which the past must be preserved and celebrated in full-scale authentic copy; a philosophy of immortality as duplication. It dominates the relation with the self, with the past, not infrequently with the present, always with

History and, even, with the European tradition.
'Travels in Hyperreality: The Fortresses of Solitude' (1975), repr. in *Travels in Hyperreality* (1986)

2 Because learning does not consist only of knowing what we must or we can do, but also of knowing what we could do and perhaps should not do.
Brother William, in *The Name of the Rose*, 'First Day: Compline' (1980)

3 Until then I had thought each book spoke of the things, human or divine, that lie outside books. Now I realized that not infrequently books speak of books: it is as if they spoke among themselves.
Narrator (Adso), ibid., 'Fourth Day: Terce'

4 The good of a book lies in its being read. A book is made up of signs that speak of other signs, which in their turn speak of things. Without an eye to read them, a book contains signs that produce no concepts; therefore it is dumb.
Brother William, ibid., 'Fifth Day: Vespers'

5 Perhaps the mission of those who love mankind is to make people laugh at the truth, *to make truth laugh*, because the only truth lies in learning to free ourselves from insane passion for the truth.
Ibid., 'Seventh Day: Night'

6 I have never doubted the truth of signs, Adso; they are the only things man has with which to orient himself in the world.
Ibid.

7 I would define the poetic effect as the capacity that a text displays for continuing to generate different readings, without ever being completely consumed.
Reflections on the Name of the Rose, 'Telling the Process' (1983)

8 The postmodern reply to the modern consists of recognizing that the past, since it cannot really be destroyed, because its destruction leads to silence, must be revisited: but with irony, not innocently. I think of the postmodern attitude as that of a man who loves a very cultivated woman and knows he cannot say to her, 'I love you madly', because he knows that she knows (and that she knows that he knows) that these words have already been written by Barbara Cartland. Still, there is a solution. He can say, 'As Barbara Cartland would put it, I love you madly.'
Ibid., 'Postmodernism, Irony, the Enjoyable'

(Sir) Arthur Stanley Eddington
(1882–1944)
BRITISH ASTRONOMER AND PHYSICIST
He was the first to confirm EINSTEIN's *theory of*

relativity, while observing the stars during the solar eclipse of 1919. His books helped to popularize science, especially* The Nature of the Physical World (1928).

1 Let us draw an arrow arbitrarily. If as we follow the arrow we find more and more of the random element in the world, then the arrow is pointing towards the future; if the random element decreases the arrow points towards the past ... I shall use the phrase 'time's arrow' to express this one-way property of time which has no analogue in space.
The Nature of the Physical World, ch. 4 (1928). 'Time's Arrow' was the title MARTIN AMIS gave to his 1991 novel in which the sequence of time is reversed.

2 I ask you to look both ways. For the road to a knowledge of the stars leads through the atom; and important knowledge of the atom has been reached through the stars.
Stars and Atoms, 'Lecture 1' (1928)

3 It cannot be denied that for a society which has to create scarcity to save its members from starvation, to whom abundance spells disaster, and to whom unlimited energy means unlimited power for war and destruction, there is an ominous cloud in the distance though at present it be no bigger than a man's hand.
New Pathways in Science, ch. 8 (1935)

Leon Edel (1907–97)
US BIOGRAPHER AND CRITIC
The foremost authority on HENRY JAMES, *he published the definitive biography (5 vols., 1953–72) and numerous editions of letters.*

1 The secret of biography resides in finding the link between talent and achievement. A biography seems irrelevant if it doesn't discover the overlap between what the individual did and the life that made this possible. Without discovering that, you have shapeless happenings and gossip.
Interview in *Writers at Work* (eighth series, ed. George Plimpton, 1988)

(Sir) Anthony Eden (1897–1977)
BRITISH POLITICIAN AND PRIME MINISTER
First Earl of Avon. Elected a Conservative MP in 1923, he served as Foreign Secretary twice under CHURCHILL, *whom he succeeded as Prime Minister (1955–7). He resigned following criticism of his conduct in the Suez crisis. See* MALCOLM MUGGERIDGE 9.

1 Everybody is always in favour of general economy and particular expenditure.
Quoted in the *Observer* 17 June 1956

2 We are in an armed conflict; that is the

phrase I have used. There has been no declaration of war.

Speech to House of Commons, 1 November 1956, publ. in *Hansard*. British and French planes had bombed Egyptian airfields on the preceding day, provoking protests in Britain and abroad. Eden justified the action: 'We best avoid wars by taking even physical action to stop small ones.'

3 It is either him [Colonel Nasser] or us, don't forget that.

Quoted in *We, the Nation*, ch. 14 (1995) by A. J. Davies

Clarissa Eden (1920–85)

WIFE OF ANTHONY EDEN

Countess of Avon. Originally Clarissa Spencer Churchill, she was the niece of WINSTON CHURCHILL, *marrying* ANTHONY EDEN *in 1952.*

1 For the past few weeks I have really felt as if the Suez Canal was flowing through my drawing room.

Speech at Gateshead, 20 November 1956, quoted in the *Gateshead Post* 23 November 1956

Jerry Edmonton (b. 1946)

CANADIAN ROCK MUSICIAN

Also known as Mars Bonfire, he was drummer with the rock band Steppenwolf in the 1960s and '70s, and occasional composer of their lyrics.

1 *Born to be wild.*

'Born to be Wild' (song) on the album *Steppenwolf* (1968) by Steppenwolf. The song, which became a biker anthem, featured in DENNIS HOPPER's film, *Easy Rider* (1969).

Edward VIII (1894–1972)

KING OF GREAT BRITAIN AND NORTHERN IRELAND

Though succeeding to the throne in 1936, he was never crowned, abdicating after eleven months in order to marry Wallis Simpson, a twice-divorced American. After the Second World War, the couple spent the rest of their lives in Paris as Duke and Duchess of Windsor.

1 These works brought all these people here. Something should be done to get them at work again.

Comment at the derelict Dowlais Iron and Steel Works in South Wales, 18 November 1936, quoted in the *Western Mail* 19 November 1936. 9000 men had recently been laid off at the works. The remark is usually quoted as 'Something must be done.'

2 I have found it impossible to carry the heavy burden of responsibility and to discharge my duties as King as I would wish to do without the help and support of the woman I love. . . . I now quit altogether public affairs, and I lay down my burden.

Abdication speech, 11 December 1936, publ. in

The Times 12 December 1936. WINSTON CHURCHILL is said to have had a hand in composing the speech, which was broadcast on radio.

3 The thing that impresses me most about America is the way parents obey their children.

Quoted in *Look* 5 March 1957

Barbara Ehrenreich (b. 1941)

US AUTHOR AND COLUMNIST

She is best known for her outspoken and humorous newspaper columns, mainly on issues of health, sex and class and from a feminist angle.

1 Exercise is the yuppie version of bulimia.

'Food Worship', first publ. 1985, repr. in *The Worst Years of Our Lives* (1991)

2 Personally, I have nothing against work, particularly when performed, quietly and unobtrusively, by someone else. I just don't happen to think it's an appropriate subject for an 'ethic'.

'Goodbye to the Work Ethic', first publ. 1988, repr. ibid.

3 America is addicted to wars of distraction.

The Times 22 April 1991

John Ehrlichman (1925–99)

PRESIDENTIAL ASSISTANT TO RICHARD NIXON

As Chief Adviser on Domestic Policy under President NIXON, *he attempted to block investigations into the Watergate break-in, for which he and* H. R. HALDEMAN *were nicknamed the 'Berlin Wall'. He served an eighteen-month prison term for conspiracy, perjury and obstruction of justice.*

1 I think we ought to let him hang there. Let him twist slowly, slowly in the wind.

Telephone conversation with John Dean, March 1973, quoted in the *Washington Post* 27 July 1973. The words refer to Patrick Gray, a nominee for director of the FBI from whom President NIXON had tacitly withdrawn his support.

2 It'll play in Peoria.

Attributed quip regarding the selling of political policy in 'middle America' (Peoria is in Illinois). Ehrlichman claimed to have originated the catch-phrase during Nixon's 1968 election campaign, though other sources suggest it was current much earlier, used in US variety shows in the 1930s.

Albert Einstein (1879–1955)

GERMAN-BORN US THEORETICAL PHYSICIST

A giant in the fields of space, time and gravitation, he was, in the words of C. P. Snow, 'the symbol of science, the master of the twentieth-century intellect'. His theory of relativity was published in 1905, his general theory of relativity in 1915. See ROLAND BARTHES 4.

1 By an application of the theory of relativity

to the taste of readers, today in Germany I am called a German man of science, and in England I am represented as a Swiss Jew. If I come to be regarded as a *bête noire* the descriptions will be reversed, and I shall become a Swiss Jew for the Germans and a German man of science for the English!

The Times 28 November 1919. Einstein expressed variations of this idea on different occasions.

2 God is subtle, but he is not malicious.

Quoted in *Einstein*, ch. 14 (1973) by R. W. Clark. The remark was made in April/May 1921, during Einstein's first visit to Princeton University, in response to the news that a 'nonzero aether drift' had been found at Mount Vernon observatory. The words were later carved above the fireplace of the Common Room of Fine Hall in Princeton's former Mathematical Institute. In 1946 Einstein gave a freer translation: 'God is slick, but he ain't mean.'

3 Quantum mechanics is certainly imposing. But an inner voice tells me that it is not yet the real thing. The theory says a lot, but does not really bring us any closer to the secret of the 'old one'. I, at any rate, am convinced that *He* is not playing at dice.

Letter to Max Born, 4 December 1926, publ. in *The Born–Einstein Letters* (ed. Max Born, 1971). The version usually remembered is 'God does not play dice [with the universe]'. Nearly twenty years later, Einstein wrote to Born: 'You believe in the God who plays dice, and I in complete law and order in a world which objectively exists, and which I, in a wildly speculative way, am trying to capture. . . . Even the great initial success of the quantum theory does not make me believe in the fundamental dice-game, although I am well aware that our younger colleagues interpret this as a consequence of senility. No doubt the day will come when we will see whose instinctive attitude was the correct one.'
(7 September 1944)

4 It has often been said, and certainly not without justification, that the man of science is a poor philosopher.

'Physics and Reality', publ. in the *Franklin Institute Journal* March 1936, repr. in *Out of My Later Years*, ch. 12, sect. 1 (1950)

5 The whole of science is nothing more than a refinement of everyday thinking.
Ibid.

6 One may say 'the eternal mystery of the world is its comprehensibility' . . . The fact that it is comprehensible is a miracle.
Ibid.

7 Science without religion is lame, religion without science is blind.

From a scientific paper at conference in New York City, September 1940, repr. ibid., ch. 7, sect. 2, 'Science and Religion'

8 We should take care not to make the intel-

lect our god; it has, of course, powerful muscles, but no personality.

From a broadcast for the United Jewish Appeal, 11 April 1943, publ. ibid., ch. 50

9 The unleashed power of the atom has changed everything save our modes of thinking and we thus drift toward unparalleled catastrophe.

Telegram sent to prominent Americans, 24 May 1946, publ. in *The New York Times* 25 May 1946. Various versions of this statement exist, probably translations from the German which Einstein always preferred to use: see *Albert Einstein: A Documentary Biography*, ch. 8 (1956) by Carl Seelig, and *Albert Einstein: A Biography*, ch. 14 (1954) by Antonina Valentin.

10 One has to divide one's time between politics and our equations. Equations are much more important to me, because politics is for the present, while . . . an equation is for eternity.

Remark at Princeton, late 1940s, quoted in *Albert Einstein*, ch. 38 (1993) by Albrecht Fösling. Einstein was then involved with the Emergency Committee of Atomic Scientists (set up to inform the public about the atomic bomb and its effects), of which he became Chairman in May 1946.

11 The most beautiful emotion we can experience is the mystical. It is the power of all true art and science. He to whom this emotion is a stranger, who can no longer wonder and stand rapt in awe, is as good as dead. To know that what is impenetrable to us really exists, manifesting itself as the highest wisdom and the most radiant beauty, which our dull faculties can comprehend only in their most primitive forms – this knowledge, this feeling, is at the center of true religiousness. In this sense, and in this sense only, I belong to the rank of devoutly religious men.

Quoted in *Einstein: His Life and Times*, ch. 12, sect. 5 (1947) by Philip Frank

12 I cannot seriously believe in it [quantum theory] because the theory cannot be reconciled with the idea that physics should represent a reality in time and space, free from spooky actions at a distance.

Letter to Max Born, 3 March 1947, publ. in *The Born–Einstein Letters* (ed. Max Born, 1971)

13 When you are courting a nice girl an hour seems like a second. When you sit on a red-hot cinder a second seems like an hour. That's relativity.

Quoted in the *News Chronicle* 14 March 1949

14 Perfection of means and confusion of goals seem – in my opinion – to characterize our age.

Out of My Later Years, ch. 14 (1950)

15 People like us, who believe in physics,

know that the distinction between past, present and future is only a stubbornly persistent illusion.

Letter 21 March 1955, publ. in *Albert Einstein, Michele Besso: Correspondence 1903–1955*, no. 215 (1972)

16 A (Success) = X (Work) + Y (Play) + Z (Keep your mouth shut).

Quoted in *Albert Einstein: A Documentary Biography*, ch. 3 (1956) by Carl Seelig

17 As far as the laws of mathematics refer to reality, they are not certain; and as far as they are certain, they do not refer to reality.

Quoted by Fritjof Capra in *The Tao of Physics*, ch. 2 (1975)

18 Two things are infinite: the universe and human stupidity. But I'm not sure about the universe.

Attributed

Dwight D. Eisenhower (1890–1969)

US GENERAL, REPUBLICAN POLITICIAN AND PRESIDENT

Dwight David Eisenhower. Supreme Commander of the Allied Forces leading the D-Day invasions in 1944, 'Ike' was given command over all NATO forces in Europe in 1951, and subsequently served two terms as Republican president (1953–61). The journalist Murray Kempton called him 'the great tortoise upon whose back the world sat for eight years'. See ADLAI STEVENSON 19.

1 Humility must always be the portion of any man who receives acclaim earned in the blood of his followers and the sacrifices of his friends.

Speech at Guildhall, London, 12 July 1945, publ. in *Eisenhower Speaks* (ed. Rudolph L. Treunfels, 1948)

2 Every gun that is made, every warship launched, every rocket fired, signifies, in the final sense, a theft from those who hunger and are not fed, those who are cold and are not clothed. The world in arms is not spending money alone. It is spending the sweat of its labourers, the genius of its scientists, the hopes of its children.

'The Chance for Peace', speech to the American Society of Newspaper Editors, Washington DC, 16 April 1953, publ. in *Public Papers of the Presidents of the United States* (1953)

3 Politics ought to be the part-time profession of every citizen who would protect the rights and privileges of free people and who would preserve what is good and fruitful in our national heritage.

Speech broadcast 28 January 1954, publ. ibid. (1954)

4 You have a row of dominoes set up; you knock over the first one, and what will hap-pen to the last one is that it will go over very quickly.

Press conference 7 April 1954, publ. ibid. Referring to the situation in south-east Asia following the defeat of the French by the Viet-Minh.

5 In the councils of government, we must guard against the acquisition of unwarranted influence, whether sought or unsought, by the military-industrial complex. The potential for the disastrous rise of misplaced power exists and will persist. We must never let the weight of this combination endanger our liberties or democratic processes. We should take nothing for granted.

Farewell broadcast on radio and television 17 January 1961, quoted in *The New York Times* 18 January 1961

6 In preparing for battle I have always found that plans are useless, but planning is indispensable.

One of Eisenhower's favourite maxims, quoted by RICHARD NIXON in *Six Crises*, 'Khrushchev' (1962)

T. S. Eliot (1888–1965)

ANGLO-AMERICAN POET AND CRITIC

Thomas Stearns Eliot. By the time The Waste Land *appeared (1922), he was regarded as the voice of a disillusioned post-First World War generation. His later verse plays and poetry, including* Murder in the Cathedral *(1935) and the* Four Quartets *(1936–42), reflect his conversion to Anglo-Catholicism. See* TOM PAULIN 4.

1 *Let us go then, you and I,*
When the evening is spread out against the sky
Like a patient etherised upon a table.

'The Love Song of J. Alfred Prufrock', publ. in *Prufrock and Other Observations* (1917). Opening lines of poem.

2 *In the room the women come and go*
Talking of Michelangelo.

Ibid.

3 *And indeed there will be time*
To wonder, 'Do I dare?' and, 'Do I dare?'
Time to turn back and descend the stair,
With a bald spot in the middle of my hair. . . .
Do I dare
Disturb the universe?

Ibid.

4 *I have measured out my life with coffee spoons.*

Ibid.

5 *No! I am not Prince Hamlet, nor was meant to be:*
Am an attendant lord, one that will do

To swell a progress, start a scene or two,
Advise the prince.
Ibid.

6 *I grow old . . . I grow old . . .*
I shall wear the bottoms of my trousers
rolled.
Ibid.

7 *Shall I part my hair behind? Do I dare to*
eat a peach?
I shall wear white flannel trousers, and
walk upon the beach.
I have heard the mermaids singing, each to
each.
I do not think that they will sing to me.
Ibid.

8 It [tradition] cannot be inherited, and if
you want it you must obtain it by great
labour.
'Tradition and the Individual Talent', sect. 1,
first publ. in *Egoist* September and December
1919, repr. in *Selected Prose of T. S. Eliot* (ed.
Frank Kermode, 1975)

9 Art never improves, but . . . the material of
art is never quite the same.
Ibid.

10 The progress of an artist is a continual self-
sacrifice, a continual extinction of personality.
Ibid.

11 Poetry is not a turning loose of emotion,
but an escape from emotion; it is not the
expression of personality, but an escape
from personality. But, of course, only
those who have personality and emotions
know what it means to want to escape
from these things.
Ibid.

12 *Uncorseted, her friendly bust*
Gives promise of pneumatic bliss.
'Whispers of Immortality', publ. in *Poems* (1919).
Grishkin – the character described here – is
thought to be a portrayal of Serafima Astafieva
(1876–1934), a Russian dancer with the Diaghilev
company who opened her own ballet school in
London. EZRA POUND also referred to her in his
Pisan Cantos 77 and 79 (1945).

13 Immature poets imitate; mature poets steal.
The Sacred Wood, 'Philip Massinger' (1920)

14 *Here I am, an old man in a dry month,*
Being read to by a boy, waiting for rain.
'Gerontion', publ. in *Ara Vos Prec* (1920). Open-
ing lines of poem.

15 In the seventeenth century a dissociation
of sensibility set in, from which we have
never recovered; and this dissociation, as is
natural, was due to the influence of the
two most powerful poets of the century,
Milton and Dryden.
'The Metaphysical Poets', first publ. in *The
Times Literary Supplement* 20 October 1921, repr.

in *Selected Prose of T. S. Eliot* (ed. Frank Kermode, 1975)

16 Poets in our civilization, as it exists at present, must be *difficult*.
Ibid.

17 *April is the cruellest month, breeding*
Lilacs out of the dead land, mixing
Memory and desire, stirring
Dull roots with spring rain.
The Waste Land, pt 1, 'The Burial of the Dead'
(1922). Opening lines of poem.

18 *I will show you fear in a handful of dust.*
Ibid.

19 *Unreal City,*
Under the brown fog of a winter dawn.
Ibid. The lines are repeated in pt 3 of the poem,
with 'noon' substituted for 'dawn'.

20 *I had not thought death had undone so*
many.
Ibid.

21 *I Tiresias, though blind, throbbing between*
two lives,
Old man with wrinkled female breasts, can
see
At the violet hour, the evening hour that
strives
Homeward, and brings the sailor home
from sea,
The typist home at teatime, clears her break-
fast, lights
Her stove, and lays out food in tins.
Ibid., pt 3, 'The Fire Sermon'

22 *O City city, I can sometimes hear*
Beside a public bar in Lower Thames Street,
The pleasant whining of a mandoline
And a clatter and a chatter from within
Where fishmen lounge at noon.
Ibid.

23 *Who is the third who walks always beside*
you?
When I count, there are only you and I
together
But when I look ahead up the white road
There is always another one walking beside
you.
Ibid., pt 5, 'What the Thunder Said'

24 *The awful daring of a moment's surrender*
Which an age of prudence can never retract.
Ibid.

25 *These fragments I have shored against my*
ruins.
Ibid.

26 *Between the conception*
And the creation
Between the emotion
And the response
Falls the Shadow.
'The Hollow Men', sect. 5, publ. in *Poems 1909–*
1925 (1925)

27　*This is the way the world ends*
　　This is the way the world ends
　　This is the way the world ends
　　Not with a bang but a whimper.
　　Ibid. Concluding lines of poem.

28　*The dreamcrossed twilight between birth*
　　　and dying.
　　'Ash-Wednesday', pt 6 (1930), repr. in *Collected
　　Poems 1909–1935* (1936)

29　*So far as we are human, what we do must
　　be either evil or good: so far as we do evil
　　or good, we are human: and it is better, in
　　a paradoxical way, to do evil than to do
　　nothing: at least we exist.*
　　'Baudelaire', first publ. as Introduction to *The
　　Intimate Journals of Charles Baudelaire* (transl.
　　CHRISTOPHER ISHERWOOD, 1930), repr. in
　　Selected Prose of T. S. Eliot (ed. Frank Kermode,
　　1975)

30　*Where is the Life we have lost in living?
　　Where is the wisdom we have lost in
　　　knowledge?
　　Where is the knowledge we have lost in
　　　information?*
　　'Choruses from "The Rock" ', pt 1 (1934), repr.
　　in *Collected Poems 1909–62* (1962)

31　*And the wind shall say 'Here were decent
　　　godless people;
　　Their only monument the asphalt road
　　And a thousand lost golf balls.'*
　　Ibid., pt 3

32　*And meanwhile we have gone on living,
　　Living and partly living,
　　Picking together the pieces,
　　Gathering faggots at nightfall,
　　Building a partial shelter,
　　For sleeping and eating and drinking and
　　　laughter.*
　　The Chorus of Women of Canterbury, in *Mur-
　　der in the Cathedral*, pt 1 (1935)

33　*The last temptation is the greatest treason:
　　To do the right deed for the wrong reason.*
　　Thomas, ibid.

34　*Time past and time future
　　What might have been and what has been
　　Point to one end, which is always present.*
　　'Burnt Norton', pt 1 (1936), the first of *Four
　　Quartets* (1935–42)

35　*Footfalls echo in the memory
　　Down the passage which we did not take
　　Towards the door we never opened
　　Into the rose-garden.*
　　Ibid.

36　*Human kind
　　Cannot bear very much reality.*
　　Ibid. The words also appeared in Eliot's *Murder
　　in the Cathedral* pt 2 (spoken by Thomas), and
　　have been evoked or echoed by numerous other
　　writers; for example GRAHAM GREENE in *Our
　　Man in Havana* (1958), where Hasselbacher

states, 'Reality in our century is not something
to be faced', and in MARGARET DRABBLE's
Realms of Gold (1975): 'The human mind can
bear plenty of reality but not too much intermit-
tent gloom.'

37　*Where does one go from a world of
　　　insanity?
　　Somewhere on the other side of despair.*
　　Harry, Lord Monchensey, in *The Family
　　Reunion*, pt 2, sc. 2 (1939)

38　*The Naming of Cats is a difficult matter,
　　It isn't just one of your holiday games;
　　You may think at first I'm as mad as a
　　　hatter
　　When I tell you, a cat must have THREE
　　　DIFFERENT NAMES.*
　　'The Naming of Cats', publ. in *Old Possum's
　　Book of Practical Cats* (1939)

39　*Jellicle Cats come out tonight
　　Jellicle Cats come one come all:
　　The Jellicle Moon is shining bright –
　　Jellicles come to the Jellicle Ball.*
　　'The Song of the Jellicles', publ. ibid.

40　*Macavity's a Mystery Cat: he's called the
　　　Hidden Paw –
　　For he's the master criminal who can defy
　　　the Law.
　　He's the bafflement of Scotland Yard, the
　　　Flying Squad's despair:
　　For when they reach the scene of crime –
　　　Macavity's not there!*
　　'Macavity: the Mystery Cat', publ. ibid.

41　*In my beginning is my end.*
　　'East Coker', pt 1 (1940), the second of *Four
　　Quartets* (1936–42). Opening line of poem. The
　　motto of Mary Queen of Scots was 'In my end is
　　my beginning.'

42　*The dripping blood our only drink,
　　The bloody flesh our only food:
　　In spite of which we like to think
　　That we are sound, substantial flesh and
　　　blood –
　　Again, in spite of that, we call this Friday
　　　good.*
　　Ibid., pt 4

43　*Each venture
　　Is a new beginning, a raid on the
　　　inarticulate
　　With shabby equipment always deter-
　　　iorating
　　In the general mess of imprecision of
　　　feeling.*
　　Ibid., pt 5

44　The first condition of right thought is right
　　sensation – the first condition of under-
　　standing a foreign country is to smell it.
　　A Choice of Kipling's Verse, Introduction (1941),
　　repr. in *On Poetry and Poets*, pt 2, 'Rudyard
　　Kipling' (1957)

45 *I do not know much about gods; but I think
    that the river
    Is a strong brown god – sullen, untamed
    and intractable.*

'The Dry Salvages', pt 1 (1941), the third of *Four
Quartets* (1935–42). Opening lines of poem.

46 *War is not a life: it is a situation,
    One which may neither be ignored nor
    accepted.*

'A Note on War Poetry', first publ. in *London
Calling* (1942) by STORM JAMESON, repr. in *Collected Poems 1909–62* (1962)

47 *It seems just possible that a poem might
    happen
    To a very young man: but a poem is not
    poetry –
    That is a life.*

Ibid.

48 *And what the dead had no speech for, when
    living,
    They can tell you, being dead: the communi-
    cation
    Of the dead is tongued with fire beyond the
    language of the living.*

'Little Gidding', pt 1 (1942), the fourth of *Four
Quartets* (1935–42)

49 *There are flood and drouth
    Over the eyes and in the mouth,
    Dead water and dead sand
    Contending for the upper hand.
    The parched eviscerate soil
    Gapes at the vanity of toil,
    Laughs without mirth.
    This is the death of earth.*

Ibid., pt 2

50 *For last year's words belong to last year's
    language
    And next year's words await another voice.*

Ibid.

51 *A people without history
    Is not redeemed from time, for history is a
    pattern
    Of timeless moments.*

Ibid., pt 5

52 *We shall not cease from exploration
    And the end of all our exploring
    Will be to arrive where we started
    And know the place for the first time.*

Ibid.

53 Culture may even be described simply as
    that which makes life worth living.

Notes Towards a Definition of Culture, ch. 1
(1948)

54 The term *culture* . . . includes all the charac-
    teristic activities and interests of a people:
    Derby Day, Henley Regatta, Cowes, the
    twelfth of August, a cup final, the dog
    races, the pin table, the dart board,
    Wensleydale cheese, boiled cabbage cut
    into sections, beetroot in vinegar,

nineteenth-century Gothic churches and
the music of Elgar.

Ibid.

55 *You will find that you survive humiliation.
    And that's an experience of incalculable
    value.*

Unidentified Guest (later identified as Sir Henry
Harcourt-Reilly), in *The Cocktail Party*, act 1,
sc. 1 (1950)

56 *Hell is oneself,
    Hell is alone, the other figures in it
    Merely projections. There is nothing to
    escape from
    And nothing to escape to. One is always
    alone.*

Edward, ibid., act 1, sc. 3

57 The years between fifty and seventy are the
    hardest. You are always being asked to do
    things, and yet you are not decrepit
    enough to turn them down.

Time 23 October 1950

58 It's not wise to violate rules until you
    know how to observe them.

Interview in *Writers at Work* (second series, ed.
George Plimpton, 1963)

59 It is a medium of entertainment which
    permits millions of people to listen to the
    same joke at the same time, and yet remain
    lonesome.

Of television, in the *New York Post* 22 September
1963

Elizabeth II (b. 1926)

QUEEN OF GREAT BRITAIN AND NORTHERN
IRELAND
*Queen since 1952 and deeply committed to the con-
cept of the Commonwealth, she has upheld the traditional, formal role of the monarchy while
conceding a degree of modernization*

1 I declare before you all that my whole life,
   whether it be long or short, shall be
   devoted to your service and the service of
   our great Imperial family to which we all
   belong.

Speech to the Commonwealth, Cape Town,
21 April 1947, quoted in *The Times* 22 April 1947

2 My husband and I . . .

Opening words of her first Christmas Message,
1953, New Zealand. This introductory phrase
became a regular feature of the Queen's
speeches, though the alternative 'Prince Philip
and I . . .' was introduced in the 1960s when it
was apparent that the familiar formula was
becoming a joke. On her 25th wedding anniversary, she joked, 'I think everybody really will concede that on this, of all days, I should begin my
speech with the words "My husband and I".'

3 Like all the best families, we have our
   share of eccentricities, of impetuous and

wayward youngsters and of family dis-
agreements.
Quoted in the *Daily Mail* 19 October 1989

4 **It's all to do with the training: you can do
a lot if you're properly trained.**
Television documentary, BBC 1, 6 February 1992

5 **1992 is not a year I shall look back on with
undiluted pleasure. In the words of one of
my more sympathetic correspondents, it
has turned out to be an Annus Horribilis.**
Speech at Guildhall, 24 November 1992, quoted
in *The Times* 25 November 1992. In a speech
commemorating her forty years on the throne,
the Queen's allusion to John Dryden's long
poem 'Annus Mirabilis' (1667) was lost on much
of the nation, though the tabloid press enjoyed it
(see SUN 8). Dryden had described 1666 as a
'year of marvels', whose events included the
Great Fire of London. A fire had gutted some of
the State Apartments in Windsor Castle a few
days before the Queen's speech, while other personal disasters included the separation of the
Prince and Princess of Wales amid sustained
criticism of the royal family in the press.

6 **Some things stay there, some things go out
of the other ear, and some things don't go
in at all.**
Quoted in the *Guardian* 20 April 1996. On her
weekly meetings with prime ministers.

Elizabeth, Queen Mother
(1900–2002)
WIFE OF KING GEORGE VI OF GREAT BRITAIN
AND NORTHERN IRELAND
*Her decision to remain in London during the Blitz
earned her the lasting affection of the British
public. After her husband's death she undertook
extensive public duties. To her friend Cecil Beaton,
she was 'everyone's favourite granny', but to Princess DIANA she was 'chief leper in the leper
colony'.*

1 **I'm glad we've been bombed. It makes me
feel I can look the East End in the face.**
Quoted in *King George VI*, pt 3, ch. 6 (1958) by
John Wheeler-Bennett. Said to a policeman after
the bombing of Buckingham Palace by German
planes. The East End bore the brunt of the
destruction in London during the Second World
War.

2 **The children will not leave unless I do, I
shall not leave unless their father does, and
the King will not leave the country in any
circumstances whatever.**
Attributed response to the suggestion that she
and Princesses Elizabeth and Margaret be evacu-
ated to Canada during the Blitz.

Duke Ellington (1899–1974)
US JAZZ MUSICIAN
*Born Edward Kennedy Ellington. Hailed as a
'Harlem Dionysus', he composed numberless tunes*
*for his own big band, including 'Creole Love Call'
(1927) and 'Mood Indigo' (1930), as well as suites,
ballet and film scores. The novelist and poet Blaise
Cendrars judged his music 'not only a new art
form but a new reason for living'.*

1 **It don't mean a thing if it ain't got that
swing.**
'It Don't Mean a Thing if it Ain't Got that
Swing' (song, 1932, written with Irving Mills).
Ellington said that Bubber Miley, a trumpeter in
the band in New Orleans during the late 1920s,
was the first person he ever heard use the
expression.

2 **Playing 'bop' is like playing Scrabble with
all the vowels missing.**
Look 10 August 1954

Alice Thomas Ellis (b. 1932)
BRITISH NOVELIST
*Pseudonym of Anna Haycraft. Her novels include
The Sin Eater (1977) and her best-known work,
The Twenty-Seventh Kingdom (1982).*

1 **Death is the last enemy: once we've got past
that I think everything will be all right.**
'In the Psychiatrist's Chair', broadcast on BBC
Radio 4, 19 August 1992

Havelock Ellis (1859–1939)
BRITISH PSYCHOLOGIST
His major work, Studies in the Psychology of Sex
*(7 vols., 1897–1928), the first encyclopaedic treat-
ment of the subject, was deemed scandalous, a
'filthy publication', and until 1935 was only legally
available in the US to doctors. He also published
popular works on sex and the arts.*

1 **All civilization has from time to time
become a thin crust over a volcano of revolution.**
Little Essays of Love and Virtue, ch. 7 (1922)

2 **It has always been difficult for Man to
realise that his life is all an art. It has been
more difficult to conceive it so than to act
it so. For that is always how he has more
or less acted it.**
The Dance of Life, ch. 1 (1923)

3 **A man must not swallow more beliefs than
he can digest.**
Ibid., ch. 5

4 **The prevalence of suicide, without doubt,
is a test of height in civilization; it means
that the population is winding up its nervous and intellectual system to the utmost
point of tension and that sometimes it
snaps.**
Ibid., ch. 7

5 **The sun, the moon and the stars would
have disappeared long ago . . . had they
happened to be within the reach of preda-
tory human hands.**
Ibid.

Ralph Ellison (1914–94)

US AUTHOR

His reputation rests on his one novel, The Invisible Man (1952), the story of an idealistic young black intellectual's search for identity, set in the slums of New York.

1 I am an invisible man. . . . I am a man of substance, of flesh and bone, fiber and liquids – and I might even be said to possess a mind. I am invisible, understand, simply because people refuse to see me.
The narrator, in *The Invisible Man*, Prologue (1952)

Richard Ellmann (1918–87)

US BIOGRAPHER AND ESSAYIST

In the words of ANTHONY BURGESS, he 'brought American common sense and a European sensibility' to his portraits of nineteenth- and twentieth-century English and Irish authors, notably YEATS, JOYCE and Wilde.

1 The imagination should queen it over the mind, with reason as her obsequious butler and memory as her underpaid maid-of-all-work.
'Wallace Stevens's Ice-Cream', first publ. in *Kenyon Review* (1957), repr. in *a long the riverrun*, pt 2 (1988)

2 If we must suffer, it is better to create the world in which we suffer, and this is what heroes do spontaneously, artists do consciously, and all men do in their degree.
'Yeats Without Analogue', lecture (1964), publ. ibid., pt 1

3 Criticism prevents art from forgetting, prevents it from sinking into conformity.
'The Uses of Decadence: Wilde, Yeats, Joyce', lecture at Bennington, Vermont, 28 September 1983, repr. ibid.

4 To delight in possession is to allow the conceivability of dispossession, to rely on constancy is impossible because it can only exist as a relation to inconstancy; what is absent calls attention to what is present.
'Becoming Exiles', publ. ibid.

Ben Elton (b. 1959)

BRITISH AUTHOR AND COMIC

From the cabaret circuit he moved to television, co-writing the comedy series The Young Ones (1982, 1984) and Blackadder (1986–9). His bestselling novels include Dead Famous (2001), and he has also written the West End musical We Will Rock You (2002).

1 The appropriation of radical thinking by lazy, self-obsessed hippies is a public relations disaster that could cost the earth.
Stark, 'Court, Hippies and Love at First Sight' (1989)

2 If only the strength of the love that people

feel when it is reciprocated could be as intense and obsessive as the love we feel when it is not; then marriages would be truly made in heaven.
Ibid., 'Private Investigations'

3 People aren't greedy any more, oh no. They're shopaholics, victims of commercialism. Victims! People don't fail any more. They experience negative success. We are building a culture of gutless, spineless, self-righteous, whining cry-babies who have an excuse for everything and take responsibility for nothing.
Bruce Delamitri, in *Popcorn*, ch. 11 (1996)

4 You ain't no Pavlov, Bruce, and we ain't no dribbling dogs. There ain't nothing specific here. I am talking generally. I'm saying that you make killing cool.
Scout, to film-maker Bruce Delamitri, ibid., ch. 36

5 If we're going to teach the kids to speak badly let's at least have people doing it who know the rules that are being broken.
Tom, Head of Youth, BBC Radio, in *Inconceivable* (1999). Sam's diary entry.

6 In our sad modern world female pop stars have to be very successful indeed before it is allowable for them to perform with their clothes on.
Sam's diary entry, ibid.

Paul Éluard (1895–1952)

FRENCH POET

Pseudonym of Eugène Grindal. His Surrealist poetry was influenced by his experiences as soldier in the First World War and Resistance fighter during the Second World War. His collections include Capital of Sorrow (1926) and Poetry and Truth (1942).

1 *Farewell sadness*
Good-day sadness
You are inscribed in the lines of the ceiling.
'À Peine défigurée', publ. in *La Vie immédiate* (1932). *Bonjour tristesse* ('Good-day sadness') was the title given to FRANÇOISE SAGAN's first novel, an international bestseller in 1954.

Dick Emery (1917–83)

BRITISH COMEDIAN

After success in the BBC radio programme Educating Archie (1958), he displayed his ability for characterization and drag sketches in The Dick Emery Show (1963–71).

1 Ooh, you are awful . . . but I like you!
Catch-phrase from *The Dick Emery Show* (1963–71). Emery used the same words as the ageing sex kitten Mandy in the 1950s radio show *Educating Archie*. 'You Are Awful' was a single by him, entering the top fifty in January 1973.

Tracey Emin (b. 1963)

BRITISH ARTIST

'Bad girl' of British art, she is frequently confrontational and confessional in her work, as in her embroidered tent Everyone I Have Ever Slept With *(1995) and* My Bed *(1999).* DAVID BOWIE *likened her to 'William Blake as a woman, written by Mike Leigh'.*

1 You're not going to make it as an artist if you don't understand commerce and you work away in an attic for twenty years, slagging off people like me, complaining about never being discovered.

Quoted in *Daily Telegraph* 29 January 2000

2 I'm not an outsider at all. I'm on every bloody A-list there is in the art world.

Quoted in *The Times* 22 July 2000

Harry Enfield (b. 1960)

BRITISH COMEDIAN

An impressionist, he invented a stream of characters for his TV shows Harry Enfield's Television Programme *(1990 and 1992) and* Harry Enfield and Chums *(1994 and 1997).*

1 Loadsamoney!

Loadsamoney, in *Saturday Live* (Channel 4, 1988)

Brian Eno (b. 1948)

BRITISH MUSICIAN, PRODUCER AND ARTIST

He was the sequined synthesizer player with the band Roxy Music (1971–3), later worked with DAVID BOWIE *and Talking Heads (see* DAVID BYRNE*), and was a pioneer of ambient music.*

1 An ambience is defined as an atmosphere, or a surrounding influence: a tint. . . . Ambient Music must be able to accommodate many levels of listening attention without enforcing one in particular; it must be as ignorable as it is interesting.

Sleevenotes to *Music for Airports* (1979). Eno called this album his first 'ambient' record, though the original concept was pioneered, he said, by Muzak Inc. in the 1950s.

2 What I find we're entering into now is not death of the author but diffusion of the author. Authorship gets spread through more and more people, you don't know who makes something now, where an idea comes from. I call this 'scenious' as opposed to genius. It's the intelligence of a whole situation, a whole network.

Interview in *i-D* October 1993

3 A culture is the sum of all the things about which humanity can choose to differ.

A Year with Swollen Appendices, 'Culture' (1996)

4 New technologies have the tendency to replace skills with judgement – it's not what you *can* do that counts, but what you *choose* to do, and this invites everyone to start crossing boundaries.

Ibid., 'Sharing Music'

Hans Magnus Enzensberger (b. 1929)

GERMAN POET AND CRITIC

The best known of Germany's post-Brechtian poets, he writes in a caustic and laconic style, often employing startling metaphors. His publications include Poems for People Who Don't Read Poems *(1968) and the narrative* The Sinking of the Titanic *(1978).*

1 *That one gets used to everything –*
One gets used to that.
The usual name for it is
A learning process.

'The Force of Habit', publ. in *Gedichte 1955–70* (1971)

2 *I am playing around*
with the end, the end of the Titanic.
I've nothing better to do.
I have time, like a God.
I have nothing to lose.

The Sinking of the Titanic, *'Fourth Canto' (1978)*

3 Even if they cannot name their own goal, people's self-directed activity expresses a practical critique of existing conditions.

'Swedish Autumn', first publ. 1982, repr. in *Europe, Europe* (1989)

4 Whenever anyone says that something or other is 'typically Italian', I want to jump up with impatience, overturn my chair, and run out of the room. Could anything be more barren than the study of 'national psychology', that mouldy garbage heap of stereotypes, prejudices, and accepted ideas?

'Italian Extravagances', first publ. 1983, repr. ibid.

5 The painter who dips his brush in the pot knows that his work is futile and that only one thing can be relied on: really existing time, which takes hold of and conserves everything, even as it wears it down. History is a process of erosion. What we call socialism is only its viceroy.

'Hungarian Confusions', first publ. 1985, repr. ibid.

6 *Slowly*
the scab peels off. A new tobacconist,
a new address. Pariahs, horribly
* relieved.*
Shades growing paler. These are the
* documents.*
This is the bunch of keys. This is the scar.

'The Divorce', publ. in *Gedichte 1950–85* (1986),

repr. in *Selected Poems* (1994, transl. Michael Hamburger)

7 **Pleasure and terror have given way to normality, and normality, wherever time is on its side, conquers everything.**
Europe, Europe, 'Epilogue: The Seacoast of Bohemia' (1989). Referring to Berlin.

8 **Mediocrity in politics is not to be despised. Greatness is not needed.**
The Late Show, BBC2, 5 November 1990

Nora Ephron (b. 1941)
US AUTHOR AND SCREENWRITER
Sex, marriage and middle-class crises are her primary subject matter, deftly and wittily treated. Her screenplays include Heartburn *(1986), from her own 1983 novel based on the break-up of her marriage to Watergate journalist* CARL BERNSTEIN, *When Harry Met Sally (1989) and* Sleepless in Seattle *(1993), which she also directed.*

1 **I am continually fascinated at the difficulty intelligent people have in distinguishing what is controversial from what is merely offensive.**
'Barney Collier's Book', publ. in *Esquire* January 1976

2 **If pregnancy were a book they would cut the last two chapters.**
Rachel Samstat (Meryl Streep), in *Heartburn* (film, 1986, screenplay by Nora Ephron adapted from her own novel, directed by Mike Nichols)

3 **No man can be friends with a woman he finds attractive. He always wants to have sex with her. Sex is always out there. Friendship is ultimately doomed and that is the end of the story.**
Harry Burns (Billy Crystal), in *When Harry Met Sally* (film, 1989, screenplay by Nora Ephron, directed and co-produced by Rob Reiner)

4 **I'll have what she's having.**
Woman diner to waiter, after observing Sally Albright (Meg Ryan) act out an orgasm, ibid.

5 **Verbal ability is a highly overrated thing in a guy, and it's our pathetic need for it that gets us into so much trouble.**
Becky (Rosie O'Donnell), in *Sleepless in Seattle* (film, 1993, screenplay by Jeff Ward, Nora Ephron and David S. Ward, directed by Nora Ephron)

Susan Ertz (1894–1985)
BRITISH NOVELIST
Her novels, which largely deal with family relationships, include Madame Claire *(1923),* Now We Set Out *(1935) and* Charmed Circle *(1956).*

1 **Millions long for immortality who do not know what to do with themselves on a rainy Sunday afternoon.**
Mrs A., in *Anger in the Sky*, ch. 5 (1943)

Linda Evangelista (b. 1965)
ITALIAN-CANADIAN MODEL
Along with Christy Turlington and Naomi Campbell, she was one of the three models for whom the term 'Supermodel' was coined in the late 1980s.

1 **We don't wake up for less than $10,000 a day.**
Quoted in *Vogue*, fall 1991, repr. in *Model*, '$10,000 a Day' (1995) by Michael Gross. She later commented, 'I feel that quote is going to be engraved on my tombstone. It was tongue-in-cheek, but it backfired. How many times do I have to apologise for a few careless words?'

2 **Nobody is born with perfect eyebrows.**
Daily Telegraph 13 August 1992

(Dame) Edith Evans (1888–1976)
BRITISH ACTRESS
She made her name playing roles in Shakespeare and Shaw, and was a majestic Lady Bracknell in Wilde's The Importance of Being Earnest. KENNETH TYNAN *described her later acting style as 'tranquillized benevolence cascading from a great height, like royalty opening a bazaar'.*

1 **When a woman behaves like a man why doesn't she behave like a nice man?**
Quoted in the *Observer* 30 September 1956

Gavin Ewart (1916–95)
BRITISH POET
He published his first collection in 1939, but it was not until the 1970s that he devoted himself to writing full-time. His light verse is often parodic in style, as in The Pleasures of the Flesh *(1966) and* Penultimate Poems *(1989).*

1 *There are sorrows in herds that are too deep for words.*
'How Tragedy is Impossible', publ. in *Or Where a Young Penguin Lies Screaming* (1977)

2 *Many an actor is funtastically handicapped by the*
superphysical triviality of his profession.
'Pros', publ. ibid.

3 *The path of true love isn't smooth,*
the ruffled feathers sex can soothe
ruffle again – for couples never
spend all their lives in bed together.
'24th March 1986', publ. in *Late Pickings* (1987)

4 *If men's lives are worth giving, they're also worth saving.*
Who let them start the bloody thing?
That's the question, there's the sting.
'The Falklands, 1982', publ. in *Selected Poems* (1996). Closing lines of poem.

W. N. Ewer (1885–1976)
BRITISH JOURNALIST
William Norman Ewer, nicknamed 'Trilby'.

Recruited as one of 'Lansbury's Lambs', he was
Foreign Correspondent on the Daily Herald 1919–
64 and Overseas Service correspondent for the
BBC.

1 *I gave my life for freedom – this I know:*
   For those who bade me fight had told me so.
   'Five Souls', publ. in *Five Souls and Other Verses*
   (1917)

Clifton Fadiman (1904–99)

US ESSAYIST

Calling himself an 'odd job man', he has written widely, including literary criticism and children's books.

1 I encountered the mama of dada again ... and as usual withdrew worsted.
Party of One (1955). Referring to GERTRUDE STEIN.

2 A cheese may disappoint. It may be dull, it may be naive, it may be oversophisticated. Yet it remains cheese, milk's leap toward immortality.
Any Number Can Play (1957)

Marianne Faithfull (b. 1946)

BRITISH SINGER

She was a wistful singer of the 1960s, acted in a number of plays and films and was the much publicized girlfriend of MICK JAGGER, later reviving her musical career with the album Broken English (1979).

1 Maybe the most you can expect from a relationship that goes bad is to come out of it with a few good songs.
Faithfull, 'Colston Hall' (1994). Referring to her relationship with MICK JAGGER.

Giovanni Falcone (1939–92)

ITALIAN JUDGE

His investigations into organized crime in Sicily led to the conviction of over 300 members of the Mafia in 1987, and also to his own assassination.

1 One usually dies because one is alone, or because one has got into something over one's head. One often dies because one does not have the right alliances, because one is not given support. In Sicily the Mafia kills the servants of the State that the State has not been able to protect.
Men of Honour, ch. 6 (1992). Closing words of book. The car containing Falcone, his wife and three bodyguards was blown up 23 May 1992.

Oriana Fallaci (b. 1930)

ITALIAN JOURNALIST AND AUTHOR

Renowned for her hard-nosed interviewing techniques, she has published The Useless Sex (1960) and Interview with History (1976), as well as novels including A Man (1979).

1 We do not understand these Americans who, like adolescents, always speak of sex, and who, like adolescents, all of a sudden have discovered that sex is good not only for procreating children.
The Egotists, 'Hugh Hefner'(1963)

2 The bitter discovery that God does not exist has destroyed the concept of fate. But to deny fate is arrogance, to declare that

we are the sole shapers of our existence is madness; if you deny fate, life becomes a series of missed opportunities, a regret for what never was and could have been, a remorse for what was not done and could have been done, and the present is wasted, twisted into another missed opportunity.

A Man, pt. 2, ch. 1 (1971)

3 All banners, even the most noble, the most pure, are filthy with blood and shit. When you look at the glorious banners displayed in museums, in churches, venerated as relics to kneel before in the name of ideals, dreams, have no illusions: those brownish stains are not traces of rust, they are dried blood, dried shit, and more often shit than blood.

Ibid., pt. 5, ch. 1

4 Death is a thief that never turns up by surprise . . . Death always announces itself by a kind of scent, impalpable perceptions, silent sounds.

Ibid., pt. 6, ch. 1

Frantz Fanon (1925–61)

FRENCH WEST INDIAN PSYCHIATRIST, PHILOSOPHER AND POLITICAL ACTIVIST
His experiences during the Algerian revolution led him to write The Wretched of the Earth *(1961), which, urging a 'collective catharsis', became a manifesto for liberation struggles against colonial powers*

1 Fervour is the weapon of choice of the impotent.
Black Skins White Masks, Introduction (1952, transl. 1967)

2 However painful it may be for me to accept this conclusion, I am obliged to state it: for the black man there is only one destiny. And it is white.
Ibid.

3 Colonialism is not a thinking machine, nor a body endowed with reasoning faculties. It is violence in its natural state, and it will only yield when confronted with greater violence.
The Wretched of the Earth, ch. 1 (1961)

4 Nationalism, that magnificent song that made the people rise against their oppressors, stops short, falters and dies away on the day that independence is proclaimed.
Ibid., ch. 3

Eleanor Farjeon (1881–1965)

BRITISH CHILDREN'S AUTHOR
She wrote prolifically for children, for instance Martin Pippin in the Apple Orchard *(1921) and, with her brother Herbert Farjeon, the educational* Kings and Queens *(1932).*

1 *Morning has broken*
Like the first morning,
Blackbird has spoken
Like the first bird.
'A Morning Song (for the First Day of Spring)', publ. in *Children's Bells* (1957). The song was a hit for Cat Stevens in 1972.

Farouk I (1920–65)

KING OF EGYPT
Increasingly absorbed in his hedonistic lifestyle, the last reigning king of Egypt (1936–52) was forced to abdicate in the coup d'état of 1952. He went into exile and became a citizen of Monaco in 1959.

1 The whole world is in revolt. Soon there will be only five kings left – the King of England, the King of Spades, the King of Clubs, the King of Hearts and the King of Diamonds.
Remark in 1948, quoted in *Life* 10 April 1950. The words were addressed to John (later Lord) Boyd-Orr, first director of the FAO, at a conference in Cairo, also quoted in Boyd-Orr's memoirs, *As I Recall*, ch. 21 (1966).

The Fast Show

Television series on BBC 2 (1994–7), consisting of short sketches written and produced by Paul Whitehouse and Charlie Higson, with contributions from actors including John Thomson, Simon Day, Arabella Weir, Caroline Aherne and Mark Williams.

1 Does my bum look big in this?
(Arabella Weir)

2 Ooh, suits you sir!
Paul Whitehouse and Mark Williams as tailors

3 Scorchio!
Weathergirl (Caroline Aherne)

4 This week, I 'ave been mostly eatin' . . .
'Jesse' (Paul Williams)

5 Very, very drunk.
'Rowley Birkin, QC' (Paul Whitehouse)

6 Which was nice.
'Patrick Nice' (Mark Williams)

William Faulkner (1897–62)

US NOVELIST
His novels, including The Sound and the Fury *(1929) and* Absalom! Absalom! *(1936), are primarily narratives of 'the tragic fable of southern history' set in the fictional Mississippi county of Yoknatapawpha. 'Mr Faulkner is interested in making your mind rather than your flesh creep,' wrote* CLIFTON FADIMAN.

1 Poor man. Poor mankind.
Hightower, in *Light in August*, ch. 4 (1932). Referring to Joe Christmas, suspected of murder and liable to be lynched.

2 I believe that man will not merely endure: he will prevail. He is immortal, not because he alone among creatures has an inexhaustible voice, but because he has a soul, a spirit capable of compassion and sacrifice and endurance. The poet's, the writer's, duty is to write about these things.

Nobel Prize acceptance speech in Stockholm, 10 December 1950, publ. in *The Penguin Book of Twentieth-Century Speeches* (ed. Brian MacArthur, 1999)

3 Maybe the only thing worse than having to give gratitude constantly . . . is having to accept it.

Temple Drake, in *Requiem for a Nun*, act 2, sc. 1 (1951)

4 If a writer has to rob his mother, he will not hesitate; the 'Ode on a Grecian Urn' is worth any number of old ladies.

Interview in the *Paris Review* spring 1956, repr. in *Writers at Work* (first series, ed. Malcolm Cowley, 1958)

5 The best job that was ever offered to me was to become a landlord in a brothel. In my opinion it's the perfect milieu for an artist to work in.

Ibid.

Mohamed al-Fayed (b. 1933)

EGYPTIAN BUSINESSMAN
Flagships of his business empire are the Ritz Hotel in Paris (acquired in 1979) and London's Harrods (1985). His son Dodi was killed with Princess DIANA in 1997.

1 For me, he [Neil Hamilton] is nothing, he is not a human, he is someone who would sell his mother for money – no dignity, no honour, nothing.

Statement in libel trial, quoted in the *Guardian* 20 November 1999. Hamilton, who was suing al-Fayed, was accused of having taken advantage of the latter's generosity while a Conservative MP. 'He had discovered a golden goose,' declared the businessman. 'The eggs came in gold.'

Jules Feiffer (b. 1929)

US CARTOONIST
He published his first collection of cartoons Sick, Sick, Sick in 1958, and attracted a following during the 1960s with his satirical comic strip Feiffer.

1 I used to think I was poor. Then they told me I wasn't poor, I was needy. Then they told me it was self-defeating to think of myself as needy, I was deprived. Then they told me deprived was a bad image, I was underprivileged. Then they told me underprivileged was overused, I was disadvan-taged. I still don't have a dime. But I sure have a great vocabulary.

Cartoon caption, 1965, quoted in *Political Dictionary*, 'Disadvantaged' (1968, rev. 1978) by William Safire

2 Much has been written about her enemies. She picked them with care, and God knows they deserved her.

Graveside eulogy of LILLIAN HELLMAN, quoted in *Lilly: Reminiscences of Lillian Hellman*, pt. 4, 'Kidding on the Square' (1988) by Peter Feibleman

Elaine Feinstein (b. 1930)

BRITISH AUTHOR AND POET
Her disparate writings are concerned with the 'persistence of the past' and reflect her Russian background. Prominent works include Badlands (1986), a poetry collection, and the novels The Survivors (1982) and Dreamers (1984).

1 She imagines herself clean as a fish,
    evasive, solitary, dumb. Her prayer:
    to make peace with her own monstrous
        nature.

'Patience', publ. in *Some Unease and Angels* (1977)

2 Poetry is
powerless as grass.
How then should it defend us?
unless by strengthening
our fierce and obstinate centres.

'Muse', publ. in *Badlands* (1986)

Marty Feldman (1933–82)

BRITISH COMEDIAN
Known for his pop-eyed appearance ('like Dada on legs' as he put it), he had his own TV shows in the 1960s and '70s, and went on to star in the MEL BROOKS films Young Frankenstein (1973) and Silent Movie (1976).

1 I looked him up in the *Cattle-breeder's Guide* – he wasn't in there; I looked him up in the *Standard Book of British Birds* – he wasn't in there either; I finally found him in the Book of Revelations.

Sketch 17 March 1969, on *Marty* (TV show, BBC 2, 1968–9), publ. in *From Fringe to Flying Circus*, ch. 8 (1980) by Roger Wilmut. Referring to the creature (never revealed) in a large basket in a vet's waiting room. The sketch won the Silver Rose award at that year's Montreux Light Entertainment Festival.

2 Comedy, like sodomy, is an unnatural act.

The Times 9 June 1969

Federico Fellini (1920–93)

ITALIAN FILM-MAKER
His idiosyncratic films, which he always scripted

himself, include La Dolce Vita *(1960),* 8 *(1963)
and* Amarcord *(1973), all partly autobiographical.
'Although my father wanted me to become an
engineer and my mother a bishop,' he stated, 'I
myself am quite content to have succeeded in
becoming an adjective.'*

1 Would you be able to give up everything,
to start life all over again . . . to choose one
thing, just one thing, and be faithful to it
. . . to make it the thing that gives meaning
to your life . . . something that contains
everything else . . . that becomes everything else just because of your boundless
faith in it?
Guido Anselmi (Marcello Mastroianni), in 8
(film, 1963, screenplay co-written by Fellini,
Ennio Flaiano, Tullio Pinelli and Brunello
Rondi, directed by Fellini)

2 It's better to destroy than to create when
you're not creating those few things which
are truly necessary.
Daumier, the critic (Jean Rougeul), ibid.

3 The movie business is macabre. Grotesque.
It is a combination of a football game and
a brothel.
New Yorker 30 October 1965, repr. in *Fellini on
Fellini*, 'Miscellany II', 'Like a puppet-master
who falls in love with his puppets', sect. 21 (ed.
Anna Keel and Christian Strich, 1974)

4 Cinéma-vérité? I prefer 'cine-mendacity'. A
lie is always more interesting than the
truth. Lies are the soul of showmanship
and I adore shows.
L'Arc 45 (1971), repr. ibid., sect. 6

5 I have invented myself entirely: a childhood, a personality, longings, dreams and
memories, all in order to enable me to tell
them.
Fellini on Fellini, 'Miscellany I', 'I'm a liar, but
an honest one', sect. 10 (ed. Anna Keel and Christian Strich, 1974)

6 Censorship is a way of admitting our own
weakness and intellectual insufficiency.
Censorship is always a political tool: certainly not an intellectual one. Criticism is
an intellectual tool: it presupposes a knowledge of what one judges and opposes.
Criticism does not destroy; it puts an
object in its proper place among other
objects.
To censor is to destroy, or at least to
oppose the process of reality.
Ibid., 'Notes on Censorship'

7 What is an artist? A provincial who finds
himself somewhere between a physical
reality and a metaphysical one. . . . It's this
in-between that I'm calling a province, this
frontier country between the tangible
world and the intangible one – which is
really the realm of the artist.
Quoted by JOHN BERGER in 'Ev'ry Time We Say

Goodbye', publ. in *Sight and Sound* June 1991,
repr. in *Keeping a Rendezvous* (1992)

James Fenton (b. 1949)
BRITISH POET AND CRITIC
*His experience as a freelance journalist and foreign
correspondent informs his poetry, which is strongly
influenced by* W. H. AUDEN. *His poetry collections
include* The Memory of War *(1982) and* Out of
Danger *(1993).*

1 It is not what they built. It is what they
knocked down.
It is not the houses. It is the spaces between
the houses.
It is not the streets that exist. It is the streets
that no longer exist.
'German Requiem' (1980), repr. in *The Memory
of War* (1982). Opening lines.

2 He tells you, in the sombrest notes,
If poets want to get their oats,
The first step is to slit their throats.
The way to divide
The sheep of poetry from the goats
Is suicide.
'Letter to John Fuller', publ. in *Children in Exile*
(1983)

3 I didn't exist at Creation,
I didn't exist at the Flood,
And I won't be around for Salvation
To sort out the sheep from the cud –
Or whatever the phrase is. The fact is
In soteriological terms
I'm a crude existential malpractice
And you are a diet of worms.
'God, a Poem', publ. ibid.

4 One does not become a guru by accident.
The Times 9 August 1984. Referring to playwright SAMUEL BECKETT.

5 Saigon was an addicted city, and we were
the drug: the corruption of children, the
mutilation of young men, the prostitution
of women, the humiliation of the old, the
division of the family, the division of the
country – it had all been done in our
name.
'The Fall of Saigon', first publ. in *Granta* no. 15,
1985, repr. in *All the Wrong Places* (1988)

6 Imitation, if it is not forgery, is a fine
thing. It stems from a generous impulse,
and a realistic sense of what can and cannot be done.
'Ars Poetica', no. 47, in the *Independent on Sunday* 16 December 1990

7 Tienanmen
Is broad and clean
And you can't tell
Where the dead have been
And you can't tell
When they'll come again

They'll come again
To Tienanmen

'Tienanmen', publ. in *Out of Danger* (1993). The
poem is dated 15 June 1989, written in response
to the savage suppression of protesters that had
just taken place in Beijing's Tienanmen Square.
Fenton later revealed that he wrote it to the tune
of 'Strange Fruit' (see BILLIE HOLIDAY 1).

Edna Ferber (1887–1968)

US AUTHOR

*A prolific writer of short stories and novels that
vividly evoke America in the 1920s and '30s, she is
best remembered for* Show Boat *(1926), which
became a hit on Broadway and as a film.*

1 Wasn't marriage, like life, unstimulating
and unprofitable and somewhat empty
when too well ordered and protected and
guarded? Wasn't it finer, more splendid,
more nourishing, when it was, like life
itself, a mixture of the sordid and the magnificent; of mud and stars; of earth and
flowers; of love and hate and laughter and
tears and ugliness and beauty and hurt?
Show Boat, ch. 19 (1926, musical show 1927,
filmed 1936 and 1951)

2 I am not belittling the brave pioneer men
but the sunbonnet as well as the sombrero
has helped to settle this glorious land of
ours.
Sabra Cravat, in *Cimarron*, ch. 23 (1929, filmed
1931 and 1960)

3 It was part of the Texas ritual. We're rich
as son-of-a-bitch stew but look how
homely we are, just as plain-folksy as
Grandpappy back in 1836. We know about
champagne and caviar but we talk hog and
hominy.
Giant, ch. 2 (1952, filmed 1956)

4 A woman can look both moral and exciting – if she also looks as if it was quite a
struggle.
Quoted in *Reader's Digest* December 1954

5 Being an old maid is like death by drowning, a really delightful sensation after you
cease to struggle.
Quoted in *The Algonquin Wits* (ed. Robert E.
Drennan, 1968)

Lawrence Ferlinghetti (b. 1919)

US POET AND PUBLISHER

*Associated with the Beat movement in the 1950s,
he co-founded San Francisco's City Lights Bookstore. He has published over forty volumes of
poetry, generally political and declamatory in style,
including* An Eye on the World *(1967) and* When
I Look at Pictures *(1990).*

1 *Constantly risking absurdity*
and death

whenever he performs
above the heads
of his audience
the poet like an acrobat
climbs on rime
to a high wire of his own making.
'A Coney Island of the Mind', sect. 15, publ. in
A Coney Island of the Mind (1958)

2 *I once started out*
to walk around the world
but ended up in Brooklyn.
That Bridge was too much for me.
'Autobiography', publ. ibid.

3 *I see another war is coming*
but I won't be there to fight it.
I have read the writing
on the outhouse wall.
I helped Kilroy write it.
Ibid.

Leslie Fiedler (1917–2003)

US CRITIC

In his major book Love and Death in the American Novel *(1960) – which identified a homoerotic
strain in nineteenth-century fiction – and in other
works, he aimed to 'define the myths which give a
special character to art and life in America'. He
also wrote novels and short stories.*

1 The 'text' is merely one of the contexts of a
piece of literature, its lexical or verbal one,
no more or less important than the sociological, psychological, historical, anthropological or generic.
Love and Death in the American Novel, Preface
(1960)

2 To be an American (unlike being English
or French or whatever) is precisely to
imagine a destiny rather than to inherit
one; since we have always been, insofar as
we are Americans at all, inhabitants of
myth rather than history.
'Cross the Border – Close the Gap', first publ. in
Playboy December 1969, repr. in *Collected Essays*
vol. 2 (1971)

Sally Field (b. 1946)

US SCREEN ACTRESS

*After making her name in TV series in the 1960s,
she starred in Hollywood movies, notably* Norma
Rae *(1979) and* Steel Magnolias *(1989).*

1 I happen to believe you make your own
destiny. You have to do the best with what
God gave you . . . Life is a box of chocolates, Forrest. You never know what
you're goin' to get.
Mrs Gump (Sally Field), in *Forrest Gump* (film,
1994, screenplay by Eric Roth adapted from
Winston Groom's novel, directed by Robert
Zemeckis)

Helen Fielding (b. 1958)

BRITISH AUTHOR

Creator of the Bridget Jones Diary *in the* Independent *in 1995, she successfully transferred her thirty-something heroine, obsessed with men and diets, to novel form in* Bridget Jones's Diary *(1996, filmed 2001) and a sequel* The Edge of Reason *(1999).*

1 Being a woman is worse than being a farmer – there is so much harvesting and crop spraying to be done: legs to be waxed, underarms shaved, eyebrows plucked, feet pumiced, skin exfoliated and moisturized, spots cleansed, roots dyed, eyelashes tinted, nails filed, cellulite massaged, stomach muscles exercised. The whole performance is so highly tuned you only need to neglect it for a few days for the whole thing to go to seed. . . . Is it any wonder girls have no confidence?
   Bridget Jones's Diary, 'Tuesday 3 January' (1996)

2 You should have said 'I'm not married because I'm a *Singleton,* you smug, prematurely ageing, narrow-minded morons. And because there's more than one bloody way to live: one in four households are single, most of the royal family are single, the nation's young men have been proved by surveys to be *completely unmarriageable,* and as a result there's a whole generation of single girls like me with their own incomes and homes who have lots of fun and don't need to wash anyone else's socks. We'd be as happy as sandboys if people like you didn't conspire to make us feel stupid just because you're jealous.'
   Shazzer, ibid., 'Wednesday 1 February'. Bridget responds: 'Singletons! Hurrah for the Singletons!'

Dorothy Fields (1904–74)

US SONGWRITER

A prolific lyricist of such enduring songs as 'On the Sunny Side of the Street' (1930), she also wrote libretti for musicals, including Annie Get Your Gun *(1946) for* IRVING BERLIN.

1 *Grab your coat, and get your hat,*
   Leave your worry on the doorstep,
   Just direct your feet
   To the sunny side of the street.
   'On the Sunny Side of the Street' (song, co-written with Jimmy McHugh) in *The International Revue* (musical show, 1930)

2 *You're calmer than the seals in the Arctic Ocean*
   At least they flap their fins to express emotion . . .
   'A Fine Romance' (song, with music by Jerome Kern) in *Swing Time* (film, 1936)

3 *So let me get right to the point.*
   I don't pop my cork for every guy I see.

Hey! big spender, spend a little time with me.
   'Big Spender' (song, with music by Cy Coleman) in *Sweet Charity* (stage musical 1966, film 1969). The song was a hit for Shirley Bassey in 1967.

W. C. Fields (1879–1946)

US ACTOR

Originally William Claude Dukinfield. 'I am free of all prejudices – I hate everybody equally,' declared this red-nosed, gravel-voiced, hard drinking misogynist of a comedian. He memorably played Micawber in David Copperfield *(1934) and he wrote many of the numerous comedies he appeared in, including* My Little Chickadee *(with* MAE WEST, *1940). See also* LEO ROSTEN 1.

1 Here lies W. C. Fields. I would rather be living in Philadelphia.
   Suggested epitaph, as told to *Vanity Fair* June 1925. Fields, who was born in Philadelphia, may have had in mind an anecdote about George Washington, who was reported to have uttered a similar sentiment regarding the choice of New York as federal capital in 1789. Fields's words (which were never actually used as his epitaph) are usually remembered, 'I'd rather be in Philadelphia', the form in which RONALD REAGAN quoted them when recovering in hospital from an assassination attempt in 1981.

2 And remember, dearie, never give a sucker an even break.
   Professor Eustace McGargle, in *Poppy* (film, 1936, screenplay by Waldemar Young and Virginia Van Upp from play by Dorothy Donnelly, directed by A. Edward Sutherland). Fields is earlier reported to have uttered these words on stage in the musical comedy *Poppy* (1923), though they do not appear in the libretto. 'Never give a sucker an even break' became Fields's catchphrase and the title of one of his last films, made in 1941 (called *What a Man* in Britain).

3 I was in love with a beautiful blonde once, she drove me to drink. 'Tis the one thing I'm indebted to her for.
   The Great Man (W. C. Fields), in *Never Give a Sucker an Even Break* (film, 1941, screenplay by John T. Neville and Prescott Chaplin based on a story by W. C. Fields, directed by Edward F. Cline)

4 Hell, I never vote *for* anybody. I always vote *against.*
   Quoted in *W. C. Fields: His Follies and Fortunes,* ch. 25 (1950) by Robert Lewis Taylor. Said to Gene Fowler who wrote two books about him.

5 If at first you don't succeed, try again. Then quit. No use being a damn fool about it.
   Quoted in *Halliwell's Who's Who in the Movies* (ed. John Walker, 1999)

6 Fish fuck in it.
   Attributed. On why he never drank water.

Eva Figes (b. 1932)
GERMAN-BORN BRITISH AUTHOR AND
TRANSLATOR
*She has produced a diverse body of work of fiction
and feminist criticism, including the novels* Winter's Journey *(1968) and* The Tree of Knowledge
*(1990), the latter written in a seventeenth-century
prose style.*

1 Providing for one's family as a good husband and father is a water-tight excuse for
making money hand over fist. Greed may
be a sin, exploitation of other people
might, on the face of it, look rather nasty,
but who can blame a man for 'doing the
best' for his children?

'A View of My Own', publ. in *Nova* January 1973

2 If each man takes his conscience as his
guide he is like to become a law unto himself, and conscience often tells us that
which we would hear.

Mrs Deborah Clarke, in *The Tree of Knowledge*,
ch. 4 (1990)

Zlata Filipovič (b. 1980)
BOSNIAN DIARIST
*Her diary, written during the Bosnian conflict
1991–3, became a bestseller throughout Europe.
Zlata and her parents left Sarajevo for France at
the end of 1993.*

1 Life goes on. The past is cruel, and that's
exactly why we should forget it. The present is cruel too and I can't forget it.
There's no joking with war. My present
reality is the cellar, fear, shells, fire.

Journal entry, 13 May 1993, publ. in *Zlata's Diary*
(1993)

2 The political situation? A STUPID MESS.
The 'kids' are trying to come to some agreement again. They're drawing maps, colouring with their crayons, but I think they're
crossing out human beings, childhood and
everything that's nice and normal. They
are really just like kids.

Ibid., 21 August 1993

Ernst Fischer (1899–1972)
AUSTRIAN EDITOR, POET AND CRITIC
*A member of the Communist Party from 1934
until 1969, when he was expelled for his criticism
of the Soviet invasion of Czechoslovakia, he was
Minister of Culture and Education in the Austrian
National Assembly.* The Necessity of Art *(1959)
and* Art Against Ideology *(1966) are regarded as
his major works of 'Marxist aesthetics'.*

1 As machines become more and more
efficient and perfect, so it will become clear
that *imperfection is the greatness of man*.

The Necessity of Art, ch. 5 (1959)

2 Man, became man through work, who
stepped out of the animal kingdom as
transformer of the natural into the artificial, who became therefore the magician,
man the creator of social reality, will
always stay the great magician, will always
be Prometheus bringing fire from heaven
to earth, will always be Orpheus enthral-
ling nature with his music. Not until
humanity itself dies will art die.

Ibid.

3 To provoke dreams of terror in the slumber of prosperity has become the moral
duty of literature.

Art Against Ideology, ch. 1 (1966)

Michael Fish (b. 1944)
BRITISH METEOROLOGIST
*Britain's longest-serving TV weatherman (since
1974) joined the Meteorological Office in 1962 and
the London Weather Centre in 1967.*

1 A woman rang to say she heard there was a
hurricane on the way. Well, don't worry,
there isn't.

Weather forecast on BBC TV, 15 October 1987.
The 'Great Storm' which struck southern England that night claimed seventeen lives and
caused approximately £300 million of damage.
Winds gusted up to 110 mph, falling within the
scale of hurricane force.

Carrie Fisher (b. 1956)
US ACTRESS, AUTHOR AND SCREENWRITER
*Daughter of Eddie Fisher and Debbie Reynolds,
she has had a varied career in Hollywood that has
included appearances in the films* Star Wars *(as
Princess Leia, 1977) and* The Blues Brothers
*(1980). Hollywood is usually the milieu of her caus-
tic and witty novels.*

1 My extroversion is a way of managing my
introversion.

Dinah, in *Surrender the Pink*, ch. 3 (1990)

2 Who am I? I'm with him, that's who.

Ibid., ch. 7

3 Look at us we're chicks lost in the netherworld of our gender, absorbed in the world
of potential purchase.

Ibid., ch. 9

H. A. L. Fisher (1865–1940)
BRITISH HISTORIAN AND POLITICIAN
*Herbert Albert Laurens Fisher. He was Liberal MP
for Hallam, Sheffield (1916–18), and the English
Universities (1918–26). As President of the Board
of Education, he introduced the 1918 Education
Act, state scholarships to universities and the
School Certificate.*

1 Men wiser and more learned than I have
discerned in history a plot, a rhythm, a

predetermined pattern. These harmonies are concealed from me. I can see only one emergency following upon another as wave follows upon wave, only one great fact with respect to which, since it is unique, there can be no generalizations, only one safe rule for the historian: that he should recognize in the development of human destinies the play of the contingent and the unforeseen.

A History of Europe, Preface (1935)

2 Purity of race does not exist. Europe is a continent of energetic mongrels.

Ibid., ch. 1

3 Politics is the art of human happiness.

Ibid., ch. 31

Lord Fisher (1841–1920)

BRITISH NAVAL COMMANDER

John Arbuthnot Fisher, First Baron of Kilverstone. Appointed First Sea Lord in 1904, he was responsible for introducing Dreadnought battleships and Invincible battle cruisers in preparation for the First World War.

1 Never contradict.
Never explain.
Never apologize.

The 'secrets of a happy life', in letter to *The Times*, 5 September 1919

M. F. K. Fisher (1908–92)

US CULINARY WRITER

Mary Frances Kennedy Fisher. One of the most highly regarded of food writers, she drew on her experiences in California and France to present food as a metaphor for life and love. Her books, autobiographical in style, include The Gastronomical Me *(1943) and* An Alphabet for Gourmets *(1949).*

1 Central heating, French rubber goods, and cookbooks are three amazing proofs of man's ingenuity in transforming necessity into art, and, of these, cookbooks are perhaps most lastingly delightful.

Serve It Forth, 'The Curious Nose' (1937)

2 Once at least in the life of every human, whether he be brute or trembling daffodil, comes a moment of complete gastronomic satisfaction.

Ibid., 'The Pale Yellow Glove'

3 Sharing food with another human being is an intimate act that should not be indulged in lightly.

An Alphabet for Gourmets, 'A is for Dining Alone' (1949)

4 The things men come to eat when they are alone are, I suppose, not much stranger than the men themselves.

Ibid., 'M is for Monastic'

5 Gastronomical perfection can be reached in these combinations: one person dining alone, usually upon a couch or a hillside; two people, of no matter what sex or age, dining in a good restaurant; six people, of no matter what sex or age, dining in a good home.

Ibid., 'From A–Z: The Perfect Dinner'

6 It was there [Dijon], I now understand, that I started to grow up, to study, to make love, to eat and drink, to be me and not what I was expected to be. It was there that I learned it is blessed to receive, as well as that every human being, no matter how base, is worthy of my respect and even my envy because he knows something that I may never be old or wise or kind or tender enough to know.

Long Ago in France, Preface (1991)

Robert Fisk (b. 1946)

BRITISH JOURNALIST AND AUTHOR

Since covering events in Northern Ireland in the early 1970s, he has worked as foreign correspondent in Lebanon for The Times *and the* Independent. *His books include* Pity the Nation *(1990), on the war in Lebanon.*

1 Journalism is about watching and witnessing history and recording it as honestly as we can. . . . At best, journalists sit at the edge of history as vulcanologists might clamber to the lip of a smoking crater . . . to peer over . . . at what happens within.

Pity the Nation, Preface (1990)

2 'Terrorists' are those who use violence against the side that is using the word.

Ibid., ch. 12

3 It might be as well for the West to remember that history in the Middle East rarely rewards the just. It never favours the foreigner and it always takes its revenge upon those who see the region through their own eyes. Not once has a foreign military adventure in the Middle East achieved its end.

Quoted in the *Guardian* 14 August 1990

4 Its pages are final proof – if the contents are true – that a massive crime against humanity has been committed in Iraq . . . It means that our massive, obstructive, brutal policy of UN sanctions has totally failed. In other words, half a million Iraqi children were killed by us – for nothing. . . . How's that for a war crime?

Independent 25 September 2002. On the Iraq dossier, published by the British government to reveal the extent of Iraqi rearmament.

F. Scott Fitzgerald (1896–1940)

US AUTHOR

Francis Scott Fitzgerald. Considered the 'white hope of American letters' by H. L. MENCKEN, *he evoked the hedonism of the Jazz Age in his short stories and the novels* The Great Gatsby *(1925) and* Tender is the Night *(1934). He was married to* ZELDA FITZGERALD. *'Sometimes I don't know whether Zelda and I are real or whether we are characters in one of my novels,' he once confessed.*

1 At eighteen our convictions are hills from which we look; at forty-five they are caves in which we hide.
Bernice Bobs Her Hair, sect. 2 (1920)

2 [Of Beatrice Blaine] She had once been a Catholic, but discovering that priests were infinitely more attentive when she was in process of losing or regaining faith in Mother Church, she maintained an enchantingly wavering attitude.
This Side of Paradise, bk. 1, ch. 1 (1920)

3 My idea is always to reach my generation. The wise writer . . . writes for the youth of his own generation, the critics of the next, and the schoolmasters of ever afterward.
'Self-interview', publ. in the *New York Tribune* 7 May 1920, repr. in *Some Sort of Epic Grandeur*, ch. 16 (biography, 1981) by Matthew J. Bruccoli. The text was also used by Fitzgerald in 'The Author's Apology', a letter to the American Booksellers Convention, May 1920.

4 Everybody's youth is a dream, a form of chemical madness.
John, in *The Diamond as Big as the Ritz*, ch. 11 (1922). Kismine replies: 'How pleasant then to be insane!'

5 Personality is an unbroken series of successful gestures.
Narrator (Nick Carraway), in *The Great Gatsby*, ch. 1 (1925)

6 One of those men who reach such an acute limited excellence at twenty-one that everything afterward savors of anti-climax.
Ibid. Referring to Tom Buchanan.

7 Every one suspects himself of at least one of the cardinal virtues.
Ibid., ch. 3

8 There are only the pursued, the pursuing, the busy, and the tired.
Ibid., ch. 4

9 What'll we do with ourselves this afternoon? And the day after that, and the next thirty years?
Daisy Buchanan, ibid., ch. 7

10 Her voice is full of money.
Gatsby, ibid. ch. 7. Referring to Daisy Buchanan. The narrator (Nick Carraway) adds, 'that was the inexhaustible charm that rose and fell in it, the jingle of it, the cymbals' song of it . . .'

11 They were careless people, Tom and Daisy – they smashed up things and creatures and then retreated back into their money or their vast carelessness, or whatever it was that kept them together, and let other people clean up the mess they had made.
Ibid., ch. 9

12 For a transitory enchanted moment man must have held his breath in the presence of this continent, compelled into an aesthetic contemplation he neither understood nor desired, face to face for the last time in history with something commensurate to his capacity for wonder.
Ibid., ch. 9

13 So we beat on, boats against the current, borne back ceaselessly into the past.
Ibid. Closing words of book.

14 Let me tell you about the very rich. They are different from you and me. They possess and enjoy early, and it does something to them, makes them soft where we are hard, and cynical where we are trustful, in a way that, unless you were born rich, it is very difficult to understand. They think, deep in their hearts, that they are better than we are because we had to discover the compensations and refuges of life for ourselves. Even when they enter deep into our world or sink below us, they still think that they are better than we are. They are different.
All the Sad Young Men, 'The Rich Boy' (1926). The story's first sentence also occurs in Fitzgerald's notebooks (*The Crack-Up*, 'Notebook E', 1945) and was taken up by Hemingway in 'The Snows of Kilimanjaro' (1936) (see ERNEST HEMINGWAY 16).

15 I hear you were seen running through Portugal in used B.V.D.'s, chewing ground glass and collecting material for a story about boule players; that you were publicity man for Lindbergh; that you have finished a novel a hundred thousand words long consisting entirely of the word 'balls' used in new groupings; that you have been naturalized a Spaniard, dress always in a wine-skin with 'zipper' vent and are engaged in bootlegging Spanish Fly between St. Sebastian and Biarritz where your agents sprinkle it on the floor of the Casino. I hope I have been misinformed but, alas!, it all has too true a ring.
Letter to Ernest Hemingway, December 1927, publ. in *The Letters of F. Scott Fitzgerald* (ed. Andrew Turnbull, 1963)

16 The early twenties when we drank wood alcohol and every day in every way grew better and better, and there was a first abortive shortening of the skirts, and girls

all looked alike in sweater dresses, and people you didn't want to know said 'Yes, we have no bananas,' and it seemed only a question of a few years before the older people would step aside and let the world be run by those who saw things as they were – and it all seems rosy and romantic to us who were young then, because we will never feel quite so intensely about our surroundings any more.

'Echoes of the Jazz Age', first publ. in *Scribner's* November 1931. The passage also appeared in *The Crack-Up* (ed. Edmund Wilson, 1945). 'Though the Jazz Age continued,' Fitzgerald wrote, 'it became less and less an affair of youth. The sequel was like a children's party taken over by the elders.'

17 The hangover became a part of the day as well allowed-for as the Spanish siesta.

'My Lost City', first publ. in *Esquire* July 1932, repr. in *The Crack-Up* (ed. Edmund Wilson, 1945)

18 One writes of scars healed, a loose parallel to the pathology of the skin, but there is no such thing in the life of an individual. There are open wounds, shrunk sometimes to the size of a pin-prick but wounds still. The marks of suffering are more comparable to the loss of a finger, or the sight of an eye. We may not miss them, either, for one minute in a year, but if we should there is nothing to be done about it.

Tender is the Night, bk. 2, ch. 11 (1934)

19 The test of a first-rate intelligence is the ability to hold two opposed ideas in the mind at the same time, and still retain the ability to function.

'The Crack-Up', article first publ. in *Esquire* February 1936, repr. in *The Crack-Up* (ed. Edmund Wilson, 1945). See also GEORGE ORWELL 47.

20 In a real dark night of the soul it is always three o'clock in the morning, day after day.

'Handle with Care', first publ. in *Esquire* March 1936, repr. ibid. The article constituted the second part of Fitzgerald's *Crack-Up* series. *The Dark Night of the Soul* is the title of a poem and commentary by the sixteenth-century Spanish mystic San Juan de la Cruz (St John of the Cross).

21 I am not a great man, but sometimes I think the impersonal and objective quality of my talent and the sacrifices of it, in pieces, to preserve its essential value has some sort of epic grandeur.

Letter to his daughter Frances Scott Fitzgerald, spring 1940, publ. ibid. The words 'some sort of epic grandeur' were used by Matthew J. Bruccoli as a title for his 1981 biography of Fitzgerald.

22 There are no second acts in American lives.

The Last Tycoon, 'Hollywood, ETC.' (ed. Edmund Wilson, 1941)

23 Show me a hero and I will write you a tragedy.

The Crack-Up, 'Notebook E' (ed. Edmund Wilson, 1945)

24 No grand idea was ever born in a conference, but a lot of foolish ideas have died there.

Ibid.

25 Men get to be a mixture of the charming mannerisms of the women they have known.

Ibid.

26 Listen, little Elia: draw your chair up close to the edge of the precipice and I'll tell you a story.

Ibid.

27 It is in the thirties that we want friends. In the forties we know they won't save us any more than love did.

Ibid., 'Notebook O'

28 All good writing is *swimming under water and holding your breath*.

Letter (undated) to his daughter Frances Scott Fitzgerald, publ. ibid.

Penelope Fitzgerald (1916–2000)
BRITISH AUTHOR
Her biographies include The Knox Brothers *(1977), an account of her father, E. V. A. Knox, Editor of* Punch, *and his three eminent brothers (one of them the theologian* RONALD KNOX*). Among her novels are* Offshore *(1979) and* Human Voices *(1980).*

1 It's very good for an idea to be commonplace. The important thing is that a new idea should develop out of what is already there so that it soon becomes an old acquaintance. Old acquaintances aren't by any means always welcome, but at least one can't be mistaken as to who or what they are.

Fred Fairly, in a lecture to his students at Cambridge, in *The Gate of Angels*, ch. 20 (1990)

Robert Fitzgerald (1910–85)
US SCHOLAR AND TRANSLATOR
His translations of classical texts, including Antigone *(1939),* The Odyssey *(1961) and* The Iliad *(1974), have become classics in their own right. He also wrote poetry, as in* A Wreath for the Sea *(1943) and* Spring Shade *(1972).*

1 Is encouragement what the poet needs? Open question. Maybe he needs discouragement. In fact, quite a few of them need more discouragement, the most discouragement possible.

Interview in *Writers at Work* (eighth series, ed. George Plimpton, 1988)

Zelda Fitzgerald (1900–1948)

US WRITER

Wife of F. SCOTT FITZGERALD, *she wrote a series of sketches (1928–9) which were published in* College Humor, *and a novel* Save Me the Waltz *(1932). In 1930 she suffered the first of her mental breakdowns. She died in a hospital fire.*

1 We grew up founding our dreams on the infinite promise of American advertising.

Alabama Beggs, in *Save Me the Waltz,* ch. 4, sect. 3 (1932). She continued: 'I *still* believe that one can learn to play the piano by mail and that mud will give you a perfect complexion.'

2 I wish I could write a beautiful book to break those hearts that are soon to cease to exist: a book of faith and small neat worlds and of people who live by the philosophies of popular songs.

Letter to her psychiatrist, May 1934, quoted in *Zelda,* pt. 3, ch. 17 (1970) by Nancy Milford

3 Ernest, don't you think Al Jolson is greater than Jesus?

Quoted by ERNEST HEMINGWAY in *A Moveable Feast,* ch. 18 (1964). Her remark anticipates John Lennon's famous claim (see JOHN LENNON 2).

Bud Flanagan (1896–1968)

BRITISH SINGER AND COMEDIAN

Born Reeven Weintrop. With his partner Chesney Allen he formed one of the most popular comedy duos of the 1930s and '40s, whose numbers included 'Underneath the Arches' (1932) and 'Run, Rabbit, Run' (1939). In 1929 they joined the anarchic comedy team, the Crazy Gang.

1 *Underneath the Arches,*
   I dream my dreams away,
   Underneath the Arches,
   On cobble-stones I lay.

'Underneath the Arches' (song, 1932, written with Chesney Allen). According to his autobiography, *My Crazy Life,* ch. 8 (1961), Flanagan conceived what was to be Flanagan and Allen's signature tune while backstage at the Derby Hippodrome in 1926. The 'Arches' were underneath London's Charing Cross station, a gathering-place for tramps. The song was renamed 'Underneath The Bridges' in America, where it was thought 'arches' might be misconstrued as 'feet'.

Oliver Flanagan (1920–87)

IRISH POLITICIAN

He joined Fine Gael in 1950 and rose to become Minister for Local Government 1975–6 and for Defence 1976–7. He was strongly opposed to changes in the contraceptive and divorce laws and a supporter of the pro-life amendment in the 1983 referendum.

1 Let us hope and trust that there are sufficient proud and ignorant people left in this country to stand up to the intellectuals who are out to destroy faith and fatherland.

Quoted in the *Irish Times* 10 April 1971

2 There was no sex in Ireland until the BBC came.

Quoted in *Ireland and the Irish: Portrait of a Changing Society,* ch. 6 (1994) by John Ardagh

Michael Flanders (1922–75) and Donald Swann (1923–94)

BRITISH SONGWRITERS AND ENTERTAINERS

Between 1956 and 1967 their songwriting partnership produced such shows as At the Drop of a Hat *(1956) and* At the Drop of Another Hat *(1963). Swann, who was confined to a wheelchair through polio, likened their collaboration to a 'cooking process', with the piano taking the place of the kitchen stove.*

1 *Mud, mud, glorious mud,*
   Nothing quite like it for cooling the blood!
   So follow me, follow,
   Down to the hollow
   And there let us wallow
   In glorious mud!

'The Hippopotamus' (song, written 1952), in *At the Drop of a Hat* (revue, 1956). The song was entirely written by Flanders who took the tune from 'Beer, Beer, Glorious Beer!', a familiar song of the time.

2 *I'm a G-nu, I'm a G-nu,*
   The g-nicest work of g-nature at the zoo!
   I'm a G-nu, how do you do?
   You really ought to k-now w-ho's w-ho.

'The Gnu' (song), ibid. According to Swann's autobiography *A Life in Song* (1991), the ditty derived from the frustrations of parking in central London: Kensington Borough Council had dug up the pavement outside Flanders' studio in order to facilitate wheel-chair access for him, but the path was often blocked by a car with the number plate letters GNU.

3 *That monarch of the road,*
   Observer of the Highway Code,
   That big six-wheeler
   Scarlet-painted
   London Transport
   Diesel-engined
   Ninety-seven horse power
   Omnibus!

'A Transport of Delight' (song) ibid.

4 Have Some Madeira, M'dear.

Title of song, ibid.

5 *Eating people is wrong!*

'The Reluctant Cannibal' (song), ibid. The words also formed the title of a novel (1959) by MALCOLM BRADBURY.

6 *Pee – Po – Belly – Bum – Drawers!*
   Let's write rude words all down our street,

Stick out our tongues at the people we meet,
Let's have an intellectual treat.
'P**, P*, B****, B**, D******' (song), from *Exti-*
ary (1961)

Ian Fleming (1908–64)
BRITISH AUTHOR
He achieved worldwide success with his spy
thrillers featuring the suave agent 007, James
Bond, who first appeared in Casino Royale *(1953).*
He referred to his books, most of which were later
filmed, as 'straight pillow fantasies of the bang-
bang, kiss-kiss variety'.

1 **Bond, James Bond.**
James Bond introduces himself, in *Casino*
Royale, ch. 7 (1953). Bond's introduction of himself occurs in various similar forms in Fleming's
books and in the film adaptations. James Bond
was the name of an ornithologist who wrote
Field Guide to Birds of the West Indies (1936), still
considered the definitive guide.

2 **A medium Vodka dry Martini – with a**
slice of lemon peel. Shaken and not stirred,
please. I would prefer Russian or Polish
vodka.
James Bond, in *Dr No*, ch. 14 (1958). Bond's
favourite tipple made its first appearance in
Casino Royale, ch. 7 (1953), where it is served 'in
a deep champagne goblet'. He instructs the bar-
man: 'Three measures of Gordon's, one of
vodka, half a measure of Kina Lillet. Shake it
very well until it's ice-cold, then add a large slice
of lemon-peel.' Fellow spy Felix Leiter calls it a
'Molotov Cocktail'. The words 'shaken and not
stirred' also occur in *Diamonds are Forever*
(1956).

3 **Some women respond to the whip, some to**
the kiss. Most of them like a mixture of
both, but none of them answer to the mind
alone, to the intellectual demand, unless
they are man dressed as woman.
From his notebooks, quoted in *The Life of Ian*
Fleming, ch. 8, sect. 1 (1966) by John Pearson.
See ROSAMOND LEHMANN 1.

4 **The older women are best, because they**
always think they may be doing it for the
last time.
Ibid.

Peter Fleming (1907–71)
BRITISH TRAVEL WRITER
Called 'an astringent narrator of romantic and
dangerous voyages' by HAROLD NICOLSON, *he*
established himself as one of the greatest exponents
of the genre with his Brazilian Adventure *(1933).*
He was the elder brother of IAN FLEMING.

1 **Long Island represents the American's idea**
of what God would have done with Nature
if he'd had the money.
Letter to his brother Rupert, 29 September 1929,
quoted in *Peter Fleming*, ch. 4 (1974) by Rupert
Hart-Davis

Dario Fo (b. 1926)
ITALIAN PLAYWRIGHT
His plays, usually co-written and co-produced with
his wife Franca Rame, blend satire and farce with
a strong left-wing slant and were frequently cen-
sored. His company, formed in 1957, scored an
international success with Accidental Death of an
Anarchist *(1970).*

1 **Accidental Death of an Anarchist.**
Title of play (1970). The play, which was first performed in Italy in 1970 and in Britain in 1979,
concerns the death of a suspect who fell, or was
pushed, from the fourth-floor window of a
police station during questioning. The title is
adapted usually to suggest official corruption or
suspicious circumstances.

2 **Feletti: So scandal is an effective means of**
maintaining power and clearing the
public's conscience.
Madman: Exactly. It is the catharsis that
liberates tension . . . And you reporters
are its worthy priesthood.
Accidental Death of an Anarchist, act 2

3 **We're up to our necks in shit, it's true, and**
that's why we walk with our heads held
high.
Madman, ibid.

4 **Can't Pay? Won't Pay!**
Title of play (1974, transl. 1978). The original
title of *Non si paga, non si paga* was the slogan
used in the play by a group of housewives in a
working-class suburb of Milan protesting against
supermarket prices by stealing the goods. First
translated as *We Can't Pay? We Won't Pay!*, the
revised English title became *Can't Pay? Won't*
Pay! for its 1981 London production and as such
was adopted as a slogan by anti-Poll Tax protesters in the 1990s.

Ferdinand Foch (1851–1929)
FRENCH GENERAL
He was Supreme Commander of the Allied Forces
on the Western front in 1918 and dictated the terms
of the armistice, achieving his lifelong ambition of
restoring Alsace and Lorraine to France.

1 **If defeat comes from moral causes, victory**
may come from moral causes also, and one
may say: 'A battle won is a battle we will
not acknowledge to be lost.'
Quoted in *Reputations*, 'Ferdinand Foch' (1928)
by B. H. Liddell Hart. Foch's conclusion was
reached from musing on his favourite aphorism
by the French political philosopher Joseph de
Maistre (1753–1821): 'A lost battle is a battle
which one believes lost: in a material sense no
battle can be lost.'

2 **My centre is giving way, my right is in**
retreat; situation excellent. I shall attack.
Attributed, ibid. Allegedly a message sent to General Joffre during the Battle of the Marne,
8 September 1914, the words are probably apocry-

phal, reflecting the grim obstinacy with which Foch was associated, indicated also by the repeated exhortation he made to his troops, even in the most hopeless conditions: *Attaquez!* According to Liddell Hart, his reckless insistence during this battle resulted in the decimation of the companies under his command, and the eventual German withdrawal astonished the exhausted French troops. Other versions of the quote include: 'My right gives way, my centre yields, everything's fine – I shall attack.'

J. Foley (1906–70)

BRITISH SONGWRITER

1 *Old soldiers never die,*
They simply fade away.
'Old Soldiers Never Die' (song, 1920). The song may have originated in or prior to the First World War.

Barbara Follett (b. 1942)

BRITISH POLITICIAN

A founder member of 'Emily's List' in the UK, which promoted women's candidacy for parliamentary office (1992), she was elected Labour MP for Stevenage in 1997.

1 Lipstick is power.
Attributed in the *Observer* 25 February 1996. Follett repudiated her most quoted soundbite.

Jane Fonda (b. 1937)

US SCREEN ACTRESS

Daughter of Henry Fonda and sister of Peter, she was cast in the 1960s as a 'sex kitten', but later films such as Coming Home *(1973) cast her in a more radical stance, reflecting her opposition to the Vietnam War. During the 1980s became known for her health and fitness books and videos.*

1 I am not a do-gooder. I am a revolutionary. A revolutionary woman.
Statement in 1972, quoted in the *Los Angeles Weekly* 28 November 1980. Fonda is also quoted as declaring: 'To be a revolutionary you have to be a human being. You have to care about people who have no power.'

2 Today I'd be a dyed blonde, a numb and dumb pill-popping star, if I hadn't taken up a cause. I could very well be dead like Marilyn. Not through drugs but dead just the same.
Daily Mail 14 April 1980

3 A man has every season while a woman only has the right to spring. That disgusts me.
Daily Mail 13 September 1989

Michael Foot (b. 1913)

BRITISH POLITICIAN

*A journalist and the author of literary and politi-*cal biographies, he was a Labour MP 1945–92 and party leader 1980–83, stepping down after a crushing electoral defeat by MARGARET THATCHER.

1 It is not necessary that every time he [Norman Tebbit] rises he should give his famous imitation of a semi-house-trained polecat.
Speech to House of Commons, 2 March 1978, publ. in *Hansard*

2 It's quite a change to have a Prime Minister who hasn't got any political ideas at all.
Quoted in the *Observer* 24 February 1991. Referring to JOHN MAJOR.

3 No rising hope on the political scene who offered his services to Labour when I happened to be its leader can be dismissed as an opportunist.
Quoted in the *Independent on Sunday* 19 February 1995. Referring to TONY BLAIR.

Malcolm Forbes (1919–90)

US MEDIA TYCOON

He took over the Forbes Magazine business empire after his father's death in 1954. An advocate of laissez-faire capitalism, he unsuccessfully ran for governorship of New Jersey in 1957.

1 What's the answer to ninety-nine questions out of a hundred? Money.
Attributed. Said to be a frequent remark made to his sons.

Anna Ford (b. 1943)

BRITISH BROADCASTER

Having presented Man Alive *and* Tomorrow's World *for the BBC (1976–8), she became an ITN newscaster and later a presenter with TV-am (1978–82).*

1 Let's face it, there are no plain women on television.
Quoted in the *Observer* 23 September 1979

2 The world men inhabit . . . is rather bleak. It is a world full of doubt and confusion, where vulnerability must be hidden, not shared; where competition, not co-operation, is the order of the day; where men sacrifice the possibility of knowing their own children and sharing in their upbringing, for the sake of a job they may have chosen by chance, which may not suit them and which in many cases dominates their lives to the exclusion of much else.
Men, concluding chapter (1985)

Gerald Ford (b. 1913)

US POLITICIAN AND PRESIDENT

A Republican, he was appointed vice-president under NIXON in 1973 and became President the following year in the wake of the Watergate scandal. The subsequent economic depression contributed to

his defeat in the 1976 election. See LYNDON
JOHNSON 10.

1 **I am a Ford, not a Lincoln.**
Address on taking vice-presidential oath,
6 December 1973, quoted in *A Ford, Not a Lincoln*, ch. 2 (1975) by Richard Reeves. Ford
explained: 'My addresses will never be as eloquent as Lincoln's. But I will do my best to equal
his brevity and plain speaking.' Eight months
later, Ford was sworn in as president. He told
Congress: 'The truth is I am the people's man.'
(12 August 1974)

2 **Our long national nightmare is over. Our
Constitution works; our great Republic is a
government of laws and not of men. Here
the people rule.**
Speech on succeeding RICHARD NIXON as President, 9 August 1974, publ. in *Public Papers of the
Presidents of the United States* (1974)

3 **Truth is the glue that holds government
together.**
Ibid. Ford used these words on various
occasions.

4 **There is no Soviet domination of Eastern
Europe and there never will be under a
Ford administration. . . . The United States
does not concede that those countries are
under the domination of the Soviet Union.**
TV debate with presidential contender JIMMY
CARTER, 6 October 1976, publ. in *Great Debates*
(1979) by S. Kraus. When asked to explain this
statement, Ford admitted: 'I was perhaps not as
precise as I should have been.'

Henry Ford (1863–1947)
US INDUSTRIALIST
*Hailed as the 'demi-god of the machine age', he
was the pioneer of mass production. In 1903 he
founded the Ford Motor Company, which by 1909
had produced the famous Model T, of which 15 million were sold in the next nineteen years.*

1 **History is more or less bunk. It's tradition.
We don't want tradition. We want to live
in the present and the only history that is
worth a tinker's damn is the history we
make today.**
Interview in the *Chicago Tribune* 25 May 1916.
Ford had to defend his views of history during
an eight-day cross-examination in the course of
a libel suit he had initiated against the *Tribune*,
after an editorial had described him as an
'anarchist' and 'ignorant idealist'.

2 **Luck and destiny are the excuses of the
world's failures.**
Quoted in the *Observer* 16 March 1930

Lena Guilbert Ford (1870–1916)
US POET
*She became famous for her song 'Keep the Home
Fires Burning' (1914), which she wrote in England
and was a great success during the First World
War. She was killed during a German Zeppelin
raid on London.*

1 **Keep the home fires burning,
While your hearts are yearning,
Though your lads are far away
They dream of home.
There's a silver lining
Through the dark cloud shining;
Turn the dark cloud inside out,
Till the boys come home.**
'Till the Boys Come Home!' (song, 1914). Music
by IVOR NOVELLO, who is credited with the
song's first line.

Richard Ford (b. 1944)
US AUTHOR
*An occasional exponent of 'Dirty Realism', he is
known for the novels* The Sportswriter *(1986) and
its sequel* Independence Day *(1995), and the
short-story collection* Rock Springs *(1987).*

1 **Married life requires shared mystery even
when all the facts are known.**
The Sportswriter, ch. 5 (1986)

2 **Construed . . . as turf, home just seems a
provisional claim, a designation you make
upon a place, not one it makes on you. A
certain set of buildings, a glimpsed,
smudged window-view across a school-
yard, a musty aroma sniffed behind a garage when you were a child, all of which
come crowding in upon your latter-day
senses – those are pungent things and
vivid, even consoling.**
'An Urge for Going', publ. in *Harper's* February
1992. 'But to me', Ford added, 'they are also
inert and nostalgic and unlikely to connect you
to the real, to that essence art can sometimes
achieve, which is permanence.'

George Foreman (b. 1948)
US BOXER
*He lost his world heavyweight title to MUHAM-
MAD ALI in the so-called 'Rumble in the Jungle' in
Zaire (1974), but regained it in 1994 at the age of
45, the oldest world heavyweight champion ever.*

1 **I want to keep fighting because it is the
only thing that keeps me out of the hamburger joints. If I don't fight, I'll eat this
planet.**
The Times 17 January 1990

Howell Forgy (1908–83)
US NAVAL CHAPLAIN

1 **Praise the Lord and pass the ammunition!**
Quoted in *The New York Times* 1 November
1942, said during the Japanese attack on Pearl
Harbor, 7 December 1941. The words have also
been attributed to William Maguire, and were
used as the title of a Frank Loesser song in 1942.

George Formby (1904–61)

BRITISH ENTERTAINER AND ACTOR

Portraying himself as a gormless working-class Lancashire lad, he accompanied himself on the ukelele on jaunty songs teeming with innuendo. He appeared in a string of successful films in the 1930s and '40s, and was Britain's highest paid entertainer during the Second World War.

1 *With my little ukelele in my hand.*

'With my Little Ukelele in My Hand' (song, 1933, with music by Jack Cottrell). Formby's record company Decca withdrew the first issue of the recording after protests at the song, particularly the last verse, which tells of the birth of a baby: 'My heart did jump with joy/I could see he was a boy/For he had a ukelele in his hand.'

2 *If you could see what I can see
When I'm cleaning windows!*

'When I'm Cleaning Windows' (song, 1937, written by Fred E. Cliffe with music by Harry Clifford) sung by Formby in *Keep Your Seats, Please* (film, 1937). The record was marked NTBB ('Not to be broadcast') by the BBC, whose controller, Lord Reith, labelled it a 'disgusting little ditty'. Particular offence was caused by the lines 'Ladies' nighties I have spied/I've often seen what goes inside/When I'm cleaning windows!'

3 *I'm leaning on a lamp-post at the corner of the street,
In case a certain little lady comes by.*

'Leaning on a Lamp-Post' (song, written by NOEL GAY) in the film *Feather Your Nest* (1937). The song was revived in 1966 by Herman's Hermits.

4 *With my little stick of Blackpool rock.
Along the Promenade I stroll
It may be sticky but I never complain
It's nice to have a nibble at it now and again.*

'With My Little Stick of Blackpool Rock' (song, 1937, written by Fred E. Cliffe with music by Harry Clifford)

5 *Auntie Maggie's Remedy
It's guaranteed never to fail
Now that's the stuff that will do the trick
It's sold at every chemist for one and a kick.*

'Auntie Maggie's Remedy' (song, written by George Formby with music by Eddie Latta) in the film *Turned Out Nice Again!* (1941). A 'kick' was sixpence.

E. M. Forster (1879–1970)

BRITISH NOVELIST AND ESSAYIST

Edward Morgan Forster. His fiction often describes the 'muddles' created by the English abroad, as in A Room with a View *(1908) and* A Passage to India *(1924), both later adapted as films. For* KATHERINE MANSFIELD, *however, he never got further than 'warming the teapot', while* VIRGINIA WOOLF *called him 'limp and damp and milder than the breath of a cow'. See* ANTHONY BURGESS 6.

1 It is not that the Englishman can't feel – it is that he is afraid to feel. He has been taught at his public school that feeling is bad form. He must not express great joy or sorrow, or even open his mouth too wide when he talks – his pipe might fall out if he did.

'Notes on the English Character', first publ. 1920, repr. in *Abinger Harvest* (1936)

2 The Germans are called brutal, the Spanish cruel, the Americans superficial, and so on; but we are perfide Albion, the island of hypocrites, the people who have built up an Empire with a Bible in one hand, a pistol in the other, and financial concessions in both pockets. Is the charge true? I think it is.

Ibid. Forster defined English hypocrisy as 'unconscious deceit' and 'muddle-headedness'.

3 Ideas are fatal to caste.

A Passage to India, pt. 1, ch. 7 (1924)

4 The so called white races are really pinko-grey.

Mr Fielding, ibid. This 'silly aside' caused scandal at Fielding's Anglo-Indian club, Forster explained, for Fielding 'did not realize that "white" has no more to do with a colour than "God Save the King" with a god, and that it is the height of impropriety to consider what it does connote'.

5 Nothing in India is identifiable, the mere asking of a question causes it to disappear or to emerge in something else.

Ibid., pt. 1, ch. 8

6 Hope, politeness, the blowing of a nose, the squeak of a boot, all produce 'boum'.

Ibid. pt. 2, ch. 14. This sound of the echo in the Marabar caves, 'entirely devoid of distinction', seemed to murmur to Mrs Moore, 'Pathos, piety, courage – they exist, but are identical, and so is filth. Everything exists, nothing has value.'

7 The final test for a novel will be our affection for it, as it is the test of our friends, and of anything else which we cannot define.

Aspects of the Novel, 'Introductory' (1927)

8 Yes – oh dear yes – the novel tells a story.

Ibid., ch. 2. Closing words of chapter.

9 Curiosity is one of the lowest of the human faculties. You will have noticed in daily life that when people are inquisitive they nearly always have bad memories and are usually stupid at bottom.

Ibid., ch. 5, 'The Plot'

10 Logic! Good gracious! What rubbish! How can I tell what I think till I see what I say?

Ibid. Riposte of 'that old lady in the anecdote who was accused by her nieces of being illogical'. Almost the same words also appeared in *The Art of Thought* (1926) by the political scientist

Graham Wallas, this time ascribed to a 'little girl' who had been told to be sure of her meaning before she spoke.

11 *Ulysses* . . . is a dogged attempt to cover the universe with mud, an inverted Victorianism, an attempt to make crossness and dirt succeed where sweetness and light failed, a simplification of the human character in the interests of Hell.

Ibid., ch. 6, 'Fantasy'. Forster also called *Ulysses* 'perhaps the most interesting literary experiment of our day'.

12 One always tends to overpraise a long book, because one has got through it.

Abinger Harvest, 'T. E. Lawrence' (1936)

13 Lord I disbelieve – help thou my unbelief.

'What I Believe', written 1939, publ. in *Two Cheers for Democracy* (1951). A reference to Mark 9:24, 'Lord, I believe, help thou mine unbelief.'

14 My law-givers are Erasmus and Montaigne, not Moses and St Paul.

Ibid.

15 I hate the idea of causes, and if I had to choose between betraying my country and betraying my friend, I hope I should have the guts to betray my country.

Ibid.

16 Two cheers for Democracy: one because it admits variety and two because it permits criticism.

Ibid. Forster thought two cheers were 'quite enough'; three he reserved for 'Love the Beloved Republic' (from Swinburne's poem, 'Hertha'). KINGSLEY AMIS commented: 'Two cheers were probably as many as Forster could manage in favour of anything, from democracy to stamp-collecting . . . The Forsters of this world go on as if they would prefer us to be spared the vulgarities entailed in running a decent society, one which deserves four cheers for its citizens and others too.'

17 The more highly public life is organized the lower does its morality sink.

Ibid.

18 Tolerance is a very dull virtue. It is boring. Unlike love, it has always had a bad press. It is negative. It merely means putting up with people, being able to stand things.

'Tolerance', written 1941, publ. ibid. The essay looked ahead to the post-war world, and the necessity to accept former enemies. 'I don't . . . regard tolerance as a great eternally established divine principle,' Forster wrote. 'It is just a make-shift, suitable for an overcrowded and overheated planet.'

19 The only books that influence us are those for which we are ready, and which have gone a little farther down our particular path than we have yet got ourselves.

'A Book that Influenced Me', written 1941, publ. ibid.

20 The humanist has four leading characteristics – curiosity, a free mind, belief in good taste, and belief in the human race.

'Gide and George', written 1943, publ. ibid.

21 Creative writers are always greater than the causes that they represent.

Ibid.

22 Art for art's sake? I should think so, and more so than ever at the present time. It is the one orderly product which our middling race has produced. It is the cry of a thousand sentinels, the echo from a thousand labyrinths, it is the lighthouse which cannot be hidden . . . it is the best evidence we can have of our dignity.

Address to PEN Club Congress, quoted in *Monitor* (ed. Huw Weldon, 1962)

Bruce Forsyth (b. 1928)

BRITISH ENTERTAINER

Originally Bruce Forsyth-Johnson. He became a national celebrity as host of Sunday Night at the London Palladium *(1958–60) and ATV's* Bruce Forsyth Show *(1960s), and as compère of the BBC's* Generation Game *(1971–8, 1990–4).*

1 Nice to see you, to see you nice.

Catchphrase from *The Bruce Forsyth Show* (1960s)

2 Didn't he do well!

Catchphrase from the *The Generation Game* (from 1970s)

Michel Foucault (1926–84)

FRENCH ESSAYIST AND PHILOSOPHER

Influenced both by Nietzsche and by structuralist philosophy, he explored the 'principles of exclusion' by which society operates, with particular reference to the sick, the insane and the criminal. Major works include Madness and Civilization *(1961) and* The Order of Things *(1966).*

1 Freedom of conscience entails more dangers than authority and despotism.

Madness and Civilization, ch. 7 (1961)

2 Marxism exists in nineteenth-century thought as a fish exists in water; that is, it ceases to breathe anywhere else.

The Order of Things, ch. 7 (1966)

3 As the archeology of our thought easily shows, man is an invention of recent date. And one perhaps nearing its end.

Ibid., ch. 10

4 Sexuality is a part of our behaviour. It's part of our world freedom. Sexuality is something that we ourselves create. It is our own creation, and much more than the discovery of a secret side of our desire. We have to understand that with our desires go new forms of relationships, new forms

of love, new forms of creation. Sex is not a fatality; it's a possibility for creative life. It's not enough to affirm that we are gay but we must also create a gay life.

'Sex, Power and the Politics of Identity', interview October 1982, first publ. in *Advocate* 7 August 1984, repr. in *Michel Foucault* (1989) by Didier Eribon

5 Modernity is the attitude that makes it possible to grasp the 'heroic' aspect of the present moment.

The Foucault Reader, 'What is Enlightenment?', pt. 2 (ed. Paul Rabinow, 1984)

H. W. Fowler (1859–1933)

BRITISH LEXICOGRAPHER

Henry Watson Fowler. With his brother Frank he compiled the first Concise Oxford Dictionary *(1911), but he is most associated with his* Modern English Usage *(1926), which became a landmark household reference work.*

1 A writer expresses himself in words that have been used before because they give his meaning better than he can give it himself, or because they are beautiful or witty, or because he expects them to touch a chord of association in his reader, or because he wishes to show that he is learned or well read. Quotations due to the last motive are invariably ill advised; the discerning reader detects it & is contemptuous; the undiscerning is perhaps impressed, but even then is at the same time repelled, pretentious quotations being the surest road to tedium.

A Dictionary of Modern English Usage, 'Quotation' (1926). Referring to 'literary or decorative quotation'.

2 The English-speaking world may be divided into (1) those who neither know nor care what a split infinitive is; (2) those who do not know, but care very much; (3) those who know & condemn; (4) those who know & approve; & (5) those who know & distinguish.

Ibid., 'Split Infinitive'. Fowler defined the first category as 'the vast majority . . . a happy folk, to be envied by most of the minority classes'.

(Sir) Norman Fowler (b. 1938)

BRITISH POLITICIAN

Elected a Conservative MP in 1970, he rose to be Minister of Employment (1987–90), special adviser to JOHN MAJOR *during the 1992 election, and Chairman of the Conservative Party (1992–4).*

1 I have a young family and for the next few years I should like to devote more time to them.

Resignation letter to the Prime Minister, publ. in the *Guardian* 4 January 1990. MARGARET

THATCHER's reply was: 'I am naturally very sorry to see you go, but understand your reasons for doing so, particularly your wish to be able to spend more time with your family.' The expression 'spend more time with his family' immediately became a euphemism for getting sacked, though there was no official indication that Fowler had been dismissed.

John Fowles (b. 1926)

BRITISH NOVELIST

His experimental novels include The Collector *(1963, filmed 1965),* The Magus *(1966, rev. 1977) and his pastiche of a Victorian romance,* The French Lieutenant's Woman *(1969, filmed 1981).*

1 Duty largely consists of pretending that the trivial is critical.

The Magus, ch. 18 (1965)

2 There is only one good definition of God: the freedom that allows other freedoms to exist.

The French Lieutenant's Woman, ch 13 (1969)

3 You do not even think of your own past as quite real; you dress it up, you gild it or blacken it, censor it, tinker with it . . . fictionalize it, in a word, and put it away on a shelf – your book, your romanced autobiography. We are all in flight from the real reality. That is the basic definition of Homo sapiens.

Ibid.

4 And so are we all novelists, that is, we have a habit of writing fictional futures for ourselves, although perhaps today we incline more to put ourselves into a film. We screen in our minds hypotheses about how we might behave, about what might happen to us. And these novelistic or cinematic hypotheses often have very much more effect on how we actually do behave, when the real future becomes the present, than we generally allow.

Ibid., ch. 45

5 Serious modern fiction has only one subject: the difficulty of writing serious modern fiction.

Miles Green, in *Mantissa* (1982)

Edward Fox (b. 1937)

BRITISH ACTOR

Often cast in restrained aristocratic roles, he has appeared in numerous TV dramas as well as such films as The Day of the Jackal *(1973) and* The Dresser *(1983).*

1 Being a gentleman is the number one priority, the chief question integral to our national life.

Daily Telegraph 14 February 1992

Janet Frame (b. 1924)

NEW ZEALAND NOVELIST AND POET
Misdiagnosed as a schizophrenic, she spent the years 1947–54 in mental hospitals, as recounted in her autobiography (3 vols., 1982–5), filmed as An Angel at My Table *(1990). Her novels include* Owls Do Cry *(1957).*

1 Every morning I woke in dread, waiting for the day nurse to go on her rounds and announce from the list of names in her hand whether or not I was for shock treatment, the new and fashionable means of quieting people and of making them realize that orders are to be obeyed and floors are to be polished without anyone protesting and faces are made to be fixed into smiles and weeping is a crime.
Faces in the Water, ch. 1 (1961). Referring to her life in a psychiatric institution.

2 For your own good is a persuasive argument that will eventually make a man agree to his own destruction.
Ibid., ch. 4

3 It would be nice to travel if you knew where you were going and where you would live at the end or do we ever know, do we ever live where we live, we're always in other places, lost, like sheep.
You Are Now Entering the Human Heart, 'The Day of the Sheep' (1983)

4 Writing a novel is not merely going on a shopping expedition across the border to an unreal land: it is hours and years spent in the factories, the streets, the cathedrals of the imagination.
The Envoy from Mirror City, ch. 20 (first volume of autobiography, 1985)

Anatole France (1844–1924)

FRENCH AUTHOR
Roused into politics by the Dreyfus case (1896), he inveighed against Church and State in such works as The Angels' Revolt *(1914), a satire on Christian theology.*

1 You think you are dying for your country; you die for the industrialists.
L'Humanité 18 July 1922

Anne Frank (1929–45)

GERMAN JEWISH REFUGEE AND DIARIST
Her diary, an account of the years 1942–4 when she and her family were in hiding in Nazi-occupied Amsterdam, was published in 1947 by her father, the only member of the family to survive. It has since been translated into over fifty languages.

1 One must apply one's reason to everything here, learning to obey, to shut up, to help, to be good, to give in, and I don't know what else. I'm afraid I shall use up all my brains too quickly, and I haven't got so

very many. Then I shall not have any left for when the war is over.
Journal entry 22 December 1942, publ. in *The Diary of a Young Girl* (1947)

2 They mustn't know my despair, I can't let them see the wounds which they have caused, I couldn't bear their sympathy and their kind-hearted jokes, it would only make me want to scream all the more. If I talk, everyone thinks I'm showing off; when I'm silent they think I'm ridiculous; rude if I answer, sly if I get a good idea, lazy if I'm tired, selfish if I eat a mouthful more than I should, stupid, cowardly, crafty, etc. etc.
Journal entry 30 January 1943, ibid.

3 I want to go on living even after my death! And therefore I am grateful to God for giving me this gift, this possibility of developing myself and of writing, of expressing all that is in me.
Journal entry 4 April 1944, ibid.

4 I don't believe that the big men, the politicians and the capitalists alone are guilty of the war. Oh, no, the little man is just as keen, otherwise the people of the world would have risen in revolt long ago! There is an urge and rage in people to destroy, to kill, to murder, and until all mankind, without exception, undergoes a great change, wars will be waged, everything that has been built up, cultivated and grown, will be destroyed and disfigured, after which mankind will have to begin all over again.
Journal entry 3 May 1944, ibid.

5 I have often been downcast, but never in despair; I regard our hiding as a dangerous adventure, romantic and interesting at the same time. In my diary I treat all the privations as amusing. I have made up my mind now to lead a different life from other girls and, later on, different from ordinary housewives. My start has been so very full of interest, and that is the sole reason why I have to laugh at the humorous side of the most dangerous moments.
Ibid.

6 Is discord going to show itself while we are still fighting, is the Jew once again worth less than another? Oh, it is sad, very sad, that once more, for the umpteenth time, the old truth is confirmed: 'What *one* Christian does is his own responsibility, what *one* Jew does is thrown back at all Jews.'
Journal entry 22 May 1944, ibid. Referring to anti-Semitism in Holland.

7 It's really a wonder that I haven't dropped all my ideals because they seem so absurd and impossible to carry out. Yet, I keep

them, because in spite of everything I still believe that people are really good at heart. I simply can't build up my hopes on a foundation consisting of confusion, misery, and death. I see the world gradually being turned into a wilderness, I hear the ever-approaching thunder, which will destroy us too, I can feel the sufferings of millions and yet, if I look up into the heavens, I think that it will all come right, that this cruelty too will end, and that peace and tranquillity will return again.

Journal entry 15 July 1944, ibid. Less than three weeks after writing this entry, on 4 August 1944, Anne along with the other occupants of the secret annexe in which they had been hiding were arrested by the Nazis and sent to concentration camps in Germany.

Hans Frank (1900–1946)
GERMAN NAZI POLITICIAN
Nazi Germany's leading lawyer, he was appointed in 1939 Governor-General of Poland, where he ran a brutally repressive régime and established concentration camps. He was tried at Nuremberg and hanged.

1 Our Constitution is the will of the Führer.
Völkischer Beobachter 20 May 1936, quoted in *Hitler: A Study in Tyranny*, ch. 7, sect. 6 (1952, rev. 1962) by Alan Bullock

2 There is no independence of law against National Socialism. Say to yourselves at every decision which you make: 'How would the Führer decide in my place?' In every decision ask yourselves: 'Is this decision compatible with the National Socialist conscience of the German people?' Then you will have a firm iron foundation which, allied with the unity of the National Socialist People's State and with your recognition of the eternal nature of the will of Adolf Hitler, will endow your own sphere of decision with the authority of the Third Reich, and this for all time.
Speech to jurists in 1936, quoted in *The Rise and Fall of the Third Reich*, ch. 8, 'Justice in the Third Reich' (1959) by William L. Shirer. Frank was at the time Commissioner of Justice and President of the German Law Academy

Felix Frankfurter (1882–1965)
US ACADEMIC AND JUDGE
He taught at Harvard Law School (1914–39), co-founded the American Civil Liberties Union (1920) and served as Associate Justice of the US Supreme Court (1939–62).

1 The words of the Constitution ... are so unrestricted by their intrinsic meaning or by their history or by tradition or by prior decisions that they leave the individual Justice free, if indeed they do not compel him,

to gather meaning not from reading the Constitution but from reading life.
'The Supreme Court', quoted in *Parliamentary Affairs* vol. 3, no. 1 winter 1949

2 Judicial judgment must take deep account ... of the day before yesterday in order that yesterday may not paralyze today.
Quoted in the *National Observer* 1 March 1965

Aretha Franklin (b. 1942)
US SOUL SINGER
Known as 'Lady Soul' for her impassioned delivery, she sang gospel songs in the Detroit church of her father, C. L. Franklin, the most celebrated gospel preacher of the 1950s, before recording a series of hits in the 1960s.

1 R-E-S-P-E-C-T
Find out what it means to me.
'Respect' (song, written by Otis Redding), on the album *I Never Loved a Man the Way I Loved You* (1967). The song was a hit for Otis Redding in 1965.

Michael Franti (b. 1966)
US RAPPER
A six-foot-six ex-baseball player, he composed and sang with Disposable Heroes of Hiphoprisy, a band on the 'liberal' wing of 1990s rap.

1 TV is the place
Where the pursuit of happiness has become the pursuit of trivia
Where toothpaste and cars have become sex objects
Where imagination is sucked out of children
by a cathode ray nipple.
TV is the only wet nurse that would create a cripple.
Television, the drug of the nation,
Breeding ignorance and feeding radiation.
'Television, the Drug of the Nation' (song) on the album *Hypocrisy is the Greatest Luxury* (1992) by the Disposable Heroes of Hiphoprisy

2 If ever I would stop thinking about music and politics
I would tell you that music is the expression of emotion
and that politics is merely the decoy of perception
'Music and Politics' (song) on ibid.

Michael Frayn (b. 1933)
BRITISH PLAYWRIGHT, NOVELIST AND JOURNALIST
A satirical wit pervades his many successful comedies for the stage, for example Noises Off (1982). He has also written novels, screenplays and translations.

1 It's not excellence which leads to celebrity, but celebrity which leads to excellence.

One makes one's reputation, and one's reputation enables one to achieve the conditions in which one can do good work.
John Dyson, in *Towards the End of the Morning*, ch. 4 (1967)

2 Happily married couples stood not face to face, absorbed in each other, but back to back looking outwards upon the world.
Bob Bell (musing to himself), ibid., ch. 8

3 So I want to tell you how important it is to make things. That's how man lives, by making. To be is to make. To make food, to make drink, to make shelter – yes, but also to make thought. Because to think is to make.
Horvath, in *Make or Break*, act 1 (1980)

4 That's what it's all about. Doors and sardines. Getting on – getting off. Getting the sardines on – getting the sardines off. That's farce. That's the theatre. That's life.
Lloyd (the director), in *Noises Off*, act 1 (1982)

Jonathan Freedland (b. 1967)
BRITISH JOURNALIST
A columnist and leader writer for the Guardian, *he compares US and British political and social institutions in his book* Bring Home the Revolution *(1998).*

1 We simultaneously disdain and covet American culture, condemning it as junk food, even as we reach for another helping – a kind of binge-and-puke social bulimia.
Bring Home the Revolution, Introduction (1998)

Max Freedman See BILL HALEY 1.

Matt Frei (b. 1963)
BRITISH JOURNALIST
A foreign correspondent for the BBC, he has also been a regular contributor to newspapers and periodicals. His first book was Italy: The Unfinished Revolution *(1995).*

1 It's like the Beatles coming together again – let's hope they don't go on a world tour.
Listener 21 June 1990. Refering to German reunification.

Marilyn French (b. 1929)
US AUTHOR
She is best known for her first novel The Women's Room *(1977), one of the earliest books to tackle radical feminist issues in easily accessible fiction. Other novels include* The Bleeding Heart *(1981).*

1 I hate discussions of feminism that end up with who does the dishes, she said. So do I. But at the end, there are always the damned dishes.
Isolde, in *The Women's Room*, ch. 1, sect. 21 (1977)

2 Whatever they may be in public life, whatever their relations with men, in their relations with women, all men are rapists and that's all they are. They rape us with their eyes, their laws, their codes.
Valerie, ibid., ch. 5, sect. 19

Sigmund Freud (1856–1939)
AUSTRIAN PSYCHIATRIST
He developed the basic techniques of psychoanalysis through free association and the analysis of dreams, as expounded in such volumes as The Interpretation of Dreams *(1899),* Totem and Taboo *(1913) and* The Ego and the Id *(1923). See* W. H. AUDEN 16; JOHN IRVING 1; R. D. LAING 1.

1 A strong egoism is a protection against disease, but in the last resort we must begin to love in order that we may not fall ill, and must fall ill if, in consequence of frustration, we cannot love.
'On Narcissism: An Introduction' (1914), repr. in *Complete Works, Standard Edition*, vol. 14 (ed. James Strachey and Anna Freud, 1954)

2 We believe that civilization has been created under the pressure of the exigencies of life at the cost of satisfaction of the instincts.
Introductory Lectures on Psychoanalysis, Lecture 1 (1915), repr. ibid., vol. 15 (1963)

3 The analytic psychotherapist thus has a threefold battle to wage – in his own mind against the forces which seek to drag him down from the analytic level; outside the analysis, against opponents who dispute the importance he attaches to the sexual instinctual forces and hinder him from making use of them in his scientific technique; and inside the analysis, against his patients, who at first behave like opponents but later on reveal the overvaluation of sexual life which dominates them, and who try to make him captive to their socially untamed passion.
'Observations on Transference-Love', first publ. 1915, repr. ibid., vol. 12 (1958)

4 If a man has been his mother's undisputed darling he retains throughout life the triumphant feeling, the confidence in success, which not seldom brings actual success along with it.
'A Childhood Recollection from Dichtung und Wahrheit', first publ. 1917, repr. ibid., vol. 17 (1955)

5 The ego is not master in its own house.
'A Difficulty in the Path of Psycho-Analysis', first publ. 1917, repr. ibid. Freud's conclusion was reached in the light of his conviction that sexual instincts could not be wholly tamed, and that mental processes were unconscious and could 'only reach the ego and come under its

control through incomplete and untrustworthy perceptions'.

6 I have found little that is 'good' about human beings on the whole. In my experience most of them are trash, no matter whether they publicly subscribe to this or that ethical doctrine or to none at all. That is something that you cannot say aloud, or perhaps even think.

Letter, 9 October 1918, publ. in *Psycho-Analysis and Faith: The Letters of Sigmund Freud and Oscar Pfister* (1963)

7 Incidentally, why was it that none of all the pious ever discovered psycho-analysis? Why did it have to wait for a completely godless Jew?

Ibid.

8 We know less about the sexual life of little girls than of boys. But we need not feel ashamed of this distinction; after all, the sexual life of adult women is a 'dark continent' for psychology.

The Question of Lay Analysis, pt. 4 (1926). The phrase 'dark continent' was written in English.

9 A civilization which leaves so large a number of its participants unsatisfied and drives them into revolt neither has nor deserves the prospect of a lasting existence.

The Future of an Illusion, ch. 2 (1927)

10 Devout believers are safeguarded in a high degree against the risk of certain neurotic illnesses; their acceptance of the universal neurosis spares them the task of constructing a personal one.

Ibid., ch. 8

11 It is always possible to bind together a considerable number of people in love, so long as there are other people left over to receive the manifestations of their aggression.

Civilization and its Discontents, ch. 5 (1930)

12 Civilization is a process in the service of Eros, whose purpose is to combine single human individuals, and after that families, then races, peoples and nations, into one great unity, the unity of mankind. Why this has to happen, we do not know; the work of Eros is precisely this.

Ibid., ch. 6

13 The only bodily organ which is really regarded as inferior is the atrophied penis, a girl's clitoris.

New Introductory Lectures on Psychoanalysis, Lecture 31, 'The Dissection of the Psychical Personality' (1933). Freud was refuting the claims of 'Individual Psychologists' that the 'inferiority complex' can be traced back to self-perceived organic defects.

14 Where id was, there ego shall be.

Ibid. The intention of psychoanalysis, Freud

explained, is 'to strengthen the ego, to make it more independent of the super-ego, to widen its field of perception and enlarge its organization, so that it can appropriate fresh portions of the id ... It is a work of culture,' he added in the closing words of the lecture, 'not unlike the draining of the Zuider Zee.'

15 I do not think our successes can compete with those of Lourdes. There are so many more people who believe in the miracles of the Blessed Virgin than in the existence of the unconscious.

Ibid. Lecture 34, 'Explanations, Applications and Orientations'

16 What progress we are making. In the Middle Ages they would have burned me. Now they are content with burning my books.

Remark in 1933, quoted in *Sigmund Freud: Life and Work*, vol. 3, pt. 1, ch. 4 (1957) by Ernest Jones. Referring to the public burning of his books in Berlin.

17 A certain degree of neurosis is of inestimable value as a drive, especially to a psychologist.

Quoted in *Fragments of an Analysis with Freud*, ch. 3, '22 January 1935' (1954) by Joseph Wortis

18 Homosexuality is assuredly no advantage, but it is nothing to be ashamed of, no vice, no degradation; it cannot be classified as an illness; we consider it to be a variation of the sexual function, produced by a certain arrest of sexual development. Many highly respectable individuals of ancient and modern times have been homosexuals, several of the greatest men among them (Plato, Michelangelo, Leonardo da Vinci, etc.). It is a great injustice to persecute homosexuality as a crime – and a cruelty, too. If you do not believe me, read the books of Havelock Ellis.

Letter to a woman requesting treatment for her son, 9 April 1935, publ. in *The Letters of Sigmund Freud* (1961)

19 Every normal person, in fact, is only normal on the average. His ego approximates to that of the psychotic in some part or other and to a greater or lesser extent.

'Analysis Terminable and Interminable', sect. 5 (1937), repr. in *Complete Works, Standard Edition*, vol. 23 (ed. James Strachey and Anna Freud, 1964)

20 The great question that has never been answered, and which I have not yet been able to answer, despite my thirty years of research into the feminine soul, is 'What does a woman want?' [*Was will das Weib?*]

Quoted in *Sigmund Freud: Life and Work*, vol. 2, pt. 3, ch. 16 (1955) by Ernest Jones. Freud's views on women are summarized in Peter Gay's biography, *Freud: A Life of Our Time*, pt. 10 (1988).

21 Yes, America is gigantic, but a gigantic mistake.

Quoted in *Memories of a Psycho-analyst*, ch. 9 (1959) by Ernest Jones. 'America is the most grandiose experiment the world has seen,' Freud said on another occasion, 'but, I am afraid, it is not going to be a success.' (*Freud: the Man and his Cause*, pt. 3, ch. 12, 1980, by Ronald W. Clark)

Nancy Friday (b. 1937)

US AUTHOR

After My Secret Garden *(1973), a study of female sexuality, she published* Men in Love *(1980) and* Women on Top *(1991), chronicles of sexual fantasies, which she describes as 'the triumph of love over rage'.*

1 Women are learning that nobody gives you an orgasm, nobody makes you sexual, except yourself.

Men in Love, ch. 1 (1980)

2 I have always believed that our erotic daydreams are the true X-rays of our sexual souls . . . An analyst collects his patients' dreams like gold coins. We should value our erotic reveries no less seriously, because they are the complex expressions of what we consciously desire and unconsciously fear. To know them is to know ourselves better.

Women on Top, pt. 1, 'Report from the Erotic Interior' (1991)

3 For the mating game to even begin, the animal must abandon at least momentarily the search for nuts and berries to pick up the erotic scent. In the very simplest of terms, there is no time for sex in a materially greedy world.

Ibid.

4 Early twentieth-century man lived in a dizzying, swivel-headed attitude toward women's sexuality. He needed to see woman as chaste, passive, spiritual, she who was so close to heaven she could save his very soul after a murderous day of competition in the new industrial society. This was known as 'the cult of the household nun'.

Ibid., pt. 2, 'A Little History'

5 The meaning of what it is to be a woman has never been more open-ended and therefore more filled with anxiety. We want to be independent/we want to be taken care of. We want men to treat us as sexual equals/we want men to sweep us away into sexual oblivion. We seduce men/we expect them to know, without being told, what it is we want done to our bodies. Men do their best, some better than others, but all work in the dark.

Ibid., pt. 2, 'What is a Real Woman?'

Betty Friedan (b. 1921)

US FEMINIST ACTIVIST AND AUTHOR

Her book, The Feminine Mystique *(1963) was a seminal influence in the women's movement. She was a founder of the National Organization for Women (NOW) (1966) and called the first International Feminist Congress in 1973, though later repudiated some aspects of contemporary feminism.*

1 The problem that has no name stirring in the minds of so many American women today is not a matter of loss of femininity or too much education, or the demands of domesticity. It is far more important than anyone recognizes. It is the key to these other new and old problems which have been torturing women and their husbands and children, and puzzling their doctors and educators for years. It may well be the key to our future as a nation and a culture. We can no longer ignore that voice within women that says: 'I want something more than my husband and my children and my home.'

The Feminine Mystique, ch. 1 (1963)

2 Instead of fulfilling the promise of infinite orgiastic bliss, sex in the America of the feminine mystique is becoming a strangely joyless national compulsion, if not a contemptuous mockery.

Ibid., ch. 11

3 The feminine mystique has succeeded in burying millions of American women alive.

Ibid., ch. 13

4 It is easier to live through someone else than to become complete yourself.

Ibid., ch. 14

5 The women's movement has for years been the scapegoat for the rage of threatened, insecure housewives who can no longer count on husbands for lifelong support.

The Second Stage, ch. 1 (1981)

6 Make policy, not coffee.

Ibid. The slogan was adopted during the National Organization for Women's Political Caucus in 1971.

Milton Friedman (b. 1912)

US ECONOMIST

A convinced monetarist, he was adviser to President REAGAN *(1981–9) and the inspiration for the economic policies of the Conservative government under* MARGARET THATCHER. *See also* ANONYMOUS 18.

1 History suggests that capitalism is a necessary condition for political freedom. Clearly it is not a sufficient condition.

Capitalism and Freedom, ch. 1 (1962)

2 **We are all Keynesians now.**

Quoted in *Time* 31 December 1965. In a letter to the magazine's editor 4 February 1966, Friedman protested that the quote was taken out of context, since he had added 'in another [sense], nobody is any longer a Keynesian'.

3 **People are out of work. Interest rates go up. Money gets tight. It's unpleasant. Only later do the good effects of an end to rising prices show up. The problem is getting through the painful cure without wanting another drink. The greatest difficulty in curtailing inflation is that, after a while, people begin to think they'd rather have the sickness than the cure.**

Playboy February 1973, repr. as Introduction to *There's No Such Thing as a Free Lunch* (1975)

4 **Perfect competition is a theoretical concept like the Euclidean line, which has no width and no depth. Just as we've never seen that line there has never been truly free enterprise.**

Ibid.

5 **What kind of society isn't structured on greed?**

Ibid.

Brian Friel (b. 1929)

IRISH PLAYWRIGHT AND AUTHOR

He gained recognition with Philadelphia, Here I Come! *(1964), which, like his later plays* Translations *(1980) and* Dancing at Lughnasa *(1990), deals with the land, its customs and emigration.*

1 **People with a culture of poverty suffer much less from repression than we of the middle class suffer and indeed, if I may make the suggestion with due qualification, they often have a hell of a lot more fun than we have.**

Dodds, in *The Freedom of the City*, act 1 (1973)

2 **It is not the literal past, the 'facts' of history, that shape us, but images of the past embodied in language. . . . We must never cease renewing those images; because once we do, we fossilize.**

Hugh, in *Translations*, act 3 (1981)

3 **The Troubles are a pigmentation in our lives here, a constant irritation that detracts from real life. But life has to do with something else as well, and it's the other things which are the more permanent and real.**

Interview in *Vanity Fair* October 1991. Referring to Northern Ireland.

Max Frisch (1911–91)

SWISS NOVELIST AND PLAYWRIGHT

He adopted an Expressionist style in his examinations of the moral dilemmas of the mid-twentieth century, as in the novels Stiller *(1954) and* Homo

Faber *(1957), and the plays* Andorra *(1961) and* The Fire Raisers *(1962).*

1 **It's precisely the disappointing stories, which have no proper ending and therefore no proper meaning, that sound true to life.**

Stiller, in *I'm Not Stiller*, 'First Notebook' (1954)

2 **Technology . . . the knack of so arranging the world that we don't have to experience it.**

Hanna, in *Homo Faber*, 'Second Stop' (1957)

Erich Fromm (1900–1980)

GERMAN-BORN US PSYCHOLOGIST

His books, which blend psychoanalysis with sociology and philosophy, show the influences of Marx and existentialism. His principal works are Escape from Freedom *(1941),* The Sane Society *(1955), and* The Art of Loving *(1956).*

1 **Man is the only animal for whom his own existence is a problem which he has to solve.**

Man for Himself, ch. 3 (1947)

2 **Man's main task in life is to give *birth* to himself, to become what he potentially is. The most important product of his effort is his own personality.**

Ibid., ch. 4

3 **To die is poignantly bitter, but the idea of having to die without having lived is unbearable.**

Ibid.

4 **Reason is man's instrument for arriving at the truth, intelligence is man's instrument for manipulating the world more successfully; the former is essentially human, the latter belongs to the animal part of man.**

The Sane Society, ch. 3 (1955)

5 **By alienation is meant a mode of experience in which the person experiences himself as an alien. He has become, one might say, estranged from himself. He does not experience himself as the center of his world, as the creator of his own acts – but his acts and their consequences have become his masters, whom he obeys, or whom he may even worship. The alienated person is out of touch with himself as he is out of touch with any other person.**

Ibid., ch. 5, 'Alienation'

6 **In the nineteenth century the problem was that *God is dead*; in the twentieth century the problem is that *man is dead*. In the nineteenth century inhumanity meant cruelty; in the twentieth century it means schizoid self-alienation. The danger of the past was that men became slaves. The danger of the future is that men may become robots.**

Ibid., ch. 9. Fromm was echoing a speech made

by ADLAI STEVENSON at Columbia University in 1954: 'We are not in danger of becoming slaves any more, but of becoming robots.'

7 Just as modern mass production requires the standardization of commodities, so the social process requires standardization of man, and this standardization is called equality.
  The Art of Loving, ch. 2 (1956)

(Sir) David Frost (b. 1939)
BRITISH BROADCASTER
Having 'risen without trace', as Kitty Muggeridge famously told her husband MALCOLM MUG-GERIDGE, he established himself as an incisive interviewer on British and American TV, co-founded London Weekend Television and in 1983 co-founded and presented TV-am.

1 Vote Labour and you build castles in the air. Vote Conservative and you can live in them.
  That Was the Week That Was, BBC TV, 31 December 1962

2 Hello, good evening, and welcome.
  The Frost Report (TV show, 1966–7). The words were used to open each show in this and subsequent Frost series.

Robert Frost (1874–1963)
US POET
His lyrical poetry was traditional in form and inspired by rural New England, as in the volume, New Hampshire (1923). He won four Pulitzer prizes and in later life was regarded as the unofficial US poet laureate. The critic YVOR WIN-TERS described him as a 'poet of the minor theme, the casual approach, and the discreetly eccentric attitude'.

1 *Something there is that doesn't love a wall, And wants it down.*
  'Mending Wall', publ. in *North of Boston* (1914)

2 *My apple trees will never get across And eat the cones under his pines, I tell him.*
  He only says, 'Good fences make good neighbors'.
  Ibid.

3 *And nothing to look backward to with pride, And nothing to look forward to with hope.*
  'The Death of the Hired Man', publ. ibid.

4 *Home is the place where, when you have to go there, They have to take you in.*
  Husband, ibid. Wife replies: 'I should have called it/Something you somehow haven't to deserve.'

5 *Most of the change we think we see in life Is due to truths being in and out of favor.*
  'The Black Cottage', publ. ibid.

6 *The best way out is always through.*
  'A Servant to Servants', publ. ibid.

7 *Pressed into service means pressed out of shape.*
  'The Self-Seeker', publ. ibid.

8 *I shall be telling this with a sigh Somewhere ages and ages hence: Two roads diverged in a wood, and I – I took the one less traveled by, And that has made all the difference.*
  'The Road Not Taken', publ. in *Mountain Interval* (1916)

9 *One could do worse than be a swinger of birches.*
  'Birches', publ. ibid.

10 A poem . . . begins as a lump in the throat, a sense of wrong, a homesickness, a love-sickness. . . . It finds the thought and the thought finds the words.
  Letter to poet and anthologist Louis Unter-meyer, 1 January 1916, publ. in *The Letters of Robert Frost to Louis Untermeyer* (1963)

11 *I met a Californian who would Talk California – a state so blessed He said, in climate, none had ever died there A natural death, and Vigilance Committees Had had to organize to stock the graveyards And vindicate the state's humanity.*
  'New Hampshire', publ. in *New Hampshire* (1923)

12 *No wonder poets sometimes have to seem So much more business-like than business men. Their wares are so much harder to get rid of.*
  Ibid.

13 *Some say the world will end in fire, Some say in ice. From what I've tasted of desire I hold with those who favor fire. But if it had to perish twice, I think I know enough of hate To say that for destruction ice Is also great And would suffice.*
  'Fire and Ice', publ. ibid.

14 *The woods are lovely, dark and deep. But I have promises to keep, And miles to go before I sleep, And miles to go before I sleep.*
  'Stopping by Woods on a Snowy Evening', publ. ibid. The lines were found on a scrap of paper on the desk of Indian Prime Minister JAWA-HARLAL NEHRU when he died – presumed to be the last words he read – and they were regularly quoted by JOHN F. KENNEDY to wind up speeches during his 1960 presidential campaign.

15 *Tree at my window, window tree, My sash is lowered when night comes on;*

*But let there never be curtain drawn
Between you and me.*
'Tree at My Window', publ. in *West-Running
Brook* (1928)

16 *I have been one acquainted with the night.*
'Acquainted with the Night', publ. ibid.

17 **Writing free verse is like playing tennis
with the net down.**
Address to Milton Academy, Massachusetts,
17 May 1935, publ. in *Interviews with Robert Frost*
(1966) by Edward Latham

18 *They cannot scare me with their empty
spaces
Between stars – on stars where no human
race is.
I have it in me so much nearer home
To scare myself with my own desert places.*
'Desert Places', publ. in *A Further Range* (1936)

19 *Two such as you with such a master speed
Cannot be parted nor be swept away
From one another once you are agreed
That life is only life forevermore
Together wing to wing and oar to oar.*
'The Master Speed', publ. ibid. The verse was
inscribed on the gravestone of Frost and his wife
Elinor in 1963.

20 *No memory of having starred
Atones for later disregard,
Or keeps the end from being hard.*
'Provide, Provide', publ. ibid.

21 *I never dared be radical when young
For fear it would make me conservative
when old.*
'Precaution', publ. ibid.

22 **No tears in the writer, no tears in the
reader.**
'The Figure a Poem Makes', Preface to *Collected
Poems* (1939)

23 *The land was ours before we were the
land's.
She was our land more than a hundred
years
Before we were her people.*
'The Gift Outright', publ. in *The Witness Tree*
(1942). Frost recited this poem at the inaugur-
ation of President KENNEDY, 20 January 1961.

24 **Happiness makes up in height what it lacks
in length.**
Poem title, ibid.

25 *And were an epitaph to be my story
I'd have a short one ready for my own.
I would have written of me on my stone:
I had a lover's quarrel with the world.*
'The Lesson for Today', publ. ibid.

26 *We dance round in a ring and suppose,
But the Secret sits in the middle and knows.*
'The Secret Sits', publ. ibid.

27 **Poetry is a way of taking life by the throat.**
Quoted in *Robert Frost: the Trial by Existence*,
ch. 18 (1960) by Elizabeth S. Sergeant

28 *Forgive, O Lord, my little jokes on Thee
And I'll forgive Thy great big one on me.*
'Cluster of Faith', publ. in *In the Clearing* (1962)

29 **You don't have to deserve your mother's
love. You have to deserve your father's.
He's more particular. . . . The father is
always a Republican towards his son, and
his mother's always a Democrat.**
Interview in *Writers at Work* (second series, ed.
George Plimpton, 1963)

30 **Thinking isn't agreeing or disagreeing.
That's voting.**
Ibid.

31 **Always fall in with what you're asked to
accept. Take what is given, and make it
over your way. My aim in life has always
been to hold my own with whatever's
going. Not against: with.**
Vogue 14 March 1963

32 **Poetry is what is lost in translation.**
Quoted in *Robert Frost: a Backward Look*, ch. 1
(1964) by Louis Untermeyer. In similar vein,
Samuel Taylor Coleridge wrote, in *Biographia Lit-
eraria* (1817): 'In poetry, in which every line,
every phrase, may pass the ordeal of deliberation
and deliberate choice, it is possible, and barely
possible, to attain that *ultimatum* which I have
ventured to propose as the infallible test of a
blameless style; namely: its *untranslatableness* in
words of the same language without injury to
the meaning.'

Christopher Fry (b. 1907)
BRITISH PLAYWRIGHT
*Born Christopher Fry Harris. Described by John
Mason Brown as 'a fellow who has wandered from
one Elizabethan Age into another', he specializes
in free-verse dramas that combine comedy and an
underlying mysticism, as in* The Lady's Not for
Burning *(1948) and* Venus Observed *(1950).*

1 *It is the individual man
In his individual freedom who can mature
With his warm spirit the unripe world.*
Moses, in *The Firstborn*, act 1, sc. 1 (1946)

2 *I travel light; as light,
That is, as a man can travel who will
Still carry his body around because
Of its sentimental value.*
Thomas, in *The Lady's Not for Burning*, act 1
(1949). The play's title was famously adapted: see
MARGARET THATCHER 10

3 *What after all
Is a halo? It's only one more thing to keep
clean.*
Ibid.

4 *Religion*
  Has made an honest woman of the super-
     natural,
  And we won't have it kicking over the traces
     again.
  Tappercoom, ibid., act 2

5 *The moon is nothing*
  But a circumambulating aphrodisiac
  Divinely subsidized to provoke the world
  Into a rising birth-rate.
  Thomas Mendip, ibid., act 3

6 Poetry is the language in which man
  explores his own amazement . . . says
  heaven and earth in one word . . . speaks of
  himself and his predicament as though for
  the first time. It has the virtue of being
  able to say twice as much as prose in half
  the time, and the drawback, if you do not
  give it your full attention, of seeming to
  say half as much in twice the time.
  Time 3 April 1950

7 Comedy is an escape, not from truth but
  from despair; a narrow escape into faith.
  Time 20 November 1950

8 Coffee in England is just toasted milk.
  New York Post 29 November 1962

Roger Fry (1866–1934)
BRITISH CRITIC AND PAINTER
A member of the Bloomsbury group, he organized
the first London exhibition of Post-Impressionists
(1910) and set up the Omega Workshops (1913–19)
for the benefit of young artists. BRIAN SEWELL
called him 'the father of foolish criticism'.

1 Art is significant deformity.
  Quoted in *Roger Fry*, ch. 8 (1940) by VIRGINIA
  WOOLF

Stephen Fry (b. 1957)
BRITISH ACTOR AND AUTHOR
Television appearances in the comedy series A Bit
of Fry & Laurie *(1989–94) and* Jeeves and Wooster *(1991–3) were followed by the lead part in the*
film Wilde *(1997). He placed himself 'somewhere*
between Alan Bennett and the Queen Mother, a
sort of public kitten'.

1 We are more afraid of being pretentious
  than of being dishonest.
  Quoted in the *Guardian* 31 December 1994

2 There is no logical explanation for despair.
  You can no more reason yourself into
  cheerfulness than you can reason yourself
  an extra six inches in height. You can only
  be better prepared.
  Speech to launch the Samaritans' annual report,
  17 May 1996, quoted in the *Guardian* 18 May
  1996. Speaking of the breakdown which caused
  him to abandon a play in mid-production.

Northrop Frye (1912–91)
CANADIAN LITERARY CRITIC
He established his reputation with Fearful Sym-
metry *(1947) and* Anatomy of Criticism *(1957),*
which deal with literary archetypes. The Great
Code *(1982) examines the symbolism of the Bible.*

1 It is clear that all verbal structures with
  meaning are verbal imitations of that elusive psychological and physiological process
  known as thought, a process stumbling
  through emotional entanglements, sudden
  irrational convictions, involuntary gleams
  of insight, rationalized prejudices, and
  blocks of panic and inertia, finally to reach
  a completely incommunicable intuition.
  Anatomy of Criticism, 'Formal Phase: Symbol as
  Image' (1957)

2 Popular art is normally decried as vulgar
  by the cultivated people of its time; then it
  loses favor with its original audience as a
  new generation grows up; then it begins to
  merge into the softer lighting of 'quaint',
  and cultivated people become interested in
  it, and finally it begins to take on the
  archaic dignity of the primitive.
  Ibid., 'Mythical Phase: Symbol as Archetype'

Carlos Fuentes (b. 1928)
MEXICAN AUTHOR AND CRITIC
Since winning recognition for his first collection of
short stories, The Masked Days *(1954), he has writ-*
ten numerous works of fiction and criticism as well
as a study of Latin America's Spanish heritage,
Terra Nostra *(1975).*

1 What the United States does best is to
  understand itself. What it does worst is
  understand others.
  Time 16 June 1986

2 By its very nature, the novel indicates that
  we are becoming. There is no final solution. There is no last word.
  Guardian 24 February 1989

3 If the Soviet Union can give up the
  Brezhnev Doctrine for the Sinatra Doc-
  trine, the United States can give up the
  James Monroe Doctrine for the Marilyn
  Monroe Doctrine: Let's all go to bed wear-
  ing the perfume we like best.
  Quoted in *The Times* 23 February 1990

4 I don't think any good book is based on
  factual experience. Bad books are about
  things the writer already knew before he
  wrote them.
  International Herald Tribune 5 November 1991

Francis Fukuyama (b. 1952)
US HISTORIAN
His chief work, The End of History and the Last

Man *(1992), asserts that liberal democracy will triumph over all other forms of government, and was commonly cited as a description of the world in the wake of the Cold War.*

1 **What we may be witnessing is not just the end of the Cold War but the end of history as such: that is, the end point of man's ideological evolution and the universalization of Western liberal democracy.**
Independent 20 September 1989

2 **While it is often the enemy of democracy, nationalism has also been democracy's handmaiden, from the time of the French Revolution.**
Independent 3 March 1992

J. William Fulbright (1905–95)

US POLITICIAN

James William Fulbright. Elected as a Democrat to Congress in 1942 and to the Senate in 1944, he established a system of exchange programmes for teachers and students between the US and other countries (1946). He opposed McCarthyism and the Vietnam War.

1 **In the long course of history, having people who understand your thought is much greater security than another submarine.**
The New York Times 26 June 1986. Speaking of the Fulbright scholarship programme.

R. Buckminster Fuller (1895–1983)

US ENGINEER AND POET

Richard Buckminster Fuller. A designer and inventor, he developed the geodesic dome (from 1945), and in 1962 he became Professor of Poetry at Harvard

1 **Here is God's purpose –
for God, to me, it seems,
is a verb
not a noun,
proper or improper.**
Untitled poem, written 1940, publ. in *No More Secondhand God* (1963)

2 **Either war is obsolete or men are.**
New Yorker 8 January 1966

3 **Dare to be naïve.**
Synergetics, 'Moral of the Work' (1975)

Paul Fussell (b. 1924)

US HISTORIAN

Called a 'thinking man's John Wayne' for his vigorous prose, he has written on both world wars, as in The Boy Scout Handbook and Other Observations *(1982), and on American society in* Class: A Guide through the American Status System *(1983).*

1 **The worst thing about war was the sitting around and wondering what you were doing morally.**
The Times 28 November 1991

Rose Fyleman (1877–1957)

BRITISH CHILDREN'S AUTHOR

A formidable character who had little time for children, she nevertheless devoted a career to writing for them. Her first collection of verse 'Fairies and Chimneys' (1918) proved her most popular.

1 **There are fairies at the bottom of our garden!**
'The Fairies', publ. in *Punch* 23 May 1917, repr. in *Fairies and Chimneys* (1918)

Jostein Gaarder (b. 1952)

NORWEGIAN PHILOSOPHER

A former teacher of philosophy, he writes fiction for children and adults. Sophie's World (1991) was his first book to be published in English, and was an international success.

1 A lot of people experience the world with the same incredulity as when a magician pulls a rabbit out of a hat. . . . We know that the world is not all sleight of hand and deception because we are in it, we are part of it. Actually we *are* the white rabbit being pulled out of the hat. The only difference between us and the white rabbit is that the rabbit does not realize it is taking part in a magic trick.

   Sophie's World, 'The Top Hat' (1991)

Clark Gable (1901–60)

US SCREEN ACTOR

By the time he played Fletcher Christian in Mutiny on the Bounty *(1935) he was hailed as 'the King of Hollywood'. His most famous roles were in* Gone with the Wind *(1939) and his last film,* The Misfits *(1961).*

1 Frankly, my dear, I don't give a damn!

   Rhett Butler (Clark Gable), in *Gone with the Wind* (film, 1939, screenplay by Sidney Howard based on the 1936 novel by Margaret Mitchell, directed by Victor Fleming and others). The final words of Rhett's farewell to Scarlett O'Hara (Vivien Leigh), in answer to her lament, 'Where shall I go? What shall I do?' Because of the wish not to offend the censors, the words were spoken with the emphasis on 'give' to soften the impact of the oath. Producer DAVID O. SELZNICK was still fined $5,000, however. For Margaret Mitchell's version, see MARGARET MITCHELL 8.

Zsa Zsa Gabor (b. 1919)

HUNGARIAN-BORN US ACTRESS

Despite an undistinguished acting career, she became a denizen of gossip columns for her wealth and numerous marriages and affairs. Her liaison with the dictator Rafael Trujillo provoked the comment, 'the most expensive courtesan since Madame de Pompadour'.

1 I never hated a man enough to give him diamonds back.

   Quoted in the *Observer* 25 August 1957

2 A man in love is incomplete until he has married – then he's finished.

   Quoted in *Newsweek* 28 March 1960

3 Husbands are like fires. They go out when unattended.

   Ibid.

4 The only place men want depth in a woman is in her cleavage.

   Quoted in the *Guardian* 19 December 1998

Serge Gainsbourg (1928–91)
FRENCH SINGER, SONGWRITER AND
FILM-MAKER
*Originally Lucien Ginzburg. He wrote for Johnny
Hallyday, Juliette Greco and Petula Clark, among
other singers, and also recorded many of his own
songs. According to his biographer, he 'acted out
the country's post-war vices: alcoholism, nicotine,
exhibitionism, incest, sex-mania and self-love'.*

1 *Je t'aime . . . moi non plus.*
'Je t'aime . . . moi non plus' (song with Jane
Birkin, 1969). The erotic duet by Gainsbourg
and Birkin was formally condemned by the Vatican and banned by many radio stations, even in
its instrumental version, though it still reached
no. 2 in the British charts in July 1969, and no. 1
on its reissue in October. The song was originally recorded in December 1967 by BRIGITTE
BARDOT, then romantically involved with
Gainsbourg, after she had asked him to write for
her 'the most beautiful love song that you could
imagine, dedicated to me'. However when the
press got wind of the recording with its moaning
and heavy breathing, she begged him to withdraw the record, which was consequently not
released until 1986 in aid of an animal charity.
Gainsbourg directed a film titled *Je t'aime . . .
moi non plus*, giving GÉRARD DEPARDIEU one
of his first film roles in 1976.

2 **Ugliness is superior to beauty, because ugliness lasts.**
Quoted in *GQ* January 2000. Gainsbourg himself was described as having 'the face of a
squashed frog', and refused to have mirrors in
his home.

Hugh Gaitskell (1906–63)
BRITISH POLITICIAN
*He became Labour leader in 1955, in which
capacity he opposed EDEN's Suez policy as well as
his own party's vote for unilateral disarmament
(1960). ROY JENKINS called him 'that very rare
phenomenon, a great politician who was also an
unusually agreeable man', but for TONY BENN he
was a 'divisive leader' with 'a real civil servant's
mind'. See also ANEURIN BEVAN 10.*

1 I have never had a great many baths and I
can assure those that have them as a habit
that it does not make a great difference to
their health if they have fewer. . . . As for
appearance, most of that is underneath
and nobody sees it.
Speech at Hastings, 1947, quoted in *The Fine Art
of Political Wit*, ch. 8 (1964) by Leon Harris. Gaitskell, who was then Minister for Fuel and Power,
was proposing an economy drive; his remark
elicited the rejoinder by WINSTON CHURCHILL
in the House of Commons: 'When Ministers
of the Crown speak like this . . . the Prime
Minister and his friends have no need to wonder
why they are getting increasingly into bad
odour.'

2 **There are some of us, Mr Chairman, who
will fight and fight and fight again to save
the Party we love.**
Speech at Labour Party Conference, Scarborough, 5 October 1961, publ. in *The Penguin
Book of Twentieth-Century Speeches* (ed. Brian
MacArthur, 1999). The plea referred to calls to
reject the Party's defence policy in favour of unilateral nuclear disarmament, which Gaitskell
believed would tear the Party asunder. The vote
resulted in a defeat of the official policy,
although this was overturned at the following
year's Conference.

3 **It does mean . . . the end of Britain as an
independent European state. . . . It means
the end of a thousand years of history. You
may say, 'Let it end', but, my goodness, it
is a decision that needs a little care and
thought.**
Speech at Labour Party Conference, Brighton,
3 October 1962, publ. ibid. Referring to Britain's
membership of the EEC. MACMILLAN's Conservative government had initiated negotiations
for joining the European Community, although
DE GAULLE's declared intention in 1963 to veto
any application by Britain made the issue a less
pressing concern.

J. K. Galbraith (b. 1908)
US ECONOMIST
*John Kenneth Galbraith. A Keynesian, he was
adviser to Presidents KENNEDY and JOHNSON.
His books had a popular appeal, particularly* The
Affluent Society *(1958) and* The Age of Uncer-
tainty *(1977).*

1 In the usual (though certainly not in
every) public decision on economic policy,
the choice is between courses that are
almost equally good or equally bad. It is
the narrowest decisions that are most
ardently debated. If the world is lucky
enough to enjoy peace, it may even one
day make the discovery, to the horror of
doctrinaire free-enterprisers and doctrinaire planners alike, that what is called
capitalism and what is called socialism are
both capable of working quite well.
'The American Economy: Its Substance and
Myth', first publ. in *Years of the Modern* (ed.
J. W. Chase, 1949), repr. in *The Galbraith Reader*
(1979)

2 **Wealth is not without its advantages and
the case to the contrary, although it has
often been made, has never proved widely
persuasive.**
The Affluent Society, ch. 1, sect. 1 (1958). Opening
words.

3 Consumer wants can have bizarre, frivolous, or even immoral origins, and an
admirable case can still be made for a
society that seeks to satisfy them. But the

case cannot stand if it is the process of satisfying wants that creates the wants.

Ibid., ch. 11, sect. 2

4 It is a far, far better thing to have a firm anchor in nonsense than to put out on the troubled seas of thought.

Ibid., ch. 11, sect. 4. Of the resistance of conventional wisdom to the 'economics of affluence'.

5 In a community where public services have failed to keep abreast of private consumption things are very different. Here, in an atmosphere of private opulence and public squalor, the private goods have full sway.

Ibid., ch. 18, sect. 2

6 Meetings are a great trap. Soon you find yourself trying to get agreement and then the people who disagree come to think they have a right to be persuaded. Thus they acquire power; thus meetings become a source of opposition and trouble. However, they are indispensable when you don't want to do anything.

Journal entry, 22 April 1961, in *Ambassador's Journal*, ch. 5 (1969). The journal was written while Galbraith was serving as US ambassador to India 1961–3.

7 Politics is not the art of the possible. It consists in choosing between the disastrous and the unpalatable.

Letter to President Kennedy, 2 March 1962, publ. ibid., ch. 15. Galbraith was referring to Bismarck's celebrated saying, *Die Politik ist die Lehre von Möglichen* ('Politics is the art of the possible').

8 By all but the pathologically romantic, it is now recognized that this is not the age of the small man.

The New Industrial State, ch. 3 (1967)

9 There are few ironclad rules of diplomacy but to one there is no exception. When an official reports that talks were useful, it can safely be concluded that nothing was accomplished.

'The American Ambassador', publ. in *Foreign Service Journal* June 1969

10 All successful revolutions are the kicking in of a rotten door. The violence of revolutions is the violence of men who charge into a vacuum.

The Age of Uncertainty, ch. 3 (1977)

11 All of the great leaders have had one characteristic in common: it was the willingness to confront unequivocally the major anxiety of their people in their time. This, and not much else, is the essence of leadership.

Ibid., ch. 12

12 In any great organization it is far, far safer to be wrong with the majority than to be right alone.

Guardian 28 July 1989

13 There's a certain part of the contented majority who love anybody who is worth a billion dollars.

Guardian 23 May 1992. Referring to millionaire presidential candidate H. ROSS PEROT.

14 The Third Way is a purely political concept. The increase in numbers and power of the middle-income groups means that governments choose to meet their needs first. The Third Way is a justification of that necessity.

Interview with ROY HATTERSLEY in the *Guardian* 17 October 1998

Noel Gallagher (b. 1967)

BRITISH ROCK MUSICIAN

He is lead singer and main songwriter of Oasis, whose 'mad for it' image has attracted much press attention. Hit albums by Oasis include Definitely Maybe *(1994) and* (What's the Story) Morning Glory? *(1995).*

1 What people have got to understand is that we are lads. We have burgled houses and nicked car stereos, and we like girls and we swear and we go to the football and take the piss.

Interview in *Melody Maker* 30 March 1996. The confession prompted an investigation by Greater Manchester police, and a defence by the mother of Noel and Liam Gallagher: 'As far as I know they were never involved in any crime. They were just normal boys. . . . Really, they are very thoughtful and kind and all they think about are their family and friends.'

2 Drugs is like getting up and having a cup of tea in the morning.

Radio interview 28 January 1997, quoted in the *Daily Telegraph* 31 January 1997

3 I would hope we mean more to people than putting money in a church basket and saying ten Hail Marys on a Sunday. Has God played Knebworth recently?

Interview in the *New Musical Express* 12 July 1997

4 We were supposed to be the ones who turned up at the awards ceremony poking fun at the Establishment and getting pissed and getting on everyone's nerves. As it panned out we became the Establishment, and I didn't particularly like that.

Interview in *GQ* February 2000

Paul Gallico (1897–1976)

US NOVELIST

Of his forty-odd books, best known is The Snow Goose *(1941), set in the Lincolnshire Fens. The*

Poseidon Adventure (1969) was made into one of the first big-budget disaster movies (1972).

1 No one can be as calculatedly rude as the British, which amazes Americans, who do not understand studied insult and can only offer abuse as a substitute.

The New York Times 14 January 1962. Gallico lived in England from 1936.

2 If there is any larceny in a man, golf will bring it out.

The New York Times 6 March 1977

José Antonio Viera Gallo (b. 1943)

CHILEAN POLITICIAN
He served as Under-Secretary of Justice (1970–72) in the government of SALVADOR ALLENDE.

1 Socialism can only arrive by bicycle.

Quoted in Energy and Equity, Foreword (1974) by Ivan Illich

Indira Gandhi (1917–84)

INDIAN POLITICIAN
Daughter of JAWAHARLAL NEHRU, she was leader of the Congress Party (1966–77) and Prime Minister (1966–77, 1980–4). She was assassinated by members of her Sikh bodyguard. 'My father was a statesman, I'm a political woman,' she is quoted as saying. 'My father was a saint. I'm not.'

1 I myself, in my heart, say that people should have all the children they want. But it's a mistaken idea, like many of our ideas that go back thousands of years, and it must be rooted out. . . . But how can you change . . . an age-old habit? The only way is to plan births by one means or another. And the sterilization of men is one method of birth control. The surest, most radical method.

Interview in February 1972, publ. in Interview with History, ch. 7 (1976) by ORIANA FALLACI

2 There exists no politician in India daring enough to attempt to explain to the masses that cows can be eaten.

Quoted by ORIANA FALLACI in 'Indira's Coup', publ. in the New York Review of Books 18 September 1975

3 Even if I died in the service of the nation, I would be proud of it. Every drop of my blood . . . will contribute to the growth of this nation and make it strong and dynamic.

Speech in Delhi, 30 October 1984. Said on the eve of her assassination.

Mahatma Gandhi (1869–1948)

INDIAN POLITICAL AND SPIRITUAL LEADER
Mohandas Karamchand Gandhi, called Mahatma ('Great Soul'). As the driving force behind India's struggle for independence, he advocated non-violent civil disobedience, fasts and passive resistance, for which he came to be regarded popularly as a saint. He was assassinated by a Hindu fanatic. According to EINSTEIN, 'In our time of utter moral decadence he was the only statesman to stand for a higher human relationship in the political sphere.' See also JAWAHARLAL NEHRU 3.

1 I claim that in losing the spinning wheel we lost our left lung. We are, therefore, suffering from galloping consumption. The restoration of the wheel arrests the progress of the fell disease.

Young India 13 October 1921

2 A policy is a temporary creed liable to be changed, but while it holds good it has got to be pursued with apostolic zeal.

Letter to the General Secretary of the Congress Party, India, 8 March 1922, publ. in Gandhi's Letters on Indian Affairs, 'To Co-workers' (1923)

3 Non-violence is the first article of my faith. It is the last article of my faith.

Speech in defence trial, Ahmedabad, 18 March 1922, publ. in Young India 23 March 1922, repr. in The Penguin Book of Twentieth-Century Speeches (ed. Brian MacArthur, 1999). Gandhi was charged with sedition for three articles published in his newspaper Young India. Pleading guilty and demanding of the judge 'the highest penalty that can be inflicted upon me for what in law is a deliberate crime and what appears to me to be the highest duty of a citizen', he was sentenced to six years' imprisonment, but released after two years on grounds of ill health.

4 I have nothing new to teach the world. Truth and Non-violence are as old as the hills. All I have done is to try experiments in both on as vast a scale as I could.

Harijan 28 March 1936

5 An unjust law is itself a species of violence. Arrest for its breach is more so.

Non-Violence in Peace and War, vol. 2, ch. 150 (1949)

6 Reporter: 'Mr Gandhi, what do you think of Western civilization?'
Gandhi: 'I think it would be a very good idea.'

Attributed. There is no evidence of any such exchange having taken place, although E.F. SCHUMACHER in Good Work, ch. 2, 1979) mentions seeing a film of Gandhi disembarking at Southampton, England, in 1930, in which Gandhi is asked his opinion on modern civilization, and gives the answer as above

Greta Garbo (1905–90)

SWEDISH-BORN US SCREEN ACTRESS
Originally Greta Lovisa Gustafsson. 'The only one who has ever been really mysterious', according to Joan Crawford, she possessed a compelling screen presence both in silent films and the talkies. She

was acclaimed for her starring roles in Mata Hari *(1931)*, Anna Karenina *(1935) and* Camille *(1937), but retired in 1941. Her famous reclusiveness enhanced her image as 'the Swedish Sphinx'. See* KENNETH TYNAN 1.

1 I want to be alone.

Grusinskaya (Greta Garbo), in *Grand Hotel* (film, 1932, screenplay by William A. Drake based on *Menschen im Hotel*, the German play and novel by Vicki Baum, directed by Edmund Goulding). The phrase was associated with Garbo although she claims never to have said it word for word: 'I only said I want to be *left* alone.' However the screenplay shows that she spoke the words three times to the Baron (John Barrymore), and she expressed the same sentiment in the film, *The Single Standard* (1929): 'I am walking alone because I want to be alone.'

2 Tomorrow I got to work with a lot of people who are dead. It's so sad. I'm an onlooker. I've passed being active in life. It's not a question of time and age – but it's just what you are yourself. One doesn't do the things one doesn't want to do.

Remark, February 1932, quoted in *Self-Portrait with Friends: The Selected Diaries of Cecil Beaton*, ch. 4 (ed. Richard Buckle, 1979)

3 What a waste of the best years of my life – always alone – it was so stupid not being able to partake more. Now I'm just a gipsy, living a life apart, but I know my ways and I must not see people.

Remark, 4 March 1948, ibid., ch. 16

Jerry Garcia *(1942–95)*

US ROCK MUSICIAN

Jerome John Garcia. He was a founder member of the Grateful Dead (1966), whose albums include Workingman's Dead *(1970)*, Europe 72 *(1972) and* Built to Last *(1989). Nicknamed Captain Trips, he had increasing drug and alcohol problems, culminating in a fatal overdose.*

1 Nobody stopped thinking about those psychedelic experiences. Once you've been to some of those places, you think, 'How can I get back there again but make it a little easier on myself?'

Interview in *Rolling Stone* 30 November 1989

2 What we do is as American as lynch mobs. America has always been a complex place.

Ibid. Speaking of the Grateful Dead.

3 We're like bad architecture or an old whore. If you stick around long enough, eventually you get respectable.

Quoted in *Captain Trips*, ch. 9 (1994) by Sandy Troy. Speaking of the Grateful Dead. The expression was not new: in the film *Chinatown* (1974, screenplay by Robert Towne), Noah Cross (played by John Huston) declares, 'Politicians, ugly buildings and whores all get respectable if they last long enough.'

Federico García Lorca *(1898–1936)*

SPANISH POET AND PLAYWRIGHT

He drew on the folk and flamenco traditions of Andalusia in his poems such as Gypsy Ballads *(1928) and his trilogy of plays,* Blood Wedding *(1933)*, Yerma *(1934) and* The House of Bernarda Alba *(1936). He was assassinated by Nationalist partisans during the Spanish Civil War.*

1 *Green oh how I love you green.*
Green wind. Green boughs.

'Sleepwalking Ballad', publ. in *Gypsy Ballads* (written 1924–7, publ. 1928, transl. 1995). Opening lines.

2 *They ride the roads*
with souls of patent leather.
Hunched and nocturnal,
they command, where they appear,
the silence of dark rubber
and fears of fine sand.

'Ballad of the Spanish Civil Guard', publ. ibid.

3 *To see you naked is to recall the earth.*

'Qasida of the Recumbent Woman', publ. in *The Divan of the Tamarit* (written 1931–4, publ. 1940, transl. 1990)

4 The two elements the traveller first captures in the big city are extrahuman architecture and furious rhythm. Geometry and anguish.

'A Poet in New York', lecture in Madrid, March 1932, publ. in *Poet in New York* (1940, transl. 1988). 'At first glance, the rhythm may be confused with gaiety,' Lorca continued, 'but when you look more closely at the mechanism of social life and the painful slavery of both men and machines, you see that it is nothing but a kind of typical, empty anguish that makes even crime and gangs forgivable means of escape.'

5 The only things that the United States has given to the world are skyscrapers, jazz, and cocktails. That is all. And in Cuba, in *our* America, they make much better cocktails.

Interview, 1933, publ. in *Obras Completas*, vol. 3 (1986)

6 I'm hurt, hurt and humiliated beyond endurance, seeing the wheat ripening, the fountains never ceasing to give water, the sheep bearing hundreds of lambs, the she-dogs, until it seems the whole country rises to show me its tender sleeping young while I feel two hammer-blows here instead of the mouth of my child.

Yerma, in *Yerma*, act 2, sc. 2 (1934)

7 *At five in the afternoon.*
It was exactly five in the afternoon.
A boy brought the white sheet
at five in the afternoon.

'The Goring and the Death', publ. in *Lament for Ignacio Sánchez Mejías* (1935, transl. 1995). The poem describes the death of a bullfighter.

Gabriel García Márquez (b. 1928)
COLOMBIAN AUTHOR

His most famous novel, One Hundred Years of Solitude *(1967), was one of the earliest works to be labelled 'magic realist'. Later books include* Love in the Time of Cholera *(1985) and* Strange Pilgrims *(1992).*

1 They felt that they had been the victims of some new and showy gypsy business and they decided not to return to the movies, considering that they already had too many troubles of their own to weep over the acted-out misfortunes of imaginary beings.

 One Hundred Years of Solitude (1967). Referring to the people of Macondo, who have learned from the mayor's proclamation that the movies are not real and that 'the cinema was a machine of illusion and did not merit the emotional outbursts of the audience'.

2 The only difference today between Liberals and Conservatives is that the Liberals go to mass at five o'clock and the Conservatives at eight.

 Colonel Aureliano Buendía, ibid.

3 The world must be all fucked up when men travel first class and literature goes as freight.

 The Catalan bookstore owner in Macondo, ibid.

4 Necessity has the face of a dog.

 Mina, in *In Evil Hour* (1968)

5 No, not rich. I am a poor man with money, which is not the same thing.

 Uncle Leo XII, in *Love in the Time of Cholera* (1985)

6 The problem with marriage is that it ends every night after making love, and it must be rebuilt every morning before breakfast.

 Dr Urbino, ibid.

John Garfield (1913–52)
US ACTOR

Originally Julius Garfinkle. His film roles often reflected his own experiences on the wrong side of the tracks. He formed his own production company in the late 1940s but was blacklisted shortly after for failing to name friends as Communists.

1 With my brains and your looks, we could go places.

 Frank Chambers (John Garfield), in *The Postman Always Rings Twice* (film, 1946, screenplay by Harry Ruskin and Niven Busch adapted from James M. Cain's novel, directed by Tay Garnett)

2 I wasn't strong enough to resist corruption, but I was strong enough to fight for a piece of it.

 Joe Morse (John Garfield), in *Force of Evil* (film, 1948, screenplay by Abraham Polonsky and Ira Wolfert adapted from Ira Wolfert's novel, directed by Abraham Polonsky)

Alex Garland (b. 1970)
BRITISH NOVELIST

His first book, The Beach *(1996, filmed 2000), became a backpacker's rites-of-passage tale, quickly became a cult bestseller and was followed by* The Tesseract *(1998). 'Everything I know about writing, I learned through drawing comic strips,' he stated.*

1 I had ambiguous feelings about the differences between tourists and travellers – the problem being that the more I travelled, the smaller the differences became. But the one difference I could still latch on to was that tourists went on holidays while travellers did something else. They *travelled.*

 Richard, in *The Beach*, 'Getting There: Talk' (1996)

Judy Garland (1922–69)
US SCREEN ACTRESS AND SINGER

Originally Frances Gumm. She was the child star of The Wizard of Oz *(1939), and, under the direction of her husband Vincente Minnelli, the lead in* Meet Me in St Louis *(1944). She was later caught in a spiral of depression and drugs but returned to the screen with* A Star Is Born *(1954).*

1 *Somewhere over the rainbow*
 Way up high,
 There's a land that I heard of
 Once in a lullaby.

 'Over the Rainbow' (song, written by YIP HARBURG with music by Harold Arlen), sung as Dorothy in *The Wizard of Oz* (film, 1939). The song was re-recorded by Garland on the album *The London Sessions* (1960), by which time, according to her biographer, 'the song no longer belonged to Dorothy; it belonged, forever, to Judy Garland'. Other artists to have recorded it include FRANK SINATRA, Ella Fitzgerald, WILLIE NELSON and ARETHA FRANKLIN.

2 Toto, I've a feeling we're not in Kansas anymore. . . . Now I know we're not in Kansas.

 Dorothy, in *The Wizard of Oz* (film, 1939, screenplay by Noel Langley, Florence Ryerson and Edgar Allan Wolfe from book by L. Frank Baum, directed by Victor Fleming. The words, uttered on arriving in the Land of Oz and addressed to Dorothy's dog, do not appear in L. Frank Baum's original book, *The Wonderful Wizard of Oz* (1900).

3 I was born at the age of twelve on a Metro-Goldwyn-Mayer lot.

 Quoted in the *Observer* 18 February 1951

John Garner (1868–1967)
US POLITICIAN

A Democratic leader in the House of Representatives, he was chosen as Speaker in 1931 and served as Vice-President (1933–41) under FRANKLIN D. ROOSEVELT.

1 The vice-presidency isn't worth a pitcher

of warm piss. It doesn't amount to a hill of beans.

Quoted in *Cactus Jack*, ch. 11 (1978) by O. C. Fisher. The words are commonly misquoted '. . . pitcher of warm spit'. In 1963 Garner declared, 'Worst damnfool mistake I ever made was letting myself be elected Vice President of the United States. Should have stuck . . . as Speaker of the House. . . . Gave up the second most important job in Government for eight long years as Roosevelt's spare tire.'

Marcus Garvey (1887–1940)

JAMAICAN CIVIL RIGHTS CAMPAIGNER

Calling himself a 'black Napoleon', he founded the Universal Negro Improvement Association in 1914, and from New York led the first American black nationalist movement, which rejected integration and favoured resettlement in Liberia.

1 Look for me in the whirlwind or the storm, look for me all around you, for, with God's grace, I shall come and bring with me countless millions of Black slaves who have died in America and the West Indies and the millions in Africa to aid you in the fight for Liberty, Freedom and Life.

'First Message to the Negroes of the World from Atlanta Prison' 10 February 1925, publ. in *The Philosophy and Opinions of Marcus Garvey*, vol. 2 (ed. Amy Jacques Garvey, 1923, rev. 1986)

2 No race has the last word on culture and on civilization. You do not know what the black man is capable of; you do not know what he is thinking and therefore you do not know what the oppressed and suppressed Negro, by virtue of his condition and circumstance, may give to the world as a surprise.

Speech at Royal Albert Hall, London, 6 June 1928, publ. in *Marcus Garvey and the Vision of Africa*, pt 5 (ed. John Henrik Clarke, 1974)

3 Day by day we hear the cry of AFRICA FOR THE AFRICANS. This cry has become a positive, determined one. It is a cry that is raised simultaneously the world over because of the universal oppression that affects the Negro.

Quoted in *The Philosophy and Opinions of Marcus Garvey*, vol. 1, ch. 1 (ed. Amy Jacques Garvey, 1923, rev. 1986)

Bill Gates (b. 1955)

US SOFTWARE ENGINEER AND ENTREPRENEUR

One of the world's richest men, he is Chairman and Chief Software Architect of the Microsoft Corporation which he co-founded in 1975.

1 One thing is clear: We don't have the option of turning away from the future.

No one gets to vote on whether technology is going to change our lives.

The Road Ahead, ch. 1 (1995, rev. 1996)

2 Success is a lousy teacher. It seduces smart people into thinking they can't lose.

Ibid., ch. 3

3 People often overestimate what will happen in the next two years and underestimate what will happen in ten.

Ibid., 'Afterword'

Noel Gay (1898–1954)

BRITISH COMPOSER

Pseudonym of Richard Moxon Armitage. A classically trained musical prodigy, he was responsible for the stage musical Me and My Girl *(1937), the longest running show of the 1930s, and novelty songs such as 'Run Rabbit Run' (1939). See also* GEORGE FORMBY 3.

1 *The sun has got its hat on*
Hip hip hip hooray
The sun has got its hat on
And it's coming out to play.

'The Sun Has Got Its Hat On' (song, 1932, with lyrics by Ralph Butler). The song was sung by Jack Hulbert in 1932, and was a hit for Jonathan King in 1971.

2 *Any time you're Lambeth way,*
Any evening any day,
You'll find us all
Doin' the Lambeth walk.

'The Lambeth Walk' (song, with lyrics by Arthur Rose, music by Noel Gay and Douglas Furber) in *Me and My Girl* (stage musical, 1937). Sung on stage by Lupino Lane as Bill Snibson, the song was popularized by Russ Morgan and his Orchestra. Lane also starred in the 1939 film version of the show, titled *The Lambeth Walk*.

3 *Run, rabbit, run, rabbit, run, run, run.*
Run, rabbit, run, rabbit, run, run, run.
Bang, bang, bang, bang, goes the farmer's gun,
Run, rabbit, run, rabbit, run, run, run.

'Run Rabbit Run!' (song, with lyrics by Ralph Butler) in *The Little Dog Laughed* (musical show, 1939). The song was performed by BUD FLANAGAN, who starred alongside the Crazy Gang and the Hoffman Sisters. The song and show were a smash hit during the 'phoney war' (1939–40).

Gloria Gaynor (b. 1949)

US SOUL SINGER

With her powerful voice backed by disco rhythms, the 'Queen of Soul' had hits during the 1970s but lost favour with the advent of electronic dance music.

1 *I never can say goodbye.*

'Never Can Say Goodbye' (song, written by Clifton Davis) on the album *Never Can Say Goodbye* (1974). The song had been a hit for Isaac Hayes and the Jackson Five, both in 1971. It reached no. 1 for Gaynor, helping to ignite the disco boom.

2 *As long as I know how to love, I know I'll stay alive,*
I've got all my life to live, I've got so much love to give,
I will survive! I will survive!

'I Will Survive' (song, written by Dino Fekaris and Freddie Perren) on the album *Love Tracks* (1979). The top-selling disco hit became an enduring feminist and gay anthem and is said to be the most requested karaoke song.

Carlo Gébler (b. 1954)
IRISH AUTHOR
The son of writers EDNA O'BRIEN *and Ernest Gébler, he explores family issues in his novels, as in his first,* The Eleventh Summer *(1985), and in the memoir* Father and I *(2001). He has also written screenplays.*

1 Life's a series of blows. What is born a drum is beaten till death.
Narrator (Katherine Baring), in *Life of a Drum,* Prologue (1991)

(Sir) Eric Geddes (1875–1937)
BRITISH POLITICIAN
He was elected Conservative MP for Cambridge in 1917, and while Minister of Transport (1919–21) oversaw the amalgamation of the railways. As chairman of the 'Geddes Axe' committee, he was responsible for drastic cuts in the economy and for devising ways of increasing revenue.

1 The Germans, if this Government is returned, are going to pay every penny; they are going to be squeezed as a lemon is squeezed – until the pips squeak. My only doubt is not whether we can squeeze hard enough, but whether there is enough juice.
Speech at Cambridge, 10 December 1918, quoted in the *Cambridge Daily News* 11 December 1918
On German war reparations following the First World War.

(Sir) Bob Geldof (b. 1954)
IRISH ROCK SINGER
Lead singer of the Boomtown Rats (1975–86), he raised £8 million for African famine relief through the Band Aid record 'Do They Know It's Christmas?' in 1984, and a year later a further £48 million through Live Aid charity concerts. He has also campaigned to cancel Third World debt.

1 Most people get into bands for three very simple rock and roll reasons: to get laid, to get fame, and to get rich.
Melody Maker 27 August 1977

2 I don't like Mondays.
'I Don't Like Mondays' (song) on the album *The Fine Art of Surfacing* (1979) by the Boomtown Rats. The lyrics were inspired by the story of schoolgirl Brenda Spencer who went on a shoot-

ing spree in San Diego, California, in January 1979, giving these words as the reason. Spencer's parents attempted to have the record banned and many US radio stations refused to play it.

3 Feed the world
Let them know it's Christmas time again.
'Do They Know it's Christmas?' (song, 1984, co-written with Midge Ure). The record became the biggest-selling British single of all time.

4 Irish Americans are about as Irish as black Americans are African.
Quoted in the *Observer* 22 June 1986

Henry Geldzahler (b. 1935)
BELGIAN-BORN US CURATOR AND ART CRITIC
He has written extensively on contemporary art and was the first curator of the department of twentieth-century art at the Metropolitan Museum of Art, New York (1967–78).

1 The history of modern art is also the history of the progressive loss of art's audience. Art has increasingly become the concern of the artist and the bafflement of the public.
'The Art Audience and the Critic', first publ. in the *Hudson Review* spring 1965, repr. in *The New Art: A Critical Anthology* (ed. Gregory Battcock, 1966, rev. 1973)

2 The thing that's extraordinary is that no art remains shocking for more than ten or twelve years. There is no shocking art that doesn't reduce itself to triviality or beauty.
Looking at Pictures (1990)

Martha Gellhorn (1908–98)
US JOURNALIST AND AUTHOR
Her reportage from the Spanish Civil War, the Second World War, Vietnam and Central America is collected in The Face of War *(1959, rev. 1967, 1986 and 1993), and she also wrote fiction. She was married to* ERNEST HEMINGWAY *1940–45.*

1 Serious, careful, honest journalism is essential, not because it is a guiding light but because it is a form of honorable behavior, involving the reporter and the reader.
The Face of War, Introduction (1959)

2 It is in our ancient tradition to murder each other; but only we, in the present, should pay the price of our abominable stupidity. Nothing that concerns us, in our brief moment of history, gives us the right to stop time, to blot out the future, to end the continuing miracles and glories and tragedies and wretchedness of the human race.
Ibid.

3 The vital interests of the state, which are always about power, have nothing to do with the vital interests of the citizens,

which are private and simple and are always about a better life for themselves and their children. You do not kill for such interests, you work for them.

Ibid., Introduction (1959, rev. 1967)

4 After a lifetime of war-watching, I see war as an endemic human disease, and governments are the carriers.

The Face of War, Introduction (1959, rev. 1986)

Jean Genet (1910–86)

FRENCH PLAYWRIGHT AND NOVELIST

Dealing chiefly with the alienated and marginalized underworld of Paris, his novels, beginning with Our Lady of the Flowers *(1943), and plays, such as* The Maids *(1947), explore the nature of good and evil. His reputation was enhanced by the book* Saint Genet *(1952) by* JEAN-PAUL SARTRE.

1 To achieve harmony in bad taste is the height of elegance.

The Thief's Journal (1949, transl. 1965)

2 Excluded by my birth and tastes from the social order, I was not aware of its diversity. . . . Nothing in the world was irrelevant: the stars on a general's sleeve, the stock-market quotations, the olive harvest, the style of the judiciary, the wheat exchange, flower-beds. . . . Nothing. This order, fearful and feared, whose details were all inter-related, had a meaning: my exile.

Ibid.

3 What we need is hatred. From it our ideas are born.

Bobo, in *The Blacks* (1958)

4 Are you there, Africa with the bulging chest and oblong thigh? Sulking Africa, wrought of iron, in the fire, Africa of the millions of royal slaves, deported Africa, drifting continent, are you there? Slowly you vanish, you withdraw into the past, into the tales of castaways, colonial museums, the works of scholars.

Felicity, ibid.

5 Crimes of which a people is ashamed constitute its real history. The same is true of man.

Notes for *The Screens* (1961, transl. 1973)

6 Anyone who hasn't experienced the ecstasy of betrayal knows nothing about ecstasy at all.

Prisoner of Love, pt 1 (1986)

George V (1865–1936)

KING OF GREAT BRITAIN AND IRELAND

Prior to succeeding to the throne in 1910 'he did nothing at all but kill animals and stick in stamps', according to his biographer HAROLD NICOLSON.

As king, he was instrumental in the formation of the national government of 1931, and instigated the tradition of the Christmas Day broadcasts in 1932. 'I march with the times' was his watchword.

1 How is the Empire?

Attributed last words, as reported to the nation 21 January 1936 – the day after the king's death – in a broadcast tribute by prime minister STANLEY BALDWIN. Other accounts deny this was the king's last utterance, although a memorandum of Lord Wigram, the king's private secretary, was made at 11 am, 20 January: 'He murmured something about the Empire, and I replied that "All is well, Sir, with the Empire" ' (quoted in *Dawson of Penn*, 1950, by Francis Watson). The time of his death was given as 11.55 pm.

2 Bugger Bognor.

Attributed deathbed remark, in *King George V*, ch. 9 (1983) by Kenneth Rose. The king apparently spoke the words on being assured by a courtier that he would soon be in Bognor. However, according to the king's librarian, Owen Morshead, the exclamation was made much earlier, in 1929, in response to a suggestion that the town should be named Bognor Regis in commemoration of George V's convalescence there following a serious illness.

3 My father was frightened of his mother, I was frightened by my father, and I'm damned well going to see to it that my children are frightened of me.

Remark to a friend, quoted in *Charles and Diana*, ch. 2 (1985) by Ralph G. Martin

George VI (1895–1952)

KING OF GREAT BRITAIN AND NORTHERN IRELAND

He succeeded to the throne following the abdication of his brother EDWARD VIII *in 1936. His many wartime broadcasts and his insistence on remaining in London during the Blitz won him popular support.*

1 It is not the walls that make the city, but the people who live within them. The walls of London may be battered, but the spirit of the Londoner stands resolute and undismayed.

Radio broadcast to the Empire, 23 September 1940, during the German bomber offensive

2 Abroad is bloody.

Attributed, in *A Certain World*, 'Royalty' (1970) by W. H. AUDEN. See also NANCY MITFORD 1.

Gladys George (c. 1898–1954)

US ACTRESS

Having starred in vaudeville and on Broadway, she enjoyed success in Hollywood in the films The Roaring Twenties *(1939) and* The Maltese Falcon *(1941).*

1 He used to be a big shot.

Panama Smith (Gladys George), in *The Roaring Twenties* (film, 1939, screenplay by Jerry Wald,

Richard Macaulay and Robert Rossen based on a story by MARK HELLINGER, directed by Raoul Walsh). These last words of the movie refer to the character played by JAMES CAGNEY, who has been fatally wounded.

Ira Gershwin (1896–1983)
US LYRICIST
Originally Israel Gershvin. The elder brother of George Gershwin, he wrote the sophisticated lyrics to most of his brother's songs in more than twenty successful Broadway musicals. After George's death in 1937, he worked with Jerome Kern, Kurt Weill and Harold Arlen.

1 *I got rhythm,*
  I got music,
  I got my man
  Who could ask for anything more?
  'I Got Rhythm' (song, with music by George Gershwin) in *Girl Crazy* (stage musical 1930, film 1932 and 1943). Originally sung by Ethel Merman, the number was performed in the 1943 film version by JUDY GARLAND, and by Gene Kelly in the movie *An American in Paris* (1951).

2 *Summertime and the living is easy,*
  Fish are jumping, and the cotton is high.
  'Summertime' (song, co-written with Du Bose Heyward with music by George Gershwin) in *Porgy and Bess* (stage musical 1935, film 1959). The lyrics from this opener for *Porgy and Bess*, like those of other songs in the show, were based on an original poem in the novel *Porgy* (1926) by Du Bose Heyward. It was a hit for BILLIE HOLIDAY in 1936.

3 *It ain't necessarily so,*
  The things that you're liable
  To read in the Bible,
  It ain't necessarily so.
  'It Ain't Necessarily So', ibid. The song was recorded by BING CROSBY in 1938, among others, and sung by SAMMY DAVIS JR in the film adaptation.

4 *A foggy day in London Town*
  Had me low and had me down.
  I viewed the morning with alarm,
  The British Museum had lost its charm.
  'A Foggy Day' (song, with music by George Gershwin) in *A Damsel in Distress* (film, 1937). The number is performed in the film by Fred Astaire.

5 *Holding hands at midnight*
  'Neath a starry sky,
  Nice work if you can get it,
  And you can get it if you try.
  'Nice Work if You Can Get It', ibid.

6 *You like potato and I like po-tah-to,*
  You like tomato and I like to-mah-to;
  Potato, po-tah-to, tomato, to-mah-to –
  Let's call the whole thing off!
  'Let's Call the Whole Thing Off' (song, with music by George Gershwin) in *Shall We Dance*

(film, 1937). Sung by Fred Astaire and Ginger Rogers.

J. Paul Getty (1892–1976)
US OIL MILLIONAIRE AND ART COLLECTOR
The oil business made him one of the world's richest men, with a personal wealth estimated at over $1 billion in 1968. He exhibited items from his extensive art collection in the museum founded by and named after him in California (1953).

1 If you can actually count your money, then you are not really a rich man.
  Quoted in the *Observer* 3 November 1957

Stella Gibbons (1902–89)
BRITISH AUTHOR
She worked for much of her life as a journalist and wrote numerous novels and short stories, but is best known for her parody on rural life, Cold Comfort Farm *(1933).*

1 Something nasty in the woodshed.
  Cold Comfort Farm, ch. 8 and *passim* (1932). This recurring motif of some unspecific secret and shameful act witnessed in the past was used in the novel as an ironic symbol of corrupting knowledge.

Kahlil Gibran (1883–1931)
SYRIAN-BORN US POET AND NOVELIST
His writings both in Arabic and English combine romanticism with mysticism, influenced by the Bible, Sufism and William Blake. His most enduring work, The Prophet *(1923), has sold more than 20 million copies.*

1 *Love gives naught but itself and takes*
  naught but from itself.
  Love possesses not nor would it be possessed;
  For love is sufficient unto love.
  The Prophet, 'On Love' (1923)

2 *You may give them your love but not your thoughts,*
  For they have their own thoughts.
  You may house their bodies but not their souls,
  For their souls dwell in the house of tomorrow, which you cannot visit, not even in your dreams.
  Ibid., 'On Children'

3 *Life is indeed darkness save when there is urge,*
  And all urge is blind save when there is knowledge,
  And all knowledge is vain save when there is work,
  And all work is empty save when there is love.
  Ibid., 'On Work'

4 The lust for comfort, that stealthy thing

208 Gibson

that enters the house a guest, and then becomes a host, and then a master.
Ibid., 'On Houses'

5 Beauty is eternity gazing at itself in a mirror.
Ibid., 'On Beauty'

6 *Verily the kindness that gazes upon itself in a mirror turns to stone,*
And a good deed that calls itself by tender names becomes the parent to a curse.
Ibid., 'The Farewell'

7 A little knowledge that *acts* is worth infinitely more than much knowledge that is idle.
The Voice of the Master, pt 2, ch. 8 (1960)

8 When we turn to one another for counsel we reduce the number of our enemies.
Ibid., pt 2, ch. 10

William Gibson (b. 1948)
US SCIENCE FICTION AUTHOR
His acclaimed first novel Neuromancer *(1984) helped to establish the genre of 'cyberpunk' and popularized the notion of computer cyberspace. The 'high-tech lowlifes' of this and other novels also feature in his short stories collected in* Burning Chrome *(1986).*

1 I think that the computer as some sort of discrete object that one owns and is very, very aware of . . . will become a very quaint and antique concept.
Interview in *Rapid Eye 3* (ed. Simon Dwyer, 1995). Gibson predicted computers becoming 'small and transparent and finally invisible'.

2 The old futures have a way of hanging around. . . . I think now that everyone sort of knows that the real future is going to be cluttered with all the same junk we have today, except it will be old and beat up and there will be more of it.
Interview in *Sight and Sound* July 1995

André Gide (1869–1951)
FRENCH AUTHOR
With the declared intention of 'disturbing' his readers, he founded his reputation on his novels such as The Immoralist *(1902) and* Strait is the Gate *(1909). He also published literary and social criticism and helped found the* Nouvelle revue française *(1908). The author Peter Quennell once called him 'an elderly fallen angel travelling incognito'.*

1 The most decisive actions of our life – I mean those that are most likely to decide the whole course of our future – are, more often than not, unconsidered.
Hildebrant, in *The Counterfeiters*, pt 3, ch. 16 (1925)

2 Old hands soil, it seems, whatever they caress, but they too have their beauty when

they are joined in prayer. Young hands were made for caresses and the sheathing of love. It is a pity to make them join too soon.
Journal entry, 21 January 1929, publ. in *Journals 1889–1949* (ed. Justin O'Brien, 1951)

3 The sole art that suits me is that which, rising from unrest, tends toward serenity.
Ibid., 23 November 1940

Gilbert
(of Gilbert and George) See GILBERT PROESCH.

George Gilder (b. 1939)
US EDITOR, SPEECHWRITER AND AUTHOR
Conservative in outlook, he was speechwriter for Rockefeller (1964), NIXON *(1968) and Dole (1976), and labelled 'the nation's leading male chauvinist-pig author' by* Time *magazine in 1974.*

1 Sexuality, family unity, kinship, masculine solidarity, maternity, motivation, nurturing, all the rituals of personal identity and development, all the bonds of community, seem 'sexist', 'superstitious', 'mystical', 'inefficient', 'discriminatory'. And, of course, they are – and they are also indispensable to a civilized society.
Sexual Suicide, Introduction (1973)

2 Unlike femininity, relaxed masculinity is at bottom empty, a limp nullity. While the female body is full of internal potentiality, the male is internally barren. . . . Manhood at the most basic level can be validated and expressed only in action.
Ibid., pt 1, ch. 1

Terry Gilkyson (1916–99)
US SONGWRITER AND ACTOR
Hamilton H. Gilkyson III. Although he acted in several films in the 1950s, he became better known as songwriter for such films as Swiss Family Robinson *(1960) and* The Jungle Book *(1967).*

1 *The bare necessities, the simple bare necessities*
Forget about your worries and your strife.
'Bare Necessities' (song) in *The Jungle Book* (film, 1967). Sung by Phil Harris as Baloo and Bruce Reitherman as Mowgli.

Eric Gill (1882–1940)
BRITISH SCULPTOR, ENGRAVER, WRITER AND TYPOGRAPHER
A Catholic whose private life provoked calls for his work to be withdrawn, he carved the sculptures Stations of the Cross *in Westminster Cathedral (1914–18) and* Prospero and Ariel *(1930) at the BBC's Broadcasting House. He illustrated for the Golden Cockerell Press, and devised typefaces, including the first sanserif type, Gill Sans.*

1 That state is a state of Slavery in which a

man does what he likes to do in his spare time and in his working time that which is required of him. This state can only exist when what a man likes to do is to please himself.

'Slavery and Freedom', first publ. 1918, repr. in *Art-Nonsense and Other Essays* (1929). Opening paragraph.

2 Art is skill, that is the first meaning of the word.

Art, ch. 1 (1934). Yet in his essay, 'Art and Love' (1927), Gill pointed out, 'As no one would think it an adequate definition of Man to say that he is a two-legged mammal, so no one should be satisfied with the definition of Art that it is simply skill, or that it is skill in the imitation of nature.'

3 Man cannot live on the human plane, he must be either above or below it.

Autobiography, 'Conclusion' (1940)

4 Culture is a sham if it is only a sort of Gothic front put on an iron building – like Tower Bridge – or a classical front put on a steel frame – like the *Daily Telegraph* building in Fleet Street. Culture, if it is to be a real thing and a holy thing, must be the product of what we actually do for a living – not something added, like sugar on a pill.

Essays, 'Education for What?' (1948)

5 Catholics are necessarily at war with this age. That we are not more conscious of the fact, that we so often endeavour to make an impossible peace with it – that is the tragedy. You cannot serve God and Mammon.

Ibid., 'Idiocy or Ill-Will'

6 Man does not live by bread alone, but by science he attempts to do so. Hence the deadliness of all that is purely scientific.

Ibid., 'Art'

Penelope Gilliatt (1932–93)

BRITISH AUTHOR
Her novels include A State of Change *(1967) and* The Cutting Edge *(1978), and she also wrote short stories, the screenplay for* Sunday, Bloody Sunday *(1971) and critical works on the cinema and theatre.*

1 Boston is one of the few American cities that regrets the past. . . . Boston's like England. Up to its ears in yellowing photographs.

A State of Change, pt 1, ch. 7 (1967)

2 Why is it that beautiful women never seem to have any curiosity? Is it because they know they're classical? With classical things the Lord finished the job. Ordinary ugly people know they're deficient and they go on looking for the pieces.

Ibid., pt 2, ch. 8

3 Russians have always been hugely concerned with ethics and hardly at all with conduct.

Don, ibid. The remark follows the observation by Christabel, 'Russia does at least try to conduct its life so as to make the good things available to everyone.'

Gary Gilmore (1941–77)

US CONVICT
Convicted for the murder of two students, he was the first person to be executed in the USA after the reinstatement of the death penalty in 1976, a sentence which he requested in preference to life imprisonment.

1 Your Honor, I don't want to take up a lot of your time with my words. I believe I was given a fair trial and I think the sentence is proper and I am willing to accept it like a man. I don't wish to appeal. . . . I desire to be executed on schedule, and I just wish to accept that with the grace and dignity of a man.

Speech to the Supreme Court, 9 November 1976, quoted in *The Executioner's Song*, bk 2, pt 1, ch. 1, sect. 7 (1979) by Norman Mailer. Gilmore's last words to the firing squad were 'Let's do it!'

(Sir) Ian Gilmour (b. 1926)

BRITISH POLITICIAN
A Conservative MP, he was a cabinet minister in the HEATH *and* THATCHER *governments until 1981, holding posts in defence in government and in opposition.*

1 Conservatives do not worship democracy. For them majority rule is a device. . . . And if it is leading to an end that is undesirable or inconsistent with itself, then there is a theoretical case for ending it.

Inside Right, pt 3, ch. 5 (1977)

Newt Gingrich (b. 1943)

US POLITICIAN
A confrontational spokesman for the Republican Party and a convinced Reaganite, he was elected Speaker of the House of Representatives in 1994. In 1997 he was fined $300,000 for misleading the House.

1 In every election in American history both parties have their clichés. The party that has the clichés that ring true wins.

International Herald Tribune 1 August 1988

Allen Ginsberg (1926–97)

US POET
His Howl and Other Poems *(1956) was claimed by the Beat generation as its poetic manifesto. He*

became a 'spiritual godfather' of the counterculture in the 1960s and '70s (the phrase 'flower power' came from him), and he was outspoken on civil rights and gay liberation.

1 Fortunately art is a community effort – a small but select community living in a spiritualized world endeavoring to interpret the wars and the solitudes of the flesh.

Journal entry, 11 July 1954, publ. in *Journals: Early Fifties Early Sixties*, 'Mexico and Return to US' (ed. Gordon Ball, 1977)

2 *I saw the best minds of my generation destroyed by madness, starving hysterical naked,*
dragging themselves through the negro streets at dawn looking for an angry fix,
angelheaded hipsters burning for the ancient heavenly connection to the starry dynamo in the machinery of night,
who poverty and tatters and hollow-eyed and high sat up smoking in the supernatural darkness of cold-water flats floating across the tops of cities contemplating jazz.

'Howl', publ. in *Howl and Other Poems* (1956). Opening lines.

3 *What thoughts I have of you tonight, Walt Whitman, for I walked down the sidestreets under the trees with a headache self-conscious looking at the full moon.*
In my hungry fatigue, and shopping for images, I went into the neon fruit supermarket, dreaming of your enumerations!

'A Supermarket in California', publ. ibid. Opening lines of poem.

4 *A perfect beauty of a sunflower! a perfect excellent lovely sunflower*
existence! a sweet natural eye to the new hip moon, woke up alive and excited grasping in the sunset shadow sunrise golden monthly breeze.

'Sunflower Sutra', publ. ibid.

5 *America I'm putting my queer shoulder to the wheel.*

'America', publ. ibid. Last line of poem.

6 *Downtown Manhattan, clear winter noon, and I've been up all night, talking, talking, reading the Kaddish aloud, listening to Ray Charles blues shout blind on the phonograph*

'Kaddish', sect. 1, publ. in *Kaddish and Other Poems* (1960)

7 *This is the end, the redemption from Wilderness, way for the Wonderer, House sought for All, black handkerchief washed clean by weeping – page beyond Psalm – Last change of mine and Naomi*

– to God's perfect Darkness – Death, stay thy phantoms!

Ibid.

8 *Democracy! Bah! When I hear that word I reach for my feather Boa!*

'Subliminal', written in journal, October 1960, publ. in *Journals: Early Fifties Early Sixties*, 'New York City' (ed. Gordon Ball, 1977). See HERMANN GOERING 2.

9 *No monster vibration, no snake universe hallucinations. Many tiny jeweled violet flowers along the path of a living brook that looked like Blake's illustration for a canal in grassy Eden: huge Pacific watery shore, Orlovsky dancing naked like Shiva long-haired before giant green waves, titanic cliffs that Wordsworth mentioned in his own Sublime, great yellow sun veiled with mist hanging over the planet's oceanic horizon. No harm.*

Letter, 2 June 1966, publ. in *Paris Review* summer 1966. On an LSD experience in Big Sur, California.

10 *What if someone gave a war and Nobody came?*
Life would ring the bells of Ecstasy and Forever be Itself again.

'Graffiti 12th Cubicle Men's Room Syracuse Airport', publ. in *The Fall of America* (1972). The words of the first line were current during the anti-war protests of the 1960s, and were adapted as the title of a 1970 film, *Suppose They Gave a War and Nobody Came?* starring Brian Keith and Tony Curtis. The original inspiration was probably a poem by Carl Sandburg: see CARL SANDBURG 7.

11 *Nobody saves America by sniffing cocaine Jiggling yr knees blankeyed in the rain When it snows in yr nose you catch cold in yr brain.*

Lines publ. in *Ginsberg: A Biography*, ch. 16 (1989) by Barry Miles

12 Poetry is not an expression of the party line. It's that time of night, lying in bed, thinking what you really think, making the private world public, that's what the poet does.

Quoted ibid., ch. 17

Natalia Ginzburg (1916–91)

ITALIAN NOVELIST
She wrote unsentimentally about family relationships in her novels, which include The Dry Heart *(1947),* Family Sayings *(1963) and* The Manzoni Family *(1987).*

1 You aren't ill: it is just that you are made of second-rate materials.

Alberto to his wife Miranda, in *Family Sayings* (1963, rev. 1984)

Nikki Giovanni (b. 1943)

US POET

Originally Yolande Giovanni. Called the 'Princess of Black Poetry', she was prominent in the black literary movement of the late 1960s. Among her collections are Black Feeling, Black Talk *(1968) and* Cotton Candy on a Rainy Day *(1978).*

1 it's a sex object if you're pretty
and no love
or love and no sex if you're fat
'Woman Poem', publ. in *Black Judgment* (1969)

2 There're two people in the world that are not likeable: a master and a slave.
A Dialogue (with JAMES BALDWIN, 1973). The book is a transcription of a discussion between Giovanni and Baldwin in London, 4 November 1971.

3 I think one of the nicest things that we created as a generation was just the fact that we could say, Hey, I don't like white people.
Ibid.

George Gipp See RONALD REAGAN 24.

Jean Giraudoux (1882–1944)

FRENCH AUTHOR AND DIPLOMAT

He combined a career in the diplomatic service (1910–40) with a writing vocation. Many of his novels and plays, which include Judith *(1931) and* Tiger at the Gates *(1935), are retellings of biblical stories and Greek myths.*

1 I tell you, sir, the only safeguard of order and discipline in the modern world is a standardized worker with interchangeable parts. That would solve the entire problem of management.
The President, in *The Madwoman of Chaillot*, act 1 (1945)

Maurice Girodias (1919–90)

FRENCH PUBLISHER

The Olympia Press, which he founded in Paris in 1953, was responsible for the publication of works by GENET, BECKETT, HENRY MILLER *and* WILLIAM BURROUGHS *and was the first to publish* NABOKOV's Lolita.

1 Conservatism, colonialism, racism, and religious intolerance are part of the make-up of the French bourgeois, who is just as bigoted, brainlessly selfish, and frightened as his counterparts in the other countries. . . . France is now entirely dominated, owned, manipulated, exploited, milked, policed, by *les bourgeois* for *les bourgeois*.
The Olympia Reader, Introduction (ed. Maurice Girodias, 1965)

Edna Gladney

US PHILANTHROPIST

She made a career of rescuing illegitimate children and raising them in her private orphanage in Texas. She was instrumental in passing a law to eliminate from public record whether or not orphans are born illegitimately.

1 There are no illegitimate children, there are only illegitimate parents.
Quoted in *Kiss Hollywood Goodbye*, ch. 18 by ANITA LOOS. MGM paid Gladney a large sum for this widely quoted line which was to form the basis of the 1941 film *Blossoms in the Dust*, starring Greer Garson (screenplay by Loos, directed and produced by Mervyn LeRoy). It is not clear whether the words originated with Gladney, however. The lawyer Léon Yankwich was supposed to have made a similar remark in June 1928, during a hearing at the State District Court, Southern District of California, and he was quoting the journalist O. O. McIntyre. The words have also been ascribed to BERNADETTE MCALISKEY in 1971.

Ellen Glasgow (1874–1945)

US NOVELIST

Her unsentimental novels, for example Barren Ground *(1925) and* The Sheltered Life *(1932), describe the social divisions and hypocrisies of Virginia and the plight of women in the American South.* CARL VAN DOREN *mourned: 'Southern romance is dead. Ellen Glasgow has murdered it.'*

1 Women like to sit down with trouble as if it were knitting.
Jenny Blair, in *The Sheltered Life*, pt 3, sect. 3 (1932)

2 I have observed with wonder so many intellectual and literary fashions that I have come at last to rely positively upon one conviction alone. No idea is so antiquated that it was not once modern. No idea is so modern that it will not some day be antiquated. . . . To seize the flying thought before it escapes us is our only touch with reality.
'Empty American Novels', address to the Modern Language Association (1936), repr. in *The New York Times* 1 January 1937

3 No matter how vital experience might be while you lived it, no sooner was it ended and dead than it became as lifeless as the piles of dry dust in a school history book.
In This Our Life, pt 3, ch. 9 (1941)

George Glass (1910–84)

US FILM EXECUTIVE

Sometimes known as Georges Glass, he worked extensively as a film producer in Europe and Hollywood in a career spanning over thirty years.

1 An actor is a kind of guy who if you ain't talking about him ain't listening.
Quoted in *Brando*, ch. 8 (1973) by Bob Thomas. The quote is frequently ascribed to MARLON BRANDO, who may have heard it from Glass. The actor Michael Wilding is similarly quoted as saying, 'You can pick out actors by the glazed look that comes into their eyes when the conversation wanders away from themselves.'

Misha Glenny (b. 1958)
BRITISH JOURNALIST, AUTHOR AND BROADCASTER
An expert on Central and Eastern Europe, he was a BBC foreign correspondent (1989–95), and has published The Rebirth of History *(1990) and* The Fall of Yugoslavia *(1992), among other titles.*

1 After the end of the Cold War, some governments have tended to forget Eastern Europe, allowing the new democracies to stew in the gelatinous leftovers of communism. But the peoples of the new democracies will not forget the West – Europe has become the most unstable continent in the world.
The Rebirth of History, ch. 9 (1990, rev. 1993)

Jean-Luc Godard (b. 1930)
FRENCH FILM-MAKER AND AUTHOR
His first feature film À bout de souffle *(Breathless, 1959) established him as a leader of the nouvelle vague movement in cinema. In subsequent films he made use of free improvisation and anti-narration, adopting an increasingly political stance, as in* Wind from the East *(1969).*

1 The cinema is not a craft. It is an art. It does not mean team-work. One is always alone; on the set as before the blank page.
'Bergmanorama', first publ. in *Cahiers du Cinéma* July 1958, repr. in *Godard on Godard* (ed. Tom Milne, 1972)

2 I don't know if I'm free because I'm unhappy or unhappy because I'm free.
Patricia Franchini (Jean Seberg), in *Breathless* (film, 1959, written and directed by Jean-Luc Godard)

3 Photography is truth . . . and the cinema is the truth twenty-four times a second.
Bruno Forestier (Michel Subor), in *Le Petit soldat* (film, 1960, written and directed by Jean-Luc Godard)

4 When I hear the word culture, I take out my chequebook.
Jeremy Prokosh (Jack Palance), a film producer, in *Le Mépris* (film, 1963, adapted by Jean-Luc Godard from *A Ghost at Noon* by Alberto Moravia, directed by Jean-Luc Godard). See HERMANN GOERING 2.

5 More and more I see the human predicament as a dialogue between lovers.
Natasha von Braun (Anna Karina), in *Alphaville* (film, 1965, written and directed by Jean-Luc Godard)

6 Give us this day our television, and an automobile, but deliver us from freedom.
Madeleine (Chantal Goya), in *Masculin-féminin* (film, 1966, adapted by Jean-Luc Godard from two short stories by Guy de Maupassant, directed by Jean-Luc Godard)

7 To me style is just the outside of content, and content the inside of style, like the outside and the inside of the human body – both go together, they can't be separated.
Quoted in *Godard*, Introduction (1967) by Richard Roud

8 All you need for a movie is a gun and a girl.
Journal entry, 16 May 1991, quoted in *Projections* (ed. John Boorman and Walter Donohue, 1992)

Alfred Godley (1856–1925)
BRITISH SCHOLAR
Deemed 'an almost perfect writer of elegant Latin', he wrote humorous and satirical prose and verse as well as publishing on classical authors.

1 What is this that roareth thus?
Can it be a Motor Bus?
Yes, the smell and hideous hum
Indicat Motorem Bum . . .
Domine, defende nos
Contra hos Motores Bos!
'The Motor Bus', in letter, 10 January 1914, publ. in *Reliquiae*, vol. 1 (1926)

Joseph Goebbels (1897–1945)
GERMAN NAZI LEADER
As HITLER's *Minister of Propaganda from 1933, he was given extensive powers in government in 1943. Committed to Hitler to the last, he killed his six children and, with his wife, committed suicide.*

1 We enter parliament in order to supply ourselves, in the arsenal of democracy, with its own weapons. . . . If democracy is so stupid as to give us free tickets and salaries for this bear's work, that is its affair. . . . We do not come as friends, nor even as neutrals. We come as enemies. As the wolf bursts into the flock, so we come.
Der Angriff 30 April 1928

2 We can do without butter, but, despite all our love of peace, not without arms. One cannot shoot with butter, but with guns.
Speech in Berlin, 17 January 1936, quoted in *Allgemeine Zeitung* 18 January 1936. The origin of the 'guns or butter' quote is unverifiable. In the summer of 1936, in a radio broadcast on the Four Year Plan, HERMANN GOERING announced, 'Guns will make us powerful; butter will only make us fat.'

Hermann Goering (1893–1946)

GERMAN NAZI LEADER

Having joined the Nazi government in 1933, he was responsible for founding the Gestapo, establishing concentration camps and building up the Luftwaffe. In 1940 he became Marshal of the Reich but was dismissed in 1945. He committed suicide after being sentenced at Nuremberg.

1 I herewith commission you to carry out all preparations with regard to . . . a total solution of the Jewish question in those territories of Europe which are under German influence . . . I furthermore charge you to submit to me as soon as possible a draft showing the . . . measures already taken for the execution of the intended final solution of the Jewish question.

Military directive to Reinhard Heydrich, 31 July 1941, quoted in *The Rise and Fall of the Third Reich*, ch. 27 (1960) by William L. Shirer. According to Shirer, the German word *Endloesung* was erroneously rendered 'desired solution' at Goering's trial at Nuremberg, thus allowing the judge to accept Goering's insistence that he had never used the terms 'total' or 'final solution'; 'the first time I learned of these terrible exterminations was right here at Nuremberg', Goering declared. Heydrich, Deputy Chief of the Gestapo, has also been associated with the phrase.

2 Whenever I hear the word culture, I reach for my revolver.

Attributed. Whether or not Goering ever uttered these words, the only recorded reference to them is in the play *Schlageter* (1933) by Hanns Johst (1890–1978), Nazi playwright and President of the Reich Chamber of Literature. The line is spoken by a stormtrooper in act 1, sc. 1: 'When I hear the word culture, I cock my Browning.' Many variations have been coined (see ALLEN GINSBERG 8, JEAN-LUC GODARD 4).

Isaac Goldberg (1887–1938)

US CRITIC

The literary editor of American Freeman (1923–32), he was instrumental in introducing the modern literature of Latin America to English-speaking readers.

1 Diplomacy is to do and say
The nastiest things in the nicest way.
The Reflex October 1927

Whoopi Goldberg (b. 1949)

US SCREEN ACTRESS AND COMEDIENNE

Originally Caryn Johnson. Formerly a stand-up comedienne, she is known for her roles in The Color Purple (1985), Ghost (1990) and Sister Act (1992).

1 I'm not an African. The Africans know I'm not an African. I'm an American. This is my country. My people helped to build it

and we've been here for centuries. Just call me black if you want to call me anything.
Interview in the *Daily Telegraph* 20 April 1998. On the label 'African-American'.

(Sir) William Golding (1911–93)

BRITISH AUTHOR

He achieved success with his first novel Lord of the Flies (1954), whose themes of human fallibility and the potential of evil recurred in such later works as The Spire (1964) and Rites of Passage (1980).

1 Sleep is when all the unsorted stuff comes flying out as from a dustbin upset in a high wind.
Pincher Martin, ch. 6 (1956)

2 Marx, Darwin and Freud are the three most crashing bores of the Western world. The simplistic popularization of their ideas has thrust our world into a mental straitjacket from which we can only escape by the most anarchic violence.
'Belief and Creativity', lecture given in Hamburg, Germany, April 1980, repr. in *A Moving Target* (1982)

3 It may be – I hope it is – redemption to guess and perhaps perceive that the universe, the hell which we see for all its beauty, vastness, majesty, is only part of a whole which is quite unimaginable.
Ibid.

4 The writer probably knows what he meant when he wrote a book, but he should immediately forget what he meant when he's written it.
Novelists in Interview (ed. John Haffenden, 1985)

5 Childhood is a disease – a sickness that you grow out of.
Quoted in the *Guardian* 22 June 1990. Golding worked for many years as a school-teacher.

Albert Goldman (1927–94)

US AUTHOR AND CRITIC

Called by Newsweek 'half scholarly intellectual and half funky pop rock schlock freak', he wrote iconoclastic biographies of LENNY BRUCE (1974), ELVIS PRESLEY (1981) and JOHN LENNON (1988).

1 Commercial to the core, Elvis was the kind of singer dear to the heart of the music business. For him to sing a song was to sell a song. His G clef was a dollar sign
Elvis, ch. 14 (1981)

Emma Goldman (1869–1940)

LITHUANIAN-BORN US ANARCHIST

Imprisoned for inciting unemployed workers to riot in 1893 and for opposing conscription during the First World War, she was deported from the USA in 1919 and subsequently lived in Russia and

France. She wrote numerous political articles and her autobiography Living My Life *(1931).*

1 The individual whose vision encompasses the whole world often feels nowhere so hedged in and out of touch with his surroundings as in his native land.

'The Individual, Society and the State', first publ. c. 1940, repr. in *Red Emma Speaks*, pt 1 (ed. Alix Kates Shulman, 1972)

William Goldman (b. 1931)

US SCREENWRITER AND NOVELIST

He won Academy Awards for his screenplays of Butch Cassidy and the Sundance Kid *(1970) and* All the President's Men *(1983). He has also adapted his own novels for the screen, including* Marathon Man *(1975, filmed 1976).*

1 As far as the filmmaking process is concerned, stars are essentially worthless – and absolutely essential.

Adventures in the Screen Trade, ch. 1 (1983)

2 Studio executives are intelligent, brutally overworked men and women who share one thing in common with baseball managers: They wake up every morning of the world with the knowledge that sooner or later they're going to get fired.

Ibid.

3 Whoever invented the meeting must have had Hollywood in mind. I think they should consider giving Oscars for meetings: Best Meeting of the Year, Best Supporting Meeting, Best Meeting Based on Material from Another Meeting.

Ibid., ch. 2

(Sir) James Goldsmith (1933–97)

ANGLO-FRENCH BUSINESSMAN

His business empire made him one of the wealthiest men in Britain, while his flamboyant lifestyle led to his being regularly pilloried in Private Eye. *He was elected a French MEP (1995–7) and financed and led the Referendum Party in the British general election of 1997.*

1 In my lifetime there has never been a moment when the establishment has been right. The slaves of this world are those who wish to belong to its ranks.

Quoted in the *Observer* 20 July 1997

Barry Goldwater (1909–98)

US POLITICIAN

As a Republican Senator (1953–64, 1969–87) he held an extreme anti-Communist stance. He was defeated as presidential candidate in the 1964 election, and in 1969 chaired the Armed Services Commission.

1 I would remind you that extremism in the defense of liberty is no vice! And let me remind you also that moderation in the pursuit of justice is no virtue!

Speech accepting presidential nomination at Republican National Convention, San Francisco, 16 July 1964, quoted in *The New York Times* 17 July 1964. Goldwater later attributed these words to Cicero. LYNDON B. JOHNSON, as Democratic nominee for the presidency, replied in a speech in New York, 31 October 1964: 'Extremism in the pursuit of the Presidency is an unpardonable vice. Moderation in the affairs of the nation is the highest virtue.' Johnson won a sweeping victory against Goldwater in the presidential election three days later.

Samuel Goldwyn (1882–1974)

POLISH-BORN US FILM PRODUCER

Originally Samuel Goldfish. As head of one of Hollywood's mightiest film studios, he had the knack of assembling creative teams, including William Wyler, who directed such films as Wuthering Heights *(1939) and* The Best Years of Our Lives *(1946) for Samuel Goldwyn Productions. He was notorious for his malapropisms, although some of the most famous were apocryphal.*

1 Gentlemen, include me out!

Attributed in *The Goldwyn Touch*, ch. 10 (1986) by Michael Freedland. The remark is supposed to have been made in October 1933, on resigning from the Motion Picture Producers and Distributors of America over a labour dispute, but Goldwyn himself denied ever having used the words, claiming instead to have said, 'Gentlemen, I'm withdrawing from the association.'

2 That is the kind of ad I like. Facts, facts, facts.

Quoted in *Goldwyn: The Man Behind the Myth*, ch. 16 (1976) by Arthur Marx. Goldwyn was referring to an advertisement for the film *We Live Again* (1934), which described it as: 'The greatest motion picture in all history, by the world's most outstanding writer. The directorial genius of Mamoulian, the beauty of Anna Sten and the producing genius of Goldwyn have combined to make the greatest entertainment in the world.' The film flopped.

3 A verbal contract isn't worth the paper it is written on.

Attributed in *The Great Goldwyn*, ch. 1 (1937) by Alva Johnston. In *They Never Said It* (1989) by Paul F. Boller Jr and John George, Goldwyn's actual words are reported as, 'His verbal contract is worth more than the paper it's written on', referring to movie executive Joseph M. Schenck, who was regarded as completely trustworthy. This popular version is probably one of the many 'Goldwynisms' cooked up by Goldwyn's own staff.

4 That's the way with these directors, they're always biting the hand that lays the golden egg.

Ibid.

5 I had a monumental idea this morning,
but I didn't like it.
Ibid.

6 [Too caustic?] To hell with the cost. If it's a
good picture, we'll make it.
To a director who was asked his opinion of a
script, quoted ibid.

7 God makes stars. I just produce them.
Quoted in the *Daily Express* 16 May 1939

8 Any man who goes to a psychiatrist should
have his head examined.
Quoted in *Moguls*, ch. 3 (1969) by Norman
Zierold

9 I don't think anybody should write his
autobiography until after he's dead.
Quoted in *Goldwyn: The Man Behind the Myth*,
Prologue (1976) by Arthur Marx

10 Pictures are for entertainment, messages
should be delivered by Western Union.
Quoted ibid. ch. 15

11 I read part of it all the way through.
Quoted ibid. ch. 27

(Sir) E. H. Gombrich (1909–2001)

AUSTRIAN-BORN BRITISH ART CRITIC AND
HISTORIAN
*Ernst Hans Joseph Gombrich. He emigrated to Eng-
land in 1936 to work at the Warburg Institute, University of London. Publications include his popular
works* The Story of Art *(1950) and* Art and Illusion *(1960).*

1 There really is no such thing as Art. There
are only artists.
The Story of Art, Introduction (1950). Opening
words.

2 For that strange precinct we call 'art' is like
a hall of mirrors or a whispering gallery.
Each form conjures up a thousand mem
ories and after-images. No sooner is an
image presented as art than, by this very
act, a new frame of reference is created
which it cannot escape.
'Aspects of Form: A Symposium on Form in
Nature and Art' (ed. L. L. Whyte, 1951), repr. as
'Meditations on a Hobby Horse' in *Meditations
on a Hobby Horse and Other Essays on the Theory
of Art* (1963)

F. Gonzalez-Crussi (b. 1936)

MEXICAN PROFESSOR OF PATHOLOGY AND
AUTHOR
*Frank Gonzalez-Crussi. His collections of pithy
and humorous essays are drawn from his experience as a practising pathologist. They include*
Three Forms of Sudden Death and Other Reflections on the Grandeur and Misery of the Body
(1986).

1 Ceremony and ritual spring from our
heart of hearts: those who govern us know
it well, for they would sooner deny us

bread than dare alter the observance of tradition.
Notes of an Anatomist, 'On Embalming' (1985)

Linda Goodman (c. 1925–95)

US ASTROLOGER
Born Mary Alice Kemery. Her books Sun Signs
(1968) and Love Signs *(1978), which incorporated
popular psychology, were bestsellers. She has also
published poetry.*

1 The stars which shone over Babylon and
the stable in Bethlehem still shine as
brightly over the Empire State Building
and your front yard today. They perform
their cycles with the same mathematical
precision, and they will continue to affect
each thing on earth, including man, as
long as the earth exists.
Linda Goodman's Sun Signs, Afterword (1968)

Lord Goodman (1913–95)

BRITISH LAWYER AND PUBLIC FIGURE
*Arnold Goodman. Chairman of the Arts Council
of Great Britain (1965–72), and Director of the
Royal Opera House (1972–83), he was adviser to
three prime ministers, and honoured by both*
HAROLD WILSON *and* EDWARD HEATH.

1 That is one of the great advantages of the
arts: they are a consolation for loneliness.
Interview in *Singular Encounters*, 'Lord Goodman' (1990) by Naim Attallah

Paul Goodman (1911–72)

US AUTHOR, POET AND CRITIC
*In his prolific output he championed the cause of
the individual against institutions, as in* Growing
Up Absurd *(1960) and* The Individual and Culture *(1969).*

1 Here we have the beautiful British compromise: a man can say anything, he mustn't
do anything; a man can listen to anything,
but he mustn't be roused to do anything.
By freedom of speech is meant freedom to
talk *about*; speech is not saying-as-an-
action.
'Censorship and Pornography on the Stage',
pt 2, lecture, 1959, published in *Creator Spirit
Come* (1977)

2 When the Devil quotes Scriptures, it's not,
really, to deceive, but simply that the
masses are so ignorant of theology that
somebody has to teach them the elemen-
tary texts before he can seduce them.
Five Years, 'Spring and Summer 1956', sect. 6
(1966)

3 When a village ceases to be a community,
it becomes oppressive in its narrow conformity. So one becomes an individual and
migrates to the city. There, finding others
likeminded, one re-establishes a village

community. Nowadays only New Yorkers are yokels.

Ibid., 'Winter and Spring 1956–1957', sect. 8

4 To translate, one must have a style of his own, for otherwise the translation will have no rhythm or nuance, which come from the process of artistically thinking through and molding the sentences; they cannot be reconstituted by piecemeal imitation. The problem of translation is to retreat to a simpler tenor of one's own style and creatively adjust this to one's author.

Ibid., 'Summer 1957, in Europe', sect. 8

Mikhail Gorbachev (b. 1931)

RUSSIAN POLITICAL LEADER
General Secretary of the Soviet Communist Party (1985–91) and President of the USSR (1990–91), he introduced perestroika, *and* glasnost, *which transformed the Soviet Union and led to its demise in 1991. See* MARGARET THATCHER 17.

1 The essence of perestroika lies in the fact that *it unites socialism with democracy* . . . We want more socialism and, therefore, more democracy.

Perestroika, pt 1, ch. 1 (1987)

2 I am a Communist, a convinced Communist! For some that may be a fantasy. But to me it is my main goal.

Speech at Second National Congress of People's Deputies, Moscow, December 1989, quoted in *The New York Times* 26 Dec 1989. A week earlier, however, *Newsweek* had quoted Gorbachev as confiding to MARGARET THATCHER, 'I don't even know if I'm a Communist any more.' Both pronouncements are discussed in *Gorbachev*, pt 6, 'Sakharov's Warning' (1991) by Gail Sheehy.

3 I believe, as Lenin said, that this revolutionary chaos may yet crystallise into new forms of life.

Quoted in *The Times* 18 May 1990. Referring to the secession of the Baltic republics and other regional disputes.

4 The market came with the dawn of civilization and it is not an invention of capitalism. . . . If it leads to improving the well-being of the people there is no contradiction with socialism.

Quoted in the *Guardian* 21 June 1990

5 My life's work has been accomplished. I did all that I could.

Quoted in the *Observer* 15 December 1991. On being ousted as Soviet President.

Nadine Gordimer (b. 1923)

SOUTH AFRICAN AUTHOR
Apartheid and its destructive effects, both on the privileged and the oppressed, are the main themes of her short stories and novels. Her works include the autobiographical The Lying Days *(1953),* The Conservationist *(1974) and* Burger's Daughter *(1979), which was banned in South Africa.*

1 The country of the tourist pamphlet always is another country, an embarrassing abstraction of the desirable that, thank God, does not exist on this planet, where there are always ants and bad smells and empty Coca-Cola bottles to keep the grubby finger-print of reality upon the beautiful.

A World of Strangers, ch. 1 (1958)

2 If you live in Europe . . . things change . . . but continuity never seems to break. You don't have to throw the past away.

Madame Bagnelli, in *Burger's Daughter*, pt 2 (1979)

3 If people would forget about utopia! When rationalism destroyed heaven and decided to set it up here on earth, that most terrible of all goals entered human ambition. It was clear there'd be no end to what people would be made to suffer for it.

Bernard, ibid.

4 Responsibility is what awaits outside the Eden of Creativity.

'The Essential Gesture', lecture at University of Michigan, 12 October 1984, first publ. in *The Tanner Lectures on Human Values* (ed. Sterling M. McMurrin, 1985), repr. in *The Essential Gesture* (ed. Stephen Clingman, 1988)

5 There is no moral authority like that of sacrifice.

Ibid.

6 Censorship is never over for those who have experienced it. It is a brand on the imagination that affects the individual who has suffered it, forever.

'Censorship and its Aftermath', address at International Writers' Day conference, London, June 1990, publ. in *Index on Censorship* August 1990

Mack Gordon (1904–59)

POLISH-BORN US SONGWRITER
Originally Morris Gittler. He teamed up with Harry Revel to create numbers for Hollywood films in the 1930s, and with Harry Warren to produce such songs as 'Chattanooga Choo-Choo' (1941) and 'Kalamazoo' (1942), both hits for Glenn Miller.

1 *Pardon me boy,*
Is that the Chattanooga Choo-Choo?
Track twenty-nine,
Boy you can give me a shine.

'Chattanooga Choo-Choo' (song, written 1934 with music by Harry Warren) in *Sun Valley Serenade* (musical show and film, 1941). Sung by Dorothy Dandridge in the film, the number was recorded by Glenn Miller and his Orchestra, for whom it sold a million and became the first record to be awarded a gold disc.

(Sir) David Gore-Booth (b. 1943)
BRITISH DIPLOMAT
He was Ambassador to Saudi Arabia (1993) and British High Commissioner to India (1996–8).

1 Diplomacy is made up of equal parts of protocol, vitriol and alcohol.
Attributed

Teresa Gorman (b. 1931)
BRITISH POLITICIAN
A right-wing libertarian and businesswoman, she was elected Conservative MP in 1987 and has been outspoken on women's issues and against Britain's membership of the EU.

1 The Conservative Establishment has always treated women as nannies, grannies and fannies.
Quoted in the *Guardian* 27 December 1998

Stuart Gorrell (1902–63)
US SONGWRITER
A schoolfriend of Hoagy Carmichael, he was later an editor at the Miami Herald.

1 *Georgia, Georgia, no peace I find,*
Just an old sweet song keeps Georgia on my mind.
'Georgia on my Mind' (song, 1930, with music by Hoagy Carmichael). The song was first sung by Hoagy Carmichael, was a hit for Mildred Bailey (1932), Ray Charles (1960) and WILLIE NELSON (1978), and has been adopted as the state song of Georgia.

Stephen Jay Gould (1941–2002)
US PALAEONTOLOGIST AND AUTHOR
His award-winning books, including Hens' Teeth and Horses' Toes *(1983),* Wonderful Life *(1989) and* Eight Little Piggies *(1993), propose the theory of 'punctuated equilibrium' – evolution in stops and starts – and argue against biological determinism.*

1 *Homo Sapiens . . . a tiny twig on an improbable branch of a contingent limb on a fortunate tree.*
Wonderful Life: The Burgess Shale and the Nature of History, ch. 4, 'Walcott's Vision and the Nature of History' (1989)

2 Science is an integral part of culture. It's not this foreign thing, done by an arcane priesthood. It's one of the glories of human intellectual tradition.
Independent 24 January 1990

3 We think that we are reading nature by applying rules of logic and laws of matter to our observations. But we are often tell-

ing stories – in the good sense, but stories nonetheless.
Bully for Brontosaurus, ch. 5 (1991)

4 Knowledge and wonder are the dyad of our worthy lives as intellectual beings.
Ibid., ch. 35

5 Progress in knowledge is not a tower to heaven built of bricks from the bottom up, but a product of impasse and breakthrough, yielding a bizarre and circuitous structure that ultimately rises nonetheless.
Eight Little Piggies, pt 3, essay 9 (1993)

6 The real tragedy of human existence is not that we are nasty by nature, but that a cruel structural asymmetry grants to rare events of meanness such power to shape our history.
Ibid., pt 5, essay 19

7 People in the past, in religious civilizations, had a real, profound terror of apocalyptic catastrophe. What frightens us in our secular age is the computer breakdown that'll occur if computers interpret the 00 of the year 2000 as a return to 1900.
'Time Scales and the Year 2000', Introduction to *Conversations About the End of Time* (ed. Catherine David, Frédéric Lenoir and Jean-Philippe de Tonnac, 1999)

Philip Gourevitch (b. 1961)
US JOURNALIST AND AUTHOR
A staff writer at the New Yorker, *he reported on the Rwanda massacres of 1994, the subject of his acclaimed account,* We Wish to Inform You that Tomorrow We Will be Killed with Our Families *(1998).*

1 Genocide, after all, is an exercise in community building. A vigorous totalitarian order requires that the people be invested in the leaders' scheme, and while genocide may be the most perverse and ambitious means to this end, it is also the most comprehensive.
We Wish to Inform You that Tomorrow We Will be Killed with Our Families, pt 1, ch. 7 (1998)

2 Rwanda had presented the world with the most unambiguous case of genocide since Hitler's war against the Jews, and the world sent blankets, beans, and bandages to camps controlled by the killers, apparently hoping that everybody would behave nicely in the future.
Ibid., ch. 11

Lew Grade (1906–98)
UKRAINIAN-BORN BRITISH FILM AND TV ENTREPRENEUR
Baron Grade of Elstree, born Louis Winogradsky.

Once a champion tap-dancer, he became a theatri-
cal agent (from 1943), Managing Director of ATV
(1962–76) and a film producer.

1 **All my shows are great. Some of them are**
bad. But they are all great.
Quoted in the *Observer* 14 September 1975

2 **It would have been cheaper to lower the**
Atlantic.
Attributed comment on his film *Raise the*
Titanic (1980), which took only $7 million at the
box office, having cost $40 million to make.

Michael Grade (b. 1943)
BRITISH BROADCASTING EXECUTIVE
Nephew of LORD GRADE, *he was the BBC's young-*
est ever Controller in 1984, and head of Channel 4
(1988–97). He became Executive Chairman of
Pinewood and Shepperton Studios in 2000 and
Chairman of the Camelot group in 2002.

1 **The BBC keeps us all honest.**
Quoted in the *Independent on Sunday*
19 February 1995

Graffiti

1 **Kilroy was here.**
First World War, left by US servicemen, particularly Air Transport Command. The words may
have originated with a shipyard inspector in
Massachusetts, who left his name on goods he
had passed.

2 **Imagination has seized power.**
(*L'imagination prend le pouvoir.*)
Paris, 1968, quoted in *Paris '68*, ch. 2 (1988) by
Marc Rohan

3 **One non-revolutionary weekend is infi-**
nitely more bloody than a month of perma-
nent revolution.
School of Oriental Languages, London, 1968,
publ. in *Leaving the 20th Century: The Incomplete*
Work of the Situationist International (ed./transl.
Christopher Gray, 1974)

4 **Clapton is God.**
London, late 1960s. Referring to guitarist Eric
Clapton. 'I never ever saw that written anywhere
or heard people say it after gigs,' Clapton later
stated in an interview. 'I would think that it had
just got out of proportion . . . I completely
ignored it, really.'

5 **A woman needs a man like a fish needs a**
bicycle.
1970s. See also GLORA STEINEM 9.

6 **God made us Catholics but the armalite**
made us equal.
Graffiti in Belfast, 1970s

7 **It doesn't matter who you vote for, the**
government always gets in.
London, 1970s

8 *Liberté! Fraternité! Sexualité!*
Paris Métro, 1980s

9 **If voting changed anything, they'd abolish**
it.
1980s. The words were taken as the title of a
book by KEN LIVINGSTONE in 1987.

10 **They came, they saw, they did a little**
shopping.
Berlin wall, following the influx of thousands of
East Berliners into West Berlin after the lifting of
travel restrictions, reported in *Newsweek*
4 December 1989

11 **Workers of the world forgive me.**
On the bust of Karl Marx in Bucharest, reported
in the *The Times* 4 May 1990

12 **Dead twat.**
On the statue of WINSTON CHURCHILL in
Parliament Square, London, daubed by 'anti-
capitalist' rioters, 1 May 2000

13 **Smoke Bush not Iraq.**
On the Iraq crisis, 2002–2003

Harry Graham (1874–1936)
BRITISH AUTHOR AND RHYMESTER

1 *Weep not for little Leonie,*
Abducted by a French Marquis!
Though loss of honour was a wrench,
Just think how it's improved her French.
'Compensation', publ. in *More Ruthless Rhymes*
for Heartless Homes (1930)

Martha Graham (1894–1991)
US DANCER AND CHOREOGRAPHER
Providing the first real alternative to classical
ballet, she started the Martha Graham School of
Contemporary Dance in 1927, becoming America's
leading exponent of Expressionist dance. Among
her most famous works are Appalachian Spring
(1944) and Clytemnestra *(1958).*

1 **Nothing is more revealing than movement.**
'The American Dance', publ. in *Modern Dance*
(ed. Virginia Stewart, 1935)

2 **We look at the dance to impart the sen-**
sation of living in an affirmation of life, to
energize the spectator into keener aware-
ness of the vigor, the mystery, the humor,
the variety, and the wonder of life. This is
the function of the American dance.
Ibid.

3 **There is a supreme lucidity, which is the**
precisely calculated awareness which is
called madness.
The Notebooks of Martha Graham, 'The Trysting
Tent' (1973)

4 **No artist is ahead of his time. He *is* his**
time; it is just that others are behind the
times.
Quoted in the *Observer* 8 July 1979

Philip L. Graham (1915–63)

US NEWSPAPER PUBLISHER

Known as a talented fixer, he took control of the Washington Post in 1946, turning it into a leading newspaper of the day.

1 News is the first rough draft of history.

Attributed. The aphorism has also been ascribed to *Washington Post* editor Ben C. Bradlee, but Bradlee himself, in an interview in *Vanity Fair* September 1991, credited it to Graham, formerly his boss at the *Post*.

Gloria Grahame (1924–81)

US SCREEN ACTRESS

Originally Gloria Hallward. A blonde leading lady, she found her niche in film noir playing morally ambiguous women. Her films include In a Lonely Place *(1950) and* The Bad and the Beautiful *(1952).*

1 I was born when you kissed me. I died when you left me. I lived a few weeks while you loved me.

Laurel Gray (Gloria Grahame), quoting the unfinished script of screenwriter Dixon Steele (Humphrey Bogart) at the end of *In a Lonely Place* (film, 1950, screenplay by Andrew Solt adapted from novel by Dorothy B. Hughes, directed by Nicholas Ray)

2 I've been rich and I've been poor. Believe me, rich is better.

Debby Marsh (Gloria Grahame), in *The Big Heat* (film, 1953, screenplay by Sidney Boehm from novel by William P. McGivern, directed by Fritz Lang). See also SOPHIE TUCKER 1.

3 We're all sisters under the mink.

Ibid.

Percy Grainger (1882–1961)

AUSTRALIAN-BORN US COMPOSER AND PIANIST

He settled in America in 1914 after collecting folk tunes in England and Europe. His orchestral works Shepherd's Hey *(1911) and* Molly on the Shore *(1914) contributed to a folk revival.*

1 Salvation Army Booth objected to the devil having all the good tunes. I object to jazz and vaudeville having all the best instruments.

Spoon River, Preface (1939). The quotation referred to is usually associated with the clergyman Rowland Hill (1744–1833), who 'did not see any reason why the devil should have all the good tunes'.

Antonio Gramsci (1891–1937)

ITALIAN POLITICAL THEORIST

Having established the Italian Communist Party in 1921, he became its leader in 1924, but was arrested when MUSSOLINI *banned the party in 1926. He spent the rest of his life in prison, where he wrote thirty notebooks published posthumously as* Letters from Prison *(1947).*

1 I would like you to understand completely, also emotionally, that I'm a political detainee and will be a political prisoner, that I have nothing now or in the future to be ashamed of in this situation. That, at bottom, I myself have in a certain sense asked for this detention and this sentence, because I've always refused to change my opinion, for which I would be willing to give my life and not just remain in prison. That therefore I can only be tranquil and content with myself.

Letter to his mother, 10 May 1928, publ. in *Gramsci: Letters from Prison* (1947, transl. 1993)

2 I'm a pessimist because of intelligence, but an optimist because of will.

Letter, 19 December 1929, publ. ibid.

3 If you think about it seriously, all the questions about the soul and the immortality of the soul and paradise and hell are at bottom only a way of seeing this very simple fact: that every action of ours is passed on to others according to its value, of good or evil, it passes from father to son, from one generation to the next, in a perpetual movement.

Letter to his mother, 15 June 1931, publ. ibid.

4 I turn and turn in my cell like a fly that doesn't know where to die.

Letter, 20 July 1931, publ. ibid.

Grandmaster Flash (b. 1958)

US RAP SINGER

Originally Joseph Saddler. A top DJ of the 1970s and one of the pioneers of hip-hop, he worked with the rap and break-dancing team, the Furious Five. His single 'Freedom' (1980) earned a gold disc.

1 It's like a jungle sometimes,
It makes me wonder
How I keep from going under.

'The Message' (song, written by Sylvia Robinson and Duke Bootee, 1982) on the album *Greatest Messages* (1984) by Grandmaster Flash and the Furious Five

Bernie Grant (1944–2000)

BRITISH POLITICIAN

Branded 'the high priest of race conflict' by Douglas Hurd, he was the first black council leader in Britain (Haringey, 1985–7), and was one of the first three black MPs in the House of Commons when elected Labour MP for Tottenham in 1987.

1 The police were to blame for what happened on Sunday night and what they got was a bloody good hiding.

Press statement outside Tottenham Town Hall, 8 October 1985, quoted in *The Times* 9 October 1985. Grant was speaking in the wake of the

Broadwater Farm riots in north London, during which PC Keith Blakelock was murdered.

Cary Grant (1904–86)

BRITISH-BORN US ACTOR

Originally Archibald Leach. For over three decades he was a debonair leading man ranging from light comedic roles as in Bringing up Baby *(1938) to parts in* HITCHCOCK *thrillers, including* Notorious *(1946) and* North by Northwest *(1959).*

1 Old Cary Grant fine. How you?

Attributed telegram, quoted in *Cary Grant* (1983) by R. Schickel. The words are supposed to be in response to a cable sent by a journalist to Grant's press agent, 'How old Cary Grant?'

Günter Grass (b. 1927)

GERMAN NOVELIST

Often cast in the role of the 'conscience of his generation', he caused controversy with his first novel The Tin Drum *(1959) for its depiction of the Nazis. He was speechwriter for Willy Brandt when Brandt was Mayor of West Berlin.*

1 Even bad books are books and therefore sacred.

Narrator (Oskar Matzerath), in *The Tin Drum*, bk 1, 'Rasputin and the Alphabet' (1959)

2 Art is uncompromising and life is full of compromises.

Quoted by ARTHUR MILLER, in *Paris Review* summer 1966

3 Melancholy has ceased to be an individual phenomenon, an exception. It has become the class privilege of the wage earner, a mass state of mind that finds its cause wherever life is governed by production quotas.

From the Diary of a Snail, 'On Stasis in Progress' (1972)

4 If work and leisure are soon to be subordinated to this one utopian principle – absolute busyness – then utopia and melancholy will come to coincide: an age without conflict will dawn, perpetually busy – and without consciousness.

Ibid.

5 We already have the statistics for the future: the growth percentages of pollution, overpopulation, desertification. The future is already in place.

Interview in the *New Statesman and Society* 22 June 1990

6 Art is so wonderfully irrational, exuberantly pointless, but necessary all the same. Pointless and yet necessary, that's hard for a puritan to understand.

Ibid.

7 Believing: it means believing in our own lies. And I can say that I am grateful that I got this lesson very early.

Omnibus, television broadcast on BBC1, 3 November 1992

Robert Graves (1895–1985)

BRITISH POET AND AUTHOR

Although his output included autobiography (Goodbye to All That, *1929), historical novels* (I, Claudius, *1934), studies of mythology* (The Greek Myths, *1955) and literary criticism, he regarded himself primarily as a poet, and was Professor of Poetry at Oxford (1961–6).*

1 *Children are dumb to say how hot the day is,*
How hot the scent is of the summer rose,
How dreadful the black wastes of evening sky,
How dreadful the tall soldiers drumming by.

'The Cool Web', publ. in *Poems* (1927)

2 *There's a cool web of language winds us in,*
Retreat from too much joy or too much fear.

Ibid.

3 Goodbye to All That.

Title of autobiography (1929)

4 *Down, wanton, down! Have you no shame*
That at the whisper of Love's name,
Or Beauty's, presto! up you raise
Your angry head and stand at gaze?

'Down, Wanton, Down!', publ. in *Poems 1930–1933* (1933)

5 *To evoke posterity*
Is to weep on your own grave,
Ventriloquizing for the unborn.

'To Evoke Posterity', publ. in *Collected Poems* (1938)

6 To be a poet is a condition rather than a profession.

'The Cost of Letters', reply to questionnaire in *Horizon* September 1946

7 The reason why the hairs stand on end, the eyes water, the throat is constricted, the skin crawls and a shiver runs down the spine when one writes or reads a true poem is that a true poem is necessarily an invocation of the White Goddess, or Muse, the Mother of All Living, the ancient power of fright and lust – the female spider or the queen bee whose embrace is death.

The White Goddess, ch. 1 (1948)

8 *Counting the beats,*
Counting the slow heart beats,
The bleeding to death of time in slow heart beats,
Wakeful they lie.

'Counting the Beats', publ. in *Poems and Satires* (1951)

9 *Why have such scores of lovely girls*
   Married impossible men?
   Simple sacrifice may be ruled out,
   And missionary endeavour, nine times out
      of ten.
   'A Slice of Wedding Cake', publ. in *Steps* (1958)

10 *Love, the sole Goddess fit for swearing by,*
   Concedes us graciously the little lie:
   The white lie, the half lie, the lie corrective
   Without which love's exchange might prove
      defective,
   Confirming hazardous relationships
   By kindly maquillage *of Truth's pale lips.*
   'Friday Night', publ. in *5 Pens in Hand* (1958)

11 *A difficult achievement for true lovers*
   Is to lie mute, without embrace or kiss,
   Without a rustle or a smothered sigh,
   Basking each in the other's glory.
   'The Starred Coverlet', publ. in *More Poems*
   (1961)

12 Nine-tenths of English poetic literature is
   the result either of vulgar careerism or of a
   poet trying to keep his hand in. Most poets
   are dead by their late twenties.
   Quoted in the *Observer* 11 November 1962

13 If there's no money in poetry, neither is
   there poetry in money.
   Speech at London School of Economics,
   6 December 1963, publ. in *Mammon and the
   Black Goddess*, 'Mammon' (1965)

14 *Perfect reliance on the impossible*
   By strict avoidance of all such conjecture
   As underlies the so-called possible:
   That is true love's adventure.
   'To put It Simply', publ. in *Poems 1968–70*
   (1970)

15 *Are not all centuries, like men,*
   Born hopeful too and gay,
   And good for seventy years, but then
   Hope slowly seeps away?
   'The Imminent Seventies', publ. ibid.

16 *Poets are guardians*
   Of a shadowy island
   With granges and forest
   Warmed by the Moon
   'The Title of Poet', publ. in *Poems 1970–1972*
   (1972)

Alasdair Gray (b. 1934)

SCOTTISH NOVELIST
*He writes picaresque narratives which deal with
contemporary Scotland, for example* Lanark
(1981), The Fall of Kelvin Walker *(1985) and* Poor
Things *(1992).*

1 Glasgow, the sort of industrial city where
   most people live nowadays but nobody
   imagines living.
   The Oracle, in *Lanark*, bk 3, ch. 11 (1981)

2 Everyone sees life through their job. To
   the doctor the world is a hospital, to the
   broker it is a stock exchange, to the
   lawyer a vast criminal court, to the soldier
   a barracks and area of manoeuvre, to the
   farmer soil and bad weather, to truck-
   drivers a road system, to dustmen a mid-
   den, to prostitutes a brothel, to mothers an
   inescapable nursery, to children a school,
   to film stars a looking-glass, to undertakers
   a morgue, and to myself a security installation powered by the sun and only crack-
   able by death.
   1982, Janine, ch. 4 (1984)

3 Outside babyhood hardly anyone feels
   healthy for long, but viewed in health and
   without prejudice the universe is an
   orchard of strange lovely bodies: fruit,
   stars and people freely grown for us by
   God (if we're religious) or by the universe
   itself, if we ain't.
   Dad, in *Something Leather*, ch. 11 (1990)

John Gray (b. 1951)

US PSYCHOTHERAPIST AND AUTHOR
He is best known for Men are from Mars,
Women are from Venus *(1992), which, like
his other books, discusses gender differences
and the promotion of understanding between the
sexes.*

1 Men mistakenly expect women to think,
   communicate, and react the way men do;
   women mistakenly expect men to feel, communicate and respond the way women do.
   We have forgotten that men and women
   are supposed to be different. As a result
   our relationships are filled with unnecessary friction and conflict. Clearly recognizing and respecting these differences
   dramatically reduces confusion when dealing with the opposite sex. When you
   remember that men are from Mars and
   women are from Venus, everything can be
   explained.
   Men Are from Mars, Women Are from Venus,
   ch. 1 (1992)

2 One of the big challenges for men is correctly to interpret and support a woman
   when she is talking about her feelings. The
   biggest challenge for women is correctly to
   interpret and support a man when he isn't
   talking.
   Ibid., ch. 5, 'When Martians Don't Talk'

Simon Gray (b. 1936)

BRITISH PLAYWRIGHT
*His wry and comedic plays which take as their mil-
ieu the worlds of academia and publishing include*
Wise Child *(1967),* Melon *(1987) and* Cell Mates
(1995). He has also written for television.

1 Everybody in Los Angeles lives miles away, not from anywhere, because there isn't actually an anywhere to live away from, but from each other.
   How's That for Telling 'Em, Fat Lady?, ch. 2 (1988)

2 Faith is . . . a matter of believing what's impossible to believe. Do you, um, see? Otherwise it's not faith. It's certainty.
   Ronnie, in *Hidden Laughter*, act 1, sc. 1 (1990)

3 People should worry about each other. Because worry is just love in its worst form. But it's still love.
   Louise, ibid., act 1, sc. 2

4 I'm fanatical about sport: there seems to me something almost religious about the fact that human beings can organise play, the spirit of play.
   Interview in the *Independent on Sunday* 19 February 1995

Hannah Green (b. 1932)

US AUTHOR
Originally Joanne Greenberg. She is mainly known for her autobiographical novel I Never Promised You a Rose Garden *(1964), the story of a fight against schizophrenia.*

1 I Never Promised You a Rose Garden.
   Title of novel (1964, filmed 1977). A song with this title written by Joe South was the only hit for country singer Lynn Anderson (1971).

Henry Green (1905–73)

BRITISH NOVELIST
Originally Henry Vincent Yorke. Alongside his work as an engineer, he wrote impressionistic novels that relied on dialogue rather than plot, for example Blindness *(1926),* Living *(1929) and* Loving *(1945).*

1 Prose is not to be read aloud but to oneself at night, and it is not quick as poetry, but rather a gathering web of insinuations which go further than names however shared can ever go. Prose should be a long intimacy between strangers with no direct appeal to what both may have known. It should slowly appeal to feelings unexpressed, it should in the end draw tears out of the stone.
   Pack My Bag: A Self Portrait (1940)

2 The very deaf, as I am, hear the most astounding things all round them, which have not, in fact, been said. This enlivens my replies until, through mishearing, a new level of communication is reached.
   Interview in *Writers at Work* (second series, ed. George Plimpton, 1963)

Jonathon Green (b. 1948)

BRITISH ANTHOLOGIST AND LEXICOGRAPHER
He wrote for Rolling Stone, IT *and* Oz *in the 1960s and '70s, and is the author of numerous dictionaries and anthologies on language topics, including the* Dictionary of Slang *(1998).*

1 Today, as those who were young then, or just becoming adults, are passing into middle age, the 60s seem the most inescapable of all those nostalgia-girt decades. Whether hymned by ageing hippies, still wreathed in rosy fantasies, or vilified by contemporary politicians, desperately hunting an easy scapegoat for over-complex ills, the image remains: something happened.
   Days in the Life, Introduction (1988)

2 Slang is the counter-language. A jackanapes lexicon of the dispossessed. The language of the rebel, the outlaw, the despised, the marginal, the young. Above all it is the language of the city.
   Dictionary of Slang, Introduction (1998)

3 Women? Let's get real: we called them chicks. What they did was 'chick work', which tended to be secretarial in its myriad forms. . . . Whatever their own agenda, girls were there for sex, joint-rolling and throwing together the all too mandatory slop.
   Sunday Times 7 November 1999. Referring to perceptions of women in the 1960s.

Peter Greenaway (b. 1942)

BRITISH FILM-MAKER
His films are characterized by an intellectual obliqueness that has frequently alienated critics. His first major success, The Draughtsman's Contract *(1982) was followed by, among others,* A Zed and Two Noughts *(1985) and* The Pillow-Book *(1996).*

1 The Cook, the Thief, His Wife and Her Lover
   Title of film (written and directed by Peter Greenaway, 1989)

2 We don't need books to make films. It's the last thing we want – it turns cinema into the bastard art of illustration.
   Quoted in the *Independent on Sunday* 10 July 1994

Graham Greene (1904–91)

BRITISH AUTHOR
He is best known for his 'Catholic novels' such as Brighton Rock *(1938, filmed 1947) and* The Heart of the Matter *(1948), which deal with issues of faith and failure.* EVELYN WAUGH *advised him not to give up writing about God as it would be like 'P. G. Wodehouse dropping Jeeves halfway*

through the Wooster series'. See also T. S.
ELIOT 36.

1 There is always one moment in childhood
when the door opens and lets the future in.
The Power and the Glory, pt 1, ch. 1 (1940)

2 Behind the complicated details of the
world stand the simplicities: God is good,
the grown-up man or woman knows the
answer to every question, there is such a
thing as truth, and justice is as measured
and faultless as a clock. Our heroes are
simple: they are brave, they tell the truth,
they are good swordsmen and they are
never in the long run really defeated. That
is why no later books satisfy us like those
which were read to us in childhood – for
those promised a world of great simplicity
of which we knew the rules, but the later
books are complicated and contradictory
with experience; they are formed out of
our own disappointing memories.
The Ministry of Fear, bk 1, ch. 7, sect. 1 (1943)

3 Surely we choose our death as much as we
choose our job. It grows out of our acts
and our evasions, out of our fears and out
of our moments of courage.
'The Lost Childhood' (1947), repr. in *The Lost
Childhood and Other Essays* (1951)

4 A child, after all, knows most of the game –
it is only an attitude to it that he lacks.
Ibid.

5 Against the beautiful and the clever and
the successful, one can wage a pitiless war,
but not against the unattractive: then the
millstone weighs on the breast.
The Heart of the Matter, bk 1, pt 1, ch. 2, sect. 2
(1948)

6 People talk about the courage of condemned men walking to the place of
execution: sometimes it needs as much
courage to walk with any kind of bearing
towards another person's habitual misery.
Ibid., bk 1, pt 1, ch. 2, sect. 3

7 The truth has never been of any real value
to any human being – it is a symbol for
mathematicians and philosophers to pursue. In human relations kindness and lies
are worth a thousand truths.
Scobie, ibid., bk 1, pt 1, ch. 2, sect. 4

8 Despair is the price one pays for setting
oneself an impossible aim. It is, one is told,
the unforgivable sin, but it is a sin the corrupt or evil man never practises. He always
has hope. He never reaches the freezing-
point of knowing absolute failure.
Ibid., bk 1, pt 1, ch. 2, sect. 4

9 He felt the loyalty we feel to unhappiness –
the sense that that is where we really
belong.
Of Harris, ibid., bk 2, pt 2, ch. 1, sect. 1

10 His hilarity was like a scream from a
crevasse.
Of Major Scobie, ibid., bk 3, pt 1, ch. 1, sect. 1

11 Death's at the bottom of everything,
Martins. Leave death to the professionals.
Major Calloway (Trevor Howard), in *The Third
Man* (film, 1950, screenplay by Graham Greene,
directed by Carol Reed). *The Third Man* was
first written as a preliminary draft for the film's
screenplay, and later published as a novella (in
which these lines do not appear).

12 The world doesn't make any heroes
anymore.
Major Calloway, ibid.

13 Innocence always calls mutely for protection when we would be so much wiser to
guard ourselves against it: innocence is like
a dumb leper who has lost his bell, wandering the world, meaning no harm.
The Quiet American, pt 1, ch. 3, sect. 3 (1955).
Later in the book, the narrator describes Pyle –
the idealistic 'quiet American' of the title – in
similar terms: 'What's the good? He'll always be
innocent, you can't blame the innocent, they are
always guiltless. All you can do is control them
or eliminate them. Innocence is a kind of
insanity.' (pt. 3, ch. 2, sect. 1)

14 Those who marry God can become domesticated too – it's just as hum-drum a marriage as all the others. The word 'Love'
means a formal touch of the lips as in the
ceremony of the Mass, and 'Ave Maria'
like 'dearest' is a phrase to open a letter.
A Burnt-Out Case, pt 1, ch. 1, sect. 2 (1961)

15 Cynicism is cheap – you can buy it at any
Monoprix store – it's built into all poor-
quality goods.
The Comedians, pt 1, ch. 1, sect. 3 (1966)

16 However great a man's fear of life, suicide
remains the courageous act, the clear-
headed act of a mathematician. The suicide
has judged by the laws of chance – so
many odds against one that to live will be
more miserable than to die. His sense of
mathematics is greater than his sense of
survival.
Dr Magiot, ibid., ch. 4, sect. 1

17 We mustn't complain too much of being
comedians – it's an honourable profession.
If only we could be good ones the world
might gain at least a sense of style. We
have failed – that's all. We are bad comedians, we aren't bad men.
The ambassador, ibid., ch. 5, sect. 2

18 If you have abandoned one faith, do not
abandon all faith. There is always an
alternative to the faith we lose. Or is it
the same faith under another mask?
Dr Magiot, ibid., pt 3, ch. 4, sect. 4

19 Communism, my friend, is more than

Marxism, just as Catholicism . . . is more than the Roman Curia. There is a *mystique* as well as a *politique*. . . . Catholics and Communists have committed great crimes, but at least they have not stood aside, like an established society, and been indifferent. I would rather have blood on my hands than water like Pilate.

Dr Magiot, ibid., pt 3, ch. 4, sect. 4

20 God . . . created a number of possibilities in case some of his prototypes failed – that is the meaning of evolution.

Mr Visconti, in *Travels with My Aunt*, pt 2, ch. 7 (1969)

21 Morality comes with the sad wisdom of age, when the sense of curiosity has withered.

A Sort of Life, ch. 7, sect. 1 (1971)

22 A petty reason perhaps why novelists more and more try to keep a distance from journalists is that novelists are trying to write the truth and journalists are trying to write fiction.

Letter to 'Atticus' (Stephen Pile), in the *Sunday Times* 18 January 1981, repr. in *Yours, Etc: Letters to the Press, 1945–1989* (1989)

23 Success is more dangerous than failure, the ripples break over a wider coastline.

Quoted in the *Independent* 4 April 1991. Recalled at Greene's death by critic Miriam Allot.

Germaine Greer (b. 1939)

AUSTRALIAN FEMINIST AUTHOR AND CRITIC
Her book The Female Eunuch *(1970) was a seminal influence on a generation of women. Subsequent works include* Sex and Destiny *(1984) and* The Whole Woman *(1999). She is Professor of English and Comparative Studies at Warwick University.*

1 If you think you are emancipated, you might consider the idea of tasting your menstrual blood – if it makes you sick, you've a long way to go, baby.

The Female Eunuch, 'The Wicked Womb' (1970)

2 Freud is the father of psychoanalysis. It had no mother.

Ibid., 'The Psychological Sell'

3 Even crushed against his brother in the Tube the average Englishman pretends desperately that he is alone.

Ibid., 'Womanpower'

4 Every time a woman makes herself laugh at her husband's often-told jokes she betrays him. The man who looks at his woman and says 'What would I do without you?' is already destroyed.

Ibid., 'Egotism'

5 Love, love, love – all the wretched cant of it, masking egotism, lust, masochism, fantasy under a mythology of sentimental postures, a welter of self-induced miseries and joys, blinding and masking the essential personalities in the frozen gestures of courtship, in the kissing and the dating and the desire, the compliments and the quarrels which vivify its barrenness.

Ibid., 'Obsession'

6 Women have very little idea of how much men hate them.

Ibid., 'Loathing and Disgust'

7 Women's liberation, if it abolishes the patriarchal family, will abolish a necessary substructure of the authoritarian state, and once that withers away Marx will have come true willy-nilly, so let's get on with it.

Ibid., 'Revolution'

8 The surest guide to the correctness of the path that women take is *joy in the struggle*. Revolution is the festival of the oppressed.

Ibid.

9 The tragedy of machismo is that a man is never quite man enough.

'My Mailer Problem', first publ. in *Esquire* September 1971, repr. in *The Madwoman's Underclothes* (1986)

10 Where else in the world is a generous man defined as one who would give you his arsehole and shit through his ribs?

Of Australia, in 'The New Maharajahs', first publ. in the *Sunday Times* 16 January 1972, repr. ibid.

11 The compelled mother loves her child as the caged bird sings. The song does not justify the cage nor the love the enforcement.

'Abortion', first publ. in the *Sunday Times* 21 May 1972, repr. ibid.

12 We in the West do not refrain from childbirth because we are concerned about the population explosion or because we feel we cannot afford children, but because we do not like children.

Sex and Destiny, ch. 1 (1984)

13 The most threatened group in human societies as in animal societies is the unmated male: the unmated male is more likely to wind up in prison or in an asylum or dead than his mated counterpart. He is less likely to be promoted at work and he is considered a poor credit risk.

Ibid., ch. 2

14 The only perfect love to be found on earth is not sexual love, which is riddled with hostility and insecurity, but the wordless commitment of families, which takes as its model mother-love.

The Madwoman's Underclothes, Introduction (1986). Greer goes on, 'This is not to say that fathers have no place, for father-love, with its driving for self-improvement and discipline, is also essential to survival, but that uncorrected father-love, father-love as it were practised by both parents, is a way to annihilation.'

15 Human beings have an inalienable right to invent themselves; when that right is pre-empted it is called brain-washing.

The Times 1 February 1986

16 English culture is basically homosexual in the sense that the men only really care about other men.

Daily Mail 18 April 1988

17 Libraries are reservoirs of strength, grace and wit, reminders of order, calm and continuity, lakes of mental energy, neither warm nor cold, light nor dark. The pleasure they give is steady, unorgastic, reliable, deep and long-lasting. In any library in the world, I am at home, unselfconscious, still and absorbed.

Daddy, We Hardly Knew You, 'Still in Melbourne, January 1987' (1989)

18 Orgasmism is a Western neurosis, but I say once you've had one, you've had them all.

Interview in *A Little Light Friction*, 'Germaine Greer' (1989) by Val Hennessy

19 An enema under the influence of Ecstasy would probably feel much like this.

Independent on Sunday 3 June 1990. Referring to D. H. LAWRENCE's description of the female orgasm in *Lady Chatterley's Lover*.

20 The misery of the middle-aged woman is a grey and hopeless thing, born of having nothing to live for, of disappointment and resentment at having been gypped by consumer society, and surviving merely to be the butt of its unthinking scorn.

The Change: Women, Ageing and the Menopause, Introduction (1991)

21 The climacteric marks the end of apologizing. The chrysalis of conditioning has once for all to break and the female woman finally to emerge.

Ibid., ch. 17

Hubert Gregg (b. 1914)

BRITISH SONGWRITER AND ENTERTAINER
A versatile performer, he also wrote plays and composed the music and lyrics for numerous revues, including Strike a Note *(1943).*

1 *Maybe it's because I'm a Londoner*
That I love London so,
Maybe it's because I'm a Londoner –
That I think of her – wherever I go.
I get a funny feeling inside of me –
Just walking up and down, –

Maybe it's because I'm a Londoner
That I love London Town.
'Maybe It's Because I'm a Londoner' (song, 1947). The song was recorded by BILLY COTTON and his band in 1949.

Dick Gregory (b. 1932)

US COMEDIAN AND CIVIL RIGHTS ACTIVIST
He was the first black comedian to achieve success among white audiences, using satire to score his points. In the 1960s he became involved with the civil rights movement and Black Power.

1 Civil Rights: What black folks are given in the US on the installment plan, as in civil-rights bills. Not to be confused with *human rights*, which are the dignity, stature, humanity, respect, and freedom belonging to all people by right of their birth.

Dick Gregory's Political Primer (1972)

Joyce Grenfell (1910–79)

BRITISH ENTERTAINER AND AUTHOR
The daughter of one of the American Langhorne sisters (one of whom was NANCY ASTOR*), she appeared in revue until the early 1950s and subsequently presented her own one-woman shows, most famously* Joyce Grenfell Requests the Pleasure *(from 1954).*

1 George – don't do that.
Catch-phrase in various sketches in the 1950s, and the title of the collection, *George – Don't Do That* (1977)

2 *Stately as a galleon, I sail across the floor,*
Doing the military two-step, as in the days
of yore.
'Stately as a Galleon' (song), publ. in *Stately as a Galleon* (1978)

3 Progress everywhere today does seem to come so *very* heavily disguised as Chaos.
'English Lit.', publ. ibid.

Clifford Grey (1887–1941)

BRITISH SONGWRITER
Originally Percival Davis. A prolific lyricist and librettist for the London and New York stages, he provided songs for a string of shows including The Bing Boys are Here *(1916) and* Mr Cinders *(1929).*

1 *If you were the only girl in the world*
And I were the only boy.
'If You Were the Only Girl in the World' (song, with music by Nat Ayer) in the musical show *The Bing Boys are Here* (1916). The song was first performed by George Robey and Violet Lorraine, introduced in America by Rudy Vallee in the film *The Vagabond Lover* (1929), and sung by Gordon McCrae and Doris Day in the film *By the Light of the Silvery Moon* (1953).

Joel Grey (b. 1932)

US SINGER AND ACTOR

Originally Joe Katz. He created the role of the MC in both stage and screen versions of Cabaret *(1966 and 1972). He also starred in* George M!, *a musical biography of* GEORGE M. COHAN. *See also* LIZA MINNELLI 1.

1 *Meine Damen und Herren, Mesdames et Messieurs,*
Ladies und Gentlemen – comment ça va?
Do you feel good? . . . I am your host . . .
Wilkommen! Bienvenue! Welcome!
Im Cabaret! Au Cabaret! To Cabaret!
'Wilkommen' (song, written by Fred Ebb and John Kander), sung by the Master of Ceremonies (Joel Grey) in *Cabaret* (musical play by Joe Masterhoff, 1966, filmed 1972)

Lord Grey (1862–1933)

BRITISH STATESMAN

Sir Edward Grey, First Viscount of Falloden. As Foreign Secretary (1905–16), he was responsible for the Russian entente of 1907 and sided with France in the Agadir incident in 1911.

1 The lamps are going out all over Europe; we shall not see them lit again in our lifetime.
Said in London, 3 August 1914, quoted in *Twenty-Five Years*, vol. 2, ch. 18 (1925). The words were spoken on the eve of Britain's declaration of war against Germany.

D. W. Griffith (1874–1948)

US FILM-MAKER

David Wark Griffith. He originated many of the conventions of present-day cinematic technique. His masterpiece, The Birth of a Nation *(1915), was described by* WOODROW WILSON *as 'like writing history with lightning'.*

1 We do not fear censorship for we have no wish to offend with improprieties or obscenities, but we do demand, as a right, the liberty to show the dark side of wrong, that we may illuminate the bright side of virtue – the same liberty that is conceded to the art of the written word, that art to which we owe the Bible and the works of Shakespeare.
'A Plea for the Art of the Motion Picture', released as Prologue to *The Birth of a Nation* (film, 1915)

Melanie Griffith (b. 1957)

US ACTRESS

Daughter of the actress Tippi Hedren, she began appearing in films in the mid-1970s. Her greatest success came in such films as Working Girl *(1988),* Pacific Heights *(1990) and* Lolita *(1997).*

1 I have a head for business and a bod for sin. Is there anything wrong with that?
Tess McGill (Melanie Griffith), in *Working Girl* (film, 1988, screenplay by Kevin Wade, directed by Mike Nichols)

Mervyn Griffith-Jones (1909–79)

BRITISH LAWYER

He was one of the British Prosecuting Counsel at the Nuremberg trials (1945–6) and a member of the standing committee on Criminal Law Revision (1958).

1 Would you approve of your young sons, young daughters – because girls can read as well as boys – reading this book? Is it a book that you would have lying around in your own house? Is it a book that you would even wish your wife or your servants to read?
Opening address to jury during the prosecution of Penguin Books Ltd., 20 October 1961, publ. in *The Trial of Lady Chatterley* (ed. C. H. Rolph, 1961). Griffith-Jones was senior prosecuting counsel in the case brought against Penguin for publishing an unexpurgated edition of D. H. Lawrence's *Lady Chatterley's Lover*. Rolph noted the 'visible – and risible – effect on the jury' of these remarks, and surmised that this 'may well have been the first nail in the prosecution's coffin'.

John Grigg (1924–2001)

BRITISH AUTHOR AND JOURNALIST

Lord Altrincham (renounced title in 1963). He was a columnist for the Guardian *and* The Times, *and wrote on twentieth-century social history.*

1 Autobiography is now as common as adultery and hardly less reprehensible.
Sunday Times 28 February 1962

Georg Groddeck (1866–1934)

GERMAN PSYCHOANALYST

Regarded as one of the founding fathers of psychosomatic medicine, he opened the sanatorium Marienhöhe in 1900 and ran it until his death. His books were burnt by the Nazis.

1 One must not forget that recovery is brought about not by the physician, but by the sick man himself. He heals himself, by his own power, exactly as he walks by means of his own power, or eats, or thinks, breathes or sleeps.
The Book of the It, 'Letter 32' (1923)

Matt Groening (b. 1954)

US CARTOONIST

In 1987 he created The Simpsons *as a filler on* The Tracy Ullman Show *for the Fox TV network. A thirteen-episode series of half-hour slots premiered in January 1990 and became one of the hottest marketing properties of the decade.*

1 **Eat my shorts!**
Bart Simpson, in *The Simpsons* (TV cartoon, from 1987)

2 **D'oh!**
Homer Simpson's habitual expression of exasperation, ibid.

Andrei Gromyko (1909–89)

SOVIET STATESMAN AND DIPLOMAT

He was Soviet ambassador to the US from 1943 and to the UN 1946–9, during which time he exercised his right of veto no fewer than twenty-five times. He was later Foreign Minister 1957–85 and President of the USSR 1985–8.

1 Greece is a sort of American vassal; the Netherlands is the country of American bases that grow like tulip bulbs; Cuba is the main sugar plantation of the American monopolies; Turkey is prepared to kowtow before any United States pro-consul and Canada is the boring second fiddle in the American symphony.
New York Herald Tribune 30 June 1953

Walter Gropius (1883–1969)

GERMAN ARCHITECT

An early pioneer of the International Style, he was a co-founder and Director (1919–28) of the Bauhaus School of Design, and Professor of Architecture at Harvard (1938–52). By using modern techniques and materials, he aimed to bridge 'the gap between the rigid mentality of the businessman and technologist and the imagination of the creative artist'.

1 Architects, painters, and sculptors must recognize anew and learn to grasp the composite character of a building both as an entity and in its separate parts. Only then will their work be imbued with the architectonic spirit which it has lost as 'salon art' ... Together let us desire, conceive, and create the new structure of the future, which will embrace architecture and sculpture and painting in one unity and which will one day rise toward heaven from the hands of a million workers like the crystal symbol of a new faith.
'The Bauhaus Proclamation April 1919', repr. in *The Bauhaus*, ch. 2 (1962) by Hans Wingler

George Grosz (1893–1959)

GERMAN-BORN US ARTIST

A member of the Berlin Dadaists after the First World War, he produced vitriolic satirical drawings criticizing German social mores, government, militarism and Nazism, work that has been described as 'the most definitive catalogue of man's depravity in all history'. In 1938 he became a naturalized US citizen.

1 The bourgeoisie and the petty bourgeoisie have armed themselves against the rising proletariat with, among other things, 'culture'. It's an old ploy of the bourgeoisie. They keep a standing 'art' to defend their collapsing culture.
'The Art Scab' (written with John Heartfield), first publ. in *Der Gegner*, vol. 1, nos. 10–12, 1920, repr. in *Art is in Danger* (transl. 1987)

2 The cult of individuality and personality, which promotes painters and poets only to promote itself, is really a business. The greater the 'genius' of the personage, the greater the profit.
'Instead of a Biography', first publ. in *Der Gegner*, vol. 2., no. 3, 1920, repr. ibid.

John Guare (b. 1938)

US PLAYWRIGHT

Describing himself in one of his own plays as 'the world's oldest living promising young playwright', he wrote black comedies about modern America, such as The House of Blue Leaves *(1972) and* Bosoms of Neglect *(1979).*

1 Avoiding humiliation is the core of tragedy and comedy.
Independent 17 October 1988

2 We live in a world where amnesia is the most wished-for state. When did history become a bad word?
International Herald Tribune 13 June 1990

3 Show business offers more solid promises than Catholicism
Independent 25 April 1992

Bob Guccione (b. 1930)

US PUBLISHER

Chiefly identified with the magazine Penthouse *which he founded in 1965, he is the publisher of a range of magazines including* Omni *and the* Saturday Review.

1 You have to penetrate a woman's defenses. Getting into her head is a prerequisite to getting into her body.
Interview in *Speaking Frankly* (1978) by Wendy Leigh

2 If I were asked for a one line answer to the question 'What makes a woman good in bed?' I would say, 'A man who is good in bed.'
Ibid.

Philip Guedalla (1889–1944)

BRITISH AUTHOR

A writer with a taste for the epigram, he believed that historical works should be entertaining as well as conscientious. His books include Palmerston *(1926),* The Hundred Days *(1934) and* The Hundred Years *(1936).*

1 History repeats itself. Historians repeat each other.
Supers and Supermen, 'Some Historians' (1920)

2 The work of Henry James has always seemed divisible by a simple dynastic arrangement into three reigns: James I, James II, and the Old Pretender.
Ibid., 'Some Critics'

3 Any stigma, as the old saying is, will serve to beat a dogma.
Masters and Men, 'Ministers of State' (1923)

4 Biography is a very definite region bounded on the north by history, on the south by fiction, on the east by obituary, and on the west by tedium.
Quoted in the *Observer* 3 March 1929

'Che' Guevara (1928–67)

ARGENTINIAN REVOLUTIONARY LEADER
Ernesto Guevara de la Serna. The most iconized figure of the twentieth century, he was second in command to FIDEL CASTRO *during the Cuban revolution of 1959, subsequently holding government posts under him. He was captured and executed while campaigning in Bolivia.*

1 When asked whether or not we are Marxists, our position is the same as that of a physicist or a biologist who is asked if he is a 'Newtonian', or if he is a 'Pasteurian'.
'We Are Practical Revolutionaries', publ. in *Verde Olivo* 8 October 1960, repr. in *Venceremos! The Speeches and Writings of Ernesto Che Guevara* (ed. John Gerassi, 1968)

2 Many will call me an adventurer, and I am, but of a different kind – one who risks his skin in order to prove his convictions.
Letter, 1965, publ. ibid. From his last letter to his parents before leaving Cuba to set up guerrilla forces in Bolivia.

3 Let me say, with the risk of appearing ridiculous, that the true revolutionary is guided by strong feelings of love. It is impossible to think of an authentic revolutionary without this quality.
'Socialism and Man in Cuba', open letter to the editor of a Uruguayan newspaper *La Marcha*, 1967, publ. in *Che Guevara on Revolution* (ed. Jay Mallin, 1969)

Hervé Guibert (1955–91)

FRENCH AUTHOR AND PHOTOGRAPHER
A photo critic for Le Monde *and editor and photographer for* L'Autre Journal, *he also wrote novels, for example* Les Aveugles *(1985). He died from AIDS.*

1 AIDS was . . . an illness in stages, a very long flight of steps that led assuredly to death, but whose every step represented a unique apprenticeship. It was a disease that gave death time to live and its victims time to die, time to discover time, and in the end to discover life.
To the Friend Who Did Not Save My Life, ch. 61 (1991)

Texas Guinan (1884–1933)

US ACTRESS
Originally Mary Louise Cecilia Guinan. With the catch-phrase 'Hello, sucker!' she was a celebrated nightclub hostess of speakeasies in the 1920s, and as such the subject of repeated raids by Prohibition agents.

1 Fifty million Frenchmen can't be wrong.
Catch-phrase in the 1920s. This was already a popular saying among US soldiers during the First World War, and possibly dates from earlier. It was the title of a song recorded by SOPHIE TUCKER in 1927, of COLE PORTER's first Broadway hit (1929), and of a 1931 film.

Nubar Gulbenkian (1896–1972)

BRITISH OIL TYCOON AND SOCIALITE
Son of Calouste Gulbenkian, who established the Gulbenkian Foundation, he worked for his father and was commercial attaché to the Iranian Embassy (1926–51 and 1956–65).

1 The best number for a dinner party is two – myself and a dam' good head waiter.
Daily Telegraph 14 January 1965

Thom Gunn (b. 1929)

BRITISH POET
Initially regarded as a Movement poet, he developed a freer style after his move to California in 1954. He has written on his homosexuality in The Passages of Joy *(1982) and on the AIDS epidemic in* The Man with Night Sweats *(1992).*

1 *I prod, you react. Thus to and fro*
We turn, to see ourselves perform the same
Comical acts inside the tragic game.
'Carnal Knowledge', publ. in *Fighting Terms* (1954)

2 *No plausible nostalgia, no brown shame,*
I had when treating with my enemies.
And always when a living impulse came
I acted, and my action made me wise.
And I regretted nothing.
'Incident on a Journey', publ. ibid.

3 *On motorcycles, up the road, they come:*
Small, black, as flies hanging in heat, the
Boys,
Until the distance throws them forth, their
hum
Bulges to thunder held by calf and thigh.
In goggles, donned impersonality,
In gleaming jackets trophied with the dust,
They strap in doubt – by hiding it, robust –
And almost hear a meaning in their noise.
'On the Move', publ. in *The Sense of Movement* (1957)

4 *Distorting hackneyed words in hackneyed*
  *   songs*
He turns revolt into a style, prolongs
The impulse to a habit of the time.
'Elvis Presley', publ. ibid. The poem gave
GEORGE MELLY the title for his study of the pop
arts in Britain, *Revolt into Style* (1970).

5 *My thoughts are crowded with death*
and it draws so oddly on the sexual
that I am confused
confused to be attracted
by, in effect, my own annihilation.
'In Time of Plague', publ. in *The Man with Night
Sweats* (1992)

John Gunther (1901–70)
US JOURNALIST AND AUTHOR
*He became known for his series of analyses of coun-
tries, beginning with the bestselling* Inside Europe
*(1936), which combined first-hand insights with
documentary material.*

1 **Ours is the only country deliberately
founded on a good idea.**
Inside USA, Foreword (1947)

George Gurdjieff (c. 1877–1949)
GREEK-ARMENIAN RELIGIOUS TEACHER AND
MYSTIC
*Born George S. Georgiades. He founded the first of
his Institutes for the Harmonious Development of
Man in Moscow (1912) where he propounded a
system of raising consciousness called the Fourth
Way. His ideas were transmitted by his disciple
Ouspensky.*

1 **A man can only attain knowledge with the
help of those who possess it. This must be
understood from the very beginning.** *One
must learn from him who knows.*
Quoted in *In Search of the Miraculous*, ch. 2
(1949) by P. D. Ouspensky

2 **A considerable percentage of the people we
meet on the street are people who are
empty inside, that is, they are actually
already dead. It is fortunate for us that we
do not see and do not know it. If we knew
what a number of people are actually dead
and what a number of these dead people
govern our lives, we should go mad with
horror.**
Quoted ibid., ch. 8

3 **A man may be born, but in order to be
born he must first die, and in order to die
he must first awake.**
Quoted ibid., ch. 11. Gurdjieff explained: 'If a
man dies without having been awakened he cannot be born. If a man is born without having
died he may become an "immortal thing". Thus
the fact that he has not "died" prevents a man
from being "born"; the fact of his not having
awakened prevents him from "dying"; and

should he be born without having died he is prevented from "being".'

4 **A man will renounce any pleasures you
like but he will not give up his suffering.**
Quoted ibid., ch. 13

5 **Every ceremony or rite has a value if it is
performed without alteration. A ceremony
is a book in which a great deal is written.
Anyone who understands can read it. One
rite often contains more than a hundred
books.**
Quoted ibid., ch. 15

6 **A 'sin' is something which is not necessary.**
Quoted ibid., ch. 17

Ivor Gurney (1890–1937)
BRITISH POET AND COMPOSER
*After being gassed in the First World War, he pub-
lished two volumes of poetry from hospital:* Severn
and Somme *(1917) and* War's Embers *(1919).
From 1922 he was in a mental hospital. His poems
and some 300 songs dealt largely with his native
Gloucestershire.*

1 *There are strange hells within the minds
  war made*
*Not so often, not so humiliatingly afraid
As one would have expected – the racket
  and fear guns made.*
'Strange Hells' (1919–22), publ. in *Collected
Poems* (1982)

2 *Fierce indignation is best understood by
  those
Who have time or no fear, or a hope in its
  real good.
One loses it with a filed soul or in sentimental mood.*
'Sonnet – September 1922', publ. ibid.

3 *And more than he,
I paid the prices of life
Standing where Rome immortal heard Octo-
  ber's strife,
A war poet whose right of honour cuts false-
  hood like a knife.*
'Poem for End' (1922–5), publ. ibid.

4 *Only, who thought of England as two thousand years
Must keep of today's life the proper anger
  and fears:
England that was paid for by building and
  ploughing and tears.*
Ibid.

Arlo Guthrie (b. 1947)
US SINGER AND SONGWRITER
Son of WOODY GUTHRIE, *he became known for
his song 'Alice's Restaurant' (1967), from which a
film was made (1969). He appeared at festivals
and marches throughout the 1960s and '70s, and
later opened the Guthrie Center in Housatonic,
Massachusetts.*

1 **You can get anything you want at Alice's Restaurant.**

'Alice's Restaurant Massacree' (song), on the album *Alice's Restaurant* (1967)

2 *Coming into Los Angeles, bringing in a couple of keys,*
Don't touch my bags, if you please, Mister Customs Man.

'Coming into Los Angeles' (song) on the album *Running Down the Road* (1969)

Woody Guthrie (1912–67)

US SINGER AND SONGWRITER

Woodrow Wilson Guthrie. He travelled the road during the Depression, gathering many of the 'Dust Bowl ballads' that he would later perform on radio. He composed more than a thousand songs, often directed against social injustice and poverty. His autobiography, Bound For Glory *(1943), was filmed in 1976.*

1 **This machine kills fascists.**

Written on his guitar, 1940s

2 *This land is your land, this land is my land,*
From California to the New York Island.
From the redwood forest to the Gulf Stream waters
This land was made for you and me.

'This Land Is Your Land' (song, 1956). The song is said to have been written in response to the patriotic hymn, 'God Bless America' (see IRVING BERLIN 1). In *Tarantula* (1970), BOB DYLAN wrote: 'This land is your land and this land is my land – sure, but the world is run by those that never listen to music anyway.'

J. S. Habgood (b. 1927)

BRITISH ECCLESIASTIC

As Archbishop of York 1983–95, he was unashamedly liberal in his stance. His published works include Church and Nation in a Secular Age *(1983).*

1 **Movements born in hatred very quickly take on the characteristics of the thing they oppose.**

Referring to extreme feminists, quoted in the *Observer* 4 May 1986

2 **All knowledge is ambiguous.**

Observer 14 April 1991

Jean Hagen (1924–77)

US ACTRESS

Originally Jean Verhagen. She was known for her comedy roles in the films Adam's Rib *(1949) and* Singin' in the Rain *(1952).*

1 **If we bring a little joy into your humdrum lives, it makes us feel our work ain't been in vain for nothin'.**

Lina Lamont (Jean Hagen), in *Singin' in the Rain* (film musical, 1952, screenplay by BETTY COMDEN and ADOLPH GREEN, directed by Gene Kelly and Stanley Donen)

2 **Talent is an amalgam of high sensitivity; easy vulnerability; high sensory equipment (seeing, hearing, touching, smelling, tasting – *intensely*); a vivid imagination as well as a grip on reality; the desire to communicate one's own experience and sensations, to make one's self heard and seen.**

Respect for Acting, pt 1, ch. 1 (1973)

Merle Haggard (b. 1937)

US COUNTRY MUSICIAN

After his release from San Quentin prison, he topped the country charts twenty-three times, with songs mostly on hard drinking, hard living and blue-collar themes.

1 *I'm proud to be an Okie from Muskogee A place where even squares can have a ball.*

'Okie from Muskogee' (song, 1969, written by Merle Haggard and PHIL OCHS). Though a tongue-in-cheek homage to provincial American values, this song and its follow-up 'The Fighting Side of Me' (1970) won Haggard a new right-wing audience, and a reputation for being President NIXON's favourite country singer.

William Hague (b. 1961)

BRITISH POLITICIAN

Already known for his address to the Conservative Party Conference at the age of sixteen, he became a Conservative MP in 1989 and was leader of the opposition 1997–2001.

1 **Not just sleepy villages, polite manners, friendly vicars, and the novels of Scott and Austen . . . but also the ambitious, the**

bold, the brassy, the vigorous, the exciting, the leading world nation that we are and can be.

Of 'the British way', in speech to Centre for Policy Studies, quoted in the *Daily Telegraph* 19 January 1999

2 If all we had needed to govern the country was someone who repeated everything we'd said before, we could have bought a parrot.

Speech at Conservative Party Conference in Blackpool, 7 October 1999, quoted in the *Guardian* 8 October 1999. Referring to Labour prime minister TONY BLAIR.

Lord Hailsham (1907–2001)

BRITISH POLITICIAN

Quintin Hogg, Viscount Hailsham of St Marylebone. Following his father into parliament in 1938, he was Chairman of the Conservative Party 1957–9 and served two terms as Lord Chancellor (1970–74 and 1979–87). Judge Pickles called him a 'quixotic dictator'. See also REGINALD PAGET 1.

1 Being Conservative is only another way of being British.

Remark in 1967, quoted by John Barnes in 'Ideology and Factions', publ. in *Conservative Century*, pt 2 (ed. Anthony Seldon and Stuart Ball, 1994)

Peter Hain (b. 1950)

BRITISH POLITICAL ACTIVIST AND POLITICIAN

His family fled to Britain from South Africa in 1966. He campaigned against apartheid as Leader of the Young Liberals, was elected Labour MP for Neath in 1991 and in 2002 became Secretary of State for Wales.

1 A sporting system is the by-product of society and its political system, and it is just boyhood dreaming to suppose you can ever take politics out of sport.

Observer 2 May 1971. Hain had targeted sports events as a means of raising media coverage in the Young Liberals' anti-apartheid protests.

J. B. S. Haldane (1892–1964)

BRITISH-BORN INDIAN SCIENTIST

John Burdon Sanderson Haldane. He specialized in population genetics as related to evolution theory at University College, London (1937–57), and at Orissa, India, where he emigrated in 1957. His books Possible Worlds *(1927) and* Science in Everyday Life *(1939) helped to popularize general scientific issues.*

1 Until politics are a branch of science we shall do well to regard political and social reforms as experiments rather than short-cuts to the millennium.

Possible Worlds and Other Essays, 'Science and Politics' (1927)

2 While I do not suggest that humanity will ever be able to dispense with its martyrs, I cannot avoid the suspicion that with a little more thought and a little less belief their number may be substantially reduced.

Ibid., 'The Duty of Doubt'

3 The wise man regulates his conduct by the theories both of religion and science. But he regards these theories not as statements of ultimate fact but as art-forms.

Ibid., 'Science and Theology as Art-Forms'. Closing words of essay.

4 My own suspicion is that the Universe is not only queerer than we suppose, but queerer than we *can* suppose.

Ibid., 'Possible Worlds'

5 In fact, words are well adapted for description and the arousing of emotion, but for many kinds of precise thought other symbols are much better.

The Inequality of Man, 'God-Makers' (1932)

6 A fairly bright boy is far more intelligent and far better company than the average adult.

Quoted in *The New York Times* 13 June 1948

7 *I wish I had the voice of Homer To sing of rectal carcinoma.*

'Cancer's a Funny Thing', publ. in the *New Statesman* 21 February 1964. Opening lines of a poem describing Haldane's colostomy. 'The main functions of my rhyme,' Haldane wrote, 'were to induce cancer patients to be operated on early and to be cheerful about it.'

8 I'd lay down my life for two brothers or eight cousins.

Attributed in the *New Scientist* 8 August 1974

H. R. Haldeman (1926–93)

US WHITE HOUSE OFFICIAL

Harry Robbins Haldeman. He was nicknamed the 'Iron Chancellor' while White House Chief of Staff under President NIXON *(1969–73). His involvement in the Watergate cover-up led to an eighteen-month prison sentence.*

1 Once the toothpaste is out of the tube, it is awfully hard to get it back in.

Remark to John Dean, 8 April 1973, publ. in *Hearings Before the Select Committee on Presidential Campaign Activities of US Senate: Watergate and Related Activities*, vol. 4 (1973). Referring to the exposure of the White House's involvement in the bugging of the Watergate building.

Nancy Hale (b. 1908)

US AUTHOR AND EDITOR

In 1935 she became the first woman reporter at The New York Times. *She published memoirs, short stories and novels, including* The Prodigal Women *(1942), a study of motherhood and identity.*

1 The best work of artists in any age is the work of innocence liberated by technical knowledge.

Mary Cassatt: A Biography of the Great American Painter, pt 2, ch. 7 (1975)

Alex Haley (1921–92)
US AUTHOR

His Autobiography of Malcolm X *(1965) has become a classic, although he is best known for* Roots: The Saga of an American Family *(1976, televised 1977), which tracked seven generations of an African-American family.*

1 It is rightly said that when a griot dies, it is as if a library has burned to the ground. The griots symbolize how all human ancestry goes back to some place, and some time, where there was no writing. Then, the memories and the mouths of ancient elders was the only way that early histories of mankind got passed along . . . for all of us today to know who we are.

Roots, 'Acknowledgements' (1976). Referring to the transmitters of oral history in west African villages.

Bill Haley (1925–81)
US ROCK MUSICIAN

His composition 'Crazy Man Crazy' (1953), recorded with the Comets, was considered the first 'rock and roll' record to enter Billboard's *pop chart. Subsequent hits included 'Rock Around the Clock' and 'Shake, Rattle and Roll' (both 1954).*

1 One-two-three o'clock, four o'clock rock!
Five-six-seven o'clock, eight o'clock rock!
Nine-ten-eleven o'clock, twelve o'clock rock!
We're gonna rock around the clock tonight!

'Rock Around the Clock' (song, 1954, written by Max Freedman and 'Jimmy De Knight', pseudonym of Haley's publisher James Myers) by Bill Haley and His Comets. The song was a minor hit in 1952 for Sunny Dae, but became the biggest hit of the rock 'n' roll era for Haley when his recording was adopted as the title music to the film *Blackboard Jungle* (1955), selling more than 25 million copies. The 1956 film *Rock Around the Clock* featured this and Haley's other hits, and caused riots in cinemas when the song was played.

2 Shake, rattle and roll.

'Shake, Rattle and Roll' (song, 1954, written by Charles Calhoun). Originally a hit for 'blues-shouter' Big Joe Turner, it was the first hit for Haley and the Comets.

3 See you later, alligator,
After 'while, crocodile;
Can't you see you're in my way, now,
Don't you know you cramp my style?

'See You Later Alligator' (song, 1956, written by Charles Calhoun). The record was Haley's last US top-ten hit.

Gus Hall (1910–2000)
US POLITICAL ACTIVIST

Originally Arvo Gus Halberg. A communist since youth, he was imprisoned for subversive activities (1951–7) and became General Secretary of the US Communist Party in 1959. He was four times candidate for the US presidency.

1 *Perestroika* basically is creating material incentives for the individual. Some of the comrades deny that, but I can't see it any other way. In that sense human nature kinda goes backwards. It's a step backwards. You have to realize the people weren't quite ready for a socialist production system.

Interview in the *Independent* 19 May 1990

Jerry Hall (b. 1956)
US MODEL AND ACTRESS

The ex-wife of MICK JAGGER, *she has had a high-profile modelling career, and has also been a contributing editor to the* Tatler *and has acted in films and on the London stage.*

1 My mother said it was simple to keep a man, you must be a maid in the living room, a cook in the kitchen and a whore in the bedroom. I said I'd hire the other two and take care of the bedroom bit.

Quoted in the *Observer* 6 October 1985

(Sir) Peter Hall (b. 1930)
BRITISH THEATRE, OPERA AND FILM DIRECTOR

He established the Royal Shakespeare Company as a permanent company and was a key player in the formation of the National Theatre. 'We caused a revolution in the speaking of Shakespeare's verse,' he said of his work at the RSC, 'and, at the gate of heaven, if I was asked to justify myself, I would say that is the best thing I've done in my life.' He has also directed opera and films

1 Theatres have to be run on obsession.

Quoted in the *Observer* 10 August 1986

2 The English hate the arts because they are so good at them. It's the great paradox.

Quoted in the *Observer* 7 September 1997

Radclyffe Hall (1883–1943)
BRITISH NOVELIST

Marguerite Radclyffe Hall. She is best known for her novel The Well of Loneliness *(1928), banned in Britain for many years for its open treatment of lesbianism.*

1 You're neither unnatural, nor abominable, nor mad; you're as much a part of what people call nature as anyone else; only you're unexplained as yet – you've not got your niche in creation.

The Well of Loneliness, bk 2, ch. 20, sect. 3 (1928). The speech that 'Puddle' (the tutor, Miss

Puddleton) resolves to make to the book's lesbian heroine, Stephen Gordon. The book was temporarily suspended in the USA, and, after a notorious trial, banned in Britain, where the editor of the *Sunday Express* wrote that he 'would sooner give a healthy boy or girl a dose of prussic acid than a copy of it'.

2 I am one of those whom God marked on the forehead. Like Cain, I am marked and blemished. If you come to me . . . the world will abhor you, will persecute you, will call you unclean. Our love may be faithful even unto death and beyond – yet the world will call it unclean.
Stephen, ibid., ch. 37, sect. 3

Margaret Halsey (b. 1910)
US AUTHOR
Calling herself a 'humorist and a moral positivist', she wrote on topics ranging from racism and neglect of children to English foibles. Her books include With Malice Toward Some *(1938) and* The Folks at Home *(1952).*

1 The boneless quality of English conversation, which, so far as I have heard it, is all form and no content. Listening to Britons dining out is like watching people play first-class tennis with imaginary balls.
With Malice Toward Some, pt 1, 'June 12' (1938)

2 Humility is not my forte, and whenever I dwell for any length of time on my own shortcomings, they gradually begin to seem mild, harmless, rather engaging little things, not at all like the staring defects in other people's characters.
Ibid., pt 1, 'June 15'

3 Englishwomen's shoes look as if they had been made by someone who had often heard shoes described, but had never seen any.
Ibid., pt 2

Edith Hamilton (1867–1963)
US CLASSICAL SCHOLAR AND TRANSLATOR
Headmistress of Bryn Mawr preparatory school in Baltimore (1896–1922) and a devotee of classical studies, she wrote The Greek Way *(1930),* The Roman Way *(1932) and, in* Mythology *(1942), translations of classical myths.*

1 The anthropologists are busy, indeed, and ready to transport us back into the savage forest where all human things . . . have their beginnings; but the seed never explains the flower.
The Greek Way, ch. 1 (1930)

2 There are few efforts more conducive to humility than that of the translator trying to communicate an incommunicable beauty. Yet, unless we do try, something unique and never surpassed will cease to exist except in the libraries of a few inquisitive book lovers.
Three Greek Plays, Introduction (1937)

Richard Hamilton (b. 1922)
BRITISH ARTIST
His work with the Independent Group, and particularly his collage 'Just What Is It That Makes Today's Homes So Different, So Appealing?' (1956), helped to establish Pop Art in Britain.

1 If the artist is not to lose much of his ancient purpose he may have to plunder the popular arts to recover the imagery which is his rightful inheritance.
'For the Finest Art Try – POP', first publ. in *Gazette* no. 1, 1961, repr. in *Collected Words 1953–1982* (1982)

2 Any interior is a set of anachronisms, a museum with the lingering residues of decorative styles that an inhabited space collects. Banal or beautiful, exquisite or sordid, each says a lot about its owner and something about humanity in general.
'Interiors', publ. in *Vanguard* September 1978, repr. ibid.

James Hamilton-Paterson (b. 1941)
BRITISH AUTHOR
He won plaudits for his first novel Gerontius *(1989) and for* The Ghosts of Manila *(1994). His non-fiction publications include* Seven Tenths: The Sea and its Thresholds *(1992).*

1 To name something is to take control of it. It could be argued that the Old Testament story of Genesis was less a matter of creation than of naming, of God taking control of chaos.
Seven-Tenths: The Sea and Its Thresholds, ch. 1, sect. 2 (1992)

2 There is a psychological accuracy in this insistence that a proper life cannot be lived without pilgrimage, a journey, a great excursion and abandoning of towns, village, hearth. Only in this way is the unsuspected majesty of the world revealed.
Ibid., ch. 7, sect. 2

Dag Hammarskjöld (1905–61)
SWEDISH STATESMAN
Describing himself as the 'curator of the secrets of 82 nations', he was UN Secretary-General 1953–61. He died in a plane crash in Zambia while attempting to mediate in the Congo crisis.

1 We are not permitted to choose the frame of our destiny. But what we put into it is ours.
Note written 1950, publ. in *Markings*, 'Night is Drawing Nigh' (1964)

2 The UN is not just a product of do-gooders. It is harshly real. The day will

come when men will see the UN and what it means clearly. Everything will be all right – you know when? When people, just people, stop thinking of the United Nations as a weird Picasso abstraction, and see it as a drawing they made themselves.

Time 27 June 1955

3 In our era, the road to holiness necessarily passes through the world of action.

Note written 1955, publ. in *Markings*, 'Night is Drawing Nigh' (1964)

4 Your body must become familiar with its death – in all its possible forms and degrees – as a self-evident, imminent, and emotionally neutral step on the way towards the goal you have found worthy of your life.

Note written 1957, publ. ibid.

5 I don't know Who – or what – put the question, I don't know when it was put. I don't even remember answering. But at some moment I did answer *Yes* to Someone – or Something – and from that hour I was certain that existence is meaningful and that, therefore, my life, in self-surrender, had a goal.

Note written Whit Sunday 1961, publ. ibid.

Oscar Hammerstein II (1895–1960)
US SONGWRITER

His collaborators included Jerome Kern in Show Boat *(1927) and, for sixteen years, Richard Rodgers, with whom he produced such musical classics as* Oklahoma! *(1943) and* South Pacific *(1949).*

1 Ol' man river, dat ol' man river,
  He must know sumpin', but don't say nothin'
  He just keeps rollin',
  He keeps on rollin' along.

'Ol' Man River' (song, with music by Jerome Kern) in the stage musical *Show Boat* (1927, filmed 1936 and 1951)

2 The last time I saw Paris
  Her heart was warm and gay,
  I heard the laughter of her heart in every street café.

'The Last Time I Saw Paris' (song, with music by Jerome Kern) in the film *Lady Be Good* (1941). Hammerstein's last major collaboration with Jerome Kern was inspired by news of the German occupation of Paris, and won an Oscar. The movie bears no relation to the stage musical of the same name scored by George Gershwin in 1924.

3 Oh, what a beautiful mornin',
  Oh, what a beautiful day!
  I got a beautiful feelin'
  Ev'rything's goin' my way.

'Oh, What a Beautiful Mornin'' (song, with music by Richard Rodgers) in *Oklahoma!* (stage musical 1943, film 1955)

4 The corn is as high as an elephant's eye,
  And it looks like it's climbin' clear up to the sky.

Ibid.

5 June is bustin' out all over.

'June is Bustin' Out All Over' (song, with music by Richard Rodgers) in *Carousel* (stage musical 1945, film 1956)

6 You'll never walk alone.

'You'll Never Walk Alone', ibid. Recorded at various times by JUDY GARLAND, FRANK SINATRA and Gerry and the Pacemakers, the song has been adopted by crowds at British football matches, chiefly associated with Liverpool FC.

7 Some enchanted evening,
  You may see a stranger,
  You may see a stranger,
  Across a crowded room.

'Some Enchanted Evening' (song, with music by Richard Rodgers) in *South Pacific* (stage musical 1949, film 1958)

8 I'm gonna wash that man right out of my hair.

'I'm Gonna Wash That Man Right out of My Hair', ibid.

9 The hills are alive with the sound of music.

'The Sound of Music' (song, with music by Richard Rodgers) in *The Sound of Music* (stage musical 1959, film 1965)

10 Climb every mountain, ford every stream
   Follow every rainbow, till you find your dream!

'Climb Every Mountain', ibid.

Dashiell Hammett (1894–1961)
US CRIME WRITER

He was a key innovator in the 'hard-boiled' school of crime fiction. Many of his thrillers are better known as films, for example The Maltese Falcon *(1930, filmed 1941) and* The Thin Man *(1932, filmed 1934). He and* LILLIAN HELLMAN *(with whom he lived) were persecuted for their left-wing views during the McCarthy era.*

1 When a man's partner is killed he's supposed to do something about it. It doesn't make any difference what you thought of him. He was your partner, and you're supposed to do something about it.

Sam Spade, in *The Maltese Falcon*, 'If They Hang You' (1930). The words are spoken thus by HUMPHREY BOGART in the movie adaptation, scripted and directed by JOHN HUSTON (1941).

Katharine Hamnett (b. 1947)
BRITISH FASHION DESIGNER

She established her own company in 1979 to execute her designs, which are distinguished by their loose lines and use of natural fabrics. She has campaigned against both Conservative and Labour policies on various issues.

1 The origins of clothing are not practical.
They are mystical and erotic. The primitive
man in the wolf-pelt was not keeping dry;
he was saying: 'Look what I killed. Aren't I
the best?'

Independent on Sunday 10 March 1991

Christopher Hampton (b. 1946)

BRITISH PLAYWRIGHT

*He was the first resident playwright at London's
Royal Court Theatre, where most of his plays have
been produced. Highly regarded for his* Tales from
Hollywood *(1982), he scored his greatest success
with* Les Liaisons Dangereuses *(1985, filmed
1998).*

1 I have always thought of sophistication as
rather a feeble substitute for decadence.

Braham, in *The Philanthropist*, sc. 3 (1970)

2 Masturbation is the thinking man's television.

Ibid.

3 A great number of the disappointments
and mishaps of the troubled world are the
direct result of literature and the allied
arts. It is our belief that no human being
who devotes his life and energy to the
manufacture of fantasies can be anything
but fundamentally inadequate.

Celia, ibid. sc. 5

4 I always divide people into two groups.
Those who live by what they know to be a
lie, and those who live by what they
believe, falsely, to be the truth.

Don, ibid.

5 If I had to give a definition of capitalism I
would say: the process whereby American
girls turn into American women.

Carlos, in *Savages*, sc. 16 (1974)

6 Asking a working writer what he thinks
about critics is like asking a lamp-post
what it feels about dogs.

Sunday Times 16 October 1977

Han Suyin (b. 1917)

CHINESE-BORN BRITISH AUTHOR

*Pseudonym of Elizabeth Comber. She is most
associated with her autobiographical novel* A
Many-Splendoured Thing *(1952), filmed as* Love
is A Many-Splendored Thing *(1955).*

1 Exploitation and oppression is not a matter of *race*. It is the system, the apparatus
of world-wide brigandage called imperialism, which made the Powers behave the
way they did. I have no illusions on this
score, nor do I believe that any Asian
nation or African nation, in the same state
of dominance, and with the same system of

colonial profit-amassing and plunder,
would have behaved otherwise.

The Crippled Tree, pt 1, ch. 9 (vol. 1 of autobiography *China*, 1965)

Tony Hancock (1924–68)

BRITISH COMEDIAN

*He achieved fame as the pompous and lugubrious
misfit with a sardonic wit in* Hancock's Half
Hour, *on radio (1954–9) and television (1956–61).
A decline into alcoholism ended in his suicide.*

1 It's red hot, mate. I hate to think of this
sort of book getting in the wrong hands.
As soon as I've finished this, I shall recommend they ban it.

'The Missing Page', broadcast 26 February 1960,
in *Hancock's Half-Hour* (BBC TV series, 1956–
61, written by Ray Galton and Alan Simpson)

2 I don't mind giving them a reasonable
amount, but a pint . . . why that's very
nearly an armful.

'The Blood Donor', broadcast 23 June 1961, ibid.

3 The secret of my work is a knowledge of
what constitutes living in general, I think.
You take the weaknesses of your own
character and of other people's characters
and you exploit them. You show yourself
up, and you show them up.

Interview with John Freeman on *Face to Face*
(BBC TV), quoted in *Hancock's Half-Hour*, epigraph (1974) by Ray Galton and Alan Simpson

Peter Handke (b. 1942)

AUSTRIAN NOVELIST, PLAYWRIGHT AND
DIRECTOR

His first play Insulting the Audience *(1966) was
an example of his anti-theatre writing, which alternately abuses and praises the audience. His story*
The Goalie's Anxiety at the Penalty Kick *(1970)
was filmed by* WIM WENDERS *in 1972, initiating a
collaboration that included* Wings of Desire
(1989).

1 Fiction, inventing an event as a vehicle for
my information about the world, is no
longer necessary, it is just a hindrance. Progress in literature in general seems to me
to consist of a gradual removal of unneces-
ary fictions. More and more vehicles fall
away, the story becomes unnecessary. It is
more to do with the imparting of experiences, verbal and non-verbal, and it is no
longer necessary to invent a story for that.

I Am an Inhabitant of an Ivory Tower (1967)

2 If a nation loses its storytellers, it loses its
childhood.

Independent 9 June 1988

3 If Thomas Mann counts as the greatest German writer of this century, writing makes

no sense at all. Anyone who follows him is already lost as far as I'm concerned.

Quoted in the *Guardian* 13 August 1994

Terry Hands (b. 1941)

BRITISH THEATRE AND OPERA DIRECTOR

He co-founded the Everyman Theatre in Liverpool and was subsequently joint Artistic Director of the Royal Shakespeare Company (with TREVOR NUNN, *1978–86) and Chief Executive (1986–91).*

1 We may pretend that we're basically moral people who make mistakes, but the whole of history proves otherwise.

The Times 11 August 1992

Tom Hanks (b. 1956)

US SCREEN ACTOR

A versatile mainstream actor, he came to attention in Splash *(1984) and won international success with his starring roles in* Philadelphia *(1993),* Forrest Gump *(1994) and* Saving Private Ryan *(1998).*

1 The prejudice surrounding AIDS exacts a social death which precedes the actual physical one.

Andrew Beckett (Tom Hanks), in *Philadelphia* (film, 1993, screenplay by Ron Nyswaner, directed by Jonathan Demme). Hanks is reading a Supreme Court ruling from a previous case.

2 Stupid is as stupid does.

Forrest Gump (Tom Hanks) quoting his mother, in *Forrest Gump* (film, 1994, screenplay by Eric Roth based on a novel by Winston Groom, directed by Robert Zemeckis). Forrest Gump habitually repeats his mother's *bons mots*. See also SALLY FIELD 1.

3 What I do for a living is go to work and pretend I'm somebody else. . . . Acting is what I do and, unfortunately I can't do much of anything else. It's this or nothing. I can *pretend* to build automobiles.

Quoted in *Tom Hanks*, ch. 11 (1995) by Roy Trakin

4 I do think that a sense of humor gets you much farther in the movies than it does in real life. There was a long period of time where I swear to God being funny just didn't get you laid no matter how funny you were.

Ibid., ch. 15

William Hanna (1910–2001) and Joseph Barbera (b. 1911)

US ANIMATORS

They were the creators of Tom and Jerry *for MGM (1937–57) and went on to found their own company, producing cartoons such as* Yogi Bear, Huckleberry Hound *and* The Flintstones.

1 Yabba dabba do!

Fred Flintstone, in *The Flintstones* (TV cartoon,

1960–66, produced by Hanna and Barbera). Fred Flintstone (voiced by Alan Reed) and Barney Rubble were modelled on Jackie Gleason and Art Carney in the TV sitcom, *The Honeymooners* (1955–71).

Brian Hanrahan (b. 1949)

BRITISH JOURNALIST

After stints as BBC Far East correspondent (1983–5) and Moscow correspondent (1986–9), he has been a diplomatic correspondent and editor.

1 I'm not allowed to say how many planes joined the raid, but I counted them all out, and I counted them all back.

BBC news report, 1 May 1982, publ. in *'I Counted Them All Out and I Counted Them All Back'*, 'Air Battles' (1982, with Robert Fox). The broadcast from the Falkland Islands described the safe return of British Harriers to HMS *Hermes* after their first attack on the landing strip of Port Stanley.

Otto Harbach (1873–1963)

US SONGWRITER

A prolific lyricist and librettist, he collaborated with Sigmund Romberg, Jerome Kern and George Gershwin on such hits as the musical No, No, Nanette *(1925).*

1 When a lovely flame dies
   Smoke gets in your eyes.

'Smoke Gets in your Eyes' (song, with music by Jerome Kern) in *Roberta* (musical show 1933, film 1935)

Yip Harburg (1898–1981)

US SONGWRITER

Born Isidore Hochberg, changed to Edgar Y. Harburg. He is identified with such socially conscious and idealistic songs as 'Brother Can You Spare a Dime' (1932) and those he wrote for The Wizard of Oz *(1939) He was also active in civil rights movements. See also* JUDY GARLAND 1.

1 Once I built a railroad,
   Now it's done,
   Brother, can you spare a dime?

'Brother Can You Spare a Dime?' (song, with music by Jay Gorney), in *Americana* (musical show, 1932). The line has been often rendered, 'Buddy, can you spare a dime?' Asked to update the song for *The New York Times* some fifty years later, Harburg came up with: 'Once we had depression/But with a dime/A guy wasn't out of luck./Now we've got inflation, drugs and crime./Brother can you spare a buck?'

2 Say, it's only a paper moon,
   Sailing over a cardboard sea.

'It's Only a Paper Moon' (song, written with Billy Rose, music by Harold Arlen) in *The Great Magoo* (stage musical, 1932)

3 *We got no Mussolini, got no Mosley,*
We got Popeye and Gipsy Rose Lee.

'God's Country' (song) in *Hooray for What?*
(stage musical, 1937). The song also featured in
the Busby Berkeley movie *Babes in Arms* (1939),
and was covered by FRANK SINATRA and Vic
Damone.

4 *Follow the yellow brick road.*

'We're Off to See the Wizard' (song, with music
by Harold Arlen), in *The Wizard of Oz* (film,
1939)

5 *We're off to see the Wizard*
The wonderful Wizard of Oz.

Ibid.

6 *I could while away the hours*
Conversin' with the flowers,
Consultin' with the rain;
With the thoughts I'd be thinkin'
I could be another Lincoln
If I only had a brain . . .

The scarecrow (Ray Bolger), singing 'If I Only
Had a Brain' (song, with music by Harold
Arlen), ibid.

7 *Wanna cry, wanna croon.*
Wanna laugh like a loon.
It's that Old Devil Moon in your eyes.

'Old Devil Moon' (song, with music by Burton
Lane), in *Finian's Rainbow* (stage musical 1947,
filmed 1968)

Gilbert Harding (1907–60)

BRITISH BROADCASTER

He became quiz master for the BBC radio pro-
gramme Round Britain Quiz *in 1947 and also*
appeared on the radio quiz Twenty Questions *and*
TV's What's my Line? *He was famously rude and*
'difficult', as he himself remarked: 'I am full of the
milk of human kindness, damn it. My trouble is
that it gets clotted so easily.'

1 If, sir, I possessed . . . the power of convey-
ing unlimited sexual attraction through
the potency of my voice, I would not be
reduced to accepting a miserable pittance
from the BBC for interviewing a faded
female in a damp basement.

Recalled by Wynford Vaughan Thomas, in *Gil-*
bert Harding by His Friends, 'Gilbert and Outside
Broadcasts' (ed. Stephen Grenfell, 1961).
Response to a request by MAE WEST's manager
to sound more 'sexy' when interviewing the
actress.

Warren G. Harding (1865–1923)

US PRESIDENT

Warren Gamaliel Harding. As Republican Presi-
dent (1921–3) he proved to be politically naïve,
unprepared for the 'Teapot Dome Scandal' which
exposed corruption in government. WOODROW
WILSON *criticized his 'bungalow mind', while for*

H. L. MENCKEN *he was 'a tin horn politician with*
the manner of a rural corn doctor and the mien of
a ham actor'.

1 America's present need is not heroics, but
healing; not nostrums, but normalcy; not
revolution, but restoration.

Speech in Boston, 14 May 1920, quoted in *Re-*
dedicating America, ch. 17 (1920) by Frederick E.
Schortemeier. 'Back to normalcy' was Harding's
campaign slogan in that year.

Elizabeth Hardwick (b. 1916)

US CRITIC AND AUTHOR

Known mainly for her brilliant literary and social
criticism in the New York Review of Books,
which she helped to found in 1963, she also wrote
novels dealing with the fragility of human relation-
ships. She was married to ROBERT LOWELL *1949–*
72.

1 This is the unspoken contract of a wife and
her works. In the long run wives are to be
paid in a peculiar coin – consideration for
their feelings. And it usually turns out this
is an enormous, unthinkable inflation few
men will remit, or if they will, only with a
sense of being overcharged.

Seduction and Betrayal: Women and Literature,
'Amateurs' (1974)

2 The fifties – they seem to have taken place
on a sunny afternoon that asked nothing
of you except a drifting belief in the
moment and its power to satisfy.

Bartleby in Manhattan and Other Essays, 'Domestic Manners' (1983)

Oliver Hardy (1892–1957)

US COMEDIAN

Originally Norvell Hardy. He was the overbearing
and rotund member of the comedy duo Laurel and
Hardy, formed in 1926. The partnership resulted in
more than 200 films, both 'silents' and 'talkies'.

1 Here's another nice mess you've gotten me
into.

Ollie in *The Laurel–Hardy Murder Case* (film,
1930). This is the earliest use of the famous
catch-phrase which featured in various Laurel
and Hardy films, always uttered by Oliver Hardy
to Stan Laurel, although Laurel (1890–1965) is
credited with most of the scriptwork, and
directed many of the films. The words are generally misquoted as 'another fine mess', which was
the title of a Laurel and Hardy short released in
1930, but have not been traced to any dialogue in
this form.

Thomas Hardy (1840–1928)

BRITISH NOVELIST AND POET

His novels set in 'Wessex' (his native Dorset and
around) are mainly harsh rural tragedies. The

controversial Tess of the d'Urbervilles (1891) branded him an atheist, and after Jude the Obscure (1896) he confined himself to writing poetry. D. H. LAWRENCE remarked, 'What a commonplace genius he has, or a genius for the commonplace, I don't know which.'

1 Yonder a maid and her wight
Come whispering by:
War's annals will cloud into night
Ere their story die.

'In Time of "The Breaking of Nations"', written 1915, publ. in Moments of Vision (1917)

2 My opinion is that a poet should express the emotion of all the ages and the thought of his own.

Remark 1918, quoted in The Later Years of Thomas Hardy, ch. 15 (1930) by Florence Emily Hardy

3 The value of old age depends upon the person who reaches it. To some men of early performance it is useless. To others, who are late to develop, it just enables them to finish the job.

'Birthday Notes', written 1920, quoted ibid.

4 After two thousand years of mass
We've got as far as poison-gas.

'Christmas: 1924', publ. in Winter Words (1928)

5 Well, World, you have kept faith with me,
Kept faith with me;
Upon the whole you have proved to be
Much as you said you were.

'He Never Expected Much', publ. ibid. The poem is subtitled 'A Consideration on My Eighty-Sixth Birthday'.

(Sir) David Hare (b. 1947)
BRITISH PLAYWRIGHT
Resident playwright at the Royal Court Theatre (1969–71), and co-founder of the Joint Stock Theatre Company (1974), he is the author of numerous modern satires, including Teeth 'n' Smiles (1975) and the trilogy Racing Demon (1990), Murmuring Judges (1991) and The Absence of War (1994). See also HOWARD BRENTON AND DAVID HARE.

1 The theatre is the best way of showing the gap between what is said and what is seen to be done, and that is why, ragged and gap-toothed as it is, it has still a far healthier potential than some poorer, abandoned arts.

'The Playwright as Historian', publ. in the Sunday Times 26 November 1978

2 How the right wing always appropriate good manners. Yes? They always have that. Form and decorum. A permanent excuse for not addressing themselves to what people actually say, because they can always turn their heads away if a sentence is not correctly formulated.

Stephen, in A Map of the World, act 1 (1982)

3 This feeling, finally, that we may change things – this is at the centre of everything we are. Lose that . . . lose that, lose everything.

Mehta, ibid., act 2

4 England's funny. You only get the point of it eight days a year. The sun comes out and you remember. You think oh, yes, all this . . . all this around us – that's what it's for.

Anne Rice, in Strapless, pt 5 (1989)

5 Like everything in England, it turns out to be a matter of class. You just listen. Educated clerics don't like evangelicals, because evangelicals drink sweet sherry and keep budgerigars and have ducks in formations on their walls. Yes, and they also have the distressingly downmarket habit of trying to get people emotionally involved.

Tony, in Racing Demon, act 2, sc. 1 (1990)

6 Policing's largely the fine art of getting through biros.

Sandra, in Murmuring Judges, act 1, sc. 5 (1991)

7 I love its volatility. Its special beauty seems to me to come from the fact that at seven-thirty you have no idea how you will be feeling at ten-fifteen. And at ten-fifteen you will look back, as across an ocean, to the almost unrecognizable stranger who arrived at seven-thirty.

On working in the theatre, in Writing Left-Handed, ch. 3 (1991)

8 Writers always sound insufferably smug when they sit back and assert that their job is only to raise questions and not to answer them. But, in good part, it is true. And once you become committed to one particular answer, your freedom to ask new questions is seriously impaired.

Ibid.

9 Acting is a judgment of character.

Said to critic Michael Billington, quoted by him in the Guardian 2 October 1993

W. F. Hargreaves (1846–1919)
BRITISH SONGWRITER

1 I'm Burlington Bertie
I rise at ten thirty and saunter along like a toff,
I walk down the Strand with my gloves on my hand,
Then I walk down again with them off.

'Burlington Bertie from Bow' (song, 1915). The song was first performed by Ella Shields, male impersonator and Hargreaves's wife. Among the artists who covered it were ELSA LANCHESTER and JULIE ANDREWS (as Gertrude Lawrence in the 1968 film *Star!*).

Tom Harkin (b. 1939)
US SENATOR
A Senator since 1984, he was a Democratic candidate for the presidency in 1992. He co-authored Five Minutes to Midnight: Why the Nuclear Threat is Growing Faster Than Ever *(1990).*

1 The Gulf War was like teenage sex. We got in too soon and out too soon.
Quoted in the *Independent on Sunday* 29 September 1991

Lord Harlech (1918–85)
BRITISH DIPLOMAT AND BUSINESSMAN
William David Ormsby Gore. He became Conservative MP for Oswestry in 1950, later serving as British Ambassador in Washington (1961–5). His Harlech television company won a broadcasting franchise in 1967.

1 Britain will be honored by historians more for the way she disposed of an empire than for the way in which she acquired it.
The New York Times 28 October 1962

Jean Harlow (1911–37)
US ACTRESS
Originally Harlean Carpentier. The 'Blonde Bombshell' became the first sex symbol of the talkies, playing comedy roles in such films as Platinum Blonde *(1931) and* Bombshell *(1933). According to* GRAHAM GREENE, *'Her technique was the gangster's technique – she toted a breast like a man totes a gun.' See also* MARGOT ASQUITH 3.

1 Would you be shocked if I put on something more comfortable?
Helen (Jean Harlow), in *Hell's Angels* (film, 1930, screenplay by H. Behn, H. Estabrook and J. M. March based on a story by Marshall Neilan and Joseph Moncure March, produced and co-directed by Howard Hughes, J. Whale, M. Neilan and L. Reed). The line is usually misquoted: 'Excuse me while I slip into something more comfortable.' Harlow, aged just eighteen, acted the part of an English girl who, clad in a backless velvet evening gown with beaded straps, addresses the question to Ben Lyons (Monty Rutledge).

Michael Harrington (1928–89)
US SOCIAL SCIENTIST AND AUTHOR
A passionate champion of the poor and dispossessed, and a member of the Catholic Worker Movement, he is principally known for his study of poverty The Other America *(1962).*

1 That the poor are invisible is one of the

most important things about them. They are not simply neglected and forgotten as in the old rhetoric of reform; what is much worse, they are not seen.
The Other America, ch. 1, sect. 1 (1962)

2 To be a Negro is to participate in a culture of poverty and fear that goes far deeper than any law for or against discrimination. . . . After the racist statutes are all struck down, after legal equality has been achieved in the schools and in the courts, there remains the profound institutionalized and abiding wrong that white America has worked on the Negro for so long.
Ibid., ch. 4

3 Our affluent society contains those of talent and insight who are driven to prefer poverty, to choose it, rather than to submit to the desolation of an empty abundance. It is a strange part of the other America that one finds in the intellectual slums.
Ibid., ch. 5, sect. 1

4 Life is lived in common, but not in community.
Of life in the slums, ibid., ch. 7, sect. 4

5 If there is technological advance without social advance, there is, almost automatically, an increase in human misery, in impoverishment.
Ibid., Appendix, sect. 1

Frank Harris (1856–1931)
IRISH JOURNALIST AND AUTHOR
Originally James Thomas Harris. He is chiefly remembered for his scandalous autobiography My Life and Loves *(5 vols. 1922–8). Other works include biographies of Oscar Wilde and* GEORGE BERNARD SHAW, *who described him as a 'man of splendid visions, unreasonable expectations, fierce appetites'.*

1 All that is amiable and sweet and good in life, all that ennobles and chastens, I have won from women.
My Life and Loves, vol. 2, Foreword (1925)

2 There is a subtle compensation in everything, and the cheapening of books, the vulgarization of knowledge, has a great deal to answer for. We have forgotten how to use books, and they revenge themselves on us.
Ibid., vol. 3, ch. 1 (1926)

3 Stupidity and malevolence are the twin rulers of human destiny and there is no hope for the future save in the soul of man, and even there high purpose is fitful and often dwarfed by animal necessities.
Ibid., vol. 5, ch. 1 (1928)

Martyn Harris (b. 1952)
BRITISH JOURNALIST AND AUTHOR
He was a feature writer for New Society *1979–82 and subsequently on the* Daily Telegraph. *His novels include* Do It Again *(1989).*

1 Pull out a Monte Cristo at a dinner party and the political liberal turns into the nicotine fascist.
   Daily Telegraph 20 January 1989

Richard Harris (1932–2002)
IRISH ACTOR
Described by the critic Clive Barnes as having a face like 'five miles of bad Irish country road', he made his screen debut in Alive and Kicking *(1958), and established himself on the London stage the following year in* J. P. DONLEAVY's The Ginger Man. *His last role was as the headmaster Dumbledore in the first two Harry Potter films (2001 and 2002).*

1 I often sit back and think 'I wish I'd done that' and find out later that I already have.
   On his drinking, quoted in the *Sun* 19 May 1988

Robert Harris (b. 1957)
BRITISH JOURNALIST AND AUTHOR
A journalist on the Observer *and the* Sunday Times, *he became a best-selling author with his fictional reworkings of history,* Fatherland *(1992) and* Archangel *(1998).*

1 We believe in God, we believe in Germany which He created in His world, and in the Führer, Adolf Hitler, whom He has sent us.
   SS cadets, in *Fatherland*, pt 2, ch. 3 (1992)

2 There can now be no doubt that it is Stalin rather than Hitler who is the most alarming figure of the twentieth century. . . . I say this not merely because Stalin killed more people than Hitler – though clearly he did – and not even because Stalin was more of a psychopath than Hitler – although clearly he was. I say it because Stalin was not a one off like Hitler, an eruption from nowhere. Stalin stands in a historical tradition of rule by terror which existed before him, which he refined, and which could exist again. His, not Hitler's, is the spectre that should worry us.
   Kelso, in *Archangel*, ch. 11 (1998)

3 In Russia, the past carries razors and a pair of handcuffs.
   Suvorin, ibid.

4 The great western myth. . . . That just because a place has a McDonalds and MTV and takes American Express it's exactly the same as everywhere else – it doesn't have a past any more, it's Year Zero.
   Kelso, ibid., ch. 16

5 History is too important to be left to the historians.
   Quoted in the *Observer* 25 October 1998

Rolf Harris (b. 1930)
AUSTRALIAN TELEVISION PRESENTER
His fast-talking, fast-drawing style has made him a popular presenter of children's shows since 1954. His hit records include 'Sun Arise' (1962 and 1997) and 'Two Little Boys' (1969 and 1970).

1 *Tie me kangaroo down, sport.*
   'Tie Me Kangaroo Down, Sport' (song, 1960) on the album *Sun Arise* (1963)

Sydney Harris (1917–86)
US JOURNALIST
Known for his witty aphorisms, he wrote the column 'Strictly Personal' which was syndicated to some 200 newspapers in North America. His books include Pieces of Eight *(1982).*

1 People who think they're generous to a fault usually think that's their only fault.
   On the Contrary, ch. 7 (1962)

2 A cynic is not merely one who reads bitter lessons from the past; he is one who is prematurely disappointed in the future.
   Ibid.

Barbara Grizzuti Harrison (b. 1934)
US AUTHOR AND PUBLICIST
She has written travel books and studies of cults, for example Visions of Glory *(1978).*

1 Fantasies are more than substitutes for unpleasant reality; they are also dress rehearsals, plans. All acts performed in the world begin in the imagination.
   'Talking Dirty', publ. in *Ms* October 1973

2 Kindness and intelligence don't always deliver us from the pitfalls and traps: there are always failures of love, of will, of imagination. There is no way to take the danger out of human relationships.
   'Secrets Women Tell Each Other', publ. in *McCall's* August 1975

George Harrison (1943–2001)
BRITISH ROCK MUSICIAN
*He was the first ex-Beatle to secure a chart-topping album (*All Things Must Pass*) and single ('My Sweet Lord'), both in 1970. He later established the film production company HandMade Films (1978).*

1 This place has become a haven for drop-outs. The trouble is, some of our best friends are drop-outs.
   Speaking of the Apple office in London's Savile Row, quoted in *Shout! The True Story of the Beatles*, pt 4, 'May 1969' (1981) by Philip Norman

2 It's the basic nature of the bee to seek

more nectar, just as it's the soul's nature to always seek a better experience. When you've had all these experiences – met all the famous people, made some money, toured the world and got all the acclaim – you still think: 'Is that it?' Some people might be satisfied with that, but I wasn't and I'm still not.

Quoted in *The Beatles Anthology*, '1967' (2000)

Jane Harrison (1850–1928)

BRITISH CLASSICAL SCHOLAR AND AUTHOR
She is known for her writings on classical art, religion and literature, for example Prolegomena to the Study of Greek Religion *(1903).*

1 To be womanly is one thing, and one only; it is to be sensitive to man, to be highly endowed with the sex instinct; to be manly is to be sensitive to woman.

Alpha and Omega, 'Homo Sum' (1915)

2 Marriage, for a woman at least, hampers the two things that made life to me glorious – friendship and learning.

Reminiscences of a Student's Life, 'Conclusion' (1925)

Paul Carter Harrison (b. 1936)

US PLAYWRIGHT AND AUTHOR
His plays, such as The Great MacDaddy *(1973), and the play anthologies he has edited focus on African-American themes.*

1 The poor tread lightest on the earth. The higher our income, the more resources we control and the more havoc we wreak.

Guardian 1 May 1992

Tony Harrison (b. 1937)

BRITISH POET, PLAYWRIGHT AND TRANSLATOR
A classicist from a working-class background, he stirred controversy with his poems 'v.' *(1985) and* 'The Blasphemer's Banquet' *(1989). His plays include* Phaedra Britannica *(1975), and he has also made translations and adaptations for the theatre.*

1 *A language near extinction best preserves the deepest grammar of our nothingness.*

'Art & Extinction', no. 6, publ. in *Continuous: School of Eloquence* (1981)

2 Every poem is a momentary defeat of pessimism.

Interview in *Poetry Review* January 1984

3 *The ones we choose to love become our anchor*
   when the hawser of the blood-tie's hacked, or frays.

'v.' (1985)

4 *Its blasphemy enabled man*
   to break free from the Bible and Koran

with their life-denying fundamentalists
and hell fire such fanatics love to fan.

'The Blasphemers' Banquet' (BBC1, 31 July 1989), televised poem first publ. in *Tony Harrison: Bloodaxe Critical Anthologies 1* (ed. Neil Astley, 1991). Referring to *The Satanic Verses*, by SALMAN RUSHDIE.

5 *The Prospero of poisons, the Faustus of the front,*
   bringing mental magic to modern armament.

Square Rounds, pt 2 (1992). The speaker is intended to be the German chemist Fritz Haber, Nobel prizewinner and 'father' of chemical warfare.

Lorenz Hart (1895–1943)

US SONGWRITER
His twenty-five-year collaboration with the composer Richard Rodgers resulted in twenty-six Broadway musicals distinguished by their lyrical sophistication, including their masterwork Pal Joey *(1940).*

1 *We'll have Manhattan,*
   The Bronx and Staten
   Island too.

'Manhattan' (song, with music by Richard Rodgers), in *Garrick Gaieties* (revue, 1925). The show was Rodgers and Hart's first Broadway success as a songwriting team, and the song was also a hit, successfully recorded by Paul Whiteman and Ben Selvin.

2 *When love congeals*
   It soon reveals
   The faint aroma of performing seals,
   The double crossing of a pair of heels.
   I wish I were in love again!

'I Wish I Were in Love Again' (song, with music by Richard Rodgers), in *Babes in Arms* (stage show 1937, filmed 1939). The song was a hit for SOPHIE TUCKER and Peggy Lee.

3 *I get too hungry for dinner at eight.*
   I like the theatre, but never come late.
   I never bother with people I hate.
   That's why the lady is a tramp.

'The Lady is a Tramp' (song, with music by Richard Rodgers), ibid.

4 *I'm wild again*
   Beguiled again
   A simpering, whimpering child again,
   Bewitched, bothered and bewildered am I.

'Bewitched, Bothered and Bewildered' (song, with music by Richard Rodgers), in *Pal Joey* (stage show 1940, filmed 1957)

L. P. Hartley (1895–1972)

BRITISH AUTHOR
Leslie Poles Hartley. His novels, which include Eustace and Hilda *(1947) and* The Go-Between *(1953, filmed 1971), typically portray psychological*

relationships among the middle classes, often with a sinister slant.

1 The past is a foreign country; they do things differently there.
The Go-Between, Prologue (1953). Opening sentence.

Ihab Hassan (b. 1925)
EGYPTIAN-BORN US CRITIC
His preoccupations are, in his words, 'avant-garde moments, the postmodern phenomenon, travel as quest, vision and transgression, the collision and interanimation of cultures, especially Oriental and Occidental'. His books include Out of Egypt: Fragments *of an Autobiography (1986).*

1 The (post) structuralist temper requires too great a depersonalization of the writing/speaking subject. Writing becomes plagiarism; speaking becomes quoting. Meanwhile, we do write, we do speak.
'The Re-Vision of Literature', publ. in *New Literary History* autumn 1976, repr. in *The Right Promethean Fire* (1980)

(Sir) Max Hastings (b. 1945)
BRITISH JOURNALIST AND EDITOR
As a freelance journalist he covered worldwide conflicts, notably the Falklands War (1982). He was Editor of the Daily Telegraph 1986–95 and of the Evening Standard 1996–2002.

1 If you can't get a job as a pianist in a brothel you become a royal reporter.
Daily Express 9 June 1992

Roy Hattersley (b. 1932)
BRITISH POLITICIAN
Baron Hattersley of Sparkbrook. Elected a Labour MP in 1964, he held ministerial office in the CALLAGHAN *government and was later Shadow Chancellor and Deputy Leader of the Labour Party (1983–92). Describing his role as 'the great bystander, the shadowy figure', he has also published novels, biographies and memoirs.*

1 Morality and expediency coincide more than the cynics allow.
Guardian 30 September 1988

2 In my opinion, any man who can afford to buy a newspaper should not be allowed to own one.
Quoted in *Maxwell, the Outsider*, ch. 13 (1988) by Tom Bower

3 In politics, being ridiculous is more damaging than being extreme.
Evening Standard 9 May 1989. Hattersley himself was cruelly lampooned in the television puppet satire, *Spitting Image.*

4 The proposition that Muslims are welcome in Britain if, and only if, they stop behaving like Muslims is a doctrine which is

incompatible with the principles that guide a free society.
Independent 21 July 1989

5 There is no doubt that, as works of art, books that lack canine interest are incomplete.
Quoted in the *Sunday Times Review* 27 September 1998. On the publication of Hattersley's book, written in the persona of Buster, his dog.

Charles Haughey (b. 1925)
IRISH STATESMAN
He was elected a Fianna Fáil MP in 1957 and dismissed from Jack Lynch's government in 1970 for allegedly importing guns for the IRA, although subsequently acquitted. He was Prime Minister 1979–81, 1982 and 1987–92.

1 Ireland is where strange tales begin and happy endings are possible.
Daily Telegraph 14 July 1988

Václav Havel (b. 1936)
CZECH PLAYWRIGHT AND PRESIDENT
His dissidence, expressed in his plays and his support for Charter 77, resulted in two terms of imprisonment (1979–83 and 1989). Following the Velvet Revolution of 1989, he was elected President of Czechoslovakia and was President of the independent Czech Republic 1993–2003.

1 True enough, the country is calm. Calm as a morgue or a grave, would you not say?
'Letter to Dr Gustáv Husák' (8 April 1975), publ. in *Living in Truth*, pt 1 (1986)

2 You do not become a 'dissident' just because you decide one day to take up this most unusual career. You are thrown into it by your personal sense of responsibility, combined with a complex set of external circumstances. You are cast out of the existing structures and placed in a position of conflict with them. It begins as an attempt to do your work well, and ends with being branded an enemy of society.
'The Power of the Powerless', sect. 14 (1978), repr. in *Living in Truth*, pt 1 (1986)

3 There are times when we must sink to the bottom of our misery to understand truth, just as we must descend to the bottom of a well to see the stars in broad daylight.
Ibid., sect. 16

4 I think theatre should always be somewhat suspect.
Disturbing the Peace, ch. 2 (1986)

5 The truth is not simply what you think it is; it is also the circumstances in which it is said, and to whom, why, and how it is said.
Ibid.

6 [The] attempt to devote oneself to literature alone is a most deceptive thing, and

s

... often, paradoxically, it is literature that suffers for it.
Ibid., ch. 3

7 None of us knows all the potentialities that slumber in the spirit of the population, or all the ways in which that population can surprise us when there is the right interplay of events.
Ibid.

8 There's always something suspect about an intellectual on the winning side.
Ibid., ch. 5

9 Hope is definitely not the same thing as optimism. It is not the conviction that something will turn out well, but the certainty that something makes sense, regardless of how it turns out.
Ibid.

10 The exercise of power is determined by thousands of interactions between the world of the powerful and that of the powerless, all the more so because these worlds are never divided by a sharp line: everyone has a small part of himself in both.
Ibid.

11 The cliché organizes life; it expropriates people's identity; it becomes ruler, defence lawyer, judge, and the law.
Ibid.

12 I really do inhabit a system in which words are capable of shaking the entire structure of government, where words can prove mightier than ten military divisions.
Speech accepting a peace prize in Germany, October 1989, quoted in the *Independent* 9 December 1989

13 People have passed through a very dark tunnel at the end of which there was a light of freedom. Unexpectedly they passed through the prison gates and found themselves in a square. They are now free and they don't know where to go.
Address to Institute of Contemporary Arts, London, quoted in the *Independent* 24 March 1990

14 If you want to see your plays performed the way you wrote them, become President.
Ibid.

15 We are finding out that what looked like a neglected house a year ago is in fact a ruin.
On the state of Czechoslovakia and other ex-Soviet Bloc countries, in the *Daily Telegraph* 3 January 1991

16 There is no more relying on the accidents of history that lift poets into places where empires and military alliances are brought down. The warning voices of poets must be carefully listened to and taken very seriously, perhaps even more seriously than the voices of bankers or stockbrokers. But at the same time, we cannot expect that the world – in the hands of poets – will suddenly be transformed into a poem.
Speech at City University, New York, 19 September 2002, publ. in the *New York Review of Books* 24 October 2002

Jacquetta Hawkes (1910–96)

BRITISH ARCHAEOLOGIST AND AUTHOR
Before taking up writing she carried out excavations in Britain, France and Palestine and was Secretary to the UK Commission for UNESCO (1943–9). Her books, such as Early Britain (1945), did much to popularize archaeology. She was married to J. B. PRIESTLEY.

1 The only inequalities that matter begin in the mind. It is not income levels but differences in mental equipment that keep people apart, breed feelings of inferiority.
New Statesman January 1957

Stephen Hawking (b. 1942)

BRITISH THEORETICAL PHYSICIST
His work in quantum mechanics, black holes and the big bang theory of the universe was partially elucidated in his surprise bestseller A Brief History of Time *(1988). He has been severely disabled by a neuromotor disease since the 1960s.*

1 If we find the answer to that, it would be the ultimate triumph of human reason – for then we would know the mind of God.
A Brief History of Time, ch. 11 (1988). Closing words of book, referring to the question 'why it is that we and the universe exist'.

2 Have we been visited by aliens? ... I don't believe we have. I think that any such visit would be obvious and probably unpleasant. What would be the point of aliens revealing themselves only to a few cranks?
Radio Times 17 February 1996

Screamin' Jay Hawkins (b. 1929)

US ROCK SINGER
Originally Jalacy Hawkins. A boxer turned rhythm and blues performer, he was famed for his voodoo stage act which involved skulls, a flaming coffin and outlandish garb.

1 *I put a spell on you, because you're mine*
You'd better stop the things you're doing
Ha! Haa! Haa! – What's up! – I ain't lyin'!
Yeaaaaahhhh! I can't stand it, oh no,
Your runnin' around,
I can't stand no – I can't stand you putting me down.
'I Put a Spell on You' (song, 1956, co-written with Herb Slotkin). Some radio stations refused

to play the song on the grounds that it was 'cannibalistic'. Nina Simone, who covered the song in 1965, called it a song that 'no one could ignore'.

Ian Hay (1876–1952)
BRITISH PLAYWRIGHT AND NOVELIST
Originally John Hay Beith. The first of his light and humorous novels, Pip (1907), was a bestseller, although he is remembered chiefly for The First Hundred Thousand (1915). He adapted several of his own books as plays.

1 **War is hell and all that, but it has a good deal to recommend it. It wipes out all the small nuisances of peace-time.**

Wagstaffe, in *The First Hundred Thousand*, ch. 10 (1915). Among the 'small nuisances' Wagstaffe listed suffragettes, futurism, the tango, party politics and golf-maniacs.

Colin Haycraft (1929–94)
BRITISH PUBLISHER
Before assuming chairmanship of Duckworth and Co. in 1971, he was director of Weidenfeld & Nicolson and Managing Director of the World University Library.

1 **A publisher is a specialized form of bank or building society, catering for customers who cannot cope with life and are therefore forced to write about it.**

Letter to the *Sunday Times* 11 February 1990. 'Hype,' added Haycraft, 'springs eternal in every publisher's breast.'

Sterling Hayden (1916–86)
US SCREEN ACTOR
Originally John Hamilton. Billed as 'the Beautiful Blond Viking God', he numbered The Asphalt Jungle (1950) and The Killing (1956) among his most successful films. In 1951 he testified against alleged Communist sympathizers in Hollywood before House Un-American Activities Committee, to his later regret. 'I started at the top and worked my way down,' he concluded.

1 **I know you like a book, ya little tramp. You'd sell out your own mother for a piece of fudge. . . . You've got a great big dollar there where most women have a heart.**

Johnny Clay (Sterling Hayden) speaking to Sherry Peatty (Marie Windsor), in *The Killing* (film, 1956, screenplay by Stanley Kubrick and Jim Thompson adapted from the *The Clean Break* by Lionel White, directed by Stanley Kubrick)

2 **I can no longer sit back and allow Communist infiltration, Communist indoctrination, Communist subversion and the international Communist conspiracy to sap and impurify all of our precious bodily fluids.**

General D. Ripper (Sterling Hayden), in *Dr Strangelove: Or How I Learned to Stop Worrying and Love the Bomb* (film, 1963, screenplay by Stanley Kubrick, Terry Southern and Peter George based on Peter George's novel *Red Alert*, produced and directed by Stanley Kubrick)

Friedrich August von Hayek (1899–1992)
AUSTRIAN-BORN BRITISH ECONOMIST
Called the 'father of monetarism', he was a strong critic of Keynesian theory and directly opposed to government intervention in a free market. He was Professor of Economic Science at London (1931–50).

1 **Planning and competition can be combined only by planning for competition, but not by planning against competition.**

The Road to Serfdom, ch. 3 (1944)

2 **The system of private property is the most important guarantee of freedom, not only for those who own property, but scarcely less for those who do not.**

Ibid., ch. 8

3 **There are no better terms available to describe [the] difference between the approach of the natural and the social sciences than to call the former 'objective' and the latter 'subjective'. . . . While for the natural scientist the contrast between objective facts and subjective opinions is a simple one, the distinction cannot as readily be applied to the object of the social sciences. The reason for this is that the object, the 'facts' of the social sciences are also opinions – not opinions of the student of the social phenomena, of course, but opinions of those whose actions produce the object of the social scientist.**

The Counter-Revolution of Science, pt 1, ch. 3 (1952)

Denis Healey (b. 1917)
BRITISH POLITICIAN
Baron Healey of Riddlesden. Elected a Labour MP in 1952, he went on to become Minister for Defence in the WILSON government (1964–70), and subsequently Chancellor of the Exchequer (1974–9) and Deputy Leader (1980–83).

1 **Their Europeanism is nothing but imperialism with an inferiority complex.**

Of the Conservative Party, quoted in the *Observer* 7 October 1962

2 **His speech was rather like being savaged by a dead sheep.**

Speech to House of Commons, 14 June 1978,

publ. in *Hansard*. Referring to a criticism of Healey's Budget proposals by Shadow Chancellor GEOFFREY HOWE. According to Healey's memoirs (*The Time of My Life*, pt 3, ch. 21, 1989), this off-the-cuff remark was inspired by WINSTON CHURCHILL's comment that an attack by Labour politician CLEMENT ATTLEE was 'like being savaged by a pet lamb'. In 1983, after being congratulated by Healey on his appointment as Foreign Secretary, Howe commented that it was 'like being nuzzled by an old ram'. Healey's rejoinder: 'It would be the end of a beautiful friendship if he accused me of necrophilia.'

3 **I sometimes think that the critical difference between a democracy and a dictatorship is that in a dictatorship there are only two people out of every hundred who take a personal interest in politics; in a democracy there are three.**

The Time of My Life, pt 2, ch. 7 (1989)

4 **Mrs Thatcher has added the diplomacy of Alf Garnett to the economics of Arthur Daley**

Quoted in the *Observer* 31 December 1989

Seamus Heaney (b. 1939)

IRISH POET

With its allusion to Irish tradition and myth, his lyrical poetry expresses a close relationship with the land, as in his first collection, Death of a Naturalist *(1966), and also addresses the political situation in Ireland, as in* North *(1975).* GAVIN EWART *saluted him in a poem: 'He's very popular among his mates,/I think I'm Auden, he thinks he's Yeats.'*

1 *Between my finger and my thumb*
The squat pen rests.
I'll dig with it.
'Digging', publ. in *Death of a Naturalist* (1966). Closing words of poem.

2 *We have no prairies*
To slice a big sun at evening –
Everywhere the eye concedes to
Encroaching horizon,

Is wooed into the cyclops' eye
Of a tarn.
'Bogland', publ. in *Door into the Dark* (1969)

3 *The ground itself is kind, black butter*

Melting and opening underfoot,
Missing its last definition
By millions of years.
Ibid.

4 *Who would connive*
in civilised outrage
yet understand the exact
and tribal, intimate revenge.
'Punishment', publ. in *North*, pt 1 (1975)

5 *The famous*

Northern reticence, the tight gag of place
And times: yes, yes. Of the 'wee six' I sing
Where to be saved you only must save face
And whatever you say, you say nothing.
'Whatever You Say Say Nothing', publ. ibid., pt 2

6 *Elderberry? It is shires dreaming wine.*
'Glanmore Sonnets', publ. in *Field Work* (1979)

7 *Don't be surprised*
If I demur, for, be advised
My passport's green.
No glass of ours was ever raised
To toast The Queen.
'An Open Letter to Blake and Andrew' (1983). The poem is addressed to BLAKE MORRISON and ANDREW MOTION, editors of *The Penguin Book of Contemporary British Poetry* (1982), who included him in the anthology.

8 *Everywhere being nowhere,*
who can prove
one place more than another?
'Birthplace', publ. in *Station Island*, pt 1 (1984)

9 *We are earthworms of the earth, and all*
that
has gone through us is what will be our
trace.
'Station Island', publ. ibid., pt 2

10 *Passive*
Suffering makes the world go round.
Peace on earth, men of good will, all that
Holds good as long as the balance holds,
The scales stand steady and the angels' strain
Prolongs itself at an unearthly pitch.
'Weighing In', publ. in *Spirit Level* (1996)

11 **Generations of gifted northern poets have let the linguistic cat out of the sectarian bag, setting it free in the great street carnival of 'protholics and catestants'.**
Quoted in the *Observer* 12 April 1998

(Sir) Edward Heath (b. 1916)

BRITISH STATESMAN

A keen sailor and accomplished musician, he entered Parliament as a Conservative MP in 1950, and as Prime Minister (1970–74) took Britain into the Common Market, which he afterwards considered his greatest achievement. JONATHAN AITKEN *called him 'a peddler of dreams from Broadstairs-les-deux-Eglises'.*

1 **When the people said 'the miners won a great victory' or 'the Government lost that one', what did they mean? In the country we live in, there could not be any 'we' or 'they'. There was only 'us' – all of us. If the Government is defeated then the country is defeated.**
Spoken after the settlement of the miners' strike, February 1972, quoted in *Edward Heath*, pt 4, ch. 21 (1993) by John Campbell

2 **The unpleasant and unacceptable face of capitalism.**
Speech to House of Commons, 15 May 1973,

publ. in *Hansard*. Referring to the 'Lonrho affair', in which Duncan Sandys, a non-executive director of the company and Conservative MP, was paid £130,000 compensation via an offshore account during a period of deep recession. The resulting enquiry led to legislation requiring companies to disclose payments and MPs to register their private interests.

3 **We are the trades union for the pensioners and for children; we are the union for the disabled and the sick; we are the union for those who live in slums or for those who want to buy homes. We are the union for the unemployed and the low paid. We are the union for those in poverty and for the hard pressed. . . . We are the union for the nation as a whole.**

Of the Conservative Party, in election campaign speech, Manchester, 20 February 1974, quoted in *The Times* 21 February 1974

4 **Better a three-day week than a no-day week.**

Quoted in the *Observer* 28 July 1974. Heath had announced at the end of 1973 that industry would work to a three-day week during the energy crisis.

5 **I have no interest in sailing round the world. Not that there is any lack of requests for me to do so.**

Observer 19 June 1977. Heath, a skilled ocean-racing yachtsman, captained the British team to victory with his boat *Morning Cloud* in the Sydney–Hobart race (1969) and the Admiral's Cup (1971).

6 **Either you agree with everything and you just become a lackey, in which case you will be described as loyal and 'dry', or you have contrary views and express them, without in any way indulging in personalities, in which case you are disloyal and 'wet' and ought to be chucked out. I object to the whole level of political discussion at the moment, that there must never be a U-turn, that people are 'wet' or 'dry' and so on. This is childish. Why cannot we discuss the merits of these things, instead of trying to encapsulate them in words like 'wet' or 'dry' or 'U-turn'?**

Quoted in *The Times* 4 July 1981. Commenting on MARGARET THATCHER's insistence on monetarist policies at the expense of high unemployment and inflation. In September 1981, Thatcher sacked three more 'wets' – Christopher Soames, Mark Carlisle and IAN GILMOUR – in favour of NIGEL LAWSON, CECIL PARKINSON and NORMAN TEBBIT.

7 **We cannot live permanently by taking in each other's washing.**

An often-repeated remark during the 1980s, quoted in *Edward Heath*, pt 6, ch. 36 (1993) by John Campbell. Heath was concerned at the loss of Britain's manufacturing capacity, scorning the idea of a service economy.

Ben Hecht (1894–1964)

US JOURNALIST, AUTHOR AND SCREENWRITER

He was the writer of (and uncredited collaborator in) numerous screenplays, among them The Scoundrel *(1935) and* Notorious *(1946). 'Writing a good movie brings a writer about as much fame as steering a bicycle,' he once commented.*

1 **Movies are one of the bad habits that corrupted our century. Of their many sins, I offer as the worst their effect on the intellectual side of the nation. It is chiefly from that viewpoint I write of them – as an eruption of trash that has lamed the American mind and retarded Americans from becoming a cultured people.**

A Child of the Century, bk 5 'What the Movies Are' (1954). Hecht continued, 'They have slapped into the American mind more human misinformation in one evening than the Dark Ages could muster in a decade.'

2 **I discovered early in my movie work that a movie is never any better than the stupidest man connected with it. There are times when this distinction may be given to the writer or director. Most often it belongs to the producer.**

Ibid., bk 5 'Illustrations by Doré (Gustave)'. Hecht saw the producer's chief task as 'the job of turning good writers into movie hacks. These sinister fellows were always my bosses.'

Eric Heffer (1922–91)

BRITISH POLITICIAN

A socialist traditionalist, he was elected Labour MP for Walton, Liverpool, in 1964 and served as a junior minister under HAROLD WILSON *(1974–5) and in* MICHAEL FOOT*'s shadow cabinet (1981).*

1 **Jesus Christ was not a conservative. That's a racing certainty.**

Observer 20 February 1983

Hugh Hefner (b. 1926)

US PUBLISHER

He founded Playboy *magazine in 1953. Its glossy soft-porn style was later extended to* Playboy *clubs, in the face of increasing criticism by feminist groups in the 1970s.*

1 **Much of what *Playboy* is really all about is the projection of the adolescent fantasies I have never really lost. The boy has been father to the man.**

Quoted in *Hefner*, ch. 11 (1974) by Frank Brady

Martin Heidegger (1889–1976)

GERMAN PHILOSOPHER

His standing largely rests on his incomplete work
Being and Time *(1927), an analysis of human
existence and death. He was a key influence on*
SARTRE, *though his Nazi sympathies damaged his
reputation.*

1 Man acts as though *he* were the shaper and
master of language, while in fact *language*
remains the master of man.

'Building Dwelling Thinking', lecture, 5 August
1951, publ. in *Poetry, Language, Thought* (1971)

2 The German language 'speaks Being', while
all the others merely 'speak of Being'.

Quoted in Prologue to *An Appetite for Poetry:
Essays in Literary Interpretation* (1989) by Frank
Kermode

Muhammad Heikal (b. 1923)

EGYPTIAN JOURNALIST

*He gained fame as Editor-in-Chief (1957–74) of
the Cairo newspaper* Al-Ahram, *called the New
York Times of the Arab world for its standards of
objectivity.*

1 We [the Arabs] have proved we are not
modern. We have proved we are not
religious in the real sense of the word. We
have proved that we cannot afford
democracy.

Independent 11 March 1992. On the conduct of
Arab governments in the wake of the Gulf War.

Carolyn Heilbrun (b. 1926)

US AUTHOR AND ACADEMIC

Her books, such as Reinventing Womanhood
(1979) and Writing a Woman's Life *(1989),
emphasize the importance of women's fulfilment.
Writing as Amanda Cross, she satirizes literary-
academic milieux in her cerebral detective novels.*

1 In former days, everyone found the
assumption of innocence so easy; today we
find fatally easy the assumption of guilt.

Kate Fansler, in *Poetic Justice* ch. 2 (written as
Amanda Cross, 1970)

2 Women are liberated the moment they
stop caring what other women think of
them.

Emilia Airhart, ibid. ch. 7

3 We cannot guess the outcome of our
actions. . . . Which is why our actions must
always be acceptable in themselves, and
not as strategies.

Professor Frederick Clemance, ibid., ch. 11. He
adds 'Kant put it differently and better.'

4 The married are those who have taken the
terrible risk of intimacy and, having taken
it, know life without intimacy to be
impossible.

'Marriage is the Message', publ. in *Ms* August
1974

Cynthia Heimel (b. 1947)

US COLUMNIST

*She is an outspoken, humorous and feisty colum-
nist, voicing opinions on a range of subjects.*

1 The '60s, contrary to popular belief, are
not dead. . . . And deep in the heart of
every forty-year old accountant is the
secret knowledge that he was there, then.
He may not admit it, he may not want to
do anything about it, but he still gets a
twinge of fury when he hears 'Day Tripper'
in Muzak, and a hidden part of his brain
sings, 'What a drag it is to get old' at three
in the morning while he's trying to get
some sleep. He knows what's been lost.

'Highway 1967 Revisited', first publ. in *Playboy*
1987, repr. in *If You Can't Live Without Me, Why
Aren't You Dead Yet?*, 'The Writer's Life' (1991)

Piet Hein (1905–96)

DANISH INVENTOR AND POET

*Writing as Kumbel, he is known for the grook
(gruk in Danish), a short aphoristic form created
by him during the Nazi occupation, which
expresses serious concerns through humour. He has
translated many into English.*

1 *The human spirit sublimates
the impulses it thwarts:
a healthy sex life mitigates
the lust for other sports.*

'Hint and Suggestion', publ. in *Grooks* (1966)

2 *They're busy making bigger roads,
and better roads and more,
so that people can discover
even faster than before
that everything is everywhere alike.*

'Road Sense', publ. ibid.

3 *The road to wisdom? – Well, it's plain
and simple to express:
Err
and err
and err again
but less
and less
and less.*

'The Road to Wisdom', publ. ibid.

Joseph Heller (1923–99)

US NOVELIST

*Drawing on his experience in the Second World
War, he produced his bestselling satirical novel*
Catch-22 *(1961). Other works include the more
experimental* Something Happened *(1974) and*
God Knows *(1984).*

1 Death to all modifiers.

Yossarian, in *Catch-22*, ch. 1 (1961)

2 He had decided to live for ever or die in
the attempt.

Of Yossarian, ibid., ch. 3

3 **He was a self-made man who owed his lack of success to nobody.**
Of Colonel Cargill, ibid.

4 **There's a rule saying I have to ground anyone who's crazy. . . . There's a catch. Catch-22. Anyone who wants to get out of combat duty isn't really crazy.**
Doc Daneeka, ibid., ch. 5. The narrator explains: 'Orr was crazy and could be grounded. All he had to do was ask; and as soon as he did, he would no longer be crazy and would have to fly more missions.'

5 **Some men are born mediocre, some men achieve mediocrity, and some men have mediocrity thrust upon them. With Major Major it had been all three.**
Ibid., ch. 9. A reworking of Shakespeare's 'Some are born great, some achieve greatness, and some have greatness thrust upon 'em' (Malvolio, quoting Maria's letter in *Twelfth Night*)

6 **Frankly, I'd like to see the government get out of war altogether and leave the whole field to private industry.**
Milo Minderbinder, ibid., ch. 24

7 **I think that maybe in every company today there is always at least one person who is going crazy slowly.**
Narrator (Bob Slocum), in *Something Happened*, 'The office in which I work' (1974)

8 **It's a wise person, I guess, who knows he's dumb, and an honest person who knows he's a liar. And it's a dumb person, I guess, who's convinced he is wise.**
Ibid.

Mark Hellinger (1903–47)
US JOURNALIST, SCREENWRITER AND PRODUCER
Producer of more than twenty films and a writer for films such as Broadway Bill *(1934) and* Comet Over Broadway *(1938), he was also considered the first Broadway columnist.*

1 **Every murder turns on a bright hot light, and a lot of people . . . have to walk out of the shadows.**
Narrator, in *The Naked City* (film, 1948, screenplay by Albert Maltz and Malvin Wald, directed by Jules Dassin). Hellinger's last production was narrated by himself.

2 **There are eight million stories in the naked city. This has been one of them.**
Afterword, ibid. Hellinger's sign-off was used at the end of each episode of the TV series of the same name (1958–62).

Lillian Hellman (1905–84)
US PLAYWRIGHT
A left-wing activist and the leading woman playwright of her generation, she dealt with political and social issues in her plays, such as The Children's Hour *(1934) and* The Little Foxes *(1939). See* JULES FEIFFER 2, MARY MCCARTHY 12.

1 **Cynicism is an unpleasant way of saying the truth.**
Ben, in *The Little Foxes*, act 1 (1939)

2 **It's an indulgence to sit in a room and discuss your beliefs as if they were a juicy piece of gossip.**
Sara Müller, in *Watch on the Rhine*, act 2 (1941)

3 **I cannot and will not cut my conscience to fit this year's fashions.**
Letter to John S. Wood, Chairman of the House un-American Activities Committee, 19 May 1952, quoted in the *Nation* 31 May 1952. The letter contained Hellman's refusal to testify against colleagues accused of Communist affiliations.

4 **People change and forget to tell each other. Too bad – causes so many mistakes.**
Anna, in *Toys in the Attic*, act 3 (1960)

5 **They're fancy talkers about themselves, writers. If I had to give young writers advice, I would say don't listen to writers talking about writing or themselves.**
The New York Times 21 February 1960

6 **Intellectuals can tell themselves anything, sell themselves any bill of goods, which is why they were so often patsies for the ruling classes in nineteenth-century France and England, or twentieth-century Russia and America.**
Journal entry, 30 April 1967, publ. in Hellman's memoir, *An Unfinished Woman*, ch. 13 (1969)

7 **It is a mark of many famous people that they cannot part with their brightest hour: what worked once must always work.**
Pentimento, 'Theatre' (1973). Referring to TALLULAH BANKHEAD, who 'had been the nineteen-twenties' most daring girl, but what had been dashing, even brave, had become by 1939 shrill and tiring'.

8 **Every time she gets laid she gets married. Nobody told her you can do it and stay single.**
Of Elizabeth Taylor, quoted in *Lilly: Reminiscences of Lillian Hellman*, pt 4 (1988) by Peter Feibleman

Leona Helmsley (b. 1920)
US BUSINESSWOMAN
Dubbed 'the Queen of Mean' by the tabloids, she was sentenced in 1992 to four years in prison, 750 hours of community service and $7.1 million in fines for tax evasion. In 1998 she was left a second fortune by her husband.

1 **We don't pay taxes. Only the little people pay taxes.**
Quoted in *The New York Times* 12 July 1989. The words were reported by Helmsley's former housekeeper during her employer's trial for tax evasion.

Ernest Hemingway (1899–1961)
US AUTHOR

Themes of honour and masculinity recur in his novels and short stories, including A Farewell to Arms *(1929, filmed 1932 and 1957),* For Whom the Bell Tolls *(1940, filmed 1943) and* The Old Man and the Sea *(1952, filmed 1958). He took his own life with a shotgun. 'Hemingway's words strike you, each one, as if they were pebbles fetched fresh from a brook', wrote Ford Madox Ford. See also* MARLENE DIETRICH 6, MIKE TYSON 2.

1 Switzerland is a small, steep country, much more up and down than sideways, and is all stuck over with large brown hotels built on the cuckoo clock style of architecture.
Quoted in the *Toronto Star Weekly* 4 March 1922

2 *The age demanded that we dance*
And jammed us into iron pants.
And in the end the age was handed
The sort of shit that it demanded.
'The Age Demanded', publ. in *Der Querschnitt* February 1925, repr. in *Sylvia Beach and the Lost Generation*, ch. 9 (1983) by Noel Riley Fitch

3 God knows people who are paid to have attitudes toward things, professional critics, make me sick; camp following eunuchs of literature. They won't even whore. They're all virtuous and sterile. And how well meaning and high minded. But they're all camp followers.
Letter to Sherwood Anderson, 23 May 1925, publ. in *Selected Letters* (ed. Carlos Baker, 1981)

4 You're an expatriate. You've lost touch with the soil. You get precious. Fake European standards have ruined you. You drink yourself to death. You become obsessed by sex. You spend all your time talking, not working. You are an expatriate, see? You hang around cafés.
Bill Gorton to Jake Barnes, in *The Sun Also Rises*, bk 2, ch. 12 (1926, filmed 1957). Jake replies: 'It sounds like a swell life.'

5 In the fall the war was always there but we did not go to it any more.
Men Without Women, 'In Another Country' (1927). F. SCOTT FITZGERALD praised this as 'one of the most beautiful prose sentences I've ever read'.

6 I was always embarrassed by the words sacred, glorious and sacrifice and the expression in vain. We had heard them, sometimes standing in the rain almost out of earshot, so that only the shouted words came through, and had read them, on proclamations that were slapped up by billposters over other proclamations, now for a long time, and I had seen nothing sacred, and the things that were glorious had no glory and the sacrifices were like the stock-yards at Chicago if nothing was done with the meat except to bury it.
Frederic Henry, in *A Farewell to Arms*, ch. 27 (1929, filmed 1932 and 1957)

7 Grace under pressure.
Definition of 'guts', in interview by DOROTHY PARKER in the *New Yorker* 30 November 1929. The formula was invoked by JOHN F. KENNEDY at the start of his collection of essays, *Profiles of Courage* (1956), possibly originating in the Latin motto, *Fortiter in re, suaviter in modo* ('strong in deed, gentle in manner').

8 Our nada who art in nada, nada be thy name thy kingdom nada thy will be nada in nada as it is in nada. Give us this nada our daily nada and nada us our nada as we nada our nadas and nada us not into nada but deliver us from nada; pues nada. Hail nothing full of nothing, nothing is with thee.
The older waiter, in 'A Clean, Well-Lighted Place', publ. in *Winner Take Nothing* (1933)

9 About morals, I know only that what is moral is what you feel good after and what is immoral is what you feel bad after.
Death in the Afternoon, ch. 1 (1932)

10 All our words from loose using have lost their edge.
Ibid., ch. 7

11 Bullfighting is the only art in which the artist is in danger of death and in which the degree of brilliance in the performance is left to the fighter's honor.
Ibid., ch. 9

12 Madame, all stories, if continued far enough, end in death, and he is no true-story teller who would keep that from you.
Ibid., ch. 11

13 A serious writer is not to be confounded with a solemn writer. A serious writer may be a hawk or a buzzard or even a popinjay, but a solemn writer is always a bloody owl.
Ibid., ch. 16

14 All good books are alike in that they are truer than if they had really happened and after you are finished reading one you will feel that all that happened to you and afterwards it all belongs to you; the good and the bad, the ecstasy, the remorse, and sorrow, the people and the places and how the weather was.
'Old Newsman Writes: A Letter from Cuba', first publ. in *Esquire* December 1934, repr. in *By-Line Ernest Hemingway* (ed. William White, 1967)

15 All modern American literature comes from one book by Mark Twain called *Huckleberry Finn*. . . . American writing comes from that. There was nothing

before. There has been nothing as good
since.

The Green Hills of Africa, ch. 1 (1935)

16 The rich were dull and they drank too
much or they played too much back-
gammon. They were dull and they were
repetitious. He remembered poor Julian
and his romantic awe of them and how he
had started a story once that began, 'The
very rich are different from you and me.'
And how someone had said to Julian, 'Yes,
they have more money.'

'The Snows of Kilimanjaro', first publ. in *Esquire*
August 1936, repr. in *The Fifth Column and the
First Forty-Nine Stories* (1938). In its original publication, 'Julian' was named as F. Scott Fitzgerald, who in 1926 had opened a story 'Let me
tell you about the very rich. They are different
from you and me.' See also F. SCOTT
FITZGERALD 14.

17 But did thee feel the earth move?

Robert Jordan speaking to Maria, in *For Whom
the Bell Tolls*, ch. 13 (1940, filmed 1943). During
their lovemaking, Jordan had 'felt the earth
move out and away from under them'. The
words do not appear in the film version.

18 He was just a coward and that was the
worst luck any man could have.

Robert Jordan speaking of his father, ibid.,
ch. 30

19 The world is a fine place and worth fighting for.

Robert Jordan, ibid., ch. 43

20 Cowardice, as distinguished from panic, is
almost always simply a lack of ability to
suspend the functioning of the
imagination.

Men at War, Introduction (1942)

21 All my life I've looked at words as though I
were seeing them for the first time.

Letter, 9 April 1945, publ. in *Selected Letters* (ed.
Carlos Baker, 1981)

22 It wasn't by accident that the Gettysburg
address was so short. The laws of prose
writing are as immutable as those of flight,
of mathematics, of physics.

Letter, 23 July 1945, publ. ibid. Hemingway was
discussing the difficulties of sustaining an epic at
a high pitch.

23 Scott took LITERATURE so solemnly. He
never understood that it was just writing
as well as you can and finishing what you
start.

Referring to F. SCOTT FITZGERALD in letter to
Arthur Mizener, 12 May 1950, publ. ibid.
Mizener wrote a biography of Fitzgerald, and
edited his essays and short stories.

24 I started out very quiet and I beat Mr Turg-
enev. Then I trained hard and I beat Mr de
Maupassant. I've fought two draws with
Mr Stendhal, and I think I had an edge in

the last one. But nobody's going to get me
in any ring with Mr Tolstoy unless I'm
crazy or I keep getting better.

New Yorker 13 May 1950

25 Writing and travel broaden your ass if not
your mind and I like to write standing up.

Letter, 9 July 1950, publ. in *Selected Letters* (ed.
Carlos Baker, 1981)

26 Man is not made for defeat. A man can be
destroyed but not defeated.

The Old Man and the Sea (1952). Quoted as the
final words in A. E. Hotchner's biography, *Papa
Hemingway* (1966).

27 There isn't any symbolism. The sea is the
sea. The old man is an old man. The boy is
a boy and the fish is a fish. The sharks are
all sharks no better and no worse. All the
symbolism that people say is shit. What
goes beyond is what you see beyond when
you know.

Letter to the critic Bernard Berenson,
13 September 1952, publ. in *Selected Letters* (ed.
Carlos Baker, 1981). Referring to Hemingway's
novella *The Old Man and the Sea*.

28 Actually if a writer needs a dictionary he
should not write. He should have read the
dictionary at least three times from beginning to end and then have loaned it to
someone who needs it. There are only certain words which are valid and similies
(bring me my dictionary) are like defective
ammunition (the lowest thing I can think
of at this time).

Letter to Bernard Berenson, 20 March 1953,
publ. ibid. Hemingway's spelling, as manifested
in his letters, was deeply flawed. See also below
ERNEST HEMINGWAY 37.

29 Writing, at its best, is a lonely life.
Organizations for writers palliate the
writer's loneliness, but I doubt if they
improve his writing. He grows in public
stature as he sheds his loneliness and often
his work deteriorates. For he does his work
alone and if he is a good enough writer he
must face eternity, or the lack of it, each
day.

Address recorded for the Nobel Prize Committee, accepting the Nobel Prize for Literature,
10 December 1954, publ. in *Hemingway: The
Writer as Artist*, ch. 13 (1963) by Carlos Baker

30 How simple the writing of literature would
be if it were only necessary to write in
another way what has been well written. It
is because we have had such great writers
in the past that a writer is driven far out
past where he can go, out to where no one
can help him.

Ibid.

31 The most essential gift for a good writer is
a built-in, shock-proof, shit detector. This

is the writer's radar and all great writers have had it.

Interview in the *Paris Review* spring 1958, repr. in *Writers at Work* (second series, ed. George Plimpton, 1963)

32 We are all apprentices in a craft where no one ever becomes a master.

New York Journal-American 11 July 1961

33 All things truly wicked start from an innocence.

A Moveable Feast, ch. 17 (1964)

34 Never confuse movement with action

Quoted by MARLENE DIETRICH in *Papa Hemingway*, pt 1, ch. 1 (1966) by A. E. Hotchner. 'In those five words,' Dietrich commented, 'he gave me a whole philosophy.'

35 You write a book like that that you're fond of over the years, then you see that happen to it, it's like pissing in your father's beer.

After seeing DAVID O. SELZNICK's remake of *A Farewell to Arms* (1957), quoted ibid.

36 If you are lucky enough to have lived in Paris as a young man, then wherever you go for the rest of your life it stays with you, for Paris is a moveable feast.

Quoted ibid., pt 1, ch. 3. The words 'a moveable feast' were used – on Hotchner's recommendation – as the title of Hemingway's posthumously published Paris memoirs. This paragraph appears as the book's epigraph.

37 Poor Faulkner. Does he really think big emotions come from big words? He thinks I don't know the ten-dollar words. I know them all right. But there are older and simpler and better words, and those are the ones I use.

Quoted ibid., pt 1, ch. 4. Hemingway's rebuke was made after being informed (by Hotchner) that WILLIAM FAULKNER considered Hemingway 'had no courage' and 'had never been known to use a word that might send the reader to the dictionary'. For Hemingway, Faulkner was 'Old Corndrinking Mellifluous'.

38 To be a successful father . . . there's one absolute rule: when you have a kid, don't look at it for the first two years.

Quoted ibid., pt 2, ch. 5

Jimi Hendrix (1942–70)

US ROCK MUSICIAN

James Marshall Hendrix. Half-Cherokee Indian, he was the most influential rock guitarist of the 1960s, legendary for his flamboyant technique and style. He came to London from New York in 1966 and had hits the following year with 'Hey Joe' and 'Purple Haze'.

1 Hey Joe,
   Where're you going with that gun in your hand?

'Hey Joe' (song, 1966, written by Billy Roberts) on the album *Smash Hits* (1968). The song had

earlier been performed by David Crosby with the Byrds, and was a US hit for LA garage band The Leaves in 1966.

2 *Purple haze all in my brain,
   Lately things don't seem the same,
   Actin' funny, but I don't know why,
   'Scuse me while I kiss the sky.*

'Purple Haze' (song, 1967) on ibid.

3 I believe everybody should have a room where they get rid of all their . . . releases, where they can do all their releases. So my room was a stage.

Interview 12 September 1970, publ. in *Radio 1's Classic Interviews* (ed. Jeff Simpson, 1992). The interview, which has never been fully broadcast, took place two days before Hendrix was found dead in his London hotel room.

4 I'd like to take part in a change of reality.

Ibid. In answer to the question, 'Do you want to change the world?'

5 Blues is easy to play, but hard to feel.

Quoted in *Crosstown Traffic*, ch. 6 (1989) by Charles Shaar Murray

Arthur W. D. Henley

1 *Nobody loves a fairy when she's forty.*

'Nobody loves a fairy when she's forty' (song, 1934, written by Arthur le Clerq). The song was recorded by Tessie O'Shea.

Katharine Hepburn (1909–2003)

US ACTRESS

An untypical Hollywood star for her independent, feisty spirit, she made nine films with Spencer Tracy, with whom she had a long-standing relationship. Her other films include The Philadelphia Story *(1940),* The African Queen *(1951) and* On Golden Pond *(1981). See* DOROTHY PARKER 13.

1 The average Hollywood film star's ambition is to be admired by an American, courted by an Italian, married to an Englishman and have a French boyfriend.

New York Journal-American 22 February 1954

2 Only the really plain people know about love – the very fascinating ones try so hard to create an impression that they very soon exhaust their talents.

Look 18 February 1958

3 To keep your character intact you cannot stoop to filthy acts. It makes it easier to stoop the next time.

Quoted in the *Los Angeles Times* 24 November 1974

(Sir) A. P. Herbert (1890–1971)

BRITISH AUTHOR AND POLITICIAN

Alan Patrick Herbert. A brilliant librettist for such light operas as La Vie Parisienne *(1929) and* Bless the Bride *(1947), he also wrote poetry, plays and*

novels, and was an Independent MP for Oxford University 1935–50.

1 **People must not do things for fun. We are not here for fun. There is no reference to fun in any act of Parliament.**
Lord Light, in *Uncommon Law*, 'Is it a Free Country?' (1935)

2 **The critical period in matrimony is breakfast-time.**
Ibid., 'Is Marriage Lawful?'

3 **The Englishman never enjoys himself except for a noble purpose.**
Mr Justice Plush, ibid., 'Is Fox-Hunting Fun?'

4 **An Act of God was defined as *'something which no reasonable man could have expected'.***
Mr David, ibid., 'Act of God'

Oliver Herford (1863–1935)
US POET AND ILLUSTRATOR
Called the 'Charles Lamb of his day' by William Dean Howells, he contributed illustrations, caricatures, verses and essays to numerous periodicals from the 1890s to the 1930s. His collections include A Little Book of Bores *(1906).*

1 **[He] has a whim of iron.**
Excuse It Please, 'Impossible Pudding' (1929). Referring to King Barumph in the story. The remark had earlier been attributed to Herford about his wife.

Michael Herr (b. 1940)
US JOURNALIST
He covered the Vietnam war for Esquire *in 1967, later describing his impressions in* Dispatches *(1977). He was script consultant to* COPPOLA'S Apocalypse Now *(1979) and wrote the screenplay for* Full Metal Jacket *(1987).*

1 **We came to fear something more complicated than death, an annihilation less final but more complete, and we got out. Because . . . we all knew that if you stayed too long you became one of those poor bastards who had to have a war on all the time, and where was that?**
Dispatches, 'Colleagues', sect. 3 (1977)

2 **Vietnam was what we had instead of happy childhoods.**
Ibid.

3 **All the wrong people remember Vietnam. I think all the people who remember it should forget it, and all the people who forgot it should remember it.**
Observer 15 January 1989

Édouard Herriot (1872–1957)
FRENCH STATESMAN
A radical Socialist politician, he was Prime Minister 1924–5, 1926 and 1932. As President of the Chamber of Deputies, he strongly opposed the Vichy government and was gaoled by the Nazis. He was President of the National Assembly 1947–54.

1 **When it's a question of peace one must talk to the Devil himself.**
Quoted in the *Observer* 21 September 1953

John Hersey (1914–93)
US NOVELIST AND JOURNALIST
He is known for his documentary fiction of the Second World War, including A Bell for Adano *(1944), and for* Hiroshima *(1946), an account of the nuclear explosion and its aftermath.*

1 **What has kept the world safe from the bomb since 1945 has not been deterrence, in the sense of fear of specific weapons, so much as it's been memory. The memory of what happened at Hiroshima.**
Interview in *Writers at Work* (eighth series, ed. George Plimpton, 1988)

Werner Herzog (b. 1942)
GERMAN FILM-MAKER
Originally Werner Stipetic. A leading member of the New Cinema in Germany, he is associated with metaphysical films in which landscape plays a prominent role, such as Aguirre: The Wrath of God *(1973),* Heart of Glass *(1976) and* Where the Green Ants Dream *(1984).*

1 **You should look straight at a film; that's the only way to see one. Film is not the art of scholars but of illiterates.**
Interview in *The New York Times* 11 September 1977

2 **For such an advanced civilization as ours to be without images that are adequate to it is as serious a defect as being without memory.**
Ibid.

Michael Heseltine (b. 1933)
BRITISH POLITICIAN
Baron Heseltine of Thenford. Nicknamed 'Tarzan' for his outdoors image, he was a Conservative MP 1966–2001, during which time he served as Environment Secretary (1979–83), Defence Secretary (1983–6) and Deputy Prime Minister (1995–7).

1 **There you have it! The final proof. Labour's brand new, shining, modernists' economic dream. But it's not Brown's – it's Balls'!**
Speech to Conservative Party Conference, Bournemouth, 12 October 1994, quoted in the *Daily Telegraph* 13 October 1994. Heseltine was referring to Gordon Brown's recent speech on Labour's economic policy, specifically: 'Our new economic approach is rooted in ideas which stress the importance of macro-economics,

neo-classical endogenous growth theory and the symbiotic relationships between growth and investment in people and infrastructure', said by Heseltine to have been written by a '27-year-old choral-singing researcher named Ed Balls'.

Hermann Hesse (1877–1962)
GERMAN NOVELIST AND POET
Imbued with the influences of German romanticism, Eastern religion and Jungian psychoanalysis, his works, which include Steppenwolf *(1927, filmed 1974) and* The Glass Bead Game *(1943), acquired a cult readership.*

1 What constitutes a real, live human being is more of a mystery than ever these days, and men – each one of whom is a valuable, unique experiment on the part of nature – are shot down wholesale.
Narrator (Sinclair), in *Demian*, Prologue (1919)

2 In each individual the spirit is made flesh, in each one the whole of creation suffers, in each one a Saviour is crucified.
Ibid.

3 I am fond of music I think because it is so amoral. Everything else is moral and I am after something that isn't. I have always found moralizing intolerable.
Ibid., ch. 5

4 One never reaches home, but wherever friendly paths intersect the whole world looks like home for a time.
Frau Eva, ibid., ch. 7

5 Every age, every culture, every custom and tradition has its own character, its own weakness and its own strength, its beauties and cruelties; it accepts certain sufferings as matters of course, puts up patiently with certain evils. Human life is reduced to real suffering, to hell, only when two ages, two cultures and religions overlap.
Steppenwolf, Preface (1927)

6 What I always hated and detested and cursed above all things was this contentment, this healthiness and comfort, this carefully preserved optimism of the middle classes, this fat and prosperous brood of mediocrity.
Ibid., 'For Madmen Only'

7 The bourgeois treasures nothing more highly than the self. . . . And so at the cost of intensity he achieves his own preservation and security. His harvest is a quiet mind which he prefers to being possessed by God, as he prefers comfort to pleasure, convenience to liberty, and a pleasant temperature to that deathly inner consuming fire.
Ibid., 'Treatise on the Steppenwolf'

8 To study history means submitting to chaos and nevertheless retaining faith in order and meaning. It is a very serious task, young man, and possibly a tragic one.
Father Jacobus, in *The Glass Bead Game*, ch. 4 (1943, transl. 1960)

9 The call of death is a call of love. Death can be sweet if we answer it in the affirmative, if we accept it as one of the great eternal forms of life and transformation.
Letter, 1950, publ. in *Hermann Hesse: A Pictorial Biography*, 'Montagnola' (ed. Volker Michels, 1973)

Lord Hewart (1870–1943)
BRITISH JUDGE
Gordon, first Viscount Hewart. Liberal MP for Leicester (1913–22), Attorney General (1919–22) and Lord Chief Justice (1922–40), he was considered a brilliant advocate, less effective as a judge.

1 Justice should not only be done, but should manifestly and undoubtedly be seen to be done.
Remark in 'Rex v. Surrey Justices', 9 November 1923, publ. in *King's Bench Reports*, vol. 1 (1924). Ruling on the quashing of a conviction on technical grounds.

Robert Hewison (b. 1943)
BRITISH CULTURAL HISTORIAN
He is a critic and commentator on the arts, and the author of books including Ruskin in Venice *(1978) and* Culture and Consensus *(1995).*

1 Individually, museums are fine institutions, dedicated to the high values of preservation, education and truth; collectively, their growth in numbers points to the imaginative death of this country.
The Heritage Industry, Introduction (1987)

2 If the only new thing we have to offer is an improved version of the past, then today can only be inferior to yesterday. Hypnotised by images of the past, we risk losing all capacity for creative change.
Ibid.

3 Postmodernism is modernism with the optimism taken out.
Ibid., ch. 6

4 The turn of the century raises expectations. The end of a millennium promises apocalypse and revelation. But at the close of the twentieth century the golden age seems behind us, not ahead. The end game of the 1990s promises neither nirvana nor armageddon, but entropy.
Future Tense, ch. 1 (1990)

Du Bose Heyward
See IRA GERSHWIN 2, 3

George V. Higgins (b. 1939)

US NOVELIST

George Vincent Higgins. His first-hand experiences as journalist and attorney contributed to the success of his literary thrillers, which often have Boston as a backdrop. These include The Friends of Eddie Coyle *(1972) and* Outlaws *(1987).*

1 Data is what distinguishes the dilettante from the artist.

Guardian 17 June 1988

2 Politics is a choice of enemas. You're gonna get it up the ass, no matter what you do.

Ed Cobb, in *Victories*, ch. 7 (1991)

Benny Hill (1925–92)

BRITISH COMEDIAN

Originally Alfred Hawthorne. He was considered the last of the visual comics, and wrote scripts and music as well as playing most of the characters in The Benny Hill Show *on television (1957–66). His saucy sketches attracted a world-wide audience.*

1 That's what show business is – sincere insincerity.

Quoted in the *Observer* 12 June 1977

Christopher Hill (1912–2003)

BRITISH HISTORIAN

A renowned Marxist historian, he has written widely on the period of the Civil War, including The English Revolution, 1640 *(1940) and* Milton and the English Revolution *(1978).*

1 Only very slowly and late have men come to realize that unless freedom is universal it is only extended privilege.

The Century of Revolution, ch. 20 (1961)

2 History has to be rewritten in every generation, because although the past does not change the present does; each generation asks new questions of the past, and finds new areas of sympathy as it re-lives different aspects of the experiences of its predecessors.

The World Turned Upside Down, Introduction (1972)

Damon Hill (b. 1960)

BRITISH RACING DRIVER

Son of Formula One driver Graham Hill and winner of more than twenty Grands Prix, he retired from Formula One racing in 1999.

1 Winning is everything. The only ones who remember when you come second are your wife and your dog.

Quoted in the *Sunday Times* 18 December 1994

Sidney Hillman (1887–1946)

LITHUANIAN-BORN US TRADE UNIONIST

Originally Simcha Hillman. Having emigrated to the USA in 1907, he became President of the Amalgamated Clothing Workers of America in 1914, a position he held until his death.

1 Politics is the science of how who gets what, when and why.

Political Primer for all Americans (1944)

Heinrich Himmler (1900–1945)

GERMAN NAZI LEADER

He was made head of the SS in 1929 and of the Gestapo in 1936, and was responsible for directing the extermination of the Jews. He committed suicide at the end of the Second World War.

1 My honour is my loyalty.
 (Meine Ehre heisst Treue.)

Formulated as the watchword of the SS Nazi élite, translated by HANNAH ARENDT in *The Origins of Totalitarianism*, ch. 10 (1951). The US Government Printing Office's *Nazi Conspiracy and Aggression* (1946–8), vol. 5 gives an alternative translation: 'My honour signifies faithfulness.'

2 Whether nations live in prosperity or starve to death like cattle interests me only in so far as we need them as slaves to our *Kultur*; otherwise it is of no interest to me. Whether 10,000 Russian females fall down from exhaustion while digging an antitank ditch interests me only in so far as the antitank ditch for Germany is finished.

Address to SS officers at Posen, 4 October 1943, quoted in *The Rise and Fall of the Third Reich*, ch. 27 (1959) by William L. Shirer

Beatrice Hinkle (1874–1953)

US PSYCHIATRIST

She was the translator of JUNG *and first American practitioner of his analytical psychology. Her book* The Re-creating of the Individual *(1923) established her as a pioneering feminist critic of* FREUD.

1 Fundamentally the male artist approximates more to the psychology of woman, who, biologically speaking, is a purely creative being and whose personality has been as mysterious and unfathomable to the man as the artist has been to the average person.

The Recreating of the Individual, 'The Psychology of the Artist' (1923)

Hirohito (1901–89)

EMPEROR OF JAPAN

Emperor from 1926, he enjoyed the longest reign of any Japanese monarch, coinciding with the country's period of expansionism (from 1931) and the Second World War. He renounced his divinity in 1946.

1 We have resolved to endure the unendurable and suffer what is unsufferable.

Statement 15 August 1945, quoted by A. J. P.Taylor in the *Listener* 9 September 1976. The declaration was made following the dropping of the atomic bomb on Hiroshima and was the first time a Japanese emperor had made a direct address to his people.

Damien Hirst (b. 1965)

BRITISH ARTIST

His often provocative installations and most famously his pickled animals raise questions of life and mortality. He won the 1995 Turner Prize with Mother and Child Divided.

1 I sometimes feel that I have nothing to say and I want to communicate this.

Independent 21 July 1992

2 I think the idea is more important than the object. The object can look after itself. It will probably last long after I'm dead. I'm more frightened of being stabbed myself. You can always get another shark.

Interview by WILL SELF in *Modern Painters* summer 1994, repr. in *Junk Mail* (1995) by Will Self. Hirst was referring to one of his installations of a shark preserved in formaldehyde. Coincidentally, the day after this interview, one of his new exhibits at the Serpentine Gallery, also a preserved animal, was vandalized.

3 As an artist you have to reinvent yourself every day. Which I think is what you do anyway as a person, which is why people fall out, split up, get together. . . . It's like a turning over.

Interview in *The Idler* July/August 1995

4 I think there's a handful of eye people and billions of ear people. Some people go look at it and think it's great, so they buy it, and all these other people hear that they've bought it so they buy it too.

Interview in the *Big Issue* 1–7 September 1997

5 I've got two ways of looking at this. I am either a genius – hummmm, fantastic – or the art world is incapable of dealing with the kind of art that is going on today. My answer is the art world is fucked. I'm not a genius.

Quoted in the *Observer* 14 September 1997

Ian Hislop (b. 1960)

BRITISH JOURNALIST AND BROADCASTER

He was a television scriptwriter for Spitting Image *(1984–9), became Editor of* Private Eye *in 1989 and since 1991 has captained a team on the BBC TV quiz show* Have I Got News For You.

1 It's the gap between how they *think* they are coming over and how they *actually* come over. In their case, it's the *gulf* between their self-perception and the

reality. The job of a satirist is to point it out.

Interview in the *Guardian* 27 April 1996 Referring to what makes JAMES GOLDSMITH, JEFFREY ARCHER and Princess DIANA natural subjects for satire.

(Sir) Alfred Hitchcock (1899–1980)

BRITISH FILM-MAKER

Based in Hollywood from the 1940s, he was a master of the suspense thriller. His films include The Thirty Nine Steps *(1935),* Rear Window *(1954),* Psycho *(1960) and* The Birds *(1963). 'His reputation has suffered from the fact that he has given audiences more pleasure than is permissible in serious cinema,' was critic Andrew Sarris's tribute.*

1 Actors are cattle.

Quoted in the *Saturday Evening Post* 22 May 1943. The remark caused Carole Lombard, his star of the time, to lead a herd of oxen onto the set. He later told the press, 'I didn't say actors are cattle. What I said was, actors should be *treated* like cattle.'

2 Drama is life with the dull bits cut out.

Quoted in the *Observer* 10 July 1960. Speaking to FRANÇOIS TRUFFAUT in 1962, Hitchcock explained, 'Making a film means, first of all, to tell a story. That story can be an improbable one, but it should never be banal. It must be dramatic and human. What is drama, after all, but life with the dull bits cut out?'

3 Some films are slices of life. Mine are slices of cake.

Interview August 1962, publ. in *Hitchcock*, ch. 4 (1966, rev. 1984) by FRANÇOIS TRUFFAUT. The quote re-surfaced in the *Sunday Times* 6 March 1977 as 'For me, the cinema is not a slice of life, but a piece of cake'.

4 Dialogue should simply be a sound among other sounds, just something that comes out of the mouths of people whose eyes tell the story in visual terms.

Ibid., ch. 11

5 I find commercials fascinating. They are so exquisitely vulgar and so delightfully tasteless that they must be irresistible to everyone save the few who aren't enchanted by discussions of nasal passages and digestive tracts.

Screen Producers Guild dinner, 7 March 1965, publ. in *Hitchcock on Hitchcock*, 'After-Dinner Speech' (ed. Sidney Gottlieb, 1995). The television commercial, Hitchcock added, 'is the only instance where Man has invented a torture and then provided the victim with a means of escape'.

6 The invention of television can be compared to the introduction of indoor plumbing. Fundamentally it brought no change

in the public's habits. It simply eliminated the necessity of leaving the house.

Ibid.

7 One of television's greatest contributions is that it brought murder back into the home where it belongs.

Ibid.

8 Blondes are the best victims. They're like virgin snow which shows up the bloody footprints.

Sunday Times 1 September 1973

9 In the old days villains had moustaches and kicked the dog. Audiences are smarter today. They don't want their villain to be thrown at them with green limelight on his face. They want an ordinary human being with failings.

Quoted in *Filmgoer's Companion* (ed. Leslie Halliwell, 1984)

10 I'm not against the police; I'm just afraid of them.

Quoted in *New Society* 10 May 1984

11 There is no terror in a bang, only in the anticipation of it.

Quoted in *Halliwell's Who's Who in the Movies* (ed. John Walker, 1999)

Adolf Hitler (1889–1945)

GERMAN DICTATOR

By 1921 he had assumed leadership of the National Socialist German Workers' Party (Nazi Party) and after a failed attempt at overthrowing the government wrote his political manifesto, Mein Kampf, from prison (1925). Chancellor from 1933, he pursued fanatical anti-Semitic policies and initiated the expansionist policies that led to the Second World War. See HENRY MILLER 9, EZRA POUND 23.

1 If today I stand here as a revolutionary, it is as a revolutionary against the Revolution.

Speech 26 February 1924, quoted in *Hitler, a Study in Tyranny*, ch. 2, sect. 7 (1952, rev. 1962) by Alan Bullock. Hitler's statement was made while he was on trial for his part in the unsuccessful *putsch* against the Republican government in Munich, Germany, which had itself overthrown the Bavarian monarchy in 1918.

2 The broad masses of a population are more amenable to the appeal of rhetoric than to any other force.

Mein Kampf, vol. 1, ch. 3 (1925)

3 All great movements are popular movements. They are the volcanic eruptions of human passions and emotions, stirred into activity by the ruthless Goddess of Distress or by the torch of the spoken word cast into the midst of the people.

Ibid.

4 The art of leadership . . . consists in consolidating the attention of the people against a single adversary and taking care that nothing will split up that attention. . . . The leader of genius must have the ability to make different opponents appear as if they belonged to one category.

Ibid.

5 Mankind has grown strong in eternal struggles and it will only perish through eternal peace.

Ibid., ch. 4

6 As soon as by one's own propaganda even a glimpse of right on the other side is admitted, the cause for doubting one's own right is laid.

Ibid., ch. 6

7 The great mass of people . . . will more easily fall victim to a big lie than to a small one.

Ibid., ch. 10

8 Germany will either be a world power or will not be at all.

Ibid., vol. 2, ch. 14

9 Struggle is the father of all things. . . . It is not by the principles of humanity that man lives or is able to preserve himself above the animal world, but solely by means of the most brutal struggle.

Speech at Kulmbach, 5 February 1928, quoted in *Hitler, a Study in Tyranny*, ch. 1, sect. 3 (1952, rev. 1962) by Alan Bullock

10 When an opponent declares, 'I will not come over to your side,' I calmly say, 'Your child belongs to us already. . . . What are you? You will pass on. Your descendants, however, now stand in the new camp. In a short time they will know nothing else but this new community.'

Speech 6 November 1933, quoted in *The Rise and Fall of the Third Reich*, ch. 8, 'Education in the Third Reich' (1959) by William L Shirer

11 If it rests with Germany war will not come again. This country has a more profound impression than any other of the evil that war causes. . . . In our belief Germany's present-day problems cannot be settled by war.

Interview in the *Daily Mail* 6 August 1934

12 Whoever lights the torch of war in Europe can wish for nothing but chaos. We, however, live in the firm conviction that in our time will be fulfilled, not the decline, but the renaissance of the West. That Germany may make an imperishable contribution to this great work is our proud hope and our unshakeable belief.

Speech to the Reichstag, Berlin, 21 May 1935,

quoted in *Hitler, a Study in Tyranny*, ch. 6,
sect. 4 (1952, rev. 1962) by Alan Bullock

13 I go the way that Providence dictates with
the assurance of a sleepwalker.
Speech in Munich, 15 March 1936, quoted ibid.,
ch. 7, sect. 1. On Germany's reoccupation of the
Rhineland.

14 I am convinced that 1941 will be the crucial
year of a great New Order in Europe. The
world shall open up for everyone. Privileges for individuals, the tyranny of certain
nations and their financial rulers shall fall.
And, last of all, this year will help to provide the foundations of a real understanding among peoples, and with it the
certainty of conciliation among nations.
... Those nations who are still opposed to
us will some day recognize the greater
enemy within. They they will join us in a
combined front, a front against Jewish
exploitation and racial degeneration.
Speech at Berlin Sportspalast, 30 January 1941,
quoted ibid., ch. 11, sect. 4. Closing words of
speech.

15 The heaviest blow that ever struck humanity was the coming of Christianity. Bolshev-
ism is Christianity's illegitimate child.
Both are inventions of the Jew.
Remarks 11–12 June 1941, recorded by Martin
Bormann, publ. in *Hitler's Table Talk* (1953). At
a later date (10 October 1941), Hitler is reported
as saying: 'Christianity is a rebellion against natural law, a protest against nature. Taken to its logical extreme, Christianity would mean the
systematic cultivation of the human failure.'

16 After fifteen years of work I have achieved,
as a common German soldier and merely
with my fanatical will-power, the unity of
the German nation, and have freed it from
the death sentence of Versailles.
Proclamation 21 December 1941, addressing
troops after taking over as Commander-in-Chief
of the army

17 I don't see much future for the Americans.
... Everything about the behaviour of
American society reveals that it's half
Judaized, and the other half negrified. How
can one expect a State like that to hold
together?
Remarks 7 January 1942, recorded by Martin Bor-
mann, publ. in *Hitler's Table Talk* (1953)

18 Churchill is the very type of a corrupt journalist. There's not a worse prostitute in
politics. He himself has written that it's
unimaginable what can be done in war
with the help of lies. He's an utterly amoral repulsive creature. I'm convinced that
he has his place of refuge ready beyond the
Atlantic. He obviously won't seek sanctu-
ary in Canada. In Canada he'd be beaten
up. He'll go to his friends the Yankees. As

soon as this damnable winter is over, we'll
remedy all that.
Ibid., 18 February 1942

19 Is Paris burning?
[*Brennt Paris?*]
Attributed enquiry by telephone to General
Alfred Jodl, 25 August 1944, in Rastenburg, Germany. Hitler had ordered Paris to be destroyed
rather than allow it to fall into Allied hands. The
words were taken as the title of a book by Larry
Collins and Dominique Lapierre (1965) and of a
film with an all-star cast and screenplay contributions by Gore Vidal and Francis Ford
Coppola (1966). In June 1940, Hitler is reported
to have said to the architect ALBERT SPEER: 'In
the past I have often wondered whether we
would not have to destroy Paris. But when we
are finished in Berlin, Paris will only be a
shadow. So why should we destroy it?'

Edward Hoagland (b. 1932)
US AUTHOR AND ESSAYIST
*He is best known for his writings on wild animals
and nature in novels, such as* The Peacock's Tail
(1965), and non-fiction works, including The Courage of Turtles *(1971). 'In all my books witnessing
things is what counts,' he has said.*

1 Animals used to provide a lowlife way to
kill and get away with it, as they do still,
but, more intriguingly, for some people
they are an aperture through which
wounds drain. The scapegoat of olden
times, driven off for the bystanders' sins,
has become a tender thing, a running
injury. There, running away ... is me: hurt
it and you are hurting me.
'Lament the Red Wolf', first publ. in *Sports Illustrated* 14 January 1974, repr. in *Heart's Desire*
(1988)

2 In order to really enjoy a dog, one doesn't
merely try to train him to be semihuman.
The point of it is to open oneself to the
possibility of becoming partly a dog.
'Dogs and the Tug of Life', first publ. in *Harper's*
February 1975, repr. ibid.

3 There is a time of life somewhere between
the sullen fugues of adolescence and the
retrenchments of middle age when human
nature becomes so absolutely absorbing
one wants to be in the city constantly, even
at the height of summer.
'City Walking', first publ. in *The New York
Times Book Review* 1 June 1975, repr. ibid.

4 Men often compete with one another until
the day they die; comradeship consists of
rubbing shoulders jocularly with a competitor.
'Heaven and Nature', first publ. in *Harper's*
March 1988, repr. ibid.

5 The question of whether it's God's green
earth is not at centre stage, except in the

sense that if so, one is reminded with some regularity that He may be dying.

Guardian 20 January 1990

6 Like a kick in the butt, the force of events wakes slumberous talents.

Guardian 11 August 1990

Russell Hoban (b. 1925)
US AUTHOR AND ILLUSTRATOR

His many novels include Turtle Diary *(1975, filmed 1985) and* Riddley Walker *(1980), written in a post-apocalyptic language. He also writes children's books, notably the classic* The Mouse and His Child *(1969).*

1 If the past cannot teach the present and the father cannot teach the son, then history need not have bothered to go on, and the world has wasted a great deal of time.

Jachin-Boaz, in *The Lion of Boaz-Jachin and Jachin-Boaz*, ch. 1 (1973)

2 After all, when you come right down to it, how many people speak the same language even when they speak the same language?

Boaz-Jachin, ibid., ch. 27

3 Sometimes there's nothing but Sundays for weeks on end. Why can't they move Sunday to the middle of the week so you could put it in the OUT tray on your desk?

'The tightly furled man', ibid., ch. 32. 'Forgive us our Sundays,' he added, 'as we forgive those who Sunday against us.'

4 Me, what's that after all? An arbitrary limitation of being bounded by the people before and after and on either side. Where they leave off, I begin, and vice versa.

William G, in *Turtle Diary*, ch. 11 (1975)

5 Sometimes I think that the biggest difference between men and women is that more men need to seek out some terrible lurking thing in existence and hurl themselves upon it. . . . Women know where it lives but they can let it alone.

Neaera, ibid., ch. 18

6 Nothing to be done really about animals. Anything you do looks foolish. The answer isn't in us. It's almost as if we're put here on earth to show how silly they aren't.

George Fairbairn, ibid., ch. 42

7 Language is an archeological vehicle . . . the language we speak is a whole palimpsest of human effort and history.

Novelists in Interview (ed. John Haffenden, 1985)

E. J. Hobsbawm (b. 1917)
BRITISH HISTORIAN

Eric John Hobsbawm. He has chronicled the working classes in Europe in The Age of Revolution 1789–1848 *(1962) and* The Age of Capital 1848–75 *(1975), and is author of* Politics for a Rational Left *(1989).* A. J. P. TAYLOR *commented, 'He has taken to heart Lenin's dictum "patiently explain".'*

1 War has been the most convenient pseudo-solution for the problems of twentieth-century capitalism. It provides the incentives to modernization and techno-logical revolution which the market and the pursuit of profit do only fitfully and by accident, it makes the unthinkable (such as votes for women and the abolition of unemployment) not merely thinkable but practicable. . . . What is equally important, it can re-create communities of men and give a temporary sense to their lives by uniting them against foreigners and out-siders. This is an achievement beyond the power of the private enterprise economy . . . when left to itself.

Observer 26 May 1968

2 There is not much that even the most socially responsible scientists can do as individuals, or even as a group, about the social consequences of their activities.

New York Review of Books 19 November 1970

3 It seems that American patriotism measures itself against an outcast group. The right Americans are the right Americans because they're not like the wrong Americans, who are not really Americans.

Marxism Today January 1988

4 Xenophobia looks like becoming the mass ideology of the 20th-century *fin-de-siècle*. What holds humanity together today is the denial of what the human race has in common.

Lecture to the American Anthropological Association, publ. in *Anthropology Today* February 1992

5 Nations without a past are contradictions in terms. What makes a nation *is* the past, what justifies one nation against others is the past, and historians are the people who produce it.

Ibid.

David Hockney (b. 1937)
BRITISH ARTIST

Associated with the Pop Art movement in his early career, he moved to California in the 1960s, where he was inspired to use intense colours, most famously in his swimming pool series. He has experimented in many diverse media. ROBERT HUGHES *called him the 'Cole Porter of contemporary art'.*

1 Television is becoming a collage – there are so many channels that you move through them making a collage yourself. In that sense, everyone sees something a bit different.

Hockney On Photography, 'New York: November 1985' (ed. Wendy Brown, 1988)

2 Art has to move you and design does not, unless it's a good design for a bus.

Press conference, Tate Gallery, London, 25 October 1988, quoted in the *Guardian* 26 October 1988

3 We live in an age where the artist is forgotten. He is a researcher. I see myself that way.

Quoted in the *Observer* 9 June 1991

4 Tobacco may kill you but it's slow and it's rather a pleasure. People smoke for their mental health don't they? It's part of their total health, I'd say.

Interview in the *Guardian* 25 March 1995. On taking up smoking after a period of abstinence.

5 Seeing is the function of memory.

Quoted in the *Observer* 30 May 1999

Glenn Hoddle (b. 1957)

BRITISH FOOTBALL MANAGER AND PLAYER
He played for Tottenham Hotspur, Swindon Town and Chelsea before becoming England's manager (1996–9). In 2000 he was appointed manager of Southampton.

1 You and I have been physically given two hands and two legs and half decent brains. Some people have not been born like that for a reason. The karma is working from another lifetime. I have nothing to hide about that. It is not only people with disabilities. What you sow, you have to reap.

The Times 30 January 1999. This comment, together with his reliance on the healer Eileen Drewery, caused him to lose his position as England's manager. The blind Labour minister DAVID BLUNKETT commented: 'If Hoddle is right, I must have been a failed football coach in a previous incarnation.'

Ralph Hodgson (1871–1962)

BRITISH POET
Associated with the Georgian poets, he addressed the themes of England, nature and cruelty to animals in his verse, as in The Last Blackbird *(1907),* Eve *(1913) and* Poems *(1917).*

1 *'Twould ring the bells of Heaven*
The wildest peal for years,
If Parson lost his senses
And people came to theirs,
And he and they together
Knelt down with angry prayers
For tamed and shabby tigers
And dancing dogs and bears,
And wretched, blind, pit ponies,
And little hunted hares.

'Bells of Heaven', publ. in *Poems* (1917)

2 *Time, you old gypsy man,*
Will you not stay,
Put up your caravan
Just for one day?

'Time, You Old Gypsy Man', publ. ibid.

Peter Høeg (b. 1957)

DANISH AUTHOR
He established himself as one of Denmark's foremost writers with The History of Danish Dreams *(1988),* Miss Smilla's Feeling for Snow *(1992), an international bestseller, and* The Woman and the Ape *(1996).*

1 Reading snow is like listening to music. To describe what you've read is to try to explain music in writing.

Smilla, in *Miss Smilla's Feeling for Snow*, 'The City', pt 1, ch. 7 (1992)

2 Deep inside I know that trying to fathom things out leads to blindness, that the desire to understand has a built-in brutality that erases what you seek to comprehend. Only experience is sensitive.

Smilla, ibid. 'The City', pt 3, ch. 6

3 Time is no law of nature. It is a plan. When you look at it with awareness, or start to touch it, then it starts to disintegrate.

Katarina, in *Borderliners*, pt 1, ch. 14 (1993)

4 Contrary to what adults believe the joy of children at play comes not from having no knowledge of Death – every living creature has that. It comes from their divining what the grown-ups have lost sight of; that even though Death makes a fierce opponent, it is not invincible.

The Woman and the Ape, pt 3, ch. 1 (1996)

Eric Hoffer (1902–83)

US PHILOSOPHER AND APHORIST
A self-educated scholar and working-class philosopher, he held a part-time job as a dockworker while producing collections of essays and aphorisms, for example The Passionate State of Mind *(1955).*

1 More! is as effective a revolutionary slogan as was ever invented by doctrinaires of discontent. The American, who cannot learn to want what he has, is a permanent revolutionary.

The Passionate State of Mind, aph. 22 (1955)

2 Youth itself is a talent – a perishable talent.

Ibid., aph. 32

3 When people are free to do as they please, they usually imitate each other.

Ibid., aph. 33. Hoffer added, 'A society which gives unlimited freedom to the individual, more often than not attains a disconcerting sameness. On the other hand, where communal discipline is strict but not ruthless . . . originality is likely to thrive.'

4 Facts are counterrevolutionary.
Ibid., aph. 73

5 To have a grievance is to have a purpose in life.
Ibid., aph. 166. Hoffer added: 'It not infrequently happens that those who hunger for hope give their allegiance to him who offers them a grievance.'

6 The basic test of freedom is perhaps less in what we are free to do than in what we are free not to do. It is the freedom to refrain, withdraw and abstain which makes a totalitarian regime impossible.
Ibid., aph. 176

7 To know a person's religion we need not listen to his profession of faith but must find his brand of intolerance.
Ibid., aph. 215

8 Our greatest pretenses are built up not to hide the evil and the ugly in us, but our emptiness. The hardest thing to hide is something that is not there.
Ibid., aph. 217

9 To spell out the obvious is often to call it in question.
Ibid., aph. 220

10 We do not really feel grateful toward those who make our dreams come true; they ruin our dreams.
Ibid., aph. 232

11 The beginning of thought is in disagreement – not only with others but also with ourselves.
Ibid., aph. 266

12 A great man's greatest good luck is to die at the right time.
Ibid., aph. 276

13 The individual who has to justify his existence by his own efforts is in eternal bondage to himself.
The Ordeal of Change, ch. 5 (1964)

14 Our passionate preoccupation with the sky, the stars, and a God somewhere in outer space is a homing impulse. We are drawn back to where we came from.
The New York Times 21 July 1969. Commenting on the first manned moon-landing.

15 Absolute faith corrupts as absolutely as absolute power.
Reflections on the Human Condition, aph. 13 (1972)

16 Capitalism is at its liberating best in a non-capitalist environment. The crypto-businessman is the true revolutionary in a Communist country.
Ibid., aph. 73

17 An empty head is not really empty; it is stuffed with rubbish. Hence the difficulty of forcing anything into an empty head.
Ibid., aph. 88

18 People who bite the hand that feeds them usually lick the boot that kicks them.
Ibid., aph. 141

19 It is a sign of creeping inner death when we can no longer praise the living.
Ibid., aph. 147

20 The end comes when we no longer talk with ourselves. It is the end of genuine thinking and the beginning of the final loneliness.
Ibid., aph. 150

21 Unpredictability, too, can become monotonous.
Ibid., aph. 224

Abbie Hoffman (1935–89)
US POLITICAL ACTIVIST
Abbott Hoffman. As founder (1968) of the Youth International Party (Yippies), he received wide media coverage for his campaigns against Vietnam, capitalism and the US political system. He committed suicide.

1 The first duty of a revolutionary is to get away with it.
Attributed, 1970

2 Avoid all needle drugs. The only dope worth shooting is Richard Nixon.
Steal This Book (1971)

3 Sacred cows make the best hamburgers.
Attributed

Al Hoffman (1902–60) and
Dick Manning (1912–91)
US COMPOSERS AND SONGWRITERS
Hoffman was a composer of romantic ballads in the 1930s and of novelty songs in the 1940s and '50s. He wrote for JUDY GARLAND and Max Bygraves. Manning, born Samuel Medoff, was a composer as well as a songwriter, best known for novelty songs.

1 Takes two to tango.
'Takes Two to Tango' (song, 1952). Originally sung by Pearl Bailey, it was later recorded by LOUIS ARMSTRONG, Hermione Gingold and GILBERT HARDING.

Dustin Hoffman (b. 1937)
US ACTOR
He received accolades for his antiheroic screen roles in The Graduate (1967) and Midnight Cowboy (1969), going on to win an Academy Award in Rain Man (1988). See LAURENCE OLIVIER 2.

1 Mrs Robinson, you're trying to seduce me. Aren't you?

Ben Braddock (Dustin Hoffman), in *The Graduate* (film, 1967, screenplay by Calder Willingham and Buck Henry based on the novel by Charles Webb, directed by Mike Nichols)

2 One thing about being successful is that I stopped being afraid of dying. Once you're a star you're dead already. You're embalmed.

Quoted in *Filmgoer's Companion* (ed. Leslie Halliwell, 1984)

3 They sort of Europeanised us all. Before them, our society hadn't been the Great Society as much as it had been the Revlon Society.

Of the Beatles, in interview in the *Observer* 19 February 1989

4 I envy people who can just look at a sunset. I wonder how you can shoot it. There is nothing more grotesque to me than a vacation.

Ibid.

5 If you have this enormous talent, it's got you by the balls, it's a *demon*. You can't be a family man and a husband and a caring person and *be* that animal. Dickens wasn't that nice a guy.

Empire August 1992

Max Hoffman (1869–1927)
GERMAN GENERAL

An officer in the Prussian army from 1899, he was official German military observer in Manchuria on the Japanese side 1904–5 and became a general in 1917.

1 Ludendorff: The English soldiers fight like lions.
Hoffman: True. But don't we know that they are lions led by donkeys.

Attributed in *The Donkeys*, epigraph (1961) by ALAN CLARK. The saying is also attributed to Napoleon.

Gerard Hoffnung (1925–59)
BRITISH HUMORIST AND MUSICIAN

He first published his cartoons in the Evening Post *(1947), later drawing for* Punch *and other periodicals. In the mid-1950s he instigated the Hoffnung Music Festivals at the Festival Hall.*

1 Have you tried the famous echo in the Reading Room of the British Museum?

Speech to Oxford Union, 4 December 1958. Suggested advice to tourists.

Quintin Hogg See LORD HAILSHAM.

Richard Hoggart (b. 1918)
BRITISH CRITIC

Having held a number of official positions in the arts, education and at UNESCO (1971–5), he has helped to broaden the scope of literary studies. Publications include The Uses of Literacy *(1957) and* An Idea and Its Servants *(1978).*

1 My argument is . . . that we are moving towards the creation of a mass culture; that the remnants of what was at least in parts an urban culture 'of the people' are being destroyed; and that the new mass culture is in some important ways less healthy than the often crude culture it is replacing.

The Uses of Literacy, ch. 1, sect. B (1957)

2 Compared even with the pub around the corner, this is all a peculiarly thin and pallid form of dissipation, a sort of spiritual dry-rot amid the odour of boiled milk.

Ibid., ch. 8, sect. A. Referring to northern milk-bars

3 Almost all of us at some time settle for trash, even though we may know better.

Independent on Sunday 19 February 1995

Simon Hoggart (b. 1946)
BRITISH JOURNALIST

After working in various capacities at Punch *and the* Observer, *he became parliamentary reporter for the Guardian in 1993. The son of* RICHARD HOGGART, *he has chaired BBC radio's News Quiz since 1996.*

1 In Washington, the first thing people tell you is what their job is. In Los Angeles you learn their star sign. In Houston you're told how rich they are. And in New York they tell you what their rent is.

America: A User's Guide, ch. 1 (1990)

2 Reagan was a flesh and blood version of any other mute national emblem, say the Statue of Liberty. Everyone knows what she represents, but no one would dream of asking her opnion.

Ibid., ch. 11

3 Peter Mandelson is someone who can skulk in broad daylight.

Guardian 10 July 1998

Billie Holiday (1915–59)
US BLUES SINGER

Originally Eleanora Fagan. Known as 'Lady Day', she was distinguished for her intense, emotional delivery and idiosyncratic phrasing. Her later years were blighted by drug addiction. See STUDS TERKEL 1.

1 *Southern trees bear a strange fruit*
Blood on the leaf and blood at the root

Black bodies swingin' in the southern breeze
Strange fruit hangin' in the poplar trees.
'Strange Fruit' (song, 1939). Holiday closed her show for years with the song, which originated as an anti-lynching poem written by Lewis Allan, and was set to music by Danny Mendelson and pianist Sonny White.

2 *Mama may have, papa may have,*
But God bless the child that's got his own!
'God Bless the Child' (song, 1941, written with Arthur Herzog Jr)

3 I can't stand to sing the same song the same way two nights in succession, let alone two years or ten years. If you can, then it ain't music, it's close-order drill or exercise or yodeling or something, not music.
Lady Sings the Blues, ch. 4 (written with William Dufty, 1956, rev. 1975)

4 You can be up to your boobies in white satin, with gardenias in your hair and no sugar cane for miles, but you can still be working on a plantation.
Ibid., ch. 11

5 In this country, don't forget, a habit is no damn private hell. There's no solitary confinement outside of jail. A habit is hell for those you love. And in this country it's the worst kind of hell for those who love you.
Ibid., ch. 24. Referring to her addiction to drugs. Holiday spent nearly a year in jail for narcotics offences following her first solo concert in New York, 1946.

Jack Holland (b. 1947)
IRISH JOURNALIST AND AUTHOR
His political articles and analyses have appeared widely in British, Irish and US periodicals. His books include Too Long A Sacrifice: Life & Death in Northern Ireland Since 1969 *(1981).*

1 The tragedy of Northern Ireland is that it is now a society in which the dead console the living.
The New York Times Magazine 15 July 1979

Andrew Holleran (b. 1943)
US JOURNALIST AND AUTHOR
His openly autobiographical work explores gay concerns, as in his collection of essays Ground Zero *(1980), focusing on AIDS and changes in the gay community.*

1 They [club regulars] seldom looked happy. They passed one another without a word in the elevator, like silent shades in hell, hell-bent on their next look from a handsome stranger. Their next rush from a popper. The next song that turned their bones to jelly and left them all on the dance floor with heads back, eyes nearly closed, in the ecstasy of saints receiving the stigmata.
Dancer from the Dance, ch. 2 (1978)

R. J. Hollingdale (1930–2001)
BRITISH AUTHOR, CRITIC AND TRANSLATOR
Reginald John Hollingdale. Specializing in German writers and philosophers, he wrote on and translated Nietzsche, Schopenhauer and Goethe. His Western Philosophy: An Introduction *was published in 1966.*

1 I admit that the generation which produced Stalin, Auschwitz and Hiroshima will take some beating; but the radical and universal consciousness of the death of God is still ahead of us; perhaps we shall have to colonize the stars before it is finally borne in upon us that God is not out there.
Thomas Mann: A Critical Study, ch. 8 (1971)

(Sir) Ian Holm (b. 1932)
BRITISH ACTOR
Originally Ian Holm Cuthbert. He came to notice for his work with the Royal Shakespeare Company in the 1960s, and has since appeared in a range of roles on stage, film and TV.

1 You still don't know what you're dealing with, do you? . . . Perfect organism. Its structural perfection is matched only by its hostility. I admire its purity, a survivor; unclouded by conscience, remorse or delusions of morality.
Ash (Ian Holm), in *Alien* (film, 1979, screenplay by Dan O'Bannon, directed by Ridley Scott)

John Clellon Holmes (1926–88)
US POET, NOVELIST AND ESSAYIST
He gave the earliest portrait of Beat culture in his novel, Go *(1952), originally titled* The Beat Generation *(published in Britain as* The Beat Boys, *1959). He published two volumes of poetry in the 1970s and his final collection,* Dire Coasts, *in 1988.*

1 More than mere weariness, it ['Beat'] involves the feeling of having been used, of being raw. It involves a sort of nakedness of mind, and, ultimately, of soul; a feeling of being reduced to the bedrock of consciousness. In short, then being undramatically pushed up against the wall.
'This is the Beat Generation', publ. in *The New York Times* 16 November 1952, repr. in *Nothing More to Declare* (1967). See JACK KEROUAC 8.

2 Young Americans have immemorially been as uncritical in their surrender to the present as they are ruthless in their repudiation of the past.
'The Game of the Name', first publ. 1965, repr. ibid

3 I am weary of labels. Whatever lies ahead for my generation will certainly make them less and less applicable to our experience, for an inevitable part of aging seems

to be that one relentlessly becomes less representative of one's times, and more representative of oneself. Something like this, it seems to me, is happening to all of us who shared the Beat years.

Ibid.

John H. Holmes (1879–1964)

US UNITARIAN MINISTER

A 'crusading cleric' and an avowed pacifist, he helped found the National Association for the Advancement of Colored People (NAACP) in 1909 and was Chairman of the American Civil Liberties Union (ACLU) 1939–49.

1 This, now, is the judgement of our scientific age – the third reaction of man upon the universe! This universe is not hostile, nor yet is it friendly. It is simply indifferent.

The Sensible Man's View of Religion, ch. 4 (1932)

Larry Holmes (b. 1949)

US BOXER

Known as the 'Easton Assassin', he was world heavyweight champion (1978–85), winning forty-eight out of his fifty contests.

1 All fighters are prostitutes and all promotors are pimps.

Quoted in the *Guardian* 24 December 1984

Richard Holmes (b. 1945)

BRITISH BIOGRAPHER

He has specialized in the English Romantics in such works as Shelley: The Pursuit *(1974) and his two biographies of Coleridge (1989, 1998). He has also published* Footsteps: Adventures of a Romantic Biographer *(1985).*

1 A biography is like a handshake down the years, that can become an arm-wrestle.

Remark at Waterstone's Debate, 16 October 1990, quoted in the *Sunday Times* 21 October 1990

Oliver Wendell Holmes Jr
(1841–1935)

US JUDGE

Nicknamed 'The Great Dissenter', he was Supreme Court Justice (1902–32), earning a reputation for the elegance of his writings and judgments on common law and equity. 'One of my old formulas is to be an enthusiast in the front part of your heart and ironical at the back,' he stated.

1 The most stringent protection of free speech would not protect a man in falsely shouting fire in a theate and causing a panic.

Supreme Court opinion in *Schenk v. United States, Baer v. United States* (1919)

2 Oh, to be seventy again!

Attributed remark at ninety, after seeing a beautiful young woman

Robert Holmes à Court (1937–90)

SOUTH AFRICAN-BORN AUSTRALIAN BUSINESSMAN

Until the stock market crash in 1987, he was the richest person in Australia. His Bell Group held 30 per cent of Broken Hill Proprietary, Australia's largest company.

1 It's a well known proposition that you know who's going to win negotiation: it's he who pauses the longest.

Sydney Morning Herald 24 May 1986

Michael Holroyd (b. 1935)

BRITISH AUTHOR

He is chiefly known for his works of biography, notably Lytton Strachey *(2 vols. 1967–8),* Augustus John *(2 vols. 1974–5) and* Bernard Shaw *(4 vols. 1988–92), which* ANTHONY BURGESS *praised as 'the crown of an astonishing period of biographical achievement'.*

1 Death is the great enemy and the point of biography is to retrieve people on the page from death.

Desert Island Discs, BBC Radio 4, 20 February 2000

Miroslav Holub (1923–98)

CZECH BIOLOGIST AND POET

'I have a single goal but two ways to reach it,' he explained of his own dual career as both immunologist and poet. Forbidden from publishing in his home country 1968–82, he became well known abroad for such verse collections as Where the Blood Flows *(1963) and* On the Contrary *(1982).*

1 *Here in the Lord's bosom rests*
The tongues of beggars,
The lungs of generals,
The eyes of informers,
The skins of martyrs
In the absolute
Of the microscope's lenses.

'Pathology', publ. in *Day Duty* (1958)

2 *The word is the first small step*
to freedom
from oneself.

'Brief Reflection on the Word Pain', publ. in *On the Contrary* (1982)

3 *Evolution is nothing but*
a long string of false steps;
and it may happen that a severed head
will sing.

'The Minotaur's Thoughts on Poetry', publ. ibid.

4 *In laughter we stretch the mouth from ear to ear,*
or at least in that direction,

we bare our teeth and in that way reveal
long-past stages in evolution
when laughter still was an expression of
triumph over a slain neighbour.
'Brief Reflection on Laughter', publ. ibid.

5 **Humankind can generally be divided into**
hunters and people who cope with the
consequences.
'Shedding Life', essay first publ. in *Science 86*,
repr. in *The Dimension of the Present Moment*
and Other Essays (1990)

6 **Life is about trying without winning. That**
is why humanity developed the instinct for
sport.
Remark at the Cheltenham Festival of Literature,
October 1995, quoted in the *Daily Telegraph*
21 October 1995

Lord Home (1903–95)
BRITISH STATESMAN
Sir Alec Douglas-Home, Baron Home of the Hir-
sel. Elected Conservative MP in 1931, he became
Prime Minister following MACMILLAN*'s resig-*
nation in 1963, but lost the 1964 general election to
WILSON. *He was Foreign Secretary under* HEATH
(1970–74).

1 **As far as [being] the fourteenth earl is con-**
cerned, I suppose Mr Wilson, when you
come to think of it, is the fourteenth Mr
Wilson.
Television interview, 21 October 1963, quoted in
the *Daily Telegraph* 22 October 1963

2 **There are two problems in my life. The pol-**
itical ones are insoluble and the economic
ones are incomprehensible.
Quoted in *The New York Times* 9 January 1964

John Lee Hooker (1917–2001)
US BLUES MUSICIAN
His percussive guitar style could be heard on his
first record 'Boogie Chillen' (1948) and the later
hits 'Dimples' (1956) and 'Boom Boom' (1962). He
emerged from years of obscurity with his comeback
album The Healer *(1989).*

1 **It's never hard to sing the blues. Everyone**
in the world has the blues . . . poor people
have the blues because they're poor and
hungry. Rich people can't sleep at night
because they're trying to hold on to their
money and everything they have.
Detroit Free Press 8 September 1991

Herbert Hoover (1874–1964)
US PRESIDENT
Republican President 1929–33, he was called 'the
Great Engineer' for the public works projects
initiated under his administration, although his
opposition to government intervention in the after-
math of the Slump and his repeated assertion that

'prosperity cannot be restored by raids upon the
public treasury' caused him to lose popularity.

1 **The American system of rugged indi-**
vidualism.
Speech in Madison Square Garden, New York
City, 22 October 1928, quoted in *New Day*, 'New
York City: Restored under Republican Direction' (1928). Hoover was contrasting American
values with 'a European philosophy of diametri-
cally opposed doctrines – doctrines of paternal-
ism and state socialism'.

2 **The slogan of progress is changing from**
the full dinner pail to the full garage.
Ibid. 'New York City: Higher Standards of
Living'

3 **Older men declare war. But it is youth that**
must fight and die. And it is youth who
must inherit the tribulation, the sorrow
and the triumphs that are the aftermath of
war.
Speech at Republican National Convention,
Chicago, 27 June 1944, publ. in *Official Report of*
the Proceedings of the 23rd Republican National
Convention (1944)

J. Edgar Hoover (1895–1972)
US DIRECTOR OF THE FBI
John Edgar Hoover. Director of the FBI from 1924
until his death, he resisted Communism and dis-
trusted the civil rights movement. In the words of
Time *magazine, 'he fashioned his career as an*
improbable bureaucratic morality play peopled by
bad guys and G-men'.

1 **Truth-telling, I have found, is the key to**
responsible citizenship. The thousands of
criminals I have seen in forty years of law
enforcement have had one thing in
common: every single one was a liar.
Family Weekly 14 July 1963

Arthur Hopcraft (b. 1932)
BRITISH AUTHOR
He was a reporter on the Guardian *(1959–64) and*
a sportswriter for the Observer *(1964–73). His*
books include The Football Man *(1968), and he*
has written numerous television plays.

1 **The point about football in Britain is that**
it is not just a sport people take to, like
cricket or tennis or running long distances.
It is inherent in the people. It is built into
the urban psyche, as much a common
experience to our children as are uncles
and school. It is not a phenomenon; it is
an everyday matter. There is more eccen-
tricity in deliberately disregarding it than
in devoting a life to it. It has more signifi-
cance in the national character than
theatre has.
The Football Man: People and Passions in Soccer,
Introduction (1968)

Bob Hope (b. 1903)

BRITISH-BORN US COMEDIAN

Originally Leslie Thomas Hope. Famous for his
wisecracking repartee, as in the Road to . . . *films*
which he made with BING CROSBY *and Dorothy*
Lamour, he was a dedicated entertainer to the
troops during the Second World War and the con-
flicts in Korea and Vietnam.

1 **I get goose pimples. Even my goose**
pimples have goose pimples.

Wallie Campbell (Bob Hope), in *The Cat and*
the Canary (film, 1939, screenplay by Walter
DeLeon and Lynn Starling based on play by
John Willard, directed by Elliott Nugent)

2 **How did you get into that dress – with a**
spray gun?

Hot Lips Barton (Bob Hope), in *Road to Rio*
(film, 1947, screenplay by Edmund Beloin and
Jack Rose, directed by Norman McLeod). The
question is addressed to Lucia Maria De
Andrade (Dorothy Lamour).

3 **If you watch a game, it's fun. If you play it,**
it's recreation. If you work at it, it's golf.

Quoted in *Reader's Digest* October 1958

4 **I don't generally feel anything until noon,**
then it's time for my nap.

International Herald Tribune 3 August 1990

Christopher Hope (b. 1944)

SOUTH AFRICAN AUTHOR AND POET

He published his first poems in South Africa,
which he left in 1976. His novels, beginning with A
Separate Development *(1980), are satirical in*
style and mostly set in his native land.

1 **Nothing an interested foreigner may have**
to say about the Soviet Union today can
compare with the scorn and fury of those
who inhabit the ruin of a dream.

Sunday Times 15 April 1990

Dennis Hopper (b. 1935)

US ACTOR AND FILM-MAKER

He first appeared in Rebel Without a Cause
(1955) and made his mark with the archetypal
road movie Easy Rider *(1969), which he directed*
and co-starred in. He later specialized in playing
villainous psychopaths.

1 **Well let's face it, what right have you to a**
life, unless you devote it to dispelling the
confines that our parents worked so hard
to achieve . . . although don't forget that
we're all parents now.

Interview in *Blitz* May 1983

2 **Once we get out of the 80s, the 90s are**
going to make the 60s seem like the 50s.

The fugitive (Dennis Hopper), in *Flashback*
(film, 1990, screenplay by David Loughery,
directed by Franco Amurri)

3 **Sure I remember the Seventies. There were**
a lot of drawn blinds and dark rooms.

Interview in *The Face* May 1993

Nick Hornby (b. 1957)

BRITISH AUTHOR

His fiction humorously explores themes of mascu-
linity and relationships. His first three novels Fever
Pitch *(1992),* High Fidelity *(1995) and* About a
Boy *(1998) have all been filmed.*

1 **The natural state of the football fan is**
bitter disappointment, no matter what the
score.

Fever Pitch, '1968–1975: Home Début' (1992)

2 **I used to believe, although I don't now,**
that growing and growing up are analo-
gous, that both are inevitable and uncon-
trollable processes. Now it seems to me
that growing up is governed by the will,
that one can *choose* **to become an adult,**
but only at given moments.

Ibid., '1976–1986: A Fourth Division Town'.
Hornby continues, 'These moments come along
fairly infrequently – during crises in relationships, for example, or when one has been given
the chance to start afresh somewhere – and one
can ignore them or seize them.'

3 **I am not saying that the anally retentive**
woman does not exist, but she is vastly out-
numbered by her masculine equivalent;
and while there are women with obses-
sions, they are usually, I think, obsessive
about people, or the focus for their obses-
sion changes frequently.

Ibid., '1976–1986: Boys and Girls'

4 **Radio football is football reduced to its**
lowest common denominator. Shorn of the
game's aesthetic pleasures, or the comfort
of a crowd that feels the same way as you,
or the sense of security that you get when
you see that your defenders and goalkeeper
are more or less where they should be, all
that is left is naked fear.

Ibid., '1976–1986: Filling a Hole'

5 **There must be many fathers around the**
country who have experienced the
cruellest, most crushing rejection of all:
their children have ended up supporting
the wrong team.

Ibid., '1976–1986: My Brother'

6 **Even though there is no question that sex**
is a nicer activity than watching football
(no nil-nil draws, no offside trap, no cup
upsets, *and* **you're warm), in the normal**
run of things, the feelings it engenders are
simply not as intense as those brought
about by a once-in-a-lifetime last-minute
Championship winner.

Ibid., '1986–1992: The Greatest Moment Ever'

7 **Be tolerant of those who describe a sport-**

ing moment as their best ever. We do not lack imagination, nor have we had sad and barren lives; it is just that real life is paler, duller, and contains less potential for unexpected delirium.

Ibid.

8 One moment you're ticking along, cleaning the toilet bowl and expressing your feelings and doing all the other things that a modern chap is supposed to do; the next, you're manipulating and sulking and double-dealing and fibbing with the best of them. I can't work it out.

High Fidelity, ch. 5 (1995)

9 Sex is about the only grown-up thing I know how to do; it's weird, then, that it's the only thing which can make me feel like a ten-year old.

Ibid., ch. 10

10 You can never do the right thing by someone if you've stopped sleeping with them. You can't see a way back, or through, or round, however hard you try.

Ibid., ch. 25

Karen Horney (1885–1952)
GERMAN-BORN US PSYCHIATRIST

Her key works, The Neurotic Personality of Our Time *(1937) and* New Ways in Psychoanalysis *(1939), were critical of Freudian theory, especially in relation to female psycho-sexuality. She founded the Association for the Advancement of Psychoanalysis in 1941.*

1 Is not the tremendous strength in men of the impulse to creative work in every field precisely due to their feeling of playing a relatively small part in the creation of living beings, which constantly impels them to an overcompensation in achievement?

Feminine Psychology, 'The Flight from Womanhood' (1926)

Janette Turner Hospital (b. 1942)
AUSTRALIAN AUTHOR

Her novels The Ivory Swing *(1982) and* Borderline *(1985) and the short story collection* Dislocations *(1986) cross cultural and national boundaries, reflecting her own moves between Australia, Europe and America.*

1 We inherit plots. . . . There are only two or three in the world, five or six at most. We ride them like treadmills.

Independent 7 April 1990

A. E. Housman (1859–1936)
BRITISH POET AND CLASSICAL SCHOLAR

Alfred Edward Housman. His poetical reputation grew from a single volume, A Shropshire Lad *(1896), after which he wrote little verse though continued to write and lecture on poetry. He was*

appointed Professor of Latin at University College, London (1892) and at Cambridge (1911).

1 Experience has taught me, when I am shaving of a morning, to keep watch over my thoughts, because, if a line of poetry strays into my memory, my skin bristles so that the razor ceases to act.

'The Name and Nature of Poetry', lecture at Senate House, Cambridge, 9 May 1933, publ. 1933, repr. in *A.E. Housman: Selected Prose* (ed. John Carter, 1961). The seat of this sensation, Housman explained, 'is the pit of the stomach'. The lecture was his first public utterance on the subject of poetry.

2 In every American there is an air of incorrigible innocence, which seems to conceal a diabolical cunning.

Quoted in *Voices: A Memoir,* 'The Sneeze' (1983) by Frederic Prokosch. Said to Prokosch, an author and poet whose volume *The Asiatics* had been recently published to critical acclaim. Housman had asked of Prokosch, 'Is your air of simplicity just a part of your cunning, or is your cunning just an aspect of your inner simplicity?'

3 Indeed – very good. I shall – have to repeat – that – on the Golden Floor.

Last words, as reported in letter to Richard Perceval Graves, 12 May 1976, quoted in *A. E. Housman, The Scholar Poet,* ch. 12 (1979) by Richard Perceval Graves. The words were spoken to Housman's doctor, who had just recounted the response of an actor when asked what members of his profession did in their spare time: 'Well, I suppose you could say we spend half our time lying on the sands looking at the stars, and the other half lying on the Stars looking at the sands!'

Libby Houston (b. 1941)
BRITISH POET AND BOTANIST

Her verse, including the collections At the Mercy *(1981),* Necessity *(1988) and* Cover of Darkness *(1999), combines a naturalist's eye with sharp metaphysical humour.*

1 The base emotions Plato banned
  have left a radio-active and not radiant
  land.

'Judging Lear', publ. in *At the Mercy* (1981)

2 When your dreams tire, they go underground
  and out of kindness that's where they stay.

'Gold', publ. in *Necessity* (1988)

Geoffrey Howe (b. 1926)
BRITISH POLITICIAN

Baron Howe of Aberavon. Under MARGARET THATCHER, *he was Chancellor of the Exchequer (1979–83), Foreign Secretary (1983–89), and Deputy Prime Minister and Leader of the House of Commons (1989–90). Journalist Peter Freedman described him as having 'all the dash and panache of the Hush Puppies which are his favourite foot-wear'. See also* DENIS HEALEY 2.

1 It is rather like sending your opening batsmen to the crease only for them to find the moment that the first balls are bowled that their bats have been broken before the game by the team captain.
Resignation speech as Deputy Prime Minister to House of Commons, 13 November 1990, publ. in *Conflict of Loyalty*, Appendix 2 (1994). The speech refers to the difficulties he faced as Foreign Secretary as the result of MARGARET THATCHER's anti-European stance.

Kim Howells (b. 1946)
BRITISH POLITICIAN
Elected Labour MP for Pontypridd in 1992, he was a junior minister at the Department of Trade and Industry (1998–2001), and subsequently appointed 'Minister for Culture'.

1 If this is the best British artists can produce then British art is lost. It is cold, mechanical, conceptual bullshit. The attempts at contextualisation are particularly pathetic and symptomatic of a lack of conviction.
Quoted in the *Evening Standard* 31 October 2002. Howell's note was pinned to the wall at Tate Britain after his visit to the Turner Prize exhibition.

Frankie Howerd (1922–92)
BRITISH COMEDIAN
Originally Francis Alex Howard. A stand-up comedian from the 1940s, he appeared in revues in the 1950s, but is best known as the slave Lurcio in the TV series Up Pompeii *(1969–71, filmed 1971), in which he displayed his mastery of the suggestive innuendo.*

1 I was amazed.
Catchphrase from 1940s. Other phrases associated with Howerd include 'Mock ye not!' and 'Nay, nay, and thrice nay!', adapted to 'Woe, woe, and thrice woe' as spoken by the soothsayer in the TV show, *Up Pompeii*.

(Sir) Fred Hoyle (1915–2001)
BRITISH ASTRONOMER
He founded the Institute of Theoretical Astronomy in Cambridge, where he was also Professor of Astronomy (1958–72). Maintaining that life originated in bacteria and viruses in space, he has written science fiction and popular science books.

1 Space isn't remote at all. It's only an hour's drive away if your car could go straight upwards.
Observer 9 September 1979

Kin Hubbard (1868–1930)
US HUMORIST AND JOURNALIST
Frank McKinney Hubbard. Working at the Indian-apolis Sun from 1899 until his death, he became known for caricatures of political figures, and achieved national fame for his Abe Martin character (from 1904).

1 Classic music is th' kind that we keep thinkin'll turn into a tune.
Comments of Abe Martin and His Neighbors (1923)

2 Nobuddy ever fergits where he buried a hatchet.
Indianapolis News 4 January 1925, repr. in *Abe Martin's Broadcast* (1930)

3 When a fellow says, it hain't the money but the principle o' the thing, it's th' money.
Hoss Sense and Nonsense (1926)

4 Th' only way t' entertain some folks is t' listen t' 'em.
Abe Martin's Wisecracks (ed. E.V. Lucas, 1930)

5 All th' world loves a good loser.
Ibid.

6 Makin' a long stay short is a great aid t' popularity.
Ibid.

Ruth Hubbard (b. 1924)
US BIOLOGIST
Her books, such as Biological Woman – The Convenient Myth *(1983) and* The Politics of Women's Biology *(1990), explore science from a feminist perspective.*

1 Every theory is a self-fulfilling prophecy that orders experience into the framework it provides.
'Have Only Men Evolved?', publ. in *Women Look at Biology Looking At Women* (ed. Ruth Hubbard, Mary Sue Henifin and Barbara Fried, 1979)

Richard Huelsenbeck (1892–1974)
GERMAN POET AND PSYCHOANALYST
With HUGO BALL *he was the co-founder of Dadaism in 1916 and brought the movement to Berlin. In 1936 he settled in New York, where he practised as a psychoanalyst.*

1 I am firmly convinced that all art will become dadaistic in the course of time, because from Dada proceeds the perpetual urge for its renovation.
'Dada Lives', publ. in *Transition* no. 25, autumn 1936, transl. in *The Dada Painters and Poets: An Anthology* (ed. Robert Motherwell, 1951)

Arianna Huffington (b. 1950)
GREEK AUTHOR
Formerly Arianna Stassinopoulos. Her provocative work ranges from studies on the women's move-

ment (The Female Woman, 1973) and spirituality
(The Other Revolution, 1979), to biography
(Picasso: Creator and Destroyer, 1988).

1 Our current obsession with creativity is the
result of our continued striving for immortality in an era when most people no
longer believe in an after-life.
The Female Woman, 'The Working Woman'
(1973)

2 Not only is it harder to be a man, it is also
harder to become one.
Ibid., 'The Male Man'

3 Liberation is an evershifting horizon, a
total ideology that can never fulfill its
promises. . . . It has the therapeutic quality
of providing emotionally charged rituals of
solidarity in hatred – it is the amphetam-
ine of its believers.
Ibid., 'The Liberated Woman? . . . and Her Lib-
erators'

Langston Hughes (1902–67)
US POET AND AUTHOR
*Called the 'poet laureate of Harlem', he was a
major influence on the development of black litera-
ture in America. His poetry collections include* The
Weary Blues *(1926). His humorous sketches,
'Simple Stories', appeared in the 1950s in books,
comic strips and on the stage.*

1 *I got the Weary Blues
And I can't be satisfied.*
'The Weary Blues', written 1922, publ. in *The
Weary Blues* (1926). In his autobiography,
Hughes claimed these lines originated in 'the
first blues verse I'd ever heard'.

2 *I, too, sing America.
I am the darker brother.
They send me to eat in the kitchen when
    company comes.
But I laugh,
And eat well,
And grow strong.*
'I, Too', first publ. in *Survey Graphic* March
1925, repr. in *Selected Poems* (1954)

3 Jazz to me is one of the inherent expressions of Negro life in America: the
eternal tom-tom beating in the Negro soul
– the tom-tom of revolt against weariness
in a white world, a world of subway trains,
and work, work, work; the tom-tom of joy
and laughter, and pain swallowed in a
smile.
'The Negro Artist and the Racial Mountain',
publ. in *Nation* 23 June 1926

4 *I swear to the Lord
I still can't see
Why Democracy means
Everybody but me.*
'The Black Man Speaks', publ. in *Jim Crow's Last
Stand* (1943)

5 *But softly
As the tune comes from his throat
Trouble
Mellows to a golden note.*
'Trumpet Player', publ. in *Fields of Wonder*
(1947)

6 *Good morning, daddy!
Ain't you heard
The boogie-woogie rumble
Of a dream deferred?*
'Dream Boogie', publ. in *Montage of a Dream
Deferred* (1951)

7 *What happens to a dream deferred?
Does it dry up
like a raisin in the sun?
Or fester like a sore –
And then run?
Does it stink like rotten meat?
Or crust and sugar over –
like a syrupy sweet?
Maybe it just sags
like a heavy load.
Or does it explode?*
'Harlem', publ. ibid.

8 It's powerful . . . that one drop of Negro
blood – because just *one* drop of black
blood makes a man colored. One drop –
you are a Negro! . . . Black is powerful.
Simple Takes a Wife (1953)

Richard Hughes (1900–1976)
BRITISH NOVELIST AND PLAYWRIGHT
*He travelled widely and wrote the first radio
drama* Danger *(1924) for the BBC, but is best
known for his portrayal of childhood* A High
Wind in Jamaica *(1929).*

1 The yachtsman leaves no tracks. A thousand keels may plough a strait, but they
leave it virgin. Except for desert and the
snows, there is hardly an inch of land on
the round earth where man has not left his
mark again and again; but most of the surface of the ocean is to-day as if Man had
not been created.
The Saturday Book, 'Sailing' (1946)

Robert Hughes (b. 1938)
AUSTRALIAN AUTHOR AND CRITIC
Senior art critic for Time *magazine since 1970, he
has written on art in* The Shock of the New
(1980), on convict transports to Australia in The
Fatal Shore *(1987), and on political correctness in*
America *in* Culture of Complaint *(1993).*

1 Would Australians have done anything
differently if their country had not been
settled as the jail of infinite space? Certainly they would. They would have
remembered more of their own history.
The Fatal Shore, ch. 17 (1987)

2 The contest between education and TV – between argument and conviction by spectacle – has been won by television.
Culture of Complaint, ch. 1 (1993)

3 The self is now the sacred cow of American culture, self-esteem is sacrosanct.
Ibid.

Ted Hughes (1930–98)
BRITISH POET
His muscular verse is characterized by its raw nature imagery in such collections as The Hawk in the Rain *(1957) and* Crow *(1970). 'Among the grey-suited modern poets . . . he stood out like the bloodstained survivor of a Greek tragedy,' wrote* JOHN CAREY. Birthday Letters *(1998) chronicles his marriage to* SYLVIA PLATH. *He was Poet Laureate from 1984.*

1 *I saw the horses:*
Huge in the dense grey – ten together –
Megalith-still. They breathed, making no move,
With draped manes and tilted hind-hooves,
Making no sound.
I passed: not one snorted or jerked its head.
Grey silent fragments
Of a grey silent world.
'The Horses', publ. in *The Hawk in the Rain* (1957)

2 *This house has been far out at sea all night,*
The woods crashing through darkness, the booming hills,
Winds stampeding the fields under the window
Floundering black astride and blinding wet.
'Wind', publ. ibid.

3 *Russia and America circle each other;*
Threats nudge an act that were without doubt
A melting of the mould in the mother,
Stones melting about the root.
'A Woman Unconscious', publ. in *Lupercal* (1960)

4 *The future's no calamitous change*
But a malingering of now,
Histories, towns, faces that no
Malice or accident much derange.
Ibid.

5 *Daylong this tomcat lies stretched flat*
As an old rough mat, no mouth and no eyes,
Continual wars and wives are what
Have tattered his ears and battered his head.
'Esther's Tomcat', publ. ibid.

6 *My feet are locked upon the rough bark.*
It took the whole of Creation
To produce my foot, my each feather:
Now I hold Creation in my foot.
'Hawk Roosting', publ. ibid.

7 *Pike, three inches long, perfect*
Pike in all parts, green tigering the gold.
'Pike', publ. ibid.

8 *The sea cries with its meaningless voice*
Treating alike its dead and its living,
Probably bored with the appearance of heaven
After so many millions of nights without sleep,
Without purpose, without self-deception.
'Pibroch', publ. in *Wodwo*, pt 3 (1967)

9 Any form of violence, any vehement form of activity, invokes the bigger energy, the elemental power circuit of the universe.
Interview in 1971, quoted in the *Sunday Times* 1 November 1998

10 *The flame-red moon, the harvest moon,*
Rolls along the hills, gently bouncing,
A vast balloon,
Till it takes off, and sinks upward
To lie in the bottom of the sky, like a gold doubloon.
'The Harvest Moon', publ. in *Season Songs* (1976)

11 *Death invented the phone it looks like the altar of death*
Do not worship the telephone
It drags its worshippers into actual graves
With a variety of devices, through a variety of disguised voices
'Do Not Pick Up the Telephone', publ. in *Earth Numb* (1979)

12 *The river is a god*
Knee-deep among the reeds, watching men,
Or hung by the heels down at the door of a dam
It is a god, and inviolable.
And will wash itself of all deaths.
'River', publ. in *The River* (1983)

13 *You were never*
More than a step from Paradise.
You had instant access, your analyst told you,
To the core of your Inferno –
The pit of your hairy flower.
'Child's Park', publ. in *Birthday Letters* (1998). Addressed to SYLVIA PLATH, the poems were written over a period of twenty-five years following her suicide in 1963.

(Sir) Richard Hull (1907–89)
BRITISH GENERAL
He was appointed Chief of Staff, Middle East Land Forces (1953–4), and supervised the evacuation from Suez. He was Chief of Defence Staff 1965–7.

1 Conscription may have been good for the country, but it damn near killed the army.
Quoted in *Anatomy of Britain Today*, ch. 19 (1965) by Anthony Sampson. Hull oversaw the abolition of national service in 1957.

Basil Hume (1923–99)

BRITISH ECCLESIASTIC

A Roman Catholic Benedictine monk and Abbot of Ampleforth (1963–76), he was the first monk to occupy the office of Archbishop of Westminster (1976–99). Widely respected for his modesty and piety, he was called 'my cardinal' by ELIZABETH II.

1 Moral choices do not depend on personal preference and private decision but on right reason and, I would add, divine order.

The Times 16 March 1990

2 If people pray, their consciousnesses become more sensitive. It is very difficult to be a praying person and then go and be beastly to your neighbour.

Quoted in *The Times* 11 April 1998

Hubert H. Humphrey (1911–78)

US POLITICIAN

An eloquent speaker, he gained a liberal reputation but as Vice-President under LYNDON JOHNSON *from 1964 alienated many by his support for the Vietnam War. As the Democratic presidential candidate, he narrowly lost to* NIXON *in 1968.*

1 There are not enough jails, not enough policemen, not enough courts to enforce a law not supported by the people.

Speech at Williamsburg, 1 May 1965, quoted in *The New York Times* 2 May 1965

2 The right to be heard does not automatically include the right to be taken seriously.

Speech to National Student Association at Madison, 23 August 1965, quoted in *The New York Times* 24 August 1965

3 Here we are, just as we ought to be, here we are, the people, here we are in a spirit of dedication, here we are the way politics ought to be in America, the politics of happiness, the politics of purpose and the politics of joy.

Speech in Washington DC, 27 April 1968, quoted in *The New York Times* 28 April 1968. 'The Politics of Joy' was Humphrey's presidential campaign slogan in 1968.

Barry Humphries (b. 1934)

AUSTRALIAN ENTERTAINER

He created the Barry Mackenzie comic strip in Private Eye (1964–73), but is most famous for his satirical creations, Sir Les Patterson and Dame Edna Everage, 'housewife superstar'.

1 Oh, I was down by Manly Pier
 Drinking tubes of ice-cold beer
 With a bucket full of prawns upon me knee.
 But when I'd swallowed the last prawn

I had a Technicolor yawn
 And I chundered in the old Pacific sea.

'Chunder Down Under' (1964), publ. in *A Nice Night's Entertainment* (1981). In the glossary in *Bazza Pulls It Off* (1972), Humphries defines the word 'chunder', which he claims to have popularized, as 'to enjoy oneself in reverse'.

2 Feminist: a woman, usually ill-favoured . . . in whom the film-making instinct has displaced the maternal.

A Nice Night's Entertainment, Glossary (1981)

3 My work is really addressed to a provincial English audience, and whether we like it or not, and whatever American affectations we may entertain here in Australia, we are really provincial English society. Our humour touches the same nerve.

Age 19 February 1983

4 The only people really keeping the spirit of irony alive in Australia are taxi-drivers and homosexuals.

Australian Women's Weekly February 1983

Robert Hunter (b. 1938)

US ROCK LYRICIST

He wrote lyrics for the Grateful Dead, and also recorded solo albums, for example Tiger Rose *(1975) and* Jack O'Roses *(1980).*

1 What a long strange trip it's been.

'Truckin'' (song) on the album *American Beauty* (1971) by the Grateful Dead. This best-known of the Grateful Dead's lyrics ('WALSTIB' to dedicated fans) has been adopted on badges and posters and as the title of books and articles evoking the 1960s. A retrospective Grateful Dead album of 1977 also had this as the title.

Herman Hupfeld (1894–1951)

US SONGWRITER

Among the numerous songs he contributed for stage shows and films of the 1920s and '30s, he is best remembered for 'As Time Goes By' (1931). He was also responsible for 'Sing Something Simple' (1930) and 'Let's Put Out the Lights and Go To Sleep' (1932).

1 You must remember this, a kiss is still a kiss,
 A sigh is just a sigh;
 The fundamental things apply,
 As time goes by.

'As Time Goes By' (song), in *Everybody's Welcome* (show, 1931). The song was picked up and featured in the movie, *Casablanca* (1943), sung by Dooley Wilson as Sam – though the extent of Wilson's active involvement has been questioned. In *Everybody's Welcome,* the song was sung by Frances Williams. See also INGRID BERGMAN 1.

Zora Neale Hurston (1903–60)

US AUTHOR AND ANTHROPOLOGIST

A leading figure of the Harlem Renaissance, she influenced generations of black women writers with her novel Their Eyes Were Watching God *(1937) and her collections of African-American folk tales. See also* YOKO ONO 2.

1 But I am not tragically colored. There is no great sorrow dammed up in my soul, nor lurking behind my eyes. I do not mind at all. I do not belong to the sobbing school of negrohood who hold that nature some-how has given them a lowdown dirty deal . . . No, I do not weep at the world – I am too busy sharpening my oyster knife.

'How It Feels to Be Colored Me', essay first publ. 1928, repr. in *I Love Myself When I Am Laughing* (1979)

2 Ships at a distance have every man's wish on board.

Their Eyes Were Watching God, ch. 1 (1937)

Saddam Hussein (b. 1937)

IRAQI PRESIDENT

As president and head of the armed forces of Iraq from 1979, he waged war against Iran (1980–88), and invaded Kuwait (1990), which led to his defeat by Arab and Western forces in the Gulf War (1991). He was ousted from power by the US-led invasion of Iraq in 2003. NORMAN SCHWARZ-KOPF *said of him: 'He is neither a strategist, nor is he schooled in the operational art, nor is he a tacti-cian, nor is he a general, nor is he a soldier. Other than that, he is a great military man.'*

1 The great, the jewel and the mother of battles has begun.

Speech at the start of the Gulf War, 6 January 1991, quoted in the *Independent* 19 January 1991

2 Baghdad, its people and leadership, is determined to force the Mongols of our age to commit suicide at its gates.

Speech in Baghdad, 17 January 2003, quoted in the *Daily Telegraph* 18 January 2003. The speech, which marked the twelfth anniversary of the onset of the Gulf War, compared Britain and America to the Mongol hordes which destroyed Baghdad in 1258.

John Huston (1906–87)

US FILM-MAKER AND ACTOR

Prolific but unpredictable, he excelled in adventure pictures and film noir. He made his debut with The Maltese Falcon *(1941) and won an Oscar for* The Treasure of the Sierra Madre *(1948).*

1 After all, crime is only a lefthanded form of human endeavor.

Emmerich (Louis Calhern), in *The Asphalt Jungle* (film, 1950, written and directed by John Huston from novel by W. R. Burnett)

2 Talk to them [actors] about things they don't know. Try to give them an inferiority complex. If the actress is beautiful, screw her. If she isn't, present her with a valuable painting she will not understand. If they insist on being boring, kick their asses or twist their noses. And that's about all there is to it.

Quoted in *Things I Did . . . and Things I Think I Did* (1984) by Jean Negulesco. Advice to a young director on how to handle actors.

3 Hollywood has always been a cage . . . a cage to catch our dreams.

Quoted in the *Sunday Times* 27 December 1987

Lauren Hutton (b. 1943)

US ACTRESS AND MODEL

Originally Mary Hutton. A former Playboy Bunny, she became one of America's highest paid models in the 1960s, and also acted in films, for example A Wedding *(1978) and* American Gigolo *(1979).*

1 Models are the physical mirror of feminin-ity. They *should* come in all sizes, shapes, and ages, and now they do. If my two careers mean anything, it's that.

Quoted in *Model*, pt 2 (1995) by Michael Gross

Will Hutton (b. 1950)

BRITISH JOURNALIST AND AUTHOR

An influential thinker on government and society, he was Editor-in-Chief of the Observer (1998–9). His books include The State We're In *(1995), on the economic, social and political degeneration of Britain.*

1 There needs to be fear and greed in the system in order to make it tick.

The State We're In, ch. 7 (1995)

2 Private schools, in short, are one of the most important economic and social insti-tutions in these islands. Everybody knows it, but to say so is taboo.

Observer 6 September 1998. 'The drift to private schools is becoming a stampede,' Hutton con-tinued. 'We are building one of the most unequal and nastiest societies on earth – and nobody is protesting.'

Aldous Huxley (1894–1963)

BRITISH AUTHOR

His early novels of the 1920s were brilliant satires of upper class and intellectual life; but he produced his best work in the 1930s, including the dystopic Brave New World *(1932). The Doors of Percep-tion (1954) recorded his experiments with psycho-tropic drugs in California, where he lived from 1937.*

1 I can sympathise with people's pains, but not with their pleasures. There is some-thing curiously boring about somebody else's happiness.

Limbo, 'Cynthia' (1920)

2 *Beauty for some provides escape,*
Who gain a happiness in eyeing
The gorgeous buttocks of the ape
Or Autumn sunsets exquisitely dying.
'Ninth Philosopher's Song', in *Leda* (1920)

3 Most of one's life is one prolonged effort
to prevent oneself thinking.
Mr Topes, in *Mortal Coils*, 'Green Tunnels'
(1922)

4 There are few who would not rather be
taken in adultery than in provincialism.
Mr Boldero, in *Antic Hay*, ch. 10 (1923)

5 I have discovered the most exciting, the
most arduous literary form of all, the most
difficult to master, the most pregnant in
curious possibilities. I mean the advertisement. . . . It is far easier to write ten passably effective Sonnets, good enough to take
in the not too inquiring critic, than one
effective advertisement that will take in a
few thousand of the uncritical buying
public.
On the Margin, 'Advertisement' (1923)

6 I'm afraid of losing my obscurity. Genuineness only thrives in the dark. Like celery.
Miss Thriplow, in *Those Barren Leaves*, pt 1, ch. 1
(1925)

7 If it were not for the intellectual snobs who
pay – in solid cash – the tribute which philistinism owes to culture, the arts would perish with their starving practitioners. Let us
thank heaven for hypocrisy.
Jesting Pilate, pt 1 (1926)

8 Thought is barred in this City of Dreadful
Joy and conversation is unknown.
Of Los Angeles, ibid., pt 4

9 Those who believe that they are exclusively
in the right are generally those who
achieve something.
Proper Studies, 'A Note on Dogma: Varieties of
Human Type' (1927)

10 It takes two to make a murder. There are
born victims, born to have their throats
cut, as the cut-throats are born to be
hanged.
Maurice Spandrell, in *Point Counter Point*, ch. 12
(1928)

11 A bad book is as much of a labour to write
as a good one; it comes as sincerely from
the author's soul.
Ibid., ch. 13 (1928)

12 Consistency is contrary to nature, contrary
to life. The only completely consistent
people are the dead.
Do What You Will, 'Wordsworth in the Tropics'
(1929)

13 Single-mindedness is all very well in cows
or baboons; in an animal claiming to

belong to the same species as Shakespeare
it is simply disgraceful.
Ibid., 'Pascal', sect. 24

14 Experience is not a matter of having actually swum the Hellespont, or danced with
the dervishes, or slept in a doss-house. It is
a matter of sensibility and intuition, of seeing and hearing the significant things, of
paying attention at the right moments, of
understanding and co-ordinating. Experience is not what happens to a man; it is
what a man does with what happens to
him.
Texts and Pretexts, Introduction (1932)

15 Official dignity tends to increase in inverse
ratio to the importance of the country in
which the office is held.
Beyond the Mexique Bay, 'Puerto Barrios'
(1934)

16 People will insist on treating the *mons Ven-
eris* as though it were Mount Everest. Too
silly!
Mary Amberly, in *Eyeless in Gaza*, ch. 30
(1936)

17 So long as men worship the Caesars and
Napoleons, Caesars and Napoleons will
duly rise and make them miserable.
Ends and Means, ch. 8 (1937)

18 There's only one corner of the universe
you can be certain of improving, and that's
your own self.
Carlo Malpighi (quoting Bruno Rontini), in
Time Must Have a Stop, ch. 7 (1944)

19 If we could sniff or swallow something that
would, for five or six hours each day, abolish our solitude as individuals, atone us
with our fellows in a glowing exaltation of
affection and make life in all its aspects
seem not only worth living, but divinely
beautiful and significant, and if this
heavenly, world-transfiguring drug were of
such a kind that we could wake up next
morning with a clear head and an undam-
aged constitution – then, it seems to me,
all our problems (and not merely the one
small problem of discovering a novel pleasure) would be wholly solved and earth
would become paradise.
Music at Night and Other Essays, 'Wanted, a
New Pleasure' (1949). Huxley's earlier writings
revealed a different attitude: 'I prefer being
sober to even the rosiest and most agreeable
intoxications,' he wrote in his Introduction to
Texts and Pretexts (1932). 'The peyotl-trances of
Swinburne, for example, have always left me perfectly *compos mentis*; I do not catch the
infection.'

20 Speed, it seems to me, provides the one
genuinely modern pleasure.
Ibid.

21 Man is an intelligence, not served by, but in servitude to his organs.
Themes and Variations, 'Variations on a Philosopher' (1950)

22 A priest's life is not supposed to be well-rounded; it is supposed to be one-pointed – a compass, not a weathercock.
The Devils of Loudun, ch. 1 (1952)

23 Pure Spirit, one hundred degrees proof – that's a drink that only the most hardened contemplation-guzzlers indulge in. Bodhisattvas dilute their Nirvana with equal parts of love and work.
Susila, in *Island*, ch. 15 (1962)

24 It's with bad sentiments that one makes good novels.
Letter, 10 July 1962, quoted in *Aldous Huxley: The Critical Heritage* (ed. Donald Watt, 1975). Huxley believed this to be the explanation for why his novel *Island* – published that year and greatly criticized – was 'so inadequate'.

25 Idealism is the noble toga that political gentlemen drape over their will to power.
Quoted in the *New York Herald Tribune* 25 November 1963

Elspeth Huxley (1907–97)
BRITISH AUTHOR
She wrote widely on her native land Kenya, as in her best-known novel, The Flame Trees of Thika *(1959).*

1 Only man is not content to leave things as they are but must always be changing them, and when he has done so, is seldom satisfied with the result.
The Mottled Lizard, ch. 4 (vol. 2 of autobiography, 1962)

(Sir) Julian Huxley (1887–1975)
BRITISH BIOLOGIST
He was the first Director of UNESCO (1946–8), helped found the World Wildlife Fund (now called World Wildlife Fund for Nature) and wrote popular science books including Essays of a Biologist *(1923).*

1 God can no longer be considered controller of the universe in any but a Pickwickian sense. Operationally, God is beginning to resemble not a ruler but the last fading smile of a cosmic Cheshire cat.
Religion without Revelation, ch. 3 (1957 edn)

Dolores Ibárruri (1895–1989)

SPANISH POLITICIAN AND JOURNALIST

Known as 'La Pasionaria' (The Passion Flower), she was the Republic's most effective propagandist during the Spanish Civil War. She was elected as a Communist deputy to the Cortes in 1936 and lived in the USSR after Franco's victory, returning to be re-elected to the Cortes at the age of eighty-one.

1 **No pasarán!**
   (They shall not pass!)
   Radio broadcast from Paris 18 July 1936, quoted in *The Spanish Civil War*, bk. 2, ch. 16 (1961, rev. 1965) by Hugh Thomas. This rallying call for the women of Spain to defend the Republic became a slogan in the ensuing Civil War. Previous attributions for the words include Marshal Pétain (1856–1951) during the defence of Verdun in 1916: *Ils ne passeront pas.*

2 **It is better to die on your feet than to live on your knees!**
   Radio broadcast from Paris 3 September 1936, quoted ibid. In her autobiography (1966), Ibárruri stated that she had first used the words in a previous broadcast in Spain, 18 July, when she had also uttered *No pasarán!* (see above). Like that slogan, this also became a slogan in the ensuing Civil War, and also has an earlier attribution, to Mexican revolutionary Emiliano Zapata (c. 1877–1919).

Ice Cube (b. 1969)

US RAP MUSICIAN

Born O'Shea Jackson. He was a founder member of the LA rap group Niggaz With Attitude (NWA), and as a solo artist released the confrontational AmeriKKKa's Most Wanted (1990). He has also starred in films, including Boyz 'n the Hood (1991).

1 *Up early in the morning, dressed in black*
   Don't ask why 'cuz I'm down in a suit and tie
   They killed a homie that I went to school with (damn)
   I tell you, life ain't shit to fool with.
   'Dead Homiez' (song) on album *AmeriKKKa's Most Wanted* (1990). Opening lines.

2 **If I'm more of an influence to your son as a rapper than you are as a father ... you got to look at yourself as a parent.**
   Interview in *Rolling Stone* 4 October 1994

Ice-T (b. 1958)

US RAP MUSICIAN

Originally Tracey Marrow. He was hailed LA's first hip hop artist with the release of 'The Coldest Rapper' (1983), and went on to become one of the West Coast's most outspoken 'gangsta' rappers. 'Cop Killer' (1992) caused a furore and was withdrawn.

1 *You're just a toy punk to mess with that junk*

*You want some real dope, come look in my
trunk
The dope I'm sellin' is life, a hundred per-
cent legit
So get real, fool, and try some real hit.*
'I'm your Pusher' (song, written by Ice-T and
Afrika Islam) on the album *Power* (1988)

2 *You better think it out
We should be able to say anything
Our lungs are meant to shout.
Say what you feel, yell out what's real
Even though it may not bring mass appeal
Your opinion is yours, mine is mine
If you don't like what I'm sayin' fine.*
'Freedom of Speech' (song, written by Ice-T and
Afrika Islam) on the album *The Iceberg/Freedom
of Speech. . . . Just Watch What You Say* (1990)

3 I started off rapping for people just like
myself, people who were in awe of wealth
and flash. It was a conversation between
me and them. But now most of those who
buy my records are listening in on others'
conversation. They are the aural equivalent
of voyeurs, thrilled at this crazy world that
has nothing to so with their experience.
Observer 27 October 1991

4 Crime is an equal-opportunity employer.
It never discriminates. Anybody can enter
the field. You don't need a college education. You don't need a G.E.D. You don't
have to be any special color. You don't
need white people to like you. You're self-
employed. As a result, criminals are very
independent people.
The Ice Opinion, ch. 3 (1994, written with Heidi
Sigmund)

5 Passion makes the world go round. Love
just makes it a safer place.
Ibid., ch. 4

Harold L. Ickes (1874–1952)
US POLITICIAN
*Harold LeClair Ickes. A Republican turned Demo-
crat, he was a lifelong supporter of President
ROOSEVELT, and was his 'hatchet man' during
presidential campaigns. As head of the Public
Works Administration, he implemented New Deal
projects (1933–9).*

1 I am against government by crony.
Speech February 1946, on resigning from his
post as Secretary of the Interior, referring to
President TRUMAN's award of government positions to old friends.

2 The trouble with Senator Long is that he
is suffering from halitosis of the intellect.
That's presuming Emperor Long has an
intellect.
Quoted in *The Politics of Upheaval*, pt 2, ch. 14,
sect. 5 (1960) by ARTHUR J. SCHLESINGER JR.
The remarks were a riposte to Long's suggestion
that Ickes could go 'slap damn to hell', during

an altercation over Roosevelt's New Deal, which
Senator Huey Long, nicknamed 'Emperor of
Louisiana', strongly opposed.

Michael Ignatieff (b. 1947)
CANADIAN AUTHOR AND CRITIC
*Once labelled 'the thinking woman's crumpet', he
describes himself as an 'academic who went over
the monastery wall'. Among his books are the
family memoir* The Russian Album *(1987), the
novel* Scar Tissue *(1993) and a biography of
ISAIAH BERLIN (1998).*

1 Most of us no longer watch television; we
graze, zapping back and forth between
channels whenever our boredom threshold
is triggered. No one does any one thing at
a time. A new culture has taken shape
which caters for people with the attention
span of a flea.
Three-Minute Culture, BBC 2, 15 January 1989

2 There's a very low contempt threshold for
TV presenters.
Daily Telegraph 22 February 1989

Ivan Illich (b. 1926)
AUSTRIAN-BORN US PHILOSOPHER AND
AUTHOR
His works such as Deschooling Society *(1971) and*
Towards a History of Need *(1978) are critiques of
economic policy, particularly in respect of the
Third World, where, he argues, new forms of
dependency have been created.*

1 The compulsion to do good is an innate
American trait. Only North Americans
seem to believe that they always should,
may, and actually can choose somebody
with whom to share their blessings. Ultimately this attitude leads to bombing
people into the acceptance of gifts.
Celebration of Awareness, Preface to ch. 2 (1969)

2 There is no greater distance than that
between a man in prayer and God.
Ibid., ch. 4

3 School divides life into two segments,
which are increasingly of comparable
length. As much as anything else, school-
ing implies custodial care for persons who
are declared undesirable elsewhere by the
simple fact that a school has been built to
serve them.
Ibid., ch. 8

4 My friends, it is your task to surprise yourselves, and us, with the education you succeed in inventing for your children. Our
hope of salvation lies in our being surprised by the Other. Let us learn always to
receive further surprises.
Ibid., ch. 9

5 Man must choose whether to be rich in things or in the freedom to use them.
Deschooling Society, ch. 4 (1971)

Gary Indiana
US AUTHOR
After Scar Tissue *(1987), a collection of fictional commentaries on contemporary culture, he turned to novel writing with such works as* Horse Crazy *(1989).* Three Month Fever *(1999), on Andrew Cucanan,* VERSACE'*s killer, brought him wider recognition.*

1 Affection is the mortal illness of lonely people.
Horse Crazy, ch. 1 (1989)

2 We listen to the hum and throb of the hospital and watch the soundless river shatter light into thousands of white drops. It isn't fair. We used to say: How can we live like this? And now the question really is: How can we die like this?
On dying from AIDS, ibid., ch. 5

William Ralph Inge (1860–1954)
BRITISH PHILOSOPHER AND ECCLESIASTIC
As Dean of St Paul's, London (1911–34), he was known as the 'Gloomy Dean' on account of his pessimistic sermons and newspaper articles. Among his popular works are Outspoken Essays *(1919 and 1922). He also wrote studies of Plotinus on whom he was an expert.*

1 It takes in reality only one to make a quarrel. It is useless for the sheep to pass resolutions in favour of vegetarianism, while the wolf remains of a different opinion.
'Patriotism', first publ. 1915, repr. in *Outspoken Essays* (first series, 1919)

2 Public opinion, a vulgar, impertinent, anonymous tyrant who deliberately makes life unpleasant for anyone who is not content to be the average man.
'Our Present Discontents', ibid.

3 A man may build himself a throne of bayonets, but he cannot sit on it.
Lecture given at St Andrews, Scotland, 1918, repr. in *The Philosophy of Plotinus*, vol. 2, Lecture 22 (1923). The words were quoted by BORIS YELTSIN from a tank during the failed military coup in Russia, August 1991.

4 Every institution not only carries within it the seeds of its own dissolution, but prepares the way for its most hated rival.
'The Victorian Age', Rede Lecture, Cambridge University, 1922, publ. ibid.

5 Literature flourishes best when it is half a trade and half an art.
Ibid.

6 Events in the past may be roughly divided into those which probably never happened and those which do not matter. This is what makes the trade of historian so attractive.
Assessments and Anticipations, 'Prognostications' (1929)

7 I think middle-age is the best time, if we can escape the fatty degeneration of the conscience which often sets in at about fifty.
Quoted in the *Observer* 8 June 1930

8 Worry is interest paid on trouble before it falls due.
Observer 14 February 1932

(Sir) Bernard Ingham (b. 1932)
BRITISH GOVERNMENT PRESS OFFICER
He was Chief Information Officer under TONY BENN *(1975–8) and Chief Press Secretary to* MARGARET THATCHER *(1979–90). Gruff and forthright, he was called a 'truculent, arrogant bully' by Tam Dalyell, and 'the sewer rather than the sewage' by John Biffen, but was highly esteemed by Thatcher, to whom he was devotedly loyal.*

1 What greatly concerns me and many other Socialists is that there are thousands of highly moral, upright and indeed religious people who are nevertheless Tory to the bone. They are quite frankly enigmas to simple souls like me.
Column as 'Albion' in the *Leeds Weekly Citizen* 11 June 1965, quoted in *Good and Faithful Servant*, Preface (1990) by ROBERT HARRIS. When asked in 1990 about his earlier vitriol vis-à-vis the Conservative Party, he answered: 'I don't think I loathed it. I just didn't like what it represented. It stood for privilege and I think Mrs Thatcher has changed all that.'

2 I . . . have never regarded the Official Secrets Act as a constraint on my operations. Indeed, I regard myself as licensed to break that law as and when I judge necessary; and I suppose it is necessary to break it every other minute of every working day.
Speech to IBA, 1981, quoted ibid. ch. 8. 'I'm the man who is licensed to leak,' he told a gathering in 1990.

3 I sometimes compare press officers to riflemen on the Somme – mowing down wave upon wave of distortion, taking out rank upon rank of supposition, deduction and gossip.
Address at Press Gallery luncheon, quoted in the *Independent* 8 February 1990

Richard Ingrams (b. 1937)
BRITISH JOURNALIST AND EDITOR
In 1962 he co-founded the satirical magazine Private Eye *of which he was Editor 1963–86. He subsequently founded and edited the* Oldie *(from 1992), which he saw as an antidote to 'yoof' culture.*

1 **Publish and be sued.**
Personal motto, as suggested on *Quote . . . Unquote*, BBC Radio 4, 4 May 1977. The words echo those attributed to the Duke of Wellington, 'Publish and be damned!', said to have been the Duke's response in 1842 to an attempt to blackmail him over the publication of letters to his mistress Harriet Wilson.

2 **If your lawyers tell you that you have a very good case, you should settle immediately.**
Quoted in *Maxwell: The Outsider*, ch. 14 (1988, rev. 1991) by Tom Bower. On losing a libel action taken out by ROBERT MAXWELL against *Private Eye*, November 1985, concerning allegations in July 1985 that Maxwell had paid for Labour Party leader NEIL KINNOCK's travel expenses in the hope of a peerage. Ingrams blamed the jury for his losing the case, who 'while good and true [are] immensely thick'.

3 **It's important for people not to hold a high opinion of politicians, and one of the strengths of the British is that they don't on the whole. Even Mrs Thatcher, the most successful politician of our time, who has done more than anyone, is not liked very much in her own country, and that's a good attitude. The danger begins when people start admiring politicians.**
Interview in *Singular Encounters* (1990) by Naim Attallah

Eugène Ionesco (1912–94)
ROMANIAN-BORN FRENCH PLAYWRIGHT
Regarding humour as his 'outlet, release and salvation', he was a prominent figure of the Theatre of the Absurd. His early one-act plays, such as The Bald Prima Donna *(1950), deal with self-estrangement and failure of communication. Later full-length plays feature the semi-autobiographical character Bérenger.*

1 **Yoghurt is very good for the stomach, the lumber regions and apotheosis.**
Mr Smith, in *The Bald Prima Donna* (1950)

2 **Life is an abnormal business.**
Jean, in *The Rhinoceros*, act 1 (1959)

3 **An avant-garde man is like an enemy inside a city he is bent on destroying, against which he rebels; for like any system of government, an established form of expression is also a form of oppression.**
'A Talk about the Avant-Garde', lecture, Helsinki, June 1959, publ. in *Notes and Counter Notes* (1962)

4 **Banality is a symptom of non-communication. Men hide behind their clichés.**
'Further Notes, 1960', publ. ibid.

5 **All history is nothing but a succession of 'crises' – of rupture, repudiation and resistance. . . . When there is no 'crisis', there is stagnation, petrification and death.**
'Have I Written Anti-Theatre?' publ. ibid.

6 **Since the death instinct exists in the heart of everything that lives, since we suffer from trying to repress it, since everything that lives longs for rest, let us unfasten the ties that bind us to life, let us cultivate our death wish, let us develop it, water it like a plant, let it grow unhindered. Suffering and fear are born from the repression of the death wish.**
Fragments of a Journal (1967)

7 **Beauty is a precious trace that eternity causes to appear to us and that it takes away from us. A manifestation of eternity, and a sign of death as well.**
Present Past – Past Present, ch. 5 (1968)

8 **The light of memory, or rather the light that memory lends to things, is the palest light of all. . . . Just as dreams do, memory makes me profoundly aware of the unreality, the evanescence of the world, a fleeting image in the moving water.**
Ibid.

9 **Boredom! I've got used to that. You get used to it, or rather, you don't get used to it, but you get used to not getting used to it.**
Jean, in *Journeys Among The Dead* (1981)

10 **Shakespeare was the great one before us. His place was between God and despair.**
International Herald Tribune 17 June 1988

(Sir) Muhammad Iqbal (1873–1938)
INDIAN POET AND PHILOSOPHER
His writings, classical in style and intended for recitation, were formative on the movement which led to the creation of the separate Muslim state of Pakistan. His best known work is Secrets of the Self *(1915).*

1 *Thou didst create the night, but I made the lamp.*
Thou didst create clay, but I made the cup.
Thou didst create the deserts, mountains and forests,
I produced the orchards, gardens and groves.
It is I who made the glass out of stone,
And it is I who turn a poison into an antidote.
Quoted in *The Clear Light of Day*, ch. 2 (1980) by Anita Desai

Clifford Irving (b. 1930)
US AUTHOR AND HOAXER
He is best known for his fake 'autobiography' of Howard Hughes, which he revealed before

publication (1972) as an elaborate hoax and for which he was sentenced to two and a half years' imprisonment and fined $10,000; his book Hoax *(1981) tells the story. Among his other works are* Fake! *(1968), the story of a Hungarian art forger, and books written under the pen-name John Luckless.*

1 A criminal trial is like a Russian novel: it starts with exasperating slowness as the characters are introduced to a jury, then there are complications in the form of minor witnesses, the protagonist finally appears and contradictions arise to produce drama, and finally as both jury and spectators grow weary and confused the pace quickens, reaching its climax in passionate final argument.

Sunday Times 14 August 1988

John Irving (b. 1942)
US AUTHOR

He is noted for his surreal yet plausible black comedies, often with a homicidal thread, notably The World According to Garp *(1978, filmed 1982) and* The Cider House Rules *(1985, filmed 2000).*

1 Sigmund Freud was a novelist with a scientific background. He just didn't know he was a novelist. All those damn psychiatrists after him, they didn't know he was a novelist either.

Interview in *Writers at Work* (eighth series, ed. George Plimpton, 1988)

2 It is a game with a lot of waiting in it; it is a game with increasingly heightened anticipation of increasingly limited results.

Of baseball, in *A Prayer for Owen Meany*, ch. 1 (1989)

Christopher Isherwood (1904–86)
BRITISH-BORN US AUTHOR

His life as a teacher in Germany (1929–33) inspired the sketches of social disintegration in Mr Norris Changes Trains *(1935) and* Goodbye to Berlin *(1939). He emigrated to the USA in 1946 with* W.H. AUDEN, *with whom he collaborated on three verse plays.*

1 I am a camera with its shutter open, quite passive, recording, not thinking.

Goodbye to Berlin, 'A Berlin Diary (Autumn 1930)' (1939) . Opening sentence of story. Isherwood's collection was later to form the basis of John Van Druten's play *I Am a Camera* (1951) and the Broadway musical *Cabaret* (1966, filmed 1972).

2 California is a tragic country – like Palestine, like every Promised Land.

'Los Angeles', first publ. in *Horizon*, 1947, repr. in *Exhumations* (1966)

Kazuo Ishiguro (b. 1954)
JAPANESE-BORN BRITISH NOVELIST

Set in Japan or Britain, Ishiguro's novels are a melancholy reassessment of the past. The best known are An Artist of the Floating World *(1986) and* The Remains of the Day *(1989, filmed 1993).*

1 By the very nature of a witticism, one is given very little time to assess its various possible repercussions before one is called to give voice to it, and one gravely risks uttering all manner of unsuitable things if one has not first acquired the necessary skill and experience.

Mr Stevens, in *The Remains of the Day*, 'Day Three – Morning. Taunton, Somerset' (1989)

2 I can't even say I made my own mistakes. Really – one has to ask oneself – what dignity is there in that?

Mr Stevens, ibid. 'Day Six – Evening. Weymouth'

Eddie Izzard (b. 1962)
BRITISH COMEDIAN

Best known as a debonair cross-dresser, he delivers his quizzical and original observations on his one-man shows. 'The only reason I've got where I am today is because of saying "Errrrr . . ." and wearing make-up,' he once said.

1 How to survive boarding school. Do not express emotion, do not feel emotion, do not have emotion. If someone hits you, hit them back; if someone argues with you, argue back – never give an inch, never look vulnerable and you will survive.

Interview in the *Observer* 5 October 1997. Izzard was sent to boarding school at the age of six when his mother was dying of cancer. He says that he cried for a year.

2 Women have this vast variety of lingerie, stockings and tights and different patterns, and shoes, with different-sized heels, in red and black, and skirts – short, long, with slits – push-the-boob things . . . there's so much around in women's things that is erotic. While men have: shirt shirt shirt jumper shirt jumper jacket jumper shirt jacket trousers trousers shirt trousers flat shoes.

Interview in *The Times* 10 December 1999

George Jackson (1941–71)

US BLACK ACTIVIST AND AUTHOR

Sentenced in 1960 for armed robbery, he became a convinced Communist and black activist as a prisoner in St Quentin and Soledad. He was accused with three others (together known as the Soledad Brothers) of the murder of a prison guard, and was later killed in controversial circumstances.

1 If we are to be men again we must stop working for nothing, competing against each other for the little they allow us to possess, stop selling our women or allowing them to be used and handled against their will, stop letting our children be educated by the barbarian, using their language, dress, and customs, and most assuredly stop turning our cheeks.
Letter to his father from Soledad Prison, 30 March 1965, publ. in *Soledad Brother* (1970)

2 Nonviolent theory is practicable in civilized lands among civilized people, the Asians and Africans, but a look at European history shows that anything of great value that ever changed hands was taken by force of arms.
Letter to his mother from Soledad Prison, March 1967, publ. ibid.

3 Every time I hear the word 'law' I visualize gangs of militiamen or Pinkertons busting strikes, pigs wearing sheets and caps that fit over their pointed heads. I see a white oak and a barefoot black hanging, or snake-eyes peeping down the lenses of telescopic rifles, or conspiracy trials.
Blood in my Eye, 'Classes at War' (1972)

Glenda Jackson (b. 1936)

BRITISH ACTRESS AND POLITICIAN

Renowned as a performer on stage and in film (winning Oscars for her roles in Women in Love, *1969, and* A Touch of Class, *1974), she was elected Labour MP for Hampstead and Highgate in 1992. Her former husband, Roy Hodges, once said of her: 'If she went into politics she'd be prime minister.'*

1 Acting is not about dressing up. Acting is about stripping bare. The whole essence of learning lines is to forget them so you can make them sound like you thought of them that instant.
Sunday Telegraph 26 July 1992

Holbrook Jackson (1874–1948)

BRITISH AUTHOR AND CRITIC

He wrote on literary figures, particularly William Morris in whom he had a lifelong interest, in such books as On Art and Socialism *(1947). He was also a passionate bibliophile.*

1 Pedantry is the dotage of knowledge.
Anatomy of Bibliomania, vol. 1, pt 7, 'A Cure for Pedantry' (1930)

Jesse Jackson (b. 1941)

US CLERGYMAN AND CIVIL RIGHTS
LEADER

*A persuasive Baptist preacher and black civil rights
activist, he worked with* MARTIN LUTHER KING
*and founded the National Rainbow Coalition in
1984. The same year, and again in 1988, he was a
candidate for the Democratic Party's presidential
nomination, the first African-American to bid for
the office.*

1 I hear that melting-pot stuff a lot, and all I
can say is that we haven't melted.

Playboy November 1969

2 When we're unemployed, we're called lazy;
when the whites are unemployed it's called
a depression.

Interview in *The Americans*, 'When Whites Are
Unemployed, It's Called a Depression' (1970) by
David Frost

3 Racism as a form of skin worship, and as a
sickness and a pathological anxiety for
America, is so great, until the poor whites
– rather than fighting for jobs or education
– fight to remain pink and fight to remain
white. And therefore they cannot see an
alliance with people that they feel to be
inherently inferior.

Ibid.

4 The burden of being black is that you have
to be superior just to be equal. But the
glory of it is that, once you achieve, you
have achieved, indeed.

Christian Science Monitor 26 September
1979

5 I am not a perfect servant. I am a public
servant doing my best against the odds. As
I develop and serve, be patient. God is not
finished with me yet.

Speech at Democratic National Convention, San
Francisco, 16 July 1984, quoted in the *New Left
Review*, vol. 149, 1985

6 Our flag is red, white, and blue, but our
nation is a rainbow – red, yellow, brown,
black and white, we are *all* precious in
God's sight!

Speech at Democratic National Convention, San
Francisco, 17 July 1984, quoted in *Jesse: The Life
and Pilgrimage of Jesse Jackson*, ch. 15 (1996) by
Marshall Frady. Jackson – who also compared
America to a quilt: 'many pieces, many colors,
many sizes, all woven and held together by a
common thread' – named his political organization the 'National Rainbow Coalition'.

7 My constituency is the desperate, the
damned, the disinherited, the disrespected
and the despised.

Speech at Democratic National Convention, San
Francisco, 17 July 1984, quoted in *Jesse Jackson*,
ch. 8 (1991) by Robert Jakoubek

8 Great things happen in small places. Jesus

was born in Bethlehem. Jesse Jackson was
born in Greenville.

Daily Mail 9 March 1988

9 A cheque or credit card, a Gucci bag strap,
anything of value will do. Give as you live.

Quoted in the *Daily Telegraph* 6 April 1988. Comments while fund-raising in Aspen, Colorado.

10 We've removed the ceiling above our
dreams. There are no more impossible
dreams.

Independent 9 June 1988

11 If you wake up in the morning and think
you're white, you're bound to meet someone before five o'clock who will let you
know you are just another nigger.

Sun 20 September 1989

Mahalia Jackson (1911–72)

US GOSPEL SINGER

*The 'Queen of the Gospel Song' was already a
popular recording star by the 1940s. In 1947 'Move
On Up a Little Higher' became the first gospel
record to sell a million copies. From 1955 she was
active in the civil rights movement.*

1 It's easy to be independent when you've
got money. But to be independent when
you haven't got a thing – that's the Lord's
test.

Movin' On Up, ch. 1 (1966, written with Evan
McLoud Wylie)

2 This musical thing has been here since
America been here. This is trial and tribulation music.

Quoted in *Time* magazine 28 June 1968

Michael Jackson (b. 1958)

US SINGER AND DANCER

*The youngest member of the soul pop family group
the Jackson Five, he sold a world record 40 million
copies of his album* Thriller *(1982), helped by
state-of-the-art videos which featured his deft dancing. His reclusive lifestyle and cosmetic makeover
have generated much press interest.*

1 I love *E. T.* 'cos it reminds me of me. Someone from another world coming down and
you becoming friends with them and this
person is, like, 800 years old and he's filling you with all kinds of wisdom and he
can teach you how to fly. That whole fantasy thing which I think is great. I mean,
who don't wanna fly?

Interview in *Smash Hits* 20 January 1983. Jackson
collaborated with *E.T.* director Steven Spielberg
on the 'E.T. Storybook' album and also narrated
it.

2 *Well they say the sky's the limit
And to me that's really true
But my friend you have seen nothing*

Just wait 'til I get through . . .
Because I'm bad, I'm bad.
'Bad' (song) on the album *Bad* (1987)

3 *I'm not going to spend*
My life being a color
Don't tell me you agree with me
When I saw you kicking dirt in my eye
But, if you're thinkin' about my baby
It don't matter if you're black or white.
'Black or White' (song) on the album *Dangerous*
(1991)

Bianca Jagger (b. 1944)
NICARAGUAN MODEL AND HUMAN RIGHTS
ACTIVIST
Called the world's best dressed human rights cam-
paigner, she was MICK JAGGER'*s first wife, and*
has since dedicated herself to good causes.

1 My marriage ended on my wedding day.
Quoted in *The Life and Good Times of the Rolling*
Stones (1989) by Philip Norman. Referring to her
wedding to MICK JAGGER in St Tropez in 1971.
The chaotic event had attracted a mob of
reporters and photographers, eliciting the com-
ment from him: 'I am not in a goldfish bowl and
I am not the king of France.'

Mick Jagger (b. 1943)
BRITISH ROCK MUSICIAN
The once rebellious lead singer with the Rolling
Stones, he has taken on a number of acting roles
and released solo albums, always returning to the
band that launched him. See GEORGE MELLY 3.

1 The only performance that makes it, that
really makes it, is the one that ends in
madness.
Turner (Mick Jagger), in *Performance* (film,
1970, screenplay by Donald Cammell, directed
by Donald Cammell and Nicolas Roeg,)

2 People have this obsession. They want you
to be like you were in 1969. They want you
to, because otherwise their youth goes with
you. . . . It's very selfish, but it's understandable.
Quoted in the *Observer* 10 January 1993

Mick Jagger (b. 1943) and
Keith Richards (b. 1943)
BRITISH ROCK MUSICIANS
The Jagger–Richards partnership produced nearly
all of the Rolling Stones' original material. Their
r-'n'-b-driven songs such as 'The Last Time' and
'(I Can't Get No) Satisfaction' (both 1965) articu-
lated the energy and sexuality of the 1960s. See also
KEITH RICHARDS.

1 I can't get no satisfaction.
'(I Can't Get No) Satisfaction' (song, 1965) on
the album *Big Hits (High Tide and Green Grass)*
(1966) by the Rolling Stones

2 *Get off of my cloud.*
'Get Off of My Cloud' (song, 1965) on ibid.

3 *She goes running for the shelter*
Of a mother's little helper,
And it helps her on her way,
Gets her through her busy day.
'Mother's Little Helper' (song) on the album
Aftermath (1966) by the Rolling Stones

4 *I shouted out, 'Who killed the Kennedy's?'*
When after all, it was you and me.
'Sympathy for the Devil' (song) on the album
Beggars' Banquet (1969) by the Rolling Stones.
The song, whose lyrics were inspired by Jagger's
reading of Mikhail Bulgakov's *The Master and*
Margarita, was the subject of a film by JEAN-
LUC GODARD, *Sympathy for the Devil* (1969).

5 *But what can a poor boy do*
Except to sing for a rock 'n' roll band,
'Cause in sleepy London town
There's just no place for a street fighting
man!
'Street Fighting Man' (song) on ibid.

6 *You can't always get what you want*
But if you try sometimes
You just might find
You get what you need.
'You Can't Always Get What You Want' (song)
on the album *Let It Bleed* (1970) by the Rolling
Stones

7 *I know it's only rock 'n' roll but I like it.*
'It's Only Rock 'n' Roll' (song) on the album *It's*
Only Rock 'n' Roll (1974) by the Rolling Stones

Tom Jaine (b. 1943)
BRITISH COOKERY WRITER
He has edited the Good Food Guide *(1989–93)*
and is the proprietor of Prospect Books, which pub-
lishes his cookery books.

1 If cooking becomes an art form rather
than a means of providing a reasonable
diet, then something is clearly wrong.
Daily Telegraph 19 October 1989

Lord Jakobovits (1921–99)
BRITISH RABBI
Emmanuel Jakobovits. As Chief Rabbi of the
Commonwealth (1967–91), he was conservative in
outlook but instrumental in mending rifts within
Britain's Jewish community.

1 Silence, indifference and inaction were
Hitler's principal allies.
Independent 5 December 1989. Referring to the
prosecution of war criminals.

2 We must pursue the peace efforts as if
there were no terrorism, and fight the terrorists as if there were no peace efforts.
Letter to *The Times* 5 March 1996, following a
spate of bomb attacks by Hamas in Tel Aviv and
Jerusalem

Clive James (b. 1939)

AUSTRALIAN AUTHOR, CRITIC AND
BROADCASTER

*He has published several volumes of criticism,
mock-epic verse and 'unreliable memoirs', and displays his wise-cracking wit in his frequent TV
appearances.*

1 Prejudices are useless. Call Los Angeles any
dirty name you like – Six Suburbs in
Search of a City, Paradise with a Lobot-
omy, anything – but the fact remains that
you are already living in it before you get
there.

'Postcard from Los Angeles 1', first publ. in the
Observer 16 June 1979, repr. in *Flying Visits*
(1984)

2 All television ever did was shrink the
demand for ordinary movies. The demand
for extraordinary movies increased. If any
one thing is wrong with the movie industry
today, it is the unrelenting effort to
astonish.
Ibid.

3 As a work of art it has the same status as a
long conversation between two not very
bright drunks.

'A Blizzard of Tiny Kisses', first publ. in the
London Review of Books, 1980, repr. in *From the
Land of Shadows* (1982). Referring to *Princess
Daisy* by Judith Krantz, which fetched what was
then a record advance of $3,208,875 when the
rights were sold at auction in New York.

4 A sceptic finds *Dallas* absurd. A cynic
thinks the public doesn't.
Glued to the Box, Introduction (1983). Referring
to the US soap opera that captured a world-wide
market (1978–91).

5 Anyone afraid of what he thinks television
does to the world is probably just afraid of
the world.
Ibid.

C. L. R. James (1901–89)

TRINIDADIAN JOURNALIST AND AUTHOR
*Cyril Lionel Robert James. He came to England in
1933 to work as cricket correspondent on the Manchester Guardian. His essentially Marxist political
ideas evolved during his time in the US 1938–53.
He is best known for* Beyond a Boundary *(1963), a
blend of sport and politics.*

1 Cricket is first and foremost a dramatic
spectacle. It belongs with the theatre,
ballet, opera and the dance.
Beyond a Boundary, pt 6, ch. 16 (1963)

Henry James (1843–1916)

US AUTHOR
*An American transplanted to Europe, he returned
frequently to the theme of the old and new worlds
and the collision between them. His major works*

include The Portrait of a Lady *(1881) and* The
Ambassadors *(1903).* WILLIAM FAULKNER *called
him 'the nicest old lady I ever met', while for* VIR-
GINIA WOOLF *he was 'that courtly, worldly, sentimental old gentleman [who] can still make us
afraid of the dark'. See also* NEWS OF THE
WORLD 1.

1 However British you may be, I am more
British still.
Quoted in *Henry James at Home*, ch. 7, sect. 5
(1969) by H. Montgomery Hyde. The remark
addressed to two English friends in August 1914
was reported in a letter written to *The Times*
4 March 1916 by the poet and critic Edmund
Gosse. James had lived in England since 1876
and took British citizenship in 1915 as a gesture
of support for Britain's war effort.

2 It is art that *makes* life, makes interest,
makes importance . . . and I know of no
substitute whatever for the force and
beauty of its process.
Letter to H. G. WELLS, 10 July 1915, publ. in
Henry James Letters, vol. 4 (ed. Leon Edel, 1984).
Wells replied (13 July): 'I don't clearly understand your concluding phrases . . . I can only
read sense into it by assuming that you are using
"art" for every conscious human activity. I use
the word for a research and attainment that is
technical and special.'

3 Happy you poets who can be present and
so present by a simple flicker of your
genius, and not, like the clumsier race,
have to lay a train and pile up faggots that
may not after prove in the least combustible!
Letter to poet W.B. YEATS, 25 August 1915, in private collection. This observation was later incorporated into Yeats's poem, 'In Memory of Major
Robert Gregory'.

4 So here it is at last, the distinguished thing!
Quoted in *A Backward Glance*, ch. 14 (1934) by
EDITH WHARTON. The words are often claimed
to be James's last words, but were actually
reported to have been *heard* by him 2 December
1915, when he suffered a stroke at the beginning of
his last illness. This version of the anecdote, which
was recounted to Wharton by James's friend Lady
Prothero, was described by his biographer LEON
EDEL as 'a beautiful bit of apocrypha'.

5 Tell the boys to follow, to be faithful, to
take me seriously.
Last words, quoted in *Henry James at Home*,
ch. 7, sect. 4 (1969) by H. Montgomery Hyde.
James is said to have uttered the words in one of
his last conscious moments when his mind was
dwelling on his work. He died 28 February 1916.

P. D. James (b. 1920)

BRITISH AUTHOR
*Phyllis Dorothy White, Baroness James of Holland
Park. Her work in the forensic science and criminal law departments of the Home Office provided
useful background for her chilling detective novels,*

such as Death of an Expert Witness *(1977) and* Devices and Desires *(1989).*

1 What the detective story is about is not murder but the restoration of order.
Interview in *The Face* December 1986

2 Great literature cannot grow from a neglected or impoverished soil. Only if we actually tend or care will it transpire that every hundred years or so we might get a *Middlemarch*.
Daily Telegraph 14 April 1988

3 A man who lives with nature is used to violence and is companionable with death. There is more violence in an English hedgerow than in the meanest streets of a great city.
Jonah the tramp, in *Devices and Desires*, ch. 40 (1989)

4 Creativity doesn't flourish in an atmosphere of despotism, coercion and fear.
Quoted in the *Sunday Times* 7 March 1999. Commenting on management practices in the BBC under JOHN BIRT.

Storm Jameson (1891–1986)
BRITISH NOVELIST
She made her name with two trilogies describing the lives of a family of Yorkshire shipbuilders between the wars, The Triumph of Time *(1927–31) and* The Mirror in Darkness *(1934–6).*

1 Mere human beings can't afford to be fanatical about anything. . . . Not even about justice or loyalty. The fanatic for justice ends by murdering a million helpless people to clear a space for his law-courts. If we are to survive on this planet, there must be compromises.
Vancura, in *A Cup of Tea for Mr Thorgil*, ch. 28 (1957)

Kathleen Jamie (b. 1962)
BRITISH POET
In addition to her poetry, which is characterized by its strong Scottish flavour, she has written travel books about Asia. Her collections include Black Spiders *(1982).*

1 Pass the tambourine, let me bash out the praises
to the Lord God of movement, to Absolute non-friction, flight, and the scary side: death by avalanche, birth by failed contraception.
'The Way We Live', publ. in *The Way We Live* (1987)

Elizabeth Janeway (1913–93)
US AUTHOR
A major spokeswoman for the women's movement, she is remembered as a balanced, sometimes ironic

commentator on shifting gender roles. *Her books include* Men's World – Woman's Place *(1971).*

1 As long as mixed grills and combination salads are popular, anthologies will undoubtedly continue in favor.
The Writer's Book, ch. 32 (ed. Helen Hull, 1950)

2 I am not sure how many 'sins' I would recognize in the world. Some would surely be defused by changed circumstances. But I can imagine none that is more irredeemably sinful than the betrayal, the exploitation, of the young by those who should care for them.
'Incest: A Rational Look at the Oldest Taboo', publ. in *Ms.* November 1981

Tama Janowitz (b. 1957)
US AUTHOR
She is known for her postmodernist and humorous fiction depicting the inner life of New York City, for example American Dad *(1981) and* Slaves of New York *(1986, filmed 1989). The* Hudson Review *called her 'a literary Cyndi Lauper, a connoisseur of kitsch'.*

1 I was like a social worker for lepers. My clients had a chunk of their body they wanted to give away; for a price I was there to receive it. Crimes, sins, nightmares, hunks of hair: it was surprising how many of them had something to dispose of. The more I charged, the easier it was for them to breathe freely once more.
Slaves of New York, 'Modern Saint 271' (1986)

2 Long after the bomb falls and you and your good deeds are gone, cockroaches will still be here, prowling the streets like armored cars.
Ibid.

3 With publicity comes humiliation.
International Herald Tribune 8 September 1992

Derek Jarman (1942–94)
BRITISH FILM-MAKER, THEATRE DIRECTOR AND ARTIST
He was experimental in his work for the theatre and in his films, the first of which, Sebastiane *(1976), had Latin dialogue, while one of his last,* Blue *(1993), showed an unchanging blue screen. He also painted and designed sets.*

1 Now is the time of departure. The last streamer that ties us to what is known, parts. We drift into a sea of storms.
Narrator in *Jubilee* (film, 1977, written and directed by Derek Jarman)

2 Understand that sexuality is as wide as the sea. Understand that your morality is not law. Understand that we are you. Understand that if we decide to have sex whether

safe, safer, or unsafe, it is our decision and you have no rights in our lovemaking.

At Your Own Risk: A Saint's Testament, '1940's' (1992)

3 All men are homosexual, some turn straight. It must be very odd to be a straight man because your sexuality is hopelessly defensive. It's like an ideal of racial purity.

Ibid.

4 An orgasm joins you to the past. Its timelessness becomes the brotherhood; the brethren are lovers; they extend the 'family'. I share that sexuality. It was then, is now and will be in the future.

Ibid., '1950's'

5 The modern queer was invented by Tennessee Williams. Brando in blue jeans, sneakers, white T-shirt and leather jacket. When you saw that, you knew they were available.

Ibid., '1960's'

6 I wouldn't wish the eighties on anyone, it was the time when all that was rotten bubbled to the surface. If you were not at the receiving end of this mayhem you could be unaware of it. It was possible to live through the decade preoccupied by the mortgage and the pence you saved on your income tax. It was also possible for those of us who saw what was happening to turn our eyes in a different direction; but what, in another decade, had been a trip to the clap clinic was now a trip to the mortuary.

Ibid., '1980's'

7 I'm not afraid of death but I am afraid of dying. Pain can be alleviated by morphine but the pain of social ostracism cannot be taken away.

Ibid. On being HIV positive.

8 Paradise haunts gardens, and some gardens are paradises. Mine is one of them. Others are like bad children – spoilt by their parents, over-watered and covered with noxious chemicals.

Derek Jarman's Garden (text by Derek Jarman, photographs by Howard Sooley, 1995). Jarman created his own garden at Prospect Cottage, on an inhospitable stretch of shingle on the Kent coast, within sight of the nuclear power station at Dungeness. He incorporated driftwood, shells and sculptures made from stones and other flotsam found on the beach.

Randall Jarrell (1914–65)
US POET AND CRITIC
His often harrowing poetry was written, according to Time *magazine, in 'plain American, which dogs and cats can read'. Verse collections include* The Woman at the Washington Zoo *(1960) and* The Lost World *(1965).*

1 *Six miles from earth, loosed from its dream of life,*
I woke to black flak and the nightmare fighters.
When I died they washed me out of the turret with a hose.

'The Death of the Ball Turret Gunner' (1945), repr. in *Selected Poems* (1955)

2 When you begin to read a poem you are entering a foreign country whose laws and language and life are a kind of translation of your own; but to accept it because its stews taste exactly like your old mother's hash, or to reject it because the owl-headed goddess of wisdom in its temple is fatter than the Statue of Liberty, is an equal mark of that want of imagination, that inaccessibility to experience, of which each of us who dies a natural death will die.

Poetry and the Age, 'The Obscurity of the Poet' (1953)

3 The work of art is as done as it will ever get, and all the critics in the world can't make its crust a bit browner; they may help *us*, the indigent readers, but they haven't done a thing to it. Around the throne of God, where all the angels read perfectly, there are no critics – there is no need for them.

Ibid., 'The Age of Criticism'

4 His voice not only took you into his confidence, it laid a fire for you and put your slippers by it and then went into the other room to get into something more comfortable.

Pictures from an Institution, pt 1, ch. 10 (1954). Referring to President Robbins.

5 Old faces are forbidding or beautiful for what is expressed in them; in a face that is young enough almost everything but the youth is hidden, so that it is beautiful both for what is there and what cannot yet be there.

Ibid., pt 4, ch. 4

6 It is better to entertain an idea than to take it home to live with you for the rest of your life.

Ibid., ch. 9

7 Europeans and Americans are like men and women: they understand each other worse, and it matters less, than either of them suppose.

Ibid.

Antony Jay (b. 1930)
BRITISH AUTHOR AND JOURNALIST
Having worked as a director and producer for the BBC (1955–64), he co-scripted with JONATHAN

LYNN *the BBC television series satirizing high politics,* Yes Minister *(1980–82) and* Yes Prime Minister *(1986–8).*

1 *You gave the world the guillotine*
But still we don't know why the heck
You have to drop it on our neck.
We're glad of what we did to you,
At Agincourt and Waterloo.
And now the Franco-Prussian War
Is something we are strongly for.
So damn your food and damn your wines,
Your twisted loaves and twisting vines,
Your table d'hôte, *your* à la carte,
Your land, your history, your art.
From now on you can keep the lot.
Take every single thing you've got,
Your land, your wealth, your men, your
dames,
Your dream of independent power,
And dear old Konrad Adenauer,
And stick them up your Eiffel Tower.

Time *magazine 8 February 1963. Referring to France's rejection of Britain's entry into the Common Market.*

2 Jim Hacker: Don't tell me about the press. I know exactly who reads the papers. The *Daily Mirror* is read by people who think they run the country. The *Guardian* is read by people who think they ought to run the country. *The Times* is read by people who actually do run the country. The *Daily Mail* is read by the wives of the people who run the country. The *Financial Times* is read by people who own the country. The *Morning Star* is read by people who think the country ought to be run by another country. And the *Daily Telegraph* is read by people who think it is.
Sir Humphrey: Prime Minister, what about the people who read the *Sun*?
Bernard Woolley: *Sun* readers don't care who runs the country, as long as she's got big tits.

Yes Prime Minister *(BBC TV series co-written with* JONATHAN LYNN*), 'A Conflict of Interest', broadcast 29 December 1987*

Douglas Jay (1907–96)
BRITISH POLITICIAN
Baron Jay of Battersea. Labour MP 1945–83, he was Financial Secretary to the Cabinet 1950–51 and President of the Board of Trade 1964–7, dismissed from the WILSON *Cabinet for his opposition to British entry into the EEC.*

1 In the case of nutrition and health, just as in the case of education, the gentleman in Whitehall really does know better what is good for people than the people know themselves.
The Socialist Case, ch. 30 (1937)

(Sir) James Jeans (1877–1946)
BRITISH ASTROPHYSICIST AND MATHEMATICIAN
His Dynamical Theory of Gases (1904) became a standard technical text, while The Universe Around Us *(1929) and* Through Space and Time *(1934) did much to popularize astronomy.*

1 From the intrinsic evidence of his creation, the Great Architect of the Universe now begins to appear as a pure mathematician.
The Mysterious Universe, ch. 5 (1930)

(Sir) Geoffrey Jellicoe (1900–96)
BRITISH ARCHITECT AND HISTORIAN
His writings, notably Landscape of Man *(1975), were influential on the development of landscapes and gardens. His designs often incorporate water and sculpture.*

1 Architecture is to make us know and remember who we are.
International Herald Tribune 6 November 1989

David Jenkins (b. 1925)
BRITISH ECCLESIASTIC
He was Professor of Theology at Leeds (1979–84) before becoming Bishop of Durham (1984–94), in which capacity he caused controversy over his interpretation of basic biblical tenets.

1 I wouldn't put it past God to arrange a virgin birth if He wanted, but I very much doubt if He would.
Church Times 4 May 1984

2 No statement about God is simply, literally true. God is far more than can be measured, described, defined in ordinary language, or pinned down to any particular happening.
Guardian 24 December 1984

3 As I get older I seem to believe less and less and yet to believe what I do believe more and more.
Daily Telegraph 2 November 1988

Roy Jenkins (1920–2003)
BRITISH POLITICIAN AND AUTHOR
Baron Jenkins of Hillhead. Elected a Labour MP in 1948, he was Home Secretary (1965–7 and 1974–6) and Chancellor of the Exchequer (1967–70). He was the first leader of the Social Democratic Party in 1981 but lost his seat in 1987, subsequently becoming Chancellor of Oxford University. He was noted for his biographies and his patrician tastes. ROBERT HARRIS *called him 'the most clubbable Coriolanus British politics has ever produced'.*

1 There is nobody in politics I can remember and no case I can think of in history where a man combined such a powerful

political personality with so little intelligence.

Of JAMES CALLAGHAN, quoted in *The Crossman Diaries*, 5 September 1969 (1979). Remark to RICHARD CROSSMAN, who demurred: 'I think Jim Callaghan is a wonderful political personality, easily the most accomplished politician in the Labour Party.'

2 **The politics of the left and centre of this country are frozen in an out-of-date mould which is bad for the political and economic health of Britain and increasingly inhibiting for those who live within the mould. Can it be broken?**

Speech to Parliamentary Press Gallery, 9 June 1980, quoted in *The Times* 10 June 1980. The Social Democratic Party, which Jenkins co-founded in 1981, was said to have 'broken the mould of British politics'.

Elizabeth Jennings (b. 1926)

BRITISH POET

Writing in traditional verse form, she explores personal themes of suffering and isolation, influenced by her Roman Catholic faith and by a period of mental illness. Her collections include The Mind Has Mountains *(1966),* Moments of Grace *(1979) and* Tributes *(1989).*

1 *But every season is a kind*
  Of rich nostalgia. We give names –
  Autumn and summer, winter, spring –
  As though to unfasten from the mind
  Our moods and give them outward forms.
  We want the certain, solid thing.

  'Song at the Beginning of Autumn', publ. in *A Way of Looking* (1955)

2 *Do they know they're old,*
  These two who are my father and my mother
  Whose fire from which I came, has now grown cold?

  'One Flesh', publ. in *The Mind Has Mountains* (1966)

3 *Two people, yes, two lasting friends.*
  The giving comes, the taking ends.
  There is no measure for such things.
  For this all Nature slows and sings.

  'Friendship', publ. in *Relationships* (1972)

4 *At last now you can be*
  What the old cannot recall
  And the young long for in dreams,
  Yet still include them all.

  'Accepted', publ. in *Growing Pains* (1975)

5 *I have come into the hour of a white healing.*
  Grief's surgery is over and I wear
  The scar of my remorse and of my feeling.

  'Into the Hour', publ. in *Moments of Grace* (1979)

6 *Never to possess,*
  Therefore never lose, –

This is a creed of fire,
The burning of excess,
The cold ash of loss,
Continual desire.

'Ways', publ. in *Extending the Territory* (1985)

Jiang Qing (1914–91)

CHINESE PARTY OFFICIAL

The third wife of MAO ZEDONG, *she played a prominent role in the Cultural Revolution (1966–9) and was the leading member of the 'Gang of Four' after Mao's death in 1976. Arrested for treason, she received a death sentence which was commuted to life imprisonment, but reportedly committed suicide.*

1 **There cannot be peaceful coexistence in the ideological realm. Peaceful coexistence corrupts.**

  Said in April 1967, quoted in *Mao and China: From Revolution to Revolution*, ch. 15 (1972) by Stanley Karnow

C. E. M. Joad (1891–1953)

BRITISH PHILOSOPHER AND AUTHOR

Cyril Edwin Mitchinson Joad. Author of more than forty books, he made the subject of philosophy accessible to the general reader, as in Guide to Philosophy *(1936), often incorporating his own controversial views.*

1 **It all depends what you mean by . . .**

  Typical intervention when answering questions on 'The Brains Trust', BBC radio (1941–8).

2 **A good soul like a good body should be as unobtrusive as possible; in so far as it functions properly, it should not be noticed for good or for ill.**

  The Book of Joad, ch. 2, 'Food and Women' (1932)

3 **Conscience was the barmaid of the Victorian soul. Recognizing that human beings were fallible and that their failings, though regrettable, must be humoured, conscience would permit, rather ungraciously perhaps, the indulgence of a number of carefully selected desires.**

  Ibid., ch. 11, 'Morals and My Lack of Them'

(Sir) Elton John (b. 1947)

BRITISH ROCK MUSICIAN

Originally Reginald Kenneth Dwight. A regular chart-topper from the 1970s to the 1990s, he is known for his flamboyant performances and extravagant lifestyle. Bestselling albums include Goodbye Yellow Brick Road *(1973).*

1 *And it seems to me you lived your life*
  Like a candle in the wind.

  'Candle in the Wind' (song, with lyrics by Bernie Taupin), on the album *Goodbye Yellow Brick Road* (1973). The song, which was about MARILYN MONROE, was re-released in 1997 with new words addressed to Princess DIANA (see 4 below). *Candle in the Wind* was the title of a 1941 play by Maxwell Anderson.

2 *Saturday night's alright for fighting.*
'Saturday Night's Alright for Fighting' (song, with lyrics by Bernie Taupin), on ibid.

3 I cannot bear successful people who are miserable.
Quoted in the *Sydney Morning Herald* 4 January 1986

4 *Goodbye English rose,*
May you ever grow in our hearts
'Candle in the Wind '97' (song, 1997, with lyrics by Bernie Taupin). The 1973 song was re-written to mark the death of Princess DIANA and performed by Elton John at her funeral in Westminster Abbey.

Pope John XXIII (1881–1963)
ITALIAN ECCLESIASTIC
Angelo Giuseppe Roncalli. Elected Pope in 1958, he was responsible for convening the Second Vatican Council in 1962 by which he intended to update and reform the Church, but died after the first session. The Council was continued by Pope Paul VI.

1 In order to imbue civilization with sound principles and enliven it with the spirit of the gospel, it is not enough to be illumined with the gift of faith and enkindled with the desire of forwarding a good cause. For this end it is necessary to take an active part in the various organizations and influence them from within. And since our present age is one of outstanding scientific and technical progress and excellence, one will not be able to enter these organizations and work effectively from within unless he is scientifically competent, technically capable and skilled in the practice of his own profession.
Encyclical 10 April 1963: *Pacem in Terris*, pt 5

2 Learn how to be a policeman, because that cannot be improvised. As regards being pope, you will see later. Anybody can be pope; the proof of this is that I have become one.
Letter to a young boy, publ. in *The Wit and Wisdom of Good Pope John* (ed. Henri Fesquet, 1963)

Pope John Paul II (b. 1920)
POLISH ECCLESIASTIC
Karol Jozef Wojtyla. The first non-Italian to be elected Pope (1978) since 1522, he has travelled extensively, speaking out against married priests, birth control, abortion, genetic manipulation and capital punishment. In 2000 he made a public apology for the historic sins of the Catholic Church.

1 As the family goes, so goes the nation and so goes the whole world in which we live.
Quoted in the *Observer* 7 December 1986

2 The question confronting the Church today is not any longer whether the man in the street can grasp a religious message, but how to employ the communications media so as to let him have the full impact of the Gospel message.
International Herald Tribune 8 May 1989

3 The cemetery of the victims of human cruelty in our century is extended to include yet another vast cemetery, that of the unborn.
Quoted in the *Observer* 9 June 1991

4 It would be simplistic to say that Divine Providence caused the fall of Communism. In a certain sense Communism as a system fell by itself. It fell as a consequence of its own mistakes and abuses. *It proved to be a medicine more dangerous than the disease itself.* It did not bring about true social reform, yet it did become a powerful threat and challenge to the entire world. But *it fell by itself, because of its own inherent weakness.*
Crossing the Threshold of Hope, 'Was God at Work in the Fall of Communism?' (1994)

5 *It is not possible to speak of the right to choose when a clear moral evil is involved, when what is at stake is the commandment Do not kill!*
Of abortion, ibid. 'The Defense of Every Life'

Gerald W. Johnson (1890–1980)
US AUTHOR
Gerald White Johnson. He was an authority on American history and government. His prolific writing career spanned six decades.

1 Heroes are created by popular demand, sometimes out of the scantiest materials, or none at all.
American Heroes and Hero-Worship, ch. 1 (1943)

James Weldon Johnson
(1871–1938)
US AUTHOR AND DIPLOMAT
He was consul in Venezuela and Nicaragua (1906–12) and prominent in the National Association for the Advancement of Colored People (1916–30). His novel The Autobiography of an Ex-Colored Man *(1912), his poetry and his anthologies contributed to the Harlem Renaissance of the 1920s.*

1 *And God stepped out on space,*
And He looked around and said,
'I'm lonely –
I'll make me a world.'
'The Creation', st. 1, written and first publ. 1918, repr. in *God's Trombones: Seven Negro Sermons in Verse* (1927)

2 *Young man –*
Young man –
Your arm's too short to box with God.
'The Prodigal Son', publ. ibid.

3 It is from the blues that all that may be called American music derives its most distinctive character.
Black Manhattan, ch. 11 (1930)

Lady Bird Johnson (b. 1912)
US FIRST LADY
Claudia Alta Taylor Johnson. She owned and operated KTBC radio and TV station in Austin, Texas, and was active in the political campaigns of her husband, LYNDON B. JOHNSON.

1 It all began so beautifully. After a drizzle in the morning, the sun came out bright and clear. We were driving into Dallas. In the lead car were President and Mrs Kennedy . . .
First entry, 22 November 1963, in *A White House Diary* (1970)

2 The first lady is, and always has been, an unpaid public servant elected by one person, her husband.
Journal entry, 14 March 1968, publ. ibid.

Linton Kwesi Johnson (b. 1952)
ANGLO-JAMAICAN POET AND SINGER
Since the 1970s he has been the voice of dub poetry. Among his collections, written in Jamaican patois, are Dread Beat 'n' Blood *(1975, album 1978) and* Mi Revalueshanary Fren: Selected Poems *(2002).*

1 *Brothers and sisters rocking,*
a dread beat pulsing fire, burning.
'Dread Beat 'n' Blood' (poem, 1975), set to music and released on the album *Dread Beat 'n' Blood* (1978) by Poet and the Roots

2 *Inglan is a bitch*
There's no escapin' it.
'Inglan is a Bitch' on the album *Bass Culture* (1980)

Lyndon B. Johnson (1908–73)
US POLITICIAN AND PRESIDENT
Lyndon Baines Johnson. A Texan Democrat, he served as President (1963–9) following KENNEDY's *assassination. His passing of the Civil Rights Act (1964) and Voting Rights Act (1965) led* RALPH ELLISON *to call him 'the greatest American president for the poor and for the Negroes', but his escalation of the Vietnam War lost him popularity. See also* BARRY GOLDWATER 1, POLITICAL SLOGANS 9.

1 Son, in politics you've got to learn that overnight chicken shit can turn to chicken salad.
Quoted in *Richard Nixon: The Shaping of his Character*, ch. 25 (1983) by FAWN BRODIE. Johnson, who had previously referred to RICHARD

NIXON as 'chicken shit', was replying to a reporter who had questioned him on his embracing Nixon on the latter's return from a vice-presidential tour of South America in May 1958, during which he had been mobbed by an angry crowd in Caracas. WALTER LIPPMANN called the tour 'a diplomatic Pearl Harbor' and the *Boston Globe* said it was 'one of the most ineptly handled episodes in this country's foreign relations'.

2 The world has narrowed to a neighborhood before it has broadened to a brotherhood.
Speech in New York City, 17 December 1963, publ. in *Public Papers of the Presidents of the United States, Lyndon B. Johnson: 1963–64*

3 This administration today, here and now, declares unconditional war on poverty in America.
State of the Union address to Congress, 8 January 1964, publ. ibid.

4 I don't believe in labels. I want to do the best I can. I want to be progressive without getting both feet off the ground at the same time. I want to be prudent without having my mind closed to anything that is new or different. I have often said that I was proud that I was a free man first and an American second, and a public servant third and a Democrat fourth, in that order, and I guess as a Democrat, if I had to place a label on myself, I would want to be a progressive who is prudent.
TV and radio interview, 15 March 1964, publ. ibid.

5 The Great Society is a place where every child can find knowledge to enrich his mind and to enlarge his talents. . . . It is a place where the city of man serves not only the needs of the body and the demands of commerce but the desire for beauty and the hunger for community. . . . It is a place where men are more concerned with the quality of their goals than the quantity of their goods.
Speech in Ann Arbor, Michigan, 22 May 1964, publ. ibid. The slogan 'Great Society' had been current for several years, possibly originating as the title of a book by economist Graham Wallas in 1914. As suggested by Richard N. Goodwin, Secretary General of the International Peace Corps Secretariat and occasional speechwriter, it became closely associated with Johnson's presidency, featuring in his acceptance speech at the Democratic Party National Convention, August 1964 (see Hugh Sidey's *A Very Personal Presidency*, 1968).

6 This is not a jungle war, but a struggle for freedom on every front of human activity.
Of the Vietnam War, in television broadcast 4 August 1964

7 We are not about to send American boys

9 or 10,000 miles away from home to do what Asian boys ought to be doing for themselves.

Speech at Akron University, Ohio, 21 October 1964, publ. in *Public Papers of the Presidents of the United States, Lyndon B. Johnson: 1963–64.*

8 I don't want loyalty. I want *loyalty*. I want him to kiss my ass in Macy's window at high noon and tell me it smells like roses. I want his pecker in my pocket.

Quoted in *The Best and the Brightest*, ch. 20 (1972) by David Halberstam. Referring to a prospective assistant.

9 Better to have him inside the tent pissing out, than outside pissing in.

Of J. EDGAR HOOVER, ibid.

10 Jerry Ford is so dumb he can't fart and chew gum at the same time.

Quoted in *A Ford, Not a Lincoln*, ch. 1, by Richard Reeves (1975). Reeves asserts that Johnson's put-down was 'cleaned up' by 'the late President's aides and history'.

Pamela Hansford Johnson

(1912–81)

BRITISH AUTHOR AND CRITIC

She published psychological novels, such as the trilogy Too Dear for My Possessing *(1940–48), but also wrote in a lighter vein, as in* The Unspeakable Skipton *(1959). According to* ANTHONY BURGESS, *'Some of her books are characterized by a sort of grave levity, others by a sort of light gravity.' She was married to* C. P. SNOW.

1 There are few things more disturbing than to find, in somebody we detest, a moral quality which seems to us demonstrably superior to anything we ourselves possess. It augurs not merely an unfairness on the part of creation, but a lack of artistic judgement. . . . Sainthood is acceptable only in saints.

Night and Silence, Who is Here? – An American Comedy, ch. 23 (1963)

Paul Johnson (b. 1928)

BRITISH JOURNALIST AND AUTHOR

He was Editor of the New Statesman *in the 1960s but later retreated from his socialist position. His books include* A History of Christianity *(1976),* Enemies of Society *(1977) and* A History of the Jews *(1987).*

1 While the music is performed, the cameras linger savagely over the faces of the audience. What a bottomless chasm of vacuity they reveal! Those who flock round the Beatles, who scream themselves into hysteria, whose vacant faces flicker over the TV screen, are the least fortunate of their

generation, the dull, the idle, the failures . . .

'The Menace of Beatlism', publ. in *New Statesman* 28 February 1964

2 The most socially subversive institution of our time is the one-parent family.

Quoted in the *Sunday Correspondent* 24 December 1989

Philip Johnson (b. 1906)

US ARCHITECT

He coined the term 'International Style' in 1932, and, following the theories of MIES VAN DER ROHE, *embraced postmodernism. He was Director of Architecture and Design at New York's Museum of Modern Art 1932–54, and published* Architecture 1949–65 *in 1966.*

1 The automobile is the greatest catastrophe in the entire history of City architecture.

'The Town and the Automobile, or the Pride of Elm Street' (1955), repr. in *Writings* (1979)

2 Architecture is the art of how to waste space.

The New York Times 27 December 1964

3 All architects want to live beyond their deaths.

Quoted in the *Observer* 27 December 1987

R. W. Johnson (b. 1916)

US JOURNALIST AND NEWSPAPER EXECUTIVE

1 Any solution to a problem changes the problem.

Washingtonian November 1979

Al Jolson (1886–1950)

RUSSIAN-BORN US SINGER AND ENTERTAINER

Originally Asa Yoelson. He wooed vaudeville audiences of the 1920s as a blackface comedian and singer of sentimental songs such as 'Mammy', 'Sonny Boy' and 'Swanee'. GEORGE BURNS *observed that it was easy to make him happy: 'You just had to cheer him for breakfast, applaud wildly for lunch, and give him a standing ovation for dinner.'*

1 *California here I come.*

'California Here I Come' (song, co-written by Jolson, BUDDY DE SYLVA and Joseph Mayer) in the stage musical *Bombo* (1921)

2 Wait a minute, wait a minute, you ain't heard nothing yet. Wait a minute I tell you. You ain't heard nothing yet. Do you want to hear 'Toot, Toot, Tootsie'?

Jakie Rabinowitz (Al Jolson), in *The Jazz Singer* (film, 1927, screenplay by Alfred A. Cohen, directed by Louis Silver). These were Al Jolson's first spoken words in the first talking picture. The screenplay was based on *The Day of Atone-*

ment, a story written and adapted for the stage by Samson Raphaelson and supposedly based on Al Jolson's own life. 'You ain't heard nothing yet' had been Jolson's slogan since 1906 and was the title of a song recorded by him in 1919, written by BUDDY DE SYLVA and GUS KAHN (Kahn also co-wrote 'Toot, Toot, Tootsie').

Beverly Jones (b. 1927)
US FEMINIST WRITER

1 Now, as always, the most automated appliance in a household is the mother.
'The Dynamics of Marriage and Motherhood', publ. in *The Florida Paper on Women's Liberation* (1970)

Chuck Jones (1912–2002)
US ANIMATOR AND CARTOON DIRECTOR
Originally Charles Jones. He worked for Warner Bros from 1933, creating the characters Road Runner and Wile E. Coyote and directing Bugs Bunny and Daffy Duck cartoons.

1 Beep! Beep!
The Road Runner, in *Looney Tunes/Merrie Melodies* (Warner Brothers cartoon, 1949–66). This only line of dialogue between the Road Runner at full sprint and Wile E. Coyote was voiced by Mel Blanc. The characters were created by Chuck Jones (who directed most of the episodes) and Michael Maltese and first introduced in a Warner Brothers' *Looney Tunes* cartoon called *Fast and Furry-Ous* (1949).

Quincy Jones (b. 1933)
US MUSICIAN, ARRANGER AND PRODUCER
The producer of three of MICHAEL JACKSON'*s biggest-selling albums (1980–87) as well as the all-star charity recording 'We Are the World' (1985), he has worked in jazz, pop and rock and composed scores for more than forty films.*

1 When you get your ass kicked that hard, it makes you go to the innermost depths of what you are all about as a human being. Now, maybe most people have not been kicked that hard, but it's still in everybody, and this music rings a bell that you can hear throughout the fucking world.
On the blues, quoted in *Rolling Stone* 1 July 1976

Steve Jones (b. 1944)
BRITISH GENETICIST
Called the 'Charles Darwin of the television era', he is Professor of Genetics at London University and a noted popularizer of science. His publications include The Language of Genes *(1993) and* Almost Like a Whale *(1999).*

1 Evolution is to the social sciences as statues are to birds: a convenient platform upon which to deposit badly digested ideas.
Almost Like a Whale: The Origin of the Species

Updated, 'An Historical Sketch of the Progress of Opinion on the Origin of Species' (1999). Jones had earlier used the aphorism in another context: 'Evolution is to allegory as statues are to birdshit: a convenient platform upon which to deposit badly digested ideas' (quoted in the *Guardian* 31 July 1997).

2 Evolution is, for most of the time, a race to stay in the same place.
Ibid., ch. 6

3 When we no longer look at an organic being as a savage looks at a ship, as at something wholly beyond his comprehension; when we regard every production of nature as one which has had a history; when we contemplate every complex structure and instinct as the summing up of many contrivances, each useful to the possessor, nearly in the same way as when we look at any great mechanical invention as the summing up of the labour, the experience, the reason, and even the blunders of numerous workmen; when we thus view each organic being, how far more interesting, I speak from experience, will the study of natural history become!
Ibid., ch. 14

4 Gravity is the universal glue that makes the cosmos stick together.
Quoted in the *Daily Telegraph* 6 January 1999

Erica Jong (b. 1942)
US AUTHOR AND POET
Her first volume of poetry, Fruits and Vegetables *(1971), won her a reputation as a feminist writer, although she is best known for her first novel* Fear of Flying *(1973) and its sequel* How to Save Your Own Life *(1977), which wittily chronicled the sexual adventures of Isadora Wing.*

1 Perhaps all artists were, in a sense, housewives: tenders of the earth household.
'The Artist as Housewife: The Housewife as Artist', publ. in *The First Ms. Reader* (ed. Francine Klagsbrun, 1972)

2 Solitude is un-American. . . . There is simply no dignified way for a woman to live alone. Oh, she can get along financially perhaps (though not nearly as well as a man), but emotionally she is never left in peace. Her friends, her family, her fellow workers never let her forget that her husbandlessness, her childlessness – her selfishness, in short – is a reproach to the American way of life.
Narrator (Isadora Wing), in *Fear of Flying*, ch. 1 (1973)

3 The zipless fuck is absolutely pure. It is free of ulterior motives. There is no power game. The man is not 'taking' and the woman is not 'giving'. No one is attempting to cuckold a husband or humiliate a

wife. No one is trying to prove anything or get anything out of anyone. The zipless fuck is the purest thing there is. And it is rarer than the unicorn. And I have never had one.

Ibid. Jong explained, 'Zipless . . . because the incident has all the swift compression of a dream and is seemingly free of all remorse and guilt.'

4 Men have always detested women's gossip because they suspect the truth: their measurements are being taken and compared. . . . Men can mock it, but they can't prevent it. Gossip is the opiate of the oppressed.

Ibid., ch. 6

5 There is nothing fiercer than a failed artist. The energy remains, but, having no outlet, it implodes in a great black fart of rage which smokes up all the inner windows of the soul. Horrible as successful artists often are, there is nothing crueler or more vain than a failed artist.

Ibid., ch. 9

6 Men and women, women and men. It will never work.

Ibid., ch. 16

7 *Each month*
the blood sheets down
like good red rain.

'Gardener', publ. in *Half Lives* (1973)

8 Jealousy is all the fun you *think* they had . . .

How to Save Your Own Life, epigraph to 'Bennett tells all in Woodstock . . .' (1977)

9 Advice is what we ask for when we already know the answer but wish we didn't.

Ibid., epigraph to 'A day in the life . . .'

10 In a bad marriage, friends are the invisible glue. If we have enough friends, we may go on for years, intending to leave, talking about leaving – instead of actually getting up and leaving.

Ibid., 'A day in the life . . .'

11 There is a rhythm to the ending of a marriage just like the rhythm of a courtship – only backward. You try to start again but get into blaming over and over. Finally you are both worn out, exhausted, hopeless. Then lawyers are called in to pick clean the corpses. The death has occurred much earlier.

Ibid., 'There is a rhythm to the ending . . .'

12 Where is Hollywood located? Chiefly between the ears. In that part of the American brain lately vacated by God.

Ibid., epigraph to 'Hello to Hollywood . . .'

13 Every country gets the circus it deserves.

Spain gets bullfights. Italy gets the Catholic Church. America gets Hollywood.

Ibid., epigraph to 'Take the Red-Eye . . .'

14 What does a woman want? She wants what she has been told she ought to want. . . . Orgasm is no proof of anything. Orgasm is proof of orgasm. Someday every woman will have orgasms – like every family has color TV – and we can all get on with the real business of life.

Ibid., 'The street where I lived . . .'

15 Do you want me to tell you something really subversive? Love *is* everything it's cracked up to be. That's why people are so cynical about it. . . . It really *is* worth fighting for, being brave for, risking everything for. And the trouble is, if you don't risk anything, you risk even *more*.

Hans, ibid. 'Intuition, extuition . . .'

16 Sex as an illness is a concept Americans can love. We may be afraid of pleasure, but we love diseases. With disease we know what to do: declare war.

Quoted in the *Sunday Telegraph* 27 December 1998

Janis Joplin (1943–70)

US ROCK SINGER

An impassioned blues-style singer ('I'd rather not sing than sing quiet'), she performed with the band Big Brother and the Holding Company before going solo in 1968. Her career was cut short by her addiction to alcohol and drugs, and her biggest hit 'Me and Bobby McGee' was released posthumously in 1971.

1 Fourteen heart attacks and he had to die in my week. In MY week.

Quoted in the *New Musical Express* 12 April 1969. Referring to former President EISENHOWER, whose death prevented Joplin's photograph appearing on the cover of *Newsweek*.

2 *Oh, Lord, won't you buy me a Mercedes Benz?*
My friends all drive Porsches,
I must make amends.

'Mercedes Benz' (song) on the album *Pearl* (1971)

3 On stage I make love to 25,000 people, then I go home alone.

Quoted in the *New Yorker* 14 August 1971

4 It's not what isn't, it's what you wish *was* that makes unhappiness. . . . I think I think too much. That's why I drink.

Quoted in *Rock 'n' Roll Babylon*, ch. 3 (1982) by Gary Herman

June Jordan (b. 1936)

US POET AND CIVIL RIGHTS ACTIVIST

She has campaigned on issues of feminism and racism, and for the inclusion of black studies on

university curricula. Her poetry collections include
Things That I Do in the Dark *(1977) and* Passion
(1980).

1 Body and soul, Black America reveals the
extreme questions of contemporary life,
questions of freedom and identity: *How
can I be who I am?*

'Black Studies: Bringing Back the Person', first
publ. in *The Evergreen Review* October 1969,
repr. in *Moving Towards Home: Political Essays*
(1989)

2 In the name of motherhood and
fatherhood and education and good
manners, we threaten and suffocate and
bind and ensnare and bribe and trick children into wholesale emulation of our ways.

'Old Stories: New Lives', keynote address to
Child Welfare League of America, 1978, publ.
ibid.

3 I am a feminist, and what that means to
me is much the same as the meaning of the
fact that I am Black: it means that I must
undertake to love myself and to respect
myself as though my very life depends
upon self-love and self-respect.

'Where is the Love?', address to Black Writers'
Conference, Howard University, 1978, publ.
ibid.

4 *We are the wrong people of
the wrong skin in the wrong continent and
what
in the hell is everybody being reasonable
about*

'Poem about My Rights', publ. in *Passion* (1980)

5 In America, you can segregate the people,
but the problems will travel. From slavery
to equal rights, from state suppression of
dissent to crime, drugs and unemployment, I can't think of a supposedly Black
issue that hasn't wasted the original Black
target group and then spread like measles
to outlying white experience.

'Problems of Language in a Democratic State',
first publ. 1982, repr. in *Moving Towards Home:
Political Essays* (1989)

Jenny Joseph (b. 1932)
BRITISH POET

Among her poetry collections are Rose in the Afternoon *(1974),* Beyond Descartes *(1983) and*
Extended Similes *(1997). She has also written for
children.*

1 *When I am an old woman I shall wear
purple
With a red hat which doesn't go, and
doesn't suit me.
And I shall spend my pension on brandy
and summer gloves
And satin sandals, and say we've got no
money for butter.*

'Warning', publ. in *Rose in the Afternoon* (1974)

2 *I shall go out in my slippers in the rain
And pick the flowers in other people's
gardens
And learn to spit.*

Ibid.

Michael Joseph (1897–1958)
BRITISH PUBLISHER

*He founded Michael Joseph Ltd in 1935, publishing
C. S. Forester and* H. E. BATES, *among others.*

1 Authors are easy enough to get on with – if
you are fond of children.

Quoted in the *Observer* 29 May 1949

Marcel Jouhandeau (1888–1979)
FRENCH AUTHOR

*Almost entirely autobiographical, his novels usu-
ally portray inhabitants of Chaminadour, a fictionalized version of his native town, and include*
La Jeunesse de Théophile *(1921) and* Marcel et
Élise *(1953).*

1 To really know someone is to have loved
and hated him in turn.

Défense de l'enfer, 'Erotologie' (1935)

James Joyce (1882–1941)
IRISH AUTHOR

*He revolutionized the novel with his use of experi-
mental language and writing techniques in* Ulysses
*(1922, banned in Britain and the US until 1936)
and* Finnegans Wake *(1939), both written in self-
imposed exile from Ireland. He shocked many of
his contemporaries (see* E. M. FORSTER 11, D. H.
LAWRENCE 17, VIRGINIA WOOLF 8*), but for*
SAMUEL BECKETT, *'his writing is not about something. It is the thing itself.'*

1 Love (understood as the desire of good for
another) is in fact so unnatural a phenomenon that it can scarcely repeat itself, the
soul being unable to become virgin again
and not having energy enough to cast itself
out again into the ocean of another's
soul.

Notes to the play *Exiles* (notes written 1914–15,
publ. 1952; *Exiles* publ. 1918)

2 What did that mean, to kiss? You put your
face up like that to say goodnight and then
his mother put her face down. That was to
kiss. His mother put her lips on his cheek;
her lips were soft and they wetted his
cheek; and they made a tiny little noise:
kiss. Why did people do that with their
two faces?

Stephen Dedalus, in *A Portrait of the Artist as a
Young Man,* ch. 1 (1916)

3 When the soul of a man is born in this
country there are nets flung at it to hold it

back from flight. You talk to me of nationality, language, religion. I shall try to fly by those nets.

Stephen Dedalus, ibid., ch. 5. Speaking to the young patriot Davin.

4 Do you know what Ireland is? Ireland is the old sow that eats her farrow.

Ibid.

5 Pity is the feeling which arrests the mind in the presence of whatsoever is grave and constant in human sufferings and unites it with the human sufferer. Terror is the feeling which arrests the mind in the presence of whatsoever is grave and constant in human sufferings and unites it with the secret cause.

Ibid.

6 To speak of these things and to try to understand their nature and, having understood it, to try slowly and humbly and constantly to express, to press out again, from the gross earth or what it brings forth, from sound and shape and colour which are the prison gates of our soul, an image of the beauty we have come to understand – that is art.

Ibid.

7 Art is the human disposition of sensible or intelligible matter for an aesthetic end.

Ibid. The definition appeared earlier in Joyce's 'Paris Notebook' dated 28 March 1903.

8 The artist, like the God of the creation, remains within or behind or beyond or above his handiwork, invisible, refined out of existence, indifferent, paring his fingernails.

Ibid.

9 Whatever else is unsure in this stinking dunghill of a world a mother's love is not.

Cranly, ibid.

10 I will tell you what I will do and what I will not do. I will not serve that in which I no longer believe, whether it call itself my home, my fatherland, or my church: and I will try to express myself in some mode of life or art as freely as I can and as wholly as I can, using for my defence the only arms I allow myself to use – silence, exile and cunning.

Stephen Dedalus, ibid.

11 Welcome, O life! I go to encounter for the millionth time the reality of experience and to forge in the smithy of my soul the uncreated conscience of my race. . . . Old father, old artificer, stand me now and ever in good stead.

Ibid. Said by Stephen departing from Ireland, in the closing lines of the book. 'Old artificer' is a reference to Daedalus, the mythical craftsman, whose flight from Crete ended in the drowning

of his son. Joyce's own experience on fleeing Ireland was largely of debt and penury.

12 While you have a thing it can be taken from you . . . but when you give it, you have given it. No robber can take it from you. It is yours then for ever when you have given it. It will be yours always. That is to give.

Richard Rowan, in *Exiles*, act 1 (1918)

13 You forget that the kingdom of heaven suffers violence: and the kingdom of heaven is like a woman.

Robert Hand, ibid. act 2

14 Writing in English is the most ingenious torture ever devised for sins committed in previous lives. The English reading public explains the reason why.

Letter, 5 September 1918, publ. in *Selected Letters of James Joyce* (ed. Richard Ellmann, 1975)

15 The snotgreen sea. The scrotumtightening sea.

Buck Mulligan, in *Ulysses*, ch. 1 ('Telemachus') (1922)

16 It is a symbol of Irish art. The cracked looking glass of a servant.

Stephen Dedalus, ibid. Referring to Buck Mulligan's purloined mirror.

17 I fear those big words which make us so unhappy.

Stephen Dedalus, ibid., ch. 2 ('Nestor')

18 History is a nightmare from which I am trying to awake.

Ibid.

19 A man of genius makes no mistakes. His errors are volitional and are the portals of discovery.

Stephen Dedalus, ibid., ch. 9 ('Scylla and Charybdis')

20 A nation is the same people living in the same place.

Leopold Bloom, ibid., ch. 12 ('Cyclops')

21 Greater love than this, he said, no man hath that a man lay down his wife for his friend. Go thou and do likewise. Thus, or words to that effect, said Zarathustra, sometime regius professor of French letters to the university of Oxtail nor breathed there ever that man to whom mankind was more beholden.

Stephen Dedalus, ibid., ch. 14 ('Oxen of the Sun'). 'Greater love . . .' parodies John 15:13. Joyce's passage refers to 'those delicate poets' Francis Beaumont and John Fletcher, who 'had but the one doxy between them'.

22 British Beatitudes! . . . Beer, beef, business, bibles, bulldogs, battleships, buggery and bishops.

Ibid.

23 frseeeeeeeefronnnng train somewhere

whistling the strength those engines have
in them like big giants and the water rolling all over and out of them all sides like
the end of Loves old sweeeetsonnnng the
poor men that have to be out all the night
from their wives and families in those
roasting engines

Molly Bloom's soliloquy, ibid., ch. 18
('Penelope')

24 He kissed me under the Moorish wall and I
thought well as well him as another and
then I asked him with my eyes to ask again
yes and then he asked me would I yes to
say yes my mountain flower and first I put
my arms around him yes and drew him
down to me so he could feel my breasts all
perfume yes and his heart was going like
mad and yes I said yes I will Yes.

Ibid. Closing words of book.

25 riverrun, past Eve and Adam's, from
swerve of shore to bend of bay, brings us
by a commodious vicus of recirculation
back to Howth Castle and Environs.

Finnegans Wake, pt 1, ch. 1 (1939). Opening
words of book. The book's closing words ('A
way a lone a last a loved a long the') form the
first part of this sentence, which provided a title
for a volume of essays by RICHARD ELLMANN,
Joyce's biographer: *a long the riverrun* (1988).

26 That ideal reader suffering from an ideal
insomnia.

Ibid., ch. 5

27 You have become of twosome twiminds
forenenst gods, hidden and discovered,
nay, condemned fool, anarch, egoarch, hire-
siarch, you have reared your disunited
kingdom on the vacuum of your own most
intensely doubtful soul.

Ibid., ch. 7. Part of Shaun's diatribe against his
wastrel brother Shem, whose loose counterpart
in real life was Stanislaus Joyce (James's younger
brother) berating James.

28 O, you were excruciated, in honour bound
to the cross of your own cruelfiction!

Ibid.

29 Oft in the smelly night will they wallow for
a clutch of the famished hand, I say, them
bearded jezabelles you hired to rob you,
while on your sodden straw impolitely you
encored (Airish and nawboggaleesh!) those
hornmade ivory dreams you reved of the
Ruth you called your companionate, a
beauty from the bible, of the flushpots of
Euston and the hanging garments of Marylebone.

Ibid.

30 All moanday, tearsday, wailsday, thumps-
day, frightday, shatterday till the fear of
the Law.

Ibid., pt 2, ch. 2

31 Three quarks for Muster Mark!

Ibid., ch. 4. This seabirds' chorus song is the
origin of the name 'quark' given to the hypothetical particle postulated by the physicists Murray
Gell-Mann and George Zweig in 1963.

32 I should tell you that honestly, on my
honour of a Nearwickcd, I always think in
a wordworth's of that primed favourite
continental poet, Daunty, Gouty and Shop-
keeper, A.G., whom the generality admoy-
ers in this that is and that this is to come.

Humphrey Chimpden Earwicker, making an
incoherent speech in his defence, ibid., pt 3, ch. 3

33 When I hear the word 'stream' uttered
with such a revolting primness, what I
think of is urine and not the contemporary
novel. And besides, it isn't new, it is far
from the *dernier cri*. Shakespeare used it
continually, much too much in my
opinion, and there's *Tristam Shandy*, not
to mention the *Agamemnon* . . .

On 'the stream of consciousness', quoted in
Voices: A Memoir, 'At Sylvia's' (1983) by Frederic
Prokosch. Joyce was replying to the assertion by
the young author and poet Prokosch that Molly
Bloom's final monologue in *Ulysses* exemplified
this form. 'Molly Bloom was a down-to-earth
lady,' Joyce said. 'She would never have indulged
in anything so refined as a stream of consciousness.'

William Joyce (1906–46)

BRITISH FASCIST

*'Lord Haw-Haw', as he came to be known, was
expelled from OSWALD MOSLEY's Fascist Party in
1937 and founded the British Nationalist Socialist
League. He broadcast propaganda against Britain
throughout the Second World War and was
hanged for treason after his capture.*

1 Germany calling! Germany calling!

Opening words of propaganda broadcasts from
Hamburg, September 1939–April 1945

Mike Judge (b. 1963)

ECUADOR-BORN US ANIMATOR AND
FILM-MAKER

*He is best known for the animated TV series
Beavis and Butt-head (1992–7) and King of the
Hill (1997). The film Beavis and Butt-head Do
America appeared in 1996.*

1 I like stuff that's cool, I don't like stuff that
sucks.

Butt-head, in *Beavis and Butt-head* (cartoon
created and voiced by Mike Judge, written by
Sam Johnson and Chris Marcil, shown on MTV
from Sept 1992)

Walid Jumblatt (b. 1949)

LEBANESE POLITICIAN

He has been leader of the Druze and Progressive

Socialist Party since 1977 and was Minister of Public Works 1989–92.

1 Here, even the law of the jungle has broken down.

Quoted in the *Sunday Times* 29 December 1985. Speaking of events in Lebanon in the wake of the Israeli army's withdrawal.

Carl Jung (1875–1961)
SWISS PSYCHIATRIST

He was a collaborator with FREUD *from 1907, but his work* The Psychology of the Unconscious *(1912) instigated a rift with him over the relevance of sexuality in psychological problems. Jung's 'analytical psychology' emphasized the 'collective unconscious' and 'individuation', and his* Psychological Types *(1921) introduced the concept of introversion and extroversion.*

1 So often among so-called 'primitives' one comes across spiritual personalities who immediately inspire respect, as though they were the fully matured products of an undisturbed fate.

'Marriage as a Psychological Relationship' (1925), repr. in *Collected Works*, vol. 17 (ed. William McGuire, 1954)

2 Nothing is more repulsive than a furtively prurient spirituality; it is just as unsavoury as gross sensuality.

Ibid.

3 The wine of youth does not always clear with advancing years; sometimes it grows turbid.

The Stages of Life (1930), repr. ibid., vol. 8 (1960)

4 The psychiatrist knows only too well how each of us becomes the helpless but not pitiable victim of his own sentiments. Sentimentality is the superstructure erected upon brutality.

Ulysses: A Monologue (1932), repr. ibid., vol. 15 (1966)

5 If there is anything that we wish to change in the child, we should first examine it and see whether it is not something that could better be changed in ourselves.

The Development of Personality (1934), repr. ibid., vol. 17 (1954)

6 Personality is the supreme realization of the innate idiosyncrasy of a living being. It is an act of high courage flung in the face of life, the absolute affirmation of all that constitutes the individual, the most successful adaptation to the universal conditions of existence coupled with the greatest possible freedom for self-determination.

Ibid.

7 Instead of being at the mercy of wild beasts, earthquakes, landslides, and inundations, modern man is battered by the elemental forces of his own psyche. This is

the World Power that vastly exceeds all other powers on earth. The Age of Enlightenment, which stripped nature and human institutions of gods, overlooked the God of Terror who dwells in the human soul.

Ibid.

8 From the middle of life onward, only he remains vitally alive who is ready to *die with life.*

The Soul and Death (1934), repr. ibid., vol. 8 (1960)

9 I cannot love anyone if I hate myself. That is the reason why we feel so extremely uncomfortable in the presence of people who are noted for their special virtuousness, for they radiate an atmosphere of the torture they inflict on themselves. That is not a virtue but a vice.

Basel seminar (1934), multigraphed for private circulation by the Psychology Club, Zurich, repr. ibid. vol. 18 (1977)

10 Neurosis is always a substitute for legitimate suffering.

Psychology and Religion (1938), repr. ibid., vol. 11 (1958)

11 Our blight is ideologies – they are the long-expected Antichrist!

'Psychological Commentary on "The Tibetan Book of the Great Liberation" ' (1939, rev. 1954), repr. ibid.

12 Yoga in Mayfair or Fifth Avenue, or in any other place which is on the telephone, is a spiritual fake.

Ibid.

13 Masses are always breeding grounds of psychic epidemics.

Concerning Rebirth (1940), repr. ibid., vol. 9, pt 1 (1959)

14 An inflated consciousness is always egocentric and conscious of nothing but its own existence. It is incapable of learning from the past, incapable of understanding contemporary events, and incapable of drawing right conclusions about the future. It is hypnotized by itself and therefore cannot be argued with. It inevitably dooms itself to calamities that must strike it dead.

Psychology and Alchemy, Epilogue (1944) repr. ibid. vol. 12 (1968)

15 It is a fact that cannot be denied: the wickedness of others becomes our own wickedness because it kindles something evil in our own hearts.

After the Catastrophe (1945), repr. ibid., vol. 10 (1964)

16 The wise man who is not heeded is counted a fool, and the fool who proclaims the general folly first and loudest passes

for a prophet and Führer, and sometimes it is luckily the other way round as well, or else mankind would long since have perished of stupidity.

Mysterium Coniunctionis (1955–6), repr. ibid., vol. 14 (1963)

17 Resistance to the organized mass can be effected only by the man who is as well organized in his individuality as the mass itself.

The Undiscovered Self, ch. 4 (1957)

18 Because the European does not know his own unconscious, he does not understand the East and projects into it everything he fears and despises in himself.

Foreword to *Beelden uit het onbewuste* (1957) by R. J. Van Helsdingen, repr. in *The Collected Works*, vol. 18 (ed. William McGuire, 1977)

19 In all chaos there is a cosmos, in all disorder a secret order.

'Archetypes of the Collective Unconscious' (1935, rev. 1954), repr. ibid., vol. 9, pt 1 (1959)

20 The word 'belief' is a difficult thing for me. I don't *believe*. I must have a reason for a certain hypothesis. Either I *know* a thing, and then I know it – I don't need to believe it.

Interview in 1959, publ. in *Face to Face* (1964) by Hugh Burnett. Jung's statement helps to explain the answer he gave when asked if he believed in God: 'I do not believe . . . I know' (quoted by LAURENS VAN DER POST in *Jung and the Story of Our Time*, 1976)

21 The images of the unconscious place a great responsibility upon a man. Failure to understand them, or a shirking of ethical responsibility, deprives him of his wholeness and imposes a painful fragmentariness on his life.

Memories, Dreams, Reflections, ch. 6 (1962)

22 A man who has not passed through the inferno of his passions has never overcome them.

Ibid., ch. 9, sect. 4

23 As far as we can discern, the sole purpose of human existence is to kindle a light in the darkness of mere being.

Ibid., ch. 11

24 Every form of addiction is bad, no matter whether the narcotic be alcohol or morphine or idealism.

Ibid., ch. 12

25 Life is – or has – meaning and meaninglessness. I cherish the anxious hope that meaning will preponderate and win the battle.

Ibid., 'Retrospect'

26 I am incapable of determining ultimate worth or worthlessness; I have no judgement about myself and my life. There is nothing I am quite sure about. I have no definite convictions – not about anything really. I only know that I was born and exist, and it seems to me that I have been carried along.

Ibid.

Theodore Kaczynski (b. 1942)

US TERRORIST

Known as 'Unabomber' and called the 'Luddite King' by the media, he killed three people and injured twenty-three others in his campaign of random bombings inspired by his hatred of technology. After seventeen years in hiding he was caught and sentenced to life imprisonment (1998).

1 The positive ideal that we propose is Nature. That is, WILD nature; those aspects of the functioning of the Earth and its living things that are independent of human management and free of human interference and control. And with wild nature we include human nature.
The Industrial Society and Its Future, 'Strategy', sect. 183, publ. in the Washington Post 19 September 1995

2 The only points on which we absolutely insist are that the single overriding goal must be the elimination of modern technology, and that no other goal can be allowed to compete with this one.
Ibid., sect. 206

Pauline Kael (1919–2001)

US FILM CRITIC

'The sanest, saltiest, most resourceful and least attitudinizing movie critic in the USA', according to writer and producer Richard Schickel, she reviewed for the New Yorker 1968–91.

1 The United States has now achieved what critics of socialism have always posited as the end result of a socialist state: a prosperous, empty, uninspiring uniformity. (If we do not have exactly what Marx meant by a classless society, we do have something so close to it that the term is certainly no longer an alluring goal.)
'The Glamour of Delinquency', first publ. 1955, repr. in I Lost it at the Movies (1965)

2 The first prerogative of an artist in any medium is to make a fool of himself.
'Is There a Cure for Film Criticism?' first publ. 1962, repr. ibid.

3 Regrettably, one of the surest signs of the Philistine is his reverence for the superior tastes of those who put him down.
'Zeitgeist and Poltergeist', first publ. 1964, repr. ibid.

4 It seems likely that many of the young who don't wait for others to call them artists, but simply announce that they are, don't have the patience to make art.
'Movie Brutalists', first publ. 1966, repr. in Kiss Kiss Bang Bang (1968)

5 The words 'Kiss Kiss Bang Bang', which I saw on an Italian movie poster, are perhaps the briefest statement imaginable of the basic appeal of movies. This appeal is

what attracts us, and ultimately what makes us despair when we begin to understand how seldom movies are more than this.

Kiss Kiss Bang Bang, 'A Note on the Title' (1968)

6 Watching old movies is like spending an evening with those people next door. They bore us, and we wouldn't go out of our way to see them; we drop in on them because they're so close. If it took some effort to see old movies, we might try to find out which were the good ones, and if people saw only the good ones maybe they would still respect old movies. As it is, people sit and watch movies that audiences walked out on thirty years ago. Like Lot's wife, we are tempted to take another look, attracted not by evil but by something that seems much more shameful – our own innocence.

Ibid., 'Movies on Television'

7 Irresponsibility is part of the pleasure of all art, it is the part the schools cannot recognize.

'Trash, Art, and the Movies', first publ. 1968, repr. in *Going Steady* (1970)

8 In the arts, the critic is the only independent source of information. The rest is advertising.

Quoted in *Newsweek* 24 December 1973

9 Robert Redford . . . has turned almost alarmingly blond – he's gone past platinum, he must be into plutonium; his hair is coordinated with his teeth.

Reeling, pt 2, 'The Sting' (1976)

Franz Kafka (1883–1924)

CZECH AUTHOR

His short stories, notably The Metamorphosis *(1915), and his novels, for example* The Trial *(1925) and* The Castle *(1926), depicted a 'Kafkaesque' world where the individual is overwhelmed by incomprehensible labyrinths of totalitarian bureaucracy. All were written in German.*

1 As Gregor Samsa awoke one morning from uneasy dreams he found himself transformed in his bed into a gigantic insect.

The Metamorphosis, ch. 1 (1915, transl. 1933). Opening sentence.

2 All human errors are impatience, a premature breaking off of methodical procedure, an apparent fencing-in of what is apparently at issue.

The Collected Aphorisms, no. 2 (October 1917–February 1918), publ. in *Shorter Works*, vol. 1 (ed. and transl. Malcolm Pasley, 1973)

3 A first sign of the beginning of understanding is the wish to die.

Ibid., no. 13

4 In theory there is a possibility of perfect happiness: To believe in the indestructible element within one, and not to strive towards it.

Ibid., no. 68

5 A belief is like a guillotine, just as heavy, just as light.

Ibid., no. 87

6 It is not necessary that you leave the house. Remain at your table and listen. Do not even listen, only wait. Do not even wait, be wholly still and alone. The world will present itself to you for its unmasking, it can do no other, in ecstasy it will writhe at your feet.

Ibid., no. 109

7 My guiding principle is this: Guilt is never to be doubted.

Officer, in *In the Penal Settlement* (1920, transl. 1933), repr. in *Metamorphosis and Other Stories* (1961)

8 Life's splendour forever lies in wait about each one of us in all its fullness, but veiled from view, deep down, invisible, far off. It *is* there, though, not hostile, not reluctant, not deaf. If you summon it by the right word, by its right name, it will come.

Journal entry, 18 October 1921, publ. in *The Diaries of Franz Kafka: 1910–23* (ed. Max Brod, 1948 and 1949)

9 Anyone who cannot come to terms with his life while he is alive needs one hand to ward off a little his despair over his fate . . . but with his other hand he can note down what he sees among the ruins.

Journal entry, 19 October 1921, publ. ibid.

10 If there is a transmigration of souls then I am not yet on the bottom rung. My life is a hesitation before birth.

Journal entry, 24 January 1922, publ. ibid.

11 Someone must have been telling lies about Joseph K., for without having done anything wrong he was arrested one fine morning.

The Trial, ch. 1 (1925, transl. 1935). Opening words.

12 You may object that it is not a trial at all; you are quite right, for it is only a trial if I recognize it as such.

Joseph K., ibid. ch. 2

13 It's often safer to be in chains than to be free.

The Advocate, ibid. ch. 8. An allusion to Rousseau's famous dictum, 'Man is born free, and everywhere he is in chains' (from *The Social Contract*, 1762).

14 Human nature, essentially changeable, unstable as the dust, can endure no restraint; if it binds itself it soon begins to tear madly at its bonds, until it rends

everything asunder, the wall, the bonds
and its very self.
The Great Wall of China (1931, transl. 1949), repr.
in *Metamorphosis and Other Stories* (1961)

15 Try with all your might to comprehend the
decrees of the high command, but only up
to a certain point; then avoid further meditation.
Ibid. A 'very wise maxim' regarding the rationale
behind the construction of the Great Wall of
China.

Gus Kahn (1886–1941)
US SONGWRITER
*A Tin Pan Alley writer for films and Broadway
shows, he collaborated successfully with Walter
Donaldson and provided a number of hit songs for*
AL JOLSON. *Other compositions include 'Yes, Sir,
That's My Baby' (1925) and 'My Baby Just Cares
for Me' (1930).*

1 *All God's chillun got rhythm.*
'All God's Chillun Got Rhythm' (song, with
music by Bronislaw Kaper and Walter Jurmann)
in the Marx Brothers' film, *A Day at the Races*
(1937). The number was sung by Ivie Andersen
in the film, and subsequently recorded by Benny
Bergan and his Orchestra, JUDY GARLAND and
June Christy.

Kaixi Wuer
CHINESE STUDENT LEADER
*Prominent during the student demonstrations in
Tiananmen Square (1989), he headed the Auton-
omous Student Association, and later escaped to
France.*

1 A black sun has appeared in the sky of my
motherland.
Quoted in the *Independent* 29 June 1989. On the
massacre in Tienanmen Square, Beijing, 3 June.

Ryszard Kapuśński (b. 1932)
POLISH JOURNALIST
*His work focuses on Poland, and the revolutions
and civil wars of the Third World and includes a
portrait of Haile Selassie,* The Emperor *(1978),
and writings on Africa and Kyrghistan.*

1 When is a crisis reached? When questions
arise that can't be answered.
'A Warsaw Diary', publ. in *Granta* no. 15 (1985)

2 Our salvation is in striving to achieve what
we know we'll never achieve.
Ibid.

3 We follow the mystics. They know where
they are going. They, too, go astray, but
when they go astray they do so in a way
that is mystical, dark, and mysterious.
Ibid.

4 Do not be misled by the fact that you are

at liberty and relatively free; that for the
moment you are not under lock and key:
you have simply been granted a reprieve.
Ibid.

5 In Poland a man must be one thing: white
or black, here or there, with us or against
us – clearly, openly, without hesitations.
. . . We lack the liberal, democratic tradition rich in all its gradations. We have
instead the tradition of struggle: the
extreme situation, the final gesture.
Ibid.

6 First you destroy those who create values.
Then you destroy those who know what
the values are, and who also know that
those destroyed before were in fact the
creators of values. But real barbarism
begins when no one can any longer judge
or know that what he does is barbaric.
Ibid.

7 Our job is like a baker's work – his rolls
are tasty as long as they're fresh; after two
days they're stale; after a week, they're
covered with mould and fit only to be
thrown out.
On journalism, in *The Soccer War*, 'The Plan of
the Never-Written Book', sect. 33 (1990)

8 Although a system may cease to exist in
the legal sense or as a structure of power,
its values (or anti-values), its philosophy,
its teachings remain in us. They rule our
thinking, our conduct, our attitude to
others. The situation is a demonic paradox: we have toppled the system but we
still carry its genes.
Independent on Sunday 1 September 1991

9 The so-called new Russian man is characterized mainly by his complete exhaustion.
You may find yourself wondering if he has
the strength to enjoy his new-found freedom. He is like a long-distance runner
who, on reaching the finishing line, is
incapable even of raising his hands in a
gesture of victory.
Ibid. 27 October 1991

Yousuf Karsh (1908–2002)
ARMENIAN-BORN CANADIAN
PHOTOGRAPHER
*Famous for his studies of world personalities, he
first caught attention for his portrait of* WINSTON
CHURCHILL *(1941), reputedly the most repro-
duced photograph of all time.* ROY STRONG *said
of his subjects that 'Karsh supplies the halo'.*

1 If there is a single quality that is shared by
all great men, it is vanity. But I mean by
'vanity' only that they appreciate their own
worth. Without this kind of vanity they

would not be great. And with vanity alone, of course, a man is nothing.

Cosmopolitan December 1955

Gary Kasparov (b. 1963)

AZERBAIJANI CHESS PLAYER

Born Harry Weinstein. At twenty-two he was the youngest person to win a world chess championship (1985). In 1993, he led the breakaway Professional Chess Association in forming a rival championship, which he won.

1 When your house is on fire, you can't be bothered with the neighbours. Or, as we say in chess, if your king is under attack you don't worry about losing a pawn on the queen's side.

Interview in the *Observer* 3 December 1989. Referring to MIKHAIL GORBACHEV's attitude to changes in Eastern Europe.

George S. Kaufman (1889–1961)

US PLAYWRIGHT AND DIRECTOR

He was a theatrical lion of New York in the 1920s and '30s, author of many Broadway hits which he often directed. He collaborated with EDNA FERBER in Dinner at Eight *(1932, filmed 1933) and with Moss Hart in* You Can't Take It With You *(1936, filmed 1938).*

1 Satire is what closes Saturday night.

Quoted in *George S. Kaufman and his Friends*, ch. 6 (1974) by Scott Meredith

Gerald Kaufman (b. 1930)

BRITISH POLITICIAN

Elected Labour MP for Manchester in 1970, he was political press adviser to HAROLD WILSON before becoming Under-Secretary of State in the Department of Industry (1975–9) and later Shadow Foreign Secretary (1987–92).

1 The longest suicide note in history.

Quoted in *The Time of My Life*, ch. 23 (1989) by DENIS HEALEY. Referring to the Labour Party's manifesto for the 1983 general election, 'New Hope For Britain'. 'The scale of our defeat was devastating,' Healey wrote of the results of the subsequent election.

Kenneth Kaunda (b. 1924)

ZAMBIAN POLITICIAN AND PRESIDENT

He led Zambia to independence, becoming its first President (1964–91), and rallied other southern African nations in opposition to the white minority governments of South Africa and Rhodesia. He survived several coups in the 1980s, but lost the 1991 election.

1 When (the Englishman) wants a new market for his adulterated Manchester goods, he sends a missionary to teach the Natives the Gospel of Peace. The Natives kill the missionary, he flies to arms in defence of Christianity, fights for it, conquers for it, and takes the market as a reward from heaven.

Letter to missionaries, March 1952, publ. in *Zambia Shall Be Free*, ch. 16 (1962)

2 The moment you have protected an individual you have protected society.

Quoted in the *Observer* 6 May 1962

3 Some people draw a comforting distinction between 'force' and 'violence'. They define 'violence' as the improper use of 'force', and 'force' as 'violence sanctioned by the law'. I refuse to cloud the issue by such word-play. . . . With some exceptions, the power which establishes a state is violence; the power which maintains it is violence; the power which eventually overthrows it is violence – or if you prefer a nicer word 'force'. . . . Call an elephant a rabbit only if it gives you comfort to feel that you are about to be trampled to death by a rabbit.

Kaunda on Violence, pt 1, 'Living by the Sword' (1980)

4 I fear that the drama can only be brought to its climax in one of two ways – through the selective brutality of terrorism or the impartial horrors of war.

Ibid., pt 2, 'Illusion of Innocence'. Referring to the situation in South Africa.

Patrick Kavanagh (1904–67)

IRISH POET AND AUTHOR

Initially labelled a 'peasant poet' after the publication of his first collection Ploughman and Other Poems *(1936), he achieved wider recognition for the new realism of 'The Great Hunger' (1942), an epic poem of the Irish famine.*

1 *I have what every poet hates in spite*
   Of all the solemn talk of contemplation.

'Inniskeen Road: July Evening', publ. in *Ploughman and Other Poems* (1936)

2 *Clay is the word and clay is the flesh*
   Where the potato-gatherers like mechanized
      scarecrows move
   Along the side-fall of the hill – Maguire and
      his men.

'The Great Hunger' (1942), repr. in *Soul for Sale* (1947)

3 *I had a very pleasant journey, thank you sincerely*
   For giving me my madness back, or nearly.

'Come Dance with Kitty Stobling', publ. in *Come Dance with Kitty Stobling* (1960). Closing lines of poem.

4 A sweeping statement is the only statement worth listening to. The critic without faith gives balanced opinions, usually about second-rate writers.

Collected Pruse, 'Signposts' (1967)

5 Malice is only another name for
mediocrity.
Ibid.

Nikos Kazantzakis (1883–1957)
GREEK AUTHOR
The best known of his many novels are Zorba the
Greek *(1946, filmed 1964) and* The Last Temptation of Christ *(1959, filmed 1988). His 'principal
anguish', he once said, was 'the incessant, merciless
battle between the spirit and the flesh'.*

1 Life is trouble. Death, no. To live – do you
know what that means? To undo your belt
and look for trouble.
Zorba, in *Zorba the Greek*, ch. 8 (1946)

Jonathan Keates (b. 1946)
BRITISH AUTHOR AND CRITIC
*He has written biographies of Stendhal, Handel
and Purcell and also books on Italy, for example*
Italian Journeys *(1991).*

1 In classical antiquity he would have been
blinded and castrated, dressed as a woman
and kept in a temple, his pronouncements
delivered to the people by a special college
of priests.
Of Prince CHARLES, in the *Observer* 7 January
1990

Diane Keaton (b. 1946)
US SCREEN ACTRESS
Originally Diane Hall. She has appeared in The
Godfather *(1972, 1974, 1990) and opposite* WOODY
ALLEN *in* Annie Hall *(1977). The critic John
Simon compared her acting style to a 'nervous
breakdown in slow motion'.*

1 Well, la-de-da!
Annie, in *Annie Hall*, (film, 1977, screenplay by
Woody Allen and Marshall Brickman, directed
by Woody Allen)

Barrie Keeffe (b. 1945)
BRITISH PLAYWRIGHT
*His work for the theatre, film, TV and radio pre-
sents punchy and humorous snapshots of the
British class system and of London's East End
where he grew up. His plays include the trilogy*
Gimme Shelter *(1977) and* Wild Justice *(1992).*

1 I write plays for people who wouldn't be
seen dead in the theatre.
Evening Standard 8 June 1989

Brian Keenan (b. 1950)
IRISH HOSTAGE IN LEBANON AND AUTHOR
*Kidnapped while a lecturer at the American Uni-
versity in Beirut, he spent four and a half years
(1986–90) held captive by a fundamentalist
Shi'ite group, as recounted in* An Evil Cradling
(1992).

1 Hostage is a crucifying aloneness. It is a
silent, screaming slide into the bowels of
ultimate despair. Hostage is a man hanging
by his fingernails over the edge of chaos,
feeling his fingers slowly straightening.
Hostage is the humiliating stripping away
of every sense and fibre of body and mind
and spirit that make us what we are.
Hostage is a mutant creation filled with
fear, self-loathing, guilt and death-wishing.
But he is a man, a rare, unique and beautiful creation of which these things are no
part.
News conference in Dublin, 30 August 1990,
quoted in the *Independent* 31 August 1990.
Following his relase from captivity in
Lebanon.

Garrison Keillor (b. 1942)
US BROADCASTER AND AUTHOR
*His wry and laconic tales of Lake Wobegon, based
on his memories of semi-rural Minnesota, were
first heard on his live, weekly radio show 'A Prairie
Home Companion' (1974–87).*

1 It has been a quiet week in Lake
Wobegon.
Opening to each broadcast of *A Prairie Home
Companion*

2 Lake Wobegon . . . where all the
women are strong, all the men are good-
looking, and all the children are above
average.
Ibid.

3 Nothing you do for children is ever
wasted. They seem not to notice us, hover-
ing, averting our eyes, and they seldom
offer thanks, but what we do for them is
never wasted.
Leaving Home, 'Easter' (1987)

4 A lovely thing about Christmas is that it's
compulsory, like a thunderstorm, and we
all go through it together.
Ibid., 'Exiles'

5 Humor, a good sense of it, is to Americans
what manhood is to Spaniards and we will
go to great lengths to prove it. Experiments with laboratory rats have shown
that, if one psychologist in the room
laughs at something a rat does, all of the
other psychologists in the room will laugh
equally. Nobody wants to be left holding
the joke.
We Are Still Married, Introduction (1989)

6 Even in a time of elephantine vanity and
greed, one never has to look far to see the
campfires of gentle people.
Ibid., 'The Meaning of Life'

7 A good newspaper is never nearly good

enough but a lousy newspaper is a joy forever.

'That Old "Picayune-Moon" ', publ. in *Harper's* September 1990

Penelope Keith (b. 1939)
BRITISH ACTRESS
Most famous for her parts in the TV sitcoms The Good Life *(1976–8) and* To the Manor Born *(1979–81), she has also played numerous parts on stage and in film.*

1 Shyness is just egotism out of its depth.
Daily Mail 27 June 1988

Helen Keller (1880–1968)
US AUTHOR AND LECTURER
Profoundly blind and deaf since infancy, she devoted her life to campaigning and raising funds for the deaf and blind, as related in The Story of My Life *(1902) and other books.*

1 Science may have found a cure for most evils; but it has found no remedy for the worst of them all – the apathy of human beings.
My Religion, pt 1, ch. 6 (1927)

Petra Kelly (1947–92)
GERMAN POLITICIAN
Originally Petra Lehmann. She co-founded Die Grünen (Green Party) in 1979, which entered the Bundestag in 1983 with twenty-eight seats. She died in an apparent joint suicide pact with her lover, an ex-general.

1 We, the generation that faces the next century, can add the . . . solemn injunction 'If we don't do the impossible, we shall be faced with the unthinkable.'
Quoted in *Vanity Fair* January 1993

Thomas Keneally (b. 1935)
AUSTRALIAN NOVELIST
His 'faction' novels chart critical moments in history, as in Confederates *(1979). His Holocaust tale* Schindler's Ark *(1982) was filmed as* Schindler's List *(1993). He is a leading figure in the Australian Republican Movement.*

1 We have found that it *is* possible for Australians to have literary ideas about the place, that Australia is not outside the universe. In short Australia – which used to have one unifying rite, cricket – has now become pluralist. I cannot but predict it will be a disaster for Australian cricket.
Summer Days, 'The Cyclical Supremacy of Australia in World Cricket' (1981)

2 In a way Australia is like Catholicism. The company is sometimes questionable and the landscape is grotesque. But you always come back.
Woman's Day 4 July 1983

Florynce R. Kennedy (1916–2000)
US LAWYER AND CIVIL RIGHTS ACTIVIST
Florynce Rae Kennedy. She was a forthright champion of African-Americans, women, the poor, homosexuals and prostitutes. In 1966 she founded the Media Workshop to combat racism in the media.

1 Niggerization is the result of oppression – and it doesn't just apply to the black people. Old people, poor people, and students can also get niggerized.
Quoted by GLORIA STEINEM, in 'The Verbal Karate of Florynce R. Kennedy, Esq.', publ. in *Ms.* March 1973

2 If men could get pregnant, abortion would be a sacrament.
Ibid.

3 There are very few jobs that actually require a penis or vagina. All other jobs should be open to everybody.
Quoted by John Brady, in 'Freelancer with No Time to Write', publ. in *Writer's Digest* February 1974

G. A. Studdert Kennedy (1883–1929)
BRITISH CLERIC AND POET
(Rev.) Geoffrey Anketell Studdert Kennedy. He was awarded the Military Cross for his service as chaplain in the First World War and later became chaplain to GEORGE V. *Under the pseudonym 'Woodbine Willie', he published* Rough Rhymes of a Padre *(1918).*

1 Waste of Blood, and waste of Tears,
Waste of youth's most precious years,
Waste of ways the saints have trod,
Waste of Glory, waste of God,
War!
'Waste', publ. in *More Rough Rhymes of a Padre* (1918)

Jacqueline Kennedy (1929–94)
US FIRST LADY
Later Jacqueline Kennedy Onassis. Admired for her elegance and style, she married JOHN F. KENNEDY *in 1953 and as First Lady promoted arts, history and conservation issues. After her husband's death she married shipping magnate Aristotle Onassis in 1968.*

1 If you bungle raising your children, I don't think whatever else you do well matters very much.
Quoted in *Kennedy*, pt 4, ch. 15 (1965) by Theodore C. Sorenson

Jimmy Kennedy (1902–84)
BRITISH SONGWRITER
Before teaming up with Michael Carr (see below), he had hits with 'The Teddy Bears' Picnic' (1932) and 'The Isle of Capri' (1934) sung by Gracie Fields. He co-wrote 'Red Sails in the Sunset' (1935)

and had success in America with 'South of the Border' (1940).

1 *If you go down in the woods today*
You're sure of a big surprise
If you go down in the woods today
You'd better go in disguise
For every Bear that ever there was
Will gather there for certain because,
Today's the day the Teddy Bears have their
   Picnic.

'Teddy Bear's Picnic' (song, 1932). The words, set to a 1904 tune by John W. Bratton, were supposed to be about THEODORE ROOSEVELT taking time off from his presidential campaigning to go bear-hunting. The song was recorded by Henry Hall in 1933, quickly becoming a children's classic.

2 *In out in out shake it all about,*
You do the Hokey Cokey
And you turn around,
That's what it's all about.

'Hokey Cokey' (song, 1942). The 'Cockney' lyrics were set to a traditional tune.

Jimmy Kennedy (1902–84) and
Michael Carr (1904–68)
BRITISH SONGWRITERS
Their string of hits began in 1935 and ranged from cowboy songs to show tunes. Carr, born Maurice Cohen, later composed 'Man of Mystery' (1960) and 'Kon-Tiki' (1961) for the Shadows.

1 We're going to hang out our washing on the Siegfried Line.

'We're Going to Hang out Our Washing on the Siegfried Line' (song, 1939). This 'Tipperary' of the Second World War was the last of the numerous hits enjoyed by the Kennedy/Carr partnership. The Siegfried Line was Germany's main belt of militarization on its western frontier in 1939.

John F. Kennedy (1917–63)
US POLITICIAN AND PRESIDENT
John Fitzgerald Kennedy. A Democrat, he was, in 1960, the first Roman Catholic and youngest man to become President. Popular for his wit, charm and youth, he was assassinated in Dallas. Said by one senator to combine the best qualities of ELVIS PRESLEY *and* FRANKLIN D. ROOSEVELT, *he called himself 'an idealist without illusions'.*

1 I just received the following wire from my generous Daddy – 'Dear Jack, Don't buy a single vote more than is necessary. I'll be damned if I'm going to pay for a landslide.'
Speech at Gridiron Dinner, Washington DC, 15 March 1958, quoted in *The Wit of President Kennedy*, 'The Family' (1964) by Bill Adler

2 We stand today on the edge of a new frontier – the frontier of the 1960s – a frontier of unknown opportunities and perils – a frontier of unfulfilled hopes and threats.

. . . The New Frontier of which I speak is not a set of promises – it is a set of challenges.
Acceptance speech at the Democratic Convention, Los Angeles, 15 July 1960, publ. in *The Penguin Book of Twentieth-Century Speeches* (ed. Brian MacArthur, 1999). Theodore C. Sorensen in his biography *Kennedy* (1965) took credit for drafting this speech.

3 Do you realize the responsibility I carry? I'm the only person between Nixon and the White House.
Teasing remark to a liberal supporter during the 1960 election campaign. Quoted in *Kennedy*, pt 2, ch. 7 (1965) by Theodore C. Sorensen. In the event, NIXON won 49.6 per cent of the total vote, giving Kennedy the narrowest victory in a presidential election since 1888.

4 Our growing softness, our increasing lack of physical fitness, is a menace to our security.
'The Soft America' (1960), repr. in *Sport and Society: an Anthology* (ed. John T. Talamini and Charles H. Page, 1973)

5 To those people in the huts and villages across the globe struggling to break the bonds of mass misery, we pledge our best efforts to help them help themselves, for whatever period is required – not because the Communists may be doing it, not because we seek their votes, but because it is right. If a free society cannot help the many who are poor, it cannot save the few who are rich.
Inaugural address, Washington DC 20 January 1961, publ. in *The Penguin Book of Twentieth-Century Speeches* (ed. Brian MacArthur, 1999)

6 We dare not tempt them with weakness. For only when our arms are sufficient beyond doubt can we be certain beyond doubt that they will never be employed.
Ibid.

7 Let us never negotiate out of fear. But let us never fear to negotiate.
Ibid.

8 All this will not be finished in the first 100 days. Nor will it be finished in the first 1,000 days, nor in the life of this Administration, nor even perhaps in our lifetime on this planet. But let us begin.
Ibid. On his reform programme. Kennedy's administration lasted a little over 1,000 days.

9 And so, my fellow Americans, ask not what your country can do for you – ask what you can do for your country. My fellow citizens of the world, ask not what America will do for you, but what together we can do for the freedom of man.
Ibid. Kennedy had previously expressed the same idea in a televised campaign address 20 September 1960. Among the many ante-

cedents which have been cited, Oliver Wendell Holmes Sr stated in his Memorial Day Address (1884): 'It is now the moment . . . to recall what our country has done for each of us, and to ask ourselves what we can do for our country in return.'

10 I do not think it altogether inappropriate to introduce myself to this audience. I am the man who accompanied Jacqueline Kennedy to Paris, and I have enjoyed it.

Speech at SHAPE Headquarters, Paris, 2 June 1961, publ. in *Public Papers of the Presidents of the United States: 1961*. Referring to the massive publicity generated by the Kennedys' visit to Paris – focused particularly on JACKIE KENNEDY.

11 Conformity is the jailer of freedom and the enemy of growth.

Address to UN General Assembly, 25 September 1961, publ. ibid.

12 Washington is a city of Southern efficiency and Northern charm.

Remark in November 1961, quoted in *Portrait of a President* (1962) by William Manchester

13 We must use time as a tool, not as a couch.

Quoted in the *Observer* 10 December 1961

14 We test and then they test and we have to test again. And you build up until somebody uses them.

Remark in 1961, quoted in *A Thousand Days*, ch. 17 (1965) by ARTHUR M. SCHLESINGER JR

15 Those who make peaceful revolution impossible will make violent revolution inevitable.

Speech at the White House, 13 March 1962, publ. in *Public Papers of the Presidents of the United States: 1962*. Addressing diplomats who represented Latin American republics.

16 There is always inequity in life. Some men are killed in a war and some men are wounded, and some men never leave the country. . . . Life is unfair.

Press conference 21 March 1962, quoted in *A Thousand Days*, ch. 4 (1965) by ARTHUR M. SCHLESINGER JR

17 I think this is the most extraordinary collection of talent, of human knowledge, that has ever been gathered together at the White House – with the possible exception of when Thomas Jefferson dined alone.

Remark at a dinner for Nobel prize-winners, 29 April 1962, Washington DC, publ. in *Public Papers of the Presidents of the United States: 1962*

18 Most of us are conditioned for many years to have a political viewpoint – Republican or Democratic, liberal, conservative, or moderate. The fact of the matter is that most of the problems . . . that we now face are technical problems, are administrative problems. They are very sophisticated judgments, which do not lend themselves to

the great sort of passionate movements which have stirred this country so often in the past. [They] deal with questions which are now beyond the comprehension of most men.

Press conference, May 1962, quoted in 'Policy-Planning for the Establishment' by David Eakins, publ. in *A New History of Leviathan* (ed. Ronald Radosh and Murray Rothbard, 1972)

19 If we cannot end now our differences, at least we can help make the world safe for diversity.

Commencement address, American University, Washington D.C., 10 June 1963, publ. in *Public Papers of the Presidents of the United States: 1963*. Referring to Soviet-American relations.

20 No one has been barred on account of his race from fighting or dying for America – there are no 'white' or 'colored' signs on the foxholes or graveyards of battle.

Message to Congress, 19 June 1963, quoted in *The New York Times* 20 June 1963. Referring to the proposed civil rights bill.

21 All free men, wherever they may live, are citizens of Berlin. And therefore, as a free man, I take pride in the words 'Ich bin ein Berliner'.

Speech in West Berlin, 26 June 1963, publ. in *The Penguin Book of Twentieth-Century Speeches* (ed. Brian MacArthur, 1999). Kennedy's words recalled Cicero, *Civis Romanus sum* ('I am a Roman citizen'), from *In Verrem*, speech 5. Kennedy should more correctly have said *Ich bin Berliner; ein Berliner* suggests a local type of doughnut.

22 The United States has to move very fast to even stand still.

Quoted in the *Observer* 21 July 1963

23 I never know when I press these whether I am going to blow up Massachusetts or start the project . . .

Speech at Salt Lake City, September 1963, quoted in *The Wit of President Kennedy*, 'The Presidency' (ed. Bill Adler, 1964). Kennedy was supposed to pull a switch to activate generators in the Colorado River basin, 150 miles distant.

24 When power leads man towards arrogance, poetry reminds him of his limitations. When power narrows the area of man's concern, poetry reminds him of the richness and diversity of existence. When power corrupts, poetry cleanses.

Speech at Amherst College, 26 October 1963, quoted in *The New York Times* 27 October 1963. The occasion of Kennedy's last major public address was the dedication of the Robert Frost Library at the college. Previously, in a speech at Harvard, 14 June 1956, Kennedy said: 'If more politicians knew poetry, and more poets knew politics, I am convinced the world would be a little better place to live.'

25 In free society art is not a weapon. . . .
Artists are not engineers of the soul.

Speech at Amherst College, 26 October 1963,
quoted in *The New York Times* 27 October 1963.
The phrase 'Engineers of human souls' had been
previously used by JOSEF STALIN and Maxim
Gorky in the 1930s.

26 It was involuntary. They sank my boat.

Quoted in *A Thousand Days*, ch. 4 (1965) by
Arthur M. Schlesinger Jr. Answer to small boy
who asked how he became a war hero.

27 I suppose if you had to choose just one
quality to have that would be it: vitality.

Quoted ibid., ch. 25

28 There is a terrific disadvantage in not having the abrasive quality of the press
applied to you daily. . . . Even though we
never like it, and even though we wish they
didn't write it, and even though we disapprove, there isn't any doubt that we
could not do the job at all in a free society
without a very, very active press.

Quoted in *Kennedy*, pt 3, ch. 12 (1965) by Theodore C. Sorensen. With reference to KHRUSH-
CHEV's control of the Soviet press.

29 Domestic policy can only defeat us; foreign
policy can kill us.

Quoted in *The Imperial Presidency*, ch. 11, sect. 7
(1973) by Arthur M. Schlesinger Jr

30 You never know what's hit you. A gunshot
is the perfect way.

Quoted in *The Kennedys*, pt 3, ch. 3 (1984) by
Peter Collier and David Horowitz. Remark when
asked how he would choose to die.

31 Forgive your enemies, but never forget
their names.

Attributed. The quote has also been ascribed to
ROBERT F. KENNEDY.

Joseph P. Kennedy (1888–1969)

US TYCOON AND DIPLOMAT

*Joseph Patrick Kennedy. A self-made millionaire
by the age of thirty, he was Ambassador to Britain
(1937–40) and subsequently concentrated on
grooming his sons JOHN F. KENNEDY, ROBERT F.
KENNEDY and Edward for political careers.*

1 When the going gets tough, the tough get
going.

Quoted in *Honey Fitz* (1962), ch. 20, by J. H.
Cutler. The quotation has also been ascribed to
US football coach Knute Rockne (1888–1931).

Nigel Kennedy (b. 1956)

BRITISH VIOLINIST

*He is credited with helping to create a new audi-
ence for classical music in Britain with his recordings of Vivaldi and Beethoven. His punk-ish
appearance and commercial instincts (he re-
branded himself 'Kennedy' in 1999) led John*

*Drummond, former head of Radio 3 and Proms
director, to call him 'the Liberace of the 1990s'.*

1 When I get those really intense moments it
doesn't feel like it's the violin that's giving
them to me, it's like I'm in touch with
some realm of consciousness which is
much bigger than I am. . . . It's the music
which takes over.

Interview in the *Guardian* 1 March 1997

Robert F. Kennedy (1925–68)

US POLITICIAN AND LAWYER

*Robert Francis Kennedy. He was presidential cam-
paign manager for his brother JOHN F. KENNEDY
and as Attorney-General (1961–4) promoted the
Civil Rights Act of 1964. He was assassinated while
campaigning for presidential nomination. The journalist Murray Kempton called him 'the highest
ranking withdrawn adolescent since Alexander
Hamilton in 1794'.*

1 Every society gets the kind of criminal it
deserves. What is equally true is that every
community gets the kind of law enforcement it insists on.

The Pursuit of Justice, pt 3, 'Eradicating Free
Enterprise in Organized Crime' (1964)

2 What is objectionable, what is dangerous,
about extremists is not that they are
extreme, but that they are intolerant. The
evil is not what they say about thair cause,
but what they say about their opponents.

Ibid., pt 3, 'Extremism, Left and Right'

3 The free way of life proposes ends, but it
does not prescribe means.

Ibid., pt 5, 'Berlin East and West'

4 One-fifth of the people are against everything all the time.

Speech at University of Pennsylvania, 6 May
1964, quoted in the *Philadelphia Inquirer* 7 May
1964

Elizabeth Kenny (1886–1952)

AUSTRALIAN NURSE

*She pioneered the use of muscle therapy to treat
poliomyelitis, establishing clinics in Britain,
America and Australia.*

1 The record of one's life must needs prove
more interesting to him who writes it than
to him who reads what has been written.

And They Shall Walk, Foreword (1943, written
with Martha Ostenso)

Corita Kent (1918–86)

US ARTIST

*A member of the Sisters of the Immaculate Heart
of Mary, she was branded a 'guerrilla with a paint
brush' and pressured into leaving the sisterhood.*

1 Women's liberation is the liberation of the

feminine in the man and the masculine in the woman.

Quoted in the *Los Angeles Times* 11 July 1974

Alvin Kernan (b. 1923)
US ACADEMIC
He has written widely on English literature, particularly on Shakespeare and Ben Jonson. His publications include The Plot of Satire *(1965) and* The Death of Literature *(1990).*

1 In the electronic age, books, words and reading are not likely to remain sufficiently authoritative and central to knowledge to justify literature.
International Herald Tribune 12 December 1990

Jack Kerouac (1922–69)
US AUTHOR
Originally Jean Louis Kerouac. He published his first novel The Town and the City *in 1950, but it was* On the Road *(1957) that established him as the voice of the Beat generation. Later books failed to achieve the same impact. 'My work comprises one vast book like Proust's* Remembrance of Things Past,' *he once said, 'except that my remembrances are written on the run instead of afterwards in a sickbed.'*

1 I must change my life, now, I have reached 21 and I am indeed earnest about all things. This does not mean I will cease my debauching.
Undated letter, 1943, publ. in *Selected Letters 1940–1956* (ed. Ann Charters, 1995)

2 All of life is a foreign country.
Letter, 24 June 1949, publ. in *The Beat Vision: A Primary Sourcebook* (ed. Arthur and Kit Knight, 1987)

3 The requirements for prose and verse are the same, i.e. *blow* What a man most wishes to hide, revise, and unsay, is precisely what Literature is waiting and bleeding for. Every doctor knows, every Prophet knows the convulsion of truth.
Letter to Malcolm Cowley, 11 September 1955, publ. in *Selected Letters 1940–1956* (ed. Ann Charters, 1995). The critic Malcolm Cowley was then an editorial adviser for Viking Press, which he later persuaded to publish *On the Road*.

4 But then they danced down the street like dingledodies, and I shambled after as I've been doing all my life after people who interest me, because the only people for me are the mad ones, the ones who are mad to live, mad to talk, mad to be saved, desirous of everything at the same time, the ones who never yawn or say a commonplace thing, but burn, burn, burn, like fabulous yellow roman candles exploding like spiders across the stars and in the middle

you see the blue centerlight pop and everybody goes 'Awww!'
Narrator (Sal Paradise), in *On the Road*, pt 1, ch. 1 (1957)

5 We wandered around, carrying our bundles of rags in the narrow romantic streets. Everybody looked like a broken-down movie extra, a withered starlet; disenchanted stunt-men, midget auto-racers, poignant California characters with their end-of-the-continent sadness, handsome, decadent, Casanova-ish men, puffy-eyed motel blondes, hustlers, pimps, whores, masseurs, bellhops – a lemon lot, and how's a man going to make a living with a gang like that?
Ibid., pt 2, ch. 9. On arriving in San Francisco.

6 Standing in front of everybody, ragged and broken and idiotic, right under the lightbulbs, his bony mad face covered with sweat and throbbing veins, saying, 'Yes, yes, yes,' as though tremendous revelations were pouring into him all the time now, and I am convinced they were, and the others suspected as much and were frightened. He was BEAT – the root, the soul of Beatific.
Ibid., pt 3, ch. 3. Of Dean Moriarty. The character of Moriarty was modelled on that of NEAL CASSADY.

7 Do you know there's a road that goes down to Mexico and all the way to Panama? – and maybe all the way to the bottom of South America where the Indians are seven feet tall and eat cocaine on the mountainside? Yes! You and I, Sal, we'd dig the whole world with a car like this because, man, the road must eventually lead to the whole world. Ain't nowhere else it can go – right?
Dean Moriarty, ibid , pt 3, ch 9

8 John Clellon Holmes . . . and I were sitting around trying to think up the meaning of the Lost Generation and the subsequent Existentialism and I said, 'You know, this is really a beat generation' and he leapt up and said 'That's it, that's right!'
Interview in *Playboy* June 1959, explaining the origin of the label 'Beat Generation'. On another occasion, Kerouac ascribed the expression's origin to Herbert Huncke, a Times Square hustler he'd met a decade earlier. The words also appeared as the title of an article by Holmes and in his novel, *Go* (1952), originally entitled *The Beat Generation* and published in Britain as *The Beat Boys* (1959); see JOHN CLELLON HOLMES 1.

9 It is not my fault that certain so-called bohemian elements have found in my writings something to hang their peculiar beatnik theories on.
New York Journal-American 8 December 1960

Jean Kerr (b. 1923)

US AUTHOR AND PLAYWRIGHT

In her own words, she wrote 'realistic comedy' set in an affluent suburbia, for example the play Mary, Mary *(1961). She was married to* WALTER KERR, *with whom she sometimes collaborated.*

1 As someone pointed out recently, if you can keep your head when all about you are losing theirs, it's just possible you haven't grasped the situation.

Please Don't Eat the Daisies, Introduction (1957)

2 I'm tired of all this nonsense about beauty being only skin-deep. That's deep enough. What do you want – an adorable pancreas?

The Snake Has All the Lines, 'Mirror, Mirror on the Wall' (1958)

3 Even though a number of people have tried, no one has yet found a way to drink for a living.

Sydney, in *Poor Richard*, act 1 (1963)

4 Hope is the feeling you have that the feeling you have isn't permanent.

Felicia, in *Finishing Touches*, act 3 (1973)

Walter Kerr (1913–96)

US CRITIC

Drama critic with the New York Herald Tribune *(1951–66) and* The New York Times *(1966–83), he was praised by* KENNETH TYNAN *for 'vaulting over the barrier we erect between "serious" and "light" criticism'.*

1 Me no Leica.

Attributed review of *I Am A Camera* (1951), John Van Druten's dramatization of 'Sally Bowles' from *Goodbye to Berlin* by CHRISTOPHER ISHERWOOD, quoted in *No Turn Unstoned*, ch. 5 (1982) by Diana Rigg

Gerald Kersh (1911–68)

BRITISH AUTHOR AND JOURNALIST

A best-selling writer of crime fiction, he gained fame with his third book, Harry Fabian: Night and the City *(1938) and was also known for his short stories featuring Karmesin.*

1 Now, you mummy's darlings, get a rift on them boots. Definitely shine 'em, my little curly-headed lambs, for in our mob, war or no war, you die with clean boots on.

They Die With Their Boots Clean, Prologue (1941)

2 I can't believe in the God of my Fathers. If there is one Mind which understands all things, it will comprehend me in my unbelief. I don't know whose hand hung Hesperus in the sky, and fixed the Dog Star, and scattered the shining dust of Heaven, and fired the sun, and froze the darkness between the lonely worlds that spin in space.

Old Silence, ibid., pt 3, 'The Tempering'

Ken Kesey (1935–2001)

US AUTHOR

His experience as an aide in a mental hospital formed the basis for his bestselling satirical novel One Flew Over the Cuckoo's Nest *(1962, filmed 1975). He later became leader of the 'Merry Pranksters', an itinerant hippie group whose exploits were recorded in* The Electric Kool-Aid Acid Test *(1968) by* TOM WOLFE.

1 I've watched her get more and more skilful over the years. Practice has steadied and strengthened her until now she wields a sure power that extends in all directions on hairlike wires too small for anybody's eye but mine; I see her sit in the center of this web of wires like a watchful robot, tend her network with mechanical insect skill, know every second which wires run where and just what current to send up to get the results she wants.

Narrator (Chief Bromden), referring to 'the Big Nurse', Miss Ratched, in *One Flew Over the Cuckoo's Nest*, pt 1 (1962). The book's title derives from a children's folk rhyme, 'One flew east, one flew west,/One flew over the cuckoo's nest.'

2 I'd rather be a lightning rod than a seismograph.

Quoted in *The Electric Kool-Aid Acid Test*, ch. 1 (1968) by TOM WOLFE

3 You're either on the bus or off the bus. If you're on the bus, and you get left behind, then you'll find it again. If you're off the bus in the first place – then it won't make a damn.

Quoted ibid., ch. 6

Ellen Key (1849–1926)

SWEDISH AUTHOR AND FEMINIST

She wrote on a range of women's issues, most famously in The Century of the Child *(1900).*

1 Art, that great undogmatized church.

The Renaissance of Motherhood, pt 2, ch. 1 (1914)

John Maynard Keynes (1883–1946)

BRITISH ECONOMIST

Baron Keynes of Tilton. Regarding himself as 'a voice crying in the wilderness' who 'had, therefore, to cry loudly', he was a pioneer of macroeconomics, arguing in favour of increased government spending as a cure for rising unemployment. His major works are A Treatise on Money *(1930) and* The General Theory of Employment, Interest and Money *(1936).*

1 The disruptive powers of excessive national fecundity may have played a

greater part in bursting the bonds of convention than either the power of ideas or the errors of autocracy.

The Economic Consequences of Peace (1919), repr. in *Collected Writings*, vol. 2 (1971)

2 Lenin was right. There is no subtler, no surer means of overturning the existing basis of society than to debauch the currency. The process engages all the forces of economic law on the side of destruction, and does it in a manner which not one man in a million is able to diagnose.

Ibid., ch. 6. Keynes repeated this assertion in *Essays in Persuasion*, ch. 2 (1931): 'The best way to destroy the capitalist system is to debauch the currency. By a continuing process of inflation governments can confiscate, secretly and unobserved, an important part of the wealth of their citizens.' The words attributed to Lenin have never been found in his writings.

3 *Long run* is a misleading guide to current affairs. *In the long run* we are all dead.

A Tract on Monetary Reform, ch. 3 (1923)

4 The Labour Party . . . is a class party, and the class is not my class. . . . The *class* war will find me on the side of the educated *bourgeoisie*.

Am I a Liberal? (1925), repr. in *Collected Writings*, vol. 9 (1972)

5 A study of the history of opinion is a necessary preliminary to the emancipation of the mind. I do not know which makes a man more conservative – to know nothing but the present, or nothing but the past.

The End of Laissez-Faire, ch. 1 (1926)

6 Marxian Socialism must always remain a portent to the historians of Opinion – how a doctrine so illogical and so dull can have exercised so powerful and enduring an influence over the minds of men, and, through them, the events of history.

Ibid., ch. 3

7 I think that Capitalism, wisely managed, can probably be made more efficient for attaining economic ends than any alternative system yet in sight, but that in itself it is in many ways extremely objectionable.

Ibid., ch. 5

8 Most men love money and security more, and creation and construction less, as they get older.

Essays in Persuasion, ch. 5, 'The Future' (1931)

9 For at least another hundred years we must pretend to ourselves and to every one that fair is foul and foul is fair; for foul is useful and fair is not. Avarice and usury and precaution must be our gods for a little longer still.

Ibid. Keynes argued that the 'detestable . . . love of money' and other vices of greed must con-

tinue until the economy has grown enough to satisfy human wants and provide the potential for removing poverty.

10 If economists could manage to get themselves thought of as humble, competent people on a level with dentists, that would be splendid.

Ibid.

11 Nothing mattered except states of mind, chiefly our own.

Essays in Biography, ch. 39 (1933). Referring to the 'Apostles' group at Cambridge University.

12 The decadent international but individualistic capitalism in the hands of which we found ourselves after the war is not a success. It is not intelligent. It is not beautiful. It is not just. It is not virtuous. And it doesn't deliver the goods.

National Self-Sufficiency, sect. 3 (1933), repr. in *Collected Writings*, vol. 11 (1982)

13 Words ought to be a little wild for they are the assault of thoughts on the unthinking.

New Statesman and Nation 15 July 1933

14 The difficulty lies, not in the new ideas, but in escaping from the old ones, which ramify, for those brought up as most of us have been, into every corner of our minds.

The General Theory of Employment, Interest and Money, Preface (1936)

15 The social object of skilled investment should be to defeat the dark forces of time and ignorance which envelope our future.

Ibid., bk 4, ch. 12, sect. 5

16 It is better that a man should tyrannize over his bank balance than over his fellow-citizens and whilst the former is sometimes denounced as being but a means to the latter, sometimes at least it is an alternative.

Ibid., ch. 24, 'Concluding Notes'

17 The ideas of economists and political philosophers, both when they are right and when they are wrong, are more powerful than is commonly understood. Indeed the world is ruled by little else. Practical men, who believe themselves to be quite exempt from any intellectual influence, are usually the slaves of some defunct economist.

Ibid.

18 It is ideas, not vested interests, which are dangerous for good or evil.

Ibid., ch. 24

19 The day is not far off when the economic problem will take the back seat where it belongs, and the arena of the heart and the head will be occupied or reoccupied, by our real problems – the problems of life and of human relations, of creation and behaviour and religion.

First Annual Report of the Arts Council (1945–6)

Imran Khan (b. 1952)

PAKISTANI CRICKETER

He played eighty-eight test matches for Pakistan, forty-eight as captain, and led his country to victory in the 1992 World Cup. In the same year he retired and took up politics, leading the Movement for Justice Party.

1 There is no essential discrepancy between the game's time-honoured virtues and the world we live in. It is a matter of creatively adapting the form in order to preserve the content. So far much valuable time has been wasted on quibbling over what 'isn't cricket', and not much has been devoted to what cricket should become.

Of cricket, in *All Round View*, ch. 13 (1988)

Ayatollah Ruhollah Khomeini

(1900–1989)

IRANIAN RELIGIOUS AND POLITICAL LEADER

Originally Ruhollah Musawi. After the Iranian Revolution of 1979, he established a fundamentalist Islamic republic and was named Iran's political and religious leader for life.

1 I would like to inform all the intrepid Muslims in the world that the author of the book entitled *The Satanic Verses*, which has been compiled, printed and published in opposition to Islam, the prophet and the Qur'an, as well as those publishers who were aware of its contents, have been declared *madhur el dam* ['those whose blood must be shed']. I call on all zealous Muslims to execute them quickly, wherever they find them, so that no one will dare to insult Islam again. Whoever is killed in this path will be regarded as a martyr.

Fatwa, or legal ruling, issued 14 February 1989, quoted in *A Satanic Affair*, ch. 5 (1990) by Malise Ruthven

Nikita Khrushchev (1894–1971)

SOVIET POLITICIAN AND PREMIER

During his terms as First Secretary of the Communist Party (1953–64) and Premier (1958–64), he broke with Stalinist policies and laid the basis for liberalizing Soviet Communism and for the independence of European communist parties.

1 If anyone believes that our smiles involve abandonment of the teaching of Marx, Engels and Lenin he deceives himself. Those who wait for that must wait until a shrimp learns to whistle.

Speech in Moscow, 17 September 1955, quoted in *The New York Times* 18 September 1955

2 Comrades! We must abolish the cult of the individual decisively, once and for all.

Speech to the secret session of the Twentieth Congress of the Soviet Communist Party, 25 February 1956, quoted in the *Manchester Guardian* 11 June 1956. Khrushchev used the occasion to identify STALIN as the chief exponent of the cult of the individual (also translated 'cult of the personality') by 'the glorification of his own person'.

3 Everyone can err, but Stalin considered that he never erred, that he was always right. He never acknowledged to anyone that he made any mistake, large or small, despite the fact that he made not a few mistakes in the matter of theory and in his practical activity.

Speech to the Twentieth Congress of the Soviet Communist Party, February 1956, quoted in *Stalin*, pt 2, ch. 6 (ed. T. H. Rigby, 1966)

4 It doesn't depend on you whether or not we exist. If you don't like us, don't accept our invitations and don't invite us to come to see you. Whether you like it or not, history is on our side. We will bury you.

Speech to Western diplomats at the Kremlin, 18 November 1956, quoted in *The Times* 19 November 1956. Khrushchev later explained this remark as an idiomatic expression to mean 'we will outlive you' (i.e. communism will triumph). On another occasion, 24 August 1963, addressing a group of Westerners in Split in the former Yugoslavia, he referred to his controversial statement: 'Of course we will not bury you with a shovel. Your own working class will bury you.'

5 If one cannot catch a bird of paradise, better take a wet hen.

Quoted in *Time* 6 January 1958

6 When you are skinning your customers you should leave some skin on to grow again so that you can skin them again.

Quoted in the *Observer* 28 May 1961. Advice to British businessmen.

7 They talk about who won and who lost. Human reason won. Mankind won.

Quoted in the *Observer* 11 November 1962. Referring to the Cuban missile crisis.

8 Politicians are the same all over: they promise to build a bridge even where there is no river.

Quoted in the *New York Herald-Tribune* 22 August 1963. Khrushchev used the same figure of speech at a press conference, Glen Cove, New York, October 1960.

9 He who cannot eat horsemeat need not do so. Let him eat pork. But he who cannot eat pork, let him eat horsemeat. It's simply a question of taste.

New York World-Telegram and Sun 25 August 1964

10 If you live among wolves you have to act like a wolf.

Quoted in the *Observer* 20 September 1964

11 If we were to promise people nothing
better than only revolution, they would
scratch their heads and say: 'Is it not better
to have good goulash?'

Quoted in the *Observer* 27 December 1964

Jean Kierans (b. 1930)
FORMER GIRLFRIEND OF JOHN MAJOR
*Her affair with MAJOR lasted 1963–70, and
became public in 1995.*

1 It makes me laugh now when I hear him
called a grey man. That's just a cover. It's a
mask.

Quoted in the *Independent on Sunday*
19 February 1995

Krzysztof Kieślowski (1941–96)
POLISH FILM-MAKER
*He established himself as an innovative director
with a series of films on the ten commandments,
including* A Short Film about Killing *(1988).*
Three Colours: Blue, White, Red *(1993–4) furthered his reputation. He summed up his work, 'I
simply wanted to show that life was complicated'.*

1 I'm frightened of all those people who
show you the way, who know. Because
really . . . nobody really knows, with a few
exceptions. Unfortunately, the actions of
these people usually end in tragedy – like
the Second World War or Stalinism or
something. I'm convinced that Stalin and
Hitler knew exactly what they were to do.
They knew very well. But that's how it is.
That's fanaticism. That's knowing. That's
the feeling of absolutely knowing. And the
next minute, it's army boots. It always
ends up like that.

Kieślowski on Kieślowski, ch. 1 (1993)

2 I think they're just as unhappy as we are,
except that we still talk about it sometimes
. . . they only say that everything's fine,
that it's fantastic. . . . If I had to be confronted for a whole year with people saying
that everything's fantastic then I simply
couldn't stand it.

On Americans, ibid., ch. 4

3 Our mouths are full of such words as freedom, but what does it really mean? Does it
not perhaps mean being totally alone, living in a total vacuum?

Quoted in appreciation in the *Guardian*
14 March 1996

Dorothy Kilgallen (1913–65)
US COLUMNIST AND TELEVISION
PERSONALITY
*She wrote for newspapers and magazines, and
appeared on* What's My Line? *on television and*
Breakfast with Dorothy and Dick *on radio.*

1 Doorman – a genius who can open the
door of your car with one hand, help you
in with the other, and still have one left for
the tip.

Quoted in *Violets and Vinegar,* 'Come Away,
Poverty's Catching' (ed. Jilly Cooper and Tom
Hartman, 1980)

B. B. King (b. 1925)
US BLUES MUSICIAN
*Originally Riley King, known as B.B. (Blues Boy).
Distinguished by a powerful voice and the sparse
riffs played on his guitar 'Lucille', he has been a
major figure in blues for more than forty years.*

1 The blues was like that problem child that
you may have had in the family. You was a
little bit ashamed to let anybody see him,
but you loved him. You just didn't know
how other people would take it.

Interview in the *Sunday Times* 4 November 1984

Don King (b. 1931)
US BOXING PROMOTER
*From a criminal background he became boxing's
most successful promoter, numbering among his clients MUHAMMAD ALI, Sugar Ray Leonard and
MIKE TYSON. According to LARRY HOLMES: 'He
doesn't care about black or white. He just cares
about green.'*

1 I'm one of the world's great survivors. I'll
always survive because I've got the right
combination of wit, grit and bullshit.

Quoted in the *Sunday Times* 18 December 1994

2 I dare to be great. The man without imagination stands unhurt and hath no wings.
This is my credo, this is my forte.

Interview in the *Independent on Sunday*
10 March 1996

Florence King (b. 1936)
US AUTHOR
*Calling herself a woman who 'rips the teats off
sacred cows', she has written* Southern Ladies and
Gentlemen *(1975) and* When Sisterhood Was in
Flower *(1978), as well as essays and erotic novels.*

1 He travels fastest who travels alone, and
that goes double for she. Real feminism is
spinsterhood.

Reflections in a Jaundiced Eye, 'Spinsterhood is
Powerful' (1989). Referring to KIPLING, 'He
travels the fastest who travels alone' (from 'The
Winners' in *The Story of the Gadsbys,* 1890).

2 For men who want to flee Family Man
America and never come back, there is a
guaranteed solution: homosexuality is the
new French Foreign Legion.

Ibid., 'From Captain Marvel to Captain Valium'

3 We want a president who is as much like
an American tourist as possible. Someone
with the same goofy grin, the same innocent intentions, the same naive trust; a

president with no conception of foreign policy and no discernible connection to the US government, whose Nice Guyism will narrow the gap between the US and us until nobody can tell the difference.

Ibid., 'Nice Guyism'

4 The witty woman is a tragic figure in American life. Wit destroys eroticism and eroticism destroys wit, so women must choose between taking lovers and taking no prisoners.

Ibid., 'The State of the Funny Bone'

Martin Luther King Jr (1929–68)

US CLERGYMAN AND CIVIL RIGHTS LEADER

An inspiring orator, he was a leader of the civil rights movement of the 1950s and '60s, and instrumental in the bus boycott in Montgomery, Alabama (1955), and the march of 200,000 demonstrators on Washington DC (1963). His non-violent policy of passive resistance was conditioned by his Baptist upbringing. He was assassinated in Memphis.

1 It is my hope that as the Negro plunges deeper into the quest for freedom and justice he will plunge even deeper into the philosophy of non-violence. The Negro all over the South must come to the point that he can say to his white brother: 'We will match your capacity to inflict suffering with our capacity to endure suffering. We will meet your physical force with soul force. We will not hate you, but we will not obey your evil laws. We will soon wear you down by pure capacity to suffer.'

Letter, 28 October 1957

2 I want to be the white man's brother, not his brother-in-law.

New York Journal-American 10 September 1962

3 It may be true that the law cannot make a man love me, but it can keep him from lynching me, and I think that's pretty important.

Quoted in the *Wall Street Journal* 13 November 1962

4 Nothing in all the world is more dangerous than sincere ignorance and conscientious stupidity.

Strength to Love, ch. 4, sect. 3 (1963)

5 The means by which we live have out-distanced the ends for which we live. Our scientific power has outrun our spiritual power. We have guided missiles and mis-guided men.

Ibid., ch. 7

6 We have genuflected before the god of science only to find that it has given us the atomic bomb, producing fears and anxieties that science can never mitigate.

Ibid., ch. 13

7 Freedom is never voluntarily given by the oppressor; it must be demanded by the oppressed.

'Letter from Birmingham Jail', open letter to clergymen, 16 April 1963, first publ. in *Atlantic Monthly* August 1963, repr. in *Why We Can't Wait* (1963)

8 I submit that an individual who breaks a law that conscience tells him is unjust, and who willingly accepts the penalty of imprisonment in order to arouse the conscience of the community over its injustice, is in reality expressing the highest respect for law.

Ibid.

9 I have almost reached the regrettable conclusion that the Negro's great stumbling block in his stride toward freedom is not the White Citizen's Counciler or the Ku Klux Klanner, but the white moderate.

Ibid.

10 Shallow understanding from people of good will is more frustrating than absolute misunderstanding from people of ill will.

Ibid.

11 Law and order exist for the purpose of establishing justice, and . . . when they fail in this purpose they become the danger-ously structured dams that block the flow of social progress.

Ibid.

12 We who engage in nonviolent direct action are not the creators of tension. We merely bring to the surface the hidden tension that is already alive.

Ibid.

13 We will have to repent in this generation not merely for the hateful words and actions of the bad people but for the appal-ling silence of the good people.

Ibid.

14 The question is not whether we will be extremist but what kind of extremist will we be.

Ibid.

15 There can be no deep disappointment where there is not deep love.

Ibid. Speaking of the church which 'we have blemished and scarred . . . through social neglect and through fear of being nonconformists'.

16 Abused and scorned though we may be, our destiny is tied up with America's destiny. Before the pilgrims landed at Ply-mouth, we were here. Before the pen of Jefferson etched the majestic words of the Declaration of Independence across the pages of history, we were here. For more than two centuries our forebears labored in this country without wages; they made

cotton king; they built the homes of their masters while suffering gross injustice and shameful humiliation – and yet out of a bottomless vitality they continued to thrive and develop. If the inexpressible cruelties of slavery could not stop us, the opposition we now face will surely fail.

Ibid. The first sentence of this extract recalls a speech by abolitionist Frederick Douglass, in Boston, 12 February 1862: 'The destiny of the colored American . . . is the destiny of America.'

17 If a man hasn't discovered something that he will die for, he isn't fit to live.

Speech in Detroit, 23 June 1963, quoted in *The Days of Martin Luther King*, ch. 4 (1971) by James Bishop

18 No, no, we are not satisfied, and we will not be satisfied until justice rolls down like waters and righteousness like a mighty stream.

'I Have a Dream', speech at civil rights march, Washington DC, 28 August 1963, publ. in *A Testament of Hope: Essential Writings* (ed. James Melvin Washington, 1986). King was quoting the Old Testament, Amos 5:24.

19 I have a dream that one day on the red hills of Georgia the sons of former slaves and the sons of former slave owners will be able to sit down together at the table of brotherhood. I have a dream that one day even the state of Mississippi, a desert state sweltering with the heat of injustice and oppression, will be transformed into an oasis of freedom and justice. I have a dream that my four little children will one day live in a nation where they will not be judged by the color of their skin but by the content of their character. I have a dream today.

Ibid.

20 A riot is at bottom the language of the unheard.

Where Do We Go from Here? ch. 4 (1967)

21 It doesn't matter with me now. Because I've been to the mountaintop. And I don't mind. Like anybody, I would like to live a long life. Longevity has its place. But I'm not concerned about that now. I just want to do God's will. And He's allowed me to go up to the mountain. And I've looked over, and I've seen the Promised Land. . . . Mine eyes have seen the glory of the coming of the Lord.

'I See the Promised Land', speech in Memphis, 3 April 1968, publ. in *A Testament of Hope: Essential Writings* (ed. James Melvin Washington, 1986). The last words are from Julia Ward Howe's 'Battle Hymn of the Republic'. The speech was made on the day preceding King's assassination.

22 Free at last, Free at last
Thank God Almighty
I'm free at last

Epitaph on King's tomb, in South View Cemetery, Atlanta, Georgia. The words are from the spiritual with which he often closed his speeches.

Stephen King (b. 1947)
US AUTHOR
His prolific output of horror fiction, for example Carrie *(1974, filmed 1976) and* The Shining *(1977, filmed 1980), has made his name synonymous with the genre.*

1 Talent is cheaper than table salt. What separates the talented individual from the successful one is a lot of hard work.

Quoted in the *Independent on Sunday* 10 March 1996

Miles Kington (b. 1941)
BRITISH HUMORIST AND MUSICIAN
A frequent broadcaster and contributor to periodicals, he was literary editor of Punch *1967–80. His books include* Let's Parler Franglais *(1982).*

1 Most English conversation is not conversation at all, but the exchange of little ritual expressions which only work if you know the exact context.

Independent 6 December 1989

Neil Kinnock (b. 1942)
BRITISH POLITICIAN
Labelled a Welsh firebrand, he was leader of the Labour Party 1983–92, and became a European Commissioner in 1994. See SUN 6.

1 If Margaret Thatcher wins – I warn you not to be ordinary. I warn you not to be young. I warn you not to fall ill. I warn you not to get old.

Speech at Bridgend, 7 June 1983, publ. in *The Penguin Book of Twentieth-Century Speeches* (ed. Brian MacArthur, 1999). The eve-of-election speech made a strong impact, contributing to Kinnock's election as Labour leader four months later.

2 I would die for my country, but I could never let my country die for me.

Speech to Labour Party Conference, 30 September 1986, quoted in the *Guardian* 1 October 1986. On the issue of nuclear disarmament.

3 The enemy of idealism is zealotry.

Quoted in the *Observer* 27 December 1987

Michael Kinsley (b. 1951)
US JOURNALIST
He has been Editor of Harper's *and* New Republic, *where he wrote the 'TRB from Washington' column, and Managing Editor of the* Washington Monthly.

1 He's nice enough not to want to be associated with a nasty remark but not nice enough not to make it. Lacking the courage of one's nastiness does not make one nice.

On GEORGE BUSH, in *Time* magazine 16 July 1990

2 A gaffe is when a politician tells the truth.

Guardian 14 January 1992

Rudyard Kipling (1865–1936)

BRITISH AUTHOR AND POET

He worked as a journalist in India (1882–9), where he set his Plain Tales from the Hills *(1888) and* The Jungle Book *(1894). His popular poetry reflected the concerns of the common man.* T. S. ELIOT *called him 'a laureate without laurels'.*

1 **Power without responsibility – the prerogative of the harlot throughout the ages.**

Quoted in *The Kipling Journal* December 1971, repr. in *Kipling: Interviews and Recollections* (ed. Harold Orel, 1983). The remark was quoted at a dinner by Arthur Windham Baldwin, son of STANLEY BALDWIN, having been made originally *c.* 1917 in reply to Max Aitken (Lord Beaverbrook), who had said to Kipling, regarding his recent acquisition of the *Daily Express*: 'What I want is power. Kiss 'em one day and kick 'em the next.' The words were borrowed (with Kipling's permission) by his cousin Stanley Baldwin in a speech, 17 March 1931, attacking press barons Lord Beaverbrook and Lord Rothermere, whose newspapers he described as 'engines of propaganda'.

2 *If any question why we died,*
Tell them, because our fathers lied.

'Common Form', publ. in *The Years Between* (1919)

3 **Words are, of course, the most powerful drug used by mankind.**

Speech 14 February 1923, quoted in *The Times* 15 February 1923

4 *For the female of the species is more deadly than the male.*

'The Female of the Species', publ. in *Rudyard Kipling's Verse* (1927)

5 **A people always ends by resembling its shadow.**

Quoted in *The Art of Writing*, 'The Writer's Craft', sect. 2 (1960) by André Maurois. Said to the author and critic ANDRÉ MAUROIS *c.* 1930, on the subject of the transformation of Germany.

Jeane Kirkpatrick (b. 1926)

US PUBLIC OFFICIAL AND DIPLOMAT

She joined the REAGAN *cabinet as Ambassador to the United Nations (1981–5), where she became known for her forthright promotion of US interests.*

1 **Vietnam presumably taught us that the**

United States could not serve as the world's policeman; it should also have taught us the dangers of trying to be the world's midwife to democracy when the birth is scheduled to take place under conditions of guerrilla war.

'Dictatorship and Double Standards' publ. in *Commentary* November 1979

Henry Kissinger (b. 1923)

GERMAN-BORN US POLITICIAN AND DIPLOMAT

Considered the second most powerful member of the NIXON *administration, he served as National Security Adviser (1968–73) and as Secretary of State (1973–7). His 'shuttle diplomacy' was crucial in Arab–Israeli peace negotiations and he was jointly awarded the Nobel Peace Prize (1973) for his work in resolving the Vietnam War. 'Satire died the day they gave Henry Kissinger the Nobel Peace Prize,'* TOM LEHRER *declared. 'There were no jokes left after that.'*

1 **The conventional army loses if it does not win. The guerrilla wins if he does not lose.**

Foreign Affairs January 1969. Writing of the Vietnam War.

2 **There can't be a crisis next week. My schedule is already full.**

The New York Times Magazine 1 June 1969

3 **Intelligence is not all that important in the exercise of power, and often actually doesn't help. . . . A fellow who does my job doesn't need to be too intelligent.**

Interview in *Interview with History* (1970) by ORIANA FALLACI

4 **I've always acted alone. Americans like that enormously. Americans like the cowboy who leads the wagon train by riding ahead alone on his horse, the cowboy who rides all alone into the town, the village, with his horse and nothing else. Maybe even without a pistol, since he doesn't shoot. He acts, that's all, by being in the right place at the right time.**

Ibid.

5 **We are all the President's men.**

Said in 1970, after the invasion of Cambodia, quoted in the *Sunday Times* 4 May 1975. Kissinger's statement inspired the title of the book by *Washington Post* reporters CARL BERNSTEIN and Bob Woodward, *All the President's Men* (1974, filmed 1976), describing their investigation into the Watergate break-in.

6 **Power is the great aphrodisiac.**

Quoted in *The New York Times* 19 January 1971

7 **Even a paranoid can have enemies.**

Quoted in *Time* magazine 24 January 1977. The words have also been ascribed to the poet Delmore Schwartz, among others.

8 **Some of the critics viewed Vietnam as a morality play in which the wicked must be**

punished before the final curtain and where any attempt to salvage self-respect from the outcome compounded the wrong. I viewed it as a genuine tragedy. No one had a monopoly on anguish.

The White House Years, ch. 8 (1979)

9 We cannot always assure the future of our friends; we have a better chance of assuring our future if we remember who our friends are.

Ibid., ch. 29. Referring to the changing US policy towards the Shah of Iran.

10 The superpowers often behave like two heavily-armed blind men feeling their way around a room, each believing himself in mortal peril from the other, whom he assumes to have perfect vision.

Quoted in the *Observer* 30 September 1979

11 Most foreign policies that history has marked highly, in whatever country, have been originated by leaders who were opposed by experts. . . . It is, after all, the responsibility of the expert to operate the familiar and that of the leader to transcend it.

Years of Upheaval, ch. 10, 'The Foreign Service' (1982)

12 To have striven so hard, to have molded a public personality out of so amorphous an identity, to have sustained that superhuman effort only to end with every weakness disclosed and every error compounding the downfall – that was a fate of biblical proportions. Evidently the Deity would not tolerate the presumption that all can be manipulated; an object lesson of the limits of human presumption was necessary.

Ibid., ch. 25, 'The End of the Road'. On the downfall of RICHARD NIXON.

13 Blessed are the people whose leaders can look destiny in the eye without flinching but also without attempting to play God.

Ibid.

14 Moderation is a virtue only in those who are thought to have an alternative.

Quoted in the *Observer* 24 January 1982

15 I am being frank about myself in this book. I tell of my first mistake on page 850.

Quoted in the *Observer* 2 January 1983. Referring to the second volume of his memoirs, *Years of Upheaval*.

16 The American foreign policy trauma of the sixties and seventies was caused by applying valid principles to unsuitable conditions.

Guardian 16 December 1992. Arguing against a role for the USA as 'world policeman'.

17 Mr Clinton does not have the strength of character to be a war criminal.

Independent 16 January 1999

Carolyn Kizer (b. 1925)

US POET

Her verse uses often grotesque imagery to explore feminist themes. Her first collection, Poems, *appeared in 1959.*

1 Our masks, always in peril of smearing or cracking,
In need of continuous check in the mirror or silverware,
Keep us in thrall to ourselves, concerned with our surfaces.

'Pro Femina', publ. in *Knock Upon Silence* (1965)

Paul Klee (1879–1940)

SWISS ARTIST

He joined the Expressionist group Der Blaue Reiter *(1911–12) and taught at the Bauhaus (1920–31). His paintings, such as* Twittering Machine *(1922), suggest a childlike innocence and were hugely influential.*

1 Colour possesses me. I don't have to pursue it. It will possess me always, I know it. That is the meaning of this happy hour: Colour and I are one. I am a painter.

Journal entry, written in Tunisia, 16 April 1914, publ. in *The Diaries of Paul Klee 1898–1918*, no. 926 (1957, transl. 1965)

2 One eye sees, the other feels.

Journal entry, 1914, publ. ibid., no. 937

3 The more horrible this world . . . the more abstract our art, whereas a happy world brings forth an art of the here and now.

Journal entry, 1915, publ. ibid., no. 951

4 Everything vanishes around me, and works are born as if out of the void. Ripe, graphic fruits fall off. My hand has become the obedient instrument of a remote will.

Journal entry, January/February 1918, publ. ibid., no. 1104

5 Art does not reproduce the visible; rather, it makes visible.

'Creative Credo', sect. 1, written 1918, publ. 1920, repr. in *The Inward Vision* (1957)

6 The creative impulse suddenly springs to life, like a flame, passes through the hand onto the canvas, where it spreads farther until, like the spark that closes an electric circuit, it returns to the source: the eye and the mind.

Ibid., sect. 4

7 Standing at his appointed place, the trunk of the tree, he does nothing other than gather and pass on what comes to him from the depths. He neither serves nor rules – he transmits. His position is

humble. And the beauty at the crown is not his own. He is merely a channel.
On Modern Art (1924). On the role of the artist.

8 An active line on a walk, moving freely without a goal. A walk for a walk's sake.
Pedagogical Sketchbook, ch. 1 (1925). On his hieroglyphic drawing style.

Joe Klein (b. 1946)
US JOURNALIST AND AUTHOR
A journalist for three decades, notably at the New Yorker *and* Newsweek, *he first denied, then confirmed his authorship of the anonymously published bestseller* Primary Colors *(1996, filmed 1998), a political novel closely modelled on the rise of the Clintons to the White House.*

1 It was interesting how even mediocre politicians reflexively found their way to the elemental rules of the game – in this case: Never attack an opponent when he is in the process of killing himself.
Primary Colors, ch. 4 (1996)

2 We tell them [politicians] what they want to hear – and when we tell them something they *don't* want to hear, it's usually because we've calculated that's what they really want. We live an eternity of false smiles – and why? Because it's the price you pay to lead.
Jack Stanton, ibid., ch. 9

Richard Klein (b. 1941)
US AUTHOR
He has written perceptively and humorously on food, wine and smoking, as in Cigarettes are Sublime *(1993) and* Eat Fat *(1996).*

1 It is their uselessness that ensures the aesthetic appeal of cigarettes – the sublimely, darkly beautiful pleasure that cigarettes bring to the lives of smokers. It is a pleasure that is democratic, popular, and universal; it is a form of beauty that the world of high as well as popular culture has for more than a century recognized and explicitly celebrated, in prose and poetry, in images both still and moving.
Cigarettes Are Sublime, Introduction (1993)

2 Fat is beautiful, sexy, and strong. Politicians cultivate it, singers require it, gourmets appreciate it, and lovers play with it. *Fat* is a fabulous three-letter word.
Eat Fat, 'A Preface in Conclusion' (1996)

Mark Knopfler (b. 1949)
BRITISH ROCK MUSICIAN
He was lead singer, guitarist and songwriter with Dire Staits, one of the most successful bands of the 1980s, later reverting to a rootsier sound with the Notting Hillbillies.

1 *That ain't working, that's the way you do it Get your money for nothing and chicks for free.*
'Money For Nothing' (song, co-written with STING) on the album *Brothers in Arms* (1985)

2 My idea of heaven is a place where the Tyne meets the Delta, where folk music meets the blues.
Interview in *Mojo* April 1996

Ronald Knox (1888–1957)
BRITISH SCHOLAR AND PRIEST
An Anglican chaplain, he converted to Roman Catholicism and became Catholic chaplain to Oxford University (1926–39). He wrote an authorized translation of the Bible (1945–9), apologetics, and detective novels.

1 *There was once a man who said, 'God Must think it exceedingly odd If he finds that this tree Continues to be When there's no one about in the Quad.'*
The Complete Limerick Book (1924) by Langford Reed. Knox's limerick was anonymously answered: 'Dear Sir, Your astonishment's odd:/I am always about in the Quad./And that's why the tree/Will continue to be,/Since observed by Yours faithfully, God.'

2 Only man has dignity; only man, therefore, can be funny.
Essays in Satire, Introduction (1928)

3 It is stupid of modern civilization to have given up believing in the devil, when he is the only explanation of it.
Let Dons Delight, ch. 8 (1939)

4 A loud noise at one end and no sense of responsibility at the other.
Of babies, quoted by C. Blackmore in 1976 Reith lecture. RONALD REAGAN adapted Knox's definition during his campaign for the governorship of California in 1965, when he described government as 'an alimentary canal with a big appetite at one end and no responsibility at the other'.

Ted Koehler (1894–1973)
US SONGWRITER
He wrote for such films as My Wild Irish Rose *(1947), and in collaboration with Harold Arlen, Burton Lane and other composers had such hits as 'I Love a Parade' (1931) and 'Stormy Weather' (1933).*

1 *Don't know why There's no sun up in the sky, Stormy weather Since my man and I ain't together It keeps raining all the time.*
'Stormy Weather' (song, 1933, music by Harold Arlen). Originally sung by Ethel Walters in *Cotton Club Review* (musical show, 1933), the song was later performed by Lena Horne in the film *Stormy Weather* (1943) and by Connee Boswell in the film *Swing Parade* (1946).

Arthur Koestler (1905–83)

HUNGARIAN-BORN BRITISH AUTHOR

A journalist and one-time member of the Communist Party, he escaped to England in 1940 where he published Darkness at Noon *(1940), a fictional account of the Stalinist purges. He also wrote on politics, parapsychology and the history of science.*

1 The ultimate truth is penultimately always a falsehood. He who will be proved right in the end appears to be wrong and harmful before it.

Extract from Rubashov's diary, in *Darkness at Noon*, 'The Second Hearing' (1940)

2 Politics can be relatively fair in the breathing spaces of history; at its critical turning points there is no other rule possible than the old one, that the end justifies the means.

Extract from Rubashov's diary, ibid.

3 The definition of the individual was: a multitude of one million divided by one million.

Ibid., 'The Grammatical Fiction'. On the teaching of the Party.

4 Space-ships and time machines are no escape from the human condition. Let Othello subject Desdemona to a lie-detector test; his jealousy will still blind him to the evidence. Let Oedipus triumph over gravity; he won't triumph over his fate.

'The Boredom of Fantasy', first publ. 1953, repr. in *The Trail of the Dinosaur*, pt 2 (1955)

5 One question that people always ask at home is never asked here: 'What happened to Communism in Russia?' Everybody yawns when a visitor brings it up, because the answer is so obvious to every Russian. The answer is that there never was Communism in Russia; there were only Communists.

'The Shadow of a Tree', first publ. 1953, repr. ibid. Koestler continued: 'The régime did not want Communists; it wanted robots. It will take at least a generation to change them back into humans again.'

6 If conquerors be regarded as the engine-drivers of History, then the conquerors of thought are perhaps the pointsmen who, less conspicuous to the traveller's eye, determine the direction of the journey.

The Sleepwalkers, pt 1, ch. 2 sect. 4 (1959)

7 Nobody before the Pythagoreans had thought that mathematical relations held the secret of the universe. Twenty-five centuries later, Europe is still blessed and cursed with their heritage. To non-European civilizations, the idea that numbers are the key to both wisdom and power, seems never to have occurred.

Ibid.

8 True creativity often starts where language ends.

The Act of Creation, bk 1, pt 2, ch. 7 (1964)

9 The moment of truth, the sudden emergence of a new insight, is an act of intuition. Such intuitions give the appearance of miraculous flashes, or short-circuits of reasoning. In fact they may be likened to an immersed chain, of which only the beginning and the end are visible above the surface of consciousness. The diver vanishes at one end of the chain and comes up at the other end, guided by invisible links.

Ibid., ch. 8

10 God seems to have left the receiver off the hook, and time is running out.

The Ghost in the Machine, ch. 18 (1967)

11 Prometheus is reaching out for the stars with an empty grin on his face.

The New York Times 21 July 1969. On the first manned moon-landing.

12 The most persistent sound which reverberates through man's history is the beating of war drums.

Janus: A Summing Up, 'Prologue: The New Calendar', sect. 1 (1978)

Helmut Kohl (b. 1930)

GERMAN POLITICIAN

The longest-serving post-war German leader, he became Chairman of the Christian Democratic Party in 1973, Chancellor of West Germany in 1982 and Chancellor of a united Germany (1990–98). His reputation was later damaged by his refusal to reveal the source of party donations.

1 Everybody should know that Germany will not go it alone: there will be no restless Reich.

International Herald Tribune 3 October 1990

2 I doubt that the evil spirits of the past, under which we in Europe have already suffered more than enough this century, have been banished for ever.

Independent 28 October 1992

Barbara Kolb (b. 1939)

US COMPOSER

Her music has been called a fusion of Debussy with jazz. Her best known piece is Soundings *(1971–2); later works take their inspiration from the visual arts.*

1 Composing a piece of music is very feminine. It is sensitive, emotional, contemplative. By comparison, doing housework is positively masculine.

Quoted in *Time* 10 November 1975

Käthe Kollwitz (1867–1945)

GERMAN ARTIST

Once described as the last great German Expressionist, she articulated her radical and pacifist sympathies in her bold and powerful lithographs, etchings and woodcuts, which often focused on victims of poverty and war.

1 Where do all the women who have watched so carefully over the lives of their beloved ones get the heroism to send them to face the cannon?

Journal entry, 27 August 1914, publ. in *Diaries and Letters* (ed. Hans Kollwitz, 1955)

2 Bisexuality is almost a necessary factor in artistic production; at any rate, the tinge of masculinity within me helped me in my work.

Journal entry, 1942, publ. ibid.

George Konrád (b. 1933)

HUNGARIAN AUTHOR

His novels include The Case Worker *(1969) and* The City Builder *(1977). Believing that his duty as a writer was to remain in Hungary, he was briefly imprisoned in 1974 for subversive agitation.*

1 Many people feel empty, a world that seemed so strong just collapsed. Forty years have been wasted on stupid strife for the sake of an unsuccessful experiment. The values gathered together have vanished, the strategies for survival have become ridiculous. And so forty years of our lives have become a story, a bad anecdote. But it may be possible to remember these adventures with a kind of irony.

Sunday Correspondent 15 April 1990. Referring to the collapse of Soviet power in Eastern Europe.

2 You take a number of small steps which you believe are right, thinking maybe tomorrow somebody will treat this as a dangerous provocation. And then you wait. If there is no reaction, you take another step: courage is only an accumulation of small steps.

Ibid. On surviving as a writer in Communist Hungary.

Wladyslaw Kozdra (1920–86)

POLISH COMMUNIST PARTY OFFICIAL

1 The trumpets of the Beatles are not the trumpets of Jericho which will cause the walls of socialism to come tumbling down.

Speech at Eighth Plenary Session of the Central Committee of the Polish Communist Party, 16–17 May 1967, quoted in *Rock Around the Bloc*, ch. 6 (1990) by Timothy Ryback

Larry Kramer (b. 1935)

US PLAYWRIGHT AND NOVELIST

He produced and scripted Ken Russell's film Women in Love *(1969), but became better known for his writings on New York's gay scene. His play* The Normal Heart *(1985) was an indictment of the responses to AIDS.*

1 We're all going to go crazy, living this epidemic every minute, while the rest of the world goes on out there, all around us, as if nothing is happening, going on with their own lives and not knowing what it's like, what we're going through. We're living through war, but where they're living it's peacetime, and we're all in the same country.

Ned, in *The Normal Heart*, act 2, sc. 11 (1985)

2 The only way we'll have real pride is when we demand recognition of a culture that isn't just sexual. It's all there – all through history we've been there; but we have to claim it, and identify who was in it, and articulate what's in our minds and hearts and all our creative contributions to this earth. And until we do that, and until we organize ourselves block by neighborhood by city by state into a united visible community that fights back, we're doomed.

Ned, ibid., act 2, sc. 13

Karl Kraus (1874–1936)

AUSTRIAN SATIRIST

He edited his own satirical journal Die Fackel *(1899–1936), in which he waged a one-man war against all forms of corruption. He was particularly scathing about the liberal press and the bourgeoisie, which he also attacked in his poetry and plays.*

1 In these great times which I knew when they were this small; which will become small again, provided they have time left for it; and which, because in the realm of organic growth, no such transformation is possible, we had better call fat times and, truly hard times as well; in these times in which things are happening that could not be imagined and in which what can no longer be *imagined* must *happen*, for if one could imagine it, it would not happen; in these serious times which have died laughing at the thought that they might become serious; which, surprised by their own tragedy, are reaching for diversion and, catching themselves redhanded, are groping for words; in these loud times which boom with the horrible symphony of actions which produce reports and of reports which cause actions: in these times you should not expect any words of my own from me – none but these words which

barely manage to prevent silence from being misinterpreted.

'In These Great Times', speech in Vienna, 19 November 1914, first publ. in *Die Fackel* December 1914, repr. in *In These Great Times: A Karl Kraus Reader* (ed. Harry Zohn, 1976)

2 Culture is the tacit agreement to let the means of subsistence disappear behind the purpose of existence. Civilization is the subordination of the latter to the former.
Ibid.

3 If one reads a newspaper only for information, one does not learn the truth, not even the truth about the paper. The truth is that the newspaper is not a statement of contents but the contents themselves; and more than that, it is an instigator.
Ibid.

4 The heroes of obtrusiveness, people with whom no soldier would lie down in the trenches, though he has to submit to being interviewed by them, break into recently abandoned royal castles so that they can report, 'We got there first!' It would be far less shameful to be paid for committing atrocities than for fabricating them. . . . If the reporter has killed our imagination with his truth, he threatens our life with his lies.
On war correspondents, ibid.

5 The esthete stands in the same relation to beauty as the pornographer stands to love, and the politician stands to life.
Die Fackel 5 October 1915, repr. in *Anti-Freud: Karl Kraus's Criticism of Psychoanalysis and Psychiatry*, ch. 8 (1976) by THOMAS SZASZ

6 News reports stand up as people, and people wither into editorials. Clichés walk around on two legs while men are having theirs shot off.
Grumbler, in Prologue (1917) to *The Last Days of Mankind* (1919), repr. in *In These Great Times: A Karl Kraus Reader* (ed. Harry Zohn, 1976)

7 My unconscious knows more about the consciousness of the psychologist than his consciousness knows about my unconscious.
Die Fackel 18 January 1917, repr. in *Anti-Freud: Karl Kraus's Criticism of Psychoanalysis and Psychiatry*, ch. 6 (1976) by Thomas Szasz

8 War: first, one hopes to win; then one expects the enemy to lose; then, one is satisfied that he too is suffering; in the end, one is surprised that everyone has lost.
Die Fackel 9 October 1917, repr. ibid., ch. 8

Jiddu Krishnamurti (1895–1986)
INDIAN MYSTIC
As an obscure youth he was hailed as a 'world teacher' and messiah by the Theosophical Society's President, Annie Besant, but in 1929 he renounced organized religion in favour of complete spiritual freedom.

1 I maintain that Truth is a pathless land, and you cannot approach it by any path whatsoever, by any religion, by any sect.
Speech in Holland, 3 August 1929, quoted in *Krishnamurti*, ch. 2 (1931) by Lilly Heber

Kris Kristofferson (b. 1936)
US SINGER, SONGWRITER AND ACTOR
He made his name with two songs, 'Me and Bobby McGhee' (1969) and 'Help Me Make It Through the Night' (1971). He went on to record country albums and star in films.

1 Freedom's just another word for nothing left to lose.
'Me and Bobby McGhee' (song, 1969, written with Fred Foster). The song, first recorded by ROGER MILLER in 1969, was a posthumous hit for JANIS JOPLIN in 1971, and the title track of a Kristofferson album later that year.

Arthur Kroker (b. 1945),
Marilouise Kroker and
David Cook (b. 1946)
CANADIAN SOCIOLOGISTS
Arthur and Marilouise Kroker have edited cultural and political studies and wrote The Postmodern Scene *(1986). David Cook is an academic at the University of Toronto.*

1 The future of America may or may not bring forth a black President, a woman President, a Jewish President, but it most certainly always will have a suburban President. A President whose senses have been defined by the suburbs, where lakes and public baths mutate into back yards and freeways, where walking means driving, where talking means telephoning, where watching means TV, and where living means real, imitation life.
Panic Encyclopedia, 'Panic Suburbs' (1989)

Louis Kronenberger (1904–80)
US CRITIC, EDITOR AND AUTHOR
He is best known for his biographies, and has also written novels and essays on English and American history and culture.

1 The trouble with our age is that it is all signpost and no destination.
Company Manners, 'The Spirit of the Age' (1954)

Joseph Wood Krutch (1893–1970)
US AUTHOR AND CRITIC
He was drama critic for The Nation *(1924–52) and also published essays, biographies and works on nature. 'Maybe the most I can claim,' he wrote,*

'is that I know more about botany than any other New York critic, and more about the theatre than any other botanist.'

1 Cats seem to go on the principle that it never does any harm to ask for what you want.
Twelve Seasons, February (1949)

2 The most serious charge which can be brought against New England is not Puritanism but February.
Ibid.

Elisabeth Kübler-Ross (b. 1926)
SWISS-BORN US PSYCHIATRIST
Her books have been instrumental in highlighting the psychological needs of terminally ill patients.

1 Guilt is perhaps the most painful companion of death.
On Death and Dying, ch. 9 (1969)

Stanley Kubrick (1928–99)
US FILM-MAKER
Famed for his meticulous procedures and ambitious technique, he worked in a range of genres from science fiction (2001: A Space Odyssey, 1968) to youth violence (A Clockwork Orange, 1971) and horror (The Shining, 1979). See also STERLING HAYDEN 1, 2; GEORGE C. SCOTT 1.

1 The great nations have always acted like gangsters, and the small nations like prostitutes.
Guardian 5 June 1963

2 Confront a man in his office with a nuclear alarm, and you have a documentary. If the news reaches him in his living room, you have a drama. If it catches him in the lavatory, the result is comedy.
Quoted in *Stanley Kubrick Directs* (1972) by Alexander Walker. Discussing comic method in his film *Dr. Strangelove* (1964).

3 Ghost stories appeal to our craving for immortality. If you can be afraid of a ghost, then you have to believe that a ghost may exist. And if a ghost exists then oblivion might not be the end.
Newsweek 26 May 1980. Referring to his film *The Shining*.

4 Somebody has said that man is the missing link between primitive apes and civilized human beings. You might say that the idea is inherent in *2001*. We are semi-civilized, capable of cooperation and affection, but needing some sort of transfiguration into a higher form of life.
Quoted in *Stanley Kubrick: A Film Odyssey* (1975) by Gene D. Phillips

Milan Kundera (b. 1929)
CZECH-BORN FRENCH AUTHOR AND CRITIC
The writer EDMUND WHITE *described him as 'currently the favored spokesman for the uneasy conscience of the French intellectual'. He moved to France in 1975 after being banned in his home country. His novels blend fact with fiction, philosophy and politics and include* The Joke *(1967) and* Immortality *(1991).*

1 Optimism is the opium of the people.
The Joke, pt 3, ch. 3 (1967, transl. 1982). The line, written by Ludvik on a postcard, was used by the Party as incriminating evidence against him, though it was only meant as 'a joke'.

2 No great movement designed to change the world can bear to be laughed at or belittled. Mockery is a rust that corrodes all it touches.
Kostka, ibid., pt 6, ch. 18

3 The struggle of man against power is the struggle of memory against forgetting.
Mirek, in *The Book of Laughter and Forgetting*, pt 1, sect. 2 (1978)

4 The reason we write books is that our kids don't give a damn. We turn to an anonymous world because our wife stops up her ears when we talk to her.
Ibid., pt 4, sect. 9

5 There is nothing heavier than compassion. Not even one's own pain weighs so heavy as the pain one feels with someone, for someone, a pain intensified by the imagination and prolonged by a hundred echoes.
The Unbearable Lightness of Being, pt 1, ch. 15 (1984)

6 Her drama was a drama not of heaviness but of lightness. What fell to her lot was not the burden but the unbearable lightness of being.
Of Sabina, ibid., pt 3, ch. 10

7 No matter how much we scorn it, kitsch is an integral part of the human condition.
Ibid., pt 6, ch. 12

8 Mankind's true moral test, its fundamental test (which lies deeply buried from view), consists of its attitude towards those who are at its mercy: animals.
Ibid., pt 7, ch. 2

9 A novel that does not uncover a hitherto unknown segment of existence is immoral. Knowledge is the novel's only morality.
The New York Review of Books 19 July 1984

10 For a novelist, a given historic situation is an *anthropologic laboratory* in which he explores his basic question: *What is human existence?*
Postscript to 1986 edn of *Life Is Elsewhere* (first publ. 1973)

11 The light that radiates from the great

novels time can never dim, for human existence is perpetually being forgotten by man and thus the novelists' discoveries, however old they may be, will never cease to astonish.
Guardian 3 June 1988

12 Without the meditative background that is criticism, works become isolated gestures, ahistorical accidents, soon forgotten.
'On Criticism, Aesthetics, and Europe', publ. in *Review of Contemporary Fiction* summer 1989

13 The serial number of a human specimen is the face, that accidental and unrepeatable combination of features. It reflects neither character nor soul, nor what we call the self. The face is only the serial number of a specimen.
Immortality, pt 1, ch. 3 (1991)

14 Hate traps us by binding us too tightly to our adversary.
Ibid., pt 1, ch. 5

15 Listening to a news broadcast is like smoking a cigarette and crushing the butt in the ashtray.
Paul, ibid., pt 3, 'The Brilliant Ally of His Own Gravediggers'

16 War and culture, those are the two poles of Europe, her heaven and hell, her glory and shame, and they cannot be separated from one another. When one comes to an end, the other will end also and one cannot end without the other. The fact that no war has broken out in Europe for fifty years is connected in some mysterious way with the fact that for fifty years no new Picasso has appeared either.
Ibid.

17 *I think, therefore I am* is the statement of an intellectual who underrates toothaches.
Ibid., pt 4, ch. 11. Referring to the famous formula by Descartes.

18 All great novels, all true novels, are bisexual.
The Times 16 May 1991

Akira Kurosawa (1910–98)

JAPANESE FILM-MAKER

He introduced Japanese cinema to the West with Rashomon *(1950), and his samurai epics such as* The Seven Samurai *(1954) were the inspiration for Hollywood and spaghetti westerns.*

1 We have survived again.
The samurai Kanbei to Shichiroji, after they have battled to save a village from a bandit attack, in *The Seven Samurai* (film, 1954, screenplay by Shinobu Hashimoto, Hideo Oguni and Akira Kurosawa, directed by Akira Kurosawa)

Labour Party Constitution

1 To secure for the workers by hand or by
brain the full fruits of their industry, and
the most equitable distribution thereof
that may be possible, upon the basis of the
common ownership of the means of production, distribution, and exchange.

Clause 4, drafted in 1918 by SIDNEY WEBB and
Arthur Henderson, and revised in 1926. There
were regular attempts to drop this commitment
to nationalization, including by HUGH GAIT-
SKELL after Labour's defeat in 1959, and ROY
HATTERSLEY in 1993; it was finally rescinded by
New Labour in 1995.

Christian Lacroix (b. 1951)

FRENCH FASHION DESIGNER

*He opened his own couture and ready-to-wear
business in 1987. He is known for his ornate
designs, including the puffball skirt, low necklines,
and use of ethnic fabrics.*

1 So much contemporary art and design is a
parody, a joke, and full of allusions to the
past. It's like that because it is the end of
an era, like the end of the nineteenth century. Not such a comfortable period to live
in. Everything must be a kind of caricature
to register, everything must be larger than
life.

Quoted in the *Sunday Times* October 1987, repr.
in *Sultans of Style*, 'Christian Lacroix' (1990) by
Georgina Howell

2 Haute Couture should be fun, foolish and
almost unwearable.

Quoted in the *Observer* 27 December 1987

3 For me, elegance is not to pass unnoticed
but to get to the very soul of what one is.

International Herald Tribune 21 January 1992

Suzanne LaFollette (1893–1983)

US EDITOR AND AUTHOR

*As a committed libertarian and feminist, she advo-
cated economic freedom for both sexes in such
works as* Concerning Women *(1926). She became
an ardent anti-Communist in the 1940s, and in
1955 founded, with William F. Buckley, the*
National Review. *'I haven't moved,' she commented, 'the world has moved to the left of me.'*

1 There is nothing more innately human
than the tendency to transmute what has
become customary into what has been
divinely ordained.

Concerning Women, 'The Beginnings of Emancipation' (1926)

2 Most people, no doubt, when they espouse
human rights, make their own mental res-
ervations about the proper application of
the word 'human'.

Ibid.

3 Laws are felt only when the individual comes into conflict with them.
Ibid.

Karl Lagerfeld (b. 1938)

GERMAN-BORN FRENCH FASHION DESIGNER
Design director for Chanel, he showed his first collection under his own label in 1984.

1 Only the minute and the future are interesting in fashion – it exists to be destroyed. If everybody did everything with respect, you'd go nowhere.
Quoted in *Vanity Fair* February 1992

John Lahr (b. 1941)

US AUTHOR AND CRITIC
Theatre critic for the Village Voice *and since 1992 the* New Yorker, *he has written biographies of* JOE ORTON, *his father Bert Lahr, the actor, and* FRANK SINATRA.

1 Society drives people crazy with lust and calls it advertising.
Guardian 2 August 1989

R. D. Laing (1927–89)

BRITISH PSYCHIATRIST
Ronald David Laing. The leading light of the antipsychiatry movement, he made extensive studies of schizophrenia, believing it to spring from tensions within the nuclear family. His books include The Divided Self *(1959) and* The Politics of the Family *(1971).*

1 Freud was a hero. He descended to the 'Underworld' and met there stark terrors. He carried with him his theory as a Medusa's head which turned these terrors to stone.
The Divided Self, pt 1, ch. 1 (1959)

2 Schizophrenia cannot be understood without understanding despair.
Ibid., ch. 2

3 True guilt is guilt at the obligation one owes to oneself to be oneself. False guilt is guilt felt at not being what other people feel one ought to be or assume that one is.
The Self and Others, ch. 10 (1961)

4 We are all murderers and prostitutes – no matter to what culture, society, class, nation one belongs, no matter how normal, moral, or mature, one takes oneself to be.
The Politics of Experience, Introduction (1967)

5 Alienation as our present destiny is achieved only by outrageous violence perpetrated by human beings on human beings.
Ibid.

6 From the moment of birth, when the stone-age baby confronts the twentieth-century mother, the baby is subjected to these forces of violence, called love, as its mother and father have been, and their parents and their parents before them. These forces are mainly concerned with destroying most of its potentialities. This enterprise is on the whole successful.
Ibid., ch. 3

7 The brotherhood of man is evoked by particular men according to their circumstances. But it seldom extends to all men. In the name of our freedom and our brotherhood we are prepared to blow up the other half of mankind and to be blown up in our turn.
Ibid., ch. 4

8 There is no such 'condition' as 'schizophrenia', but the label is a social fact and the social fact a *political event*.
Ibid., ch. 5

9 The experience and behaviour that gets labelled schizophrenic is a special strategy that a person invents in order to live in an unlivable situation.
Ibid.

10 Madness need not be all breakdown. It may also be break-through. It is potential liberation and renewal as well as enslavement and existential death.
Ibid., ch. 6

Constant Lambert (1905–51)

BRITISH COMPOSER
He is best known for his jazz concert piece Rio Grande *(1929), written for voices and orchestra. As musical director of Sadler's Wells (1930–47) he was a major force in establishing British ballet.*

1 To put it vulgarly, the whole trouble with a folk song is that once you have played it through there is nothing much you can do except play it over again and play it rather louder.
Music Ho!, ch. 3 (1934)

George Lamming (b. 1927)

BARBADIAN AUTHOR
He was born and brought up in Carrington's Village, Barbados, the inspiration for his first novel, In the Castle of My Skin *(1953), an account of emergence from a colonial ideology. His essays are published in* The Pleasures of Exile *(1960).*

1 No black boy wanted to be white, but it was also true that no black boy liked the idea of being black. . . . When you asked Boy Blue why he was so black he would answer 'Just as I was goin' to born the light went out.' The light had gone out for many of us.
Narrator (G), in *In the Castle of My Skin*, ch. 6 (1953)

Norman Lamont (b. 1942)

BRITISH POLITICIAN

Baron Lamont of Lerwick. He was elected Conservative MP in 1972 and became Chancellor of the Exchequer in 1990. Following Britain's withdrawal from the European Exchange Rate Mechanism, he was replaced in 1993 and became a trenchant critic of the Conservative government's policies.

1 The green shoots of economic spring are appearing once again.

Speech at Conservative Party Conference, Blackpool, 9 October 1991, quoted in *The Times* 10 October 1991. The phrase is usually remembered 'green shoots of economic recovery'.

2 We give the impression of being in office but not in power.

Resignation statement to House of Commons, 9 June 1993, publ. in *The Times* 10 June 1993. Lamont had been replaced as Chancellor of the Exchequer in a Cabinet reshuffle two weeks earlier.

Giuseppe Tomasi di Lampedusa (1896–1957)

SICILIAN AUTHOR

His only novel, The Leopard *(1958, filmed 1963), tells the nostalgic but cynical tale of an aristocratic family in Sicily in the aftermath of Italy's unification.*

1 If we want everything to remain as it is, it will be necessary for everything to change.

Prince Tancredi, in *The Leopard*, ch. 1 (1958)

Burt Lancaster (1913–94)

US SCREEN ACTOR

Burton Stephen Lancaster. He became established in underworld roles from his first film The Killers *(1946). 'Most people seem to think I'm the kind of guy who shaves with a blowtorch,' he once said. 'Actually I'm bookish and worrisome.'*

1 My right hand hasn't seen my left hand in thirty years.

J. J. Hunsecker (Burt Lancaster), in *Sweet Smell of Success* (film, 1957, screenplay by Clifford Odets and Ernest Lehman, adapted from short story by Ernest Lehman, directed by Alexander Mackendrick)

Elsa Lanchester (1902–86)

BRITISH-BORN US ACTRESS

Originally Elizabeth Sullivan. Among her films are The Bride of Frankenstein *(1935) and* Witness for the Prosecution *(1957). She was married to the actor Charles Laughton.*

1 She looked as though butter wouldn't melt in her mouth – or anywhere else.

Attributed. Referring to actress Maureen O'Hara.

(Sir) Osbert Lancaster (1908–86)

BRITISH AUTHOR AND CARTOONIST

Described by JOHN BETJEMAN *as writing 'deliciously convoluted prose', he was a satirist of mores and architecture, coining the phrase 'stockbroker Tudor'. He drew cartoons for the* Daily Express *from 1939 until his death.*

1 For self-revelation, whether it be a Tudor villa on the by-pass or a bomb-proof chalet at Berchtesgaden, there's no place like home.

Homes Sweet Homes, Preface (1939)

Martin Landau (b. 1931)

US SCREEN ACTOR

He played hoods in a variety of Hollywood films, such as HITCHCOCK's North by Northwest *(1959), and appeared on television in* Mission Impossible *(1966–8).*

1 Captains go down with their ships, not businessmen.

Abe Karatz (Martin Landau), in *Tucker – the Man and His Dream* (film, 1988, screenplay by Arnold Schulman, directed by Francis Ford Coppola)

Ann Landers (1918–2002)

US COLUMNIST

Originally Esther Pauline Lederer. She was a long-running agony aunt for the Chicago Sun-Times *(1955–87), trusted for her plain and sensible advice.*

1 All married couples should learn the art of battle as they should learn the art of making love. Good battle is objective and honest – never vicious or cruel. Good battle is healthy and constructive, and brings to a marriage the principle of equal partnership.

Ann Landers Says Truth Is Stranger . . ., ch. 11 (1968)

2 At every party there are two kinds of people – those who want to go home and those who don't. The trouble is, they are usually married to each other.

International Herald Tribune 19 June 1991

Baron Lane (b. 1918)

BRITISH JUDGE

Baron Geoffrey Lane of St Ippollitts. He was made a QC in 1962 and served as Lord Justice of Appeal (1974–9) and Lord Chief Justice of England (1980–92).

1 Loss of freedom seldom happens overnight. Oppression doesn't stand on the doorstep with toothbrush moustache and swastika armband – it creeps up insidiously . . . step by step, and all of a sudden

the unfortunate citizen realises that it is gone.

Quoted in the *Independent* 3 February 1990. Referring to proposed legal reforms.

Helmut Lang (b. 1956)

AUSTRIAN FASHION DESIGNER

Associated with an urban minimalist style, he designs clothes that are 'cool for grownups'. He was the first designer to show his collection on the Internet (1998–9).

1 Fashion designers must give a social reflection of the things which are going on. Fashion is a kind of communication. It's a language without words. Fashion is about attitude, not hemlines.

Interview in *i-D* December 1993

Julia Lang (b. 1921)

BRITISH BROADCASTER

1 Are you sitting comfortably? Then I'll begin.

Introductory words to *Listen with Mother* (daily children's stories on BBC radio, 1950–82). She also used the words '. . . Then we'll begin'.

Dorothea Lange (1895–1979)

US PHOTOGRAPHER

Her photographs in An American Exodus: A Record of Human Erosion *(1939), produced in collaboration with her husband, the economist Paul Taylor, memorably documented the homeless of San Francisco and the migrant workers of the Depression.*

1 The camera is an instrument that teaches people how to see without a camera.

Quoted in the *Los Angeles Times* 13 August 1978

Halvard Lange (1902–70)

NORWEGIAN HISTORIAN AND POLITICIAN

A Labour politician, he was Foreign Minister of Norway (1946–65) and as a founding father of NATO was responsible for Norway's entry into that organization.

1 We do not regard Englishmen as foreigners. We look on them only as rather mad Norwegians.

Quoted in the *Observer* 9 March 1957

Susanne K. Langer (1895–1985)

US PHILOSOPHER

Susanne Knauth Langer. She wrote on aesthetics and linguistic analysis, as in Feeling and Form *(1953) and* Mind: An Essay on Human Feeling *(3 vols., 1967–82).*

1 Art is the objectification of feeling, and the subjectification of nature.

Mind: An Essay on Human Feeling, vol. 1, pt 2, ch. 4 (1967)

Lewis H. Lapham (b. 1935)

US ESSAYIST AND EDITOR

Lewis Henry Lapham. Calling himself a 'novelist manqué and a historian manqué', he has been Editor of Harper's magazine since 1975, and has commentated extensively on US materialism and the world economy, as in The Agony of Mammon *(1999).*

1 Under the rules of a society that cannot distinguish between profit and profiteering, between money defined as necessity and money defined as luxury, murder is occasionally obligatory and always permissible.

Money and Class in America, ch. 4 (1988)

2 To the United States the Third World often takes the form of a black woman who has been made pregnant in a moment of passion and who shows up one day in the reception room on the forty-ninth floor threatening to make a scene. The lawyers pay the woman off, sometimes uniformed guards accompany her to the elevators.

Ibid., ch. 5, sect. 1

3 I never can pass by the Metropolitan Museum of Art in New York without thinking of it not as a gallery of living portraits but as a cemetery of tax-deductible wealth.

Ibid., ch. 9

4 The more prosperous and settled a nation, the more readily it tends to think of war as a regrettable accident; to nations less fortunate the chance of war presents itself as a possible bountiful friend.

Harper's March 1991

5 Thirty years ago it was 'the conservative establishment' that was at fault, a conspiracy largely composed of university professors, bureaucrats, and TV executives who couldn't play guitar and trembled at the sound of Dylan's harmonica. Now it is 'the liberal establishment' that is at fault, a conspiracy largely composed of university professors, bureaucrats, and TV executives who tremble before the wisdom of Arianna Huffington.

Ibid. March 1996

Frances Moore Lappé (b. 1944)

US ECOLOGIST AND AUTHOR

Her arguments for more equitable control over food production and distribution to prevent world hunger are expressed in Diet for a Small Planet *(1971) and* Food First: Beyond the Myth of Scarcity *(1977).*

1 The act of putting into your mouth what the earth has grown is perhaps your most direct interaction with the earth.

Diet for a Small Planet, pt 1 (1971)

Philip Larkin (1922–85)

BRITISH POET

A librarian all his life (at Hull from 1955), he was preoccupied with transience and death at the cost of being, as he put it, a 'gloomy old sod'. His volumes include The Less Deceived *(1955) and* High Windows *(1974).* JOHN CAREY *observed: 'His attitude to most accredited sources of pleasure would make Scrooge seem unduly frolicsome.'*

1 I have just farted with the sound of an iron ruler twanging in a desk-lid and the smell of a west wind over a decaying patch of red cabbages.
Letter to J. B. Sutton, 31 December 1941, publ. in *Selected Letters of Philip Larkin 1940–1985* (ed. Anthony Thwaite, 1992)

2 Poetry = heightened talking. Novel = heightened story. Painting = a heightened seeing.
Ibid. 23 May 1947

3 I search myself for illusions like a monkey looking for fleas.
Ibid., 13 July 1949

4 Most people, I'm convinced, don't think about life at all. They grab what they think they want and the subsequent consequences keep them busy in an endless chain till they're carried out feet first.
Ibid., 30 October 1949

5 I am beginning to think of the creative imagination as a fruit-machine on which victories are rare and separated by much vain expense, and represent a rare alignment of mental and spiritual qualities that normally are quite at odds.
Letter to Alan Pringle, 26 February 1950, publ. ibid.

6 I have no ideas about poetry at all. For me, a poem is the crossroads of my thoughts, my feelings, my imaginings, my wishes, & my verbal sense: normally these run parallel; often two or more cross; but only when all cross at one point do you get a poem.
Letter to J. B. Sutton, 10 July 1951, publ. ibid.

7 *What are days for?*
Days are where we live.
They come, they wake us
Time and time over.
'Days', written August 1953, publ. in *The Whitsun Weddings* (1964)

8 *A serious house on serious earth it is,*
In whose blent air all our compulsions meet,
Are recognised, and robed as destinies.
'Church Going', publ. in *The Less Deceived* (1955)

9 *Why should I let the toad* work
Squat on my life?

Can't I use my wit as a pitchfork
And drive the brute off?
'Toads', publ. ibid.

10 *Home is so sad. It stays as it was left,*
Shaped to the comfort of the last to go
As if to win them back.
'Home is so Sad', written 1958, publ. in *The Whitsun Weddings* (1964)

11 The only way of getting shut of your family is to put your neck into the noose of another one. Such is nature's abhorrence of a vacuum.
Letter to Judy Egerton, 25 May 1958, publ. in *Selected Letters of Philip Larkin 1940–1985* (ed. Anthony Thwaite, 1992)

12 Life doesn't wait to be asked: it comes grinning in, sits down uninvited & helps itself to bread & cheese, & comments uninhibitedly on the decorations.
Ibid.

13 Above all, though, children are linked to adults by the simple fact that they are in process of turning into them. For this they may be forgiven much. Children are bound to be inferior to adults, or there is no incentive to grow up.
'The Savage Seventh', essay publ. in the *Spectator* 10 October 1959, repr. in *Required Writing* (1983)

14 *Selflessness is like waiting in a hospital*
In a badly-fitting suit on a cold wet morning.
Selfishness is like listening to good jazz
With drinks for further orders and a huge fire.
'None of the books have time', written 1960, publ. in *Collected Poems* (1988)

15 A poem is usually a highly professional artificial thing, a verbal device designed to reproduce a thought or emotion indefinitely: it shd have no dead parts, & every word should be completely unchangeable and unmoveable.
Letter to Pamela Kitson, 12 March 1965, publ. in *Selected Letters* (ed. Anthony Thwaite, 1992)

16 Marriage, well. I think of it as a marvellous thing for other people, like going to the stake.
Ibid. Larkin had earlier written, in a letter dated 30 July 1950, 'There is no hell like marriage. The hell of loneliness, while still hell, is not so bad as the hell of marriage. And all for what, eh, you tell me that? . . . To put forward all one's self-control and resilience *just to go on living with someone* – by God!'

17 *The trees are coming into leaf*
Like something almost being said.
'The Trees', written 1967, publ. in *High Windows* (1974)

18 *Sexual intercourse began*
In nineteen sixty-three

(Which was rather late for me) –
Between the end of the Chatterley ban
And the Beatles' first LP.
'Annus Mirabilis', written 1967, publ. ibid.

19 *The hardness and the brightness and the*
plain
Far-reaching singleness of that wide stare
Is a reminder of the strength and pain
Of being young; that it can't come again,
But is for others undiminished somewhere.
'Sad Steps', written 1968, publ. ibid.

20 *They fuck you up, your mum and dad.*
They may not mean to, but they do.
They fill you with the faults they had
And add some extra, just for you.
'This Be The Verse', written 1971, publ. ibid. In
a letter, 6 June 1982, Larkin complained of the
notoriety of this poem, which 'will clearly be
my "Lake Isle of Innisfree". I fully expect to
hear it recited by a thousand Girl Guides before
I die.'

21 *Man hands on misery to man.*
It deepens like a coastal shelf.
Get out as early as you can,
And don't have any kids yourself.
Ibid.

22 *Quarterly, is it, money reproaches me:*
'Why do you let me lie here wastefully?
I am all you never had of goods and sex.
You could get them still by writing a few
cheques.'
'Money', publ. ibid.

23 *Perhaps being old is having lighted*
rooms
Inside your head, and people in them,
acting.
People you know, yet can't quite name.
'The Old Fools', publ. ibid.

24 *Deprivation is for me what daffodils were*
for Wordsworth.
Interview in the *Observer* 1979, repr. in *Required*
Writing (1983)

25 I see life more as an affair of solitude diversified by company than an affair of company diversified by solitude.
Ibid.

26 *One of the sadder things, I think,*
Is how our birthdays slowly sink:
Presents and parties disappear,
The cards grow fewer year by year,
Till, when one reaches sixty five,
How many care we're still alive?
'Dear CHARLES, My Muse, asleep or dead',
written for the poet CHARLES CAUSLEY (1982),
publ. in *Collected Poems* (1988)

27 The diatonic scale is what you use if you
want to write a national anthem, or a love
song, or a lullaby. The chromatic scale is
what you use to give the effect of drinking

a quinine martini and having an enema at
the same time.
Interview in the *Paris Review* 1982, repr. in
Required Writing (1983)

Christopher Lasch (1932–94)
US HISTORIAN
The Culture of Narcissism *(1977) is the best*
known of his powerful indictments of the consumer
society, which he blamed for eroding community
values and the work ethic.

1 A society that has made 'nostalgia' a marketable commodity on the cultural
exchange quickly repudiates the suggestion
that life in the past was in any important
way better than life today.
The Culture of Narcissism, Preface (1977)

2 Today Americans are overcome not by the
sense of endless possibility but by the
banality of the social order they have
erected against it.
Ibid., ch. 1, 'The Therapeutic Sensibility'

3 Every age develops its own peculiar forms
of pathology, which express in exaggerated
form its underlying character structure.
Ibid., ch. 2, 'Social Influences on Narcissism'

4 The job of the press is to encourage debate,
not to supply the public with information.
'Journalism, Publicity, and the Lost Art of Political Argument', first publ. in the *Gannett Center*
Journal spring 1990, repr. in *Harper's* September
1990. According to Lasch, 'Information, usually
seen as the precondition of debate, is better
understood as its by-product.'

Stan Laurel See OLIVER HARDY 1.

James Laver (1899–1975)
BRITISH ART CRITIC AND AUTHOR
A keeper at London's Victoria and Albert Museum
(1922–59), he wrote on art criticism, but is chiefly
known for his works on the history of fashion, such
as Taste and Fashion *(1937).*

1 The same costume will be

Indecent	10 years before its time
Shameless	5 years before its time
Outré (daring)	1 year before its time
Smart	
Dowdy	1 year after its time
Hideous	10 years after its time
Ridiculous	20 years after its time
Amusing	30 years after its time
Quaint	50 years after its time
Charming	70 years after its time
Romantic	100 years after its time
Beautiful	150 years after its time.

Taste and Fashion, ch. 18 (1937)

2 The erogenous zone is always shifting, and

it is the business of fashion to pursue it, without ever catching it up.

Quoted in *New Society* 2 February 1984

Denis Law (b. 1940)

BRITISH FOOTBALLER

Known as 'the King' to his fans, he was a consistent goal-scorer for Manchester City (1960–61 and 1973–4) and Manchester United (1962–73).

1 The one thing that has never changed in the history of the game is the shape of the ball.

Quoted in the *Sunday Times* 18 December 1994

D. H. Lawrence (1885–1930)

BRITISH AUTHOR

David Herbert Lawrence. Although acclaimed for his novel Sons and Lovers *(1913), he was forced abroad by hostile reaction to subsequent work such as* The Rainbow *(1915). Both* Women in Love *(1921) and* Lady Chatterley's Lover *(1928) provoked outrage for their frank treatment of sexuality. He is also remembered for his poetry. He liked to write when he was feeling spiteful, he admitted, as it was like 'having a good sneeze'. See* ANGELA CARTER 8, GERMAINE GREER 19.

1 Primarily I am a passionately religious man, and my novels must be written from the depth of my religious experience.

Letter to writer and critic Edward Garnett, 22 April 1914, publ. in *The Letters of D.H. Lawrence*, vol. 2 (ed. George J. Zytaruk and James T. Boulton, 1981). 'I shall always be a priest of love,' Lawrence had earlier written (letter, 25 December 1912).

2 The source of all life and knowledge is in man and woman, and the source of all living is in the interchange and the meeting and mingling of these two: man-life and woman-life, man-knowledge and woman-knowledge, man-being and woman-being.

Letter, 2 June 1914, publ. ibid.

3 I can only see death and more death, till we are black and swollen with death.

Ibid. 2 June 1915

4 You must drop all your democracy. You must not believe in 'the people'. One class is no better than another. It must be a case of Wisdom, or Truth. Let the working classes *be* working classes. That is the truth. There must be an aristocracy of people who have wisdom, and there must be a Ruler: a Kaiser: no Presidents and democracies.

Letter to BERTRAND RUSSELL, c. 14 July 1915, publ. ibid. 'The more I see of democracy the more I dislike it,' wrote Lawrence seven years later in Australia. 'It just brings everything down to the mere vulgar level of wages and prices, electric light and water closets, and nothing else' (letter, 13 June 1922).

5 The deadly Hydra now is the hydra of Equality. Liberty, Equality and Fraternity is the three-fanged serpent.

Letter, 16 July 1915 to BERTRAND RUSSELL, publ. ibid.

6 *Not I, not I, but the wind that blows through me!*
A fine wind is blowing the new direction of Time.

'Song of a Man Who has Come Through', publ. in *Look! We Have Come Through!* (1917)

7 Comes over one an absolute necessity to move. And what is more, to move in some particular direction. A double necessity then: to get on the move, and to know whither.

Sea and Sardinia, ch. 1 (1923). Opening words of book.

8 How beautiful maleness is, if it finds its right expression.

Ibid. ch. 3

9 Never trust the artist. Trust the tale. The proper function of a critic is to save the tale from the artist who created it.

Studies in Classic American Literature, ch. 1 (1923)

10 Be still when you have nothing to say; when genuine passion moves you, say what you've got to say, and say it hot.

Ibid., ch. 2

11 *A snake came to my water-trough*
On a hot, hot day, and I in pyjamas for the heat,
To drink there.

'Snake', publ. in *Birds, Beasts and Flowers* (1923). Opening lines.

12 I can't bear art that you can walk round and admire. A book should be either a bandit or a rebel or a man in the crowd.

Letter, 22 January 1925, publ. in *The Letters of D. H. Lawrence*, vol. 5 (ed. James T. Boulton, 1987)

13 To the Puritan, all things are impure, as somebody says.

Etruscan Places, ch. 1 (written 1927, publ. 1932). Probably referring to St Paul's words in Titus 1:15, 'Unto the pure all things are pure'.

14 Museums, museums, museums, object-lessons rigged out to illustrate the unsound theories of archaeologists, crazy attempts to co-ordinate and get into a fixed order that which has no fixed order and will not be co-ordinated! It is sickening! Why must all experience be systematized?

Ibid., ch. 6. Bemoaning the removal of excavated Etruscan tombs to the archaeological museum in Florence. 'A museum is not a first-hand contact', continued Lawrence, 'it is an illustrated lecture. And what one wants is the actual vital touch.'

15 Ours is essentially a tragic age, so we refuse to take it tragically.
Lady Chatterley's Lover, ch. 1 (1928). Opening words of book.

16 John Thomas says good-night to lady Jane, a little droopingly, but with a hopeful heart.
Ibid., ch. 19. Closing words of letter from Mellors to Connie Chatterley, and last words of book. An expurgated version of the book that first appeared in 1932 was published in 1972 with the title *John Thomas and Lady Jane*.

17 My God, what a clumsy *olla putrida* James Joyce is! Nothing but old fags and cabbage-stumps of quotations from the Bible and the rest, stewed in the juice of deliberate, journalistic dirty-mindedness.
Letter to Maria and ALDOUS HUXLEY, 15 August 1928, publ. in *The Letters of D. H. Lawrence*, vol. 6 (ed. James T. Boulton, Margaret H. Boulton and Gerald M. Lacy, 1991). *Olla putrida* is Latin for 'putrid pot', or incongruous mixture.

18 *The upshot was, my paintings must burn that English artists might finally learn.*
'Innocent England', publ. in *Collected Poems*, vol. 2 (1964). Poem written 1928 on the suppression of an exhibition of his paintings in London, on grounds of obscenity.

19 *How beastly the bourgeois is especially the male of the species – presentable, eminently presentable.*
'How Beastly the Bourgeois Is', publ. in *Pansies* (1929)

20 *I never saw a wild thing Sorry for itself. A small bird will drop frozen dead From a bough Without ever having felt sorry for itself.*
'Self-Pity', publ. ibid.

21 *When I read Shakespeare I am struck with wonder That such trivial people should muse and thunder In such lovely language.*
'When I Read Shakespeare', publ. ibid.

22 If a woman hasn't got a tiny streak of a harlot in her, she's a dry stick as a rule.
Pornography and Obscenity (1930), repr. in *Phoenix: The Posthumous Papers of D. H. Lawrence*, pt 3 (ed. E. McDonald, 1936)

23 Pornography is the attempt to insult sex, to do dirt on it.
Ibid. Lawrence admitted, however, that the definition of pornography varied according to the individual: 'What is pornography to one man is the laughter of genius to another.'

24 The one thing that it seems impossible to escape from, once the habit is formed, is masturbation. It goes on and on, on into old age, in spite of marriage or love affairs or anything else. And it always carries this

secret feeling of futility and humiliation, futility and humiliation. And this is, perhaps, the deepest and most dangerous cancer of our civilization. Instead of being a comparatively pure and harmless vice, masturbation is certainly the most dangerous sexual vice that a society can be afflicted with, in the long run. Comparatively pure it may be – purity being what it is. But harmless!!!
Ibid.

25 *And if tonight my soul may find her peace in sleep, and sink in good oblivion, and in the morning wake like a new-opened flower then I have been dipped again in God, and new-created.*
'Shadows', publ. in *Last Poems* (1932)

T. E. Lawrence (1888–1935)
BRITISH SOLDIER AND SCHOLAR
Thomas Edward Lawrence. He was known as Lawrence of Arabia after leading the Arab revolt against the Turks in the First World War, as recorded in The Seven Pillars of Wisdom *(1926). He was killed in a motorcycle accident.*

1 Often I wish I had known at the beginning the weary lag that any sudden reputation brings. I should have refrained from doing even the little that I did; and now I would be left alone and able to live as I chose. To have news value is to have a tin can tied to one's tail.
Letter, 1 April 1935, publ. in *The Letters of T.E. Lawrence* (ed. Malcolm Brown, 1988). Written a few weeks before his death.

Nigel Lawson (b. 1932)
BRITISH POLITICIAN
Baron Lawson of Blaby. Before entering politics as a Conservative MP in 1974, he was a financial journalist and Editor of the Spectator *(1966–70). He was appointed Chancellor of the Exchequer in 1983, resigning in 1989.*

1 To govern is to choose. To appear to be unable to choose is to appear to be unable to govern.
Daily Mail 26 March 1991

Nigella Lawson (b. 1960)
BRITISH JOURNALIST AND BROADCASTER
The daughter of NIGEL LAWSON, she writes for various newspapers and is famous for her cookery programmes and spin-off books.

1 Pregnancy is the ultimate display of potency, just as potency, in another sense, is said to be the ultimate aphrodisiac. No wonder, then, that a private sexual act should be interpreted as the greatest public come on. Perhaps it's good to see that,

even in politics, life insistently asserts itself.

Observer 21 November 1999. Commenting on the announcement of the pregnancy of CHERIE BLAIR.

2 Sometimes . . . we want to feel not like a postmodern, post feminist, overstretched modern woman but, rather, a domestic goddess, trailing nutmeggy fumes of baking pie in our languorous wake.

How To Be a Domestic Goddess, Preface (2000)

Irving Layton (b. 1912)
CANADIAN POET

Originally Israel Lazarovitch. His verse, encompassing both satirical digs against the bourgeoisie and explicitly erotic love poetry, appears in Here and Now *(1945) and* The Swinging Flesh *(1961), among other collections.*

1 If poetry is like an orgasm, an academic can be likened to someone who studies the passion-stains on the bedsheets.

The Whole Bloody Bird, 'Obs II' (1969)

2 In Pierre Elliot Trudeau, Canada has at last produced a political leader worthy of assassination.

Ibid.

3 *Conscience: self-esteem with a halo.*

Ibid., 'Aphs'

4 *When you argue with your inferiors, you convince them of only one thing: they are as clever as you.*

Ibid.

5 *Idealist: a cynic in the making.*

Ibid.

6 *My neighbour*
doesn't want to be loved
as much as
he wants to be envied.

Ibid.

7 *An aphorism*
should be
like a burr:
sting,
stick,
and leave
a little soreness
afterwards.

Ibid.

John Le Carré (b. 1931)
BRITISH AUTHOR

Pen name of David Cornwell. He was a member of the Foreign Service (1960–64) before becoming a full-time writer of complex spy thrillers featuring the self-effacing agent George Smiley. Titles include The Spy Who Came in From the Cold *(1963, filmed 1965) and* The Russia House *(1989, filmed 1991).*

1 What do you think spies are: priests, saints and martyrs? They're a squalid procession of vain fools, traitors too, yes; pansies, sadists and drunkards, people who play cowboys and Indians to brighten their rotten lives.

Leamas, in *The Spy Who Came in From the Cold*, ch. 25 (1963)

2 It's easy to forget what intelligence consists of: luck and speculation. Here and there a windfall, here and there a scoop.

Leclerc, in *The Looking-Glass War*, pt 2, ch. 9 (1965)

3 A committee is an animal with four back legs.

Smiley (quoting Karla), in *Tinker, Tailor, Soldier, Spy*, pt 3, ch. 34 (1974)

4 For decades to come the spy world will continue to be the collective couch where the subconscious of each nation is confessed.

Quoted in the *Observer* 19 November 1989

5 It was *man* who ended the Cold War in case you didn't notice. It wasn't weaponry, or technology, or armies or campaigns. It was just *man*. Not even Western man either, as it happened, but our sworn enemy in the East, who went into the streets, faced the bullets and the batons and said: we've had enough. It was *their* emperor, not ours, who had the nerve to mount the rostrum and declare he had no clothes. And the ideologies trailed after these impossible events like condemned prisoners, as ideologies do when they've had their day. . . . One day, history may tell us who really won.

Smiley, in *The Secret Pilgrim*, ch. 12 (1990)

6 You ask can we ever trust the Bear? . . . I will give you several answers at once. The first is no, we can never trust the Bear. For one reason, the Bear doesn't trust himself. The Bear is threatened and the Bear is frightened and the Bear is falling apart. The Bear is disgusted with his past, sick of his present and scared stiff of his future. He often was. The Bear is broke, lazy, volatile, incompetent, slippery, dangerously proud, dangerously armed, sometimes brilliant, often ignorant. Without his claws, he'd be just another chaotic member of the Third World. . . . The second answer is yes, we can trust the Bear completely. The Bear has never been so trustworthy. The Bear is begging to be part of us, to submerge his problems in us, to have his own bank account with us, to shop in our High Street and be accepted as a dignified member of our forest as well as his. . . . The Bear needs us so desperately that we may safely trust him to need us.

Smiley, ibid., ch. 12,

7 I don't think it is given to any of us to be impertinent to great religions with impunity.

International Herald Tribune 23 May 1989. Referring to SALMAN RUSHDIE and his book *The Satanic Verses*, which was considered offensive to Islam.

Le Corbusier (1887–1965)

SWISS-BORN FRENCH ARCHITECT

Pseudonym of Charles-Édouard Jeanneret. He was a pioneer of the International Style, characterized by the use of steel and reinforced concrete, open-plan interiors and geometric forms. His theories are set out in Towards a New Architecture *(1923) and* Le Modulor *(1948).*

1 A house is a machine for living in.
(Une maison est une machine-à-habiter.)

Towards a New Architecture, ch. 1, 'Eyes Which Do Not See: Airplanes' (1923, transl. 1946)

2 Our own epoch is determining, day by day, its own style. Our eyes, unhappily, are unable yet to discern it.

Ibid.

3 A hundred times have I thought New York is a catastrophe . . . it is a beautiful catastrophe.

Quoted in the *New York Herald Tribune* 6 August 1961

Ursula Le Guin (b. 1929)

US AUTHOR

Her science fiction and fantasy novels depict alternative worlds analogous to our own, as in The Left Hand of Darkness *(1969) and* The Dispossessed *(1974). Her books for children include the allegorical 'Earthsea' trilogy (1968–72).*

1 When action grows unprofitable, gather information; when information grows unprofitable, sleep.

'Ekumenical' saying, in *The Left Hand of Darkness*, ch. 3 (1969)

2 It is a terrible thing, this kindness that human beings do not lose. Terrible, because when we are finally naked in the dark and cold, it is all we have. We who are so rich, so full of strength, we end up with that small change. We have nothing else to give.

Narrator (Estraven), ibid. ch. 13

3 In so far as one denies what is, one is possessed by what is not, the compulsions, the fantasies, the terrors that flock to fill the void.

The Lathe of Heaven, ch. 10 (1971)

4 Let the athletes die young and laurel-crowned. Let the soldiers earn the Purple Hearts. Let women die old, white-crowned, with human hearts.

'The Space Crone', first publ. in *The*

Co-Evolution Quarterly summer 1976, repr. in *Dancing at the Edge of the World* (1989)

5 The children of the revolution are always ungrateful, and the revolution must be grateful that it is so.

'Reciprocity of Prose and Poetry', address in Washington DC, 1983, publ. in *Dancing at the Edge of the World* (1989)

6 If science fiction is the mythology of modern technology, then its myth is tragic.

'The Carrier Bag Theory of Fiction', written 1986, first publ. in *Women of Vision* (ed. Denise M. Du Pont, 1988), repr. ibid.

7 We are volcanoes. When we women offer our experience as our truth, as human truth, all the maps change. There are new mountains.

Bryn Mawr Commencement Address, 1986, publ. ibid.

8 If you want your writing to be taken seriously, don't marry and have kids, and above all, don't die. But if you have to die, commit suicide. They approve of that.

'Prospects for Women in Writing', speech in Portland, Maine, September 1986, publ. ibid.

9 My imagination makes me human and makes me a fool; it gives me all the world and exiles me from it.

'Winged: The Creatures on my Mind', publ. in *Harper's* August 1990

Jean-Marie Le Pen (b. 1928)

FRENCH NATIONALIST POLITICIAN

He formed the French National Front in 1972, whose policies include the repatriation of immigrants. Elected to the European Parliament in 1984, he has made unsuccessful bids for the French presidency in 1988, 1995 and 2002.

1 I have not made a study of it, but believe that it is a minor point in the history of the war.

Quoted in the *Sunday Times* 27 December 1987. Referring to the Holocaust.

Eda J. Le Shan (b. 1922)

US ACADEMIC AND AUTHOR

As well as works of social commentary, she has written self-help books, for example How to Survive Parenthood *(1965).*

1 In all our efforts to provide 'advantages' we have actually produced the busiest, most competitive, highly pressured and over-organized generation of youngsters in our history – and possibly the unhappiest. We seem hell-bent on eliminating much of childhood.

The Conspiracy Against Childhood, ch. 1 (1967)

Bernard Leach (1887–1979)

BRITISH POTTER

A leading figure of twentieth-century ceramics for more than fifty years, he aimed to combine functionality with beauty. After a period of study in Japan, he established his pottery in St Ives, Cornwall.

1 Do not pursue skills, technique will follow the idea. The idea will find technique, it is included in the real gift.

The Potter's Challenge, ch. 1 (1976)

2 The pot is the man: his virtues and his vices are shown therein – no disguise is possible.

Ibid., ch. 4

Stephen Leacock (1869–1944)

BRITISH-BORN CANADIAN HUMORIST AND ECONOMIST

He lectured and wrote on political economics but is best known for his humorous observations of social foibles, including Literary Lapses *(1910) and* Frenzied Fiction *(1917).*

1 Advertising may be described as the science of arresting the human intelligence long enough to get money from it.

The Garden of Folly, 'The Perfect Salesman' (1924)

2 Writing is simple: you just jot down amusing ideas as they occur to you. The jotting presents no problem; it is the occurring that is difficult.

Quoted by ROBERTSON DAVIES in Introduction to *The Penguin Stephen Leacock* (1981)

Timothy Leary (1920–96)

US PSYCHOLOGIST

He was branded by RICHARD NIXON *'the most dangerous man in America' for his advocacy of psychotropic drugs, for which he was several times imprisoned. In later life he was a zealot of new technology.*

1 My advice to people today is as follows: If you take the game of life seriously, if you take your nervous system seriously, if you take your sense organs seriously, if you take the energy process seriously, you must turn on, tune in, and drop out.

Lecture, 1966, publ. in *The Politics of Ecstasy*, ch. 21 (1968). Nearly thirty years later, Leary suggested a variation of this slogan, 'Tune in, turn on, boot up' (*Guardian* 2 December 1995).

2 I declare that the Beatles are mutants. Prototypes of evolutionary agents sent by God with a mysterious power to create a new species – a young race of laughing freemen.... They are the wisest, holiest, most effective avatars the human race has ever produced.

Quoted in *Shout! The True Story of the Beatles*, pt 4, 'August 1967' (1981) by Philip Norman

3 I declare that World War III is now being waged by short-haired robots whose deliberate aim is to destroy the complex web of free wild life by the imposition of mechanical order.

Manifesto (1970), repr. in *Counterculture and Revolution* (ed. David Horowitz, Michael P. Lerner and Craig Pykes, 1972). Leary's *Manifesto* was written after escaping from prison and fleeing to Algeria.

4 Science is all metaphor.

Interview 24 September 1980, publ. in *Contemporary Authors*, vol. 107 (1983)

5 In the information age, you don't teach philosophy as they did after feudalism. You perform it. If Aristotle were alive today he'd have a talk show.

Evening Standard 8 February 1989

6 How you die is the most important thing you ever do. It's the exit, the final scene of the glorious epic of your life. It's the third act and, you know, everything builds up to the third act.

Interview in the *Guardian* 2 December 1995. Leary, who had been diagnosed as suffering from cancer, intended to expire live on the Internet, although this was not in the end carried out. His last wish was to have his remains launched into space.

William Least Heat-Moon (b. 1939)

US AUTHOR

Originally William Trogdon. Of mixed Native American blood, he writes about those parts of America 'where time and men and deeds connect', as in Blue Highways *(1983) and* River Horse *(1999).*

1 Beware thoughts that come in the night. They aren't turned properly; they come in askew, free of sense and restriction, deriving from the most remote of sources.

Blue Highways: A Journey into America, pt 1, ch. 1 (1983). Opening sentences of book.

2 To say nothing is out here is incorrect; to say the desert is stingy with everything except space and light, stone and earth is closer to the truth.

Ibid., pt 4, ch. 8

3 Whoever the last true cowboy in America turns out to be, he's likely to be an Indian.

Ibid., pt 5, ch. 2

F. R. Leavis (1895–1978)

BRITISH LITERARY CRITIC

Frank Raymond Leavis. A devotee of high standards in English literature and criticism, he

founded and edited the quarterly Scrutiny (1932–53) with his wife Q. D. Leavis. His works include The Great Tradition (1948) and The Common Pursuit (1952).

1 The opposition to the Georgians was already at the time in question (just after the war) Sitwellism. But the Sitwells belong to the history of publicity rather than of poetry.
On Georgian poetry, in New Bearings in English Poetry, ch. 2 (1932)

2 One of the supreme debts one great writer can owe another is the realization of unlikeness.
The Great Tradition, ch. 1 (1948)

3 I have, then, given my hostages. What I think and judge I have stated as responsibly and clearly as I can. Jane Austen, George Eliot, Henry James, Conrad, and D. H. Lawrence: the great tradition of the English novel is there.
Ibid.

Fran Lebowitz (b. 1951)
US JOURNALIST
Her satirical essays, tart and light-hearted in style, appear in the collections Metropolitan Life (1978) and Social Studies (1981).

1 All God's children are not beautiful. Most of God's children are, in fact, barely presentable.
Metropolitan Life, 'Manners' (1978)

2 There is no such thing as inner peace. There is only nervousness or death. Any attempt to prove otherwise constitutes unacceptable behavior.
Ibid.

3 If you are of the opinion that the contemplation of suicide is sufficient evidence of a poetic nature, do not forget that actions speak louder than words.
Ibid., 'Letters'

4 Being a woman is of special interest only to aspiring male transsexuals. To actual women it is merely a good excuse not to play football.
Ibid.

5 Original thought is like original sin: both happened before you were born to people you could not have possibly met.
Social Studies, 'People' (1981)

6 The opposite of talking isn't listening. The opposite of talking is waiting.
Ibid.

7 Do not, on a rainy day, ask your child what he feels like doing, because I assure you that what he feels like doing, you won't feel like watching.
Ibid., 'Parental Guidance'

8 Remember that as a teenager you are at the last stage in your life when you will be happy to hear that the phone is for you.
Ibid., 'Tips for Teens'

9 Stand firm in your refusal to remain conscious during algebra. In real life, I assure you, there is no such thing as algebra.
Ibid.

10 To put it rather bluntly, I am not the type who wants to go back to the land; I am the type who wants to go back to the hotel.
Ibid., 'Things'

11 If you are a dog and your owner suggests that you wear a sweater . . . suggest that he wear a tail.
Ibid., 'Pointers for Pets'

Huddie 'Leadbelly' Ledbetter
(1889–1949)
US FOLK AND BLUES MUSICIAN
Of black and Cherokee Indian origins, he worked as a cotton-picker and labourer but spent much of his life in prison, where he was recorded by the archivists John and Alan Lomax, who later launched him on the New York folk scene.

1 Look a here people, listen to me,
Don't try to find no home in Washington DC
Lord, it's a bourgeois town, it's a bourgeois town.
'Bourgeois Blues' (song, c. 1933, written with Alan Lomax) on the album Easy Rider (1962). The song was recorded in Louisiana State Prison by musicologist Alan Lomax, who helped to obtain Leadbelly's release in 1934.

2 Let the Midnight Special
Shine her light on me.
'Midnight Special' (song, traditional), recorded 1940, publ. in Our Singing Country (1941) by John A. and Alan Lomax. Already known as a southern prison ballad when Leadbelly recorded it, the song refers to a train running past Sugarland Prison, Texas, whose headlight shining on an inmate supposedly indicated that he would soon be free.

Gypsy Rose Lee (1914–70)
US STRIPTEASE ARTISTE
Originally Rose Louise Hovick. She was the most famous stripper of the 1930s and appeared in the Ziegfeld Follies (1936). Her autobiography (1957) was adapted for the stage musical Gypsy (1959, filmed 1962).

1 God is love, but get it in writing.
Attributed

Harper Lee (b. 1926)
US AUTHOR
A descendant of Robert E. Lee, she won the Pulitzer Prize for literature for her first and only novel

To Kill a Mockingbird *(1960, filmed 1962), a tale
of racial injustice in the American south narrated
by a six-year-old girl.*

1 Until I feared I would lose it, I never loved
to read. One does not love breathing.
Scout, in *To Kill a Mockingbird*, pt 1, ch. 2 (1960)

2 The one thing that doesn't abide by majority rule is a person's conscience.
Atticus Finch, ibid., ch. 11

3 Folks don't like to have somebody around
knowin' more than they do. It aggravates
'em. You're not gonna change any of them
by talkin' right, they've got to want to
learn themselves, and when they don't
want to learn there's nothing you can do
but keep your mouth shut or talk their
language.
Calpurnia, ibid., pt 2, ch. 12

4 I'm no idealist to believe firmly in the
integrity of our courts and in the jury
system – that is no ideal to me, it is a living, working reality. Gentlemen, a court
is no better than each man of you sitting
before me on this jury. A court is only as
sound as its jury, and a jury is only as
sound as the men who make it up.
Speech to the jury by Atticus Finch, ibid., ch. 20

5 As you grow older, you'll see white men
cheat black men every day of your life, but
let me tell you something and don't you
forget it – whenever a white man does that
to a black man, no matter who he is, how
rich he is, or how fine a family he comes
from, that white man is trash.
Atticus Finch to his son Jem, ibid., ch. 23

Spike Lee (b. 1956)
US FILM-MAKER
*Originally Shelton Jackson Lee. He has aroused
controversy for his depictions of racial tensions in
such films as* Do the Right Thing *(1989), while*
Malcolm X *(1992) was criticized for its alleged
bias. He once remarked: 'There are so few black
films that when you do one it has to represent
every black person in the world.'*

1 This [racism] is something that white
America is going to have to work out themselves. If they decide they want to stop it,
curtail it, or to do the right thing . . . then
it will be done, but not until then.
Interview in *Roger Ebert's Home Movie Companion* (1990)

2 If we became students of Malcolm X, we
would not have young black men out there
killing each other like they're killing each
other now. Young black men would not be
impregnating young black women at the
rate going on now. We'd not have the
drugs we have now, or the alcoholism.
Interview in *i-D* January 1993. Lee's lengthy

biopic, *Malcolm X* (1992), was described as 'a
movie about the need for religion, or moral
steadfastness'.

Tommy Lee (b. 1962)
US ROCK MUSICIAN
*Born Thomas Lee Bass. From 1981 he was drum-
mer with the LA heavy metal band Mötley Crüe,
whose mission statement was 'sex, drugs, pizza and
more sex'. He achieved further fame for his showbiz relationship with wife Pamela Anderson.*

1 You rip! Boom! Boom! Boom! Let's get
together.
Chat-up line to Pamela Anderson, whom he married five days later, quoted in *FHM* March 1996

Henri Lefebvre (1901–91)
FRENCH PHILOSOPHER
*He was artistic director of the radio broadcasting
company Radiodiffusion Français 1944–9, and
also wrote widely on philosophy, notably on Marx,
as in* The Sociology of Marx *(1966).*

1 The most remarkable aspect of the transition we are living through is not so much
the passage from want to affluence as the
passage from labour to leisure. . . . Leisure
contains the future, it is the new horizon.
Everyday Life in the Modern World (1962) ch. 1,
'What Should the New Society be Called?'
Lefebvre continued: 'The prospect then is one of
unremitting labour to bequeath to future generations a chance of founding a society of leisure
that will overcome the demands and compulsions of productive labour so that time may be
devoted to creative activities or simply to pleasure and happiness.'

David Lehman (b. 1948)
US POET, EDITOR AND CRITIC
He was book critic for Newsweek *and has published the poetry collections* Some Nerve *(1973)
and* Day One *(1979), as well as a study of crime
fiction,* The Perfect Murder *(1989).*

1 Words can have no single fixed meaning.
Like wayward electrons, they can spin
away from their initial orbit and enter a
wider magnetic field. No one owns them or
has a proprietary right to dictate how they
will be used.
Signs of the Times, ch. 1 (1991)

2 There is an air of last things, a brooding
sense of impending annihilation, about so
much deconstructive activity, in so many
of its guises; it is not merely postmodernist
but preapocalyptic.
Ibid.

3 Obscurantism is the academic theorist's
revenge on society for having consigned

him or her to relative obscurity – a way of proclaiming one's superiority in the face of one's diminished influence.

Ibid., ch. 3

Rosamond Lehmann (1903–90)
BRITISH AUTHOR
Her fiction is characterized by sensitive portrayals of young women undergoing the 'torment of loving', as in An Invitation to the Waltz *(1932) and its sequel* The Weather in the Streets *(1936).*

1 **The trouble with Ian [Fleming] is that he gets off with women because he can't get on with them.**

Quoted in *The Life of Ian Fleming*, ch. 8, sect. 1 (1966) by John Pearson. The novelist Ian Fleming was famed for his voracious and cynical sexual appetite (see IAN FLEMING 3 and 4). Lehmann's description is said to be borrowed from ELIZABETH BOWEN (untraced).

Tom Lehrer (b. 1928)
US HUMORIST
The sharply satirical songs he wrote and performed throughout the 1950s and '60s were famous for their black humour, pastiche and parody. He deftly accompanied himself on piano.

1 *Even though the prospect sickens,*
   Brother, here we go again.
   On Christmas Day you can't get sore,
   Your fellow man you must adore,
   There's time to cheat him all the more
   The other three hundred and sixty-four.
   'A Christmas Carol' (song) on the album *An Evening Wasted with Tom Lehrer* (1959)

2 *How I ache for the touch of your lips, dear,*
   But much more for the feel of your whips, dear,
   You can raise welts,
   Like nobody else,
   As we dance to the Masochism Tango!
   'The Masochism Tango' (song), ibid.

3 **Life is like a sewer. What you get out of it depends on what you put into it.**
   Preamble to 'We Will All Go Together When We Go' (song), ibid.

Jerry Leiber and
Mike Stoller See ELVIS PRESLEY 1.

Fred W. Leigh (1870–1924)
BRITISH SONGWRITER
He joined the publishing firm Francis Day and Hunter c. 1900 and became literary editor there, a post he held until his death. He wrote songs associated with Marie Lloyd, among others.

1 *I always hold in having it if you fancy it,*
   If you fancy it that's understood!

And suppose it makes you fat? I don't worry over that,
'Cos a little of what you fancy does you good!
'A Little of What You Fancy Does You Good' (song, 1915, written with George Arthurs)

2 *Why am I always the bridesmaid,*
   Never the blushing bride?
   'Why Am I Always the Bridesmaid?' (song, 1917, written with Charles Collins and Lily Morris)

3 *My old man said, 'Follow the van,*
   Don't dilly-dally on the way!'
   'Don't Dilly-Dally on the Way' (song, 1919, written with Charles Collins). The song, which was also known as 'My Old Man Says "Follow the Van" ' and 'The Cock-linnet Song', was popularized by Marie Lloyd.

Mike Leigh (b. 1943)
BRITISH FILM-MAKER
His work on stage and screen is in turns mundane, poignant, funny and bleak. His best known television play is Abigail's Party *(1977), and his films include* Life is Sweet *(1991) and* Secrets and Lies *(1996). His task, he said, is 'to reproduce the real world with some kind of semblance of reality'.*

1 **Thanks for the mammaries.**
   Johnny (David Thewlis), with his hand inside Sophie's top, in *Naked* (film, 1993, written and directed by Mike Leigh)

2 **Was I bored? No, I wasn't fuckin' bored. I'm never bored. That's the trouble with everybody – you're all so bored. You've 'ad nature explained to you and you're bored with it. You've 'ad the living body explained to you and you're bored with it. You've 'ad the universe explained to you and you're bored with it. So now you just want cheap thrills and like plenty of 'em, and it dun't matter 'ow tawdry or vacuous they are as long as it's new, as long as it's new, as long as it flashes and fuckin' bleeps in forty fuckin' different colours. Well, whatever else you can say about me, I'm not fuckin' bored!**
   Johnny (David Thewlis) to Louise, ibid.

3 **I don't 'ave a future. Nobody 'as a future. The party's over. Take a look around you, man. It's all breakin' up.**
   Johnny (David Thewlis), ibid.

4 **Morals are a matter of taste.**
   Interview in *Naked and Other Screenplays* (1995)

5 **Making a film is a political act because life is about how you live it in the smallest way from moment to moment as well as the great movements which are actually easy to talk about.**
   Interview in *Salon* 16 September 1996

Michel Leiris (1901–90)

FRENCH ANTHROPOLOGIST AND AUTHOR

After an association with the Surrealists (1925–9), he worked as an anthropologist and published several confessional autobiographies, including Manhood (1939) and The Rules of the Game (4 vols. 1948–76).

1 Dream is not a revelation. If a dream affords the dreamer some light on himself, it is not the person with closed eyes who makes the discovery but the person with open eyes lucid enough to fit thoughts together. Dream – a scintillating mirage surrounded by shadows – is essentially poetry.

Quoted by Roger Shattuck in Introduction to *Nights as Day, Days as Night* (1961)

Prue Leith (b. 1940)

BRITISH CHEF, CATERER AND AUTHOR

Regarded as the 'doyenne of British cookery', she has been a writer and broadcaster on cookery for thirty years.

1 When you get to fifty-two food becomes more important than sex.

Guardian 11 November 1992

Curtis E. LeMay (1906–90)

US AIR FORCE GENERAL

Curtis Emerson LeMay. He commanded the bombers that dropped the atom bombs on Japan in 1945 and was subsequently the first head of the USAF's élite nuclear bomber strike force (1948–57) and Air Force Chief of Staff (1961–5). He was said to be the inspiration for the gung-ho General Jack D. Ripper in KUBRICK's *film* Dr. Strangelove *(1963) (see* STERLING HAYDEN 2*).*

1 My solution to the problem would be to tell them [the North Vietnamese] they've got to draw in their horns and stop aggression or we're going to bomb them back into the Stone Age.

Quoted in *Mission with LeMay* (1965). The words inspired the ironic slogan 'Bombs Away with Curt LeMay!'

Jack Lemmon (1925–2001)

US ACTOR

Often cast in comedy films such as Some Like It Hot (1959), the start of a seven-film collaboration with BILLY WILDER, *he also won acclaim for Save the Tiger (1973) and Missing (1982).*

1 Look at that! Look how she moves! That's just like jell-O on springs. She must have some sort of built-in motor or something, huh? I tell you it's a whole different sex.

Jerry/Daphne (Jack Lemmon) in *Some Like It Hot* (film, 1959, screenplay by Billy Wilder and I.A.L. Diamond, directed and produced by Billy

Wilder). Said to Joe/Josephine (Tony Curtis) on the station platform, the first time they set eyes on Sugar Kane (Marilyn Monroe).

Vladimir Ilyich Lenin (1870–1924)

RUSSIAN REVOLUTIONARY LEADER

Originally Vladimir Ilyich Ulyanov. He was the leading figure in the Bolshevik revolution of 1917 and became the first head of a Soviet government. The Marxist-Leninist policies that he established came to be the basis of communist ideology everywhere.

1 Imperialism is capitalism at that stage of development at which the dominance of monopolies and finance capitalism is established; in which the export of capital has acquired pronounced importance; in which the division of the world among the international trusts has begun, in which the division of all territories of the globe among the biggest capitalist powers has been completed.

Imperialism, the Highest Stage of Capitalism, ch. 7 (1916). The formulation has been paraphrased: 'Imperialism is the monopoly stage of capitalism.'

2 Capitalists are no more capable of self-sacrifice than a man is capable of lifting himself up by his own bootstraps.

Letters From Afar, ch. 4 (1917)

3 While the State exists there can be no freedom; when there is freedom there will be no State.

The State and Revolution, ch. 5, sect. 4 (1919)

4 When one makes a Revolution, one cannot mark time; one must always go forward – or go back. He who now talks about the 'freedom of the press' goes backward, and halts our headlong course towards Socialism.

Speech at Smolny, 17 November 1917, quoted in *Ten Days That Shook the World*, ch. 11 (1926) by JOHN REED

5 If Socialism can only be realized when the intellectual development of all the people permits it, then we shall not see Socialism for at least five hundred years.

Speech at Peasants' Congress, Petrograd, 27 November 1917, quoted ibid., ch. 12

6 Politics begin where the masses are, not where there are thousands, but where there are millions, that is where serious politics begin.

Report to Seventh Congress of the Russian Communist Party, 7 March 1918, publ. in *Selected Works*, vol. 7 (1937)

7 All our lives we fought against exalting the individual, against the elevation of the single person, and long ago we were over and done with the business of a hero, and

here it comes up again: the glorification of one personality. This is not good at all. I am just like everybody else.

Remark after being shot in 1918, quoted in *Not By Politics Alone*, ch. 2 (1973) by Tamara Deutsche. See also NIKITA KHRUSHCHEV 2.

8 **You cannot make a revolution in white gloves.**

Lenin to Kropotkin in May 1919, quoted ibid.

9 **A good man fallen among Fabians.**

Of GEORGE BERNARD SHAW, quoted in *Six Weeks in Russia in 1919*, 'Notes of a Conversation with Lenin' (1919) by Arthur Ransome. Remark made to Arthur Ransome.

10 **You all know that even when women have full rights, they still remain fatally down-trodden because all housework is left to them. In most cases housework is the most unproductive, the most barbarous and the most arduous work a woman can do. It is exceptionally petty and does not include anything that would in any way promote the development of the woman.**

'The Tasks of the Working Women's Movement in the Soviet Republic', first publ. 1919, repr. in *Collected Works*, vol. 30 (1965)

11 **Communism is Soviet power plus the electrification of the whole country.**

Report on the Work of the Council of People's Commissars, 22 December 1920, repr. in *Collected Works*, vol. 31 (1966). The words were used as a slogan to promote the plans of the State Committee for the Electrification of Russia.

12 **It is true that liberty is precious – so precious that it must be rationed.**

Attributed in *Soviet Communism: A New Civilisation?* (1936) by Beatrice and SIDNEY WEBB

John Lennon (1940–80)
BRITISH ROCK MUSICIAN
After separating from the Beatles in 1970 he pursued a solo career in tandem with his wife YOKO ONO. His most successful albums were Imagine *(1971) and* Double Fantasy *(1980). He was murdered by a fan outside his apartment in New York. See* BONO 2, JOHN LENNON AND PAUL MCCARTNEY, YOKO ONO 4.

1 **Will people in the cheaper seats clap your hands? All the rest of you, if you'll just rattle your jewellery.**

To the audience at Royal Command Performance, London, 4 November 1963, quoted in *Shout! The True Story of the Beatles*, pt 2, 'November 1963' (1981) by Philip Norman. Lennon, here announcing the band's final number of their performance, 'Twist and Shout', had earlier warned manager Brian Epstein that he was going to ad lib if the audience proved unresponsive: 'I'll just tell 'em to rattle their fuckin' jewellery.'

2 **Christianity will go. It will vanish and**

shrink. I needn't argue with that; I'm right and I will be proved right. We're more popular than Jesus now; I don't know which will go first – rock and roll or Christianity.

Interview in the *Evening Standard* 4 March 1966. 'Jesus was all right', Lennon explained, 'but his disciples were thick and ordinary. It's them twisting it that ruins it for me.' His remarks provoked an angry reaction, especially in the USA, causing Lennon to explain himself at a press conference in Chicago, 11 August 1966: 'I'm not saying that we're better or greater, or comparing us with Jesus Christ as a person, or God as a thing, or whatever it is. I just said what I said, and it was wrong, or it was taken wrong. And now it's all this.' See also ZELDA FITZGERALD 3.

3 *Christ, you know it ain't easy,*
You know how hard it can be,
The way things are going
They're going to crucify me.

'The Ballad of John and Yoko' (song, 1969) on the album *Hey Jude* (1970) by the Beatles. The song, which was banned by some radio stations for its perceived blasphemy, is also credited to PAUL MCCARTNEY, who played piano, bass and drums on the record.

4 *All we are saying is give peace a chance.*

'Give Peace a Chance' (song) on the album *Live Peace in Toronto* (1969) by the Plastic Ono Band. The song (credited also to PAUL MCCARTNEY), was originally recorded during the eight-day 'bed-in' by Lennon and YOKO ONO in an Amsterdam hotel in May 1969, with participation by ALLEN GINSBERG and TIMOTHY LEARY, among others. It became an anthem for anti-Vietnam and other peace protesters.

5 **The Blue Meanies, or whatever they are, still preach violence all the time in every newspaper, every TV show and every magazine. The least Yoko and I can do is hog the headlines and make people laugh. We're quite willing to be the world's clowns if it will do any good. For reasons known only to themselves, people print what I say. And I say 'peace'.**

Quoted in *Shout! The True Story of the Beatles*, pt 4, 'May 1969' (1981) by Philip Norman. On the peace campaign waged by Lennon and YOKO ONO.

6 **Lots of people who complained about us receiving the MBE received theirs for heroism in the war – for killing people. We received ours for entertaining other people. I'd say we deserve ours more.**

Quoted in *Beatles Illustrated Lyrics*, vol. 1 (ed. Alan Aldridge, 1969)

7 *A working class hero is something to be*
If you want to be a hero then just follow me.

'Working Class Hero' (song) on the album *John Lennon/Plastic Ono Band* (1970) by John Lennon and the Plastic Ono Band

8 *God is a concept by which we measure our pain.*
'God' (song) on ibid.

9 **You have to be a bastard to make it, and that's a fact. And the Beatles are the biggest bastards on earth.**
Interview in *Lennon Remembers* (ed. Jann Wenner, 1970)

10 *Imagine there's no heaven,*
It's easy if you try,
No hell below us,
Above us only sky,
Imagine all the people
Living for today.
'Imagine' (song) on the album *Imagine* (1971)

11 **One has to completely humiliate oneself to be what the Beatles were, and that's what I resent. I didn't know, I didn't foresee. It happened bit by bit, gradually, until this complete craziness is surrounding you, and you're doing exactly what you don't want to do with people you can't stand – the people you hated when you were ten.**
Interview in *Rolling Stone* 7 January 1971

12 **We were all on this ship in the sixties, our generation, a ship going to discover the New World. And the Beatles were in the crow's nest of that ship.**
Interview for French TV, March 1974, publ. in *Imagine* (ed. Andrew Solt and Sam Egan, 1988)

13 **New York is what Paris was in the twenties . . . the centre of the art world. And we want to be in the centre. It's the greatest place on earth . . . I've got a lot of friends here and I even brought my own cash.**
The Tomorrow Show, NBC-TV, April 1975 publ. ibid. Lennon was given his long-awaited green card (residency permit) in the USA the following year.

14 *Life is what happens to you while you're busy making other plans.*
'Beautiful Boy' (song) on the album *Starting Over* (1980). The line has also been attributed to Betty Talmadge (divorced wife of Senator Herman Talmadge) and Thomas La Mance (unknown).

15 **My defences were so great. The cocky rock and roll hero who knows all the answers was actually a terrified guy who didn't know how to cry. Simple.**
Interview in *Playboy* September 1980

16 **I've had the boyhood thing of being Elvis. Now I want to be with my best friend, and my best friend's my wife. Who could ask for anything more?**
Interview for KFRC RKO Radio (San Francisco), 8 December 1980, the day of Lennon's murder, publ. in *Imagine* (ed. Andrew Solt and Sam Egan, 1988)

17 **My role in society, or any artist or poet's**
role, is to try and express what we all feel. Not to tell people how to feel. Not as a preacher, not as a leader, but as a reflection of us all.
Ibid.

18 **It's amazing how low you go to get high.**
Skywriting by Word of Mouth, 'The Art of Deception is in the Eye of the Beholder' (ed. Yoko Ono, 1986)

John Lennon (1940–80) and Paul McCartney (b. 1942)
BRITISH ROCK MUSICIANS
Hailed by the critic William Mann as the most important songwriters since Schubert, they co-wrote most of the songs recorded by the Beatles, Lennon's mordant and surreal wit a foil for McCartney's pop sensibility. See also JOHN LENNON *and* PAUL MCCARTNEY.

1 *She loves you, yeh, yeh, yeh.*
'She Loves You' (song, 1963) on the album *A Collection of Beatles Oldies (But Goldies)* (1966) by the Beatles. The song was the group's all-time top-selling UK single.

2 *It's been a hard day's night,*
And I've been working like a dog.
'A Hard Day's Night' (song) on the album *A Hard Day's Night* (1964) by the Beatles. The phrase 'hard day's night' originated with RINGO STARR's comment on a heavy schedule shooting the film which was later given this title. It was called a typical 'Ringoism' by John Lennon, who also used the words in his book, *In His Own Write*.

3 *I don't care too much for money,*
For money can't buy me love.
'Can't Buy Me Love' (song) on ibid.

4 *She's got a ticket to ride, but she don't care.*
'Ticket to Ride' (song) on the album *Help!* (1965) by the Beatles

5 *Yesterday, all my troubles seemed so far away,*
Now it looks as though they're here to stay.
Oh I believe in yesterday.
'Yesterday' (song) on ibid. The song, wholly written by McCartney and originally entitled 'Scrambled Eggs' ('. . . Oh my baby how I love your legs'), became the most covered song in history.

6 *He's a real nowhere man*
Sitting in his nowhere land
Making all his nowhere plans for nobody.
'Nowhere Man' (song) on the album *Rubber Soul* (1966) by the Beatles

7 *Waits at the window,*
Wearing the face that she keeps in a jar by the door.
Who is it for?
'Eleanor Rigby' (song) on the album *Revolver* (1966) by the Beatles. For novelist A. S. BYATT,

the lyric has 'the minimalist perfection of a Beckett story'.

8 *We all live in a yellow submarine.*
'Yellow Submarine' (song) on ibid.

9 *The Magical Mystery Tour*
Is coming to take you away.
'Magical Mystery Tour' (song) on TV film and album *Magical Mystery Tour* (1967) by the Beatles

10 *What do you see when you turn out the light?*
I can't tell you but I know it's mine.
Oh, I get by with a little help from my friends.
'With a Little Help from my Friends' (song) on the album *Sgt. Pepper's Lonely Hearts Club Band* (1967) by the Beatles

11 *I've got to admit it's getting better.*
'Getting Better' (song) on ibid.

12 *Will you still need me,*
Will you still feed me,
When I'm sixty-four?
'When I'm Sixty-four' (song) on ibid.

13 *I heard the news today, oh boy.*
Four thousand holes in Blackburn Lancashire.
And though the holes were rather small,
They had to count them all.
'A Day in the Life' (song) on ibid.

14 *I'd love to turn you on.*
Ibid.

15 *All you need is love.*
'All You Need is Love' (song, 1967) on the album *Yellow Submarine* (1969) by the Beatles. The song was written specially for 'Our World', the first worldwide satellite TV broadcast, 25 July 1967, in which it was performed and transmitted live to 400 million viewers. The words were used as the title of both a book and TV documentary by Tony Palmer charting the history of popular music (1976).

16 *When I hold you in my arms*
And I feel my finger on your trigger
I know no one can do me no harm
Because happiness is a warm gun.
'Happiness is a Warm Gun' (song), on *The Beatles* (1968). The title was inspired by an advertising slogan for the National Rifle Association in the USA.

17 *And in the end, the love you take*
Is equal to the love you make.
'The End' (song), on the album *Abbey Road* (1970) by the Beatles. Lennon once called these the best lines McCartney had ever written.

Annie Lennox (b. 1954)
BRITISH SINGER
Born Griselda Anne Lennox. Her powerful voice

helped to make the Eurythmics one of the most successful bands of the 1980s.

1 *Sisters are doing it for themselves,*
Standing on their own two feet,
Ringing on their own bells.
'Sisters Are Doing It For Themselves' (song, written by Dave Stewart) on the album *Be Yourself Tonight* (1985) by the Eurythmics. Sung as a duet with soul diva ARETHA FRANKLIN.

2 **There are two kinds of artists left: those who endorse Pepsi and those who simply won't.**
Guardian 30 November 1990

(Sir) Graham Leonard (b. 1921)
BRITISH ECCLESIASTIC
He argued against the proposed unification of Anglicans and Methodists in the 1970s, and as Bishop of London (1981–91) opposed the ordination of women to the priesthood. He converted to Roman Catholicism in 1994.

1 **The purpose of population is not ultimately peopling earth. It is to fill heaven.**
Speech to Church of England Synod, 10 February 1983, quoted in the *Observer* 13 February 1983

Alan Jay Lerner (1918–86)
US SONGWRITER
He collaborated with Frederick Loewe to produce Broadway musicals such as Paint Your Wagon *(1951, filmed 1969),* My Fair Lady *(1956, filmed 1964) and the film* Gigi *(1958). See also* MAURICE CHEVALIER 1.

1 *Wouldn't it be loverly . . .*
'Wouldn't it be Loverly?' (song) in *My Fair Lady* (stage show 1956, film 1964). Sung by Eliza Doolittle.

2 *The rain in Spain stays mainly in the plain.*
'The Rain in Spain' (song) ibid. The words are a phonetic exercise devised by Henry Higgins for Eliza Doolittle.

3 *I could have danced all night.*
'I Could Have Danced All Night' (song) ibid. Sung by Eliza Doolittle.

4 *I'm getting married in the morning,*
Ding! dong! the bells are gonna chime.
Pull out the stopper;
Let's have a whopper;
But get me to the church on time!
'Get Me to the Church on Time' (song) ibid. Sung by Alfred Doolittle.

5 *Ask every person if he's heard the story,*
And tell it strong and clear if he has not,
That once there was a fleeting wisp of glory
Called Camelot . . .
Don't let it be forgot
That once there was a spot
For one brief shining moment that was known
As Camelot.
'Camelot' (song), in *Camelot* (musical show

1960, film 1967). The song was named by JACQUELINE KENNEDY in an interview shortly after JOHN F. KENNEDY's assassination as having had particular significance for her husband's presidency: 'Camelot had suddenly become the symbol of those thousand days when people the world over saw a bright new light of hope shining from the White House. For myself, I have never been able to see a performance of *Camelot* again.' Official Kennedy biographer William Manchester called his book *One Brief Shining Moment* (1983).

Max Lerner (1902–92)
RUSSIAN-BORN US JOURNALIST, AUTHOR AND ACADEMIC
Born Mikhail Lerner. His liberal views were aired in his articles for The Nation *(which he edited 1936–8) and other periodicals, and in his* New York Post *columns (from 1949). He taught political science and published books on diverse subjects.*

1 A President is best judged by the enemies he makes when he has really hit his stride.
'The Education of Harry Truman', first publ. in the *New York Post* 9 January 1949, repr. in *The Unfinished Country*, pt 4 (1959)

2 There is a hate layer of opinion and emotion in America. There will be other McCarthys to come who will be hailed as its heroes.
'McCarthyism: The Smell of Decay', first publ. in the *New York Post* 5 April 1950, repr. ibid. pt 4. The article saw the first coining of the word 'McCarthyism', as Lerner affirmed in a later column, 3 February 1954, in which he commented: 'For my own part I doubt seriously whether the word will outlast the political power of the man from whom it derives.'

3 Having a thirteen-year-old in the family is like having a general-admission ticket to the movies, radio and TV. You get to understand that the glittering new arts of our civilization are directed to the teenagers, and by their suffrage they stand or fall.
'Teen-ager', first publ. in the *New York Post* 4 June 1952, repr. ibid., pt 1

4 The real sadness of fifty is not that you change so much but that you change so little.
'Fifty', first publ. in the *New York Post* 18 December 1952, repr. ibid., pt 1

5 The crime of book purging is that it involves a rejection of the word. For the word is never absolute truth, but only man's frail and human effort to approach the truth. To reject the word is to reject the human search.
'The Vigilantes and the Chain of Fear', first publ. in the *New York Post* 24 June 1953, repr.

ibid., pt 4. Referring to the McCarthy book burnings.

6 I am neither an optimist nor pessimist, but a possibilist.
Entry in *Who's Who in America* (1992)

Doris Lessing (b. 1919)
BRITISH NOVELIST
Brought up in Rhodesia, she moved to London in 1949 where she published her first novel The Grass is Singing *(1950), a study of interracial relationships in Africa. Subsequent works include* The Golden Notebook *(1962), considered a milestone of feminist literature.*

1 When old settlers say 'One has to understand the country,' what they mean is, 'You have to get used to our ideas about the native.' They are saying, in effect, 'Learn our ideas, or otherwise get out; we don't want you.'
The Grass is Singing, ch. 1 (1950)

2 It is terrible to destroy a person's picture of himself in the interests of truth or some other abstraction.
Ibid., ch. 2

3 If a fish is the movement of water embodied, given shape, then cat is a diagram and pattern of subtle air.
Particularly Cats, ch. 2 (1967)

4 What is charm then? The free giving of a grace, the spending of something given by nature in her role of spendthrift . . . something extra, superfluous, unnecessary, essentially a power thrown away.
Ibid., ch. 9

5 This world is run by people who know how to do things. They know how things work. They are *equipped*. Up there, there's a layer of people who run everything. But we – we're just peasants. We don't understand what's going on, and we can't do anything.
Dorothy, in *The Good Terrorist* (1985)

6 Space or science fiction has become a dialect for our time.
Guardian 7 November 1988

7 The great secret that all old people share is that you really haven't changed in seventy or eighty years. Your body changes, but you don't change at all. And that, of course, causes great confusion.
Sunday Times 10 May 1992

8 Political correctness is the natural continuum from the party line. What we are seeing once again is a self-appointed group of vigilantes imposing their views on others. It is a heritage of communism, but they don't seem to see this.
Ibid.

Kathy Lette (b. 1958)
AUSTRALIAN NOVELIST

Her books, including Girls' Night Out *(1988) and* Nip 'n' Tuck *(2001), are rapid-fire wisecracking tales of independent women. 'I like a female character who's got a bit of armpit stubble and occasionally goes for gold in the hypocrisy olympics,' she declared.*

1 I didn't 'fall' pregnant! I was bloody well pushed.

Madeline Wolfe, in *Foetal Attraction*, pt 1, 'First Stage' (1993)

2 I speak as your native guide to the mysterious tribe called the English. Dress code is everything. You can be a card-carrying Nazi, you can pay gigolos to eat gnocchi out of your navel and you won't be pilloried – as long as you never, ever wear linen with tweed.

Gillian Cassells, ibid., pt 1, 'A New Taste Sensation'

3 What a woman needs is to marry a rich old boy, the sort of human handbag you can put down by the door at parties and pick up on the way home for the cab fare. With a complementary toy boy on the side.

Ibid.

4 All this male angst over size. It's *attitude* women are interested in. Women like a penis which says, 'G'day! God, am I glad to see *you*.'

Maddy, in *Mad Cows*, ch. 10 (1996)

Oscar Levant (1906–72)
US PIANIST AND COMPOSER

Witty and eccentric, he was a respected interpreter of Gershwin and wrote film scores for Hollywood in the 1920s and '30s. He appeared as himself in the films Rhapsody in Blue *(1945) and* An American in Paris *(1951).*

1 Epigram: a wisecrack that played Carnegie Hall.

Coronet Magazine September 1958

2 Strip away the phony tinsel of Hollywood and you find the real tinsel underneath.

Inquisition in Eden (1965)

Leslie Lever (1903–77)
BRITISH SOLICITOR AND POLITICIAN

Baron Lever of Ardwick. He was senior partner in Leslie Lever and Co., Lord Mayor of Manchester (1957–8) and Labour MP for the Ardwick division of Manchester (1950–70).

1 Generosity is a part of my character, and I therefore hasten to assure this Government that I will never make an allegation of dishonesty against it wherever a simple explanation of stupidity will suffice.

Speech to House of Commons, quoted in *The Fine Art of Political Wit*, ch. 12 (1964) by Leon Harris

Denise Levertov (b. 1923)
BRITISH-BORN US POET

She came under the influence of WILLIAM CARLOS WILLIAMS *and the Black Mountain poets in the 1950s and was later active in anti-Vietnam War protests. Her collections include* With Eyes at the Back of Our Heads *(1959) and* Footprints *(1972).*

1 *Two by two in the ark of*
   the ache of it.

'The Ache of Marriage', publ. in *O Taste and See* (1964)

2 *If woman is inconstant,*
   good, I am faithful to
   ebb and flow, I fall
   in season and now
   is a time of ripening.

'Stepping Westward', publ. in *The Sorrow Dance* (1967)

Carlo Levi (1902–75)
ITALIAN AUTHOR AND PAINTER

His first and most successful novel, Christ Stopped at Eboli *(1945, filmed 1979), was based on his experience of internment during the Second World War as a consequence of his anti-fascist activities. Later works include* The Linden Tree *(1959).*

1 Christ never came this far, nor did time, nor the individual soul, nor hope, nor the relation of cause to effect, nor reason nor history.

Christ Stopped at Eboli, ch. 1 (1945). Referring to Basilicata, in southern Italy. The book was the first to publicize the true plight of the Italian south.

2 We always find tedious places, languid and dark places, in books, in the best books. And especially in paintings, which are mythical landscapes of the soul, no matter what subject they represent, and cannot be without intricate pathless woods, without swamps, without this idle and nocturnal tedium.

The Watch, ch. 3, sect. 2 (1950)

3 Here in Italy every tree, every stone in the street has a history, something's happened, perhaps a thousand years ago, but there's always someone who remembers it or has heard about it and can tell you about it. Over there a tree is a tree, a stone is a stone, and a man is nothing but a man. They are honest and simple but you might feel that something is missing.

Ibid., ch. 9, sect. 2

Primo Levi (1919–87)

ITALIAN CHEMIST AND AUTHOR

His survival of the concentration camp at Ausch-
witz was a constant theme in his books, and
formed the basis for his autobiographical trilogy
beginning with If This Is a Man *(1947). His scien-*
tific background was evident in most of his works,
for example The Periodic Table *(1975).*

1 *Consider whether this is a man,*
   Who labours in the mud
   Who knows no peace
   Who fights for a crust of bread
   Who dies at a yes or a no.
   'Shemà', written 1946, publ. in *Shemà: Collected*
   Poems of Primo Levi (1976)

2 Sooner or later in life everyone discovers
   that perfect happiness is unrealizable, but
   there are few who pause to consider the
   antithesis: that perfect unhappiness is
   equally unattainable. The obstacles preventing the realization of both these
   extreme states are of the same nature: they
   derive from our human condition which is
   opposed to everything infinite.
   If This Is a Man, ch. 1 (1947)

3 But consider what value, what meaning is
   enclosed even in the smallest of our daily
   habits, in the hundred possessions which
   even the poorest beggar owns: a handkerchief, an old letter, the photo of a cherished person. These things are part of us,
   almost like limbs of our body; nor is it conceivable that we can be deprived of them
   in our world, for we immediately find
   others to substitute the old ones, other
   objects which are ours in their personification and evocation of our memories.
   Ibid., ch. 2

4 For me chemistry represented an indefinite
   cloud of future potentialities which envel-
   oped my life to come in black volutes
   torn by fiery flashes, like those which had
   hidden Mount Sinai. Like Moses, from that
   cloud I expected my law, the principle of
   order in me, around me, and in the world.
   . . . I would watch the buds swell in spring,
   the mica glint in the granite, my own
   hands, and I would say to myself: 'I will
   understand this, too, I will understand
   everything.'
   The Periodic Table, 'Hydrogen' (1975)

5 In order for the wheel to turn, for life to
   be lived, impurities are needed, and the
   impurities of impurities in the soil, too, as
   is known, if it is to be fertile. Dissension,
   diversity, the grain of salt and mustard are
   needed: Fascism does not want them, forbids them, and that's why you're not a Fascist; it wants everybody to be the same,
   and you are not. But immaculate virtue

does not exist either, or if it exists it is
detestable.
Ibid., 'Zinc'

6 *Every man is the enemy*
      of every other,
   With everyone split by an inner border,
   The right hand enemy of the left.
   On your feet, old men, enemies of your-
      selves:
   Our war is never over.
   'Partisan', written 1981, publ. in *Collected Poems*
   (1988)

7 The future of humanity is uncertain, even
   in the most prosperous countries, and the
   quality of life deteriorates; and yet I believe
   that what is being discovered about the
   infinitely large and infinitely small is
   sufficient to absolve this end of the century
   and millennium. What a very few are
   acquiring in knowledge of the physical
   world will perhaps cause this period not to
   be judged as a pure return of barbarism.
   Other People's Trades, 'News from The Sky'
   (1985)

8 To be considered stupid and to be told so
   is more painful than being called glutton-
   ous, mendacious, violent, lascivious, lazy,
   cowardly: every weakness, every vice, has
   found its defenders, its rhetoric, its
   ennoblement and exaltation, but stupidity
   hasn't.
   Ibid., 'The Irritable Chess-players'

9 The bond between a man and his profession is similar to that which ties him
   to his country; it is just as complex, often
   ambivalent, and in general it is understood
   completely only when it is broken: by exile
   or emigration in the case of one's country,
   by retirement in the case of a trade or profession.
   Ibid., 'Ex-Chemist'

10 Anyone who has obeyed nature by transmitting a piece of gossip experiences the
   explosive relief that accompanies the
   satisfying of a primary need.
   'About Gossip', first publ. in *La Stampa* 24 June
   1986, repr. in *The Mirror Maker* (1989)

11 The aims of life are the best defence
   against death.
   The Drowned and the Saved, ch. 6 (1988)

Bernard Levin (b. 1928)

BRITISH JOURNALIST AND CRITIC

He has written political commentary and criticism
for numerous newspapers and magazines, and has
also been a radio scriptwriter and broadcaster. His
books include The Way We Live Now *(1984).*

1 In every age of transition men are never so
   firmly bound to one way of life as when

they are about to abandon it, so that fanaticism and intolerance reach their most intense forms just before tolerance and mutual acceptance come to be the natural order of things.

The Pendulum Years, ch. 4 (1970). Referring to John Profumo, 'the last victim of the old, unpermissive standards'.

2 Between them, then, Walrus and Carpenter, they divided up the Sixties.

Ibid., ch. 12. Referring to HAROLD MACMILLAN and HAROLD WILSON.

Emmanuel Levinas (1905–95)
FRENCH PHILOSOPHER

He is regarded as one of the foremost exponents of the work of Husserl, and an influence on SARTRE *and* DERRIDA. *His philosophy of ethics is explained in* Existence and Existents *(1947) and* Totality and Infinity *(1961), among other works.*

1 If the 1945 victory demonstrates that in history, vice is ultimately punished and virtue recognized, we do not wish once more to bear the brunt of this demonstration.

'The Diary of Leon Brunschvicg', first publ. 1949, repr. in *Difficult Freedom*, pt 1 (1990)

2 The faith that moves mountains and conceives of a world without slaves immediately transports itself to utopia, separating the reign of God from the reign of Caesar. This reassures Caesar.

'Place and Utopia', first publ. 1950, repr. ibid., pt 3

3 Evil is not a mystical principle that can be effaced by a ritual, it is an offence perpetrated on man by man. No one, not even God, can substitute himself for the victim.

'A Religion for Adults', first publ. 1957, repr. ibid., pt 1

4 Monotheism has not only a horror of idols, but a nose for false prophecy. A special patience – Judaism – is required to refuse all premature messianic claims.

'Judaism and the Present', first publ. 1969, repr. ibid., pt 5

Joseph E. Levine (1905–87)
US FILM PRODUCER AND EXECUTIVE

He was known for his use of intensive advertising and saturation booking, and for importing European films. He also produced his own films, including The Carpetbaggers *(1963).*

1 You can fool all the people all the time if the advertising is right and the budget is big enough.

Quoted in *Halliwell's Who's Who in the Movies* (ed. John Walker, 1999)

Claude Lévi-Strauss (b. 1908)
FRENCH ANTHROPOLOGIST

Defining his position as one of 'serene pessimism', he formulated the principles of structuralism through his studies of kinship, myth and religion. His theories are set down in Mythologies *(4 vols.) 1964–71).*

1 Being human signifies, for each one of us, belonging to a class, a society, a country, a continent and a civilization.

Tristes tropiques, ch. 38 (1955)

2 The world began without man, and it will end without him.

Ibid., ch. 40

3 Language is a form of human reason, which has its internal logic of which man knows nothing.

The Savage Mind, ch. 9 (1962)

4 The scientific mind does not so much provide *the right answers as ask the right questions.*

The Raw and the Cooked, 'Overture' (1964)

5 I therefore claim to show, not how men think in myths, but how myths operate in men's minds without their being aware of the fact.

Ibid.

6 Since music is a language with some meaning at least for the immense majority of mankind, although only a tiny minority of people are capable of formulating a meaning in it, and since it is the only language with the contradictory attributes of being at once intelligible and untranslatable, the musical creator is a being comparable to the gods, and music itself the supreme mystery of the science of man, a mystery that all the various disciplines come up against and which holds the key to their progress.

Ibid.

7 Journeys, those magic caskets full of dreamlike promises, will never again yield up their treasures untarnished. . . . The first thing we see as we travel around the world is our own filth, thrown into the face of mankind.

Quoted in the *Independent on Sunday* 4 August 1991

Bernard-Henri Lévy (b. 1948)
FRENCH PHILOSOPHER

As a 'New Philosopher', he came to the forefront of radical French thought in the mid-1970s. His Barbarism with a Human Face *(1977) was a denunciation of Marxism.*

1 The only successful revolution of this century is totalitarianism.

Time 12 September 1977

2 I think enthusiasm is one of the worst

temptations for an intellectual. It is almost a rule that when intellectuals enthuse, they are wrong.
International Herald Tribune 21 January 1991

3 Between the barbarity of capitalism, which censures itself much of the time, and the barbarity of socialism, which does not, I guess I would choose capitalism.
Quoted in the *Independent on Sunday* 31 March 1991

Monica Lewinsky (b. 1973)
US FORMER WHITE HOUSE AIDE
She was catapulted to fame over her sexual relationship with President CLINTON, *begun in 1995, testifying at the Senate Hearing Committee in 1998.*

1 I would just like to say that no one ever asked me to lie, and I was never promised a job for my silence. And I am sorry, I'm really sorry for everything that's happened. And I hate Linda Tripp.
Concluding her evidence to the Grand Jury, quoted in the *Daily Telegraph* 23 September 1998. Linda Tripp was a colleague at the White House who taped Lewinsky's confidences regarding her affair with President CLINTON.

C. S. Lewis (1898–1963)
BRITISH AUTHOR
Clive Staples Lewis. He published more than forty works on Christian subjects, notably the satirical Screwtape Letters *(1942). Christian allegory also runs through his classic series for children* The Chronicles of Narnia *(1950–56) and his works of science fiction.*

1 There are two equal and opposite errors into which our race can fall about the devils. One is to disbelieve in their existence. The other is to believe, and to feel an excessive and unhealthy interest in them. They themselves are equally pleased by both errors and hail a materialist or a magician with the same delight.
The Screwtape Letters, Preface (1942)

2 The safest road to Hell is the gradual one – the gentle slope, soft underfoot, without sudden turnings, without milestones, without signposts.
Screwtape, ibid., 'Letter 12'

3 Much of the modern resistance to chastity comes from men's belief that they 'own' their bodies – those vast and perilous estates, pulsating with the energy that made the worlds, in which they find themselves without their consent and from which they are ejected at the pleasure of Another!
Ibid., 'Letter 21'

4 Courage is not simply *one* of the virtues

but the form of every virtue at the testing point, which means at the point of highest reality.
Quoted in *The Unquiet Grave*, pt 3 (1944, rev. 1951) by CYRIL CONNOLLY

5 I remember summing up what I took to be our destiny, in conversation with my best friend at Chartres, by the formula, 'Term, holidays, term, holidays, till we leave school, and then work, work, work till we die.'
Surprised by Joy, ch. 4 (1955)

6 Literary experience heals the wound, without undermining the privilege, of individuality. There are mass emotions which heal the wound; but they destroy the privilege. . . . Like a night sky in the Greek poem, I see with a myriad eyes, but it is still I who see. Here, as in worship, in love, in moral action, and in knowing, I transcend myself; and am never more myself than when I do.
An Experiment in Criticism (1961). Last words of book.

7 No one ever told me that grief felt so like fear.
A Grief Observed, pt 1 (1961). Opening words of book of mourning for Lewis's dead wife. Their affair and marriage, her death from cancer and his bereavement were recounted in *Shadowlands*, a play (1979), TV film (1985) and film for the cinema (1993).

8 It is hard to have patience with people who say 'There is no death' or 'Death doesn't matter.' There is death. And whatever is matters. And whatever happens has consequences, and it and they are irrevocable and irreversible. You might as well say that birth doesn't matter.
Ibid.

9 Talk to me about the truth of religion and I'll listen gladly. Talk to me about the duty of religion and I'll listen submissively. But don't come talking to me about the consolations of religion or I shall suspect that you don't understand.
Ibid., pt 2

10 There is, hidden or flaunted, a sword between the sexes till an entire marriage reconciles them.
Ibid., pt 3

11 If, as I can't help suspecting, the dead also feel the pains of separation (and this may be one of their purgatorial sufferings), then for both lovers, and for all pairs of lovers without exception, bereavement is a universal and integral part of our experience of love.
Ibid.

12 Can a mortal ask questions which God finds unanswerable? Quite easily, I should

think. All nonsense questions are unanswerable.

Ibid., pt 4

Jerry Lee Lewis (b. 1935)

US ROCK MUSICIAN

His piano-pounding on 'Whole Lotta Shakin' Going On' and 'Great Balls of Fire' (both 1957) caught the public imagination, although his career was set back by the scandal surrounding his marriage to his fourteen-year-old cousin in 1958.

1 You shake my nerves and you rattle my
    brain.
   Too much love drives a man insane.
   You broke my will, but what a thrill.
   Goodness gracious, great balls of fire!

'Great Balls of Fire' (song, 1957, written by Jack Hammer and Otis Blackwell) on the album *The Golden Hits of Jerry Lee Lewis* (1964). *Great Balls of Fire!* was the title of a 1989 film based on his life.

2 I'm not putting Elvis down, but he was a
    shitass, a yellow belly, and I hated the
    fucker.

Said in 1988, quoted in the *New Musical Express* 4 February 1995

Sinclair Lewis (1885–1951)

US NOVELIST

He caused a sensation with his first novel Main Street *(1920), an exposé of small-town life in the Midwest, and continued in the same satirical vein with* Babbitt *(1922),* Arrowsmith *(1925) and* Elmer Gantry *(1927). In 1930 he was the first American to be awarded the Nobel Prize for Literature.*

1 In other countries, art and literature are
   left to a lot of shabby bums living in attics
   and feeding on booze and spaghetti, but in
   America the successful writer or picture-
   painter is indistinguishable from any other
   decent businessman.

George Follansbee Babbitt, in *Babbitt*, ch. 14, sect. 3 (1922). Addressing the Zenith Real Estate Board.

2 Damn the great executives, the men of
   measured merriment, damn the men with
   careful smiles, damn the men that run the
   shops, oh, damn their measured merriment.

Martin Arrowsmith, in *Arrowsmith*, ch. 25 (1925)

3 Our American professors like their literature clear and cold and pure and very
   dead.

Speech to Swedish Academy in Stockholm, 12 December 1930, on accepting the Nobel Prize for Literature, quoted in *Literature 1901–1967* (1969) by H. Frenz

(Percy) Wyndham Lewis (1882–1957)

BRITISH AUTHOR AND PAINTER

He was a leader of the Vorticist school of abstract painting and served as a war artist in the First World War. His writings include the satires The Apes of God *(1930) and* The Revenge for Love *(1937). His reputation suffered on account of his pro-Fascist sympathies, later recanted. 'I do not think I had ever seen a nastier-looking man,'* ERNEST HEMINGWAY *remembered. 'Under the black hat, when I had first seen them, the eyes had been those of an unsuccessful rapist.'*

1 If you do not regard feminism with an
   uplifting sense of the gloriousness of
   woman's industrial destiny, or in the way,
   in short, that it is prescribed, by the rules
   of the political publicist, that you should,
   that will be interpreted by your opponents
   as an attack on *woman*.

The Art of Being Ruled, 'The Family and Feminism', sect. 6 (1926)

2 Almost anything that can be praised or
   advocated has been put to some disgusting
   use. There is no principle, however
   immaculate, that has not had its compromising manipulator.

Ibid., sect. 8

3 The ideas of a time are like the clothes of a
   season: they are as arbitrary, as much
   imposed by some superior will which is seldom explicit. They are utilitarian and political, the instruments of smooth-running
   government.

Ibid., 'Beyond Action and Reaction', sect. 3

4 We are the first men of a Future that has
    not materialized. We belong to a 'great age'
    that has not 'come off'. We moved too
    quickly for the world. We set too sharp a
    pace.

Blasting and Bombardiering, pt 5, 'The Period of "Ulysses", "Blast", "The Waste Land" ' (1937)

5 I feel most at home in the United States,
   not because it is intrinsically a more interesting country, but because no one really
   belongs there any more than I do. We are
   all there together in its wholly excellent
   vacuum.

America and Cosmic Man, 'The Case Against Roots' (1948)

Liberace (1919–87)

US ENTERTAINER

Originally Wladziu Valentino Liberace. With his rhinestones, candelabra, gold lamé and coiffed hair, he played romantic arrangements of popular classics. Cassandra of the Daily Mail *called him 'a superb piece of calculating candyfloss'.*

1 When the reviews are bad I tell my staff

that they can join me as I cry all the way to the bank.

Liberace: An Autobiography, ch. 2. (1973). The catch-phrase 'I cried all the way to the bank' was used in Liberace's stage act from the 1950s.

R. M. Lindner (1914–56)

US NOVELIST

Robert Mitchell Lindner. Among his books are Rebel without a Cause: the Hypnoanalysis of a Criminal Psychopath *(1944) and* Must You Conform? *(1956).*

1 **Rebel without a Cause.**

Title of book (1944, filmed 1955). The phrase is most associated with the film's star James Dean, whose role was touted in the publicity as 'the bad boy from a good family'.

Maureen Lipman (b. 1946)

BRITISH COMEDY ACTRESS

Her performances on stage include the one-woman show Re: Joyce *(1988) about* JOYCE GRENFELL. *She appears regularly on television and writes magazine columns and humorous books.*

1 **Men are . . . a mystery. After all, they spit, they punch, they scream, they rant, they kick each other when they're down and think nothing of putting their hands down their shorts and fiddling about. Of course, if they did it in the street they'd be arrested – but if they do it on a pitch they're worth £7 million!**

You Can Read Me Like a Book, ch. 6 (1995)

Walter Lippmann (1889–1974)

US JOURNALIST

The newspaper column was for him 'the laboratory or clinic in which I test the philosophy and keep it from becoming too abstract'. His daily columns were syndicated through the New York Herald Tribune, *and in 1962 he won the Pulitzer Prize for international reporting.*

1 **The great social adventure of America is no longer the conquest of the wilderness but the absorption of fifty different peoples.**

A Preface to Politics, ch. 6 (1914)

2 **The best servants of the people, like the best valets, must whisper unpleasant truths in the master's ear. It is the court fool, not the foolish courtier, whom the king can least afford to lose.**

Ibid., ch. 6

3 **In making the great experiment of governing people by consent rather than by coercion, it is not sufficient that the party in power should have a majority. It is just as necessary that the party in power should never outrage the minority.**

'The Indispensable Opposition', publ. in the

Atlantic Monthly (1939), repr. in *The Essential Lippmann*, pt 6, sect. 2 (ed. Clinton Rossiter and James Lare, 1982)

4 **The final test of a leader is that he leaves behind him in other men the conviction and the will to carry on.**

'Roosevelt Is Gone', first publ. in the *New York Herald Tribune* 14 April 1945, repr. ibid. pt 10, sect. 5. 'The genius of a good leader,' Lippmann added, 'is to leave behind him a situation which common sense, without the grace of genius, can deal with successfully.'

5 **When distant and unfamiliar and complex things are communicated to great masses of people, the truth suffers a considerable and often a radical distortion. The complex is made over into the simple, the hypothetical into the dogmatic, and the relative into an absolute.**

The Public Philosophy ch. 2, sect. 3 (1955)

6 **Successful democratic politicians are insecure and intimidated men. They advance politically only as they placate, appease, bribe, seduce, bamboozle, or otherwise manage to manipulate the demanding and threatening elements in their constituencies.**

Ibid., sect. 4

Little Richard (b. 1932)

US ROCK 'N' ROLL MUSICIAN

Originally Richard Penniman. Raised a Seventh-Day Adventist in Georgia, he had one of the most powerful voices in rock 'n' roll, coupled with an outrageously camp stage presence. A run of hit singles, including 'Tutti-Frutti' (1955) and 'Long Tall Sally' (1956), ended when he turned to religion.

1 *Awop-bop-a-loo-mop alop-bam-boom!*

'Tutti-Frutti' (song, 1955, written with J. Lubin and Dorothy La Bostrie) on the album *Here's Little Richard* (1957)

2 **The Girl Can't Help It.**

Song title (1956, written by BOBBY TROUP) on ibid. The title was also used for what has been called the best rock 'n' roll film ever (1956), in which Little Richard made an explosive cameo performance.

Joan Littlewood (1914–2002)

BRITISH THEATRE DIRECTOR

With EWAN MACCOLL *she set up the Theatre Union in the 1930s and Theatre Workshop in 1945, based in London's Stratford East from 1953. Her experimental techniques were acclaimed in such productions as* The Good Soldier Schweik *(1955).*

1 **Oh What a Lovely War!**

Song and title of stage show (1963, filmed 1969, written with Charles Chilton and Gerry Raffles)

Liu Shao-Ch'i (1898–1969)
CHINESE LEADER
He was elected to China's politburo in 1934, and in 1959 rose to become Chairman of the People's Republic of China. His recovery programme following the failure of the Great Leap Forward was denounced, and in 1967 he was stripped of his post.

1 There is no such thing as a perfect leader either in the past or present, in China or elsewhere. If there is one, he is only pretending, like a pig inserting scallions into its nose in an effort to look like an elephant.
   Remark, 13 July 1947, quoted in *Mao and China: From Revolution to Revolution*, ch. 4 (1972) by Stanley Karnow

Penelope Lively (b. 1933)
BRITISH NOVELIST
A vivid sense of the past and of place pervades her writing, both in her work for children and in her adult fiction. Notable are her children's book The Ghost of Thomas Kempe *(1973) and the memoir* Oleander, Jacaranda *(1994).*

1 Wars are fought by children. Conceived by their mad demonic elders, and fought by boys.
   Moontiger, ch. 8 (1987)

2 I believe that the experience of childhood is irretrievable. All that remains, for any of us, is a headful of brilliant frozen moments, already dangerously distorted by the wisdoms of maturity.
   Oleander, Jacaranda, Preface (1994)

Ken Livingstone (b. 1945)
BRITISH POLITICIAN AND MAYOR
The left-wing leader of the Greater London Council (1981–6), he was elected Labour MP for Brent East, London in 1987. He was expelled from the Labour Party when he ran as an independent candidate for the London mayoral election in 2000, which he won.

1 What a squalid and irresponsible little profession it is. . . . Nothing prepares you for how bad Fleet Street really is until it craps on you from a great height.
   Quoted in *City Limits* 1 May 1986.

2 The problem is that many MPs never see the London that exists beyond the wine bars and brothels of Westminster.
   The Times 19 February 1987

3 Anybody who enjoys being in the House of Commons probably needs psychiatric care.
   Evening Standard 26 February 1988

4 Politics is a marathon not a sprint.
   New Statesman 10 October 1997

5 You can judge politicians by how they treat refugees; they do to them what they would like to do to everyone else if they could get away with it.
   Quoted in the *Independent on Sunday* 13 June 1999

Llosa See VARGAS LLOSA.

David Lloyd George (1863–1945)
BRITISH POLITICIAN AND PRIME MINISTER
First Earl of Dwyfor. A Liberal MP from 1890, he was Chancellor of the Exchequer 1908–15 and head of the coalition government 1916–22. JOHN MAYNARD KEYNES *referred to him as 'this extraordinary figure of our time, this syren, this goatfooted bard, this half-human visitor to our age'. See also* MARGOT ASQUITH 2.

1 We have been living in a sheltered valley for generations. We have been too comfortable and too indulgent – many, perhaps, too selfish – and the stern hand of fate has scourged us to an elevation where we can see the great everlasting things that matter for a nation – the great peaks we had forgotten, of Honour, Duty, Patriotism, and, clad in glittering white, the great pinnacle of Sacrifice pointing like a rugged finger to Heaven.
   Speech at Queen's Hall, London, 21 September 1914, publ. in *The Penguin Book of Twentieth-Century Speeches* (ed. Brian MacArthur, 1999)

2 At eleven o'clock this morning came to an end the cruellest and most terrible war that has ever scourged mankind. I hope we may say that thus, this fateful morning, came to an end all wars.
   Speech to House of Commons, London, 11 November 1918, publ. in *Hansard*. The speech was made on the day that the armistice was signed between the allied powers and Germany. *The War That Will End War* was the title of a novel by H. G. WELLS (1914).

3 What is our task? To make Britain a fit country for heroes to live in.
   Speech at Wolverhampton, 24 November 1918, publ. in *The Penguin Book of Twentieth-Century Speeches* (ed. Brian MacArthur, 1999). The words were frequently recalled in the years of low wages and unemployment that followed

4 The finest eloquence is that which gets things done and the worst is that which delays them.
   Speech at Paris Peace Conference, 18 January 1919, quoted in *The Times* 20 January 1919

5 He will be just like the scent on a pocket handkerchief.
   Remark, 9 June 1922, quoted in *Whitehall Diary*, vol. 1 (1969) by Thomas Jones. On A. J. BALFOUR's place in history.

6 In business a refusal to face disagreeable

facts leads to bankruptcy; in war it leads to defeat; in science it leads to false conclusions; in theology it is commonly believed to lead to perdition; in politics it lands you in all these unpleasant consequences.

Speech at National Liberal Club, London, 12 May 1924, publ. in *Slings and Arrows*, 'Maxims' (1929)

(Sir) Robert Lockhart (1886–1970)
BRITISH AUTHOR, DIPLOMAT AND JOURNALIST
As the unofficial British representative to the Bolshevik government in 1918, he narrowly escaped a death sentence after being accused of conspiring to kill Lenin. He wrote for the Evening Standard, *and served in the Foreign Office during the Second World War.*

1 As a cure for the cold, take your toddy to bed, put one bowler hat at the foot, and drink until you see two.

Quoted in the *Independent* 25 November 1989

David Lodge (b. 1935)
BRITISH AUTHOR, CRITIC AND ACADEMIC
His literary criticism applies structuralist analysis, while his fiction mixes realism and parody, as in Changing Places *(1975),* Small World *(1984) and* Thinks . . . *(2001), all of which have academic settings.*

1 Literature is mostly about having sex and not much about having children. Life is the other way round.

Adam Appleby, in *The British Museum Is Falling Down*, ch. 4 (1965)

2 As to our universities . . . they are élitist where they should be egalitarian and egalitarian where they should be élitist.

Charles, in *Nice Work*, pt 5, ch. 4 (1988)

Henry Cabot Lodge Jr (1902–85)
US POLITICIAN AND DIPLOMAT
He held a Republican seat in the Senate 1937–44 and 1947–52 and subsequently served as US ambassador to the United Nations (1953–60), to South Vietnam (1963–4 and 1965–7) and to West Germany (1968–9).

1 This organization is created to prevent you from going to hell. It isn't created to take you to heaven.

Of the United Nations, in *The New York Times* 28 January 1954

Haniel Long (1888–1956)
US AUTHOR, POET AND JOURNALIST
Among his poetical works are Atlantides *(1933) and* The Grist Mill *(1945). His novels include* Interlinear to Cabeza de Vaca *(1936) and* Malinche *(1939).*

1 And who is any of us, that without starvation he can go through the kingdoms of starvation?

Interlinear to Cabeza de Vaca (1936)

2 Our deeds disguise us. People need endless time to try on their deeds, until each knows the proper deeds for him to do. But every day, every hour, rushes by. There is no time.

Malinche (1939)

3 Has a man any fault a woman cannot weave with and try to change into something better, if the god her man prays to is a mother holding a baby?

Ibid.

Anita Loos (1888–1981)
US NOVELIST AND SCREENWRITER
In six decades she wrote 150 screenplays and scenarios as well as Broadway plays and memoirs, although her name is chiefly associated with the novel Gentlemen Prefer Blondes *(1925, filmed 1928 and 1953), a witty portrait of the Roaring Twenties.*

1 I really think that American gentlemen are the best after all, because kissing your hand may make you feel very very good but a diamond and a sapphire bracelet lasts forever.

Gentlemen Prefer Blondes, 'Paris is Divine' (1925). Lorelei Lee's journal entry 27 April.

2 Pleasure that isn't paid for is as insipid as everything else that's free.

Kiss Hollywood Good-by, ch. 2 (1974)

3 Show business is the best possible therapy for remorse.

Ibid., ch. 13

4 That our popular art forms have become so obsessed with sex has turned the USA into a nation of hobbledehoys; as if grown people don't have more vital concerns, such as taxes, inflation, dirty politics, earning a living, getting an education, or keeping out of jail.

Ibid., ch. 21

5 If we have to tell Hollywood good-by, it may be with one of those tender, old-fashioned, seven-second kisses exchanged between two people of the *opposite* sex, with all their clothes on.

Ibid., ch. 21. Last lines of book.

Lorca See GARCÍA LORCA

Konrad Lorenz (1903–89)
AUSTRIAN ETHOLOGIST
Known as the father of ethology, he contributed to the knowledge of behavioural patterns in animals, particularly in birds, and in 1935 recorded the

phenomenon of imprinting. His books include Man Meets Dog *(1950) and* On Aggression *(1963).*

1 It is a good morning exercise for a research scientist to discard a pet hypothesis every day before breakfast. It keeps him young.
   On Aggression, ch. 2 (1963)

2 Historians will have to face the fact that natural selection determined the evolution of cultures in the same manner as it did that of species.
   Ibid., ch. 13

Joe Louis (1914–81)

US BOXER

Originally Joseph Louis Borrow. 'The Brown Bomber' won sixty-seven out of seventy professional fights, and was World Heavyweight Champion 1937–49, defending his title a record twenty-five times.

1 He can run. But he can't hide.
   Quoted in *Louis: My Life Story* (1947). The threat was addressed to Billy Conn, his opponent in a World Championship match, 19 June 1946, which Louis won.

(Sir) Bernard Lovell (b. 1913)

BRITISH ASTRONOMER

A pioneer in the study of radio astronomy, he founded Jodrell Bank Experimental Station (now Nuffield Radio Astronomy Laboratories) and was its Director 1951–81. His publications include Voice of the Universe *(1987).*

1 The pursuit of the good and evil are now linked in astronomy as in almost all science. . . . The fate of human civilization will depend on whether the rockets of the future carry the astronomer's telescope or a hydrogen bomb.
   'Fourth Reith Lecture', publ. in *The Individual and the Universe* (1959)

James Lovell (b. 1928)

US ASTRONAUT

Crew member of the Gemini 7 (1965), Gemini 12 (1966) and Apollo 8 (1968) space missions, and commander of the unsuccessful Apollo 13 moon mission (1970), he was Deputy Director of the Johnson Space Center in Houston, Texas 1971–3.

1 Houston, we've had a problem.
   Radio transmission from Apollo 13, 14 April 1970, quoted in *The Times* 15 April 1970. The message was given following an explosion in the service module which led to the abandonment of the moon landing, although the crew was able to return safely to earth three days later. The words have also been ascribed to another crew member, John Swigert, and are often misquoted 'Houston, we've got a problem', the title of a TV movie in 1974.

Amy Lowell (1874–1925)

US POET

After her first collection, A Dome of Many-Colored Glass *(1912), she became the leader of the Imagist movement in America, writing what she called 'polyphonic prose' and 'unrhymed cadence'. Other works include* What's O'Clock *(1925).*

1 *All books are either dreams or swords,*
   You can cut, or you can drug, with words.
   'Sword Blades and Poppy Seed', publ. in *Sword Blades and Poppy Seed* (1914)

2 *For the man who should loose me is dead,*
   Fighting with the Duke in Flanders,
   In a pattern called a war.
   Christ! What are patterns for?
   'Patterns', publ. in *Men, Women and Ghosts* (1916)

3 *Moon!*
   Moon!
   I am prone before you.
   Pity me,
   And drench me in loneliness.
   'On a Certain Critic' (1919), repr. in *Complete Poetical Works* (1955)

4 *A man must be sacrificed now and again*
   To provide for the next generation of men.
   'A Critical Fable' (1922), repr. ibid.

Robert Lowell (1917–77)

US POET

His early collections reflected his conversion to Roman Catholicism in conflict with his Boston ancestry. Life Studies *(1959), which dealt with episodes from his personal life, indicated a new ironic style, developed in such later collections as* The Old Glory *(1965).*

1 *I saw the spiders marching through the air,*
   Swimming from tree to tree that mildewed day
   In latter August when the hay
   Came creaking to the barn.
   'Mr Edwards and the Spider', written 1946, publ. in *Poems 1938–1949* (1950)

2 *This is death.*
   To die and know it. This is the Black Widow, death.
   Ibid.

3 *These are the tranquilized Fifties,*
   and I am forty. Ought I to regret my seedtime?
   'Memories of West Street and Lepke', publ. in *Life Studies* (1959)

4 *I was a fire-breathing Catholic C.O.,*
   and made my manic statement,
   telling off the state and president, and then
   sat waiting sentence in the bull pen
   beside a Negro boy with curlicues
   of marijuana in his hair.
   Ibid. Lowell was an ardent convert to Roman Catholicism in the 1940s.

5 *At forty-five,*
What next, what next?
I meet my father,
my age, still alive.
'Middle Age', publ. in *For The Union Dead* (1964)

6 *Their monument sticks like a fishbone*
in the city's throat.
'For The Union Dead', publ. ibid.

7 *The Aquarium is gone. Everywhere,*
giant finned cars nose forward like fish;
a savage servility
slides by on grease.
Ibid.

8 *If we see light at the end of the tunnel,*
It's the light of the oncoming train.
'Since 1939', publ. in *Day by Day* (1977)

9 *Folly comes from something –*
the present, yes,
we are in it,
it's the infection
of things gone.
'We Took Our Paradise', publ. ibid.

Malcolm Lowry (1909–57)
BRITISH NOVELIST
His best-known novel, Under the Volcano *(1947), which narrates the last day of a British consul in Mexico, drew on his own experience as a nomadic alcoholic. He lived mainly in British Columbia, returning to Britain in 1954 where he died of barbiturate poisoning.*

1 What I have absolutely no sympathy with is the legislator, the man who seeks, for his own profit, to exploit the weaknesses of those who are unable to help themselves and then to fasten some moral superscription upon it. This I loathe so much that I cannot conceivably explain how much it is.
Letter, 1937, publ. in *Selected Letters of Malcolm Lowry* (1967). Lowry was fulminating against his persecution by 'spies and dogs' in Oaxaca, Mexico, where he was drinking heavily while writing *Under the Volcano*.

2 How alike are the groans of love to those of the dying.
Narrator, in *Under the Volcano*, ch. 12 (1947)

E. V. Lucas (1868–1938)
BRITISH JOURNALIST AND ESSAYIST
Edward Verrall Lucas. He was a prolific writer of novels, travel books, and essays in the style of Charles Lamb, on whom he was an authority. His essay collections include Adventures and Misgivings *(1938).*

1 I have noticed that the people who are late are often so much jollier than the people who have to wait for them.
365 Days and One More, 'October 3' (1926). 'I am

a believer in punctuality,' Lucas wrote in 1932, 'though it makes me very lonely.'

2 There can be no defence like elaborate courtesy.
Reading, Writing and Remembering, ch. 8 (1932)

George Lucas (b. 1944)
US FILM-MAKER
Called 'Walt Disney's version of a mad scientist' by STEVEN SPIELBERG, *he co-wrote and directed* American Graffiti *(1973) and wrote and directed* Star Wars *(1977), also contributing to the latter's various sequels.*

1 Star Wars.
Title of film (written and directed by George Lucas, 1977). The film won seven Academy Awards, and was the highest grossing film at the time. In 1983 President REAGAN announced the Strategic Defense Initiative, a missile defence system based in space which was immediately nicknamed the Star Wars defence.

2 May the Force be with you!
Ben 'Obi-wan' Kenobi (Alec Guinness), ibid.

3 The Empire Strikes Back.
Title of film (1980, screenplay by Leigh Brackett and Laurence Kasdan from original story by George Lucas, directed by Irvin Kershner)

Clare Boothe Luce (1903–87)
US PLAYWRIGHT AND POLITICIAN
Born Clare Boothe. She was Managing Editor of Vanity Fair *(1930–34) and author of the Broadway hits* The Women *(1936, filmed 1939) and* Kiss the Boys Goodbye *(1938, filmed 1941). In 1942 she was elected to the House of Representatives as a Republican, and was US ambassador to Italy 1953–7.*

1 Lying increases the creative faculties, expands the ego, lessens the friction of social contacts. . . . It is only in lies, wholeheartedly and bravely told, that human nature attains through words and speech the forebearance, the nobility, the romance, the idealism, that – being what it is – it falls so short of in fact and in deed.
Vanity Fair October 1930

2 A man has only one escape from his old self: to see a different self – in the mirror of some woman's eyes.
Mrs Morehead, in *The Women*, act 1, sc. 3 (1936). Directed by George Cukor, the film version achieved some notoriety with a cast of 135 women and no men.

3 You know, that's the only good thing about divorce; you get to sleep with your mother.
Little Mary, ibid., act 2, sc. 4

4 Much of what Mr Wallace calls his global thinking is, no matter how you slice it, still 'globaloney'. Mr Wallace's warp of sense

and his woof of nonsense is very tricky cloth out of which to cut the pattern of a post-war world.

Speech to Congress, 9 February 1943, publ. in *Congressional Record*, vol. 89. Referring to Vice-president Henry Wallace's views on foreign policy, in Boothe Luce's maiden speech in the House, in which she first coined the term *globaloney*.

5 To put a woman on the ticket would challenge the loyalty of women everywhere to their sex, because it would be made to seem that the defeat of the ticket meant the defeat for a hundred years of women's chance to be truly equal with men in politics.

Quoted in the *New York World-Telegram* 28 June 1948

6 Communism is the opiate of the intellectuals [with] no cure except as a guillotine might be called a cure for dandruff.

Newsweek 24 January 1955

7 But if God had wanted us to think just with our wombs, why did He give us a brain?

Nora, in *Slam the Door Softly* (1970)

John Lukacs (b. 1924)
HUNGARIAN-BORN US HISTORIAN
Known as a 'philosopher historian', he has published Decline and Rise of Europe *(1965) and* Outgrowing Democracy: A History of the United States in the Twentieth Century *(1984), among other works.*

1 All the isms are wasms – except one, the most powerful ism of this century, indeed, of the entire democratic age, which is nationalism.

'The Stirrings of History', publ. in *Harper's* August 1990

Alison Lurie (b. 1926)
US AUTHOR
EDMUND WHITE *praised her work for its 'seamless progressions of effects'. Her novels, such as* Foreign Affairs *(1984), recount the lives of the sophisticated and academic upper middle class. She has also written non-fictional commentary.*

1 Conspicuous consumption in dress still survives in two locations: the private lives of the urban rich and the public lives of the urban poor.

The Language of Clothes, Preface (1981, rev. 1992)

Witold Lutoslawski (1913–94)
POLISH COMPOSER AND CONDUCTOR
A prolific composer and a conductor of his own pieces, he is best known for his orchestral work, which developed from traditional pieces such as Symphonic Variations *(1938) to aleatory and* improvisational compositions, *for example* Venetian Games *(1961).*

1 One can create a masterpiece by using any means of expression, no matter how absurd, just as one can make a beautiful gesture lying at the edge, or even the bottom, of a precipice.

Conversations with Witold Lutoslawski, ch. 9 (ed. Tadeusz Kaczynski, 1972, transl. 1984)

2 The collection of antiques which is a symphony orchestra belongs more properly to the past. A modern composer is forced to translate into the language of these old instruments what his imagination proposes to him in a form which has nothing in common with them.

Ibid., ch. 13

3 People whose sensibility is destroyed by music in trains, airports, lifts, cannot concentrate on a Beethoven quartet.

Independent on Sunday 13 January 1991

Rosa Luxemburg (1870–1919)
POLISH-BORN GERMAN REVOLUTIONARY
Known as 'Red Rosa', she co-founded what would later be the Polish Communist Party before moving to Germany in 1898, where she helped set up the Spartacus League in 1916, the precursor of the German Communist Party. She was murdered after helping to organize an uprising in Berlin.

1 Freedom is always and exclusively freedom for the one who thinks differently.

Prison notes, 1918, publ. in *The Russian Revolution*, ch. 6 (1922, transl. 1961)

2 Without general elections, without unrestricted freedom of press and assembly, without a free struggle of opinion, life dies out in every public institution, becomes a mere semblance of life, in which only the bureaucracy remains as the active element. Public life gradually falls asleep, a few dozen party leaders of inexhaustible energy and boundless experience direct and rule. . . . Such conditions must inevitably cause a brutalization of public life: attempted assassinations, shootings of hostages, etc.

Ibid.

Gavin Lyall (1932–2003)
BRITISH JOURNALIST AND NOVELIST
His thrillers include The Secret Servant *(1980) and a quartet of novels featuring the SAS officer Harry Maxim. He also wrote on military aviation.*

1 Opinionated writing is always the most difficult . . . simply because it involves retaining in the cold morning-after crystal

of the printed word the burning flow of
molten feeling.
Introduction to *Roundabout* (1962) by Katharine
Whitehorn

John Lydon (b. 1957)

BRITISH ROCK MUSICIAN
*As Johnny Rotten, he joined the seminal punk
band the Sex Pistols in 1975 as singer and leering
agent provocateur. The group inspired a generation of punk rockers with such vitriolic anthems as
'Anarchy in the UK' (1976).*

1 *I am an Anti-Christ*
I am an anarchist
Don't know what I want but I know where
to get it
I wanna destroy passers-by
Because I wanna be anarchy!
'Anarchy in the U.K.' (song, 1976, written by
Johnny Rotten, Steve Jones, Glen Matlock and
Paul Cook) on the album *Never Mind the Bol-
locks* (1977) by the Sex Pistols

2 There's no love at all. . . . You can't love
anything. Love is what you feel for a dog
or a pussy cat. It doesn't apply to humans,
and if it does it just shows how low you
are.
Interview, 19 November 1976, publ. in *1988: The
New Wave Punk Rock Explosion*, 'The Sex Pistols'
(1977) by Caroline Coon

3 *When there's no future*
How can there be sin
We're the flowers in the dustbin
We're the poison in your human machine
We're the future
Your future
God Save the Queen.
'God Save the Queen/No Future' (song, written
by Johnny Rotten, Steve Jones, Glen Matlock
and Paul Cook) on the album *Never Mind the
Bollocks* (1977) by the Sex Pistols. Despite a
broadcasting ban on the song, which was
released to coincide with the twenty-fifth anni-
versary celebrations of Queen Elizabeth II's
accession, it reached no. 2 in the British charts.

4 *We're pretty . . . pretty vacant*
And we don't care.
'Pretty Vacant' (song, written by Johnny Rotten,
Steve Jones, Glen Matlock and Paul Cook) on
ibid.

5 I'm not here for your amusement. You're
here for mine.
To audience in Memphis, Tennessee, 1978,
quoted in *Sex Pistols File* (ed. Ray Stevenson,
1984)

6 No one in this band is a musician. We all
hate the term. We're something close to
factory workers. Machinists. Skilled
operators.
Quoted in *Rock 'N' Roll Babylon*, ch. 4 (1982) by
Gary Herman

7 Punks in their silly leather jackets are a cliché. I have never liked the term and have
never discussed it. I just got on with it and
got out of it when it became a competition.
Observer 4 May 1986

8 Sex is two minutes of squelching.
Quoted in *Vox* March 1994

David Lynch (b. 1946)

US FILM-MAKER
His first film, Eraserhead *(1977), established him
as a film-maker of dark and bizarre originality.
Subsequent films include* Blue Velvet *(1986) and*
Wild at Heart *(1990), but he is probably known
best for the cult TV series* Twin Peaks *(1989–91).*

1 When you sleep, you don't control your
dream. I like to dive into a dream world
that I've made, a world I chose and that I
have complete contol over.
La Revue du Cinéma February 1987, quoted in
David Lynch, ch. 5 (1992) by Michel Chion

2 Damned fine cup of coffee!
Agent Dale Cooper (Kyle MacLachlan), in *Twin
Peaks* (TV series, 1989–91, written and created
by David Lynch and Mark Frost). 'Damned fine
cheese cake!' and 'Damned fine pie!' are other
frequent remarks associated with Agent Cooper.

3 This whole world is wild at heart and
weird on top.
Lula (Laura Dern), in *Wild at Heart* (film, 1990,
written by David Lynch adapted from Barry
Gifford's novel, directed by David Lynch)

Robert Lynd (1879–1949)

ANGLO-IRISH ESSAYIST AND JOURNALIST
Literary Editor of the Daily News *(later the* News
Chronicle*) 1912–47, he also contributed articles to
the* New Statesman *as 'YY' (1913–45). He was a
leading campaigner for the reprieve of* ROGER
CASEMENT.

1 There are some people who want to throw
their arms round you simply because it is
Christmas; there are other people who
want to strangle you simply because it is
Christmas.
The Book of This and That, 'On Christmas' (1915)

Russell Lynes (1910–91)

US EDITOR AND CRITIC
*Most of his journalistic career was devoted to
Harper's magazine, of which he became Assistant
Editor in 1944. His books include* Snobs *(1950)
and* The Tastemakers *(1954), both critiques on
social pretension in America.*

1 It is always well to accept your own shortcomings with candor but to regard those
of your friends with polite incredulity.
'The Art of Accepting', publ. in *Vogue*
1 September 1952

2 The art of acceptance is the art of making

someone who has just done you a small favor wish that he might have done you a greater one.

Reader's Digest December 1954

3 A lady is nothing very specific. One man's lady is another man's woman; sometimes, one man's lady is another man's wife. Definitions overlap but they almost never coincide.

'Is There a Lady in the House?', publ. in *Look* 22 July 1958

Jonathan Lynn (b. 1943)

BRITISH SCREENWRITER AND FILM-MAKER

He co-scripted with ANTONY JAY *the BBC television series* Yes Minister *(1980–82) and* Yes Prime Minister *(1986–8) (see* RICHARD CROSSMAN 1*) and has written and directed the films* Clue *(1985) and* Nuns on the Run *(1990). See also* ANTONY JAY 2.

1 Husbands should be like kleenex: soft, strong, and disposable.

Mrs White (Madeline Kahn), in *Clue* (film, 1985, written and directed by Jonathan Lynn)

(Dame) Vera Lynn (b. 1917)

BRITISH SINGER

She became 'the Forces' Sweetheart' during the Second World War, catching the mood of the moment with her optimistic and patriotic songs. She broadcast her own radio show Sincerely Yours *1941–7.*

1 *We'll meet again*
Don't know where, don't know when,
But I know we'll meet again
Some sunny day.

'We'll Meet Again' (song, 1941, written by ROSS PARKER and HUGH CHARLES)

Jean François Lyotard (1924–98)

FRENCH PHILOSOPHER

He abandoned his position as a Marxist in the 1950s and '60s to become a leading theorist of postmodernism. His book The Postmodern Condition *(1979) argued against the 'grand narratives' of political, religious, historical and scientific theories in favour of the 'small narratives' which focus on the individual.*

1 Knowledge in the form of an informational commodity indispensable to productive power is already, and will continue to be, a major – perhaps *the* major – stake in the worldwide competition for power. It is conceivable that the nation-states will one day fight for control of information, just as they battled in the past for control over territory, and afterwards for control over access to and exploitation of raw materials and cheap labour.

The Postmodern Condition: A Report on Knowledge, Introduction (1979, rev. 1986)

2 Eclecticism is the degree zero of contemporary general culture: one listens to reggae, watches a western, eats McDonald's food for lunch and local cuisine for dinner, wears Paris perfume in Tokyo and 'retro' clothes in Hong Kong; knowledge is a matter for TV games. It is easy to find a public for eclectic works.

'Answering the Question: What is Postmodernism?', first publ. in *Critique* April 1982, repr. ibid.

3 A work can become modern only if it is first postmodern. Postmodernism thus understood is not modernism at its end but in the nascent state, and this state is constant.

Ibid.

Bernadette McAliskey (b. 1947)

NORTHERN IRISH POLITICIAN

Originally Bernadette Devlin. In 1969 she became the youngest MP in the House of Commons since William Pitt the Younger when she won the Mid-Ulster seat for the Independent Unity Party. See also EDNA GLADNEY 1.

1 To gain that which is worth having, it may be necessary to lose everything else.

The Price of my Soul, Preface (1969)

Douglas MacArthur (1880–1964)

US GENERAL

He was Supreme Commander of the South West Pacific Area in the Second World War, and led UN forces during the Korean War (1950–51), but was dismissed when he advocated extending the war against China. EISENHOWER *remarked, 'I studied dramatics under him for twelve years.'*

1 I came through and I shall return.

Statement in Adelaide, Australia, 20 March 1942, quoted in *The New York Times* 21 March 1942. The pledge was made on disembarking from the Philippines, which he had been ordered to evacuate following an unsuccessful defence of the Bataan peninsula. MacArthur subsequently pursued a brilliant 'leap-frogging' strategy which enabled him to return to the Philippines in October 1944. His men celebrated his victory with the song, 'By the grace of God and a few Marines/MacArthur returned to the Philippines.'

2 Like the old soldier of the ballad, I now close my military career and just fade away, an old soldier who tried to do his duty as God gave him the light to see that duty. Goodbye.

Speech to Congress, 19 April 1951, publ. in *Congressional Record*, vol. 97. Referring to his dismissal as commander of UN forces in Korea, for dissenting from the Truman administration's conduct of the war. TRUMAN called the speech 'nothing but a bunch of damn bullshit' (in Merle Miller's *Plain Speaking: Conversations with Harry S. Truman*, ch. 25, 1973). The 'ballad' referred to by MacArthur was a barrack-room ditty which originated as a British army song in the First World War.

(Dame) Rose Macaulay (1881–1958)

BRITISH AUTHOR AND ESSAYIST

She was a writer of humorous and urbane novels, for example Potterism *(1920),* The World My Wilderness *(1950) and* The Towers of Trebizond *(1956). She also published travel books and journalism.*

1 Sleeping in a bed – it is, apparently, of immense importance. Against those who sleep, from choice or necessity, elsewhere society feels righteously hostile. It is not done. It is disorderly, anarchical.

A Casual Commentary, 'Beds and 'Omes' (1925)

2 Cranks live by theory, not by pure desire. They want votes, peace, nuts, liberty, and spinning-looms not because they love these things, as a child loves jam, but because they think they ought to have them. That is one element which makes the crank.
Ibid., 'Cranks'

3 As to the family, I have never understood how that fits in with the other ideals – or, indeed, why it should be an ideal at all. A group of closely related persons living under one roof; it is a convenience, often a necessity, sometimes a pleasure, sometimes the reverse; but who first exalted it as admirable, an almost religious ideal?
The World My Wilderness, ch. 20 (1950)

Eugene J. McCarthy (b. 1916)
US POLITICIAN AND AUTHOR
Eugene Joseph McCarthy. He was elected to the Senate in 1958 and unsuccessfully stood for the Democratic presidential nomination in 1968 on a platform of opposition to the Vietnam War, and again in 1972.

1 The only thing that saves us from the bureaucracy is inefficiency. An efficient bureaucracy is the greatest threat to liberty.
Time 12 February 1979

Joseph McCarthy (1908–57)
US POLITICIAN
Elected a Republican senator in 1946, he created controversy in 1950 with unproven allegations of infiltration of the State Department by communists. The ensuing investigations ended in 1954 when he was officially censured by the Senate for unbecoming conduct. HARRY S. TRUMAN *called him 'a pathological character assassin'. See also* ED MURROW 1.

1 McCarthyism is Americanism with its sleeves rolled.
Speech in Wisconsin, 1952, quoted in *Senator Joe McCarthy*, ch. 1 (1973) by Richard Rovere

Mary McCarthy (1912–89)
US AUTHOR AND CRITIC
She was a contributor to the Partisan Review, *among other publications, and the writer of satirical novels such as* The Groves of Academe *(1952) and* The Group *(1963, filmed 1966). She was married to the critic Edmund Wilson 1938–46.*

1 When an American heiress wants to buy a man, she at once crosses the Atlantic. The only really materialistic people I have ever met have been Europeans.
'America the Beautiful: The Humanist in the Bathtub', first publ. in *Commentary* September 1947, repr. in *On the Contrary* (1961)

2 The American character looks always as if it had just had a rather bad haircut, which gives it, in our eyes at any rate, a greater humanity than the European, which even among its beggars has an all too professional air.
Ibid.

3 The happy ending is our national belief.
Ibid.

4 The immense popularity of American movies abroad demonstrates that Europe is the unfinished negative of which America is the proof.
Ibid.

5 In verity . . . we are the poor. This humanity we would claim for ourselves is the legacy, not only of the Enlightenment, but of the thousands and thousands of European peasants and poor townspeople who came here bringing their humanity and their sufferings with them. It is the absence of a stable upper class that is responsible for much of the vulgarity of the American scene. Should we blush before the visitor for this deficiency?
Ibid.

6 Liberty, as it is conceived by current opinion, has nothing inherent about it; it is a sort of gift or trust bestowed on the individual by the state pending *good behavior*.
'The Contagion of Ideas', speech, 1952, publ. ibid.

7 Every age has a keyhole to which its eye is pasted.
'My Confession', first publ. 1953, repr. ibid.

8 There are no new truths, but only truths that have not been recognized by those who have perceived them without noticing. A truth is something that everybody can be shown to know and to have known, as people say, all along.
'The Vita Activa', first publ. in the *New Yorker* 18 October 1958, repr. ibid.

9 The labor of keeping house is labor in its most naked state, for labor is toil that never finishes, toil that has to be begun again the moment it is completed, toil that is destroyed and consumed by the life process.
Ibid.

10 In violence we forget who we are.
On the Contrary, pt 3, 'Characters in Fiction' (1961)

11 I suppose everyone continues to be interested in the quest for the self, but what you feel when you're older, I think, is that . . . you really must *make* the self. It is absolutely useless to look for it, you won't find it, but it's possible in some sense to make

it. I don't mean in the sense of making a mask, a Yeatsian mask. But you finally begin in some sense to make and choose the self you want.

Interview in *Writers at Work* (second series, ed. George Plimpton, 1963)

12 Every word she [Lillian Hellman] writes is a lie, including 'and' and 'the'.

Interview on *Dick Cavett Show*, January 1980, quoted in *The New York Times* 16 February 1980. McCarthy was quoting herself referring to LIL-LIAN HELLMAN in the 1930s. McCarthy's remark resulted in a row and prolonged law-suit which probably contributed to the wasting illness that eventually killed her; see Carol Brightman, *Writing Dangerously: Mary McCarthy and Her World* (1993).

(Sir) Paul McCartney (b. 1942)

BRITISH ROCK MUSICIAN

Labelled as the gentler, more melodic half of the LENNON–MCCARTNEY *partnership, he was bass-guitarist with the Beatles and went on to found the band Wings. He later co-wrote (with Colin Davis) the classical 'Liverpool Oratorio' (1991) and co-founded the Liverpool Institute of Performing Arts (1996).*

1 I really wish people who look with anger at the weirdos, at the happenings and psychedelic freakouts, would instead of looking with anger look with nothing. If they could be unbiased about it, they'd realise that what these people are talking about is something they'd really like for themselves: personal freedom.

Interview on Granada TV, 1967, quoted in *It Was Twenty Years Ago Today*, ch. 5 (1987) by DEREK TAYLOR

2 I didn't leave The Beatles. The Beatles have left The Beatles but no one wants to be the one to say the party's over.

Said in 1970, quoted in *The Beatles . . . After the Break-up*, 'You Say Goodbye and I Say Hello . . .' (1991) by David Bennahum

3 It's a drag.

Response to reporters asking him to comment on JOHN LENNON's death, 9 December 1980, quoted in *Paul McCartney: Many Years From Now*, ch. 14, 'How Do You Sleep?' (1997) by Barry Miles. 'It looked so callous in print,' he later explained. 'You can't take the print back and say, "Look, let me just rub that print in shit and pee over it and then cry over it for three years, then you'll see what I meant when I said that word" . . . What I meant was "Fuck off! Don't invade my privacy."'

4 What's wrong with sentimental? Sentimental means you *love*, you *care*, you *like* stuff. The thing is, we're *frightened* to be sentimental.

Interview in *Smash Hits* 24 November 1983

5 It's like if you've been an astronaut and you've been to the moon, what do you do with the rest of your life?

Said in 1990, quoted in *The Beatles . . . After the Break-up*, 'I Am the Walrus' (1991) by David Bennahum

6 Ballads and babies. That's what happened to me.

Time 8 June 1992. On his fiftieth birthday.

7 You say you're trying to 'make it', but at that time you just mean 'do well', to get this music thing to feel good so you enjoy it and other people enjoy it, so you'll get asked back.

Quoted in *Paul McCartney: Many Years From Now*, 'Afterword' (1997) by Barry Miles. On starting off in a band.

8 I'm a smoke screen expert . . . I lie all the time. It is the price of fame.

Quoted in the *Observer* 26 April 1998

Ewan MacColl (1915–89)

BRITISH FOLK SINGER AND SONGWRITER

Originally James Miller. After forming the influential Theatre Workshop with JOAN LITTLEWOOD *in 1945, he became a leading figure in the folk revival of the 1950s and '60s. With his wife Peggy Seeger he devised the innovatory Radio Ballads series, a combination of interviews, narration and songs broadcast on the BBC 1958–65.*

1 *I found my love by the gasworks crofts*
Dreamed a dream by the old canal
Kissed my girl by the factory wall
Dirty old town, dirty old town.

'Dirty Old Town' (song, 1950). MacColl wrote the song (which refers to Salford) to facilitate a scene change in his play *Landscape with Chimneys*. It became the signature tune of the Spinners folk group, and was revived by Shane MacGowan's band the Pogues in 1985.

2 Dylan is to me the perfect symbol of the anti-artist in our society. He is against everything – the last resort of someone who doesn't really want to change the world. . . . Dylan's songs accept the world as it is.

Interview in *Melody Maker* September 1965, quoted in *No Direction Home*, ch. 8 (1989) by Robert Shelton. MacColl was one of BOB DYLAN's most outspoken critics.

Frank McCourt (b. 1931)

US AUTHOR

Of Irish parentage, he worked as a teacher and lecturer in New York for thirty years before his first book Angela's Ashes *became an international bestseller (1996, filmed 1999). This bleak memoir of his Irish childhood was followed by a sequel* 'Tis *in 1999.*

1 When I look back on my childhood I wonder how I survived at all. It was, of

course, a miserable childhood: the happy childhood is hardly worth your while. Worse than the ordinary miserable childhood is the miserable Irish childhood, and worse yet is the miserable Irish Catholic childhood.

Angela's Ashes, ch. 1 (1996)

Carson McCullers (1917–67)

US AUTHOR

Described as 'Southern Gothic' in style, her fiction focuses on the misfits and outcasts of society, as in her first novel The Heart Is a Lonely Hunter *(1940) and her novella* The Ballad of the Sad Café *(1951). She was confined to a wheelchair from the age of twenty-nine.*

1 All men are lonely. But sometimes it seems to me that we Americans are the loneliest of all. Our hunger for foreign places and new ways has been with us almost like a national disease. Our literature is stamped with a quality of longing and unrest, and our writers have been great wanderers.

'Look Homeward, Americans', first publ. in *Vogue* 1 December 1940, repr. in *The Mortgaged Heart* (ed. Margarita G. Smith, 1972)

2 There's nothing that makes you so aware of the improvisation of human existence as a song unfinished. Or an old address book.

Ferris, in 'The Sojourner', publ. in *The Ballad of the Sad Café* (1951)

Hugh MacDiarmid (1892–1978)

SCOTTISH POET AND CRITIC

Originally Christopher Murray Grieve. With its use of Scots dialect and colloquialisms, his major work A Drunk Man Looks at the Thistle *(1926) established him as the leading figure of the 'Scottish Renaissance'. He was an ardent Marxist, and co-founder of the Scottish Nationalist Party (1928).*

1 *There is no such excuse for this Brummagen 'peace-maker',*
This ig-Nobel prizewinner,
This ersatz-Christian,
This 'J'aime Berlin'!
Never were accessories to crime more cold-blooded;
The callous and irresponsible betrayal
Of the Czech Republic has brought not peace
But a new and sharper sword . . .

Of NEVILLE CHAMBERLAIN, in 'When the Gangs Came to London: On the Recent Thanksgiving for "Peace"', first publ. in *The Times Literary Supplement* 17 March 2000. The recently unearthed poem was sent to Catherine Carswell, 17 October 1938 (dedicated to her and KAREL ČAPEK). The last lines recall Matthew 10:34: 'Think not that I came to send peace on the earth: I came not to send peace, but a sword.'

2 *Auden, MacNeice, Day Lewis, I have read them all,*
Hoping against hope to hear the authentic call.
. . .
And I know the explanation I must pass is this
– You cannot light a match on a crumbling wall.

'British Leftish Poetry, 1930–1940', from poem sequence *Impavidi Progrediamur* (*c.* 1940–60), publ. in *Collected Poems* (1962)

3 *Man does not cease to interest me*
When he ceases to be miserable.
Quite the contrary!
That it is important to aid him
In the beginning goes without saying,
Like a plant it is essential
To water at first,
But this is in order to get it to flower
And I am concerned with the blossom.

'Reflections in a Slum', ibid. Concluding lines of poem.

Country Joe McDonald (b. 1942)

US SINGER AND SONGWRITER

Performing politically inspired songs from c. 1960, he formed Country Joe and the Fish in 1965, a band combining protest with West Coast psychedelic rock.

1 *And it's one, two, three what are we fightin' for?*
Don't ask me I don't give a damn, next stop is Vietnam!
And it's five, six, seven, open up the pearly gates,
There ain't no time to wonder why,
Whoopee! – we're all going to die.

'I-Feel-Like-I'm-Fixin'-to-Die-Rag' (song, 1965) on the album *I-Feel-Like-I'm-Fixin'-to-Die-Rag* (1968) by Country Joe and the Fish. The song became a feature of the anti-war rallies and festivals at which Country Joe appeared.

(Sir) Trevor McDonald (b. 1939)

TRINIDAD-BORN BRITISH JOURNALIST AND BROADCASTER

A dedicated cricket enthusiast who has written biographies of the cricketers Clive Lloyd (1985) and Viv Richards (1987), he was a newscaster on ITN's News at Ten *(1990–99).*

1 Men of my age live in a state of continual desperation.

Today 8 December 1989

2 I am a West Indian peasant who has drifted into this business and who has survived. If I knew the secret, I would bottle it and sell it.

Quoted in the *Independent* 20 April 1996

Ian McEwan (b. 1948)

BRITISH AUTHOR

His early work, beginning with the stories First Love, Last Rites *(1975), is often erotic and macabre in style. Later novels include* The Child in Time *(1987),* Black Dogs *(1992) and* Amsterdam *(1998).*

1 One has to have the courage of one's pessimism.

Interview in the *Guardian* 26 May 1983

2 By concentrating on what is good in people, by appealing to their idealism and their sense of justice, and by asking them to put their faith in the future, socialists put themselves at a severe disadvantage.

Interview in *City Limits* 27 May 1983

3 For children, childhood is timeless. It's always the present. Everything is in the present tense. Of course they have memories. Of course, time shifts a little for them and Christmas comes round in the end. But they don't *feel* it. Today is what they feel, and when they say 'When I grow up . . .' there's always an edge of disbelief – how could they ever be other than what they are?

Charles Darke, in *The Child in Time*, ch. 2 (1987)

4 A disruptive minority of humankind regarded journeys, even short ones, as the occasion for pleasant encounters. There were people ready to inflict intimacies on strangers. Such travellers were to be avoided if you belonged to the majority for whom a journey was the occasion for silence, reflection, daydream. The requirements were simple: an unobstructed view of a changing landscape, however dull, and freedom from the breath of other passengers, their body warmth, sandwiches and limbs.

Narrator, ibid. ch. 3

5 You enter a state of controlled passivity, you relax your grip and accept that even if your declared intention is to justify the ways of God to man, you might end up interesting your readers rather more in Satan.

A Move Abroad, Preface (1989). On writing novels.

6 It is not the first duty of the novelist to provide blueprints for insurrection, or uplifting tales of successful resistance for the benefit of the opposition. The naming of what is there is what is important.

Ibid.

7 It is photography itself that creates the illusion of innocence. Its ironies of frozen narrative lend to its subjects an apparent unawareness that they will change or die. It is the future they are innocent of. Fifty years on we look at them with the godly knowledge of how they turned out after all – who they married, the date of their death – with no thought for who will one day be holding the photographs of us.

Jeremy, in *Black Dogs*, pt 1 (1992)

8 It's an opportunity to fly first-class, sit around the pool and be betrayed.

Quoted in the *Independent on Sunday* 22 August 1993. On screenwriting.

9 This is our mammalian conflict – what to give to the others, and what to keep for yourself. Treading that line, keeping the others in check, and being kept in check by them, is what we call morality.

Enduring Love, ch. 1 (1997)

10 Mostly, we are good when it makes sense. A good society is one that makes sense of being good.

Ibid.

11 There is only love, and then oblivion. Love was all they had to set against the hatred of their murderers.

Guardian 15 September 2001. On the last calls to loved ones made by people in the World Trade Center before it collapsed.

12 It is hard to be cruel once you permit yourself to enter the mind of your victim. Imagining what it is like to be someone other than yourself is at the core of our humanity. It is the essence of compassion, and it is the beginning of morality. The hijackers used fanatical certainty, misplaced religious faith, and dehumanising hatred to purge themselves of the human instinct for empathy. Among their crimes was a failure of the imagination.

Ibid.

John McGinley (b. 1959)

US SCREEN ACTOR

After his debut in Sweet Liberty *(1986) he appeared in several of* OLIVER STONE's *films such as* Wall Street *(1987) and* Nixon *(1995). Other films include* Seven *(1995).*

1 You're a real blue flame special, aren't you son? Young, dumb and full of come, I know. What I don't know is how you got assigned here. Guess we must have ourselves an asshole shortage, huh?

Ben Harp (John McGinley), in *Point Break* (film, 1991, screenplay by Pete Iliff, directed by KATHRYN BIGELOW). McGinley is grilling FBI agent Keanu Reeves, newly posted to an LA police department.

Phyllis McGinley (1905–78)

US POET AND AUTHOR

A wry essayist and deftly humorous versifier, she was praised by W. H. AUDEN *among others. Her poetry collections include* A Pocketful of Wry *(1940) and* Times Three *(1960).*

1 Gossip isn't scandal and it's not merely malicious. It's chatter about the human race by lovers of the same. Gossip is the tool of the poet, the shop-talk of the scientist, and the consolation of the housewife, wit, tycoon and intellectual. It begins in the nursery and ends when speech is past.
'A New Year and No Resolutions', publ. in *Woman's Home Companion* January 1957

2 Our bodies are shaped to bear children, and our lives are a working out of the processes of creation. All our ambitions and intelligence are beside that great elemental point.
The Province of the Heart, 'The Honor of Being a Woman' (1959)

3 Say what you will, making marriage work is a woman's business. The institution was invented to do her homage; it was contrived for her protection. Unless she accepts it as such – as a beautiful, bountiful, but quite unequal association – the going will be hard indeed.
Ibid.

4 Frigidity is largely nonsense. It is this generation's catchword, one only vaguely understood and constantly misused. Frigid women are few. There is a host of diffident and slow-ripening ones.
Ibid.

5 Women are the fulfilled sex. Through our children we are able to produce our own immortality, so we lack that divine restlessness which sends men charging off in pursuit of fortune or fame or an imagined Utopia. That is why we number so few geniuses among us. The wholesome oyster wears no pearl, the healthy whale no ambergris, and as long as we can keep on adding to the race, we harbor a sort of health within ourselves.
Ibid., 'Some of My Best Friends . . .'

6 *A Mother's hardest to forgive.*
Life is the fruit she longs to hand you,
Ripe on a plate. And while you live,
Relentlessly she understands you.
'The Adversary', publ. in *A Certain Age* (1960)

7 *The knowingness of little girls*
Is hidden underneath their curls.
'What Every Woman Knows', publ. in *Times Three* (1960)

8 *For little boys are rancorous*
When robbed of any myth,
And spiteful and cantankerous
To all their kin and kith.
But little girls can draw conclusions
And profit from their lost illusions.
Ibid.

Patrick McGoohan (b. 1928)
US-BORN BRITISH ACTOR
He has appeared in numerous adventure films, but is best known for his TV personae as secret agent John Drake in Danger Man *(1960–67) and as Number Six in the cult series* The Prisoner *(1967–8).*

1 I am not a number – I am a free man!
Number Six (Patrick McGoohan), in preamble to each episode of *The Prisoner* (TV series, 1967–8, created by Patrick McGoohan, George Markstein and David Tomblin). Number Six (who is never named) states during one episode: 'I will not be pushed, stamped, filed, indexed, briefed, debriefed, or numbered. My life is my own.'

2 But what is the greatest evil? If you are going to epitomize evil, what is it? Is it the bomb? The greatest evil that one has to fight constantly, every minute of the day until one dies, is the worse part of oneself.
Quoted in *The Prisoner and Danger Man*, 'I Am Not a Number, I Am a Free Man' (1989) by Dave Rogers

Roger McGough (b. 1937)
BRITISH POET
With BRIAN PATTEN *and Adrian Henri, he was one of the 'Liverpool Poets'. His off-beat, punning humour is shown in such collections as* Gig *(1973) and* Waving at Trains *(1982). He also writes for children, and presents* Poetry Please *on BBC Radio 4.*

1 *Let me die a youngman's death*
Not a free from sin tiptoe in
Candle wax & waning death
Not a curtains drawn by angels borne
'What a nice way to go' death
'Let Me Die a Youngman's Death', publ. in *The Mersey Sound* (1967)

2 *Teach me, o Lord, to be permissive*
the 'sixties way to save the soul
three leers for sexual freedom
let the good times rock'n'roll.
'My little plastic mac', publ. in *Watchwords* (1969)

3 *May your poems run away from home*
and live between the lines.
May they break and enter, assault and batter,
and loiter in the mind with intent.
'the most unforgettable character I've ever met gives advice to the young poet', publ. in *Gig* (1973)

George McGovern (b. 1922)
US POLITICIAN
A radical reforming Democrat, he was elected to the House of Representatives in 1956 and was Senator 1963–81. He was a leading opponent of the war

in Vietnam, and as Democratic presidential candidate was heavily defeated by NIXON in 1972.

1 You know, sometimes, when they say you're ahead of your time, it's just a polite way of saying you have a real bad sense of timing.
Guardian 14 March 1990

(Sir) Ian MacGregor (1912–98)
BRITISH INDUSTRIALIST
As Chairman of the National Coal Board (1983–6), he instigated a programme of drastic cut-backs which were heavily opposed by trades unions and led to the miners' strike of 1984–5.

1 People are now discovering the price of insubordination and insurrection. And boy, are we going to make it stick!
Quoted in the *Sunday Telegraph* 10 March 1985. Referring to the miners' strike.

Thomas McGuane (b. 1939)
US NOVELIST
Known for their black humour targeted at what he terms the 'snivelization' of America, his novels feature anti-heroes grappling with the conditions of contemporary society, as in The Sporting Club *(1969) and* Nobody's Angel *(1979).*

1 America is like one of those old-fashioned six-cylinder truck engines that can be missing two sparkplugs and have a broken flywheel and have a crankshaft that's 5000 millimetres off fitting properly, and two bad ball-bearings, and still runs. We're in that kind of situation. We can have substantial parts of the population committing suicide, and still run and look fairly good.
Sunday Correspondent 1 April 1990

Roger McGuinn (b. 1942)
US ROCK MUSICIAN
Born Jim McGuinn. In 1964 he founded the folk-rock West Coast group the Byrds, whose album Sweetheart of the Rodeo *(1968) set the pattern for country rock.*

1 Eight miles high,
And when you touch down
You'll find that
It's stranger than known.
'Eight Miles High' (song, written by Roger McGuinn, Gene Clark and David Crosby) on the album *Fifth Dimension* (1966) by the Byrds. The song was one of the first to be banned for its drugs allusions.

Barry McGuire (b. 1937)
US SINGER AND SONGWRITER
The lead vocalist with the New Christy Minstrels, he had an international solo hit with the protest

song 'Eve of Destruction' (1965). He later became a religious singer as a born-again Christian.

1 Marches alone can't bring integratin'
When human respect is disintegratin'
This whole crazy world is just too frustratin'
And you tell me
Over and over and over again my friend
That you don't believe we're on the eve of destruction.
'Eve of Destruction' (song, written by P. F. Sloan) on the album *Eve of Destruction* (1965). The song was countered soon afterwards by the conservative 'Dawn of Correction' by the Spokesmen (1965).

William McIlvanney (b. 1936)
BRITISH NOVELIST
Many of his novels reflect the tough working-class culture of his childhood in Scotland, and he has also published a series of thrillers featuring the Glasgow detective Jack Laidlaw, including Laidlaw *(1977) and* Strange Loyalties *(1991).*

1 Who thinks the law has anything to do with justice? It's what we have because we can't have justice.
Laidlaw, in *Laidlaw*, ch. 35 (1977)

Jay McInerney (b. 1955)
US AUTHOR
His first novel Bright Lights, Big City *(1984, filmed 1988) gained him popularity and a reputation for preppy debauchery. Subsequent novels include* Brightness Falls *(1992) and* The Last of the Savages *(1996).*

1 Don't ask a writer what he's working on. It's like asking someone with cancer about the progress of his disease.
Jeff, in *Brightness Falls*, ch. 1 (1992)

2 A party is like a marriage . . . making itself up while seeming to follow precedent, running on steel rails into uncharted wilderness while the promises shiver and wobble on the armrests like crystal stemware.
Corrine, ibid.

3 I think men talk to women so they can sleep with them and women sleep with men so they can talk to them.
Jeff, ibid. ch. 8

4 The new puritanism. Sloth, gluttony, recreational drugs were out. Narcissism, blind ambition and greed by contrast were free of side- or after-effects, at least in this life, and who was counting on the other anymore?
Narrator, ibid. ch. 10

5 I think writing does come out of a deep well of loneliness and a desire to fill some

kind of gap. No one in his right mind would sit down to write a book if he were a well-adjusted, happy man.

Interview in the *Independent on Sunday* 19 April 1992

Colin MacInnes (1914–76)

BRITISH AUTHOR AND CRITIC

According to GEORGE MELLY *he was 'the first adult to recognize the significance of pop'. He is most remembered for his 'London' trilogy,* City of Spades *(1957),* Absolute Beginners *(1959, filmed 1986) and* Mr Love and Justice *(1960).*

1 In England, pop art and fine art stand resolutely back to back.

'Pop Songs and Teenagers', first publ. in *Twentieth Century* February 1958, repr. in *England, Half English* (1961)

2 Today, age is needy and, as its powers decline, so does its income; but full-blooded youth has wealth as well as vigour. In this decade, we witness the second Children's Crusade, armed with strength and beauty, against all 'squares', all adult naysayers.

Ibid.

3 Yes, I tell you, it had a real savage splendour in the days when we found that no one couldn't sit on our faces any more because we'd love to spend at last, and our world was to be our world, the one we wanted and not standing on the doorstep of somebody else's waiting for honey, perhaps.

Narrator, in *Absolute Beginners*, 'in June' (1959)

4 As for the boys and girls, the dear young absolute beginners, I sometimes feel that if they only *knew* this fact, this very simple fact, namely how powerful they really are, then they could rise up overnight and enslave the old tax-payers, the whole damn lot of them – toupets and falsies and rejuvenators and all – even though they number millions and sit in the seats of strength.

Ibid. The narrator adds: 'Youth has power, a kind of divine power straight from mother nature.'

5 The great thing about the jazz world, and all the kids that enter into it, is that no one, not a soul, cares what your class is, or what your race is, or what your income, or if you're a boy, or girl, or bent, or versatile, or what you are – so long as you dig the scene and can behave yourself, and have left all that crap behind you, too, when you come in the jazz club door.

Ibid.

Alasdair MacIntyre (b. 1929)

BRITISH PHILOSOPHER

His writings underline the role of eighteenth- and nineteenth-century Scottish philosophy and the influence of Greek schools of thought. Titles include After Virtue *(1981) and* Three Versions of Moral Enquiry *(1989).*

1 A striking feature of moral and political argument in the modern world is the extent to which it is innovators, radicals, and revolutionaries who revive old doctrines, while their conservative and reactionary opponents are the inventors of new ones.

A Short History of Ethics, ch. 17 (1966)

(Sir) Ian McKellen (b. 1939)

BRITISH ACTOR

Recognized as one of the leading Shakespearian actors of his generation, he established his reputation in such roles as Richard II (1968) and Macbeth (1976). His films include Scandal *(1989) and* Richard III *(1996).*

1 Constant conditioning in my youth and social pressure in every department of my life all failed to convert me to heterosexuality.

The Times 5 December 1991

Kelvin MacKenzie (b. 1946)

BRITISH JOURNALIST

Known as a Murdoch man, he was Editor of the SUN *newspaper 1981–94, reinforcing the paper's populist appeal and taking its circulation to more than 4.5 million. He became Managing Director of Mirror Group Newspapers in 1998.*

1 If they have a popular thought they have to go into a darkened room and lie down until it passes.

Independent 19 September 1989. On editors of the 'quality press'.

Catharine A. MacKinnon (b. 1946)

US LAWYER AND FEMINIST CRITIC

Since her first book Sexual Harassment of Working Women *(1979), she has fought for women's legal and social equality. In 1983 she campaigned (unsuccessfully) with* ANDREA DWORKIN *to have pornography legally recognized as a violation of human rights.*

1 Politically, I call it rape whenever a woman has sex and feels violated.

Feminism Unmodified (1987)

2 If pornography is part of your sexuality, then you have no right to your sexuality.

Quoted in the *San Francisco Examiner* 29 November 1992

3 In a society in which equality is a fact, not merely a word, words of racial or sexual

assault and humiliation will be nonsense syllables.

Only Words, ch. 3 (1993)

Shirley MacLaine (b. 1934)

US ACTRESS

Born Shirley MacLean Beaty, sister of WARREN BEATTY. *Specializing in comedy roles, she made her screen debut in* HITCHCOCK*'s* The Trouble with Harry *(1955). Later films include* The Apartment *(1960) and* Terms of Endearment *(1983).*

1 I do not see plays because I can nap at home for free, and I don't see movies because they're trash and they've got nothing but naked people in 'em, and I don't read books because if they're any good they're going to make them into miniseries.

Ouiser Boudreaux (Shirley MacLaine), in *Steel Magnolias* (film, 1989, screenplay by Robert Harling adapted from his play, directed by Herbert Ross)

Malcolm McLaren (b. 1946)

BRITISH ROCK IMPRESARIO

The Chelsea boutique he opened in 1971 with VIVIENNE WESTWOOD *sold the bondage designs that typified the punk era. He managed punk bands the New York Dolls (1974–5), the Sex Pistols (1976–8) and Bow Wow Wow (1980–84) and recorded his own eclectic albums.*

1 Our culture has become something that is completely and utterly in love with its parent. It's become a notion of boredom that is bought and sold, where nothing will happen except that people will become more and more terrified of tomorrow, because the new continues to look old, and the old will always look cute.

'Punk and History', transcript of discussion in New York City, 24 September 1988, publ. in *Discourses: Conversations in Postmodern Art and Culture* (ed. Russell Ferguson *et al.*, 1990)

2 Rock and roll doesn't necessarily mean a band. It doesn't mean a singer, and it doesn't mean a lyric, really. . . . It's that question of trying to be immortal.

Ibid.

3 This is the end of an era in pop music. It's the end of ideology. Everything is branded. It began with the compilation album – 'music to drive to', 'music to eat to' – thus denying each artist their own ideological spirit. Pop is now given away with a few Esso coupons at your local garage.

Quoted in the *Observer* 20 September 1998

Mignon McLaughlin (b. c. 1915)

US AUTHOR AND EDITOR

A contributor to magazines and periodicals, she

wrote The Neurotic's Notebook *(1963) and a follow-up in 1966.*

1 Every society honors its live conformists and its dead troublemakers.

The Neurotic's Notebook (1963)

2 It's innocence when it charms us, ignorance when it doesn't.

Ibid.

3 For the happiest life, days should be rigorously planned, nights left open to chance.

Atlantic Monthly July 1965

Don McLean (b. 1945)

US SINGER AND SONGWRITER

Appointed 'Hudson River Troubadour' by the New York State Council on the Arts, he toured schools and small communities around the eastern USA 1968–70. His song 'American Pie' became an unexpected radio hit, as did 'Vincent' (both 1971).

1 *Bye bye, Miss American Pie,*
   Drove my Chevy to the levee but the levee was dry,
   And the good old boys were drinking whiskey and rye
   Singing 'This'll be the day that I die.'

'American Pie' (song) on the album *American Pie* (1971). The song charted for McLean in 1971 and again on its re-release in 1991, and was an international hit for MADONNA in 2000.

2 *And the three men I admire the most,*
   The Father, Son and Holy Ghost,
   They caught the last train for the coast
   The day the music died.

Ibid. On the deaths of rock 'n' rollers Buddy Holly, the Big Bopper and Richie Valens in a plane crash while on tour, 2 February 1959.

Archibald MacLeish (1892–1982)

US POET AND POLITICIAN

After publishing volumes of short verse and the narrative poem Conquistador *(1932), he turned to writing political verse plays, including* Air Raid *(1938). He had a parallel career as an academic and public official and contributed to the draft of* UNESCO*'s constitution.*

1 *A poem should not mean*
   But be.

'Ars Poetica', publ. in *Streets in the Moon* (1926)

2 *America is promises to*
   Take!
   America is promises to
   Us
   To take them
   Brutally
   With love but
   Take them.

'America Was Promises', publ. in *America Was Promises* (1939)

3 The dissenter is every human being at

those moments of his life when he resigns momentarily from the herd and thinks for himself.

'In Praise of Dissent', publ. in *The New York Times* 16 December 1956

4 To see the earth as we now see it, small and beautiful in that eternal silence where it floats, is to see ourselves as riders on the earth together, brothers on that bright loveliness in the unending night – brothers who *see* now they are truly brothers.

'Riders on Earth Together, Brothers in Eternal Cold', first publ. in *The New York Times* 25 December 1968, repr. in *Riders on Earth* (1978) as 'Bubble of Blue Air'. Referring to the first pictures of the earth from the moon.

5 Poets . . . are literal-minded men who will squeeze a word till it hurts.

'Apologia', first publ. in *Harvard Law Review* June 1972, repr. ibid. as 'Art and Law'

6 We are as great as our belief in human liberty – no greater. And our belief in human liberty is only ours when it is larger than ourselves.

'Now Let Us Address the Main Question: Bicentennial of What?', publ. in *The New York Times* 3 July 1976, repr. ibid. as 'The Ghost of Thomas Jefferson'

Micheál MacLiammóir (1899–1978)

IRISH ACTOR, THEATRE DIRECTOR AND PLAYWRIGHT

He co-founded Dublin's Gate Theatre and the Galway Theatre (both 1928) and enjoyed international success as an actor and in his one-man show The Importance of Being Oscar *(1960). He also painted and wrote.*

1 We are born at the rise of the curtain and we die with its fall, and every night in the presence of our patrons we write our new creation, and every night it is blotted out forever; and of what use is it to say to audience or to critic, 'Ah, but you should have seen me last Tuesday'?

'Hamlet in Elsinore', publ. in *The Bell* October 1952. Referring to acting in the theatre.

2 He knew that he was precisely what he himself would have chosen to be had God consulted him on the subject of his birth; he fully appreciated and approved what had been bestowed, and realized that he couldn't have done the job better himself, in fact he would not have changed a single item.

Of ORSON WELLES, in *All For Hecuba*, ch. 4, 'Changes' (autobiography, 1947). Impressions on first meeting Welles. MacLiammóir's most celebrated film role was playing Iago in Welles' *Othello* (1952).

Marshall McLuhan (1911–80)

CANADIAN COMMUNICATIONS THEORIST

He wrote epigrammatically on the effects of mass media on contemporary society in The Gutenberg Galaxy *(1962) and* Understanding Media *(1964), concluding that 'all media work us over completely'.*

1 Today the tyrant rules not by club or fist, but, disguised as a market researcher, he shepherds his flocks in the ways of utility and comfort.

The Mechanical Bride, Preface (1951)

2 Today it is not the classroom nor the classics which are the repositories of models of eloquence, but the ad agencies.

Ibid., 'Plain Talk'

3 For tribal man space was the uncontrollable mystery. For technological man it is time that occupies the same role.

Ibid., 'Magic that Changes Mood'

4 It is the weak and confused who worship the pseudosimplicities of brutal directness.

Ibid., 'The Tough as Narcissus'

5 The new electronic interdependence recreates the world in the image of a global village.

The Gutenberg Galaxy, 'Chapter Gloss' (1962). GUY DEBORD commented on this famous phrase: 'The Sage of Toronto . . . spent several decades marvelling at the numerous freedoms created by a "global village" instantly and effortlessly accessible to all. Villages, unlike towns, have always been ruled by conformism, isolation, petty surveillance, boredom and repetitive malicious gossip about the same families. Which is a precise enough description of the global spectacle's present vulgarity.'

6 A point of view can be a dangerous luxury when substituted for insight and understanding.

Ibid., 'Typographic Man Can Express but is Helpless to Read the Configuration of Print Technology'

7 If the nineteenth century was the age of the editorial chair, ours is the century of the psychiatrist's couch.

Understanding Media, Introduction (1964)

8 The mark of our time is its revulsion against imposed patterns.

Ibid.

9 The medium is the message. This is merely to say that the personal and social consequences of any medium – that is, of any extension of ourselves – result from the new scale that is introduced into our affairs by each extension of ourselves, or by any new technology.

Ibid., ch. 1

10 The name of a man is a numbing blow from which he never recovers.
Ibid., ch. 2

11 Money: The poor man's credit card.
Ibid., title of ch. 14

12 Where the whole man is involved there is no work. Work begins with the division of labor.
Ibid., ch. 14

13 The car has become the carapace, the protective and aggressive shell, of urban and suburban man.
Ibid., ch. 22

14 Ideally, advertising aims at the goal of a programmed harmony among all human impulses and aspirations and endeavors. Using handicraft methods, it stretches out toward the ultimate electronic goal of a collective consciousness.
Ibid., ch. 23

15 The more the data banks record about each one of us, the less we exist.
Playboy March 1969

16 Diaper backward spells repaid. Think about it.
Remark at American Booksellers Association luncheon, Washington DC, June 1969, quoted in the Vancouver Sun 7 June 1969

17 Politics will eventually be replaced by imagery. The politician will be only too happy to abdicate in favor of his image, because the image will be much more powerful than he could ever be.
Ibid.

18 Television brought the brutality of war into the comfort of the living room. Vietnam was lost in the living rooms of America – not on the battlefields of Vietnam.
Quoted in the Montreal Gazette 16 May 1975

19 Advertising is the greatest art form of the twentieth century.
Advertising Age 3 September 1976

Harold Macmillan (1894–1986)

BRITISH POLITICIAN AND PRIME MINISTER
Lord Stockton. He was elected Conservative MP in 1926 and was Prime Minister 1957–63. Nicknamed 'Supermac' by the cartoonist Vicky, he was intellectual and aristocratic in style, and famously imperturbable. See ANEURIN BEVAN 11, 13.

1 Forever poised between a cliché and an indiscretion.
Newsweek 30 April 1956. On the role of a foreign secretary.

2 Let us be frank about it: most of our people have never had it so good.
Speech in Bedford, 20 July 1957, quoted in The Times 22 July 1957. The slogan was already cur-

rent in the USA at the end of the Second World War.

3 I thought the best thing to do was to settle up these little local difficulties, and then turn to the wider vision of the Commonwealth.
Statement at London airport, 7 January 1958, quoted in The Times 8 January 1958. The remark, made when Macmillan was preparing to leave on a Commonwealth tour, referred to the resignation of the Chancellor of the Exchequer Peter Thorneycroft and treasury ministers ENOCH POWELL and Nigel Birch in protest against public spending increases. His words furthered Macmillan's reputation for 'unflappability'.

4 At home you always have to be a politician. When you're abroad you almost feel yourself a statesman.
Speech in Melbourne, 17 February 1958, quoted in Look 15 April 1958. Remark made during the first visit to Australia by a British prime minister.

5 We have seen the awakening of national consciousness in peoples who have for centuries lived in dependence upon some other power. . . . The wind of change is blowing through the continent, and, whether we like it or not, this growth of national consciousness is a political fact.
Speech to South African Parliament, Cape Town, 3 February 1960, publ. in The Penguin Book of Twentieth-Century Speeches (ed. Brian MacArthur, 1999)

6 As usual the Liberals offer a mixture of sound and original ideas. Unfortunately none of the sound ideas is original and none of the original ideas is sound.
Speech in London, 7 March 1961, quoted in The Times 8 March 1961

7 Power? It's like a dead sea fruit. When you achieve it, there's nothing there.
Quoted in The New Anatomy of Britain, ch. 37 (1971) by Anthony Sampson

8 If you don't believe in God, all you have to believe in is decency. . . . Decency is very good. Better decent than indecent. But I don't think it's enough.
Said to William F. Buckley Jr on Firing Line, New York, 20 November 1980, quoted in Macmillan, vol. 2, ch. 19 (1989) by Alistair Horne

9 Memorial services are the cocktail parties of the geriatric set.
Quoted ibid., ch. 20

10 It is the duty of Her Majesty's Government neither to flap nor to falter.
Attributed

Larry McMurtry (b. 1936)

US SCREENWRITER, NOVELIST AND
ESSAYIST

*He helped to establish western fiction as a serious
literary genre with such works as* Horseman, Pass
By *(1961, filmed as* Hud, *1963), and adapted his
own* The Last Picture Show *(1966) and* Terms of
Endearment *(1975) for the film versions (1971 and
1983).*

1 Self-parody is the first portent of age.

Danny Deck, in *Some Can Whistle*, pt 1, ch. 14
(1989)

2 True maturity is only reached when a man
realizes he has become a father figure to
his girlfriends' boyfriends – and he accepts
it.

Ibid., ch. 12

3 The lives of happy people are dense with
their own doings – crowded, active, thick.
. . . But the sorrowing are nomads, on a
plain with few landmarks and no boundaries; sorrow's horizons are vague and its
demands are few.

Ibid., pt 4, ch. 9

Louis MacNeice (1907–63)

IRISH POET

*Associated with the left-wing poets of the 1930s, he
combined lyricism and colloquial speech patterns
in such collections as* Autumn Journal *(1938) and*
Solstices *(1961). He also worked as a radio producer and wrote many innovative documentaries
and dramas for the BBC.*

1 *World is crazier and more of it than we
think,*
Incorrigibly plural. I peel and portion
A tangerine and spit the pips and feel
The drunkenness of things being various.

'Snow', publ. in *Poems* (1935). The Belfast poet
Michael Longley has commented that the line
'The drunkenness of things being various' could
be the motto for the whole of MacNeice's life
and work.

2 *The sunlight on the garden*
Hardens and grows cold,
We cannot cage the minute
Within its net of gold,
When all is told
We cannot beg for pardon.

'Sunlight on the Garden', publ. in *Earth Compels*
(1938)

3 *It's no go the merrygoround, it's no go the
rickshaw,*
*All we want is a limousine and a ticket for
the peepshow.*

'Bagpipe Music', publ. ibid.

4 *It's no go the Government grants, it's no go
the elections,*

*Sit on your arse for fifty years and hang
your hat on a pension.*

Ibid.

5 *Some on commission, some for the love of
learning,*
*Some because they have nothing better to
do*
*Or because they hope these walls of books
will deaden*
*The drumming of the demon in their
ears.*

'The British Museum Reading Room', publ. in
Plant and Phantom (1941)

Madonna (b. 1959)

US SINGER AND ACTRESS

*Madonna Louise Ciccone. She made the first of
many dance-driven albums in 1983, since when she
has established herself as an icon of female independence and sexuality. She has also starred in films,
for example* Evita *(1996).*

1 *You know that we are living in a material
world*
And I am a material girl.

'I Am a Material Girl' (song, written by Peter
Brown and Robert Rans) on the album *Like a
Virgin* (1984)

2 *Like a virgin*
Touched for the very first time
Like a virgin
When your heart beats
Next to mine.

'Like a Virgin' (song, written by Billy Steinberg
and Tom Kelly), ibid.

3 *Express yourself*
So you can respect yourself

'Express Yourself' (song, written by Madonna
and Stephen Bray) on the album *Like a Prayer*
(1989)

4 Catholicism is not a soothing religion. It's
a painful religion. We're all gluttons for
punishment.

Interview in *Rolling Stone* 23 March 1989

5 To me, the whole process of being a brush-
stroke in someone else's painting is a little
difficult.

Interview in *Vanity Fair* April 1991

6 Everyone probably thinks that I'm a raving
nymphomaniac, that I have an *insatiable*
sexual appetite, when the truth is I'd rather
read a book.

Q Magazine June 1991

7 I always thought of losing my virginity as a
career move.

Quoted in *Madonna Unauthorized*, Epilogue
(1991) by Christopher Andersen

John Gillespie Magee (1922–41)

US-BORN PILOT WITH ROYAL CANADIAN AIR FORCE

He died while on a bombing mission over Germany, leaving as a legacy the poem 'High Flight', made famous when quoted by RONALD REAGAN *following the Challenger space shuttle disaster in 1986.*

1 Oh! I have slipped the surly bonds of earth,
   And danced the skies on laughter-silvered
   wings.

'High Flight', written 1941, publ. in *More Poems from the Forces* (ed. K. Rhys, 1943). Opening lines of sonnet.

2 And while with silent lifting mind I've trod
   The high, untrespassed sanctity of space,
   Put out my hand and touched the face of
   God.

Ibid. Last lines of sonnet.

Anna Magnani (1908–73)

EGYPTIAN-BORN ITALIAN ACTRESS

She had her first big break in Roberto Rossellini's film Rome, Open City *(1945) and was acclaimed for her first Hollywood role in* The Rose Tattoo *(1955). For Jean Renoir, she was 'the complete animal – an animal created for the stage and screen'.*

1 Great passions, my dear, don't exist: they're liars' fantasies. What do exist are little loves that may last for a short or a longer while.

Quoted in *The Egotists*, 'Anna Magnani' (1963) by Oriana Fallaci

Magnus Magnusson (b. 1929)

BRITISH WRITER AND BROADCASTER

He is known for his popular television documentaries and books on archaeology, and for chairing the inquisitorial TV quiz programme Mastermind *(1972–97).*

1 I've started, so I'll finish.

Mastermind quiz series (BBC, 1972–97). Magnusson's words after his final show were: 'I've started, now I've finished.'

René Magritte (1898–1967)

BELGIAN SURREALIST PAINTER

Joining the Paris Surrealists in 1927, he became a leading practitioner and theorist of Surrealism. He is probably best known for his images of figures in bowler hats, as in the painting Threatened Assassin *(1927).*

1 To be a surrealist . . . means barring from your mind all remembrance of what you have seen, and being always on the lookout for what has never been.

Time 21 April 1947

2 The mind loves the unknown. It loves images whose meaning is unknown, since the meaning of the mind itself is unknown.

Quoted in *Magritte*, ch. 1 (1970) by Suzi Gablik

3 The present reeks of mediocrity and the atom bomb.

Quoted ibid., ch. 5. 'I don't want to belong to my own time, or for that matter, to any other,' Magritte added.

Naguib Mahfouz (b. 1911)

EGYPTIAN NOVELIST

He established his reputation with his epic of family and social history, Cairo Trilogy *(1956–7), and* Miramar *(1967). In 1988 he was the first Egyptian to be awarded the Nobel Prize for Literature.*

1 Inwardly art is a means of expurgation, outwardly a means of battle, incumbent on men born and reared in sin and determined to rebel against it. Nothing else matters.

Wedding Song, 'Abas Karam Younis' (1981)

Norman Mailer (b. 1923)

US AUTHOR

He won immediate fame with The Naked and the Dead *(1948), a war novel that was primarily a critique of American society.* Armies of the Night *(1968) and* Executioner's Song *(1979) were examples of his 'new journalism'.* GORE VIDAL *remarked: 'He is now what he wanted to be: the patron saint of bad journalism.'*

1 For jazz is orgasm, it is the music of orgasm, good orgasm and bad, and so it spoke across a nation, it had the communication of art even where it was watered, perverted, corrupted, and almost killed, it spoke in no matter what laundered popular way of instantaneous existential states to which some whites could respond, it was indeed a communication by art because it said, 'I feel this, and now you do too'.

'The White Negro', sect. 2, first publ. in *Dissent*, summer 1957, repr. in *Advertisements for Myself* (1959)

2 Hip is the sophistication of the wise primitive in a giant jungle.

Ibid., sect. 3

3 The final purpose of art is to intensify, even, if necessary, to exacerbate, the moral consciousness of people.

'Hip, Hell, and the Navigator', first publ. in the *Western Review* winter 1959, repr. in *Conversations with Norman Mailer* (ed. J. Michael Lennon, 1988)

4 Each day a few more lies eat into the seed with which we are born, little institutional lies from the print of newspapers, the

shock waves of television, and the sentimental cheats of the movie screen.

Advertisements for Myself, 'First Advertisement for Myself' (1959)

5 There is probably no sensitive heterosexual alive who is not preoccupied with his latent homosexuality.

Ibid., 'The Homosexual Villain'

6 The White Protestant's ultimate sympathy must be with science, factology, and committee rather than with sex, birth, heat, flesh, creation, the sweet and the funky; they must vote, manipulate, control, and direct, these Protestants who are the center of power in our land, they must go for what they believe is reason when it is only the Square logic of the past.

Ibid., 'Advertisement for "Games and Ends".'

7 Masculinity is not something given to you, but something you gain. And you gain it by winning small battles with honor.

'Petty Notes on Some Sex in America', first publ. 1961–2, repr. in *Cannibals and Christians* (1966). 'Because there is very little honor left in American life,' Mailer continued, 'there is a certain built-in tendency to destroy masculinity in American men.'

8 A modern democracy is a tyranny whose borders are undefined; one discovers how far one can go only by traveling in a straight line until one is stopped.

The Presidential Papers, Preface (1963)

9 Ultimately a hero is a man who would argue with the gods, and so awakens devils to contest his vision. The more a man can achieve, the more he may be certain that the devil will inhabit a part of his creation.

Ibid.

10 Writing books is the closest men ever come to childbearing.

'Mr Mailer Interviews Himself', first publ. in *The New York Times Book Review* 17 September 1965, repr. in *Conversations with Norman Mailer* (ed. J. Michael Lennon, 1988)

11 Sentimentality is the emotional promiscuity of those who have no sentiment.

Cannibals and Christians, 'My Hope for America' (1966)

12 New York is one of the capitals of the world and Los Angeles is a constellation of plastic, San Francisco is a lady, Boston has become Urban Renewal, Philadelphia and Baltimore and Washington blink like dull diamonds in the smog of Eastern Megalopolis, and New Orleans is unremarkable past the French Quarter. Detroit is a one-trade town, Pittsburgh has lost its golden triangle, St Louis has become the golden arch of the corporation, and nights in Kansas City close early. The oil depletion allowance makes Houston and Dallas naught but checkerboards for this sort of game. But Chicago is a great American city. Perhaps it is the last of the great American cities.

Miami and the Siege of Chicago, 'The Siege of Chicago' (1969). Opening paragraph.

13 The horror of the Twentieth Century was the size of each new event, and the paucity of its reverberation.

A Fire on the Moon, pt 1, ch. 1 (1970)

14 So we think of Marilyn who was every man's love affair with America. Marilyn Monroe who was blonde and beautiful and had a sweet little rinky-dink of a voice and all the cleanliness of all the clean American backyards.

Marilyn, ch. 1 (1973)

15 There is nothing safe about sex. There never will be.

International Herald Tribune 24 January 1992

John Major (b. 1943)

BRITISH POLITICIAN AND PRIME MINISTER

Succeeding MARGARET THATCHER *as Conservative Prime Minister in 1990, he won the 1992 general election but, dogged by criticism over the economy and European policy, suffered the greatest ever Tory election defeat in 1997. He retired from parliament in 2000. See* MICHAEL FOOT 2, JEAN KIERANS 1.

1 The first requirement of politics is not intellect or stamina but patience. Politics is a very long run game and the tortoise will usually beat the hare.

Daily Express 25 July 1989

2 The harsh truth is that if the policy isn't hurting, it isn't working. I know there is a difficult period ahead but the important thing is that we cannot and must not fudge the determination to stop inflation in its tracks.

Speech at Northampton, 27 October 1989, quoted in *The Times* 28 October 1989. This was Major's first speech as Chancellor of the Exchequer after the resignation of NIGEL LAWSON.

3 The politician who never made a mistake never made a decision.

Interview on 'The World This Weekend', BBC Radio 4, 25 November 1990

4 I want to see us build a country that is at ease with itself, a country that is confident, and a country that is prepared and willing to make the changes necessary to provide a better quality of life for all our citizens. I don't promise you that it will be easy, and I don't promise you that it will be quick, but I believe it is an immensely worthwhile job. Now, if you will forgive me, because it will be neither easy nor quick, I will go

into Number 10 straight away and make a start right now.

Speech outside No. 10 Downing Street, 28 November 1990, quoted in *John Major*, ch. 1 (1991) by Nesta Wyn Ellis. Major had won the Conservative Party leadership election, thereby becoming Prime Minister.

5 A consensus politician is someone who does something that he doesn't believe is right because it keeps people quiet when he does it.

Daily Mail 4 January 1991

6 Only in Britain could it be thought a defect to be 'too clever by half'. The probability is that too many people are too stupid by three-quarters.

Quoted in the *Observer* 7 July 1991

7 Society needs to condemn a little more and understand a little less.

Interview in the *Mail on Sunday* 21 February 1993. On the killing of James Bulger.

8 Fifty years on from now, Britain will still be the country of long shadows on county grounds, warm beer, invincible green suburbs, dog lovers and – as George Orwell said – old maids bicycling to Holy Communion through the morning mist.

Speech to Conservative Group for Europe, Inter-continental Hotel, London, 22 April 1993, quoted in the *Daily Telegraph* 23 April 1993. See GEORGE ORWELL 17.

9 It is time to get back to basics: to self-discipline and respect for the law, to consideration for others, to accepting responsibility for yourself and your family, and not shuffling it off on the state.

Speech to Conservative Party Conference, Black-pool, 8 October 1993, quoted in *The Times* 9 October 1993

Janet Malcolm (b. 1934)

US JOURNALIST, ESSAYIST AND CRITIC
Her wide-ranging books include Diana and Nikon: Essays on the Aesthetic of Photography *(1980) and* Reading Chekhov: A Critical Journey *(2003).*

1 Every journalist who is not too stupid or too full of himself to notice what is going on knows that what he does is morally indefensible. He is a kind of confidence man, preying on people's vanity, ignorance, or loneliness, gaining their trust and betraying them without remorse.

The Journalist and the Murderer, pt 1 (1990). Opening paragraph of book, which discusses the case of journalist Joe McGinniss, who won the trust of an alleged murderer, then wrote a best-seller, *Fatal Vision* (1984), proclaiming his guilt.

2 Fidelity to the subject's thought and to his

characteristic way of expressing himself is the sine qua non of journalistic quotation.

Ibid. Malcolm, who had been accused in a legal dispute of fabricating quotations, argued in her book that capturing the gist of a statement is primary, while accurate quotation is impossible. 'When we talk with somebody, we are not aware of the language we are speaking,' she wrote. 'Our ear takes it in as English, and only if we see it transcribed verbatim do we realize that it is a kind of foreign tongue.'

Malcolm X (1925–65)

US BLACK CIVIL RIGHTS ACTIVIST
Originally Malcolm Little. He converted to Islam and joined the Black Muslims (Nation of Islam) while in prison for burglary (1946–53). On his release he attracted a following through his advocacy of black separatism and self-defence, but his founding of the Organization of Afro-American Unity in 1964 caused a rift with the Black Muslims which led to his assassination.

1 If you're born in America with a black skin, you're born in prison, and the masses of black people in America today are beginning to regard our plight or predicament in this society as one of a prison inmate.

Interview in June 1963, publ. in *Malcolm X: The Man and His Times*, pt 3, 'Malcolm X Talks with Kenneth B. Clark' (ed. John Henrik Clarke, 1969)

2 There is nothing in our book, the Koran, that teaches us to suffer peacefully. Our religion teaches us to be intelligent. Be peaceful, be courteous, obey the law, respect everyone; but if someone puts his hand on you, send him to the cemetery. That's a good religion.

'Message to the Grass Roots', speech in Detroit, November 1963, publ. in *Malcolm X Speaks*, ch. 1 (1965). See also ALICE WALKER 18.

3 It's just like when you've got some coffee that's too black, which means it's too strong. What do you do? You integrate it with cream, you make it weak. But if you pour too much cream in it, you won't even know you ever had coffee. It used to be hot, it becomes cool. It used to be strong, it becomes weak. It used to wake you up, now it puts you to sleep.

Ibid.

4 Sitting at the table doesn't make you a diner, unless you eat some of what's on that plate. Being here in America doesn't make you an American. Being born here in America doesn't make you an American.

'The Ballot or the Bullet', speech in Cleveland, Ohio, 3 April 1964, publ. ibid., ch. 3

5 We have formed an organization known as the Organization of Afro-American Unity . . . To fight whoever gets in our way, to bring about the complete independence of

people of African descent here in the Western hemisphere, and first here in the United States, and bring about the freedom of these people by any means necessary. That's our motto. We want freedom by any means necessary. We want justice by any means necessary. We want equality by any means necessary.

Speech at OAAU Founding Rally, Audubon Ballroom, New York, 28 June 1964, publ. in *Malcolm X By Any Means Necessary* (ed. George Breitman, 1970). The words 'by any means necessary' became a rallying call among radical movements in the 1960s.

6 The common goal of 22 million Afro-Americans is respect as *human beings*, the God-given right to be a *human being*. Our common goal is to obtain the *human rights* that America has been denying us. We can never get civil rights in America until our *human rights* are first restored. We will never be recognized as citizens there until we are first recognized as *humans*.

'Racism: the Cancer that is Destroying America', publ. in the *Egyptian Gazette* 25 August 1964. See DICK GREGORY 1.

7 I believe in the brotherhood of man, all men, but I don't believe in brotherhood with anybody who doesn't want brotherhood with me. I believe in treating people right, but I'm not going to waste my time trying to treat somebody right who doesn't know how to return the treatment.

Speech in New York, 12 December 1964, publ. in *Malcolm X: The Man and His Times*, pt 5, 'Communication and Reality' (ed. John Henrik Clarke, 1969)

8 You can't separate peace from freedom because no one can be at peace unless he has his freedom.

'Prospects for Freedom in 1965', speech in New York, 7 January 1965, publ. in *Malcolm X Speaks*, ch. 12 (1965)

John Malkovich (b. 1953)
US ACTOR
He was co-founder of the Steppenwolf Theatre Company in Chicago (1976), making his cinematic debut in Places in the Heart *(1984). In 1999 he played himself in* Being John Malkovich.

1 Where women are concerned, the rule is never to go out with anyone better dressed than you.

Interview in the *Independent on Sunday* 5 April 1992

George Leigh Mallory (1886–1924)
BRITISH MOUNTAINEER
Assistant Master of Charterhouse College, Cambridge (1910–15), he lost his life during his third

attempt to climb Everest after previous ventures in 1921 and 1922.

1 Because it's there.

Interview in *The New York Times* 18 March 1923. On being asked why he wanted to climb Mount Everest.

David Malouf (b. 1934)
AUSTRALIAN NOVELIST AND POET
His fiction frequently takes on historical themes, as in An Imaginary Life *(1978) about Ovid, and his epic* The Great World *(1990). He has also written librettos.*

1 *All safe as houses, fire*
   kennelled in a matchbox,
   the water of drowned valleys
   dammed behind taps.
   Barring accidents, or malice
   nothing's disaster-proof.

'On Refusing an All-risk Insurance Policy', publ. in *Bicycle and Other Poems* (1970)

André Malraux (1901–76)
FRENCH STATESMAN AND MAN OF LETTERS
He fought in Indochina, Spain and France, and held a number of cabinet positions in post-war Gaullist administrations. His writings include history, philosophy and the novels Man's Fate *(1933) and* Man's Hope *(1937, filmed 1938).*

1 There are not fifty ways of fighting, there's only one, and that's to win. Neither revolution nor war consists in doing what one pleases

Man's Hope, pt 2, sect. 2, ch. 12 (1937)

2 All art is a revolt against man's fate.

The Voices of Silence, pt 4, ch. 7 (1951)

3 Remote from ourselves in dream and in time, India belongs to the Ancient Orient of our soul. . . . What is Zeus, compared with Shiva? The only god of antiquity whose language is worthy of India is the god without temples – Fate.

Anti-Memoirs, 'The Temptation of the West', sect. 1 (1967)

4 The attempt to force human beings to despise themselves. That is what I call hell.

Ibid., 'The Human Condition', sect. 2. Referring to the concentration camps in Nazi Germany.

David Mamet (b. 1947)
US PLAYWRIGHT
His breakthrough play was American Buffalo *(1975), and he subsequently won the Pulitzer Prize for* Glengarry Glen Ross *(1984). His 1992 play about sexual harassment* Oleanna *(filmed 1994) provoked accusations of misogyny. He has also written screenplays and essays.*

1 We respond to a drama to that extent to which it corresponds to our dreamlife.

Writing in Restaurants, 'A National Dream-Life' (1986)

2 The product of the artist has become less important than the *fact* of the artist. We wish to absorb this person. We wish to devour someone who has experienced the tragic. In our society this person is much more important than anything he might create.

Ibid., 'Exuvial Magic: An Essay Concerning Fashion'

3 The poker player learns that sometimes both science and common sense are wrong; that the bumblebee *can* fly; that, perhaps, one should never trust an expert; that there are more things in heaven and earth than are dreamt of by those with an academic bent.

Ibid., 'Things I Have Learned Playing Poker on the Hill'

4 The art of the theater is action. It is the study of commitment. The word is an act. To *say* the word in such a way as to make it heard and understood by all in the theater is a commitment – it is the highest art to see a human being out on a stage speaking to a thousand of his or her peers saying, 'These words which I am speaking are the *truth* – they are not an approximation of any kind. They are the God's truth, and I support them with my life,' which is what the actor does on stage. Without this commitment, acting becomes prostitution and writing becomes advertising.

Ibid., 'Against Amplification'

5 Life in the movie business is like the beginning of a new love affair: it's full of surprises and you're constantly getting fucked.

Charlie Fox, in *Speed-the-Plow*, sc. 1 (1988)

6 A good film script should be able to do completely without dialogue.

Independent 11 November 1988

7 I can envision no device more capable of spreading ignorance and illiteracy than the computer. It is, I think, like the atom bomb, a naturally evolved engine of destruction, a sign, like the Tower of Babel, that civilization has run its course.

Jafsie and John Henry, 'Why Don't You Write With a Computer?' (2000)

Nelson Mandela (b. 1918)

SOUTH AFRICAN POLITICAL LEADER

The international symbol of the anti-apartheid movement, he spent the years 1964–90 in prison for his role in the banned African National Congress. On his release he was elected President of the ANC and South Africa's first black president (1994–9). He received the Nobel Peace Prize in 1993.

1 For my own part I have made my choice. I will not leave South Africa, nor will I surrender. Only through hardship, sacrifice and militant action can freedom be won. The struggle is my life. I will continue fighting for freedom until the end of my days.

Press statement, 26 June 1961, publ. by the ANC in London, repr. in *The Struggle Is My Life*, pt 2 'The Struggle Is My Life' (1978)

2 Whatever he himself may say in his defence, the white man's moral standards in this country must be judged by the extent to which he has condemned the vast majority of its inhabitants to serfdom and inferiority.

Defence statement at trial in Pretoria, 15 October–7 November 1962, publ. ibid., 'Black Man in a White Court'

3 The whole life of any thinking African in this country drives him continuously to a conflict between his conscience on the one hand and the law on the other.

Address to court after closure of prosecution case, ibid.

4 Only free men can negotiate. Prisoners cannot enter into contracts.

Statement from prison, 10 February 1985, quoted in *Higher than Hope*, ch. 30 (1988) by Fatima Meer. Refusing the terms set for his release by South African president P. W. BOTHA. The statement was read by Zindzi Mandela, Nelson's daughter, at a United Democratic Front rally at the Jabulani Stadium, Soweto.

5 The prison . . . operates to break the human spirit, to exploit human weakness, undermine human strength, destroy initiative, individuality, negate intelligence and process an amorphous, robot-like mass. The great challenge is how to resist, how not to adjust, to keep intact the knowledge of the society outside and to live by its rules, for that is the only way to maintain the human and the social within you.

Quoted ibid., ch. 25

6 There is nothing more terrifying than to be alone with sheer time. Then the ghosts come crowding in. They can be very sinister, very mischievous, raising a thousand doubts in your mind about the people outside, their loyalty. Was your sacrifice worth the trouble? What would your life have been like if you hadn't got involved?

Ibid. On solitary confinement

7 To be father of a nation is a great honour, but to be the father of a family is a greater joy.

Long Walk to Freedom, ch. 109 (1994)

Winnie Mandela (b. 1934)

SOUTH AFRICAN POLITICAL LEADER

Nomzano Zaniewe Winifred Mandela. During her husband NELSON MANDELA*'s imprisonment, she campaigned for his release and for the African National Congress. She was charged with kidnapping in 1991 and with fraud in 2002. She separated from her husband in 1992 and they divorced in 1996.*

1 Together, hand in hand, with that stick of matches, with our necklace, we shall liberate this country.

Speech in black townships, quoted in the *Guardian* 15 April 1986

Osip Mandelstam (1891–1938)

RUSSIAN POET

Associated with the Acmeist movement, he published the collections Kamen (Stone, *1913) and* Tristia (Sad Things, *1922). He was harshly criticized by the Bolsheviks and in 1934 was arrested and exiled for a poem denouncing* STALIN. *He died en route to a forced labour camp.*

1 I have studied the science of good-byes, the bare-headed laments of night.

'Tristia', st. 1, publ. in *Tristia* (1922), repr. in *Selected Poems* (1973)

2 O indigence at the root of our lives, how poor is the language of happiness! Everything's happened before and will happen again, but still the moment of each meeting is sweet.

Ibid., st. 3

3 In poetry, war is always being waged. It is only in periods of social imbecility that there is peace or a peace treaty is concluded. Like generals, the bearers of word roots take up arms against each other. Word roots battle in the darkness, depleting each other's food supplies and the juices of the earth.

'Vulgata: Some Notes on Poetry', essay, first publ. 1923, repr. in *The Complete Critical Prose and Letters* (ed. Jane Gary Harris et al., 1979)

4 To read Pasternak's verse is to clear your throat, to fortify your breathing, to fill your lungs; surely such poetry could provide a cure for tuberculosis. No poetry is more healthful at the present moment! It is like *koumiss* after evaporated milk.

'Boris Pasternak', essay, first publ. 1923, repr. ibid. as 'Some Notes on Poetry'

5 No matter how you stars want to shine, First apply on the dotted line, We're sure to renew your permission For shining or writing or extinction.

Untitled poem, written October 1930, publ. in *Osip Mandelstam: 50 poems* (1977)

6 Poetry, you put storms to good use.

'To the German Language', written August 1932, publ. in *Selected Poems* (1973)

7 But whenever there's a snatch of talk it turns to the Kremlin mountaineer, the ten thick worms his fingers, his words like measures of weight, the huge laughing cockroaches on his top lip the glitter of his boot-rims.

'The Stalin Epigram', written 1933, publ. in *Selected Poems* (1973). Referring to Stalin. The private circulation of the poem led to Mandelstam's first arrest in 1934.

8 A quotation is not an excerpt. A quotation is a cicada. Its natural state is that of unceasing sound. Having once seized hold of the air, it will not let it go.

'Conversation About Dante', sect. 2, written 1933–4, publ. in *The Complete Critical Prose and Letters* (ed. Jane Gary Harris et al., 1979)

Christopher Manes (b. 1957)

US ECOLOGIST

He is prominent among environmental activists for the video documentary Earth First! The Politics of Radical Environmentalism *(1988) and for his book* Green Rage *(1990).*

1 Such is the scope of the environmental crisis that it makes us question our entire history on Earth, back to the origins of civilization. People in the future may very well look back and wonder how the last generations could have gotten caught up in such minor distractions as two world wars, space flight, and the nuclear arms race.

Green Rage, ch. 2 (1990)

2 It entered the seventies as a vague critic of our society and exited as an institution, wrapped in the consumerism and political ambitions it once condemned. In their drive to win credibility with the government agencies and corporations . . . the new professional environmentalists seemed to have wandered into the ambiguous world of George Orwell's *Animal Farm*, where it was increasingly difficult to tell the farmers from the pigs.

Of the ecology movement, ibid., ch. 3

Michael Manley (1924–97)

JAMAICAN POLITICIAN AND PRIME MINISTER

He succeeded his father Norman Manley as President of the People's National Party in 1969, and served as Prime Minister 1972–80 and 1989–92.

1 You know people exaggerate that all is wild in Jamaica. I think that sometimes people fire a shot to try to make you nervous. They are not trying to hurt you.

Daily Telegraph 8 February 1989

Golo Mann (1909–94)

GERMAN HISTORIAN

Diverging from the literary careers of his father
THOMAS MANN *and his brother* KLAUS MANN,
*he established a reputation as a historian, chiefly
known for his* History of Germany Since 1789
(1968) and the biography, Wallenstein: His Life
Narrated *(1971).*

1 Closest to the truth are those who deal
  lightly with it because they know it is
  inexhaustible.
  Quoted in *Thomas Mann and His Family*, 'Golo
  Mann: The Liberation of an Unloved One'
  (1987) by Marcel Reich-Ranicki. Writing of satirist Heinrich Heine.

2 Man is always more than he can know of
  himself; consequently, his accomplishments, time and again, will come as a surprise to him.
  Ibid. An insight gleaned from philosopher Karl
  Jaspers.

Klaus Mann (1906–49)

GERMAN AUTHOR

After he and family members THOMAS MANN
and GOLO MANN *settled in America, he founded
the literary magazine* Decision *and published* The
Turning Point, *an autobiography (1942), and*
Pathetic Symphony, *about Tchaikovsky (1948).*

1 One cannot serve this Eros without becoming a stranger in society as it is today; one
  cannot commit oneself to this form of love
  without incurring a mortal wound.
  Quoted in *Thomas Mann and His Family*, 'Klaus
  Mann' (1987) by Marcel Reich-Ranicki. Referring to his homosexuality.

Thomas Mann (1875–1955)

GERMAN-BORN US AUTHOR AND CRITIC

His most celebrated works include Buddenbrooks
(1901), Tonio Kröger *(1902),* Death in Venice
(1913, filmed 1971) and The Magic Mountain
*(1924). Much of his fiction examines the role of the
artist in society. A supporter of the Weimar Republic, he fled Nazi Germany and in 1940 became an
American citizen. See* PETER HANDKE 3.

1 A man lives not only his personal life, as
  an individual, but also, consciously or
  unconsciously, the life of his epoch and his
  contemporaries.
  The Magic Mountain, ch. 2, 'At Tienappels''
  (1924)

2 There is something suspicious about
  music, gentlemen. I insist that she is, by
  her nature, equivocal. I shall not be going
  too far in saying at once that she is politically suspect.
  Herr Settembrini, ibid., ch. 4, 'Politically
  Suspect'

3 Time has no divisions to mark its passage,
  there is never a thunderstorm or blare of
  trumpets to announce the beginning of a
  new month or year. Even when a new century begins it is only we mortals who ring
  bells and fire off pistols.
  Ibid., ch. 5, 'Whims of Mercurius'

4 Opinions cannot survive if one has no
  chance to fight for them.
  Ibid., ch. 6, 'Of The City of God'

5 A man's dying is more the survivors' affair
  than his own.
  Ibid., 'A Soldier, And Brave'

6 We, when we sow the seeds of doubt
  deeper than the most up-to-date and mod-
  ish free-thought has ever dreamed of
  doing, we well know what we are about.
  Only out of radical skepsis, out of moral
  chaos, can the Absolute spring, the
  anointed Terror of which the time has
  need.
  Leo Naphta, ibid., ch. 7, 'Hysterica Passio'

7 An art whose medium is language will
  always show a high degree of critical creativeness, for speech is itself a critique of
  life: it names, it characterizes, it passes
  judgment, in that it creates.
  'Lessing speech', Prussian Academy of Art,
  Berlin, 22 January 1929, first publ. 1930, repr. in
  Essays of Three Decades (1942)

8 Unhappy German nation, how do you like
  the Messianic rôle allotted to you, not by
  God, nor by destiny, but by a handful of
  perverted and bloody-minded men?
  'This War', first publ. 1939, repr. in *Order of the
  Day* (1942)

9 The Freudian theory is one of the most
  important foundation stones for an edifice
  to be built by future generations, the dwelling of a freer and wiser humanity.
  The New York Times 21 June 1939

10 It is a strange fact that freedom and
  equality, the two basic ideas of democracy,
  are to some extent contradictory. Logically
  considered, freedom and equality are mutually exclusive, just as society and the individual are mutually exclusive.
  'The War and the Future', speech 1940, publ. in
  Order of the Day (1942)

11 What we call National-Socialism is the
  poisonous perversion of ideas which have
  a long history in German intellectual life.
  Ibid.

12 I have always been an admirer, I regard the
  gift of admiration as indispensable if one is
  to amount to something; I don't know
  where I would be without it.
  Letter, 1950, quoted in *Thomas Mann and His
  Family*, 'Thomas Mann – The Birth of Criticism'
  (1987) by Marcel Reich-Ranicki

13 Every reasonable human being should be a moderate Socialist.

The New York Times 18 June 1950, quoted in *Thomas Mann: A Critical Study*, ch. 2 (1971) by R. J. Hollingdale

Dick Manning See AL HOFFMAN AND DICK MANNING.

Katherine Mansfield (1888–1923)
NEW ZEALAND-BORN BRITISH AUTHOR

Her stories, collected in Bliss (1919) and The Garden Party (1920) among other titles, are noted for their psychological realism, though they did not meet with the approval of VIRGINIA WOOLF, who remarked: 'Her mind is a very thin soil, laid an inch or two upon very barren rock.' She also wrote poetry, posthumously edited and published by her husband JOHN MIDDLETON MURRY. See LOUISE BOGAN 2.

1 To work – to work! It is such infinite delight to know that we still have the best things to do.

Letter to BERTRAND RUSSELL, 7 December 1916, publ. in *Collected Letters*, vol. 1 (ed. Vincent O'Sullivan and Margaret Scott, 1984)

2 It's a terrible thing to be alone – yes it is – it is – but don't lower your mask until you have another mask prepared beneath – as terrible as you like – but a *mask*.

Letter to JOHN MIDDLETON MURRY, July 1917, publ. ibid. Referring to Murry's current writing which she found 'indecent' for his tendency to 'abase' himself, during a period when he was most influenced by the style of D. H. LAWRENCE.

3 I'm a writer first & a woman after.

Ibid., 3 December 1920

4 Everything in life that we really accept undergoes a change. So suffering must become Love. That is the mystery.

Journal entry, 19 December 1920, publ. in *The Journal of Katherine Mansfield* (1927)

Mao Zedong (1893–1976)
CHINESE LEADER

One of the founders of the Chinese Communist Party in 1921, he became its leader in 1943 and Chairman of the People's Republic of China in 1949. His 'Thoughts' became doctrine in China and were cited by radicals everywhere, although his name is also associated with the oppression of the Cultural Revolution (1966–9).

1 A revolution is not a dinner party, or writing an essay, or painting a picture, or doing embroidery; it cannot be so refined, so leisurely and gentle, so temperate, kind, courteous, restrained and magnanimous. A revolution is an insurrection, an act of violence by which one class overthrows another.

Report, March 1927, publ. in *Selected Works*, vol. 1 (1954)

2 Politics is war without bloodshed while war is politics with bloodshed.

'On Protracted War', lecture, May 1938, publ. ibid., vol. 2 (1961)

3 Weapons are an important factor in war, but not the decisive factor; it is people, not things, that are decisive. The contest of strength is not only a contest of military and economic power, but also a contest of human power and morale. Military and economic power is necessarily wielded by people.

Ibid.

4 Our attitude towards ourselves should be 'to be insatiable in learning' and towards others 'to be tireless in teaching'.

'The Role of the Chinese Communist Party in the National War' (October 1938), publ. ibid.

5 Every Communist must grasp the truth, 'Political power grows out of the barrel of a gun.'

'Problems of War and Strategy', speech, 6 November 1938, publ. ibid. JEAN GENET observed: 'Power may be at the end of a gun, but sometimes it's also at the end of the shadow or the image of a gun.'

6 War can only be abolished through war, and in order to get rid of the gun it is necessary to take up the gun.

Ibid.

7 So long as a person who has made mistakes does not hide his sickness for fear of treatment or persist in his mistakes until he is beyond cure, so long as he honestly and sincerely wishes to be cured and to mend his ways, we should welcome him and cure his sickness so that he can become a good comrade. We can never succeed if we just let ourselves go and lash out at him. In treating an ideological or a political malady, one must never be rough and rash but must adopt the approach of 'curing the sickness to save the patient', which is the only correct and effective method.

'Rectify the Party's Style of Work' (1 February 1942), publ. ibid., vol. 3 (1961)

8 There is in fact no such thing as art for art's sake, art that stands above classes, art that is detached from or independent of politics. Proletarian literature and art are part of the whole proletarian revolutionary cause.

'Talks at the Yenan Forum on Literature and Art' (May 1942), publ. ibid.

9 Take the ideas of the masses (scattered and

unsystematic ideas) and concentrate them (through study turn them into concentrated and systematic ideas), then go to the masses and propagate and explain these ideas until the masses embrace them as their own, hold fast to them and translate them into action, and test the correctness of these ideas in such action. Then once again concentrate ideas from the masses and once again go to the masses so that the ideas are persevered in and carried through. And so on, over and over again in an endless spiral, with the ideas becoming more correct, more vital and richer each time. Such is the Marxist theory of knowledge.

'Some Questions Concerning Methods of Leadership' (1 June 1943), publ. ibid.

10 An army without culture is a dull-witted army, and a dull-witted army cannot defeat the enemy.

'The United Front in Cultural Work' (30 October 1944), publ. ibid.

11 The people, and the people alone, are the motive force in the making of world history.

'On Coalition Government' (24 April 1945), publ. ibid.

12 All reactionaries are paper tigers. In appearance, the reactionaries are terrifying, but in reality they are not so powerful. From a long-term point of view, it is not the reactionaries but the people who are really powerful.

'Talk with the American correspondent Anne Louise Strong', August 1946, publ. ibid., vol. 4 (1961). Mao returned to this theme in a later speech in Moscow, 18 November 1957: 'Was not Hitler a paper tiger? Was Hitler not overthrown? ... US imperialism has not yet been overthrown and it has the atomic bomb. I believe it also will be overthrown. It, too, is a paper tiger.'

13 Classes struggle, some classes triumph, others are eliminated. Such is history; such is the history of civilization for thousands of years.

Said in August 1949, quoted in Mao and China: From Revolution to Revolution (1972) by Stanley Karnow

14 Communism is not love. Communism is a hammer which we use to crush the enemy.

Quoted in Time 18 December 1950

15 Letting a hundred flowers blossom and a hundred schools of thought contend is the policy for promoting the progress of the arts and the sciences and a flourishing socialist culture in our land.

Speech in Beijing, 27 February 1957, quoted in Quotations from Chairman Mao Tse-Tung, ch. 32 (1966)

16 Apart from their other characteristics, the

outstanding thing about China's 600 million people is that they are 'poor and blank'. This may seem a bad thing, but in reality it is a good thing. Poverty gives rise to the desire for change, the desire for action and the desire for revolution. On a blank sheet of paper free from any mark, the freshest and most beautiful characters can be written, the freshest and most beautiful pictures can be painted.

'Introducing a Co-operative' (15 April 1958), quoted ibid., ch. 3

Diego Maradona (b. 1960)
ARGENTINIAN FOOTBALLER
A brilliant and controversial striker, he became the world's most expensive footballer on joining Barcelona for £5 million in 1982. He played a key role in Argentina's victory in the 1986 World Cup, although his career was marred by cocaine use.

1 The goal was scored a little bit by the hand of God, a little by the head of Maradona.

Quoted in the Observer 29 June 1986. Referring to the goal bounced off his fist, thereby ousting England from the World Cup finals in Mexico.

Marcel Marceau (b. 1923)
FRENCH MIME ARTIST
Internationally recognized for his mastery of mime, he extended the possibilities of the art in such works as the mime-drama Don Juan *(1964) and the ballet* Candide *(1971).*

1 Do not the most moving moments of our lives find us all without words?

Reader's Digest June 1958

2 I have spent more than half a lifetime trying to express the tragic moment.

Guardian 11 August 1988

Paul Marcinkus (b. 1922)
US ECCLESIASTIC
He was director of the Institute of Religious Works, or Vatican bank, which became implicated in the scandal surrounding the Banco Ambrosiano in 1982. The Holy See resisted all attempts by investigating magistrates to force him to submit to Italian justice.

1 You can't run the Church on Hail Marys.

Quoted in the Observer 25 May 1986

Imelda Marcos (b. 1929)
FILIPINO FIRST LADY
The wife of Ferdinand Marcos, President of the Philippines (1965–86), she was publicly disgraced by revelations of nepotism, embezzlement of state funds and a prodigious collection of shoes. She was elected to the Philippines House of Representatives in 1995.

1 I get so tired listening to one million

dollars here, one million dollars there, it's
so petty.

Quoted in *The Times* 22 June 1990. Marcos was
complaining of the numerous witnesses called to
testify to her financial profligacy during her trial
on charges of embezzlement in New York.

Greil Marcus (b. 1945)

US ROCK JOURNALIST
A contributor of articles and reviews to The New
York Times, Village Voice *and* Rolling Stone,
*where he was Associate Editor (1969–70) and
Book Editor (1975–80), he wrote the classic* Mys-
tery Train: Images of America in Rock 'n' Roll
Music *(1975).*

1 We make the oldest stories new when we
succeed, and we are trapped by the old
stories when we fail.

Mystery Train, Prologue (1975)

2 It may be that the most interesting American struggle is the struggle to set oneself
free from the limits one is born to, and
then to learn something of the value of
those limits.

Ibid., 'Robert Johnson, 1938'

3 No failure in America, whether of love or
money, is ever simple; it is always a kind of
betrayal, of a mass of shadowy, shared
hopes.

Ibid.

4 Rock 'n' roll is a combination of good
ideas dried up by fads, terrible junk, hideous failings in taste and judgment, gullibility and manipulation, moments of
unbelievable clarity and invention, pleasure, fun, vulgarity, excess, novelty and
utter enervation.

Ibid., 'Randy Newman: Pop'

5 We fight our way through the massed and
leveled collective safe taste of the Top 40,
just looking for a little something we can
call our own. But when we find it and jam
the radio to hear it again it isn't just ours –
it is a link to thousands of others who are
sharing it with us. As a matter of a single
song this might mean very little; as culture,
as a way of life, you can't beat it.

Ibid.

6 It is a sure sign that a culture has reached a
dead end when it is no longer intrigued by
its myths.

Ibid., 'Elvis: Presliad: Fanfare'

7 Punk to me was a form of free speech. It
was a moment when suddenly all kinds of
strange voices that no reasonable person
could ever have expected to hear in public
were being heard all over the place.

'Punk and History', transcript of discussion,
24 September 1988, New York, publ. in

*Discourses: Conversations in Postmodern Art and
Culture* (ed. Russell Ferguson *et al.*, 1990)

Herbert Marcuse (1898–1979)

GERMAN-BORN US POLITICAL PHILOSOPHER
*The blend of psychoanalytic theory and libertarian
left-wing thought in such works as* Eros and Civilization *(1955) and* One-Dimensional Man *(1964)
was a major influence on young intellectuals in the
1960s.*

1 If the worker and his boss enjoy the same
television program and visit the same
resort places, if the typist is as attractively
made up as the daughter of her employer,
if the Negro owns a Cadillac, if they all
read the same newspaper, then this assimilation indicates not the disappearance of
classes, but the extent to which the needs
and satisfactions that serve the preservation of the Establishment are shared by
the underlying population.

One-Dimensional Man, ch. 1 (1964)

2 The web of domination has become the
web of Reason itself, and this society is
fatally entangled in it.

Ibid., ch. 5

3 Self-determination, the autonomy of the
individual, asserts itself in the right to race
his automobile, to handle his power tools,
to buy a gun, to communicate to mass
audiences his opinion, no matter how
ignorant, how aggressive, it may be.

An Essay on Liberation, ch. 1 (1969)

Jacques Maritain (1882–1973)

FRENCH PHILOSOPHER
*As a neo-Thomist philosopher and Catholic theo-
logian, he drew controversy for his liberal and left-
wing interpretation of Roman Catholic doctrine.
Published works include* The Degrees of Knowledge *(1932) and* Scholasticism in Politics *(1940).*

1 I don't see America as a mainland, but as a
sea, a big ocean. Sometimes a storm arises,
a formidable current develops, and it
seems it will engulf everything. Wait a
moment, another current will appear and
bring the first one to naught.

Reflections on America, ch. 4 (1948)

(Dame) Alicia Markova (b. 1910)

BRITISH BALLERINA
*Born Lilian Alicia Marks. She joined Diaghilev's
Ballets Russes in 1924 and was prima ballerina of
the Vic-Wells (now the Royal Ballet) 1933–5. She
toured extensively, notably in Giselle, and in 1950
founded the Festival Ballet Company.*

1 Glorious bouquets and storms of applause
. . . are the trimmings which every artist
naturally enjoys. But to *move* an audience
in such a role, to hear in the applause that

unmistakable note which breaks through good theatre manners and comes from the heart, is to feel that you have won through to life itself. Such pleasure does not vanish with the fall of the curtain, but becomes part of one's own life.

Giselle and I, ch. 18 (1960)

Bob Marley (1945–81)
JAMAICAN REGGAE MUSICIAN
He made his first record in 1961, but it was not until the albums Catch a Fire *(1972) and* Natty Dread *(1975), recorded with the Wailers, that he achieved international success. His songs drew heavily on his Rastafarian beliefs.*

1 *Get up, stand up,*
Stand up for your rights.
Get up, stand up,
Don't give up the fight.
'Get Up, Stand Up' (song, written with PETER TOSH) on the album *Burnin'* (1973) by the Wailers

2 *Them belly full but we 'ungry*
A hungry mob is a angry mob.
'Them Belly Full' (song, written by Legon Cogil and Carlton Barrett) on the album *Natty Dread* (1975) by Bob Marley and the Wailers

3 Until the philosophy which holds one race superior and another inferior is finally and permanently discredited and abandoned, everywhere is war . . . and until there are no longer first-class and second-class citizens of any nation, until the colour of a man's skin is of no more significance than the colour of his eyes, me seh war. And until the basic human rights are equally guaranteed to all without regard to race, there is war. And until that day, the dream of lasting peace, world citizenship, rule of international morality, will remain but a fleeting illusion to be pursued, but never attained . . . now everywhere is war.
'War' (song) on the album *Rastaman Vibration* (1976) by Bob Marley and the Wailers. The words of the song are based on a speech given to the United Nations by the Ethiopian emperor Haile Selassie in 1968.

4 The real reggae must come from Jamaica, because other people could not play it all the while, anyway – it would go against the whole life. Reggae has t' be inside you. . . . Reggae music is simple, all the while. . . . Cannot be taught, that's a fact.
Interview in *Melody Maker* 12 June 1976, repr. in *Melody Maker: Classic Rock Interviews* (ed. Allan Jones, 1994)

5 *Emancipate yourselves from mental slavery.*
None but ourselves can free our minds.
'Redemption Song' (song) on the album *Uprising* (1980) by Bob Marley and the Wailers

Don Marquis (1878–1937)
US HUMORIST AND JOURNALIST
Known for his poems, essays and humorous writings, he was the creator in 1927 of archy and mehitabel, a cat and a literary-minded cockroach who debate life's complexities in light verse.

1 *A fierce unrest seethes at the core*
Of all existing things:
It was the eager wish to soar
That gave the gods their wings.
'Unrest', publ. in *Dreams and Dust* (1915)

2 *my youth i shall never forget*
but there s nothing i really regret
wotthehell wotthehell
there s a dance in the old dame yet
toujours gai toujours gai
'the song of mehitabel', publ. in *archy and mehitabel* (1927)

3 *persian pussy from over the sea*
demure and lazy and smug and fat
none of your ribbons and bells for me
ours is the zest of the alley cat
'mehitabels extensive past', publ. ibid.

4 *procrastination is the*
art of keeping
up with yesterday
'certain maxims of archy', publ. ibid.

5 *every cloud*
has its silver
lining but it is
sometimes a little
difficult to get it to
the mint
Ibid.

6 *an optimist is a guy*
who has never had
much experience
Ibid.

7 *did you ever*
notice that when
a politician
does get an idea
he usually
gets it all wrong
'mehitabel again', publ. in *archys life of mehitabel* (1933)

8 *now and then*
there is a person born
who is so unlucky
that he runs into accidents
which started out to happen
to somebody else
'archy says', publ. ibid.

9 Bores bore each other too; but it never seems to teach them anything.
Quoted in *A Little Book of Aphorisms* (1947) by Frederic B. Wilcox

10 The art of newspaper paragraphing is to

stroke a platitude until it purrs like an epigram.

Ibid. ADLAI STEVENSON borrowed this idea when he quipped: 'The Republicans stroke platitudes until they purr like epigrams' (quoted in *The Fine Art of Political Wit*, ch. 1, 1964 by Leon Harris).

11 Middle age is the time when a man is always thinking that in a week or two he will feel as good as ever.

Ibid.

12 A demagogue is a person with whom we disagree as to which gang should mismanage the country.

Ibid.

13 I get up in the morning with an idea for a three-volume novel and by nightfall it's a paragraph in my column.

Quoted in *O Rare Don Marquis*, ch. 6 (1962) by E. Anthony

14 Writing a book of poetry is like dropping a rose petal down the Grand Canyon and waiting for the echo.

Ibid. This aphorism emerged as the distillation of what had been a long piece on the futility of writing poetry for Don Marquis's 'Sun Dial' column, which he rejected on the grounds of it being too much a plaint, publishing instead this one sentence.

15 Poetry is what Milton saw when he went blind.

Ibid., ch. 11. 'That line would have pleased Milton himself,' observed the poet Louis Untermeyer.

16 By the time a bartender knows what drink a man will have before he orders, there is little else about him worth knowing.

Ibid. FRANKLIN P. ADAMS cited this aphorism to illustrate Marquis's gift for 'telling a whole story in a sentence'.

Anthony Marriott (b. 1931) and Alistair Foot

BRITISH PLAYWRIGHTS

They collaborated on a number of plays, including Uproar in the House (1967) and No Sex Please – We're British (1971), a long-running West End farce.

1 No Sex Please – We're British.

Title of play (1971)

Wynton Marsalis (b. 1961)

US JAZZ MUSICIAN

He emerged in the 1980s with a trumpet style equally at home with the classical and jazz repertoires. His jazz albums include Soul Gestures in Southern Blue (1991).

1 Jazz is music that really deals with what it means to be an American. The irony is when they wrote the Declaration of Independence and the United States Constitution, they didn't even think of a Black man. Yet Louis Armstrong, the grandson of a slave, is the one more than anybody else [who] could translate into music that feeling of what it is to be an American.

'We Must Preserve Our Jazz Heritage', publ. in *Ebony* February 1986

Thomas R. Marshall (1854–1925)

US POLITICIAN

A Democratic governor of Indiana (1909–13), he served two terms as vice-president under WOODROW WILSON (1913–17 and 1917–21).

1 What this country needs is a really good 5-cent cigar.

Quoted in the *New York Tribune* 4 January 1920

Steve Martin (b. 1945)

US COMEDIAN AND COMIC ACTOR

Starting out as a stand-up comic, he has appeared in numerous films including Roxanne (1987) and LA Story (1991), both of which he wrote, produced and starred in.

1 All dames are alike. They reach down your throat so they can grab your heart, they pull it out, they throw it on the floor and they step on it with their high heels. They spit on it. They shove it in the oven and they cook the shit out of it. Then they slice it into little pieces, slam it on a hunk of toast and serve it to you. And they expect you to say: thanks honey, it's delicious!

Rigby Reardon (Steve Martin), in *Dead Men Don't Wear Plaid*, (film, 1982, screenplay by George Gipe, Carl Reiner and Steve Martin, directed by Carl Reiner)

2 I believe entertainment can aspire to be art, and can become art, but if you set out to make art you're an idiot.

Today 17 May 1989

Strother Martin (1919–80)

US SCREEN ACTOR

He played character parts in numerous films and on television from the 1950s, such as the westerns True Grit and Butch Cassidy and the Sundance Kid (both 1969).

1 What we've got here is a failure to communicate.

Camp commandant (Strother Martin), in *Cool Hand Luke* (film, 1967, screenplay and original novel by Donn Pearce, directed by Stuart Rosenberg). The words appeared as a publicity slogan for the movie.

Groucho Marx (1895–1977)

US COMIC ACTOR

Originally Julius Marx. Called the 'Oscar Wilde of the wisecrack' by critic Philip French, he was the most garrulous of the Marx Brothers, famous for his cigar, moustache, sloping walk and caustic asides. In the opinion of S. J. PERELMAN, *'The man was a major comedian, which is to say that he had the compassion of an icicle, the effrontery of a carnival shill and the generosity of a pawn-broker.'*

1   I hope all your teeth have cavities, and don't forget; abscess makes the heart grow fonder.

Hammer (Groucho Marx), in *The Cocoanuts* (film, 1929, screenplay by Morrie Ryskind based on the play by GEORGE KAUFMAN and IRVING BERLIN, directed by Robert Florey and Joseph Santley)

2   One morning I shot an elephant in my pajamas. How he got into my pajamas I'll never know.

Capt Jeffrey Spaulding (Groucho Marx), in *Animal Crackers* (film, 1930, screenplay by Morrie Ryskind based on a musical by Morrie Ryskind and GEORGE KAUFMAN, directed by Victor Heerman)

3   That's what I always say. Love flies out the door when money comes innuendo.

Groucho as himself, in *Monkey Business* (film, 1931, screenplay by Arthur Sheekman based on a story by S. J. PERELMAN, W.B. Johnstone and Roland Pertwee, directed by Norman McLeod)

4   Oh, why can't we break away from all this, just you and I, and lodge with my fleas in the hills? I mean, flee to my lodge in the hills.

Ibid.

5   Oh, I realize it's a penny here and a penny there, but look at me: I've worked myself up from nothing to a state of extreme poverty.

Ibid.

6   Remember, you're fighting for this woman's honor, which is probably more than she ever did.

Rufus T. Firefly (Groucho Marx), in *Duck Soup* (film, 1933, screenplay by Bert Kalmar, Arthur Sheekman, Nat Perrin and Harry Ruby, directed by Leo McCarey). Referring to Mrs Teasdale (Margaret Dumont).

7   Either he's dead or my watch has stopped.

Dr. Hackenbush (Groucho Marx), in *A Day at the Races* (film, 1937, screenplay by Robert Pirosh, George Seaton and George Oppenheimer, directed by Sam Wood)

8   Emily, I've a little confession to make. I really am a horse doctor. But marry me, and I'll never look at another horse.

Ibid. Proposing to Mrs Upjohn (Margaret Dumont).

9   The trouble with writing a book about yourself is that you can't fool around. If you write about someone else, you can stretch the truth from here to Finland. If you write about yourself the slightest deviation makes you realize instantly that there may be honor among thieves, but *you* are just a dirty liar.

Groucho and Me, ch. 1 (1959). Opening sentence of book.

10   Although it is generally known, I think it's about time to announce that I was born at a very early age.

Ibid.

11   From the moment I picked your book up until I laid it down I was convulsed with laughter. Someday I intend reading it.

Quoted in *Life* 9 February 1962. Referring to *Dawn Ginsbergh's Revenge* by S. J. PERELMAN.

12   Please accept my resignation. I don't care to belong to any club that will have me as a member.

Quoted in *The Groucho Letters*, Introduction (1967). WOODY ALLEN paraphrases the quote in the opening scene of *Annie Hall* (1977), where he attributes it to SIGMUND FREUD and remarks: 'That's the key joke of my adult life in terms of my relationship with women.'

13   I never forget a face, but in your case I'll be glad to make an exception.

Quoted in *People I Have Loved, Known or Admired*, 'Groucho', sect. 2 (1970) by LEO ROSTEN

14   I find television very educational. Every time someone switches it on I go into another room and read a good book.

Quoted in *Halliwell's Filmgoer's Companion* (1984)

15   I've been around so long I can remember Doris Day before she was a virgin.

Attributed in *Halliwell's Who's Who in the Movies* (ed. John Walker, 1999)

Harpo Marx (1888–1964)
US COMIC ACTOR
Originally Adolph Marx. The silent member of the Marx Brothers, he took his stage-name from the harp he played. His main props consisted of a red wig and an oversized coat holding a collection of bizarre bric-a-brac.

1   Join the Army and See the Navy.

Sign paraded by Brownie (Harpo Marx) in *Duck Soup* (film, 1933, screenplay by Bert Kalmar, Arthur Sheekman, Nat Perrin and Harry Ruby, directed by Leo McCarey)

Hugh Masakela (b. 1939)
SOUTH AFRICAN JAZZ TRUMPETER
Having left South Africa in 1960, he introduced township jazz to audiences in London and New York and recorded albums such as Trumpet Africa *(1962). He did not return to South Africa until 1990.*

1   The Afro-American experience is the only real culture that America has. Basically,

every American tries to walk, talk, dress and behave like African Americans.
International Herald Tribune 17 May 1990

Jackie Mason (b. 1931)

US COMIC

Originally Jacob Moshe Maza. He studied to become a rabbi before becoming a stand-up comedian, famous for his rapid-fire Brooklyn-Jewish wisecracks. His one-man shows include The World According to Me! (New York, 1986).

1 This is the only country in the world where the food is more dangerous than sex.
Of England, in the *Daily Telegraph* 17 February 1989

2 If an Englishman gets run down by a truck he apologizes to the truck.
Independent 20 September 1990

Allan Massie (b. 1938)

BRITISH AUTHOR

A novelist and journalist of Scottish background, he draws on historical themes, often from classical Rome. His fiction includes Change and Decay in All Around I See (1978) and Caesar (1993).

1 Do you know what a soldier is, young man? He's the chap who makes it possible for civilised folk to despise war.
Colonel Fernie, in *A Question of Loyalties*, pt 2, ch. 1 (1989)

2 Blunders are an inescapable feature of war, because choice in military affairs lies generally between the bad and the worse.
Marshal Pétain, ibid., pt 3, ch. 11

Brian Masters (b. 1939)

BRITISH AUTHOR

He earned critical plaudits for his biographies of Marie Corelli (1978) and Georgiana, Duchess of Devonshire (1981).

1 Evil is something you recognize immediately you see it: it works through charm.
Daily Telegraph 31 May 1991

Harry Mathews (b. 1930)

US NOVELIST

Also a poet and translator, he is best known for his fiction, notably his witty cult classics The Conversions (1962), Tlooth (1966) and The Sinking of the Odradek Stadium (1971–2).

1 Translation is the paradigm, the exemplar of all writing. . . . It is translation that demonstrates most vividly the yearning for transformation that underlies every act involving speech, that supremely human gift.
Country Cooking & Other Stories, 'The Dialect of the Tribe' (1980)

2 Syntax and vocabulary are overwhelming

constraints – the rules that run us. Language is using *us* to talk – we think we're using the language, but language is doing the thinking, we're its slavish agents.
Interview in *City Limits* 26 May 1988

Henri Matisse (1869–1954)

FRENCH ARTIST

A leading Post-Impressionist and Fauvist painter, his work was characterized by sinuous lines and flamboyant colour, as in Portrait of Madame Matisse (1905) and The Dance (1910). 'What I dream of,' he wrote, 'is an art of balance, of purity and serenity devoid of troubling and depressing submatter.'

1 You study, you learn, but you guard the original naïveté. It has to be within you, as desire for drink is within the drunkard or love is within the lover.
Quoted in *Time* 26 June 1950

2 There is nothing more difficult for a truly creative painter than to paint a rose, because before he can do so he has first to forget all the roses that were ever painted.
Comment recalled in obituaries, 5 November 1954

W. Somerset Maugham (1874–1965)

BRITISH AUTHOR

William Somerset Maugham. An immensely prolific novelist, essayist and short story writer, he earned popular fame for such works as Of Human Bondage (1915), Cakes and Ale (1930) and The Razor's Edge (1944).

1 Like all weak men he laid an exaggerated stress on not changing one's mind.
Of Human Bondage, ch. 39 (1915). Referring to the Vicar of Blackstable.

2 Money is like a sixth sense without which you cannot make a complete use of the other five.
Monsieur Foinet, ibid., ch. 51

3 Impropriety is the soul of wit
The Moon and Sixpence, ch. 4 (1919)

4 It is not true that suffering ennobles the character; happiness does that sometimes, but suffering, for the most part, makes men petty and vindictive.
Ibid., ch. 17. Nearly twenty years later, Maugham used almost identical words to describe the suffering he witnessed as a medical student, in *The Summing Up*, ch. 19 (1938).

5 Hypocrisy is the most difficult and nerve-racking vice that any man can pursue; it needs an unceasing vigilance and a rare detachment of spirit. It cannot, like adultery or gluttony, be practised at spare moments; it is a whole-time job.
Cakes and Ale, ch. 1 (1930)

6 The Americans . . . have invented so wide
a range of pithy and hackneyed phrases
that they can carry on an amusing and animated conversation without giving a
moment's reflection to what they are saying and so leave their minds free to consider the more important matters of big
business and fornication.
Ibid., ch. 2

7 The ideal has many names, and beauty is
but one of them.
Ibid., ch. 11

8 From the earliest times the old have
rubbed it into the young that they are
wiser than they, and before the young had
discovered what nonsense this was they
were old too, and it profited them to carry
on the imposture.
Ashenden, ibid., ch. 11

9 Poor Henry, he's spending eternity wandering round and round a stately park and the
fence is just too high for him to peep over
and they're having tea just too far away for
him to hear what the countess is saying.
Edward Driffield referring to HENRY JAMES,
ibid. James, he said, 'had turned his back on one
of the great events of the world's history, the rise
of the United States, in order to report tittle-
tattle at tea parties in English country houses'. In
a notebook entry in 1937, Maugham wrote of
James: 'He did not live, he observed life from a
window, and too often was inclined to content
himself with no more than what his friends told
him they saw when *they* looked out of a
window.'

10 The common idea that success spoils
people by making them vain, egotistic, and
self-complacent is erroneous; on the contrary, it makes them, for the most part,
humble, tolerant, and kind. Failure makes
people cruel and bitter.
Ibid., ch. 48

11 There is no explanation for evil. It must
be looked upon as a necessary part of the
order of the universe. To ignore it is childish, to bewail it senseless.
Ibid., ch. 73

12 Sentimentality is only sentiment that rubs
you up the wrong way.
Entry 1941 in *A Writer's Notebook* (1949)

13 I made up my mind long ago that life was
too short to do anything for myself that I
could pay others to do for me.
Ibid.

14 I am told that today rather more than 60
per cent of the men who go to university
go on a Government grant. This is a new
class that has entered upon the scene. It is
the white-collar proletariat. . . . They do
not go to university to acquire culture but
to get a job, and when they have got one,
scamp it. They have no manners and are
woefully unable to deal with any social predicament. Their idea of a celebration is to
go to a public house and drink six beers.
They are mean, malicious and envious. . . .
They are scum.
Sunday Times 25 December 1955. Referring to the
generation of 'Angry Young Men' as portrayed
in KINGSLEY AMIS's 1954 novel *Lucky Jim*. These
people, Maugham continued, 'will in due course
leave the university. Some will doubtless sink
back, perhaps with relief, into the modest social
class from which they emerged; some will take
to drink, some to crime and go to prison. . . . A
few will go into Parliament, become Cabinet
Ministers and rule the country. I look upon
myself as fortunate that I shall not live to see it.'

15 The crown of literature is poetry. It is its
end and aim. It is the sublimest activity of
the human mind. It is the achievement of
beauty and delicacy. The writer of prose
can only step aside when the poet passes.
Saturday Review 20 July 1957

16 What has influenced my life more than
any other single thing has been my stam-
mer. Had I not stammered I would probably . . . have gone to Cambridge as my
brothers did, perhaps have become a don
and every now and then published a dreary
book about French literature.
Newsweek 23 May 1960

Armistead Maupin (b. 1944)
US JOURNALIST AND AUTHOR
*He wrote for various newspapers, including the
San Francisco Chronicle (1976–7), before pub-
lishing the six-novel sequence* Tales of the City
*(1978–90), a sympathetic portrait of gay life in
San Francisco.*

1 Too much of a good thing is wonderful.
More Tales of the City, 'The Road to Ruin'
(1980). Motto inscribed on a brass plaque outside the Pinus club.

2 Mona's Law. That's what she calls it. She
says you can have a hot job, a hot lover
and a hot apartment, but you can't have all
three at the same time.
Michael, ibid., 'Mona's Law'

3 I think a lot of gay people who are not dealing with their homosexuality get into
right-wing politics.
Guardian 22 April 1988

François Mauriac (1885–1970)
FRENCH AUTHOR
*In his own words, he set out 'to make the Catholic
universe of evil palpable, tangible, odorous' in such
novels as* Flesh and Blood *(1920),* The Knot of
Vipers *(1932) and* La Pharisienne *(1941).*

1 I love Germany so dearly that I hope there will always be two of them.
Quoted in *Newsweek* 20 November 1989

André Maurois (1885–1967)
FRENCH AUTHOR AND CRITIC
Born Emile Salomon Wilhelm Herzog. A prominent man of letters for fifty years, he wrote the novels The Thought Reading Machine *(1938) and* Woman without Love *(1945), as well as histories, essays and fictionalized biographies such as* Ariel *(1923), a life of Shelley.*

1 Self-pity comes so naturally to all of us, that the most solid happiness can be shaken by the compassion of a fool.
Ariel, ch. 16 (1923)

2 A successful marriage is an edifice that must be rebuilt every day.
The Art of Living, 'The Art of Marriage' (1940)

3 Growing old is no more than a bad habit which a busy man has no time to form.
Ibid., 'The Art of Growing Old'. 'The true evil,' Maurois wrote, 'is not the weakening of the body, but the indifference of the soul.'

4 The difficult part in an argument is not to defend one's opinion, but rather to know it.
Quoted in *A Little Book of Aphorisms* (1947) by Frederic B. Wilcox

5 Style [is] the hallmark of a temperament stamped on the material in hand.
The Art of Writing, 'The Writer's Craft', sect. 2 (1960)

6 A great biography should, like the close of a great drama, leave behind it a feeling of serenity. We collect into a small bunch the flowers, the few flowers, which brought sweetness into a life, and present it as an offering to an accomplished destiny.
Ibid., 'The Writer's Craft', sect. 5

Robert Maxwell (1923–91)
CZECH-BORN BRITISH PUBLISHER
Originally Jan Ludvik Hoch. As a self-made communications tycoon, he had worldwide business interests and acted as adviser to government and industry. In Britain he was Chairman of the Mirror Group from 1984, from which, following his mysterious death at sea, it emerged that he had siphoned money from employee pension funds to offset business losses.

1 It's the editors who interfere in the publisher's prerogative, not the other way round.
Said in July 1985, quoted in *Maxwell: The Outsider*, ch. 13 (1988, rev. 1991) by Tom Bower. Referring to his relations with Mirror Group Newspapers.

2 Ordinary people may not understand the meaning of democracy but they've a passionate regard for fair play.
Quoted in *Maxwell*, ch. 1 (1988) by Joe Haines

3 When I fire someone it is like a thunderclap. My primary duty is to hire and fire editors. I treat them like a Field Marshal.
Independent 13 May 1990

4 When I pass a belt, I can't resist hitting below it.
International Herald Tribune 18 March 1991

Vladimir Mayakovsky (1893–1930)
RUSSIAN POET AND DRAMATIST
A founder of the Russian Futurist movement, he embraced the Bolshevik cause with 'Ode to Revolution' (1918) and 'Left March' (1919), and with his play 150,000,000 *(1920). Five years after he took his own life,* STALIN *declared that 'indifference to his memory and works is a crime'.*

1 Or if you prefer
as the sky changes tone
I'll be absolutely tender
not a man but a cloud in trousers.
'The Cloud in Trousers' (1915), repr. in *Russian Poetry: the Modern Period* (ed. John Glad and Daniel Weissbort, 1978)

2 No gray hair in my soul
no doddering tenderness,
I rock the world with the thunder of my voice,
strolling, looking good –
twenty-two.
Ibid.

3 The bull of the days is skewballed.
The cart of the years is slow.
Our god is speed. The heart is our drum.
'Our March' st. 2 and 6, written 1917, publ. in *The Heritage of Russian Verse* (ed. and transl. Dimitri Obolensky, 1962)

4 My verse
has brought me
no roubles to spare:
no craftsmen have made
mahogany chairs for my house.
'At the top of my voice', written 1929–30, repr. in *Twentieth-Century Russian Poetry* (ed. Albert C. Todd and Max Hayward, 1993)

5 Comrade life,
let us
march faster,
March
faster through what's left
of the five-year plan.
Ibid.

6 The ship of love has foundered on life's reef. You and I are even. And why should we list our mutual grievances, our hurts, our griefs? See how the world has grown.
Unfinished poem in letter written 12 April 1930,

publ. ibid. Mayakovsky's last poem was found in his papers after his suicide.

Curtis Mayfield (b. 1942)
US SINGER AND SONGWRITER

After eleven years leading the gospel-influenced soul group the Impressions, he had solo hits with 'Move On Up' (1970) and his soundtrack to the film Superfly *(1972).*

1 *People get ready*
There's a train a-coming
You don't need no baggage
You just get on board
All you need is faith to hear the diesels humming
Don't need no ticket you just thank the Lord.
'People Get Ready' (song, 1964) by the Impressions

Margaret Mead (1901–78)
US ANTHROPOLOGIST

Described by JACOB BRONOWSKI *as 'splendidly sensible', she popularized anthropology through her studies of the people of Samoa and New Guinea, notably with the classic* Coming of Age in Samoa *(1928). She was outspoken on women's rights and environment issues.*

1 As the traveler who has once been from home is wiser than he who has never left his own doorstep, so a knowledge of one other culture should sharpen our ability to scrutinize more steadily, to appreciate more lovingly, our own.
Coming of Age in Samoa, Introduction (1928)

2 A society which is clamoring for choice, which is filled with many articulate groups, each urging its own brand of salvation, its own variety of economic philosophy, will give each new generation no peace until all have chosen or gone under, unable to bear the conditions of choice. The stress is in our civilization.
Ibid., ch. 14

3 Coming to terms with the rhythms of women's lives means coming to terms with life itself, accepting the imperatives of the body rather than the imperatives of an artificial, man-made, perhaps transcendentally beautiful civilization. Emphasis on the male work-rhythm is an emphasis on infinite possibilities; emphasis on the female rhythms is an emphasis on a defined pattern, on limitation.
Male and Female, ch. 8 (1949)

4 The suffering of either sex – of the male who is unable, because of the way in which he was reared, to take the strong initiating or patriarchal role that is still demanded of him, or of the female who has been given

too much freedom of movement as a child to stay placidly within the house as an adult – this suffering, this discrepancy, this sense of failure in an enjoined role, is the point of leverage for social change.
Ibid., ch. 15

5 Each home has been reduced to the bare essentials – to barer essentials than most primitive people would consider possible. Only one woman's hands to feed the baby, answer the telephone, turn off the gas under the pot that is boiling over, soothe the older child who has broken a toy, and open both doors at once. She is a nutritionist, a child psychologist, an engineer, a production manager, an expert buyer, all in one. Her husband sees her as free to plan her own time, and envies her; she sees him as having regular hours and envies him.
Ibid., ch. 16

6 I was brought up to believe that the only thing worth doing was to add to the sum of accurate information in the world.
The New York Times 9 August 1964

7 It is an open question whether any behavior based on fear of eternal punishment can be regarded as ethical or should be regarded as merely cowardly.
Quoted in *Redbook* February 1971

8 The mind is not sex-typed.
Blackberry Winter, ch. 5 (1972)

9 The city as a center where, any day in any year, there may be a fresh encounter with a new talent, a keen mind or a gifted specialist – this is essential to the life of a country. To play this role in our lives a city must have a soul – a university, a great art or music school, a cathedral or a great mosque or temple, a great laboratory or scientific center, as well as the libraries and museums and galleries that bring past and present together. A city must be a place where groups of women and men are seeking and developing the highest things they know.
Quoted in *Redbook* August 1978

(Sir) Peter Medawar (1915–87)
BRITISH IMMUNOLOGIST

He shared a Nobel Prize in 1960 for his work on immunology and was Director of the Institute for Medical Research 1962–75. His publications include general essays on science, collected in The Art of the Soluble *(1967) and* The Limits of Science *(1985).*

1 If politics is the art of the possible, research is surely the art of the soluble. Both are immensely practical-minded affairs.
'The Act of Creation', first publ. in the *New*

Statesman 19 June 1964, repr. in *The Art of the Soluble* (1967)

2 Considered in its entirety, psychoanalysis won't do. It's an end product, moreover, like a dinosaur or a zeppelin; no better theory can ever be erected on its ruins, which will remain for ever one of the saddest and strangest of all landmarks in the history of twentieth-century thought.
The Hope of Progress, 'Further Comments on Psychoanalysis' (1972)

3 Today the world changes so quickly that in growing up we take leave not just of youth but of the world we were young in. . . . Fear and resentment of what is new is really a lament for the memories of our childhood.
Pluto's Republic, 'On "The Effecting of All Things Possible" ' (1982)

Golda Meir (1898–1978)
UKRAINIAN-BORN ISRAELI POLITICIAN AND PRIME MINISTER
Originally Goldie Myerson. After emigrating to the USA in 1906, she moved to Palestine in 1921 where she was prominent in the Labour Movement. She held government posts following the creation of the state of Israel and was Prime Minister 1966–74.

1 There was no such thing as a Palestinian people . . . it is not as though there was a Palestinian people and we came and threw them out and took their country away from them. They did not exist.
Sunday Times 15 June 1969

2 We have always said that in our war with the Arabs we had a secret weapon – no alternative.
Life 3 October 1969

3 To be or not to be is not a question of compromise. Either you be or you don't be.
Quoted in *The New York Times* 12 December 1974. On the future of Israel.

4 Pessimism is a luxury that a Jew can never allow himself.
Quoted in the *Observer* 29 December 1974

David Mellor (b. 1949)
BRITISH POLITICIAN
Elected Conservative MP for Putney in 1979, he was Minister for the Arts in 1990 and Chief Secretary to the Treasury 1990–92. Revelations about an extra-marital affair forced him to resign from his position as Secretary of State for National Heritage in 1992.

1 The popular press is drinking in the last chance saloon.
Interview on Channel 4, 21 December 1989, quoted in *The Times* 22 December 1989. The comment was sparked by intrusive press coverage of the recent Hillsborough disaster. 'What is of interest to the public is not always in the public interest,' he added.

2 The tabloids are like animals, with their own behavioural patterns. There's no point in complaining about them, any more than complaining that lions might eat you.
Independent 3 November 1992

3 Lawyers are like rhinoceroses: thick-skinned, short-sighted, and always ready to charge.
Question Time, BBC1, 3 December 1992

George Melly (b. 1926)
BRITISH JAZZ MUSICIAN, CRITIC AND AUTHOR
He has sung blues and jazz with John Chilton's Feetwarmers since the 1970s, worked as a television and film reviewer and published memoirs and books of social history.

1 The mistake which most critics make is to persist in trying to evaluate pop culture as if it were something else: the equivalent of insisting on considering a bicycle as if it were a horse.
Revolt into Style, Introduction (1970)

2 The pop manner has become respectable, pop matter is suspect. In the mass media too the revolt has turned into a style.
Ibid., 'Film, TV, Radio, Theatre: All My Hating'. The phrase 'revolt into style' is borrowed from lines by Thom Gunn: see THOM GUNN 4.

3 Surely nothing could be that funny.
Quoted in the *Independent on Sunday* 1 January 1995. On being told by MICK JAGGER that his wrinkles were laughter lines.

4 Who wants to be 98? Someone who's 97.
Quoted by ANTHONY CLARE in *In the Psychiatrist's Chair*, Radio 4, 24 October 1999

H.L. Mencken (1880–1956)
US JOURNALIST
Henry Louis Mencken. Known as 'the sage of Baltimore' for his lifelong association with the Baltimore Sun, he used his columns to lambast hypocrisy and provincialism in middle-class America. His writings are collected in Prejudices (6 vols. 1919–27). WALTER LIPPMANN called him 'the most powerful personal influence on this whole generation of educated people'.

1 Democracy is the theory that the common people know what they want, and deserve to get it good and hard.
Little Book in C Major (1916)

2 Conscience is the inner voice which warns us that someone may be looking.
Ibid.

3 Time is a great legalizer, even in the field of morals.
A Book of Prefaces, ch. 4, sect. 6 (1917)

4 Philadelphia has always been one of the most Pecksniffian of American cities, and thus probably leads the world.
The American Language, note (1919). Referring to the replacement of 'a virgin' by 'a young girl' in the city's public ledger describing characters in a play in 1916. 'Pecksniffian', meaning hypocritically benevolent, alludes to Seth Pecksniff in Dickens's *Martin Chuzzlewit* (1843).

5 The public, with its mob yearning to be instructed, edified and pulled by the nose, demands certainties; it must be told definitely and a bit raucously that this is true and that is false. But there *are* no certainties.
Prejudices, ch. 3 (first series, 1919)

6 All successful newspapers are ceaselessly querulous and bellicose. They never defend anyone or anything if they can help it; if the job is forced upon them, they tackle it by denouncing someone or something else.
Ibid., ch. 13

7 Every man sees in his relatives, and especially in his cousins, a series of grotesque caricatures of himself.
Smart Set August 1919, repr. in *Prejudices*, 'The Relative' (third series, 1922)

8 Puritanism: The haunting fear that someone, somewhere, may be happy.
A Book of Burlesques, 'Sententiae' (1920)

9 An idealist is one who, on noticing that a rose smells better than a cabbage, concludes that it will also make better soup.
Ibid.

10 Adultery is the application of democracy to love.
Ibid.

11 It is the dull man who is always sure, and the sure man who is always dull.
Prejudices, ch. 1 (second series, 1920)

12 To sum up:
1. The cosmos is a gigantic fly-wheel making 10,000 revolutions a minute.
2. Man is a sick fly taking a dizzy ride on it.
3. Religion is the theory that the wheel was designed and set spinning to give him the ride.
Smart Set December 1920, repr. in *A Mencken Chrestomathy*, pt 1, 'Coda' (1949)

13 Injustice is relatively easy to bear; what stings is justice.
Prejudices, ch. 3 (third series, 1922)

14 Faith may be defined briefly as an illogical belief in the occurrence of the improbable. . . . A man full of faith is simply one who has lost (or never had) the capacity for clear and realistic thought. He is not a mere ass: he is actually ill.
Ibid., ch. 14

15 No one in this world, so far as I know . . . has ever lost money by underestimating the intelligence of the great masses of the plain people.
Chicago Tribune 19 September 1926

16 It [New York] is the place where all the aspirations of the Western World meet to form one vast master aspiration, as powerful as the suction of a steam dredge. It is the icing on the pie called Christian civilization.
Prejudices, ch. 9 (sixth series, 1927)

17 If Los Angeles is not the one authentic rectum of civilization, then I am no anatomist. Any time you want to go out again and burn it down, count me in.
Letter, 15 March 1927, to F. SCOTT FITZGERALD and ZELDA FITZGERALD on their return from working in Hollywood, quoted in *Invented Lives* (1984) by James R. Mellon

18 When women kiss it always reminds one of prize-fighters shaking hands.
A Mencken Chrestomathy, ch. 30 (1949)

19 Whenever you hear a man speak of his love for his country, it is a sign that he expects to be paid for it.
Ibid., 'Sententiae: The Mind of Men'

20 Self-respect – the secure feeling that no one, as yet, is suspicious.
Ibid.

21 Whenever a husband and wife begin to discuss their marriage they are giving evidence at a coroner's inquest.
Ibid., 'Sententiae: Masculum et Feminam Creavit Eos'

22 No matter how happily a woman may be married, it always pleases her to discover that there is a nice man who wishes that she were not.
Ibid.

23 Husbands never become good; they merely become proficient.
Ibid.

24 Archbishop – A Christian ecclesiastic of a rank superior to that attained by Christ.
Ibid., 'Sententiae: Arcana Coelestia'

25 Theology – An effort to explain the unknowable by putting it into terms of the not worth knowing.
Ibid.

26 A society made up of individuals who were all capable of original thought would probably be unendurable.
Minority Report: H. L. Mencken's Notebooks, no. 13 (1956)

27 It is now quite lawful for a Catholic woman to avoid pregnancy by a resort to mathematics, though she is still forbidden to resort to physics and chemistry.

Ibid., no. 62

28 There are people who read too much: bibliobibuli. I know some who are constantly drunk on books, as other men are drunk on whiskey or religion. They wander through this most diverting and stimulating of worlds in a haze, seeing nothing and hearing nothing.

Ibid., no. 71

29 The chief contribution of Protestantism to human thought is its massive proof that God is a bore.

Ibid., no. 309

Carlos Menem (b. 1935)
ARGENTINIAN POLITICIAN AND PRIME MINISTER
He was President of Argentina 1989–99, the first Peronist to hold the office since the overthrow of Juan Perón in 1973.

1 The conflict should never have happened, we deeply regret it.

Sun 23 October 1998. Contrary to the *Sun*'s headline, 'Argentina says: We're sorry for the Falklands', Menem denied making an apology. 'Saying sorry is something completely different,' he was reported in the *Guardian* 24 October 1998. 'That is not the way I expressed it.' Some detected the hand of TONY BLAIR's press secretary, Alastair Campbell, in the article. Menem was due to make a state visit to Britain the following week.

(Sir) Robert Menzies (1894–1978)
AUSTRALIAN POLITICIAN AND PRIME MINISTER
Leader of the Australian Liberal Party, he was Prime Minister 1939–1941 and 1949–66, making him Australia's longest serving prime minister.

1 Men of genius are not to be analyzed by commonplace rules. The rest of us who have been or are leaders, more commonplace in our quality, will do well to remember two things. One is *never to forget posterity when devising a policy.* The other is *never to think of posterity when making a speech.*

The Measure of the Years, ch. 1 (1970)

2 A Prime Minister exercises his greatest public influence by creating a public impression of himself, hoping all the time that the people will be generous rather than just.

Quoted in *Australian Politics. A Third Reader*, ch. 60 (1973) by Henry Mayer and Helen Nelson

Johnny Mercer (1909–76)
US SONGWRITER
A highly prolific lyricist, he collaborated with Harold Arlen on the musicals St Louis Woman *(1946) and* Saratoga *(1959), and also recorded his own compositions, such as 'Baby It's Cold Outside' (1949). He founded Capitol Records in 1942.*

1 That old black magic.

Title of song (with music by Harold Arlen) in *Star Spangled Rhythm* (film, 1943). First sung by Johnny Johnston, the song was later identified with singer Billy Daniels.

2 *You've got to ac-cent-tchu-ate the positive Elim-my-nate the negative Latch on to the affirmative Don't mess with Mister In-between.*

'Ac-cent-tchu-ate the Positive' (song, with music by Harold Arlen) in the musical film *Here Come the Waves* (1944). The song was originally sung by BING CROSBY, and was also recorded by Mercer himself.

3 *We're after the same rainbow's end Waiting round the bend My Huckleberry friend Moon River and me.*

'Moon River' (song, with music by Henry Mancini) in the film *Breakfast at Tiffany's* (1961)

Maurice Merleau-Ponty (1908–61)
FRENCH PHILOSOPHER
Influenced by Husserl, he made significant contributions to phenomenology in such works as Phenomenology of Perception *(1945). He co-edited, with* SARTRE *and* DE BEAUVOIR, *the monthly review* Les Temps modernes *1945–9.*

1 The world is . . . the natural setting of, and field for, all my thoughts and all my explicit perceptions. Truth does not 'inhabit' only 'the inner man,' or more accurately, there is no inner man, man is in the world, and only in the world does he know himself.

Phenomenology of Perception, Preface (1945)

Thomas Merton (1915–68)
US AUTHOR AND MONK
A trappist monk from 1941, he was also a prolific writer of poetry, essays and religious works. His autobiographical The Seven Storey Mountain *(1948) became an international bestseller and later books revealed his interest in Oriental mysticism.*

1 Death is someone you see very clearly with eyes in the center of your heart: eyes that see not by reacting to light, but by reacting to a kind of a chill from within the marrow of your own life.

The Seven Storey Mountain, pt 1, ch. 3 (1948)

2 The logic of worldly success rests on a fallacy: the strange error that our perfection

depends on the thoughts and opinions and applause of other men! A weird life it is, indeed, to be living always in somebody else's imagination, as if that were the only place in which one could at last become real!

Ibid., pt 3, ch. 2

Oliver Messiaen (1908–92)

FRENCH COMPOSER AND ORGANIST

His music, much of it written for organ, is mystical in character and often makes use of transcriptions of birdsong. Major works include Quartet for the End of Time *(1941).*

1 My faith is the grand drama of my life. I'm a believer, so I sing words of God to those who have no faith. I give bird songs to those who dwell in cities and have never heard them, make rhythms for those who know only military marches or jazz, and paint colours for those who see none.

Independent 9 December 1988

George Michael (b. 1963)

BRITISH SINGER AND SONGWRITER

Originally Giorgos Kyriacou Panayiotou. He scored numerous hits as a member of the white soul duo Wham!, going on to have a successful solo career with songs such as 'Faith' (1987).

1 If you don't want people to think you're gay, you don't grow a moustache that makes you look like you've failed a Village People audition.

Daily Telegraph 7 November 1998

James A. Michener (1907–97)

US NOVELIST

James Albert Michener. The sweeping narrative of his lengthy, fact-filled novels such as Hawaii *(1959) and* Chesapeake *(1978) led* Newsweek *to describe him as 'the literary world's Cecil B. DeMille'.*

1 I was brought up in the great tradition of the late nineteenth century: that a writer never complains, never explains and never disdains.

Quoted in the *Observer* 26 November 1989

Ludwig Mies Van Der Rohe

(1886–1969)

GERMAN-BORN US ARCHITECT

Originally Ludwig Mies. He was Director of the Bauhaus (1930–33) before moving to America, where he became the leading figure of the International Style, and pioneer of the glass and steel skyscraper.

1 Less is more.

Quoted in the *New York Herald Tribune* 28 June 1959. Mies Van Der Rohe was an advocate of

'skin and bones construction'. His famous dictum had been associated with him since much earlier. Among the many rejoinders to it, FRANK LLOYD WRIGHT wrote, 'Less is only more where more is no good' (*The Future of Architecture*, 1953).

George Mikes (1912–87)

HUNGARIAN-BORN BRITISH HUMORIST

Settling in Britain in 1938, he recorded his observations on his adopted country in a series of satirical books including How to be an Alien *(1946) and* As Others See You *(1961).).*

1 On the Continent people have good food; in England people have good table manners.

How to be an Alien: A Handbook for Beginners and More Advanced Pupils, ch. 1, sect. 1 (1946)

2 Continental people have sex lives; the English have hot-water bottles.

Ibid., sect. 6. Thirty years later, Mikes referred to this notorious pronouncement: 'Things *have* progressed. Not on the continent, where people still have sex lives; but they have progressed here because the English now have electric blankets' (*How to be Decadent*, 1977).

3 An Englishman, even if he is alone, forms an orderly queue of one.

Ibid., sect. 14. Mikes expanded on this in *How to be Decadent* (1977): 'In shops the English stand in queues; in government offices they sit in queues; in churches they kneel in queues; at sale times, they lie in queues all night.'

4 Whatever else an Italian may lack, he has an Ego. Sometimes two. It is nice to think that even the poorest Italian may possess two Egos while even the richest Englishman, as a rule, has none.

Italy for Beginners, 'Tourists and Natives: Two Redeeming Sins' (1956)

Edna St Vincent Millay

(1892–1950)

US POET

The foremost American woman poet of the 1920s and a skilful sonneteer, she epitomized the free spirit of the Jazz Age in such volumes as A Few Figs from Thistles *(1920) and* The Harp-Weaver and Other Poems *(1923).*

1 God, I can push the grass apart
   And lay my finger on Thy heart.

'Renascence', publ. in *Renascence and Other Poems* (1917)

2 The soul can split the sky in two,
   And let the face of God shine through.

Ibid.

3 My candle burns at both ends;
   It will not last the night;

But ah, my foes, and oh, my friends –
It gives a lovely light.
'First Fig', publ. in *A Few Figs From Thistles*
(1920)

4 *Safe upon the solid rock the ugly houses
stand:
Come and see my shining palaces built
upon the sand!*
'Second Fig', publ. ibid.

5 *Death devours all lovely things;
Lesbia with her sparrow
Shares the darkness – presently
Every bed is narrow.*
'Passer Mortuus Est', publ. in *Second April*
(1921). Alluding to the poems dedicated to Les-
bia by Catullus.

6 *After all, my erstwhile dear,
My no longer cherished,
Need we say it was not love,
Now that love is perished?*
Ibid.

7 *I know I am but summer to your heart,
And not the full four seasons of the year.*
'I Know I Am But Summer to Your Heart', publ.
in *The Harp-Weaver and Other Poems* (1923)

8 *Euclid alone
Has looked on Beauty bare. Fortunate they
Who, though once only and then but far
away,
Have heard her massive sandal set on stone.*
'Euclid Alone Has Looked on Beauty Bare',
publ. ibid.

9 *Childhood is the kingdom where nobody
dies.
Nobody that matters, that is.*
'Childhood is the Kingdom Where Nobody
Dies', publ. in *Wine From These Grapes* (1934)

10 *Set the foot down with distrust on the crust
of the world – it is thin.*
'The Underground System', publ. in *Huntsman,
What Quarry?* (1939)

Alice Duer Miller (1874–1942)
US AUTHOR AND POET
*Her short stories and novellas appeared in the col-
lection* Summer Holiday *(1941), and her most
famous poem is* The White Cliffs *(1940). She was
active in the women's suffrage movement.*

1 *They make other nations seem pale and
flighty,
But they do think England is God almighty,
And you must remind them now and then
That other countries breed other men.*
The White Cliffs (1940). Part of a long narrative
poem extolling Britain's resistance during the
Second World War.

2 *I am American bred,
I have seen much to hate here – much to
forgive,*

*But in a world where England is finished
and dead,
I do not wish to live.*
Ibid. Closing lines of poem.

Arthur Miller (b. 1915)
US PLAYWRIGHT
*He established himself as a master dramatist with
his plays* Death of a Salesman *(1949) and* The
Crucible *(1953), which took the Salem witch trials
of 1692 as an allegory for the McCarthyism of
which Miller had personal experience in the 1950s.
His marriage (1956–61) to* MARILYN MONROE
was the inspiration for his screenplay for The Misfits *(1960), in which she starred.*

1 He's liked, but he's not well liked.
Biff, in *Death of a Salesman*, act 1 (1949). Referring to Bernard, his schoolfriend.

2 A small man can be just as exhausted as a
great man.
Linda, ibid. Referring to her husband Willy
Loman.

3 I don't say he's a great man. Willy Loman
never made a lot of money. His name was
never in the paper. He's not the finest
character that ever lived. But he's a human
being, and a terrible thing is happening to
him. So attention must be paid.
Ibid.

4 For a salesman, there is no rock bottom to
the life. He don't put a bolt to a nut, he
don't tell you the law or give you medicine. He's a man way out there in the blue,
riding on a smile and a shoeshine. And
when they start not smiling back – that's
an earthquake. And then you get yourself a
couple of spots on your hat, and you're
finished. Nobody dast blame this man. A
salesman is got to dream, boy. It comes
with the territory.
Charley, ibid., 'Requiem'

5 You must understand, sir, that a person
is either with this court or he must be
counted against it, there be no road
between. This is a sharp time, now, a precise time – we live no longer in the dusky
afternoon when evil mixed itself with good
and befuddled the world. Now, by God's
grace, the shining sun is up, and them that
fear not light will surely praise it. I hope
you will be one of those.
Judge Danforth (addressing Francis), in *The Crucible*, act 3 (1953)

6 By whatever means it is accomplished, the
prime business of a play is to arouse the
passions of its audience so that by the
route of passion may be opened up new
relationships between a man and men, and
between men and Man.
Collected Plays, Introduction, sect. 7 (1958)

7 A good newspaper, I suppose, is a nation talking to itself.

Quoted in the *Observer* 26 November 1961

8 A suicide kills two people, Maggie. That's what it's for.

Quentin, in *After the Fall*, act 2 (1964)

9 A playwright . . . is . . . the litmus paper of the arts. He's got to be, because if he isn't working on the same wave length as the audience, no one would know what in hell he was talking about. He is a kind of psychic journalist, even when he's great.

Interview in the *Paris Review* summer 1966

10 The concentration camp is the final expression of human separateness and its ultimate consequence. It is organized abandonment.

Ibid. Miller regarded this concept as underpinning his 1964 play *After the Fall*, which included a concentration camp in its staging.

11 In the theater, while you recognized that you were looking at a house, it was a house in quotation marks. On screen, the quotation marks tend to be blotted out by the camera.

The New York Times 15 September 1985. On a television production of *Death of a Salesman*.

12 Without alienation, there can be no politics.

Interview in *Marxism Today* January 1988

13 I'm the end of the line; absurd and appalling as it may seem, serious New York theatre has died in my lifetime.

The Times 11 January 1989

14 I love her too, but our neuroses just don't match.

Lyman, in *The Ride Down Mount Morgan*, act 1 (1991). Discussing his wife.

15 Maybe all one can do is hope to end up with the right regrets.

Tom, ibid.

16 Look, we're all the same; a man is a fourteen-room house – in the bedroom he's asleep with his intelligent wife, in the living-room he's rolling around with some bareass girl, in the library he's paying his taxes, in the yard he's raising tomatoes, and in the cellar he's making a bomb to blow it all up.

Lyman, ibid., act 2

Henry Miller (1891–1980)

US AUTHOR

While in Paris (1930–39) he wrote the books for which he is best known, Tropic of Cancer *(1934),* Black Spring *(1936) and* Tropic of Capricorn *(1938). Autobiographical in tone and overtly sexual, they were banned in the UK and USA until the 1960s. The author Gerald Brenan remarked: 'Miller is not really a writer but a non-stop talker to whom someone has given a typewriter.' See also* KATE MILLETT 5, EZRA POUND 19.

1 It is true I swim in a perpetual sea of sex but the actual excursions are fairly limited.

Letter, 1 February 1932, publ. in *Letters to Anaïs Nin*, pt 1 (1965)

2 This is not a book. This is libel, slander, defamation of character. This is not a book, in the ordinary sense of the word. No, this is a prolonged insult, a gob of spit in the face of Art, a kick in the pants to God, Man, Destiny, Time, Love, Beauty . . . what you will. I am going to sing for you, a little off key perhaps, but I will sing.

Tropic of Cancer (1934).

3 An artist is always alone – if he *is* an artist. No, what the artist needs is *loneliness*.

Ibid.

4 Every man with a bellyful of the classics is an enemy to the human race.

Ibid.

5 What is not in the open street is false, derived, that is to say, *literature*.

Black Spring, 'The Fourteenth Ward' (1936)

6 Confusion is a word we have invented for an order which is not understood.

Tropic of Capricorn, 'On the Ovarian Trolley: An Interlude' (1939)

7 What does it matter how one comes by the truth so long as one pounces upon it and lives by it?

Tropic of Capricorn (1938)

8 What holds the world together, as I have learned from bitter experience, is sexual intercourse.

Ibid.

9 Hitler is no worse, nay better, in my opinion, than the other lugs. He makes the German mistake of being tactless, that's all.

Letter to LAWRENCE DURRELL, March 1939, publ. in *The Durrell–Miller Letters 1935–80* (1988). Written shortly after the Nazis had marched into Czechoslovakia.

10 Why are we so full of restraint? Why do we not give in all directions? Is it fear of losing ourselves? Until we do lose ourselves there is no hope of finding ourselves.

The World of Sex (1940)

11 Moralities, ethics, laws, customs, beliefs, doctrines – these are of trifling import. All that matters is that the miraculous become the norm.

Ibid.

12 **The aim of life is to live, and to live means to be aware, joyously, drunkenly, serenely, divinely aware.**
The Wisdom of the Heart, 'Creative Death' (1941)

13 **In expanding the field of knowledge, we but increase the horizon of ignorance.**
Ibid., 'The Wisdom of the Heart'

14 **The American ideal is youth – handsome, empty youth.**
Ibid., 'Raimu'. In America, Miller explained, 'youth means simply athleticism, disrespect, gangsterism, or sickly idealism expressing itself through thinly disguised and badly digested social science theories acted out by idiots who are desperadoes at heart.'

15 **Life, as it is called, is for most of us one long postponement.**
Ibid., 'The Enormous Womb'

16 **I have never been able to look upon America as young and vital but rather as prematurely old, as a fruit which rotted before it had a chance to ripen.**
The Air-Conditioned Nightmare, 'Dr Souchon: Surgeon-Painter' (1945)

17 **Music is a beautiful opiate, if you don't take it too seriously.**
Ibid., 'With Edgar Varèse in the Gobi Desert'

18 **Sex is one of the nine reasons for reincarnation. The other eight are unimportant.**
Sexus, ch. 21 (1949)

19 **I didn't have to think up so much as a comma or a semicolon; it was all given, straight from the celestial recording room. Weary, I would beg for a break, an intermission, time enough, let's say, to go to the toilet or take a breath of fresh air on the balcony. Nothing doing!**
Big Sur and the Oranges of Hieronymus Bosch, pt 2, 'A Fortune in Francs' (1957). On the composition of *Tropic of Capricorn*. Miller went on: 'How could I possibly imagine then that some few years later a judicial triumvirate, eager to prove me a sinner, would accuse me of having written such passages "for gain"?'

20 **Obscenity is a cleansing process, whereas pornography only adds to the murk.**
Interview in the *Paris Review* summer 1961, repr. in *Writers at Work* (second series, ed. George Plimpton, 1963). Miller is quoted as saying: 'I am for obscenity and against pornography.'

21 **Whenever a taboo is broken, something good happens, something vitalizing. . . . Taboos after all are only hangovers, the product of diseased minds, you might say, of fearsome people who hadn't the courage to live and who under the guise of morality and religion have imposed these things upon us.**
Ibid.

Jonathan Miller (b. 1934)
BRITISH DOCTOR, HUMORIST AND DIRECTOR
Combining careers in medical research and the arts, he came to notice in the Beyond the Fringe *revues (1961–4), and subsequently as an innovative director of Shakespeare and opera.*

1 **I wasn't driven into medicine by a social conscience but by rampant curiosity.**
Quoted in the *Observer* 5 February 1983

2 **Jokes have little to do with spontaneous humour. The teller has the same relationship to them that he or she might have to Hertz Rent-a-Car. A joke is a hired object, with many previous users, and very often its ashtrays are filled with other people's cigarettes, and its gears are worn and slipping, because other people have driven this joke very badly before you got behind the wheel.**
'Among Chickens', publ. in *Granta* no. 23, spring 1988

3 **What makes literature interesting is that it does not survive its translation. The characters in a novel are made out of the sentences. That's what their substance is.**
Sunday Times 12 February 1989

4 **Attitudes to museums have changed. If it had Marilyn Monroe's knickers or Laurence Olivier's jockstrap they would flock to it.**
Daily Telegraph 7 June 1989. On the low attendances at his recently opened Theatre Museum.

5 **Errors of taste are very often the outward sign of a deep fault of sensibility.**
Guardian 21 May 1992

6 **There are no élitist people there are only élitist ideas**
Interview in the *Guardian* 12 September 1998

Roger Miller (1936–92)
US COUNTRY SINGER AND SONGWRITER
His self-penned songs 'Dang Me' (1964) and 'King of the Road' (1965) were million-sellers, notching up eight Grammy awards between them. Later hits included 'Little Green Apples' (1968).

1 *I'm a man of means by no means King of the road.*
'King of the Road' (song) on the album *The Return of Roger Miller* (1965)

2 *England swings like a pendulum do Bobbies on bicycles two by two Westminster Abbey, the tower of Big Ben, The rosy red cheeks of the little children.*
'England Swings' (song) on the album *Golden Hits* (1965)

Kate Millett (b. 1934)
US FEMINIST AUTHOR
Her first book, Sexual Politics *(1970), was an indictment of the patriarchal value systems which she perceived in politics and literature. She was active in civil rights movements in the 1970s.*

1 However muted its present appearance may be, sexual dominion obtains nevertheless as perhaps the most pervasive ideology of our culture and provides its most fundamental concept of power.
   Sexual Politics, ch. 2 (1970)

2 Because of our social circumstances, male and female are really two cultures and their life experiences are utterly different.
   Ibid., ch. 2, sect. 2

3 The concept of romantic love affords a means of emotional manipulation which the male is free to exploit, since love is the only circumstance in which the female is (ideologically) pardoned for sexual activity.
   Ibid., sect. 4

4 Perhaps nothing is so depressing an index of the inhumanity of the male-supremacist mentality as the fact that the more genial human traits are assigned to the underclass: affection, response to sympathy, kindness, cheerfulness.
   Ibid., ch. 4. Referring to a table of character traits assignable to male and female roles.

5 Miller does have something highly important to tell us; his virulent sexism is beyond question an honest contribution to social and psychological understanding which we can hardly afford to ignore. But to confuse this neurotic hostility, this frank abuse, with sanity, is pitiable. To confuse it with freedom were vicious, were it not so very sad.
   Referring to HENRY MILLER, ibid., ch. 6

6 To be a rebel is not to be a revolutionary. It is more often but a way of spinning one's wheels deeper in the sand.
   Ibid., ch. 8, sect. 2

Spike Milligan (1918–2002)
BRITISH COMEDIAN AND HUMOROUS WRITER
Born Terence Alan Milligan. He co-scripted and performed in The Goon Show *for BBC radio (1951–60), which* JOHN LENNON *called 'a conspiracy against reality, a coup d'état of the mind'. His many humorous books of verse, fiction and autobiography include* Puckoon *(1963, filmed 2003) and* Adolf Hitler, My Part in His Downfall *(1971).*

1 Ying tong iddle I po.
   Ned Seagoon (Harry Secombe), in *The Goon Show* (BBC radio comedy series, 1951–60, written by Spike Milligan), publ. in *The Goon Show*

Scripts (ed. Spike Milligan, 1972). The words were set to music and released as 'The Ying Tong Song' in 1956.

2 I'm a hero wid coward's legs, I'm a hero from the waist up.
   Puckoon, ch. 2 (1963, filmed 2003)

3 Money couldn't buy friends, but you got a better class of enemy.
   Mrs Doonan, ibid., ch. 6

4 Her protruding breasts were pressed flat between his body and hers. He had felt them, he had fondled them, he lifted them, he pressed them, he weighed them, he valued them, he counted them, he massaged them, he stood back from them, he pulled them, he sat on them and picking up a banjo he played them.
   Ibid., ch. 10

5 Contraceptives should be used on every conceivable occasion.
   Camden Theatre, London, 30 April 1972, publ. in *The Last Goon Show of Them All* (1972)

C. Wright Mills (1916–62)
US SOCIOLOGIST
Charles Wright Mills. Influenced by Marx and MAX WEBER *in his critique of the American establishment, he contributed to the popular understanding of sociology with such books as* White Collar *(1951).*

1 Commercial jazz, soap opera, pulp fiction, comic strips, the movies set the images, mannerisms, standards, and aims of the urban masses. In one way or another, everyone is equal before these cultural machines; like technology itself, the mass media are nearly universal in their incidence and appeal. They are a kind of common denominator, a kind of scheme for pre-scheduled, mass emotions.
   White Collar, ch. 15, sect. 3 (1951)

2 By the power elite, we refer to those political, economic, and military circles which as an intricate set of overlapping cliques share decisions having at least national consequences. In so far as national events are decided, the power elite are those who decide them.
   The Power Elite, ch. 1 (1956)

3 The life-fate of the modern individual depends not only upon the family into which he was born or which he enters by marriage, but increasingly upon the corporation in which he spends the most alert hours of his best years.
   Ibid.

4 Power is not of a man. Wealth does not center in the person of the wealthy. Celebrity is not inherent in any personality. To

be celebrated, to be wealthy, to have power requires access to major institutions.

Ibid.

5 In the world of the celebrity, the hierarchy of publicity has replaced the hierarchy of descent and even of great wealth.

Quoted in *Talking to Myself*, bk 4, ch. 1 (1977) by STUDS TERKEL

A. A. Milne (1882–1958)

BRITISH AUTHOR

Alan Alexander Milne. Although well known during the 1920s as a writer for Punch and of light comedies, he is now remembered for his classic children's stories and poems written for his son, Christopher Robin, and the play Toad of Toad Hall *(1929), based on Kenneth Grahame's* Wind in the Willows.

1 *James James*
  Said to his Mother,
  'Mother,' he said, said he;
  'You must never go down to the end of the town, if you don't go down with me.'

'Disobedience', publ. in *When We Were Very Young* (1924)

2 *Nobody,*
  My darling
  Could call me
  A fussy man –
  BUT
  I do like a little bit of butter to my bread!

'The King's Breakfast', publ. ibid.

3 *A bear, however hard he tries,*
  Grows tubby without exercise.

'Teddy Bear', publ. ibid.

4 *How sweet to be a Cloud*
  Floating in the Blue!

Winnie-the-Pooh, in *Winnie-the-Pooh*, ch. 1 (1926)

5 I am a Bear of Very Little Brain, and long words Bother me.

Ibid., ch. 4

6 Pathetic. That's what it is. Pathetic.

Eeyore, ibid., ch. 6

7 Now then, Pooh, time for a little something.

Piglet, ibid.

8 My spelling is Wobbly. It's good spelling but it Wobbles, and the letters get in the wrong places.

Winnie-the-Pooh, ibid.

Czeslaw Milosz (b. 1911)

LITHUANIAN-BORN POLISH POET

During the 1930s he established himself as Poland's leading avant-garde poet but subsequently spent thirty-five years in exile in France and America. His collections include Bells in Winter *(1978).*

1 *Grow your tree of falsehood from a small grain of truth.*
  Do not follow those who lie in contempt of reality.
  Let your lie be even more logical than the truth itself,
  So the weary travellers may find repose.

'Child of Europe', sect. 4, publ. in *Selected Poems* (1973)

2 *Blessed be jubilation.*
  Vintages and harvests.
  Even if not everyone
  Is granted serenity.

'A Poem for the End of the Century', publ. in *Provinces* (1991)

Liza Minnelli (b. 1946)

US ACTRESS

The daughter of JUDY GARLAND *and director Vincente Minnelli, she inherited her mother's powerful and vibrant singing voice, used to effect in her greatest successes, the films* Cabaret *(1972) and* New York, New York *(1977).*

1 *Money makes the world go round*
  the world go round
  the world go round,
  Money makes the world go round
  That clinking clanking sound!

'Money' (song, written by Fred Ebb and John Kander) in *Cabaret* (musical play by Joe Masterhoff, 1966, filmed 1972). The words are sung by Sally Bowles (Liza Minnelli) and the Master of Ceremonies (JOEL GREY).

2 In Hollywood now when people die they don't say, 'Did he leave a will?' but 'Did he leave a diary?'

Interview in the *Observer* 13 August 1989

(Dame) Helen Mirren (b. 1945)

BRITISH ACTRESS

Admired for her cool sexuality, she has acted on stage with the Royal Shakespeare Company, in numerous films, and on television in Prime Suspect *(1991–3 and 1996).*

1 The part never calls for it [nudity]. And I've never ever used that excuse. The box office calls for it.

Quoted in the *Guardian* 31 December 1994

Yukio Mishima (1925–70)

JAPANESE AUTHOR

Originally Kimitake Hiraoka. He published novels, poetry and versions of Noh and Kabuki plays. The Sea of Fertility *tetralogy (1972–4) evokes, in his own words, 'the old beautiful tradition of Japan, which is disappearing very quickly day by day'. Increasingly obsessed with death and sacrifice, he committed a ritual Samurai suicide, seppuku.*

1 The sound of the rain is like the voices of tens of thousands of monks reading sutras.

. . . No-one's words can compete with this mercilessly powerful rain. The only thing that can compete with the sound of this rain, that can smash this deathlike wall of sound, is the shout of a man who refuses to stoop to this chatter, the shout of a simple spirit that knows no words.

Thirst for Love, ch. 4 (*Ai No Kawaki*, 1950, transl. 1969)

2 From the moment that a man no longer responds in the slightest to the motives that regulate the material world, that world appears to be at complete repose.

Death in Midsummer and Other Stories, 'The Priest of Shiga Temple and His Love' (1966)

3 Literary art takes its materials from life, but although life is thus the mother of literature, it is also her bitter enemy; although life is inherent in the author himself, it is also the eternal antithesis of art.

Mishima on Hagakure, 'Hagakure and I' (1977)

4 Ours is an age in which everything is based on the premise that it is best to live as long as possible. The average life span has become the longest in history, and a monotonous plan for humanity unrolls before us.

Ibid., 'Hagakure is Alive Today'

5 Youth possesses the impulse to resist and the impulse to surrender, in equal measure. One might re-define these as the impulse to be free and the impulse to die. The manifestation of these impulses, no matter how political the form it assumes, is like an electric current that results from a difference in electrical charge – in other words, from the fundamental contradictions of human existence.

Ibid.

6 If we value so highly the dignity of life, how can we not also value the dignity of death? No death may be called futile.

Ibid., 'How to Read *Hagakure*'

Mistinguett (1874–1956)
FRENCH DANCER AND SINGER
Originally Jeanne Marie Bourgeois. A popular and vivacious music hall artiste until her seventies, she performed at the Folies-Bergère with her partner MAURICE CHEVALIER, *and at the Moulin Rouge.*

1 A kiss can be a comma, a question mark or an exclamation point. That's basic spelling that every woman ought to know.

Theatre Arts December 1955

Adrian Mitchell (b. 1932)
BRITISH POET AND AUTHOR
A leading figure of the Underground Poetry and performance poetry of the 1960s, he describes himself: 'My brain socialist/My heart anarchist/My

eyes pacifist/My blood revolutionary.' *Among his collections are* Out Loud (1968) *and* On the Beach at Cambridge (1986).

1 Most people ignore most poetry
     because
  most poetry ignores most people.

Poems, Epigraph (1964)

2 I was run over by the truth one day.
  Ever since the accident I've walked this way
  So stick my legs in plaster
  Tell me lies about Vietnam.

'To Whom it May Concern', publ. in *Out Loud* (1968). Opening lines of poem.

3 Retire, retire into a fungus basement
  Where nothing moves except the draught
  And the light and dark grey figures
  Doubling their money on the screen;
  Where the cabbages taste like the mummy's
     hand
  And the meat tastes of feet;
  Where there is nothing to say except:
  'Remember?' or 'Your turn to dust the cat'.

'Old Age Report', publ. in *Ride the Nightmare* (1971)

Elma Mitchell (1919–2000)
BRITISH POET
Elizabeth Manuel Mitchell. Her collections include The Human Cage (1979) *and* Furnished Room (1983).

1 Women reminded him of lilies and roses.
  Me they remind rather of blood and soap,
  Armed with a warm rag, assaulting noses,
  Ears, neck, mouth and all the secret places.

'Thoughts after Ruskin', publ. in *The Poor Man in the Flesh* (1976)

Joni Mitchell (b. 1943)
CANADIAN-BORN US SINGER AND SONGWRITER
Originally Roberta Joan Anderson. She set the pattern for musical introspection in the late 1960s and '70s with her folk-based albums such as Blue (1971). *Later recordings, for example* Mingus (1979), *mixed jazz and rock.*

1 I've looked at life from both sides now
  From up and down, and still somehow
  It's life illusions I recall
  I really don't know life at all.

'Both Sides Now' (song) on the album *Clouds* (1969). The song was covered by Judy Collins in 1970.

2 We are stardust,
  We are golden,
  And we got to get ourselves
  Back to the garden.

'Woodstock' (song, 1969) on the album *Ladies of the Canyon* (1970). The song was a hit for Matthews Southern Comfort.

3 *They paved paradise*
And put up a parking lot
With a pink hotel,
A boutique, and a swinging hot spot.
'Big Yellow Taxi' (song) on ibid.

4 *All the people at this party, they've got a lot*
of style,
They've got stamps of many countries,
they've got passport smiles.
Some are friendly, some are cutting, some
are watchin' it from the wings,
Some are standin' in the center givin' to get
something.
'People's Parties' (song) on the album *Court and Spark* (1974)

5 There are things to confess that enrich the world, and things that need not be said.
Independent 13 May 1988

6 I'm not a pitiable creature. It's just that I suffer very eloquently.
Interview in the *Observer* 18 October 1998

Juliet Mitchell (b. 1940)
NEW ZEALAND-BORN BRITISH AUTHOR
An editor with New Left Review, *she wrote her early books such as* Women's Estate *(1971) from a Marxist-feminist perspective. Other works include* Psychoanalysis and Feminism *(1974).*

1 A fixed image of the future is in the worst sense ahistorical.
'Women – The Longest Revolution', publ. in *New Left Review* November–December 1966

2 'Leaders' are rarely ousted by anyone other than would-be leaders. In not wishing to act like 'men', there is no need for us to act like 'women'. The rise of the oppressed should not be a glorification of oppressed characteristics.
Women's Estate, ch. 10 (1971)

Margaret Mitchell (1900–1949)
US NOVELIST
Over a period of ten years she wrote her only novel Gone with the Wind *(1936, filmed 1939), a romantic drama set in the American Civil War. It was, she said, 'basically just a simple yarn of fairly simple people'.*

1 Land is the only thing in the world that amounts to anything, for 'tis the only thing in this world that lasts. . . . 'Tis the only thing worth working for, worth fighting for – worth dying for.
Gerald O'Hara, in *Gone with the Wind*, vol. 1, pt 1, ch. 2 (1936)

2 I'm tired of everlastingly being unnatural and never doing anything I want to do. I'm tired of acting like I don't eat more than a bird, and walking when I want to run and saying I feel faint after a waltz, when I could dance for two days and never get

tired. I'm tired of saying, 'How wonderful you are!' to fool men who haven't got one-half the sense I've got, and I'm tired of pretending I don't know anything, so men can tell me things and feel important while they're doing it.
Scarlett O'Hara, ibid., ch. 5

3 Until you've lost your reputation, you never realize what a burden it was or what freedom really is.
Ibid.

4 What most people don't seem to realize is that there is just as much money to be made out of the wreckage of a civilization as from the upbuilding of one.
Rhett Butler, ibid., pt 2, ch. 9

5 Fighting is like champagne. It goes to the heads of cowards as quickly as of heroes. Any fool can be brave on a battlefield when it's be brave or else be killed.
Ashley Wilkes, ibid., vol. 2, pt 4, ch. 31

6 Southerners can never resist a losing cause.
Rhett Butler, ibid., ch. 34

7 Death and taxes and childbirth! There's never any convenient time for any of them!
Scarlett O'Hara, ibid., ch. 38

8 I was never one to patiently pick up broken fragments and glue them together again and tell myself that the mended whole was as good as new. What is broken is broken – and I'd rather remember it as it was at its best than mend it and see the broken places as long as I lived. . . . I wish I could care what you do or where you go, but I can't. My dear, I don't give a damn.
Rhett Butler, ibid., pt 5, ch. 63. See CLARK GABLE 1 for the film version of this speech.

9 After all, tomorrow is another day.
Scarlett O'Hara, ibid. Closing words of book and film.

Warren Mitchell (b. 1926)
BRITISH ACTOR
Originally Warren Misell. Best known as the foul-mouthed bigot Alf Garnett in the TV sitcom Till Death Us Do Part *(1965–75), he is also noted for his theatre performances.*

1 Comedy comes from conflict, from hatred.
The Times 31 December 1990

Robert Mitchum (1917–97)
US ACTOR
He played tough guys for over thirty years in such films as Night of the Hunter *(1955) and* Farewell My Lovely *(1975). Always self-deprecating of his talents, he claimed to have survived because 'I work cheap and don't take up much time'.*

1 **You know something – you're a pretty nice guy, for a girl.**
Frank Jessup (Robert Mitchum), in *Angel Face* (film, 1953, screenplay by Frank Nugent and Oscar Millard, directed and produced by Otto Preminger)

Nancy Mitford (1904–73)
BRITISH AUTHOR
The eldest of the six aristocratic Mitford sisters, she wrote the autobiographical novels The Pursuit of Love *(1945) and* Love in a Cold Climate *(1949). Her sister Jessica described her as having the 'aspect of an elegant pirate's moll'.*

1 **Uncle Matthew's four years in France and Italy between 1914 and 1918 had given him no great opinion of foreigners. 'Frogs,' he would say, 'are slightly better than Huns or Wops, but abroad is unutterably bloody and foreigners are fiends.'**
The Pursuit of Love, ch. 15 (1945)

2 **Ancestry has never counted much in England. The English lord knows himself to be such a very genuine article that, when looking for a wife, he can rise above such baubles as seize quartiers. Kind hearts, in his view, are more than coronets, and large tracts of town property more than Norman blood.**
'The English Aristocracy', first publ. in *Encounter*, repr. in *Noblesse Oblige* (1956)

Issey Miyake (b. 1938)
JAPANESE FASHION DESIGNER
He began showing his collections in New York and Paris in the early 1970s. His designs blend East with West and emphasize a layered and textured look.

1 **Design is not for philosophy – it's for life.**
International Herald Tribune 23 March 1992

Wilson Mizner (1876–1933)
US DRAMATIST AND WIT
Before becoming a playwright, he was a hustler for a medicine show, a professional cardsharp, a boxing manager and a gold prospector. His most successful plays were co-written, including The Only Law *(1909, with G. Bronson Howard) and* The Deep Purple *(1910, with Paul Armstrong).*

1 **Be nice to people on your way up because you'll meet them on your way down.**
Quoted in *The Legendary Mizners*, ch. 4 (1953) by Alva Johnson. Also attributed to the comic Jimmy Durante.

2 **A trip through a sewer in a glass-bottomed boat.**
Ibid. Mizner's description of Hollywood was reworked in a speech by James J. Walker, Mayor of New York, in 1928: 'A reformer is a guy who rides through a sewer in a glass-bottomed boat.'

3 **If you steal from one author, it's plagiarism; if you steal from many, it's research.**
Ibid.

4 **Working for Warner Brothers is like fucking a porcupine: it's a hundred pricks against one.**
Quoted in *Bring on the Empty Horses*, 'Degrees of Friendliness' (1975) by David Niven

Walter Mondale (b. 1928)
US POLITICIAN AND VICE-PRESIDENT
A Democratic senator 1964–76, he was JIMMY CARTER'*s vice-president (1977–81) and won the Democratic presidential nomination in 1984, but was heavily defeated by* RONALD REAGAN.

1 **Where's the beef?**
Campaign slogan for 1984 Democratic presidential nomination. Originally an advertising slogan for Wendy's Hamburgers, the words were taken up by Mondale's campaign team after a televised debate 11 March 1984, in which the candidate told rival Gary Hart, 'When I hear your new ideas I'm reminded of that ad, *Where's the beef?*'

2 **Political image is like mixing cement. When it's wet, you can move it around and shape it, but at some point it hardens and there's almost nothing you can do to reshape it.**
Quoted in the *Independent on Sunday* 12 May 1991

Le Monde
1 *Nous sommes tous Américains.*
(We are all Americans now.)
Headline, 13 September 2001. Referring to the worldwide solidarity with and sympathy for the United States in the wake of '9/11'.

Marilyn Monroe (1926–62)
US SCREEN ACTRESS
Originally Norma Jean Mortenson or Baker. Described by LAURENCE OLIVIER *as a 'professional amateur', she was the supreme 1950s sex icon and the archetypal 'dumb blonde' in the comedies* Gentlemen Prefer Blondes *(1953) and* Some Like It Hot *(1959). Deeply insecure, she died from a drugs overdose. See* NORMAN MAILER 14, BILLY WILDER 5.

1 **Does this boat go to Europe, France?**
Lorelei Lee (Marilyn Monroe), in *Gentlemen Prefer Blondes* (film, 1953, screenplay by Charles Lederer based on novel by ANITA LOOS, directed by Howard Hawkes). The words do not appear in the 1925 novel.

2 **Diamonds are a girl's best friend.**
'Diamonds are a Girl's Best Friend' (song, written by Leo Robin with music by Jule Styne), ibid. The song first appeared in the 1949 stage show of *Gentlemen Prefer Blondes*.

3 **I don't care how rich he is – as long as he**

has a yacht, his own private railroad car, and his own toothpaste.

Sugar Kane (Marilyn Monroe), in *Some Like It Hot* (film, 1959, screenplay by Billy Wilder and I. A. L. Diamond, produced and directed by Billy Wilder)

4 I always get the fuzzy end of the lollipop.

Ibid.

5 Unfortunately, I am involved in a freedom ride protesting the loss of the minority rights belonging to the few remaining earthbound stars. All we demanded was our right to twinkle.

Telegram, to Mr and Mrs Robert Kennedy, turning down a party invitation, 13 June 1962, shown on *Marilyn: Something's Got to Give*, Channel 4, 2 August 1992

6 Fame will go by and, so long, I've had you, fame. If it goes by, I've always known it was fickle. So at least it's something I experienced, but that's not where I live.

Life 3 August 1962. Conclusion of taped conversation, published on the day that Monroe died.

7 My work is the only ground I've ever had to stand on . . . To put it bluntly I seem to have a whole superstructure with no foundation.

Quoted in *Marilyn*, ch. 7 (1973) by NORMAN MAILER

8 Hollywood's a place where they'll pay you a thousand dollars for a kiss, and fifty cents for your soul. I know, because I turned down the first offer often enough and held out for the fifty cents.

Quoted in *Marilyn Monroe In Her Own Words*, 'Acting' (1990)

9 Husbands are chiefly good as lovers when they are betraying their wives.

Ibid., 'Weddings & Divorces'

10 I always felt I was a nobody, and the only way for me to be somebody was to be – well, somebody else. Which is probably why I wanted to act.

Quoted in *Marilyn Monroe: The Biography*, ch. 15 (1993) by Donald Spoto

C. E. Montague (1867–1928)

BRITISH AUTHOR AND JOURNALIST

Charles Edward Montague. A journalist with the Manchester Guardian from 1898, he wrote numerous books including Disenchantment (1922), which recounts his experience of the First World War, and the novel Rough Justice (1926).

1 There is no limit to what a man can do so long as he does not care a straw who gets the credit for it.

Disenchantment, ch. 15, sect. 3 (1922)

2 A lie will easily get you out of a scrape, and yet, strangely and beautifully, rapture pos-sesses you when you have taken the scrape and left out the lie.

Ibid., sect. 4

3 War hath no fury like a non-combatant.

Ibid., ch. 16

Eugenio Montale (1896–1981)

ITALIAN POET

Director of the Italian Scientific-Literary Cabinet 1929–38, he was literary and music editor of the Milan newspaper Corriere della Sera *from 1947. His poems, in* Le Occasioni *(1939) and* Satura *(1962), among other collections, focus on the 'pain of living'.*

1 To make one, too many lives are needed.

'Summer', publ. in *Le Occasioni* (1939), repr. in *Selected Poems* (1964). This last line of the poem was remembered by ITALO CALVINO in a newspaper tribute to Montale after the poet's death.

2 All religions of the only God
are one: just the cooks and the cooking vary.

'The Death of God', publ. in *Satura* (1962), repr. in *New Poems* (1976). Opening words of poem.

3 Words
are everyone's property and in vain
do they hide in dictionaries,
for there's always a rogue
who digs up the rarest
and most stinking truffles.

'Words', ibid.

4 The new man is born too old to tolerate the new world. The present conditions of life have not yet erased the traces of the past. We run too fast, but we still do not move enough. . . . He looks but he does not contemplate, he sees but he does not think.

Poet in Our Time (1972)

5 Youth is the vilest of all illusions.

'Sorapis, 40 Years Ago', publ. in *Diario del '71 e del '72* (1973), repr. in *New Poems* (1976)

6 Tear up your pages, throw them in a sewer,
take no degree in anything,
and you will be able to say that you were
perhaps alive for a moment or an instant.

'The Decline of Values', ibid.

Maria Montessori (1870–1952)

ITALIAN EDUCATIONIST

The first woman in Italy to gain a medical degree (1894), she gave her name to a system of education for children aged from three to six, which emphasizes freedom of expression and self-direction.

1 If education is always to be conceived along the same antiquated lines of a mere transmission of knowledge, there is little to be hoped from it in the bettering of man's future. For what is the use of transmitting

knowledge if the individual's total development lags behind?

The Absorbent Mind, ch. 1 (1949)

2 If help and salvation are to come, they can only come from the children, for the children are the makers of men.

Ibid.

3 There is . . . in every child a painstaking teacher, so skilful that he obtains identical results in all children in all parts of the world. The only language men ever speak perfectly is the one they learn in babyhood, when no one can teach them anything!

Ibid.

4 We teachers can only help the work going on, as servants wait upon a master.

Ibid.

Viscount Montgomery (1887–1976)

BRITISH SOLDIER

Bernard Montgomery, First Viscount Montgomery of Alamein. As commander of the Eighth Army he defeated Rommel at the battle of El Alamein (1942) and played a key role in the invasion of Italy the following year. In 1944 he commanded the allied forces in the Normandy invasion. See WINSTON CHURCHILL 52.

1 Rule 1, on page 1 of the book of war, is: 'Do not march on Moscow'. Various people have tried it, Napoleon and Hitler, and it is no good. . . . Rule 2 of war . . . is: 'Do not go fighting with your land armies in China'. It is a vast country, with no clearly defined objectives, and an army fighting there would be engulfed by what is known as the Ming Bing, the people's insurgents.

Speech to House of Lords, 30 May 1962, publ. in *Hansard* (Lords)

2 Far from helping these unnatural practices along, surely our task is to build a bulwark which will defy evil influences which are seeking to undermine the very foundations of our national character – defy them; do not help them. I have heard some say . . . that such practices are allowed in France and in other NATO countries. We are not French, and we are not other nationals. We are British, thank God!

On homosexual practices, ibid., 26 May 1965, debating the Sexual Offences Bill

Monty Python's Flying Circus

The surreal BBC TV comedy series (1969–74) was written and performed by Graham Chapman (1941–89), JOHN CLEESE *(b. 1939), Terry Gilliam (b. 1940), Eric Idle (b. 1943), Terry Jones (b. 1942) and* MICHAEL PALIN *(b. 1943), and spawned several films.*

1 And now for something completely different.

John Cleese, as newsreader. The words became a catch-phrase used by various characters as a link between sketches in different episodes.

2 Nudge, nudge, wink, wink, say no more, know what I mean . . .

Eric Idle, in first series, episode 3, first broadcast 19 October 1969

3 This parrot is no more! It has ceased to be! It's expired and gone to meet its maker! This is a late parrot! It's a stiff! . . . THIS IS AN EX-PARROT!

John Cleese, ibid., episode 8, first broadcast 7 December 1969

4 *I'm a lumberjack*
And I'm OK,
I sleep all night
And I work all day.
I cut down trees, I skip and jump,
I like to press wild flowers.
I put on women's clothing
And hang around in bars.

'The Lumberjack Song' ibid., episode 9, first broadcast 14 December 1969

5 Nobody expects the Spanish Inquisition!

Michael Palin, in second series, episode 2, first broadcast 22 September 1970

6 One minute I'm a leper with a trade, next minute my livelihood's gone. Not so much as a by-your-leave. You're cured, mate. Bloody do-gooder!

Beggar (Michael Palin), in *Monty Python's Life of Brian* (film, 1979, written by John Cleese, Graham Chapman, Terry Gilliam, Eric Idle, Terry Jones and Michael Palin, directed by Terry Jones). On being cured by Jesus.

7 Apart from the sanitation, the medicine, education, wine, public order, irrigation, roads, the fresh water system and public health, what have the Romans ever done for us?

The leader of the People's Front of Judaea (John Cleese), ibid. A voice pipes up, 'Brought peace?'

8 *When you're chewing on life's gristle*
Don't grumble, give a whistle
And this'll help turn things out for the best . . .
And . . . always look on the bright side of life.

Mr Frisbee III (Eric Idle), ibid.

Brian Moore (1921–99)

IRISH-BORN CANADIAN NOVELIST

Misfits, Catholicism and sectarian conflict are recurrent themes in his work, in which women are frequently protagonists, as in The Lonely Passion of Judith Hearne *(1955, filmed 1987) and* I Am Mary Dunne *(1968).*

1 There comes a point in many people's lives

when they can no longer play the role they have chosen for themselves. When that happens, we are like actors finding that someone has changed the play.

Sunday Times 15 April 1990. 'What I write about,' Moore added, 'is the mess that follows.'

2 The world's made up of individuals who don't want to be heroes.

Ibid.

3 Research is usually a policeman stopping a novel from progressing.

Ibid.

Clayton Moore (1914–99)

US SCREEN ACTOR

Originally Jack Carlton Moore. He played small roles in Hollywood throughout the 1940s, and in 1949 he was assigned the role of the Lone Ranger when the radio hit was transferred to television, continuing in the part until the series ended in 1957.

1 Hi-yo, Silver, away!

The Lone Ranger (Clayton Moore), in *The Lone Ranger* (TV series, 1949–57, created by Fran Striker and George Trendle). Heard at the beginning of each episode of the show, which ran for sixteen years on radio before making its TV debut with Moore as the Masked Man on his 'fiery horse with the speed of light'.

Jo Moore (b. 1963)

BRITISH GOVERNMENT ADVISER

She was appointed adviser to STEPHEN BYERS *at the Department of Trade and Industry in 2000, and resigned in controversial circumstances in 2002.*

1 It is now a very good day to get out anything we want to bury.

E-mail to members of her department, sent thirty minutes after the attack on the World Trade Center in New York, 11 September 2001, quoted in the *Guardian* 9 October 2001. Often misquoted as 'A good day to bury bad news'.

Marianne Moore (1887–1972)

US POET

T. S. ELIOT *praised the 'swift dissolving image' of her verse, which is characterized by its individual metrical style and her sharp wit. Her publications include* Observations *(1924) and* Nevertheless *(1944).*

1 *nor till the poets among us can be*
  'literalists of
the imagination' – above
insolence and triviality and can present
for inspection, 'imaginary gardens with real
    toads in them,' shall we have
    it.

'Poetry', first publ. in *Others* July 1919, repr. in *Selected Poems* (1935)

2 *with its baby rivers and little towns, each*
    with its abbey or its cathedral,
with voices – one voice perhaps, echoing
    through the transept – the
criterion of suitability and convenience.

'England', first publ. in *The Dial* April 1920, repr. ibid.

3 *My father used to say,*
  'Superior people never make long visits,
  have to be shown Longfellow's grave
  or the glass flowers at Harvard.'

'Silence', first publ. in *The Dial* October 1924, repr. ibid.

4 *The deepest feeling always shows itself in*
    silence;
not in silence, but restraint.

Ibid.

5 Poetry, that is to say the poetic, is a primal necessity.

'Comment', first publ. in *The Dial* August 1926, repr. in *Complete Prose* (1987)

6 When one cannot appraise out of one's own experience, the temptation to blunder is minimized, but even when one can, appraisal seems chiefly useful as appraisal of the appraiser.

'Comment', first publ. in *The Dial* October 1928, repr. ibid.

7 The catnip that art is, or *ignis fatuus*, or drop on the cactus, does seem worth the martyrdom of pursuit.

Letter to WILLIAM CARLOS WILLIAMS, 26 January 1934, publ. in *The Selected Letters of Marianne Moore*, 'The Poet in Brooklyn: 1930–1934' (ed. Bonnie Costello, 1998)

8 *O to be a dragon*
a symbol of the power of Heaven – of
    silkworm
size or immense; at times invisible.
Felicitous phenomenon!

'O To Be a Dragon', publ. in *O To Be a Dragon* (1959)

9 *Camels are snobbish*
and sheep, unintelligent;
water buffaloes, neurasthenic –
even murderous.
Reindeer seem over-serious.

'The Arctic Ox (Or Goat)', publ. ibid.

10 I see no reason for calling my work poetry except that there is no other category in which to put it.

Quoted in the *New York Mirror* 31 May 1959. On accepting the National Book Award for poetry.

11 A writer is unfair to himself when he is unable to be hard on himself.

Interview in *Writers at Work* (second series, ed. George Plimpton, 1963)

Michael Moore (b. 1954)

US AUTHOR, FILM-MAKER AND POLITICAL ACTIVIST

Regarded as a fearless political commentator, he has made the documentary films Roger and Me *(1989) and* Bowling for Columbine *(2002) and is the author of* Downsize This: Random Threats from an Unarmed American *(1996) and* Stupid White Men *(2002).*

1 I want us all to face our fears and stop behaving like our goal in life is to merely survive. 'Surviving' is for wimps and game show contestants stranded in the jungle or on a desert island. You are not stranded. You own the store. The bad guys are just a bunch of silly, stupid white men. And there's a helluva lot more of us than there are of them. Use your power. You deserve better.

  Stupid White Men, ch. 12 (2002). Closing words of book.

Roger Moore (b. 1927)

BRITISH SCREEN ACTOR

Previously a model for knitted cardigans, he played suave action men in the television series The Saint *(1962–9) and as agent 007 in seven James Bond films (1973–85).*

1 Left eyebrow raised, right eyebrow raised.

  Of his acting range, quoted in *Star Billing*, 'Seven Comments on the Art of Acting' (1985) by David Brown

Alberto Moravia (1907–90)

ITALIAN AUTHOR

Originally Alberto Pincherle. He made his mark with The Time of Indifference *(1929, filmed 1964), a portrayal of middle-class decadence. This theme, along with those of alienation and loveless sexuality, permeates his other works, for example* The Woman of Rome *(1947, filmed 1954).*

1 Although not all men possess the same intellectual capacity and the same knowledge, they all, even the most wretched, have their own moral world in its entirety.

  The Woman of Rome, Preface (1947)

Jeanne Moreau (b. 1928)

FRENCH ACTRESS

Her sensual beauty and sensitive acting were utilized by directors of the French New Wave, for example Louis Malle in Les Amants *(1958),* ROGER VADIM *in* Les Liaisons dangereuses *(1959) and* TRUFFAUT *in* Jules et Jim *(1961).*

1 Acting deals with very delicate emotions. It is not putting up a mask. Each time an actor acts he does not hide; he exposes himself.

  The New York Times 30 June 1976

Robin Morgan (b. 1941)

US FEMINIST AUTHOR AND POET

As a chronicler of the women's movement in the USA, she edited the seminal collection of essays Sisterhood is Powerful *(1970), followed by a wider-ranging collection from different countries,* The Anatomy of Freedom *(1982).*

1 It isn't until you begin to fight in your own cause that you (a) become really committed to winning, and (b) become a genuine ally of other people struggling for their freedom.

  Sisterhood Is Powerful, Introduction (1970)

2 *Don't accept rides from strange men, and remember that all men are as strange as hell.*

  Ibid., 'Letter to a Sister Underground'

Christopher Morley (1890–1957)

US NOVELIST, JOURNALIST AND POET

Best known for his novel Kitty Foyle *(1939), he also published poetry and essay collections. As editor he promoted the works of Joseph Conrad.*

1 Life is a foreign language: all men mispronounce it.

  Thunder on the Left, ch. 14 (1925)

2 Dancing is a wonderful training for girls, it's the first way you learn to guess what a man is going to do before he does it.

  Kitty Foyle, ch. 11 (1939)

Robert Morley (1908–92)

BRITISH ACTOR AND HUMORIST

He remained a committed stage actor while also pursuing a screen career from 1938, appearing in such films as Oscar Wilde *(1960). His humorous observations and anecdotes are collected in* A Musing Morley *(1974) and* The Pleasures of Ages *(1988).*

1 The British tourist is always happy abroad as long as the natives are waiters.

  Quoted in the *Observer* 20 April 1958

2 The French are a logical people, which is one reason the English dislike them so intensely. The other is that they own France, a country which we have always judged to be much too good for them.

  A Musing Morley, 'France and the French' (1974)

Desmond Morris (b. 1928)

BRITISH ZOOLOGIST

He was presenter of television's Zoo Time *in the late 1950s and keeper of mammals for the Zoological Society 1959–67 before his bestsellers* The Naked Ape *(1967) and* The Human Zoo *(1969) made him a household name.*

1 We never stop investigating. We are never satisfied that we know enough to get by. Every question we answer leads on to

another question. This has become the greatest survival trick of our species.

The Naked Ape, ch. 4 (1967)

2 We are, to put it mildly, in a mess, and there is a strong chance that we shall have exterminated ourselves by the end of the century. Our only consolation will have to be that, as a species, we have had an exciting term of office.

Ibid., ch. 5

3 The city is not a concrete jungle, it is a human zoo.

The Human Zoo, Introduction (1969)

Blake Morrison (b. 1950)
BRITISH POET AND AUTHOR
He is known for his poem collections including The Ballad of the Yorkshire Ripper *(1987), his study of fatherhood in* And When Did You Last See Your Father? *(1993) and his reflections on the James Bulger murder,* As If *(1997).*

1 The selective memory isn't selective enough.

Independent on Sunday 16 June 1991

2 Every age has its own story, or rewrites the same story; every Age too.

As If, ch. 1 (1997)

3 Some deaths are emblematic, tipping the scales, and little James's death – green fruit shaken from the bough, an ear of grain sown back in the earth – seemed like the murder of hope: the unthinkable thought of, the undoable done. If child-killings are the worst killings, then a child child-killing must be worse than worst, a new superlative in horror.

Ibid. On the James Bulger case.

4 By sparing the rod we've bred a generation of hoodlums. Cherub-faced muggers. Rapists who don't have pubic hair yet. Pre-pubescents with glittering knives. What's childhood coming to? Keep your kids well back. Childhood's not a place for children.

Ibid., ch. 2. Articulating popular reactions to the Bulger case.

5 Without art, confessionalism is masturbation.

Too True, Introduction (1998)

6 Certainly, porn has its uses: like a pet dog, it can console the lonely; like oysters, it can sharpen a lover's appetite; like cocoa, it can get the restless off to sleep.

Ibid., 'The Trouble With Porn', sect. 3

Jim Morrison (1943–71)
US ROCK MUSICIAN
Styling himself the Lizard King, he was the singer and main inspiration of the Doors, a Los Angeles rock group formed in 1966. Increasingly erratic and

in thrall to drugs, he died in mysterious circumstances in Paris.

1 *Come on baby light my fire.*

'Light My Fire' (song, written by the Doors) on the album *The Doors* (1967) by the Doors

2 *This is the end,*
Beautiful friend.
This is the end,
My only friend, the end.
It hurts to set you free
But you'll never follow me.

'The End' (song, written by the Doors), on ibid. The song was featured in FRANCIS FORD COPPOLA's film *Apocalypse Now* (1979).

3 *'Father?'*
'Yes, son?'
'I want to kill you.'
'Mother, I want to . . .'

Ibid.

4 *We want the world and we want it now!*

'When the Music's Over' (song, written by the Doors) on the album *Strange Days* (1967) by the Doors

5 *I am the Lizard King*
I can do anything.

'The Celebration of the Lizard' (poem and song) on the album *Waiting For the Sun* (1968) by the Doors

6 *They got the guns but we got the numbers.*

'Five to One' (song, written by the Doors), ibid.

7 I'm interested in anything about revolt, disorder, chaos, especially activity that appears to have no meaning. It seems to me to be the road toward freedom.

Quoted in *Time* 24 January 1968

8 The Lords appease us with images. They give us books, concerts, galleries, shows, cinemas. Especially the cinemas. Through art they confuse us and blind us to our enslavement. Art adorns our prison walls, keeps us silent and diverted and indifferent.

'The Lords: Notes on Vision' (1969), repr. in *The Lords and the New Creatures* (1970)

9 The most loving parents and relatives commit murder with smiles on their faces. They force us to destroy the person we really are: a subtle kind of murder.

Quoted in *In Their Own Words: The Doors*, ch. 1 (1988) by Andrew Doe and John Tobler

Toni Morrison (b. 1931)
US NOVELIST AND EDITOR
Chloe Anthony Morrison. Her novels use the history and culture of African-Americans as the basis for explorations of emotions and relationships, and include Tar Baby *(1981),* Beloved *(1987) and* Jazz *(1992). In 1993 she was the first African-American to win the Nobel Prize for Literature.*

1 Like any artist with no art form, she [Sula] became dangerous.
Sula (1973)

2 Grab this land! Take it, hold it, my brothers, make it, my brothers, shake it, squeeze it, turn it, twist it, beat it, kick it, kiss it, whip it, stomp it, dig it, plow it, seed it, reap it, rent it, buy it, sell it, own it, build it, multiply it, and pass it on – can you hear me? Pass it on!
Macon Dead, in *Song of Solomon*, pt 1, ch. 10 (1977)

3 At some point in life the world's beauty becomes enough. You don't need to photograph, paint or even remember it. It is enough.
Tar Baby, ch. 8 (1981)

4 An innocent man is a sin before God. Inhuman and therefore untrustworthy. No man should live without absorbing the sins of his kind, the foul air of his innocence, even if it did wilt rows of angel trumpets and cause them to fall from their vines.
Ibid.

5 Of course I'm a black writer. . . . I'm not *just* a black writer, but categories like black writer, woman writer and Latin American writer aren't marginal anymore. We have to acknowledge that the thing we call 'literature' is more pluralistic now, just as society ought to be. The melting pot never worked. We ought to be able to accept on equal terms everybody from the Hasidim to Walter Lippmann, from the Rastafarians to Ralph Bunche.
Quoted in *Newsweek* 30 March 1981

6 How soon country people forget. When they fall in love with a city it is forever, and it is like forever. As though there never was a time when they didn't love it. The minute they arrive at the train station or get off the ferry and glimpse the wide streets and the wasteful lamps lighting them, they know they are born for it. There, in a city, they are not so much new as themselves: their stronger, riskier selves.
Jazz, ch. 2 (1992)

7 In this country American means white. Everybody else has to hyphenate.
Guardian 29 January 1992

Van Morrison (b. 1945)
IRISH ROCK MUSICIAN
Originally George Ivan Morrison. He formed the R'n'B band Them in 1963, which had hits with his compositions 'Here Comes the Night' and 'Gloria' (both 1965). Astral Weeks (1968) and Moondance (1970) were the first of a long series of solo albums.

1 Music is spiritual. The music business is not.
The Times 6 July 1990

Morrissey (b. 1959)
BRITISH ROCK MUSICIAN
Stephen Patrick Morrissey. Described by Melody Maker as 'the Peregrine Worsthorne of pop', he was singer with the Smiths, an influential Manchester band which split in 1987.

1 *I was happy in the haze of a drunken hour But heaven knows I'm miserable now.*
'Heaven Knows I'm Miserable Now' (song, 1984, written with Johnny Marr) on the album *Hatful of Hollow* by the Smiths (1985)

2 *Hang the deejay.*
'Panic' (song, 1986, written with Johnny Marr) on the album *The World Won't Listen* (1987)

3 Everything went downhill from the moment McDonald's was given a licence to invade England. . . . To me, it was like the outbreak of war and I couldn't understand why English troops weren't retaliating.
Quoted in the *Guardian* 26 February 1994

John Mortimer (b. 1923)
BRITISH BARRISTER AND AUTHOR
He is best known for his novels featuring the amiable and eccentric lawyer Rumpole and adapted for television as Rumpole of the Bailey (1978–80). The light-hearted style of his novels such as Paradise Postponed (1985) and Summer's Lease (1988) cushions his biting satire of the English upper-middle class. He has also written plays, including A Voyage Round My Father (1970, televised 1982), screenplays and translations.

1 The shelf life of the modern hardback writer is somewhere between the milk and the yoghurt.
Quoted in the *Sunday Times* 27 December 1987

2 When you get to my age life seems little more than one long march to and from the lavatory.
Haverford Downs, in *Summer's Lease*, pt 2, ch. 3 (1988)

3 The worst fault of the working classes is telling their children they're not going to succeed, saying: 'There is life, but it's not for you.'
Daily Mail 31 May 1988

4 The freedom to make a fortune on the Stock Exchange has been made to sound more alluring than freedom of speech.
Quoted in the *Independent* 29 October 1988

5 Farce is tragedy played at a thousand revolutions per minute.
The Times 9 September 1992

6 At Harrow, you could have any boy for a box of Cadbury's milk chocolate.

Quoted in the *Sunday Times* 27 September 1998. Referring to his schooldays at Harrow.

7 The main aim of education should be to send children out into the world with a reasonably sized anthology in their heads so that, while seated on the lavatory, waiting in doctors' surgeries, on stationary trains or watching interviews with politicians, they may have something interesting to think about.

Quoted in *The Times* 30 December 2000

8 Champagne socialist.

Attributed description of himself, as a Labour-supporting member of the upper-middle classes

(Sir) Claus Moser (b. 1922)
GERMAN-BORN BRITISH ACADEMIC

A public figure in the arts and the academic world, he has been Chairman of the Royal Opera House (1974–87) and Warden of Wadham College, Oxford (1984–93).

1 Education costs money, but then so does ignorance.

Daily Telegraph 21 August 1990

2 For hundreds of years Britain has been brilliant at educating an élite: the problem is the other eighty per cent.

Broadcast on BBC Radio 4, 16 November 1990

(Sir) Oswald Mosley (1896–1980)
BRITISH FASCIST LEADER

He was successively a Conservative, Independent and Labour MP (1918–31) before founding the British Union of Fascists ('the Blackshirts') in 1932. Interned during the Second World War, he founded the right-wing Union Movement in 1948. His second wife was Diana Mitford.

1 I have always felt a clear choice existed between two states of mind, the writing of history and the making of history. He who is interested in the latter should only be detained by the former just long enough to absorb its lessons.

My Life, ch. 3 (1968)

2 Great men of action . . . never mind on occasion being ridiculous; in a sense it is part of their job, and at times they all are. A prophet or an achiever must never mind an occasional absurdity, it is an occupational risk.

Ibid., ch. 12

3 When the bystanders see an elephant coming down the street, it is idle to tell them it is a pleasant Sunday afternoon outing organised by the Young Men's Christian Association. We were a distinctive movement of intense national patriotism, but in the age of fascism it was clearly

jejune and possibly dishonest to deny that we were fascist.

Ibid., ch. 16

4 Ideas in a void have never appealed to me; action must follow thought or political life is meaningless.

Ibid., ch. 17

5 I am not, and never have been, a man of the right. My position was on the left and is now in the centre of politics.

Letter to *The Times* 26 April 1968

Robert Motherwell (1915–91)
US ARTIST

He was a key member of the New York Abstract Expressionists in the 1940s, producing massive painted images and collages which retained figurative and narrative elements, such as Elegies to the Spanish Republic *(1949–76). He also wrote on the theory of modern art.*

1 The public history of modern art is the story of conventional people not knowing what they are dealing with.

The Dada Painters and Poets: An Anthology, Preface (ed. Robert Motherwell, 1951)

Andrew Motion (b. 1952)
BRITISH POET AND BIOGRAPHER

His reflective, highly personal verse, published in Love in a Life *(1991) among other collections, shows the influence of Keats,* EDWARD THOMAS *and* PHILIP LARKIN, *all of whom have been subjects of critical studies and biographies by him. He was created Poet Laureate in 1999.*

1 *I admit that I also yearn to leave my mark*
   on society,
and not see machines or people trample it
   foolishly.
On the one hand it's only shit; on the other,
   shit's shit,
and what we desire in the world is less, not
   more, of it.

'It is an Offence', publ. in *Love in a Life* (1991)

2 *For a million years one life simply turns*
   into the next –
The spider hangs between driftwood and
   sea holly,
the sparrow hawk balances exactly over a
   shrew,
the hare sits bolt upright and urgent, all
   ears:
there is no reason why any of this should
   change.

'Salt Water', publ. in *Salt Water* (1997)

3 *Beside the river, swerving under ground,*
your future tracked you, snapping at your
   heels:
Diana, breathless, hunted by your own
   quick hounds.

'Mythology', publ. in *The Times* 6 September

1997, repr. in *News That Stays News* (ed. Simon Rae, 1999)

4 The fact of the matter is that it is a difficult time in our history for white, straight, middle-aged, middle-class males.

Quoted in the *Daily Telegraph* 20 May 1999. Said on his appointment as Poet Laureate.

Louis Mountbatten (1900–79)

BRITISH NAVAL COMMANDER AND STATESMAN

First Earl Mountbatten of Burma. The great-grandson of Queen Victoria, he was Supreme Allied Commander in South-East Asia (1941–3), the last Viceroy of India (1947) and Chief of Defence Staff (1959–65). He was assassinated by an IRA bomb.

1 If the Third World War is fought with nuclear weapons, the fourth will be fought with bows and arrows.

Maclean's 17 November 1975

Malcolm Muggeridge (1903–90)

BRITISH JOURNALIST AND BROADCASTER

He worked for the Manchester Guardian, *the* Evening Standard *and the* Daily Telegraph *and was Editor of* Punch *1953–7. His views were iconoclastic and informed by his Christian beliefs, which earned him the nickname 'Saint Mug'.* KENNETH TYNAN *compared him to a 'garden gnome expelled from Eden . . . come to rest as a gargoyle brooding over a derelict cathedral'.*

1 Good taste and humour are a contradiction in terms, like a chaste whore.

Time 14 September 1953. Defending his editorship of *Punch*.

2 There's nothing in this world more instinctively abhorrent to me than finding myself in agreement with my fellow-humans.

Any Questions?, BBC radio broadcast, 29 April 1955, publ. in *Muggeridge Through the Microphone*, 'Mini-Mania' (1967)

3 This horror of pain is a rather low instinct and . . . if I think of human beings I've known and of my own life, such as it is, I can't recall any case of pain which didn't, on the whole, enrich life.

Meeting Point, BBC1 television broadcast, 11 August 1963, publ. ibid., 'The Problem of Pain'

4 There is something ridiculous and even quite indecent in an individual *claiming* to be happy. Still more a people or a nation making such a claim. . . . This lamentable phrase 'the pursuit of happiness' is responsible for a good part of the ills and miseries of the modern world.

Woman's Hour, BBC radio broadcast, 5 October 1965, publ. ibid., 'Happiness'

5 Sex is the mysticism of materialism and the only possible religion in a materialistic society.

Television broadcast, BBC1, 21 October 1965, quoted ibid., 'The American Way of Sex'

6 The orgasm has replaced the Cross as the focus of longing and the image of fulfilment.

Tread Softly For You Tread on My Jokes, 'Down with Sex' (1966)

7 Television was not invented to make human beings vacuous, but is an emanation of their vacuity.

Ibid., 'I Like Dwight'

8 The genius of Man in our time has gone into jet-propulsion, atom-splitting, penicillin-curing, etc. There is none over for works of imagination; of spiritual insight or mystical enlightenment. I asked for bread and was given a tranquilliser. It is important to recognise that in our time man has not written one word, thought one thought, put two notes or two bricks together, splashed colour on to canvas or concrete into space, in a manner which will be of any conceivable *imaginative* interest to posterity.

Ibid.

9 As has been truly said in his days as an active politician, he was not only a bore; he bored for England.

Ibid., 'Boring for England'. Referring to ANTHONY EDEN.

10 One of the peculiar sins of the twentieth century which we've developed to a very high level is the sin of credulity. It has been said that when human beings stop believing in God they believe in nothing. The truth is much worse: they believe in anything.

Woman's Hour, BBC radio broadcast, 23 March 1966, publ. in *Muggeridge Through the Microphone*, 'An Eighth Deadly Sin' (1967)

11 The trouble with kingdoms of heaven on earth is that they're liable to come to pass, and then their fraudulence is apparent for all to see. We need a kingdom of heaven in Heaven, if only because it can't be realised.

Jesus Rediscovered, 'Me and Myself' (1979)

12 Civilisation – a heap of rubble scavenged by scrawny English Lit vultures.

Quoted in *New Society* 6 October 1983

Edwin Muir (1887–1959)

BRITISH POET

Brought up on the island of Orkney, he later lived in Prague where he produced translations of KAFKA. *His poetry collections, including* The Voyage *(1946) and* The Labyrinth *(1949), combine myth and dreams.*

1 *Late in the summer the strange horses*
     came.
  We heard a distant tapping on the road,
  A deepening drumming; it stopped, went on
     again
  And at the corner changed to hollow
     thunder.
  We saw the heads
  Like a wild wave charging and were afraid.
  'The Horses', publ. in *One Foot in Eden* (1956)

Frank Muir (1920–98)

BRITISH HUMORIST
With DENIS NORDEN *he formed a successful*
comedy-writing team responsible for such series as
Take It From Here *(1947–58) and* Whack-O!
(1958–60). He appeared regularly on radio and
television shows such as My Word *and* Call My
Bluff.

1 Wit is a weapon. Jokes are a masculine way
  of inflicting superiority. But humour is the
  pursuit of a gentle grin, usually in solitude.
  Daily Mail 26 April 1990

2 The thinking man's crumpet.
  Attributed description of Joan Bakewell

Arthur Mullard (1910–95)

BRITISH COMIC ACTOR AND BOXER
Previously a boxer, rag-and-bone man and
bouncer, he played comic roles as a burly Cockney
in numerous films, and became a popular tele-
vision performer in the 1960s and '70s.

1 Boxing got me started on philosophy. You
  bash them, they bash you and you think,
  what's it all for?
  Quoted in the *Independent on Sunday*
  17 December 1995

Lewis Mumford (1895–1990)

US SOCIAL PHILOSOPHER
His books Technics and Civilization *(1934) and*
Myth and Machine *(1967, 1970) analyzed the*
impact of technology on society, while The Culture
of Cities *(1938) and* The City in History *(1961)*
were celebrated studies on urbanism.

1 Every generation revolts against its fathers
  and makes friends with its grandfathers.
  The Brown Decades, ch. 1 (1931)

2 The clock, not the steam-engine, is the
  key-machine of the modern industrial age.
  Technics and Civilization, ch. 1, sect. 2 (1934)

3 War is the supreme drama of a completely
  mechanized society.
  Ibid., ch. 6, sect. 11

4 Today, the notion of progress in a single
  line without goal or limit seems perhaps
  the most parochial notion of a very parochial century.
  Ibid., ch. 8, sect. 12

5 However far modern science and technics
  have fallen short of their inherent possibilities, they have taught mankind at least one
  lesson: Nothing is impossible.
  Ibid., sect. 13

6 The city is a fact in nature, like a cave, a
  run of mackerel or an ant-heap. But it is
  also a conscious work of art, and it holds
  within its communal framework many simpler and more personal forms of art. Mind
  takes form in the city; and in turn, urban
  forms condition mind.
  The Culture of Cities, Introduction (1938)

7 By his very success in inventing labor-
  saving devices, modern man has manufactured an abyss of boredom that only the
  privileged classes in earlier civilizations
  have ever fathomed.
  The Conduct of Life, 'The Challenge of Renewal'
  (1951)

8 Every new baby is a blind desperate vote
  for survival: people who find themselves
  unable to register an effective political protest against extermination do so by a biological act.
  The City in History, ch. 18 (1961)

(Dame) Iris Murdoch (1919–99)

BRITISH NOVELIST AND PHILOSOPHER
A fellow in philosophy at Oxford (1948–63), she
wove intricate plots around the emotions and
relationships of her characters in such novels as
The Bell *(1958),* The Sea, the Sea *(1978) and* The
Green Knight *(1993). She was married to the*
author John Bayley.

1 In almost every marriage there is a selfish
  and an unselfish partner. A pattern is set
  up and soon becomes inflexible, of one
  person always making the demands and
  one person always giving way.
  Martin Lynch-Gibbon, in *A Severed Head*, ch. 2
  (1961)

2 One doesn't have to get anywhere in a marriage. It's not a public conveyance.
  Ibid., ch. 3

3 You cannot have both truth and what you
  call civilization.
  Honor Klein, ibid., ch. 9

4 Falling out of love is chiefly a matter of *for-*
  getting how charming someone is.
  Anderson Palmer, ibid., ch. 24

5 I think being a woman is like being Irish.
  . . . Everyone says you're important and
  nice, but you take second place all the
  same.
  Frances Bellman, in *The Red and the Green*, ch. 2
  (1965). Iris Murdoch was born in Dublin of
  Anglo-Irish parents.

6 Being good is just a matter of temperament in the end.
Kate Gray, in *The Nice and the Good*, ch. 14
(1968)

7 Happiness is a matter of one's most ordinary everyday mode of consciousness
being busy and lively and unconcerned
with self. To be damned is for one's ordinary everyday mode of consciousness to be
unremitting agonizing preoccupation with
self.
Willy Kost, ibid., ch. 22

8 No love is entirely without worth, even
when the frivolous calls to the frivolous
and the base to the base.
Narrator, ibid., ch. 39

9 Writing is like getting married. One should
never commit oneself until one is amazed
at one's luck.
The Black Prince, 'Bradley Pearson's Foreword'
(1972). The narrator is here discussing his own
literary output: three short books in forty years.

10 A good man often appears *gauche* simply
because he does not take advantage of the
myriad mean little chances of making himself look stylish. Preferring truth to form,
he is not constantly at work upon the
façade of his appearance.
Bradley Pearson, ibid., pt 1

11 Bereavement is a darkness impenetrable to
the imagination of the unbereaved.
Montague Small, in *The Sacred and Profane Love
Machine* (1974)

12 The priesthood is a marriage. People often
start by falling in love, and they go on for
years without realizing that that love must
change into some other love which is so
unlike it that it can hardly be recognised as
love at all.
Brendan Craddock, in *Henry and Cato*, pt 2,
'The Great Teacher' (1976)

13 Human affairs are not serious, but they
have to be taken seriously.
Ibid.

14 Art is the final cunning of the human soul
which would rather do anything than face
the gods.
Plato, in *Acastos: Two Platonic Dialogues*, 'Art
and Eros: A Dialogue about Art' (first performed
on stage 1980, publ. 1986)

15 In philosophy if you aren't moving at a
snail's pace you aren't moving at all.
Socrates, ibid. 'Above the Gods: A Dialogue
about Religion'

16 Possibly, more people kill themselves and
others out of hurt vanity than out of envy,
jealousy, malice or desire for revenge.
The Philosopher's Pupil, 'The Events in Our
Town' (1983)

17 He was a sociologist; he had got into an
intellectual muddle early on in life and
never managed to get out.
Ibid. Referring to Whit Meynell.

18 As for truth – well, it's like brown – it's not
in the spectrum. . . . Truth is *sui generis*.
Rozanov, ibid.

19 All art is a struggle to be, in a particular
sort of way, virtuous.
Novelists in Interview (ed. John Haffenden, 1985)

20 Philosophy! Empty thinking by ignorant
conceited men who think they can digest
without eating!
Levquist, in *The Book and the Brotherhood*, pt 1,
'Midsummer' (1987)

21 Perhaps misguided moral passion is better
than confused indifference.
Jenkin Riderhood, ibid., pt 2, 'Midwinter'

22 We shall be better prepared for the future
if we see how terrible, how *doomed* the present is.
David Crimond, ibid.

23 But fantasy *kills* imagination, pornography
is death to art.
Alfred Ludens, in *The Message to the Planet*, pt 1
(1989)

24 I daresay anything can be made holy by
being sincerely worshipped.
Maisie Tether, ibid., pt 5

25 Perhaps when distant people on other
planets pick up some wave-length of ours
all they hear is a continuous scream.
Alfred Ludens, ibid., pt 6

26 A bad review is even less important than
whether it is raining in Patagonia.
The Times 6 July 1989

Rupert Murdoch (b. 1931)
AUSTRALIAN-BORN US MEDIA TYCOON
His newspaper empire in Britain ranges from the
Sun, *where he introduced the 'page three girl', to*
The Times, *while in America, he acquired the*
New York Post *and* Twentieth-Century Fox *film
studios. In 1989 he set up the satellite network Sky
Television (now BSkyB).*

1 William Shakespeare wrote for the masses.
If he were alive today, he'd probably be the
chief scriptwriter on *All in the Family* or
Dallas.
Quoted in the *Sunday Express* 30 December 1984

2 Much of what passes for quality on British
television is no more than a reflection of
the narrow élite which controls it and has
always thought that its tastes were synonymous with quality.
Address to the Edinburgh Television Festival,
25 August 1989, quoted in the *Guardian*
1 January 1990

3 Modernization is Americanization. It is the American way of organizing society that is prevailing in the world.

'The Wriston Lecture', Manhattan Institute, New York, 9 November 1989, quoted in *Rupert Murdoch: Ringmaster of the Information Circus*, ch. 14 (1992) by William Shawcross

Bill Murray (b. 1950)
US SCREEN ACTOR
Since coming to notice on TV's Saturday Night Live, he has appeared in the films Ghost Busters (1984), Little Shop of Horrors (1986) and Groundhog Day (1993).

1 We're Americans with a capital A. Do you know what that means? That means that our forefathers were kicked out of every decent country in the world. We are the wretched refuse. We're underdogs. We're mutts. . . . We're all very, very different. But there is one thing we all have in common: we are all stupid enough to enlist in the army.

John Winger (Bill Murray), in *Stripes* (film, 1981, screenplay by Len Blum, Dan Goldberg and Harold Ramis, directed and co-produced by Ivan Reitman)

Les Murray (b. 1938)
AUSTRALIAN POET
His rural upbringing gave him a close acquaint-ance with the Australian landscape which he cele-brates in his verse. His collections include The Vernacular Republic: Poems 1961–1981 (1982) *and* Translations from the Natural World (1992).

1 *Axe-fall, echo and silence. It will be cen-turies*
before many men are truly at home in this country,
and yet, there have always been some, in each generation,
there have always been some who could live in the presence of silence.

'Noonday Axeman', publ. in *The Ilex Tree* (1965)

2 *Men must have legends, else they will die of strangeness.*
Ibid.

3 *Nothing's said till it's dreamed out in words and nothing's true that figures in words only.*

'Poetry and Religion', publ. in *The Daylight Moon* (1987)

4 *Then, strung out and spotty, you wriggle and sigh*
and kiss all the fellows and make them all die.

'Midnight Lake', publ. in *Dog Fox Field* (1991). Final couplet of poem.

5 *Australians are like most who won't read this poem*

or any, since literature turned on them
and bodiless jargons without reverie
scorn their loves as illusion and biology,
compared with bloody History, the opposite of home.

'A Brief History', publ. in *Subhuman Redneck Poems* (1996). Last stanza of poem.

6 *Sex is a Nazi. The students all knew this at your school. To it, everyone's subhuman*
for parts of their lives. Some are all their lives.
You'll be one of those if these things worry you.

'Rock Music', publ. ibid.

7 *For the truth, we are silent. For the flatter-ing dream,*
in massed farting reassurance, we spasm and scream.

Ibid. Last stanza of poem.

Ed Murrow (1908–65)
US NEWSCASTER
An esteemed figure in American broadcasting, he reported on wartime Britain for CBS and pro-duced and presented the current affairs shows See It Now (1951–8) *and* Person to Person (1953–60). *His exposé of* JOSEPH McCARTHY *in 1954 contrib-uted to the latter's downfall.*

1 No one can terrorize a whole nation, unless we are all his accomplices.

Of JOSEPH McCARTHY, in 'See It Now', CBS television broadcast, 7 March 1954

2 He mobilized the English language and sent it into battle to steady his fellow countrymen and hearten those Europeans upon whom the long dark night of tyranny had descended.

Of WINSTON CHURCHILL, in TV broadcast to mark Churchill's eightieth birthday, 30 November 1954, publ. in *In Search of Light* (1967)

John Middleton Murry (1889–1957)
BRITISH CRITIC AND EDITOR
Founder and editor of the journal The Adelphi (1923–48), *he was married to* KATHERINE MANS-FIELD, *editing her poems, stories and correspon-dence, and publishing her biography in 1933. He became a radical Christian and a prominent paci-fist, editing* Peace News 1940–46.

1 If the Nazis have really been guilty of the unspeakable crimes circumstantially imputed to them, then – let us make no mistake – pacifism is faced with a situation with which it cannot cope. The conven-tional pacifist conception of a reasonable or generous peace is irrelevant to this reality.

Peace News 22 September 1944

Benito Mussolini (1883–1945)

ITALIAN DICTATOR

He helped found the Italian fascist movement in 1919, and by 1925 had established himself as dictator, or 'Duce', of Italy. He annexed Abyssinia (1936) and entered the Second World War on HITLER*'s side. He was killed while attempting to flee Italy.* ERNEST HEMINGWAY *remarked, 'There is something wrong, even histrionically, with a man who wears white spats with a black shirt.' See also* EZRA POUND 18.

1 I could have transformed this grey hall into an armed camp of Blackshirts, a bivouac for corpses. I could have nailed up the doors of Parliament.

Speech, 16 November 1922, quoted in *Benito Mussolini*, pt 1, ch. 4 (1962, rev. 1965 and 1975) by Christopher Hibbert. First speech to the Italian Chamber of Deputies after becoming Prime Minister.

2 Fascism, the more it considers and observes the future and the development of humanity, quite apart from political considerations of the moment, believes neither in the possibility nor the utility of perpetual peace.

'The Political and Social Doctrine of Fascism', publ. in *Enciclopedia Italiana* (1932)

3 War alone brings up to their highest tension all human energies and imposes the stamp of nobility upon the peoples who have the courage to make it.

Ibid.

4 It is humiliating to remain with our hands folded while others write history. It matters little who wins. To make a people great it is necessary to send them to battle even if you have to kick them in the pants. That is what I shall do.

Quoted in journal entry by Galeazzo Ciano, 11 April 1940, publ. in *Diary 1939–1943* (1946) by Galeazzo Ciano. Said to Count Ciano, Mussolini's son-in-law and Minister for Foreign Affairs. Italy entered the Second World War on 10 June 1940.

Mike Myers (b. 1964)

CANADIAN COMIC ACTOR AND SCREENWRITER

Coming to notice on NBC's Saturday Night Live *(1989–94), he adapted his 'Wayne's World' sketch into two successful films* Wayne's World *(1992) and* Wayne's World 2 *(1993). He subsequently starred in a sequence of films as the spoof spy* Austin Powers.

1 No way dude.

Wayne Campbell (Mike Myers), in *Wayne's World* (film, 1992, screenplay by Mike Myers, Bonnie Turner and Terry Turner, directed by Penelope Spheeris). The oft-repeated line was featured regularly on *Saturday Night Live*.

2 Garth, marriage is punishment for shoplifting, in some countries.

Ibid.

3 Shall we shag now, or shall we shag later?

Austin Powers (Mike Myers), in *Austin Powers: International Man of Mystery* (film, 1997, screenplay by Mike Myers, directed by Jay Roach)

Vladimir Nabokov (1899–1977)

RUSSIAN-BORN US NOVELIST AND POET

He gained instant notoriety for Lolita *(1955, filmed 1962 and 1997), a showcase for his wit and erudition. Other novels include* Pnin *(1957) and* Pale Fire *(1962). 'He writes prose the only way it should be written,'* JOHN UPDIKE *commented: '– that is ecstatically.'*

1 There are aphorisms that, like airplanes, stay up only while they are in motion.
Koncheyev, in *The Gift*, ch. 1 (1937, transl. 1963)

2 Lolita, light of my life, fire of my loins. My sin, my soul. Lo-lee-ta: the tip of the tongue taking a trip of three steps down the palate to tap, at three, on the teeth. Lo. Lee. Ta.
Humbert Humbert (narrator), in *Lolita*, pt 1, ch. 1 (1955). Opening lines of book.

3 You can always count on a murderer for a fancy prose style.
Ibid.

4 My very photogenic mother died in a freak accident (picnic, lightning) when I was three, and, save for a pocket of warmth in the darkest past, nothing of her subsists within the hollows and dells of memory.
Ibid., ch. 2

5 Between the age limits of nine and fourteen there occur maidens who, to certain bewitched travelers, twice or many times older than they, reveal their true nature which is not human, but nymphic (that is, demoniac); and these chosen creatures I propose to to designate as 'nymphets'.
Ibid., ch. 5. This passage was cut in the 1962 film directed by STANLEY KUBRICK.

6 The tiny madman in his padded cell.
Ibid., ch. 11. Describing an embryo.

7 The cradle rocks above an abyss, and common sense tells us that our existence is but a brief crack of light between two eternities of darkness.
Speak, Memory, ch. 1, sect. 1 (1955, rev. 1966). Opening words of Nabokov's autobiography.

8 Imagination, the supreme delight of the immortal and the immature, should be limited. In order to enjoy life, we should not enjoy it too much.
Ibid.

9 Let me say at once that I reject completely the vulgar, shabby, fundamentally medieval world of Freud, with its crankish quest for sexual symbols (something like searching for Baconian acrostics in Shakespeare's works) and its bitter little embryos spying, from their natural nooks, upon the love life of their parents.
Ibid.

10 Treading the soil of the moon, palpating

its pebbles, tasting the panic and splendor
of the event, feeling in the pit of one's
stomach the separation from terra . . .
these form the most romantic sensation
an explorer has ever known . . . this is the
only thing I can say about the matter. The
utilitarian results do not interest me.
The New York Times 21 July 1969. Referring to
the first manned moon-landing.

11 A novelist is, like all mortals, more fully at
home on the surface of the present than in
the ooze of the past.
Strong Opinions, ch. 20 (1977)

12 Style and Structure are the essence of a
book; great ideas are hogwash.
Interview in *Writers at Work* (fourth series, ed.
George Plimpton, 1977)

Ralph Nader (b. 1934)
US CONSUMER RIGHTS AND GREEN ACTIVIST
*Called the 'scourge of corporate morality', he has
led numerous consumer campaigns and pressure
groups including 'Nader's Raiders'. He stood for
the US presidency in 1996 and 2000.*

1 For almost seventy years the life insurance
industry has been a smug sacred cow feeding the public a steady line of sacred bull.
Testimony to US Senate subcommittee, quoted
in *The New York Times* 19 May 1974

(Sir) V. S. Naipaul (b. 1932)
TRINIDAD-BORN BRITISH AUTHOR
*Vidiadhar Surajprasad Naipaul. Describing him-
self as 'content to be a colonial, without a past,
without ancestors', he explores themes of alienation and the experience of 'universal wanderers' in
his books, which include* A House for Mr Biswas
(1961) and Among the Believers *(1981).*

1 I'm the kind of writer that people think
other people are reading.
Radio Times 24–30 March 1979

2 To read a newspaper for the first time is
like coming into a film that has been on
for an hour. Newspapers are like serials.
To understand them you have to take
knowledge to them; the knowledge that
serves best is the knowledge provided by
the newspaper itself.
The Enigma of Arrival (1987), 'The Journey'. On
reading *The New York Times* for the first time.

3 My writing is like fine wine; the more you
read, the more you get from it. Reading it
once is like taking a dog to the theatre.
Quoted in *The Times* 20 October 2001

Ogden Nash (1902–71)
US POET
A frequent contributor to the New Yorker, *he
caused both scandal and amusement with his
puns, parodies and clever rhymes. His collections*

include Free Wheeling *(1931) and* Everyone But
Thee and Me *(1962).*

1 *Candy*
Is dandy
But Liquor
Is quicker.
'Reflections on Ice-Breaking', publ. in *Hard
Lines* (1931)

2 *The cow is of the bovine ilk;*
One end is moo, the other, milk.
'The Cow', publ. in *Free Wheeling* (1931)

3 *No matter how deep and dark your pit, how*
dank your shroud,
Their heads are heroically unbloody and
unbowed.
'Look For the Silver Lining', publ. in *Happy
Days* (1933). Describing 'The cheery souls who
drop around after every catastrophe and think
they are taking the curse off/By telling you about
somebody who is even worse off'.

4 *I don't mind their having a lot of money,*
and I don't care how they employ it,
But I do think that they damn well ought to
admit they enjoy it.
'The Terrible People', publ. ibid.

5 *Man is a victim of dope*
In the incurable form of hope.
'Good-by, Old Year, You Oaf or Why Don't
They Pay the Bonus?', publ. in *The Primrose
Path* (1935)

6 *Every New Year is the direct descendant, isn't*
it, of a long line of proven criminals?
Ibid.

7 *Here is a pen and here is a pencil,*
Here's a typewriter, here's a stencil,
Here is a list of today's appointments,
And all the flies in all the ointments,
The daily woes that a man endures –
Take them, George, they're yours!
'Let George Do It, If You Can Find Him', publ.
ibid.

8 *If you are really Master of your Fate,*
It shouldn't make any difference to you
whether Cleopatra or the Bearded Lady
is your mate.
'The Anatomy of Happiness', publ. in *I'm a
Stranger Here Myself* (1938)

9 *The most exciting happiness is the happi-*
ness generated by forces beyond your
control.
Ibid.

10 *I think remorse ought to stop biting the con-*
sciences that feed it.
'A Clean Conscience Never Relaxes', publ. ibid.

11 *Every Englishman is convinced of one thing,*
viz.:
That to be an Englishman is to belong to
the most exclusive club there is.
'England Expects', publ. ibid.

12 *How easy for those who do not bulge*
To not overindulge!
'A Necessary Dirge', publ. ibid.

13 *Whether elected or appointed*
He considers himself the Lord's anointed,
And indeed the ointment lingers on him
So thick you can't get your fingers on him.
'The Politician', publ. ibid.

14 *I do not like to get the news, because there*
has never been an era when so many
things were going so right for so many of
the wrong persons.
'Everybody Tells Me Everything', publ. in *The*
Face is Familiar (1940)

15 *And one of his partners asked 'Has he ver-*
tigo?' and the other glanced out and
down and said 'Oh no, only about ten
feet more.'
'Mr Artesian's Conscientiousness', publ. ibid.

16 *I have a bone to pick with Fate.*
Come here and tell me, girlie,
Do you think my mind is maturing late,
Or simply rotted early?
'Lines on Facing Forty', publ. in *Good Intentions*
(1942)

17 *The further through life I drift*
The more obvious it becomes that I am lack-
ing in thrift.
'A Penny Saved is Impossible from Good Intentions', publ. ibid.

18 *You scour the Bowery, ransack the Bronx,*
Through funeral parlors and honky-tonks.
From river to river you comb the town
For a place to lay your family down.
'Nature Abhors a Vacancy', publ. in *Versus*
(1949)

19 *Indoors or out, no one relaxes*
In March, that month of wind and taxes,
The wind will presently disappear,
The taxes last us all the year.
'Thar She Blows', publ. ibid.

20 *Your hair may be brushed, but your mind's*
untidy,
You've had about seven hours' sleep since
Friday,
No wonder you feel that lost sensation;
You're sunk from a riot of relaxation.
'We'll All Feel Better By Wednesday', publ. ibid.

21 *A door is what a dog is perpetually on the*
wrong side of.
'A Dog's Best Friend is his Illiteracy', publ. in
The Private Dining Room (1953)

22 *Good wine needs no bush,*
And perhaps products that people really
want need no hard-sell or soft-sell TV
push.
Why not?
Look at pot.
'Most Doctors Recommend or Yours For Fast

Fast Fast Relief', publ. in *The Old Dog Barks*
Backwards (1972)

Paul Nash (1889–1946)
BRITISH ARTIST
He was the official war artist of both world wars
and remembered above all for the Cubist-
influenced The Menin Road *(1918), and* Totes
Meer *(Dead Sea, 1940–41).*

1 I am no longer an artist, interested and
curious. I am a messenger who will bring
back word from the men who are fighting
to those who want the war to go on for
ever. Feeble, inarticulate, will be my message, but it will have a bitter truth, and
may it burn their lousy souls.
Letter to his wife, 13 November 1917, publ. in
Outline: An Autobiography and Other Writings
(1949)

Taslima Nasreen (b. 1962)
BANGLADESHI AUTHOR
Her novel Shame *(1993), an account of the per-*
secution of Muslim women, led to death threats
from Islamic fundamentalists and forced her into
exile. My Childhood Days *(1999) and* Strong
Breeze *(2002) were subsequently banned by the*
Bangladeshi government.

1 Our religion doesn't give women any
human dignity. Women are considered
slaves. . . . I write against the religion
because if women want to live like human
beings, they will have to live outside the
religion and Islamic law.
The Times 22 June 1994

George Jean Nathan (1882–1958)
US EDITOR AND CRITIC
Said to be the highest paid drama critic ever, he
co-edited the magazine Smart Set *with* H. L.
MENCKEN *and in 1924 founded with Mencken*
the American Mercury, *to which he was a regular*
contributor. He also wrote plays and edited the
annual Theatre Book of the Year *(1943–51).*

1 The aim of great drama is not to make
men happy with themselves as they are,
but with themselves as they might, yet alas
cannot, be.
The Critic and the Drama, ch. 2, sect. 1 (1922)

2 In the words of a friend of mine, I drink to
make other people interesting.
The Autobiography of an Attitude, 'On Alcohol'
(1925). The joke is usually ascribed to Nathan
himself.

3 To speak of morals in art is to speak of
legislature in sex. Art is the sex of the
imagination.
American Mercury July 1926, repr. in *The World*
of George Jean Nathan (ed. Charles S. Angoff,
1998)

4 All criticism, after all, is a criticism of the critic himself before it is one of the criticized.

Art of the Night, 'Advice to a Young Critic', no. 18 (1928)

5 The test of a real comedian is whether you laugh at him before he opens his mouth.

American Mercury September 1929, repr. in *The World of George Jean Nathan* (ed. Charles S. Angoff, 1998)

6 All really great drama is a form of scandal.

Ibid.

Terry Nation (1930–97)

BRITISH SCREENWRITER
He began as a stand-up comedian but made his reputation as the creator of science fiction adventures on TV, notably the BBC series Dr Who *(1963–89).*

1 We will obey! . . . Exterminate! Exterminate!

The Daleks, in *Doctor Who* (BBC television series, 1963–89). The original voices of the Daleks, which appeared in some eighty episodes of *Dr Who*, were Peter Hawkins, who also voiced the Flowerpot Men, and David Graham, who also voiced the chauffeur Parker in *Thunderbirds*.

Myron 'Grim' Natwick (1890–1990)

US ANIMATOR
He started as an animator at William Randolph Hearst's International Film Studio in New York in 1916, and subsequently worked at Fleischer Studios and Walt Disney Studios, where he was responsible for animating Snow White *(1937).*

1 Boop-boop-a-doop.

Betty Boop's catchphrase, in *Talkartoons* (cartoon series), created by Grim Natwick in 1930 for the Fleischer Studios. Betty starred in her own show 1932–9, and was dropped following a wave of puritanical attacks, mostly by women's clubs. The character was said to have been modelled on the actress Helen Kane, who later sued the studio for $250,000 and lost.

Yitzhak Navon (b. 1921)

ISRAELI POLITICIAN AND PRESIDENT
Having served as a Deputy in the Knesset (1965–78), he spent five years as Israeli President and after 1984 was Deputy Prime Minister and Minister of Education and Culture in the national unity government.

1 It's not that I don't have opinions, rather that I'm paid not to think aloud.

Quoted in the *Observer* 16 January 1983

Martina Navratilova (b. 1956)

CZECH-BORN US TENNIS PLAYER
The dominant woman player of the 1980s, she won a record nine Wimbledon singles titles before retiring from competitive singles tennis in 1994.

1 I'm not just involved in tennis but committed. Do you know the difference between involvement and commitment? Think of ham and eggs. The chicken is involved. The pig is committed.

Quoted in the *International Herald Tribune* 3 September 1982

2 The moment of victory is much too short to live for that and nothing else.

Guardian 21 June 1989

Jawaharlal Nehru (1889–1964)

INDIAN POLITICIAN AND PRIME MINISTER
Known as 'Pandit' ('Teacher') Nehru, and the father of INDIRA GANDHI, *he led the socialist wing of the Indian National Congress. Despite a total of eighteen years spent in prison, he was instrumental in achieving Indian independence in 1947, and served as the country's first prime minister until his death.*

1 The British Government in India is like a tooth that is decaying but is still strongly embedded. It is painful, but it cannot be easily pulled out.

Towards Freedom (1935)

2 At the stroke of the midnight hour, while the world sleeps, India will awake to life and freedom.

Speech to Indian Assembly, 14 August 1947, quoted in *Freedom at Midnight*, Preface (1975) by Larry Collins and Dominique LaPierre. Spoken on the eve of independence.

3 The light has gone out of our lives and there is darkness everywhere and I do not quite know what to tell you and how to say it. Our beloved leader, Bapu as we call him, the father of the nation, is no more.

Broadcast on All-India Radio, 30 January 1948, quoted in *The Life of Mahatma Gandhi*, ch. 1 (1951) by Louis Fischer. Speech following the assassination of GANDHI by a Hindu fanatic, an event which provoked nationwide rioting.

4 I shall be the last Englishman to rule in India.

Quoted in *A Life in Our Times*, ch. 26 (1981) by J. K. GALBRAITH. Nehru spent the years 1905–12 in England: at Harrow School and Trinity College, Cambridge, and at the Inner Temple, London, where he qualified as a barrister.

Andrew Neil (b. 1949)

BRITISH JOURNALIST AND EDITOR
As Editor of the Sunday Times *1983–94, he modernized the paper and gave it a marked Thatcherite political stance. He was subsequently*

publisher and Editor-in-chief of The Scotsman *and* Scotland on Sunday.

1 Our establishment has presided over economic decline and bequeathed a culture of mediocrity. Why join a bunch of losers?

Evening Standard 26 May 1993

Paula Nelson (b. 1945)

US BUSINESS CONSULTANT

Her financial self-help books include The Joy of Money *(1975), a guide to women's financial freedom, and* Paula Nelson's Guide to Getting Rich *(1986).*

1 Women's battle for financial equality has barely been joined, much less won. Society still traditionally assigns to woman the role of money-handler rather than money-maker, and our assigned specialty is far more likely to be home economics than financial economics.

The Joy of Money, ch. 1 (1975)

Richard Nelson (b. 1950)

US PLAYWRIGHT

The clash of personal beliefs with political ideologies is the theme of many of his plays, which include Conjuring an Event *(performed 1976),* Jungle Coup *(1978) and* Principia Scriptoriae *(1986).*

1 If you take away ideology, you are left with a case by case ethics which in practice ends up as me first, me only, and in rampant greed.

Independent 12 July 1989

Willie Nelson (b. 1933)

US SINGER AND SONGWRITER

Already known as a songwriter in Nashville, he cut his first LP in 1962, and enjoyed greatest success in the 1970s, notably with Red Headed Stranger *(1975). He was a famous exponent of the 'outlaw' style of country music.*

1 I'm a country songwriter and we write cry-in-your-beer songs. That's what we do. Something that you can slow dance to.

Interview in the *Independent* 11 May 1996

Howard Nemerov (1920–91)

US POET, NOVELIST AND CRITIC

Best known for his poetry, which takes in nature and philosophical issues, he also wrote novels, such as The Melodramatist *(1949), and works of criticism.* JOYCE CAROL OATES *called him unclassifiable, being a 'romantic, realist, comedian, satirist, relentless and indefatigable brooder upon the most ancient mysteries'.*

1 *And I speak to you now with the land's voice,*
It is the cold wild land that says to you

A knowledge glimmers in the sleep of things:
The old hills hunch before the north wind blows.

'A Spell Before Winter', publ. in *Collected Poems* (1977)

2 The only way out is the way through, just as you cannot escape from death except by dying. Being unable to write, you must examine in writing this being unable, which becomes for the present – henceforth? – the subject to which you are condemned.

Journal of the Fictive Life, 'Reflexions of the Novelist Felix Ledger', sect. B (1965)

3 Obvious enough that generalities work to protect the mind from the great outdoors; is it possible that this was in fact their first purpose?

Ibid., sect. C

4 I've never read a political poem that's accomplished anything. Poetry makes things happen, but rarely what the poet wants.

International Herald Tribune 14 October 1988.
See also W. H. AUDEN 18

Pablo Neruda (1904–73)

CHILEAN POET AND DIPLOMAT

Born Ricardo Eliezer Neftalí Reyes. He was well known for his Twenty Love Poems and a Song of Despair *(1924) before serving as a diplomat and Senator (1927–48). His major work, the epic* General Song *(1950), was a wide-ranging hymn to Latin America.* GARCÍA LORCA *called him 'a poet closer to death than to philosophy, closer to pain than to insight, closer to blood than to ink'.*

1 *If you should ask me where I've been all this time*
I have to say 'Things happen'.

'There is No Forgetting: Sonata' (1935), repr. in *Selected Poems* (ed. Nathaniel Tarn, 1970). Opening lines of poem.

2 *The dark of a day gone by*
Grown fat on our grieving blood.
Ibid.

3 *Night, snow, and sand make up the form of my thin country,*
all silence lies in its long line,
all foam flows from its marine beard,
all coal covers it with mysterious kisses.
Gold burns in its fingers like an ember
and silver illuminates like a green moon
its thickened shadow of a sullen planet.
'Discoverers of Chile' (1950), repr. ibid.

4 Many of the creative spirits of our time do not realize that what seems to them to be the deepest expression of their being is often deadly poison injected into them by their most implacable enemies. Dying

capitalism is filling the cup of human creation with a bitter brew.

'Our Duty Toward Life', publ. in *Let the Rail Splitter Awake and Other Poems* (1950)

5 *No one can claim the name of Pedro,*
nobody is Rosa or Maria,
all of us are dust or sand,
all of us are rain under rain.
They have spoken to me of Venezuelas,
of Chiles and Paraguays;
I have no idea what they are saying.
I know only the skin of the earth
and I know it has no name.

'Too Many Names' (1958), repr. in *Selected Poems* (ed. Nathaniel Tarn, 1970)

6 *The word*
was born in the blood,
grew in the dark body, beating,
And flew through the lips and the mouth.

'The Word' (1962), repr. ibid. Opening lines of poem.

7 *And it was at that age . . . Poetry arrived*
in search of me. I don't know, I don't know
where
it came from, from winter or a river.
I don't know how or when,
no, they were not voices, they were not
words, nor silence,
but from the street I was summoned,
from the branches of night,
abruptly from the others,
among violent fires
or returning alone,
there I was without a face
and it touched me.

'Poetry' (1964), repr. ibid. The words appeared at the end of *Il Postino*, the 1994 film by Michael Radford which dramatized Neruda's exile on an Italian island.

8 As for me, I am – or think I am – hard-nosed, small-eyed, sparse of hair, swollen in the abdomen, long-legged, broad-footed, yellow-complexioned, generous in love, impossible at figures, confused by words, tender-handed, slow-walking, pure-hearted, fond of stars and tides and swells, an admirer of beetles, a walker of sands, institutionally dull, perpetually Chilean, friend to my friends, silent to my enemies, meddlesome among birds, bad-mannered at home, timid in gatherings, daring in solitude, repentant without reason . . . persistently in disorder, brave out of necessity, a coward without guilt, lazy by vocation, lovable to women, congenitally active, a poet by curse, and a first-rate fool.

'Panorama', publ. in *Defectos escogidos* (1973), quoted in *Neruda: An Intimate Biography*, pt 8, sect. 182 (1985) by Volodia Teitelboim

9 I can live only in my own country. I cannot live without having my feet and my hands on it and my ear against it, without feeling the movement of its waters and its shadows, without feeling my roots reach down into its soil for maternal nourishment.

Memoirs, ch. 8 (1974). Referring to his work and travels abroad 1940–43.

10 Using language like clothes or the skin on your body, with its sleeves, its patches, its transpirations, and its blood and sweat stains, that's what shows a writer's mettle. This is style.

Ibid., ch. 11

11 Latin America is very fond of the word 'hope'. We like to be called the 'continent of hope'. Candidates for deputy, senator, president, call themselves 'candidates of hope'. This hope is really something like a promise of heaven, an IOU whose payment is always being put off. It is put off until the next legislative campaign, until next year, until the next century.

Ibid.

12 The human crowd has been the lesson of my life. I can come to it with the born timidity of the poet, with the fear of the timid, but once I am in its midst, I feel transfigured. I am part of the essential majority, I am one more leaf on the great human tree.

Ibid.

Julia Neuberger (b. 1950)

BRITISH RABBI, WRITER AND BROADCASTER
Britain's first female rabbi, she is known for her liberal views and her support of the hospice movement.

1 We don't like children much. We tend to fear our young.

Quoted in the *Daily Telegraph* 21 October 1995

Richard Neville (b. 1941)

AUSTRALIAN JOURNALIST
He co-founded Oz in 1963 and started its English counterpart after moving to England in 1966. In 1971 he was charged with publishing a magazine likely 'to corrupt public morals' and spent fifteen months in prison.

1 Is marijuana addictive? Yes, in the sense that most of the really pleasant things in life are worth endlessly repeating.

Playpower, 'Johnny Pot Wears Gold Sandals and a Black Derby Hat' (1971)

Andrea Newman (b. 1938)

BRITISH AUTHOR
Her novels, which track the cut and thrust of personal relationships, include A Bouquet of Barbed Wire *(1969, televised 1976) and* A Share of the World *(1992).*

1 **I love the male body, it's better designed than the male mind.**

Today 30 September 1988

Barnett Newman (1905–70)

US ARTIST

Originally Baruch Newman. In 1948 he was one of the founders of the 'Subject of the Artist' school in New York. In the same year he painted Onement I, *the first of his 'zip paintings', and he is also known for the 'Stations of the Cross' series (exhibited 1966).*

1 **The human in language is literature, not communication. Man's first cry was a song. Man's first address to a neighbor was a cry of power and solemn weakness, not a request for a drink of water.**

'The First Man Was an Artist', publ. in *Tiger's Eye* October 1947, repr. in *Art in Theory*, pt 5A (ed. Charles Harrison and Paul Wood, 1992)

News of the World

1 **All human life is there.**

Slogan from the 1950s. The words were possibly derived from HENRY JAMES in his short story 'The Madonna of the Future' (1873): 'Cats and monkeys, monkeys and cats – all human life is there!'

Ngo Dinh Diem (1901–63)

VIETNAMESE POLITICIAN

He became Prime Minister in 1954 under Emperor Bao Dai, whom he ousted in 1955, establishing himself as President of the newly declared Republic of Vietnam (South Vietnam). He was assassinated in a military coup.

1 **Follow me if I advance! Kill me if I retreat! Revenge me if I die!**

On becoming President of Vietnam in 1955, reported in *Time* 8 November 1963. The same exhortation had been made by MUSSOLINI to his officers after an attempt on his life in 1926.

Jack Nicholson (b. 1937)

US SCREEN ACTOR

Usually cast in roguish parts, he rose to fame as the wired lawyer in Easy Rider *(1969) and has since starred in numerous films, including* The Shining *(1980) and* About Schmidt *(2002).*

1 **I mean, it's real hard to be free when you're bought and sold in the market place.**

George Hanson (Jack Nicholson), in *Easy Rider* (film, 1969, written by DENNIS HOPPER, Peter Fonda and Terry Southern, directed by Dennis Hopper)

2 **All work and no play makes Jack a dull boy.**

Jack Torrance (Jack Nicholson), in *The Shining* (film, 1980, screenplay by STANLEY KUBRICK

and Diane Johnson, produced and directed by Stanley Kubrick). The proverb typed by Nicholson covers the pages of the manuscript he is supposed to be working on.

3 **Americans don't like sexual movies – they like sexy movies.**

Quoted in *Rolling Stone* March 1984

4 **Our generation are the new old. I remember what someone of 60 looked like when I was a kid. They didn't look like me.**

Quoted in the *Daily Telegraph* 21 February 1998

5 **There's so much darn porn out there, I never got out of the house.**

Quoted in *The Times* 6 March 1999. On why he is giving up using the Internet.

Jack Nicklaus (b. 1940)

US GOLFER

Nicknamed the 'Golden Bear', he has won eighteen professional major titles (1962–86), a world record. He has also designed and built golf courses.

1 **The older you get the stronger the wind gets – and it's always in your face.**

Quoted in the *International Herald Tribune* 28 February 1990. Said on his fiftieth birthday.

(Sir) Harold Nicolson (1886–1968)

BRITISH DIPLOMAT, JOURNALIST AND AUTHOR

He held a variety of diplomatic posts until 1929, when he took up journalism. His publications include histories, biographies and political studies, but he is best remembered for his Diaries and Letters 1930–62 (1968). He was married to VITA SACKVILLE-WEST.

1 **We shall have to walk and live a Woolworth life hereafter.**

Journal entry, 4 June 1941, publ. in *Diaries and Letters 1939–45* (ed. Nigel Nicolson, 1968). On post-war Britain.

2 **God how I loathe these communists! My hatred for Mussolini was just a passing dislike, my fear of Hitler but a momentary apprehension, compared to my deep and burning detestation of the Marxists.**

Letter to his wife, VITA SACKVILLE-WEST, 25 September 1947, publ. in *Diaries and Letters 1945–62* (ed. Nigel Nicolson, 1968)

Reinhold Niebuhr (1892–1971)

US THEOLOGIAN AND HISTORIAN

He was a Lutheran pastor before becoming an influential teacher at the Union Theological Seminary, New York (1928–60). He worked to obtain social justice from within the Socialist and subsequently Democratic parties. His many works include The Nature and Destiny of Man *(2 vols. 1941–3).*

1 **A wise architect observed that you could break the laws of architectural art provided**

you had mastered them first. That would apply to religion as well as to art. Ignorance of the past does not guarantee freedom from its imperfections.

Entry, 1928, in *Leaves from the Notebook of a Tamed Cynic* (1930)

2 Life is a battle between faith and reason in which each feeds upon the other, drawing sustenance from it and destroying it.

Ibid.

3 Man's capacity for justice makes democracy possible, but man's inclination to injustice makes democracy necessary.

The Children of Light and the Children of Darkness, Foreword (1944)

4 O God, give us serenity to accept what cannot be changed, courage to change what should be changed, and wisdom to distinguish the one from the other.

'Serenity Prayer', ascribed to Niebuhr in *Courage to Change* (1961) by June Bingham. The prayer, which exists in varying forms, has been used by Alcoholics Anonymous since the 1940s. 'It may have been spooking around for years, even centuries, but I don't think so,' Niebuhr stated. 'I honestly do believe that I wrote it myself.' However, claims have been made of previous versions from both fourteenth-century England and eighteenth-century Germany.

Martin Niemöller (1892–1984)
GERMAN PROTESTANT PASTOR AND THEOLOGIAN
Having spent time in concentration camps for his criticisms of the Nazis, he was responsible for the Evangelical Church's 'Stuttgart Confession of Guilt' (1945), an apology for not opposing HITLER *more forcefully. He was President of the World Council of Churches 1961–8.*

1 When Hitler attacked the Jews . . . I was not a Jew, therefore, I was not concerned. And when Hitler attacked the Catholics, I was not a Catholic, and therefore, I was not concerned. And when Hitler attacked the unions and the industrialists, I was not a member of the unions and I was not concerned. Then, Hitler attacked me and the Protestant church – and there was nobody left to be concerned.

Attributed. The original passage has never been traced.

Anaïs Nin (1903–77)
FRENCH-BORN US NOVELIST AND DIARIST
She was known principally for her journals (7 vols. 1966–80), a chronicle of avant-garde society in Paris and New York. Her fiction, which reflects her interest in dreams and psychoanalysis, includes House of Incest *(1936) and the stories* Under a Glass Bell *(1948).*

1 Woman does not forget she needs the

fecundator, she does not forget that everything that is born of her is planted in her.

Journal entry, August 1937, publ. in *The Diary of Anaïs Nin*, vol. 2 (1967)

2 Electric flesh-arrows . . . traversing the body. A rainbow of color strikes the eyelids. A foam of music falls over the ears. It is the gong of the orgasm.

Ibid. October 1937

3 The violence and obscenity are left unadulterated, as manifestation of the mystery and pain which ever accompanies the act of creation.

Preface to *Tropic of Cancer* (1934) by HENRY MILLER

4 I stopped loving my father a long time ago. What remained was the slavery to a pattern.

Under a Glass Bell, 'Birth' (1948)

5 I never liked the language of Henry Miller. I don't think pornography has added to our sensual life.

Quoted in *The Times* 1 June 1970. Nin had a ten-year relationship with Miller in France and America.

Richard Nixon (1913–92)
US POLITICIAN AND PRESIDENT
As Republican president (1969–74) he oversaw American withdrawal from Vietnam and the resumption of diplomatic relations with China. In 1974 he became the first and only US president to resign, thereby saving himself from impeachment in the wake of the Watergate scandal. He was given a full pardon by GERALD FORD. *See* JOHN F. KENNEDY 3, ADLAI STEVENSON 9, HUNTER S. THOMPSON 1.

1 Once you get into this great stream of history you can't get out. You can drown. Or you can be pulled ashore by the tide. But it is awfully hard to get out when you are in the middle of the stream – if it is intended that you stay there.

Quoted in *Richard Nixon: A Political and Personal Portrait*, ch. 10 (1959) by Earl Mazo. On revoking his decision to retire in 1954.

2 The one thing sure about politics is that what goes up comes down and what goes down often comes up.

Quoted ibid., ch. 17

3 A public man must never forget that he loses his usefulness when he as an individual, rather than his policy, becomes the issue.

Life 8 June 1959. The remark appeared in a tribute to JOHN FOSTER DULLES on his death. Dulles, Nixon asserted, recognized this 'fundamental truth'.

4 The more you stay in this kind of job, the

more you realize that a public figure, a major public figure, is a lonely man.

Interview as vice-president, quoted in *Nixon and Rockefeller: A Double Portrait*, 'A Talk with Nixon' (1960) by Stewart Alsop

5 The easiest period in a crisis situation is actually the battle itself. The most difficult is the period of indecision – whether to fight or run away. And the most dangerous period is the aftermath. It is then, with all his resources spent and his guard down, that an individual must watch out for dulled reactions and faulty judgment.

Six Crises, Introduction (1962). 'Crisis can indeed be an agony,' Nixon observed. 'But it is the exquisite agony which a man might not want to experience again – yet would not for the world have missed.'

6 As I leave you I want you to know – just think how much you're going to be missing. You won't have Nixon to kick around any more because, gentlemen, this is my last press conference.

Press conference, 5 November 1962, quoted in *The New York Times* 8 November 1962, following defeat in the California gubernatorial election.

7 The Cold War isn't thawing; it is burning with a deadly heat. Communism isn't sleeping; it is, as always, plotting, scheming, working, fighting.

'Cuba, Castro and John F. Kennedy', publ. in *Reader's Digest* November 1964

8 Let us begin by committing ourselves to the truth, to see it like it is and tell it like it is, to find the truth, to speak the truth and to live the truth.

Speech accepting the Republican presidential nomination, 8 August 1968, Miami, quoted in *The New York Times* 9 August 1968

9 This is the greatest week in the history of the world since the Creation, because as a result of what happened in this week, the world is bigger, infinitely.

Remarks on USS *Hornet*, 24 July 1969, welcoming back the crew of Apollo 11 four days after the first manned moon-landing, quoted in *Nixon: The Triumph of a Politician*, vol. 2, ch. 13 (1989) by Stephen Ambrose. A few days later, Ambrose relates, the evangelist Billy Graham mentioned three greater days: Christ's birth, Christ's death, and Christ's resurrection. Nixon's scribbled response was. 'Tell Billy RN referred to a *week* not *a day*.'

10 Let us understand: North Vietnam cannot defeat or humiliate the United States. Only Americans can do that.

Television address, 3 November 1969, quoted ibid., ch. 14. In his *Memoirs*, Nixon commented: 'Very few speeches actually influence the course of history. The November 3 speech was one of them.'

11 Expletive deleted.

Taped transcripts of conversations September 1972–April 1973, publ. in *The Presidential Transcripts* (1974). The tapes, which were played for the judicial committee of the House of Representatives 30 April 1974, were edited transcripts of meetings between Nixon and his advisers in the Oval Office over a period of seven months. Public reaction seemed more shocked by the sleazy language used by the President and his inner circle than by the revelations of Nixon appearing to condone corrupt practices. The first recorded meeting took place between Nixon, H. R. HALDEMAN and John Dean on 15 September 1972, when Nixon, referring to a bug that Dean had found in a telephone at the Watergate Building, declared: '[expletive deleted] do they really want to believe that we planted that?'

12 There can be no whitewash at the White House.

On Watergate, in television address, 30 April 1973, quoted in *The New York Times* 1 May 1973. In July 1972 agents of Nixon's re-election committee were arrested in the Democratic Party headquarters after an attempt to tap telephones there, of which Nixon denied all knowledge.

13 I welcome this kind of examination because people have got to know whether or not their President is a crook. Well, I'm not a crook.

Press conference, 17 November 1973, publ. in *The New York Times* 18 November 1973

14 Defeat doesn't finish a man – quit does. A man is not finished when he's defeated. He's finished when he quits.

Note written with reference to Edward Kennedy and the Chappaquiddick Bridge incident, July 1969, quoted in *Before the Fall*, pt 3, ch. 4 (1975) by WILLIAM SAFIRE

15 When the President does it, that means that it is not illegal.

TV interview with DAVID FROST, 20 May 1977, publ. in *I Gave Them a Sword*, ch. 8 (1978) by David Frost

16 Castro couldn't even go to the bathroom unless the Soviet Union put the nickel in the toilet.

Remark to interviewer September 1980, quoted in *Exile: The Unquiet Oblivion of Richard M. Nixon*, ch. 17 (1984) by Robert Sam Anson

17 No event in American history is more misunderstood than the Vietnam War. It was misreported then, and it is misremembered now.

'No More Vietnams', publ. in *The New York Times* 28 March 1985

18 Finishing second in the Olympics gets you silver. Finishing second in politics gets you oblivion.

Quoted in the *Sunday Times* 13 November 1988.

On the defeat of Michael Dukakis by GEORGE BUSH in the presidential election.

19 I played by the rules of politics as I found them.

Quoted in *The Times* 26 March 1990

Kwame Nkrumah (1909–72)

GHANAIAN PRESIDENT

Called the 'Gandhi of Africa', he was the leader of the Gold Coast's struggle for independence and was Prime Minister of Ghana, as it was re-named, 1957–60. As President (1960–66), he established an authoritarian regime until his overthrow in a coup.

1 The best way of learning to be an independent sovereign state is to be an independent sovereign state.

Speech to Legislative Assembly, Accra, 18 May 1956, quoted in *Axioms of Kwame Nkrumah* (1967)

2 Revolutions are brought about by men, by men who think as men of action and act as men of thought.

Consciencism, ch. 2 (1964)

3 It is far easier for the proverbial camel to pass through the needle's eye, hump and all, than for an erstwhile colonial administration to give sound and honest counsel of a *political* nature to its liberated territory.

Ibid., ch. 4

(Sir) Sidney Nolan (1917–92)

AUSTRALIAN ARTIST

He is noted for his paintings of the Australian outback, most famously the 'Ned Kelly' series (1946). He also painted subjects taken from his travels and from mythology, as in the 'Leda and the Swan' series (1961).

1 When the critics come around it's always too late.

Quoted in the *Daily Telegraph* 15 September 1992

Peggy Noonan (b. 1950)

US AUTHOR AND PRESIDENTIAL SPEECHWRITER

She was special assistant and speechwriter to RONALD REAGAN and GEORGE BUSH, recording her experiences in her memoir What I Saw at the Revolution *(1990). See also* GEORGE BUSH 7.

1 You don't have to be old in America to say of a world you lived in, That world is gone.

What I Saw at the Revolution, ch. 1 (1990)

2 A speech is poetry: cadence, rhythm, imagery, sweep! A speech reminds us that words, like children, have the power to make dance the dullest beanbag of a heart.

Ibid., ch. 5

3 The battle for the mind of Ronald Reagan was like the trench warfare of World War I: Never have so many fought so hard for such barren terrain.

Ibid., ch. 14

4 What did I learn in my time in government?

If you join government, calmly make your contribution and move on. Don't go along to get along; do your best and when you have to – and you will – leave, and be something else.

Don't fall in love with politicians, they're all a disappointment. They can't help it, they just are.

Beware the politically obsessed. They are often bright and interesting, but they have something missing in their natures; there is a hole, an empty place, and they use politics to fill it up. It leaves them somehow misshapen.

Ibid., 'Another Epilogue'

Denis Norden (b. 1922)

BRITISH HUMORIST

With his long-standing partner FRANK MUIR he wrote extensively for BBC radio, for example Take It From Here *(1947–58). He also appeared on radio and TV quiz shows and presented LWT's* It'll Be Alright on the Night *(1977–97).*

1 It's a funny kind of month, October. For the really keen cricket fan it's when you discover that your wife left you in May.

She October 1977

Edward Norman (b. 1938)

BRITISH ECCLESIASTIC AND ACADEMIC

He was Dean of Peterhouse, Cambridge (1971–88) and since 1999 has been Chancellor at York Minster. His publications include Church and Society in Modern England *(1976).*

1 Many are called but few are chosen. There are sayings of Christ which suggest that the Church he came to establish will always be a minority affair.

The Times 20 February 1992

Oliver North (b. 1943)

US MARINE OFFICER

He was appointed by RONALD REAGAN to the staff of the National Security Council in 1981. Implicated in the Iran–Contra scandal, he resigned in 1986 but successfully appealed against his conviction and in 1991 all charges were dropped.

1 I'm trusting in the Lord and a good lawyer.

Quoted in the *Observer* 7 December 1986. On investigations into the Iran–Contra affair, whereby funds from arms sales to Iran were transferred to Contra guerrillas in Nicaragua.

Ivor Novello (1893–1951)

WELSH ACTOR, COMPOSER AND PLAYWRIGHT

Originally David Ivor Davies. He combined careers as actor-manager and composer, acquiring matinée idol status in romantic musical shows such as Perchance to Dream *(1945). See also* LENA GUILBERT FORD 1.

1 There's something Vichy about the French.

Quoted by Edward Marsh in letter, March 1941, publ. in *Ambrosia and Small Beer*, ch. 4 (ed. Christopher Hassall, 1964)

(Sir) Trevor Nunn (b. 1940)

BRITISH STAGE DIRECTOR

While Artistic Director of the Royal Shakespeare Theatre Company (1968–87), he was responsible for two new theatres in Stratford. He was Director of the Royal National Theatre 1997–2003.

1 Soundbite and slogan, strapline and head-line: at every turn we meet hyperbole. The soaring inflation of the English language is more urgently in need of control than the economic variety.

Independent 6 June 1998

Jeff Nuttall (b. 1933)

BRITISH POET, PAINTER AND MUSICIAN

His contribution to the sex and drugs ethos of the 1960s was, he said, to 'fertilize this very scorched earth for those yet to come'. His book Bomb Culture *(1968) was one of the key works of that decade.*

1 Not one of us, no solitary one, had any serious political preoccupation or any belief in the changeability of society and events. No single solitary one amongst us had the slightest spark of hope or gave a damn about a thing except the crackling certainty of Now.

Bomb Culture, 'Pop', sect. 2 (1968). On post-war youth culture.

2 What is missed by the mystics . . . is that there is a purpose, and a *divine* purpose, to the human alienation from the cosmos. The recognition, definition of Being, in wonderment and ecstasy can only be carried out by a conscious entity alienated from the eternal totality. You can't dig It if you *are* It. No man beholds his own face.

Ibid., 'The Underground', sect. 4

Julius Nyerere (1922–99)

TANZANIAN PRESIDENT

From 1954 he organized the Tanganyika African National Union, and he became first President of Tanzania in 1964. His efforts to establish an African socialism failed, and he retired in 1985. 'The Prime Minister is like the great banyan tree,' remarked the politician Kanoji Patel. 'Thousands shelter beneath it, but nothing grows.'

1 When we were at school we were taught to sing the songs of the Europeans. How many of us were taught the songs of the Wanyamwezi or of the Wahehe? Many of us have learnt to dance the rumba, or the cha cha, to rock and roll and to twist and even to dance the waltz and fox-trot. But how many of us can dance, or have even heard of the gombe sugu, the mangala, nyang'umumi, kiduo, or lele mama?

Tanzania National Assembly Official Reports (1962), quoted in *African All-Stars*, pt 1 (1987) by Chris Stapleton and Chris May

2 Our mistake was in the assumption that freedom – real freedom – would neces-sarily and with little trouble follow libera-tion from alien rule. . . . Our countries are effectively being governed by people who have only the most marginal interest in our affairs.

Quoted by CHRISTOPHER HILL in the *Guardian Weekly* 6 May 1984

Ann Oakley (b. 1944)
BRITISH SOCIOLOGIST AND AUTHOR

Her non-fiction work examines the roles of house-wives and mothers, as in Woman's Work: The Housewife, Past and Present *(1974). Her best known novel,* The Men's Room *(1988, televised 1991), is a steamy tale of academic adultery.*

1 Clearly, society has a tremendous stake in insisting on a woman's natural fitness for the career of mother: the alternatives are all too expensive.
   Woman's Work: The Housewife, Past and Present, ch. 8 (1974)

2 Housework is work directly opposed to the possibility of human self-actualization.
   Ibid., ch. 9

3 If love . . . means that one person absorbs the other, then no real relationship exists any more. Love evaporates; there is nothing left to love. The integrity of self is gone.
   Taking It Like a Woman, 'Love: Irresolution' (1984)

4 Families are nothing other than the idolatry of duty.
   Ibid., 'The War Between Love and the Family II'

5 There are always women who will take men on their own terms. If I were a man I wouldn't bother to change while there are women like that around.
   Quoted in the *Observer* 27 October 1991

Joyce Carol Oates (b. 1938)
US AUTHOR

Using a range of genres from Gothic horror fiction to social commentary, she exposes the violence and decay in American life. Her novels include Them *(1969),* A Bloodsmoor Romance *(1982) and* Blonde *(2000), based on the life of* MARILYN MONROE.

1 The worst cynicism: a belief in luck.
   Do What You Will, pt 2 ch. 15 (1970)

2 Nothing is accidental in the universe – this is one of my Laws of Physics – except the entire universe itself, which is Pure Accident, pure divinity.
   Ibid., 'The Summing Up: Meredith Dawe'

3 It is not her body that he wants but it is only through her body that he can take possession of another human being, so he must labor upon her body, he must enter her body, to make his claim.
   Unholy Loves, 'In the Founders' Room' (1979)

4 Our enemy is by tradition our savior, in preventing us from superficiality.
   Quoting an aphorism, in 'Master Race', publ. in *Partisan Review 50th Anniversary Edition* (ed. William Phillips, 1985)

5 The television screen, so unlike the movie

screen, sharply reduced human beings, revealed them as small, trivial, flat, in two banal dimensions, drained of color. Wasn't there something reassuring about it! – that human beings were in fact merely images of a kind registered in one another's eyes and brains, phenomena composed of microscopic flickering dots like atoms. They *were* atoms – nothing more. A quick switch of the dial and they disappeared and who could lament the loss?
You Must Remember This, pt 1, ch. 13 (1987)

6 When you're fifty you start thinking about things you haven't thought about before. I used to think getting old was about vanity – but actually it's about losing people you love. Getting wrinkles is trivial.
Interview in the *Guardian* 18 August 1989

Conor Cruise O'Brien (b. 1917)
IRISH HISTORIAN, DIPLOMAT AND CRITIC
Once described by the New Statesman *as 'a modern version of that nineteenth-century radical phenomenon, the Only White Man the Natives Trust', he published a powerful eyewitness account of the Congo crisis,* To Katanga and Back *(1962). He held a seat in the Irish parliament 1969–77, and is a regular commentator on international affairs.*

1 Irishness is not primarily a question of birth or blood or language; it is the condition of being involved in the Irish situation, and usually of being mauled by it.
'Irishness', publ. in the *New Statesman* 17 January 1959, written as Donat O'Donnell

2 The United Nations cannot do anything, and never could; it is not an animate entity or agent. It is a place, a stage, a forum and a shrine . . . a place to which powerful people can repair when they are fearful about the course on which their own rhetoric seems to be propelling them.
New Republic 4 November 1985

3 Nothing does more to activate Christian divisions than talk about Christian unity.
The Times 3 October 1989

Edna O'Brien (b. 1932)
IRISH AUTHOR
Her novels, some of which were banned in Ireland for their treatment of sex, typically narrate attempts to escape repressive situations, and include The Country Girls *(1960) and* A Pagan Place *(1970).*

1 I am committing suicide through lack of intelligence, and through not knowing, not learning to know, how to live.
Narrator (Martha), in 'The Love Object', first publ. in the *New Yorker* (1963), repr. in *The Love Object* (1968)

2 After the rich, the most obnoxious people in the world are those who serve the rich.
Ellen, in *August Is a Wicked* Month, ch. 8 (1965)

3 Countries are either mothers or fathers, and engender the emotional bristle secretly reserved for either sire.
Mother Ireland, ch. 1 (1976)

4 Irish? In truth I would not want to be anything else. It is a state of mind as well as an actual country. It is being at odds with other nationalities, having a quite different philosophy about pleasure, about punishment, about life, and about death. At least it does not leave one pusillanimous.
Ibid., ch. 7

5 Oh shadows of love, inebriations of love, foretastes of love, trickles of love, but never yet the one true love.
Narrator (Mary Hooligan), in *Night* (1972)

6 In every question and every remark tossed back and forth between lovers who have not played out the last fugue, there is one question and it is this: 'Is there someone new?'
Lantern Slides, 'Long Distance' (1990)

Flann O'Brien (1911–66)
IRISH AUTHOR
Pseudonym of Brian O'Nolan. Influenced by JAMES JOYCE, *he published the experimental* At Swim-Two-Birds *(1939) and* The Poor Mouth *(1941), originally written in Gaelic. As Myles na Gopaleen, he wrote a lively column for the* Irish Times *from 1940.*

1 *When money's tight and is hard to get
And your horse has also ran,
When all you have is a heap of debt –
A PINT OF PLAIN IS YOUR ONLY
MAN.*
At Swim-Two-Birds, ch. 1 (1939)

2 The gross and net result of it is that people who spent most of their natural lives riding iron bicycles over the rocky roadsteads of this parish get their personalities mixed up with the personalities of their bicycle as a result of the interchanging of the atoms of each of them and you would be surprised at the number of people in these parts who nearly are half people and half bicycles.
Sergeant, in *The Third Policeman*, ch. 6 (written 1940, publ. 1967)

Richard O'Brien (b. 1942)
BRITISH ACTOR AND SCREENWRITER
Originally Richard Timothy Smith. He was the creator of the cult Rocky Horror Show *(1973, filmed as* The Rocky Horror Picture Show, *1975), which he called 'a mix of sex, rock 'n' roll and*

gothic horror'. He later hosted The Crystal Maze
for Channel 4 TV (1990–93).

1 **Give yourself over to absolute pleasure.**
Dr Frank N. Furter (Tim Curry), in *The Rocky
Horror Picture Show* (film, 1975, screenplay by
Jim Sharman and Richard O'Brien, based on
Richard O'Brien's stage musical, directed by Jim
Sharman)

2 **It's not easy having a good time . . . even
smiling makes my face ache.**
Dr Frank N. Furter, ibid.

3 **Don't dream it. Be it.**
Dr Frank N. Furter, ibid.

Sean O'Casey (1880–1964)
IRISH PLAYWRIGHT
*Originally John Casey. He is best remembered for
his early realist works documenting Ireland's
troubled modern history, notably* Juno and the
Paycock *(1924) and* The Plough and the Stars
(1926). After The Silver Tassie *(1929) was rejected
by Dublin's Abbey Theatre, he lived in England.*

1 **You cannot put a rope around the neck of
an idea; you cannot put an idea up against
a barrack-square wall and riddle it with
bullets; you cannot confine it in the strongest prison cell that your slaves could ever
build.**
The Story of Thomas Ashe, ch. 4 (1917)

2 **Th' whole worl's in a state o' chassis!**
Jack Boyle, in *Juno and the Paycock*, act 1 and *passim* (1924). Also the last words of play.

3 **As far as I can see, the Polis as Polis, in this
city, is Null an' Void!**
Mrs Madigan, ibid. act 3. Referring to Dublin
during the Irish Civil War in 1922

4 **There's no reason to bring religion into it.
I think we ought to have as great a regard
for religion as we can, so as to keep it out
of as many things as possible.**
Fluther Good, in *The Plough and the Stars*, act 1
(1926)

5 **It's my rule never to lose me temper till it
would be dethrimental to keep it.**
Ibid.

6 **Work! Labour, the *aspergas me* of life; the
one great sacrament of humanity from
which all other things flow – security,
leisure, joy, art, literature, even divinity
itself.**
Rose and Crown, 'In New York Now' (fifth volume of autobiography, 1952)

7 **Wealth often takes away chances from men
as well as poverty. There is none to tell the
rich to go on striving, for a rich man
makes the law that hallows and hollows his
own life.**
Ibid., 'Pennsylvanian Visit'

8 **Jesus, Buddha, Mahommed, great as each**

may be, their highest comfort given to the
sorrowful is a cordial introduction into
another's woe. Sorrow's the great community in which all men born of woman
are members at one time or another.
Ibid., 'Wild Life in New Amsterdam'

9 **What time has been wasted during man's
destiny in the struggle to decide what
man's next world will be like! The keener
the effort to find out, the less he knew
about the present one he lived in.**
Sunset and Evening Star, 'Shaw's Corner' (sixth
volume of autobiography, 1954)

10 **The flame from the angel's sword in the
garden of Eden has been catalysed into the
atom bomb; God's thunderbolt became
blunted, so man's dunderbolt has become
the steel star of destruction.**
Ibid., 'And Evening Star'

11 **Here, with whitened hair, desires failing,
strength ebbing out of him, with the sun
gone down and with only the serenity and
the calm warning of the evening star left to
him, he drank to Life, to all it had been, to
what it was, to what it would be. Hurrah!**
Ibid. Final paragraph of book.

12 **Laughter is wine for the soul – laughter
soft, or loud and deep, tinged through with
seriousness . . . the hilarious declaration
made by man that life is worth living.**
Green Crows, 'Saturday Night' (1956)

13 **Here we have bishops, priests, and
deacons, a Censorship Board, vigilant lib-
rarians, confraternities and sodalities,
Duce Maria, Legions of Mary, Knights of
this Christian order and Knights of that
one, all surrounding the sinner's free will
in an embattled circle.**
Letter to the *Irish Times* 8 June 1957

14 **What a terrible thing has happened to us
all! To you there, to us here, to all everywhere. Peace who was becoming bright-
eyed, now sits in the shadow of death; her
handsome champion has been killed as he
walked by her very side. Her gallant boy is
dead. What a cruel, foul, and most unnatural murder!**
Of the assassination of JOHN F. KENNEDY, in
letter publ. in *The New York Times* 27 November
1963

Flannery O'Connor (1925–64)
US AUTHOR
*Raised a devout Roman Catholic in the Protestant
fundamentalist South, she took as her main theme
the nature of evil. Her 'Southern Gothic' novels
and short stories, often peopled by the marginalized and the violent, include* Wise Blood
(1952) and A Good Man is Hard to Find *(1955).*

1 **I preach there are all kinds of truth, your**

truth and somebody else's. But behind all of them there is only one truth and that is that there's no truth.

The preacher Hazel Motes, in *Wise Blood*, ch. 10 (1952)

2 Manners are of such great consequence to the novelist that any kind will do. Bad manners are better than no manners at all, and because we are losing our customary manners, we are probably overly conscious of them; this seems to be a condition that produces writers.

'The Fiction Writer and His Country', publ. in *The Living Novel: A Symposium* (ed. Granville Hicks, 1957)

3 I have found that anything that comes out of the South is going to be called grotesque by the Northern reader, unless it *is* grotesque, in which case it is going to be called realistic.

'Some Aspects of The Grotesque in Southern Fiction', lecture in Macon, Georgia, autumn 1960, first publ. 1965, repr. in *Mystery and Manners* (ed. Sally and Robert Fitzgerald, 1972)

4 While the South is hardly Christ-centered, it is most certainly Christ-haunted.

Ibid.

5 Being a Georgia author is a rather specious dignity, on the same order as, for the pig, being a Talmadge ham.

'The Regional Writer', first publ. 1963, repr. ibid.

6 It seems that the fiction writer has a revolting attachment to the poor, for even when he writes about the rich, he is more concerned with what they lack than with what they have.

'The Teaching of Literature', publ. ibid.

Sinéad O'Connor (b. 1966)
IRISH SINGER AND SONGWRITER
Described by the New Musical Express *as 'the Johnny Rotten of the Eighties' for her rebellious, publicity-conscious antics, she had an international hit with the Prince song 'Nothing Compares 2 U' in 1990.*

1 I believe our purpose is to inspire and guide the human race.

Independent 12 February 1991. On popular music.

2 Loneliness is a crowded room.

Interview in the *Observer* 13 September 1998

Wendy O'Connor
KURT COBAIN'S MOTHER

1 Now he's gone and joined that stupid club.

On her son's suicide, quoted in the *Daily Telegraph* 14 April 1994. Referring to the number of other deaths by young rock stars.

Cristina Odone (b. 1960)
ITALIAN JOURNALIST AND AUTHOR
She was Editor of the Catholic Herald *(1992–6) and joined the* New Statesman *as Deputy Editor in 1998. Her novels include* The Shrine *(1996) and* A Perfect Wife *(1997).*

1 Catholicism is like a bowl of spaghetti, full of different strands. It is only if you eat them all together that it will do you any good.

Independent 21 October 1992

Georgia O'Keeffe (1887–1986)
US ARTIST
A pioneer of American abstract art, she went on to produce more figurative work, often inspired by the desert landscape of New Mexico, as in Black Iris *(1926) and* Cow's Skull, Red, White and Blue *(1931).*

1 Marks on paper are free – free speech – press – pictures all go together I suppose.

Letter, 14 January 1916, quoted in *Portrait of an Artist*, ch. 3 (1986) by Laurie Lisle

2 Before I put a brush to canvas, I question, 'Is this mine? . . . Is it influenced by some idea which I have acquired from some man?' . . . I am trying with all my skill to do a painting that is all of women, as well as all of me.

Debate reported in the *New York World* 16 March 1930, quoted ibid., ch. 9

3 When you take a flower in your hand and really look at it, it's your world for the moment. I want to give that world to someone else. Most people in the city rush around so, they have no time to look at a flower. I want them to see it whether they want to or not.

New York Post 16 May 1946, quoted ibid., ch. 6. Flowers were a favourite subject of O'Keeffe.

4 I hate flowers – I paint them because they're cheaper than models and they don't move.

Quoted in the *New York Herald Tribune* 18 April 1954, repr. ibid. O'Keeffe was responding to the remark, 'How perfect to meet you with flowers in your hands!'

5 I don't very much enjoy looking at paintings in general. I know too much about them. I take them apart.

Quoted in the *San Francisco Examiner and Chronicle* 16 March 1971

Ben Okri (b. 1959)
NIGERIAN AUTHOR
The New York Times *likened his work to 'a continent dreamed up, in tandem, by Hieronymus Bosch and Jorge Luis Borges', although Okri himself describes it as 'a kind of realism, but a realism with many more dimensions'. His novels include*

The Famished Road *(1991) and* Astonishing the Gods *(1995).* An African Elegy *(1992) is a poetry collection.*

1 The sun bared the reality of our lives and everything was so harsh it was a mystery that we could understand and care for one another or for anything at all.
   The Famished Road, bk 2, ch. 10 (1991)

2 Many people have walked out of life because they stopped seeing it. Many have fallen into the abyss because they were looking for solid ground, for certainties. Happy are those who are still, and to whom things come.
   Ibid., bk 4, ch. 13

3 I think our childhood goes back thousands of years, farther back than the memory of any race.
   Astonishing the Gods, bk 4, ch. 17 (1995)

4 Each moment offered us clarity and liberation but we settled for the comforting shapes of legends, no matter how monstrous or useless.
   Infinite Riches, bk 1, ch. 11 (1998)

5 Suffering is an aspect of the great Promethean will, the thing in us which most makes the spirit wake up. Modern literature is the product of too much false suffering, too much false pain. Real suffering is like the dirt that miners dig up and carry away. It is necessary if we are to find the true gold that writers seek.
   Quoted in the Guardian 21 August 1999

Claes Oldenburg (b. 1929)
SWEDISH-BORN US ARTIST
A member of the Pop Art movement, he began his 'happenings' in 1962, from which developed his giant soft sculptures of everyday objects. His 'Colossal Monuments' include Clothespin *in Philadelphia and* Colossal Ashtray with Fag-ends *in Paris.*

1 *I am for an art that is political-erotical-mystical, that does something other than sit on its ass in a museum.*
   I am for an art that grows up not knowing it is art at all, an art given the chance of having a starting point of zero.
   I am for an art that employs itself with everyday crap & still comes out on top.
   I am for an art that imitates the human, that is comic, if necessary, or violent, or whatever is necessary.
   'I Am For an Art', catalogue for exhibition in New York, June 1961, repr. in Store Days (1966)

2 Basically collectors want nudes. So I have supplied for them nude cars, nude telephones, nude electric plugs, nude switches, nude fans, newd electretcetera and sew on.
   Quoted in Moderna Museet Gallery catalogue,
   Stockholm, 1966, repr. in Icons and Images of the Sixties, 'Pop Art: Claes Oldenburg's Contented Objects' (1971) by Nicholas and Elena Calas

(Sir) Laurence Olivier (1907–89)
BRITISH ACTOR AND DIRECTOR
Baron Olivier of Brighton. Regarded by many as the greatest actor of his generation, he played all the major Shakespearian roles on the stage and also starred in the films Henry V *(1944) and* Hamlet *(1948), among many others. He was the first director of the National Theatre (1963–73) and the first actor to be made a life peer (1970).*

1 Shakespeare – the nearest thing in incarnation to the eye of God.
   Kenneth Harris Talking To, 'Sir Laurence Olivier' (1971)

2 Why don't you try acting, dear boy – it's so much easier.
   Attributed advice to DUSTIN HOFFMAN, his co-star in the film Marathon Man (1976), who stayed awake for days on end in order to 'inhabit' his role

3 Acting is a masochistic form of exhibitionism. It is not quite the occupation of an adult.
   Time 3 July 1978

Charles Olson (1910–70)
US POET AND CRITIC
Spokesman of the Black Mountain Poets, he argued that poetry should depend on the rhythms of breathing rather than rhyme and metre in his influential essay 'Projective Verse' (1950). He is also known for the The Maximus Poems *(1953–70) and a study of Herman Melville,* Call Me Ishmael *(1947).*

1 I take SPACE to be the central fact to man born in America. . . . I spell it large because it comes large here. Large and without mercy.
   Call Me Ishmael, sect. 1 (1947)

2 Get on with it, keep moving, keep in, speed, the nerves, their speed, the perceptions, theirs, the acts, the split second acts, the whole business, keep it moving as fast as you can, citizen. . . . So there we are, fast, there's the dogma.
   'Projective Verse', first publ. in Poetry New York (1950), repr. in Selected Writings of Charles Olson (ed. Robert Creeley, 1951)

Jacqueline Kennedy Onassis
See JACQUELINE KENNEDY.

Michael Ondaatje (b. 1943)
SRI LANKAN-BORN CANADIAN NOVELIST AND POET
He has published numerous volumes of verse,

including The Cinnamon Peeler *(1990)*, *but he is best known for his novels, notably* The English Patient *(1992, filmed 1996).*

1 The first sentence of every novel should be: 'Trust me, this will take time but there is order here, very faint, very human.' Meander if you want to get to town.
In the Skin of a Lion, bk 2, 'Palace of Purification' (1987)

2 The past is still, for us, a place that is not safely settled.
The Faber Book of Contemporary Canadian Short Stories, Introduction (1990)

3 The desert could not be claimed or owned – it was a piece of cloth carried by winds, never held down by stones, and given a hundred shifting names long before Canterbury existed, long before battles and treaties quilted Europe and the East. Its caravans, those strange rambling feasts and cultures, left nothing behind, not an ember.
The English Patient, ch. 4 (1992)

4 *A libertine was one who made love before nightfall*
Or without darkening the room.
'A Gentleman Compares His Virtue to a Piece of Jade', publ. in *Handwriting* (1994)

Eugene O'Neill (1888–1953)
US PLAYWRIGHT
The first American dramatist to win the Nobel Prize for Literature (1936), he also won a total of four Pulitzer Prizes including one for the autobiographical Long Day's Journey into Night *(1956), generally considered his finest work. On hearing he was giving up drinking,* GEORGE BERNARD SHAW *remarked: 'He'll probably never write a good play again.'*

1 Life is for each man a solitary cell whose walls are mirrors.
Lazarus, in *Lazarus Laughed*, act 2, sc. 1 (1927)

2 When men make gods, there is no God!
Lazarus, ibid., sc. 2

3 Man's loneliness is but his fear of life.
Lazarus, ibid., act 3, sc. 2

4 The old – like children – talk to themselves, for they have reached that hopeless wisdom of experience which knows that though one were to cry it in the streets to multitudes, or whisper it in the kiss to one's beloved, the only ears that can ever hear one's secrets are one's own!
Tiberius, ibid., act 4, sc. 1

5 Life is perhaps most wisely regarded as a bad dream between two awakenings, and every day is a life in miniature.
Chu-Yin, in *Marco Millions*, act 2, sc. 2 (1928)

6 The only living life is in the past and future – the present is an interlude – strange interlude in which we call on past and future to bear witness we are living.
Nina, in *Strange Interlude*, pt 2, act 8 (1928)

7 The sea hates a coward!
Bryant, in *Mourning Becomes Electra*, pt 2, act 4 (1931)

8 It is like acid always burning in my brain that the stupid butchering of the last war taught men nothing at all, that they sank back listlessly on the warm manure pile of the dead and went to sleep, indifferently bestowing custody of their future, their fate, into the hands of State departments, whose members are trained to be conspirators, card sharps, double-crossers and secret betrayers of their own people; into the hands of greedy capitalist ruling classes so stupid they could not even see when their own greed began devouring itself; into the hands of that most debased type of pimp, the politician, and that most craven of all lice and job-worshippers, the bureaucrats.
Letter to his son, June 1942, publ. in *Selected Letters of Eugene O'Neill* (ed. Travis Bogard and Jackson R. Bryer, 1988)

9 The lie of a pipe dream is what gives life to the whole misbegotten mad lot of us, drunk or sober.
Larry, in *The Iceman Cometh*, act 1 (1946). 'It is a play about pipe dreams,' O'Neill remarked about this work. 'And the philosophy is that there is always one dream left, one final dream, no matter how low you have fallen, down there at the bottom of the bottle. I know, because I saw it.'

10 None of us can help the things life has done to us. They're done before you realize it, and once they're done they make you do other things until at last everything comes between you and what you'd like to be, and you've lost your true self forever.
Mary, in *Long Day's Journey into Night*, act 2, sc. 1 (1956)

11 We fought so long against small things that we became small ourselves.
Quoted by VÁCLAV HAVEL in *Disturbing the Peace*, ch. 3 (1986)

12 I knew it. I knew it. Born in a hotel room – and God damn it – died in a hotel room.
Attributed, shortly before his death in the Shelton Hotel, Boston, 27 November 1953

Yoko Ono (b. 1933)
JAPANESE-BORN US ARTIST
Yoko Ono Lennon. As painter, sculptor and performance artist, she was a prominent member of New York's neo-Dadaist Fluxus group in the 1960s. Her work developed pacifist themes following her marriage to JOHN LENNON *in 1969.*

1 Everybody's an artist. Everybody's God. It's just that they're inhibited. I believe in people so much that if the whole of civilization is burned so we don't have any memory of it, even then people will start to build their own art. It is a necessity – a function. We don't need history.
Interview for Dutch TV, October 1968, publ. in *Imagine* (ed. Andrew Solt and Sam Egan, 1988)

2 Woman is the nigger of the world.
Interview in *Nova* 1968, quoted in *The Lennon Tapes* (1981). The words were the basis of the eponymously titled song by JOHN LENNON on the album *Some Time in New York City* (1972), and recall those of ZORA NEALE HURSTON: 'De nigger woman is de mule uh de world so fur as Ah can see.' (*Their Eyes Were Watching God*, ch. 2, 1937)

3 The odds of not meeting in this life are so great that every meeting is like a miracle. It's a wonder that we don't make love to every single person we meet.
Sleevenotes on *Feeling the Space* (album, 1973)

4 If all of us just loved and cared for one person each. That is all it takes. Love breeds love. Maybe then we will be able to prevent each other from going insane. Maybe then we will be able to prevent each other from becoming violent, as violence is in our hearts and not in our weapons. Guilt is not in the one who pulls the trigger, but in each of us who allows it.
Letter to the world's press, following the murder of JOHN LENNON in 1980

Lord Onslow (b. 1938)
BRITISH PEER
Sir Michael Onslow, Baron Cranley. An outspoken Tory maverick with liberal leanings, he was one of the ninety-two hereditary peers to keep their seats after reform of the House of Lords in 1999.

1 I will be sad if I look up or down after my death and don't see my son asleep on the same benches on which I slept.
Quoted in the *Guardian* 26 October 1998. Speaking against Labour's plans for reforming the House of Lords. He threatened that he would 'go out like a football hooligan' if he lost his seat.

J. Robert Oppenheimer (1904–67)
US PHYSICIST
Julius Robert Oppenheimer. In 1943 he became Director at the Los Alamos laboratory, overseeing the Manhattan Project to develop the atomic bomb. Horrified at the bomb's destructive power, he resigned in 1945, later arguing unsuccessfully for joint US–Soviet control of atomic energy.

1 In some sort of crude sense, which no vulgarity, no humor, no overstatement can quite extinguish, the physicists have

known sin; and this is a knowledge which they cannot lose.
'Physics in the Contemporary World', lecture at Massachusetts Institute of Technology, 25 November 1947, first publ. in *Technology Review* no. 50, 1948, repr. in *Open Mind* (1955). Oppenheimer's remark became notorious after it was quoted in *Time* magazine 23 February 1948 and 8 November 1948.

2 When you see something that is technically sweet, you go ahead and do it and you argue about what to do about it only after you have had your technical success. That is the way it was with the atomic bomb.
In the Matter of J. Robert Oppenheimer: USAEC Transcript of Hearing Before Personnel Security Board (1954). Statement during hearings investigating allegations of former communist associations, in connection with Oppenheimer's involvement in the Los Alamos project to develop the atomic bomb.

Martin Oppenheimer (b. 1930)
GERMAN-BORN US SOCIOLOGIST
He had a wide influence on non-violent protest in the 1960s through his articles and the books A Manual for Direct Action (1964, with George Lakey) and The Urban Guerrilla (1969).

1 Today's city is the most vulnerable social structure ever conceived by man.
The Urban Guerrilla, ch. 7 (1969)

Susie Orbach (b. 1946)
BRITISH PSYCHOTHERAPIST AND AUTHOR
Her work is directed to understanding eating disorders, which she discusses in her books, notably Fat is a Feminist Issue (1978).

1 Fat is a social disease, and fat is a feminist issue.
Fat is a Feminist Issue, Introduction (1978). 'Fat,' wrote Orbach, 'is a way of saying "no" to powerlessness and self-denial.'

Tony O'Reilly (b. 1936)
IRISH ENTREPRENEUR
After a career as a rugby international, he went into business and was Chairman (1987–2000) of the Heinz International Corporation and subsequently Chairman of Independent News and Media.

1 Truly great brands are far more than just labels for products; they are symbols that encapsulate the desires of consumers; they are standards held aloft under which the masses congregate.
Speech to British Council of Shopping Centres, 1990, quoted in 'Brand Leader' by Fintan O'Toole, publ. in *Granta* no. 53, spring 1996

Leoluca Orlando (b. 1947)
SICILIAN POLITICIAN
Mayor of Palermo 1985–2001, he was expelled from the Christian Democrat Party in 1990 and formed his own party, La Rete ('network'), dedicated to eradicating Mafia influence and reinvigorating the city.

1 In Italy it is not important who you are but whom you belong to.
  Quoted in the *International Herald Tribune* 25 April 1991

P. J. O'Rourke (b. 1947)
US JOURNALIST
Patrick John O'Rourke. He is notorious for his acidic sketches of public affairs from a humorous right-wing perspective, collected in Holidays in Hell (1988) and The Enemies List (1996), among other titles. Time magazine called him 'an acerbic master of gonzo journalism'.

1 Name me, if you can, a better feeling than the one you get when you've half a bottle of Chivas in the bag with a gram of coke up your nose and a teenage lovely pulling off her tube top in the next seat over while you're doing a hundred miles an hour in a suburban side street.
  Republican Party Reptile, 'How to Drive Fast on Drugs while Getting Your Wing Wang Squeezed and Not Spill Your Drink' (1987)

2 Western civilization not only provides a bit of life, a pinch of liberty and the occasional pursuance of happiness, it's also the only thing that's ever tried to. Our civilization is the first in history to show even the slightest concern for average, undistinguished, none-too-commendable people like us.
  Holidays in Hell, Introduction (1988)

3 In the end we beat them with Levi 501 jeans. Seventy-two years of Communist indoctrination and propaganda was drowned out by a three-ounce Sony Walkman. A huge totalitarian system . . . has been brought to its knees because nobody wants to wear Bulgarian shoes. . . . Now they're lunch, and we're number one on the planet.
  'The Death of Communism', first publ. in *Rolling Stone* November 1989, repr. in *Give War A Chance* (1992)

4 We spend all day broadcasting on the radio and TV telling people back home what's happening here. And we learn what's happening here by spending all day monitoring the radio and TV broadcasts from back home.
  On reporting the Gulf War, in 'Gulf Diary', 31 January 1991, first publ. in *Rolling Stone*, repr. ibid.

5 Politics are for foreigners with their endless wrongs and paltry rights. Politics are a lousy way to get things done. Politics are, like God's infinite mercy, a last resort.
  Parliament of Whores, Preface to British edn (1991)

6 Maybe a nation that consumes as much booze and dope as we do and has our kind of divorce statistics should pipe down about 'character issues'. Either that or just go ahead and determine the presidency with three-legged races and pie-eating contests. It would make better TV.
  Ibid., 'Attack of the Midget Vote Suckers'

7 Whatever it is that the government does, sensible Americans would prefer that the government do it to somebody else. This is the idea behind foreign policy.
  Ibid., 'Very Foreign Policy'

8 The neo-hippie-dips, the sentimentality-crazed iguana anthropomorphizers, the Chicken Littles, the three-bong-hit William Blakes – thank God these people don't actually go outdoors much, or the environment would be even worse than it is already.
  On ecologists, ibid., 'Dirt of the Earth: The Ecologists'

9 Every government is a parliament of whores. The trouble is, in a democracy the whores are us.
  Ibid., 'At Home in the Parliament of Whores'

10 No drug, not even alcohol, causes the fundamental ills of society. If we're looking for the sources of our troubles, we shouldn't test people for drugs, we should test them for stupidity, ignorance, greed and love of power.
  Give War A Chance, 'Studying for Our Drug Test' (1992)

11 At forty-seven the things which really matter and the things which are really fun are the dreadful things that our parents really said mattered. Family and work and duty. Crap like that.
  Interview in the *Guardian* 25 November 1995

José Ortega y Gasset (1883–1955)
SPANISH ESSAYIST AND PHILOSOPHER
He played a significant part in introducing Spanish readers to modernist fiction. His major work, The Revolt of the Masses (1930), denounced the anti-intellectualism and intolerance of both left and right in the years preceding the Spanish Civil War.

1 I am I plus my surroundings and if I do not preserve the latter, I do not preserve myself.
  Meditations on Quixote, 'To the Reader' (1914)

2 I do not deny that there may be other well-founded causes for the hatred which various classes feel toward politicians, but the *main one seems to me that politicians are symbols of the fact that every class must take every other class into account.*
Invertebrate Spain, ch. 2, 'Direct Action' (1921)

3 Poetry has become the higher algebra of metaphors.
The Dehumanization of Art, 'More About the Dehumanization of Art' (1925)

4 The characteristic of the hour is that the commonplace mind, knowing itself to be commonplace, has the assurance to proclaim the rights of the commonplace and to impose them wherever it will.
The Revolt of the Masses, ch. 1 (1930)

5 Civilization is nothing else than the attempt to reduce force to being the *ultima ratio*.
Ibid., ch. 8

6 Liberalism – it is well to recall this today – is the supreme form of generosity; it is the right which the majority concedes to minorities and hence it is *the noblest cry that has ever resounded in this planet*. It announces the determination to share existence with the enemy; more than that, with an enemy which is weak.
Ibid.

7 We have need of history in its entirety, not to fall back into it, but to see if we can escape from it.
Ibid., ch. 10

8 A revolution does not last more than fifteen years, the period which coincides with the flourishing of a generation.
Ibid.

9 Youth does not require reasons for living, it only needs pretexts.
Ibid., ch. 14, sect. 3

10 Biography is: a system in which the contradictions of a human life are unified.
'In Search of Goethe from Within', first publ. in *Partisan Review* December 1949, repr. in *The Dehumanization of Art and Other Essays* (1968)

11 Poetry is adolescence fermented, and thus preserved.
Ibid.

Joe Orton (1933–67)
BRITISH PLAYWRIGHT
Originally John Kingsley. The hallmarks of his farces, such as Entertaining Mr Sloane *(1964) and* Loot *(1966), were black humour, bad taste and cutting dialogue. He was murdered by his lover, Kenneth Halliwell, who then took his own life.*

1 I always say to myself that the theatre is the Temple of Dionysus, and not Apollo.

You do the Dionysus thing on your typewriter, and then you allow a little Apollo in, just a little to shape and guide it along certain lines you may want to go along. But you can't allow Apollo in completely.
Interview on BBC Radio, 28 July 1964, quoted in *Prick up Your Ears: The Biography of Joe Orton*, ch. 1 (1978) by John Lahr

2 Every luxury was lavished on you – atheism, breast-feeding, circumcision.
Hal, in *Loot*, act 1 (1966)

3 Reading isn't an occupation we encourage among police officers. We try to keep the paper work down to a minimum.
Truscott, ibid., act 2

4 I was enraged that there were so many rubbishy novels and rubbishy books. It reminded me of the Bible: 'Of the making of books, there is no end', because there isn't. Libraries might as well not exist; they've got endless shelves of rubbish and hardly any space for good books.
Evening News 9 June 1967, quoted in *Prick up Your Ears: The Biography of Joe Orton*, ch. 3 (1978) by John Lahr. Orton was explaining his defacement of library books, for which he and his lover Halliwell received a six-month jail sentence in 1962.

5 You were born with your legs apart. They'll send you to the grave in a Y-shaped coffin.
Dr Prentice to his wife, in *What the Butler Saw*, act 1 (1969)

6 In an age of declining faith, sir, surely it's enough for the young to hold spiritual convictions. It's an act of pedantry to ask that they should be the right ones.
Notes for dialogue in *What the Butler Saw*, quoted in *Prick up Your Ears: The Biography of Joe Orton*, ch. 6 (1978) by John Lahr

George Orwell (1903–50)
BRITISH AUTHOR AND ESSAYIST
After working as an Imperial Police officer in Burma, he travelled and wrote in Europe, often performing menial jobs. The Road to Wigan Pier (1937) and Homage to Catalonia *(1938) expressed his socialist sympathies, while* Animal Farm *(1945, filmed 1954) and* Nineteen Eighty-Four *(1949, filmed 1956 and 1984) indicated his disillusionment with the socialist experiment.* CYRIL CONNOLLY *remarked, 'He could not blow his nose without moralising on conditions in the handkerchief industry.'*

1 He was an embittered atheist (the sort of atheist who does not so much disbelieve in God as personally dislike Him).
Down and Out in Paris and London, ch. 30 (1933). Referring to Bozo, a London 'screever' or pavement artist. In later years, Bozo was heard

to remark that Orwell 'always had £50 in his pocket' during his 'down-and-out' experiences.

2 **I sometimes think that the price of liberty is not so much eternal vigilance as eternal dirt.**

The Road to Wigan Pier, ch. 4 (1937). A reference to John Philpot Curran, 'The condition upon which God hath given liberty to man is eternal vigilance' (1790).

3 **As with the Christian religion, the worst advertisement for Socialism is its adherents.**

Ibid., ch. 11

4 **The high-water mark, so to speak, of Socialist literature is W. H. Auden, a sort of gutless Kipling, and the even feebler poets who are associated with him.**

Ibid. In his essay 'Inside the Whale' (1940), Orwell wrote: 'Some years ago I described Auden as "a sort of gutless Kipling". As criticism this was quite unworthy, indeed it was merely a spiteful remark, but it is a fact that in Auden's work, especially his earlier work, an atmosphere of uplift – something rather like Kipling's *If* or Newbolt's *Play up, Play up, and Play the Game!* – never seems to be very far away.'

5 **We of the sinking middle class . . . may sink without further struggles into the working class where we belong, and probably when we get there it will not be so dreadful as we feared, for, after all, we have nothing to lose but our aitches.**

Ibid., ch. 13

6 **And then England – southern England, probably the sleekest landscape in the world. It is difficult when you pass that way . . . to believe that anything is really happening anywhere. Earthquakes in Japan, famines in China, revolutions in Mexico? Don't worry, the milk will be on the doorstep tomorrow morning, the *New Statesman* will come out on Friday. . . . And then the huge peaceful wilderness of outer London, the barges on the miry river, the familiar streets, the posters telling of cricket matches and Royal weddings, the men in bowler hats, the pigeons in Trafalgar Square, the red buses, the blue policemen – all sleeping the deep, deep sleep of England, from which I sometimes fear that we shall never wake till we are jerked out of it by the roar of bombs.**

Homage to Catalonia, ch. 14 (1938). Describing Orwell's return from Spain in closing words of book.

7 **I'm fat, but I'm thin inside. Has it ever struck you that there's a thin man inside every fat man, just as they say there's a statue inside every block of stone?**

Coming Up for Air, pt 1, ch. 3 (1939). See also KINGSLEY AMIS 4, CYRIL CONNOLLY 18.

8 **To say 'I accept' in an age like our own is to say that you accept concentration camps, rubber truncheons, Hitler, Stalin, bombs, aeroplanes, tinned food, machine guns, putsches, purges, slogans, Bedaux belts, gas masks, submarines, spies, provocateurs, press-censorship, secret prisons, aspirins, Hollywood films and political murder.**

Inside the Whale and Other Essays, 'Inside the Whale', sect. 1 (1940).

9 **Of course there is much more in *Ulysses* than this ['commonplaceness of material'], because Joyce is a kind of poet and also an elephantine pedant, but his real achievement has been to get the familiar on to paper.**

Ibid.

10 **The 'Communism' of the English intellectual is something explicable enough. It is the patriotism of the deracinated.**

Ibid., sect. 2

11 **So much of left-wing thought is a kind of playing with fire by people who don't even know that fire is hot.**

Ibid.

12 **Good novels are not written by orthodoxy-sniffers, nor by people who are conscience-stricken about their own orthodoxy. Good novels are written by people who are *not frightened*.**

Ibid.

13 **For a creative writer possession of the 'truth' is less important than emotional sincerity.**

Ibid., sect. 3

14 **Progress is not an illusion, it happens, but it is slow and invariably disappointing.**

Ibid., 'Charles Dickens', sect. 1

15 **Men are only as good as their technical development allows them to be.**

Ibid., sect. 4

16 **Most revolutionaries are potential Tories, because they imagine that everything can be put right by altering the *shape* of society; once that change is effected, as it sometimes is, they see no need for any other.**

Ibid., sect. 6

17 **The clatter of clogs in the Lancashire mill towns, the to-and-fro of the lorries on the Great North Road, the queues outside the Labour Exchanges, the rattle of pin-tables in the Soho pubs, the old maids biking to Holy Communion through the through the mists of the autumn mornings – all these are not only fragments, but *characteristic* fragments, of the English scene. How**

can one make a pattern out of this muddle?

The Lion and the Unicorn, pt 1, 'England Your England', sect. 1 (1941). John Major nostalgically evoked this passage; see JOHN MAJOR 8.

18 England . . . resembles a family, a rather stuffy Victorian family, with not many black sheep in it but with all its cupboards bursting with skeletons. It has rich relations who have to be kowtowed to and poor relations who are horribly sat upon, and there is a deep conspiracy of silence about the source of the family income. It is a family in which the young are generally thwarted and most of the power is in the hands of irresponsible uncles and bed-ridden aunts. Still, it is a family. It has its private language and its common memories, and at the approach of an enemy it closes its ranks. A family with the wrong members in control – that, perhaps, is as near as one can come to describing England in a phrase.

Ibid., sect. 3

19 Probably the battle of Waterloo *was* won on the playing-fields of Eton, but the opening battles of all subsequent wars have been lost there.

Ibid., sect. 4. Referring to words attributed to the Duke of Wellington.

20 Whatever is funny is subversive, every joke is ultimately a custard pie, and the reason why so large a proportion of jokes centre round obscenity is simply that all societies, as the price of survival, have to insist on a fairly high standard of sexual morality. A dirty joke is not, of course, a serious attack upon morality, but it is a sort of mental rebellion, a momentary wish that things were otherwise.

'The Art of Donald McGill', publ. in *Horizon* September 1941, repr. in *Collected Essays* (1961)

21 The high sentiments always win in the end, the leaders who offer blood, toil, tears and sweat always get more out of their followers than those who offer safety and a good time. When it comes to the pinch, human beings are heroic.

Ibid.

22 I know it is the fashion to say that most of recorded history is lies anyway. I am willing to believe that history is for the most part inaccurate and biased, but what is peculiar to our own age is the abandonment of the idea that history *could* be truthfully written.

'Looking Back on the Spanish War', sect. 4, written 1943, publ. in *England Your England* (1953), repr. in *Homage to Catalonia* (1966 edn)

23 To a surprising extent the war-lords in shining armour, the apostles of the martial virtues, tend not to die fighting when the time comes. History is full of ignominious getaways by the great and famous.

'Who Are the War Criminals?', publ. in *Tribune* 22 October 1943, repr. in *The Collected Essays, Journalism and Letters of George Orwell*, vol. 2 (ed. Sonia Orwell and Ian Angus, 1968)

24 Autobiography is only to be trusted when it reveals something disgraceful. A man who gives a good account of himself is probably lying, since any life when viewed from the inside is simply a series of defeats.

'Benefit of Clergy: Some Notes on Salvador Dali', written for *The Saturday Book* (1944), publ. ibid., vol. 3. The essay was suppressed by the publishers of *The Saturday Book* and appeared in *Dickens, Dali and Others* (ed. George Orwell, 1946).

25 As a rule they will refuse even to sample a foreign dish, they regard such things as garlic and olive oil with disgust, life is unliveable to them unless they have tea and puddings.

On the English attitude to food, in 'The English People: England at First Glance', written 1944, publ. in *Britain in Pictures* (1947), repr. ibid. vol. 3

26 To write or even speak English is not a science but an art. There are no reliable words. . . . Whoever writes English is involved in a struggle that never lets up even for a sentence. He is struggling against vagueness, against obscurity, against the lure of the decorative adjective, against the encroachment of Latin and Greek, and, above all, against the worn-out phrases and dead metaphors with which the language is cluttered up.

'The English People: The English Language', ibid. Consequently, Orwell explained, 'the peculiarities of the English language make it almost impossible for anyone who has left school at fourteen to learn a foreign language after he has grown up.'

27 Language ought to be the joint creation of poets and manual workers.

'The English People: The Future of the English People', ibid.

28 The English are probably more capable than most peoples of making revolutionary change without bloodshed. In England, if anywhere, it would be possible to abolish poverty without destroying liberty.

Ibid.

29 For all I know, by the time this book is published my view of the Soviet régime may be the generally accepted one. But what use would that be in itself? To exchange one orthodoxy for another is not necessarily an advance. The enemy is the gramophone

mind, whether or not one agrees with the record that is being played at the moment.

'The Freedom of the Press', proposed preface to *Animal Farm* (1945), first publ. in *The Times Literary Supplement* 15 September 1972, repr. in *Animal Farm* fiftieth anniversary edn (1995)

30 If liberty means anything at all it means the right to tell people what they do not want to hear. The common people still vaguely subscribe to that doctrine and act on it. In our country – it is not the same in all countries: it was not so in republican France, and it is not so in the USA today – it is the liberals who fear liberty and the intellectuals who want to do dirt on the intellect.

Ibid.

31 Four legs good, two legs bad.

Animal Farm, ch. 3 (1945). By the end of the story, the animals' revolutionary maxim has changed to 'Four legs good, two legs *better*' (ch. 10).

32 All animals are equal but some animals are more equal than others.

Ibid., ch. 10. The animals' commandment as it appeared at the end of the story, originally 'All animals are equal.'

33 To walk through the ruined cities of Germany is to feel an actual doubt about the continuity of civilization.

Observer 8 April 1945

34 Serious sport has nothing to do with fair play. It is bound up with hatred, jealousy, boastfulness, and disregard of all the rules and sadistic pleasure in witnessing violence: in other words it is war minus the shooting.

'Sporting Spirit', publ. in *Tribune* 14 December 1945, repr. in *Shooting an Elephant* (1950)

35 He is a man of thirty-five, but looks fifty. He is bald, has varicose veins and wears spectacles, or would wear them if his only pair were not chronically lost. If things are normal with him, he will be suffering from malnutrition, but if he has recently had a lucky streak, he will be suffering from a hangover. At present it is half past eleven in the morning, and according to his schedule he should have started work two hours ago; but even if he had made any serious effort to start he would have been frustrated by the almost continuous ringing of the telephone bell, the yells of the baby, the rattle of an electric drill out in the street, and the heavy boots of his creditors clumping up the stairs. The most recent interruption was the arrival of the second post, which brought him two circulars and an income tax demand printed in red. Needless to say this person is a writer.

'Confessions of a Book Reviewer' (1946), repr. in *The Collected Essays, Journalism and Letters of George Orwell*, vol. 4 (ed. Sonia Orwell and Ian Angus, 1968)

36 The Catholic and the Communist are alike in assuming that an opponent cannot be both honest and intelligent.

'The Prevention of Literature', first publ. in *Polemic* January 1946, repr. in *Collected Essays* (1961)

37 In our time, political speech and writing are largely the defence of the indefensible.

'Politics and the English Language', first publ. in *Horizon* April 1946, repr. in *Shooting an Elephant* (1950)

38 The great enemy of clear language is insincerity. When there is a gap between one's real and one's declared aims, one turns as it were instinctively to long words and exhausted idioms, like a cuttlefish squirting out ink.

Ibid.

39 The quickest way of ending a war is to lose it.

'Second Thoughts on James Burnham', first publ. in *Polemic* May 1946, repr. in *Shooting an Elephant* (1950)

40 No one can look back on his schooldays and say with truth that they were altogether unhappy.

'Such, Such were the Joys', written 1947, first publ. in *Partisan Review* September/October 1952, repr. in *The Collected Essays, Journalism and Letters of George Orwell*, vol. 4 (ed. Sonia Orwell and Ian Angus, 1968). Orwell himself attended Eton.

41 It was a bright, cold day in April and the clocks were striking thirteen.

Nineteen Eighty-Four, pt 1, ch. 1 (1949). Opening words of book.

42 BIG BROTHER IS WATCHING YOU.

Caption to 'Ingsoc' poster, ibid. The poster is described as 'one of those pictures which are so contrived that the eyes follow you about when you move'.

43 War is peace. Freedom is slavery. Ignorance is strength.

Ingsoc party slogan, ibid.

44 Who controls the past controls the future: who controls the present controls the past.

Ingsoc party slogan, ibid., ch. 3

45 Don't you see that the whole aim of Newspeak is to narrow the range of thought? In the end we shall make thoughtcrime literally impossible, because there will be no words in which to express it.

Symes, ibid., ch. 5

46 Freedom is the freedom to say that two plus two make four. If that is granted, all else follows.

Winston Smith writing in his diary, ibid., pt 2, ch. 7

47 *Doublethink* means the power of holding two contradictory beliefs in one's mind simultaneously, and accepting both of them.
Extract from Goldstein's book, ibid., ch. 9

48 Power is not a means, it is an end. One does not establish a dictatorship in order to safeguard a revolution; one makes the revolution in order to establish the dictatorship.
O'Brien, ibid., pt 3, ch. 3

49 If you want a vision of the future, imagine a boot stamping on a human face – forever.
Ibid.

50 Saints should always be judged guilty until they are proved innocent.
'Reflections on Gandhi', first publ. in *Partisan Review* January 1949, repr. in *Shooting an Elephant* (1950). Orwell expressed scepticism of all forms of sainthood: 'It is probable,' he wrote, 'that some who achieve or aspire to sainthood have never felt much temptation to be human beings.'

51 One cannot really be a Catholic and grown-up.
Manuscript Notebook (1949), repr. in *The Collected Essays, Journalism and Letters of George Orwell*, vol. 4 (ed. Sonia Orwell and Ian Angus, 1968)

52 At 50, everyone has the face he deserves.
Ibid. Last entry in Orwell's notebook, 17 April 1949. ALBERT CAMUS, in *The Fall* (1956), expressed much the same notion: 'After a certain age every man is responsible for his face.'

John Osborne (1929–94)
BRITISH PLAYWRIGHT

His character Jimmy Porter in Look Back in Anger *(1956, filmed 1958) became the mouthpiece of a generation of 'angry young men'. Milton Shulman, in the* Evening Standard, *wrote that the play 'aims at being a despairing cry but achieves only the stature of a self-pitying snivel', but for others it resonated strongly and revitalized British theatre. The* Entertainer *(1957, filmed 1960) was equally successful.*

1 Why do I do this every Sunday? Even the book reviews seem to be the same as last week's. Different books – same reviews.
Jimmy Porter, in *Look Back in Anger*, act 1 (1956). Opening words of play.

2 Oh heavens, how I long for a little ordinary human enthusiasm. Just enthusiasm – that's all. I want to hear a warm, thrilling voice cry out Hallelujah! Hallelujah! I'm alive!
Ibid.

3 I don't think one 'comes down' from

Jimmy's university. According to him, it's not even red brick, but white tile.
Alison, ibid., act 2, sc.1

4 Anyone who's never watched somebody die is suffering from a pretty bad case of virginity.
Jimmy Porter, ibid.

5 The whole point of a sacrifice is that you give up something you never really wanted in the first place . . . People are doing it around you all the time. They give up their careers, say – or their beliefs – or sex.
Ibid., act 3, sc. 1

6 There aren't any good, brave causes left. If the big bang does come, and we all get killed off, it won't be in aid of the old-fashioned grand design. It'll just be for the Brave New-nothing-very-much-thank-you. About as pointless and inglorious as stepping in front of a bus. No, there's nothing left for it, me boy, but to let yourself be butchered by the women.
Ibid.

7 It's no good trying to fool yourself about love. You can't fall into it like a soft job, without dirtying up your hands. It takes muscle and guts. And if you can't bear the thought of messing up your nice, clean soul, you'd better give up the whole idea of life, and become a saint. Because you'll never make it as a human being. It's either this world or the next.
Ibid., sc.2

8 What are we hoping to get out of it, what's it all in aid of – is it really just for the sake of a gloved hand waving at you from a golden coach?
Jean, in *The Entertainer*, no. 10 (1957)

9 Here we are, we're alone in the universe, there's no God, it just seems that it all began by something as simple as sunlight striking on a piece of rock. And here we are. We've only got ourselves. Somehow, we've just got to make a go of it. *We've only got ourselves.*
Ibid., no.12

10 It's easy to answer the ultimate questions – it saves you bothering with the immediate ones.
George, in *Epitaph for George Dillon*, act 2 (1958, written with Anthony Creighton)

11 Damn you, England. You're rotting now, and quite soon you'll disappear. My hate will outrun you yet if only for a few seconds. I wish it could be eternal.
Letter to *Tribune* 18 August 1961

12 Inside every playwright there is a Falstaff,

gathering like a boil to be lanced by his
liege employers – fashion and caprice.

Almost a Gentleman, ch. 18 (autobiography,
1991)

13 What we remember is what we become.
What we have forgotten is more kindly
and disturbs only our dreams. We become
resemblances of our past.

Ibid., ch. 26

14 I have only one regret remaining now in
this matter of Adolf. It is simply that I was
unable to look down upon her open coffin
and, like that bird in the Book of Tobit,
drop a good, large mess in her eye.

Ibid., ch. 28. 'Adolf' was Osborne's name for his
wife, JILL BENNETT. Tobit, a pious Jew in the
Apocrypha's Book of Tobit, was blinded by sparrows' droppings.

15 Homophobia may be offensive but the
other side of the coin is just as noisome,
whatever they may tell you in Euroboy or
Zipper.

Spectator 17 December 1994

Peter O'Toole (b. 1932)

IRISH-BORN BRITISH ACTOR

*An established Shakespearian actor, he achieved
international recognition in the title role of the
film* Lawrence of Arabia *(1962). He later played
the dissipated Jeffrey Bernard on stage (1990s), a
part ideally suited to his erratic and often inebriated style.*

1 The only exercise I get these days is walking behind the coffins of my friends who
take exercise.

Quoted in the *Observer* 1 August 1999

John Otway (b. 1953)

BRITISH ROCK MUSICIAN

*He achieved short-lived stardom in 1977 when,
together with Wild Willy Barrett, he had a hit with
the punk-ish 'Really Free'. He repeated his chart
success in 2002 with the cheesy 'Bunsen Burner'.*

1 There's no point in success if you don't let
it go to your head. That's what it's for.

Quoted in the *Sunday Correspondent* 6 May
1990. Otway spent recklessly after signing a
record contract with a record company aged
twenty-four, including the purchase of a Bentley
which he was never able to drive.

Wilfred Owen (1893–1918)

BRITISH POET

*He received the Military Cross as an infantry
officer in the First World War, although he was
traumatized by the experience of trench warfare.*
SIEGFRIED SASSOON *encouraged him to write
about what Owen called 'the pity of war', and published his poems after Owen's death in action, a
week before the Armistice.* YEATS *characterized
him as 'all blood, dirt and sucked sugar stick'.*

1 *What passing-bells for these who die as
cattle?*
Only the monstrous anger of the guns.

'Anthem for Doomed Youth', written 1917, publ.
in *The Poems of Wilfred Owen* (ed. Edmund
Blunden, 1931)

2 *Red lips are not so red*
*As the stained stones kissed by the English
dead.*

'Greater Love', written 1917, publ. ibid. Opening
lines of poem.

3 *If you could hear, at every jolt, the blood*
*Come gargling from the froth-corrupted
lungs,*
Bitter as the cud
*Of vile, incurable sores on innocent
tongues, –*
*My friend, you would not tell with such
high zest*
To children ardent for some desperate glory,
The old Lie: Dulce et decorum est
Pro patria mori.

'Dulce et Decorum Est', written 1918, publ. ibid.

4 *Was it for this the clay grew tall?*
O what made fatuous sunbeams toil
To break earth's sleep at all?

'Futility', written 1918, publ. ibid.

5 *Courage was mine, and I had mystery,*
Wisdom was mine, and I had mastery.

'Strange Meeting', written 1918, publ. ibid.

6 *I am the enemy you killed, my friend.*
I knew you in this dark; for so you frowned
*Yesterday through me as you jabbed and
killed.*
*I parried; but my hands were loath and
cold.*
Let us sleep now . . .

Ibid. Closing lines of poem, of which variant versions exist.

7 Above all I am not concerned with Poetry.
My subject is War, and the pity of War.
The Poetry is in the pity.

Draft preface, written 1918, publ. ibid. The lines
were the motto for Benjamin Britten's *War
Requiem* (1962), which combined Owen's poems
with the Latin Mass for the Dead.

8 All a poet can do to-day is warn. That is
why the true Poets must be truthful.

Ibid.

Amos Oz (b. 1939)

ISRAELI NOVELIST

*Originally Amos Klausner. Called 'Israel's most
persuasive spokesman to the outside world' by the
poet D. J. Enright, he is the author of novels and
short stories dealing with modern and historical
Israel, notably* My Michael *(1972).*

1 Zionism is not a first name but a surname,
a family name, and this family is divided,

feuding over the question of a 'master plan' for the enterprise.

In the Land of Israel, 'An Argument on Life and Death (B)' (1983)

2 It is crystal clear to me that if Arabs put down a draft resolution blaming Israel for the recent earthquake in Iran it would probably have a majority, the US would veto it and Britain and France would abstain.

The Times 24 October 1990. Referring to Israel's refusal to cooperate with UN attempts to carry out an inquiry after Israeli police fired on demonstrators at Temple Mount, Jerusalem.

Cynthia Ozick (b. 1928)

US AUTHOR

Her work, deeply rooted in Jewish culture and folklore, has been praised by A. ALVAREZ *for its* 'crooked flights of imagination'. *Her novels include her first,* Trust *(1966), and her short stories are published in* The Pagan Rabbi *(1971).*

1 Wondrous hole! Magical hole! Dazzlingly influential hole! Noble and effulgent hole! From this hole everything follows logically: first the baby, then the placenta, then, for years and years and years until death, a way of life. It is all logic, and she who lives by the hole will live also by its logic. It is, appropriately, logic with a hole in it.

'The Hole/Birth Catalog', publ. in *Ms.* October 1972, repr. in *The First Ms. Reader* (ed. Francine Klagsbrun, 1972)

2 The usefulness of madmen is famous: they demonstrate society's logic flagrantly carried out down to its last scrimshaw scrap.

Ibid.

Vance Packard (1914–96)
US AUTHOR AND JOURNALIST

Described as 'a blend of amateur sociologist and crusading journalist', he addresses anxieties raised by rapid social change. His most influential work, The Hidden Persuaders *(1957), highlights the incursions of consumer advertising.*

1 The professional persuaders . . . see us as bundles of day-dreams, misty hidden yearnings, guilt complexes, irrational emotional blockages. We are image lovers given to impulsive and compulsive acts. We annoy them with our seemingly senseless quirks, but we please them with our growing docility in responding to their manipulation of symbols that stir us to action.

The Hidden Persuaders, ch. 1 (1957)

Reginald Paget (1908–90)
BRITISH POLITICIAN

Baron Paget of Northampton. The scion of five generations of Conservative politicians, he held the Labour seat for Northampton 1945–74. He was outspoken against HAROLD WILSON *and was said to be the slowest speaker in the House.*

1 When sexual indulgence has reduced a man to the shape of Lord Hailsham, sexual continence involves no more than a sense of the ridiculous.

Speech to House of Commons, 17 June 1963, during a debate on the Profumo affair, quoted in *The Fine Art of Political Wit,* ch. 12 (1964) by Leon Harris. Paget was one of the few who spoke up for Profumo during the scandal. BERNARD LEVIN called his words 'of such deadly and elegant cruelty that its like had not been fashioned in England since the death of Pope'.

Camille Paglia (b. 1947)
US AUTHOR AND CRITIC

In her magnum opus Sexual Personae *(1990) and subsequent books, she berates orthodox feminist theory for downplaying the role of eroticism. Her fast-talking, contentious style has alienated many. 'I'm an egomaniac,' she admitted. 'I have no rivals . . . I was born with the killer instinct.'*

1 Men know they are sexual exiles. They wander the earth seeking satisfaction, craving and despising, never content. There is nothing in that anguished motion for women to envy.

Sexual Personae ch. 1 (1990)

2 Male urination really *is* a kind of accomplishment, an arc of transcendence. A woman merely waters the ground she stands on.

Ibid.

3 Pornography is human imagination in tense theatrical action; its violations are a

protest against the violations of our freedom by nature.
Ibid.

4 Out with stereotypes, feminism proclaims.
But stereotypes are the west's stunning
sexual personae, the vehicles of art's
assault against nature. The moment there
is imagination, there is myth.
Ibid.

5 Popular culture is the new Babylon, into
which so much art and intellect now flow.
It is our imperial sex theater, supreme
temple of the western eye. We live in the
age of idols. The pagan past, never dead,
flames again in our mystic hierarchies of
stardom.
Ibid., ch. 4

6 Television is actually closer to reality than
anything in books. The madness of TV is
the madness of human life.
Harper's March 1991

7 There is no female Mozart because there is
no female Jack the Ripper.
International Herald Tribune 26 April 1991

8 Gay men may seek sex without emotion;
lesbians often end up in emotion without
sex.
'Homosexuality at the Fin de Siècle', publ. in
Esquire October 1991, repr. in Sex, Art, and
American Culture (1992)

9 Gay men are guardians of the masculine
impulse. To have anonymous sex in a dark
alleyway is to pay homage to the dream of
male freedom. The unknown stranger is a
wandering pagan god. The altar, as in pre-
history, is anywhere you kneel.
Ibid.

10 If you live in rock and roll, as I do, you see
the reality of sex, of male lust and women
being aroused by male lust. It attracts
women. It doesn't repel them.
Interview in Playboy October 1991, repr. ibid.
'The Rape Debate'

11 When anything goes, it's women who lose.
Observer 15 December 1991

12 The prostitute is not, as feminists claim,
the victim of men but rather their conqueror, an outlaw who controls the sexual
channel between nature and culture.
'Elizabeth Taylor: Hollywood's Pagan Queen',
publ. in Penthouse March 1992, repr. in Sex, Art,
and American Culture (1992)

13 We need a new kind of feminism, one that
stresses personal responsibility and is open
to art and sex in all their dark, unconsoling
mysteries.
Sex, Art, and American Culture, Introduction
(1992)

14 If civilization had been left in female hands
we would still be living in grass huts.
Quoting herself in ibid.

Marcel Pagnol (1895–1974)

FRENCH DRAMATIST AND FILM DIRECTOR
His plays and films are rooted in his upbringing in
Marseille and rural Provence, for example Manon
des Sources (film, 1953). He founded Cahiers du
film in 1931, and in 1946 was the first film-maker
to be elected to the Académie Française.

1 One has to look out for engineers – they
begin with sewing machines and end up
with the atomic bomb.
Critique des critiques, ch. 3 (1949)

Ian Paisley (b. 1926)

NORTHERN IRISH POLITICIAN
Founder in 1951 of the Free Presbyterian Church
of Ulster, he is leader of the Democratic Unionist
Party, and has been an MP in Westminster since
1970 and an MEP since 1979. He is known for his
anti-nationalist political stance and fundamentalist religious beliefs.

1 I would rather be British than just.
Quoted in Ulster, ch. 3 (1972) by the Sunday
Times Insight Team. The remark was addressed
to Bernadette Devlin (see BERNADETTE MCALIS-
KEY) in October 1969.

2 I would be quite happy to see the Devil's
buttermilk banned from society.
Quoted in the Irish Times 14 March 1998. Referring to draught Guinness.

3 There are various ways to martyr a man.
You can lie about him, and I have been
lied about. You can ostracise him, and the
fundamentalists have been ostracised. You
can defame him. You can seek to destroy
him. You can, first of all, kill his character.
And my character has been assassinated
across the world by the media.
Quoted in the Guardian 25 April 1998. 'They're
not against me personally,' he continued, 'I
recognise that. They're against my preaching,
because I won't give in . . . But I am not sacrific-
ing my religious views for anybody. I am a captive to the Bible.'

Michael Palin (b. 1943)

BRITISH ACTOR, AUTHOR AND TELEVISION
PRESENTER
Since working as a member of the MONTY
PYTHON'S FLYING CIRCUS team (1969–74), he
has appeared in the film A Fish Called Wanda
(1988), presented travelogues for BBC TV and
written the novel Hemingway's Chair (1995, televised 1999).

1 Travel, at its best, is a process of continually conquering disbelief.
Pole to Pole, 'Day 20' (1992)

Arnold Palmer (b. 1929)
US GOLFER

A popularizer of golf in the 1950s and '60s, he won all the major professional titles except for the USA PGA championship, and was the first golfer to earn $1 million prize-money.

1 Concentration comes out of a combination of confidence and hunger.

Quoted in 'Stairway to Heaven' (1993) by Timothy O'Grady, repr. as 'Playing Handball with Zeus' in *The Esquire Book of Sports Writing* (ed. Greg Williams, 1995)

Vance Palmer (1885–1959)
AUSTRALIAN AUTHOR AND POET

Best known for his novel The Passage *(1930), he also wrote stories, plays and essays, and with his wife, the critic Nettie Palmer, helped set up the Pioneer Players in Melbourne.*

1 It is the business of Art to give things shape. Anyone who takes no delight in the firm outline of an object, or in its essential character, has no artistic sense. . . . He cannot even be nourished by Art. Like Ephraim, he feeds upon the East wind, which has no boundaries.

'On Boundaries' (1921), repr. in *Intimate Portraits* (ed. H. P. Heseltine, 1969)

2 The truth is that literature, particularly fiction, is not the pure medium we sometimes assume it to be. Response to it is affected by things other than its own intrinsic quality; by a curiosity or lack of it about the people it deals with, their outlook, their way of life.

'Fragment of Autobiography' (1958), repr. ibid.

Tara Palmer-Tomkinson (b. 1971)
BRITISH SOCIALITE

Dubbed the original 'It girl', and a media celebrity, she has been a bra model and gossip columnist, and makes frequent television appearances.

1 I am a drug addict, not a paedophile.

Quoted in *The Times* 16 October 1999. Denying that she had slept with Prince William.

Emmeline Pankhurst (1857–1928)
BRITISH SUFFRAGETTE

She founded the Women's Franchise League in 1889 and, supported by her daughters Christabel and SYLVIA PANKHURST, *the Women's Social and Political Union in 1903. Their campaign to obtain the vote for women led to her arrest and imprisonment on several occasions.*

1 We never went to prison in order to be martyrs. We went there in order that we might obtain the rights of citizenship. We were willing to break laws that we might force men to give us the right to make laws.

My Own Story, pt 2, ch. 8 (1914)

Sylvia Pankhurst (1882–1960)
BRITISH POLITICAL ACTIVIST

With her mother EMMELINE PANKHURST *and sister Christabel she co-founded the Women's Social and Political Union, but broke with it to form the East London Federation. In 1914 she established* The Women's Dreadnought *(later called* The Workers' Dreadnought*).*

1 Some people say that the lives of working women are too hard and their education too small for them to become a powerful voice in winning the vote. Such people have forgotten their history.

The Women's Dreadnought 8 March 1914, quoted in *Sylvia Pankhurst: A Life in Radical Politics*, ch. 3 (1999) by Mary Davis

2 International solidarity is a sentiment which only attains a sturdy growth amongst those who are fully convinced that capitalism has had its day.

India and the Earthly Paradise (1926), quoted ibid., ch. 6

Charlie Parker (1920–55)
US JAZZ MUSICIAN

Nicknamed 'Bird' or 'Yardbird', he was a master alto sax player, composer and bandleader, who, along with trumpeter Dizzy Gillespie, helped to create the bebop style of jazz with such recordings as 'Ornithology' (1944–7).

1 Music is your own experience, your own thoughts, your wisdom. If you don't live it, it won't come out of your horn. They teach you there's a boundary line to music. But, man, there's no boundary line to art.

Quoted in *Hear Me Talkin' to Ya*, 'Coda' (ed. Nat Shapiro and Nat Hentoff, 1955)

Dorothy Parker (1893–1967)
US HUMOROUS WRITER

Described by ALEXANDER WOOLLCOTT *as 'a combination of Little Nell and Macbeth', she became drama critic at Vanity Fair in 1917, moving to* Life *soon after with* ROBERT BENCHLEY *and* ROBERT SHERWOOD. *All three became key figures of the Algonquin literary circle in the 1920s. Her popular writings include* Enough Rope *(poetry, 1926) and* Here Lies *(short stories, 1939).*

1 Brevity is the soul of lingerie.

Caption publ. in *Vogue*, 1916, quoted in *While Rome Burns*, 'Our Mrs Parker' (1934) by Alexander Woollcott. An allusion to Shakespeare, 'Brevity is the soul of wit' (*Hamlet* act 2, sc. 2).

2 Where's the man could ease a heart
Like a satin gown?

'The Satin Dress', publ. in *Enough Rope* (1926)

3 *Oh, life is a glorious cycle of song,*
  A medley of extemporanea;
  And love is a thing that can never go wrong;
  And I am Marie of Roumania.
  'Comment', publ. ibid.

4 *Razors pain you;*
  Rivers are damp;
  Acids stain you;
  And drugs cause cramp.
  Guns aren't lawful;
  Nooses give;
  Gas smells awful;
  You might as well live.
  'Résumé', publ. ibid.

5 *Scratch a lover, and find a foe.*
  'Ballade of a Great Weariness', publ. ibid.

6 *Why is it no one ever sent me yet*
  One perfect limousine, do you suppose?
  Ah no, it's always just my luck to get
  One perfect rose.
  'One Perfect Rose', publ. ibid.

7 *Men seldom make passes*
  At girls who wear glasses.
  'News Item', publ. ibid.

8 *If, with the literate, I am*
  Impelled to try an epigram,
  I never seek to take the credit;
  We all assume that Oscar said it.
  'A Pig's-Eye View of Literature', publ. in *Sunset Gun* (1928)

9 *Tonstant Weader fwowed up.*
  New Yorker 20 October 1928, repr. in *The Collected Dorothy Parker*, pt 2 (1973). Closing words of review of *The House at Pooh Corner*, in Parker's 'Constant Reader' column.

10 *Drink, and dance and laugh and lie,*
   Love the reeling midnight through,
   For tomorrow we shall die!
   (But, alas, we never do.)
   'The Flaw in Paganism', publ. in *Death and Taxes* (1931)

11 **How do they know?**
   Remark on hearing the announcement that CALVIN COOLIDGE had died (1933), quoted in the *Paris Review* summer 1956, repr. in *Writers at Work* (first series, ed. Malcolm Cowley, 1958)

12 *The House Beautiful* **is the play lousy.**
   New Yorker, 1933, quoted ibid. Review of *The House Beautiful* by Channing Pollock.

13 **She runs the gamut of emotions from A to B.**
   Of KATHARINE HEPBURN, in theatre review of *The Lake* (1933), quoted in obituary, *Publishers Weekly* 19 June 1967

14 **Excuse my dust.**
   Suggested epitaph, quoted in *While Rome Burns*, 'Our Mrs Parker' (1934) by ALEXANDER WOOLLCOTT

15 **That woman speaks eighteen languages and can't say No in any of them.**
   Of a departing guest, quoted ibid.

16 **And there was that wholesale libel on a Yale prom. If all the girls attending it were laid end to end, Mrs Parker said, she wouldn't be at all surprised.**
   Ibid.

17 **Good work, Mary. We all knew you had it in you.**
   Quoted ibid. Telegram to a friend (Mrs Robert Sherwood) who had become a mother after a prolonged pregnancy.

18 **Sorrow is tranquility remembered in emotion.**
   'Sentiment', publ. in *Here Lies* (1939). Adapting Wordsworth, 'Poetry . . . takes its origin from emotion recollected in tranquillity' (*Lyrical Ballads*, Preface to second edn, 1801).

19 **All those writers who write about their childhood! Gentle God, if I wrote about mine you wouldn't sit in the same room with me.**
   Interview in the *Paris Review* summer 1956, repr. in *Writers at Work* (first series, ed. Malcolm Cowley, 1958)

20 **As artists they're rot, but as providers they're oil wells; they gush. Norris said she never wrote a story unless it was fun to do. I understand Ferber whistles at her typewriter. And there was that poor sucker Flaubert rolling around on his floor for three days looking for the right word.**
   On women writers, ibid.

21 **There's a helluva distance between wisecracking and wit. Wit has truth in it; wisecracking is simply calisthenics with words.**
   Ibid.

22 **Hollywood money isn't money. It's congealed snow, melts in your hand, and there you are.**
   Ibid. 'I can't talk about Hollywood,' Parker declared. 'It was a horror to me when I was there and it's a horror to look back on. I can't imagine how I did it. When I got away from it I couldn't even refer to the place by name. "Out there," I called it.'

23 **It's not the tragedies that kill us, it's the messes.**
   Ibid.

24 **This is not a novel to be tossed aside lightly. It should be thrown with great force.**
   Book review, quoted in *The Algonquin Wits* (ed. Robert E. Drennan, 1968)

25 **Enjoyed it! One more drink and I'd have been under the host.**
   Quoted ibid. On being asked whether she had enjoyed a party.

26 **You can lead a horticulture, but you can't make her think.**

Quoted in *You Might As Well Live* (1970) by John Keats. On being challenged to make a sentence using the word 'horticulture'.

27 **It serves me right for putting all my eggs in one bastard.**

On her abortion, quoted ibid., pt 2, ch. 3

Lord Parker (1900–1972)

BRITISH JUDGE

Hubert Lister, Baron Parker of Waddington. He was made a Lord Justice of Appeal in 1954 and was Lord Chief Justice of England 1958–71.

1 **A judge is not supposed to know anything about the facts of life until they have been presented in evidence and explained to him at least three times.**

Quoted in the *Observer* 12 March 1961

Ross Parker (1914–74) and Hugh Charles (1907–95)

BRITISH SONGWRITERS

The two collaborated on songs throughout the Second World War. Hugh Charles also worked with NOEL GAY, *among others, and later concentrated on theatre productions. See also* VERA LYNN 1.

1 *There'll always be an England*
While there's a country lane,
Wherever there's a cottage small
Beside a field of grain.

'There'll Always Be an England' (song, 1939). Originally performed by BILLY COTTON and his Orchestra.

C. Northcote Parkinson (1909–93)

BRITISH HISTORIAN AND POLITICAL SCIENTIST

Cyril Northcote Parkinson. He wrote a number of historical, political and economic works, but is best known for Parkinson's Law *(1957), a tongue-in-cheek look at businesses and bureaucracies.*

1 **Work expands so as to fill the time available for its completion. General recognition of this fact is shown in the proverbial phrase 'It is the busiest man who has time to spare'.**

Parkinson's Law or The Pursuit of Progress, 'Parkinson's Law or the Rising Pyramid' (1957). Opening words of book.

2 **A committee is organic rather than mechanical in its nature: it is not a structure but a plant. It takes root and grows, it flowers, wilts, and dies, scattering the seed from which other committees will bloom in their turn.**

Ibid., 'Directors and Councils or Coefficient of Inefficiency'

3 **The Law of Triviality . . . briefly stated, it** means that the time spent on any item of the agenda will be in inverse proportion to the sum involved.

Ibid., 'High Finance or the Point of Vanishing Interest'

4 **The man who is denied the opportunity of taking decisions of importance begins to regard as important the decisions he is allowed to take.**

Ibid., 'Pension Point or the Age of Retirement'

5 **Expenditure rises to meet income.**

The Law and the Profits, ch. 1 (1960). Opening sentence of book.

6 **Expansion means complexity, and complexity decay.**

In-laws and Outlaws, 'The Third Law' (1962)

Cecil Parkinson (b. 1931)

BRITISH POLITICIAN

Baron Parkinson of Carnforth. Elected a Conservative MP in 1970, he rose to become party Chairman (1981–3) and a close confidant of MARGARET THATCHER. *He resigned following revelations about his private life, but rejoined the cabinet 1987–90, and was again party Chairman 1997–8.*

1 **From the days when the miners' leaders thought they owned the Government to the day when every miner owns part of his own mine – that's the British revolution.**

Quoted in the *Daily Mail* 13 October 1988

2 **It is better to be a has-been than a never-was.**

Quoted in the *Guardian* 29 June 1990

3 **In politics people give you what they think you deserve and deny you what they think you want.**

Television interview, ITV, 19 November 1990

Michael Parkinson (b. 1935)

BRITISH JOURNALIST AND BROADCASTER

Renowned for his smooth style and professional composure, he hosted the television chat show Parkinson (1971–82 and from 1998), and was co-founder and presenter of TV-am (1983–4). He has also written widely on sport.

1 **The kind of show I do consists of two consenting adults performing unnatural acts in public.**

Quoted in the *Sunday Times* 27 December 1987. On his new chat show, *One to One*, on Yorkshire TV 1987–8.

2 **Generally speaking, being famous is a bit like having measles. It is a minor affliction and the rash soon disappears. But for some it never goes away. It dictates their life and shapes their circumstance. They and their family are forever on display.**

Quoted in the *Observer* 11 March 2001

Norman Parkinson (1913–90)

BRITISH FASHION PHOTOGRAPHER

Originally Ronald William Parkinson Smith. For fifty years he was one of Britain's most famous fashion and portrait photographers, noted for his official portraits of the royal family.

1 I could never bear to be buried with people to whom I had not been introduced.

Quoted in obituary in the *Guardian* 16 February 1990

Matthew Parris (b. 1949)

BRITISH POLITICIAN AND JOURNALIST

Since his parliamentary career as a Conservative MP (1979–86), he has been presenter of LWT's Weekend World (1986–8), parliamentary sketch-writer for The Times and columnist for the Spectator.

1 Being an MP feeds your vanity and starves your self-respect.

The Times 9 February 1994

2 Since the dawn of man every politician has been torn between a wish to say something memorable, and a terror of saying something which is remembered.

Introduction to *Read My Lips* (1996) by Matthew Parris and Phil Mason

3 As we ridicule the po-faced puritans of the Left, we forget how ripe for ridicule are the sniffy certainties of our own creed. . . . We too, we who are PS – the politically sound – have our thought police, our pursed lips and our mental phrasebook of sound (and unsound) expressions, sound (and unsound) attitudes, sound (and unsound) belief.

Spectator 19 February 2000. Examples given by Parris of 'non-PS' expressions are 'ethnicity', 'gender' and 'sexuality', for which the equivalent 'PS' terms would be, respectively, 'race', 'sex' and 'which team is he playing for?'

Elsie Clews Parsons (1874–1941)

US ANTHROPOLOGIST AND FEMINIST CRITIC

Dubbed 'the Left's favourite anthropologist', she was the first woman president of the American Anthropological Association (1940–41). Her writings include The Old-Fashioned Woman (1913) and Fear and Conventionality (1914).

1 I wonder if this notion that women have had a free scope in the arts is not due to a misunderstanding of the arts themselves, to ignorance of their ritualistic origins and conditions, to oversight of the apprenticeship they demand, in short to an amateurish or dilettante notion of the nature of art? Is it not possible that art, true to its

origin in priestcraft, has been pre-eminently exclusive of women . . . ?

Narrator (Cynthia), in *The Journal of a Feminist*, March 1914 (1994)

2 Some day there may be a 'masculism' movement to allow men to act 'like women'.

Ibid. April 1914

Talcott Parsons (1902–79)

US SOCIOLOGIST

His principal works The Structure of Social Action (1937) and The Social System (1951) proposed a functionalist view of society that prevailed in US sociology from the 1940s until the 1960s.

1 It is a fact that social existence depends to a large extent on a moral consensus of its members and that the penalty of its too radical breakdown is social extinction. This fact is one which the type of liberal whose theoretical background is essentially utilitarian is all too apt to ignore.

The Structure of Social Action, vol. 1, ch. 10 (1937)

2 Science is intimately integrated with the whole social structure and cultural tradition. They mutually support one other – only in certain types of society can science flourish, and conversely without a continuous and healthy development and application of science such a society cannot function properly.

The Social System, ch. 8 (1951)

Tony Parsons (b. 1955)

BRITISH JOURNALIST AND NOVELIST

A 'street-wise' writer on popular culture, he was, at the age of eighteen, a leader writer on the New Musical Express and one of the first champions of punk. Proceeding to the Daily Telegraph, the Daily Mirror and GQ, he had success with his New Man novel Man and Boy (1999).

1 The trouble with the working class today is that they are such peasants. Something has died in them – a sense of grace, all feelings of community, their intelligence, decency and wit. Socialism is finished here because it is no longer possible to feel sentimental about the workers.

'The Tattooed Jungle', publ. in *Arena* September/October 1989, repr. in *Dispatches from the Front Line of Popular Culture* (1994)

2 Begging defaces the city, degrades the spirit. It dehumanises you as well as them; it brutalises us all. You learn to walk past these people, you have to, and it makes it easier to turn away from the truly needy. These professional leeches, big strapping lads some of them, harden your heart, put

calloused on your soul. They make every cry for help seem like junk mail.

'Street Trash', publ. in *Arena* September/October 1991, repr. ibid.

3 **Being middle class means always having to say you're sorry.**

'The Polenta Jungle', publ. in *Arena* March/April 1993, repr. ibid. See ERICH SEGAL 1

4 **The discreet charms of the bourgeoisie have been underrated for too long. They are the most cultured class. The hardest working. They believe in the welfare state but are aware of its corrupting nature. Yes, there are many things to despise about the middle class. But, unlike the nobs and the riff-raff, they do not know their place. They believe in self-improvement.**

Ibid.

5 **There are few things in this world more reassuring than an unhappy Lottery winner.**

Observer 8 November 1998

6 **Pornography is many things to many men. But it is never adult. Pornography exists in a state of perpetual adolescence. . . . Planet porn is Disneyland for habitual monkey-spankers.**

GQ January 2000

Frances Partridge (b. 1900)

BRITISH TRANSLATOR AND AUTHOR

Born in Bloomsbury, she was for years at the centre of the Bloomsbury literary set whose exploits she portrayed in her memoirs Love in Bloomsbury *(1981) and* A Bloomsbury Album *(1987). She was a literary translator for much of her life.*

1 **It is a purely relative matter where one draws the plimsoll-line of condemnation, and . . . if you find the whole of humanity falls below it you have simply made a mistake and drawn it too high. And are probably below it yourself.**

Journal entry, 3 September 1959, publ. in *Julia*, ch. 17 (1983)

Pier Paolo Pasolini (1922–75)

ITALIAN FILM-MAKER AND AUTHOR

Themes of violence, depravity and eroticism run through his early novels about slum life in Rome and his films, which include The Gospel According to St Matthew *(1964) and* The Canterbury Tales *(1972). 'I do nothing to console, nothing to embellish reality, nothing to sell the goods,' he stated. He was murdered in Ostia, allegedly by a homosexual prostitute.*

1 **In my desperation there is no more purity, no more innocence. . . . Now I am a desert completely explored; there is no way to save me. I am all consciousness.**

Entry for 21 November 1946, in the second of Pasolini's 'Red Notebooks', publ. in *Pasolini Requiem*, ch. 9 (1992) by David Barth Schwartz

2 **Don't think for a moment that the middle-class journalist cares at all for the truth; to be in some way honest; to be personal. He completely depersonalizes himself, to allow himself to speak to a hypothetical public, one which he naturally considers right-thinking but idiotic, normal but ferocious, uncensored but vile.**

'Le belle bandiere', column in *Vie Nuove* 15 October 1960, repr. ibid. ch. 16

3 **Too often a great mistake is made in discussions about censorship: that of putting the debate in the terms proposed by the censors: that is of the moralistic–sexual. Instead it is quite otherwise: one must completely ignore their hypocritical pretext, and see what should be obvious to a child, that censorship is a political issue, with sex as a simple and shameless pretext.**

Ibid. 17 December 1960

4 **The atheism of a militant Communist is the essence of religion compared to the cynicism of a capitalist: in the first, one can always find those moments of idealism, of desperation, of psychological violence, of conscious will, of faith – which are elements, even degraded, of religion – in the second one finds only Mammon.**

Ibid. 29 October 1964, ch. 18

5 **The relationship between a son and his mother is not a historical relationship, it is a purely interior, private relationship which is outside history, indeed it is meta-historical, and therefore ideologically unproductive, whereas what produces history is the relationship of hatred and love between father and son.**

'Perché quella di Edipo è una storia', Introduction to *Oedipus Rex* (film, 1967), repr. in *Pasolini Requiem*, ch. 20 (1992) by David Barth Schwartz

6 **Death does determine life. . . . Once life is finished it acquires a sense; up to that point it has not got a sense; its sense is suspended and therefore ambiguous.**

Pasolini On Pasolini: Interviews with Oswald Stack, ch. 3 (1969)

7 **The sexual freedom of today for most people is really only a convention, an obligation, a social duty, a social anxiety, a necessary feature of the consumer's way of life.**

'Sono Contro l'Aborto', first publ. in *Il Corriere della Sera* 19 January 1975, repr. in *Scritti Corsari* (1975)

8 **Hope? I have none and furthermore I condemn it with everything in my power. Hope is the flag, the special marker of**

hypocrisy . . . I don't believe in it. I believe
only in my own vitality.

Quoted in *Pasolini Requiem*, ch. 19 (1992) by
David Barth Schwartz

Boris Pasternak (1890–1960)

RUSSIAN POET, NOVELIST AND TRANSLATOR
*He began his literary career as a poet and author
of short fiction, but his reputation in the West was
established with his only novel Dr Zhivago (1957,
filmed 1965), an epic of the Russian Revolution
and its aftermath that was banned in the Soviet
Union. See* OSIP MANDELSTAM 4.

1 *We live in days to come, I tell them firmly,*
  And share one lot in common now. If
    crippled,
  No matter! Stay. We are in fact run over
  By the New Man in the wagon of his Plan.

  'When I Grow Weary', publ. in *Second Birth*
  (1932), repr. in *Poems* (transl. Eugene M.
  Kayden, 1959)

2 *My soul, you are a mourner*
  Of all where I survive.
  You are a mausoleum
  Of those tortured alive.

  'My Soul' (1957), repr. in *Modern Russian Poetry*
  (ed. Vladimir Markov and Merrill Sparks, 1966)

3 *The snow was falling soft and slow*
  From land to land.
  A candle flamed upon a table;
  A candle flamed.

  'Winter Night' (1957). repr. in *Poems* (transl.
  Eugene M. Kayden, 1959)

4 What is history? Its beginning is that of the
  centuries of systematic work devoted to
  the solution of the enigma of death, so that
  death itself may eventually be overcome.
  That is why people write symphonies, and
  why they discover mathematical infinity
  and electromagnetic waves.

  Nikolay Nikolayevich, in *Doctor Zhivago*, ch. 1,
  sect. 5 (1957)

5 That's metaphysics, my dear fellow. It's forbidden me by my doctor, my stomach
  won't take it.

  Ivan Ivanovich, ibid.

6 No deep and strong feeling, such as we
  may come across here and there in the
  world, is unmixed with compassion. The
  more we love, the more the object of our
  love seems to us to be a victim.

  Ibid., ch. 12, sect. 7

7 I don't like people who have never fallen
  or stumbled. Their virtue is lifeless and it
  isn't of much value. Life hasn't revealed its
  beauty to them.

  Zhivago, ibid., ch. 13, sect. 12

8 Everything established, settled, everything
  to do with home and order and the
  common round, has crumbled into dust

and been swept away in the general
upheaval and reorganization of the whole
of society. The whole human way of life
has been destroyed and ruined. All that's
left is the bare, shivering human soul,
stripped to the last shred, the naked force
of the human psyche for which nothing
has changed because it was always cold and
shivering and reaching out to its nearest
neighbour, as cold and lonely as itself.

Lara, describing life in Communist Russia, ibid.,
sect. 13

9 As far as modern writing is concerned, it is
  rarely rewarding to translate it, although it
  might be easy. . . . Translation is very
  much like copying paintings.

  Interview in *Writers at Work* (second series, ed.
  George Plimpton, 1963). 'The only interesting
  sort of translating is that of classics,' Pasternak
  declared.

10 It is no longer possible for lyric poetry to
   express the immensity of our experience.
   Life has grown too cumbersome, too complicated. We have acquired values which
   are best expressed in prose.

   Ibid.

Jan Patocka (1907–77)

CZECH PHILOSOPHER AND ACTIVIST
*Specializing in phenomenology, hermeneutics and
the philosophy of science, he lectured at Prague's
Charles University until 1948 when he was banned
following the Communist takeover. He was professor there 1965–70.*

1 The real test of a man is not how well he
  plays the role he has invented for himself,
  but how well he plays the role that destiny
  assigned to him.

  Quoted in *Disturbing the Peace*, ch. 2 (1986) by
  Václav Havel. Advice given to HAVEL.

Brian Patten (b. 1946)

BRITISH POET
*With the other 'Liverpool poets', Adrian Henri and
ROGER MCGOUGH, he was committed to poetry
as live performance. His lyrical, observational and
accessible poems are published in* Notes to the
Hurrying Man *(1969) and* Storm Damage *(1988)
among other collections.*

1 When in public poetry should take off its
  clothes and wave to the nearest person in
  sight; it should be seen in the company of
  thieves and lovers rather than that of journalists and publishers.

  'Prose Poem Towards a Definition of Itself',
  publ. in *Little Johnny's Confession* (1967)

2 *You ask for a poem.*
  And so I write you a tragedy about
  How a blade of grass
  Becomes more and more difficult to offer,
  And about how as you grow older

A blade of grass
Becomes more difficult to accept.
'A Blade of Grass', publ. in *Vanishing Trick* (1976). Closing lines of poem.

Chris Patten (b. 1944)

BRITISH POLITICIAN
Before serving as Conservative Party Chairman (1990–92), he was Minister for Overseas Development and Environment Secretary. After losing his seat as an MP he was Governor of Hong Kong (1992–7).

1 Green politics at its worst amounts to a sort of Zen fascism; less extreme, it denounces growth and seeks to stop the world so that we can all get off.
Independent 19 April 1989

2 In a democracy everybody has a right to be represented, including the jerks.
Evening Standard 2 May 1991

3 There is a sort of exotic preposterousness about a lot of elections, the way arguments are made even cruder.
Quoted in the *Observer* 30 June 1991. Patten managed the electoral campaign of 1992 which led to a fourth successive Conservative victory, though he himself lost his seat.

Tom Paulin (b. 1949)

BRITISH POET
Although born in Leeds, he is known as an Ulster poet, whose vision of a non-sectarian Ireland is expressed in such works as A State of Justice *(1977) and* The Liberty Tree *(1983).*

1 Puritan metaphor is a form of irony which has a habit of becoming literal: a dynamic millenarian rhetoric can inspire men to place actual dynamite under the status quo.
'Paisley's Progress' (1982), repr. in *Writing to the Moment* (1996)

2 *I live in the half-light*
of a strange
shivering translation
where the kingdom of letters
is like the postal system
of a frozen state
and your last question
slips through like code.
'What Kind of Formation are B Specials?', publ. in *The Liberty Tree* (1983)

3 *Maybe the true taste of it*
is knowing the limits of your own fraud-
ulence
'Middle Age', publ. in *Walking a Line* (1994)

4 His work seems endlessly subtle and intelligent, many of his cadences are perfect, but there is a malignity in it which is terrifying. It's so firm and so quiet, because like a

true politician Eliot never apologizes and he never explains.
Of T. S. ELIOT, in 'T. S. Eliot and Anti-Semitism' (review of Anthony Julius, *T. S. Eliot, Anti-Semitism and Literary Form*, 1996), publ. in *Writing to the Moment* (1996). 'I can think of no other modern writer whose prejudices have been treated with such tolerance,' wrote Paulin of Eliot.

Luciano Pavarotti (b. 1935)

ITALIAN TENOR
Along with José Carreras and Placido Domingo he is one of the 'Three Tenors' who have helped to popularize opera. His rendition of 'Nessun Dorma' was adopted as the theme tune for the 1990 football World Cup.

1 I am not a musician. I don't go in too deep. If you have the music in your head, and you sing it with your body, then you'll be all right.
Quoted in the *Observer* 27 July 1997

Cesare Pavese (1908–50)

ITALIAN POET, NOVELIST AND TRANSLATOR
His translations helped to popularize modern English and American literature in Italy. His novels include The Moon and the Bonfires *(1950) and* The House on the Hill *(1961). Regarded by some as an anti-Fascist hero, he considered himself a coward and grew disillusioned with politics.*

1 Living is like working out a long addition sum, and if you make a mistake in the first two totals you will never find the right answer. It means involving oneself in a complicated chain of circumstances.
Journal entry, 5 May 1936, publ. in *This Business of Living: Diary 1935–1950* (1952, transl. 1961)

2 Literature is a defence against the attacks of life. It says to life: 'You can't deceive me. I know your habits, foresee and enjoy watching all your reactions, and steal your secret by involving you in cunning obstructions that halt your normal flow.'
Journal entry, 10 November 1938, publ. ibid.

3 Perfect behaviour is born of complete indifference.
Ibid., 21 February 1940

4 Artists are the monks of the bourgeois state.
Ibid., 25 July 1940

5 A man is never completely alone in this world. At the worst, he has the company of a boy, a youth, and by and by a grown man – the one he used to be.
Ibid. winter 1941–2

6 The richness of life lies in memories we have forgotten.
Ibid. 13 February 1944

7 At great periods you have always felt, deep

within you, the temptation to commit suicide. *You gave yourself to it*, breached your own defences. You were a child. The idea of suicide was a protest against life; by dying, you would escape this longing for death.

Ibid. 1 January 1950. Suicide was a continuing theme in Pavese's diaries. 'No one ever lacks a good reason for suicide,' he wrote in 1938. He took his own life in a Turin hotel, shortly after being awarded the Strega Prize.

8 I have knocked about the world enough to know that one lot of flesh and blood is as good as another. But that's why you get tired and try to put down roots. To find somewhere where you belong so that you are worth more than the usual round of the seasons and last a bit longer.

Narrator (Anguilla), in *The Moon and the Bonfires*, ch. 1 (1950)

9 When they're dealing with the dead, priests are always right.

Ibid., ch. 12

Jeremy Paxman (b. 1950)
BRITISH TELEVISION PRESENTER AND JOURNALIST

Famous for his probing and abrasive style on BBC2's Newsnight, *he once asked Conservative Home Secretary Michael Howard the same question thirteen times in succession. He has also authored reflections on British society, for example* The English *(1998).*

1 The BBC is rather like a cross between the Church of England and the Post Office.

Friends in High Places, ch. 4 (1990)

2 It's very difficult to remain calm when you're listening to someone talk complete bollocks.

Quoted in the *Observer* 6 April 1997

3 I hate the word 'sneering'. I can't help the way my face looks.

Ibid.

4 It sometimes seems the Church of England thinks God is just the ultimate 'good chap'.

The English: A Portrait of a People, ch. 6 (1998)

5 The English approach to ideas is not to kill them, but to let them die of neglect.

Independent 24 October 1998

6 Things rush on [to television] at a fantastic speed, get recycled, pushed out and not thought about again. The fight is about controlling what goes through that sausage machine, which is what the spin doctors are about.

Interview in the *Guardian* 24 January 2000

Cynthia Payne (b. 1934)
BRITISH HOUSEWIFE AND HOSTESS

Revelations about her suburban 'vicarage tea-parties with sex thrown in' led to a court case and prison sentence in 1980 and formed the basis of the film Personal Services *(1987).*

1 To me it's just like having a cup of tea. After two abortions I am not particularly interested in sex, but I know it makes other people happy.

The Times 4 February 1987. Remark after being acquitted of running a brothel in Streatham, South London.

Octavio Paz (1914–98)
MEXICAN POET AND ESSAYIST

Among his poetry collections are Eagle or Sun? *(1951) and* Salamandra *(1962), which includes the long poem 'Sal'. His most important prose work is* The Labyrinth of Solitude *(1950), an analysis of Mexican culture and history. He served as a diplomat 1945–68.*

1 Modern man likes to pretend that his thinking is wide-awake. But this wide-awake thinking has led us into the mazes of a nightmare in which the torture chambers are endlessly repeated in the mirrors of reason.

The Labyrinth of Solitude, ch. 9 (1950)

2 Man, even man debased by the neo-capitalism and pseudosocialism of our time, is a marvellous being because he sometimes *speaks*. Language is the mark, the sign, not of his fall but of his original innocence. Through the Word we may regain the lost kingdom and recover powers we possessed in the far-distant past.

Alternating Current, 'André Breton or the Quest of the Beginning' (1967)

3 Art is an invention of aesthetics, which in turn is an invention of philosophers. . . . What we call art is a game.

Ibid.

4 To read a poem is to hear it with our eyes; to hear it is to see it with our ears.

Ibid., 'Recapitulations'

5 Social criticism begins with grammar and the re-establishing of meanings.

The Other Mexico: Critique of the Pyramid, 'Development and Other Mirages' (1972)

6 Wisdom lies neither in fixity nor in change, but in the dialectic between the two.

The Times 8 June 1989

7 Writers, you know, are the beggars of Western society.

Quoted in the *Independent on Sunday* 30 December 1990

Mervyn Peake (1911–68)

BRITISH AUTHOR AND ILLUSTRATOR

His fantasy trilogy, Titus Groan (1946), Gormenghast (1950) and Titus Alone (1959), became a cult classic (televised 2000), and spawned the word 'Gormenghastian'. He also wrote verse and illustrated. His ambition, he declared, was to 'create arabesques, abstracts, of thrilling colour, worlds on their own, landscapes and roofscapes and skyscapes peopled with hierophants and lords'.

1 They resemble rubber, your ladyship, ha, ha, ha. Just a core of india-rubber, with an elastic centre. Oh yes, they are. Very, very much so. Resilience is no word for it – oh dear me, no. Every ounce, a bounce, ha, ha! Every ounce, a bounce.

    Doctor Prunesquallor describing babies to the Countess of Groan, in *Titus Groan*, 'Titus is Christened' (1946)

2 My memory is so very untrustworthy. It's as fickle as a fox. Ask me to name the third lateral bloodvessel that runs east to west when I lie on my face at sundown, or the percentage of chalk to be found in the knuckles of an average spinster in her fifty-seventh year, ha, ha, ha! – or even ask me, my dear boy, to give details of the pulse rate of frogs two minutes before they die of scabies – these things are no tax upon my memory, ha, ha, ha! but ask me to remember exactly what you said your problems were, a minute ago, and you will find that my memory has forsaken me utterly.

    Doctor Prunesquallor to Steerpike, ibid., 'At the Prunesquallors'

3 There is a kind of laughter that sickens the soul. Laughter when it is out of control: when it screams and stamps its feet, and sets the bells jangling in the next town. Laughter in all its ignorance and cruelty. Laughter with the seed of Satan in it.

    Sometime, Never, 'Boy in Darkness' (1956)

4 *Each day I live in a glass room*
    Unless I break it with the thrusting
    Of my senses and pass through
    The splintered walls to the great landscape.
    'Each Day I Live in a Glass Room', publ. in *A Reverie of Bone* (1967)

Norman Vincent Peale (1898–1993)

US CLERGYMAN AND AUTHOR

He helped establish the American Foundation of Religion and Psychiatry next to the church where he was a minister in New York (1932–84), publishing his insights in his bestselling books, notably The Power of Positive Thinking (1952).

1 One of the greatest tragedies of the average person is the tendency to spend our whole lives perfecting our faults.

    The Power of Positive Thinking, ch. 15 (1952)

Patrick Henry Pearse (1879–1916)

IRISH NATIONALIST LEADER

He joined the Irish Republican Brotherhood in 1915, was appointed Commander-in-Chief of the 1916 Easter Rising and was proclaimed President of a provisional Irish government. He was shot after the failure of the Rising.

1 There are in every generation those who shrink from the ultimate sacrifice, but there are in every generation those who make it with joy and laughter and these are the salt of the generations.

    Commemoration address, 2 March 1914, Brooklyn, New York. The speech was in honour of Irish patriot Robert Emmet, executed in 1803 for his part in an abortive invasion of Ireland.

2 Life springs from death and from the graves of patriot men and women spring living nations. The Defenders of this Realm have worked well in secret and in the open. They think that they have pacified Ireland. They think that they have pacified half of us and intimidated the other half. They think that they have foreseen everything, think that they have provided against everything; but the fools, the fools, the fools! – they have left us our Fenian dead, and while Ireland holds these graves, Ireland unfree shall never be at peace.

    Graveside oration 1 August 1915, quoted in *Patrick Pearse: The Triumph of Failure*, 'Politics' (1977) by Ruth Dudley Edwards. The last part of this speech was incorporated into SEAN O'CASEY's *The Plough and the Stars*, act 2 (1926)

Hesketh Pearson (1887–1964)

BRITISH BIOGRAPHER

Having been a successful actor and theatre director, he turned to biography in 1931. His subjects included Gilbert and Sullivan (1935), GEORGE BERNARD SHAW (1942) and Benjamin Disraeli (1951).

1 Misquotation is, in fact, the pride and privilege of the learned. A widely-read man never quotes accurately, for the rather obvious reason that he has read too widely.

    Common Misquotations, Introduction (1934). 'Misquotations,' Pearson wrote, 'are the only quotations that are never misquoted.'

D. A. Pennebaker (b. 1930)

US FILM-MAKER

Don Alan Pennebaker. He is best known for his documentaries and performance footage, often linked to rock music, such as Don't Look Back (1967), a record of BOB DYLAN's 1965 English tour.

1 Films have to be made totally by fascists – there's no room for democracy in making film.

    Independent 29 July 1988

S. J. Perelman (1904–79)

US HUMORIST

Sidney Joseph Perelman. Describing himself as 'button cute, rapier keen, wafer-thin and pauper-poor', he contributed regular articles to the New Yorker. *His Hollywood screenplays included* Monkey Business *(1931) and* Horse Feathers *(1932) for the* MARX *brothers.*

1 There is nothing like a good, painstaking survey full of decimal points and guarded generalizations to put a glaze like a Sung vase on your eyeball.

Keep It Crisp (1946)

2 English life, while very pleasant, is rather bland. I expected kindness and gentility and I found it, but there is such a thing as too much couth.

Quoted in the *Observer* 24 September 1971

Shimon Peres (b. 1923)

POLISH-BORN ISRAELI POLITICIAN AND PRIME MINISTER

Originally Shimon Perski. In 1994, he shared the Nobel Peace Prize with Itzhak Rabin and YASSER ARAFAT *for helping to bring about the Israel–PLO peace accord. He was Labour Prime Minister 1984–6 and 1995–6 and Deputy Prime Minister 2001–03.*

1 Television has made dictatorship impossible, but democracy unbearable.

Quoted in the *Financial Times* 31 January 1995

Gabriel Péri (d. 1942)

FRENCH COMMUNIST DEPUTY

1 I will soon be going out to shape all the singing tomorrows.

Letter written shortly before his execution by the Germans, July 1942, quoted in *The New York Times* 11 April 1943

Anthony Perkins (1932–92)

US SCREEN ACTOR

He specialized in roles as a troubled young man before achieving international fame as Norman Bates in the film Psycho *(1960). Later films include* Catch-22 *(1970).*

1 A boy's best friend is his mother.

Norman Bates (Anthony Perkins), in *Psycho* (film, 1960, screenplay by Joseph Stefano based on novel by Robert Bloch, produced and directed by ALFRED HITCHCOCK)

2 We all go a little mad sometimes.

Ibid.

3 I have learned more about love, selflessness and human understanding in this great adventure in the world of Aids

than I ever did in the cut-throat, competitive world in which I spent my life.

Posthumous statement, publ. in the *Independent on Sunday* 20 September 1992

Carl Perkins (1932–98)

US COUNTRY AND ROCK MUSICIAN

His hit 'Blue Suede Shoes' (1956), a blend of black beat and country, became the anthem of rockabilly music. His songs were recorded by The Beatles, and he enjoyed periodic revivals of interest.

1 It's one for the money,
Two for the show,
Three to get ready,
Now go, cat, go!
But don't you step on my Blue Suede Shoes.
You can do anything but lay off my Blue Suede Shoes.

'Blue Suede Shoes' (song, 1956). A million-seller, Perkins's recording topped both Country and Rhythm 'n' Blues charts, and reached no. 2 in the pop charts, although his version was eventually eclipsed by the cover released shortly afterwards by ELVIS PRESLEY.

Eva Perón (1919–52)

ARGENTINIAN POLITICIAN

An actress before marrying JUAN PERÓN *(1945), 'Evita', as she was popularly known, became his chief adviser when he was elected President in 1946. She founded the Peronista Feminist Party in 1949 and undertook considerable work for the poor, who idolized her. See also* TIM RICE 1.

1 You will all have clothes like these some day. . . . Some day you will be able to sit next to any rich woman on a basis of complete equality. What we are fighting for is to destroy the inequality between you and the wives of your bosses.

Presidential campaign speech, 1946, quoted in *The Perón Era, 'Evita'* (1965) by Robert J. Alexander. As wife of the President, Eva Perón reportedly spent an average of 40,000 dollars annually on her dresses alone.

2 Almsgiving tends to perpetuate poverty; aid does away with it once and for all. Almsgiving leaves a man just where he was before. Aid restores him to society as an individual worthy of all respect and not as a man with a grievance. Almsgiving is the generosity of the rich; social aid levels up social inequalities. Charity separates the rich from the poor; aid raises the needy and sets him on the same level with the rich.

'My Labor in the Field of Social Aid', speech to the American Congress of Industrial Medicine, 5 December 1949

3 Never abandon the poor – they are the only ones who know how to be loyal.

Quoted in *Evita: An Intimate Portrait of Eva*

Perón (1997) by Tomás de Elia and Juan Pablo Queiroz. Spoken to Juan Perón, 25 July 1952, the day before her death.

4 When I die, take off the red varnish and replace it with a plain varnish.

Quoted by her maid, in *Eva Perón*, ch. 13 (1978) by John Barnes. Among her last words.

5 Fanaticism is the wisdom of the spirit. What matter if one is a fanatic, if one is that in the company of martyrs and heroes . . . ? In any case life has its real value not when it is lived in a spirit of egotism, just for oneself, but when one surrenders oneself, completely and fanatically, to an ideal which has more value than life itself.

Evita: The Real Lives of Eva Perón, ch. 7 (1996) by Nicholas Fraser and Marysa Navarro

6 I will come again, and I will be millions.

Quoted ibid., Epilogue

Juan Perón (1895–1974)

ARGENTINIAN POLITICIAN

Elected President in 1946, he won the support of the masses through a programme of social reforms known as 'justicialismo'. He was overthrown and went into exile in 1955, returning to power in 1973.

1 I never killed anybody. Nobody died with his shoes on.

Quoted in *Eva Perón*, Epilogue (1978) by John Barnes

Laurence J. Peter (1919–90)

US-CANADIAN AUTHOR

Laurence Johnston Peter. His book The Peter Principle (1969) argues that people are promoted to positions for which they are incompetent. He also published sequels and anthologies of quotations.

1 In a hierarchy every employee tends to rise to his level of incompetence.

The 'Peter Principle', in *The Peter Principle*, ch. 1 (1969, written with Raymond Hull). Compare with the 'Paula Principle': 'Women stay below their level of competence, because they hold back from promotion' (Liz Filkin, quoted in the *Observer* 19 October 1986).

Kim Philby (1912–88)

BRITISH INTELLIGENCE OFFICER AND SOVIET SPY

Harold Adrian Russell Philby. Recruited by the Soviets before being employed by British intelligence in 1940, he was dismissed from the service in 1955 for his Communist sympathies. He defected to the USSR in 1963 and took Russian citizenship.

1 To betray, you must first belong. I never belonged.

Sunday Times 17 December 1967

Philip, Duke of Edinburgh (b. 1921)

The Greek-born Philip Mountbatten adopted British nationality in 1947, marrying the future ELIZABETH II *the same year. Notorious for his insensitive remarks, he has set up the Duke of Edinburgh Award Scheme for training young people.*

1 Dentopedalogy is the science of opening your mouth and putting your foot in it. I've been practising it for years.

Address to General Dental Council, quoted in *Time* 21 November 1960

2 I never see any home cooking. All I get is fancy stuff.

Quoted in the *Observer* 28 October 1962

3 All money nowadays seems to be produced with a natural homing instinct for the Treasury.

Quoted in the *Observer* 26 May 1963

4 We live in what virtually amounts to a museum – which does not happen to a lot of people.

Remark, 25 February 1964, quoted in *Anatomy of Britain Today*, pt 1, ch. 2 (1965) by Anthony Sampson

5 When a man opens the car door for his wife, it's either a new car or a new wife.

Today 2 March 1988

6 I don't think a prostitute is more moral than a wife, but they are doing the same thing.

Speech 6 December 1988, quoted in the *Daily Mail* 7 December 1988. Prince Philip was dismissing claims that those who sell slaughtered meat have greater moral authority than those who participate in blood sports.

Philip Morris cigarettes

1 There is no 'safe' cigarette. These are and have been the messages of public health authorities worldwide. Smokers and potential smokers should rely on these messages in making all smoking-related decisions.

Posted on the Philip Morris website, 13 October 1999, quoted in the *Independent* 14 October 1999. First public admission by the Philip Morris company that smoking is not harmless.

Adam Phillips (b. 1954)

BRITISH PSYCHOANALYST AND AUTHOR

He believes in widening the appeal of his subject, of which he has written in literary and aphoristic vein in On Kissing, Tickling and Being Bored *(1993).*

1 All of us may be surrealists in our dreams, but in our worries we are incorrigibly bourgeois.

'Worrying and its Discontents', first publ. in *Raritan* vol. 9, no. 9, 1989, repr. in *On Kissing, Tickling and Being Bored* (1993)

Julia Phillips (b. 1945)

US FILM PRODUCER

She gained the distinction of being the first woman producer to be awarded an Oscar, for The Sting (1973), co-produced with her husband Michael Phillips. Taxi Driver *(1976) and* Close Encounters of the Third Kind *(1977) were other co-productions, before a cocaine habit and divorce ended her film career.*

1 Hollywood is a place that attracts people with massive holes in their souls.

The Times 3 April 1991

Edith Piaf (1918–63)

FRENCH SINGER

Originally Edith Giovanna Gassion. Helped to a mainstream career by MAURICE CHEVALIER, *she was known for her powerful voice and waif-like appearance, to which she owed her name Piaf (Parisian slang for 'little sparrow'). Her funeral brought Paris traffic to a standstill.*

1 *Quand il me prend dans ses bras*
Il me parle tout bas
Je vois la vie en rose.
(When he takes me in his arms
He speaks to me in a low voice
I see *la vie en rose*.)

'La Vie en rose' (song, 1946, written by Louiguy, Piaf and Mal Davis)

2 *Non! Rien de rien* . . .
Non, je ne regrette rien!
Ni le bien qu'on m'a fait,
Ni le mal. Tout ça m'est bien égal!
(No, I regret nothing . . .
Neither the good nor the bad,
It's all the same for me.)

'Non, je ne regrette rien' (song, 1961, written by Charles Dumont and Michael Vaucaire)

Francis Picabia (1878–1953)

FRENCH PAINTER AND POET

He was linked to all the principal art movements of the early twentieth century. With MARCEL DUCHAMP *and* MAN RAY *he introduced Dadaism to New York, and he edited the anti-art magazine variously titled* 291, 391, 491 *and* 591.

1 My arse contemplates those who talk behind my back.

391 10 July 1921, repr. in *Yes No: Poems and Sayings,* 'Sayings' (ed. Rémy Hall, 1990)

2 Men have always need of god! A god to defend them against other men.

'Trompettes de Jericho', first publ. in *Comoedia* 19 January 1922, repr. in *Écrits,* vol. 2, '1922' (ed. Olivier Revault d'Allones and Dominique Bouissou, 1978)

3 Let us never forget that the greatest man is never more than an animal disguised as a god.

'Jésus dit à ces Juifs', first publ. in *La Vie moderne* 25 February 1923, repr. ibid., '1923'

4 Wherever art appears, life disappears.

'L'Humour poétique', first publ. in *La Nef* December 1950/January 1951, repr. ibid.

5 Nature is unfair? So much the better, inequality is the only bearable thing, the monotony of equality can only lead us to boredom.

Ibid.

Pablo Picasso (1881–1973)

SPANISH ARTIST

Associated with Cubism, of which his Les Demoiselles d'Avignon *(1906–7) is generally considered the first major example, he explored many other areas of painting and sculpture, incorporating harlequins, minotaurs and African imagery in his work.* Guernica *(1937), showing the bombing of a Basque town during the Spanish Civil War, achieved iconic status.*

1 We all know that Art is not truth. Art is a lie that makes us realize truth, at least the truth that is given us to understand. The artist must know the manner whereby to convince others of the truthfulness of his lies.

'Picasso Speaks', publ. in *Arts* May 1923, repr. in *Picasso: Fifty Years of His Art* (1946) by Alfred H. Barr Jr

2 Through art we express our conception of what nature is not.

Ibid.

3 Everything is a miracle. It is a miracle that one does not dissolve in one's bath like a lump of sugar.

Quoted in *Opium* (1929) by JEAN COCTEAU

4 They ought to put out the eyes of painters as they do goldfinches in order that they can sing better.

Intransigeant 15 June 1932, repr. in *Picasso on Art* (1972) by Dore Ashton

5 When you start with a portrait and search for a pure form, a clear volume, through successive eliminations, you arrive inevitably at the egg. Likewise, starting with the egg and following the same process in reverse, one finishes with the portrait.

Ibid.

6 Painting is a *jeu d'esprit*.

Arts 29 June 1935, quoted in *Picasso: Fifty Years of His Art* (1946) by Alfred H. Barr Jr

7 Art is not the application of a canon of beauty but what the instinct and the brain can conceive beyond any canon. When we

love a woman we don't start measuring her
limbs.

'Conversation avec Picasso', publ. in *Cahiers
d'art*, vol. 10, no. 10 (1935), repr. ibid.

8 There ought to be an absolute dictatorship
... a dictatorship of painters ... a dictatorship of one painter ... to suppress all
those who have betrayed us, to suppress
the cheaters, to suppress the tricks, to suppress mannerisms, to suppress charms, to
suppress history, to suppress a heap of
other things. But common sense always
gets away with it. Above all, let's have a revolution against that!

Ibid.

9 To finish a work? To finish a picture? What
nonsense! To finish it means to be through
with it, to kill it, to rid it of its soul, to give
it its final blow ... the *coup de grâce* for
the painter as well as for the picture.

Quoted in *Picasso: portraits et souvenirs*, ch. 7
(1946) by Jaime Sabartés

10 It [genius] is personality with a penny's
worth of talent. Error which chances to
rise above the commonplace.

Quoted ibid., ch. 9

11 The genius of Einstein leads to Hiroshima.

Remark to Françoise Gilot in 1946, quoted in
Life with Picasso, pt 2 (1964) by Françoise Gilot
and Carlton Lake

12 Youth has no age.

Arts de France no. 6, 1946, repr. in *Picasso on Art*
(1972) by Dore Ashton

13 Now at least we know everything that
painting isn't.

Said in Rome 1949, quoted in *Scritti di Picasso*
(1964) by Mario De Micheli. In answer to
whether figurative painting was still possible
after the advances made by photography and
cinema, reported by artist Renato Guttuso in his
journals.

14 Painting is a blind man's profession. He
paints not what he sees, but what he feels,
what he tells himself about what he has
seen.

Quoted in *Journals*, pt 1, 'War and Peace' (1956)
by JEAN COCTEAU

15 One does a whole painting for one peach
and people think just the opposite – that
that particular peach is but a detail.

Quoted in *Vogue* 1 November 1956

16 Success is dangerous. One begins to copy
oneself, and to copy oneself is more dangerous than to copy others. It leads to
sterility.

Ibid.

17 Art is never chaste. It ought to be forbidden to ignorant innocents, never
allowed into contact with those not

sufficiently prepared. Yes, art is dangerous.
Where it is chaste, it is not art.

Quoted in *Pablo Picasso*, ch. 11 (1957) by
Antonina Vallentin

18 Ah, good taste! What a dreadful thing!
Taste is the enemy of creativeness.

Quoted in *Quote Magazine* 24 March 1957

19 If all the ways I have been along were
marked on a map and joined up with a
line, it might represent a minotaur.

Official catalogue of the Musée d'Antibes,
known as the Musée Picasso, quoted in *Picasso
in Antibes* (1960) by Dor de la Souchère

20 Today, as you know, I am famous and very
rich. But when I am alone with myself, I
haven't the courage to consider myself an
artist, in the great and ancient sense of that
word ... I am only a public entertainer,
who understands his age.

Le Spectacle du monde November 1962, repr. in
The Trousered Ape, ch. 2 (1971) by Duncan
Williams

21 One starts to get young at the age of sixty
and then it is too late.

Quoted in the *Sunday Times* 20 October 1963

22 God is really only another artist. He
invented the giraffe, the elephant, and the
cat. He has no real style. He just keeps on
trying other things.

Quoted in *Life with Picasso*, pt 1 (1964) by Françoise Gilot and Carlton Lake

23 Is there anything more dangerous than
sympathetic understanding?

Quoted in *Picasso Says ...*, 'Solitude' (1966) by
Hélène Parmelin

Marge Piercy (b. 1936)
US NOVELIST AND POET

*Her stated aim 'to be useful' is reflected in her
visionary political and feminist fiction and verse.
Novels include* Woman on the Edge of Time
(1976) and Body of Glass *(1992), and her poetry is
collected in* Hard Loving *(1969) and* Stone, Paper,
Knife *(1983), among other titles.*

1 Many of my generation and ... suspect the
Age of Greed and Waste to be ... crudely
overdrawn. But to burn your compost! To
pour your shit into the water down-
stream must drink! That fish must live in!
Into rivers whose estuaries and marshes
are links in the whole offshore food chain
... Nobody's going to believe this. It all
goes to show you can be too smart to see
the middle step and fall on your face
leaping!

Luciente, in *Woman on the Edge of Time*, ch. 2
(1976)

2 We have limited resources. We plan co-
operatively. We can afford to waste ...
nothing. You might say our – you'd say

religion? – ideas make us see ourselves as partners with water, air, birds, fish, trees.
Ibid., ch. 6

3 I write to change consciousness, to reach those people who don't agree already. Cultural work is one of the most effective ways of reaching people. If you don't support alternate ways of imagining things, people aren't going to be able to imagine a better world.
Vida, flyleaf (1979)

Harold Pinter (b. 1930)
BRITISH PLAYWRIGHT
When asked what his plays were about, he once answered, 'the weasel under the cocktail cabinet'. Early works include The Birthday Party *(1957),* The Caretaker *(1960, filmed 1963) and* The Homecoming *(1965), while later plays are more explicitly political, for example* Mountain Language *(1988).*

1 If only I could get down to Sidcup! I've been waiting for the weather to break. He's got my papers, this man I left them with, it's got it all down there, I could prove everything.
Davies, in *The Caretaker*, act 1 (1960)

2 You're nothing else but a wild animal, when you come down to it. You're a barbarian. And to put the old tin lid on it, you stink from arse-hole to breakfast time.
Mick, speaking to Davies, ibid., act 3

3 I have never been loved. From this I derive my strength.
Spooner, in *No Man's Land*, act 1 (1975)

4 You are in no man's land. Which never moves, which never changes, which never grows older, but which remains forever, icy and silent.
Spooner, ibid., act 2

5 I tend to believe that cricket is the greatest thing that God ever created on earth.
'Pinter on Pinter', in the *Observer* 5 October 1980

6 I hate despair. I find it intolerable. The stink of it gets up my nose. It's a blemish. Despair, old fruit, is a cancer. It should be castrated. Indeed I've often found that that works. Chop the balls off and despair goes out the window.
Nicholas, in *One for the Road* (1985)

7 You have to look very carefully at your motives if you become a public figure. The danger is that you become an exhibitionist, self-important, pompous. . . . Before you know where you are you're having make-up put on, your eyelashes are being tinted.
'A Play and its Politics', conversation, February 1985, publ. with play *One for the Road* (1985)

8 Now hear this. You are mountain people. You hear me? Your language is dead. It is forbidden. It is not permitted to speak your mountain language in this place.
Officer, in *Mountain Language*, sc. 1 (1988)

9 The US is without doubt the greatest show on the road. Brutal, indifferent, scornful and ruthless it may be, but it's also very smart. As a salesman it's out on its own. And its most saleable commodity is self-love. The US has actually educated itself to be in love with itself.
'It Never Happened', publ. in the *Guardian* 4 December 1996, repr. in *Various Voices* (1998)

10 That the torturers listen to music and are very kind to their children has been well established throughout twentieth-century history. This is one of the very complex states of affairs in the psychology of our social and political lives.
'Writing, Politics and *Ashes to Ashes*', interview in Barcelona, 6 December 1996, publ. ibid.

11 It comes easily for the English people to mock. It's a very odd situation indeed in England; you try to address real facts of life that surround you and are treated with great hostility.
Ibid. On the public response to his political involvement.

Luigi Pirandello (1867–1936)
ITALIAN AUTHOR AND PLAYWRIGHT
His novel The Late Mattia Pascal *(1903) and the plays* Six Characters in Search of an Author *(1921) and* Henry IV *(1922) share the themes of tragic alienation and the illusion of personality. He established his own theatre, the Teatro d'Arte, in 1925.*

1 Anyone can be heroic from time to time, but a gentleman is something you have to be all the time.
Maurizio, in *The Pleasure of Honesty* act 1 (1918)

2 In bed my real love has always been the sleep that rescued me by allowing me to dream.
Silia, in *The Rules of the Game* act 2 (1919, transl. 1959)

3 But you must play your part, just as I am playing mine. It's all in the game. . . . Each of us must play his part through to the end.
Leone, ibid.

4 Six Characters in Search of an Author.
Play title (1921)

5 Nature uses human imagination to lift her work of creation to even higher levels.
The Father, in *Six Characters in Search of an Author*, act 1 (1921)

6 Whoever has the luck to be born a charac-

ter can laugh even at death. Because a
character will never die! A man will die, a
writer, the instrument of creation: but
what he has created will never die!

Ibid.

7 Each of us, face to face with other men, is
clothed with some sort of dignity, but we
know only too well all the unspeakable
things that go on in the heart.

Ibid.

8 When the characters are really alive before
their author, the latter does nothing but
follow them in their action, in their words,
in the situations which they suggest to
him.

Ibid., act 3

9 Every true man, sir, who is a little above
the level of the beasts and plants does not
live for the sake of living, without knowing
how to live; but he lives so as to give a
meaning and a value of his own to life.

Ibid.

10 You know what it means to be with a madman? To be with someone who shakes the
foundations, the logic of the whole structure of everything you've built in and
around yourselves.

Henry IV, in *Henry IV*, act 2 (1922)

Robert M. Pirsig (b. 1928)
US AUTHOR
He had a cult hit with Zen and the Art of Motorcycle Maintenance *(1974), an account of a motorcycle journey across America narrated as both a
physical expedition and a psychological quest,
which he subtitled 'An Inquiry into Values'.*

1 The Buddha, the Godhead, resides quite as
comfortably in the circuits of a digital computer or the gears of a cycle transmission
as he does at the top of a mountain or in
the petals of a flower.

Zen and the Art of Motorcycle Maintenance, pt 1,
ch. 1 (1974)

2 A motorcycle functions entirely in accordance with the laws of reason, and a study
of the art of motorcycle maintenance is
really a miniature study of the art of ration-
ality itself.

Ibid., pt 2, ch. 8

3 One geometry cannot be more true than
another; it can only be more *convenient*.
Geometry is not true, it is advantageous.

Ibid., pt 3, ch. 22

4 Traditional scientific method has always
been at the very *best*, 20–20 hindsight. It's
good for seeing where you've been. It's
good for testing the truth of what you

think you know, but it can't tell you where
you *ought* to go.

Ibid., pt 3, ch. 24

Brad Pitt (b. 1963)
US SCREEN ACTOR
*William Bradley Pitt. One of Hollywood's highest-
banking stars, he has appeared in* True Romance
(1993) Twelve Monkeys *(1995), Meet Joe Black
(1998) and* Snatch *(2000). He is famous for his dislike of personal publicity.*

1 Celebrity is bestial. It is the worst type of
karma because of the huge solitude it
brings. You are like a gazelle that finds
itself straying from the flock. And soon
your path is cut off by lions.

Quoted in the *Daily Telegraph* 24 December 1998

Walter B. Pitkin (1878–1953)
US AUTHOR, EDITOR AND PSYCHOLOGIST
His numerous works of popular psychology include
The Psychology of Happiness *(1929) and* Let's
Get What We Want *(1935).*

1 Life Begins at Forty.

Book title (1932)

Pius XI (1857–1939)
ITALIAN ECCLESIASTIC AND POPE
*Ambrogio Damiano Achille Ratti. Pope from 1922,
he was responsible for signing the Lateran Treaty
(1929) with* MUSSOLINI, *a concordat that established the independence of the Vatican State.*

1 Whether considered as a doctrine, or as an
historical fact, or as a movemement, socialism, if it really remains socialism, cannot
be brought into harmony with the dogmas
of the Catholic church. . . . Religious socialism, Christian socialism, are expressions
implying a contradiction in terms.

Quadragesimo Anno (encyclical, 1931)

Pius XII (1876–1958)
ITALIAN ECCLESIASTIC AND POPE
*Eugenio Pacelli. He was made Pope in 1939 and is
remembered for his conservative approach to doctrine and politics. He maintained diplomatic
relations with both Allied and Axis governments,
but failed to speak out against Nazi atrocities.*

1 The Church welcomes technological progress and receives it with love, for it is an
indubitable fact that technological progress comes from God and, therefore, can
and must lead to Him.

Christmas message, 1953, publ. in *The Harvest of
a Quiet Eye* (ed. Alan L. Mackay, 1977)

Erin Pizzey (b. 1939)

BRITISH ACTIVIST AND AUTHOR

In 1971 she founded Chiswick Women's Aid, the first shelter in Britain for battered wives and their children. She has written on domestic violence as well as works of fiction.

1 To me, a good family is the basis of democracy and is democratic to the core. That's why the feminists had to destroy it.
Quoted in the *Observer* 11 February 1996

Max Planck (1858–1947)

GERMAN PHYSICIST

Professor at Berlin (1892–1926), he broke with classical physics when he proposed his revolutionary quantum theory (1900), one of the main foundations of twentieth-century physics.

1 A new scientific truth does not triumph by convincing its opponents and making them see the light, but rather because its opponents eventually die, and a new generation grows up that is familiar with it.
Scientific Autobiography and Other Papers, 'Scientific Autobiography' (1948)

Sylvia Plath (1932–63)

US POET

Her best known works are the partly autobiographical novel The Bell Jar *(1963) and* Ariel *(1965), a collection of her late poems. Her suicide, a year after separating from her husband* TED HUGHES, *was the culmination of a series of attempts on her own life.*

1 *How frail the human heart must be –*
  a mirrored pool of thought . . .
'I Thought I Could Not Be Hurt', first poem written aged fourteen, quoted in *Letters Home: Correspondence 1950–1963*, Introduction (1975) by Aurelia Schober Plath

2 *Prim, pink-breasted, feminine, she nurses*
  Chocolate fancies in rose-papered rooms.
'Female Author', publ. in *Collected Poems*, 'Juvenilia' (ed. Ted Hughes, 1981)

3 Apparently, the most difficult feat for a Cambridge male is to accept a woman not merely as feeling, not merely as thinking, but as managing a complex, vital interweaving of both.
Isis (Oxford students' magazine) 6 May 1956. Written while Plath was a student at Cambridge.

4 *Overnight, very*
  Whitely, discreetly,
  Very quietly
  Our toes, our noses
  Take hold on the loam,
  Acquire the air.
'Mushrooms', written 1959, publ. in *The Colossus* (1960)

5 *These poems do not live: it's a sad*
  diagnosis.

They grew their toes and fingers well
  enough,
Their little foreheads bulged with concentration.
If they missed out on walking about like
  people
It wasn't for any lack of mother-love.
'Stillborn', written 1960, publ. in *Crossing the Water* (1971)

6 *Love set you going like a fat gold watch.*
  The midwife slapped your footsoles, and
    your bald cry
  Took its place among the elements.
'Morning Song', first publ. in the *Observer* 21 May 1961, repr. in *Ariel* (1965)

7 *Widow. The word consumes itself . . .*
'Widow', written 1961, publ. in *Crossing the Water* (1971)

8 *Is there no way out of the mind?*
'Apprehensions', written 1962, publ. ibid.

9 If neurotic is wanting two mutually exclusive things at one and the same time, then I'm neurotic as hell. I'll be flying back and forth between one mutually exclusive thing and another for the rest of my days.
Narrator (Esther Greenwood), in *The Bell Jar*, ch. 8 (1963)

10 *Every woman adores a Fascist,*
   The boot in the face, the brute
   Brute heart of a brute like you.
'Daddy', first publ. in *Encounter* October 1963, repr. in *Ariel* (1965)

11 *Dying*
   Is an art, like everything else.
   I do it exceptionally well.
   I do it so it feels like hell.
   I do it so it feels real.
   I guess you could say I've a call.
'Lady Lazarus', ibid.

12 *Kindness glides about my house.*
   Dame Kindness, she is so nice!
   The blue and red jewels of her rings smoke
   In the windows, the mirrors
   Are filling with smiles.
'Kindness', written 1963, publ. in *Ariel* (1965)

13 *Perfection is terrible, it cannot have*
   children.
'The Munich Mannequins', ibid.

14 *The woman is perfected.*
   Her dead
   Body wears the smile of accomplishment.
'Edge', ibid. Opening lines of Plath's last poem, written a week before her suicide.

William Plomer (1903–73)

SOUTH AFRICAN AUTHOR AND POET

His first novel Turbott Wolfe *(1925) dealt with*

racism. *In 1929 he settled in London where he published both light and serious verse and wrote librettos for* BENJAMIN BRITTEN. STEPHEN SPENDER *described his work as 'wind-blown, sun-saturated, sparkling'.*

1 *When her guests were awash with champagne and with gin*
   She was recklessly sober, as sharp as a pin.
   An abstemious man would reel at her look
   As she rolled a bright eye and praised his last book.
   'Slightly Foxed, or The Widower of Bayswater', publ. in *Collected Poems* (1960)

2 *Peristalsis calls for roughage,*
   Haulms and fibres, husks and grit,
   Nature's way to open bowels,
   Maybe – let them practise it.
   'The Flying Bum', publ. ibid.

3 *The commonplace needs no defence,*
   Dullness is in the critic's eye,
   Without a licence life evolves
   From some dim phase its own surprise.
   'The Bungalows', publ. ibid.

4 *Everything sings*
   in snowy stillness
   in marble wonder,
   in formal myth,
   believed because
   impossible,
   believed as only
   a poem can be,
   the anti-fact
   of a holy spore
   spreading the Word
   unsaid before.
   'A Church in Bavaria', publ. ibid.

5 *The dead are non-living*
   the hungry are non-fed:
   don't think because you're non-unconscious
   that you're alive – you're non-dead.
   'Bureaucratic Negatives', publ. ibid.

Norman Podhoretz (b. 1930)
US EDITOR, CRITIC AND ESSAYIST
In a style that he admitted 'could be characterized as provocative', his writings emphasized the cultural roots of political issues, as in the critique The Present Danger: Do We Have the Will to Reverse the Decline of American Power? *(1980).*

1 Our culture is ill-equipped to assert the bourgeois values which would be the salvation of the under-class, because we have lost those values ourselves
   Daily Mail 10 November 1989

Political slogans
See also STOKELY CARMICHAEL 1, DARIO FO 4, JOHN LENNON 4, MALCOLM X 5

1 Land. Bread. Peace.
   Revolutionary slogan of 1917 calling for land

reform, access to food, and Russian withdrawal from the First World War. Taken up and promoted by the Bolsheviks

2 Our day will come.
   (*Tiocfaidh Ar La.*)
   IRA slogan, 1920s

3 We shall not be moved.
   Title of labour and civil rights song, 1930s, adapted from an earlier gospel hymn

4 One realm, one people, one leader.
   (*Ein Reich, ein Volk, ein Führer.*)
   Nazi Party slogan, early 1930s

5 Strength through joy.
   (*Kraft durch Freude.*)
   German Labour Front slogan from 1933, credited to Robert Ley (1890–1945), German Nazi and head of the Labour Front 1933–45

6 War will cease when men refuse to fight. What are *you* going to do about it?
   Pacifist slogan, c. 1936. In May 1940, the Peace Pledge Union was prosecuted under Defence Regulation 39a for a poster with these words. The editor, Canon Stuart Morris, told the court that the poster was 'two-year-old stock' and 'inappropriate at the present time' as activists were anxious 'not to be thought to be obstructing the war effort'. The slogan is often quoted used as 'Wars will cease . . .'

7 A bayonet is a weapon with a worker at each end.
   British pacifist slogan, 1940s

8 Ban the bomb.
   US anti-nuclear slogan, from 1953, adopted in Britain by the Campaign for Nuclear Disarmament

9 Hey, hey, LBJ, how many kids did you kill today?
   Anti-Vietnam slogan, opposing LYNDON B. JOHNSON's continuation of the war.

10 Hell no, we won't go.
   Chant of US draft resisters refusing to serve in the Vietnam War

11 Make love not war.
   Hippie slogan of the 1960s

12 Burn, baby, burn!
   Slogan linked to the race riots in Watts, Los Angeles, August 1965, in *I Hear America Talking*, 'The Blacks' (1976) by Stuart Berg Flexner

13 Black is Beautiful.
   Slogan of the Black Power movement, 1960s

14 Power to the people.
   Slogan of the Black Panther movement, from c. 1968. Also the title of a song by JOHN LENNON in 1971.

15 Every mother a willing mother. Every child a wanted child.
   Abortion rights slogan, early 1970s

16 Who governs Britain?
   Conservative slogan for 1974 general election. In

the wake of the industrial disputes, in particular the long miners' strike, which had undermined the government of EDWARD HEATH and which had precipitated the election, the Conservative Party made the struggle with the unions the central issue of their electoral campaign. The Labour Party, under HAROLD WILSON, concentrated instead on creating a harmonious 'social contract' with the unions, as highlighted in their manifesto 'Let Us Work Together'. The result of the election was a marginal Labour victory and a government heavily dependent on the unions.

17 **Save the whale.**
Greenpeace slogan from 1970s

18 **It takes up to 40 dumb animals to make a fur coat but only one to wear it.**
Slogan of anti-fur trade group Lynx, mid-1980s. The words appeared on a banner in DAVID BAILEY's celebrated video in support of the group.

19 **Let Nicaragua Live.**
Slogan opposing the Reagan administration's campaign against Nicaragua's Sandinista government, mid-1980s

20 *The people united*
Will never be defeated.
(El pueblo unido
Jamás será vencido.)
Chanted on demonstrations against US intervention in Central America, 1980s. Also used in the Seattle protests against the World Trade Organization, in November 1999

21 **Ulster says no.**
Unionist slogan opposing the Anglo-Irish Agreement of 15 November 1985

22 **Think globally, act locally.**
Friends of the Earth slogan, mid-1980s

23 **Better to break the law than break the poor.**
Slogan of the British anti-Poll Tax campaign, late 1980s, thought to have been coined by members of Militant Tendency

24 **If not us, who? If not now, when?**
Slogan by Czech university students in Prague, November 1989

25 **Coal not dole.**
Slogan early 1990s, protesting against plans of the Conservative government to close British coal mines.

26 **Reclaim the Streets.**
Slogan used by direct action groups in London, early 1990s, and adopted internationally

27 **Freedom to drive or freedom to breathe.**
Anti-roads slogan from early 1990s

28 **Keep your rosaries out of our ovaries.**
Women's Action Committee against anti-abortionists, 1992

29 **Fight for your right to party.**
Slogan of the Advance Party, formed to resist the provisions of the Criminal Justice Act of

1994 banning open-air raves. Also the title of a song by the Beastie Boys which charted in 1987.

30 **No compromise in defence of the earth.**
Slogan of the international direct action movement, Earth First, 1990s

31 **Under the tarmac, the trees.**
Road protester slogan, 1990s

32 **Resistance as global as capital.**
Slogan of 'anti-capitalist' protesters, from late 1990s. Directed against policies of the World Trade Organization and the International Monetary Fund which were seen to be sustaining global capitalism by suppressing poor economies. The slogan is sometimes rendered 'Resistance Transnational as Capital'.

33 **Not in my name.**
Pacifist slogan in the US and Britain, 2002–3, protesting against war against Iraq

Jackson Pollock (1912–56)
US ARTIST
Paul Jackson Pollock. At first influenced by Surrealists such as Miró, he was a leading Abstract Expressionist, earning the nickname 'Jack the Dripper' for his use of dripped or poured paint to achieve his 'action paintings'. Examples of his work are Number Ten, 1949 (1949) and Blue Poles (1952).

1 When I say artist I don't mean in the narrow sense of the word – but the man who is building things – creating molding the earth – whether it be the plains of the west – or the iron ore of Penn. It's all a big game of construction – some with a brush – some with a shovel – some choose a pen.
Letter to his father, 1932, publ. in *Jackson Pollock: A Catalogue Raisonné of Paintings, Drawings and Other Works*, vol. 4 (ed. Francis V. O'Connor and Eugene V. Thaw, 1978)

2 The method of painting is the natural growth out of a need. I want to express my feelings rather than illustrate them. Technique is just a means of arriving at a statement. . . . I *can* control the flow of paint: there is no accident, just as there is no beginning and no end.
Narrative to *Jackson Pollock* (film, 1951, made by Hans Nemuth and Paul Falkenberg), publ. in *Jackson Pollock* (1960) by Bryan Robertson

Georges Pompidou (1911–74)
FRENCH PRESIDENT
Holding government posts since 1946, he was Gaullist Prime Minister 1962–8 and President 1969–74.

1 There are three roads to ruin: women,

gambling and technicians. The most pleasant is with women, the quickest is with gambling, but the surest is with technicians.

Quoted in the *Sunday Telegraph* 26 May 1968

Iggy Pop (b. 1947)
US ROCK MUSICIAN
Originally James Newell Osterberg. Founder of the proto-punk band the Stooges in 1967, he gained a reputation as an anarchic self-mutilator and self-exposer in the band's live sets. His solo albums include Lust for Life *(1978).*

1 *No fun, my babe. No Fun.*
No fun to hang around feeling the same old way.
No fun to hang around, freaked out for another day.
No fun to be all alone, walking by myself.
No fun to be alone in love with nobody else.
'No Fun' (song, written by Iggy Pop and Ron Asheton) on the album *The Stooges* (1969) by Iggy Pop and the Stooges

2 *Nihilism is best done by professionals.*
Independent 12 July 1990

3 *I spent most of the Eighties, most of my life, riding around in somebody else's car, in possession of, or ingested of, something illegal, on my way from something illegal to something illegal with many illegal things happening all around me.*
Interview in the *Guardian* 17 February 1996

(Sir) Karl Popper (1902–94)
AUSTRIAN-BORN BRITISH PHILOSOPHER
His first and major book The Logic of Scientific Discovery *(1934) posits the doctrine that true scientific theories must pass the test of 'falsifiability'. Later works criticized Plato, Hegel and Marx. He was professor at the London School of Economics 1949–69.*

1 We may become the makers of our own fate when we have ceased to pose as its prophets.
The Open Society and its Enemies, Introduction (1945)

2 All science is cosmology, I believe, and for me the interest of philosophy, no less than that of science, lies solely in the contributions which it has made to it.
Preface (1959) to *The Logic of Scientific Discovery* (1934)

3 For this, indeed, is the true source of our ignorance – the fact that our knowledge can only be finite, while our ignorance must necessarily be infinite.
Lecture to British Academy, 20 January 1960, publ. in *Proceedings of the British Academy*, vol. 4 (1960)

4 Science may be described as the art of systematic over-simplification.
Quoted in the *Observer* 1 August 1982

Cole Porter (1893–1964)
US COMPOSER AND LYRICIST
The epitome of suave sophistication, he was unequalled for his deft and witty wordplay set to perfectly adapted melodies. His hit musical shows include Anything Goes *(1934) and* Kiss Me Kate *(1948).*

1 *If you want to buy my wares*
Follow me and climb the stairs . . .
Love for sale.
'Love for Sale' (song) in *The New Yorkers* (stage musical, 1930)

2 *Night and day, you are the one,*
Only you beneath the moon and under the sun.
'Night and Day' (song) in *The Gay Divorce* (stage musical, 1932, filmed as *The Gay Divorcee*, 1934). Originally sung by Fred Astaire.

3 *Oh, give me land, lots of land*
Under starry skies above
Don't fence me in.
'Don't Fence Me In' (song, 1934). The song, first recorded by Roy Rogers and The Sons of Pioneers, was later a hit for Bing Crosby with the Andrews sisters and revived in *Hollywood Canteen* (film musical, 1944)

4 *I've got you under my skin.*
'I've Got You under My Skin' (song, 1934), in *Born to Dance* (film musical, 1936)

5 *In olden days a glimpse of stocking*
Was looked on as something shocking
But now, God knows,
Anything goes.
'Anything Goes' (song), in *Anything Goes* (stage musical 1934, film 1956). Sung by Ethel Merman in the musical and by Mitzi Gaynor in the film version.

6 *Good authors, too, who once knew better words*
Now only use four-letter words
Writing prose . . .
Anything goes.
Ibid.

7 *At words poetic, I'm so pathetic*
That I always have found it best
Instead of getting 'em off my chest,
To let 'em rest unexpressed
'You're the Top' (song), ibid. Sung by William Gaxton and Ethel Merman in the original show, the song was recorded by Porter himself and later covered by Ella Fitzgerald and Buddy Greco, among others. The lyrics were adapted by P. G. WODEHOUSE for the 1935 London show.

8 *You're the Nile,*
You're the Tower of Pisa,
You're the smile

On the Mona Lisa . . .
But if, baby, I'm the bottom,
You're the top!
Ibid.

9 *I get no kick from champagne.*
Mere alcohol doesn't thrill me at all,
So tell me why should it be true
That I get a kick out of you.
'I Get a Kick Out of You' (song), ibid.

10 *Miss Otis regrets (she's unable to lunch*
today).
'Miss Otis Regrets' (song), in *Hi Diddle Diddle*
(stage musical, 1934)

11 *There's no love song finer,*
But how strange the change from major to
minor
Every time we say goodbye.
'Ev'ry Time We Say Goodbye' (song), in *Seven*
Lively Arts (stage musical, 1944). The song was a
hit for Benny Goodman (1945) and recorded by
Ella Fitzgerald (1956), in a version described by
her biographer Stuart Nicholson as 'a "We'll
Meet Again" for the Cold War generation'.

12 *He may have hair upon his chest*
But, sister, so has Lassie.
'I Hate Men' (song), in *Kiss Me Kate* (stage musi-
cal 1948, filmed 1953)

13 *I love Paris in the springtime.*
'I Love Paris' (song) in *Can-Can* (stage musical,
1953, film 1960)

14 *Birds do it, bees do it,*
Even educated fleas do it.
Let's do it, let's fall in love.
'Let's Do It' (song, 1954). The song was first fea-
tured in a 1928 show, *Paris*, without this verse.

Katherine Anne Porter (1890–1980)
US AUTHOR
Her first short story collection, Flowering Judas,
appeared in 1928. Her best known work, Ship of
Fools *(1962), stirred public controversy for its alle-*
gorical depiction of inter-war Germany.

1 They had both noticed that a life of dissipation sometimes gave to a face the look of
gaunt suffering spirituality that a life of
asceticism was supposed to give and quite
often did not.
Ship of Fools, pt 3 (1962). Referring to Herr Freytag and Mrs Treadwell.

2 The real sin against life is to abuse and
destroy beauty, even one's own – even
more, one's own, for that has been put in
our care and we are responsible for its
well-being.
Herr Freytag, ibid.

3 Human life itself may be almost pure
chaos, but the work of the artist – the only
thing he's good for – is to take these hand-
fuls of confusion and disparate things,

things that seem to be irreconcilable, and
put them together in a frame to give them
some kind of shape and meaning. Even if
it's only his view of a meaning. That's what
he's for – to give his view of life.
Interview in *Writers at Work* (second series, ed.
George Plimpton, 1963)

4 A cultivated style would be like a mask.
Everybody knows it's a mask, and sooner
or later you must show yourself – or at
least, you show yourself as someone who
could not afford to show himself, and so
created something to hide behind.
Ibid.

5 If it is not perfect, it is not love, and if it is
not love, it is bound to be hate sooner or
later. This is perhaps a not too exaggerated
statement of the extreme position of
Romantic Love, more especially in
America, where we are all brought up on
it, whether we know it or not.
'The Necessary Enemy', publ. in *The Collected*
Essays and Occasional Writings of Katherine Anne
Porter (1970)

Peter Porter (b. 1929)
AUSTRALIAN POET
Since 1951 he has lived outside Australia, mainly in
Britain. His verse collections include Preaching to
the Converted *(1972) and* English Subtitles
(1981). CLIVE JAMES *once quipped that Porter's*
poems are 'so freighted with learned references
that I can't even tell if I don't know what they
mean'.

1 *When I dream of God I see*
A Massacre of Cats. Why
should they insist on their own
language and religion, who
needs to purr to make his point?
Death to all cats! The Rule
of Dogs shall last a thousand years!
'Mort aux chats', publ. in *Preaching to the Con-*
verted (1972)

2 *Sparrows acclimatize but I still seek*
The permanently upright city where
Speech is nature, and plants conceive in
pots,
Where one escapes from what one is and
who
One was, where home is just a postmark
And country wisdom clings to calendars,
The opposite of the sunburned truth-teller's
World, haunted by precepts and the
Pleiades.
'On First Looking into Chapman's Hesiod',
publ. in *Living in a Calm Country* (1975)

3 *The channels of our lives are blocked,*
The hand is stopped upon the clock,
No one can say why hearts will break
And marriages are all opaque:

A map of loss, some posted cards,
The living house reduced to shards,
The abstract hell of memory,
The pointlessness of poetry.

'An Exequy', publ. in *The Cost of Seriousness* (1978)

4 *Nobody feels well after his fortieth birthday*
But the convalescence is touched by glory.

'Returning', publ. in *English Subtitles* (1981)

Dennis Potter (1935–94)

BRITISH DRAMATIST AND SCREENWRITER
The writer of controversial and innovative plays for the BBC for nearly thirty years, he often evoked memories of his own youth in his work, as in Pennies from Heaven *(1978),* Blue Remembered Hills *(1979) and* The Singing Detective *(1986).*

1 The TV play . . . is not *necessarily* a miserable compromise between theatre and cinema. It need be neither the photographed stage play nor the thumbnail film. There are strengths and potentialities which belong to television alone, and I think it is an exhilarating medium for the young writer as well as being the nearest thing we are ever likely to get to a 'theatre of the people'.

The Nigel Barton Plays, Introduction (1967)

2 In the last resort, politics don't count for you. Your brave new society will never come because you are incapable of working for it, incapable of telling lies for it, cheating for it, humiliating yourself for it. When you actually talk to real people you cower away from their ignorance and their apathy, don't you? Your condescending Hampstead Socialism collapses at the first belch of wind from a navvy's guts. You can't stand the stink of life, sweetheart!

Nigel Barton, addressing his wife Anne, in *Vote Vote Vote for Nigel Barton*, sc. 20, BBC play, broadcast 15 December 1965

3 To be a candidate is to submit to a personally humiliating experience, in which the set smile freezes on your face like a grin on a corpse. Dead ideas. Dead thoughts. Dead slogans. All of them sicked up on your doorstep. No wonder people are disgusted by this gruesome charade.

Nigel Barton, addressing a council dinner, ibid., sc. 24

4 Blimey, I can almost taste it! It's looking for the blue, ennit, and the gold. The patch of blue sky. The gold of the, of the bleed'n dawn, or – the light in somebody's eyes – Pennies From Heaven, that's what it is. And we can't see 'em, clinking and clink-

ing, all around, all over the place . . . just bend down and pick 'em up.

Arthur, in *Pennies from Heaven*, episode 2 (BBC television series, 1978)

5 Even in a future land of Muzak, monosodium glutamate and melamined encounters, the old resilient dreams will insist on making metaphors and finding illumination in the midst of surrounding dross. There is, then, no place where 'God' cannot reach.

Brimstone and Treacle, Introduction (1987). The play *Brimstone and Treacle* was originally written to be broadcast in 1976 but was banned on grounds of taste and not shown until 1989.

6 There's no way that you, nor any other man, could ever understand what it is that you men make us women think of our bodies.

Jessica, in *Blackeyes* (BBC television series, 1989)

7 The trouble with words is that you never know whose mouths they've been in.

Guardian 15 February 1993

8 Things are both more trivial than they ever were, and more important than they ever were, and the difference between the trivial and the important doesn't seem to matter – but the *nowness* of everything is absolutely wondrous. . . . The fact is, that if you see the present tense, boy do you see it, and boy can you celebrate it!

Interview with Melvyn Bragg, Channel 4, 5 April 1994. Referring to the terminal stages of his illness.

9 Religion to me has always been the wound, not the bandage.

Ibid.

10 I find the word 'British' harder and harder to use as time passes.

Ibid.

11 I think we should always look back on our own past with a sort of tender contempt. As long as the tenderness is there but also please let some of the contempt be there, because we know what we're like, we know how we hustle and bustle and shove and push, and you sometimes use grand words to cloak it.

Ibid.

12 Cheap songs, so called, actually do have something of the Psalms of David about them. They do say the world is other than it is. They do illuminate. This is why people say, 'Listen, they're playing our song'. It's not because that particular song actually expresses the depth of the feelings that they felt when they met each other and heard it. It is that somehow it re-evokes it, but with a different coating of

irony and self-knowledge. Those feelings come bubbling back.

Ibid.

13 **The closer writing approaches to therapy, the worse it becomes.**

Quoted in *Dennis Potter: A Life on Screen*, ch. 3 (1995) by John R. Cook

Ezra Pound (1885–1972)

US POET AND CRITIC

A founder of the Imagist movement while in London (1908–20), he settled in Italy in 1925, from where he broadcast Fascist propaganda during the Second World War. He was judged insane by a US psychiatric committee and confined to a mental hospital 1945–58. His main works are the Cantos *(written 1917–70), and he also translated widely.* GERTRUDE STEIN *described him as 'a village explainer, excellent if you were a village, but if you were not, not'.*

1 **Humanity is the rich effluvium, it is the waste and the manure and the soil, and from it grows the tree of the arts.**

Poetry October 1914. Objecting to the motto on the cover of the magazine *Poetry*, that 'To have great poets, there must be great audiences too', a quote by Walt Whitman ('Ventures on an Old Theme', 1881). Pound upheld that the arts were dependent on no one.

2 **The Image is more than an idea. It is a vortex or cluster of fused ideas and is endowed with energy.**

'Affirmations – As for Imagisme', publ. in *New Age* 28 January 1915, repr. in *Selected Prose 1909– 1965*, pt 7 (ed. William Cookson, 1973)

3 **If a patron buys from an artist who needs money (needs money to buy tools, time, food), the patron then makes himself equal to the artist; he is building art into the world; he creates.**

Letter, 8 March 1915, publ. in *The Letters of Ezra Pound 1907–1941* (ed. D. D. Paige, 1951). Pound was urging US collector John Quinn to support the new renaissance of the arts that Pound believed was imminent.

4 **There are few things more difficult than to appraise the work of a man suddenly dead in his youth; to disentangle 'promise' from achievement; to save him from that sentimentalizing which confuses the tragedy of the interruption with the merit of the work actually performed.**

Gaudier-Brzeska: A Memoir, ch. 13 (1916). Of French sculptor and Vorticist Henri Gaudier-Brzeska, killed in action in France, 1915.

5 *The apparition of these faces in the crowd;*
Petals on a wet, black bough.

'In a Station of the Metro', publ. in *Lustra* (1916)

6 *Winter is icummen in,*
Lhude sing Goddamm,
Raineth drop and staineth slop,

And how the wind doth ramm!
Sing: Goddamm.

'Ancient Music', publ. in *Lustra* (1917 edn). Pound's pastiche of the medieval song ('Sumer is icumen in,/Lhude sing cuccu!') was originally dropped from the 1916 edition of *Lustra*, having been considered offensive.

7 **A great age of literature is perhaps always a great age of translations.**

Egoist October 1917, quoted in *A Serious Character*, pt 2, ch. 20 (1988) by Humphrey Carpenter

8 **A man of genius has a right to any mode of expression.**

Letter to the painter J. B. Yeats (father of w. b. yeats), 4 February 1918, quoted in *A Serious Character*, pt 2, ch. 10 (1988) by Humphrey Carpenter

9 *The age demanded an image*
Of its accelerated grimace,
Something for the modern stage,
Not, at any rate, an Attic grace;
Not, not certainly, the obscure reveries
Of the inward gaze;
Better mendacities
Than the classics in paraphrase!

'E. P. Ode pour l'élection de son sépulcre', pt 2, publ. in *Hugh Selwyn Mauberley* (1920)

10 *There died a myriad,*
And of the best, among them,
For an old bitch gone in the teeth,
For a botched civilization.

Ibid., pt 5

11 **The curse of me & my nation is that we always think things can be bettered by immediate action of some sort,** *any* **sort rather than no sort.**

Letter to JAMES JOYCE, 7–8 June 1920, publ. in *Pound/Joyce: The Letters of Ezra Pound to James Joyce* (ed. Forrest Read, 1968)

12 **It is more than likely that the brain itself is, in origin and development, only a sort of great clot of genital fluid held in suspense or reserved ... This hypothesis ... would explain the enormous content of the brain as a maker or presenter of images.**

'Translator's Postscript' to *Physique de l'amour* (1922) by Rémy de Gourmont

13 **I consider criticism merely a preliminary excitement, a statement of things a writer has to clear up in his own head sometime or other, probably antecedent to writing; of no value unless it come to fruit in the created work later.**

'On Criticism in General', publ. in *Criterion* January 1923

14 **Great literature is simply language charged with meaning to the utmost possible degree.**

How to Read, pt 2 (1931)

15 **The author's conviction on this day of**

New Year is that music begins to atrophy when it departs too far from the dance; that poetry begins to atrophy when it gets too far from music; but this must not be taken as implying that all good music is dance music or all poetry lyric. Bach and Mozart are never too far from physical movement.

ABC of Reading, 'Warning' (1934)

16 Literature is news that STAYS news.

Ibid., ch. 2

17 Good writers are those who keep the language efficient. That is to say, keep it accurate, keep it clear.

Ibid., ch. 3

18 AS A MIND, who the hell else is there left for me to take an interest IN??

Of MUSSOLINI, in letter, 28 August 1934, quoted in *A Serious Character*, pt 3, ch. 13 (1988) by Humphrey Carpenter. Interviewed in May 1945, Pound described MUSSOLINI as 'a very human, imperfect character who lost his head', and in the opening lines of canto 74 (first of his *Pisan Cantos*, written in 1948 while he was awaiting trial for treason), he spoke of 'the enormous tragedy of the dream in the peasant's bent shoulders'.

19 Here is a dirty book worth reading . . . a bawdy which will be very useful to put Wyndham and JJ into their proper cubby holes; cause Miller is sore and without kinks.

Referring to HENRY MILLER's *Tropic of Cancer*, in letter, 1 December 1934, quoted by Karl Shapiro in 'The Greatest Living Author', preface to *Tropic of Cancer* (1960 edn) by Henry Miller. The book was first published in Paris in 1934, but suppressed in the US and Britain. 'Wyndham' was WYNDHAM LEWIS, 'JJ' JAMES JOYCE.

20 Man is an over-complicated organism. If he is doomed to extinction he will die out for want of simplicity.

Guide to Kulchur, pt 3, sect. 5, ch. 19 (1938)

21 In our time, the curse is monetary illiteracy, just as inability to read plain print was the curse of earlier centuries.

Ibid., pt 4, sect. 8, ch. 31

22 Mass ought to be in Latin, unless you cd. do it in Greek or Chinese. In fact, *any* abracadabra that no bloody member of the public or half-educated ape of a clargimint cd. think he understood.

Letter, 7 March 1940, publ. in *The Letters of Ezra Pound 1907–1941* (ed. D. D. Paige, 1951)

23 Adolf Hitler was a Jeanne d'Arc, a saint. He was a martyr. Like many martyrs, he held extreme views.

Interview in the *Philadelphia Record* and *Chicago Sun* 9 May 1945

24 I guess the definition of a lunatic is a man surrounded by them.

Quoted in *Charles Olson and Ezra Pound*, 'Canto 3, January 24 1946' (1975) by Catherine Seelye. Said to CHARLES OLSON in 1945, when Olson visited Pound in St Elizabeth's Hospital, Washington, the institution for the criminally insane in which Pound was detained pending a judgment on his wartime broadcasts from Rome.

25 With one day's reading a man may have the key in his hands.

Pisan Cantos, canto 74 (1948)

26 As a lone ant from a broken ant-hill from the wreckage of Europe, ego scriptor.

Ibid., canto 76

27 WOT IZZA COMIN'?
'I'll tell you wot izza comin'
Sochy-lism is a-comin''

Ibid., canto 77

28 There once was a brainy baboon
Who always breathed down a bassoon,
For he said, 'It appears
That in billions of years
I shall certainly hit on a tune.'

Letter, 21 July 1949, quoted in *A Serious Character*, pt 2, ch. 16 (1988) by Humphrey Carpenter. Pound himself took up the bassoon for a few months in 1921.

29 I have always thought the suicide shd bump off at least one swine before taking off for parts unknown.

Letter to ARCHIBALD MACLEISH, 10 September 1956, quoted ibid., pt 5, ch. 3

30 Technique is the test of sincerity. If a thing isn't worth getting the technique to say, it is of inferior value.

Interview in *Writers at Work* (second series, ed. George Plimpton, 1963)

31 No verse is *libre* for the man who wants to do a good job.

Ibid.

32 There is natural ignorance and there is artificial ignorance. I should say at the present moment the artificial ignorance is about eighty-five per cent.

Ibid.

33 If the individual, or heretic, gets hold of some essential truth, or sees some error in the system being practised, he commits so many marginal errors himself that he is worn out before he can establish his point.

Ibid. Pound was obliquely referring to his own 'heresy' which resulted in his incarceration in a US mental institution.

34 It is difficult to write a paradiso when all the superficial indications are that you ought to write an apocalypse. It is obviously much easier to find inhabitants for an inferno or even a purgatorio.

Ibid.

35 Somebody said that I am the last American living the tragedy of Europe.
Ibid.

36 You let *me* throw the bricks through the front window. You go in at the back door and take the swag.
Remark to T. S. ELIOT, reported by Pound acolyte and critic Hugh Kenner, quoted in *A Serious Character*, pt 2, ch. 13 (1988) by Humphrey Carpenter

37 The worst mistake I made was that stupid, suburban prejudice of anti-Semitism.
In conversation with ALLEN GINSBERG in June 1968, quoted ibid., pt 5, ch. 5

Anthony Powell (1905–2000)
BRITISH NOVELIST
He is best known for his novel sequence A Dance to the Music of Time *(12 vols. 1951–75), in which he surveys and satirizes the upper middle classes over a period of fifty years.*

1 Slowly, but very deliberately, the brooding edifice of seduction, creaking and incongruous, came into being, a vast Heath Robinson mechanism, dually controlled by them and lumbering gloomily down vistas of triteness. With a sort of heavy-fisted dexterity the mutually adapted emotions of each of them became synchronised, until the unavoidable anti-climax was at hand.
Afternoon Men, ch. 9 (1931). Referring to Lola and Atwater.

2 Parents . . . are sometimes a bit of a disappointment to their children. They don't fulfil the promise of their early years.
Stringham, in *A Buyer's Market*, ch. 2 (1952, second book of *A Dance to the Music of Time*)

3 Self-love seems so often unrequited.
Narrator (Nicholas Jenkins), in *The Acceptance World*, ch. 1 (1955, third book of *A Dance to the Music of Time*)

4 Growing old's like being increasingly penalized for a crime you haven't committed.
Dick Umfraville, in *Temporary Kings*, ch. 1 (1973, eleventh book of *A Dance to the Music of Time*)

5 Few persons who have ever sat for a portrait can have felt anything but inferior while the process is going on.
Quoted in the *Observer* 9 January 1983

Colin Powell (b. 1937)
US GENERAL AND POLITICIAN
A professional soldier for thirty-five years, he became Chairman of the Joint Chiefs of Staff (1989–93) and Secretary of State in 2001.

1 A great tragedy has struck our country. It will not affect the nature of our society.
Press conference in Lima, quoted in *The Times* 12 September 2001. Referring to the terrorist

attacks on the World Trade Center and the Pentagon, 11 September 2001.

Enoch Powell (1912–98)
BRITISH POLITICIAN
A classical scholar, austere intellectual and devotee of High Toryism, he became a Conservative MP in 1950 and was Minister of Health (1960–63). His outspoken views on immigraton caused him to lose his position in the shadow cabinet in 1968, and he resigned from the Conservative Party in 1974 to serve as an Ulster Unionist MP.

1 History is littered with the wars which everybody knew would never happen.
Speech to Conservative Party Conference, Scarborough, 19 October 1967, quoted in *The Times* 20 October 1967

2 Those whom the gods wish to destroy, they first make mad. We must be mad, literally mad, as a nation to be permitting the annual inflow of some fifty thousand dependants, who are for the most part the material of the future growth of the immigrant-descended population. It is like watching a nation busily engaged in heaping up its own funeral pyre.
Speech to West Midlands Conservatives, Birmingham, 20 April 1968, publ. in *The Penguin Book of Twentieth-Century Speeches* (ed. Brian MacArthur, 1999). Powell was dropped from EDWARD HEATH's shadow cabinet the day after making this notorious warning about the consequences of immigration into Britain from Commonwealth countries.

3 As I look ahead, I am filled with foreboding. Like the Roman, I seem to see 'the River Tiber foaming with much blood'.
Ibid. Quoting the Sybil's prophecy in Virgil's *Aeneid*, bk 6: 'Et Thybrim multo spumantem sanguine cerno.' The phrase 'rivers of blood' had been used previously in different contexts by Thomas Jefferson and WINSTON CHURCHILL, among others.

4 Remove advertising, disable a person or firm from preconising its wares and their merits, and the whole of society and of the economy is transformed. The enemies of advertising are the enemies of freedom.
Listener 31 July 1969

5 I do not keep a diary. Never have. To write a diary every day is like returning to one's own vomit.
Sunday Times 6 November 1977

6 All political lives, unless they are cut off in mid-stream at a happy juncture, end in failure, because that is the nature of politics and of human affairs.
Joseph Chamberlain, Epilogue (1977)

7 There is one thing you can be sure of with the Conservative Party, before anything

else – they have a grand sense for where the votes are.

Listener 28 May 1981

8 No battle is worth fighting except the last one.

Quoted in the *Observer* 2 January 1983

9 Command and obedience, Establishment and deference, they're two sides of the same coin. The Establishment is unacknowledged power. It is *the power that need not speak its name.*

Quoted in *Friends in High Places*, Introduction (1990) by JEREMY PAXMAN.

Vince Powell and Harry Driver

BRITISH TV COMEDY SCRIPTWRITERS

Among the numerous series co-scripted by the pair are Bless this House, Love Thy Neighbour *and, their greatest success,* Never Mind the Quality, Feel the Width *(1967–71).*

1 Never Mind the Quality, Feel the Width.

Title of comedy series, ITV (1967–71). The series began as a single play for ABC TV's *Armchair Theatre.*

John Cowper Powys (1872–1963)

BRITISH AUTHOR AND CRITIC

A prolific writer of poetry, essays and fiction, he is best known for his novels A Glastonbury Romance *(1932),* Weymouth Sands *(1934) and* Maiden Castle *(1936), all drawing on themes from his West Country childhood.*

1 The strongest of all psychic forces in the world is unsatisfied desire.

A Glastonbury Romance, vol. 1, ch. 4 (1932)

2 If you give up *possession*, if you give up trying to possess what attracts you, a lovely, thrilling happiness flows through you and you feel you're in touch with the secret of everything. There are only two mortal sins in the world; one of these is to be cruel and the other is *to possess*, and they are both destructive of happiness.

Sam Dekker, ibid., ch. 7

3 Every human creature is a terror to every other human creature. Human minds are like unknown planets, encountering and colliding. Every one of them contains jagged precipices, splintered rock-peaks, ghastly crevasses, smouldering volcanoes, scorched and scorching deserts, blistering sands, evil dungeons from behind whose barred windows mad and terrible faces peer out.

Ibid., ch. 14

4 What's Poetry if it isn't something that has to fight for the unseen against the seen, for the dead against the living, for the mysteri-

ous against the obvious? Poetry always takes sides. It's the only Lost Cause we've got left! It fights for the . . . for the . . . for the Impossible!

Lady Rachel Zoyland, ibid., ch. 17

5 It is an old and bitter experience of the human race that when once a gulf-stream of a particular evil has got started, it is always being whipped forward by some new little breeze, or enlarged by some new little stream emptying itself into it. A magnetic power, it seems, in such a gulf-stream of evil, attracts these casual and accidental encouragements.

Ibid., vol. 2, ch. 10

Elvis Presley (1935–77)

US SINGER

Fusing a country and western sound with rhythm and blues, he was the first white singer to introduce overt sexuality into his act. In the 1960s he concentrated mainly on films, while his act moved increasingly towards the high kitsch of Las Vegas. 'Everything starts and ends with him,' said BRUCE SPRINGSTEEN. *'He wrote the book.' See also* ALBERT GOLDMAN 1, THOM GUNN 4, JERRY LEE LEWIS 2.

1 *You ain't nothin' but a hound dog, Cryin' all the time.*

'Hound Dog' (song, 1952, written by Jerry Leiber and Mike Stoller). The song was the Leiber/Stoller partnership's first hit when recorded by Big Mama Thornton in 1952, though Presley's 1956 recording was a much bigger success.

2 *Now since my baby left me I've found a new place to dwell Down at the end of Lonely Street At Heartbreak Hotel.*

'Heartbreak Hotel' (song, 1956, written by Mae Boren Axton, Tommy Durden and Elvis Presley). Presley's first no. 1 hit is mainly credited to Mae Boren Axton, mother of HOYT AXTON.

3 I wish not to be given a title or an appointed position. I can and will do more good if I were made a Federal Agent at Large, and I will help best by doing it my way through my communications with people of all ages. First and foremost I am an entertainer but all I need is the Federal Credentials.

Letter to President NIXON, 19 December 1970, offering Presley's services as a Federal Agent to work to curb drug abuse by young people. Elvis was made an agent of the Bureau of Narcotics and Dangerous Drugs by Nixon, receiving an enamel shield which, according to biographer Albert Goldman, became one of his most treasured possessions.

4 I don't aim to let this fame business get

me. God gave me a voice. If I turned
against God, I'd be finished.

Quoted in *All You Need is Love*, 'Hail! Hail!
Rock 'n' Roll!' (1976) by Tony Palmer

Jacques Prévert (1900–1977)

FRENCH POET, CRITIC AND SCREENWRITER

*Influenced by Surrealism, he became popular in
the 1920s with humorous 'song poems' about Paris
street life. His verse collections include* Paroles
(1946) *and* Imaginaires (1970). *He was also an
eminent film critic and supplied the screenplay for*
Les Enfants du Paradis (1944) *among other films.*

1 *Our Father which art in heaven*
  Stay there
  And we will stay on earth
  Which is sometimes so pretty.

  'Pater Noster', publ. in *Paroles* (1946, rev. 1949,
  transl. Lawrence Ferlinghetti, 1958). Opening
  lines of poem.

2 *An orange on the table*
  Your dress on the rug
  And you in my bed
  Sweet present of the present
  Cool of night
  Warmth of my life.

  'Alicante', publ. ibid.

3 *Man*
  You beheld the saddest and dreariest of all
      the flowers of the earth
  And as with other flowers you gave it a
      name
  You called it Thought.

  'Flowers and Wreaths', publ. ibid.

4 When truth is no longer free, freedom is
  no longer real: the truths of the police are
  the truths of today.

  'Intermède', publ. in *Spectacle* (1951)

5 Even if happiness forgets you a little bit,
  never completely forget about it.

  Ibid.

Gerald Priestland (1927–1991)

BRITISH BROADCASTER

*He was religious correspondent for BBC TV and
radio, and the author of* America (1968) *and*
Dilemmas of Journalism (1979), *among other
writings.*

1 Journalists belong in the gutter because
  that is where the ruling classes throw their
  guilty secrets.

  Radio London, 19 May 1988

J. B. Priestley (1894–1984)

BRITISH AUTHOR

*John Boynton Priestley. Cambridge-educated, but
tied to his Yorkshire roots, he published numerous
works of literary criticism before having success
with his humorous novel* The Good Companions

(1929) *and the plays* Time and the Conways
(1937) *and* An Inspector Calls (1947).

1 Find a street without a flower, and you
  may be sure that there the English are in
  exile, still hoping and planning behind the
  lace curtain and the aspidistra for a time
  and place that will break into living
  blossom.

  English Journey, ch. 2, sect. 3 (1934)

2 This is the age, among other things, of
  chocolate.

  Ibid., ch. 4, sect. 3

3 Men are much better than their ordinary
  life allows them to be.

  Ibid., ch. 6, sect. 3. Referring to the contrast
  between the comradeship of soldiers in war and
  'the civilian life to which they returned, a condition of things in which they found their manhood stunted, their generous impulses baffled,
  their double instinct for leadership and loyalty
  completely checked'.

4 The Theatre is no place to think in. You
  can think much better quietly at home. An
  intelligent book will make more people
  think than the most exquisite production
  of the finest play. But what the dramatist
  can do . . . is to make his audience feel.

  Two Time Plays, Introduction (1937)

5 Our trouble is that we drink too much tea.
  I see in this the slow revenge of the Orient,
  which has diverted the Yellow River down
  our throats.

  Quoted in the *Observer* 15 May 1949

6 Already we Viewers, when not viewing,
  have begun to whisper to one another that
  the more we elaborate our means of communication, the less we communicate.

  Thoughts in the Wilderness, 'Televiewing' (1957)

7 I can't help feeling wary when I hear anything said about the masses. First you take
  their faces from 'em, calling them the
  masses, and then you accuse 'em of not
  having any faces.

  Narrator (Henry Sulgrave), in *Saturn Over the
  Water*, ch. 5 (1961)

8 It is hard to tell where the MCC ends and
  the Church of England begins.

  New Statesman 20 July 1962

J. A. Primo de Rivera (1903–36)

SPANISH POLITICIAN

*José Antonio Primo de Rivera. Son of the military
dictator who ruled Spain 1923–30, he founded the
Spanish Fascist Party, Falange Española, in 1933.
He was executed by the Republicans at the start of
the Civil War.*

1 Fascism is a European inquietude. It is a
  way of knowing everything – history, the
  State, the achievement of the proletarianiz-

ation of public life, a new way of knowing the phenomena of our epoch.

Quoted in *The Spanish Civil War*, bk 1, ch. 8 (1961) by Hugh Thomas

2 We, who have already borne on the road to Paradise the lives of the best among us, want a difficult, erect, implacable Paradise; a Paradise where one can never rest and which has, beside the threshold of the gates, angels with swords.

Quoted in *Falange*, ch. 7 (1962) by Stanley Payne

(Sir) V. S. Pritchett (1900–1997)
BRITISH AUTHOR AND CRITIC
Victor Sawdon Pritchett. The 'wise, foxy and kindly grandfather of present English letters' was literary critic at the New Statesman *for twenty years. His fiction expresses a sympathetic but sceptical view of human illusions, as in his novels* Dead Man Leading *(1937) and* Mr. Beluncle *(1951) and his short stories.*

1 The principle of procrastinated rape is said to be the ruling one in all the great best-sellers.

The Living Novel, 'Clarissa' (1946)

2 The detective novel is the art-for-art's-sake of our yawning Philistinism, the classic example of a specialized form of art removed from contact with the life it pretends to build on.

'The Roots of Detection', publ. in the *New Statesman* 16 June 1951, repr. in *Books in General* (1953)

3 In our family, as far as we are concerned, we were born and what happened before that is myth.

A Cab at the Door (1968). Opening words of first volume of autobiography

4 It is often said that in Ireland there is an excess of genius unsustained by talent; but there is talent in the tongues.

Midnight Oil, ch. 6 (second volume of autobiography, 1971)

5 Life – how curious is that habit that makes us think it is not here, but elsewhere.

Ibid. 'Life is elsewhere' is a loose translation of Rimbaud's line *La vraie vie est absente. Nous ne sommes pas au monde* from his poem 'Délires'. The words were used by MILAN KUNDERA as the title of his novel (written 1969, publ. 1973) in which he cites André Breton's Surrealist Manifesto (see ANDRÉ BRETON 2) and the adoption of the words as a slogan by students in Paris, May 1968.

6 Well, youth is the period of assumed personalities and disguises. It is the time of the sincerely insincere.

Ibid., ch. 8

7 How extraordinary it is that one feels most guilt about the sins one is unable to commit.

Ibid., ch. 10

Gilbert Proesch (b. 1943)
ITALIAN-BORN BRITISH ARTIST
He and George Passmore, together known as Gilbert and George, came to notice in the late 1960s, when they presented themselves as 'singing' and 'living sculptures'. The two usually portray themselves in their own panelled photo-works.

1 We try not to have ideas, preferring accidents. To create, you must empty yourself of every artistic thought.

Independent 17 April 1989

Marcel Proust (1871–1922)
FRENCH NOVELIST
After his mother's death in 1905 he became a recluse, exploring in fictional form the psychology of human memory. Remembrance of Things Past *(title also transl.* In Search of Lost Time, *1913–27) was influenced by Bergson's observations on time. 'After Proust, there are certain things that simply cannot be done again,'* FRANÇOISE SAGAN *declared. 'He marks off for you the boundaries of your talent.'*

1 One becomes moral as soon as one is unhappy.

Within a Budding Grove, 'Madame Swann at Home' (vol. 1 of *Remembrance of Things Past*, transl. C. K. Scott Moncrieff and Terence Kilmartin, 1981)

2 The charms of the passing stranger are generally in direct ratio to the swiftness of our passage.

Ibid., 'Place-Names: The Place'

3 If a little day dreaming is dangerous, the cure for it is not to dream less but to dream more, to dream all the time.

Elstir, ibid.

4 Our memory is like one of those shops in the window of which is exposed now one, now another photograph of the same person. And as a rule the most recent exhibit remains for some time the only one to be seen.

Narrator, ibid.

5 The features of our face are hardly more than gestures which force of habit made permanent. Nature, like the destruction of Pompeii, like the metamorphosis of a nymph, has arrested us in an accustomed movement.

Ibid.

6 For one disorder that doctors cure with medicaments (as I am assured they do

occasionally succeed in doing) they produce a dozen others in healthy subjects by inoculating them with that pathogenic agent a thousand times more virulent than all the microbes in the world, the idea that one is ill.

Dr du Boulbon, in *The Guermantes Way*, ch. 1 (vol. 2 of *Remembrance of Things Past*, transl. C. K. Scott Moncrieff and Terence Kilmartin, 1981)

7 Everything we think of as great has come to us from neurotics. It is they and they alone who found religions and create great works of art.

Ibid.

8 We may, indeed, say that the hour of death is uncertain, but when we say this we think of that hour as situated in a vague and remote expanse of time; it does not occur to us that it can have any connexion with the day that has already dawned and can mean that death – or its first assault and partial possession of us, after which it will never leave hold of us again – may occur this very afternoon, so far from uncertain, this afternoon whose time-table, hour by hour, has been settled in advance.

Narrator, ibid.

9 A change in the weather is sufficient to create the world and ourselves anew.

Ibid., ch. 2

10 Illness is the most heeded of doctors: to kindness and wisdom we make promises only; pain we obey.

Cities of the Plain, pt 2, ch. 1, ibid.

11 The regularity of a habit is generally in proportion to its absurdity.

The Captive (vol. 3 of *Remembrance of Things Past*, transl. C. K. Scott Moncrieff and Terence Kilmartin, 1981)

12 No banishment, indeed, to the South Pole, or to the summit of Mont Blanc, can separate us so entirely from our fellow creatures as a prolonged sojourn in the seclusion of an inner vice.

Ibid.

13 That translucent alabaster of our memories.

Ibid.

14 When two people part it is the one who is not in love who makes the tender speeches.

Ibid.

15 We find a little of everything in our memory; it is a sort of pharmacy, a sort of chemical laboratory, in which our groping hand may come to rest, now on sedative drug, now on a dangerous poison.

Ibid.

16 The human plagiarism which is most

difficult to avoid, for individuals . . . is self-plagiarism.

The Fugitive, ibid.

17 Let us leave pretty women to men with no imagination.

Ibid. The line originally appeared in Proust's early novel *Jean Santeuil* (1899).

18 The true paradises are paradises we have lost.

Time Regained (vol. 4 of *Remembrance of Things Past*, transl. C. K. Scott Moncrieff, Terence Kilmartin and Andreas Mayor, 1981)

19 A work in which there are theories is like an object which still has its price-tag on it.

Ibid.

20 I understood that all these materials for a work of literature were simply my past life; I understood that they had come to me, in frivolous pleasures, in indolence, in tenderness, in unhappiness, and that I had stored them up without divining the purpose for which they were destined or even their continued existence any more than a seed does when it forms within itself a reserve of all the nutritious substances from which it will feed a plant.

Ibid.

21 If unhappiness develops the forces of the mind, happiness alone is salutary to the body.

Ibid.

22 As for happiness, that is really useful to us in one way only, by making unhappiness possible.

Ibid.

Mario Puzo (1920–99)

US NOVELIST

His novel of the Sicilian Mafia in New York, The Godfather *(1969, filmed 1972), brought him huge success. He also co-scripted the two film sequels (1974 and 1980).*

1 He's a businessman. . . . I'll make him an offer he can't refuse.

Don Vito Corleone, in *The Godfather*, bk 1, ch. 1 (1969). The line also appears in FRANCIS FORD COPPOLA's film version of the book, written in collaboration with Puzo (1972).

2 A lawyer with his briefcase can steal more than a hundred men with guns.

Ibid. A favourite saying of the Don, dropped from the screenplay.

3 Like many businessmen of genius he [Don Corleone] learned that free competition was wasteful, monopoly efficient. And so he simply set about achieving that efficient monopoly.

Ibid., bk 3, ch. 14

4 He [Jordan Hawley] was . . . a degenerate

gambler. That is, a man who gambled simply to gamble and must lose. As a hero who goes to war must die. Show me a gambler and I'll show you a loser, show me a hero and I'll show you a corpse.

Fools Die, ch. 2 (1978)

5 What we think of as our sensitivity is only the higher evolution of terror in a poor dumb beast. We suffer for nothing. Our own death wish is our only real tragedy.

Merlyn, ibid., ch. 55

Thomas Pynchon (b. 1937)

US NOVELIST

Experimental, esoteric, and crammed with mathematical and scientific information, his novels include his first book V (1963), The Crying of Lot 49 (1966) and his magnum opus Gravity's Rainbow (1973), a darkly farcical anti-war satire.

1 Living inside the System is like riding across the country in a bus driven by a maniac bent on suicide . . .

Gravity's Rainbow, pt 3 (1973)

2 If there is something comforting – religious, if you want – about paranoia, there is still also anti-paranoia, where nothing is connected to anything, a condition not many of us can bear for long.

Ibid.

3 There's nothing so loathsome as a sentimental surrealist.

Ibid., pt 4

Muhammar Qaddafi (b. 1942)

LIBYAN LEADER

Described in turn as 'the mad dog of the Middle East' by RONALD REAGAN *and 'my brother leader' by* NELSON MANDELA, *he deposed King Idris in 1969 and became Chairman of the Revolutionary Command Council, and President of Libya in 1977.*

1 Nations whose nationalism is destroyed are subject to ruin.

The Green Book, pt. 3, 'The Social Basis of the Third Universal Theory' (1976–9)

Mary Quant (b. 1934)

BRITISH FASHION DESIGNER

A prime mover in 1960s 'swinging London', she opened one of the capital's first boutiques, Bazaar, in Chelsea, which sold her 'mod' and affordable designs, including the mini-skirts which she is credited with inventing.

1 I saw no reason why childhood shouldn't last for ever. I wanted everyone to retain the grace of a child and not to have to become stilted, confined, ugly beings. So I created clothes that worked and moved and allowed people to run, to jump, to leap, to retain their precious freedom.

Interview in *Harper's & Queen* May 1973

2 Having money is rather like being a blond. It is more fun but not vital.

Quoted in the *Observer* 2 Nov. 1986

Dan Quayle (b. 1947)

US POLITICIAN AND VICE-PRESIDENT

He was elected as a Republican to the House of Representatives in 1976 and to the Senate in 1980. As vice-president under GEORGE BUSH *(1989–93), he was mocked for his gaffes, and called a 'twink' by* P. J. O'ROURKE. *See also* LLOYD BENTSEN 1.

1 Space is almost infinite. As a matter of fact, we think it is infinite.

Daily Telegraph 8 March 1989

2 Let's ask ourselves, does America really need seventy percent of the world's lawyers?

Quoted in the *International Herald Tribune* 15 August 1991

3 You do the policy, I'll do the politics.

Remark to aide, quoted in the *International Herald Tribune* 13 January 1992

Jonathan Raban (b. 1942)

BRITISH AUTHOR AND CRITIC

He is known primarily for his travelogues, for example Old Glory *(1981),* Coasting *(1986) and* Passage to Juneau: A Sea and Its Meanings *(1999). He has also published literary criticism.*

1 The city as we imagine it, then, soft city of illusion, myth, aspiration, and nightmare, is as real, maybe more real, than the hard city one can locate on maps in statistics, in monographs on urban sociology and demography and architecture.

   Soft City, ch. 1 (1974)

2 Life, as the most ancient of all metaphors insists, is a journey; and the travel book, in its deceptive simulation of the journey's fits and starts, rehearses life's own fragmentation. More even than the novel, it embraces the contingency of things.

   For Love and Money, pt 5 (1987)

(Sir) Sarvepalli Radhakrishnan

(1888–1975)

INDIAN PHILOSOPHER AND PRESIDENT

Professor of Eastern Religions and Ethics at Oxford (1936–52) and Chancellor of the University of Delhi (1953–62), he was Indian Ambassador to the Soviet Union (1949–52) and later India's President (1962–7).

1 It is not God that is worshipped but the group or authority that claims to speak in His name. Sin becomes disobedience to authority not violation of integrity.

   Quoted in *Techniques of Persuasion,* ch. 11 (1965) by J. A. C. Brown. Referring to organized religion.

James Rado (b. 1939) and Gerome Ragni (b. 1942)

US SONGWRITERS

They are known principally as lyricists for the first rock musical Hair *(1967), which prompted the reaction by Brendan Gill of the* New Yorker: *'One can't not consent to this merry mind-blowing exercise in holy gibberish.'*

1 This is the dawning of the age of Aquarius.

   'Aquarius' (song, with music by Galt MacDermot) in *Hair* (stage musical 1967, filmed 1979)

Craig Raine (b. 1944)

BRITISH POET AND CRITIC

He is chief exponent of what JAMES FENTON *named the 'Martian' school, which treats familiar objects from an alien perspective, as in* A Martian Sends a Postcard Home *(1979). Other collections include* Rich *(1984) and* Whereabouts Unknown *(1996).*

1 *The mind is a museum*
to be looted at night.
'The Grey Boy', publ. in *Rich* (1984)

2 **The task of the artist at any time is uncompromisingly simple – to discover what has not yet been done, and to do it.**
Guardian 19 August 1988

3 **Great writers arrive among us like new diseases – threatening, powerful, impatient for patients to pick up their virus, irresistible.**
Independent on Sunday 18 November 1990

Kathleen Raine (1908–2003)
BRITISH POET
Her meditative and lyrical work, much of it inspired from the natural world, includes Stone and Flower *(1943) and* The Hollow Hill *(1965). She is an authority on William Blake and in 1981 founded the journal Temenos.*

1 *Unwise we feel, but wise we know*
Living in time is but to seem –
Like green leaves on a tree we grow,
But each must fall and fade alone.
'Seen in a Glass', dated 21 June 1941, publ. in *Living in Time* (1946)

2 *The ghosts are hungry, the ghosts are*
divine,
but the pigs eat the meal, and the priests
drink the wine.
'Maternal Grief', publ. in *Stone and Flower* (1943). Closing lines of poem.

3 *Cameras and motor-cars*
Spin on the hub of nothingness
On which revolve the years and stars.
'Ex nihilo', publ. in *The Pythoness* (1949)

4 *Love mourns its dead*
Not by number, but, one by one, each by
name.
'Statistical Grief', publ. in *The Oracle in the Heart (Poems 1975–1978)* (1980)

5 **I couldn't claim that I have never felt the urge to explore evil, but when you descend into hell you have to be very careful.**
The Times 18 April 1992

(Sir) Walter Raleigh (1861–1922)
BRITISH SCHOLAR AND CRITIC
His confessed aim in writing was 'to explain people', as in his studies of William Blake and Samuel Johnson. His lighter pieces were collected in Laughter from a Cloud *(1923).*

1 *I wish I loved the Human Race;*
I wish I loved its silly face;
I wish I liked the way it walks;
I wish I liked the way it talks;
And when I'm introduced to one
I wish I thought What Jolly Fun!
'Wishes of an Elderly Man', publ. in *Laughter from a Cloud* (1923)

(Sir) David Ramsbotham (b. 1934)
BRITISH GENERAL AND PRISONS INSPECTOR
After an army career, he was Inspector of Prisons for England and Wales (1995–2001). In 1999 he caused controversy when he called for the early release of James Bulger's killers.

1 **Prison *is* punishment, it is not *for* punishment.**
Interview on BBC Radio 4, 'The World at One', 14 March 1996. Opposing calls for harsher prison regimes.

Jeannette Rankin (1880–1973)
US SUFFRAGIST AND POLITICIAN
She was the first woman to be elected to Congress, serving two terms (1917–19 and 1941–3). A Republican and a pacifist, she campaigned vigorously for women's rights and in 1941 was the only member to vote against war with Japan.

1 **The individual woman is required . . . a thousand times a day to choose either to accept her appointed role and thereby rescue her good disposition out of the wreckage of her self-respect, or else follow an independent line of behavior and rescue her self-respect out of the wreckage of her good disposition.**
Quoted in *Jeannette Rankin: First Lady in Congress*, ch. 3 (1974) by Hannah Josephson

2 **You can no more win a war than you can win an earthquake.**
Quoted ibid., ch. 8

Frederic Raphael (b. 1931)
BRITISH AUTHOR AND CRITIC
A writer of novels and plays which explore contemporary social issues, he is best known for The Graduate Wife *(1962) and* The Glittering Prizes *(1976). He has also written screenplays for film and television.*

1 **The great networks are there to prove that ideas can be canned like spaghetti. If everything ends up by tasting like everything else, is that not the evidence that it has been properly cooked?**
'The Language of Television', publ. in *The State of the Language* (ed. Christopher Ricks, 1980)

2 **The party of God and the party of Literature have more in common than either will admit; their texts may conflict, but their bigotries coincide. Both insist on being the sole custodians of the true word and its only interpreters.**
Sunday Times 12 February 1989

Gerald Ratner (b. 1949)
BRITISH BUSINESSMAN
He was Chief Executive of the Ratners Group from

1986 until 1992, resigning after his remarks about the poor quality of Ratners products received widespread publicity.

> 1 We also do cut-glass sherry decanters complete with six glasses on a silver plated tray – that your butler can serve you drinks on – all for £4.95. People say how can you sell this for such a low price. I say because it is total crap. . . . We even sell a pair of earrings for under £1, which is cheaper than a prawn sandwich from Marks & Spencers. But I have to say the earrings probably won't last as long.
>
> Speech to the Institute of Directors, Albert Hall, 23 April 1991, quoted in *The Times*, 24 April 1991

(Sir) Terence Rattigan (1911–77)
BRITISH PLAYWRIGHT
The comedy French Without Tears (1936) was the first of numerous West End successes. His more serious plays include The Winslow Boy (1946, filmed 1948 and 1999), The Deep Blue Sea (1952) and Separate Tables (1954).

> 1 It is easy to do justice – very hard to do right. Unfortunately while the appeal of justice is intellectual, the appeal of right appears for some odd reason to induce tears in court.
>
> Sir Robert Morton, in *The Winslow Boy*, act 4 (1946)
>
> 2 The headmaster said you ruled them with a rod of iron. He called you the Himmler of the lower fifth.
>
> Peter Gilbert, addressing Andrew Crocker-Harris, in *The Browning Version* (1948)

(Sir) Simon Rattle (b. 1955)
BRITISH CONDUCTOR
He turned the City of Birmingham Symphony Orchestra into a world-class orchestra during his time as Conductor (1980–91) and Director (1991–8). In 2002 he took up the post of Chief Conductor and Artistic Director of the Berlin Philharmonic Orchestra.

> 1 If anyone has conducted a Beethoven performance, and then doesn't have to go to an osteopath, then there's something wrong.
>
> *Guardian* 31 May 1990

Irina Ratushinskaya (b. 1954)
RUSSIAN POET
Her campaigning for human rights led to a term in a labour camp (1982–6). Her poems are collected in No, I'm Not Afraid (1986) and Grey is the Colour of Hope (1988). 'For a poet,' she said, 'it is more important to keep in touch with God than politicians.'

> 1 *In order to understand birds*
> *You have to be a convict.*

> *And if you share your bread –*
> *It means your time is done.*
>
> 'The Sparrows of Butyrki', written 1981, publ. in *No, I'm Not Afraid* (1986)

Man Ray (1890–1976)
US PAINTER AND PHOTOGRAPHER
Originally Emanuel Rabinovitch. With MARCEL DUCHAMP *and* FRANCIS PICABIA *he formed a Dadaist group in New York, before moving to Paris in 1921. He took up photography to finance his painting, and also made Surrealist films, returning to the USA in 1940.*

> 1 It has never been my object to record my dreams, just the determination to realize them.
>
> Julien Levy exhibition catalogue, April 1945, quoted in *Man Ray*, Introduction (1988) by Neil Baldwin
>
> 2 To me, a painter, if not the most useful, is the least harmful member of our society.
>
> *Self Portrait*, ch. 6 (1963)
>
> 3 I paint what cannot be photographed, that which comes from the imagination or from dreams, or from an unconscious drive. I photograph the things that I do not wish to paint, the things which already have an existence.
>
> Interview publ. in *Caméra*, repr. in *Man Ray: Photographer* (ed. Philippe Sers, 1981). Man Ray repeated this remark in slightly different forms on various occasions.
>
> 4 *An original is a creation*
> *motivated by desire.*
> *Any reproduction of an original*
> *is motivated be necessity . . .*
> *It is marvelous that we are*
> *the only species that creates*
> *gratuitous forms*
> *To create is divine, to reproduce*
> *is human.*
>
> 'Originals Graphic Multiples', publ. in *Objets de mon affection* (1983), repr. in *Man Ray*, ch. 24 (1988) by Neil Baldwin

Sam Rayburn (1882–1961)
US LEGISLATOR AND POLITICIAN
Describing himself as 'without prefix, without suffix, and without apology', he was a Democrat in the House of Representatives 1913–61 and an architect of ROOSEVELT's *New Deal programme. He served as Speaker of the House from 1940.*

> 1 If you want to get along, go along.
>
> Quoted in *Forge of Democracy*, ch. 6 (1963) by Neil MacNeil. Rayburn's forty-eight years in Congress was the longest term on record, which together with his political influence earned him the sobriquet 'Mr Democrat'.

Piers Paul Read (b. 1941)

BRITISH AUTHOR

Praised by MALCOLM BRADBURY *as 'a densely social novelist who knows that public and private worlds intersect at every point', he had success with* A Married Man *(1979) and* On the Third Day *(1990).*

1 Sins become more subtle as you grow older: you commit sins of despair rather than lust.

Daily Telegraph 3 October 1990

Peter Reading (b. 1946)

BRITISH POET

Called by TOM PAULIN *'the unofficial laureate of a decaying England', he writes of the degradation of contemporary life in uncompromising language. His collections include* Ukulele Music *(1985) and* Eschatological *(1996).*

1 *This is unclean: to eat turbots on Tuesdays, tying the turban unclockwise at cockcrow, cutting the beard in a south-facing mirror, wearing the mitre while sipping the Bovril, chawing the pig and the hen and the ox-tail.*

Going On (1985). First lines of untitled poem.

2 Anyone who lives in this time is concerned with grottiness.

International Herald Tribune 10 March 1988

3 *Nothing can ever be done; things are intractably thus; all know the bite of grief, all will be brought to destiny's issue; those who have precognition suffer sorrow beforehand; bodies are bankrupt, the main Expedition has left us behind it.*

Concluding lines of untitled poem, publ. in *Perduta Gente* (1989)

Nancy Reagan (b. 1923)

US SCREEN ACTRESS AND FIRST LADY

Named Nancy Davis before her marriage to RONALD REAGAN *in 1952, she appeared in* The Next Voice You Hear *(1950), Donovan's Brain (1953) and, opposite her husband, Hellcats of the Navy (1957).*

1 A woman is like a teabag – only in hot water do you realize how strong she is.

Quoted in the *Observer* 29 March 1981. The quote has also been ascribed to ELEANOR ROOSEVELT, as cited by HILLARY CLINTON.

2 I see the first lady as another means to keep a president from becoming isolated.

Quoted in the *International Herald Tribune* 26 May 1988

3 Just say no.

Slogan for campaign to persuade people not to take illegal drugs, 1980s

Ronald Reagan (b. 1911)

US SCREEN ACTOR, POLITICIAN AND PRESIDENT

The 'Great Communicator' was a sportscaster before signing a Hollywood contract in 1937 and appearing in some fifty films. As President of the Screen Actors' Guild (1947–52), he was politically a liberal Democrat but he switched to the Republican Party in 1962. He was elected Governor of California in 1966 and was US President 1980–89. See also JACK DEMPSEY 1, RONALD KNOX 4, GORE VIDAL 16, 17.

1 Randy – where's the rest of me?

Drake McHugh (Ronald Reagan) to Randy Monaghan (Ann Sheridan), in *Kings Row* (film, 1942, screenplay by Casey Robinson, based on the novel by Henry Bellamann, directed by Sam Wood). The words are spoken by McHugh, a war veteran who wakes to find his legs amputated by a malicious doctor, in what is generally regarded as Reagan's best film performance. They provided him with a title for his 1965 autobiography, *Where's the Rest of Me?*

2 We are at war with the most dangerous enemy that has ever faced mankind in his long climb from the swamp to the stars, and it has been said if we lose that war, and in so doing lose this way of freedom of ours, history will record with the greatest astonishment that those who had the most to lose did the least to prevent its happening.

Referring to the war in Vietnam, in 'A Time for Choosing', television address, 27 October 1964, publ. in *Speaking My Mind* (1989).

3 No government ever voluntarily reduces itself in size. Government programs, once launched, never disappear. Actually, a government bureau is the nearest thing to eternal life we'll ever see on this earth! Ibid.

4 A tree's a tree. How many more do you need to look at?

Speech 12 September 1965, quoted in the *Sacramento Bee* 12 March 1966. Reagan later denied having made this statement.

5 Politics is just like show business, you have a hell of an opening, coast for a while, and then have a hell of a close.

Remark in 1966, quoted in *There He Goes Again* (ed. Mark Green and Gail MacColl, 1983)

6 Government does not solve problems; it subsidizes them.

Speech 11 December 1972, publ. in *Speaking My Mind*, 'The Wit and Wisdom of Ronald Reagan' (1989)

7 Inflation is as violent as a mugger, as fright-

ening as an armed robber and as deadly as a hit man.

Speech at Republican Party fund-raising dinner, quoted in the *Los Angeles Times* 20 October 1978

8 Of the four wars in my lifetime, none came about because the US was too strong.

Quoted in the *Observer* 29 June 1980

9 Approximately 80% of our air pollution stems from hydrocarbons released by vegetation, so let's not go overboard in setting and enforcing tough emission standards from man-made sources.

Sierra 10 September 1980, quoted in *Reagan's Reign of Error*, 'Killer Trees' (ed. Mark Green and Gail MacColl, 1987). Reagan later amended this figure to 93 per cent.

10 You can tell a lot about a fellow's character by his way of eating jelly beans.

Quoted in *The New York Times* 15 January 1981

11 There is nothing better for the inside of a man than the outside of a horse.

Remark 13 August 1987, North Platte, Nebraska, quoted in *Time* 28 December 1987. Said to be one of Reagan's favourite expressions, uttered on various occasions, and probably not original.

12 Well, I learned a lot. . . . You'd be surprised. They're all individual countries.

Quoted in the *Washington Post* 6 December 1982. Following a tour of South America.

13 We might come closer to balancing the Budget if all of us lived closer to the Commandments and the Golden Rule.

Quoted in the *Observer* 5 February 1983

14 So, in your discussions of the nuclear freeze proposals, I urge you to beware the temptation of pride – the temptation of blithely declaring yourselves above it all and label both sides equally at fault, to ignore the facts of history and the aggressive impulses of an evil empire, to simply call the arms race a giant misunderstanding and thereby remove yourself from the struggle between right and wrong, good and evil.

Speech at Annual Convention of the National Association of Evangelicals, Orlando, Florida, 8 March 1983, publ. in *Speaking My Mind* (1989). In the same speech, Reagan declared, speaking of those who live in 'totalitarian darkness': 'Let us be aware that while they preach the supremacy of the state, declare its omnipotence over individual man, and predict its eventual domination of all peoples of the earth – they are the focus of evil in the modern world.'

15 If the Soviet Union let another political party come into existence, they would still be a one-party state, because everybody would join the other party.

Said to Polish Americans in Chicago, 23 June 1983, publ. ibid. 'The Wit and Wisdom of Ronald Reagan'

16 My fellow Americans, I am pleased to tell you I just signed legislation which outlaws Russia forever. The bombing begins in five minutes.

Microphone test for radio broadcast, 11 August 1984, quoted in *The New York Times* 13 August 1984

17 They [Nicaraguan Contras] are our brothers, these freedom fighters. . . . They are the moral equal of our Founding Fathers and the brave men and women of the French Resistance. We cannot turn away from them, for the struggle here is not right versus left; it is right versus wrong.

Speech to Conservative Political Action Conference, Washington DC, 1 March 1985, publ. in *Speaking My Mind* (1989)

18 Freedom-loving people around the world must say: I am a Berliner. I am a Jew in a world still threatened by anti-Semitism. I am an Afghan, and I am a prisoner of the gulag. I am a refugee in a crowded boat foundering off the coast of Vietnam. I am Laotian, a Cambodian, a Cuban, and a Miskito Indian in Nicaragua. I, too, am a potential victim of totalitarianism.

Speech at Bitburg, West Germany, 27 May 1985, publ. ibid.

19 After seeing *Rambo* last night I know what to do next time this happens.

Following the hijack of an aeroplane carrying US passengers in 1985, quoted in *City Limits* 16 December 1987. *Rambo* star SYLVESTER STALLONE was quoted in the *Sunday Express* 17 July 1988 as saying, 'When President Reagan stood up and said: "Having seen *Rambo* I know what to do with Libya", it was the kiss of death. He made Rambo a Republican.'

20 We know that this mad dog of the Middle East has a goal of a world revolution, Muslim fundamentalist revolution, which is targeted on many of his own Arab compatriots and where we figure in that I don't know.

Of Libyan leader Colonel QADDAFI, at press conference, 9 April 1986, quoted in *The New York Times* 10 April 1986. Six days later, Reagan launched a bombing raid on Tripoli, killing about a hundred civilians.

21 No one can kill Americans and brag about it. No one.

Quoted in the *Observer* 27 April 1986, after the US attack on Libya, 15 April 1986. The attack followed the bombing of a discotheque in West Berlin, at which two American servicemen were killed and 200 injured.

22 Surround yourself with the best people you can find, delegate authority, and don't interfere.

Quoted in *Fortune* September 1986

23 That's the nice thing about this job. You

get to quote yourself shamelessly. If you don't, Larry Speakes will.

Quoted in the *Daily Telegraph* 14 April 1988. SPEAKES was then Press Secretary at the White House.

24 **Would you go out there and win one for the Gipper?**

Speech in San Diego, 7 November 1988, publ. in *Speaking My Mind* (1989). One of Reagan's favourite sayings, this is associated with the football star George Gipp (1895–1931), whom he played in the 1940 film *Knute Rockne – All-American*.

25 **Information is the oxygen of the modern age. It seeps through the walls topped by barbed wire, it wafts across the electrified borders.**

Quoted in the *Guardian* 14 June 1989

Helen Reddy (b. 1941)
AUSTRALIAN-BORN US SINGER AND SONGWRITER
Her song 'I am Woman' (1972) became an anthem for the women's liberation movement of the 1970s. Later hits included 'Angie Baby' (1974).

1 Yes, I am wise, but it's wisdom born of pain
  Yes, I've paid the price, but look how much I've gained
  If I have to, I can do anything
  I am strong, I am invincible, I am woman.
  'I am Woman' (song) on the album *I am Woman* (1972)

Florence Reece
She was the wife of a rank and file organizer for the National Miners' Union in Harlan County, Kentucky, and composer of the workers' anthem, 'Which Side are You On?' (1931).

1 Come all of you good workers,
  Good news to you I'll tell
  Of how the good old union
  Has come in here to dwell.
  Which side are you on?
  'Which Side are You On?' (song, 1931). Reece recounted how she wrote the words to this song after a raid on her home by the High Sheriff and his deputies ('they were really company gun thugs') in search of her husband during the year-long coal strike at the Brookside Mine in Harlan. Set to a traditional hymn tune, it was sung by her daughters in the union hall and later became an anthem of diverse left-wing causes. The events of the strike were portrayed in the film *Harlan County, USA* (1976).

Henry Reed (1914–86)
BRITISH POET AND PLAYWRIGHT
He established his reputation as a poet with A Map of Verona *(1946) and later went on to write a series of witty radio plays including* The Private Life of Hilda Tablet *(1954).*

1 Today we have naming of parts. Yesterday,
  We had daily cleaning. And tomorrow morning,
  We shall have what to do after firing. But today,
  Today we have naming of parts. Japonica
  Glistens like coral in all of the neighbouring gardens,
  And today we have naming of parts.
  'Lessons of the War: 1. Naming of Parts', publ. in *A Map of Verona* (1946). First verse.

2 They call it easing the Spring: it is perfectly easy
  If you have any strength in your thumb: like the bolt,
  And the breech, and the cocking-piece, and the point of balance,
  Which in our case we have not got.
  Ibid. Last verse.

John Reed (1887–1920)
US JOURNALIST AND AUTHOR
He wrote Insurgent Mexico *(1914), based on his experience of the Mexican Revolution, and* Ten Days That Shook the World *(1919), an eyewitness account of the Russian Revolution. After helping to found the Communist Labor Party in the US, he worked in the Soviet propaganda bureau and was buried in the Kremlin.*

1 In the relations of a weak Government and a rebellious people there comes a time when every act of the authorities exasperates the masses, and every refusal to act excites their contempt.
  Ten Days That Shook the World, ch. 3 (1919)

2 The devout Russian people no longer needed priests to pray them into heaven. On earth they were building a kingdom more bright than any heaven had to offer, and for which it was a glory to die.
  Ibid., ch. 10

Lou Reed (b. 1944)
US ROCK MUSICIAN
His often dark and sombre songs defined the sound of the Velvet Underground, the proto-punk New York art band which he co-founded in 1965. Since 1970 he has had a successful solo career. See also NELSON ALGREN 1.

1 I'm waiting for my man
  Twenty-six dollars in my hand
  Up to Lexington 125
  Feeling sick and dirty more dead than alive
  I'm waiting for my man.
  'I'm Waiting for the Man' (song) on the album *The Velvet Underground and Nico* (1967) by the Velvet Underground and Nico

2 I don't know just where I'm going
  But I'm gonna try for the kingdom if I can
  'Cause it makes me feel like I'm a man

When I put a spike into my vein
And I'll tell ya, things aren't quite the same.
'Heroin' (song) on ibid.

3   *You're so vicious.*
'Vicious' (song) on the album *Transformer* (1972)

4   *It's such a perfect day*
I'm glad I spent it with you
Oh such a perfect day
You just keep me hanging on.
'Perfect Day' (song), ibid. The song was a million-seller when released as a single recorded by various artists for charity in 1997.

5   *The currents rage deep inside us*
This is the age of video violence.
'Video Violence' (song) on the album *Mistrial* (1986)

6   *I don't like nostalgia unless it's mine.*
Evening Standard 8 June 1989

7   *When you're growing up in a small town*
You know you'll grow down in a small town
There is only one good use for a small town
You hate it and you know you'll have to
leave.
'Small Town' (song) on the album *Songs for Drella* (1990) by Lou Reed and John Cale

8   *Life is like Sanskrit read to a pony.*
'What's Good' (song) on the album *Magic and Loss* (1992)

Oliver Reed (1938–99)
BRITISH ACTOR
A symbol of unreconstructed masculinity, he was a powerful presence in such films as Women in Love *(1969) and* The Devils *(1971).*

1   I do not live in the world of sobriety.
Quoted in the *Sunday Times* 27 December 1987. Reed was famous for his drunken off-screen behaviour. He died in a Maltese bar.

William Rees-Mogg (b. 1928)
BRITISH JOURNALIST AND PUBLIC FIGURE
Baron Rees-Mogg of Hinton Blewitt. After editing The Times *(1967–81), he was Chairman of the Arts Council (1982–9) and first head of the Broadcasting Standards Council (1988–93).*

1   In the end you must either allow people liberty or you must shoot them. If a man claims a vote you must either give him a vote or be prepared to take his life.
Quoted by TONY PARSONS in *Arena* September/October 1989, 'The Tattooed Jungle'

2   As long as Archer remained the candidate the dormant Ethics and Integrity Committee was as much a sign of virtue as an unread Bible in a brothel.
The Times 22 November 1999. JEFFREY ARCHER was forced to withdraw from the London mayoral election following the revelation that he

lied in a previous libel case in 1986. WILLIAM HAGUE had earlier endorsed Archer as 'a candidate of probity and integrity'.

Martha Reeves (b. 1941)
US SINGER
A secretary to Tamla Motown A&R executive William 'Mickey' Stevenson, she had hits with the Vandellas, including 'Heatwave' (1963), 'Dancing in the Street' (1964) and 'Nowhere to Run' (1965).

1   *Calling out around the world*
Are you ready for a brand new beat?
Summer's here and the time is right
For dancing in the street.
'Dancing in the Street' (song, 1964, written by William 'Mickey' Stevenson and Marvin Gaye) on the album *Dance Party* (1965) by Martha and the Vandellas

Wilhelm Reich (1897–1957)
AUSTRIAN-BORN US PSYCHOANALYST AND BIOPHYSICIST
In his principal work, The Function of the Orgasm *(1927), he argued that neuroses resulted from sexual repression and could be released through regular orgasm. He emigrated to the USA in 1939, where he founded the Orgone Institute, was prosecuted for fraudulent practices and died in gaol.*

1   The pleasure of living and the pleasure of the orgasm are identical. Extreme orgasm anxiety forms the basis of the general fear of life.
The Function of the Orgasm, ch. 5, sect. 4 (1927, transl. 1942)

Jamie Reid (b. 1947)
BRITISH ARTIST
He came to notice in the 1970s for his contributions to the iconography of punk, such as his depiction of the Queen pierced with a safety pin.

1   Please wash your hands before leaving the 20th century.
Title of multi-media exhibition, 1970s, quoted in *The Incomplete Works of Jamie Reid*, 'Death' (1987) by Jamie Reid and Jon Savage

Jimmy Reid (b. 1932)
BRITISH TRADE UNION OFFICIAL
A Communist shop steward, he was prominent in industrial disputes in the early 1970s, notably at the Upper Clyde Shipyard.

1   A rat race is for rats. We're not rats. We're human beings. Reject the insidious pressures in society that would blunt your critical faculties to all that is happening around you, that would caution silence in the face of injustice lest you jeopardize your chances of promotion and self-advancement. This is how it starts and,

before you know where you are, you're a
fully paid-up member of the rat pack. The
price is too high.

Rectorial address, Glasgow University, April
1972, quoted in *Writings on the Wall*, pt 1 (ed.
Tony Benn, 1984)

Keith Reid (b. 1946)

BRITISH SONGWRITER

*He was lyricist with the progressive rock group Pro-
col Harum on all their major hits, including 'A
Whiter Shade of Pale', 'Homburg' (both 1967) and
'A Salty Dog' (1969). He later managed bands.*

1 Her face at first just ghostly
Turned a whiter shade of pale.

'A Whiter Shade of Pale' (song, 1967, with music
by Gary Brooker). Procol Harum's single was a
worldwide hit, and charted again on its re-issue
in 1972.

Theodor Reik (1888–1969)

US PSYCHOLOGIST

Although a lifelong friend of FREUD, *he differed
from him in his belief that neuroses developed
from a weakness in the ego. His books include*
Myth and Guilt *(1957) and* The Need To Be
Loved *(1963).*

1 In our civilization, men are afraid that
they will not be men enough and women
are afraid that they may be considered
only women.

Esquire November 1958

Ad Reinhardt (1913–67)

US ARTIST

*Adolf Reinhardt. He joined the avant-garde Ameri-
can Abstract Artists association in 1937. His later
minimal, monochrome style was typified in his
series of 'Black Paintings' (from the late 1950s).*

1 Art is art-as-art and everything else is
everything else. Art-as-art is nothing but
art. Art is not what is not art.

'Art-as-art', publ. in *Art International*,
December 1962, repr. in *The Selected Writings of
Ad Reinhardt*, ch. 2 (ed. Barbara Rose, 1975)

2 Art is too serious to be taken seriously.

Quoted in *Ad Reinhardt*, pt 1 (1981) by Lucy R.
Lippard

Erich Maria Remarque (1898–1970)

GERMAN-BORN US NOVELIST

*Drafted into the German army at the age of eigh-
teen, he described his wartime experiences in his
major work* All Quiet on the Western Front
*(1929). He emigrated to the USA in 1939, and was
naturalized in 1947.*

1 All Quiet on the Western Front.

English title of novel, *Im Westen nichts Neues*
(1929), which describes the daily routine of soldiers fighting in the trenches in the First World
War.

June Reinisch (b. 1943)

US PSYCHOLOGIST

She was joint editor and contributor to Mascu-
linity/Femininity *(1987) and* AIDS and Sex
(1990), and co-authored the Kinsey Institute New
Report on Sex *(1991).*

1 When people say women can't be trusted
because they cycle every month, my
response is that men cycle every day, so
they should only be allowed to negotiate
peace treaties in the evening.

The Times 20 January 1992

Agnes Repplier (1858–1950)

US AUTHOR AND SOCIAL CRITIC

*A humorous and popular speaker and essayist on
diverse subjects, she published numerous works
including* Books and Men *(1888),* Points of Fiction *(1920) and an autobiography,* Eight Decades
(1937).

1 Anyone, however, who has had dealings
with dates knows that they are worse than
elusive, they are perverse. Events do not
happen at the right time, nor in their
proper sequence. That sense of harmony
with place and season which is so strong in
the historian – if he be a readable historian
– is lamentably lacking in history, which
takes no pains to verify his most convincing statements.

To Think of Tea!, ch. 1 (1932)

2 Humor brings insight and tolerance. Irony
brings a deeper and less friendly understanding.

In Pursuit of Laughter, ch. 9 (1936)

James Reston (1909–95)

SCOTTISH-BORN US JOURNALIST

He was associated with The New York Times *for
fifty years, winning Pulitzer Prizes in 1945 and 1957
for national reporting. For* ALISTAIR COOKE *he
was 'the most agile filcher of confidential agreements, the most alert, the most probing, the most
knowledgeable – the best – of all Washington correspondents'.*

1 The conflict between the men who make
and the men who report the news is as old
as time. News may be true, but it is not
truth, and reporters and officials seldom
see it the same way. . . . In the old days,
the reporters or couriers of bad news were
often put to the gallows; now they are
given the Pulitzer Prize, but the conflict
goes on.

The Artillery of the Press, 'The Tug of History'
(1966)

2 Europe has a press that stresses opinions;

America a press, radio, and television that emphasize news.

Ibid., 'The President and the Press'

3 All politics . . . are based on the indifference of the majority.

The New York Times 12 June 1968

4 In foreign policy you have to wait twenty-five years to see how it comes out.

International Herald Tribune 18 November 1991

David Reuben (b. 1933)
US PSYCHIATRIST

GORE VIDAL *called him a 'relentlessy cheery, often genuinely funny writer . . . a moralist, expressing the hang-ups of today's middle-aged, middle-class American Jews'. His most famous work is* Everything You Always Wanted To Know About Sex, But Were Afraid To Ask *(1969).*

1 Everything You Always Wanted to Know about Sex, but Were Afraid to Ask.

Book title (1969). Reuben's manual became America's number-one non-fiction bestseller, and gave the title to WOODY ALLEN's satirical movie released in 1972.

Kenneth Rexroth (1905–82)
US POET, CRITIC AND TRANSLATOR

Known as the 'Godfather of the Beats', he covered diverse themes and poetic techniques in his collections The Phoenix and the Tortoise *(1944),* The Signature of All Things *(1950) and* The Morning Star *(1979).*

1 Into the gap between technology and environment, a black and fearsome chasm, man pours himself.

'The Mirror of Magic', publ. in *New Republic* (1948), repr. in *With Eye and Ear* (1970)

2 Man thrives where angels die of ecstasy and pigs die of disgust. The contemporary situation is like a long-standing, fatal disease. It is impossible to recall what life was like without it. We seem always to have had cancer of the heart.

Bird in the Bush: Obvious Essays by Kenneth Rexroth, 'Kenneth Patchen, Naturalist of the Public Nightmare' (1959)

3 *Inside, the hideous British Necrophilia and the rancid Stink of the Church of England.*

'The Dragon and the Unicorn', pt 1, publ. in *Collected Longer Poems* (1968). Referring to Salisbury Cathedral.

Malvina Reynolds See PETE SEEGER.

Zandra Rhodes (b. 1940)
BRITISH FASHION DESIGNER

She showed her first collection in 1969, making use of chiffons and silks in her designs. In 1975 she branched out into cosmetics and jewellery.

1 The advantage of being female is that once you're past 65, you can be a dowager empress. After the difficult part in the middle, you're allowed to be eccentric.

Quoted in the *Guardian* 19 September 1998

Jean Rhys (c. 1890–1979)
BRITISH AUTHOR

Born Ella Gwendoline Rees Williams. Her early novels include Voyage in the Dark *(1934) and* Good Morning, Midnight *(1939). Her best known work,* Wide Sargasso Sea *(1966), developed the story of Rochester's mad wife in Charlotte Brontë's* Jane Eyre.

1 The feeling of Sunday is the same everywhere, heavy, melancholy, standing still. Like when they say, 'As it was in the beginning, is now, and ever shall be, world without end.'

Narrator (Anna Morgan), in *Voyage in the Dark,* pt 1, ch. 4 (1934)

2 She [Audrey] could give herself up to the written word as naturally as a good dancer to music or a fine swimmer to water. The only difficulty was that after finishing the last sentence she was left with a feeling at once hollow and uncomfortably full. Exactly like indigestion.

'The Insect World', publ. in *Sleep It off, Lady* (1976)

Ruggiero Ricci (b. 1918)
US VIOLINIST

Noted for his command of the nineteenth-century bravura repertoire, he toured widely in America and Europe, and in 1971 introduced Paganini's rediscovered Concerto No. 4.

1 A specialist is someone who does everything else worse.

Quoted in the *Daily Telegraph* 25 May 1990

Grantland Rice (1880–1954)
US SPORTSWRITER

The first American sportswriter, he is associated with the 'gee-whiz' school of writing. He worked for the New York Tribune *(1919–30) and also published prose and poetry on other topics.*

1 *For when the One Great Scorer comes to mark against your name,*
He writes – not that you won or lost – but how you played the Game.

'Alumnus Football', publ. in *Only the Brave* (1941).

(Sir) Tim Rice (b. 1944)
BRITISH SONGWRITER

His collaborations with composer Andrew Lloyd Webber include Jesus Christ Superstar *(1971) and* Evita *(1978). He was also the lyricist for* Chess *(1984) and* The Lion King *(1994).*

1 *Don't cry for me Argentina.*
Title of song (1976, music by Andrew Lloyd
Webber) in *Evita* (stage musical 1978, filmed
1996). The song was a hit for Julie Covington in
1976 and 1978, and for MADONNA in 1996.

Mandy Rice-Davies (b. 1944)
BRITISH MODEL AND CLUB HOSTESS
*As a show girl in Murray's Cabaret Club in
London, she met Christine Keeler, mistress of both
Conservative cabinet minister John Profumo and
the Soviet naval attaché in London, and in 1963
gave evidence in subsequent investigations of poss-
ible breaches of national security.*

1 *He would, wouldn't he?*
Remark in court, 29 June 1963, quoted in the
Guardian 1 July 1963. In response to the statement that Lord Astor, one of her alleged clients,
had denied having had sex with her. The
exchange took place in the wake of the Profumo
affair.

2 *My life has been one long descent into
respectability.*
Quoted by LYNN BARBER in the *Independent on
Sunday* 31 March 1991. Referring to reports that
Rice-Davies was on social terms with Sir Denis
Thatcher, husband of MARGARET THATCHER.

Adrienne Rich (b. 1929)
US POET AND AUTHOR
She addresses feminist themes in such volumes as
Snapshots of a Daughter-in-Law *(1963) and* The
Will to Change *(1971), and in her prose writings,
which include* Of Woman Born *(1976) and the
essays* Blood, Bread, and Poetry *(1986).*

1 *We who were loved will never
unlive that crippling fever.*
'After a Sentence in "Malte Laurids Brigge"',
publ. in *Snapshots of a Daughter-in-Law* (1963)

2 *Only to have a grief
equal to all these tears!*
'Peeling Onions', publ. ibid.

3 *The mind's passion is all for singling out.
Obscurity has another tale to tell.*
'Focus', publ. in *Necessities of Life* (1966)

4 *Now, again, poetry
violent, arcane, common,
hewn of the commonest living substance
into archway, portal, frame
I grasp for you, your bloodstained splinters,
your
ancient and stubborn poise
– as the earth trembles –
burning out from the grain*
'The Fact of a Doorframe', publ. in *The Fact of a
Doorframe* (1974)

5 *Every journey into the past is complicated
by delusions, false memories, false nam-
ings of real events.*
Of Woman Born, Foreword (1976)

6 *The worker can unionize, go out on strike;
mothers are divided from each other in
homes, tied to their children by compassionate bonds; our wildcat strikes have
most often taken the form of physical or
mental breakdown.*
Ibid., ch. 2

7 *No one lives in this room
without confronting the whiteness of the
wall
behind the poems, planks of books,
photographs of dead heroines.
Without contemplating last and late
the true nature of poetry. The drive
to connect. The dream of a common
language.*
'Origins and History of Consciousness', publ. in
The Dream of a Common Language (1978)

8 *They can rule the world while they can persuade us
our pain belongs in some order.
Is death by famine worse than death by
suicide,
than a life of famine and suicide . . . ?*
'Hunger', publ. ibid.

9 *How we dwelt in two worlds
the daughters and the mothers
in the kingdom of the sons.*
'Sibling Mysteries', publ. ibid.

10 *Rape is a part of war; but it may be more
accurate to say that the capacity for
dehumanizing another which so corrodes
male sexuality is carried over from sex into
war.*
'Caryatid', first publ. in *American Poetry Review*
May/June 1973, repr. in *On Lies, Secrets, and
Silence* (1979)

11 *The connections between and among
women are the most feared, the most prob-
lematic, and the most potentially transforming force on the planet.*
'Disloyal To Civilization: Feminism, Racism,
Gynophobia', first publ. in *Chrysalis*, no. 7
(1979), repr. ibid.

Frank Rich (b. 1949)
US CRITIC
He has been a New York Times *columnist since
1994 and from 1999 senior writer for* The New
York Times Magazine. *His publications include*
Ghost Light: A Memoir *(2000).*

1 *Yesterday's 'Revolution' can always be
tomorrow's Nike commercial.*
Quoted in *The New York Times Magazine*
16 November 2002

(Sir) Cliff Richard (b. 1940)
BRITISH SINGER
*Originally Harry Webb. Backed by the Shadows he
was promoted as Britain's answer to* ELVIS

PRESLEY. *'Move It' (1958) was the first of a series of hits, and he also appeared in such family films as* Summer Holiday *(1963).*

1 *The young ones*
Darling we're the young ones
And the young ones should never be afraid.

'The Young Ones' (song, written by Sid Tepper and Roy Bennett) on the album *The Young Ones* (1961) by Cliff Richard and the Shadows. The song featured in the film of the same name (1962), and the title was used for the TV comedy *The Young Ones* (1982–4).

2 *He said, 'Son, you are a bachelor boy*
And that's the way to stay.
Son, you'll be a bachelor boy
Until your dying day.'

'Bachelor Boy' (song, written by Bruce Welch and Cliff Richard, 1962) on the album *More Hits By Cliff* (1965) by Cliff Richard and the Shadows

3 *We're all going on a summer holiday,*
No more worries for a week or two.

'Summer Holiday' (song, written by Bruce Welch and Brian Bennett) on the album *Summer Holiday* by Cliff Richard and the Shadows and in the eponymous film (both 1963)

4 **If you have got the public in the palm of your hand, you can be sure that is where they want to be.**

Quoted in the *Observer* 4 December 1988

Keith Richards (b. 1943)
BRITISH ROCK MUSICIAN
Originally Keith Richard. The lean rhythm guitarist of the Rolling Stones, and an enduring symbol of rock 'n' roll debauchery, he has co-written (with MICK JAGGER*) most of the band's material.*

1 **Music for the neck downwards.**

Of rock 'n' roll, quoted in *Sound Effects: Youth, Leisure and the Politics of Rock*, ch. 7 (1979) by Simon Frith

Miranda Richardson (b. 1958)
BRITISH ACTRESS
Often typecast as a neurotic, she was praised for her roles in the films Damage *(1992) and* Tom and Viv *(1994). She has also appeared on television.*

1 **Insecurity, commonly regarded as a weakness in normal people, is the basic tool of the actor's trade.**

Guardian 5 December 1990

Christopher Ricks (b. 1933)
BRITISH CRITIC
He has edited English Poetry and Prose 1540–1674 *(1970), among other works, and is author of* The Force of Poetry *(1984).*

1 **When a language creates – as it does – a community within the present, it does so**

only by courtesy of a community between the present and the past.

The State of the Language, Preface (1980)

Laura Riding (1901–91)
US POET AND AUTHOR
Originally Laura Reichenthal. Associated with the Fugitives, a group of Southern writers, she used unconventional rhythms and concrete imagery in her verse. With ROBERT GRAVES*, she established the Seizin Press (1927–38) and the journal* Epilogue *(1935–8).*

1 *The next world is*
As near to this
As time is similar
To truth familiar.

'From Later to Earlier', publ. in *The Poems of LR* (1938). Last lines of poem.

2 **Art, whose honesty must work through artifice, cannot avoid cheating truth.**

Selected Poems: In Five Sets, Preface (1975)

Anne Ridler (1912–2001)
BRITISH POET
Her work, appearing in such collections as The Nine Bright Shiners *(1943) and* A Matter of Life and Death *(1959), evokes everyday life in a metaphysical frame.*

1 *And when our baby stirs and struggles to be born*
It compels humility: what we began
Is now its own.

'For a Child Expected', publ. in *The Nine Bright Shiners* (1943)

2 *To mark time is not to move:*
Only the unkempt hours drip from the clock
Or pull at the cord coiled in its groove,
The marker moveless, and the change illusion.

'To Mark Time', publ. in *The Golden Bird* (1951)

3 *Nothing is lost.*
We are too sad to know that, or too blind;
Only in visisted moments do we understand:
It is not that the dead return –
They are about us always, though unguessed.

'Nothing is Lost', publ. in *A Matter of Life and Death* (1959)

4 *In every generation*
The young acquire an image of their elders
Tranquil, assured, with every day mapped out
From punctual meals to reading by the fire.
Threescore and ten is not like that at all
We find on getting there.

'Threescore and Ten', publ. in *New and Selected Poems* (1988)

5 *Immortality*
Is not mere repetition:

It is a blue flash,
A kingfisher vision
It is a new-feathered
And procreant love,
Seen where the halcyon
Nests on the waves.
'The Halcyons', publ. ibid.

Joan Rivers (b. 1935)

US COMIC

Originally Joan Alexandra Molinsky. Starting out as an acid-tongued stand-up comedienne, she gained wider success on television from 1965, hosting The Tonight Show *(1971–86),* The Late Show *(1986–7) and* The Joan Rivers Show *(1989–94).*

1 I hate housework! You make the beds, you do the dishes – and six months later you have to start all over again.
Quoted in *Woman Talk*, 'Work' (ed. Michèle Brown and Ann O'Connor, 1984)

2 My routines come out of total unhappiness. My audiences are my group therapy.
BBC 2 television broadcast 23 February 1990

Leonard Robbins (1877–1947)

US AUTHOR

Among his works are Jersey Jingles *(1907),* Mountains and Men *(1931) and* Cure It With a Garden *(1933). He wrote for* The New York Times *from 1923.*

1 How a minority,
Reaching majority,
Seizing authority,
Hates a minority!
'Minorities'

Tom Robbins (b. 1936)

US AUTHOR

His novels, which initially won a following among California's counterculture, include Another Roadside Attraction *(1971),* Even Cowgirls Get the Blues *(1976, filmed 1994) and* Jitterbug Perfume *(1984).*

1 Life is too small a container for certain individuals.
Jitterbug Perfume, pt 3 (1984)

2 Zippers are primal and modern at the very same time. On the one hand, your zipper is primitive and reptilian, on the other, mechanical and slick. A zipper is where the Industrial Revolution meets the Cobra Cult, don't you think? Ahh. Little alligators of ecstasy, that's what zippers are. Sexy, too. Now your button, a button is slim and persnickety. There's somethin' Victorian about a row o' buttons. But a zipper, why a zipper is the very snake at the gate of Eden, waitin' to escort a true believer into the Garden.
Dr Dannyboy, ibid., pt 4

Paul Robeson (1898–1976)

US SINGER AND ACTOR

He was famous for both his acting and singing prowess, as in Show Boat *(1927), in which he sang 'Ol' Man River' (see* OSCAR HAMMERSTEIN II 1*), and Othello in London (1930). His left-wing sympathies caused him to be ostracized and to leave America 1958–63.*

1 Songs of liberation – who can lock them up? The spirit of freedom – who can jail it? A people's unity – what lash can beat it down? Civil rights – what doubletalk can satisfy our needs?
'A Lesson from Our South African Brothers and Sisters', publ. in *Freedom* September 1952

Anne Robinson (b. 1944)

BRITISH TV PRESENTER AND JOURNALIST

Called 'as cuddly as a cornered ferret' by LYNN BARBER*, she presented the BBC TV programme* Points of View *(1988–94), and in 2000 became the acerbic host of the show* The Weakest Link.

1 You are the weakest link. Goodbye.
Catch-phrase used when expelling contestants on *The Weakest Link* (BBC1 game show, from 2000)

2 What are they for? They are always so pleased with themselves.
Quoted in the *Observer* 11 March 2001. Referring to the Welsh on BBC2's Room 101. The remarks provoked an outcry.

Bruce Robinson (b. 1946)

BRITISH FILM-MAKER

He wrote the screenplay for The Killing Fields *(1984) and wrote and directed* Withnail and I *(1987) and* How to Get Ahead in Advertising *(1989), both of which attracted a cult following.*

1 We are indeed drifting into the arena of the unwell, making an enemy of our own future.
Marwood (Paul McGann), in *Withnail and I* (film, 1987, written and directed by Bruce Robinson)

2 All right, this is the plan. We'll get in there and get wrecked. Then we'll eat a pork pie. Then we'll go home and drop a couple of Surmontil 50s each. That means we'll miss out Monday, but come up smiling Tuesday morning.
Withnail (Richard E. Grant), ibid.

3 I don't advise a haircut, man. All hairdressers are in the employment of the government. Hairs are your aerials. They pick up signals from the cosmos, and transmit them directly into the brain. This is the reason bald-headed men are uptight.
Danny (Ralph Brown), ibid.

4 We've gone on holiday by mistake.
Withnail (Richard E. Grant), ibid.

5 We want the finest wines available to humanity. And we want them *here*, and we want them *now*.
Ibid.

6 We're living in a shop. The world is one magnificent fucking shop, and if it hasn't got a price tag, it isn't worth having. There is no greater freedom than freedom of choice.
Dennis Bagley (Richard E. Grant), in *How to Get Ahead in Advertising* (film, 1989, written and directed by Bruce Robinson)

7 You sit in front of the typewriter and the first thing you have to deal with is the government of the mind, the super-ego, sitting up there on top of your head.
Interview in *The Idler* November/December 1995

Edward G. Robinson (1893–1973)
ROMANIAN-BORN US ACTOR
Originally Emmanuel Goldenberg. A prolific stage performer, he gained stardom with his screen portrayal of the vicious gangster Rico in Little Caesar (1930), which led on to similar roles in films such as Key Largo (1948). 'Some people have youth,' he once said, 'some have beauty – I have menace.'

1 Mother of Mercy, is this the end of Rico?
Rico Bandello (Edward G. Robinson), in *Little Caesar* (film, 1931, screenplay by Francis E. Faragoh and Robert W. Lee based on novel by W. R. Burnett, directed by Mervyn LeRoy). Dying words, having been gunned down by the police.

2 Murder is never perfect. It always falls apart sooner or later. When two people are involved, it's usually sooner. . . . They're stuck with each other and they've got to ride all the way to the end of the line and it's a one-way trip and the last stop is the cemetery.
Barton Keyes (Edward G. Robinson), in *Double Indemnity* (film, 1944, screenplay by Billy Wilder and Raymond Chandler based on James M. Cain's novel, directed by Billy Wilder)

Edwin Arlington Robinson
(1869–1935)
US POET
He was the first person to receive a Pulitzer Prize for poetry for his Collected Poems (1922), which he followed with The Man Who Died Twice (1924) and the narrative Tristram (1927).

1 *I shall have more to say when I am dead.*
'John Brown', publ. in *The Three Taverns* (1920). Last line of poem.

Mary Robinson (b. 1944)
IRISH POLITICIAN AND PRESIDENT
As an Irish Senator (1969–89), she campaigned for reform of the laws on contraception, abortion and homosexuality. She was Ireland's first woman president 1990–97, and subsequently UN Commissioner on Human Rights.

1 Instead of rocking the cradle, they rocked the system.
Referring to Irish women, in speech on becoming President, quoted in *The Times* 10 November 1990. The words allude to William Ross Wallace's poem, 'The Hand That Rules the World' (1865): 'The hand that rocks the cradle/Is the hand that rules the world.'

Gene Roddenberry (1921–91)
US TV PRODUCER AND WRITER
A police officer in Los Angeles, he wrote TV scripts in his spare time for the crime serial Dragnet, before writing full-time for shows including Dr Kildare. He is best known as creator of the science fiction series Star Trek (1966–9) and Star Trek: the Next Generation (1987–94).

1 Space – the final frontier. These are the voyages of the starship *Enterprise*. Its five-year mission: to explore strange new worlds, to seek out new life and new civilizations, to boldly go where no man has gone before.
Voiceover in *Star Trek* (TV series 1966–9, created and produced by Gene Roddenberry). This preamble to each episode includes what is probably the most famous split infinitive ever recorded.

2 Beam me up, Scotty.
Attributed to Captain James T. Kirk (William Shatner), ibid. These words were never actually spoken in the series: the nearest is 'Beam us up, Mr Scott,' said by Captain Kirk to his chief engineer.

3 It's life, Jim, but not life as we know it.
Spock (Leonard Nimoy) to Kirk (William Shatner), in *Star Trek: The Motion Picture* (film, 1979, written by Gene Roddenberry, Alan Dean Foster and Harry Livingston, directed by Robert Wise). Often misquoted 'It's life, Jim, but not as we know it', as in 'Star Trekkin', a UK no. 1 hit by the Firm.

4 We are, in many ways . . . two people. As long as the inner person believes and admits that decency is good, the outer person who has to deal with the world – a world that is not always fair – is allowed to slip from time to time. I suppose that I have thought all my life that the only real person was the inner me.
Interview in *The Humanist* March/April 1991, quoted in *Gene Roddenberry. The Man Behind the Myth*, ch. 5 (1994) by Joel Engel

Anita Roddick (b. 1942)
BRITISH BUSINESSWOMAN
With her husband she opened the first Body Shop in Brighton in 1976, since when it has grown into an international retailer of beauty products

adhering to ethical and ecological principles. She was Chief Executive of the company 1994–8.

1 It is immoral to trade on fear. It is immoral constantly to make women feel dissatisfied with their bodies. It is immoral to deceive a customer by making miracle claims for a product. It is immoral to use a photograph of a glowing sixteen-year-old to sell a cream aimed at preventing wrinkles in a forty-year-old.
Body and Soul, ch. 1 (1991)

2 I think that business practices would improve immeasurably if they were guided by 'feminine' principles – qualities like love and care and intuition.
Ibid.

3 We will compromise on almost anything, but not on our values, or our aesthetics, or our idealism, or our sense of curiosity.
Ibid., ch. 11

4 The most important principle of my life is moving out of the comfort zone. It's not just a junkie fix of experience: this is the majority world; reality.
Quoted in the *Observer* 26 April 1998. On travelling in remote parts.

Richard Rodriguez (b. 1944)
US AUTHOR AND JOURNALIST
Raised in California but with his roots in Mexico, he describes his writing as a 'marriage of journalism and literature'. He has published two volumes of autobiography and Brown: The Last Discovery of America *(2002).*

1 Mexico is a nineteenth-century country arranged for gaslight. Once brought into the harsh light of the twentieth-century media, Mexico can only seem false. In its male, in its public, in its city aspect, Mexico is an arch-transvestite, a tragic buffoon. Dogs bark and babies cry when Mother Mexico walks abroad in the light of day. The policeman, the Marxist mayor – Mother Mexico doesn't even bother to shave her mustachios. Swords and rifles and spurs and bags of money chink and clatter beneath her skirts. A chain of martyred priests dangles from her waist, for she is an austere, pious lady. Ay, how much – clutching her jangling bosoms; spilling cigars – how much she has suffered.
Frontiers, 'Night and Day' (1990)

2 In tragic cultures, the old have something to teach the young. And they are believed.
Ibid.

3 In America, the Indian is relegated to the obligatory first chapter – the Once Great Nation chapter – after which the Indian is

cleared away as easily as brush, using a very sharp rhetorical tool called an 'alas'.
'Mixed Blood', publ. in *Harper's Magazine* November 1991

Theodore Roethke (1908–63)
US POET
Influenced by YEATS, *his poems are characterized by ironic lyricism and an empathy for landscape and nature, as in* The Lost Son and Other Poems *(1948) and* The Waking *(1953).*

1 My secrets cry aloud.
I have no need for tongue.
My heart keeps open house,
My doors are widely flung.
'Open House', st. 1 publ. in *Open House* (1941).

2 I wake to sleep, and take my waking slow.
I feel my fate in what I cannot fear.
I learn by going where I have to go.
'The Waking', publ. in *The Waking: Poems, 1933–1953* (1953)

3 All finite things reveal infinitude.
'The Far Field', publ. in *The Far Field* (1964)

Ginger Rogers (1911–95)
US SCREEN ACTRESS
Originally Virginia Katherine McMath. She appeared in more than seventy films, in ten of them as the dancing partner of Fred Astaire, for example The Gay Divorcee *(1934) and* Shall We Dance *(1937). As* KATHARINE HEPBURN *remarked, 'He gives her class and she gives him sex.'*

1 Cigarette me, big boy.
Young Man of Manhattan (film, 1930, screenplay by Robert Presnell based on story by Katherine Brush, directed by Monta Bell). Rogers's first screen role.

(Sir) Richard Rogers (b. 1933)
BRITISH ARCHITECT
Baron Rogers of Riverside. His notable buildings include the Pompidou Centre, Paris (with Renzo Piano, 1979), and the Lloyds (1985) and Reuters (1992) buildings in London.

1 Form follows profit is the aesthetic principle of our times.
The Times 13 February 1991

Will Rogers (1879–1935)
US HUMORIST
Wise-cracking and homespun philosophy were his hallmarks in the Ziegfeld Follies (1916–25). He later became a national institution for his aphoristic columns in The New York Times *(from 1922), radio broadcasts and films such as* Connecticut Yankee *(1931).*

1 People are getting smarter nowadays; they

are letting lawyers, instead of their conscience, be their guide.

The Illiterate Digest, 'Helping the Girls with their Income Taxes' (1924)

2 Everything is funny as long as it is happening to somebody else.

Ibid., 'Warning to Jokers: Lay Off the Prince'

3 The United States never lost a war or won a conference.

Wit and Wisdom (ed. Jack Lait, 1936). Remark following the Versailles Peace Conference, at which President WOODROW WILSON spurned all suggestions that the US should take territory or payment as a result of participating in the First World War.

4 Communism to me is one-third practice and two-thirds explanation.

Ibid.

5 There's only one thing that can kill the movies, and that's education.

The Autobiography of Will Rogers, ch. 6 (1949)

6 You can't say that civilization don't advance . . . for in every war they kill you a new way.

Ibid., ch. 14

7 When you put down the good things you ought to have done, and leave out the bad ones you did do – well, that's Memoirs.

Ibid., ch. 16

8 I don't know jokes; I just watch the government and report the facts.

Quoted in 'A Rogers Thesaurus', in the *Saturday Review* 25 August 1962

Ernst Röhm (1887–1934)
GERMAN NAZI LEADER

An early supporter of HITLER, he was the leader of the Nazi 'Brownshirts' but was executed, along with 100 others, on the Night of the Long Knives, for his alleged part in the plot to assassinate Hitler.

1 All revolutions devour their own children.

Remark to HANS FRANK, 30 June 1933, recorded by Frank in his memoirs (1955), quoted in *The Face of the Third Reich*, 'Ernst Röhm and the Lost Generation' (1963, transl. 1970) by Joachim C. Fest. The words echo those attributed to French revolutionary Pierre Vergniaud, who was guillotined along with others of the Girondin faction in 1793.

Katie Roiphe (b. 1968)
US FEMINIST WRITER

She caused controversy with her study of date or acquaintance rape on college campuses, The Morning After: Sex, Fear and Feminism on Campus *(1993), which rejected stereotypes of men as 'sexual beasts' and of women as 'delicate vessels'.*

1 In this era of Just Say No and No Means No, we don't have many words for embracing experience. Now instead of liberation and libido, the emphasis is on trauma and disease.

The Morning After, 'The Blue-Light System' (1993)

2 The idea that men don't know what women mean when women say no stems from something deeper and more complicated than feminist concerns about rape. The conservative thrust of the movement against date rape is that women need to be protected from men who don't share their social background.

Ibid., 'The Rape-Crisis, or "Is Dating Dangerous?" '

Ida Rolf (1896–1979)
US BIOCHEMIST AND PHYSICAL THERAPIST

His deep massage therapy, disseminated through an international network of schools in the 1960s and '70s, emphasized the effects of posture on the body and mind.

1 An effective human being is a whole that is greater than the sum of its parts.

Rolfing: The Integration of Human Structures, Preface (1977)

Mickey Rooney (b. 1920)
US ACTOR AND ENTERTAINER

Originally Joe Yule. Described by critic James Agee as 'a rope-haired, kazoo-voiced kid with a comic strip face', he reached the peak of his success in the 1940s. His short stature fitted him for a series of juvenile roles, as in Boys Town *(1938) and* National Velvet *(1944).*

1 Women liked me because I made them laugh. And what is an orgasm, except laughter of the loins?

Life is Too Short, ch. 32 (autobiography, 1991). Rooney was married eight times, first to Ava Gardner.

Eleanor Roosevelt (1884–1962)
US DIPLOMAT AND FIRST LADY

After her marriage to FRANKLIN D. ROOSEVELT in 1905, she became a public figure in her own right and a champion of liberal causes. She stood in for her husband during his illness and after his death was delegate to the UN Assembly (1946–52). See ADLAI STEVENSON 17.

1 No one can make you feel inferior without your consent.

This Is My Story (1937)

2 A trait no other nation seems to possess in quite the same degree that we do – namely, a feeling of almost childish injury and resentment unless the world as a whole recognizes how innocent we are of anything

but the most generous and harmless intentions.

'My Day', syndicated newspaper column, 11 November 1946

3 You always admire what you really don't understand.

'Meet the Press', on NBC-TV, 16 September 1956

4 You will feel that you are no longer clothing yourself, you are dressing a public monument.

Quoted in the *New York Herald Tribune* 27 October 1960. Warning to wives of future presidents.

5 I think, at a child's birth, if a mother could ask a fairy godmother to endow it with the most useful gift, that gift would be curiosity.

Quoted in *Today's Health* 2 October 1966

Franklin D. Roosevelt (1882–1945)

US POLITICIAN AND PRESIDENT
Franklin Delano Roosevelt. Although paralysed from polio in 1921, he rose to become the only US president to win four elections (1933–45). A Democrat, he countered the Depression with the New Deal economic programme, and was the first president to broadcast over the radio, using his 'Fireside Chats' to explain issues and policies.

1 These unhappy times call for the building of plans that . . . build from the bottom up and not from the top down, that put their faith once more in the forgotten man at the bottom of the economic pyramid.

Radio broadcast 7 April 1932, publ. in *Public Papers and Addresses of Franklin D. Roosevelt*, vol. 1 (1938)

2 But while they prate of economic laws, men and women are starving. We must lay hold of the fact that economic laws are not made by nature. They are made by human beings.

Acceptance speech at Democratic national convention, Chicago, 2 July 1932, publ. ibid.

3 I pledge you, I pledge myself, to a new deal for the American people.

Ibid. At the height of the economic crisis, Roosevelt's 'New Deal' became the slogan of his successful campaign for the presidency.

4 Let me assert my firm belief that the only thing we have to fear is fear itself – nameless, unreasoning, unjustified terror which paralyzes needed efforts to convert retreat into advance.

Inaugural address, 4 March 1933, publ. in *The Penguin Book of Twentieth-Century Speeches* (ed. Brian MacArthur, 1999). Roosevelt used the expression 'the only thing we have to fear is fear itself' on previous occasions, and it has numerous earlier attributions, including the Duke of Wellington, Montaigne, Thoreau and the Bible.

WINSTON CHURCHILL in his wartime broadcasts is also associated with the words.

5 In the field of world policy I would dedicate this nation to the policy of the good neighbor.

Ibid.

6 I see one-third of a nation ill-housed, ill-clad, ill-nourished.

Second inaugural address, 20 January 1937, publ. in *Public Papers and Addresses of Franklin D. Roosevelt*, vol. 6 (1941)

7 War is a contagion.

Speech in Chicago, 5 October 1937, quoted in *The Wit and Wisdom of Franklin D. Roosevelt*, 'War' (ed. Maxwell Meyersohn, 1950)

8 A radical is a man with both feet firmly planted in the air. A conservative is a man with two perfectly good legs, who, however, has never learned to walk forward. A reactionary is a somnambulist walking backwards. A liberal is a man who uses his legs and his hands at the behest . . . of his head.

Radio broadcast 26 October 1939, publ. in *Public Papers and Addresses of Franklin D. Roosevelt*, vol. 8 (1941)

9 And while I am talking to you mothers and fathers, I give you one more assurance. I have said this before, but I shall say it again and again and again: Your boys are not going to be sent into any foreign wars.

Speech in Boston, 30 October 1940, publ. ibid. vol. 9. Roosevelt made the speech while campaigning for his third term as president. He declared war against Japan just over a year later (see below).

10 We have the men – the skill – the wealth – and above all, the will. . . . We must be the great arsenal of democracy.

'Fireside Chat' radio broadcast, 29 December 1940, publ. in *The Penguin Book of Twentieth-Century Speeches* (ed. Brian MacArthur, 1999)

11 We look forward to a world founded upon four essential human freedoms. The first is freedom of speech and expression – everywhere in the world. The second is freedom of every person to worship God in his own way – everywhere in the world. The third is freedom from want . . . everywhere in the world. The fourth is freedom from fear . . . anywhere in the world.

Annual Message to Congress, Washington DC, 6 January 1941, publ. ibid.

12 Yesterday, December 7, 1941 – a date which will live in infamy – the United States of America was suddenly and deliberately attacked by naval and air forces of the Empire of Japan.

Address to Congress, 8 December 1941, publ. in *Public Papers and Addresses of Franklin D. Roosevelt* vol. 10 (1950). The attack on Pearl Harbor precipitated an immediate declaration of war on Japan by both the US and Britain.

13 **It is fun to be in the same decade with you.**
Telegram to WINSTON CHURCHILL, 30 January 1942, in response to sixtieth birthday greetings, quoted in *The Hinge of Fate*, ch. 4 (1950) by Winston Churchill

14 **More than an end to war, we want an end to the beginnings of all wars.**
Speech prepared for Jefferson Day broadcast, 13 April 1945, quoted in *The Wit and Wisdom of Franklin D. Roosevelt*, 'War' (ed. Maxwell Meyersohn, 1950). Roosevelt died suddenly the day before the speech was due to be made, at Warm Springs, Georgia.

Theodore Roosevelt (1858–1919)
US POLITICIAN AND PRESIDENT
A Republican, he was the youngest US president (1901–1909) to date, remembered for his Square Deal programme of social reform and regulation of business monopolies. He unsuccessfully stood for president in the 1912 election as head of the newly-formed Progressive Party.

1 **There is no room in this country for hyphenated Americanism. . . . The one absolutely certain way of bringing this nation to ruin, of preventing all possibility of its continuing to be a nation at all, would be to permit it to become a tangle of squabbling nationalities.**
Speech in New York, 12 October 1915, publ. in *Works*, vol. 20 (Memorial edn, 1923–6)

2 **One of our defects as a nation is a tendency to use what have been called 'weasel words'. When a weasel sucks eggs the meat is sucked out of the egg. If you use a 'weasel word' after another there is nothing left of the other.**
Speech in St Louis, Missouri, 31 May 1916, publ. ibid., vol. 24 (1926). Referring to WOODROW WILSON's proposal for 'universal voluntary military training'.

3 **There can be no fifty-fifty Americanism in this country. There is room here for only 100% Americanism, only for those who are Americans and nothing else.**
Speech at State Republican Party Convention, Saratoga, New York, 19 July 1918, publ. in *Roosevelt Policy*, vol. 3 (1919)

Richard Rorty (b. 1931)
US PHILOSOPHER
Influenced by the work of John Dewey and Jürgen Habermas, his books include Philosophy and the Mirror of Nature *(1979), an attack on the aims of Cartesian philosophy, and* Contingency, Irony, and Solidarity *(1989).*

1 **There is nothing deep down inside us except what we have put there ourselves.**
Consequences of Pragmatism, 'Pragmatism and

Philosophy' (1982). Refuting the notion that there is some innate metaphysical 'truth' about human beings.

2 **Openmindedness should not be fostered because, as Scripture teaches, Truth is great and will prevail, nor because, as Milton suggests, Truth will always win in a free and open encounter. It should be fostered for its own sake.**
Contingency, Irony, and Solidarity, ch. 3, 'The Contingency of Community' (1989)

3 **Truth is simply a compliment paid to sentences seen to be paying their way.**
Quoted in *The New York Times Magazine* 12 February 1990

4 **Always strive to excel, but only on weekends.**
Ibid.

Richard Dean Rosen (b. 1949)
US JOURNALIST AND AUTHOR
He published his first book, 'a premature memoir', while still an undergraduate, and later worked as an editor and critic. He writes crime fiction as R. D. Rosen.

1 **It's apparent that we can't proceed any further without a name for this institutionalized garrulousness, this psychological patter, this need to catalogue the ego's condition. Let's call it psychobabble, this spirit which now tyrannizes conversation in the seventies.**
Psychobabble: Fast Talk and Quick Cure in the Era of Feeling, 'Psychobabble' (1977). Rosen invented the word 'psychobabble' to describe the idiom that emerged in the Bay area of San Francisco in the 1970s. The jargon of 'psychobabble', he explained, 'is now spoken by magazine editors, management consultants, sandal makers, tool and die workers, chiefs of state, Ph.D.s in clinical psychology, and just about everyone else.' It consists of 'a set of repetitive verbal formalities that kills off the very spontaneity, candor, and understanding it pretends to promote. It's an idiom that reduces psychological insight to a collection of standardized observations, that provides a frozen lexicon to deal with an infinite variety of problems.'

2 **Confession, alas, is the new handshake.**
Ibid.

Harold Rosenberg (1906–78)
US ART CRITIC AND AUTHOR
In 1952 he coined the phrase 'action painting' to describe the work of a group of American Abstract Expressionists including POLLOCK *and* DE KOONING. *He discussed his theories in* The Anxious Object *(1964). From 1966 he was art critic of the* New Yorker.

1 **Whoever undertakes to create soon finds himself engaged in creating himself.**

Self-transformation and the transformation of others have constituted the radical interest of our century, whether in painting, psychiatry, or political action.
The Tradition of the New, Preface (1960)

2 Revolution in art lies not in the will to destroy but in the revelation of what has already been destroyed. Art kills only the dead.
Ibid., ch. 6

3 Kitsch is the daily art of our time, as the vase or the hymn was for earlier generations. For the sensibility it has that arbitrariness and importance which works take on when they are no longer noticeable elements of the environment. In America kitsch is Nature. The Rocky Mountains have resembled fake art for a century.
Ibid., ch. 18

4 Only conservatives believe that subversion is still being carried on in the arts and that society is being shaken by it. . . . Advanced art today is no longer a cause – it contains no moral imperative. There is no virtue in clinging to principles and standards, no vice in selling or in selling out.
'The Cultural Situation Today', first publ. in the *Partisan Review* summer 1972, repr. as Introduction to *Discovering the Present* (1973)

5 What better way to prove that you understand a subject than to make money out of it?
Ibid.

6 Art is the laboratory for making new men.
Discovering the Present, ch. 24 (1973)

7 The story of Americans is the story of arrested metamorphoses. Those who achieve success come to a halt and accept themselves as they are. Those who fail become resigned and accept themselves as they are.
Ibid.

Alan S. C. Ross (1907–80)
BRITISH LINGUISTICS SCHOLAR
Alan Strode Campbell Ross. Author of numerous scholarly studies on German and Scandinavian etymology, he is popularly remembered for coining the expressions 'U' and 'non-U' to denote upper-class and non-upper-class linguistic usage, in a lightly satirical essay first published in 1954.

1 There are, it is true, still a few minor points of life which may serve to demarcate the upper class, but they are only minor ones. . . . When drunk, gentlemen often become amorous or maudlin or vomit in public, but they never become truculent.
'U and Non-U: An Essay in Sociological Linguis-

tics' (1954), repr. in *Noblesse Oblige* (1956) by NANCY MITFORD

2 It must be remembered that, in these matters, U-speakers have ears to hear, so that one single pronunciation, word, or phrase will suffice to brand an apparent U-speaker as originally non-U (for U-Speakers themselves never make 'mistakes').
Ibid.

Andrew Ross (b. 1956)
BRITISH SOCIAL THEORIST
In works such as The Chicago Gangster Theory of Life *(1995) he extends conventional notions of ecology to explore issues of social justice. Other works include* No Sweat *(1997), which highlights the global exploitation of garment workers.*

1 The powerful appeal of ecology as a practical politics lies in its capacity to encourage people to make consistent links between the social and emotional shape of everyday actions and a quantitative world-picture of physical causes and effects. Above all, it is a politics of information and knowledge, exceptional among social and political movements in its overriding appeal to science for proof of the justice of ecological claims.
Strange Weather: Culture, Science and Technology in the Age of Limits, ch. 6 (1991)

Harold Ross (1892–1951)
US EDITOR
As the New Yorker's *gifted and eccentric first editor (1925–51), he established a tone of intelligence and sophistication and nurtured such talents as* JAMES THURBER, EDMUND WILSON *and* TRUMAN CAPOTE.

1 The *New Yorker* will be the magazine which is not edited for the old lady from Dubuque.
Attributed, from prospectus for the *New Yorker* (1925), later quoted '. . . little old lady from Dubuque'. The prospectus, however, 'bears neither the stamp of Ross's hand nor, read aloud, the sound of Ross's voice', according to JAMES THURBER. The magazine, he wrote, was 'whatever else, first and foremost the magazine of the young man from Aspen'.

2 Editing is the same as quarreling with writers – same thing exactly.
Time 6 March 1950

3 Is Moby Dick the whale or the man?
Quoted in *The Years With Ross*, ch. 4 (1959) by James Thurber

Jean Rostand (1894–1977)
FRENCH BIOLOGIST AND AUTHOR
Alongside his books for the scientific community,

*he wrote popular works for a wider audience, such
as* Life and Its Problems *(1939) and* A Biologist's
View *(1954). He was known for his astute insights
into the social and psychological context of scientific research.*

1 Kill a man, one is a murderer; kill a
million, a conqueror; kill them all, a
God.
   Pensées d'un biologiste (1939), repr. in *The Substance of Man*, ch. 5 (1962)

2 To be adult is to be alone.
   Ibid., ch. 6

3 I still understand a few words in life, but I
no longer think they make a sentence.
   Ibid.

4 Nothing leads the scientist so astray as a
premature truth.
   Ibid., ch. 7

5 Greatness, in order to gain recognition,
must all too often consent to ape greatness.
   Ibid., ch. 8

6 Beauty in art is often nothing but ugliness
subdued.
   Ibid.

7 To reflect is to disturb one's thoughts.
   Ibid., ch. 10

8 I should have no use for a paradise in
which I should be deprived of the right to
prefer hell.
   Ibid.

9 Hatred, for the man who is not engaged in
it, is a little like the odour of garlic for one
who hasn't eaten any.
   Ibid.

10 There are moments when very little
truth would be enough to shape opinion.
One might be hated at extremely low cost.
   Ibid.

11 Far too often the choices reality proposes
are such as to take away one's taste for
choosing.
   Ibid.

12 To love an idea is to love it a little more
than one should.
   Carnets d'un biologiste, repr. ibid.

13 Certain brief sentences are peerless in their
ability to give one the feeling that nothing
remains to be said.
   Ibid.

14 God, that checkroom of our dreams.
   Ibid. Other translations give '. . . dumping
   ground of our dreams'.

15 The ideal, without doubt, varies, but its
enemies, alas, are always the same.
   Ibid.

Leo Rosten (1908–97)
US AUTHOR

*Variously writing short fiction, screenplays and
biography 'as my interests guide and seduce me',
he is best known for his humorous sketches about
a new immigrant in the US,* The Education of
H*y*m*a*n K*a*p*l*a*n *(1937) and its sequels,
and for* The Joys of Yiddish *(1968).*

1 Anybody who hates dogs and babies can't
be all bad.
   Of W. C. FIELDS, in speech in honour of Fields
   at Masquers' Club Dinner, Hollywood,
   16 February 1939, quoted in the *Saturday Review*
   12 June, 1976. Often erroneously ascribed to
   Fields, with the words: 'Anyone who hates children and dogs can't be all bad.'

Theodore Roszak (b. 1933)
US SOCIAL CRITIC

*He is a powerful critic of industrial capitalism in
works such as* The Making of a Counter-Culture
(1969) and Personal Planet *(1977). The Gendered
Atom *(1999) examines 'the sexual psychology of
science'.*

1 There are dragons buried beneath our
cities, primordial energies greater than the
power of our bombs. Two thousand years
of Judeo-Christian soul-shaping and three
centuries of crusading scientific intellect
have gone into their interment. . . . But
now they wake and stir.
   Where the Wasteland Ends, Introduction (1972)

2 Technological optimism is the snake oil of
urban-industrialism.
   Ibid., ch. 2

3 If God has at last died in our culture, he
has not been buried. For the casually
religious, he lingers on like a fond old relative who has been so expertly embalmed
that we may prop him up in the far corner
of the living room and pretend the old fellow is still with us.
   Ibid., ch. 6

Philip Roth (b. 1933)
US NOVELIST

*An irreverent satirist, he portrays a love–hate
relationship with the Jewish faith of his ancestors
in his books, which blend autobiography with fiction and include* Portnoy's Complaint *(1969),*
Zuckerman Unbound *(1981) and* American Pastoral *(1997).*

1 Only in America . . . do these peasants, our
mothers, get their hair dyed platinum at
the age of sixty, and walk up and down
Collins Avenue in Florida in pedalpushers
and mink stoles – and with opinions on
every subject under the sun. It isn't their
fault they were given a gift like speech –

look, if cows could talk, they would say things just as idiotic.

Portnoy's Complaint, 'Cunt Crazy' (1969)

2 A Jewish man with parents alive is a fifteen-year-old boy, and will remain a fifteen-year-old boy until *they die!*

Ibid.

3 My God! The English language is a *form of communication*! Conversation isn't just crossfire where you shoot and get shot at! Where you've got to duck for your life and aim to kill! Words aren't only bombs and bullets – no, they're little gifts, containing *meanings*!

Ibid., 'The Most Prevalent Form of Degradation in Erotic Life'

4 To become a celebrity is to become a brand name. There is Ivory Soap, Rice Krispies, and Philip Roth. Ivory is the soap that floats; Rice Krispies the breakfast cereal that goes snap-crackle-pop; Philip Roth the Jew who masturbates with a piece of liver.

'Interview with Le Nouvel Observateur', May 1981, repr. in *Reading Myself and Others* (1975, rev. 1985)

5 When you publish a book, it's the world's book. The world edits it.

The New York Times Book Review 2 September 1979

6 Is an intelligent human being likely to be much more than a large-scale manufacturer of misunderstanding?

Nathan Zuckerman, in *The Counterlife*, ch. 5 (1986)

7 All I can tell you with certainty is that I, for one, have no self, and that I am unwilling or unable to perpetrate upon myself the joke of a self. . . . What I have instead is a variety of impersonations I can do, and not only of myself – a troupe of players that I have internalised, a permanent company of actors that I can call upon when a self is required. . . . I am a theater and nothing more than a theater.

Ibid., Zuckerman writing to Maria.

8 England's made a Jew of me in only eight weeks, which, on reflection, might be the least painful method. A Jew without Jews, without Judaism, without Zionism, without Jewishness, without a temple or an army or even a pistol, a Jew clearly without a home, just the object itself, like a glass or an apple.

Ibid.

9 Obviously the facts are never just coming at you but are incorporated by an imagination that is formed by your previous experience. Memories of the past are not memories of facts but memories of your imaginings of the facts.

The Facts, opening letter to Zuckerman (1988)

10 Family indivisibility, the first commandment.

Ibid., Prologue

11 I write fiction and I'm told it's autobiography, I write autobiography and I'm told it's fiction, so since I'm so dim and they're so smart, let *them* decide what it is or it isn't.

Philip, in *Deception* (1990)

12 I cannot and do not live in the world of discretion, not as a writer, anyway. I would prefer to, I assure you – it would make life easier. But discretion is, unfortunately, not for novelists.

Ibid. Said to his wife.

Mark Rothko (1903–70)

LATVIAN-BORN US PAINTER

Originally Marcus Rothkovich. From 1938 he experimented with 'automatism' and produced increasingly abstract paintings. From 1958 to 1966 he worked on a series of fourteen immense canvases which were placed in a nondenominational chapel in Houston, Texas, re-named the Rothko Chapel after his death by suicide.

1 Both the sense of community and of security depend on the familiar. Freed of them, transcendental experience becomes possible.

'The Romantics Were Prompted', publ. in *Possibilities*, winter 1947–8, repr. in *Theories of Modern Art*, ch. 9 (1968) by Herschel B. Chipp

2 Pictures must be miraculous: the instant one is completed, the intimacy between the creation and the creator is ended. He is an outsider. The picture must be for him, as for anyone experiencing it later, a revelation, an unexpected and unprecedented resolution of an eternally familiar need.

Ibid.

Guy de Rothschild (b. 1909)

FRENCH BANKER

Born into the most famous family in international banking, he was President of the Compagnie du Chemin de Fer du Nord (1949–68) and of the Banque Rothschild (1968–78).

1 I have no idea what a poor Rothschild would look like. I suppose he would vanish in anonymity.

The Whims of Fortune, ch. 1 (autobiography, 1985)

Constance Rourke (1885–1941)

US AUTHOR

In 1915 she retired from university teaching to concentrate on her studies of American literature and popular culture. Her American Humor *(1931) and* The Roots of American Culture *(1942) are now considered forerunners of contemporary cultural studies.*

1 An emotional man may possess no humor, but a humorous man usually has deep pockets of emotion, sometimes tucked away or forgotten.

American Humor, ch. 1 (1931)

Rowan and Martin's Laugh-In

The show started as a one-hour special for TV in 1967 and proved so popular that it was developed into a series (1968–73). Scripted by an extensive roster of writers, its sketches featuring familiar characters were interspersed with routines by its two frontmen Dan Rowan (1922–87) and Dick Martin (b. 1923).

1 Very interesting . . . but stupid!

Catchphrase by German soldier (Arte Johnson), in *Rowan and Martin's Laugh-In* (TV comedy series, 1968–73)

2 Sock it to me!

Catchphrase by Judy Carne, ibid. She was usually hit by pies, drenched with water or dropped through a trap door on uttering this.

Helen Rowland (1875–1950)

US JOURNALIST

Her humorous observations on the subject of marriage and the single life were published in Reflections of a Bachelor Girl *(1903)*, The Sayings of Mrs Solomon *(1920) and* A Guide to Men *(1922).*

1 A husband is what is left of a lover, after the nerve has been extracted.

A Guide to Men, Prelude (1922)

2 Somehow, a bachelor never quite gets over the idea that he is a thing of beauty and a boy for ever!

Ibid., 'Bachelors'. An allusion to Keats, 'A thing of beauty is a joy for ever' (*Endymion*, 1818).

3 A fool and her money are soon courted.

Ibid., 'First Interlude'

4 Oh yes, there is a vast difference between the savage and the civilized man, but it is never apparent to their wives until after breakfast.

Ibid., 'Cymbals and Kettle-drums'

5 A widow is a fascinating being with the flavor of maturity, the spice of experience, the piquancy of novelty, the tang of practised coquetry, and the halo of one man's approval.

Ibid., 'Widows'

Richard Rowland (1880–1947)

US FILM PRODUCER

1 The lunatics have taken charge of the asylum.

Comment in 1920, quoted in *A Million and One Nights*, vol. 2, ch. 79 (1926) by Terry Ramsaye. On the formation of *United Artists* film production company by CHARLIE CHAPLIN, Douglas Fairbanks, D. W. GRIFFITH and Mary Pickford.

Tiny Rowland (1917–98)

BRITISH BUSINESSMAN

Originally Roland Walter Fuhrhop. Mine owner and newspaper publisher, he was Managing Director (1961–95) and Chief Executive (1962–95) of Lonrho, *and Chairman of the* Observer *1983–93.*

1 Europe and the U.K. are yesterday's world. Tomorrow is in the United States.

Quoted in the *Observer* 16 January 1983

2 There is no jungle in the whole of Africa like the jungle of the City of London.

Quoted in *My Life With Tiny*, ch. 8 (1987) by Richard Hall

J. K. Rowling (b. 1966)

BRITISH AUTHOR

Joanne Kathleen Rowling. Her first book, the children's fantasy Harry Potter and the Philosopher's Stone *(1997, filmed 2001), became an international bestseller and was followed by equally popular sequels.*

1 There are all kinds of courage. It takes a great deal of bravery to stand up to our enemies, but just as much to stand up to our friends.

Albus Dumbledore, in *Harry Potter and the Philosopher's Stone*, ch. 17 (1997)

2 It is our choices, Harry, that show what we truly are, far more than our abilities.

Albus Dumbledore, in *Harry Potter and the Chamber of Secrets*, ch. 18 (1998)

A. L. Rowse (1903–97)

BRITISH HISTORIAN AND CRITIC

Alfred Leslie Rowse. A fellow of All Souls College, Oxford, he was known for his studies of sixteenth-century England, as well as for biographies, memoirs and general works such as The Use of History *(1946).*

1 In an imperfect world, it seems to me that, of all human institutions, the university of Oxford, and in it the college of All Souls, come nearest to perfection.

The Saturday Book, 'All Souls' (1945)

2 This filthy twentieth century. I hate its guts.

Time 13 November 1978

Arundhati Roy (b. 1961)

INDIAN NOVELIST

Her upbringing in the minority Syrian Christian community in the state of Kerala forms the setting for her award-winning novel The God of Small Things *(1997). Her outspoken support of environmental causes and her political protests have made her a controversial figure in India.*

1 It is curious how sometimes the memory of death lurks on for so much longer than the memory of life that it purloined.
The God of Small Things, ch. 1 (1997)

2 Men's bums never grow up. Like school satchels, they evoke in an instant memories of childhood.
Ibid., ch. 3

3 It is after all so easy to shatter a story. To break a chain of thought. To ruin a fragment of a dream being carried around carefully like a piece of porcelain.
Ibid., ch. 9

4 If there is a nuclear war, our foes will not be China or America or even each other. Our foe will be the earth herself. The very elements – the sky, the air, the land, the wind and water – will all turn against us. Their wrath will be terrible.
'The End of Imagination', publ. in *Outlook* August 1998 and *Frontline* August 1998, repr. in *The Cost of Living* (1999)

5 If protesting against having a nuclear bomb implanted in my brain is anti-Hindu and anti-national, then I secede. I hereby declare myself an independent, mobile republic. I am a citizen of the earth. I own no territory. I have no flag. I'm female, but have nothing against eunuchs. My policies are simple. I'm willing to sign any nuclear non-proliferation treaty or nuclear test ban treaty that's going. Immigrants are welcome. You can help me design our flag.
Ibid.

6 If you are religious, then remember that this bomb is Man's challenge to God. It's worded quite simply: *We have the power to destroy everything that You have created.* If you're not (religious), then look at it this way. This world of ours is four thousand, six hundred million years old. It could end in an afternoon.
Ibid. Closing words of essay.

7 To slow a beast, you break its limbs. To slow a nation, you break its people. You rob them of volition. You demonstrate your absolute command over their destiny. You make it clear that ultimately it falls to you to decide who lives, who dies, who prospers, who doesn't. To exhibit your capability you show off all that you can do, and how easily you can do it. How easily you could press a button and annihilate the earth. How you can start a war, or sue for peace. How you can snatch a river away from one and gift it to another. How you can green a desert, or fell a forest and plant one somewhere else. You use caprice to fracture a people's faith in ancient things – earth, forest, water, air.
'The Greater Common Good', publ. in *Outlook* June 1999 and *Frontline* June 1999, repr. ibid.

8 Big Dams are to a Nation's 'Development' what Nuclear Bombs are to its Military Arsenal. They're both weapons of mass destruction. They're both weapons governments use to control their own people. Both twentieth-century emblems that mark a point in time when human intelligence has outstripped its own instinct for survival.
Ibid.

9 What we need to search for and find, what we need to hone and perfect into a magnificent, shining thing, is a new kind of politics. Not the politics of governance, but the politics of resistance. The politics of opposition. The politics of forcing accountability. The politics of slowing things down. The politics of joining hands across the world and preventing certain destruction. In the present circumstances, I'd say that the only thing worth globalizing is dissent. It's India's best export.
Power Politics, ch. 1 (2001)

Jerry Rubin (1938–94)

US ESSAYIST AND RADICAL LEADER

Aiming to marry hippy culture with radical politics, he helped found the Youth International Party (the 'Yippies'), organizing rallies, teach-ins and theatrical events in opposition to the Vietnam War.

1 The left demands full employment for all – we demand full unemployment for all. The world owes us a living!
Do It!, 'Yippie!', Extract 13 (1970)

2 Our message: Don't grow up. Growing up means *giving up your dreams.*
Ibid.

3 Our parents are waging a genocidal war against their own kids. The economy has no use or need for youth. Everything is already built. *Our existence is a crime.*
Ibid., Extract 14

4 Most men act so tough and strong on the outside because on the inside, we are scared, weak, and fragile. Men, not women, are the weaker sex.
Chicago Tribune 16 March 1978

Volker Ruhe (b. 1942)

GERMAN POLITICIAN

He was Germany's Defence Minister 1992–8, responsible for merging East and West Germany's forces following re-unification.

1 I am not willing to risk the lives of German soldiers for countries whose names we cannot spell properly.

Independent 28 August 1992. On intervening in the Bosnian conflict.

Donald Rumsfeld (b. 1932)

US POLITICIAN AND BUSINESS EXECUTIVE

He was elected a Republican congressman in 1962, has held various posts in the private business sector and became the youngest US Secretary for Defense (1974–75), taking up the office again in 2001.

1 If you are not criticized, you may not be doing much.

Rumsfeld's Rules, ch. 2 (1974)

2 You are thinking of Europe as Germany and France. I don't. I think that's old Europe . . . If you look at the entire NATO Europe today, the center of gravity is shifting to the east. And there are a lot of new members.

Washington Post 24 January 2003

Robert Runcie (1921–2000)

BRITISH ECCLESIASTIC

Baron Runcie of Cuddesden. Decorated in the Second World War, he was ordained in 1951 and was Archbishop of Canterbury 1980–91, during which time he criticized the THATCHER *government's 'pharisaical attitudes' to the poor.*

1 Those who dare to interpret God's will must never claim Him as an asset for one nation or group rather than another. War springs from the love and loyalty which should be offered to God being applied to some God substitute, one of the most dangerous being nationalism.

Sermon at the Falkland Islands Thanksgiving Service, St Paul's Cathedral, London, 26 July 1982, publ. in *The Times* 27 July 1982. Runcie refused to treat the commemorative service at the end of the Falklands War as a victory celebration, instead urging reconciliation.

2 Without centuries of Christian antisemitism, Hitler's passionate hatred would never have been so fervently echoed.

Daily Telegraph 10 November 1988

3 I never liked the prospect of enquiring into what happened in a man's bedroom unless he's prepared to tell me.

The Purple, the Blue and the Red, BBC Radio 4, 16 May 1996. Interview with Anthony Howard, who asked him whether he had ever knowingly ordained practising homosexuals.

Damon Runyon (1884–1946)

US AUTHOR

Previously a war correspondent and a sports reporter, he wrote lively tales of New York street-life, published in Guys and Dolls *(1931, stage musical 1950, film 1955),* Blue Plate Special *(1934) and* Take it Easy *(1939).*

1 My boy . . . always try to rub up against money, for if you rub up against money long enough, some of it may rub off on you.

Feet Samuels, in 'A Very Honorable Guy', publ. in *Cosmopolitan* August 1929, repr. in *Guys and Dolls* (1931)

2 I long ago come to the conclusion that all life is six to five against.

Sam the Gonoph, in 'A Nice Price', publ. in *Collier's* 8 September 1934, repr. in *Money from Home* (1935)

Salman Rushdie (b. 1947)

INDIAN-BORN BRITISH AUTHOR

He has used allegory, symbolism and verbal ingenuity to depict both Western and Indian society in such works as Midnight's Children *(1981) and* The Ground Beneath Her Feet *(1999). Publication of* The Satanic Verses *(1988) led to a death sentence for blasphemy issued by Iran's* AYATOLLAH KHOMEINI *and a life in hiding, from which he has gradually re-entered public life.*

1 Sometimes legends make reality, and become more useful than the facts.

Midnight's Children, bk 1, 'Hit-the-spittoon' (1981)

2 Reality is a question of perspective; the further you get from the past, the more concrete and plausible it seems – but as you approach the present, it inevitably seems more and more incredible.

Ibid., bk 2, 'All-India Radio'

3 The real risks for any artist are taken . . . in pushing the work to the limits of what is possible, in the attempt to increase the sum of what it is possible to think. Books become good when they go to this edge and risk falling over it – when they endanger the artist by reason of what he has, or has not, *artistically* dared.

'Imaginary Homelands' (1982), repr. in *Imaginary Homelands*, pt 1 (1991)

4 To explain why we become attached to our birthplaces we pretend that we are trees and speak of roots. Look under your feet. You will not find gnarled growths sprouting through the soles. Roots, I sometimes think, are a conservative myth, designed to keep us in our places.

Shame, ch. 5 (1983)

5 We who have grown up on a diet of honour and shame can still grasp what

must seem unthinkable to peoples living in the aftermath of the death of God and of tragedy: that men will sacrifice their dearest love on the implacable altars of their pride. . . . Between shame and shamelessness lies the axis upon which we turn; meteorological conditions at both these poles are of the most extreme, ferocious type. Shamelessness, shame: the roots of violence.

Ibid., ch. 7

6 In this world without quiet corners, there can be no easy escapes from history, from hullabaloo, from terrible, unquiet fuss.

'Outside the Whale' (1984), repr. in *Imaginary Homelands* (1991)

7 Such is the miraculous nature of the future of exiles: what is first uttered in the impotence of an overheated apartment becomes the fate of nations.

Ibid., 'Ayesha'. Referring to the Imam, exiled in London.

8 Your blasphemy, Salman, can't be forgiven. . . . To set your words against the Words of God.

Mahound, ibid. 'Return to Jahilia'. Addressing Salman the Persian who, despite his crime of pitting 'his Word against mine', is spared the death-sentence.

9 Where there is no belief, there is no blasphemy.

Narrator, ibid.

10 Whores and writers, Mahound. We are the people you can't forgive.

The 'famous satirist' Baal, ibid. 'Return to Jahilia'. Mahound, Prophet of Jahilia, replies, 'Writers and whores. I see no difference . . .'

11 If Woody Allen were a Muslim, he'd be dead by now.

Quoted in the *Independent* 18 February 1989. Of the death threats by Muslim extremists following the publication of *The Satanic Verses*.

12 A poet's work is to name the unnameable, to point at frauds, to take sides, start arguments, shape the world, and stop it going to sleep.

Ibid.

13 Literature is where I go to explore the highest and lowest places in human society and in the human spirit, where I hope to find not absolute truth but the truth of the tale, of the imagination and of the heart.

Quoted in the *Observer* 19 February 1989

14 Writers and politicians are natural rivals. Both groups try to make the world in their own images; they fight for the same territory.

Ibid.

15 Doubt, it seems to me, is the central con-

dition of a human being in the twentieth century.

Ibid.

16 Throughout human history, the apostles of purity, those who have claimed to possess a total explanation, have wrought havoc among mere mixed-up human beings.

'In Good Faith', publ. in the *Independent on Sunday* 4 February 1990, repr. in *Imaginary Homelands*, pt 12 (1991)

17 Books choose their authors; the act of creation is not entirely a rational and conscious one.

Ibid.

18 The idea of the sacred is quite simply one of the most conservative notions in any culture, because it seeks to turn other ideas – uncertainty, progress, change – into crimes.

'Is Nothing Sacred?', Herbert Read Memorial Lecture, ICA, London, 6 February 1990, publ. in the *Guardian* 7 February 1990, repr. ibid. In the wake of Khomeini's fatwa, the lecture was read by HAROLD PINTER.

19 Not even the visionary or mystical experience ever lasts very long. It is for art to capture that experience, to offer it to, in the case of literature, its readers; to be, for a secular, materialist culture, some sort of replacement for what the love of god offers in the world of faith.

Ibid.

20 Literature is the one place in any society where, within the secrecy of our own heads, we can hear *voices talking about everything in every possible way.* The reason for ensuring that that privileged arena is preserved is not that writers want the absolute freedom to say and do whatever they please. It is that we, all of us, readers and writers and citizens and generals and godmen, need that little, unimportant-looking room. We do not need to call it sacred, but we do need to remember that it is necessary.

Ibid.

21 Free speech is the whole thing, the whole ball game. Free speech is life itself.

Interview in the *Guardian* 8 November 1990

22 I used to say: 'there is a God-shaped hole in me.' For a long time I stressed the absence, the hole. Now I find it is the shape which has become more important.

Quoted in the *Independent on Sunday* 30 December 1990. Referring to his conversion to Islam after being branded an 'enemy of Islam'.

23 I . . . can claim to be, in some sense, an exile from Sarajevo, even though it is a city I do not know. There is a Sarajevo of the

mind, an imagined Sarajevo whose ruination and torment exiles us all.
Index on Censorship May/June 1994

24 Mother India with her garishness and her inexhaustible motion, Mother India who loved and betrayed and ate and destroyed and again loved her children, and with whom the children's passionate conjoining and eternal quarrel stretched long beyond the grave; who stretched into great mountains like exclamations of the soul and along vast rivers full of mercy and disease, and across harsh drought-ridden plateaux on which men hacked with pickaxes at the dry infertile soil.
The Moor's Last Sigh, ch. 5 (1995)

25 Civilisation is the sleight of hand that conceals our natures from ourselves.
Ibid., ch. 18

26 In the waking dreams our societies permit, in our myths, our arts, our songs, we celebrate the non-belongers, the different ones, the outlaws, the freaks. What we forbid ourselves we pay good money to watch, in a playhouse or movie theatre, or to read about between the secret covers of a book.
The Ground Beneath Her Feet, ch. 3 (1999)

27 In a time of constant transformation, beatitude is the joy that comes with belief, with certainty.
Ibid., ch. 12

28 As human knowledge has grown, it has also become plain that every religious story ever told about how we got here is quite simply wrong. This, finally, is what all religions have in common. They didn't get it right. There was no celestial churning, no maker's dance, no vomiting of galaxies, no snake or kangaroo ancestors, no Valhalla, no Olympus, no six-day conjuring trick followed by a day of rest. Wrong, wrong, wrong.
'Imagine No Heaven', publ. in the *Guardian* 16 October 1999, repr. in *Step Across This Line* (2002)

29 The real wars of religion are the wars religions unleash against ordinary citizens within their 'sphere of influence'.
Ibid.

30 To choose unbelief is to choose mind over dogma, to trust in our humanity instead of all these dangerous divinities.
Ibid.

31 The Islamic world today is being held prisoner, not by Western but by Islamic captors, who are fighting to keep closed a world that a badly outnumbered few are trying to open.
The New York Times 27 November 2002

Dean Rusk (1909–94)
US POLITICIAN
A Democrat, he held a succession of foreign affairs posts in the TRUMAN administration (1947–51) and was Secretary of State under JOHN F. KENNEDY and LYNDON JOHNSON. A vehement anti-Communist, he was instrumental in escalating the Vietnam War.

1 One of the best ways to persuade others is with your ears – by listening to them.
Reader's Digest July 1961

2 We're eyeball to eyeball, and I think the other fellow just blinked.
Remark 24 October 1962, quoted in the *Saturday Evening Post* 8 December 1962. Referring to the Cuban missile crisis, in which Rusk played a key role.

Bertrand Russell (1872–1970)
BRITISH PHILOSOPHER AND MATHEMATICIAN
Earl Russell of Kingston. Influential both as a thinker and a liberal activist, he first came to notice with Principia Mathematica *(1910–13), co-authored with his former tutor A.N. WHITEHEAD. Later publications include* A History of Western Philosophy *(1945) and his* Autobiography *(1967–9). A lifelong pacifist, he was gaoled for his stand against conscription in the First World War and again as an anti-nuclear campaigner when almost ninety. See* KATHARINE TAIT 1.

1 A hallucination is a fact, not an error; what is erroneous is a judgment based upon it.
'On the Nature of Acquaintance: Neutral Monism' (1914), repr. in *Logic and Knowledge* (1956)

2 And all this madness, all this rage, all this flaming death of our civilization and our hopes, has been brought about because a set of official gentlemen, living luxurious lives, mostly stupid, and all without imagination or heart, have chosen that it should occur rather than that any one of them should suffer some infinitesimal rebuff to his country's pride.
Letter to the *Nation* 16 August 1914, repr. in *The Autobiography of Bertrand Russell*, vol. 2, ch. 1 (1968). The letter was written 12 August 1914, eight days after the declaration of war.

3 Organic life, we are told, has developed gradually from the protozoon to the philosopher, and this development, we are assured, is indubitably an advance. Unfortunately it is the philosopher, not the protozoon, who gives us this assurance.
Mysticism and Logic, ch. 6 (1917)

4 It is clear that thought is not free if the profession of certain opinions makes it impossible to earn a living. It is clear also that thought is not free if all the arguments on one side of a controversy are perpetually presented as attractively as possible, while

the arguments on the other side can only be discovered by diligent search.

Moncure Conway Lecture, 1922, publ. in *Sceptical Essays*, 'Free Thought and Official Propaganda' (1928)

5 Machines are worshipped because they are beautiful and valued because they confer power; they are hated because they are hideous and loathed because they impose slavery.

Sceptical Essays, 'Machines and the Emotions' (1928)

6 It is obvious that 'obscenity' is not a term capable of exact legal definition; in the practice of the Courts, it means 'anything that shocks the magistrate'.

Ibid., 'The Recrudescence of Puritanism'

7 Advocates of capitalism are very apt to appeal to the sacred principles of liberty, which are all embodied in one maxim: *The fortunate must not be restrained in the exercise of tyranny over the unfortunate.*

Ibid., 'Freedom in Society'

8 The fundamental defect of fathers, in our competitive society, is that they want their children to be a credit to them.

Ibid., 'Freedom versus Authority in Education'

9 Marriage is for women the commonest mode of livelihood, and the total amount of undesired sex endured by women is probably greater in marriage than in prostitution.

Marriage and Morals, 'Prostitution' (1929)

10 Men who are unhappy, like men who sleep badly, are always proud of the fact.

The Conquest of Happiness, ch. 1 (1930)

11 Boredom is . . . a vital problem for the moralist, since at least half the sins of mankind are caused by the fear of it.

Ibid., ch. 4

12 Conventional people are roused to fury by departures from convention, largely because they regard such departures as a criticism of themselves.

Ibid., ch. 9

13 Many people when they fall in love look for a little haven of refuge from the world, where they can be sure of being admired when they are not admirable, and praised when they are not praiseworthy.

Ibid., ch. 12

14 To be able to fill leisure intelligently is the last product of civilization.

Ibid., ch. 14. At present, Russell added, 'very few people have reached this level.'

15 The fundamental concept in social science is Power, in the same sense in which

Energy is the fundamental concept in physics.

Power, ch. 1 (1938)

16 To acquire immunity to eloquence is of the utmost importance to the citizens of a democracy.

Ibid., ch. 18, sect. 4

17 Religions, which condemn the pleasures of sense, drive men to seek the pleasures of power. Throughout history power has been the vice of the ascetic.

New York Herald Tribune Magazine 6 May 1938

18 The essence of the Liberal outlook lies not in *what* opinions are held, but in *how* they are held: instead of being held dogmatically, they are held tentatively, and with a consciousness that new evidence may at any moment lead to their abandonment.

Unpopular Essays, 'Philosophy and Politics' (1950)

19 Admiration of the proletariat, like that of dams, power stations, and aeroplanes, is part of the ideology of the machine age.

Ibid., 'The Superior Virtue of the Oppressed'

20 Man is a credulous animal, and must believe *something*; in the absence of good grounds for belief, he will be satisfied with bad ones.

Ibid., 'An Outline of Intellectual Rubbish'

21 For my part I distrust *all* generalizations about women, favourable and unfavourable, masculine and feminine, ancient and modern; all alike, I should say, result from paucity of experience.

Ibid.

22 We used to think that Hitler was wicked when he wanted to kill all the Jews, but Kennedy and Macmillan and others both in the East and in the West pursue policies which will probably lead to killing not only all the Jews but all the rest of us too. They are much more wicked than Hitler and this idea of weapons of mass extermination is utterly and absolutely horrible and it is a thing which no man with one spark of humanity can tolerate and I will not pretend to obey a government which is organising the massacre of the whole of mankind. I will do anything I can to oppose such Governments in any non-violent way that seems likely to be fruitful, and I should exhort all of you to feel the same way. We cannot obey these murderers. They are wicked and abominable. They are the wickedest people that ever lived in the history of man and it is our duty to do what we can.

Extempore comment added to speech at disarmament conference, Birmingham, 15 April 1961, publ. in *The Autobiography of Bertrand Russell*, vol. 3, ch. 3 (1967). The closing words of this speech made headlines in the press in the following days.

23 Three passions, simple but overwhelmingly strong, have governed my life: the longing for love, the search for knowledge, and unbearable pity for the suffering of mankind.

The Autobiography of Bertrand Russell, vol. 1, Prologue: 'What I Have Lived For' (1967). Opening words.

24 I had supposed until that time that it was quite common for parents to love their children, but the war persuaded me that it is a rare exception. I had supposed that most people liked money better than almost anything else, but I discovered that they liked destruction even better. I had supposed that intellectuals frequently loved truth, but I found here again that not ten per cent of them prefer truth to popularity.

Ibid., vol. 2, ch. 1. Referring to the First World War.

Dora Russell (1894–1986)
BRITISH AUTHOR AND ACTIVIST
Founder of the Workers' Birth Control Group (1924), she helped establish the National Council for Civil Liberties (now Liberty), and with her former husband BERTRAND RUSSELL *was a leading member of CND in the 1950s.*

1 We want better reasons for having children than not knowing how to prevent them.

Hypatia, ch. 4 (1925)

2 All my life I have tried to do too many different things. I wonder if this is not a perpetual dilemma for women. A man enters on a job or profession, needs to stick to it to earn his living, and is unlikely to have to change it on marriage. For a woman marriage presents not only practical problems, but she finds herself emotionally pulled all ways, and tends by tradition and impulse to put the needs of others

before her own. What is more, opening her eyes on the world, she feels intensely responsible for setting it to rights.

The Tamarisk Tree, ch. 9 (1975)

3 Women must not merely imitate men. Women have more to give than performing any job in society like neutered robots. Those who talk today of rousing the 'consciousness' of women contribute an idea of real importance. It was such a grievous mistake to leave out women. For whence can come love, compassion and understanding if not out of the relations of men and women and of them to their children?

Ibid., ch. 14

4 We have never yet had a Labour Government that knew what taking power really means; they always act like second-class citizens.

Quoted in the *Observer* 30 January 1983

5 We do not want our world to perish. But in our quest for knowledge, century by century, we have placed all our trust in a cold, impartial intellect which only brings us nearer to destruction. We have heeded no wisdom offering guidance. Only by learning to love one another can our world be saved. Only love can conquer all.

Challenge to the Cold War, ch. 14 (1985). Final words of final volume of autobiography.

Gilbert Ryle (1900–76)
BRITISH PHILOSOPHER
Known for his work in linguistic philosophy at Oxford, he was author of The Concept of Mind *(1949),* Dilemmas *(1954) and* On Thinking *(1979), among other writings.*

1 A myth is, of course, not a fairy story. It is the presentation of facts belonging to one category in the idioms appropriate to another. To explode a myth is accordingly not to deny the facts but to re-allocate them.

The Concept of Mind, Introduction (1949)

Saatchi and Saatchi

The advertising agency created in 1970 by the brothers Charles Saatchi (b. 1943) and Maurice Saatchi (b. 1946) became famous for its compelling slogans and images, and counted the Conservative Party among its clients.

1 **Labour isn't working.**

British Conservative Party slogan, 1978–9. A 1999 survey in *Campaign* ranked the poster on which it appeared as the most memorable of the century. The long dole queue pictured was made up of members of the Young Conservatives, not Saatchi employees, as DENIS HEALEY suggested at the time. The poster was cited as instrumental in the downfall of JAMES CALLAGHAN's Labour administation, partly because he rose to the gibe and complained, and it marked the beginning of a new era of 'aggressive' advertising, aimed at traditional Labour voters who feared for their jobs.

2 **Australians wouldn't give a XXXX for anything else.**

Advertisement for Castlemaine lager, from 1986

3 **Tell Sid.**

Advertising slogan for the privatization of British Gas, 1986

4 **An ace caff with quite a nice museum attached.**

Advertisement for Victoria and Albert Museum, London, 1989. The most visible feature of a marketing drive spearheaded by museum director Elisabeth Esteve-Coll, the advertisement created great negative publicity by suggesting that culture took second place at the museum.

Rafael Sabatini (1875–1950)

BRITISH AUTHOR

He achieved international success with Scaramouche (1921), set in the French Revolution. His other historical novels include The Sea Hawk (1915) and Captain Blood (1922).

1 **He was born with a gift of laughter and a sense that the world was mad. And that was all his patrimony.**

Scaramouche, bk 1, ch. 1 (1921). These opening words which describe the book's hero André-Louis Moreau, are inscribed on the gate of the Hall of Graduate Studies, Yale University.

Ernesto Sábato (b. 1911)

ARGENTINIAN NOVELIST AND ESSAYIST

His criticism of Peronism led to his dismissal from his post as Professor of Theoretical Physics in 1944, following which he took up writing. His essays and novels, such as The Outsider (1950) and On Heroes and Tombs (1961), address metaphysical and existential issues.

1 **Just as the office worker dreams of murdering his hated boss and so is saved from really murdering him, so it is with the author; with his great dreams he helps his readers to survive, to avoid their worst**

intentions. And society, without realizing it . . . respects and even exalts him, albeit with a kind of jealousy, fear and even repulsion, since few people want to discover the horrors that lurk in the depths of their souls. This is the highest mission of great literature, and there is no other.

Interview in the *Independent* 20 June 1992

Jonathan Sacks (b. 1948)

BRITISH CHIEF RABBI

He has been rabbi of Golders Green (1978–82) and Marble Arch (1983–90) synagogues. His books include The Persistence of Faith *(1991) and* The Politics of Hope *(1997).*

1 Modernity is the transition from fate to choice.

'The Persistence of Faith', 1990 Reith Lecture, publ. in *The Persistence of Faith*, ch. 1, 'Liberation or Privation' (1991)

2 We no longer talk of virtues but of values, and values are tapes we play on the Walkman of the mind: any tune we choose so long as it does not disturb others.

Ibid., ch. 2, 'The Eclipse of Morality'

Oliver Sacks (b. 1933)

BRITISH NEUROLOGIST

He has found a wide readership for his accounts of unusual neurological conditions, Awakenings *(1973, filmed 1990) and* The Man Who Mistook His Wife for a Hat *(1985).*

1 The Man Who Mistook His Wife for a Hat.

Title of book (1985)

Margaret Sackville (1881–1963)

BRITISH POET

Her poetical career extended from her first collection, Poems (1901), to Quatrains (1960).

1 When all is said and done, monotony may after all be the best condition for creation.

The Works of Susan Ferrier, vol. 1, Introduction (1929)

Vita Sackville-West (1892–1962)

BRITISH AUTHOR, POET AND GARDENER

Victoria Mary Sackville-West. A prolific writer of poetry, fiction, history and biography, she was the wife of HAROLD NICOLSON *and a close friend of* VIRGINIA WOOLF. *She travelled widely before settling at Sissinghurst Castle, whose gardens she made famous.*

1 Women ought to have freedom the same as men when they are young. It is a rotten and ridiculous system at present; it's simply cheating of one's youth. It was alright for Victorians. But this generation is discarding, and the next one will have discarded, the chrysalis. Women, like men, ought to have their youth so glutted with

freedom that they hate the very idea of freedom.

Letter to her husband HAROLD NICOLSON, 1 June 1919, quoted in *Portrait of a Marriage*, pt 4 (1973) by Nigel Nicolson

2 Travel is the most private of pleasures. There is no greater bore than the travel bore. We do not in the least want to hear what he has seen in Hong-Kong.

Passenger to Teheran, ch. 1 (1926)

3 It is necessary to write, if the days are not to slip emptily by. How else, indeed, to clap the net over the butterfly of the moment?

Twelve Days, ch. 1 (1928)

William Safire (b. 1929)

US JOURNALIST

He was special assistant to President NIXON *(1969–73) and has been a respected columnist on* The New York Times *since 1973.*

1 To 'know your place' is a good idea in politics. That is not to say 'stay in your place' or 'hang on to your place', because ambition or boredom may dictate upward or downward mobility, but a sense of place – a feel for one's own position in the control room – is useful in gauging what you should try to do.

Before The Fall, Prologue (1975)

Françoise Sagan (b. 1935)

FRENCH NOVELIST

Originally Françoise Quoirez. She became an overnight phenomenon with her first book, written aged eighteen, Bonjour Tristesse *(1954, filmed 1957), which she followed with* A Certain Smile *(1956, filmed 1958), both testaments of the emotions and disillusions of adolescence.*

1 Jazz music is an intensified insouciance.

Dominique, in *A Certain Smile*, pt 1, ch. 7 (1956)

2 Writing is a question of finding a certain rhythm. I compare it to the rhythms of jazz. Much of the time life is a sort of rhythmic progression of three characters. If one tells oneself that life is like that, one feels it less arbitrary.

Interview in *Writers at Work* (first series, ed. Malcolm Cowley, 1958)

3 Of course the illusion of art is to make one believe that great literature is very close to life, but exactly the opposite is true. Life is amorphous, literature is formal.

Ibid.

4 To jealousy, nothing is more frightful than laughter.

Lucile, in *La Chamade*, ch. 9 (1965)

Edward Said (b. 1935)

PALESTINIAN-BORN US SOCIAL AND
LITERARY CRITIC

*A critic of US foreign policy, he has discoursed
forcefully on Middle Eastern issues in such works
as* Orientalism *(1978),* Culture and Imperialism
(1993) and Reflections on Exile and Other Essays
(2000).

1 Taking the late eighteenth century as a
very roughly defined starting point Orientalism can be discussed and analyzed as the
corporate institution for dealing with the
Orient – dealing with it by making statements about it, authorizing views of it,
describing it, by teaching it, settling it,
ruling over it: in short, Orientalism as a
Western style for dominating, restructur-
ing, and having authority over the Orient.
   Orientalism, Introduction (1978)

2 The web of racism, cultural stereotypes,
political imperialism, dehumanizing ideology holding in the Arab or the Muslim is
very strong indeed, and it is this web
which every Palestinian has come to feel as
his uniquely punishing destiny.
   Ibid.

3 Culture is a sort of theatre where various
political and ideological causes engage one
another. Far from being a placid realm of
Apollonian gentility, culture can even be a
battleground on which causes expose themselves to the light of day and contend with
one another.
   Culture and Imperialism, Introduction (1993)

4 There are far too many politicized people
on earth today for any nation readily to
accept the finality of America's historical
mission to lead the world.
   Ibid., ch. 4, sect. 1

5 Reading and writing texts are never neutral
activities: there are interests, powers, pleasures entailed no matter how aesthetic or
entertaining the work. Media, political
economy, mass institutions – in fine, the
tracings of secular power and the influence
of the state – are part of what we call
literature.
   Ibid., sect. 2

6 Truly this has been the age of Ayatollahs,
in which a phalanx of guardians (Kho-
meni, the Pope, Margaret Thatcher) simplify and protect one or another creed,
essence, primordial faith. One fundamentalism invidiously attacks the others in the
name of sanity, freedom, and goodness.
   Ibid., sect. 3

7 Power, after all, is not just military
strength. It is the social power that comes
from democracy, the cultural power that
comes from freedom of expression and
research, the personal power that entitles
every Arab citizen to feel that he or she is
in fact a citizen, and not just a sheep in
some great shepherd's flock.
   'A Powerless People', publ. in the *Guardian*
   25 April 1996. Discussing Arab 'powerlessness'.

8 I have no other explanation for our situation, which cannot be extenuated or
explained away by appeals to the ravages
of imperialism, or to corrupt regimes, or
any of the other litanies of self-
exculpation. The problem is Arab powerlessness.
   Ibid.

Lisa St Aubin de Terán (b. 1953)

BRITISH AUTHOR

*Exotic locales in South America and Europe form
the backdrop of much of her work, for example her
first novel* Keepers of the House *(1982). She has
also written memoirs, travelogues and poetry.*

1 Travelling is like flirting with life. It's like
saying, 'I would stay and love you, but I
have to go; this is my station.'
   Off the Rails, ch. 2 (1989)

Iberico Saint Jean

ARGENTINIAN SOLDIER AND POLITICIAN

*As general, he was governor of the province of
Buenos Aires during the military rule in
Argentina.*

1 First we kill all the subversives; then, their
collaborators; later, those who sympathize
with them; afterward, those who remain
indifferent; and finally, the undecided.
   Quoted in *Boletin de las Madres de Plaza de
   Mayo*, May 1985, repr. in *The Demon Lover*, ch. 4
   (1989) by ROBIN MORGAN

Adela Rogers St Johns (1894–1988)

US AUTHOR AND JOURNALIST

*She was a veteran reporter for various Hearst news-
papers, and was also known for her celebrity interviews, screenplays and short stories.*

1 I think every woman's entitled to a middle
husband she can forget.
   Quoted in the *Los Angeles Times* 13 October 1974

Yves Saint Laurent (b. 1936)

FRENCH FASHION DESIGNER

Having worked with CHRISTIAN DIOR *from 1954,
he established his own house in 1962, created
'power dressing', and launched the Rive Gauche
chain of boutiques in 1966 to retail his ready-to-
wear clothes.*

1 Fashions fade, style is eternal.
   Andy Warhol's Interview 13 April 1975

2 I knew the youthfulness of the sixties: Tali-
tha and Paul Getty lying on a starlit terrace

in Marrakesh, beautiful and damned, and a whole generation assembled as if for eternity where the curtain of the past seemed to lift before an extraordinary future.
Interview in *Ritz*, no. 85, 1984

3 I have often said that I wish I had invented blue jeans: the most spectacular, the most practical, the most relaxed and nonchalant. They have expression, modesty, sex appeal, simplicity – all I hope for in my clothes.
Ibid.

4 We must never confuse elegance with snobbery.
Ibid.

5 It pains me physically to see a woman victimized, rendered pathetic, by fashion.
Ibid.

6 A designer who is not also a couturier, who hasn't learned the most refined mysteries of physically creating his models, is like a sculptor who gives his drawings to another man, an artisan, to accomplish. For him the truncated process of creating will always be an interrupted act of love, and his style will bear the shame of it, the impoverishment.
Ibid.

7 A good model can advance fashion by ten years.
Ibid.

Antoine de Saint-Exupéry
(1900–44)
FRENCH AVIATOR AND AUTHOR
He recounted his adventurous life as a pilot in Wind, Sand and Stars *(1939), and also wrote the novel* Night Flight *(1931) and the allegory* The Little Prince *(1943). He disappeared on a wartime reconnaissance mission.*

1 Each man must look to himself to teach him the meaning of life. It is not something discovered: it is something moulded.
Wind, Sand and Stars, ch. 2, sect. 1 (publ. in France as *Terre des hommes*, 1939)

2 Only the unknown frightens men. But once a man has faced the unknown, that terror becomes the known.
Ibid., ch. 2, sect. 2

3 Perfection is finally attained not when there is no longer anything to add but when there is no longer anything to take away, when a body has been stripped down to its nakedness.
Ibid., ch. 3

4 The machine does not isolate man from the great problems of nature but plunges him more deeply into them.
Ibid.

5 Transport of the mails, transport of the

human voice, transport of flickering pictures – in this century as in others our highest accomplishments still have the single aim of bringing men together.
Ibid.

6 The aeroplane has unveiled for us the true face of the earth.
Ibid., ch. 5

7 Love does not consist in gazing at each other but in looking together in the same direction.
Ibid., ch. 8

8 Night, the beloved. Night, when words fade and things come alive. When the destructive analysis of day is done, and all that is truly important becomes whole and sound again. When man reassembles his fragmentary self and grows with the calm of a tree.
Flight to Arras, ch. 1 (1942)

9 War is not a true adventure. It is a mere ersatz. Where ties are established, where problems are set, where creation is stimulated – there you have adventure. But there is no adventure in heads-or-tails, in betting that the toss will come out of life or death. War is not an adventure. It is a disease. It is like typhus.
Ibid., ch. 8

10 If France is to be judged, judge her not by the effects of her defeat but by her readiness to sacrifice herself.
Ibid., ch. 15

11 When the body sinks into death, the essence of man is revealed. Man is a knot, a web, a mesh into which relationships are tied. Only those relationships matter. The body is an old crock that nobody will miss. I have never known a man to think of himself when dying. Never
Ibid., ch. 19

12 Grown-ups never understand anything for themselves, and it is tiresome for children to be always and forever explaining things to them.
The Little Prince, ch. 1 (1943)

13 It is only with the heart that one can see rightly; what is essential is invisible to the eye.
Ibid., ch. 21

J. D. Salinger (b. 1919)
US AUTHOR
Jerome David Salinger. Called 'the greatest mind ever to stay in prep school' by NORMAN MAILER, *he is known for his first and only novel* The Catcher in the Rye *(1951), which quickly became a classic text of adolescent rebellion.*

1 If you really want to hear about it, the first

thing you'll probably want to know is where I was born, and what my lousy childhood was like, and how my parents were occupied and all before they had me, and all that David Copperfield kind of crap, but I don't feel like going into it.

Narrator (Holden Caulfield), in *The Catcher in the Rye*, ch. 1 (1951). Opening lines of book.

2 What I like best is a book that's at least funny once in a while. . . . What really knocks me out is a book that, when you're all done reading it, you wish the author that wrote it was a terrific friend of yours and you could call him up on the phone whenever you felt like it. That doesn't happen much, though.

Ibid., ch. 3

3 I don't know about bores. Maybe you shouldn't feel too sorry if you see some swell girl getting married to them. They don't hurt anybody most of them, and maybe they're all terrific whistlers or something. Who the hell knows? Not me.

Ibid., ch. 17

4 I don't even like *old* cars. I mean they don't even interest me. I'd rather have a goddam horse. A horse is at least *human*, for God's sake.

Ibid.

5 I keep picturing all these little kids playing some game in this big field of rye and all. . . . If they're running and they don't look where they're going I have to come out from somewhere and *catch* them. That's all I'd do all day. I'd just be the catcher in the rye and all. I know it's crazy, but that's the only thing I'd really like to be.

Ibid., ch. 22

Anthony Sampson (b. 1926)

BRITISH JOURNALIST AND AUTHOR

His many books of commentary and analysis include The Arms Bazaar *(1977), but he is probably best known for his ongoing guide to British society,* Anatomy of Britain *(from 1962).*

1 Once you touch the trappings of monarchy, like opening an Egyptian tomb, the inside is liable to crumble.

Anatomy of Britain Today, ch. 2 (1965)

2 In America journalism is apt to be regarded as an extension of history: in Britain, as an extension of conversation.

Ibid., ch. 9

3 Members rise from CMG (known sometimes in Whitehall as 'Call Me God') to KCMG ('Kindly Call Me God') to GCMG ('God Calls Me God').

Ibid., ch. 18. The joke has appeared in various forms, including in the TV political comedy Yes

Minister, written by ANTONY JAY and JONATHAN LYNN.

Carl Sandburg (1878–1967)

US POET AND AUTHOR

In the words of Louis Untermeyer: 'The great mid-West, that vast region of steel mills and slaughterhouses, of cornfields and prairies, of crowded cities and empty skies, spoke through Carl Sandburg.' His reputation was established with his first volumes of poetry, Chicago Poems *(1916) and* Cornhuskers *(1918). He also wrote prose works.*

1 *Hog Butcher for the World,*
Tool Maker, Stacker of Wheat,
Player with Railroads and the Nation's
*   Freight Handler;*
Stormy, husky, brawling,
City of the Big Shoulders.

'Chicago', publ. in *Chicago Poems* (1916)

2 *The fog comes*
on little cat feet.
It sits looking
over harbour and city
on silent haunches
and then moves on.

'Fog', publ. ibid.

3 *I tell you the past is a bucket of ashes.*

'Prairie', publ. in *Cornhuskers* (1918)

4 *Pile the bodies high at Austerlitz and*
*   Waterloo.*
Shovel them under and let me work –
I am the grass; I cover all.

'Grass', publ. ibid.

5 Poetry is the opening and closing of a door, leaving those who look through to guess about what is seen during a moment.

'Poetry Considered', publ. in the *Atlantic Monthly* March 1923

6 *The sea speaks a language polite people*
*   never repeat.*
It is a colossal scavenger slang and has no
*   respect.*
Is it a terrible thing to be lonely?

'Two Nocturns', publ. in *Good Morning, America* (1928)

7 *The girl held still and studied.*
'Do you know . . . I know something?'
'Yes, what is it you know?'
'Sometime they'll give a war and nobody
*   will come.'*

The People, Yes, sect. 23 (1936). Referring to a girl watching a military parade. The words were popularized during the anti-war protests of the 1960s and were adapted for the film *Suppose They Gave a War and Nobody Came?* (1970). See ALLEN GINSBERG 10.

8 *The greatest cunning is to have none at all.*

Ibid., sect. 94

9 *In the darkness with a great bundle of grief*
*   the people march. In the night, and over-*

head a shovel of stars for keeps, the
people march:
'Where to? What next?'

Ibid., sect. 107. Closing lines of book.

10 A baby is God's opinion that life should go
on.

Remembrance Rock, ch. 2 (1948)

11 Slang is a language that rolls up its sleeves,
spits on its hands and goes to work.

The New York Times 13 February 1959

12 In these times you have to be an optimist
to open your eyes when you wake in the
morning.

New York Post 9 September 1960

13 Ordering a man to write a poem is like
commanding a pregnant woman to give
birth to a red-headed child.

Quoted in Reader's Digest February 1978

George Sanders (1906–72)

BRITISH ACTOR

'I was beastly but never coarse. A high-class sort of
heel,' he commented on his usual roles as cad,
crook and bounder for more than thirty years in
Hollywood. He had slightly more demanding parts
in the films Rebecca (1940) and All About Eve
(1950).

1 Miss Caswell is an actress, a graduate of
the Copacabana school of dramatic arts.

Addison De Witt (George Sanders), introducing
his protégée Miss Caswell (Marilyn Monroe) to
Margo Channing (Bette Davis), in All About Eve
(film, 1950, written and directed by Joseph L.
Mankiewicz). Sanders won an Oscar as Best Supporting Actor for his part as the venomous
drama critic, one of six Academy Awards collected by the film.

2 Dear World, I am leaving because I am
bored. I feel I have lived long enough. I am
leaving you with your worries in this sweet
cesspool. Good luck.

Suicide note, publ. in George Sanders: An Exhausted Life, ch. 20 (1991) by Richard Vanderbeets

Margaret Sanger (1883–1966)

US PIONEER OF BIRTH CONTROL MOVEMENT
Having been imprisoned for setting up a birth-
control clinic in 1916, she founded the American
Birth Control League in 1921, serving as its Presi-
dent until 1928. Her writings include What Every
Mother Should Know (1917).

1 A mutual and satisfied sexual act is of great
benefit to the average woman, the magnet-
ism of it is health giving. When it is not
desired on the part of the woman and she
gives no response, it should not take place.
The submission of her body without love
or desire is degrading to the woman's finer

sensibility, all the marriage certificates on
earth to the contrary notwithstanding.

Family Limitation, 'Coitus Interruptus' (1914)

2 No woman can call herself free who does
not own and control her body. No woman
can call herself free until she can choose
consciously whether she will or will not be
a mother.

Parade 1 December 1963

George Santayana (1863–1952)

SPANISH-BORN US PHILOSOPHER, POET AND
NOVELIST
Originally Jorge de Santayana. His reputation
rests mainly on his work as a materialist sceptic
philosopher, notably The Sense of Beauty (1896),
Scepticism and Animal Faith (1923) and Realms
of Being (1927–40). He also published poetry and
fiction.

1 Oxford, the paradise of dead philosophies.

Egotism in German Philosophy (1916). Santayana
settled in Oxford during the First World War.

2 He carries his English weather in his heart
wherever he goes, and it becomes a cool
spot in the desert, and a steady and sane
oracle amongst all the delirium of
mankind.

On the Englishman, in Soliloquies in England,
'The British Character' (1922)

3 There is no cure for birth and death save
to enjoy the interval.

Ibid., 'War Shrines'

4 Scepticism is the chastity of the intellect,
and it is shameful to surrender it too soon
or to the first comer; there is nobility in
preserving it coolly and proudly through
a long youth, until at last, in the ripeness
of instinct and discretion, it can be safely
exchanged for fidelity and happiness.

Scepticism and Animal Faith, ch. 9 (1923)

5 The young man who has not wept is a savage, and the old man who will not laugh is
a fool.

Dialogues in Limbo, ch. 3 (1925)

6 Chaos is a name for any order that produces confusion in our minds.

Dominations and Powers, bk 1, pt 1, ch. 1 (1951)

Sapphire (b. 1950)

US AUTHOR AND POET
An unsentimental chronicler of the raw experiences
of black American women, she is author of the
poetry collection American Dreams (1994) and a
novel Push (1998).

1 The farmer takes Jill down the well
& all the king's horses
& all the king's men
can't put that baby together again.

crooked man
crooked man
pumpkin eater
childhood stealer.

'Mickey Mouse Was a Scorpio', publ. in *American Dreams* (1994). Sapphire recalled that it was the writing of this poem that first made her suspect she had been abused as a child.

2 *death is where*
jimi hendrix is,
where our revolution
ended up.

'where jimi is', publ. ibid.

Susan Sarandon (b. 1946)
US SCREEN ACTRESS
She made an impact as Janet in the film of the cult classic The Rocky Horror Picture Show *(1975), and went on to star in* Atlantic City *(1980),* Thelma and Louise *(1991) and* Dead Man Walking *(1995).*

1 Do you really have to be the ice queen intellectual or the slut whore? Isn't there some way to be both?

Observer 14 September 1991

Ken Saro-Wiwa (1941–95)
NIGERIAN AUTHOR AND ACTIVIST
Kenule Saro-Wiwa. He wrote novels and the TV satire Basi and Company *(1980s). As leader of the Movement for the Survival of the Ogoni People, he campaigned against the environmental damage and expropriations he ascribed to the oil industry, for which he was arrested and executed.*

1 Lord take my soul, but the struggle continues.

Quoted in the *Daily Telegraph* 13 November 1995. Among his last words before being hanged.

May Sarton (1912–95)
US POET AND NOVELIST
Her work has been praised for its insight and sensitive handling of feminist and lesbian themes. Collected Poems *(1974), containing material from her first publications in the 1930s, consolidated her reputation as a poet.*

1 May we agree that private life is irrelevant? Multiple, mixed, ambiguous at best – out of it we try to fashion the crystal clear, the singular, the absolute, and that is what *is* relevant; that is what matters.

Hilary Stevens, in *Mrs Stevens Hears the Mermaids Singing*, pt 2 (1965)

2 The creative person, the person who moves from an irrational source of power, has to face the fact that this power antagonizes. Under all the superficial praise of the 'creative' is the desire to kill. It is the old war between the mystic and the nonmystic, a war to the death.

Narrator, ibid.

3 Self-respect is nothing to hide behind. When you need it most it isn't there.

Hilary Stevens, ibid., 'Epilogue: Mar'

Jean-Paul Sartre (1905–80)
FRENCH PHILOSOPHER AND AUTHOR
The leading exponent of Existentialism, he co-founded with SIMONE DE BEAUVOIR *the journal* Les Temps modernes *in 1946. As well as his philosophical writings, his works include the novels* Nausea *(1938) and* Roads to Freedom *(1945–9) and the plays* The Flies *(1943) and* No Exit *(1944). See* CHARLES DE GAULLE 13.

1 I am condemned to be free.

Being and Nothingness, pt 4, ch. 1, sect. 1 (1943, transl. 1956)

2 Existence precedes and commands essence.

Ibid. Sartre ascribes the notion to HEIDEGGER, although the latter specifically repudiated Sartre's reading of his maxim.

3 I am responsible for everything . . . except for my very responsibility, for I am not the foundation of my being. Therefore everything takes place as if I were compelled to be responsible. I am *abandoned* in the world . . . in the sense that I find myself suddenly alone and without help, engaged in a world for which I bear the whole responsibility without being able, whatever I do, to tear myself away from this responsibility for an instant.

Ibid., pt 4, ch. 1, sect. 3

4 Man is a useless passion.

Ibid., pt 4, ch. 2, sect. 2

5 All human actions are equivalent . . . and . . . all are on principle doomed to failure.

Ibid., 'Conclusion', sect. 2

6 Human life begins on the far side of despair.

Orestes, in *The Flies*, act 3, sc. 2 (*Les Mouches*, 1943)

7 Hell is other people.
(*L'enfer, c'est les autres.*)

Garcin, in *No Exit*, sc. 5 (*Huis clos*, 1944)

8 What then did you expect when you unbound the gag that muted those black mouths? That they would chant your praises? Did you think that when those heads that our fathers had forcibly bowed down to the ground were raised again, you would find adoration in their eyes?

'Orphée noir', Preface to *Anthologie de la nouvelle poésie nègre et malgache* (1948)

9 Every age has its own poetry; in every age the circumstances of history choose a nation, a race, a class to take up the torch by creating situations that can be

expressed or transcended only through poetry.

Ibid.

10 One is still what one is going to cease to be and already what one is going to become. One lives one's death, one dies one's life.

Saint Genet: Actor and Martyr, bk 2, 'The Melodious Child Dead in Me . . .' (1952, transl. 1963)

11 The French bourgeois doesn't dislike shit, provided it is served up to him at the right time.

Ibid., bk 2, 'To Succeed in Being All, Strive to be Nothing in Anything'

12 Fascism is not defined by the number of its victims, but by the way it kills them.

Libération 22 June 1953. Referring to the execution of Julius and Ethel Rosenberg.

13 Communism I like, but Communist intellectuals are savages.

Quoted in the *Observer* 25 March 1956

14 I hate victims who respect their executioners.

Leni, in *The Condemned of Altona*, act 1, sc. 1 (1960)

15 You can see it's the end; Europe is springing leaks everywhere. What then has happened? It simply is that in the past we made history and now it is being made of us. The ratio of forces has been inverted.

The Wretched of the Earth, Preface (1961)

16 She [my grandmother] believed in nothing; only her scepticism kept her from being an atheist.

Les Mots, 'Lire' (1964)

17 I confused things with their names: that is belief.

Ibid., 'Écrire'

18 One does not *adopt* an idea, one slips into it.

Notebooks for an Ethics, Notebook 1 (1983)

Siegfried Sassoon (1886–1967)

BRITISH POET

Remembered above all for his powerfully outspoken anti-war poems of the First World War, published in Counter-Attack *(1918) and* Satirical Poems *(1926), he also wrote a semi-fictionalized autobiography,* The Complete Memoirs of George Sherston *(3 vols, 1928–36).*

1 I am making this statement as an act of wilful defiance of military authority, because I believe that the War is being deliberately prolonged by those who have the power to end it.

'A Soldier's Declaration' (1917), widely publ. in the press and repr. in *Memoirs of an Infantry Officer*, pt 10, ch. 2 (1930). ROBERT GRAVES, who thought Sassoon 'quite right in his views

but absolutely wrong in his action', persuaded the medical board of the War Office that Sassoon was in a state of mental collapse and thus averted a court martial, though Sassoon himself actually desired one.

2 *Soldiers are citizens of death's grey land,*
Drawing no dividend from time's
tomorrows.

'Dreamers', publ. in *Counter-Attack and Other Poems* (1918)

3 *Soldiers are sworn to action; they must win*
Some flaming, fatal climax with their lives.
Soldiers are dreamers; when the guns begin
They think of firelit homes, clean beds and wives.

Ibid.

4 *'Good-morning; good morning!' the General said*
When we met him last week on our way to the line.
Now the soldiers he smiled at are most of 'em dead,
And we're cursing his staff for incompetent swine.
'He's a cheery old card,' grunted Harry to Jack
As they slogged up to Arras with rifle and pack.
But he did for them both by his plan of attack.

'The General', publ. ibid.

5 *But the past is just the same, – and War's a bloody game . . .*
Have you forgotten yet? . . .
Look down, and swear by the slain of the War that you'll never forget.

'Aftermath', publ. in *The War Poems of Siegfried Sassoon* (1919)

6 *Everyone suddenly burst out singing;*
And I was filled with such delight
As prisoned birds must find in freedom.

'Everyone Sang', publ. ibid.

7 *The song was wordless; the singing will never be done.*

Ibid.

8 *In me the tiger sniffs the rose.*

The Heart's Journey, no. 7 (1928)

9 *Who will remember, passing through this Gate,*
The unheroic Dead who fed the guns?
Who shall absolve the foulness of their fate, –
Those doomed, conscripted, unvictorious ones?

'On Passing the New Menin Gate', publ. ibid., no. 21

10 *Here was the world's worst wound. And here with pride*
'Their name liveth for ever' the Gateway claims.

Was ever an immolation so belied
As these intolerably nameless names?
Ibid.

Erik Satie (1866–1925)
FRENCH COMPOSER AND PIANIST
Mentor of the group of composers known as Les
Six, he pioneered the break with nineteenth-
century French Romanticism. His music is charac-
terized by parody, novel harmony and an aesthetic
of simplicity, as in Trois Gnossiennes *(1890).*

1 The brain of the critic is like a shop, a big
shop. Everything is to be found there:
orthopaedics, science, bedding, arts, travelling rugs . . . The critic knows all, sees all,
says all, hears all, touches all, stirs all, eats
all, confuses all, and still keeps on thinking. What a man!!!
'In Praise of Critics', lecture, February 1918,
publ. in *The Writings of Erik Satie* (ed. Nigel
Wilkins, 1980)

Salvatore Satta (1902–75)
ITALIAN LAWYER AND NOVELIST
As one of Italy's foremost jurists, he was respon-
sible for rewriting the Italian Penal Code after the
Second World War to rid it of its Fascist aspects.
His novel The Day of Judgment *(1979), on which*
he had worked for more than thirty years, was
found among his papers after his death.

1 If we really think about it, God exists for
any single individual who puts his trust in
Him, not for the whole of humanity, with
its laws, its organizations, and its violence.
Humanity is the demon which God does
not succeed in destroying.
The Day of Judgment, ch. 15 (1979)

2 The most important things in their lives
. . . was to have a lawsuit going. It was not
a question of winning or losing it, and
indeed it was vital to do neither, for otherwise the suit would be over and done with.
A lawsuit was part of the personality, if not
the only visible sign of it, to such an extent
that there was often no real animosity
between the litigants, because they both
needed each other.
Ibid., ch. 20. Referring to the people of Nuoro,
an inland mountain town in Sardinia, at the
turn of the twentieth century.

Jennifer Saunders (b. 1957)
BRITISH COMEDIAN
With Dawn French, she scripted and acted in Girls
on Top *(1985–6) for BBC2. She later developed*
her own series, Absolutely Fabulous *(1992–5), a*
satire on the world of fashion and media.

1 Not instant, darling. Grind some beans.
That's not proper coffee . . . that's just

beans that have been cremated. I want
them entire with life force.
Edina (Jennifer Saunders), in *Absolutely Fabu-*
lous, 'Fashion', first broadcast 12 November 1992

2 Mum, you've absolved yourself of responsibility. You live from self-induced crisis to
self-induced crisis. Someone chooses what
you wear. Someone does your brain. Someone tells you what to eat, and, three times
a week, someone stuffs a hose up your
bum and flushes it all out for you.
Saffron (Julia Sawalha), ibid. Edina replies: 'It's
called colonic irrigation, darling, and it's not to
be sniffed at.'

Dorothy L. Sayers (1893–1957)
BRITISH AUTHOR AND TRANSLATOR
Dorothy Leigh Sayers. She is best known for her
popular detective novels featuring the elegant and
erudite Lord Peter Wimsey, such as Whose Body?
(1923) and Murder Must Advertise *(1933). As a*
Christian apologist she wrote The Man Born to Be
King *(1941–2), a controversial sequence of radio*
plays about the life of Christ.

1 Lawyers enjoy a little mystery, you know.
Why, if everybody came forward and told
the truth, the whole truth, and nothing but
the truth straight out, we should all retire
to the workhouse.
Sir Impey Biggs, in *Clouds of Witness*, ch. 3
(1926)

2 She always says, my lord, that facts are like
cows. If you look them in the face hard
enough they generally run away.
Bunter, ibid., ch. 4

3 Time and trouble will tame an advanced
young woman, but an advanced old
woman is uncontrollable by any earthly
force.
Sir Impey Biggs, ibid., ch. 16

4 Death seems to provide the minds of the
Anglo-Saxon race with a greater fund of
amusement than any other single subject.
The Third Omnibus of Crime, Introduction
(1935)

5 *If it were not for the war,*
This war
Would suit me down to the ground.
'London Calling: Lord I Thank Thee'

6 Except ye become as little children, except
you can wake on your fiftieth birthday
with the same forward-looking excitement
and interest in life that you enjoyed when
you were five, 'ye cannot enter the kingdom of God'. One must not only die daily,
but every day we must be born again.
Creed or Chaos? and Other Essays in Popular
Mythology, 'Strong Meat' (1947)

Alexei Sayle (b. 1952)

BRITISH COMEDIAN, ACTOR AND PRESENTER
*He performed in the Comedy Store in the late
1970s and gained a television audience in* The
Young Ones *(1982) and Alexei Sayle's Stuff
(1988).*

1 'Ullo John Got a New Motor?
Song title (1984)

Arthur Scargill (b. 1938)

BRITISH TRADE UNION LEADER
*A coal miner from the age of eighteen, he was
elected NUM national President in 1981 and led
the 1984–5 national protest strike against pit
closures.*

1 If the church to which you went decided to
stop worshipping God and started worshipping the devil, you would have second
thoughts. The leadership of New Labour
has abandoned their socialist faith and
embraced capitalism which is tantamount
to embracing the devil!
Interview in the *Guardian* 4 May 1996. On his
disenchantment with the Labour Party, of which
he had been a member for thirty years, and his
creation of the Socialist Labour Party.

Simon Schama (b. 1945)

BRITISH HISTORIAN
*His evocative descriptions and racy narrative style,
both on the page and in his television programmes,
have drawn a wide audience. His books include*
Citizens: A Chronicle of the French Revolution
(1989) and Rembrandt's Eyes *(1999).*

1 Historians are left forever chasing
shadows, painfully aware of their inability
ever to reconstruct a dead world in its com-
pleteness however thorough or revealing
their documentation. . . . We are doomed
to be forever hailing someone who has just
gone around the corner and out of earshot.
Dead Certainties, 'Afterword' (1991)

2 Landscapes are culture before they are
nature; constructs of the imagination pro-
jected onto wood and water and rock.
Landscape and Memory, ch. 1, sect. 3 (1995)

3 Never confuse a genius with a Saint.
Rembrandt's Eyes, pt 5, ch. 10, sect. 3 (1999)

4 So instead of listening to cowboy pieties
. . . we turn to those who . . . understand,
especially when they hear the word
'revenge' thundered out by talk-show warriors, that the best, the only revenge, when
you're fighting a cult that fetishises death,
is life.
Guardian 14 September 2001. Referring to The
responses to '9/11'.

Felix E. Schelling (1858–1935)

US ACADEMIC
*A specialist in English Renaissance literature, he
published, among other works,* English Literature
During the Lifetime of Shakespeare *(1910) and* A
History of English Drama *(1914).*

1 True education makes for inequality; the
inequality of individuality, the inequality
of success, the glorious inequality of talent,
of genius; for inequality, not mediocrity,
individual superiority, not standardization, is the measure of the progress of the
world.
Pedagogically Speaking, ch. 8 (1929)

Elsa Schiaparelli (1890–1973)

ITALIAN-BORN FRENCH FASHION DESIGNER
*She opened her Paris salon in 1928 and quickly
became famed for her striking use of bright colours,
shoulder pads and flamboyant hats. She introduced 'shocking pink' in 1947 and opened a salon
in New York in 1949.*

1 Fashion is born by small facts, trends, or
even politics, never by trying to make little
pleats and furbelows, by trinkets, by
clothes easy to copy, or by the shortening
or lengthening of a skirt.
Shocking Life, ch. 9 (1954)

Arthur M. Schlesinger Jr (b. 1917)

US HISTORIAN AND ACADEMIC
*Arthur Meier Schlesinger. He was adviser to presi-
dents* KENNEDY *and* JOHNSON, *but quit in opposition to the Vietnam War. His works include* The
Age of Jackson *(1945),* A Thousand Days: John F.
Kennedy in the White House *(1965) and* The Age
of Roosevelt *(3 vols., 1957–60).*

1 The choice we face is not between progress
with conflict and progress without conflict.
The choice is between conflict and stagnation. You cannot expel conflict from
society any more than you can from the
human mind. When you attempt it, the
psychic costs in schizophrenia or torpor
are the same. The totalitarians regard the
toleration of conflict as our central weakness. So it may appear to be in an age of
anxiety. But we know it to be basically our
central strength.
The Vital Center: The Politics of Freedom (1949)

2 I trust that a graduate student some day
will write a doctoral essay on the influence
of the Munich analogy on the subsequent
history of the twentieth century. Perhaps
in the end he will conclude that the multitude of errors committed in the name of
'Munich' may exceed the original error of
1938.
*The Bitter Heritage: Vietnam and American
Democracy*, 'The Inscrutability of History' (1967)

3 Science and Technology revolutionize our lives, but memory, tradition and myth frame our response. Expelled from individual consciousness by the rush of change, history finds its revenge by stamping the collective unconscious with habits, values, expectations, dreams. The dialectic between past and future will continue to form our lives.

'The Challenge of Change', publ. in *The New York Times Magazine* 27 July 1986

4 Only a cad tells the truth about his love affairs.

Sunday Times Review 27 September 1998. Referring to BILL CLINTON's affair with MONICA LEWINSKY.

Artur Schnabel (1882–1951)

GERMAN-BORN US PIANIST

Making his concert début at the age of eight, he became an international celebrity, specializing in Beethoven, Mozart and Schubert. He also composed extensively for the piano. Fleeing the Nazis, he settled in the USA in 1939.

1 Applause is a receipt, not a bill.

Quoted in *The Musical Life*, 'Ovation and Triumph' (1958) by Irving Kolodin. Explaining why he did not render applause the tribute of encores.

2 The notes I handle no better than many pianists. But the pauses between the notes – ah, that is where the art resides.

Quoted in the *Chicago Daily News* 11 June 1958

Paul Schrader (b. 1946)

US FILM-MAKER

His film work often addresses themes of violence and redemption. He has worked extensively with MARTIN SCORSESE, *as in* Taxi Driver *(1976) and* The Last Temptation of Christ *(1988), and has also directed films. See also* ROBERT DE NIRO 1 *and* 2.

1 Movies are about people who *do* things. The number one fantasy of the cinema is that we can do something – we are relatively impotent in our own lives so we go to movies to watch people who are in control of their lives.

Interview in *Schrader on Schrader*, ch. 5 (ed. Kevin Jackson, 1990)

2 I could be just a writer very easily. I am not a writer. I am a *screen*writer, which is half a film-maker. . . . But it is *not* an art form, because screenplays are not works of art. They are invitations to others to collaborate on a work of art.

Quoted in *Writers in Hollywood 1915–1951*, Preface (1990) by Ian Hamilton

3 Saving someone's life is like falling in love, the best drug in the world. You wonder if

you've become immortal. It's as if God has passed through you. Why deny it? God *was* you.

Frank Pierce (Nicholas Cage), in *Bringing out the Dead* (film, 1999, screenplay by Paul Schrader, based on novel by Joe Connolly, directed by Martin Scorsese)

Charles Schulz (1922–2000)

US CARTOONIST

A freelancer for the Saturday Evening Post, he created the characters Charlie Brown, Snoopy and others for his Li'l Folks cartoon strip, which was eventually bought and re-named Peanuts by United Features in 1950, and became an international phenomenon.

1 Big sisters are the crab grass in the lawn of life.

Linus, in *Peanuts* (strip cartoon, 1952)

E. F. Schumacher (1911–77)

GERMAN-BORN BRITISH ECONOMIST

Ernst Friedrich Schumacher. A consultant on the 1942 Beveridge Report, he advised government on energy policy in the 1950s and in 1966 founded the Intermediate Technology Development Group, dedicated to developing sustainable communities. He set out his theories in the bestselling Small is Beautiful *(1973).*

1 Call a thing immoral or ugly, soul-destroying or a degradation of man, a peril to the peace of the world or to the well-being of future generations; as long as you have not shown it to be 'uneconomic' you have not really questioned its right to exist, grow, and prosper.

Small is Beautiful, pt 1, ch. 3 (1973)

2 I have no doubt that it is possible to give a new direction to technological development, a direction that shall lead it back to the real needs of man, and that also means: *to the actual size of man*. Man is small, and, therefore, small is beautiful. To go for giantism is to go for self-destruction.

Ibid., pt 2, ch. 10

Joseph Schumpeter (1883–1950)

MORAVIAN-BORN US ECONOMIST

In The Theory of Economic Development *(1912) he attributed economic growth to the activity of a few creative entrepreneurs. Other works include* Business Cycles *(1939) and the influential* Capitalism, Socialism and Democracy *(1942).*

1 For the duration of its collective life, or the time during which its identity may be assumed, each class resembles a hotel or an omnibus, always full, but always of different people.

Social Classes, ch. 3, no. 7 (1927)

2 Analyzing business cycles means neither

more nor less than analyzing the economic process of the capitalist era.
Introduction to *Business Cycles* (1939).

3 Marxism is essentially a product of the bourgeois mind.
Capitalism, Socialism and Democracy, ch. 1 (1942)

4 Economic progress, in capitalist society, means turmoil.
Ibid., ch. 3

5 The evolution of the capitalist style of life could be easily – and perhaps most tellingly – described in terms of the genesis of the modern Lounge Suit.
Ibid., ch. 11

6 Capitalism inevitably and by virtue of the very logic of its civilization creates, educates and subsidizes a vested interest in social unrest.
Ibid., ch. 13, sct. 2

7 Bureaucracy is not an obstacle to democracy but an inevitable complement to it.
Ibid., ch. 18

8 Democracy is a political *method*, that is to say, a certain type of institutional arrangement for arriving at political – legislative and administrative – decisions and hence incapable of being an end in itself.
Ibid., ch. 20, sect. 3

Arnold Schwarzenegger (b. 1947)
AUSTRIAN-BORN US SCREEN ACTOR
As 'the Austrian Oak', he was five times Mr Universe, and seven times Mr Olympia. His appearance in the documentary Pumping Iron *(1977) led to roles in* Conan the Barbarian *(1982) and* The Terminator *(1984), the film that established him.*

1 I'll be back.
The Terminator (Arnold Schwarzenegger), in *The Terminator* (film, 1984, written and directed by James Cameron). The words 'I'll be back' were uttered in seven films starring Arnold Schwarzenegger.

2 Hasta la vista, baby.
The Terminator (Arnold Schwarzenegger), in *Terminator 2: Judgment Day* (film, 1991, written, directed and produced by James Cameron).

3 Money doesn't make you happy. I now have $50 million but I was just as happy when I had $48 million.
Quoted in *Brewer's Cinema* (1995)

Norman Schwarzkopf (b. 1934)
US SOLDIER
Having joined the US army in 1956, he directed Operation Desert Storm against Iraq (1990–91), acquiring the nickname 'Stormin' Norman'.

1 A very great man once said you should love your enemies, and that's not a bad

piece of advice. We can love them, but, by God, that doesn't mean we're not going to fight them.
Daily Telegraph 1 February 1991

Albert Schweitzer (1875–1965)
GERMAN THEOLOGIAN, MISSIONARY AND MUSICIAN
In 1913, in a spirit 'not of benevolence but of atonement', he founded the leprosy hospital at Lamberéné in French-occupied Equatorial Africa where he spent the rest of his life. As well as a study of J. S. Bach and works on theology, he wrote The Philosophy of Civilization *(1923) and autobiographical works.*

1 Pessimism is depreciated will-to-live.
The Philosophy of Civilization, vol. 2: *Civilization and Ethics*, ch. 2 (1923)

2 True ethics begin where the use of language ceases.
Ibid., ch. 21

3 The African is my brother – but he is my younger brother by several centuries.
Quoted in the *Observer* 23 October 1955

Martin Scorsese (b. 1942)
US FILM-MAKER
Described by critic DAVID THOMSON *as a 'devotee of intelligence, visual beauty, and verbal style', he returns frequently in his work to the themes of masculinity and alienation.* Mean Streets *(1973),* Raging Bull *(1980) and* Goodfellas *(1990) are his acknowledged masterpieces.*

1 You don't make up for your sins in church. You do it on the streets. You do it at home. The rest is bullshit and you know it.
Voiceover, in *Mean Streets* (film, 1973, screenplay by Martin Scorsese and Mardik Martin, directed by Martin Scorsese)

2 I saw beauty in movies, usually westerns – I loved the landscape, I loved the colour of the horses and I wished I could be there. But I wasn't. So I dealt with the beauty on the streets, and the beauty was extraordinary.
Interview in the *Guardian* 11 December 1999

C. P. Scott (1846–1932)
BRITISH AUTHOR AND JOURNALIST
Charles Prestwich Scott. He became Editor of the Manchester Guardian *aged twenty-five, a position he held for fifty-nine years, the longest editorship of a national newspaper anywhere. He was a Liberal MP 1895–1906.*

1 Neither in what it gives, nor in what it does not give, nor in the mode of presentation, must the unclouded face of truth

suffer wrong. Comment is free, but facts are sacred.

Manchester Guardian 5 May 1921. Editorial marking the paper's first hundred years. TOM STOPPARD in *Night and Day* (1978) adapted the aphorism: 'Comment is free, but facts are on expenses.'

George C. Scott (b. 1926)
US SCREEN ACTOR
He has specialized in tough, authoritative roles, as in The Hustler *(1961) and* The List of Adrian Messenger *(1963), and has also directed films and worked in theatre. He was the first actor ever to refuse an Oscar (for his title role in* Patton, *1970), denouncing the selection process as a 'meat parade'.*

1 I'm not saying we wouldn't get our hair mussed, Mister President, but I do say not more than ten to twenty million dead depending on the breaks.

General 'Buck' Turgidson (George C. Scott), in *Dr Strangelove: Or How I Learned to Stop Worrying and Love the Bomb* (film, 1963, screenplay by STANLEY KUBRICK, Terry Southern and Peter George based on Peter George's novel *Red Alert*, produced and directed by Stanley Kubrick). Discussing nuclear war.

2 All this stuff you heard about America not wanting to fight, wanting to stay out of the war, is a lot of horse dung. Americans, traditionally, love to fight. All real Americans love the sting of battle. . . . Americans play to win all the time. I wouldn't give a hoot in hell for a man who lost and laughed. That's why Americans have never lost – and will never lose – a war, because the very thought of losing is hateful to Americans.

General George S. Patton Jr (George C. Scott), in *Patton: Lust for Glory* (film, 1970, screenplay by FRANCIS FORD COPPOLA and Edmund H. North, directed by Franklin J. Schaffner). In the film's opening speech, Patton addresses the audience as though they were his troops. The screenplay was based on Ladislas Farago's *Patton: Ordeal and Triumph* (1966) and *A Soldier's Story* (1951) by General OMAR BRADLEY.

3 No bastard ever won a war by dying for his country. He won it by making the other poor dumb bastard die for his country.
Ibid.

Paul Scott (1920–78)
BRITISH AUTHOR
Writing chiefly about India and Malaya, he is best known for The Raj Quartet *(1966–75, televised as* The Jewel in the Crown, *1982), a chronicle of life among the British and Anglo-Indians in the last years of the Raj.*

1 Ah, well, the truth is always one thing, but in a way it's the other thing, the gossip, that counts. It shows where people's hearts lie.

Count Bronowsky, in *The Day of the Scorpion*, bk 1, pt 3, ch. 3 (1968)

Gil Scott Heron (b. 1949)
US MUSICIAN AND AUTHOR
A novelist and poet, he set his work to music and composed political songs in a jazz-soul idiom, as on the albums Pieces of a Man *(1971) and* Free Will *(1972). He later turned to rap.*

1 *The revolution will not go better with Coke.*
The revolution will not fight the germs that may cause bad breath,
The revolution will put you in the driver's seat.
The revolution will not be televised, will not be televised,
Will not be televised, will not be televised,
The revolution will be no rerun, brother,
The revolution will be live.
'The Revolution Will Not Be Televised' (song, written with Brian Jackson) on the album *Pieces of a Man* (1971). The song was covered by Patti LaBelle.

2 *What's the word?*
Tell me brother, have you heard
from Johannesburg?
'Johannesburg' (song) on the album *From South Africa to South California* (1976)

Roger Scruton (b. 1944)
BRITISH PHILOSOPHER AND AUTHOR
A conservative thinker, he considers philosophy to be valuable only when, he says, 'connected to critical intelligence in the fields of human value'. Among his works are The Meaning of Conservatism *(1980) and* An Intelligent Person's Guide to Philosophy *(1996).*

1 Government is the primary need of every man subject to the discipline of social intercourse, and freedom the name of at least one of his anxieties.
The Meaning of Conservatism, ch. 1 (1980)

2 Once in parliament, a member, rightly subject to the discipline of party, ceases to represent his constituents in any matter of state. He is a part of the apparatus of state. What he does is determined by the established interests that seek expression through his party, and not by any 'promises' that he once made at the hustings. Democracy is simply one means of gaining power, and so of freeing oneself from the immediate demands of the multitude.
Ibid., ch. 3

3 We yearn, in fact, to *justify* the human body, to give grounds for our feeling that this is God's image. And in this yearning is

expressed our real knowledge that we are
our bodies and that they are we.
Sexual Desire: A Philosophical Investigation, ch. 9
(1986)

John Sebastian (b. 1944)

US ROCK MUSICIAN

*He was co-founder, lead singer and composer of
the folk-rock band The Lovin' Spoonful 1965–8,
and later made solo albums.*

1 *Hot town,*
  Summer in the city,
  Back o' my neck gettin' dirty and gritty.
  'Summer in the City' (song, written by John Seb-
  astian, Mark Sebastian and Steve Boone) on the
  album *Hums of The Lovin' Spoonful* (1966) by
  The Lovin' Spoonful

Alan Seeger (1888–1916)

US POET

*On the outbreak of the First World War, he joined
the French Foreign Legion and was killed in the
Somme offensive. His popular poems 'I Have a
Rendezvous with Death' and 'Ode in Memory
of the American Volunteers' were published in
Poems (1916).*

1 *I have a rendezvous with Death*
  At some disputed barricade.
  'I Have a Rendezvous with Death', publ. in the
  North American Review October 1916, repr. in
  Poems (1916)

2 *And I to my pledged word am true,*
  I shall not fail that rendezvous.
  Ibid.

Pete Seeger (b. 1919)

US FOLK SINGER AND SONGWRITER

*A Communist Party member until 1951, he co-
founded the Almanac Singers (1940–41), a campaigning folk band which included* WOODIE
GUTHRIE, *and the Weavers (1948–58). He was a
victim of the McCarthyite witch-hunt in the 1950s.*

1 *If I had a hammer, I'd hammer in the
  morning,*
  *I'd hammer in the evening all over this
  land.*
  'The Hammer Song' (song, 1949, written by Pete
  Seeger and Lee Hays) on the album *Sing Out
  with Pete* (1961). The song was successfully
  recorded by Peter, Paul and Mary in 1962 as 'If I
  Had a Hammer', becoming a staple at protests
  in the 1960s. 'We wrought better than we
  thought,' commented Seeger years later, 'the
  song has grown with time.'

2 *Where have all the flowers gone?*
  'Where Have All the Flowers Gone?' (song,
  c. 1956) on the album *The Bitter and the Sweet* by
  Pete Seeger (1963). The song, which was covered
  by the Kingston Trio as well as Peter, Paul and
  Mary in 1962, was inspired by a passage in the
  novel *And Quiet Flows the Don* (1934) by Mikhail

Sholokhov, quoting a Ukrainian folk song:
'Where are the flowers, the girls have plucked
them. Where are the girls, they've all taken husbands. Where are the men, they're all in the
army.' BOB DYLAN, apparently, spent a fruitless
year searching for this song.

3 *Little boxes on the hillside,*
  Little boxes made of ticky tacky;
  Little boxes on the hillside
  Little boxes all the same.
  There's a green one, and a pink one,
  And a blue one, and a yellow one
  And they're all made out of ticky tacky,
  And they all look just the same.
  'Little Boxes' (song, 1962, written by Malvina
  Reynolds) on the album *We Shall Overcome*
  (1963)

4 I had thought that folk music was something old, back in the library, and pop
  music was new – it was something you
  could hear on the radio. All of a sudden I
  realized that was a phony distinction. Millions of people were making music which
  grew out of the old traditions, mostly
  making up new words to fit old tunes. New
  words to fit new circumstances. This is
  what I call the folk process.
  Quoted in *All You Need is Love*, 'Go Down
  Moses!' (1976) by Tony Palmer

Erich Segal (b. 1937)

US AUTHOR

*A Yale professor who has published scholarly works
on Graeco-Roman comedy, he also wrote film
scripts, striking gold with his screenplay for* Love
Story *(1970) and his accompanying novel.*

1 Love means never having to say you're
  sorry.
  Jenny Cavilleri (Ali MacGraw), in *Love Story*
  (film, 1970, screenplay by Erich Segal, directed
  by Arthur Hiller). The words, which appear in
  ch. 13 of Segal's novelization of the film as 'Love
  means not ever having to say you're sorry', were
  used as a publicity slogan for the film, subsequently spawning numerous variations on the
  theme. See also TONY PARSONS 3.

E. C. Segar (1894–1938)

US CARTOONIST

Elzie Crisler Segar. He began the strip The
Thimble Theatre *for the New York* Evening Journal *in 1919, featuring the Oyl Family, later joined
by Popeye the sailor.*

1 I yam what I yam.
  Catch-phrase of Popeye from 1929. Originally
  created for the *Thimble Theatre* syndicated strip,
  Popeye's character took over from Olive and
  Castor Oyl, making his first official appearance
  17 January 1929, and first film appearance in 1933
  for the Fleischer Studio's *Talkartoon* series, opposite Betty Boop. After Segar's death, the strip
  was drawn by different animators in various TV

cartoons, and his character was fleshed out in ROBERT ALTMAN's *Popeye* (1980) with ROBIN WILLIAMS in the title role.

2 I likes to eat my spinach.
Ibid.

Will Self (b. 1961)
BRITISH AUTHOR
Known for his dark humour, he has drawn on his own experience of heroin addiction for his short stories The Quantity Theory of Insanity *(1991) and his novel* My Idea of Fun *(1994). Later titles include* How the Dead Live *(2000).*

1 *Wake up.* The avant-garde is dead. It's been marketed.
Interview in *The Idler* November/December 1993

2 Some people are born slack – others have slacking thrust upon them.
'Slack Attack', publ. in the *Observer* 2 January 1994, repr. in *Junk Mail* (1995)

3 As far as I can see, the history of experimental art in the twentieth century is intimately bound up with the experience of intoxification.
Quoted in *The Face* November 1994

W. C. Sellar (1898–1951) and
R. J. Yeatman (1897–1968)
BRITISH AUTHORS
Walter Carruthers Sellar and Robert Julian Yeatman. Sellar, a schoolteacher, and Yeatman, a copywriter and advertising manager, collaborated on 1066 and All That *(1930), a classic compendium of schoolroom howlers.*

1 History is not what you thought. *It is what you can remember.* All other history defeats itself.
1066 and All That, 'Compulsory Preface' (1930)

2 The Roman Conquest was, however, a Good Thing, since the Britons were only natives at the time.
Ibid., ch. 1, 'Culture Among the Ancient Britons'

3 We come at last to the Central Period of British History . . . consisting in the *utterly memorable Struggle between the Cavaliers (Wrong but Wromantic) and the Roundheads (Right but Repulsive).*
Ibid., ch. 35, 'Charles I and the Civil War'

4 King Edward's new policy of peace was very successful and culminated in the Great War to End War. This pacific and inevitable struggle was undertaken in the reign of His Good and memorable Majesty King George V and it was the cause of nowadays and the end of History.
Ibid., ch. 61, 'The Great War'

5 Do not on any account attempt to write on both sides of the paper at once.
Ibid., 'Test Paper V'. Closing words of book.

Peter Sellers (1925–80)
BRITISH COMEDIAN AND ACTOR
One of the Goons on the radio Goon Show *in the 1950s, he played a series of comedy film roles throughout the 1960s, and enjoyed a late success as the philosophical gardener in* Being There *(1979).*

1 You silly twisted boy!
Favourite expression of Lance Brigadier Grytpype-Thynne (Peter Sellers), in *The Goon Show* (BBC radio comedy series, 1951–60, written by SPIKE MILLIGAN), publ. in *The Goon Show Scripts,* ed. Spike Milligan, 1972.

2 There is no me. I do not exist. There used to be a me but I had it surgically removed.
Time 3 March 1980. Remark four months before his death.

David O. Selznick (1902–65)
US FILM PRODUCER
David Oliver Selznick. His Selznick International Pictures, founded by him in 1936, had such successes as Gone with the Wind *(1939) and* Rebecca *(1940). He was known as a hard taskmaster – 'The way I see it, my function is to be responsible for everything' – and renowned for the length of his memos.*

1 Hollywood's like Egypt, full of crumbled pyramids. It'll never come back. It'll just keep on crumbling until finally the wind blows the last studio prop across the sands.
Said in 1951 to journalist and author Ben Hecht, quoted in *A Child of the Century,* bk 5, 'Enter, the Movies' (1954) by Ben Hecht

Rod Serling (1924–75)
US SCRIPTWRITER AND TELEVISION PRODUCER
Edwin Rodman Serling. He was the creator and host of the science fiction TV series The Twilight Zone *(1959–64) and the author of more than 200 plays for television. He also wrote screenplays, and co-scripted* The Planet of the Apes *(1968).*

1 There is a fifth dimension beyond those known to man. It is a dimension vast as space and timeless as infinity. It is the middle ground between light and shadow, between the pit of his fears and the summit of his knowledge. This is the dimension of imagination. It is an area called the Twilight Zone.
The Twilight Zone, Preamble (TV series, created, written and narrated by Rod Serling, 1959–64)

Andres Serrano (b. 1950)
US PHOTOGRAPHER
He achieved notoriety in the 1980s for his use of bodily fluids in his photographs such as Piss Christ *(1989), and in the 1990s with his series* The History of Sex *(1996).*

1 **What the nuns told us in school when I was going to religious instruction was that we worship not the crucifix but Christ . . . We aren't supposed to worship the symbol or give it the same level of reverence that we give Christ because it's only a representation.**

On the depiction of the crucifix in his 1987 work, *Piss Christ*, in the *Boston Globe* 20 August 1989, quoted in *Body and Soul*, 'Andres Serrano: Invisible Power' (ed. Brian Wallis, 1995). Serrano's image aroused enormous controversy in the United States and Britain.

2 **I've always believed there was no such thing as the sacred without the profane – and in some cases it's hard to tell the difference.**

Quoted in *Contemporary Photographers* (third edn, ed. Martin Marix Evans, 1995)

Vikram Seth (b. 1952)

INDIAN AUTHOR AND POET

He has published verse, for example Mappings *(1980), and travel writing, including* From Heaven Lake *(1983), but he is best known for his long novel* A Suitable Boy *(1993), which recounts the post-independence 'India of the drawing room'.*

1 **Music is not a cheap spectacle – not the entertainment of the brothel. It is like prayer.**

Ustad Majeed Khan, in *A Suitable Boy*, ch. 6, sect. 2 (1993)

2 **Making music and making love – it's a bit too easy an equation.**

Julia, in *An Equal Music*, pt 3, sect. 16 (1999)

3 **Strange to be a man and never grow big with child. To feel a part of you opening, and a part of you leaving, and howling as if it were not a part of you. Then it puts on a green cap and a grey suit and has friends.**

Narrator (Michael), ibid., pt 8, sect 13. Observation while watching schoolchildren.

Brian Sewell

BRITISH ART CRITIC

Art critic for the Evening Standard *since the 1980s, he is alternately revered and reviled for his traditionalist stance.*

1 **There is now a universal belief that the far side of a fallen barrier is always preferable . . . and we are into new generations of artists who have never known the art of the past and have no skills or traditions by which to return to it. Time and again in the history of art, artists have broken a barrier into a cul-de-sac, and it is those who have stepped back into the past who have then, fully armed, leaped into the future.**

'Gravity and Grace', first publ. in the *Evening*

Standard (1993), repr, in *The Reviews That Caused the Rumpus*, ch. 5 (1994)

2 **She [the Queen] deserves better than to be perpetuated as an old-age pensioner about to lose her bungalow.**

Quoted in the *Independent on Sunday* 12 May 1996. On the portrait by Anthony Williams to mark the Queen's seventieth birthday.

Anne Sexton (1928–74)

US POET

Her verse, collected in Bedlam and Back *(1960) and* Live or Die *(1966) among other titles, is confessional in style and drew criticism for its candour. Afflicted by emotional breakdowns and depression, she committed suicide.*

1 **Everyone has left me
except my muse,
that good nurse.
She stays in my hand,
a mild white mouse.**

'Flee on Your Donkey', publ. in *Live or Die* (1966). The title quotes Rimbaud's *Fêtes de la faim* (1872).

2 **But suicides have a special language.
Like carpenters they want to know which tools.
They never ask why build.**

'Wanting to Die', publ. ibid.

3 **The sea is mother-death and she is a mighty female, the one who wins, the one who sucks us all up.**

Entry 19 November 1971, in 'A Small Journal', publ. in *The Poet's Story* (ed. Howard Moss, 1974)

4 **It doesn't matter who my father was; it matters who I remember he was.**

Ibid., 1 January 1972

5 **God owns heaven
but He craves the earth.**

'The Earth', publ. in *The Awful Rowing Toward God* (1975). In his essay 'A Visionary' (1891) YEATS recalls G. W. Russell (whom he refers to as 'X–') (see Æ) meeting an old peasant who, 'dumb to most men, poured out his cares for him . . . Once he burst out with, "God possesses the heavens – God possesses the heavens – but He covets the world." '

6 **My faith
is a great weight
hung on a small wire,
as doth the spider
hang her baby on a thin web.**

'Small Wire', publ. ibid.

7 **My ideas are a curse.
They spring from a radical discontent
With the awful order of things.**

'February 3rd', publ. in *Scorpio, Bad Spider, Die: the Horoscope Poems* (1978)

Yitzhak Shamir (b. 1915)

POLISH-BORN ISRAELI POLITICIAN AND
PRIME MINISTER

*Originally Yitzhak Jazernicki. A founder member
of the Israel Freedom Fighters ('the Stern Gang')
in the struggle for independence, he later became
leader of the right-wing Likud Party and served
alternately as Israel's Foreign Minister and Prime
Minister throughout the 1980s.*

1 Should there be maniacs who raise the idea
[of Palestinian self-government], they will
encounter an iron fist which will leave no
trace of such attempts.

Quoted in *The Times* 11 August 1988

2 Our image has undergone change from
David fighting Goliath to being Goliath.

Quoted in the *Daily Telegraph* 25 January 1989

The Shangri-Las

US VOCAL GROUP

*The all-girl vocal group created in 1964 consisted of
the Weiss sisters, Mary and Betty, and the twins
Mary Ann and Marge Ganser. They peaked with
such hits as 'Remember (Walking in the Sand)'
and the dramatic 'Leader of the Pack' (both 1964).*

1 *I met him at the candy store,*
He turned around and smiled at me,
You get the picture?
('Yes we see')
That's when I fell for the leader of the pack.

'The Leader of the Pack' (song, 1964, written by
George Morton, Jeff Barry and Ellie Greenwich)
on the album *Golden Hits of the Shangri-Las*
(1966)

Helen Sharman (b. 1963)

BRITISH SCIENTIST AND ASTRONAUT

*Selected from 13,000 applicants to be the British
member of the 1991 Russian space mission Project
Juno, she spent six days aboard the Mir space
station, becoming Britain's first astronaut.*

1 There is very little difference between men
and women in space.

Quoted in the *Independent on Sunday* 9 June 1991

Al Sharpton (b. 1954)

US CIVIL RIGHTS CAMPAIGNER

*A fiery polemicist and believer in direct action to
end racial discrimination, he has been President of
the National Action Network since he founded it
in 1991.*

1 What I profess to do is help the oppressed
and if I cause a load of discomfort in the
white community and the black community, that in my opinion means I'm
being effective, because I'm not trying to
make them comfortable. The job of an activist is to make people tense and cause
social change.

Independent on Sunday 21 April 1991

George Bernard Shaw (1856–1950)

IRISH PLAYWRIGHT AND CRITIC

*He was a music and drama critic before
embarking on a prodigious output of plays that
combined fierce wit with a passion for social
reform, for example* Man and Superman *(1905),
and* Pygmalion *(1913, adapted as the musical* My
Fair Lady, *1956, filmed 1964).* LENIN *called him 'a
good man fallen among Fabians'. See also* JAMES
AGATE 2, MRS PATRICK CAMPBELL 1, BERT
LESTON TAYLOR 2, W. B. YEATS 12.

1 The secret of being miserable is to have
leisure to bother about whether you are
happy or not. The cure for it is occupation.

Parents and Children, 'Children's Happiness'
(1914)

2 A perpetual holiday is a good working
definition of hell.

Ibid.

3 When our relatives are at home, we have
to think of all their good points or it would
be impossible to endure them. But when
they are away, we console ourselves for
their absence by dwelling on their vices.

Captain Shotover, in *Heartbreak House*, act 1
(1920)

4 Cruelty would be delicious if one could
only find some sort of cruelty that didn't
really hurt.

Mrs Hushabye, ibid.

5 It is a curious sensation: the sort of pain
that goes mercifully beyond our powers of
feeling. When your heart is broken, your
boats are burned: nothing matters any
more. It is the end of happiness and the
beginning of peace.

Ellie, ibid.

6 We know now that the soul is the body,
and the body the soul. They tell us they are
different because they want to persuade us
that we can keep our souls if we let them
make slaves of our bodies.

Ellie, ibid.

7 Old men are dangerous: it doesn't matter
to them what is going to happen to the
world.

Captain Shotover, ibid. Ellie responds: 'I should
have thought nothing else mattered to old men.
They can't be very interested in what is going to
happen to themselves.'

8 I feel nothing but the accursed happiness
I have dreaded all my life long: the happiness that comes as life goes, the happiness
of yielding and dreaming instead of
resisting and doing, the sweetness of the
fruit that is going rotten.

Ibid.

9 A man's interest in the world is only the
overflow from his interest in himself.
When you are a child your vessel is not yet

full; so you care for nothing but your own affairs. When you grow up, your vessel overflows; and you are a politician, a philosopher, or an explorer and adventurer. In old age the vessel dries up: there is no overflow: you are a child again.

Ibid.

10 Never waste jealousy on a real man: it is the imaginary man that supplants us all in the long run.

Hector Hushabye, ibid.

11 Go anywhere in England where there are natural, wholesome, contented, and really nice English people; and what do you always find? That the stables are the real centre of the household. . . . There are only two classes in good society in England: the equestrian classes and the neurotic classes.

Lady Utterword, ibid., act 3

12 In Ireland they try to make a cat cleanly by rubbing its nose in its own filth. Mr Joyce has tried the same treatment on the human subject. I hope it may prove successful.

Of *Ulysses*, in letter to JAMES JOYCE's publisher Sylvia Beach, 10 October 1921, publ. in *Letters of James Joyce*, vol. 3 (ed. RICHARD ELLMAN, 1966). Shaw called *Ulysses* a 'revolting record of a disgusting phase of civilisation; but it is a truthful one', though he refused the invitation to purchase a copy. In *The Table Talk of GBS* (1924), Shaw is quoted, 'I could not write the words Mr Joyce used: my prudish hand would refuse to form the letters.'

13 All the sweetness of religion is conveyed to the world by the hands of story-tellers and image-makers. Without their fictions the truths of religion would for the multitude be neither intelligible nor even apprehensible; and the prophets would prophesy and the teachers teach in vain.

Back to Methuselah, Preface, 'What to Do with the Legends' (1922)

14 You see things; and you say 'Why?' But I dream things that never were; and I say 'Why not?'

The Serpent, ibid., 'In the Beginning', act 1. These words are often associated with ROBERT F. KENNEDY after they were quoted by him in an address to the Irish Parliament in Dublin, June 1963, and attributed to him by Edward Kennedy at Robert's funeral service in 1968.

15 Life is too short for men to take it seriously.

Franklyn, ibid., 'The Gospel of the Brothers Barnabas'

16 Life is a disease; and the only difference between one man and another is the stage of the disease at which he lives. You are always at the crisis: I am always in the con-

valescent stage. I enjoy convalescence. It is the part that makes illness worth while.

Lubin, ibid. Addressing his political rival Burge.

17 A nap, my friend, is a brief period of sleep which overtakes superannuated persons whent they endeavour to entertain unwelcome visitors or to listen to scientific lectures.

The Elderly Gentleman, ibid., 'Tragedy of an Elderly Gentleman', act 1

18 It is difficult, if not impossible, for most people to think otherwise than in the fashion of their own period.

Saint Joan, Preface (1923)

19 We want a few mad people now. See where the sane ones have landed us!

Poulengey, ibid., sc.1

20 A miracle is an event which creates faith. That is the purpose and nature of miracles. . . . Frauds deceive. An event which creates faith does not deceive: therefore it is not a fraud, but a miracle.

The Archbishop, ibid., sc. 2

21 What Englishman will give his mind to politics as long as he can afford to keep a motor car?

Balbus, in *The Apple Cart*, act 1 (1929)

22 A king is not allowed the luxury of a good character. Our country has produced millions of blameless greengrocers, but not one blameless monarch.

King Magnus, ibid.

23 The national anthem belongs to the eighteenth century. In it you find us ordering God about to do our political dirty work.

A member of the Caravan of the Curious, in *The Adventures of the Black Girl in Her Search for God* (1932)

24 When Satan makes impure verses, Allah sends a divine tune to cleanse them.

The Arab, ibid.

25 Newspapers are unable, seemingly, to discriminate between a bicycle accident and the collapse of civilisation.

Preface (1933) to *Too True to be Good* (1931)

26 The trouble, Mr Goldwyn, is that you are only interested in art and I am only interested in money.

Quoted in *The Great Goldwyn*, ch. 3 (1937) by Alva Johnson. Addressed to SAMUEL GOLDWYN, according to publicity chief HOWARD DIETZ, during talks to engage Shaw as a writer for Hollywood. The words, released as a statement for the press, are probably an approximation of the original dialogue.

27 A government which robs Peter to pay Paul can always depend on the support of Paul.

Everybody's Political What's What, ch. 30 (1944)

28 [Dancing is] a perpendicular expression of a horizontal desire.

Attributed in the *New Statesman* 23 March 1962

Irwin Shaw (1913–84)

US AUTHOR

Having written plays, screenplays and short stories, he published the bestselling novel, The Young Lions *(1948, filmed 1958), based on his wartime experiences.*

1 I cringe when critics say I'm a master of the popular novel. What's an unpopular novel?

Observer 6 March 1983

Sandie Shaw (b. 1947)

BRITISH SINGER

Originally Sandra Goodrich. Famous for her bare feet and miniskirt, she had her first hits in 1964 and in 1967 was Britain's first winner of the Eurovision Song Contest with 'Puppet on a String'.

1 I'm just a normal everyday kind of goddess.

Said in 1988, quoted in the *New Musical Express* 4 February 1995

(Sir) Hartley Shawcross (1902–2003)

BRITISH LAWYER

Baron Shawcross of Friston. Attorney-General 1945–51, he was chief British prosecutor at the Nuremberg Trials (1945–6) and led the prosecution of the Klaus Fuchs 'atomic spy' case (1950).

1 You cannot do justice to the dead. When we talk about doing justice to the dead we are talking about retribution for the harm done to them. But retribution and justice are two different things.

Quoted in the *Daily Telegraph* 1 May 1991. Discussing the War Crimes Bill and the prosecution of ex-Nazis living in Britain.

Gail Sheehy (b. 1937)

US AUTHOR AND CRITIC

She has written widely on politics and social issues and has also established herself as a guide to the ageing process and the transition into what she calls the 'Flaming Fifties' and 'Serene Sixties', in such books as Passages in Men's Lives *(1998).*

1 There is no more defiant denial of one man's ability to possess one woman exclusively than the prostitute who refuses to be redeemed.

Hustling, ch. 1 (1971)

2 Democratization is not democracy; it is a slogan for the temporary liberalization handed down from an autocrat. Glasnost is not free speech; only free speech, constitutionally guaranteed, is free speech.

Gorbachev, 'Looking for Mikhail Gorbachev' (1991)

3 The secret of a leader lies in the tests he has faced over the whole course of his life and the *habit of action* he develops in meeting those tests.

Ibid.

Gilbert Shelton (b. 1940)

US CARTOONIST

His creations, the Fabulous Furry Freak Brothers, made their first appearance in The LA Free Press *in 1967, and subsequently featured in* The Fabulous Furry Freak Brothers, *the most popular underground comic, and constantly in print.*

1 We have plenty of grass, and as we all know, dope will get you through times of no money better than money will get you through times of no dope.

Freewheelin' Franklin, in 'The Freaks Pull a Heist' (1971) publ. in *The Fabulous Furry Freak Brothers* (strip cartoon, from 1968). The line became a motto for the Freak Brothers and their following.

Ron Shelton (b. 1945)

US FILM-MAKER

His films include Bull Durham *(1988),* Blaze *(1989) and* White Men Can't Jump *(1992). He appeared as himself in* Looking for Oscar *(1999).*

1 I believe in the Church of Baseball. I tried all the major religions and most of the minor ones. I've worshipped Buddha, Allah, Brahma, Vishnu, Siva, trees, mushrooms and Isadora Duncan. I know things. For instance: there are 108 beads in a Catholic rosary and there are 108 stitches in a baseball. When I learned that, I gave Jesus a chance.

Opening monologue in *Bull Durham* (film, 1988, written and directed by Ron Shelton)

2 Nobody on this planet ever really chooses each other. I mean, it's all a question of quantum physics, molecular attraction and timing.

Anne Savoy (Susan Sarandon), ibid.

3 The world is made for people who aren't cursed with self-awareness.

Anne Savoy (Susan Sarandon), ibid.

Sam Shepard (b. 1943)

US PLAYWRIGHT, SCREENWRITER AND ACTOR

Originally Samuel Shepard Rogers. His plays, often concerning spiritual vacuity and the mythology of the American West, include Buried Child *(1978) and* Simpatico *(1994). He has acted in films including* Days of Heaven *(1978), and he wrote the screenplay for* Paris Texas *(1984).*

1 A concert audience has a face. It looks worked upon. Wild eyed. Stimulated from a distant source like a laboratory experi-

ment. As though the stage event, the action being watched and heard, is only a mirror image of some unseen phenomenon.
Rolling Thunder Logbook, 'Audience' (1977)

2 Fans are more dangerous than a man with a weapon because they're after something invisible. Some imagined 'something'. At least with a gun you know what you're facing.
Ibid., 'Fans'

3 All the land has been discovered. Some parts of hidden South America maybe still lie out of sight, but this land here has been discovered. Every inch. Now the move is inner space. New religions. est. Gurus. Meditation. Outer space is too expensive and only lies within the reach of the government or corporate industry.
Ibid., 'Explore'

4 In this business we make movies, American movies. Leave the films to the French.
Saul, in *True West*, act 2, sc. 5 (1980)

5 Ideas emerge from plays, not the other way round.
'Language, Visualization and the Inner Library', publ. in *American Dreams* (ed. Bonnie Marranca, 1981)

6 I feel there are territories within us that are totally unknown. Huge, mysterious, and dangerous territories. . . . And if we don't enter those in art of one kind or another, whether it's playwriting, or painting, or music, or whatever, then I don't under stand the point of doing anything. It's the reason I write. I try to go into parts of myself that are unknown.
Quoted in *The Other American Drama*, ch. 3 (1994) by Marc Robinson

Norman Sherry (b. 1925)
BRITISH ACADEMIC AND AUTHOR
He has written on Jane Austen and GRAHAM GREENE, *but his special interest is Joseph Conrad, on whom he has published numerous works, for instance* Conrad and His World *(1972).*

1 The facts of a person's life will, like murder, come out.
International Herald Tribune 15 September 1989. Referring to his biography *Life of Graham Greene 1904–39* (1989).

Robert E. Sherwood (1896–1955)
US PLAYWRIGHT
Robert Emmet Sherwood. A member of New York's literary Algonquin Round Table, he received Pulitzer Prizes for his plays Idiot's Delight *(1936),* Abe Lincoln in Illinois *(1939) and* There Shall be No Night *(1941). He was speechwriter for* FRANKLIN D. ROOSEVELT.

1 All Coolidge had to do in 1924 was to keep his mean trap shut, to be elected. All Harding had to do in 1920 was repeat 'Avoid foreign entanglements.' All Hoover had to do in 1928 was to endorse Coolidge. All Roosevelt had to do in 1932 was to point to Hoover.
Quoted in *Wit's End* (ed. Robert E. Drennan 1968)

Carol Shields (1935–2003)
US-BORN CANADIAN AUTHOR
Coming to notice with The Republic of Love *(1992), she won wide acclaim for* The Stone Diaries *(1993), a chronicle of the life of an 'ordinary' Canadian woman.* Larry's Party *(1996) is written from a male perspective.*

1 Canada is a country where nothing seems ever to happen. A country always dressed in its Sunday go-to-meeting clothes. A country you wouldn't ask to dance a second waltz. Clean. Christian. Dull. Quiescent. But growing. Yes, it must be admitted, the Dominion is growing.
The Stone Diaries, ch. 3 (1993)

Clare Short (b. 1946)
BRITISH POLITICIAN
A popular and outspoken Labour MP for Birmingham Ladywood since 1983, she campaigned against nudity in the tabloids while in opposition and was Secretary of State for International Development 1997–2003.

1 Political correctness is a concept invented by hard-rightwing forces to defend their right to be racist, to treat women in a degrading way and to be truly vile about gay people. They invent this idea of people who are politically correct, with a rigid, monstrous attitude to life so they can attack them. But we have all had to learn to modify our language. That's all part of being a decent human being.
Interview in the *Guardian* 18 February 1995

2 It will be golden elephants next.
Quoted in the *Observer* 24 August 1997. Referring to calls to increase aid to Montserrat following the eruption there.

3 Lloyd George and Roosevelt had mistresses, no one dwelt on it. Now we have to discuss oral sex. It's not just dumbing down, it's a sort of crassness.
Interview in the *Daily Telegraph* 31 January 1998

4 Hubris is, certainly, the disease of politics. The health and safety commission should send everyone a warning.
Interview in the *Independent* 28 September 1998

Nigel Short (b. 1965)
BRITISH CHESS PLAYER

An international master from 1980, he became the youngest-ever grandmaster from Britain in 1984.

1 Chess is ruthless: you've got to be prepared to kill people.

Quoted in the *Observer* 11 August 1991

Jerry Siegel (1914–96)
US CARTOONIST

and

Joe Shuster (1914–92)
CANADIAN-BORN US CARTOONIST

Schoolmates Siegel and Shuster devised a prototype of Superman, Man of Steel, in a fanzine in 1933 and the hero was taken up by Action Comics in 1938, later appearing on radio and TV and in films. Siegel wrote Superman's adventures until 1948 and 1959–65, Shuster drew them until 1947.

1 Is it a bird? Is it a plane? No, it's SUPERMAN!

Voices in the crowd in *Superman* (cartoon, from 1933). Sometimes rendered as 'It's a bird . . . It's a plane . . .'

2 Faster than a speeding bullet! More powerful than a locomotive! Able to leap tall buildings at a single bound! . . . Strange visitor from another planet, who came to earth with powers and abilities far beyond those of mortal men. Superman! Who can change the course of mighty rivers, bend steel with his bare hands, and who . . . fights a never ending battle for truth, justice and the American way!

Voiceover in *Superman* (radio adaptation, from 1940). Spoken at the start of each radio (and later TV) broadcast.

Alan Sillitoe (b. 1928)
BRITISH AUTHOR

A factory worker who left school aged fourteen, he had immediate success with his first book Saturday Night and Sunday Morning (1958, filmed 1960), which like later works portrayed Northern working-class culture.

1 The loneliness of the long-distance runner.

Title of novel (1959)

Ignazio Silone (1900–78)
ITALIAN NOVELIST AND JOURNALIST

Originally Secondo Tranquilli. One of the founder members of the Italian Communist Party, he portrayed socialist heroes and ideological clashes in such novels as Fontamara (1930) and Bread and Wine (1937). He led the Democratic Socialist Party after the Second World War, but in 1968 referred to himself as 'a socialist without a party, a Christian without a church'.

1 Fascism was a counter-revolution against a revolution that never took place.

The School for Dictators, ch. 4 (1938)

2 The final conflict will be between the Communists and the ex-Communists.

Quoted in *The Unfinished Country*, pt 4, 'The Hero as Ex-Communist' (1959) by MAX LERNER. Remark to Communist leader Palmiro Togliatti.

Georges Simenon (1903–85)
FRENCH CRIMEWRITER

The author of over 500 novels, he made his name with the Maigret detective series (from 1931), known worldwide through film and television adaptations. 'I have no imagination,' he once admitted, 'I take everything from life.'

1 Writing is not a profession, but a vocation of unhappiness.

Interview in the *Paris Review* summer 1955, repr. in *Writers at Work* (first series, ed. Malcolm Cowley, 1958)

Paul Simon (b. 1941)
US SINGER AND SONGWRITER

He wrote most of the material performed by the Simon and Garfunkel folksinging partnership (with Art Garfunkel). His solo recordings (from 1971) have explored music from around the world, notably on the album Graceland (1986).

1 *Hello darkness, my old friend,*
I've come to talk with you again.

'The Sound of Silence' (song) on the album *Wednesday Morning 3 a.m.* (1964) by Simon and Garfunkel. Given an electric backing, the song was a hit single in 1965 and reappeared on the album *Sounds of Silence* (1966).

2 *And the sign said, 'The words of the prophets*
Are written on the subway walls
And tenement halls'
And whispered in the sounds of silence.
Ibid.

3 *Hiding in my room, safe within my womb,*
I touch no one and no one touches me.
I am a rock,
I am an island.

'I Am a Rock' (song) on the album *The Paul Simon Songbook* (1965)

4 *And here's to you, Mrs Robinson*
Jesus loves you more than you will know.
God bless you please, Mrs Robinson
Heaven holds a place for those who pray.

'Mrs Robinson' (song) in the film *The Graduate* (1967), released on the soundtrack and, in a different version, on the album *Bookends* (1968) by Simon and Garfunkel

5 *They've all gone to look for America.*

'America' (song) on the album *Bookends* (1968) by Simon and Garfunkel

6 *When times get rough,*
And friends just can't be found
Like a bridge over troubled water
I will lay me down.

'Bridge over Troubled Water' (song) on the album *Bridge over Troubled Water* (1970) by Simon and Garfunkel. The words are said to have been inspired by 'Mary Don't You Weep', a song by the gospel group the Swan Silvertones which includes the line 'I'll be a bridge over deep water if you trust in my name.'

7 *One man's ceiling is another man's floor.*

'One Man's Ceiling is Another Man's Floor' (song) on the album *There Goes Rhymin' Simon* (1973)

8 *Medicine is magical and magical is art*
The Boy in the Bubble
And the baby with the baboon heart
And I believe
These are the days of lasers in the jungle
Lasers in the jungle somewhere
Staccato signals of constant information
A loose affiliation of millionaires.

'The Boy in the Bubble' (song, with music by Paul Simon and Forere Motloheloa) on the album *Graceland* (1986)

9 *The Mississippi Delta was shining*
Like a National guitar.

'Graceland' (song) on ibid.

10 **Improvisation is too good to leave to chance.**

Quoted in the *International Herald Tribune* 12 October 1990

Nina Simone (1933–2003)
US SINGER, SONGWRITER AND PIANIST
Originally Eunice Kathleen Waymon. Her career in jazz and soul music spanned four decades, starting with the double release of 'I Love You Porgy' and 'My Baby Just Cares for Me' in 1959. In the 1960s she was the 'poet laureate of the civil rights movement'.

1 *Hey! Do you see it, can't you feel it*
It's all in the air
I can't stand oppression much longer
Somebody say a prayer.
Alabama's got me so upset
Tennessee made me lose my rest
And everybody knows about Mississippi –
Goddam.

'Mississippi – Goddam' (song) on album *Nina Simone in Concert* (1964). Inspired by the murder of Medgar Evers, one of a series of racist murders of children.

2 *To be young, gifted and black*
Is where it's at!

'Young, Gifted and Black' (song, written by Weldon J. Irvine Jr, 1969) on the album *Black Gold* (1970)

O. J. Simpson (b. 1947)
US FOOTBALLER AND COMMENTATOR
Orenthal James Simpson. One of the greatest running backs in American football, he played for the Buffalo Bills 1969–78. In 1994 he was charged with the murder of his estranged wife and her friend but was acquitted after a sensational televised trial, only to be found guilty in a civil suit in 1997.

1 **The only thing that endures is character. Fame and wealth – all that is illusion. All that endures is character.**

Remark in November 1995, quoted in the *Guardian* 30 December 1995

Frank Sinatra (1915–98)
US SINGER AND ACTOR
He first had success as a singer in the 1940s but his career peaked in the 1950s with his role in From Here to Eternity *(film, 1953) and the albums* Songs for Swinging Lovers *(1956) and* Come Fly With Me *(1959). The singer and politician Sonny Bono commented: 'Frank walks like America. Cocksure.'*

1 **Show me a guy who has feelings, and I'll show you a sucker.**

Johnny Baron (Frank Sinatra), in *Suddenly* (film, 1954, screenplay by Richard Sale, directed by Lewis Allen)

2 *Fly me to the moon,*
And let me play among the stars,
Let me see what life is like
On Jupiter and Mars.

'Fly Me to the Moon' (song, written and composed by Bart Howard) on the album *It Might as Well Be Swing* (1964)

3 *Strangers in the night, exchanging glances*
Wond'ring in the night, what were the chances
We'd be sharing love before the night was through.

'Strangers in the Night' (song, written by Charles Singleton and Eddie Snyder with music by Bert Kaempfert) on the album *Strangers in the Night* (1966)

4 *And now the end is near*
And so I face the final curtain,
I'll state my case of which I'm certain.
I've lived a life that's full, I traveled each and ev'ry highway,
And more, much more than this. I did it my way.

'My Way' (song, 1969, written by Claude François, Jacques Revaux and Paul Anka) on the album *My Way* (1969). The Canadian songwriter Paul Anka adapted the song from a French original, 'Comme d'habitude', for Sinatra, whose signature tune it became.

5 **Ol' blue eyes is back.**

Title of album (1973). Referring to a decision made in 1970 to retire.

6 **The most brutal, ugly, desperate, vicious**

form of expression it has been my misfortune to hear.

On rock 'n' roll, quoted in *Sound Effects: Youth, Leisure and the Politics of Rock*, ch. 5 (1979) by Simon Frith

7 I could go on stage and make a pizza and they'd still come to see me.

Quoted in the *Independent on Sunday* 31 May 1992

Nancy Sinatra (b. 1940)
US SINGER
The daughter of FRANK SINATRA, *she had six hits 1966–7 under the tutelage of Lee Hazlewood, including a duet with her father, 'Somethin' Stupid' (1967).*

1 These boots are made for walkin'
  And that's just what they'll do
  One of these days these boots are going to
  walk all over you.

'These Boots are Made for Walkin'' (song, 1966, written by Lee Hazlewood)

Iain Sinclair (b. 1943)
BRITISH AUTHOR
His writings include poetry, the novel White Chappell, Scarlet Tracings *(1989) and an exploration of the M25 motorway,* The Orbital *(2002).*

1 An involuntary return to the point of departure is, without doubt, the most disturbing of all journeys.

Downriver, 'Riverside Opportunities', sect. 9 (1991)

Upton Sinclair (1878–1968)
US NOVELIST AND SOCIAL REFORMER
Regarding his writing mainly as the expression of his political beliefs, he published more than eighty titles, of which the best known is The Jungle *(1906), a novel about immigrant workers in the Chicago meat industry.*

1 It is up to you to prove that human beings do not have to be prowling wolves or sly lynxes, but can be rational, just, and kindly members of a commonwealth.

I, Governor of California and How I Ended Poverty in California (Democratic Party campaign pamphlet, 1934)

2 Co-operation is the coming idea.
Co-op: A Novel of Living Together, ch. 14 (1936)

3 Concerning *The Jungle* I wrote that 'I aimed at the public's heart, and by accident I hit it in the stomach'. I helped to clean up the yards and improve the country's meat supply. Now the workers have strong unions and, I hope, are able to look out for themselves.

The Autobiography, ch. 5, sect. 14 (1963)

(Sir) Donald Sinden (b. 1923)
BRITISH ACTOR
A thespian of the old school, he has varied his work on stage from the classical, notably in Shakespearian roles, to modern comedies. His films include The Cruel Sea *(1953) and* The Day of the Jackal *(1973).*

1 Actors ought to be larger than life. You come across quite enough ordinary, nondescript people in daily life and I don't see why you should be subjected to them on the stage too.

Quoted in the *Observer* 12 February 1989

Peter Singer (b. 1946)
AUSTRALIAN PHILOSOPHER
A utilitarian philosopher who has been denounced for his views on the value of human life, he is the author of Animal Liberation *(1975), in which he coined the word 'speciesism', and* Practical Ethics *(1979).*

1 The tyranny of human over nonhuman animals ... has caused and today is still causing an amount of pain and suffering that can only be compared with that which resulted from the centuries of tyranny by white humans over black humans. The struggle against this tyranny is a struggle as important as any of the moral and social issues that have been fought over in recent years.

Animal Liberation: Towards an End to Man's Inhumanity, Preface (1975)

2 If possessing a higher degree of intelligence does not entitle one human to use another for his own ends, how can it entitle humans to exploit nonhumans for the same purpose?

Ibid., ch. 1

3 The belief that human life, and only human life, is sacrosanct is a form of speciesism.

Ibid.

4 Ethics is not an ideal system which is all very noble in theory but no good in practice. The reverse of this is closer to the truth: an ethical judgement that is no good in practice must suffer from a theoretical defect as well, for the whole point of ethical judgement is to guide practice.

Practical Ethics, ch. 1 (1979)

5 Killing them [infants], therefore, cannot be equated with killing normal human beings, or any other self-conscious beings. No infant – disabled or not – has as strong a claim to life as beings capable of seeing themselves as distinct entities, existing over time.

Ibid., ch. 7

6 The difficult issue is not whether the end

can ever justify the means, but which means are justified by which ends.

Ibid., ch. 11

(Dame) Edith Sitwell (1887–1964)
BRITISH POET AND CRITIC

Her eccentric appearance, which she herself called, 'the ordinary carried to a high degree of pictorial perfection', was made famous by the photographs of Cecil Beaton, for whom she possessed 'the mad moonstruck ethereality of a ghost'. Her experimental poetry was inspired by dance and jazz rhythms, for example in Façade (1923).

1 *Jane, Jane,*
Tall as a crane,
The morning light creaks down again.

'Aubade', publ. in *Façade* (1923). Opening lines of poem. Sitwell originally recited the poems of *Façade* through a microphone to the accompaniment of music by William Walton.

2 *Still falls the Rain –*
Dark as the world of man, black as our loss –
Blind as the nineteen hundred and forty nails
Upon the Cross.

'The Raids, 1940. Night and Dawn', publ. in *Street Songs* (1942). Opening lines of poem later set to music by BENJAMIN BRITTEN.

3 I have often wished I had time to cultivate modesty. . . . But I am too busy thinking about myself.

Quoted in the *Observer* 30 April 1950

4 Eccentricity is *not*, as dull people would have us believe, a form of madness. It is often a kind of innocent pride, and the man of genius and the aristocrat are frequently regarded as eccentrics because genius and aristocrat are entirely unafraid of and uninfluenced by the opinions and vagaries of the crowd.

Taken Care of, ch. 15 (1965)

5 Vulgarity is, in reality, nothing but a modern, chic, pert descendant of the goddess Dullness.

Ibid., ch. 19

Robert Skidelsky (b. 1939)
BRITISH HISTORIAN AND ACADEMIC

Baron Skidelsky of Tilton. His books include The World After Communism *(1994) and a biography of* JOHN MAYNARD KEYNES *(3 vols., 1983– 2000).*

1 Historians are pessimistic by nature, because the only future they can imagine is the past.

Said at Cheltenham Festival of Literature 6– 15 October 1995, quoted in the *Daily Telegraph* 21 October 1995

Cornelia Otis Skinner (1901–79)
US AUTHOR AND ACTRESS

Famous for her stage monologues and plays, such as The Pleasure of His Company *(1958), she is also known for her humorous books, notably the collections* Nuts in May *(1950) and* The Ape in Me *(1959).*

1 It's not that I don't want to be a beauty, that I don't yearn to be dripping with glamor. It's just that I can't see how any woman can find time to do to herself all the things that must apparently be done to make herself beautiful and, having once done them, how anyone without the strength of mind of a foreign missionary can keep up such a regime.

Dithers and Jitters, 'The Skin-Game' (1937)

2 That food has always been, and will continue to be, the basis for one of our greater snobbisms does not explain the fact that the attitude toward the food choice of others is becoming more and more heatedly exclusive until it may well turn into one of those forms of bigotry against which gallant little committees are constantly planning campaigns in the cause of justice and decency.

Bottoms Up!, 'Your Very Good Health' (1950)

3 It is disturbing to discover in oneself these curious revelations of the validity of the Darwinian theory. If it is true that we have sprung from the ape, there are occasions when my own spring appears not to have been very far.

The Ape in Me, 'The Ape in Me' (1959)

Wayne Sleep (b. 1948)
BRITISH DANCER AND CHOREOGRAPHER

Principal dancer with the Royal Ballet 1973–83, he performed in the original production of Cats *(1981) and adapted his TV series* The Hot Shoe Show *(1983–4) for the stage.*

1 I am the chip on my own shoulder.

Interview in *In the Psychiatrist's Chair*, BBC Radio 4, 13 September 1998

Grace Slick (b. 1939)
US ROCK MUSICIAN

Starting out with the San Francisco band the Great Society, she joined Jefferson Airplane as lead singer and songwriter in 1966, recording with them such successful albums as Surrealistic Pillow *(1967) and* Volunteers *(1969).*

1 *One pill makes you larger*
And one pill makes you small.
And the ones that mother gives you
Don't do anything at all.
Go ask Alice
When she's ten feet tall.

'White Rabbit' (song) on the album *Surrealistic*

Pillow (1967) by Jefferson Airplane. The song was originally written for Slick's band the Great Society.

2 *Remember what the dormouse said: 'Feed your head'.*

Ibid. In an interview in 1977, Slick explained: ' "Feed your head" doesn't mean take every fucking drug that comes along, 'Feed your head' means read . . . listen and read' (quoted in *Shaman Woman, Mainline Lady*, ed. Cynthia Palmer and Michael Horowitz, 1982).

Joe Slovo (1926–95)

LITHUANIAN-BORN SOUTH AFRICAN ACTIVIST

Although he was in exile for twenty-seven years, he was one of the leading figures in the African National Congress, and on his return to South Africa in 1990 a key negotiator between the nationalist parties and the government. He was Minister of Housing in MANDELA*'s government (1994–5).*

1 There are only two sorts of people in life you can trust – good Christians and good Communists.

Independent 4 November 1988

2 Let us look at the capitalist roots of the racial miseries of our own country, South Africa. The real question is not whether a system works, but for whom it works.

Quoted in obituary in the *Guardian* 7 January 1995. Criticizing the notion that capitalism works and socialism has failed.

Elizabeth Smart (1913–86)

CANADIAN NOVELIST AND POET

Her greatest work By Grand Central Station I Sat Down and Wept *(1945) was inspired by her affair with poet George Barker, narrated in highly charged language. The Assumption of the Rogues and the Rascals (1977) dealt with her experiences in England.*

1 Vanity is a vital aid to nature: completely and absolutely necessary to life. It is one of nature's ways to bind you to the earth.

Journal entry, 25 June 1933, publ. in *Necessary Secrets*, pt 1, ch. 2 (ed. Alice Van Wart, 1991)

2 O I know they make war because they want peace; they hate so that they may live; and they destroy the present to make the world safe for the future. When have they not done and said they did it for that?

Ibid. 18 February 1941

3 By Grand Central Station I Sat Down and Wept.

Title of book (1945)

4 I am over-run, jungled in my bed, I am infested with a menagerie of desires: my heart is eaten by a dove, a cat scrambles in the cave of my sex, hounds in my bed obey a whipmaster who cries nothing but havoc

as the hours test my endurance with an accumulation of tortures. Who, if I cried, would hear me among the angelic orders?

By Grand Central Station I Sat Down and Wept, pt 1 (1945)

Alfred E. Smith (1873–1944)

US POLITICIAN

Alfred Emanuel Smith, known as Al Smith. He was four times Democratic Governor of New York (1918–26) and in 1928 the first Roman Catholic to run for the presidency, but was defeated by HERBERT HOOVER.

1 All the ills of democracy can be cured by more democracy.

Speech in Albany, 27 June 1933, quoted in *The New York Times* 28 June 1933

2 No sane local official who has hung up an empty stocking over the municipal fireplace, is going to shoot Santa Claus just before a hard Christmas.

New Outlook December 1933. The phrase 'Nobody shoots at Santa Claus' was used repeatedly by Smith in campaign speeches in 1936, attacking FRANKLIN D. ROOSEVELT and what were claimed to be the spendthrift policies of the New Deal.

(Sir) Cyril Smith (b. 1928)

BRITISH POLITICIAN

Conspicuous for his twenty-seven-stone figure, he was the Liberal (1972–88) and Liberal Democrat (1988–92) MP for Rochdale.

1 This place is the longest running farce in the West End.

Of the House of Commons, said in July 1973, quoted in *Big Cyril*, ch. 8 (autobiography, 1977)

Delia Smith (b. 1941)

BRITISH COOKERY WRITER AND BROADCASTER

Bestselling cookery writer and host of a TV show, she is a household name in Britain with a devotional following.

1 A hen's egg is, quite simply, a work of art, a masterpiece of design and construction with, it has to be said, brilliant packaging!

How to Cook, bk 1, ch. 1 (1998)

2 If you sometimes feel depressed or let down, if you're suffering from the pressures of life, or simply having a plain old grey day, my advice is to roast a chicken.

How to Cook, bk 2, ch. 4 (1999)

F. E. Smith (1872–1930)

BRITISH LAWYER AND POLITICIAN

Frederick Edwin Smith, First Earl of Birkenhead. A renowned speaker and wit, he was elected a Conservative MP in 1906 and became Attorney-General (1915–19), Lord Chancellor (1919–22) and

Secretary of State for India (1924–8). MARGOT ASQUITH *thought him 'very clever, but his brains go to his head'.*

1 **The world continues to offer glittering prizes to those who have stout hearts and sharp swords.**

Rectorial Address, Glasgow University, 7 November 1923, publ. in *The Times* 8 November 1923. Smith, whose whole life was seen as a quest for 'glittering prizes', provided the title of FREDERIC RAPHAEL's novel about Cambridge graduates, *The Glittering Prizes* (1976).

Iain Duncan Smith (b. 1954)

BRITISH POLITICIAN

Elected Conservative MP for Chingford in 1992, he was appointed Shadow Defence Secretary in 1999 and became the Conservative Party's first leader to be elected by a ballot of members in 2001.

1 **Those who do not know me yet will come to understand this: When I say a thing, I mean it. When I set myself a task, I do it. When I settle on a course, I stick to it. Do not underestimate the determination of a quiet man.**

Speech to Conservative Party Conference, Bournemouth, 10 October 2002, quoted in the *Daily Telegraph* 11 October 2002. The original 'quiet man' was JOHN WAYNE, who starred in John Ford's film *The Quiet Man* (1952) as an Irish ex-boxer who returns to his native land in search of a peaceful life.

2 **I'm a great believer in free speech, but as a right, not a continuous obligation.**

Quoted in the *Guardian* 16 November 2002

Ian Smith (b. 1919)

RHODESIAN POLITICIAN AND PRIME MINISTER

He founded the Rhodesian Front (later Republican Front) in 1962, became Prime Minister of a white minority government in 1964 and unilaterally declared Rhodesian independence in 1965. He remained active in the Republican Front until 1987.

1 **We have the happiest Africans in the world.**

Quoted in the *Observer* 20 November 1971

2 **Let me say again, I don't believe in black majority rule in Rhodesia – not in a thousand years. I believe in blacks and whites working together.**

Speech broadcast 20 March 1976, quoted in the *Sunday Times* 21 March 1976. Smith finally conceded majority rule in 1979.

Joan Smith (b. 1953)

BRITISH JOURNALIST AND AUTHOR

Known as a commentator on women in society, *she has written for various newspapers and has published* Mysogynies *(1989) and* What Men Say *(1994).*

1 **What Diana seemed to have forgotten, and most people were too dazzled by her performance to recall, was the traditional fate of the women with whom she had chosen to bracket herself . . . they all wind up young, beautiful and dead.**

Different for Girls: How Culture Creates Women, pt 1 (1997)

Lillian Smith (1897–1966)

US AUTHOR

Challenging the attitudes of America's Old South, she addresses segregation and its dehumanizing effects in her fiction, notably the bestseller Strange Fruit *(1944). She worked for the Congress on Racial Equality 1946–66.*

1 **To find the point where hypothesis and fact meet; the delicate equilibrium between dream and reality; the place where fantasy and earthly things are metamorphosed into a work of art; the hour when faith in the future becomes knowledge of the past; to lay down one's power for others in need; to shake off the old ordeal and get ready for the new; to question, knowing that never can the full answer be found; to accept uncertainties quietly, even our incomplete knowledge of God; this is what man's journey is about, I think.**

The Journey, ch. 15 (1954)

2 **The human heart dares not stay away too long from that which hurt it most. There is a return journey to anguish that few of us are released from making.**

Killers of the Dream, pt 1, ch. 1 (1949, rev. 1961)

3 **Man, born of woman, has found it a hard thing to forgive her for giving him birth. The patriarchal protest against the ancient matriarch has borne strange fruit through the years.**

Ibid., pt 2, ch. 4

Liz Smith (b. 1923)

US COLUMNIST

She is famous for her gossip columns, which have appeared in the New York Daily News *(later* New York Newsday*) since 1976, among numerous other magazines and newspapers.*

1 **Gossip is news running ahead of itself in a red satin dress.**

American Way, syndicated column 3 September 1985

2 **Most good gossip columnists have a touch of Savonarola in them.**

International Herald Tribune 4 April 1991

Logan Pearsall Smith (1865–1946)

US-BORN BRITISH ESSAYIST AND APHORIST

He earned his living as a lexicographer, bibliographer and essayist, but he is chiefly remembered for his collections of aphorisms, Afterthoughts *(1931) and* All Trivia *(1933, rev. 1945).*

1 Happiness is a wine of the rarest vintage, and seems insipid to a vulgar taste.
   Afterthoughts, 'Life and Human Nature' (1931)

2 How awful to reflect that what people say of us is true!
   Ibid.

3 There are few sorrows, however poignant, in which a good income is of no avail.
   Ibid.

4 Growing old is not a gradual decline, but a series of drops, full of sorrow, from one ledge to another below it. But when we pick ourselves up we find our bones are, after all, not broken; while level enough and not unpleasing is the new terrace which lies unexplored before us.
   Ibid., 'Age and Death'

5 There is more felicity on the far side of baldness than young men can possibly imagine.
   Ibid.

6 The old know what they want; the young are sad and bewildered.
   Ibid.

7 What music is more enchanting than the voices of young people, when you can't hear what they say?
   Ibid.

8 There are people who are beautiful in dilapidation, like old houses that were hideous when new.
   Ibid.

9 The denunciation of the young is a necessary part of the hygiene of older people, and greatly assists the circulation of their blood.
   Ibid.

10 The mere process of growing old together will make the slightest acquaintance seem like bosom friends.
   Ibid.

11 I can't forgive my friends for dying; I don't find these vanishing acts of theirs at all amusing.
   Ibid.

12 Those who set out to serve both God and Mammon soon discover that there isn't a God.
   Ibid., 'Other People'

13 Most people sell their souls, and live with a good conscience on the proceeds.
   Ibid.

14 When they come downstairs from their Ivory Towers, Idealists are very apt to walk straight into the gutter.
   Ibid.

15 It is the wretchedness of being rich that you live with rich people.
   Ibid., 'In the World'

16 To suppose, as we all suppose, that we could be rich and not behave as the rich behave, is like supposing that we could drink all day and keep absolutely sober.
   Ibid.

17 The test of a vocation is the love of the drudgery it involves.
   Ibid., 'Art and Letters'

18 A best-seller is the gilded tomb of a mediocre talent.
   Ibid. See also CYRIL CONNOLLY 2

19 The notion of making money by popular work, and then retiring to do good work, is the most familiar of all the devil's traps for artists.
   Ibid.

20 Aphorisms are salted and not sugared almonds at Reason's feast.
   Ibid., 'Myself'

21 People say that life is the thing, but I prefer reading.
   Ibid.

22 We need two kinds of acquaintances, one to complain to, while to the others we boast.
   All Trivia, 'In the World' (1933)

23 What I like in a good Author isn't what he says, but what he whispers.
   Ibid., 'Art and Letters'

24 There is one thing that matters – to set a chime of words tinkling in the minds of a few fastidious people.
   Quoted by CYRIL CONNOLLY in obituary, the *New Statesman* 9 March 1946. In answer to the question, two weeks before his death, whether he had discovered any meaning in life.

Patti Smith (b. 1946)

US ROCK MUSICIAN AND POET

She wrote avant-garde poetry, for instance Seventh Heaven *(1971), and co-wrote the play* Cowboy Mouth *with* SAM SHEPARD *(1971).* Horses *(1975), by the Patti Smith Group, was one of the key albums of US punk.*

1 Jesus died for somebody's sins but not mine.
   Preamble to 'Gloria' (song, written by VAN MORRISON) on the album *Horses* (1975)

2 There's no bullshit going down with rock and roll. It's an honest form and one of the most open. It encompasses poetry, jazz

and just about anything you can imagine
... it is the highest form. It goes beyond
color, gender – anything.
Cashbox 24 January 1976

Stevie Smith (1902–71)
BRITISH POET AND NOVELIST

*Originally Florence Margaret Smith. She first came
to notice with her Novel on Yellow Paper (1936),
but became better known for her unconventional
verse, in turn humorous and serious, which she
illustrated herself. Her collections include Mother,
What Is Man? (1942) and Not Waving But
Drowning (1957). 'She looks at the world with a
mental squint,' remarked* SEAMUS HEANEY,
*'there is a discouraging wobble in the mirror she
holds up to nature.'*

1 If you cannot have your dear husband for
a comfort and a delight, for a breadwinner
and a crosspatch, for a sofa, chair or a hot-
water bottle, one can use him as a Cross to
be Borne.
Narrator (Pompey Casmilus) in *Novel on Yellow
Paper* (1936)

2 A Good Time Was Had by All.
Title of collection of verse (1937). Given as the
original source of this expression in *A Dictionary
of Catch Phrases* by Eric Partridge (ed. Paul
Beale, 1985).

3 This Englishwoman is so refined
She has no bosom and no behind.
'This Englishwoman', publ. in *A Good Time Was
Had by All* (1937)

4 I'm sorry to say my dear wife is a dreamer,
And as she dreams she gets paler and
leaner.
'Then be off to your Dream, with his fly-
away hat,
I'll stay with the girls who are happy and
fat.'
'BE OFF!', publ. in *Mother, What is Man?* (1942)

5 Fourteen-year-old, why must you giggle and
dote,
Fourteen-year-old, why are you such a
goat?
I'm fourteen years old, that is the reason,
I giggle and dote in season.
'The Conventionalist', publ. ibid.

6 I may be smelly, and I may be old,
Rough in my pebbles, reedy in my pools,
But where my fish float by I bless their
swimming
And I like people to bathe in me, especially
women.
'The River God', publ. in *Harold's Leap* (1950)

7 Oh, no no no, it was too cold always
(Still the dead one lay moaning)
I was much too far out all my life

And not waving but drowning.
'Not Waving But Drowning', publ. in *Not Waving But Drowning* (1957)

8 Marred pleasure's best, shadow makes the
sun strong.
'The Queen and the Young Princess', publ. ibid.

9 People who are always praising the past
And especially the times of faith as best
Ought to go and live in the Middle Ages
And be burnt at the stake as witches and
sages.
'The Past', publ. ibid.

10 All Poetry has to do is to make a strong
communication. All the poet has to do is
to listen. The poet is not an important fellow. There will always be another poet.
'My Muse' (1960) publ. in *Me Again: Uncollected
Writings* (ed. Jack Barbera and William
McBrien, 1981)

11 Why does my Muse only speak when she is
unhappy?
She does not, I only listen when I am
unhappy
When I am happy I live and despise writing
For my Muse this cannot but be dispiriting.
'My Muse', publ. in *Selected Poems* (1962)

12 Oh these illegitimate babies!
Oh girls, girls,
Silly little valuable things,
You should have said, No, I am valuable,
And again, It is because I am valuable
I say, No.
'Valuable', publ. in *The Frog Prince and Other
Poems* (1966)

Zadie Smith (b. 1975)
BRITISH AUTHOR

*Her bestselling debut novel White Teeth (2000,
televised 2002), written while she was still an
undergraduate, was in her own words, 'the literary
equivalent of a hyperactive ginger-haired, tap-
dancing 10-year-old'. The Autograph Man was
published in 2002.*

1 You must live life with the full knowledge
that your actions will *remain*. We are creatures of consequence ... Our children will
be born of our actions. *Our accidents will
become their destinies.*
Samad, in *White Teeth*, ch. 5 (2000, televised
2002)

2 The English are the only people who want
to teach you and steal from you at the
same time.
Alsana, in ibid., ch. 13

3 Maybe nothing that happens upon stolen
ground can expect a happy ending.
Ibid.

4 Cold, wet, miserable, terrible food, dreadful newspapers – who would want to stay?

... But you have made a devil's pact ... it drags you in and suddenly you are unsuitable to return, your children are unrecognizable, you belong nowhere.... And then you begin to give up the very *idea* of belonging.

Samad, in ibid., ch. 15

5 Creation is an act of withdrawal.

Adam, in *The Autograph Man*, bk. 1, ch. 6, sect. 3 (2002). Referring to HaShem, the Jewish God.

6 Everyone should marry a homosexual at least once. It robs a pretty girl of all her sexual vanity.

Kitty Alexander, in ibid., bk. 2, ch. 4, sect. 1

(Dame) Ethel Smyth (1858–1944)

BRITISH COMPOSER AND FEMINIST

Considered the first significant British woman composer, she is known for her operas, such as The Wreckers *(1906), as well as for songs and choral pieces. 'The March of the Women' (1911) became the anthem for the suffragette movement, of which she was an active supporter.*

1 The habit some writers indulge in of perpetual quotation is one it behoves lovers of good literature to protest against, for it is an insidious habit which in the end must cloud the stream of thought, or at least check spontaneity. If it be true that *le style c'est l'homme*, what is likely to happen if *l'homme* is for ever eking out his own personality with that of some other individual?

Streaks of Life, 'The Quotation-Fiend' (1924)

2 Because I have conducted my own operas and love sheep-dogs; because I generally dress in tweeds, and sometimes, at winter afternoon concerts, have even conducted in them; because I was a militant suffragette and seized a chance of beating time to 'The March of the Women' from the window of my cell in Holloway Prison with a tooth-brush; because I have written books, spoken speeches, broadcast, and don't always make sure that my hat is on straight; for these and other equally pertinent reasons, in a certain sense I am well known.

As Time Went on, Epilogue (1936)

Steven Soderbergh (b. 1963)

US FILM-MAKER

Since his quirky debut, sex, lies, and videotape *(1989), he has explored a variety of genres with varying success, for example* King of the Hill *(1993)* Out of Sight *(1998) and* Solaris *(2002).*

1 I think men get more and more in love with the person they're ... and women get

more and more attracted to the person they love.

Graham Dalton (James Spader), in *sex, lies, and videotape* (film, 1989, written and directed by Steven Soderbergh). The rapt Anne (Andy MacDowell) replies, 'That's beautiful ...'

2 Lying is like alcoholism. You are always recovering.

Ibid.

Bienvenida Sokolow (b. 1958)

SPANISH-BORN SOCIETY FIGURE

'Lady Buck', self-styled 'professional mistress' and the former wife of Sir Antony Buck, achieved celebrity after her affair with Sir Peter Harding forced him to resign as Chief of Defence Staff in 1994.

1 For me affection was more visible in terms of finance than in terms of words. People can talk and not mean what they say, but with money, you know it will not let you down.

Interview in *The Times* 4 March 1995

Valerie Solanas (1936–88)

US FEMINIST

An actress in ANDY WARHOL's *film* I, a Man *(1967), she achieved notoriety for shooting Warhol in 1968, and was judged schizophrenic in the ensuing trial, when she was defended by* FLORYNCE KENNEDY. *Her intended victim had been* MAURICE GIRODIAS, *whose Olympia Press later published her extremist SCUM Manifesto (1968).*

1 Life in this society being, at best, an utter bore and no aspect of society being at all relevant to women, there remains to civic-minded, responsible, thrill-seeking females only to overthrow the government, eliminate the money system, institute complete automation and destroy the male sex.

The SCUM Manifesto (1968), repr. in *Sisterhood is Powerful* (ed. Robin Morgan, 1970). The acronym *SCUM* stood for 'Society for Cutting Up Men'.

2 To call a man an animal is to flatter him; he's a machine, a walking dildo.

Ibid.

3 To be sure he's a 'Man', the male must see to it that the female be clearly a 'Woman', the opposite of a 'Man', that is, the female must act like a faggot.

Ibid.

4 Just as humans have a prior right to existence over dogs by virtue of being more highly evolved and having a superior consciousness, so women have a prior right to existence over men. The elimination of any male is, therefore, a righteous and good act, an act highly beneficial to women as well as an act of mercy.

Ibid. Her grounds for female evolutionary preeminence was her assertion that, on account of his chromosomes, 'the male is an incomplete female'.

5 I consider that a moral act. And I consider it immoral that I missed. I should have done target practice.

Of her shooting ANDY WARHOL, in interview in *Village Voice* 1 August 1977

Philippe Sollers (b. 1936)
FRENCH AUTHOR AND CRITIC

Originally Philippe Joyaux. An exponent of the nouveau roman *in the 1960s, such as* Le Parc *(1961), he has written works on Francis Bacon,* PICASSO *and Fragonard. Later novels include* Le Secret *(1992).*

1 Writing is the continuation of politics by other means.

Tel quel: théorie d'ensemble, 'Écriture et révolution' (1968). An adaptation of Karl von Clausewitz's aphorism, 'War is . . . nothing but the continuation of politics by other means' (from *On War,* 1832) *Tel Quel,* the journal edited by Sollers, was the focus for literary theories then current that proposed extending writing beyond the realm of literature.

Alexander Solzhenitsyn (b. 1918)
RUSSIAN NOVELIST

The political nature of his writing led to persecution and imprisonment, and he lived in exile 1974–94. His books include One Day in the Life of Ivan Denisovich *(1962) and* The Gulag Archipelago *(1973). 'I belong to the Russian convict world no less . . . than I do to Russian literature,' he is quoted. 'I got my education there, and it will last forever.'*

1 Here, lads, we live by the law of the *taiga.* But even here people manage to live. D'you know who are the ones the camps finish off? Those who lick other men's leftovers, those who set store by the doctors, and those who peach on their mates.

Kuziomin, in *One Day in the Life of Ivan Denisovich* (1962)

2 Literature that is not the breath of contemporary society, that dares not transmit the pains and fears of that society, that does not warn in time against threatening moral and social dangers – such literature does not deserve the name of literature; it is only a façade. Such literature loses the confidence of its own people, and its published works are used as wastepaper instead of being read.

Open letter to the Fourth Soviet Writers' Congress, 16 May 1967, repr. in *Solzhenitsyn: A Documentary Record,* 'The Struggle Intensifies' (ed. Leopold Labedz, 1970, rev. 1974)

3 Justice *is* conscience, not a personal conscience but the conscience of the whole of humanity. Those who clearly recognize the voice of their own conscience usually recognize also the voice of justice.

Letter to three students, October 1967, publ. ibid.

4 One should never direct people towards happiness, because happiness too is an idol of the market-place. One should direct them towards mutual affection. A beast gnawing at its prey can be happy too, but only human beings can feel affection for each other, and this is the highest achievement they can aspire to.

Shulubin, in *Cancer Ward,* pt 2, ch. 10 (1968)

5 You only have power over people so long as you don't take *everything* away from them. But when you've robbed a man of *everything* he's no longer in your power – he's free again.

Bobynin, in *The First Circle,* ch. 17 (1968)

6 For a country to have a great writer . . . is like having another government. That's why no régime has ever loved great writers, only minor ones.

Innokenty, ibid., ch. 57

7 Blow the dust off the clock. Your watches are behind the times. Throw open the heavy curtains which are so dear to you – you do not even suspect that the day has already dawned outside.

Letter to the Secretariat of the Soviet Writers' Union, 12 November 1969, publ. in *Solzhenitsyn: A Documentary Record,* 'Expulsion' (ed. Leopold Labedz, 1970, rev. 1974)

8 Violence finds its only refuge in falsehood, falsehood its only support in violence. Any man who has once acclaimed violence as his METHOD must inexorably choose falsehood as his PRINCIPLE.

Nobel Prize lecture, 1970, publ. ibid., 'The Struggle Continues'

9 People can live through hardship, but from hard feelings they perish.

'Asphyxiation', written 1971, publ. in *The Oak and the Calf,* 'Second Supplement' (1980)

10 There are many ways of killing a poet.

Ibid. Solzhenitsyn repeated these words on numerous occasions.

11 It is not because the truth is too difficult to see that we make mistakes. It may even lie on the surface; but we make mistakes because the easiest and most comfortable course for us is to seek insight where it accords with our emotions – especially selfish ones.

'Peace and Violence', sect. 2, first publ. in *Index* no. 4, 1973, repr. in *Solzhenitsyn: A Documentary Record,* 'Trials in Détente' (ed. Leopold Labedz, 1970, rev. 1974)

12 In our country the lie has become not just a moral category but a pillar of the State.

Time 19 January 1974, repr. in *The Oak and the Calf*, appendix (1975)

13 Woe to that nation whose literature is cut short by the intrusion of force. This is not merely interference with freedom of the press but the sealing up of a nation's heart, the excision of its memory.

Time 25 February 1974

14 For us in Russia, communism is a dead dog, while, for many people in the West, it is still a living lion.

Radio broadcast on BBC Russian service, publ. in the *Listener* 15 February 1979

15 The clock of communism has stopped striking. But its concrete building has not yet come crashing down. For that reason, instead of freeing ourselves, we must try to save ourselves from being crushed by its rubble.

'How We Must Rebuild Russia', publ. in *Komsomolskaya Pravda* 18 September 1990. Opening sentence of essay.

Anastasio Somoza (1925–80)

NICARAGUAN DICTATOR

Anastasio Somoza García. He initiated a military coup in 1936 while Commander-in-Chief of the army and assumed dictatorial powers, exiling his political opponents and amassing a personal fortune. He was assassinated and succeeded by his sons.

1 Indeed, you won the elections, but I won the count.

Quoted in the *Guardian* 17 June 1977. Addressed to an opponent who accused him of rigging the election. See also TOM STOPPARD 8.

Stephen Sondheim (b. 1930)

US SONGWRITER AND COMPOSER

Rated one of the greatest Broadway wordsmiths, he provided the lyrics to BERNSTEIN*'s West Side Story (1957) and wrote both words and music for such shows as* A Little Night Music *(1973) and* Sunday in the Park with George *(1984).*

1 *I like to be in America!*
   OK by me in America!
   Ev'rything free in America
   For a small fee in America!

'America' (song, with music by Leonard Bernstein) in *West Side Story* (stage musical 1957, film 1961)

2 *The concerts you enjoy together*
   Neighbors you annoy together
   Children you destroy together
   That make marriage a joy.

'The Little Things You Do Together' (song) in *Company* (stage musical, 1970)

3 *A toast to that invincible bunch*
   The dinosaurs surviving the crunch
   Let's hear it for the ladies who lunch.

'The Ladies Who Lunch' (song), ibid. Performed in the original cast by Elaine Stritch.

4 *Ev'ry day a little death*
   On the lips and in the eyes,
   In the murmurs, in the pauses,
   In the gestures, in the sighs.
   Ev'ry day a little dies.

'Every Day a Little Death' (song) in *A Little Night Music* (stage musical 1973, filmed 1977)

5 Send in the clowns.

Song title, ibid. The song was a hit for Judy Collins in 1975, and performed by Elizabeth Taylor in the film version. In circus or vaudeville, the words are the traditional desperate summons for some distraction for the audience when something goes badly wrong.

6 The fact is popular art dates. It grows quaint. How many people feel strongly about Gilbert and Sullivan today compared to those who felt strongly in 1890?

Quoted in the *International Herald Tribune* 20 June 1989

Susan Sontag (b. 1933)

US AUTHOR AND CRITIC

Called 'a foraging pluralist' by ELIZABETH HARDWICK *and 'probably the most intelligent woman in America' by* JONATHAN MILLER*, she has written incisively on culture and society in such works as* Against Interpretation *(1966) and* Illness as Metaphor *(1979).*

1 The truth is always something that is told, not something that is known. If there were no speaking or writing, there would be no truth about anything. There would only be what is.

The Benefactor, ch. 1 (1963)

2 The truth is balance, but the opposite of truth, which is unbalance, may not be a lie.

'Simone Weil', publ. in the *New York Review of Books* (1963), repr. in *Against Interpretation* (1966)

3 Interpretation is the revenge of the intellect upon art. Even more. It is the revenge of the intellect upon the world. To interpret is to impoverish, to deplete the world – in order to set up a shadow world of 'meanings'.

'Against Interpretation', sect. 4, publ. in the *Evergreen Review* December 1964, repr. ibid.

4 Any critic is entitled to wrong judgments, of course. But certain lapses of judgment indicate the radical failure of an entire sensibility.

'The Literary Criticism of George Lukács', first publ. in *Bookweek* (1964), repr. ibid.

5 Intelligence . . . is really a kind of taste: taste in ideas.
'Notes on "Camp" ' (1964), repr. ibid.

6 Camp is a vision of the world in terms of style – but a particular kind of style. It is the love of the exaggerated, the 'off', of things-being-what-they-are-not.
Ibid., Note 8

7 What is most beautiful in virile men is something feminine; what is most beautiful in feminine women is something masculine.
Ibid., Note 9

8 As the dandy is the nineteenth century's surrogate for the aristocrat in matters of culture, so Camp is the modern dandyism. Camp is the answer to the problem: how to be a dandy in the age of mass culture.
Ibid., Note 45

9 Jews and homosexuals are the outstanding creative minorities in contemporary urban culture. Creative, that is in the truest sense: they are creators of sensibilities. The two pioneering forces of modern sensibility are Jewish moral seriousness and homosexual aestheticism and irony.
Ibid., Note 51

10 Art is seduction, not rape.
'On Style', first publ. in the Partisan Review (1965), repr. ibid.

11 The truth is that Mozart, Pascal, Boolean algebra, Shakespeare, parliamentary government, baroque churches, Newton, the emancipation of women, Kant, Marx, and Balanchine ballets don't redeem what this particular civilization has wrought upon the world. The white race is the cancer of human history.
'What's Happening in America', publ. in the Partisan Review spring 1967, repr. in Styles of Radical Will (1969)

12 Cogito ergo boom.
Styles of Radical Will (1969), ' "Thinking Against Oneself": Reflections on Cioran'. Parenthetical comment on our sense that we stand 'in the ruins of thought, and on the verge of the ruins of history and of man himself'. From Descartes' formula, 'Cogito, ergo sum', I think therefore I am (Discours de la méthode, 1637).

13 Now there is a master scenario available to everyone. The color is black, the material is leather, the seduction is beauty, the justification is honesty, the aim is ecstasy, the fantasy is death.
'Fascinating Fascism' (1974), repr. in Under the Sign of Saturn (1980). Discussing Nazi symbolism in sado-masochism.

14 Photography is the inventory of mortality. A touch of the finger now suffices

to invest a moment with posthumous irony.
On Photography, 'Melancholy Objects' (1977)

15 The taste for quotations (and for the juxtaposition of incongruous quotations) is a Surrealist taste.
Ibid.

16 It is not altogether wrong to say that there is no such thing as a bad photograph – only less interesting, less relevant, less mysterious ones.
Ibid., 'The Heroism of Vision'

17 The painter constructs, the photographer discloses.
Ibid.

18 Illness is the night-side of life, a more onerous citizenship. Everyone who is born holds dual citizenship, in the kingdom of the well and in the kingdom of the sick. Although we all prefer to use only the good passport, sooner or later each of us is obliged, at least for a spell, to identify ourselves as citizens of that other place.
Illness as Metaphor, Preface (1978). Opening words.

19 Depression is melancholy minus its charms – the animation, the fits.
Ibid., ch. 7

20 Any important disease whose causality is murky, and for which treatment is ineffectual, tends to be awash in significance.
Ibid., ch. 8

21 The writer is either a practising recluse or a delinquent, guilt-ridden one; or both. Usually both.
'When Writers Talk Among Themselves', publ. in The New York Times 5 January 1986

22 Victims suggest innocence. And innocence, by the inexorable logic that governs all relational terms, suggests guilt.
AIDS and Its Metaphors, ch. 1 (1989)

23 Societies need to have one illness which becomes identified with evil, and attaches blame to its 'victims'.
Ibid.

24 Authoritarian political ideologies have a vested interest in promoting fear, a sense of the imminence of takeover by aliens – and real diseases are useful material.
Ibid., ch. 6

25 Fear of sexuality is the new, disease-sponsored register of the universe of fear in which everyone now lives.
Ibid., ch. 7

26 The ideology of capitalism makes us all into connoisseurs of liberty – of the indefinite expansion of possibility.
Ibid.

27 AIDS occupies such a large part in our awareness because of what it has been taken to represent. It seems the very model of all the catastrophes privileged populations feel await them.

Ibid., ch. 8

28 In a woman, beauty is something total. It is what stands, in a woman, for character. It is also, of course, a performance; something willed, designed, obtained.

Introduction to *Women*, (1999) by Annie Leibovitz

Wole Soyinka (b. 1934)

NIGERIAN AUTHOR, PLAYWRIGHT AND POET
Themes of the adaptation of his native Yoruba culture to modern westernized society and the conflicts with colonialism recur in plays such as A Dance of the Forests *(1963) and* Death and the King's Horseman *(1975). He wrote of his imprisonment (1967–9) during the Nigerian Civil War, in the journal* The Man Died *(1972) and in books of verse.*

1 The man dies in all who keep silent in the face of tyranny.

The Man Died, ch. 1 (1972)

2 Prison is only a new stage from which the struggle must be waged . . . prison, especially political prison is an artificial erection in more senses than one whose bluff must be called and whose impotence must be demonstrated.

Ibid., ch. 8

3 *I do not seek; I find.* Let actions alone be the manifestations of the authentic being in defence of its authentic visions. History is too full of failed prometheans bathing their wounded spirits in the tragic stream.

Ibid., ch. 12

4 For me, justice is the first condition of humanity.

Ibid.

5 *Life has an end. A life that will outlive Fame and friendship begs another name.*

Elesin, in *Death and the King's Horseman*, sc. 1 (1975)

(Dame) Muriel Spark (b. 1918)

BRITISH AUTHOR AND POET
She has published poetry and short stories, but is best known for her novels, notably The Prime of Miss Jean Brodie *(1961, filmed 1969), which she herself described as 'more progressive than I realised'. Her other works of fiction include* The Girls of Slender Means *(1963) and* The Driver's Seat *(1970, filmed 1974).*

1 Being over seventy is like being engaged in a war. All our friends are going or gone

and we survive amongst the dead and the dying as on a battlefield.

Miss Taylor, in *Memento Mori*, ch. 4 (1959)

2 If I had my life over again I should form the habit of nightly composing myself to thoughts of death. I would practise, as it were, the remembrance of death. There is no other practice which so intensifies life. Death, when it approaches, ought not to take one by surprise. It should be part of the full expectancy of life. Without an ever-present sense of death life is insipid. You might as well live on the whites of eggs.

Henry Mortimer, ibid., ch. 11

3 I am putting old heads on your young shoulders; all my pupils are the crème de la crème.

Miss Brodie, in *The Prime of Miss Jean Brodie*, ch. 1 (1961)

4 Give me a girl at an impressionable age, and she is mine for life!

Miss Brodie, ibid. The words echo a Jesuit maxim: 'Give me a child for the first seven years, and you may do what you like with him afterwards.'

5 One's prime is elusive. You little girls, when you grow up, must be on the alert to recognize your prime at whatever time of your life it may occur. You must then live it to the full.

Miss Brodie, ibid.

6 Art and religion first; then philosophy; lastly science. That is the order of the great subjects of life, that's their order of importance.

Miss Brodie, ibid., ch. 2

7 To me education is a leading out of what is already there in the pupil's soul. To Miss Mackay it is a putting in of something that is not there, and that is not what I call education, I call it intrusion.

Miss Brodie, ibid.

8 New York, home of the vivisectors of the mind, and of the mentally vivisected still to be reassembled, of those who live intact, habitually wondering about their states of sanity, and home of those whose minds have been dead, bearing the scars of resurrection.

The Hothouse by the East River, ch. 1 (1973)

9 I wouldn't take the Pope too seriously. He's a Pole first, a pope second, and maybe a Christian third.

International Herald Tribune 29 May 1989

10 If you're going to do a thing, you should do it thoroughly. If you're going to be a Christian, you may as well be a Catholic.

Independent 2 August 1989

Larry Speakes (b. 1939)
US EXECUTIVE AND WHITE HOUSE OFFICIAL
He was Press Secretary under Presidents FORD *(1977) and* REAGAN *(1981–7).*

1 I would dodge, not lie, in the national interest.
The New York Times 10 October 1986

Phil Spector (b. 1940)
US POP PRODUCER AND SONGWRITER
A pioneer in the use of studio techniques, he specialized in recording relatively unknown singers and groups backed by a 'wall of sound'. His biggest hits were with the Ronettes, whose lead singer he married.

1 I always went in for that Wagnerian approach to rock and roll.
Quoted in *Out of His Head*, ch. 5 (1974) by Richard Williams

Albert Speer (1905–81)
GERMAN ARCHITECT AND NAZI MINISTER
Most of his grandiose designs for HITLER *were either demolished or never realized. He was Armaments Minister from 1942 and after the war was the only leader at the Nuremberg trials to accept accountability for Nazi crimes. He was sentenced to twenty years for employing slave labour.*

1 Today, almost forty years later, I grow dizzy when I recall that the number of manufactured tanks seems to have been more important to me than the vanished victims of racism.
The Slave State, ch. 21 (1981)

Charles Spencer (b. 1964)
BRITISH JOURNALIST AND BUSINESSMAN
Earl Spencer, Viscount Althorp. He was NBC correspondent and presenter (1987–91 and 1993–6) and a reporter for Granada Television (1991–3). Following the death of his sister Princess DIANA, *he was outspoken against the press and the royal family.*

1 I . . . always believed the press would kill her in the end. But not even I could believe they would take such a direct hand in her death as seems to be the case.
On the death of Princess DIANA, in speech to press outside his home in Cape Town 31 August 1997, publ. in *The Times* 1 September 1997

2 It would appear that every proprietor and every editor of every publication that had paid for intrusive and exploitative photographs of her, encouraging greedy and ruthless individuals to risk everything in pursuit of Diana's image, has blood on his hands today.
Ibid.

3 It is a point to remember that, of all the ironies about Diana, perhaps the greatest was this: a girl given the name of the ancient goddess was, in the end, the most hunted person of the modern age.
Funeral oration at Westminster Abbey, 6 September 1997, quoted in the *Observer* 7 September 1997

Dale Spender (b. 1943)
AUSTRALIAN FEMINIST AUTHOR
She has edited anthologies of literature as well as the journal Women's Studies International Forum. Her books include Invisible Women *(1982), on the disadvantages of co-education.*

1 Paradoxically, the most constructive thing women can do . . . is to write, for in the *act* of writing we deny our mutedness and begin to eliminate some of the difficulties that have been put upon us.
Man Made Language, ch. 7 (1980)

(Sir) Stephen Spender (1909–95)
BRITISH POET
Described by Robert Craft as 'the least insular writer of his generation', he co-founded with CYRIL CONNOLLY *the magazine* Horizon *of which he was Editor (1939–41), and later co-edited* Encounter *(1953–67). His poetry collections include* Poems from Spain *(1939) and* The Edge of Darkness *(1949). See* W. H. AUDEN 53.

1 *My parents kept me from children who*
      were rough
   And who threw words like stones and who
      wore torn clothes.
'My parents kept me from children who were rough', publ. in *Poems*, no. 12 (1933). Opening lines of poem.

2 *I think continually of those who were truly*
      great.
   Who, from the womb, remembered the
      soul's history
   Through corridors of light where the hours
      are suns,
   Endless and singing.
'I Think Continually', publ. ibid., no. 23. Opening lines of poem.

3 *The names of those who in their lives fought*
      for life,
   Who wore at their hearts the fire's centre.
   Born of the sun they travelled a short while
      toward the sun
   And left the vivid air signed with their
      honour.
Ibid. Closing lines of poem.

4 *After the first powerful plain manifesto*
   The black statement of pistons, without
      more fuss

But gliding like a queen, she leaves the
station.

'The Express', publ. ibid., no. 26

5 Steaming through metal landscape on her
lines,
She plunges new eras of white happiness,
Where speed throws up strange shapes,
broad curves
And parallels clean like the steel of guns.

Ibid. Spender later amended the last line to read
'like trajectories from guns'.

6 Now over these small hills they have built
the concrete
That trails black wire:
Pylons, those pillars
Bare like nude, giant girls that have no
secret.

'The Pylons', publ. ibid., no. 28. The poem provided a label, 'the Pylon Poets', for the 1930s
poets who wrote about the modern indus-
trialized landscape, including also AUDEN and
DAY LEWIS.

7 Finally, they cease to hate: for although
hate
Bursts from the air and whips the earth like
hail
Or pours it up in fountains to marvel at,
And although hundreds fell, who can
connect
The inexhaustible anger of the guns
With the dumb patience of these tormented
animals?

'Two Armies', publ. in The Still Centre (1939)

8 The guns spell money's ultimate reason
In letters of lead on the spring hillside.

'Ultima Ratio Regum', publ. in Poems from
Spain (ed. Stephen Spender and John Lehmann,
1939). Opening lines of poem.

Oswald Spengler (1880–1936)
GERMAN HISTORIAN
His reputation rests on his major work The
Decline of the West (2 vols., 1918–22), which
argues, through what he termed a 'morphological
method', a cyclical theory of human development
in accordance with 'historical destiny'.

1 In place of a world, there is a city, a point,
in which the whole life of broad regions is
collecting while the rest dries up. In place
of a type-true people, born of and grown
on the soil, there is a new sort of nomad,
cohering unstably in fluid masses, the para-
sitical city dweller, traditionless, utterly
matter-of-fact, religionless, clever, unfruitful, deeply contemptuous of the countryman and especially that highest form of
countryman, the country gentleman.

The Decline of the West, vol. 1, ch. 1, sect. 12
(1918)

2 The last man of the world-city no longer
wants to live – he may cling to life as an

individual, but as a type, as an aggregate,
no, for it is a characteristic of this collective existence that it eliminates the terror
of death.

Ibid., vol. 2, ch. 4, sect. 5 (1922)

3 Formerly no one was allowed to think
freely; now it is permitted, but no one is
capable of it any more. Now people want
to think only what they are supposed to
want to think, and this they consider
freedom.

Ibid., ch. 12, sect. 4

The Spice Girls
BRITISH POP GROUP
Britain's most successful female vocal group shot
to fame in 1996 with their international hit 'Wan-
nabe'. The group consisted of Melanie Chisholm
('Mel C', or 'Sporty Spice'), Emma Bunton ('Baby
Spice'), Victoria Adams (later Beckham, 'Posh
Spice'), Geri Halliwell ('Ginger Spice') and
Melanie Brown ('Mel B', or 'Scary Spice').

1 I'll tell you what I want what I really really
want
(So tell me what you want, what you really
really want)
If you wanna be my lover
Gotta get with my friends
Make it last forever
Friendship never ends!

'Wannabe' (song, written by Matthew Rowbot-
tom and Richard Stannard) on the album Spice
(1996)

Steven Spielberg (b. 1947)
US FILM-MAKER
The most commercially successful director to date,
he has made a series of blockbuster films including
Jaws (1975), E.T. (1982) and Jurassic Park (1993).
J. G. BALLARD hailed him as 'the Puccini of the
cinema, a little too sweet for some tastes, but what
melodies, what orchestrations, what cathedrals of
emotion'.

1 Close Encounters of the Third Kind.

Title of film (written and directed by Steven
Spielberg, 1977)

2 The most expensive habit in the world is
celluloid, not heroin, and I need a fix every
few years.

Interview in Time 16 April 1979

Gayatri Chakravorty Spivak
(b. 1942)
INDIAN-BORN US ACADEMIC, AUTHOR AND
TRANSLATOR
She established her reputation with her 1976 translation of DERRIDA's Of Grammatology. Her own
titles include In Other Worlds (1987) and A Critique of Post-Colonial Reason (1999).

1 The fall into the abyss of deconstruction

inspires us with as much pleasure as fear. We are intoxicated with the prospect of never hitting bottom.

Translator's Preface (1976) to *Of Grammatology* (1967) by Jacques Derrida

2 The subaltern cannot speak. There is no virtue in global laundry lists with 'woman' as a pious item. Representation has not withered away. The female intellectual as intellectual has a circumscribed task which she must not disown with a flourish.

'Can the Subaltern Speak?', publ. in *Colonial Discourse and Post-Colonial Theory: A Reader* (ed. Patrick Williams and Laura Chrisman, 1994)

Benjamin Spock (1903–98)

US PAEDIATRICIAN AND AUTHOR

His seminal work The Common Sense Book of Baby and Child Care *(1946) advocated a more relaxed and sympathetic attitude to child-rearing. He later rebutted criticism of being responsible for a permissive new generation.*

1 I think that more of our children would grow up happier and more stable if they were acquiring a conviction, all through childhood, that the most important thing that human beings can do is serve humanity in some function and to live by their ideals.

Baby and Child Care, 'The Parents' Part', sect. 11 (1946, rev. 1968)

2 It is fascinating to realize that what distinguishes man so sharply from other creatures are those attitudes he develops soon after the age of 5: his inhibition and sublimation of sexuality, his interest in symbols, abstractions, systems and rules, his capacity for being inspired by heroes, God and spiritual ideals.

Ibid., sect. 13

3 Man can build a magnificent reality in adulthood out of what was only an illusion in early childhood – his loving, joyous, trusting, ingenuous, unrealistic over-idealization of his two parents.

Ibid.

4 A child loves his play, not because it's easy, but because it's hard.

Ibid., 'Managing Young Children', sect. 457

5 I was proud of the youths who opposed the war in Vietnam because they were my babies.

The Times 2 May 1988

Viola Spolin (1906–94)

US THEATRICAL DIRECTOR AND PRODUCER

Based in Chicago, she became known as the 'high priestess of improvisational theatre' and as a pioneer of games as a basis for theatre training.

1 We learn through experience and experiencing, and no one teaches anyone anything. This is as true for the infant moving from kicking to crawling to walking as it is for the scientist with his equations. If the environment permits it, anyone can learn whatever he chooses to learn; and if the individual permits it, the environment will teach him everything it has to teach.

Improvisation for the Theater, ch. 1 (1963)

2 Through spontaneity we are re-formed into ourselves. It creates an explosion that for the moment frees us from handed-down frames of reference, memory choked with old facts and information and undigested theories and techniques of other people's findings. Spontaneity is the moment of personal freedom when we are faced with reality, and see it, explore it and act accordingly. In this reality the bits and pieces of ourselves function as an organic whole. It is the time of discovery, of experiencing, of creative expression.

Ibid.

3 The audience is the most revered member of the theater. Without an audience there is no theater. Every technique learned by the actor, every curtain, every flat on the stage, every careful analysis by the director, every coordinated scene, is for the enjoyment of the audience. They are our guests, our evaluators, and the last spoke in the wheel which can then begin to roll. They make the performance meaningful.

Ibid.

John Spong (b. 1931)

US ECCLESIASTIC

Ordained an Episcopalian minister in 1955, he has stated his mission to 'write as a believing skeptic inside the structures of the church for those who have drifted outside these structures'. His books include The Living Commandments *(1977).*

1 I learned early in life that you get places by having the right enemies.

Guardian 20 July 1988

2 The priesthood in many ways is the ultimate closet in Western civilization, where gay people particularly have hidden for the past two thousand years.

Daily Telegraph 12 July 1990

Cecil Spring-Rice (1859–1918)

BRITISH DIPLOMAT

As British ambassador to Washington (1912–18), he was instrumental in persuading the Americans to enter the First World War.

1 *I vow to thee, my country – all earthly*
  things above –
  Entire and whole and perfect, the service of
  my love,
  The love that asks no question: the love that
  stands the test,
  That lays upon the altar the dearest and the
  best:
  The love that never falters, the love that
  pays the price,
  The love that makes undaunted the final
  sacrifice.

'I Vow to Thee, My Country' (1918). The hymn, which was set to the tune of 'Thaxted' (a version of 'Jupiter' from Holst's Planet Suite), was the favourite hymn of Princess DIANA.

Jerry Springer (b. 1944)

US TELEVISION HOST
He served as Mayor of Cincinnati until the day his personal cheque was found in a Kentucky brothel. His confessional Jerry Springer Show, with which he boasts he is 'proud to set a new low', has been seen globally since its inception in 1991.

1 My show is the stupidest show on TV. If
  you are watching it, get a life. I would not
  watch my show. My show is a circus.
  That's all it is.

Independent on Sunday 7 March 1999

Bruce Springsteen (b. 1949)

US ROCK MUSICIAN
Nicknamed 'The Boss', he was an icon of blue-collar rock and roll before his hit album Born to Run (1975), and he achieved global stardom with 1984's Born in the USA. He has the ability 'to make his music bleed', according to GREIL MARCUS.

1 *In the day we sweat it out in the streets of a*
  runaway American dream
  At night we ride through mansions of glory
  in suicide machines.

'Born to Run' (song) on the album *Born to Run* (1975) by Bruce Springsteen and the E Street Band

2 *Baby this town rips the bones from your*
  back,
  It's a death trap, it's a suicide rap,
  We gotta get out while we're young
  'Cause tramps like us baby we were born to
  run.

Ibid.

3 *Born down in a dead man's town*
  The first kick I took was when I hit the
  ground
  You end up like a dog that's been beat too
  much
  Till you spend half your life just covering
  up.

Born in the USA

I was born in the USA.
'Born in the USA' (song) on the album *Born in the USA* (1984) by Bruce Springsteen and the E Street Band. When REAGAN attempted to enlist the support of Springsteen for the 'message of hope' in this and other songs, Springsteen repudiated any connection with the president on stage a few days later, causing WALTER MONDALE to quip: 'Bruce may have been born to run, but he wasn't born yesterday.'

4 People want to forget. There was Vietnam,
  there was Watergate, there was Iran. We
  were beaten, we were hustled, and then we
  were humiliated. And I think people got
  a need to feel good about the country
  they live in. . . . And you see the Reagan
  reelection ads on TV. You know: 'It's
  morning in America.' And you say, well,
  it's not morning in Pittsburgh. It's not
  morning above 125th Street in New York.
  It's midnight, and, like, there's a bad moon
  risin'.

Interview in *Rolling Stone* December 1984

5 Your success story is a bigger story than
  whatever you're trying to say on stage.

Q August 1992

Josef Stalin (1879–1953)

SOVIET LEADER
Originally Josef Vissarionovich Dzhugashvili. He joined the Bolsheviks in 1903 and after the 1917 revolution became Commissar for Nationalities. By 1924 he had become General Secretary of the Central Committee and he went on to establish the USSR as a modern industrial state at the cost of millions of deaths. TROTSKY *called him 'our party's most outstanding mediocrity'. See also* JOHN F. KENNEDY 25, NIKITA KHRUSHCHEV 2, 3, OSIP MANDELSTAM 7, LEON TROTSKY 8, 21, 22, YEVGENY YEVTUSHENKO 5.

1 He who wants to lead a movement, and
  at the same time keep in touch with the
  masses, must wage a war on two fronts –
  against those who lag behind and against
  those who rush on ahead.

Pravda 2 March 1930, repr. in *Parallel Lives*, ch. 8, 'Stalin's Revolution', pt 2 (1998) by Alan Bullock

2 The Pope? How many divisions has he got?

Said 13 May 1935, quoted in *The Second World War*, vol. 1, 'The Gathering Storm', ch. 8 (1948) by WINSTON CHURCHILL. Addressed to French Foreign Minister Pierre Laval in reply to a suggestion that the Soviet Union should encourage Catholicism in order to propitiate the Pope.

3 Gratitude . . . is a sickness suffered by
  dogs.

Quoted in *Stalin's Secret War*, ch. 2 (1981) by Nikolai Tolstoy

4 Cadres determine everything.

One of his favourite watchwords, quoted in *Parallel Lives*, ch. 4, sect. 3 (1998) by Alan Bullock

5 A single death is a tragedy, a million deaths is a statistic.

Attributed

Sylvester Stallone (b. 1946)

US SCREEN ACTOR AND FILM-MAKER
Usually cast as action hero, as in Rocky *(1976), which he wrote, and* Rambo *(1985), he describes himself as the 'manifestation of his own fantasy' with 'the voice of a Mafioso pall bearer'.*

1 Rambo isn't violent. I see Rambo as a philanthropist.

Today 27 May 1988. See RONALD REAGAN 19.

Konstantin Stanislavsky (1863–1938)

RUSSIAN THEATRICAL DIRECTOR, ACTOR
AND THEORIST
He is known for his pioneering approach to acting in which actors aim, through minute study, to 'become' the characters they play. Co-founder in 1897 of the Moscow Art Theatre, he directed the first productions of Chekhov.

1 In the creative process there is the father, the author of the play; the mother, the actor pregnant with the part; and the child, the role to be born.

An Actor Prepares, ch. 16 (1936). Stanislavsky's book was a great influence on the 'method' school of acting in the US.

2 Talent is nothing but a prolonged period of attention and a shortened period of mental assimilation.

The Art of the Stage, ch. 22 (1950)

Vivian Stanshall (1943–95)

BRITISH MUSICIAN AND ENTERTAINER
A full-time English eccentric, he was a member of the Bonzo Dog Doo-Dah Band in the 1960s and later created the bufferish Sir Henry at Rawlinson End on radio, record and film.

1 Cool Britannia
Britannia take a trip
Britons ever ever ever will be hip.

'Cool Britannia' (song) on album *Gorilla* (1967) by the Bonzo Dog Doo-Dah Band. Thought to be the first use of 'Cool Britannia' subsequently used on a *Newsweek* cover and associated with Britain during TONY BLAIR's first term as prime minister.

(Dame) Freya Stark (1893–1993)

BRITISH TRAVEL WRITER
She spent most of her adult life travelling in the

Middle East, and worked for the British Ministry of Information in Aden, Egypt and Iraq during the Second World War. Her books include *The Valleys of the Assassins (1934) and* West is East *(1945).*

1 The great and almost only comfort about being a woman is that one can always pretend to be more stupid than one is and no one is surprised.

The Valleys of the Assassins, ch. 2 (1934)

2 Of the general inadequacy of intellect in the conduct of life Britain is the most majestic exponent. She is instinctively disliked by such people as French, Persians, Hindus, who are clever by nature, and think that *intellect can rule* . . . With the intellectual, it is not our stupidity, but the fact that we prove it possible to live by non-intellectual standards, which makes us disliked.

Perseus in the Wind, ch. 4 (1948)

3 The slightest living thing answers a deeper need than all the works of man because it is *transitory*. It has an evanescence of life, or growth, or change: it passes, as we do, from one stage to another, from darkness to darkness, into a distance where we, too, vanish out of sight. A work of art is static; and its value and its weakness lie in being so: but the tuft of grass and the clouds above it belong to our own travelling brotherhood.

Ibid., ch. 14

4 Pain and fear and hunger are effects of causes which can be foreseen and known: but sorrow is a debt which someone else makes for us.

Ibid., ch. 16

5 Perhaps the best function of parenthood is to teach the young creature to love with safety, so that it may be able to venture unafraid when later emotion comes; the thwarting of the instinct to love is the root of all sorrow and not sex only but divinity itself is insulted when it is repressed. To disapprove, to condemn – the human soul shrivels under barren righteousness.

Traveller's Prelude, ch. 10 (1950)

Edwin Starr (1942–2003)

US SOUL SINGER
A soul-shouter in the style of James Brown, he is best known for his song 'War' and the albums Soulmaster *(1968) and* War & Peace *(1970).*

1 War . . .
What is it good for?
Absolutely nothing.

'War' (song, 1970, written by Norman Whitfield and Barrett Strong) on the album *War & Peace* (1970)

Ringo Starr (b. 1940)

BRITISH ROCK MUSICIAN

Originally Richard Starkey. Drummer and occasional singer with the Beatles, he subsequently had hits as a solo artist and acted in films.

1 I don't like talking. Some people gab all day and some people play it smogo. I haven't got a smiling face or a talking mouth.

Quoted in *Shout! The True Story of the Beatles*, pt. 2, 'November 1963' (1981)

2 I've never really done anything to create what has happened. It creates itself. I'm here because it happened. But I didn't do anything to make it happen apart from saying 'Yes'.

Quoted in *The Beatles Illustrated Lyrics*, vol. 1 (ed. Alan Aldridge, 1969)

3 It was just like Butlins.

On India, ibid. Said after returning from meditating at Rishikesh.

(Sir) David Steel (b. 1938)

BRITISH POLITICIAN

Lord Steel of Aikwood. The youngest MP in Parliament when first elected in 1965, he led the Liberal Party 1976–88, forging the alliance with the Social Democratic Party (1983) that led to the merger of the two parties in 1989.

1 I have the good fortune to be the first Liberal leader for over half a century who is able to say to you at the end of our annual assembly: go back to your constituencies and prepare for government.

Speech at Liberal Party Assembly, Llandudno, 18 September 1981, quoted in *The Times* 19 September 1981. In the subsequent general election (1983), the Liberals won only twenty-three seats.

Tommy Steele (b. 1936)

BRITISH ACTOR AND SINGER

Originally Thomas Hicks. Starting out as Britain's first rock 'n' roll star with the hit song 'Rock With the Cavemen' (1956), he later demonstrated his Cockney pizzazz in the stage musical Half a Sixpence (1963, filmed 1967).

1 Show business is really 90 per cent luck and 10 per cent being able to handle it when it gets offered to you.

Quoted in the *Listener* 10 October 1974

Lincoln Steffens (1866–1936)

US AUTHOR AND EDITOR

One of the chief 'muckraker' journalists of his time, he set out to expose corruption in business and politics as a reporter on the New York Evening Post (1892–8) and Editor of McClure's, American, and Everybody's magazines (1902–11).

1 We Americans can't seem to get it that you can't commit rape a little.

Quoted in *Lincoln Steffens*, ch. 11, sect. 3 (1974) by Justin Kaplan. Referring to US intervention in Mexico in 1914.

2 I have been over into the future, and it works.

Autobiography, ch. 18 (1931). Remark on his return from the Soviet Union in 1919 to financier BERNARD BARUCH.

Gertrude Stein (1874–1946)

US AUTHOR

An experimental writer described by CLIFTON FADIMAN as 'a past master in making nothing happen very slowly', she is famous for her obscure repetitive word-play in works such as Three Lives (1909) and Tender Buttons (1914). The Autobiography of Alice B. Toklas (1933) is actually Stein's own fictionalized autobiography. See CLIFTON FADIMAN 1.

1 One does not get better but different and older and that is always a pleasure.

Letter to author F. SCOTT FITZGERALD, 22 May 1925, publ. in *The Crack-Up* (ed. Edmund Wilson 1945)

2 All of you young people who served in the war. You are a lost generation . . . You have no respect for anything. You drink yourselves to death.

Remark to ERNEST HEMINGWAY, quoted as epigraph to *The Sun Also Rises* (1926). Hemingway's novel describes the lives of expatriates in Paris in the 1920s. The words are also quoted in his memoir of his own time in Paris, *A Moveable Feast*, ch. 3 (1964). In Stein's *Everybody's Autobiography*, ch. 2 (1937), she recalls the origin of the expression 'lost generation': 'It was this hotelkeeper who said what it is said I said that the war generation was a lost generation. And he said it in this way. He said that every man becomes civilized between the ages of eighteen and twenty-five. If he does not go through a civilizing experience at that time in his life he will not be a civilized man. And the men who went to war at eighteen missed the period of civilizing, and they could never be civilized. They were a lost generation.'

3 The United States is just now the oldest country in the world, there always is an oldest country and she is it, it is she who is the mother of the twentieth century civilization. She began to feel herself as it just after the Civil War. And so it is a country the right age to have been born in and the wrong age to live in.

'Why I Do Not Live in America', publ. in *Transition* fall 1928, repr. in *How Writing Is Written* (ed. Robert Bartlett Haas, 1974)

4 *Pigeons on the grass alas.*
Pigeons on the grass alas.

*Short longer grass short longer longer
     shorter yellow
grass Pigeons large pigeons on the shorter
     longer yellow grass
alas pigeons on the grass.*

Four Saints in Three Acts, act 3, sc. 2 (1929), publ.
in *Operas and Plays* (1932)

5 He [Ezra Pound] was a village explainer,
    excellent if you were a village, but if you
    were not, not.

    The Autobiography of Alice B. Toklas, ch. 7
    (1933). When asked later what she meant by call-
    ing POUND (whom she 'liked . . . but did not
    find amusing') 'a village explainer', Stein told
    THORNTON WILDER, 'Ezra Pound still lives in a
    village and his world is a kind of village and
    people keep explaining things when they live in
    a village. . . . I have come not to mind if certain
    people live in villages and some of my friends
    still appear to live in villages and a village can be
    cozy as well as intuitive but must one really keep
    perpetually explaining and elucidating?' (quoted
    by Frederic Prokosch in *Voices: A Memoir*, 'The
    Evil Corner', 1983).

6 Hemingway, remarks are not literature.

    Ibid. Referring to the inclusion by HEMINGWAY
    of a comment he had made about E. E. CUM-
    MINGS' autobiographical novel *The Enormous
    Room* ('the greatest book he had ever read'),
    which he had incorporated in a manuscript of
    short stories shown to Stein.

7 The contemporary thing in art and
    literature is the thing which doesn't make
    enough difference to the people of that
    generation so that they can accept it or reject
    it.

    'How Writing is Written', publ. in *Choate
    Literary Magazine* February 1935, repr. in *How
    Writing Is Written* (ed. Robert Bartlett Haas,
    1974)

8 The unreal is natural, so natural that it
    makes of unreality the most natural of any-
    thing natural. That is what America does,
    and that is what America is.

    'I Came and Here I am', publ. in *Cosmopolitan*
    February 1936, repr. ibid.

9 In the United States there is more
    space where nobody is than where any-
    body is. That is what makes America what
    it is.

    The Geographical History of America (1936)

10 Native always means people who belong
    somewhere else, because they had once
    belonged somewhere. That shows that
    the white race does not really think that they
    belong anywhere because they think of
    everybody else as native.

    Everybody's Autobiography, ch. 1 (1937)

11 It is funny the two things most men are
    proudest of is the thing that any man can
    do and doing does in the same way, that is

being drunk and being the father of their
son.

Ibid., ch. 2

12 It takes a lot of time to be a genius, you
    have to sit around so much doing nothing,
    really doing nothing.

    Ibid.

13 The minute you or anybody else knows
    what you are you are not it, you are what
    you or anybody else knows you are and as
    everything in living is made up of finding
    out what you are it is extraordinarily
    difficult really not to know what you are
    and yet to be that thing.

    Ibid., ch. 3

14 Counting is the religion of this generation
    it is its hope and its salvation.

    Ibid.

15 There is no there there.

    Ibid., ch. 4. Referring to Oakland, California,
    where Stein spent her childhood.

16 Just before she died she asked, 'What *is* the
    answer?' No answer came. She laughed and
    said, 'In that case, what is the question?'
    Then she died.

    Quoted in *Gertrude Stein, A Biography of Her
    Work*, ch. 6 (1951) by Donald Sutherland. The
    biography concludes: 'Those were her last words,
    but they say what she had always been saying.'

17 Oh, I wish I were a miser; being a miser
    must be so occupying.

    Quoted by THORNTON WILDER in interview in
    Writers at Work (first series, ed. Malcolm
    Cowley, 1958)

18 Nature is commonplace. Imitation is more
    interesting.

    Quoted in *My Autobiography*, ch. 20 (1964) by
    CHARLIE CHAPLIN

19 In France one must adapt oneself to the fra-
    grance of a urinal.

    Quoted in *Voices: A Memoir*, 'Style' (1983) by
    Frederic Prokosch. The author and poet Pro-
    kosch had paid a visit to Stein in Paris, asking
    her opinion of the city. 'Alice deplores the
    public urinals,' Stein explained, 'I keep explain-
    ing to Alice that the Parisians are all wine-
    drinkers and for a gentleman the bladder is
    more restless than for a lady.'

20 A writer must always try to have a philos-
    ophy and he should also have a psychology
    and a philology and many other things.
    Without a philosophy and a psychology
    and all these various other things he is not
    really worthy of being called a writer. I
    agree with Kant and Schopenhauer and
    Plato and Spinoza and that is quite enough
    to be called a philosophy. But then of
    course a philosophy is not the same thing
    as a style.

    Quoted ibid.

John Steinbeck (1902–68)

US NOVELIST

He first came to notice with Tortilla Flat *(1935), a humorous portrait of California farmers. Subsequent novels were bleaker in tone, including* In Dubious Battle *(1936),* Of Mice and Men *(1937) and* The Grapes of Wrath *(1939, filmed 1940), all dealing with agricultural and migrant workers.*

1 Aw, I'm looking ahead too much. Our job's just to push along our little baby strike, if we can. But God damn it, Jim, if we could get the National Guard called out, now with the crops coming ready, we'd have the whole district organized by spring.

Mac, in *In Dubious Battle*, ch. 3 (1936). Mac, a Communist Party labour organizer, is discussing plans to strike among California's apple pickers with Jim, a new recruit. The novel's title alludes to the claim of Satan in Milton's *Paradise Lost* that he challenged God 'in dubious battle' (with an uncertain outcome) and 'shook his throne', and suggests Steinbeck's own ambivalent attitude to the methods employed by the Communist organizers.

2 Man, unlike anything organic or inorganic in the universe, grows beyond his work, walks up the stairs of his concepts, emerges ahead of his accomplishments.

The Grapes of Wrath, ch. 14 (1939)

3 Fear the time when the strikes stop while the great owners live – for every little beaten strike is proof that the step is being taken . . . fear the time when Manself will not suffer and die for a concept, for this one quality is the foundation of Manself, and this one quality is man, distinctive in the universe.

Ibid.

4 Is a tractor bad? Is the power that turns the long furrows wrong? If this tractor were ours it would be good – not mine, but ours. We could love that tractor then as we have loved this land when it was ours. But this tractor does two things – it turns the land and turns us off the land. There is little difference between this tractor and a tank. The people are driven, intimidated, hurt by both. We must think about this.

Ibid.

5 Wherever they's a fight so hungry people can eat, I'll be there. Wherever they's a cop beatin' up a guy, I'll be there . . . I'll be in the way guys yell when they're mad an' – I'll be in the way kids laugh when they're hungry an' they know supper's ready. An' when our folks eat the stuff they raise an' live in the houses they build – why, I'll be there.

Tom Joad, ibid., ch. 28. Farewell speech to his mother, in which he articulates union-organizer Jim Casy's belief that human beings make up 'one big soul ever'body's a part of'.

6 A journey is like marriage. The certain way to be wrong is to think you control it.

Travels with Charley: In Search of America, pt 1 (1961)

7 Even while I protest the assembly-line production of our food, our songs, our language, and eventually our souls, I know that it was a rare home that baked good bread in the old days. Mother's cooking was with rare exceptions poor, that good unpasteurized milk touched only by flies and bits of manure crawled with bacteria, the healthy old-time life was riddled with aches, sudden death from unknown causes, and that sweet local speech I mourn was the child of illiteracy and ignorance. It is the nature of a man as he grows older, a small bridge in time, to protest against change, particularly change for the better.

Ibid., pt 2

8 This monster of a land, this mightiest of nations, this spawn of the future, turns out to be the macrocosm of microcosm me.

Ibid., pt 3

9 It is true that we are weak and sick and ugly and quarrelsome but if that is all we ever were, we would millenniums ago have disappeared from the face of the earth.

'On Intent', publ. in *Writers at Work* (fourth series, ed. George Plimpton, 1977)

10 Time is the only critic without ambition.

'On Critics', publ. ibid.

11 Give a critic an inch, he'll write a play.

Ibid.

Gloria Steinem (b. 1934)

US FEMINIST WRITER AND EDITOR

She co-founded the Women's Action Alliance in 1970 and the National Women's Political Caucus in 1971, and was founding editor of the feminist Ms. *magazine (1981–7). Her books include* Revolution from Within *(1992) and* Moving Beyond Words *(1994).*

1 No man can call himself liberal, or radical, or even a conservative advocate of fair play, if his work depends in any way on the unpaid or underpaid labor of women at home, or in the office.

The New York Times 26 August 1971

2 Any woman who chooses to behave like a full human being should be warned that the armies of the status quo will treat her as something of a dirty joke. That's their natural and first weapon. She will *need* her sisterhood.

'Sisterhood', publ. in *Ms.* spring 1972, repr. in *Outrageous Acts and Everyday Rebellions* (1983)

3 **Pornography is about dominance. Erotica is about mutuality.**

'Erotica vs. Pornography', adapted from articles in *Ms.* August 1977 and November 1978, repr. ibid.

4 **Power can be taken, but not given. The process of the taking is empowerment in itself.**

'Far from the Opposite Shore', adapted from articles in *Ms.* July 1978 and July/August 1982, repr. in *Outrageous Acts and Everyday Rebellions* (1983)

5 **If men could menstruate . . . clearly, menstruation would become an enviable, boast-worthy, masculine event: Men would brag about how long and how much. . . . Sanitary supplies would be federally funded and free. Of course, some men would still pay for the prestige of such commercial brands as Paul Newman Tampons, Muhammed Ali's Rope-a-Dope Pads, John Wayne Maxi Pads, and Joe Namath Jock Shields – 'For Those Light Bachelor Days'.**

'If Men Could Menstruate', publ. in *Ms.* October 1978, repr. ibid.

6 **The authority of any governing institution must stop at its citizen's skin.**

'Night Thoughts of a Media-Watcher', publ. in *Ms.* November 1981

7 **We are becoming the men we wanted to marry.**

Ms. July/August 1982

8 **I have yet to hear a man ask for advice on how to combine marriage and a career.**

Radio interview, 2 April 1984, LBC

9 **A woman without a man is like a fish without a bicycle.**

Attributed. Although the quotation is usually ascribed to Steinem, the words were current as graffiti in the 1970s (see GRAFFITI 5).

George Steiner (b. 1929)
FRENCH-BORN US CRITIC AND NOVELIST

A leading figure in the study of comparative literature and of language, he is known both for his critical studies, such as The Death of Tragedy *(1960), and for his fiction, for example* The Portage to San Cristobal of A.H. *(1981), which was adapted for the stage in 1983.*

1 **We know that a man can read Goethe or Rilke in the evening, that he can play Bach and Schubert, and go to his day's work at Auschwitz in the morning.**

Language and Silence, Preface (1967)

2 **Language can only deal meaningfully with a special, restricted segment of reality. The rest, and it is presumably the much larger part, is silence.**

Ibid., 'The Retreat from the Word'

3 **Pornographers subvert this last, vital privacy; they do our imagining for us. They take away the words that were of the night and shout them over the roof-tops, making them hollow.**

Ibid., 'Nightworks'

4 **To shoot a man because one disagrees with his interpretation of Darwin or Hegel is a sinister tribute to the supremacy of ideas in human affairs – but a tribute nevertheless.**

Ibid., 'Marxism and the Literary Critic'

5 **It is not the literal past that rules us, save, possibly, in a biological sense. It is images of the past. . . . Each new historical era mirrors itself in the picture and active mythology of its past or of a past borrowed from other cultures. It tests its sense of identity, of regress or new achievement, against that past.**

In Bluebeard's Castle, ch. 1 (1971). Opening passage of book.

6 **The immense majority of human biographies are a gray transit between domestic spasm and oblivion.**

Ibid., ch. 3

7 **To many men . . . the miasma of peace seems more suffocating than the bracing air of war.**

'Has Truth a Future?', Bronowski Memorial Lecture, 1978

8 **The age of the book is almost gone.**

Daily Mail 27 June 1988

9 **There is something terribly wrong with a culture inebriated by noise and gregariousness.**

Daily Telegraph 23 May 1989

10 **Almost overwhelmingly, European culture, at the close of this millennium, is that of the museum. Who among us believes that we shall witness a new Dante, a Shakespeare of the 21st Century, a Mozart to come?**

'Modernity, Mythology and Magic', lecture at the Salzburg Festival, 1994, publ. in the *Guardian* 6 August 1994

11 **Nothing is more symptomatic of the enervation, of the decompression of the Western imagination, than our incapacity to respond to the landings on the Moon. Not a single great poem, picture, metaphor has come of this breathtaking act, of Prometheus's rescue of Icarus or of Phaeton in flight towards the stars.**

Ibid.

12 **We Jews walk closer to our children than other men . . . because to have children is possibly to condemn them.**

Interview in the *Guardian* 6 January 1996

Bruce Sterling (b. 1954)

US SCIENCE FICTION AUTHOR

His novels Involution Ocean *(1977) and* Islands in the Net *(1988) established him as the 'standard-bearer of the cyberpunks'. A short-story collection,* Globalhead, *and the non-fiction* The Hacker Crackdown *followed in 1992.*

1 If poets are the unacknowledged legislators of the world, science-fiction writers are its court jesters. We are Wise Fools who can leap, caper, utter prophecies, and scratch ourselves in public. We can play with Big Ideas because the garish motley of our pulp origins makes us seem harmless.

Preface to *Burning Chrome* (1986) by WILLIAM GIBSON

2 Technology itself has changed. Not for us the giant steam snorting wonders of the past: the Hoover Dam, the Empire State Building, the nuclear power plant. Eighties tech sticks to the skin, responds to the touch: the personal computer, the Sony Walkman, the portable telephone, the soft contact lens.

Mirrorshades, Preface (ed. Bruce Sterling, 1986). Sterling went on: 'The Eighties are an era of reassessment, of integration, of hybridized influences, of old notions shaken loose and reinterpreted with a new sophistication, a broader perspective.'

3 The hacker and the rocker are this decade's pop-culture idols, and cyberpunk is very much a pop phenomenon: spontaneous, energetic, close to its roots. Cyberpunk comes from the realm where the computer hacker and the rocker overlap, a cultural Petri dish where writhing gene lines splice.

Ibid.

Wallace Stevens (1879–1955)

US POET

He worked most of his life in law and insurance while establishing a reputation as a poet. His work, published in Harmonium *(1923),* The Man with the Blue Guitar *(1937) and* The Auroras of Autumn *(1950) among other collections, explores the transformational power of poetic language.*

1 The day of the sun is like the day of a king. It is a promenade in the morning, a sitting on the throne at noon, a pageant in the evening.

Journal entry, 20 April 1920, publ. in *Souvenirs and Prophecies: The Young Wallace Stevens,* ch. 6 (ed. Holly Stevens, 1966)

2 *Poetry is the supreme fiction, madame. Take the moral law and make a nave of it And from the nave build haunted heaven.*

'A High-Toned Old Christian Woman', publ. in *Harmonium* (1923)

3 *The only emperor is the emperor of ice-cream.*

'The Emperor of Ice-Cream', publ. ibid.

4 *Civilization must be destroyed. The hairy saints Of the North have earned this crumb by their complaints.*

'Land of Pine and Marble', publ. ibid., 'New England Verses'

5 Everything is complicated; if that were not so, life and poetry and everything else would be a bore.

Letter, 19 December 1935, publ. in *Letters of Wallace Stevens* (ed. Holly Stevens, 1967)

6 *Union of the weakest develops strength Not wisdom. Can all men, together, avenge One of the leaves that have fallen in autumn? But the wise man avenges by building his city in snow.*

'Like Decorations in a Nigger Cemetery', sect. 50, publ. in *Ideas of Order* (1936)

7 *They said, 'You have a blue guitar, You do not play things as they are.' The man replied, 'Things as they are Are changed upon the blue guitar.'*

'The Man with the Blue Guitar', publ. in *The Man with the Blue Guitar* (1937)

8 It is the unknown that excites the ardor of scholars, who, in the known alone, would shrivel up with boredom.

'The Irrational Element in Poetry', lecture (c. 1937), publ. in *Opus Posthumous* (1957)

9 *The squirming facts exceed the squamous mind, If one may say so.*

'Connoisseur of Chaos', publ. in *Parts of a World* (1942)

10 *The reason can give nothing at all Like the response to desire.*

'Dezembrum', publ. ibid. Last lines of poem.

11 All the great things have been denied and we live in an intricacy of new and local mythologies, political, economic, poetic, which are asserted with an ever-enlarging incoherence.

'The Noble Rider and the Sound of Words', lecture (1942), repr. in *The Necessary Angel* (1951)

12 We have been a little insane about the truth. We have had an obsession.

Ibid.

13 The philosopher proves that the philosopher exists. The poet merely enjoys existence.

'The Figure of the Youth as Virile Poet', lecture August 1943, publ. 1944, repr. ibid.

14 *The greatest poverty is not to live In a physical world, to feel that one's desire*

Is too difficult to tell from despair.
'Esthétique du mal', sect. 15, publ. in *Transport to Summer* (1947)

15 *The whole race is a poet that writes down The eccentric propositions of its fate.*
'Men Made out of Words', publ. ibid. Last lines of poem.

16 So, too, if, to our surprise, we should meet one of these morons whose remarks are so conspicuous a part of the folklore of the world of the radio – remarks made without using either the tongue or the brain, spouted much like the spoutings of small whales – we should recognize him as below the level of nature but not as below the level of the imagination.
'Three Academic Pieces', no. 1 (1947), repr. in *The Necessary Angel* (1951)

17 What our eyes behold may well be the text of life but one's meditations on the text and the disclosures of these meditations are no less a part of the structure of reality.
Ibid.

18 To regard the imagination as metaphysics is to think of it as part of life, and to think of it as part of life is to realize the extent of artifice. We live in the mind.
'Imagination as Value', lecture at Columbia University, 1948, publ. 1949, repr. ibid.

19 If poetry should address itself to the same needs and aspirations, the same hopes and fears, to which the Bible addresses itself, it might rival it in distribution.
Ibid.

20 Style is not something applied. It is something that permeates. It is of the nature of that in which it is found, whether the poem, the manner of a god, the bearing of a man. It is not a dress.
'Two or Three Ideas' (1951), repr. in *Opus Posthumous* (1957)

21 Thought is an infection. In the case of certain thoughts, it becomes an epidemic.
Opus Posthumous, 'Adagia' (1957)

22 As life grows more terrible, its literature grows more terrible.
Ibid.

23 Intolerance respecting other people's religion is toleration itself in comparison with intolerance respecting other people's art.
Ibid.

24 Perhaps it is of more value to infuriate philosophers than to go along with them.
Ibid.

25 One cannot spend one's time in being modern when there are so many more important things to be.
Ibid.

26 Most modern reproducers of life, even including the camera, really repudiate it. We gulp down evil, choke at good.
Ibid.

27 A poem need not have a meaning and like most things in nature often does not have.
Ibid.

28 One's ignorance is one's chief asset.
Ibid.

29 The imagination is man's power over nature.
Ibid.

Adlai Stevenson (1900–1965)

US POLITICIAN

A Democrat, he helped establish the United Nations in the 1940s, and as US ambassador to the UN (1960–65) memorably persuaded delegates of the presence of Soviet missiles in Cuba with the aid of aerial photos. He was the unsuccessful Democratic presidential candidate against EISENHOWER *in 1952 and 1956.*

1 Let's face it. Let's talk sense to the American people. Let's tell them the truth, that there are no gains without pains, that we are now on the eve of great decisions, not easy decisions.
Acceptance speech at Democratic National Convention, Chicago, 26 July 1952, publ. in *Speeches* (1953)

2 What do we mean by patriotism in the context of our times? I venture to suggest that what we mean is a sense of national responsibility . . . a patriotism which is not short, frenzied outbursts of emotion, but the tranquil and steady dedication of a lifetime.
'The Nature of Patriotism', speech to American Legion Convention, New York, 27 August 1952, publ. ibid.

3 The sound of tireless voices is the price we pay for the right to hear the music of our own opinions. But there is also, it seems to me, a moment at which democracy must prove its capacity to act. Every man has a right to be heard; but no man has the right to strangle democracy with a single set of vocal chords.
Speech in New York, 28 August 1952, publ. in *The Papers of Adlai E. Stevenson*, vol. 4 (1974). See also ADLAI STEVENSON 16.

4 A hungry man is not a free man.
'Farm Policy', speech at Kasson, Minnesota, 6 September 1952, publ. in *The Speeches of Adlai Stevenson* (1952)

5 I have been thinking that I would make a proposition to my Republican friends. That if they will stop telling lies about

Democrats, we will stop telling the truth about them.

Campaign speech, 10 September 1952, Fresno, California, quoted in *Adlai Stevenson of Illinois*, ch. 8 (1976) by John Bartlow Martin. The remark has been attributed earlier to Republican Chauncey Depew (senator 1899–1911), though with the party names reversed.

6 There is no evil in the atom; only in men's souls.

'The Atomic Future', speech at Hartford, Connecticut, 18 September 1952, publ. in *Speeches* (1953)

7 In America any boy may become President, and I suppose it's just one of the risks he takes!

Speech in Indianapolis, 26 September 1952, publ. in *Major Campaign Speeches of Adlai E. Stevenson: 1952* (1953)

8 Nothing so dates a man as to decry the younger generation.

Speech at University of Wisconsin, Madison, 8 October 1952, publ. in *Speeches* (1953)

9 The Republican Vice Presidential Candidate . . . asks you to place him a heartbeat from the Presidency.

Referring to Richard Nixon, in 'The Hiss Case', speech in Cleveland, Ohio, 23 October 1952, publ. in *Speeches* (1953). NIXON became vice-president under EISENHOWER in the November election, and was re-elected 1956. This is thought to be the first use of the phrase 'heartbeat from the presidency' to describe the position of vice-president.

10 The Republican party makes even its young men seem old; the Democratic Party makes even its old men seem young.

Quoted in *Richard Nixon: A Political and Personal Portrait*, ch. 7 (1959) by Earl Mazo. Comparing RICHARD NIXON to the septuagenarian Democratic vice-president Alben Barkley, during the 1952 presidential race.

11 A funny thing happened to me on the way to the White House.

Speech in Washington DC, 13 December 1952, quoted in *Portrait: Adlai E. Stevenson*, ch. 1 (1965) by Alden Whitman. Said after his landslide defeat in the presidential election against EISENHOWER.

12 We cannot be any stronger in our foreign policy – for all the bombs and guns we may heap up in our arsenals – than we are in the spirit which rules inside the country. Foreign policy, like a river, cannot rise above its source.

Speech in New Orleans, 4 December 1954, publ. in *What I Think* (1956)

13 We hear the Secretary of State [John Foster Dulles] boasting of his brinkmanship – the art of bringing us to the edge of the abyss.

Speech at Hartford, Connecticut, 25 February

1956, quoted in *The New York Times* 26 February 1956. See also JOHN FOSTER DULLES 1

14 Freedom is not an ideal, it is not even a protection, if it means nothing more than freedom to stagnate, to live without dreams, to have no greater aim than a second car and another television set.

'Putting First Things First', publ. in *Foreign Affairs* January 1960

15 With the supermarket as our temple and the singing commercial as our litany, are we likely to fire the world with an irresistible vision of America's exalted purpose and inspiring way of life?

Wall Street Journal 1 June 1960

16 The first principle of a free society is an untrammeled flow of words in an open forum.

The New York Times 19 January 1962

17 She [Eleanor Roosevelt] would rather light a candle than curse the darkness, and her glow has warmed the world.

Quoted in *The New York Times* 8 November 1962. Comment on learning of the death of ELEANOR ROOSEVELT, echoing the motto of the Christopher Society: 'It is better to light one candle than curse the darkness.'

18 A politician is a statesman who approaches every question with an open mouth.

Quoted in *The Fine Art of Political Wit*, ch. 10 (1964) by Leon Harris

19 The General has dedicated himself so many times, he must feel like the cornerstone of a public building.

Referring to President EISENHOWER, ibid.

20 Nixon is the kind of politician who would cut down a redwood tree, then mount the stump for a speech on conservation.

Ibid.

21 An editor is someone who separates the wheat from the chaff and then prints the chaff.

Quoted in *The Stevenson Wit* (1966). The aphorism has also been attributed to writer Elbert Hubbard.

Stephen Stills (b. 1945)
US ROCK MUSICIAN

He wrote many of the songs recorded by the LA folk-rock band Buffalo Springfield, of which he was a founder member (1966–8). He later performed with Crosby, Stills and Nash, made solo albums and formed the band Manassas.

1 *You better stop, hey,*
  What's that sound?
  Everybody look what's goin' down.

'For What it's Worth' (song, 1967) on the album *Retrospective* (1969) by Buffalo Springfield. The song, written after the 1967 riots in Los

Angeles, became a protest anthem about police brutality.

2 *If you can't be with the one you love,*
Love the one you're with.

'Love the One You're With' (song) on the album *Stephen Stills* (1970). The lyrics of the song, which was also a hit for the Isley Brothers, recall the 1947 song by YIP HARBURG, 'When I'm Not Near the Girl I Love': 'When I'm not near the girl I love,/I love the girl I'm near.'

Sting (b. 1951)
BRITISH ROCK MUSICIAN

Originally Gordon Sumner. The singer, bassist and principal songwriter with the Police until 1986, he has had a successful solo career while campaigning for Amnesty International and the Brazilian rain forest. See also MARK KNOPFLER 1.

1 Music has ceased to belong to the young ... The rock rebel is defunct. He's meaningless.

Interview in *Smash Hits* 19 August 1982

2 Humans make the mistake of believing that it's their right to survive. Species die out on this planet all the time without anybody noticing. The planet will still be here, and we must lose this attitude of divine right, that something will save us, which we've developed over the centuries. The Martians aren't going to come down and save us. God isn't going to save us.

Interview in *Rolling Stone* September 1983

3 If you love somebody set them free.

Song title on the album *The Dream of the Blue Turtles* (1985)

4 If I were a Brazilian without land or money or the means to feed my children, I would be burning the rain forest too.

International Herald Tribune 14 April 1989

5 Celebrity is good for kick-starting ideas, but often celebrity is a lead weight around your neck. It's like you pointing at the moon, but people are looking at your finger.

Interview in *Mojo* February 1995

Karlheinz Stockhausen (b. 1928)
GERMAN COMPOSER

He was a member of the Paris-based 'Musique Concrète' group and in 1953 helped found the electronic music studio at Cologne, Westdeutscher Rundfunk, becoming its director (1963–77). His work combines electronic and orchestral sounds, as in Kontakte (1960) and his operatic cycle Licht, begun in 1977.

1 Think NOTHING
Wait until it is absolutely still within you
When you have attained this
Begin to play
As soon as you start to think stop

And try to retain
The state of NON-THINKING
Then continue playing.

The New York Times 30 December 1973. Instructions to performers of his work, 'Es'.

2 The whole planning looked like Lucifer's greatest work of art.

Attributed in *Bild* 18 September 2001, referring to the terrorist attacks of '9/11'. In the resulting furore, Stockhausen insisted that his remarks, made at a press conference for the Hamburg Festival of New Music, 17 September 2001, had been 'ripped out of context'. The composer had been asked whether Lucifer, who appears in his work *Licht*, is a historical figure, and had replied that Lucifer had been present in New York. He later explained: 'Of course I used the designation "work of art" to mean the work of destruction personified in Lucifer. In the context of my other comments this was unequivocal.'

Matt Stone (b. 1971) and
Trey Parker (b. 1972)
US ANIMATORS

South Park, the controversial cartoon series created by Stone and Parker (full name Donald McKay Parker), and featuring the eight-year-olds Kyle, Stan, Kenny and Cartman, became a global hit from its debut in 1997. Asked whether he worried about offending any individual groups, Parker replied, 'You can't worry about one group. You just have to offend everyone equally, and I think we do that pretty well.'

1 Oh my God, they've killed Kenny!

South Park (cartoon series from 1997, written by Matt Stone and Trey Parker). The exclamation, or a variation of it, is made by one of the characters towards the end of most episodes.

Oliver Stone (b. 1946)
US FILM-MAKER

He was acclaimed for his films Platoon (1986) and Born on the Fourth of July (1989), both inspired by his military service in Vietnam. Other films raised controversy: JFK (1991) for its version of the KENNEDY assassination, and the ultra-violent Natural Born Killers (1994).

1 Excuses are like assholes, Taylor – everybody got one.

Sgt. O'Neill (John McGinley), in *Platoon* (film, 1986, written and directed by Oliver Stone)

2 One of the joys of going to the movies was that it was trashy, and we should never lose that.

International Herald Tribune 15 February 1988

Robert Stone (b. 1937)
US NOVELIST

He is best known for Dog Soldiers (1974, filmed

1978) and for his fictionalized study of US imperialism A Flag for Sunrise *(1981).*

1 **Life is a means of extracting fiction.**
Interview in *Writers at Work* (eighth series, ed. George Plimpton, 1988)

Sharon Stone (b. 1958)
US SCREEN ACTRESS
She made her breakthrough in the police thriller Basic Instinct *(1992), which she followed with* Casino *(1995) and* The Muse *(1999).*

1 **If you have a vagina *and* an attitude in this town, then that's a lethal combination.**
Empire June 1992. Referring to Hollywood.

2 **With women, it's dog years when you are 40. It's as if you are a thousand years old. It's over.**
Quoted in the *Observer* 7 February 1999

Marie Carmichael Stopes (1880–1958)
BRITISH SCIENTIST AND PIONEER OF BIRTH CONTROL
She published more than seventy books in her lifetime, including the controversial and influential Married Love *(1918), which advocated birth control. She founded the first British birth control clinic in London in 1921.*

1 **An impersonal and scientific knowledge of the structure of our bodies is the surest safeguard against prurient curiosity and lascivious gloating.**
Married Love, ch. 5 (1918)

(Sir) Tom Stoppard (b. 1937)
CZECH-BORN BRITISH PLAYWRIGHT
Originally Thomas Straussler. His work aspires to be, he has said, 'a perfect marriage between the play of ideas and farce'. He came to prominence with Rosencrantz and Guildenstern are Dead *(1966, filmed 1991), followed by* The Real Inspector Hound *(1968),* Jumpers *(1972) and* Travesties *(1974). He has also written fiction and screenplays.*

1 **Nothing is the history of the world viewed from a suitable distance. Revolution is a trivial shift in the emphasis of suffering; the capacity for self-indulgence changes hands. But the world does not alter its shape or its course. The seasons are inexorable, the elements constant. Against such vast immutability the human struggles take place on the same scale as the insect movement in the grass, and carnage in the streets is no more than the spider-sucked husk of a fly on a dusty window-sill.**
Lord Malquist, in *Lord Malquist and Mr Moon*, pt 1, ch. 1 (1966)

2 **My problem is that I am not frightfully interested in anything, except myself. And**

of all forms of fiction autobiography is the most gratuitous.
Lord Malquist, ibid., pt 2, ch. 3

3 **Let it be said of me that I was born appalled, lived disaffected, and died in the height of fashion.**
Lord Malquist, ibid., pt 6, ch. 2

4 **We do on stage things that are supposed to happen off. Which is a kind of integrity, if you look on every exit as being an entrance somewhere else.**
Player, in *Rosencrantz and Guildenstern are Dead*, act 1 (1966)

5 **Eternity is a terrible thought. I mean, where's it going to end?**
Rosencrantz, ibid., act 2

6 **The bad end unhappily, the good unluckily. That is what tragedy means.**
Player, ibid. The line is an adaptation of one by Oscar Wilde: 'The good ended happily, and the bad unhappily. That is what fiction means' (*The Importance of Being Earnest*, 1895).

7 **Life is a gamble at terrible odds – if it was a bet, you wouldn't take it.**
Player, ibid., act 3

8 **It's not the voting that's democracy, it's the counting.**
Dotty, in *Jumpers*, act 1 (1972). See also ANASTASIO SOMOZA 1.

9 **It's better to be quotable than honest.**
Quoted in the *Guardian* 21 March 1973

10 **War is capitalism with the gloves off and many who go to war know it but they go to war because they don't want to be a hero.**
Tzara, in *Travesties*, act 1 (1974)

11 **I'm with you on the free press. It's the newspapers I can't stand.**
Ruth, in *Night and Day*, act 1 (1978)

12 **I don't think I can be expected to take seriously any game which takes less than three days to reach its conclusion.**
On baseball, quoted in the *Guardian* 24 December 1984. Stoppard is known to be a fanatical cricket fan.

13 **I still believe that if your aim is to change the world, journalism is a more immediate short-term weapon.**
Guardian 18 March 1988

(Sir) Richard Storey (b. 1937)
BRITISH NEWSPAPER PUBLISHER
He was for over twenty-five years Chairman of, and investor in, Portsmouth and Sunderland Newspapers, resigning as Chairman shortly before PSN was bought out in 1999.

1 **The first rule of venture capitalism should be Shoot the Inventor.**
Quoted in *Eddy Shah: Today and the Newspaper*

Revolution, ch. 21 (1988) by Brian MacArthur.
Referring to entrepreneur Eddie Shah. Storey
was one of Shah's backers.

Anthony Storr (1920–2001)
BRITISH PSYCHIATRIST
*His work has been called 'psychology made prop-
erly and truly popular', as in the influential
manual* The Art of Psychotherapy *(1980).
Among his other titles are* Churchill's Black Dog
(1988) and Feet of Clay: A Study of Gurus *(1997).*

1 Self-realization is not an anti-social principle; it is firmly based on the fact that that
men need each other in order to be themselves.
The Integrity of the Personality, ch. 2 (1960)

2 A happy marriage perhaps represents the
ideal of human relationship – a setting in
which each partner, while acknowledging
the need of the other, feels free to be what
he or she by nature is: a relationship in
which instinct as well as intellect can find
expression; in which giving and taking are
equal; in which each accepts the other, and
I confronts Thou.
Ibid., ch. 9

3 The professional must learn to be moved
and touched emotionally, yet at the
same time stand back objectively: I've seen
a lot of damage done by tea and sympathy.
The Times 22 October 1992

Lytton Strachey (1880–1932)
BRITISH BIOGRAPHER AND HISTORIAN
*A member of the Bloomsbury group of writers
and artists, he was the author of* Eminent Victorians *(1918), described by* CYRIL CONNOLLY *as
'the work of a great anarch'.* T. E. LAWRENCE
*remembered him as 'an outraged wet mackerel of
a man', while* EDITH SITWELL *judged him to
have been 'cut out of very thin cardboard'.*

1 The history of the Victorian Age will
never be written: we know too much
about it.
Eminent Victorians, Preface (1918). First words of
book.

2 Ignorance is the first requisite of the historian – ignorance, which simplifies and
clarifies, which selects and omits, with a
placid perfection unattainable by the highest art.
Ibid.

Igor Stravinsky (1882–1971)
RUSSIAN-BORN US COMPOSER
*A seminal figure in twentieth-century music, he
was a composer of ballets, operas, religious pieces
and works for piano and orchestra. The* Firebird
(1910), Petrushka *(1911) and The* Rite of Spring,
which provoked a theatre riot at its first perform-
ance *in 1913, were all written for Diaghilev ballets.
'We have a duty towards music,' he asserted,
'namely to invent it.'*

1 Film music should have the same relationship to the film drama that somebody's
piano playing in my living room has to the
book I am reading.
Music Digest September 1946

2 My music is best understood by children
and animals.
Quoted in the *Observer* 8 October 1961

Jack Straw (b. 1946)
BRITISH POLITICIAN
*He was elected a Labour MP in 1979, held various
posts in the shadow cabinet, and was appointed
Home Secretary in 1997 and Foreign Secretary in
2001.*

1 Parents are responsible for their children.
That is the key belief and assertion.
Quoted in the *Daily Telegraph* 27 December
1997. Outlining the government's policy after he
had escorted his seventeen-year-old son to a
police station to be charged with trying to sell
cannabis to a reporter from the *Daily Mirror*.

Galen Strawson (b. 1952)
BRITISH PHILOSOPHER AND LITERARY
CRITIC
*In his works on the nature of mind, the Oxford-
based thinker addresses problems of causality and
human responsibility. His publications include*
Freedom and Belief *(1986) and* Secret Connexion: Causation, Realism and David Hume
(1992).

1 It is an insult to God to believe in God. For
on the one hand it is to suppose that he
has perpetrated acts of incalculable cruelty.
On the other hand, it is to suppose that he
has perversely given his human creatures
an instrument – their intellect – which
must inevitably lead them, if they are dis-
passionate and honest, to deny his existence. It is tempting to conclude that if he
exists, it is the atheists and agnostics that
he loves best, among those with any pretensions to education. For they are the ones
who have taken him most seriously.
Independent 24 June 1990

Janet Street-Porter (b. 1946)
BRITISH BROADCASTER AND JOURNALIST
*Winning a reputation as a 'mouthy' presenter and
producer for the under-25s, she was appointed the
BBC's first Commissioning Editor for youth programmes in 1988. She became Editor of the* Independent on Sunday *in 1999.*

1 I'm not bothered by the provenance of

things – to use a painter's analogy. I just think, 'Is it hot?'

Interview in the *Independent on Sunday* 20 December 1992

2 TV is not where truly innovative ideas end up any more. Why? Because TV isn't fun any more and fun is where ideas breed. A terminal blight has hit the TV industry nipping fun in the bud and stunting our growth. This blight is management – the dreaded Four Ms: male, middle class, middle-aged and mediocre.

MacTaggart Lecture, Edinburgh Television Festival, 25 August 1995, publ. in the *Guardian* 26 August 1995

3 I'm proud to say I've made a career out of being trivial. I think it's an art form.

Observer 12 November 1995. Referring to her new column.

4 We've now invented the ultimate tool for keeping the sads busy: the internet. But behind all the techno-babble about cyberspace and hyper-text and virtual worlds, behind all the promises of total immersion in a parallel universe, there's a boring reality: a bunch of screeching modems, lost jobs, and boring computer-nerds getting all excited over a glorified telephone exchange. I'm sick of the spurious claims devotees make for the internet, and I'm particularly sick of the internerds.

Without Walls: J'Accuse – Technonerds, Channel 4, 19 March 1996

(Sir) Roy Strong (b. 1935)

BRITISH HISTORIAN AND MUSEUM DIRECTOR

Flamboyant director of the National Portrait Gallery from 1967 and the Victoria and Albert Museum (1974–87) he is also a writer, broadcaster, garden expert and art historian. His many publications include Royal Gardens *(1992) and* The Tudor and Stuart Monarchy *(1995).*

1 Art history and museology have got such a death-grip that any form of educational attachment is howled down as spoon-feeding! SPOON-FEEDING, when 90% of the population still think that Botticelli is a brand of Chianti!

Journal entry, 20 September 1975, publ. in *The Roy Strong Diaries 1967–1987* (1997)

2 Good design is good housekeeping.

Creating Small Gardens, Introduction (1986)

Nadine Strossen (b. 1950)

US HUMAN RIGHTS LAWYER AND AUTHOR

Describing herself as 'a free-speech absolutist', she is the President of the American Civil Liberties Union, and author of Regulating Campus Hate Speech: A Modest Proposal? *(1990) and* Defending Pornography *(1995).*

1 The MacDworkinite idea that pornography is violence against women insults the many women who experience actual, brutal, three-dimensional violence in their real lives . . . I certainly would like nothing better than to find a simple, fast route to equality and safety for women. But censoring sexual speech is really a detour or, worse, a dead end.

Defending Pornography, ch. 13 (1995). On the anti-pornography stance of CATHARINE MACKINNON and ANDREA DWORKIN.

2 Women are not little children. Women are not weak, not victims. Pleasure and danger go together, of course they do. We want the pleasure, and we can cope with danger.

Interview in the *Observer* 28 January 1996. Referring to calls to censor negative images of women.

Joe Strummer (1952–2002)

BRITISH ROCK MUSICIAN

Originally John Graham Mellor. Chief songwriter and singer with the Clash, the most politicized of the punk groups of 1977, he went on to form the Mescaleros.

1 Going on a nostalgia trip is like going into a roomful of treacle. You think you'll pop in for a minute or two, and it tastes sweet. But before you know it, you're stuck in there for ever.

Quoted in *The Times* 24 December 2002. Strummer always resisted requests to re-form the Clash.

Joe Strummer (1952–2002) and Mick Jones (b. 1955)

BRITISH ROCK MUSICIANS

The two became torchbearers of inner-city revolt for their punk anthems written for the Clash. Jones left the band in 1983 and had hits with Big Audio Dynamite. See also JOE STRUMMER.

1 *White riot! I wanna riot!*
   White riot! a riot of my own.

'White Riot' (song) on the album *The Clash* (1977) by the Clash

2 *Career opportunities, the ones that never knock,*
   Every job they offer you is to keep you out the dock.

'Career Opportunities' (song), ibid. The song was re-recorded sung by children on the Clash album *Sandinista* (1980).

3 *Every gimmick-hungry yob digging gold from rock 'n' roll*
   Grabs the mike to tell us he'll die before he's sold
   But I believe in this – and it's been tested by research –

That he who fucks nuns will later join the church.

'Death or Glory' (song) on the album *London Calling* (1979) by the Clash

Arthur Hays Sulzberger (1891–1968)

US NEWSPAPER PROPRIETOR

Publisher of The New York Times *from 1935, he was also Chairman of the Board (1957–61). He expanded the sales of 'the good gray* Times*', as he called it, and wrote letters to the paper signed A. Aitchess (A.H.S.).*

1 We [journalists] tell the public which way the cat is jumping. The public will take care of the cat.

Quoted in *Time* 8 May 1950

Edith Summerskill (1901–80)

BRITISH POLITICIAN

Baroness Summerskill of Kenwood. A Labour MP (1938–55) and Chairman of the Party (1954–5), she was responsible for administering food rationing in ATTLEE*'s government. She campaigned for hygiene in food, good health care and women's rights.*

1 Nagging is the repetition of unpalatable truths.

Speech to Married Women's Association, House of Commons, 14 July 1960, quoted in *The Times* 15 July 1960

The Sun See ANTONY JAY 2.

1 Crisis? What crisis?

Headline, 11 January 1979. On James Callaghan's blithe denial of 'mounting chaos' in the economy. See JAMES CALLAGHAN 1.

2 Stick it up your junta!

Headline, 20 April 1982. Referring to a boycott of Argentinian corned beef during the Falklands conflict.

3 GOTCHA!

Headline, 4 May 1982. On the sinking of the Argentinian cruiser, General Belgrano. The headline appeared in the first edition only; subsequent editions were toned down, with the replacement: 'Did 1200 Argies drown?'

4 Freddie Starr ate my hamster.

Headline, 13 March 1986

5 Up yours, Delors.

Headline, 1 November 1990. On Jacques Delors, President of the European Commission, seen to be attempting to increase EU powers at the expense of British sovereignty.

6 If Kinnock wins today, will the last person to leave Britain please turn out the lights.

Headline, 9 April 1992. On election day, in which NEIL KINNOCK was the Labour challenger to JOHN MAJOR.

7 It was the Sun wot won it.

Headline, 10 April 1992. Following the unexpected Conservative victory in the general election, maintaining JOHN MAJOR in power and giving the Conservatives their fourth successive term in office.

8 One's bum year.

Headline, 25 November 1992. Reporting the Queen's speech of the preceding day, in which she had referred to her '*annus horribilis*'. *See* ELIZABETH II 5

9 Is THIS the most dangerous man in Britain?

Headline, 24 June 1998. Of Prime Minister TONY BLAIR, suspected of favouring Britain's membership of the Single European Currency.

10 *Chirac est un ver.* [Chirac is a worm.]

Headline, 20 February, 2003. Two thousand copies of a special edition of the *Sun* bearing this headline were distributed free in Paris. The accompanying article accused Chirac of being 'a disgrace to Europe by constantly threatening to veto military action to enforce the will of the UN against Iraq'.

Gloria Swanson (1897–1983)

US SCREEN ACTRESS

Originally Gloria Svensson. The highest paid star of the silent era, she appeared as a leading sophisticate in CECIL B. DE MILLE*'s films ('I acquired my expensive tastes from Mr De Mille,' she said).* Sadie Thompson *(1928) was made by her own production company and* Sunset Boulevard *revived her career in 1950. She married six times.*

1 I *am* big. It's the pictures that got small.

Norma Desmond (Gloria Swanson), in *Sunset Boulevard* (film, 1950, screenplay by Billy Wilder, Charles Brackett and D. M. Marsham Jr, directed by BILLY WILDER). Riposte to Joe Gillis (William Holden), who exclaimed in one of their opening scenes together: 'You're Norma Desmond! You used to be in silent pictures. Used to be big.'

2 I hate that word. It's *return* – a return to the millions of people who've never forgiven me for deserting the screen.

Ibid. On her 'comeback'.

3 I just want to tell you all how happy I am to be back in the studio, making a picture again! You don't know much I've missed all of you. . . . You see, this is my life. It always will be! There's nothing else. Just us, and the cameras, and those wonderful people out there in the dark. All right, Mr De Mille. I'm ready for my closeup.

Ibid. Last lines of the film, spoken while descending staircase.

4 When I die, my epitaph should read: *She Paid the Bills.* That's the story of my private life.

Quoted in the *Saturday Evening Post* 22 July 1950

Graham Swift (b. 1949)
BRITISH AUTHOR
His novels and short stories concern ordinary characters at critical points of their lives and explore themes of memory, history and landscape. His most notable works are Waterland *(1983, filmed 1992),* Last Orders *(1996, filmed 2001) and* The Light of Day *(2003).*

1 I am struck by the way people behave on the Tube. They look at each other beadily and inquisitively, and something goes on in their thoughts which must be equivalent to the way dogs and other animals, when they meet, sniff each other's arses and nuzzle each other's fur.
Shuttlecock, ch. 3 (1981)

2 All nature's creatures join to express nature's purpose. Somewhere in their mounting and mating, rutting and butting is the very secret of nature itself.
Ibid., ch. 11

3 Life is one tenth Here and Now, nine-tenths a history lesson. For most of the time the Here and Now is neither now nor here.
Waterland, ch. 8 (1983)

4 People die when curiosity goes. People have to find out, people have to know. How can there be any true revolution till we know what we are made of?
Ibid., ch. 27

5 It's the best thing that's ever been invented. If it hadn't been invented we'd've had to invent it. And it aint just a seat on wheels. It's a workmate. It's a mate. It won't ask no questions, it won't tell no lies. It's somewhere you can be and be who you are. If you aint got no place to call your own, you're okay in a motor.
Narrator (Ray) on the car, in *Last Orders,* 'Vince' (1996)

6 Crying's like pissing. You don't want to get caught short.
Narrator (Ray), ibid., 'Rochester'

Meera Syal (b. 1963)
BRITISH ACTRESS AND AUTHOR
She has appeared on television in the comedy series The Real McCoy *(1991–3) and* Goodness Gracious Me *(1998–9). Her novels include* Life Isn't All Ha Ha Hee Hee *(1999).*

1 My Aunties did not rage against fate or England when they swapped misery tales, they put everything down to the will of Bhagwan, their karma, their just deserts inherited from their last reincarnation which they had to live through with grace and dignity. In the end, they knew God was on their side. I got the feeling that most of the Tollington women assumed that He had simply forgotten them.
Meena, in *Anita and Me,* ch. 3 (1996, filmed 2002)

2 We were born here. We haven't got another world that we carry around in our heads. We have to compete. We had to take on a lot of the battles that they couldn't or wouldn't engage in. We had to redefine the image they'd given of Indians as these ethereal, exotic people, clannish, never quite involved.
Interview in the *Guardian* 6 April 1996. Contrasting the experience of British-born Asians with the attitudes of her parents' generation.

Thomas Szasz (b. 1920)
HUNGARIAN-BORN US PSYCHIATRIST
His arguments that mental illness does not exist, that psychiatry is 'neither a science nor a healing art' and that psychiatrists act as social police are set out in The Myth of Mental Illness *(1961) and* The Manufacture of Madness *(1971).*

1 In the past, men created witches; now they create mental patients.
The Manufacture of Madness, Introduction (1971). 'Institutional psychiatry is a continuation of the Inquisition,' Szasz wrote. 'All that has really changed is the vocabulary and the social style.'

2 Permissiveness is the principle of treating children as if they were adults; and the tactic of making sure they never reach that stage.
The Second Sin, 'Social Relations' (1973)

3 A child becomes an adult when he realizes that he has a right not only to be right but also to be wrong.
Ibid., 'Childhood'

4 Masturbation: the primary sexual activity of mankind. In the nineteenth century, it was a disease; in the twentieth, it's a cure.
Ibid., 'Sex'

5 A teacher should have maximal authority, and minimal power.
Ibid., 'Education'

6 Happiness is an imaginary condition, formerly often attributed by the living to the dead, now usually attributed by adults to children, and by children to adults.
Ibid., 'Emotions'

7 The proverb warns that 'You should not bite the hand that feeds you.' But maybe you should, if it prevents you from feeding yourself.
Ibid., 'Control and Self-control'

8 People often say that this or that person has not yet found himself. But the self is

not something one finds; it is something one creates.

Ibid., 'Personal Conduct'

9 The stupid neither forgive nor forget; the naïve forgive and forget; the wise forgive but do not forget.

Ibid.

10 Adulthood is the ever-shrinking period between childhood and old age. It is the apparent aim of modern industrial societies to reduce this period to a minimum.

Ibid., 'Social Relations'

11 Two wrongs don't make a right, but they make a good excuse.

Ibid.

12 The greatest analgesic, soporific, stimulant, tranquilizer, narcotic, and to some extent even antibiotic – in short, the closest thing to a genuine panacea – known to medical science is work.

Ibid., 'Medicine'

13 He who does not accept and respect those who want to reject life does not truly accept and respect life itself.

Ibid., 'Suicide'

14 Psychoanalysis is an attempt to examine a person's self-justifications. Hence it can be undertaken only with the patient's cooperation and can succeed only when the patient has something to gain by abandoning or modifying his system of self-justification.

Ibid., 'Psychoanalysis'

15 Narcissist: psychoanalytic term for the person who loves himself more than his analyst; considered to be the manifestation of a dire mental disease whose successful treatment depends on the patient learning to love the analyst more and himself less.

Ibid.

16 Aided and abetted by corrupt analysts, patients who have nothing better to do with their lives often use the psychoanalytic situation to transform insignificant childhood hurts into private shrines at which they worship unceasingly the enormity of the offenses committed against them.

Ibid., 'Psychoanalysis'. Szasz continues: 'This solution is immensely flattering to the patients – as are all forms of unmerited self-aggrandizement; it is immensely profitable for the analysts – as are all forms pandering to people's vanity; and it is often immensely unpleasant for nearly everyone else in the patient's life.'

17 Doubt is to certainty as neurosis is to psychosis. The neurotic is in doubt and has fears about persons and things; the psychotic has convictions and makes claims about them. In short, the neurotic has problems, the psychotic has solutions.

Ibid., 'Mental Illness'

18 If you talk to God, you are praying; if God talks to you, you have schizophrenia. If the dead talk to you, you are a spiritualist; if God talks to you, you are a schizophrenic.

Ibid., 'Schizophrenia'

19 There is no psychology; there is only biography and autobiography.

Ibid., 'Psychology'

Katharine Tait (b. 1923)

The daughter of BERTRAND *and* DORA RUSSELL, *she worked in the Episcopalian church, and was the author of the memoir* My Father Bertrand Russell *(1975).*

1 Reason, progress, unselfishness, a wide historical perspective, expansiveness, generosity, enlightened self-interest. I had heard it all my life, and it filled me with despair.
   Quoted in *Bertrand Russell*, Afterword (1992) by Caroline Moorehead. Referring to the writings of BERTRAND RUSSELL.

Quentin Tarantino (b. 1963)

US FILM-MAKER

After a brief acting career, he made his debut as a director with Reservoir Dogs *(1992), controversial for its violence and savage, ironic humour. Other films include* Pulp Fiction *(1994), and he wrote the screenplays for* True Romance *and* Natural Born Killers *(both 1995).*

1 Somebody's stickin' a red hot poker up our asses and we gotta find out whose name is on the handle.
   Mr Pink (Steve Buscemi), in *Reservoir Dogs* (film, 1992, written and directed by Quentin Tarantino)

2 Why am I Mr Pink? . . . Why can't we pick our own color? . . . Mr Pink sounds like Mr Pussy. Tell you what, let me be Mr Purple. That sounds good to me.
   Ibid. Mr Pink argues over the choice of alias in the run-up to the heist. Tarantino's character also objects: 'Mr Brown, that's a little too close to Mr Shit.'

3 Let's go to work.
   Joe Cabot (Lawrence Tierney), ibid. The words featured in the film's publicity.

4 I don't really give a fuck what you know or don't know, but I'm going to torture you anyway, regardless.
   Mr Blonde (Michael Madsen), ibid. Addressed to a captured policeman, whose ear he is about to slice off.

5 The worst thing about movies is, no matter how far you can go, when it comes to violence you are wearing a pair of handcuffs that novelists . . . don't wear.
   Interview May 1993, quoted in *Reservoir Dogs*, Introduction (screenplay, 1995)

6 I'm gonna git medieval on your ass.
   Marsellus Wallace (Ving Rhames), in *Pulp Fiction* (film, 1994, written and directed by Quentin Tarantino). Speaking to Zed as he prepares to sodomize him.

7 Zed's dead, baby, Zed's dead.
   Butch Coolidge (Bruce Willis), ibid.

8 I steal from every single movie ever made. I love it – if my work has anything it's that I'm taking this from this and that from

that and mixing them together. If people don't like that, then tough titty, don't go and see it, all right? I steal from everything. Great artists steal, they don't do homages.

Interview in *Empire* November 1994

9 The minute any word has that much power, everyone on the planet should scream it.

Quoted in *Quentin Tarantino: The Man and His Movies*, ch. 11 (1995) by Jami Bernard. On the frequent use of the word 'nigger' in the script of *Pulp Fiction*.

10 Everybody thought I'd gone crazy . . . I wasn't crazy. But when I was holding the shotgun, it all became clear. I realized for the first time my one true calling in life. I'm a natural born killer.

Mickey Knox (Woody Harrelson), in *Natural Born Killers* (film, 1995, screenplay by Quentin Tarantino, directed by OLIVER STONE). In a dispute with Stone, Tarantino later disowned the film.

11 Killing you and what you represent is a statement. I'm not exactly sure what it's saying.

Mickey Knox (Woody Harrelson) to a TV show host, ibid. During their interview earlier from prison, Mickey explains: 'It's just murder. All creatures and species do it. I know a lot of people who deserve to die. That's where I come in, fate's messenger.'

Booth Tarkington (1869–1946)
US AUTHOR

He was a prolific and popular writer on childhood and adolescence in Penrod *(1914),* Seventeen *(1917) and numerous plays, but received most plaudits for such novels as* The Magnificent Ambersons *(1918, filmed 1942).*

1 There are two things that will be believed of any man whatsoever, and one of them is that he has taken to drink.

Penrod, ch. 10 (1914)

2 An ideal wife is any woman who has an ideal husband.

Gallup, in 'The Hopeful Pessimist', publ. in *Looking Forward & Others* (1926)

Andrey Tarkovsky (1932–86)
RUSSIAN FILM-MAKER

His films combine an epic style and spirituality, most notably in Andrei Rublev *(1966), which was initially banned in the USSR, the science fiction* Solaris *(1972), and* The Sacrifice *(1986), made two years after he had defected to Italy. 'My purpose', he said, 'is to make films that will help people to live, even if they sometimes cause unhappiness.'*

1 Of course life has no point. If it had man would not be free, he'd become a slave to that point and his life would be governed

by completely new criteria: the criteria of slavery.

Journal entry, 5 September 1970, publ. in *Time Within Time: The Diaries 1970–1986* (1989)

2 Talent is not given to man by God; rather man is doomed to carry the cross of talent. For the artist is a being who strives (but not in secret or in hiding, nor moving in circles, nor in the spaciousness of some kind of ecological niche) to master ultimate truth. The artist masters that truth every time he creates something perfect, something whole.

Ibid., 5 December 1973

3 Time is such a simple, almost primitive idea. It is just a means of material differentiation, a way of uniting us all; for in our external, material lives we value the synchronized efforts of individual people.

Ibid., 12 December 1979

4 A person fulfils his duty to society in the name of an idea, always doing violence to someone or something.

Ibid., 22 January 1981

5 Perhaps I am an agnostic, in the sense that I reject everything that humanity presents as new to the world, on the grounds that the methods used were inappropriate. The formula $E = mc^2$ cannot be right, because there can be no such thing as positive knowledge.

Ibid., 15 July 1981

Jeffrey Tate (b. 1943)
BRITISH CONDUCTOR

He was Principal Conductor of the Royal Opera House, Covent Garden (1986–91) and Chief Conductor of the Rotterdam Philharmonic Orchestra (1991–5).

1 The most perfect expression of human behaviour is a string quartet.

New Yorker 30 April 1990

A. J. P. Taylor (1906–90)
BRITISH HISTORIAN

Alan John Percivale Taylor. Likened to Macaulay for his breadth and accessibility, he was an authority on the Habsburg monarchy and on Bismarck. His major works include The Struggle for Mastery in Europe, 1848–1918 *(1954) and* The Origins of the Second World War *(1961).*

1 There is nothing more agreeable in life than to make peace with the Establishment – and nothing more corrupting.

New Statesman 29 August 1953

2 We are apt to say that a foreign policy is successful only when the country, or at any rate the governing class, is united behind it. In reality, every line of policy is repudi-

ated by a section, often by an influential section, of the country concerned.

The Trouble Makers, ch. 1 (1957)

3 The crusade against Communism was even more imaginary than the spectre of Communism.

The Origins of the Second World War, ch. 2 (1961)

4 He aspired to power instead of influence, and as a result forfeited both.

English History, 1914–1945, ch. 1 (1965). Referring to the press magnate Lord Northcliffe, who was accused of making *The Times* and his other newspapers mouthpieces for his political ambitions.

5 Perfect soldier, perfect gentleman . . . never gave offence to anyone not even the enemy.

Of Field Marshal Alexander, in letter, 16 March 1973, publ. in *Letters to Eva* (ed. Eva Haraszti Taylor, 1991)

6 In my opinion, most of the great men of the past were only there for the beer – the wealth, prestige and grandeur that went with the power.

Quoted in *Voices 1870–1914*, Introduction (1984) by Peter Vansittart (see ADVERTISING SLOGANS 12)

Bert Leston Taylor (1866–1921)

US HUMORIST AND COLUMNIST

From 1900 he worked for the Chicago Tribune, *where his column 'A Line-o'-Type or Two' appeared for twenty years. His books include* A Line-o-Verse or Two *(1911) and* The So-Called Human Race *(1922).*

1 A bore is a man who, when you ask him how he is, tells you.

The So-Called Human Race (1922)

2 All we can get out of a Shaw play is two hours and a half of mental exhilaration. We are, inscrutably, denied the pleasure of wondering what Shaw means, or whether he is sincere.

Ibid.

D. J. Taylor (b. 1960)

BRITISH AUTHOR

David John Taylor. His works on English literature include After the War: The Novel and English Society since 1945 *(1993), and he has also written the novel* English Settlement *(1996) and the biography* Thackeray *(1999).*

1 Always in England if you had the type of brain that was capable of understanding T. S. Eliot's poetry or Kant's logic, you could be sure of finding large numbers of people who would hate you violently.

Guardian 14 September 1989

Derek Taylor (1934–97)

BRITISH JOURNALIST

A journalist in Liverpool and London, he became known as 'the Beatles man' for his enthusiasm for and connections with what he called 'the gay quartet of grammar-school boys'. He became press officer at Apple Corps in 1968, and remained close to the ex-Beatles after he left in 1970.

1 A poached egg on the Underground on the Bakerloo Line between Trafalgar Square and Charing Cross? Yes, Paul. A sock full of elephant shit on Otterspool Promenade? Give me 10 minutes, Ringo. Two Turkish dwarfs dancing the Charleston on a sideboard? Male or female, John? Pubic hair from Sonny Liston? It's early closing, George (gulp), but give me until noon tomorrow. The only gig I would do after this is the Queen. Their staff are terrified of them, and not without reason. They have fired more people than any comparable employer unit in the world. They make Lord Beaverbrook look like Jesus.

On working for the Beatles, quoted in *Shout! The True Story of the Beatles*, pt. 4, 'May 1970' (1981) by Philip Norman

Norman Tebbit (b. 1931)

BRITISH POLITICIAN

Baron Tebbit of Chingford. Elected a Conservative MP in 1970, he was labelled 'the Chingford skinhead' for his confrontational style, and according to MP Austin Mitchell possessed 'a nasty instinct for the exposed groin'. After holding Cabinet posts in employment and in trade and industry, he was Party Chairman 1985–7. A loyal Thatcherite, he was the architect of anti-trade union and privatization legislation. See MICHAEL FOOT 1.

1 He didn't riot. He got on his bike and looked for work.

Speech to Conservative Party Conference, Blackpool, 15 October 1981, quoted in the *Daily Telegraph* 16 October 1981. Tebbit's speech, which contrasted his unemployed father's self-help approach during the Depression with the attitude of rioters in Britain, was given a rousing ovation by the conference but drew criticism elsewhere in the country at a time when unemployment stood at three million.

2 It is certainly safe, in view of the movement to the right of intellectuals and political thinkers, to pronounce the brain death of socialism.

The Times 26 April 1988

3 Gradually it was becoming clear that she [Margaret Thatcher] was a Prime Minister unlike any since Churchill. Nonetheless, the 'wets', the weaker willed, the cravenhearted and the embittered failures amongst the Conservative Party still hoped

she would go away and let them go back to their old ways.

Upwardly Mobile, ch. 8 (memoirs, 1988). On MARGARET THATCHER's record by the summer of 1981.

4 The word 'conservative' is used by the BBC as a portmanteau word of abuse for anyone whose views differ from the insufferable, smug, sanctimonious, naive, guilt-ridden, wet, pink orthodoxy of that sunset home of the third-rate minds of that third-rate decade, the nineteen-sixties.

Quoted in the *Independent* 24 February 1990. In his memoirs, Tebbit lambasted the BBC for its coverage of the Falklands War: 'For me the British Broadcasting Corporation might have better called itself the Stateless Persons Broadcasting Corporation for it certainly did not reflect the mood of the British people who finance it' (ch. 8).

5 Parliament must not be told a direct untruth, but it's quite possible to allow them to mislead themselves.

Quoted in the *Observer* 17 March 1991

Shirley Temple (b. 1928)

US ACTRESS

Shirley Temple Black. The most successful child star of the 1930s, she starred in Bright Eyes *(1934), in which she sang 'On the Good Ship Lollipop', and* Curly Top *(1935). She later became involved in Republican politics and served as US ambassador to Czechoslovakia 1989–93.*

1 I stopped believing in Santa Claus when I was six. Mother took me to see him in a department store and he asked for my autograph.

Quoted in *Halliwell's Who's Who in the Movies* (ed. John Walker, 1999)

Mother Teresa (1910–97)

ALBANIAN-BORN ROMAN CATHOLIC MISSIONARY

Originally Agnes Gonxha Bojaxhin. In India since 1928, and an Indian citizen since 1949, she devoted her life to alleviating the plight of Calcutta's slum-dwellers. She founded the Congregation of the Missionaries of Charity in 1950, and by the time of her death had extended her 'missionary multi-national' to 87 countries and 160 cities. See MARK TULLY 2.

1 The biggest disease today is not leprosy or tuberculosis, but rather the feeling of being unwanted.

Quoted in the *Observer* 3 October 1971

2 To keep a lamp burning we have to keep putting oil in it.

Quoted in *Time* 29 December 1975

3 Our life of poverty is as necessary as the work itself. Only in heaven will we see how much we owe to the poor for helping us to love God better because of them.

A Gift for God, 'Carriers of Christ's Love' (1975)

4 We ourselves feel that what we are doing is just a drop in the ocean. But if that drop was not in the ocean, I think the ocean would be less because of that missing drop. I do not agree with the big way of doing things.

Ibid.

5 There must be a reason why some people can afford to live well. They must have worked for it. I only feel angry when I see waste. When I see people throwing away things that we could use.

Ibid., 'Riches'

6 I try to give to the poor people for love what the rich could get for money. No, I wouldn't touch a leper for a thousand pounds; yet I willingly cure him for the love of God.

Ibid.

7 We must have a real living determination to reach holiness. 'I will be a saint' means I will despoil myself of all that is not God; I will strip my heart of all created things; I will live in poverty and detachment; I will renounce my will, my inclinations, my whims and fancies, and make myself a willing slave to the will of God.

Ibid., 'Willing Slaves to the Will of God'

8 Many people mistake our work for our vocation. Our vocation is the love of Jesus.

From documentary film *Mother Teresa*, quoted in *The New York Times* 28 November 1986

9 So many signatures for such a small heart.

Quoted in the *Evening Standard* 3 January 1992. Referring to form-filling in a California hospital.

Studs Terkel (b. 1912)

US AUTHOR AND BROADCASTER

Called 'a national resource' by J. K. GALBRAITH, *he acted in radio soap operas and worked as a disc jockey, sports commentator and TV compère before establishing himself as a recorder of oral history. His books include* The Good War *(1984) and* Coming of Age *(1995).*

1 Something was still there, that something that distinguishes an artist from a performer: the revealing of self. Here I be. Not for long, but here I be. In sensing her mortality, we sensed our own.

Talking to Myself, bk. 4, ch. 4 (1977). On seeing BILLIE HOLIDAY perform in Chicago, 1956.

2 At a time when pimpery, lick-spittlery, and picking the public's pocket are the order of the day – indeed, officially proclaimed as virtue – the poet must play the madcap to keep his balance. And ours.

Ibid.

Mary Church Terrell (1863–1954)
US CIVIL RIGHTS ACTIVIST
Co-founder and first president of the National Association of Colored Women in 1896, she lectured against discrimination, disenfranchisement and racial violence throughout the USA.

1 Please stop using the word 'Negro'. . . . We are the only human beings in the world with fifty-seven variety of complexions who are classed together as a single racial unit. Therefore, we are really truly colored people, and that is the only name in the English language which accurately describes us.
   Letter to the editor, in the *Washington Post* 14 May 1949

Quinlan Terry (b. 1937)
BRITISH ARCHITECT
Considered one of Britain's leading exponents of neo-classical architecture, he has questioned modernist orthodoxy in The Revival of Architecture *(1986), among other works.*

1 I don't think we can ignore the Modern Movement. But I wouldn't have minded at all if it hadn't happened. I think the world would be a much nicer place.
   International Herald Tribune 25 April 1988

Margaret Thatcher (b. 1925)
BRITISH POLITICIAN AND PRIME MINISTER
Baroness Thatcher of Kesteven. Called 'the best man in England' by RONALD REAGAN, *she became Conservative Party leader in 1975 and Britain's first woman prime minister in 1979. She oversaw a transformation of large areas of society, and was eventually forced out of office in 1990 on the issue of Europe. See* KINGSLEY AMIS 10, ALAN BENNETT 4, JULIAN CRITCHLEY 2, NORMAN FOWLER 1, DENIS HEALEY 4, NEIL KINNOCK 1, NORMAN TEBBIT 3.

1 No woman in my time will be Prime Minister or Chancellor or Foreign Secretary – not the top jobs. Anyway I wouldn't want to be Prime Minister. You have to give yourself 100%.
   Interview in the *Sunday Telegraph* 26 October 1969. Mrs Thatcher was then Shadow Education Spokesman.

2 Most of us have stopped using silver for everyday.
   Quoted in the *Observer* 2 August 1970

3 One of the things being in politics has taught me is that men are not a reasoned or reasonable sex.
   Interview on BBC radio, 14 January 1972.

4 I owe nothing to Women's Lib.
   Quoted in the *Observer* 1 December 1974

5 We must have an ideology. The other side have got an ideology they can test their policies against. We must have one as well.
   Speech to the Conservative Philosophy Group, 1975, quoted in *One of Us*, ch. 18 (1989) by Hugo Young. The speech was made shortly after Thatcher was elected Conservative Party leader in February.

6 In politics if you want anything said, ask a man. If you want anything done, ask a woman.
   People 15 September 1975

7 When the next Conservative government comes to power, many trade unionists will have put it there. Millions of them vote for us at every election. I want to say this to them and to all our supporters in industry: go out and join in the work of your unions; go to their meetings and stay to the end, and learn the union rules as well as the far Left knows them. Remember that if parliamentary democracy dies, free trades unions die with it.
   Speech to Conservative Party Conference, Blackpool, 10 October 1975, publ. in *The Revival of Britain; Speeches on Home and European Affairs 1975–1988* (ed. Alistair B. Cooke, 1989)

8 Ladies and gentlemen, I stand before you tonight in my red chiffon evening gown, my face softly made up, my fair hair gently waved . . . the Iron Lady of the Western World! Me? A cold war warrior? Well, yes – if that is how they wish to interpret my defence of values and freedoms fundamental to our way of life.
   Speech at Finchley, 31 January 1976, quoted in the *Sunday Times* 1 February 1976. A week earlier, an article in the Soviet newspaper *Red Star* had branded Mrs Thatcher an 'Iron Lady'.

9 We have to get our production and our earnings into balance. There's no easy popularity in what we are proposing, but it is fundamentally sound. Yet I believe people accept there is no real alternative.
   Speech at Conservative Women's Conference, 21 May 1980, quoted in the *Daily Telegraph* 22 May 1980. Thatcher's repetition of the formula 'There is no alternative' led to her being given the acronym 'Tina'.

10 To those waiting with bated breath for that favourite media catch-phrase, the U-turn, I have only this to say. You turn, if you want; the lady's not for turning.
   Speech to the Conservative Party Conference, Brighton, 10 October 1980, publ. in *The Times* 11 October 1980. On her determination to persist in monetarist policies. The punning reference is to the play by CHRISTOPHER FRY, *The Lady's Not for Burning* (1946).

11 Just rejoice at that news and congratulate our forces and the marines.
   Quoted in *The Times* 26 April 1982. Said to

journalists on the recapture of South Georgia during the Falklands conflict, 25 April 1982, and usually remembered as 'Rejoice, rejoice . . .'

12 **When you've spent half your political life dealing with humdrum issues like the environment, it's exciting to have a real crisis on your hands.**

On the Falklands campaign, in speech to Scottish Conservative Party Conference, 14 May 1982, quoted in *One of Us*, ch. 13 (1989) by Hugo Young

13 **We have to see that the spirit of the South Atlantic – the real spirit of Britain – is kindled not only by war but can now be fired by peace. We have the first prerequisite. We know we can do it – we haven't lost the ability. That is the Falklands Factor. We have proved ourselves to ourselves. It is a lesson we must not now forget.**

Speech to Conservative women, Cheltenham, 3 July 1982, publ. in *The Penguin Book of Twentieth-Century Speeches* (ed. Brian MacArthur, 1999). The 'Falklands Factor' was widely seen as crucial in securing the Conservative Party's election win in 1983.

14 **I am extraordinarily patient provided I get my own way in the end.**

Quoted in the *Observer* 2 January 1983

15 **It was then that the iron entered my soul.**

On her time in EDWARD HEATH's cabinet, quoted in the *Observer* 27 March 1983. Thatcher and Heath were to become irreconcilable political opponents.

16 **I was asked whether I was trying to restore Victorian values. I said straight out I was. And I am.**

Speech to British Jewish Community, 21 July 1983, quoted in *Thatcher's Reign*, 'Let Our Children Grow Tall – the Family' (1984) by Melanie McFadyean and Margaret Renn. Referring to interview by Brian Walden on 'Weekend World' 17 January 1983, when she stated that Victorian values 'were the values when our country became great. . . . As our people prospered, so they used their independence and initiative to prosper others, not compulsion by the state.'

17 **We can do business together.**

Of MIKHAIL GORBACHEV, quoted in *The Times* 18 December 1984. After a meeting at which Gorbachev had declared Soviet willingness to discuss nuclear arms reductions. He became First Secretary of the Soviet Communist Party three months later.

18 **We must try to find ways to starve the terrorist and the hijacker of the oxygen of publicity on which they depend.**

Speech to American Bar Association, London, 15 July 1985, quoted in *The Times* 16 July 1985

19 **No one would remember the Good Samaritan if he'd only had good intentions – he had money as well.**

Television interview, 6 January 1986, quoted in *The Times* 12 January 1986

20 **I hope to go on and on.**

Television interview, 11 May 1987, quoted in the *Independent* 12 May 1987

21 **There is no such thing as society: there are individual men and women, and there are families.**

Interview in *Woman's Own* 31 October 1987

22 **We have not successfully rolled back the frontiers of the State in Britain only to see them reimposed at a European level, with a European super-State exercising a new dominance from Brussels.**

'The Bruges Speech', 20 September 1988, publ. in *The Penguin Book of Twentieth-Century Speeches* (ed. Brian MacArthur, 1999). The speech was drafted by Sir Charles Powell, Thatcher's adviser on foreign affairs.

23 **People think that at the top there isn't much room. They tend to think of it as an Everest. My message is that there is tons of room at the top.**

Daily Telegraph 30 September 1988. Thatcher's words recall those attributed to Daniel Webster c. 1801, rejecting advice that he stay out of the crowded legal profession: 'There is always room at the top.'

24 **We have become a grandmother.**

Quoted in *The Times* 4 March 1989

25 **The cocks may crow, but it's the hen that lays the egg.**

Quoted in the *Sunday Times* 9 April 1989

26 **Most women defend themselves. It is the female of the species – it is the tigress and lioness in you – which tends to defend when attacked.**

Daily Mail 4 May 1989

27 **I think perhaps we manage our revolutions much more quietly in this country.**

Daily Telegraph 12 July 1989. Said in the wake of the bicentenary celebrations of the French revolution in Paris.

28 **If it is once again one against forty-eight, then I am very sorry for the forty-eight.**

Quoted in the *Daily Telegraph* 25 October 1989. Referring to the pending 1989 Commonwealth Conference.

29 **I am in favour of agreement but against consensus.**

Quoted in *One of Us*, ch. 18 (1989) by Hugo Young. On one occasion Thatcher had the word 'consensus' removed from a Commonwealth conference communiqué in favour of 'agreement'. 'To me, consensus seems to be the process of abandoning all beliefs, principles, values and policies,' she explained. 'So it is something in which no one believes and to which no one objects.'

30 I am in politics because of the conflict between good and evil, and I believe that in the end good will triumph.

Quoted in the *Guardian* 23 October 1990

31 The President of the Commission, M. Delors, said at this conference the other day that he wanted the European Parliament to be the democratic body of the Community, he wanted the Commission to be the Executive, and he wanted the Council of Ministers to be the Senate. No. No. No.

Speech to House of Commons, 30 October 1990, publ. in *Hansard*. Referring to talks at the EU summit in Rome.

32 I seem to smell the stench of appeasement in the air.

On the Gulf crisis, quoted in the *Independent* 31 October 1990

33 I shan't be pulling the levers there but I shall be a very good back-seat driver.

Quoted in the *Independent* 27 November 1990. On the appointment of JOHN MAJOR as the next prime minister.

34 Home is where you come to when you have nothing better to do.

Interview in *Vanity Fair* June 1991

35 The lesson of the century has been that the people feel far more comfortable and more stable with a nation state. It is the nation state which is the unit of loyalty. Ours is the United Kingdom.

Sunday Telegraph 13 December 1992

36 Idleness, selfishness, fecklessness, envy and irresponsibility are the vices upon which socialism in any form flourishes and which it in turn encourages. But socialism's devilishly clever tactic is to play up to all those human failings, while making those who practise them feel good about it.

Nicholas Ridley Memorial Lecture, 22 August 1996, publ. in *Margaret Thatcher: The Collected Speeches* (ed. Robin Harris, 1997)

37 In my lifetime Europe has been the source of our problems, not the source of our solutions. It's America and Britain that saved the world.

Interview in *Saga Magazine* September 1998. Thatcher repeated the assertion at the following year's Conservative Party Conference: 'In my lifetime all our problems have come from mainland Europe, and the solutions have come from the English-speaking nations of the world' (*The Times* 9 October 1999).

38 Is he one of us?

Attributed, referring to candidates for office. The words gave Hugo Young the title for his biography of Thatcher, *One of Us* (1989).

Paul Theroux (b. 1941)

US NOVELIST AND TRAVEL WRITER

He has written extensively of the expatriate experience, as in his novels Jungle Lovers *(1971) and* The Mosquito Coast *(1981, filmed 1986), and of railway journeys, notably* The Great Railway Bazaar *(1975).*

1 The expatriate does not have to think; he has long since decided that nothing should change, the jungle should not alter. In Africa he is superior and should remain so. Most agree with him; all the people he works with agree with him; Africans with money and position are the most convinced of all that change means upsetting the nature of society.

'Tarzan Is an Expatriate' (1967), repr. in *Sunrise with Seamonsters* (1985)

2 I have seldom heard a train go by and not wished I was on it. Those whistles sing bewitchment: railways are irresistible bazaars, snaking along perfectly level no matter what the landscape, improving your mood with speed, and never upsetting your drink.

The Great Railway Bazaar, ch. 1 (1975)

3 Extensive traveling induces a feeling of encapsulation, and travel, so broadening at first, contracts the mind.

Ibid., ch. 21

4 The difference between travel writing and fiction is the difference between recording what the eye sees and discovering what the imagination knows.

Ibid., ch. 30

5 What interests me is the waking in the morning, the progress from the familiar to the slightly odd, to the rather strange, to the totally foreign, and finally to the outlandish. The journey, not the arrival, matters; the voyage, not the landing.

The Old Patagonian Express, ch. 1 (1979)

6 Travel is glamorous only in retrospect.

Quoted in the *Observer* 7 October 1979

7 People do not become writers out of healthy literary impulse, but out of a deep loneliness, a deficiency, a kind of dysfunction . . . and on the positive side, they turn to books for solace. It's all sorts of things. It's conceit. It's signalling for attention. People who are normal don't become writers.

Interview in the *Guardian* 11 November 1995

8 The notion of a literary quarrel – or anything that looks like a quarrel – is like catnip to literary philistines and lazy intellects.

Daily Telegraph 21 November 1998. Referring to the end of his friendship with V. S. NAIPAUL, as related in Theroux's book *Sir Vidia's Shadow* (1998)

9 **The man who is tired of London is tired of looking for a parking space.**

Interview in the *Daily Telegraph* 30 November 1998. A twist on Dr Johnson's saying 'When a man is tired of London, he is tired of life' (in Boswell's *Life*, 1791). Theroux, who moved to Hawaii after years in London, made a similar observation in *The Kingdom by the Sea*, ch. 1 (1983).

Dylan Thomas (1914–53)
WELSH POET

He published 18 Poems in 1934 and gained further recognition with Deaths and Entrances (1946). He narrated his 'play for voices', Under Milk Wood, on radio in New York shortly before his death from alcohol poisoning. 'I am in the path of Blake,' he declared, 'but so far behind that only the wings of his heels are in sight.'

1 *Never be lucid, never state,*
If you would be regarded great,
The simplest thought or sentiment
(For thought, we know, is decadent).
'A Letter to My Aunt Discussing the Correct Approach to Modern Poetry', written 1933, publ. in *The Poems* (ed. Daniel Jones, 1971)

2 *The force that through the green fuse drives the flower*
Drives my green age; that blasts the roots of trees
Is my destroyer.
'The Force that through the Green Fuse Drives the Flower', publ. in the *Sunday Referee* 29 October 1933, repr. in *18 Poems* (1934)

3 *The hand that signed the treaty bred a fever,*
And famine grew, and locusts came;
Great is the hand that holds dominion over Man by a scribbled name.
'The Hand That Signed the Paper Felled a City', publ. in *New Verse* December 1935, repr. in *25 Poems* (1936)

4 *Though lovers be lost love shall not;*
And death shall have no dominion.
'And Death Shall Have No Dominion', publ. in *25 Poems* (1936). St Paul used these words in Romans 6:9: 'Christ being raised from the dead dieth no more; death hath no more dominion over him.' An earlier version of Thomas's poem was published in the *New English Weekly* 18 May 1933, the first of his poems to be accepted by a London literary magazine.

5 I know we're not saints or virgins or lunatics; we know all the lust and lavatory jokes, and most of the dirty people; we can catch buses and count our change and cross the roads and talk real sentences. But our innocence goes awfully deep, and our discreditable secret is that we don't know anything at all, and our horrid inner secret is that we don't care that we don't.

Letter to Caitlin Macnamara, later his wife, end of 1936, publ. in *The Collected Letters of Dylan Thomas* (ed. Paul Ferris, 1985)

6 *The hunchback in the park*
A solitary mister
Propped between trees and water.
'The hunchback in the park', publ. in *Life and Letters Today* October 1941, repr. in *New Poems 1942* (1942)

7 A poet writing a poem is at peace with everything except words, which are eternal actions; only in the lulls between the warring work on words can he be at war with men.

Letter, 30 July 1945, publ. in *The Collected Letters of Dylan Thomas* (ed. Paul Ferris, 1985)

8 *Deep with the first dead lies London's daughter,*
Robed in the long friends,
The grains beyond age, the dark veins of her mother,
Secret by the unmourning water
Of the riding Thames.
After the first death, there is no other.
'A Refusal to Mourn the Death, by Fire, of a Child in London', publ. in *Horizon* October 1945, repr. in *Deaths and Entrances* (1946)

9 *In my craft or sullen art*
Exercised in the still night
When only the moon rages
And the lovers lie abed
With all their griefs in their arms,
I labour by singing light.
'In my craft or sullen art', publ. ibid.

10 *Now as I was young and easy under the apple boughs*
About the lilting house and happy as the grass was green.
'Fern Hill', publ. ibid.

11 *Do not go gentle into that good night,*
Old age should burn and rage at close of day;
Rage, rage, against the dying of the light.
'Do not go gentle into that good night', publ. in *Botteghe Oscure* November 1951, repr. in *Collected Poems* (1952)

12 **These poems, with all their crudities, doubts, and confusions, are written for the love of Man and in praise of God, and I'd be a damn' fool if they weren't.**
Collected Poems, 'Author's note' (1952)

13 **The land of my fathers. My fathers can have it.**
Referring to Wales, in *Adam* December 1953. 'Land of my Fathers' is the Welsh national anthem.

14 **Too many of the artists of Wales spend too much time talking about the position of**

the artists of Wales. There is only one position for an artist anywhere: and that is, upright.

Quite Early One Morning, 'Wales and the Artist' (1954)

15 To begin at the beginning: It is spring, moonless night in the small town, starless and bible-black, the cobblestreets silent and the hunched courters'-and-rabbits' wood limping invisible down to the sloe-black, slow, black, crowblack, fishingboat-bobbing sea.

Under Milk Wood (1954). Opening words.

16 I must put my pyjamas in the drawer marked pyjamas.

Mr Ogmore, ibid.

17 And before you let the sun in, mind it wipes its shoes.

Mrs Ogmore-Pritchard, ibid. The same character utters an almost identical line in an untitled poem in *Quite Early One Morning* (1954), which included earlier versions of *Under Milk Wood*.

18 Oh, I'm a martyr to music.

Mrs Organ Morgan, ibid.

19 You just wait. I'll sin till I blow up!

Mae Rose Cottage, ibid.

20 *We are not wholly bad or good*
Who live our lives under Milk Wood.

First Voice, ibid.

21 I've had eighteen straight whiskies. I think that's the record.

Quoted in *Dylan Thomas in America*, ch. 8 (1956) by John Malcolm Brinnin. On the day after he spoke these words in a New York hotel, Thomas fell into a coma from which he never recovered.

22 [An alcoholic is] a man you don't like who drinks as much as you do.

Quoted in *The Life of Dylan Thomas*, ch. 6 (1965) by Constantine Fitzgibbon

Edward Thomas (1878–1917)
BRITISH POET AND AUTHOR
Originally Edward Eastaway. He was encouraged by ROBERT FROST *to write poetry in 1914. Most of his verse was published in* Poems (1917) *and* Last Poems (1918) *after his death at the battle of Arras.*

1 *The past is the only dead thing that smells sweet.*

'Early One Morning', publ. in *Poems* (1917)

2 *The steam hissed. Someone cleared his throat.*
No one left and no one came
On the bare platform. What I saw
Was Adlestrop – only the name.

'Adlestrop', publ. ibid.

3 *There's none less free than who*
Does nothing and has nothing else to do,

Being free only for what is not to his mind,
And nothing is to his mind.

'Liberty', publ. ibid.

4 *I have come to the borders of sleep,*
The unfathomable deep
Forest where all must lose
Their way, however straight,
Or winding, soon or late;
They cannot choose.

'Lights Out', publ. ibid.

5 *As for myself,*
Where first I met the bitter scent is lost.
I, too, often shrivel the grey shreds,
Sniff them and think and sniff again and try
Once more to think what it is I am remembering,
Always in vain. I cannot like the scent,
Yet I would gather up others more sweet,
With no meaning, than this bitter one.

'Old Man', publ. in *Last Poems* (1918)

6 *This is no case of petty right or wrong*
That politicians or philosophers
Can judge. I hate not Germans, nor grow hot
With love of Englishmen, to please newspapers.
Beside my hate for one fat patriot
My hatred of the Kaiser is love true.

'This is no case of petty right or wrong', publ. ibid. Opening lines.

Lewis Thomas (1913–93)
US PHYSICIAN AND ACADEMIC
He found a wide readership for his reflections on biology and medicine, published in The Lives of a Cell (1974), The Medusa and the Snail (1979) *and* The Fragile Species (1992).

1 It hurts the spirit, somehow, to read the word *environments*, when the plural means that there are so many alternatives there to be sorted through, as in a market, and voted on.

The Lives of a Cell, 'Natural Man' (1974)

2 We are designed, coded, it seems, to place the highest priority on being individuals, and we must do this first, at whatever cost, even if it means disability for the group.

The Medusa and the Snail, 'On Committees' (1979)

3 We are built to make mistakes, coded for error.

Ibid. 'To Err is Human'

4 Sometimes you get a glimpse of a semicolon coming, a few lines farther on, and it is like climbing a steep path through woods and seeing a wooden bench just at a bend in the road ahead, a place where you

can expect to sit for a moment, catching your breath.
Ibid. 'Notes on Punctuation'

5 If you want to use a cliché you must take full responsibility for it yourself and not try to job it off on anon., or on society.
Ibid.

6 Music is the effort we make to explain to ourselves how our brains work. We listen to Bach transfixed because this is listening to a human mind.
Ibid., 'On Thinking About Thinking'

R. S. Thomas (1913–2000)
WELSH POET AND CLERGYMAN
Ronald Stuart Thomas. For poet Anne Stevenson, he was 'a religious poet who sees the tragedy, not the pathos, in the human condition'. A self-taught Welsh speaker and committed Welsh nationalist, he was ordained an Anglican vicar in 1936. His poems describe the Welsh landscape and those who dwell there, as in The Stones of the Field *(1946) and* Song at the Year's Turning *(1955).*

1 There is no present in Wales,
  And no future;
  There is only the past,
  Brittle with relics,
  Wind-bitten towers and castles
  With sham ghosts;
  Mouldering quarries and mines;
  And an impotent people,
  Sick with inbreeding,
  Worrying the carcase of an old song.
'Welsh Landscape', publ. in *An Acre of Land* (1952). Closing lines.

2 They chose their pastors as they chose their horses
  For hard work.
Narrator, in *The Minister* (1953), repr. in *Song at the Year's Turning* (1955)

3 There is always the thin pane of glass set up between us
  And our desires.
  We stare and stare and stare, until the night comes
  And the glass is superfluous.
The minister, ibid.

4 The pulpit is a kind of block-house
  From which to fire the random shot
  Of innuendo; but woe betide the man
  Who leaves the pulpit for the individual Assault.
The minister, ibid.

5 Stay, then, village, for round you spins
  On slow axis a world as vast
  And meaningful as any posed
  By great Plato's solitary mind.
'The Village', publ. in *Song at the Year's Turning* (1955)

6 There stood the ladies from the council houses:
  Blue eyes and Birmingham yellow
  Hair, and the ritual murder of vowels.
'Border Blues', publ. in *Poetry for Supper* (1958)

7 But what to do? Doctors in verse
  Being scarce now, most poets
  Are their own patients, compelled to treat
  Themselves first, their complaint being
  Peculiar always.
'The Cure', publ. ibid. Opening lines.

8 Sunlight's a thing that needs a window
  Before it enters a dark room.
  Windows don't happen.
'Poetry for Supper', publ. ibid.

9 Live large, man, and dream small.
'Lore', publ. in *Tares* (1961)

10 It was the mind's weight
   Kept me bent, as I grew tall.
'Sorry', publ. in *The Bread of Truth* (1963)

11 Those who crowd
   A small window dirty it
   With their breathing, though sublime
   And inexhaustible the view.
'The Small Window', publ. in *Not That He Brought Flowers* (1968)

12 I never thought other than
   That God is that great absence
   In our lives, the empty silence
   Within, the place where we go
   Seeking, not in hope to
   Arrive or find.
'Via Negativa', publ. in *H'm* (1972)

Hunter S. Thompson (b. 1939)
US JOURNALIST
Hunter Stockton Thompson. A 'New Journalist' of the 1960s, he invented the 'gonzo' genre of reporting, offering highly subjective accounts of the world with himself as protagonist. His books, including Hell's Angels *(1966) and* Fear and Loathing in Las Vegas *(1972, filmed 1998), were searing but witty indictments of American society.*

1 Richard Nixon has never been one of my favourite people, anyway. For years I've regarded his very existence as a monument to all the rancid genes and broken chromosomes that corrupt the possibilities of the American Dream; he was a foul caricature of himself, a man with no soul, no inner convictions, with the integrity of a hyena and the style of a poison toad.
'Presenting: the Richard Nixon Doll (Overhauled 1968 Model)', publ. in *Pageant* July 1968, repr. in *The Great Shark Hunt*, pt. 2 (1979)

2 Myths and legends die hard in America. We love them for the extra dimension they provide, the illusion of near-infinite possibility to erase the narrow confines of most men's reality. Weird heroes and mould-

breaking champions exist as living proof to those who need it that the tyranny of 'the rat race' is not yet final.

'Those Daring Young Men in their Flying Machines . . . Ain't What They Used to Be!', publ. in *Pageant* September 1969, repr. ibid., pt. 3

3 Fear and Loathing in Las Vegas

Book title (1972). The core of the book, whose title was frequently adapted for other publications by Thompson, originally appeared in articles in *Rolling Stone* in November 1971 under his pseudonym Raoul Duke.

4 History is hard to know, because of all the hired bullshit, but even without being sure of 'history' it seems entirely reasonable to think that every now and then the energy of a whole generation comes to a head in a long fine flash, for reasons that nobody really understands at the time – and which never explain, in retrospect, what actually happened.

Fear and Loathing in Las Vegas, ch. 8 (1972)

5 If I'd written all the truth I knew for the past ten years, about 600 people – including me – would be rotting in prison cells from Rio to Seattle today. Absolute truth is a very rare and dangerous commodity in the context of professional journalism.

'Fear and Loathing at the Superbowl', publ. in *Rolling Stone* 15 February 1973, repr. in *The Great Shark Hunt*, pt. 1 (1979)

6 *Gonzo* journalism . . . is a style of 'reporting' based on William Faulkner's idea that the best fiction is far more *true* than any kind of journalism – and the best journalists have always known this. . . . True *gonzo* reporting needs the talents of a master journalist, the eye of an artist/photographer and the heavy balls of an actor. Because the writer *must* be a participant in the scene, while he's writing it – or at least taping it, or even sketching it. Or all three. Probably the closest analogy to the ideal would be a film director/producer who writes his own scripts, does his own camera work and somehow manages to film himself in action, as the protagonist or at least a main character.

The Great Shark Hunt, 'Jacket Copy for Fear and Loathing in Las Vegas' (1979)

7 In a nation ruled by swine, all pigs are upward-mobile – and the rest of us are fucked until we can put our acts together: not necessarily to win, but mainly to keep from losing completely. We owe that to ourselves and our crippled self-image as something better than a nation of panicked sheep.

Ibid.

8 Going to trial with a lawyer who considers your whole life-style a Crime in Progress is not a happy prospect.

'A Letter to *The Champion*: a publication of the National Association of Criminal Defense Lawyers', July 1990, publ. in *Songs of the Doomed* (1991)

Jim Thompson (1906–77)

US AUTHOR

He published some thirty pulp novels, among them The Killer Inside Me *(1952, filmed 1975),* The Grifters *(1959, filmed 1990) and* The Getaway *(1963, filmed 1972).*

1 We're living in a funny world, kid, a peculiar civilization. The police are playing crooks in it, and the crooks are doing police duty. The politicians are preachers, and the preachers are politicians. The tax collectors collect for themselves. The Bad People want us to have more dough, and the Good People are fighting to keep it from us.

Lou Ford, in *The Killer Inside Me*, ch. 12 (1952)

David Thomson (b. 1941)

BRITISH FILM CRITIC AND AUTHOR

He has written widely on the film industry and its personalities, as in Movie Man *(1967),* A Biographical Dictionary of the Cinema *(1975, revised as* The Biographical Dictionary of Film *in 2002) and* America in the Dark *(1977).*

1 It [television] is on – like the light. The ordinary viewer, the average citizen, would delight the movie business if he or she saw one movie every six weeks. But he, she, we, the moblike broken family, goes back and forth, like leopards in our cage, while TV is 'on', six or seven hours a day. The world works by way of TV: that is where marketing occurs; that is how politicians play at running the country; and that is where news is defined and focused. It is lamentable, if you want to take that view. Though I suspect a greater damage to our culture and our ideas came earlier, in permitting photography. That was the first great drug, and it trained us for the others.

A Biographical Dictionary of Film, 'Dennis Potter' (1994)

John Thorne (b. 1943)

US COOKERY WRITER

Offering a holistic approach to eating and cooking, his culinary pamphlets and newsletters are collected in Simple Cooking *(1987),* Outlaw Cook *(1992) and* Serious Pig *(1996).*

1 All recipes are built on the belief that somewhere at the beginning of the chain there is a cook who does not use them. This is the great nostalgia of our cuisine, ever invok-

ing an absent mother-cook who once laid her hands on the body of the world for us and worked it into food. The promise of every cookbook is that it offers a way back onto her lap.

'Cuisine Mécanique', publ. in *The Journal of Gastronomy* spring 1990

Adam Thorpe (b. 1956)

BRITISH POET AND NOVELIST

He published two collections of poetry, Mornings in the Baltic *(1988) and* Meeting Montaigne *(1990), before his award-winning first novel* Ulverton *(1992), followed by* Pieces of Light *(1998).*

1 The tesserae of the past – Bronze-Age, Roman, mediaeval – thrown up by the coulter are as infant toys to the booming venerableness of the chalk that cradles them. And we – who are we to flail and clamour, to batter and slay, when all that surrounds us tells us of our insignificance, of our infinitesimal capacities, of our inevitable anonymity in the eternal reaches of Time?

Ulverton, ch. 10 (1992)

Jeremy Thorpe (b. 1929)

BRITISH POLITICIAN

He served as Liberal MP for North Devon (1959–79) and was a popular leader of the Party (1967–76). Forced to resign by a scandal in which he was acquitted of charges of conspiracy to murder a male lover, he lost his seat at the next general election.

1 Greater love hath no man than this, that he lay down his friends for his life.

Remark, 1962, quoted in *The General Election of 1964,* ch. 1 (1965) by D. E. Butler and Anthony King. The quip, made following a Cabinet 'reorganization' by Prime Minister HAROLD MACMILLAN in which several members of the Cabinet were sacked, is an adaptation of the words of Christ in John 15:13: 'Greater love hath no man than this, that a man lay down his life for his friends.'

Colin Thubron (b. 1939)

BRITISH TRAVEL WRITER AND NOVELIST

He has based such books as Among the Russians *(1983) and* Behind the Wall *(1987) on his travels in Asia. His novels include* Falling *(1989) and* Turning Back the Sun *(1991).*

1 Rudeness in old men is considered a sign of vitality. In fact it is quite the opposite. It springs from shrunken sympathies.

Synesius, in *Emperor,* pt. 2, ch. 13 (1978)

2 I imagine integrity as a quality of light: a kind of grey translucence, sunless. It is not at all beautiful. But it makes other lights seem disfiguring.

Constantine, ibid.

3 If a man would be happy for a week (ran a saying), he could take a wife; if he planned happiness for a month, he must kill a pig; but if he desired happiness for ever, he should plant a garden.

Behind the Wall: A Journey Through China, ch. 4 (1987)

James Thurber (1894–1961)

US HUMORIST AND ILLUSTRATOR

He was Managing Editor of the New Yorker *1927–33, to which he contributed wry sketches, cartoons and stories until his death. His short story* 'The Secret Life of Walter Mitty' *(1932, filmed 1947) prompted Larry Adler to comment: 'Freud discovered the Id, and Thurber named it Walter Mitty.'*

1 A drawing is always dragged down to the level of its caption.

New Yorker 2 August 1930

2 It takes that *je ne sais quoi* which we call sophistication for a woman to be magnificent in a drawing-room when her faculties have departed but she herself has not yet gone home.

Ibid.

3 All right, have it your way – you heard a seal bark.

Cartoon caption in the *New Yorker* 30 January 1932, repr. in *The Thurber Carnival,* pt. 8 (1945). Spoken by wife to husband in bed.

4 In an extensive reading of recent books by psychologists, psychoanalysts, psychiatrists, and inspirationalists, I have discovered that they all suffer from one or more of these expression-complexes: italicizing, capitalizing, exclamation-pointing, multiple-interrogating, and itemizing. These are all forms of what the psychos themselves would call, if they faced their condition frankly, Rhetorical-Over-Compensation.

'Peace, it's Wonderful', publ. in the *Saturday Review* 21 November 1936, repr. in *James Thurber Collecting Himself* (ed. Michael J. Rosen, 1989)

5 It's a naïve domestic Burgundy without any breeding, but I think you'll be amused by its presumption.

Cartoon caption, in the *New Yorker* 27 March 1937, repr. in *The Thurber Carnival,* pt. 9 (1945). Spoken by a pleased-looking host, to the consternation of his guests at dinner.

6 Well, if I called the wrong number, why did you answer the phone?

Woman on phone, in cartoon caption, in the *New Yorker* 5 June 1937, repr. ibid.

7 Every man is occasionally visited by the suspicion that the planet on which he is riding is not really going anywhere; that the Force which controls its measured eccen-

tricities hasn't got anything special in mind. If he broods on this somber theme long enough he gets the doleful idea that the laughing children on a merry-go-round or the thin, fine hands of a lady's watch are revolving more purposely than he is.

'Thinking Ourselves into Trouble', pt. 1, publ. in *Forum and Century* June 1939, repr. in *James Thurber Collecting Himself* (ed. Michael J. Rosen, 1989)

8 Philosophy offers the rather cold consolation that perhaps we and our planet do not actually exist; religion presents the contradictory and scarcely more comforting thought that we exist but that we cannot hope to get anywhere until we cease to exist. Alcohol, in attempting to resolve the contradiction, produces vivid patterns of Truth which vanish like snow in the morning sun and cannot be recalled; the revelations of poetry are as wonderful as a comet in the skies – and as mysterious. Love, which was once believed to contain the Answer, we now know to be nothing more than an inherited behavior pattern.

Ibid.

9 Next to reasoning, the greatest handicap to the optimum development of Man lies in the fact that this planet is just barely habitable. Its minimum temperatures are too low, and its maximum temperatures too high. Its day is not long enough, and its night is too long. The disposition of its water and earth is distinctly unfortunate (the existence of the Mediterranean Sea in the place where we find it is perhaps the unhappiest accident in the whole firmament). These factors encourage depression, fear, war, and lack of vitality. They describe a planet, which is by no means perfectly devised for the nurturing or for the perpetuation of a higher intelligence.

Ibid., pt. 2

10 Early to rise and early to bed makes a male healthy and wealthy and dead.

Fables for our Time, 'The Shrike and the Chipmunks' (1940)

11 You might as well fall flat on your face as lean over too far backward.

Ibid., 'The Bear who Let it Alone'

12 It is better to have loafed and lost than never to have loafed at all.

Ibid., 'The Courtship of Arthur and Al'. An adaptation of Tennyson's lines, ' 'Tis better to have loved and lost/Than never to have loved at all' (*In Memoriam A.H.H.*, 1850).

13 Somebody once said that I am incapable of drawing a man, but that I draw abstract things like despair, disillusion, despondency, sorrow, lapse of memory, exile, and that these things are sometimes in a shape that might be called Man or Woman.

Interview with Jack Sher in the *Detroit Free Press* 25 February 1940

14 The only rules comedy can tolerate are those of taste, and the only limitations those of libel.

'The Duchess and the Bugs' (c. 1953), repr. in *Lanterns and Lances* (1961)

15 Discussion in America means dissent.

Ibid.

16 Humor does not include sarcasm, invalid irony, sardonicism, innuendo, or any other form of cruelty. When these things are raised to a high point they can become wit, but unlike the French and the English, we have not been much good at wit since the days of Benjamin Franklin.

Letter, 25 June 1954, publ. in *Horn Book Magazine* April 1962

17 Speed is scarcely the noblest virtue of graphic composition, but it has its curious rewards. There is a sense of getting somewhere fast, which satisfies a native American urge.

A Thurber Garland, Preface (1955)

18 With sixty staring me in the face, I have developed inflammation of the sentence structure and definite hardening of the paragraphs.

Quoted in the *New York Post* 30 June 1955

19 The laughter of man is more terrible than his tears, and takes more forms – hollow, heartless, mirthless, maniacal.

The New York Times Magazine 7 December 1958

20 I consider that that 'that' that worries us so much should be forgotten. Rats desert a sinking ship. Thats infest a sinking magazine.

Memo to the *New Yorker* in 1959, first publ. in *The New York Times Book Review* 4 December 1988

21 I always begin at the left with the opening word of the sentence and read toward the right and I recommend this method.

Ibid. On his editorial technique.

22 When all things are equal, translucence in writing is more effective than transparency, just as glow is more revealing than glare.

Ibid.

23 We are a nation that has always gone in for the loud laugh, the wow, the yak, the belly laugh, and the dozen other labels for the roll-'em-in-the-aisles gagerissimo. This is the kind of laugh that delights actors, directors, and producers, but dismays writers of comedy because it is the laugh that often dies in the lobby. The appreciative smile,

the chuckle, the soundless mirth, so important to the success of comedy, cannot be understood unless one sits among the audience and feels the warmth created by the quality of laughter that the audience takes home with it.

The New York Times 21 February 1960

24 Humor is emotional chaos remembered in tranquility.

New York Post 29 February 1960. An earlier version of Thurber's quip was attributed to him by Max Eastman in *Enjoyment of Laughter* (1936): 'Humor is a kind of emotional chaos told about calmly and quietly in retrospect. There is always a laugh in the utterly familiar.' The words are adapted from Wordsworth's dictum: 'Poetry . . . takes its origin from emotion recollected in tranquillity.' (Preface to *Lyrical Ballads*, second edn, 1801).

25 I'm 65 and I guess that puts me in with the geriatrics. But if there were fifteen months in every year, I'd only be 48. That's the trouble with us. We number everything. Take women, for example. I think they deserve to have more than twelve years between the ages of 28 and 40.

Time 15 August 1960

26 From now on, I think it is safe to predict, neither the Democratic nor the Republican Party will ever nominate for President a candidate without good looks, stage presence, theatrical delivery, and a sense of timing.

Unpublished manuscript 20 March 1961, publ. in *James Thurber Collecting Himself* (ed. Michael J. Rosen, 1989). Referring to the Kennedy–Nixon TV debates.

27 My opposition [to interviews] lies in the fact that offhand answers have little value or grace of expression, and that such oral give and take helps to perpetuate the decline of the English language.

Letter to Henry Brandon, quoted in *As We Are* (1961) by Henry Brandon. Written following a lengthy interview with him.

Paul Tillich (1886–1965)

GERMAN-BORN US THEOLOGIAN

An influential Protestant thinker, he formulated a theology that incorporated existentialist themes, as set out in his major work is Systematic Theology *(3 vols., 1951–63). Other works include* The Courage to Be *(1952) and* The Eternal Now *(1963). Expelled by the Nazis, he fled to the USA in 1933.*

1 Religion is the state of being grasped by an ultimate concern, a concern which qualifies all other concerns as preliminary and which itself contains the answer to the question of a meaning of our life.

Christianity and the Encounter of the World Religions, ch. 1 (1963)

Alvin Toffler (b. 1928)

US AUTHOR

As a 'futurologist', he has written of the advent of information technology as the 'Third Wave' of civilization, after agriculture and the industrial revolution. His books include Future Shock *(1970) and* Powershift *(1990).*

1 Future shock is the dizzying disorientation brought on by the premature arrival of the future. It may well be the most important disease of tomorrow.

Future Shock, pt. 1, ch. 1, 'The Unprepared Visitor' (1970)

2 Knowledge is the most democratic source of power.

Powershift: Knowledge, Wealth, and Violence at the Edge of the 21st Century, pt. 1, ch. 2, 'The Democratic Difference' (1990)

J. R. R. Tolkien (1892–1973)

BRITISH NOVELIST AND SCHOLAR

John Ronal Reuel Tolkien. An Oxford professor and leading philologist, he was author of numerous academic publications, but is best remembered for his fantasies The Hobbit *(1937) and* The Lord of the Rings *(1954–5, filmed 1978 and 2000–2003).*

1 Curse it! Curse it! Curse it! Curse the Baggins! It's gone! What has it got in its pocketses? Oh we guess, we guess, my precious. He's found it, yes he must have. My birthday-present.

Gollum, in *The Hobbit*, ch. 5 (1937). Referring to the ring which Gollum has guessed Bilbo Baggins has in his pocket, in a game of riddles played for Bilbo's life.

2 Gandalf looked at him. 'My dear Bilbo!' he said. 'Something is the matter with you! You are not the hobbit that you were.'

Ibid., ch. 19. On Bilbo's new poetical and adventurous spirit at the end of the tale.

3 *One Ring to rule them all, One Ring to find them*
One Ring to bring them all and in the darkness bind them.

The Lord of the Rings, pt. 1: *The Fellowship of the Ring*, Epigraph (1954)

4 *The Road goes ever on and on*
Down from the door where it began
Now far ahead the Road has gone,
And I must follow, if I can,
Pursuing it with eager feet,
Until it joins some larger way
Where many paths and errands meet.
And whither then? I cannot say.

Bilbo Baggins, ibid., bk. 1, ch. 1. The rhyme recurs with variations elsewhere in the work, and a version appears at the end of *The Hobbit*.

5 Many that live deserve death. And some that die deserve life. Can you give it to

them? Then do not be too eager to deal out death in judgement. For even the very wise cannot see all ends.

Gandalf, ibid., ch. 2. Responding to Frodo's remark that Gollum's wicked actions deserve death.

6 Faithless is he that says farewell when the road darkens.

The dwarf Gimli, ibid., bk. 2, ch. 3

7 Rising swiftly up, far above the Towers of the Black Gate, high above the mountains, a vast soaring darkness sprang into the sky, flickering with fire. The earth groaned and quaked. The Towers of the Teeth swayed, tottered, and fell down; the mighty rampart crumbled; the Black Gate was hurled in ruin; and from far away, now dim, now growing, now mounting to the clouds, there came a drumming rumble, a roar, a long echoing roll of ruinous noise.
    'The realm of Sauron is ended!' said Gandalf. 'The Ring-bearer has fulfilled his Quest.'

Ibid., pt. 3: *The Return of the King*, bk. 6, ch. 4 (1955). Describing the outcome of the struggle between Frodo and Gollum on the edge of the Cracks of Doom, as Gollum topples into the abyss, taking the Ring with him to destruction.

Tatyana Tolstaya (b. 1951)
RUSSIAN AUTHOR
The great grandniece of Leo Tolstoy, she is the author of the short stories On the Golden Porch *(1989) and* Sleepwalker in a Fog *(1991).*

1 Already the writers are complaining that there is too much freedom. They need some pressure. The worse your daily life, the better your art. If you have to be careful because of oppression and censorship, this pressure produces diamonds.

On writers in Russia, in the *Independent* 31 May 1990

2 In Russia, people suffer from the stillness of time.

Ibid.

Lily Tomlin (b. 1939)
US COMEDIENNE
She came to notice on the cast of the TV show ROWAN AND MARTIN'S LAUGH-IN *(1969–72) and has since acted in numerous films, among them* Nashville *(1975) and* Tea with Mussolini *(1999). She is also known for her one-woman stage shows.*

1 The Fifties was the most sexually frustrated decade ever: ten years of foreplay. And the Sixties, well, the Sixties was like coitus interruptus. The only thing we didn't pull out of was Vietnam.

Routine on Broadway show, *Appearing Nightly* (1977), recorded on *Lily Tomlin on Stage*,

'Glenna – A Child of the Sixties' (album, 1977, material written by Lily Tomlin and Jane Wagner)

2 There will be sex after death; we just won't be able to feel it.

Quoted in *Hammer and Tongues* (ed. Michèle Brown and Ann O'Connor, 1986)

3 If love is the answer, could you rephrase the question?

Quoted in *Funny Business* (1992) by David Housham and John Frank-Keyes

Michael Torke (b. 1961)
US COMPOSER
Regarded as a rhythmic and melodic minimalist, he is one of the most widely choreographed contemporary composers, whose works include Javelin *(1994), commissioned for the Olympics, and* Brick Symphony *(1997).*

1 Why waste money on psychotherapy when you can listen to the B Minor Mass?

Independent 21 September 1990

Peter Tosh (1944–87)
JAMAICAN REGGAE MUSICIAN
Originally Winston McIntosh. With his childhood friends BOB MARLEY *and Bunny Livingston, he was one of the original Wailin' Wailers in the early 1960s, leaving the band in 1974 to pursue a solo career. See also* BOB MARLEY 1.

1 *Legalize it*
  And we will advertise it.
  'Legalize it' (song) on the album *Legalize it* (1976)

Michel Tournier (b. 1924)
FRENCH AUTHOR
His symbolist and intellectual novels such as Friday and Robinson *(1967),* The Erl King *(1970) and* Gemini *(1975) have won him an international reputation. He has been a member of the Académie Goncourt since 1972.*

1 The writer who labours on a book for four years becomes that book and assimilates all its alien elements, which add up to a structure far more impressive, vast, complex, and learned than their author. . . . The work is all-consuming, a pious labour, a parasite. And when it has fed on me and sucked my blood, when it begins to make its own way in the world, I lie wan, drained, disgusted and exhausted, and obsessed with thoughts of death.

The Wind Spirit: An Autobiography, ch. 3 (1977, transl. 1988)

2 A myth is first of all a multistoreyed structure, each storey being built according to an identical plan but at a different level of abstraction. . . . The child's tale that is the

myth's ground floor, as it were, is just as essential as its metaphysical summit.
Ibid.

3 A writer is a cottage industry. Some craftsmen make tortoiseshell combs, others make leather wallets. I make Michel Tournier manuscripts.
Independent on Sunday 17 February 1991

Sue Townsend (b. 1946)
BRITISH AUTHOR
She is best known for her satirical works The Secret Diary of Adrian Mole aged 13¾ *(1982), its sequels, and the novels* The Queen and I *(1992)* and Number 10 *(2002).*

1 My brain is hurting. I have just had two pages of *Macbeth* to translate into English.
Adrian Mole's journal entry, 21 January, in *The Secret Diary of Adrian Mole aged 13¾* (1982)

2 Marriage is nothing like being in prison! Women are let out every day to go to the shops and stuff, and quite a lot go to work.
Ibid., 2 March

3 Offal is the new black.
Adrian Mole's journal entry for 18 May, in *Adrian Mole: The Cappuccino Years* (1999). On culinary trends.

Pete Townshend (b. 1945)
BRITISH ROCK MUSICIAN
He was the guitarist and chief songwriter of the leading 'mod' band the High Numbers, renamed the Who in 1964. His guitar-smashing antics on stage epitomized the group's nihilistic image. He later composed the first 'rock opera', Tommy, in 1969.

1 *People try to put us down*
(Talkin' 'bout my generation)
Just because we get around
(Talkin' 'bout my generation)
Things they do look awful c-c-cold
(Talkin' 'bout my generation)
Hope I die before I get old.
'My Generation' (song) on the album *My Generation* (1965) by the Who

2 *I was born with a plastic spoon in my mouth.*
'Substitute' (song), ibid.

3 I . . . know what it's like to be a mod among 2 million mods, and it's incredible. It's like being the only white man at the Apollo. Someone comes up and touches you, and you become black. . . . It covered everybody, everybody looked the same, and everybody acted the same, and everybody wanted to be the same. . . . It was the closest to patriotism that I've ever felt.
Interview in *Rolling Stone* September 1968

4 It's an ordinary day for Brian. Like, he died every day, you know.
Comment to press, July 1969, quoted in *The Life and Good Times of the Rolling Stones* by Philip Norman (1989). On the drowning of Rolling Stones guitarist Brian Jones. Stung by criticism of his off-the-cuff remark, Townshend wrote a song titled 'A Normal Day for Brian, the Man Who Died Everyday', never released.

5 *I'll tip my hat to the new constitution*
Take a bow for the new revolution
Smile and grin at the change all around
Pick up my guitar and play
Just like yesterday.
Then I'll get on my knees and pray
We don't get fooled again.
'Won't Get Fooled Again' (song) on the album *Who's Next* (1971) by the Who

6 So much of what I am I got from you. I had no idea how much of it was secondhand.
Quoted in *Rolling Stone* 8 February 1990. Addressed to the Rolling Stones at the Rock and Roll Hall of Fame induction ceremony, January 1989.

7 It is amorphous, but basically it always has the same job, which is to get you through the day. And that seems to me to be a profoundly important job; it is like fresh bread.
Interview in the *Observer* 25 February 1996. In reply to the question: 'What is pop music?'

Arnold J. Toynbee (1889–1975)
BRITISH HISTORIAN
The scion of a family of historians, he was Director and Research Professor of the Royal Institute of International Affairs (1925–55) and a prolific author. His magnum opus is A Study of History *(12 vols., 1934–61).*

1 History not used is nothing, for all intellectual life is action, like practical life, and if you don't use the stuff – well, it might as well be dead.
Television broadcast on NBC-TV, 17 April 1955

2 Civilization is a movement and not a condition, a voyage and not a harbour.
Reader's Digest October 1958

3 We human beings do have some genuine freedom of choice and therefore some effective control over our own destinies. I am not a determinist. But I also believe that the decisive choice is seldom the latest choice in the series. More often than not, it will turn out to be some choice made relatively far back in the past.
'Some Great "If"s' of History', publ. in *The New York Times* 5 March 1961

4 We have been God-like in our planned breeding of our domesticated plants and

animals, but we have been rabbit-like in our unplanned breeding of ourselves.

Speech to World Food Congress, Washington DC, quoted in the *National Observer* 10 June 1963

Polly Toynbee (b. 1946)

BRITISH JOURNALIST

Granddaughter of ARNOLD TOYNBEE, *she has been writer and editor for various newspapers including the* Observer, *the* Guardian *and the* Independent.

1 Feminism is the most revolutionary idea there has ever been. Equality for women demands a change in the human psyche more profound than anything Marx dreamed of. It means valuing parenthood as much as we value banking.

Guardian 19 January 1987

2 There never could have been message or meaning in an exhibition of this kind. In the end only art transcends the platitudes of politicians, the empty exhortations and the hollow Christian attempts to impose a banality of its own. The lesson is that only those elements created by artists have meaning.

On the Millennium Dome, in the *Guardian* 5 January 2000

Violet Trefusis (1894–1972)

BRITISH NOVELIST

The daughter of Alice Keppel, mistress of Edward VII, she wrote fiction in both English and French, and two volumes of reminiscences, Prelude to Misadventure *(1942) and* Don't Look Round *(1952).*

1 You are my lover and I am your mistress and kingdoms and empires and governments have tottered and succumbed before now to that mighty combination.

Letter to VITA SACKVILLE-WEST, March 1919, publ. in *Letters to Vita Sackville-West* (1989). Closing words of letter. The two had a passionate affair between 1918 and 1921.

2 I hate men. They fill me with revulsion, even quite small boys. Marriage is an institution that ought to be confined to temperamental old maids, weary prostitutes, and royalty.

Letter to Vita Sackville-West, May/June 1919, quoted in *Portrait of a Marriage*, pt. 4 (1973) by Nigel Nicolson. Violet married Denys Trefusis on 16 June 1919.

G. M. Trevelyan (1876–1962)

BRITISH HISTORIAN

George Macaulay Trevelyan. He authored studies of Garibaldi (1907–11) before embarking on the social histories of England for which he is best known. He was Professor of Modern History at Cambridge 1927–51.

1 Socrates gave no diplomas or degrees, and would have subjected any disciple who demanded one to a disconcerting catechism on the nature of true knowledge.

History of England, bk. 2 ch. 4 (1926)

2 Social history might be defined negatively as the history of a people with the politics left out.

English Social History, Introduction (1942)

3 Disinterested intellectual curiosity is the life blood of real civilisation.

Ibid.

4 In those days, before it became scientific, cricket was the best game in the world to watch, with its rapid sequence of amusing incidents, each ball a potential crisis! Squire, farmer, blacksmith, and labourer, with their women and children came to see the fun, were at ease together and happy all the summer afternoon. If the French *noblesse* had been capable of playing cricket with their peasants, their chateaux would never have been burnt.

Ibid., ch. 8. Referring to England in the eighteenth century.

5 Education . . . has produced a vast population able to read but unable to distinguish what is worth reading, an easy prey to sensations and cheap appeals.

Ibid., ch. 18

Hugh Trevor-Roper (1914–2003)

BRITISH HISTORIAN

Baron Dacre of Glanton. An established authority on Hitler, he published The Last Days of Hitler *in 1947 but suffered loss of reputation over his authentication of Hitler's diaries in 1983, which turned out to be a forgery. He was Professor of Modern History at Oxford (1957–80).*

1 War has its priorities which the longer perspective of peace sometimes painfully deranges. The comfortable after-wisdom of the historian is a luxury. He has no responsibility. He can afford to be wrong. Therefore he can only state the facts and, like the tragedian, present rather than solve moral dilemmas.

Writing in 1974, quoted in the *Observer* 3 December 1989

Calvin Trillin (b. 1935)

US JOURNALIST AND AUTHOR

A debunker of pomposity, he was a commentator on regional stories across the USA, and he wrote as a roving gourmand in Alice, Let's Eat *(1978) and* Third Helpings *(1983).*

1 As far as I'm concerned, 'whom' is a word that was invented to make everyone sound like a butler.

'Whom Says So?', publ. in the *Nation* 8 June 1985

2 The talk shows are stuffed full of sufferers who have regained their health – congressmen who suffered through a serious spell of boozing and skirt-chasing, White House aides who were stricken cruelly with overweening ambition, movie stars and baseball players who came down with acute cases of wanting to trash hotel rooms while under the influence of recreational drugs. Most of them have found God, or at least a publisher.

'Diseases of the Mighty', publ. in the *Nation* 19 October 1985

3 Everything was blamed on Castro. Mudslides in California. The fact that you can't buy a decent tomato anymore. Was there an exceptionally high pollen count in Massapequa, Long Island, one day? It was Castro, exporting sneezes.

'Castro Forgotten, Alas', syndicated column 18 May 1986

Lionel Trilling (1905–75)
US CRITIC

His critical works, which include The Liberal Imagination *(1950) and* Sincerity and Authenticity *(1972), emphasize a moral dimension within a social context in the liberal tradition of Matthew Arnold, on whom he wrote a standard text (1939).*

1 Probably it is impossible for humor to be ever a revolutionary weapon. Candide can do little more than generate irony.

Notebook entry *c.* 1931–32, publ. in *Partisan Review 50th Anniversary Edition* (ed. William Philips, 1985)

2 We are all ill: but even a universal sickness implies an idea of health.

'Art and Neurosis', publ. in the *Partisan Review* winter 1945, repr. in *The Liberal Imagination* (1950)

3 In the American metaphysic, reality is always material reality, hard, resistant, unformed, impenetrable, and unpleasant.

'Reality in America', first publ. in the *Nation* 20 April 1946, repr. ibid.

4 Every neurosis is a primitive form of legal proceeding in which the accused carries on the prosecution, imposes judgment and executes the sentence: all to the end that someone else should not perform the same process.

Notebook entry, 1946, publ. in *Partisan Review 50th Anniversary Edition* (ed. William Philips, 1985)

5 We are at heart so profoundly anarchistic that the only form of state we can imagine living in is Utopian; and so cynical that the only Utopia we can believe in is authoritarian.

Ibid., 1948

6 We who are liberal and progressive know that the poor are our equals in every sense except that of being equal to us.

'The Princess Casamassima', first publ. as Introduction to *The Princess Casamassima* (1948) by Henry James, repr. in *The Liberal Imagination* (1950)

7 If one defends the bourgeois, philistine virtues, one does not defend them merely from the demonism or bohemianism of the artist but from the present bourgeoisie itself.

Notebook entry, *c.* 1951, publ. in *Partisan Review 50th Anniversary Edition* (ed. William Philips, 1985)

8 Immature artists imitate. Mature artists steal.

Esquire September 1962

9 A primary function of art and thought is to liberate the individual from the tyranny of his culture in the environmental sense and to permit him to stand beyond it in an autonomy of perception and judgment.

Beyond Culture, Preface (1965)

David Trimble (b. 1944)
NORTHERN IRISH POLITICIAN

MP for Upper Bann since 1990, he has been leader of the Ulster Unionist Party since 1995 and was a key figure in the Good Friday agreement in 1998, following which he became First Minister of the Northern Ireland Assembly.

1 We are not saying that, simply because someone has a past, they can't have a future. We always acknowledge that people have to change.

Quoted in the *Daily Telegraph* 2 July 1998. Acceptance speech on his election as First Minister of the Northern Ireland Assembly, Stormont, referring to the participation of Sinn Féin and other groups in the new assembly.

2 Peace is not the absence of war. Lasting peace is rooted in justice. It is rooted in a democratic culture which cherishes the rule of law and scorns the summary justice, social terrorism and gangsterism which are a fact of life for too many people in Northern Ireland.

Quoted in the *Observer* 18 October 1998. On being awarded the Nobel Peace Prize, which he shared with SDLP leader John Hume.

Alexander Trocchi (1925–83)
SCOTTISH AUTHOR

He co-founded the literary quarterly Merlin *in Paris in 1950 and was instrumental in publishing* SAMUEL BECKETT's *early work. A pivotal figure of London's underground scene in the early 1960s, he is remembered chiefly for his autobiographical novel* Cain's Book *(1960).*

1 No doubt I shall go on writing, stumbling across tundras of unmeaning, planting words like bloody flags in my wake. Loose ends, things unrelated, shifts, nightmare journeys, cities arrived at and left, meetings, desertions, betrayals, all manner of unions, adulteries, triumphs, defeats . . . these are the facts.

Cain's Book (1960)

2 All great art, and today all great artlessness, must appear extreme to the mass of men, as we know them today. It springs from the anguish of great souls. From the souls of men not formed, but deformed in factories whose inspiration is pelf.

Ibid.

Joanna Trollope (b. 1938)

BRITISH NOVELIST

A descendant of Anthony Trollope, and known as 'the queen of the Aga saga', she is the author of The Choir *(1987),* The Rector's Wife *(1991) and* Marrying the Mistress *(2002).*

1 The world's tragedy is that men love women, women love children, and children love hamsters.

Quoted in the *Observer* 7 May 2000

Leon Trotsky (1879–1940)

RUSSIAN REVOLUTIONARY

Originally Lev Davidovich Bronstein. Until the death of LENIN *he was the second most powerful man in the Soviet Union, responsible for modernizing the Red Army as Commissar for Military Affairs (1918–24). However his emphasis on world revolution alienated him from* STALIN *and he was exiled in 1929, and eventually assassinated in Mexico.*

1 The Federated Republic of Europe – the United States of Europe – that is what must be. National autonomy no longer suffices. Economic evolution demands the abolition of national frontiers. If Europe is to remain split into national groups, then Imperialism will recommence its work. Only a Federated Republic of Europe can give peace to the world.

Conversation at Smolny, 30 October 1917, quoted in *Ten Days That Shook the World*, ch. 3 (1926) by JOHN REED

2 The literary 'fellow travellers' of the Revolution.

Literature and Revolution, ch. 2 (1923). By 'fellow travellers' (*paputchiki*), a term originally used by the 'old Socialists', Trotsky referred to writers who sympathized with the Bolshevik Revolution but had no 'revolutionary past' and to whom 'the Communist ideal is foreign'. It later came to be used to mean any uncommitted sympathizers of a cause. The phrase appeared in English in an article by MAX LERNER, 'Mr Roosevelt and his Fellow-Travelers' (1936).

3 Technique is noticed most markedly in the case of those who have not mastered it.

Ibid., ch. 6. Referring to the 'breathless literary schools that followed the revolution'.

4 Learning carries within itself certain dangers because out of necessity one has to learn from one's enemies.

Ibid.

5 If the Revolution has the right to destroy bridges and art monuments whenever necessary, it will stop still less from laying its hand on any tendency in art which, no matter how great its achievement in form, threatens to disintegrate the revolutionary environment or to arouse the internal forces of the Revolution, that is, the proletariat, the peasantry and the intelligentsia, to a hostile opposition to one another. Our standard is, clearly, political, imperative and intolerant.

Ibid., ch. 7

6 Ideas that enter the mind under fire remain there securely and for ever.

My Life, ch. 35 (1930)

7 If we had had more time for discussion we should probably have made a great many more mistakes.

Ibid., ch. 36. Referring to discussions in the Central Committee of the Soviet Communist Party about the proposed development of the Red Army.

8 It was the supreme expression of the mediocrity of the apparatus that Stalin himself rose to his position.

Ibid. ch. 40. In his last book, *Stalin* (1947), drafted while in exile in Mexico, Trotsky wrote of his feelings towards STALIN: 'Our paths diverged so long ago and so far, and in my eyes he is so much the instrument of historical forces that are alien and hostile to me, that my feelings towards him differ little from those I have towards Hitler or the Mikado. The personal element burned out long ago.' Trotsky was assassinated on Stalin's orders, before the book could be finished.

9 Where force is necessary, there it must be applied boldly, decisively and completely. But one must know the limitations of force; one must know when to blend force with a manoeuvre, a blow with an agreement.

What Next?, ch. 14 (1932)

10 The slanders poured down like Niagara. If you take into consideration the setting – the war and the revolution – and the character of the accused – revolutionary leaders of millions who were conducting their party to the sovereign power – you can say without exaggeration that July 1917

was the month of the most gigantic slander in world history.

History of the Russian Revolution, vol. 2, ch. 4 (1933)

11 There is no example in history of a revolutionary movement involving such gigantic masses being so bloodless.

Ibid., vol. 2, ch. 7. Referring to the initial stages of the Russian Revolution, which included the storming of Moscow's Winter Palace.

12 Revolutions are always verbose.

Ibid., ch. 12

13 There is a limit to the application of democratic methods. You can inquire of all the passengers as to what type of car they like to ride in, but it is impossible to question them as to whether to apply the brakes when the train is at full speed and accident threatens.

Ibid., vol. 3, ch. 6

14 Insurrection is an art, and like all arts has its own laws.

Ibid.

15 From being a patriotic myth, the Russian people have become an awful reality.

Ibid., ch. 7. Referring to the chaotic aftermath of the October Revolution, 1917.

16 You [Mensheviks] are pitiful isolated individuals; you are bankrupts; your role is played out. Go where you belong from now on – into the dustbin of history!

Ibid., vol. 3, ch. 10. The Mensheviks, who participated in Kerensky's provisional government in 1917, were overthrown by the Bolsheviks and suppressed.

17 The historic ascent of humanity, taken as a whole, may be summarized as a succession of victories of consciousness over blind forces – in nature, in society, in man himself.

Ibid., vol. 3, 'Conclusions'

18 The depth and strength of a human character are defined by its moral *reserves*. People reveal themselves completely only when they are thrown out of the customary conditions of their life, for only then do they have to fall back on their reserves.

Journal entry, 5 April 1935, publ. in *Diary in Exile* (1959)

19 England is nothing but the last ward of the European madhouse, and quite possibly it will prove to be the ward for particularly violent cases.

Ibid., 11 April 1935

20 Old age is the most unexpected of all things that happen to a man.

Ibid., 8 May 1935

21 In Stalin each [Soviet bureaucrat] easily finds himself. But Stalin also finds in each

one a small part of his own spirit. Stalin is the personification of the bureaucracy. That is the substance of his political personality.

The Revolution Betrayed, ch. 11 (1937)

22 Under all conditions well-organized violence seems to him [Stalin] the shortest distance between two points.

Stalin, ch. 3 (1947)

23 The end may justify the means as long as there is something that justifies the end.

Quoted in *Antonio Gramsci: An Introduction to his Thought*, Preface (1970) by Alberto Pozzolini

Bobby Troup (1918–99)

US SONGWRITER AND ACTOR

He wrote songs for his wife, the singer and actress Julie London, as well as for FRANK SINATRA, LITTLE RICHARD, *and Tommy Dorsey, whom he played in* The Gene Krupa Story *(film, 1959). See also* LITTLE RICHARD 2.

1 If you ever plan to motor west,
  Travel my way, take the highway that's the best –
  Get your kicks on Route 66.

'Route 66' (song, 1946). The song was a hit for the Nat Cole Trio and was widely covered.

François Truffaut (1932–84)

FRENCH FILM-MAKER AND CRITIC

He was a pioneer of New Wave cinema, gaining an international reputation with The Four Hundred Blows *(1959),* Jules and Jim *(1961) and* Day for Night *(1973). 'I make films that I would like to have seen when I was a young man,' he stated.*

1 I've always had the impression that real militants are like cleaning women, doing a thankless, daily but necessary job.

Letter to JEAN-LUC GODARD, May–June 1973, publ. in *Letters* (1988)

2 When humour can be made to alternate with melancholy, one has a success, but when the *same* things are funny and melancholic at the same time, it's just wonderful.

Letter, 15 January 1980, publ. ibid.

3 All film directors, whether famous or obscure, regard themselves as misunderstood or underrated. Because of that, they all lie. They're obliged to overstate their own importance.

Letter, 8 January 1981, publ. ibid.

Harry S. Truman (1884–1972)

US POLITICIAN AND PRESIDENT

As Democratic President 1945–52, he issued the order to drop the atom bomb on Japan, initiated the Marshall Plan for European aid and helped found NATO. His 'Truman Doctrine', which

*promised US support for those threatened by the
Soviets, exacerbated the Cold War.*

1 The human animal cannot be trusted for
anything *good* except en masse. The combined thought and action of the whole
people of any race, creed or nationality,
will always point in the right direction.
Memorandum, 22 May 1945, publ. in *Mr President*, pt. 3 (1952) by William Hillman

2 There is nothing new in the world except
the history you do not know.
Quoted ibid., pt. 2, ch. 1

3 Study men, not historians.
Letter, 19 July 1950, publ. in *Off the Record* (ed.
Robert H. Ferrell, 1980)

4 A politician is a man who understands
government and it takes a politician to run
a government. A statesman is a politician
who's been dead ten or fifteen years.
Speech to Reciprocity Club, Washington DC,
11 April 1958, quoted in the *New York World-
Telegram and Sun* 12 April 1958

5 If you can't stand the heat, get out of the
kitchen.
Favourite saying of Truman's, quoted in *Mr Citizen*, ch. 15 (1960)

6 The buck stops here.
Motto on Truman's desk at the White House,
quoted in *The Man from Missouri* (1962) by
Alfred Steinberg

7 Washington is a very easy city for you to
forget where you came from and why you
got there in the first place.
*Plain Speaking: Conversations with Harry S.
Truman*, ch. 11 (1973) by Merle Miller

8 When you get to be President, there are all
those things, the honors, the twenty-one
gun salutes, all those things. You have to
remember it isn't for you. It's for the
Presidency.
Ibid., ch. 15

Dalton Trumbo (1905–76)

US SCREENWRITER AND AUTHOR

*A member of the Hollywood Ten who refused to
testify before the House Un-American Activities
Committee, he served a year in prison and was
blacklisted 1947–60. He wrote the screenplays for
Kitty Foyle (1940), Roman Holiday (1953, as Ian
McKellan Hunter) and The Brave One (1956, as
Robert Rich).*

1 Bankers, nepotists, contracts and talkies:
on four fingers one may count the leeches
which have sucked a young and vigorous
industry into paresis.
'The Fall of Hollywood', publ. in the *North
American Review* August 1933, quoted in *Writers
in Hollywood 1915–1951*, ch. 6 (1990) by Ian
Hamilton

2 Nothing is bigger than life. There's nothing noble in death. What's noble about
lying in the ground and rotting? What's
noble about never seeing the sunshine
again? What's noble about having your
arms and legs blown off? What's noble
about being an idiot? What's noble about
being blind and deaf and dumb? What's
noble about being dead?
Joe Bonham, in *Johnny Got His Gun*, bk. 1, ch. 10
(1939, filmed 1971)

Donald Trump (b. 1946)

US BUSINESSMAN

*He is a high-profile property tycoon, the owner of
real estate, an airline and casinos.*

1 Deals are my art form. Other people paint
beautifully on canvas or write wonderful
poetry. I like making deals, preferably big
deals. That's how I get my kicks.
Trump: The Art of the Deal, ch. 1 (written with
Tony Schwartz, 1987)

2 The point is that you can't be too greedy.
Ibid., ch. 2

3 I'm a bit of a P. T. Barnum. I make stars
out of everyone.
Quoted in the *Observer* 7 July 1991. Referring to
the women in his life.

Marina Tsvetaeva (1892–1941)

RUSSIAN POET AND PLAYWRIGHT

*She is best known for The Encampment of Swans
(1917–22), written in praise of counter-
revolutionaries, Craft (1923) and After Russia
(1928). She left Russia in 1922, but returned in 1939
when her husband was shot and her daughter
arrested. She later committed suicide.*

1 *Freedom! A wanton slut on a profligate's
breast!*
'Verses about Sonechka' (1917), repr. in *The
Heritage of Russian Verse* (ed. Dimitri Obolensky, 1965)

2 *Love is a stepmother, and no mother.
Then expect no justice and mercy from her.*
'Two Songs: 2' (1920), repr. in *Twentieth-
Century Russian Poetry* (ed. Albert C. Todd, Max
Hayward and Daniel Weissbort, 1993)

3 What is the main thing in love? to know
and to hide. To know about the one you
love and to hide that you love. At times the
hiding (shame) overpowers the knowing
(passion). The passion for the hidden – the
passion for the revealed.
The House at Old Pimen, ch. 2 (1934), repr. in *A
Captive Spirit: Selected Prose* (ed. and transl. J.
Marin King, 1980). Referring to her youthful
love for a girl.

4 *My desk, most loyal friend*
thank you. You've been with me on
every road I've taken.
My scar and my protection.

'Desk', written 1933–5, publ. in *Selected Poems* (1971, transl. ELAINE FEINSTEIN)

5 *It crawls, the underground snake,*
crawls, with its load of people.
And each one has his
newspaper, his skin
disease; a twitch of chewing;
newspaper caries.
Masticator of gum,
readers of newspapers.

'Readers of Newspapers', written 1935, publ. ibid.

6 There are books so alive that you're always afraid that while you weren't reading, the book has gone and changed, has shifted like a river; while you went on living, it went on living too, and like a river moved on and moved away. No one has stepped twice into the same river. But did anyone ever step twice into the same book?

Pushkin and Pugachev (1937), repr. in *A Captive Spirit: Selected Prose* (ed. and transl. J. Marin King, 1980). A reference to Heraclitus: 'You cannot step twice into the same river.'

7 A deception that elevates us is dearer than a host of low truths.

Ibid.

Barbara W. Tuchman (1912–89)
US HISTORIAN
Her bestselling books, which combine a literary and narrative approach, include The Guns of August *(1962), and* Stilwell and the American Experience in China: 1911–1945 *(1970).*

1 Dead battles, like dead generals, hold the military mind in their dead grip.

The Guns of August, ch. 2 (1962)

2 No more distressing moment can ever face a British government than that which requires it to come to a hard, fast and specific decision.

Ibid., ch. 9

3 In April 1917 the illusion of isolation was destroyed, America came to the end of innocence, and of the exuberant freedom of bachelor independence. That the responsibilities of world power have not made us happier is no surprise. To help ourselves manage them, we have replaced the illusion of isolation with a new illusion of omnipotence.

'How We Entered World War I', publ. in *The New York Times Magazine* 5 May 1967

4 Reasonable orders are easy enough to obey; it is capricious, bureaucratic or plain

idiotic demands that form the habit of discipline.

Stilwell and the American Experience in China: 1911–1945, pt. 1, ch. 1 (1970)

5 Diplomacy means all the wicked devices of the Old World, spheres of influence, balances of power, secret treaties, triple alliances, and, during the interwar period, appeasement of Fascism.

'If Mao Had Come to Washington in 1945', publ. in *Foreign Affairs* October 1972. Referring to 'the deep-seated American distrust . . . of diplomacy and diplomats'.

Sophie Tucker (1884–1966)
RUSSIAN-BORN US SINGER
Originally Sophie Abuza. With a career spanning more than sixty years, she appeared in vaudeville, burlesque, nightclubs and music halls, and became known as 'the last of the red-hot mamas' for her blues and jazz singing style.

1 I've been rich and I've been poor. Believe me, honey, rich is better.

Some of These Days (1945). See also GLORIA GRAHAME 2.

2 From birth to 18 a girl needs good parents. From 18 to 35, she needs good looks. From 35 to 55, good personality. From 55 on, she needs good cash. I'm saving my money.

Remark 1953, quoted in *Sophie*, 'When They Get Too Wild for Everyone Else' (1978) by Michael Freedland

(Sir) Mark Tully (b. 1935)
BRITISH JOURNALIST AND BROADCASTER
Associated with the BBC since 1964, he was chief of the Delhi bureau (1972–93) and Southeast Asia correspondent (1993–4). He has written and broadcast extensively on India.

1 Egalitarianism . . . in effect means equal opportunities for all to win and then ignores the inevitable losers.

No Full Stops in India, Introduction (1991)

2 She [Mother Teresa] somehow managed to combine poverty and glamour, and in that too she was like the Mahatma. They both knew that embracing poverty could be as glamorous as exhibiting wealth. It's only the middle road which is dull.

Appreciation of MOTHER TERESA, in the *Observer* 7 September 1997

(Sir) Stephen Tumim (b. 1930)
BRITISH JUDGE
He was a circuit judge 1978–96 and Chief Inspector of Prisons for England and Wales 1987–95. His book Crime and Punishment *(1997) was an indictment of the penal system.*

1 How you deal with crime depends on what sort of people you send to prison. We tend to send men, under 25, who come from broken homes and did very badly at school because they didn't try very hard and played truant, what one might call yobs . . . . These boys will come out bitter, not trained and not fit for work in the community we live in. And they're going to be with us for another 50 years.
Interview in the *Guardian* 13 April 1996. Referring to the typical prison population.

Ed Turner (b. 1935)
US TELEVISION EXECUTIVE
Managing Editor of Cable News Network, he was appointed vice-president in 1984.

1 If we had had the right technology back then, you would have seen Eva Braun on the Donahue show and Adolf Hitler on Meet the Press.
Quoted in the *Daily Telegraph* 5 September 1990

Kathleen Turner (b. 1954)
US ACTRESS
Since her debut in the film noir Body Heat *(1981), she has starred in light comedies* (Romancing the Stone, *1984) and thrillers* (V. I. Warshawski, *1991).*

1 You're not too smart, are you? I like that in a man.
Matty Walker (Kathleen Turner), in *Body Heat* (film, 1981, written and directed by Lawrence Kasdan)

2 Being a sex symbol has to do with an attitude, not looks. Most men think it's looks, most women know otherwise.
Quoted in the *Observer* 27 April 1986

Ted Turner (b. 1938)
US BROADCASTING EXECUTIVE
Robert Edward Turner. As President of Turner Broadcasting System (1963–96) he inaugurated CNN in 1980. He was vice-president of AOL Time Warner 1996–2003.

1 Life is like a B-movie. You don't want to leave in the middle of it but you don't want to see it again.
International Herald Tribune 2 March 1990

Scott Turow (b. 1949)
US LAWYER AND AUTHOR
His bestselling suspense novels, including Presumed Innocent *(1987, filmed 1990),* The Burden of Proof *(1990) and* The Laws of Our Fathers *(1996), are drawn from his inside experience as an attorney.*

1 Ladies and gentlemen, let me tell you again what you are to presume. [The defendant] is innocent. I am the judge. I am telling you that. Presume he is innocent. When you sit there, I want you to look and say to yourself, There sits an innocent man.
Judge Larren Lyttle addressing the jury, in *Presumed Innocent*, ch. 26 (1987). Judge Lyttle begins the selection of the jury by asking one member whether the defendant committed the crime, and, on receiving the answer, 'I wouldn't know, Judge,' dismissed the juror.

Desmond Tutu (b. 1931)
SOUTH AFRICAN CHURCHMAN
The first black bishop of Johannesburg (1985–6) and Archbishop of Cape Town (1986–96), he campaigned for a democratic, nonracial South Africa, advocating economic sanctions but deploring the use of violence. He was appointed Chairman of the Truth and Reconciliation Commission in 1995.

1 I am fifty-two years of age. I am a bishop in the Anglican Church, and a few people might be constrained to say that I was reasonably responsible. In the land of my birth I cannot vote, whereas a young person of eighteen can vote. And why? Because he or she possesses that wonderful biological attribute – a white skin.
Quoted in the *Guardian Weekly* 8 April 1984

2 Be nice to the whites, they need you to rediscover their humanity.
Quoted in *The New York Times* 19 October 1984

3 I am a leader by default, only because nature does not allow a vacuum.
Christian Science Monitor 20 December 1984

4 Having looked the past in the eye, having asked for forgiveness and having made amends, let us shut the door on the past – not in order to forget it but in order not to allow it to imprison us.
Report of South Africa's Truth and Reconciliation Committee, Foreword, quoted in the *Daily Telegraph* 30 October 1998

Jill Tweedie (1936–93)
BRITISH AUTHOR AND JOURNALIST
She was a broadcaster and a columnist for the Guardian *and wrote novels, including* It's Only Me *(1980),* Bliss *(1984) and* Internal Affairs *(1986).*

1 It is easy and dismally enervating to think of opposition as merely perverse or actually evil – far more invigorating to see it as essential for honing the mind, and as a positive good in itself. For the day that moral issues cease to be fought over is the

day the word 'human' disappears from the race.

Independent May 1989

Kenneth Tynan (1927–80)
BRITISH THEATRE CRITIC
Drama critic of the Observer *(1954–63) and literary manager of London's National Theatre (1963–9), he championed the work of* JOHN OSBORNE, *vigorously opposed censorship and authored the notoriously risqué revue* Oh! Calcutta! *(1969). For* GEORGE STEINER, *he was 'an anti-intellectual to the tip of his brilliant, histrionic fingers'.*

1 What, when drunk, one sees in other women, one sees in Garbo sober. . . . Most actresses in action live only to look at men, but Garbo looks at flowers, clouds and furniture with the same admiring compassion, like Eve on the morning of creation.

Sight and Sound April 1954, repr. in *Curtains*, 'The American Theatre' (1961)

2 A play . . . is basically a means of spending two hours in the dark without being bored.

Observer 7 August 1955, repr. in *The Life of Kenneth Tynan*, ch. 11 (1987) by Kathleen Tynan

3 The theatre's press-agent, asked for a description of the iconoclastic young gate-crasher, said that he was first and foremost 'an angry young man'. Before long the phrase, in itself not particularly striking, had snowballed into a cult. It did so because it defined a phenomenon that was nationally recognizable. It gave a name to a generation of young intellectuals who disliked being called intellectuals, since they thought the word phoney, affected, and 'wet'. There is nothing new in young men being angry: in fact, it would be news if they were anything else.

'The Angry Young Movement' (1958), repr. in *Tynan on Theatre* (1964). Referring to George Fearon, press agent at the Royal Court Theatre, which first staged JOHN OSBORNE's *Look Back in Anger* in 1956. Fearon is attributed with the first use of the phrase 'angry young man' in this context.

4 Art is parasitic on life, just as criticism is parasitic on art

'Ionesco and the Phantom', publ. in the *Observer* 6 July 1958, repr. in *Notes and Counter-Notes* (1962) by EUGÈNE IONESCO

5 A neurosis is a secret you don't know you're keeping.

Journal entry, 9 July 1961, publ. in *The Life of Kenneth Tynan*, ch. 18 (1987) by Kathleen Tynan

6 Satire is protest, couched in wit, against the notion that there is anything more important than the fact that all men must die.

Observer 29 April 1962, repr. ibid.

7 A good drama critic is one who perceives what is happening in the theatre of his time. A great drama critic also perceives what is not happening.

Tynan Right and Left, Foreword (1967)

8 One of the things that I promised myself that we might see at this theatre was that drama should be re-established to the same level of eminence that it attained with the Greeks; that the theatre should be a place where great matters of public concern were presented. . . . In these days, when the churches are empty, there is nowhere except the theatre where such matters can be properly debated as the Greeks debated them: matters of supreme conscience, of the highest level of importance, moral concern with great events and the motives behind them. That is what theatre is for.

Board Meeting at the National Theatre, 24 April 1967, as remembered by LAURENCE OLIVIER in *Confessions of an Actor*, appendix (1982). Olivier was Director of the National Theatre 1962–73.

Mike Tyson (b. 1966)
US BOXER
He became the youngest heavyweight champion in 1986 and was world champion 1987–90. After a prison term for rape (1992–5), he defeated FRANK BRUNO *in 1996 but was unable to repeat his former success.*

1 My objective is to be the ultimate professional. Regardless of whatever happens, the job has to be done. That's what being a professional is.

Quoted in *The New York Times* 28 June 1988

2 He [Hemingway] uses those short, sharp words just like hooks and upper cuts. You always know what he's saying 'cause he says it very clearly.

Quoted in the *Independent on Sunday* 13 February 1994. On his discovery of a liking for the works of ERNEST HEMINGWAY while in prison.

3 I have no self-esteem, but the biggest ego in the world.

Quoted in the *Independent on Sunday* 18 October 1998

Tristan Tzara (1896–1963)
ROMANIAN POET
Originally Sami Rosenstock. After launching the Dada movement in Zurich in 1916 he moved to Paris where he took part in the movement's 'happenings'. He published Vingt-cinq poèmes *(1918) and* Sept manifestes dada *(1920), and later more conventional lyrical poetry such as* Mouchoir de nuages *(1925).*

1 Art is a private thing, the artist makes it

for himself; a comprehensible work is the product of a journalist. . . . We need works that are strong, straight, precise, and forever beyond understanding.

'Dada Manifesto', publ. in *Dada* 3, 1918, repr. in *The Dada Painters and Poets* (ed. Robert Motherwell, 1951)

2 The rest, called *literature*, is a dossier of human imbecility for the guidance of future professors.

'Note on Poetry', publ. in *Dada* 4/5, May 1919, repr. in *Lampisteries* (1963)

3 DADA doubts everything. Dada is an armadillo. Everything is Dada, too. Beware of Dada. Anti-dadaism is a disease: self-kleptomania, man's normal condition, is DADA. But the real dadas are against DADA.

'Dada Manifesto on Feeble Love and Bitter Love', sect. 7, publ. in *La Vie des lettres* no. 4, 1921, repr. in *The Dada Painters and Poets* (ed. Robert Motherwell, 1951)

Harlan K. Ullman (b. 1940)
US CONSULTANT
and
James P. Wade
US POLITICIAN
After twenty years as a naval pilot, Ullman became a senior associate at the Center for Strategic and International Studies and is a columnist for the Washington Times. *Wade was a former Under-Secretary for Defense.*

1 The basis for Rapid Dominance rests in the ability to affect the will, perception, and understanding of the adversary through imposing sufficient Shock and Awe to achieve the necessary political, strategic and operational goals of the conflict or crisis that led to the use of force.
Shock and Awe, ch. 2 (1996). During the 2003 war in Iraq, Ullman conceded: 'The phrase, as used by the Pentagon now, has not been helpful. It has created a Doomsday approach. . . . The British have a much better phrase for it: effects-based operations.'

UNESCO constitution

1 Since wars begin in the minds of men, it is in the minds of men that the defences of peace must be constructed.
Preamble to constitution (1945). The wording is said to have been drafted by both CLEMENT ATTLEE and ARCHIBALD MACLEISH, who was then Chairman of the US delegation to the London conference responsible for drawing up the constitution.

John Updike (b. 1932)
US AUTHOR AND CRITIC
His many novels of middle-class alienation and adultery include Couples (1968) *and the sequences following the fortunes of car salesman 'Rabbit' Angstrom and the novelist Henry Bech.*

1 The difficulty with humorists is that they will mix what they believe with what they don't; whichever seems likelier to win an effect.
Rabbit, Run (1960)

2 The Founding Fathers in their wisdom decided that children were an unnatural strain on parents. So they provided jails called schools, equipped with tortures called an education. School is where you go between when your parents can't take you and industry can't take you.
George Caldwell, in *The Centaur,* ch. 4 (1963)

3 A healthy male adult bore consumes each year one and a half times his own weight in other people's patience.
Assorted Prose, 'Confessions of a Wild Bore' (1965)

4 If men do not keep on speaking terms
with children, they cease to be men, and
become merely machines for eating and
for earning money.
Ibid., 'A Foreword for Younger Readers'

5 Every marriage tends to consist of an
aristocrat and a peasant. Of a teacher and a
learner.
Couples, ch. 1 (1968)

6 It is not difficult to deceive the first time,
for the deceived possesses no antibodies;
unvaccinated by suspicion, she overlooks
latenesses, accepts absurd excuses, permits
the flimsiest patchings to repair great rents
in the quotidian.
Ibid., ch. 2

7 An affair wants to spill, to share its glory
with the world. No act is so private it does
not seek applause.
Ibid.

8 Sex is like money; only too much is
enough.
Piet Hanema, ibid., ch. 5

9 The first breath of adultery is the freest;
after it, constraints aping marriage
develop.
Narrator, ibid.

10 Things go bad. Food goes bad, people go
bad, maybe a whole country goes bad. The
blacks now have more than ever, but it
feels like less, maybe. We were all brought
up to want things and maybe the world
isn't big enough for all that wanting. I
don't know. I don't know anything.
Harry 'Rabbit' Angstrom, in *Rabbit Redux* (1971)

11 Confusion is just a local view of things
working out in general.
Ibid.

12 Government is either organized benevolence or organized madness; its peculiar
magnitude permits no shading.
The statesman Buchanan, in *Buchanan Dying*,
act 1 (1974)

13 To be President of the United States, sir, is
to act as advocate for a blind, venomous,
and ungrateful client; still, one must make
the best of the case, for the purposes of
Providence.
President James Polk, ibid., act 2

14 Morality . . . is a child of life, moral indignation a tool of survival. Once death has
equalized all men, worth flies from their
deeds as utility flies from their artifacts.
Buchanan, ibid., act 3

15 I think 'taste' is a social concept and not an
artistic one. I'm willing to show good taste,
if I can, in somebody else's living room,
but our reading life is too short for a writer
to be in any way polite. Since his words

enter into another's brain in silence and
intimacy, he should be as honest and
explicit as we are with ourselves.
Interview in *The New York Times Book Review*
10 April 1977, repr. in *Hugging the Shore*, Appendix (1983)

16 I would rather have as my patron a host of
anonymous citizens digging into their own
pockets for the price of a book or a magazine than a small body of enlightened and
responsible men administering public
funds. I would rather chance my personal
vision of truth striking home here and
there in the chaos of publication that exists
than attempt to filter it through a few sets
of official, honorably public-spirited
scruples.
Testimony given before the House of Representatives Committee on Education and Labor,
30 January 1978, Boston, publ. ibid.

17 That a marriage ends is less than ideal; but
all things end under heaven, and if temporality is held to be invalidating, then nothing real succeeds.
Too Far to Go, Foreword (1979)

18 America is a vast conspiracy to make you
happy.
Problems, 'How to Love America and Leave it at
the Same Time' (1980)

19 Writing criticism is to writing fiction and
poetry as hugging the shore is to sailing in
the open sea.
Hugging the Shore, Foreword (1983)

20 We must lighten ourselves to survive. We
must not cling. Safety lies in lessening, in
becoming random and thin enough for the
new to enter.
The Witches of Eastwick, pt. 1 (1984, filmed 1987).
Referring to the 'natural principle of
divestment'.

21 It [the literary interview] rots a writer's
brain, it cretinizes you. You say the same
thing again and again, and when you do
that happily you're well on the way to
being a cretin. Or a politician.
Interview by MARTIN AMIS in the *Observer*
30 August 1987, repr. in *Visiting Mrs Nabokov*,
'John Updike' (1993) by Martin Amis

22 Peace is not something we are entitled to
but an illusory respite we earn. On both
the personal and national level, islands of
truce created by balances of terror and
potential violence are the best we can hope
for.
Self-Consciousness, ch. 2 (1989)

23 Dreams come true; without that possibility, nature would not incite us to have
them.
Ibid., ch. 3

24 To say that war is madness is like saying

that sex is madness: true enough, from the standpoint of a stateless eunuch, but merely a provocative epigram for those who must make their arrangements in the world as given.

Ibid., ch. 4

25 Among the repulsions of atheism for me has been its drastic uninterestingness as an intellectual position. Where was the ingenuity, the ambiguity, the humanity (in the Harvard sense) of saying that the universe just happened to happen and that when we're dead we're dead?

Ibid.

26 Our brains are no longer conditioned for reverence and awe. We cannot imagine a Second Coming that would not be cut down to size by the televised evening news, or a Last Judgment not subject to pages of holier-than-Thou second-guessing in *The New York Review of Books*.

Ibid., ch. 6

27 The yearning for an afterlife is the opposite of selfish: it is love and praise for the world that we are privileged, in this complex interval of light, to witness and experience.

Ibid.

28 God is a word, however problematical, we do not have to look up in the dictionary. We seem to have its acquaintance from birth.

Ibid.

29 Religion enables us to ignore nothingness and get on with the jobs of life.

Ibid.

30 Looking foolish does the spirit good. The need not to look foolish is one of youth's many burdens; as we get older we are exempted from more and more, and float upward in our heedlessness, singing *Gratia Dei sum quod sum*.

Ibid. *Gratia Dei sum quod sum* ('Thanks be to God that I am what I am') is an epigraph in Updike's volume of memoirs, taken from an inscription on the tomb of Bishop West in Ely Cathedral.

31 Celebrity is a mask that eats into the face. As soon as one is aware of being 'somebody,' to be watched and listened to with extra interest, input ceases, and the performer goes blind and deaf in his overanimation. One can either see or be seen.

Ibid.

32 Customs and convictions change; respectable people are the last to know, or to admit, the change, and the ones most offended by fresh reflections of the facts in the mirror of art.

New Yorker 30 July 1990

33 In asking forgiveness of women for our mythologizing of their bodies, for being *unreal* about them, we can only appeal to their own sexuality, which is different but not basically different, perhaps, from our own. For women, too, there seems to be that that tangle of supplication and possessiveness, that descent toward infantile undifferentiation, that omnipotent helplessness, that merger with the cosmic mother-warmth, that flushed pulse-quickened leap into overestimation, projection, general mix-up.

'The Female Body', publ. in the *Michigan Quarterly Review* (1990), repr. in *The Best American Essays, 1991* (ed. Joyce Carol Oates, 1991)

34 Now that I am sixty, I see why the idea of elder wisdom has passed from currency.

New Yorker November 1992

35 Life robs us of ourselves, piece by small piece. What is eventually left is someone else.

Brazil, ch. 23 (1994)

36 For a Jew to move through post-war Europe is to move through hordes of ghosts, vast animated crowds that, since 1945, are not there at all – up in smoke. The feathery touch of the mysteriously absent is felt on all sides.

Bech at Bay, 'Bech in Czech' (1998)

Zdeněk Urbánek (b. 1917)

CZECH AUTHOR AND TRANSLATOR
As well as novels, for example Following Don Quixote *(1949), he has published collections of short stories, such as* Lives and Consciences *(1944), and essays, including* Uncommon Cases *(1993).*

1 You in the West have a problem. You are unsure when you are being lied to, when you are being tricked. We do not suffer from this; and unlike you, we have acquired the skill of reading between the lines.

Interview with John Pilger, August 1977, quoted by him in the *Guardian* 12 February 1990

(Sir) Peter Ustinov (b. 1921)

BRITISH ACTOR, WRITER AND DIRECTOR
Esteemed as a raconteur and broadcaster, he had success with his play Romanoff and Juliet *(1956, filmed 1961). Later plays include* Halfway up the Tree *(1967) and* Beethoven's Tenth *(1983). He has acted in numerous films.*

1 Laughter would be bereaved if snobbery died.

Quoted in the *Observer* 13 March 1955

2 A diplomat these days is nothing but a

head-waiter who's allowed to sit down occasionally.

The General, in *Romanoff and Juliet*, act 1 (1956). Ustinov himself played the General in the first production of the play.

3 Love is an act of endless forgiveness, a tender look which becomes a habit.

Christian Science Monitor 9 December 1958

4 If Botticelli were alive today he'd be working for *Vogue*.

Quoted in the *Observer* 21 October 1962

5 To refuse awards . . . is another way of accepting them with more noise than is normal.

Quoted in *Marlon Brando*, ch. 13 (1974, rev. 1989) by David Shipman. Of the refusal of Oscars by MARLON BRANDO and GEORGE C. SCOTT.

6 What is a more irrefutable proof of madness than an inability to have a doubt?

Dear Me, ch. 1 (1977)

7 I do not believe that friends are necessarily the people you like best, they are merely the people who got there first.

Ibid., ch. 5

8 Sex is a conversation carried out by other means. If you get on well out of bed, half the problems of bed are solved.

Interview in *Speaking Frankly* (1978) by Wendy Leigh

9 Unfortunately, the balance of nature decrees that a super-abundance of dreams is paid for by a growing potential for nightmares.

Independent 25 February 1989. Referring to the USA.

10 The truth is really an ambition which is beyond us.

International Herald Tribune 12 March 1990

11 Critics search for ages for the wrong word which, to give them credit, they eventually find.

Interview in the *Sunday Telegraph* 15 November 1998

Roger Vadim (1928–2000)
FRENCH FILM-MAKER

His glossily erotic films showcased his female stars, notably his first two wives, BRIGITTE BARDOT in And God Created Woman *(1956) and Annette Stroyberg in* Les Liaisons Dangereuses *(1959), as well as CATHERINE DENEUVE and JANE FONDA, his third wife.*

1 She [BRIGITTE BARDOT] was a wanton woman who had sacrificed her body to the god of success, perpetuating the myth of the film world in which depravity pays better than talent.

Memoirs of the Devil, ch. 8 (1975). 'From the moment I liberated Brigitte,' Vadim was earlier quoted as saying, 'the moment I showed her how to be truly herself, our marriage was all downhill' (*Sunday Express*, 2 July 1972).

Paul Valéry (1871–1945)
FRENCH POET AND ESSAYIST

After abandoning poetry for almost twenty years in favour of scientific studies, he established himself as France's leading poet with The Young Fate *(1917) and* Enchantments *(1922), which included the major poem 'The Graveyard by the Sea'.*

1 Science means simply the aggregate of all the recipes that are always successful. All the rest is literature.

Moralités (1932), repr. in *Collected Works*, vol. 14, 'Analects' (ed. J. Matthews, 1970). The last words echo Verlaine, 'All the rest is mere fine writing' ('L'Art poétique', 1882).

2 God created man and, finding him not sufficiently alone, gave him a companion to make him feel his solitude more keenly.

Tel Quel 1, 'Moralités' (1941)

3 Politics is the art of preventing people from taking part in affairs which properly concern them.

Tel Quel 2, 'Rhumbs' (1943)

Laurens van der Post (1906–96)
SOUTH AFRICAN WRITER AND PHILOSOPHER

Described by author Jan Morris as 'a mystic, disguised as a novelist and man of action', he became a mentor to PRINCE CHARLES. He wrote on ecology from a holistic viewpoint in The Lost World of the Kalahari *(1958) and* The Heart of the Hunter *(1961).*

1 Life was only possible for all of us because, in our past, there had been those who had put the claims of life itself before all else. Did it really matter whether the end came from the crab within or the hyaena without? We will have the courage to meet it

and give meaning to the manner of our dying provided we, like these humble, wrinkled old Bushmen, have not set a part of ourselves above the wholeness of life.

The Lost World of the Kalahari, ch. 10 (1958)

2 We suffer from a hubris of the mind. We have abolished superstition of the heart only to install a superstition of the intellect in its place.

The Heart of the Hunter (1961)

3 The educating of the parents is really the education of the child: children tend to live what is unlived in the parents, so it is vital that parents should be aware of their inferior, their dark side, and should press on getting to know themselves.

A Walk with a White Bushman (1986)

4 What is most threatening and destructive in human society today is the human being who is split in his own nucleus: it is the fission in the modern soul which makes nuclear fission so dangerous – he is a split atom. He has got to heal himself, make himself whole.

Ibid.

5 Somehow we should learn to know that our problems are our most precious possessions. They are the raw materials of our salvation: no problem, no redemption.

Ibid.

6 I feel that Buddhism is a religion of the high mountains. It is a religion of altitude. Christianity is a religion of serving creation in the here and now; it is very much of the earth, where man does his ploughing and sowing, his begetting and his suffering, seeking to find the great in the small, infinity in a grain of sand.

Ibid. The last words allude to William Blake, 'To see a world in a grain of sand/And a heaven in a wild flower' ('Auguries of Innocence', c. 1803).

7 The man of the Kalahari is Esau and we are Jacob, and there is a great gulf between us. This sense of property, of possession that we have is utterly foreign to the Esaus of the world. We have, he is.

Ibid.

8 The people who want sanctions remind me a lot of missionaries, who are anchored off an island full of prancing savages and cannibals whom they say they want to convert, but refuse to disembark and go among them, shouting instead, 'If you stop being cannibals, we will bring you the Bible!' This is metaphorically what they are trying to do with sanctions in South Africa.

Ibid.

Carl Van Doren (1885–1950)

US MAN OF LETTERS

Editor of the Cambridge History of American Literature *(1917–21), he helped establish the study of American letters on university curricula. He is also noted for his biographies.*

1 A classic is a book that doesn't have to be written again.

Quoted by JAMES THURBER in the *Bermudian* November 1950

Raoul Vaneigem (b. 1934)

BELGIAN PHILOSOPHER

Associated with the Situationists, he challenged what he considered the puritanism of the traditional Left with his conception of playfully subversive activism. His book The Revolution of Everyday Life *(1967) was a major influence on the New Left of the late 1960s.*

1 The organization controlling the material equipment of our everyday life is such that what in itself would enable us to construct it richly plunges us instead into a poverty of abundance, making alienation all the more intolerable as each convenience promises liberation and turns out to be only one more burden. We are condemned to slavery to the means of liberation.

'Basic Banalities II', publ. in *Internationale Situationiste* January 1963, repr. in *Situationist International Anthology* (ed. Ken Knabb, 1981)

2 Who wants a world in which the guarantee that we shall not die of starvation entails the risk of dying of boredom?

The Revolution of Everyday Life, Introduction (1967, transl. 1983)

3 There are more truths in twenty-four hours of a man's life than in all the philosophies.

Ibid., ch. 1, sect. 1

4 People who talk about revolution and class struggle without referring explicitly to everyday life, without understanding what is subversive about love and what is positive in the refusal of constraints, such people have a corpse in their mouth.

Ibid., ch. 1, sect. 4. The words were graffitoed onto walls in Paris during the 1968 revolt.

5 Never before has a civilization reached such a degree of a contempt for life; never before has a generation, drowned in mortification, felt such a rage to live.

Ibid., ch. 5

6 To be rich nowadays merely means to possess a large number of poor objects.

Ibid., ch. 7, sect. 2

7 In the kingdom of consumption the citizen is king. A democratic monarchy: equality before consumption, fraternity in consumption, and freedom through consump-

tion. The dictatorship of consumer goods has finally destroyed the barriers of blood, lineage and race.
Ibid.

8 The eruption of lived pleasure is such that in losing myself I find myself; forgetting that I exist, I realize myself.
Ibid., ch. 20, sect. 2

Nicholas Van Hoogstraten (b. 1945)
BRITISH BUSINESSMAN
An outspoken property tycoon, he was named Britain's youngest millionaire at the age of twenty-three. In 2002 he was given a ten-year prison sentence for the manslaughter of a former business associate, but he was granted a retrial the following year.

1 The Ramblers are just a bunch of the dirty mac brigade. The great unwashed. Would you have a lot of Herberts in your garden?
Quoted in the *Independent on Sunday* 6 December 1998. Referring to protesters demanding access to footpaths on his Uckfield estate. After being taken to court by the Ramblers Association, he was obliged to allow right of way in 2000.

Bartolomeo Vanzetti (1888–1927)
ITALIAN-BORN US POLITICAL ACTIVIST
Having emigrated to the United States in 1908, he was with Nicola Sacco convicted of murder in 1921, which led to a vociferous campaign alleging the two were prosecuted for their anarchist beliefs. The death sentences were carried out despite an international outcry.

1 My conviction is that I have suffered for things that I am guilty of. I am suffering because I am a radical, and indeed I am a radical; I have suffered because I was an Italian, and indeed I am an Italian; I have suffered more for my family and for my beloved than for myself; but I am so convinced to be right that if you would execute me two times, and if I could be reborn two other times, I would live again to do what I have done already.
Last speech to court, Dedham, Massachusetts, 19 April 1927, publ. in *The Penguin Book of Twentieth-Century Speeches* (ed. Brian MacArthur, 1999)

Mario Vargas Llosa (b. 1936)
PERUVIAN NOVELIST
His fiction frequently describes hypocrisy and corruption in domestic politics, and his first novel, The Time of the Hero *(1962), was publicly burned. Later titles include* Conversation in the Cathedral *(1969) and* Aunt Julia and the Scriptwriter *(1977). He stood unsuccessfully for president in Peru in 1990.*

1 Since it is impossible to know what's really happening, we Peruvians lie, invent, dream and take refuge in illusion. Because of these strange circumstances, Peruvian life, a life in which so few actually do read, has become literary.
Narrator, in *The Real Life of Alejandro Mayta*, ch. 9 (1984)

2 There is an incompatibility between literary creation and political activity.
International Herald Tribune 1 April 1988

3 Eroticism has its own moral justification because it says that pleasure is enough for me; it is a statement of the individual's sovereignty.
International Herald Tribune 23 October 1990

4 Prosperity or egalitarianism – you have to choose. I favour freedom – you never achieve real equality anyway: you simply sacrifice prosperity for an illusion.
Independent on Sunday 5 May 1991

Gianni Versace (1946–97)
ITALIAN FASHION DESIGNER
Considering himself a tailor rather than designer, he introduced his collections of men's and women's wear in 1978 and acquired a reputation for his gaudy colours and celebrity clientèle. He was shot dead outside his Florida home.

1 I like to dress egos. If you haven't got an ego today, you can forget it.
Quoted in obituary in the *Guardian* 16 July 1997

Hendrik Verwoerd (1901–66)
SOUTH AFRICAN POLITICIAN AND PRIME MINISTER
He was responsible for much of the apartheid legislation as Minister for Native Affairs (1950–58) and as Prime Minister (1958–66). In 1961 he withdrew South Africa from the Commonwealth and declared a republic. He was assassinated in the House of Assembly in Cape Town.

1 Is not our role to stand for the one thing which means our own salvation here but with which it will also be possible to save the world, and with which Europe will be able to save itself, namely the preservation of the white man and his state?
Speech in 1964, quoted in *The Oxford History of South Africa*, vol. 2, ch. 10 (ed. M. Wilson and L. Thompson, 1971)

Sid Vicious (1957–79)
BRITISH PUNK ROCKER
Originally John Ritchie. He joined the Sex Pistols on bass in 1977, and was later arrested in New York charged with murdering his girlfriend. He died of a drugs overdose while awaiting trial.

1 I've only been in love with a beer bottle and a mirror.
Quoted in *Sounds* 9 October 1976

2 I don't understand why people think it's so difficult to learn to play guitar. I found it incredibly easy. You just pick a chord, go twang, and you've got music.
Ibid.

Gore Vidal (b. 1925)
US NOVELIST AND CRITIC

An urbane and sardonic social commentator, he caused scandal for his treatment of homosexuality and transsexuality in such novels as Myra Breckin-ridge *(1968), while works such as* Julian *(1964),* Burr *(1973) and* Lincoln *(1984) fictionally explore the lives of historical figures.* FREDERIC RAPHAEL *called him 'a tribune who has little use for the plebs but no deference towards the patricians'.*

1 It is difficult to find a reputable American historian who will acknowledge the crude fact that a Franklin Roosevelt, say, wanted to be President merely to wield power, to be famed and to be feared. To learn this simple fact one must wade through a sea of evasions: history as sociology, leaders as teachers, bland benevolence as a motive force, when, finally, power *is* an end to itself, and the instinctive urge to prevail the most important single human trait, the necessary force without which no city was built, no city destroyed.
'Robert Graves and the Twelve Caesars', written 1952, publ. in the *Nation* 1959, repr. in *Rocking the Boat* (1963)

2 A talent for drama is not a talent for writing, but is an ability to articulate human relationships.
The New York Times 17 June 1956

3 Laughing at someone else is an excellent way of learning how to laugh at oneself; and questioning what seem to be the absurd beliefs of another group is a good way of recognizing the potential absurdity of many of one's own cherished beliefs.
'Satire in the 1950's', publ. in the *Nation* 26 April 1958, repr. in *Collected Essays 1952–1972* (1974)

4 Sex is. There is nothing more to be done about it. Sex builds no roads, writes no novels and sex certainly gives no meaning to anything in life but itself.
'Norman Mailer's Self-Advertisements', publ. in the *Nation* 2 January 1960, repr. ibid.

5 If most men and women were forced to rely upon physical charm to attract lovers, their sexual lives would be not only meager but in a youth-worshiping country like America painfully brief.
'Notes on Pornography', publ. in the *New York Review of Books* 31 March 1966, repr. ibid.

6 It is the spirit of the age to believe that any fact, no matter how suspect, is superior to any imaginative exercise, no matter how true.
'French Letters: Theories of the New Novel', publ. in *Encounter* December 1967, repr. ibid.

7 Always a godfather, never a god.
Quoted in *The Life of Kenneth Tynan*, ch. 27 (1987) by Kathleen Tynan. On being asked to be godfather to Kenneth and Kathleen Tynan's daughter Roxana in 1967.

8 There is something about a bureaucrat that does not like a poem.
Sex, Death and Money, Preface (1968)

9 The theater needs continual reminders that there is nothing more debasing than the work of those who do well what is not worth doing at all.
Newsweek 25 March 1968

10 I'm all for bringing back the birch, but only between consenting adults.
Television interview with DAVID FROST, quoted in the *Sunday Times* 16 September 1973

11 Whenever a friend succeeds, a little something in me dies.
Ibid.

12 Each writer is born with a repertory company in his head. Shakespeare has perhaps 20 players, and Tennessee Williams has about 5, and Samuel Beckett one – and maybe a clone of that one. I have 10 or so, and that's a lot. As you get older, you become more skillful at casting them.
Times Herald 18 June 1978

13 In America, the race goes to the loud, the solemn, the hustler. If you think you're a great writer, you must say that you are.
Interview in *Writers at Work* (fifth series, ed. George Plimpton, 1981)

14 Some writers take to drink, others take to audiences.
Ibid.

15 A narcissist is someone better looking than you are.
The New York Times 12 March 1981

16 A triumph of the embalmer's art.
Of RONALD REAGAN, quoted in the *Observer* 26 April 1981

17 As the age of television progresses the Reagans will be the rule, not the exception. To be perfect for television is all a President has to be these days.
Quoted in the *Observer* 7 February 1982

18 There is no such thing as a homosexual or a heterosexual person. There are only homo- or heterosexual acts. Most people are a mixture of impulses if not practises.
Armageddon? Essays 1983–1987, 'Tennessee Williams: Someone to Laugh at the Squares With', sect. 1 (1987). Vidal has reiterated this remark on various occasions.

19 On 16 September 1985, when the Commerce Department announced that the United States had become a debtor nation, the American Empire died.

Ibid., 'The Day the American Empire Ran out of Gas'

20 Writing fiction has become a priestly business in countries that have lost their faith.

Independent 16 August 1989

21 Think of the earth as a living organism that is being attacked by billions of bacteria whose numbers double every forty years. Either the host dies, or the virus dies, or both die.

'Gods and Greens', publ. in the *Observer* 27 August 1989, repr. in *A View from the Diner's Club* (1991)

22 I find in most novels no imagination at all. They seem to think the highest form of the novel is to write about marriage, because that's the most important thing there is for middle-class people.

Guardian 2 November 1989

23 The only thing pornography has been known to cause is solitary masturbation; as for corruption, the only immediate victim is English prose.

Quoted in the *Observer* 28 January 1996

24 What is real politics? Who collects what money from whom to spend on whom for what. That's all there is to it, but no politician in the United States dares address that subject for fear we'll discover who bought him and for how much – not to mention how the military got us $5 trillion into debt.

Interview in the *Independent* 19 August 1998

25 Everything changes except the avant-garde.
Attributed

26 He will lie even when it is inconvenient, the sign of a true artist.
Attributed

27 It is not enough to succeed. Others must fail.
Attributed

28 Never miss a chance to have sex or appear on television.
Attributed

King Vidor (1894–1982)
US FILM-MAKER

A key figure of Hollywood's silent era, he established a reputation for his films emphasizing social issues, notably The Big Parade (1925) *and* The Crowd (1928).

1 Marriage isn't a word – it's a *sentence*!
Caption in *The Crowd* (silent film, 1928)

Judith Viorst (b. 1935)
US POET AND JOURNALIST

'Married life is the rock on which I sit,' she states, and it is a recurrent theme of her light humorous verse, published in The Village Square (1965), It's Hard to Be Hip Over Thirty (1968), *and* Forever Fifty (1989).

1 With four walk-in closets to walk in,
Three bushes, two shrubs, and one tree,
The suburbs are good for the children,
But no place for grown-ups to be.
'The Suburbs Are Good For The Children', publ. in *It's Hard to Be Hip Over Thirty and Other Tragedies of Married Life* (1968)

2 But it's hard to be hip over thirty
When everyone else is nineteen,
When the last dance we learned was the Lindy,
And the last we heard, girls who looked like Barbra Streisand
Were trying to do something about it.
'It's Hard to Be Hip Over Thirty', publ. ibid.

3 It's true love because
If he said quit drinking martinis but I kept on drinking them and the next morning
I couldn't get out of bed,
He wouldn't tell me he told me.
'True Love', publ. ibid.

Viz

The comic, which features such characters as Sid the Sexist, Johnny Fartpants and The Fat Slugs, began as an enthusiasm of Chris Donald and his friends in the early 1980s. It was adopted by Virgin in 1984 and became a publishing phenomenon.

1 Buster Gonad and his Unfeasibly Large Testicles.
Comic character, inspired by 'Claude Hopper and his unfeasibly large feet'

2 Ooooh-errr.
Finbarr Saunders (and his Double Entendres)

Stephen Vizinczey (b. 1933)
HUNGARIAN NOVELIST AND CRITIC

After participating in the 1956 Hungarian uprising he fled to Canada where he became a producer in Canadian broadcasting. His best-selling novel In Praise of Older Women (1965) *was followed by his essay collections,* The Rules of Chaos (1968) *and* Truth and Lies in Literature (1986).

1 The truth is that our race survived ignorance; it is our scientific genius that will do us in.
Book review in *The Times* 21 September 1970, repr. in *Truth and Lies in Literature*, 'Leonardo's Regret' (1986)

2 Consistency is a virtue for trains: what we want from a philosopher is insights,

whether he comes by them consistently or not.

Book review in the *Sunday Telegraph* 21 April 1974, repr. ibid., 'Good Faith and Bad'

3 Strange as it may seem, no amount of learning can cure stupidity, and formal education positively fortifies it.

Book review in the *Sunday Telegraph* 2 March 1975, repr. ibid., 'Europe's Inner Demons'

4 When you close your eyes to tragedy, you close your eyes to greatness.

Book review in the *Sunday Telegraph* 5 January 1984, repr. ibid., 'Who Killed Kleist?'

5 We now have a whole culture based on the assumption that people know nothing and so anything can be said to them.

Book review in the *Observer* 24 June 1990

V. N. Volosinov (1905–60)

RUSSIAN LINGUIST

Valentin Nikolaevich Volosinov. Associated with Mikhail Bakhtin and his school of criticism which sought to strip away preconceptions about literature, he was author of Marxism and the Philosophy of Language *(1929), among other works.*

1 The domain of ideology coincides with the domain of signs. They equate with one another. Wherever a sign is present, ideology is present, too. *Everything ideological possesses semiotic value.*

Marxism and the Philosophy of Language, ch. 1 (1929)

Kurt Vonnegut (b. 1922)

US NOVELIST

He blends science fiction and fantasy with social comment in his novels, such as his first, Piano Player *(1952), and* Breakfast of Champions *(1973). His best known,* Slaughterhouse Five *(1969), is based on his experience as a prisoner of war in Germany.*

1 I have been a soreheaded occupant of a file drawer labeled 'Science Fiction' . . . and I would like out, particularly since so many serious critics regularly mistake the drawer for a urinal.

Wampeters, Foma and Granfallons, 'Science Fiction' (1974)

2 We would be a lot safer if the Government would take its money out of science and put it into astrology and the reading of palms. . . . Only in superstition is there hope. If you want to become a friend of civilization, then become an enemy of the truth and a fanatic for harmless balderdash.

Ibid., 'When I Was Twenty-One'

3 The two real political parties in America are the *Winners* and the *Losers*. The people don't acknowledge this. They claim

membership in two imaginary parties, the *Republicans* and the *Democrats*, instead.

Ibid., 'In a Manner that Must Shame God Himself'

4 Being American is to eat a lot of beef steak, and boy, we've got a lot more beef steak than any other country, and that's why you ought to be glad you're an American. And people have started looking at these big hunks of bloody meat on their plates, you know, and wondering what on earth they think they're doing.

Interview in *City Limits* 11 March 1983

5 What war has always been is a puberty ceremony. It's a very rough one, but you went away a boy and came back a man, maybe with an eye missing or whatever but godammit you were a man and people had to call you a man thereafter.

Ibid.

6 The feeling about a soldier is, when all is said and done, he wasn't really going to do very much with his life anyway. The example usually is: 'he wasn't going to compose Beethoven's Fifth.'

Ibid.

7 I was taught that the human brain was the crowning glory of evolution so far, but I think it's a very poor scheme for survival.

Quoted in the *Observer* 27 December 1987

8 The world has been ruined by appeasement. Appeasement of whom? Of the Communists? Of the Neo-Nazis? No! Appeasement of the compulsive warpreparers. I can scarcely name a nation that has not lost most of its freedom and wealth in attempts to appease its own addicts to preparations for war.

Fates Worse than Death, ch. 14 (1991)

John Vorster (1915–83)

SOUTH AFRICAN POLITICIAN AND PRIME MINISTER

Originally Balthazar Johannes Vorster. As Justice Minister (from 1961), he presided over some of the worst repression of the apartheid years. He was Prime Minister 1966–75.

1 As far as criticism is concerned, we don't resent that unless it is absolutely biased, as it is in most cases.

Quoted in the *Observer* 9 November 1969

Andrei Voznesensky (b. 1933)

RUSSIAN POET

His experimental verse, known for its use of metaphor, 'the engine of form' as he put it, has been published in Parabola *(1960),* Heart of Achilles *(1966) and* Nostalgia for the Present *(1978), among other collections.*

1 *I am Goya*
   of the bare field, by the enemy's beak
      gouged
   till the craters of my eyes gape
   I am grief
   I am the tongue
   of war, the embers of cities
   on the snows of the year 1941
   I am hunger
   'I am Goya' (1960, transl. Stanley Kunitz), repr. in *Antiworlds and the Fifth Ace* (ed. Patricia Blake and Max Hayward, 1966)

2 *Along a parabola life like a rocket flies,*
   Mainly in darkness, now and then on a
      rainbow.
   'Parabolic Ballad' (1960, transl. W. H. AUDEN), publ. in *Encounter* April 1963, repr. ibid. Opening lines of poem.

3 *The urge to kill, like the urge to beget,*
   Is blind and sinister. Its craving is set
   Today on the flesh of a hare: tomorrow it can
   Howl the same way for the flesh of a man.
   'Hunting a Hare' (1964, transl. W. H. Auden), repr. ibid.

Terry Waite (b. 1939)

BRITISH ECCLESIASTIC AND NEGOTIATOR

As special adviser to the Archbishop of Canterbury,
ROBERT RUNCIE, *he negotiated for the release of*
British and US hostages held in Beirut, but was
himself taken hostage (1987–91), an experience
described in Taken on Trust *(1993).*

1 Freeing hostages is like putting up a stage
set, which you do with the captors, agreeing on each piece as you slowly put it
together; then you leave an exit through
which both the captor and the captive can
walk with sincerity and dignity.

Television broadcast, ABC TV, 3 November
1986. On his work in Lebanon as special envoy
of the Archbishop of Canterbury to negotiate
the release of hostages, eleven weeks before his
own abduction.

2 The terrible thing about terrorism is that
ultimately it destroys those who practise it.
Slowly but surely, as they try to extinguish
life in others, the light within them dies.

Guardian 20 February 1992

Derek Walcott (b. 1930)

WEST INDIAN POET AND PLAYWRIGHT

Born in St Lucia, he has spent most of his life in
Trinidad, where he founded (1959) and for twenty-
five years ran the Trinidad Theatre Workshop. He
is best known for his verse collections such as The
Fortunate Traveller *(1981) and the epic* Omeros
(1990).

1 *I who have cursed*
   The drunken officer of British rule, how
      choose
   Between this Africa and the English tongue
      I love?
   Betray them both, or give back what they
      give?

'A Far Cry from Africa', publ. in *In a Green*
Night (1962)

2 *The peace of white horses,*
   The pastures of ports,
   The litany of islands,
   The rosary of archipelagoes.

'A Sea-Chantey', publ. ibid.

3 *Irascibility, muse of middle age.*

'The Estranging Sea', ch. 18, sect. 3, publ. in
Another Life (1973)

4 *Adam had an idea.*
   He and the snake would share
   the loss of Eden for a profit.
   So both made the New World. And it
      looked good.

'New World', publ. in *Sea Grapes* (1976)

5 *I try to forget what happiness was,*
   and when that don't work, I study the stars.

'The Schooner Flight', sect. 11, publ. in *The Star-*
Apple Kingdom (1980)

6 *I going to bite them young ladies, partner,*
like a hot dog or a hamburger
and if you thin, don't be in a fright
is only fat women I going to bite.
'The Spoiler's Return', publ. in *The Fortunate Traveller*, pt 2 (1981)

7 *Famine sighs like a scythe*
across the field of statistics and the desert
is a moving mouth. In the hold of this earth
10,000,000 shoreless souls are drifting.
Somalia: 765,000, their skeletons will go
under the tidal sand.
'The Fortunate Traveller', sect. 1, publ. ibid., pt 3

8 *To curse your birthplace is the final evil.*
Midsummer, 'Poem 29', sect. 1 (1984)

9 Any serious attempt to try to do something worthwhile is ritualistic.
Interview in *Writers at Work* (eighth series, ed. George Plimpton, 1988)

10 I come from a place that likes grandeur; it likes large gestures; it is not inhibited by flourish; it is a rhetorical society; it is a society of physical performance; it is a society of style.
Ibid.

11 The English language is nobody's special property. It is the property of the imagination: it is the property of the language itself.
Ibid.

12 Poetry, which is perfection's sweat but which must seem as fresh as the raindrops on a statue's brow, combines the natural and the marmoreal; it conjugates both tenses simultaneously: the past and the present, if the past is the sculpture and the present the beads of dew or rain on the forehead of the past.
Nobel Lecture, 1992, publ. in *The Antilles, Fragments of Epic Memory* (1993)

13 Break a vase, and the love that reassembles the fragments is stronger than that love which took its symmetry for granted when it was whole.
'Dissolving the Sigh of History', publ. in the *Guardian* 16 December 1992

George Wald (1906–97)
US BIOCHEMIST
After research work in Berlin, he was based at Harvard (1932–77), where he worked on the biochemistry of vision. He shared the 1967 Nobel Prize for Physiology or Medicine with Ragnar Granit and Haldan Hartline.

1 We are the products of editing, rather than of authorship.
'The Origin of Optical Activity', publ. in *Annals of the New York Academy of Sciences*, vol. 69 (1957)

2 It would be a poor thing to be an atom in a universe without physicists, and physicists are made of atoms. A physicist is an atom's way of knowing about atoms.
Foreword to *The Fitness of the Environment* (1959) by L. J. Henderson

George Walden (b. 1939)
BRITISH POLITICIAN
He held diplomatic posts from 1967 before being elected a Conservative MP in 1983, becoming Under-secretary of State at the Department of Education and Science (1985–7).

1 A country losing touch with its own history is like an old man losing his glasses, a distressing sight, at once vulnerable, unsure, and easily disoriented.
The Times 20 December 1986

Kurt Waldheim (b. 1918)
AUSTRIAN DIPLOMAT AND PRESIDENT
He was Secretary-General of the United Nations 1972–81 and in 1986 was elected President of Austria. He lost the 1992 election after allegations of complicity with the Nazi regime before and during the Second World War.

1 There is no such thing as collective guilt.
Quoted in the *International Herald Tribune* 11 March 1988. Referring to Austria's Nazi past.

Lech Walesa (b. 1943)
POLISH TRADE UNION LEADER AND PRESIDENT
In 1980 he founded the 'free trade union' Solidarity at the Gdansk shipyards, winning economic and political concessions from the government. He led Solidarity to victory in the 1989 election and served as Poland's President 1990–95.

1 You have riches and freedom here but I feel no sense of faith or direction. You have so many computers, why don't you use them in the search for love?
Quoted in the *Daily Telegraph* 14 December 1988. Said in Paris on his first visit outside the Soviet Bloc.

2 The supply of words in the world market is plentiful but the demand is falling. Let deeds follow words now.
Newsweek 27 November 1989

Alice Walker (b. 1944)
US AUTHOR AND CRITIC
Her novels The Third Life of Grange Copeland *(1970),* Meridian *(1976) and* The Color Purple *(1982, filmed 1985) focus on the racial and sexual oppression of black women. She has also published verse and essays, and an indictment of female circumcision,* Possessing the Secret of Joy *(1992).*

1 The gift of loneliness is sometimes a radical vision of society or one's people that

has not previously been taken into account.

Interview, publ. in *Interviews with Black Writers* (ed. John O'Brien, 1973)

2 It seems our fate to be incorrect . . . and in our incorrectness stand.

Ibid.

3 Guided by my heritage of a love of beauty and a respect for strength – in search of my mother's garden, I found my own.

'In Search of Our Mothers' Gardens', publ. in *Ms.* May 1974, repr. in *In Search of Our Mothers' Gardens* (1983)

4 How simple a thing it seems to me that to know ourselves as we are, we must know our mothers' names.

'A Letter to the Editor of *Ms.*', publ. in *Ms.* August 1974, repr. ibid.

5 All partisan movements add to the fullness of our understanding of society as a whole. They never detract; or, in any case, one must not allow them to do so. Experience adds to experience.

'Can I Be My Brother's Sister?' publ. in *Ms.* October 1975, repr. ibid., 'Brothers and Sisters'

6 It is healthier, in any case, to write for the adults one's children will become than for the children one's 'mature' critics often are.

'A Writer Because of, Not in Spite of, Her Children', publ. in *Ms.* January 1976, repr. ibid.

7 Writing saved me from the sin and inconvenience of violence.

'One Child of One's Own', publ. in *Ms.* August 1979, repr. ibid.

8 Oh those Africans!
Everywhere you look
they're bleeding
and crying
Crying and bleeding
on some of the whitest necks
in your town.

'The Diamonds on Liz's Bosom', publ. in *Horses Make a Landscape Beautiful* (1979)

9 The original 'crime' of 'niggers' and lesbians is that they prefer themselves.

'Breaking Chains and Encouraging Life', publ. in *Ms.* April 1980, repr. ibid.

10 The good news may be that Nature is phasing out the white man, but the bad news is that's who She thinks we all are.

'Nuclear Madness: What You Can Do', publ. in *Black Scholar* spring 1982, repr. ibid.

11 To me, the black black woman is our essential mother – the blacker she is the more us she is – and to see the hatred that is turned on her is enough to make me despair, almost entirely, of our future as a people.

'If the Present Looks Like the Past, What Does the Future Look Like?' publ. in *Essence* July 1982, repr. ibid.

12 The trouble with our people is as soon as they got out of slavery they didn't want to give the white man nothing else. But the fact is, you got to give 'em something. Either your money, your land, your woman or your ass.

Pa, in *The Color Purple* (1982)

13 She say, Celie, tell the truth, have you ever found God in church? I never did. I just found a bunch of folks hoping for him to show. Any God I ever felt in church I brought in with me. And I think all the other folks did too. They come to church to *share* God, not find God.

Shug, ibid.

14 Somewhere in the bible it say Jesus' hair was like lamb's wool, I say. Well, say Shug, if he came to any of these churches we talking bout he'd have to have it conked before anybody paid him any attention. The last thing niggers want to think about they God is that his hair kinky.

Narrator (Celie), ibid.

15 I think it pisses God off if you walk by the color purple in a field somewhere and don't notice it.

Shug, ibid.

16 Womanist is to feminist as purple is to lavender.

In Search of Our Mothers' Gardens, Epigraph (1983)

17 Anybody can observe the Sabbath, but making it holy surely takes the rest of the week.

Ibid., 'To the Editors of *Ms.* Magazine'

18 If Malcolm X had been a black woman his last message to the world would have been entirely different. The brotherhood of Moslem men – all colors – may exist . . . but part of the glue that holds it together is the thorough suppression of women.

Ibid.

19 There are those who believe Black people possess the secret of joy and that it is this that will sustain them through any spiritual or moral or physical devastation.

Possessing the Secret of Joy, Epigraph (1992)

George Wallace (1919–98)

US POLITICIAN

As a circuit judge in Alabama (1953–9) he made segregationist rulings in defiance of the US Civil Rights Commission, and as state Governor (1963–7) he attempted to block desegregation in Alabama schools. He was shot and paralysed while running for nomination as the Democratic Party presidential candidate in 1972.

1 **Segregation now, segregation tomorrow and segregation forever!**
Inaugural address as Governor of Alabama, January 1963, publ. in the *Birmingham World* 19 January 1963. Wallace's speechwriter, Asa Carter (1926–79), was a Ku Klux Klansman who went on to have literary success under the name of Forrest Carter, with, for example, *Gone to Texas*, filmed by CLINT EASTWOOD as *The Outlaw Josey Wales* (1976).

Mark Wallinger (b. 1959)
BRITISH ARTIST
His work, a satirical commentary on divisions in contemporary British society, varies from paintings to mixed-media installations.

1 **This century has needed witnesses more than it has needed artists. The camera asserts what it has seen. The artists are just looking.**
Guardian 13 January 1996

Michelene Wandor (b. 1940)
BRITISH POET, PLAYWRIGHT AND CRITIC
Her verse and plays, which include Spilt Milk *(1972),* Whose Greenham? *(1986) and* The Pankhursts *(1990), chiefly address themes of women's relations to a patriarchal culture. Her* Collected Poems *appeared in 1990.*

1 **Stupid word, that. Period. In America it means 'full stop', like in punctuation. That's stupid as well. A period isn't a full stop. It's a new beginning. I don't mean all that creativity, life-giving force, earth-mother stuff, I mean it's a new beginning to the month, relief that you're not pregnant, when you don't have to have a child.**
Guests in the Body, 'Mother's Pride' (1986)

2 **There is no revolutionary hope for the heterosexual, and I have therefore decided to love myself and become a lesbian.**
In conversation with her mother, in 'Meet My Mother', publ. in *Close Company: Stories of Mothers and Daughters* (ed. Christine Park and Caroline Heaton, 1987)

(Dame) Barbara Ward (1914–81)
BRITISH ECONOMIST AND JOURNALIST
Baroness Jackson of Lodsworth. She and her husband, UN official Robert Jackson, worked as advisers on development planning in India and Pakistan. Her popular writings on conservation and ecology include Spaceship Earth *(1966) and* Only One Earth *(1972, written with René Dubos).*

1 **There is no human failure greater than to launch a profoundly important endeavour and then leave it half done. This is what the West has done with its colonial system. It shook all the societies in the world loose from their old moorings. But it seems indifferent whether or not they reach safe harbour in the end.**
The Rich Nations and the Poor Nations, ch. 2 (1962)

2 **We cannot cheat on DNA. We cannot get round photosynthesis. We cannot say I am not going to give a damn about phytoplankton. All these tiny mechanisms provide the preconditions of our planetary life. To say we do not care is to say in the most literal sense that 'we choose death'.**
'Only One Earth', publ. in *Who Speaks for Earth?* (ed. Maurice F. Strong, 1973)

Andy Warhol (c. 1928–87)
US ARTIST AND FILM-MAKER
Originally Andrew Warhola. A leading figure in 1960s Pop Art, he specialized in depicting popular icons and mass-produced commodities. GORE VIDAL *called him 'a genius with the IQ of a moron', while for* EDMUND WHITE *he was 'the man whose heart is as warm as a hanky soaked in ethyl chloride'. See also* TOM WOLFE 9.

1 **My image is a statement of the symbols of the harsh, impersonal products and brash materialistic objects on which America is built today. It is a projection of everything that can be bought and sold, the practical but impermanent symbols that sustain us.**
'New Talent U.S.A.', publ. in *Art in America,* vol. 50, no. 1, 1962

2 **Those who talk about individuality the most are the ones who most object to deviation, and in a few years it may be the other way around. Some day everybody will just think what they want to think, and then everybody will probably be thinking alike; that seems to be what is happening.**
Interview in *Art News* November 1963, repr. in *Pop Art Redefined* (1969) by John Russell and Suzi Gablik

3 **I think somebody should be able to do all my paintings for me.**
Ibid.

4 **If you want to know all about Andy Warhol, just look at the surface: of my paintings and films and me, and there I am. There's nothing behind it.**
'Warhol in his Own Words', publ. in the *Los Angeles Free Press* 17 March 1967, repr. in *Andy Warhol: A Retrospective* (1986)

5 **There are beautiful sounds in rock. Very lazy, dreamlike noises. You can forget about the lyrics in most songs. Just dig the noise, and you've got our sound. . . . We're musical primitives.**
Quoted in the *New York Magazine,* 1967, repr. in *The Faber Book of Pop,* pt 5, '1966: A Quiet Evening at the Balloon Farm' (ed. Hanif Kureishi and Jon Savage, 1995). Referring to the Velvet Underground, the band that Warhol supported

from 1965, and whose first album he nominally produced (1967).

6 **In the future everybody will be world famous for fifteen minutes.**
Andy Warhol (exhibition catalogue, 1968). Ten years later, in *Andy Warhol's Exposures*, 'Studio 54' (1979), he wrote 'I'm bored with that line. I never use it any more. My new line is, "In fifteen minutes everybody will be famous." '

7 **I used to think that everything was just being funny but now I don't know. I mean, how can you tell?**
Quoted in *Vogue* 1 March 1970

8 **Sex is more exciting on the screen and between the pages than between the sheets.**
From A to B and Back Again, ch. 3 (1975)

9 **Fantasy love is much better than reality love. Never doing it is very exciting. The most exciting attractions are between two opposites that never meet.**
Ibid.

10 **Drag queens are living testimony to the way women used to want to be, the way some people still want them to be, and the way some women still actually want to be. Drags are ambulatory archives of ideal moviestar womanhood. They perform a documentary service, usually consecrating their lives to keeping the glittering alternative alive and available for (not-too-close) inspection.**
Ibid.

11 **I'm confused about who the news belongs to. I always have it in my head that if your name's in the news, then the news should be paying you. Because it's *your news* and they're taking it and selling it as their product. . . . If people didn't give the news their news, and if everybody kept their news to themselves, the news wouldn't have any news.**
Ibid., ch. 5

12 **Before I was shot, I always thought that I was more half-there than all-there – I always suspected that I was watching TV instead of living life. . . . Right when I was being shot and ever since, I knew that I was watching television. The channels switch, but it's all television.**
Ibid., ch. 6. Referring to the attempt on his life by VALERIE SOLANAS in 1968.

13 **Being good in business is the most fascinating kind of art. . . . Making money is art and working is art and good business is the best art.**
Ibid.

14 **I suppose I have a really loose interpretation of 'work', because I think that just being alive is so much work at something you don't always want to do. Being born is**

like being kidnapped. And then sold into slavery. People are working every minute. The machinery is always going. Even when you sleep.
Ibid.

15 **Since people are going to be living longer and getting older, they'll just have to learn how to be babies longer.**
Ibid., ch. 7

16 **Isn't life a series of images that change as they repeat themselves?**
Quoted in *Warhol*, 'Too Much Work 1980–84' (1989) by Victor Bokris

17 **Dying is the most embarrassing thing that can ever happen to you, because someone's got to take care of all your details.**
Ibid., 'Goodbye 1986–7'. On being admitted to hospital two days before his death, Warhol was said by a member of staff to be the only person in her experience who remembered his Blue Cross and health insurance ID numbers by heart.

Jack L. Warner (1892–1978)
US FILM PRODUCER
Originally Jack Leonard Eichelbaum. With his brothers Albert, Harry and Sam, he co-founded Warner Brothers Pictures, the first production company to introduce sound (1926). He was President of the company 1956–72.

1 **I would rather take a twenty-mile hike than crawl through a book.**
Attributed in *Writers in Hollywood 1915–1951*, ch. 5, sect. 2 (1990) by Ian Hamilton

Jack Warner (1895–1981)
BRITISH ACTOR
After working as a variety comedian, he acted in such films as The Captive Heart *(1946) and* The Blue Lamp *(1950), in which he appeared as PC Dixon, a role he extended in the TV series* Dixon of Dock Green.

1 **Evenin' all.**
George Dixon (Jack Warner), in *Dixon of Dock Green* (BBC TV series, 1955–76, created by Ted Willis). Each episode of the series started and ended with Sergeant Dixon's familiar salute and 'Evenin' all'.

Marina Warner (b. 1946)
BRITISH AUTHOR AND CRITIC
She explores the themes of sexuality and myth in her non-fiction work. Her novels include The Lost Father *(1988), and she has also published short stories, for example* The Mermaids in the Basement *(1993).*

1 **Although Mary cannot be a model for the New Woman, a goddess is better than no goddess at all, for the sombre-suited masculine world of the Protestant religion is**

altogether too much like a gentleman's club to which the ladies are only admitted on special days.

Alone of All Her Sex, Epilogue (1976)

2 I've noticed that the sign of a screen villain these days is fondling. . . . Movements of affection betoken insincerity: only the deadliest villain would reach out softly to touch an innocent face. So lethal is such a gesture that you expect him to leave a burnmark, like napalm. Sincere people never touch each other. . . . Kissers nowadays are invariably Judases.

Anna Collouthar, in *The Lost Father*, ch. 22 (1988)

3 All the soppy talk about the inner child has not laid to rest deep fantasies about the inner ogre.

No Go the Bogeyman, ch. 6 (1998)

4 Children imitate their elders: they cannot generate moral standards independently of the adults who surround them. Some will be Red Guards and denounce their grandmothers if their schoolteachers expect it of them; some will see visions of the Virgin Mary. They are not the keepers of our good conscience, and their aberrations reflect, and, in some shocking instances, magnify our own.

Ibid.

5 Fears trace a map of a society's values; we need fear to know who we are and what we do not want to be.

Ibid., Epilogue

Sylvia Townsend Warner (1893–1978)
BRITISH AUTHOR

She blended fantasy and reality in her fiction and verse. Her novels include Lolly Willowes *(1926), and* A Garland of Straw *(1943) and* Kingdoms of Elfin *(1977) are short-story collections. She was also an expert on Tudor music.*

1 There are some women . . . in whom conscience is so strongly developed that it leaves little room for anything else. Love is scarcely felt before duty rushes to encase it, anger impossible because one must always be calm and see both sides, pity evaporates in expedients, even grief is felt as a sort of bruised sense of injury, a resentment that one should have grief forced upon one when one has always acted for the best.

Autumn River, 'Total Loss' (1966)

2 When other helpers fail and comforts flee, when the senses decay and the mind moves in a narrower and narrower circle, when the grasshopper is a burden and the postman brings no letters, and even the Royal Family is no longer quite what it was, an obituary column stands fast.

Ibid., 'Their Quiet Lives'

Mary Warnock (b. 1924)
BRITISH PHILOSOPHER

Baroness Warnock of Weeke. She has advised and chaired committees on education, animal experiments and medical ethics. Her publications include The Uses of Philosophy *(1992) and* An Intelligent Person's Guide to Ethics *(1998).*

1 Oxford is, and always has been, full of cliques, full of factions, and full of a particular non-social snobbiness.

Observer 2 November 1980

Charles Marquis Warren (1917–90)
US WRITER, DIRECTOR AND PRODUCER

He is best known for writing and directing westerns during the 1950s and '60s, helping to shape the popular stereotype of the Wild West in the TV series Gunsmoke, The Virginian *and* Rawhide *as well as numerous films.*

1 Head 'em up, move 'em out, rope 'em in, head 'em off, pull 'em down, move 'em on.

Preamble to *Rawhide* (TV series, 1959–66, created by Charles Marquis Warren). The series, which ran for 217 episodes and included CLINT EASTWOOD among its stars, was based on the 1866 diary of drover and pioneer cowboy George Duffield.

Robert Penn Warren (1905–89)
US POET AND NOVELIST

A leading exponent of the New Criticism, he won three Pulitzer Prizes for the poetry collections Promises *(1957) and* Now and Then: Poems 1976–78 *(1978) and the novel* All the King's Men *(1946, filmed 1949). He became the first US Poet Laureate in 1986.*

1 Storytelling and copulation are the two chief forms of amusement in the South. They're inexpensive and easy to procure.

Newsweek 25 August 1980

Robert Warshow (1917–55)
US AUTHOR AND CRITIC

Editor of Commentary *magazine in the 1940s and '50s, he was known for his essays on popular culture, in particular cinema, published in* The Immediate Experience *(1962).*

1 In ways that we do not easily or willingly define, the gangster speaks for us, expressing that part of the American psyche which rejects the qualities and the demands of modern life, which rejects 'Americanism' itself.

'The Gangster as Tragic Hero', publ. in the *Partisan Review* 1948, repr. in *The Immediate Experience* (1962)

2 In the deeper layers of the modern consciousness ... every attempt to succeed is an act of aggression, leaving one alone and guilty and defenseless among enemies: one is *punished* for success. This is our intolerable dilemma: that failure is a kind of death and success is evil and dangerous, is – ultimately – impossible.
Ibid.

Denzel Washington (b. 1954)
US SCREEN ACTOR
He has received acclaim for his leading roles in the films Cry Freedom *(1987),* Glory *(1989),* Malcolm X *(1992) and* Philadelphia *(1993).*

1 I don't want to be in bed with anybody who's stronger than me or that has more hair on their chest than I do. Now you can call me old-fashioned, you can call me conservative ... just call me a man.
Joe Miller (Denzel Washington), in *Philadelphia*, (film, 1993, screenplay by Ron Nyswaner, directed by Jonathan Demme)

Michio Watanabe (1923–95)
JAPANESE POLITICIAN
Elected to the national House of Representatives in 1963 as a Liberal Democrat, he became Deputy Prime Minister in 1991, but failed in three attempts to become Prime Minister.

1 People with high ideals don't necessarily make good politicians. If clean politics is so important, we should leave the job to scientists and the clergy.
Quoted in *Newsweek* 12 June 1989

Keith Waterhouse (b. 1929)
BRITISH AUTHOR
Calling himself a 'journeyman writer', he drew on his Yorkshire working-class background for his whimsical novel Billy Liar *(1959). He co-wrote the screenplays for* Whistle Down the Wind *(1961) and* A Kind of Loving *(1962), and later had success with the stage show* Jeffrey Bernard is Unwell *(1989).*

1 Lying in bed, I abandoned the facts again and was back in Ambrosia.
Narrator (Billy Fisher), in *Billy Liar*, ch. 1 (1959). Opening sentence of book.

2 Jeffrey Bernard is Unwell.
Title of stage adaptation of Jeffrey Bernard's *Spectator* columns (1989). Referring to the *Spectator*'s customary notice of the non-appearance of the column written by Bernard (1932–97), whose notoriously dissolute lifestyle frequently resulted in missed editorial deadlines. The show, starring PETER O'TOOLE, ran in London's West End in 1989 and 1999.

3 We are ... entering an era of nuisance politics, where the kind of political obsessives

and hyper-activists who in the old Cold War days had no more chance of influencing events than a cabbage white has of changing back into a caterpillar, now see to their great joy a golden opportunity for bossing people about and stopping them from doing things. Put that cigarette out – the times they are a-changing.
Daily Mail 29 August 1991, repr. in *Sharon and Tracy and the Rest*, 'Joy for the Joiners' (1992)

Alan Watts (1915–73)
BRITISH-BORN US PHILOSOPHER AND AUTHOR
He was ordained an Episcopalian priest in 1944 and became known as a lecturer and broadcaster on comparative philosophy and religion. Such works as The Spirit of Zen *(1936) and* The Meaning of Happiness *(1953) labelled him 'the brain and Buddha of American Zen'.*

1 Zen ... does not confuse spirituality with thinking about God while one is peeling potatoes. Zen spirituality is just to peel the potatoes.
The Way of Zen, pt 2, ch. 2 (1957)

2 Trying to define yourself is like trying to bite your own teeth.
Life 21 April 1961

Auberon Waugh (1939–2001)
BRITISH JOURNALIST AND NOVELIST
The eldest son of EVELYN WAUGH, *he contributed to numerous newspapers and periodicals, notably* Private Eye *and the* Literary Review, *which he edited from 1986. The writer Anne Fremantle called him 'a latterday Swift, as savage, as sincere, as almost unbearably iconoclastic'.*

1 Religion was inevitably going to contract into a small nucleus of enthusiasts, and all they've achieved is to change the enthusiasts; the new enthusiasts happen to be the ones who like clapping their hands and looking soppy. They repel me.
Interview in *Singular Encounters* (1990) by Naim Attallah. Referring to new trends within the Catholic Church.

2 Anyone wishing to communicate with Americans should do so by e-mail, which has been specially invented for the purpose, involving neither physical proximity nor speech.
'Way of the World', column in the *Daily Telegraph* 1 November 1995

3 The seven million impotent American males who emerged as customers for Viagra were almost certainly the product of a changing relationship between the sexes, whereby the woman is nowadays accepted as the more important member of a partnership, being more intelligent, more

opinionated and the better judge of moral or political correctness.

Sunday Telegraph 27 September 1998

4 Novels have gone, novels are over. We don't want novels any more in this country. It's all been written. Nothing left to say. There's not a 'smart' set to emulate now, or to write about. If there's anything to say it's better done these days in newspapers or magazines.

Quoted in the *Observer* 21 November 1999

Evelyn Waugh (1903–66)

BRITISH NOVELIST

After his social satires, Decline and Fall *(1928) and* Scoop *(1938), he adopted a more serious, elegiac style in* Brideshead Revisited *(1945). He regarded his conversion to Catholicism in 1928 as the most important event of his life, once commenting: 'You don't know how much nastier I would be if I hadn't become a Catholic.'*

1 I expect you'll be becoming a schoolmaster, sir. That's what most of the gentlemen does, sir, that gets sent down for indecent behaviour.

The porter, in *Decline and Fall*, 'Prelude' (1928)

2 We schoolmasters must temper discretion with deceit.

Dr Fagan, ibid., pt 1, ch. 2

3 That's the public-school system all over. They may kick you out, but they never let you down.

Captain Grimes, ibid., pt 1, ch. 3. Paul Pennyfeather, to whom these words are addressed, had been given a letter of recommendation by his housemaster after being expelled from school.

4 We can trace almost all the disasters of English history to the influence of Wales.

Dr Fagan, ibid., pt 1, ch. 8

5 I came to the conclusion many years ago that almost all crime is due to the repressed desire for aesthetic expression.

Prison Governor Sir Wilfred Lucas-Dockery, ibid., pt 3, ch. 1. Spoken to Paul Pennyfeather, who has just been informed that he is to be put to work in the Arts and Crafts Workshop.

6 Anyone who has been to an English public school will always feel comparatively at home in prison. It is the people brought up in the gay intimacy of the slums . . . who find prison so soul-destroying.

Ibid., pt 3, ch. 4. See JONATHAN AITKEN 2.

7 If we can't stamp out literature in the country, we can at least stop its being brought in from outside.

Customs officer, in *Vile Bodies*, ch. 2 (1930)

8 All this fuss about sleeping together. For physical pleasure I'd sooner go to my dentist any day.

Nina Blount, ibid., ch. 6. Spoken to her fiancé Adam Fenwick-Symes.

9 *Feather-footed through the plashy fen passes the questing vole.*

William Boot's 'Lush Places' column, in *Scoop*, bk 1, ch. 1, sect. 4 (1938). Considered an example of 'good style' by the staff of *The Beast*.

10 News is what a chap who doesn't care much about anything wants to read. And it's only news until he's read it. After that it's dead.

Corker, ibid., bk 1, ch. 5, sect. 1

11 You should ask me whether I have any message for the British public. I have. It is this: *Might must find a way.* Not 'Force', remember; other nations use 'force'; we Britons alone use 'Might'.

Mr Baldwin, ibid., bk 2, ch. 5, sect. 1

12 If, for instance, they [journalists] have heard something from the postman, they attribute it to 'a semi-official statement'; if they have fallen into conversation with a stranger at a bar, they can conscientiously describe him as 'a source that has hitherto proved unimpeachable'. It is only when the journalist is reporting a whim of his own, and one to which he attaches minor importance, that he defines it as the opinion of 'well-informed circles'.

'Well-Informed Circles and How to Move in Them' (1939), repr. in *The Essays, Articles and Reviews of Evelyn Waugh* (ed. Donat Gallagher, 1983)

13 It is a curious thing that every creed promises a paradise which will be absolutely uninhabitable for anyone of civilised taste.

Ambrose, in *Put Out More Flags*, ch. 1, sect. 7 (1942)

14 The human mind is inspired enough when it comes to inventing horrors; it is when it tries to invent a Heaven that it shows itself cloddish. But Limbo is the place. In Limbo one has natural happiness without the beatific vision; no harps; no communal order; but wine and conversation and imperfect, various humanity. Limbo for the unbaptized, for the pious heathen, the sincere sceptic.

Ambrose, ibid.

15 Charm is the great English blight. It does not exist outside these damp islands. It spots and kills anything it touches. It kills love; it kills art; I greatly fear, my dear Charles, it has killed you.

Anthony Blanche addressing Charles Ryder, in *Brideshead Revisited*, bk. 3, ch. 2 (1945)

16 His courtesy was somewhat extravagant.

He would write and thank people who wrote to thank him for wedding presents and when he encountered anyone as punctilious as himself the correspondence ended only with death.

Life 8 April 1946

17 They are a very decent generous lot of people out here and *they don't expect you to listen.* . . . It's the secret of social ease in this country. They talk entirely for their own pleasure. Nothing they say is designed to be heard.

Sir Francis Hinsley, in *The Loved One* (1948). Referring to California, where Hinsley is a British expatriate.

18 You never find an Englishman among the under-dogs – except in England, of course.

Sir Ambrose Abercrombie, ibid.

19 That impersonal insensitive friendliness which takes the place of ceremony in that land of waifs and strays.

Ibid. Referring to Aimée Thanatogenos, an American.

20 In the dying world I come from quotation is a national vice. It used to be the classics, now it's lyric verse.

Dennis Barlow, ibid.

21 Impotence and sodomy are socially O.K. but birth control is flagrantly middle-class.

'An Open Letter . . . On a Very Serious Subject', publ. in *Encounter*, repr. in *Noblesse Oblige*, pt 3 (ed. Nancy Mitford, 1956)

22 We are American at puberty. We die French.

Journal entry, 18 July 1961, publ. in *The Diaries of Evelyn Waugh* (ed. Michael Davie, 1976)

23 Punctuality is the virtue of the bored.

Ibid., 26 March 1962

24 Manners are especially the need of the plain. The pretty can get away with anything.

Quoted in the *Observer* 15 April 1962

25 One forgets words as one forgets names. One's vocabulary needs constant fertilizing or it will die.

Journal entry, 25 December 1962, publ. in *The Diaries of Evelyn Waugh* (ed. Michael Davie, 1976)

26 It was announced that the trouble was not 'malignant'. . . . It was a typical triumph of modern science to find the only part of Randolph that was not malignant and remove it.

Ibid. March 1964. Referring to Randolph Churchill, son of WINSTON CHURCHILL and an old friend of Waugh's, with whom relations became increasingly acrimonious.

27 An artist must be a reactionary. He has to stand out against the tenor of the age and not go flopping along.

Interview in *Writers at Work* (third series, ed. George Plimpton, 1967)

Ruby Wax (b. 1953)
US TELEVISION PRESENTER

After moving to Britain in the 1970s, she worked with Dawn French and JENNIFER SAUNDERS, but is best known for her own shows, in which her angle is 'I don't kiss anyone's butt.'

1 My whole career has been an act of revenge.

Guardian 18 April 1991

John Wayne (1907–79)
US SCREEN ACTOR

Orginally Marion Michael Morrison. Known as 'The Duke', he played a succession of macho but honourable roles in westerns and war films, including Red River *(1948),* True Grit *(1969) and* The Shootist *(1976). 'I play John Wayne in every picture regardless of the character,' he once remarked, 'and I've been doing all right, haven't I?'*

1 A man oughta do what he thinks is right.

Hondo Lane (John Wayne), in *Hondo* (film, 1953, screenplay by James Edward Grant, directed by John Farrow)

2 Out here, due process is a bullet.

Col. Mike Kirby (John Wayne), in *The Green Berets* (film, 1968, screenplay by James Lee Barrett, directed by John Wayne and Ray Kellogg)

3 I'm just an ordinary goddamn American and I talk for all the ordinary goddamn Americans, the butchers and bakers and plumbers. I know these people; I know what they think.

Quoted in *The Film Greats*, 'John Wayne' (1985) by Barry Norman

4 Nobody should come to the movies unless he believes in heroes.

Quoted in *The Official John Wayne Reference Book* (1985, rev. 1993) by Charles John Kieskalt

Sigourney Weaver (b. 1949)
US SCREEN ACTRESS

The daughter of Sylvester Weaver, president of NBC, she has had leading roles in Alien *(1979) and its sequels,* The Year of Living Dangerously *(1983), and* Gorillas in the Mist *(1988), among other films.*

1 Never burn bridges. Today's junior prick, tomorrow's senior partner.

Katharine Parker (Sigourney Weaver), in

Working Girl (film, 1988, screenplay by Kevin Wade, directed by Mike Nichols)

Jack Webb (1920–87)
US ACTOR AND PRODUCER
He starred in the Dragnet *police series on radio and TV, and also in the films* Pete Kelly's Blues *(1955) and* The Last Time I Saw Archie *(1961), all of which he also produced. His first wife was the singer and actress Julie London.*

1 This is the city. Los Angeles, California. I work here. I carry a badge. My name's Friday. The story you are about to see is true; the names have been changed to protect the innocent.

Sgt. Joe Friday (Jack Webb), introducing *Dragnet* (radio and TV series, 1949–71, created by Jack Webb and Richard L. Breen, written, produced and directed by Jack Webb). Originally produced for radio, then successfully on TV for another 18 years, the crime series *Dragnet* started every episode with this monologue. Friday's speech was also characterized by such expressions as 'Just the facts, ma'am' and 'That's my job'.

Mary Webb (1881–1927)
BRITISH AUTHOR
Her romantic fiction set in the Shropshire countryside became popular after her novel Precious Bane *(1924) was praised by Prime Minister* STANLEY BALDWIN. *Her melodramatic style was satirized by* STELLA GIBBONS *in* Cold Comfort Farm *(1932).*

1 To many women marriage is . . . merely a physical change impinging on their ordinary nature, leaving their mentality untouched, their self-possession intact. They are not burnt by even the red fire of physical passion – far less by the white fire of love

The Golden Arrow, ch. 18 (1916)

2 The past is only the present become invisible and mute; and because it is invisible and mute, its memoried glances and its murmurs are infinitely precious. We are tomorrow's past.

Precious Bane, Foreword (1924)

3 'Saddle your dreams afore you ride 'em.'
Ibid., bk 1, title of ch. 6

Sidney Webb (1859–1947)
BRITISH SOCIALIST
Baron Passfield. Founder of the Fabian Society (1884) and of the London School of Economics (1895), he was instrumental in drafting the LABOUR PARTY CONSTITUTION, *entering parliament as a Labour MP in 1922. With his wife Beatrice he founded the* New Statesman *(1913) and published numerous works, including* Soviet Communism *(1935).*

1 Let me insist on what our opponents habitually ignore, and indeed, what they seem intellectually incapable of understanding, namely the inevitable gradualness of our scheme of change.

Speech to Labour Party Conference, London, 26 June 1923, publ. in *The Labour Party on the Threshold* (Fabian Tract no. 207, 1923). Referring to the programme of the Labour Party, then in opposition.

2 Marriage is the waste-paper basket of the emotions.

Quoted in *Autobiography*, vol. 1, ch. 4 (1967) by BERTRAND RUSSELL. This was a habitual saying, according to his wife Beatrice Webb, though Russell denied ever hearing it. The Webbs were, he wrote, 'the most completely married couple that I have ever known. They were, however, very averse from any romantic view of love or marriage. Marriage was a social institution designed to fit instinct into a legal framework.'

Max Weber (1864–1920)
GERMAN SOCIOLOGIST
Regarded as the founder of modern sociology, he is best known for The Protestant Ethic and the Spirit of Capitalism *(1904) and* Economy and Society *(1922).*

1 One can say that three pre-eminent qualities are decisive for the politician: passion, a feeling of responsibility, and a sense of proportion.

'Politics as a Vocation' (1919), repr. in *Essays in Sociology* (ed. H. H. Gerth and C. WRIGHT MILLS, 1946)

2 Only he has the calling for politics who is sure that he will not crumble when the world from his point of view is too stupid or base for what he wants to offer. Only he who in the face of all this can say 'In spite of all!' has the calling for politics.
Ibid.

3 A really definitive and good accomplishment is today always a specialized accomplishment. And whoever lacks the capacity to put on blinders, so to speak, and to come up to the idea that the fate of his soul depends upon whether or not he makes the correct conjecture at this passage of this manuscript may as well stay away from science. He will never have what one may call the 'personal experience' of science. Without this strange intoxication, ridiculed by every outsider; without this passion . . . you have *no* calling for science and you should do something else. For nothing is worthy of man as man unless he can pursue it with passionate devotion.

'Science as a Vocation' (1919), repr. ibid.

Jeffrey Weeks (b. 1945)

BRITISH SEXOLOGIST

His published works on sex, gender and society include Coming Out *(1977),* Invented Moralities *(1995) and* Making Sexual History *(1999).*

1 It is only possible to express the feelings of the body through the lacework of meanings that envelop it. Sexuality is as much about language as it is about sexual organs.

Against Nature, Introduction (1991)

Simone Weil (1909–43)

FRENCH PHILOSOPHER AND MYSTIC

Passionately concerned with religious matters as well as social equality and pacifism, she interspersed teaching philosophy with manual work, and died from pleurisy after restricting herself to the same diet as those in Nazi labour camps. Her works include Gravity and Grace *(1947) and* Waiting on God *(1950).*

1 I am not a Catholic; but I consider the Christian idea, which has its roots in Greek thought and in the course of the centuries has nourished all of our European civilization, as something that one cannot renounce without becoming degraded.

Letter, March 1937, publ. in *Vie de Simone Weil*, vol. 2, ch. 3 (1976) by Simone Pétrement

2 What a country calls its vital economic interests are not the things which enable its citizens to live, but the things which enable it to make war. Petrol is more likely than wheat to be a cause of international conflict.

'The Power of Words', publ. in *Nouveaux Cahiers*, 1 and 15 April 1937, repr. in *Selected Essays* (ed. Richard Rees, 1962)

3 I suffer more from the humiliations inflicted by my country than from those inflicted on her.

Letter to GEORGES BERNANOS, *c.* 1938, publ. ibid.

4 Who were the fools who spread the story that brute force cannot kill ideas? Nothing is easier. And once they are dead they are no more than corpses.

'Three Letters on History: Théophile de Viau' (1938 or 1939), publ. ibid.

5 The real stumbling-block of totalitarian régimes is not the spiritual need of men for freedom of thought; it is men's inability to stand the physical and nervous strain of a permanent state of excitement, except during a few years of their youth.

'Cold War Policy in 1939' (1939), publ. ibid.

6 If Germany, thanks to Hitler and his successors, were to enslave the European nations and destroy most of the treasures of their past, future historians would certainly pronounce that she had civilized Europe.

'The Great Beast', pt 3 (1939–40), publ. ibid.

7 It is not the cause for which men took up arms that makes a victory more just or less, it is the order that is established when arms have been laid down.

Ibid., 'Conclusion'

8 I would suggest that barbarism be considered as a permanent and universal human characteristic which becomes more or less pronounced according to the play of circumstances.

'Hitler and Roman Foreign Policy', publ. in *Nouveaux Cahiers* 1 January 1940

9 Force is as pitiless to the man who possesses it, or thinks he does, as it is to its victims; the second it crushes, the first it intoxicates. The truth is, nobody really possesses it.

'The *Iliad* or the Poem of Force', publ. in *Cahiers du Sud* December 1940/January 1941, repr. in *Simone Weil: An Anthology* (ed. Sian Miles, 1986). Translation by MARY MCCARTHY.

10 Humanism was not wrong in thinking that truth, beauty, liberty, and equality are of infinite value, but in thinking that man can get them for himself without grace.

'The Romanesque Renaissance', publ. in *Cahiers du Sud* 1941 or 1942, repr. in *Selected Essays* (ed. Richard Rees, 1962)

11 When a contradiction is impossible to resolve except by a lie, then we know that it is really a door.

New York Notebook, written 1942, publ. 1950, repr. in *First and Last Notebooks*, pt 3 (ed. Richard Rees, 1970)

12 Equality is the public recognition, effectively expressed in institutions and manners, of the principle that an equal degree of attention is due to the needs of all human beings.

'Draft for a Statement of Human Obligation' (1943), publ. in *Selected Essays* (ed. Richard Rees, 1962)

13 One cannot imagine St Francis of Assisi talking about rights.

'Human Personality' (1943), publ. in *La Table Ronde* December 1950, repr. ibid.

14 Real genius is nothing else but the supernatural virtue of humility in the domain of thought.

Ibid.

15 Beauty always promises, but never gives anything.

Ibid.

16 There is one, and only one, thing in modern society more hideous than crime – namely, repressive justice.

Ibid.

17 It is only the impossible that is possible for God. He has given over the possible to the mechanics of matter and the autonomy of his creatures.
'A War of Religions' (1943), publ. ibid.

18 We must prefer real hell to an imaginary paradise.
Ibid.

19 A test of what is real is that it is hard and rough. Joys are found in it, not pleasure. What is pleasant belongs to dreams.
Gravity and Grace, 'Illusions' (1947)

20 Purity is the power to contemplate defilement.
Ibid., 'Attention and Will'

21 A work of art has an author and yet, when it is perfect, it has something which is essentially anonymous about it.
Ibid., 'Beauty'

22 Culture is an instrument wielded by teachers to manufacture teachers, who, in their turn, will manufacture still more teachers.
The Need for Roots, pt 2, 'Uprootedness in the Towns' (1949)

23 Every time that I think of the crucifixion of Christ, I commit the sin of envy.
Waiting on God, 'Letter 4' (1950)

24 Those who are unhappy have no need for anything in this world but people capable of giving them their attention.
Ibid., 'Reflections on the Right Use of School Studies'

25 A doctrine serves no purpose in itself, but it is indispensable to have one if only to avoid being deceived by false doctrines.
Écrits de Londres, 'Fragments et notes' (1957)

26 It would seem that man was born a slave, and that slavery is his natural condition. At the same time nothing on earth can stop man from feeling himself born for liberty. Never, whatever may happen, can he accept servitude; for he is a thinking creature.
Oppression and Liberty, ch. 4 (1958)

27 In the Church, considered as a social organism, the mysteries inevitably degenerate into beliefs.
Quoted in *Simone Weil: Utopian Pessimist*, ch. 9 (1989) by David McLellan

Steven Weinberg (b. 1933)
US THEORETICAL PHYSICIST
From 1967 he developed a model of particle interaction potentially capable of providing a universal theory of nature. His publications include Dreams of a Final Theory *(1993) and* The Quantum Theory of Fields *(1995–6).*

1 The more the universe seems comprehensible, the more it also seems pointless.
The First Three Minutes, ch. 8 (1977)

2 The effort to understand the universe is one of the very few things that lifts human life a little above the level of farce, and gives it some of the grace of tragedy.
Ibid. Closing sentence of book.

George Weiss (b. 1940)
BRITISH ECCENTRIC
A feature of the London scene since the 1960s, he also goes under the name 'Captain Rainbow'.

1 Most idealistic people are skint. I have discovered that people with money have no imagination, and people with imagination have no money.
Guardian 3 November 1984

Colin Welch (b. 1924)
BRITISH JOURNALIST
As parliamentary sketch writer, columnist and editor he was long associated with the Daily Telegraph *(1950–83) and has also contributed to the* Spectator, *the* Daily Mail *and the* Independent.

1 To be conservative requires no brains whatsoever. Cabbages, cows and conifers are conservatives, and are so stupid they don't even know it. All that is basically required is acceptance of what exists.
Spectator 21 July 1967

Fay Weldon (b. 1933)
BRITISH NOVELIST AND TELEVISION PLAYWRIGHT
Formerly an advertising copywriter, she writes with astute irony of women and their struggles with men. Among her many novels are The Life and Loves of a She-Devil *(1983, televised 1985, filmed 1989) and* The Hearts and Lives of Men *(1987). She has also written numerous plays, scripts and television adaptations See also* ADVERTISING SLOGANS 8.

1 The New Women! I could barely recognise them as being of the same sex as myself, their buttocks arrogant in tight jeans, openly inviting, breasts falling free and shameless and feeling no apparent obligation to smile, look pleasant or keep their voices low. And how they live! Just look at them to know how! If a man doesn't bring them to orgasm, they look for another who does. If by mistake they fall pregnant, they abort by vacuum aspiration. If they don't like the food, they push the plate away. If the job doesn't suit them, they hand in their notice. They are satiated by everything, hungry for nothing. They are what I wanted to be; they are what I worked for

them to be: and now I see them, I hate them.

Narrator (Praxis Duveen), in *Praxis*, ch. 2 (1978)

2 We shelter children for a time; we live side by side with men; and that is all. We owe them nothing, and are owed nothing. I think we owe our friends more, especially our female friends.

Narrator (Praxis Duveen), ibid., ch. 19

3 You end up as you deserve. In old age you must put up with the face, the friends, the health, and the children you have earned.

Narrator (Praxis Duveen), ibid. ch. 21

4 Writers were never meant to be professionals. Writing is not a profession, it is an activity, an essentially amateur occupation. It is what you do when you are not living. It is something you do with your hands, like knitting.

Auntie Fay, in *Letters to Alice*, Letter 5 (1984)

5 That to be good is to be happy is not something particularly evident in any of our experiences of real life, yet how badly we want it, and need it, to be true.

Ibid. On Jane Austen's promise, 'If you are good . . . you will be happy'.

6 Young women especially have something invested in being *nice people*, and it's only when you have children that you realise you're not a nice person at all, but generally a selfish bully.

Independent on Sunday 5 May 1991

7 Your generation does too much sharing. To share grief is to double grief, not halve it.

Christabel, in 'A Good Sound Marriage' (1991), publ. in *Wicked Women* (1995)

8 Push, rend, slither, pop, baby's here. Baby cries.

'Pains' (1994), publ. ibid.

9 Therapists, New Agers and Born Again Christians seldom blink. A blink marks the mind's registration of a new idea. Converts have no intention of receiving new ideas. They know already all they want to know.

Elaine Desmond, in 'End of the Line', publ. ibid.

10 Experts are never in real danger. Everyone needs them. The chambermaid always survives the palace revolution. Someone has to make the beds.

Defoe Desmond, ibid.

11 We are all one-syllable people now, two at the most. So we mumble and stumble into our futures. But it is still our task and our reward to scavenge through the universe, picking up the detritus of lost concepts,

dusting them down, making them shine. Latin was the best polishing cloth of all, but we threw it away.

Elaine Desmond, ibid.

12 Rape isn't actually the worst thing that can happen to a woman if you're safe and alive.

Independent on Sunday 5 July 1998

13 Even God has become female. God is no longer the bearded patriarch in the sky. He has had a sex change and turned into Mother Nature.

Quoted in *The Times* 29 August 1998. On the feminization of society.

Orson Welles (1915–85)
US FILM-MAKER AND ACTOR

'A bravura personality' according to KENNETH TYNAN, *he founded the Mercury Theatre in 1937 and went on to make what many consider the greatest film ever made,* Citizen Kane *(1941), in which he was producer, director, screenwriter and leading actor. He produced and directed* The Magnificent Ambersons *(1942) and* The Lady from Shanghai *(1948), both praised by critics but commercial failures. See* MICHEÁL MACLIAMMÓIR 2.

1 Ladies and gentlemen, I have a grave announcement to make. Incredible as it may seem, strange beings who landed in New Jersey tonight are the vanguard of an invading army from Mars.

CBS radio broadcast, Hallowe'en, 1938, from a reading of *The War of the Worlds* (1898) by H. G. WELLS. According to the later reports, despite clear warnings that the broadcast was science fiction, listeners jammed switchboards and roads as they abandoned their homes in large numbers, with some people claiming they had actually seen the Martians.

2 In Italy for thirty years under the Borgias they had warfare, terror, murder, bloodshed – they produced Michelangelo, Leonardo da Vinci and the Renaissance. In Switzerland they had brotherly love, five hundred years of democracy and peace, and what did they produce? The cuckoo clock!

Harry Lime, in *The Third Man*, (film, 1949, screenplay by GRAHAM GREENE, directed by Carol Reed). Welles starred in the film and contributed the speech to Greene's screenplay; he later claimed that his words were based on a fragment of an old Hungarian play. Welles played the role of Cesare Borgia in the film *Prince of Foxes*, also released in 1949.

3 The essential is to excite the spectators. If that means playing *Hamlet* on a flying trapeze or in an aquarium, you do it.

Les Nouvelles littéraires, 1953, quoted in *Citizen Welles*, ch. 16 (1989) by Frank Brady

4 **The biggest electric train set any boy ever had!**
Of RKO studios, quoted in *The Fabulous Orson Welles*, ch. 7 (1956) by Peter Noble

5 **I hate television. I hate it as much as peanuts. But I can't stop eating peanuts.**
New York Herald Tribune 12 October 1956

6 **When you are down and out something always turns up – and it is usually the noses of your friends.**
The New York Times 1 April 1962

7 **I hate it when people pray on the screen. It's not because I hate praying, but whenever I see an actor fold his hands and look up in the spotlight, I'm lost. There's only one other thing in the movies I hate as much, and that's sex. You just can't get in bed or pray to God and convince me on the screen.**
Interview in *The Americans*, 'Can a Martian Survive by Pretending to be a Leading American Actor?' (1970) by DAVID FROST

8 **I think we're a kind of desperation. We're sort of a maddening luxury. The basic and essential human is the woman, and all that we're doing is trying to brighten up the place.**
On men, ibid.

9 **The ideal American type is perfectly expressed by the Protestant, individualist, anti-conformist, and this is the type that is in the process of disappearing. In reality there are few left.**
Interview in *Hollywood Voices* (ed. Andrew Sarris, 1971)

10 **A good artist should be isolated. If he isn't isolated, something is wrong.**
Ibid.

11 **The director is simply the audience. So the terrible burden of the director is to take the place of that yawning vacuum, to *be* the audience and to select from what happens during the day which movement shall be a disaster and which a gala night. His job is to preside over accidents.**
Speech to Hollywood Foreign Press Association, broadcast at the memorial service for Welles in Los Angeles, 4 November 1985, publ. in *Citizen Welles*, ch. 21 (1989) by Frank Brady

12 **We're born alone, we live alone, we die alone. Only through our love and friendship can we create the illusion for the moment that we're not alone.**
Danny's friend (Orson Welles), in *Someone to Love* (film, 1987, written and directed by Henry Jaglom). Speech contributed to screenplay by Welles, who appeared in the film as Henry Jaglom's unnamed mentor.

13 **I want to give the audience a *hint* of a scene. No more than that. Give them too** much and they won't contribute anything themselves. Give them just a suggestion and you get them working with you. That's what gives the theater meaning: when it becomes a social act.
Quoted in *Citizen Welles*, ch. 8 (1989) by Frank Brady

H. G. Wells (1866–1946)
BRITISH AUTHOR
Herbert George Wells. He was a pioneer of science fiction with such works as The Time Machine *(1895) and* The War of the Worlds *(1898), and the author of comic novels, including* Kipps *(1905) and* The History of Mr. Polly *(1910). He also wrote on history, science and socialism. His lover* REBECCA WEST *described him as 'the old maid among novelists', while* BRIAN ALDISS *considered him 'the Shakespeare of science fiction'. See also* HENRY JAMES 2.

1 **Moral indignation is jealousy with a halo. It is the peculiar snare of the perplexed orthodox.**
The Wife of Sir Isaac Harman, ch. 9, sect. 2 (1914)

2 **Nothing could have been more obvious to the people of the early twentieth century than the rapidity with which war was becoming impossible. And as certainly they did not see it. They did not see it until the atomic bombs burst in their fumbling hands.**
The World Set Free: A Story of Mankind, ch. 2, sect. 5 (1914). In his fantasy, Wells predicted an age of atomic energy starting with a war commencing in 1956.

3 **I had rather be called a journalist than an artist.**
Letter to HENRY JAMES, 8 July 1915, publ. in *Henry James and H. G. Wells* (ed. LEON EDEL and Gordon N. Ray, 1958)

4 **Beauty isn't a special inserted sort of thing. It is just life, pure life, life nascent, running clear and strong.**
Quoted by REBECCA WEST in book review in the *Daily News* 14 August 1915, repr. in *The History of Mr Wells*, ch. 5 (1995) by MICHAEL FOOT

5 **He was inordinately proud of England and he abused her incessantly.**
Mr Britling Sees it Through, bk 1, ch. 2, sect. 2 (1916). Referring to Mr Britling.

6 **We English are everlasting children in an everlasting nursery.**
Ibid., ch. 2, sect. 5

7 **Human history becomes more and more a race between education and catastrophe.**
The Outline of History, vol. 2, ch. 41 (1920)

8 **In England we have come to rely upon a comfortable time-lag of fifty years or a century intervening between the perception**

that something ought to be done and a serious attempt to do it.

The Work, Wealth and Happiness of Mankind, ch. 2 (1931)

9 Mankind which began in a cave and behind a windbreak will end in the disease-soaked ruins of a slum.

The Fate of Homo Sapiens, ch. 26 (1939)

10 There comes a moment in the day when you have written your pages in the morning, attended to your correspondence in the afternoon, and have nothing further to do. Then comes that hour when you are bored; that's the time for sex.

Quoted in *My Autobiography,* ch. 16 (1964) by CHARLIE CHAPLIN

John Wells (b. 1936)
BRITISH AUTHOR, ACTOR AND DIRECTOR
He was co-editor of Private Eye *(1964–7) and author of the satirical diaries of Mary Wilson and Denis Thatcher that appeared there, which he dramatized as* Mrs. Wilson's Diary *(1968) and* Anyone for Denis? *(1981).*

1 Infantilism is possibly the hallmark of our generation.

Quoted in *Beyond the Fringe . . . and Beyond,* pt 4 (1989) by Ronald Bergan

Irvine Welsh (b. 1958)
SCOTTISH AUTHOR
His novel Trainspotting *(1993, filmed 1996) accorded him cult status for its unsentimental portrayal of the subculture of heroin addicts. The* Acid House *(1994) and* Ecstasy *(1996) are collections of short stories inspired by dance culture, while the novel* Filth *(1998) was adapted for the stage.*

1 Take yir best orgasm, multiply the feeling by twenty, and you're still fuckin miles off the pace. Ma dry, cracking bones are soothed and liquefied by ma beautiful heroine's tender caresses. The earth moved, and it's still moving.

Renton, in *Trainspotting,* 'Kicking' (1993)

2 They'd rather gie a merchant school old boy with severe brain damage a job in nuclear engineering than gie a schemie wi a Ph.D. a post as a cleaner in an abbatoir.

Renton, ibid.

3 Ah don't hate the English. They're just wankers. We are colonized by wankers. We can't even pick a decent, healthy culture to be colonised by. No. We're ruled by effete arseholes. What does that make us?

Renton, ibid., 'Relapsing'

4 Choose us. Choose life. Choose mortgage payments; choose washing machines; choose cars; choose sitting oan a couch watching mind-numbing and spirit-crushing game shows, stuffing fuckin junk food intae yir mooth. Choose rotting away, pishing and shiteing yersel in a home, a total fuckin embarrassment tae the selfish, fucked-up brats ye've produced. Choose life.

Well, ah choose no tae choose life.

Renton, ibid., 'Blowing it: Searching for the Inner Man'

5 People are a wee bit fed up with the lack of substance in middle class postmodern writing. You know, that somehow the Oxbridge writer goes into this kind of supermarket and just picks whatever style or voices that they like. . . . You can't do subcultures as an Oxford twat hanging around the fucking streets, sitting in pubs and listening in on people.

Interview in *Dazed and Confused* February 1996

6 You can't afford a conscience in this life, that has become a luxury for the rich and a social ball and chain for the rest of us.

Robertson, in *Filth,* 'At Home with the Blades' (1998)

7 That's the thing with sex work, it always comes down to the most basic of formulas. If you really want to see how capitalism operates, never mind Adam Smith's pin factory, this is the place to study.

Nikki Fuller Smith, in *Porno,* ch. 16 (2002)

8 Straight actors are bigger whores than porn stars. Just letting somebody use your body, or the images of it you create, that's fuck all. It's when you let them use your emotions; that's real hooring. You can never, ever prostitute those!

Simon 'Sick Boy' Williamson, ibid., ch. 16

9 Pornography sneezes and popular culture catches cold. People want sex, violence, food, pets, DIY and humiliation. . . . in Britain we want to see people get fucked.

Simon 'Sick Boy' Williamson, ibid., ch. 29

Wim Wenders (b. 1945)
GERMAN FILM-MAKER
A key figure in the German cinema of the 1970s with such films as Summer in the City *(1970) and* Kings of the Road *(1976), he established himself in the USA with* Paris, Texas *(1984). Themes of alienation and wandering recur in his work.*

1 The Yanks have colonized our subconscious.

Robert Lander (Hans Zischler), in *Kings of the Road* (film, 1976, written and directed by Wim Wenders). Wenders himself said that he had been brought up on a diet of American movies.

2 Stories give people the feeling that there is meaning, that there is ultimately an order lurking behind the incredible confusion of appearances and phenomena that sur-

rounds them. . . . Stories are substitutes for God. Or maybe the other way round.

'Impossible Stories', talk given at a colloquium on narrative technique, 1982, publ. in *The Logic of Images* (1988)

3 A lot of my films start off with roadmaps instead of scripts. Sometimes it feels like flying blind without instruments. You fly all night and in the morning you arrive somewhere. That is: you have to try to make a landing somewhere so the film can end.

'Like Flying Blind without Instruments' (1984), publ. ibid.

4 The camera is a weapon against the tragedy of things, against their disappearing.

'Why do You Make Films?', reply to questionnaire April 1987, repr. ibid.

5 The more opinions you have, the less you see.

Quoted in *Evening Standard* 25 April 1990

6 What I fear most is an overdose of images. I fear losing the ability to discriminate between the good and the ugly.

Interview in the *Independent on Sunday* 19 April 1992

Arnold Wesker (b. 1932)

BRITISH PLAYWRIGHT

He once claimed his role to be 'that of a propagandist, direct or indirect, for world socialism'. His plays include Roots *(1959),* Chips with Everything *(1962) and* Caritas *(1981).*

1 I was never an angry young man, none of us was. On the contrary, we were all very happy young men and women. Who would not have been happy? Discovered, applauded, paid, made internationally famous overnight? But I am an angry old man.

Quoted in the *Independent on Sunday* 23 October 1994

Mae West (1892–1980)

US ACTRESS

After vaudeville appearances, she wrote and produced a play, Sex *(1926), for which she spent a week in prison for 'corrupting the morals of youth'. She transferred her vampish persona to the screen in a series of films including* I'm No Angel *(1933) and* Every Day's a Holiday *(1937). Mistress of the double entendre, she claimed to have written all her own lines.*

1 Goodness had nothing to do with it.

Night After Night (film, 1932, screenplay by Vincent Laurence, directed by Archie Mayo). Response to checkroom girl's exclamation, 'Goodness, what beautiful diamonds!', also the title of West's autobiography (1960).

2 Is that a gun in your pocket, or are you just glad to see me?

Lady Lou (Mae West), in *She Done Him Wrong* (film, 1933, screenplay by Harvey Thew and John Bright based on Mae West's play *Diamond Lil*, directed by Lowell Sherman)

3 Am I making myself clear, boys?

Lady Lou, ibid.

4 Why don't you come up sometime 'n see me? I'm home every evening . . . come on up, I'll tell your fortune.

Lady Lou, ibid.

5 When women go wrong, men go right after them.

Lady Lou, ibid.

6 I've been things and seen places.

Lady Lou, ibid.

7 It's not the men in my life, but the life in my men.

Tira (Mae West), in *I'm No Angel* (film, 1933, screenplay by Mae West and Harlan Thompson, directed by Wesley Ruggles). Rephrasing a reporter's remarks.

8 Beulah, peel me a grape.

Tira, ibid.

9 She's the kind of girl who climbed the ladder of success, wrong by wrong.

Tira, ibid.

10 When I'm good, I'm very, very good, but when I'm bad, I'm better.

Tira, ibid.

11 I believe that it's better to be looked over than it is to be overlooked.

Belle, in *Belle of the Nineties* (film, 1934, screenplay by Mae West, directed by Leo McCarey)

12 When choosing between two evils, I always like to pick the one I never tried before.

Frisco Doll (Mae West), in *Klondike Annie* (film, 1936, screenplay by Mae West, directed by Raoul Walsh)

13 Give a man a free hand and he'll try to put it all over you.

Frisco Doll, ibid.

14 I always say, keep a diary and some day it'll keep you.

Peaches O'Day (Mae West), in *Every Day's a Holiday* (film, 1937, screenplay by Mae West, directed by A. Edward Sutherland)

15 You ought to get out of those wet clothes and into a dry Martini.

Peaches O'Day, ibid. The line is said to have been borrowed by West, originally coined in the 1920s by ROBERT BENCHLEY's press agent.

16 Too much of a good thing can be wonderful.

Goodness Had Nothing to Do with It, ch. 21 (1960)

17 I think censorship is necessary; the things they're doing and saying in films right now just shouldn't be allowed. There's no dignity anymore and I think that's very important.

Interview in *Take One* 22 January 1974, quoted in *Writers in Hollywood 1915–1951*, ch. 4, sect. 2 (1990) by Ian Hamilton

18 There are no good girls gone wrong, just bad girls found out.

On Sex, Health and ESP, 'Last Word' (1975)

19 My advice to those who think they have to take off their clothes to be a star is, once you're boned, what's left to create the illusion? Let 'em wonder. I never believed in givin' them too much of me.

Quoted by David Ray Johnson in 'Biographical Study', appendix to *On Sex, Health and ESP* (1975)

20 I used to be Snow White – but I drifted.

Attributed

21 A hard man's good to find.

Attributed. Sometimes quoted with the added '. . . but you'll mostly find him asleep'.

(Dame) Rebecca West (1892–1983)
BRITISH AUTHOR
Original name Cicily Isabel Fairfield. An ardent feminist, she was the author of psychological novels, for instance The Thinking Reed *(1936), but is best known for her reports of the Nuremberg trials and for her study of the Balkans,* Black Lamb and Grey Falcon *(1942).*

1 I wonder if we are all wrong about each other, if we are just composing unwritten novels about the people we meet?

Letter, 1917, quoted as epigraph to *Rebecca West: A Life* (1987) by Victoria Glendinning

2 Most works of art, like most wines, ought to be consumed in the district of their fabrication.

Ending in Earnest, 'Journey's End Again' (1931)

3 There is no such thing as conversation. It is an illusion. There are intersecting monologues, that is all.

The Harsh Voice, 'There Is No Conversation' (1935)

4 It is queer how it is always one's virtues and not one's vices that precipitate one into disaster.

There Is No Conversation, ch. 1 (1935)

5 She [Isabelle] saw she had fallen into the hands of one of those doctors who have strayed too far from aperients in the direction of the soul.

The Thinking Reed, ch. 10 (1936)

6 All good biography, as all good fiction, comes down to the study of original sin, of our inherent disposition to choose death when we ought to choose life.

Time and Tide (1941)

7 There is no wider gulf in the universe than yawns between those on the hither and thither side of vital experience.

Black Lamb and Grey Falcon, vol. 1, 'Serbia' (1942)

8 All men should have a drop of treason in their veins, if nations are not to go soft like so many sleepy pears.

The Meaning of Treason, pt 4, 'Conclusion' (1949)

9 Just how difficult it is to write biography can be reckoned by anybody who sits down and considers just how many people know the real truth about his or her love affairs.

'The Art of Skepticism', publ. in *Vogue* 1 November 1952

10 Any authentic work of art must start an argument between the artist and his audience.

The Court and the Castle, pt 1, ch. 1 (1957)

11 Motherhood is the strangest thing, it can be like being one's own Trojan horse.

Letter, 20 August 1959, quoted in *Rebecca West: A Life*, pt 5, ch. 8 (1987) by Victoria Glendinning

12 He is every other inch a gentleman.

Quoted ibid., pt 3, ch. 5. Referring to novelist Michael Arlen. ALEXANDER WOOLLCOTT is also credited with this remark about Arlen in *Wit's End* (ed. Robert E. Drennan, 1968)

Edward Weston (1886–1958)
US PHOTOGRAPHER
Regarded by Ansel Adams as having 'recreated the mother-forms and forces of nature', he is known for his studies of landscapes, clouds, vegetables and nudes. With Adams, he founded the 'f/64' school of photography.

1 I have been photographing our toilet, that glossy enameled receptacle of extraordinary beauty. . . . Here was every sensuous curve of the 'human figure divine' but minus the imperfections. Never did the Greeks reach a more significant consummation to their culture, and it somehow reminded me, in the glory of its chaste convulsions and in its swelling, sweeping, forward movement of finely progressing contours, of the Victory of Samothrace.

Journal entry, 21 October 1925, publ. in *The Daybooks of Edward Weston*, vol. 1, pt 4, ch. 1 (ed. Nancy Newhall, 1961)

2 Photography suits the temper of this age – of active bodies and minds. It is a perfect medium for one whose mind is teeming

with ideas, imagery, for a prolific worker who would be slowed down by painting or sculpting, for one who sees quickly and acts decisively, accurately.

Journal entry, June 1934, publ. ibid., vol. 2, pt 3, ch. 10 (ed. Nancy Newhall, 1966)

Vivienne Westwood (b. 1941)

BRITISH FASHION DESIGNER

From selling punk fashions in the 1970s with MALCOLM MCLAREN, *she helped create the New Romantic look of the 1980s and later showed a long-standing interest in 'innerwear as outerwear'.*

1 Every time I hear that word, I cringe. Fun! I think it's disgusting; it's just running around. It's not my idea of pleasure.
Quoted in the *Independent on Sunday* 18 February 1990

2 It is not possible for a man to be elegant without a touch of femininity.
Quoted in the *Independent* 12 July 1990

3 The catwalk is theatre. It's about provocation and outrage.
Quoted in *Fashion and Perversity*, pt 1 (1996) by Fred Vermorel

4 What is sex after all? It's self-expression.
Quoted ibid.

5 Fashion is really about being naked.
Quoted ibid.

6 It is elegance that is potent and subversive. Elegance in a world of vulgarity.
Quoted ibid.

7 The English aristocracy is now only the middle class with knobs on.
Quoted in the *Guardian* 22 February 1997

8 The only possible effect one can have on the world is through unpopular ideas. They are the only subversion.
Quoted in *Westwood* (1999) by Catherine McDermott

9 You can say everything you want to say through tailoring – I believe that everything resides in technique. You can't teach creativity and it is from technique that one is able to be creative. This is the terrible mistake of this century – to put creativity first.
Quoted ibid.

10 The last people with any ideas are young people. The age in which we live, this non-stop distraction, is making it more impossible for the young generation to ever have the curiosity or discipline . . . because you need to be alone to find out anything.
Interview in the *Independent on Sunday* 8 November 1998

Tina Weymouth (b. 1950) and Chris Frantz (b. 1951)

US ROCK MUSICIANS

Married in 1977, they were members of the new wave/funk group Talking Heads (see DAVID BYRNE*) and in 1980 formed the spin-off Tom Tom Club, described as 'Talking Heads on vacation'.*

1 What are words worth?
Words in papers
Words in books
Words on TV
Words are crooks
Words of comfort
Words of peace
Words to make the fighting cease
Words to tell you what to do
Words are working hard for you.
'Wordy Rappinghood' (song) on the album *The Tom Tom Club* (1980)

Edith Wharton (1862–1937)

US AUTHOR

Encouraged by HENRY JAMES, *she established her reputation as a novelist of manners with* The House of Mirth *(1905). Much of her work satirized her own aristocratic class in Europe and America.*

1 Mrs Ballinger is one of the ladies who pursue Culture in bands, as though it were dangerous to meet it alone.
Xingu and Other Stories, 'Xingu' (1916)

2 How much longer are we going to think it necessary to be 'American' before (or in contradistinction to) being cultivated, being enlightened, being humane, & having the same intellectual discipline as other civilized countries? It is really too easy a disguise for our shortcomings to dress them up as a form of patriotism!
Letter, 19 July 1919, publ. in *The Letters of Edith Wharton* (ed. R. W. B. Leavis and Nancy Lewis, 1988)

3 I have never known a novel that was good enough to be good in spite of its being adapted to the author's political views.
Letter to UPTON SINCLAIR, 19 August 1927, publ. ibid.

4 There's no such thing as old age, there is only sorrow.
A Backward Glance, 'A First Word' (1934)

Charles Wheeler (b. 1923)

BRITISH JOURNALIST AND BROADCASTER

He joined the BBC in 1946 and was Chief Foreign Correspondent for America (1965–73) and Europe (1973–6) and subsequently a presenter of Panorama *and* Newsweek.

1 He smiled rather too much. He smiled at breakfast, you know.

Remembering the spy George Blake on *Inside Story* BBC 1, quoted in the *Independent* 20 September 1990

Francis Wheen (b. 1957)
BRITISH JOURNALIST AND BROADCASTER
A contributor to numerous newspapers and periodicals, he has also presented programmes for BBC radio. His books include Television: A History *(1985) and* Karl Marx *(1999).*

1 The only fetters binding the working class today are mock-Rolex watches.

Karl Marx, Introduction (1999)

E. B. White (1899–1985)
US AUTHOR AND EDITOR
Elwyn Brooks White. He began a long association with the New Yorker *in 1925, writing its 'Talk of the Town' column. His books include* Is Sex Necessary? *(1929), co-authored with* JAMES THURBER, *and his children's classic of poetry and humorous stories* Charlotte's Web *(1952).*

1 I say it's spinach, and I say the hell with it.

Cartoon caption, in the *New Yorker* 8 December 1928. Little girl in reply to her mother's remark, 'It's broccoli, dear' (drawing by Carl Rose).

2 Democracy is the recurrent suspicion that more than half of the people are right more than half of the time.

New Yorker 3 July 1944

3 The so-called science of poll-taking is not a science at all but mere necromancy. People are unpredictable by nature, and although you can take a nation's pulse, you can't be sure that the nation hasn't just run up a flight of stairs.

'Polling', publ. in the *New Yorker* 13 November 1948, repr. in *Writings from the New Yorker 1927–1976* (ed. Rebecca M. Dale, 1991)

4 Television hangs on the questionable theory that whatever happens anywhere should be sensed everywhere. If everyone is going to be able to see everything, in the long run all sights may lose whatever rarity value they once possessed, and it may well turn out that people, being able to see and hear practically everything, will be specially interested in almost nothing.

'Television', publ. in the *New Yorker* 4 December 1948, repr. ibid.

5 Commuters give the city its tidal restlessness; natives give it solidity and continuity; but the settlers give it passion.

'Here is New York', publ. in *Holiday* April 1949

6 The terror of the atom age is not the violence of the new power but the speed of man's adjustment to it – the speed of his acceptance.

The Second Tree from the Corner, 'Notes on Our Time' (1954)

7 Commuter – one who spends his life
In riding to and from his wife;
A man who shaves and takes a train,
And then rides back to shave again.

'The Commuter', publ. in *Poems and Sketches* (1982)

8 Shocking writing is like murder: the questions the jury must decide are the questions of motive and intent.

Interview in *Writers at Work* (eighth series, ed. George Plimpton, 1988)

Edmund White (b. 1940)
US AUTHOR
He is best known for his essays and criticism, and for the novel A Boy's Own Story *(1982), which describes an adolescent coming to terms with his homosexuality.*

1 In the lifelong romance each man has with himself, he should know which vows he's sworn.

'The Gay Philosopher', written 1969, publ. in *The Burning Library* (1994)

2 Perhaps sex and sentiment *should* be separated. Isn't sex, shadowed as it always is by jealousy and ruled by caprice, a rather risky basis for a sustained, important relationship?

'Fantasia on the Seventies' (1977), repr. ibid.

3 Sado-masochism is a futile effort to reduce ubiquitous cruelty to the comprehensible scope of sex.

'Sado Machismo', publ. in *New Times* 8 January 1979, repr. ibid.

4 When 'morality' is discussed I invariably discover, halfway into the conversation, that what is meant are not the great ethical questions . . . but the rather dreary business of sexual habit, which to my mind is an aesthetic rather than an ethical issue.

States of Desire: Travels in Gay America, ch. 2 (1980)

5 I feel sorry for a man who never wanted to go to bed with his father; when the father dies, how can his ghost get warm except in a posthumous embrace? For that matter, how does the survivor get warm?

A Boy's Own Story, ch. 1 (1982)

6 For my father . . . manliness was not discussable, but had it been, it would have included a good business suit, ambition, paying one's bills on time, enough knowledge of baseball to hand out like tips at the barbershop, a residual but never foolhardy degree of courage, and an unbreachable reserve; to the headmaster man-

liness . . . entailed tweeds, trust funds, graciousness to servants, a polite but slightly chilly relationship to God, a pretended interest in knowledge and an obsessive interest in sports, especially muddy, dangerous ones.
Ibid., ch. 6

7 I have no contempt for that time of life when our friendships are most passionate and our passions are incorrigible and none of our sentiments yet compromised by greed or cowardice or disappointment. The volatility and intensity of adolescence are qualities we should aspire to preserve.
'Paradise Found', publ. in *Mother Jones* June 1983, repr. in *The Burning Library* (1994)

8 We treat the failure of marriage as though it were the failure of individuals to achieve it – a decline in grit or maturity or commitment or stamina rather than the unraveling of a poorly tied knot. Bourgeois marriage was meant to concentrate friendship, romance, and sex into an institution at once familial and economic. Only the most intense surveillance could keep such a bulky, ill-assorted load from bursting at the seams.
'Sexual Culture', publ. in *Vanity Fair*, 1983, repr. ibid.

9 The right to have sex, even to look for it, has been so stringently denied to gays for so many centuries that the drive toward sexual freedom remains a bright, throbbing banner in the fierce winds whipping over the ghetto.
Ibid.

10 All men want quick, uncomplicated sexual adventure (as well as sustained romantic passion); in a world of all men, that desire is granted.
Ibid.

11 The AIDS epidemic has rolled back a big rotting log and revealed all the squirming life underneath it, since it involves, all at once, the main themes of our existence: sex, death, power, money, love, hate, disease and panic. No American phenomenon has been so compelling since the Vietnam War.
States of Desire: Travels in Gay America (1980) 'Afterword – AIDS: An American Epidemic' (added to 1986 edn)

T. H. White (1906–64)
BRITISH AUTHOR
Terence Hanbury White. Writing mostly for children, he is best known for The Once and Future King (1939–58), *based on Arthurian legend. His other works are a similar mix of medievalism, fantasy and science fiction.*

1 The Once and Future King.
Book title (1958). The words which refer to King Arthur are derived from the inscription supposed to be on his tomb, according to Sir Thomas Malory's *Le Morte d'Arthur*, bk 21, ch. 7 (1485): 'Hic iacet Arthurus, rex quondam rexque futurus.'

Alfred North Whitehead (1861–1947)
BRITISH PHILOSOPHER
He established his reputation with his work on mathematical logic, collaborating with his former pupil BERTRAND RUSSELL *to produce* Principia Mathematica (1910–13). *His metaphysical theory was published in* Process and Reality (1929) *and he also wrote numerous popular works.*

1 Uneducated clever women, who have seen much of the world, are in middle life so much the most cultured part of the community. They have been saved from this horrible burden of inert ideas.
'The Aims of Education', publ. in *The Organisation of Thought* (1917), repr. in *The Aims of Education and Other Essays* (1929)

2 Style is the ultimate morality of mind.
Ibid.

3 Every philosophy is tinged with the colouring of some secret imaginative background, which never emerges explicitly into its train of reasoning.
Science and the Modern World, ch. 1 (1926)

4 The safest general characterization of the European philosophical tradition is that it consists of a series of footnotes to Plato.
Process and Reality, pt 2, ch. 1, sect. 1 (1929)

5 In a general way the whole period of education is dominated by this threefold rhythm. Till the age of thirteen or fourteen there is the romantic stage, from fourteen to eighteen the stage of precision, and from eighteen to two and twenty the stage of generalization.
The Aims of Education and Other Essays, 'The Rhythmic Claims of Freedom and Discipline' (1929)

6 Life is an offensive, directed against the repetitious mechanism of the Universe.
Adventures of Ideas, pt 1, ch. 5 (1933)

7 It is more important that a proposition be interesting than that it be true. This statement is almost a tautology. For the energy of operation of a proposition in an occasion of experience is its interest, and is its importance. But of course a true proposition is more apt to be interesting than a false one.
Ibid., pt 4, ch. 16

8 Art is the imposing of a pattern on experi-

ence, and our aesthetic enjoyment is recognition of the pattern.

Dialogues of Alfred North Whitehead, '10 June 1943' (ed. Lucien Price, 1954)

9 There are no whole truths; all truths are half-truths. It is trying to treat them as whole truths that plays the devil.

Ibid., Prologue

Katharine Whitehorn (b. 1926)

BRITISH JOURNALIST

She became a columnist for the Observer in 1960 and was Assistant Editor 1980–88.

1 When it comes to housework the one thing no book of household management can ever tell you is how to begin. Or maybe I mean *why*.

Roundabout, 'Nought for Homework' (1962)

2 From a commercial point of view, if Christmas did not exist it would be necessary to invent it.

Ibid., 'The Office Party'

3 An office party is not, as is sometimes supposed, the Managing Director's chance to kiss the tea-girl. It is the tea-girl's chance to kiss the Managing Director (however bizarre an ambition this may seem to anyone who has seen the Managing Director face on). Bringing down the mighty from their seats is an agreeable and necessary pastime, but no one supposes that the mighty, having struggled so hard to get seated, will enjoy the dethronement.

Ibid.

4 Hats divide generally into three classes: offensive hats, defensive hats, and shrapnel.

Shouts and Murmurs, 'Hats' (1963)

5 People get a bad impression of it [the English climate] by continually trying to treat it as if it was a bank clerk, who ought to be on time on Tuesday next, instead of philosophically seeing it as a painter, who may do anything so long as you don't try to predict what.

Observer 7 August 1966

6 Any committee that is the slightest use is composed of people who are too busy to want to sit on it for a second longer than they have to.

Observations, 'Are You Sitting Comfortably?' (1970)

7 I wouldn't say when you've seen one Western you've seen the lot; but when you've seen the lot you get the feeling you've seen one.

Sunday Best, 'Decoding the West' (1976)

8 The thing has been blown up out of all proportion. PC language is *not* enjoined on one and all – there are a lot more places where you can say 'spic' and 'bitch' with impunity than places where you can smoke a cigarette.

Observer 25 August 1991

Gough Whitlam (b. 1916)

AUSTRALIAN POLITICIAN AND PRIME MINISTER

Elected the first Australian Labor prime minister for twenty-three years in 1972, he was dismissed by the Governor General in controversial circumstances in 1975, retiring from politics in 1977.

1 The punters know that the horse named Morality rarely gets past the post, whereas the nag named Self-Interest always runs a good race.

Daily Telegraph 19 October 1989

Anne Widdecombe (b. 1947)

BRITISH POLITICIAN

An outspoken Conservative MP since 1987, she was a junior minister in the Home Office (1995–7) and became Shadow Home Secretary in 1999, the same year she converted to Roman Catholicism.

1 He has something of the night in him.

Quoted in the *Sunday Times* 11 May 1997. Referring to Michael Howard, the former Home Secretary, whose candidature in the Conservative Party leadership election was said to have been seriously damaged by Widdecombe's remark.

2 Being English means, to me, tea on vicarage lawns, roses in a summer twilight, people keeping themselves to themselves, well-fed cats purring on hearthrugs, the bottom right-hand column of the 'Times' correspondence column.

Quoted in the *Big Issue* 10 August 1998

Norbert Wiener (1894–1964)

US MATHEMATICIAN

He taught at the Massachusetts Institute of Technology (1919–60), where he became interested in the 'science of control and communication in the animal and machine' for which he coined the word 'cybernetics', as described in his book Cybernetics *(1948).*

1 A painter like Picasso, who runs through many periods and phases, ends up by saying all those things which are on the tip of the tongue of the age to say, and finally sterilizes the originality of his contemporaries and juniors.

The Human Use of Human Beings, ch. 7 (1950)

2 The idea that information can be stored in a changing world without an overwhelming depreciation of its value is false. It is scarcely less false than the more plausible claim that after a war we may take our existing weapons, fill their barrels with

cylinder oil, and coat their outsides with sprayed rubber film, and let them statically await the next emergency.

Ibid.

Elie Wiesel (b. 1928)

ROMANIAN-BORN US AUTHOR

A survivor of Auschwitz, he worked in journalism in Israel and the United States. Much of his work is based on his traumatic personal experiences, including three novels Night *(1958),* Dawn *(1961) and* The Accident *(1961).*

1 The opposite of love is not hate, it's indifference. The opposite of art is not ugliness, it's indifference. The opposite of faith is not heresy, it's indifference. And the opposite of life is not death, it's indifference.

US News and World Report 27 October 1986

2 How do you describe the sorting out on arriving at Auschwitz, the separation of children who see a father or mother going away, never to be seen again? How do you express the dumb grief of a little girl and the endless lines of women, children and rabbis being driven across the Polish or Ukrainian landscapes to their deaths? No, I can't do it. And because I'm a writer and teacher, I don't understand how Europe's most cultured nation could have done that. For these men who killed with submachine guns in the Ukraine were university graduates. Afterwards they would go home and read a poem by Heine. So what happened?

Testifying at the trial of Klaus Barbie in Lyons, 2 June 1987, quoted in *Le Monde* 4 June 1987

3 Once you bring life into the world, you must protect it. We must protect it by changing the world.

Interview in *Writers at Work* (eighth series, ed. George Plimpton, 1988)

4 Nobody is stonger, nobody is weaker than someone who came back. There is nothing you can do to such a person because whatever you could do is less than what has already been done to him. We have already paid the price.

Ibid.

5 What does mysticism really mean? It means the way to attain knowledge. It's close to philosophy, except in philosophy you go horizontally while in mysticism you go vertically.

Ibid.

6 We are heading towards catastrophe. I think the world is going to pieces. I am very pessimistic. Why? Because the world hasn't been punished yet, and the only punishment that could be adequate is the nuclear destruction of the world.

Ibid.

7 When you see the abyss, and we have looked into it, then what? There isn't much room at the edge – one person, another, not many. If you are there, others cannot be there. If you are there, you become a protective wall. What happens? You become part of the abyss.

Ibid.

8 I marvel at the resilience of the Jewish people. Their best characteristic is their desire to remember. No other people has such an obsession with memory.

Daily Mail 15 July 1988. Wiesel's 'major preoccupation', he said on a previous occasion, is 'the kingdom of memory. I want to protect and enrich that kingdom, glorify that kingdom and serve it.'

9 In this place of darkness and malediction we can but stand in awe and remember its stateless, faceless and nameless victims. Close your eyes and look: endless nocturnal processions are converging here, and here it is always night. Here heaven and earth are on fire.

Address at fiftieth anniversary of liberation of Auschwitz, 27 January 1995, publ. in *The Penguin Book of Twentieth-Century Speeches* (ed. Brian MacArthur, 1999)

10 It is true that not all the victims were Jews. But all the Jews were victims.

Ibid.

Billy Wilder (1906–2002)

AUSTRIAN-BORN US FILM-MAKER

Originally Samuel Wilder. Working in Hollywood from 1934, he enjoyed a long association with co-writers Charles Brackett and later I. A. L. Diamond on films such as Double Indemnity *(1944),* Sunset Boulevard *(1950),* The Seven Year Itch *(1955) and* The Apartment *(1960).*

1 One's too many, and a hundred's not enough.

Nat the bartender (Howard Da Silva), in *The Lost Weekend* (film, 1945, screenplay by Charles Brackett and Billy Wilder based on novel by Charles Jackson, directed by Billy Wilder). Spoken to regular customer Don Birnam (Ray Milland) whose descent into alcoholic breakdown is portrayed in the film. See also BRENDAN BEHAN 6.

2 I don't go to church. Kneeling bags my nylons.

Lorraine (Jan Sterling), in *The Big Carnival* (film, 1951, screenplay by Billy Wilder, Lesser Samuel and Walter Newman, produced and directed by Billy Wilder). The movie was originally released under the title *Ace in the Hole*.

3 Well, nobody's perfect.

Osgood E. Fielding III (Joe E. Brown), in *Some Like It Hot* (film, 1959, screenplay by Billy Wilder and I. A. L. Diamond, produced and directed by Billy Wilder). On discovering that his fiancée (JACK LEMMON) is a man, in final words of film.

4 A woman without a man is like a trailer without a car; it ain't going nowhere.

Polly the Pistol (Kim Novak), in *Kiss me, Stupid* (film, 1964, written and directed by Billy Wilder)

5 Ah, Marilyn, Hollywood's Joan of Arc, our Ultimate Sacrificial Lamb. Well, let me tell you, she was mean, terribly mean. The meanest woman I have ever known in this town. I am appalled by this Marilyn Monroe cult. Perhaps it's getting to be an act of courage to say the truth about her. Well, let me be courageous. I have never met anyone as utterly mean as Marilyn Monroe. Nor as utterly fabulous on the screen.

Interview in the *Los Angeles Times*, 1968, quoted in *Billy Wilder in Hollywood*, ch. 19 (1977) by Maurice Zolotow

6 A country where the money falls apart but you can't tear the toilet paper.

Of France, quoted ibid., ch. 18

7 Hindsight is always twenty-twenty.

Quoted in *Wit and Wisdom of the Moviemakers*, ch. 7 (ed. John Robert Columbo, 1979)

8 An audience is never wrong. An individual member of it may be an imbecile, but a thousand imbeciles together in the dark – that is critical genius.

Arena TV profile, 24 January 1992, BBC2

Thornton Wilder (1897–1975)
US NOVELIST AND PLAYWRIGHT
His work dealt primarily with 'those things which repeat and repeat and repeat in the lives of millions', as he once described it. He won Pulitzer prizes for his novel The Bridge of San Luis Rey *(1927, filmed 1929) and the plays* Our Town *(1938, filmed 1940) and* The Skin of Our Teeth *(1942).*

1 I've never forgotten for long at a time that living is struggle. I know that every good and excellent thing in the world stands moment by moment on the razor-edge of danger and must be fought for – whether it's a field, or a home, or a country.

Antrobus, in *The Skin of Our Teeth*, act 3 (1942)

2 Literature is the orchestration of platitudes.

Time 12 January 1953

3 Marriage is a bribe to make a housekeeper think she's a householder.

Vendergelder, in *The Matchmaker*, act 1 (1954). The play, which was adapted from a previous work, *The Merchant of Yonkers* (1939), was later

the basis for the Broadway musical *Hello Dolly!* (1963).

4 Never support two weaknesses at the same time. It's your combination sinners – your lecherous liars and your miserly drunkards – who dishonor the vices and bring them into bad repute.

Malachi, ibid., act 3

5 The test of an adventure is that when you're in the middle of it, you say to yourself, 'Oh, now I've got myself into an awful mess; I wish I were sitting quietly at home.' And the sign that something's wrong with you is when you sit quietly at home wishing you were out having lots of adventure.

Barnaby, ibid., act 4

6 I am convinced that, except in a few extraordinary cases, one form or another of an unhappy childhood is essential to the formation of exceptional gifts.

Interview in *Writers at Work* (first series, ed. Malcolm Cowley, 1958)

7 A dramatist is one who believes that the pure event, an action involving human beings, is more arresting than any comment that can be made upon it.

Ibid.

Paul Wilkinson (b. 1937)
BRITISH ACADEMIC
Professor of International Relations from 1990 and appointed Director of the Centre for the Study of Political Violence at St Andrew's University, Scotland, in 1999, he is the author of books on terrorism and sectarian conflict.

1 Fighting terrorism is like being a goalkeeper. You can make a hundred brilliant saves but the only shot that people remember is the one that gets past you.

Daily Telegraph 1 September 1992

George F. Will (b. 1941)
US POLITICAL COLUMNIST
Long respected as a journalist and broadcaster, he has published widely, including The Pursuit of Virtue, and Other Tory Notions *(1982) and* The Leveling Wind *(1994).*

1 It is no longer enough to be lusty. One must be a sexual gourmet.

'The Ploy of Sex' (1974), repr. in *The Pursuit of Happiness, and Other Sobering Thoughts* (1978)

2 A politician's words reveal less about what he thinks about his subject than what he thinks about his audience.

Quoted in *A Ford, Not a Lincoln*, ch. 1 (1975) by Richard Reeves

3 Voters don't decide issues, they decide *who* will decide issues.

Newsweek 8 March 1976

4 Statecraft is soulcraft. Just as all education is moral education because learning conditions conduct, much legislation is moral legislation because it conditions the action and the thought of the nation in broad and important spheres of life.
Statecraft as Soulcraft: What Government Does, ch. 1 (1984)

5 Politics should share one purpose with religion: the steady emancipation of the individual through the education of his passions.
Ibid., ch. 2

6 Americans are overreaching; overreaching is the most admirable and most American of the many American excesses.
Ibid., ch. 4

7 To be an intelligent fan is to participate in something. It is an activity, a form of appreciating that is good for the individual's soul, and hence for society.
Men at Work: The Craft of Baseball, Introduction (1990)

8 Football combines the two worst things about America: it is violence punctuated by committee meetings.
International Herald Tribune 7 May 1990

Hank Williams (1923–53)
US COUNTRY MUSICIAN
Performing at southern honky-tonks in his teens, he made his first recordings in 1946 and rose to become country music's biggest star. He died of an alcohol-related heart disease.

1 Your cheatin' heart.
Title of song (1953), film biopic (1964) and biography by Chet Flippo (1981). Recorded on Williams's last session in Nashville, the song posthumously topped both *Billboard* and *Cashbox* country charts for months, and came to be covered by over 300 other artists.

2 You've got to have smelled a lot of mule manure before you can sing like a hillbilly.
Quoted in *All You Need is Love*, 'Making Moonshine' by Tony Palmer (1976)

Raymond Williams (1921–88)
WELSH NOVELIST AND CRITIC
Credited with the founding of cultural materialism as an approach to literature, he authored Culture and Society *(1958) and* The Long Revolution *(1961). He was active in the New Left and published the* May Day Manifesto *of 1968 and* Marxism and Literature *(1977), as well as novels.*

1 What breaks capitalism, all that will ever break capitalism, is capitalists. The faster they run the more strain on their heart.
Monkey Pitter, in *Loyalties*, pt 3, ch. 2 (1985)

2 It wasn't idealism that made me, from the beginning, want a more secure and

rational society. It was an intellectual judgement, to which I still hold. When I was young its name was socialism. We can be deflected by names. But the need was absolute, and is still absolute.
Norman Braose, ibid., pt 5, ch. 5

Robbie Williams (b. 1974)
BRITISH POP MUSICIAN
After leaving one of the first boy bands of the 1990s, Take That, *in 1995, he quickly became a major solo star with such hits as 'Angels' (1997) and 'Let Me Entertain You' (1998).*

1 Some say that we are players, some say that we are pawns.
But we've been making money since the day that we were born.
'Millennium' (song, co-written with Guy Chambers) on the album *I've Been Expecting You* (1998)

Robin Williams (b. 1951)
US ACTOR AND COMEDIAN
A versatile comedian, he made TV appearances in Happy Days *and* Mork and Mindy *(1978–82) and has starred in such films as* Good Morning, Vietnam *(1987),* Dead Poets Society *(1989), and* Good Will Hunting *(1997).*

1 Come on now! You kick out the gooks, the next thing you know, you have to kick out the chinks, the spicks, the spooks, the kikes and all that's going to be left is a couple of brain-dead rednecks.
Adrian Cronauer (Robin Williams), in *Good Morning, Vietnam* (film, 1987, screenplay by Mitch Markowitz, directed by Barry Levinson)

2 You're only given a little spark of madness. You mustn't lose it.
Quoted in *Funny Business* (1992) by David Housham and John Frank-Keyes

Shirley Williams (b. 1930)
BRITISH LIBERAL-DEMOCRAT POLITICIAN
Baroness Williams of Crosby. Daughter of the novelist VERA BRITTAIN, *she became the first elected MP of the new Social Democratic Party in 1981, and its President (1982–3). In 2001 she was elected Leader of the Liberal Democrats in the House of Lords.*

1 The Catholic Church has never really come to terms with women. What I object to is being treated either as Madonnas or Mary Magdalenes.
Observer 22 March 1981

Tennessee Williams (1911–83)
US PLAYWRIGHT
His background of growing up in genteel poverty in the deep South is portrayed in most of his plays, not least in his first success The Glass Menagerie

(1944). He won Pulitzer Prizes for A Streetcar Named Desire *(1947, filmed 1951) and* Cat on a Hot Tin Roof *(1955, filmed 1958).*

1 In memory everything seems to happen to music.

Tom, in *The Glass Menagerie*, sc. 1 (1944)

2 Time is the longest distance between two places.

Tom, ibid., sc. 7

3 I can't stand a naked light bulb, any more than I can a rude remark or a vulgar action.

Blanche DuBois, in *A Streetcar Named Desire*, sc. 3 (1947)

4 I have always depended on the kindness of strangers.

Blanche DuBois, ibid., sc. 11. Her final words.

5 Time rushes toward us with its hospital tray of infinitely varied narcotics, even while it is preparing us for its inevitably fatal operation.

The Rose Tattoo, 'The Timeless World of a Play' (1951)

6 When so many are lonely as seem to be lonely, it would be inexcusably selfish to be lonely alone.

Don Quixote, in *Camino Real*, Prologue (1953)

7 You said 'They're harmless dreamers and they're loved by the people.' – 'What,' I asked you, 'is harmless about a dreamer, and what,' I asked you, 'is harmless about the love of the people? – Revolution only needs good dreamers who remember their dreams.'

Gutman to the Generalissimo, ibid., Block 2

8 The most dangerous word in any human tongue is the word for brother. It's inflammatory.

Gutman, ibid.

9 We have to distrust each other. It is our only defence against betrayal.

Marguerite Gautier, ibid., Block 10

10 Oh, Jacques, we're used to each other, we're a pair of captive hawks caught in the same cage, and so we've grown used to each other. That's what passes for love at this dim, shadowy end of the Camino Real . . .

Marguerite Gautier to Jacques Casanova, ibid.

11 We're all of us guinea pigs in the laboratory of God. Humanity is just a work in progress.

The Gipsy, ibid., Block 12

12 Everyone says he's sincere, but everyone isn't sincere. If everyone was sincere who says he's sincere there wouldn't be half so many insincere ones in the world and there would be lots, lots, lots more really sincere ones!

Esmeralda, ibid.

13 Mendacity is a system that we live in. Liquor is one way out an' death's the other.

Brick, in *Cat on a Hot Tin Roof*, act 2 (1955)

14 You've got many refinements. I don't think you need to worry about your failure at long division. I mean, after all, you got through short division, and short division is all that a lady ought to be called on to cope with . . .

Silva (Karl Malden) speaking to Baby Doll (Carroll Baker), in *Baby Doll* (film, 1956, screenplay by Tennessee Williams, directed by Elia Kazan)

15 We're all of us sentenced to solitary confinement inside our own skins, for life!

Val Xavier, in *Orpheus Descending*, act 2, sc. 1 (1957)

16 I don't believe in villains or heroes, only in right or wrong ways that individuals are taken, not by choice, but by necessity or by certain still uncomprehended influences in themselves, their circumstances and their antecedents.

New York Post 17 March 1957

17 The world is a funny paper read backwards. And that way it isn't so funny.

Self-interview, in the *Observer* 7 April 1957

18 Don't look forward to the day you stop suffering, because when it comes you'll *know* you're dead.

Quoted in the *Observer* 26 January 1958

19 It haunts me, the passage of time. I think time is a merciless thing. I think life is a process of burning oneself out and time is the fire that burns you. But I think the spirit of man is a good adversary.

New York Post 30 April 1958

20 We all live in a house on fire, no fire department to call; no way out, just the upstairs window to look out of while the fire burns the house down with us trapped, locked in it.

Chris, in *The Milk Train Doesn't Stop Here Anymore*, sc. 6 (1963)

William Carlos Williams (1883–1963)

US POET

He is known for celebrating the everyday in his verse, often in unconventional rhythm and metre. His major work Paterson *(1946–58) was based on themes of the city of that name in New Jersey. His final verse collection* Pictures from Breughel *(1962) won a Pulitzer Prize.*

1 *The pure products of America*
 go crazy –
 mountain folk from Kentucky

 or the ribbed north end of
 Jersey
 with its isolate lakes and

 valleys, its deaf-mutes, thieves.
 'To Elsie', publ. in *Spring and All* (1923)

2 Afraid lest he be caught up in a net of
 words, tripped up, bewildered and so
 defeated – thrown aside – a man hesitates
 to write down his innermost convictions.
 Journal entry, 7 July 1929, publ. in *The Embodiment of Knowledge* (1974)

3 *It's the anarchy of poverty*
 delights me.
 'The Poor', publ. in *Recent Verse* (1938)

4 Say it! No ideas but in things.
 Paterson, bk 1, 'The Delineaments of the Giants',
 sect. 1 (1946, rev. 1963). Williams's poetic dictum
 – to present the subject concretely, without literary artifice – was influential on the Beat writers,
 notably ALLEN GINSBERG.

5 It is dangerous to leave written that which
 is badly written. A chance word, upon
 paper, may destroy the world. Watch carefully and erase, while the power is still
 yours, I say to myself, for all that is put
 down, once it escapes, may rot its way into
 a thousand minds, the corn become a
 black smut, and all libraries, of necessity,
 be burned to the ground as a consequence.
 Only one answer: write carelessly so that
 nothing that is not green will survive.
 Ibid. bk 3, 'The Library', sect. 3

6 *It is difficult*
 to get the news from poems
 yet men die miserably every day
 for lack
 of what is found there.
 'Asphodel, That Greeny Flower', publ. in *Journey
 to Love* (1955)

Roy Williamson (1937–90)
SCOTTISH FOLK MUSICIAN
*He was a founding member of the Corrie Folk
Trio, which formed in the 1960s and continued as
a duo, the Corries, with Ronnie Brown until 1990.*

1 *O Flower of Scotland,*
 When will we see
 Your like again,
 That fought and died for,
 Your wee bit hill and glen,
 And stood against him,
 Proud Edward's Army,
 And sent him homeward,
 Tae think again.
 'Flower of Scotland' (song, 1968) on the album
 The Corries in Concert (1969) by the Corries. The

song has come to be regarded as Scotland's
unofficial national anthem.

Wendell Willkie (1892–1944)
US LAWYER AND POLITICIAN
*He ran as Republican candidate for the presidency
in 1940 but was narrowly defeated by F. D. ROOSE-
VELT. Committed to international cooperation
and civil rights, he undertook a round-the-world
trip and published* One World *(1943) on his
return.*

1 The constitution does not provide for first
 and second class citizens.
 An American Programme, ch. 2 (1944)

A. N. Wilson (b. 1950)
BRITISH AUTHOR
*Andrew Norman Wilson. He is known for his
novels satirizing British society, such as* The
Sweets of Pimlico *(1977) and* Love Unknown
*(1986), as well as works of Christian apologia and
biographies. He is regarded as High Church Conservative.*

1 In universities and intellectual circles,
 academics can guarantee themselves
 popularity – or, which is just as satisfying,
 unpopularity – by being opinionated
 rather than by being learned.
 Book review in the *Guardian* 30 September 1989

2 The fact that logic cannot satisfy us awakens an almost insatiable hunger for the
 irrational.
 Ibid.

3 If you know somebody is going to be
 awfully annoyed by something you write,
 that's obviously very satisfying, and if they
 howl with rage or cry, that's honey.
 Quoted in the *Independent on Sunday*
 13 September 1992

4 The cult of a year ago has dwindled and
 become, as religions tend to, the preserve
 of children, homosexuals and lonely
 housewives.
 Interview with ANTHONY CLARE in *In the Psychiatrist's Chair* 13 September 1998, Radio 4.
 Referring to the reaction to the death of Princess
 DIANA.

(Sir) Angus Wilson (1913–91)
BRITISH AUTHOR
*On the staff of the British Museum Library until
1955, he had success with his stories satirizing the
middle class, and the novels* Hemlock and After
(1952) and Anglo-Saxon Attitudes *(1956).*

1 The opportunities for heroism are limited
 in this kind of world: the most people can
 do is sometimes not to be as weak as
 they've been at other times.
 Interview in *Writers at Work* (first series, ed. Mal
 colm Cowley, 1958)

Charles E. Wilson (1890–1961)

US INDUSTRIALIST AND POLITICIAN
He was President of General Motors (1941–52) and served as Secretary of Defense under EISEN-HOWER *(1953–7).*

1 For years I thought what was good for our country was good for General Motors and vice versa. The difference did not exist. Our company is too big. It goes with the welfare of the country.

Statement to US Senate committee, January 1953, quoted in *The New York Times* 24 February 1953. The words – usually quoted 'What's good for the country is good for General Motors, and vice versa' – were pounced upon by the Democrats on the committee, who were in a majority, to question his true loyalties.

Harold Wilson (1916–95)

BRITISH POLITICIAN AND PRIME MINISTER
Baron Wilson of Riveaulx. He delighted in his 'common touch', expressed in his fondness for HP sauce, Gannex raincoat and constant pipe-smoking. He was Labour Prime Minister 1964–70 and 1974–6, introducing economic sanctions against Rhodesia in 1965 and renegotiating Britain's terms of entry into the EEC in 1974.

1 This Party is a moral crusade or it is nothing.

Speech to Labour Party Conference, 1 October 1962, quoted in *The Times* 2 October 1962. The words were recalled by TONY BLAIR on Wilson's death.

2 If I had the choice between smoked salmon and tinned salmon, I'd have it tinned. With vinegar.

Quoted in the *Observer* 11 November 1962

3 We are redefining and we are restating our Socialism in terms of the scientific revolution. But that revolution cannot become a reality unless we are prepared to make far-reaching changes in economic and social attitudes which permeate our whole system of society. The Britain that is going to be forged in the white heat of this revolution will be no place for restrictive practices or for outdated methods on either side of industry.

Speech to Labour Party Conference in Scarborough, 1 October 1963, publ. in *The Penguin Book of Twentieth-Century Speeches* (ed. Brian MacArthur, 1999). In his first conference speech as party leader, Wilson attempted to associate Labour with what became known as the 'white heat of the technological revolution', in contrast to the perceived old-fashioned ideas of ALEC DOUGLAS-HOME's Conservative Party.

4 A week is a long time in politics.

Attributed, *c.* 1964. In *Sayings of the Century*, 'Prime Ministers: A Word from No. 10' (1984) by Nigel Rees, it is reported that in 1977 Wilson

was unable to remember when or even if he had uttered this aphorism always associated with him. The words were probably said off the record to lobby correspondents.

5 From now the pound abroad is worth fourteen per cent or so less in terms of other currencies. It does not mean, of course, that the pound here in Britain, in your pocket or purse, or in your bank, has been devalued.

Broadcast, 19 November 1967, BBC TV, quoted in *The Times* 20 November 1967

6 One man's wage rise is another man's price increase.

Speech at Blackburn, 8 January 1970, quoted in the *Observer* 11 January 1970

Robert Wilson (b. 1941)

US THEATRE DIRECTOR AND DESIGNER
An avant-garde director, he has cooperated with contemporary composers such as Philip Glass in Einstein on the Beach *(1976) and Tom Waits in* The Black Rider *(1990).*

1 Once something becomes discernible, or understandable, we no longer need to repeat it. We can destroy it.

Quoted in the *Sunday Times* 17 November 1991

Woodrow Wilson (1856–1924)

US POLITICIAN AND PRESIDENT
Thomas Woodrow Wilson. As Democratic president (1913–21), he reluctantly entered the First World War in 1917, contributed to the armistice with his 'Fourteen Points' plan and championed the League of Nations. 'In Wilson, the whole of mankind breaks camp, sets out from home and wrestles with the universe and its gods,' WILLIAM BOLITHO *eulogized.*

1 It is like writing history with lightning and my only regret is that it is all so terribly true.

Attributed remark at the White House, 18 February 1915, quoted in *The Image*, ch. 4 (1962) by DANIEL J. BOORSTIN. On seeing D. W. GRIFFITH's epic of the Civil War, *The Birth of a Nation*.

2 No nation is fit to sit in judgement upon any other nation.

Speech in New York, 20 April 1915, publ. in *Selected Addresses* (1918)

3 Once lead this people into war and they will forget there ever was such a thing as tolerance.

Quoted in *Mr Wilson's War*, pt 3, ch. 12 (1917) by JOHN DOS PASSOS

4 A little group of wilful men reflecting no opinion but their own have rendered the great Government of the United States helpless and contemptible.

Statement 4 March 1917, quoted in *The New*

York Times 5 March 1917. Referring to a successful filibuster against Wilson's bill to arm US merchant ships against German submarine attacks.

5 **The world must be made safe for democracy. Its peace must be planted upon the
tested foundations of political liberty.**
Speech to Congress, 2 April 1917, publ. in *The
Penguin Book of Twentieth-Century Speeches* (ed.
Brian MacArthur, 1999). Proposing a state of
war against Germany, which was almost unani-
mously voted four days later. A year earlier,
Wilson had run his re-election campaign on the
boast of having 'kept us out of war', having pursued a policy of remaining 'studiously neutral'.
See also THOMAS WOLFE 1.

6 **Sometimes people call me an idealist. Well,
that is the way I know I am an American.
. . . America is the only idealistic nation in
the world.**
Speech at Sioux Falls, North Dakota,
8 September 1919, publ. in *The Messages and
Papers of Woodrow Wilson*, vol. 2 (ed. Albert
Shaw, 1924)

R. Foster Winans (b. 1948)
US JOURNALIST
A Wall Street Journal *reporter, he was tried and
convicted for 'insider dealing'.*

1 **The only reason to invest in the market is
because you think you know something
others don't.**
Newsweek 1 December 1986

Oprah Winfrey (b. 1954)
US CHAT SHOW HOST
She hosts a daytime talk show, The Oprah Winfrey Show *(from 1985), on which controversial
problems are aired, and has also appeared in the
film* The Color Purple *(1985).*

1 **I am those women. I am every one of
them. And they are me. That's why we get
along so well.**
Quoted in *Oprah!*, 'A Day with Oprah' (1987) by
Robert Waldron. Referring to the victims and
survivors who appear on her show.

2 **What I've learned about being angry with
people is that it generally hurts you more
than it hurts them.**
Quoted ibid., ch. 2

3 **I've been guilty of misusing TV. It's a
dangerous medium and is misused all the
time.**
Radio Times 23 February 1999

Michael Winner (b. 1935)
BRITISH FILM-MAKER
*He is associated with films of revenge and vigilante
violence, particularly the three* Death Wish *films
he directed (1974, 1981, 1985).*

1 **The truth of the matter is that muggers are
very interesting people.**
Daily Express 11 May 1989

Shelley Winters (b. 1922)
US ACTRESS
*Originally Shirley Schrift. Typecast in early films
playing vulnerable characters, she extended her
roles in* The Diary of Anne Frank *(1959) and* The
Poseidon Adventure *(1972).*

1 **Every now and then, when you're on stage,
you hear the best sound a player can hear.
It's a sound you can't get in movies or in
television. It is the sound of a wonderful,
deep silence that means you've hit them
where they live.**
Theatre Arts June 1956

Yvor Winters (1900–1968)
US LITERARY CRITIC AND POET
*He was associated with New Criticism and pub-
lished* In Defense of Reason *(1947) and* The Function of Criticism *(1957). To the Holy Spirit
(1947) was his last volume of poetry.*

1 **Professors of literature, who for the most
part are genteel but mediocre men, can
make but a poor defense of their profession, and the professors of science, who
are frequently men of great intelligence but
of limited interests and education, feel a
politely disguised contempt for it; and thus
the study of one of the most pervasive and
powerful influences on human life is tra-
duced and neglected.**
In Defense of Reason, Foreword (1947)

Jeanette Winterson (b. 1959)
BRITISH AUTHOR
*She came to notice with her first novel, the autobio-
graphical* Oranges Are Not the Only Fruit *(1985),
in which she recounts her self-fulfilment as a lesbian. This was followed by* Written on the Body
(1992), Art and Lies *(1994), and* The Powerbook
(2000), among others.

1 **Oranges Are Not the Only Fruit.**
Title of novel (1985)

2 **However it is debased or misinterpreted,
love is a redemptive feature. To focus on
one individual so that their desires become
superior to yours is a very cleansing
experience.**
The Times 26 August 1992

3 **Why is it that the most unoriginal thing we
can say to one another is still the thing we
long to hear? 'I love you' is always a quotation. You did not say it first and neither
did I, yet when you say it and when I say
it we speak like savages who have found
three words and worship them.**
Written on the Body (1992)

4 Why do human beings need answers?
Partly I suppose because without one,
almost any one, the question itself soon
sounds silly.
Ibid.

5 It's awkward, in a society where the cult of
the individual has never been preached
with greater force, and where many of our
collective ills are a result of that force, to
say that it is the Self to which one must
attend. But the Self is not a random collection of stray desires striving to be satisfied,
nor is it only by suppressing such desires,
as women are encouraged to do, that any
social cohesion is possible. Our broken
society is not born out of the triumph of
the individual, but out of his effacement.
Art and Lies, 'Handel' (1994)

6 There's no such thing as autobiography
there's only art and lies.
Ibid., 'Sappho'

7 The masses are fobbed off with gadgets,
while the real science takes place behind
closed doors, the preserve of the pharma-
ceuticals and the military. Genetic control
will be the weapon of the future. Doctors
will fill the ranks of the New Model Army.
. . . The white coat will replace the khaki
fatigues as the gun gives way to the
syringe.
Ibid., 'Handel'

8 No one working in the English language
now comes close to my exuberance, my passion, my fidelity to words.
Sunday Times 13 March 1994. On naming herself
the best living author writing in English.

Ludwig Wittgenstein (1889–1951)
AUSTRIAN-BORN BRITISH PHILOSOPHER
He studied mathematics and logic under BER-
TRAND RUSSELL *at Cambridge and wrote his
seminal work on logical positivism,* Tractatus
Logico-Philosophicus *(1921), in an Italian prison
camp. He later published* Philosophical Investigations *(1953), in which he examines the uses and
inherent logic of language.*

1 Logic takes care of itself; all we have to do
is to look and see how it does it.
Entry, 13 October 1914, publ. in *Notebooks 1914–
1916* (ed. G. E. M. Anscombe, 1961). Also in
Tractatus Logico-Philosophicus, sect. 5:473 (1921)

2 When one is frightened of the truth . . .
then it is never the *whole* truth that one
has an inkling of.
Entry, 15 October 1914, publ. ibid.

3 The logic of the world is prior to all truth
and falsehood.
Entry, 18 October 1914, publ. ibid. Reformulated
in *Tractatus Logico-Philosophicus*, sect. 5:552

(1921): 'Logic is *prior* to every experience – that
something *is so*.'

4 Don't get involved in partial problems, but
always take flight to where there is a free
view over the whole *single* great problem,
even if this view is still not a clear one.
Entry, 1 November 1914, publ. ibid.

5 It is one of the chief skills of the philosopher not to occupy himself with questions which do not concern him.
Entry, 1 May 1915, publ. ibid.

6 Language is a part of our organism and no
less complicated than it.
Entry, 14 May 1915, publ. in ibid. Also in
Tractatus Logico-Philosophicus, sect. 4:002 (1921):
'Everyday language is a part of the human organ-
ism and is no less complicated than it.'

7 The philosophical I is not the human
being, not the human body or the human
soul with the psychological properties, but
the metaphysical subject, the boundary
(not a part) of the world.
Entry, 2 September 1915, publ. ibid. Also in
Tractatus Logico-Philosophicus, sect. 5:641 (1921)

8 In order to be able to set a limit to
thought, we should have to find both sides
of the limit thinkable (i.e. we should have
to be able to think what cannot be
thought).
Tractatus Logico-Philosophicus, Preface (1921)

9 I am my world. (The microcosm.)
Ibid., sect. 5:63

10 Death is not an event in life: we do not live
to experience death. If we take eternity to
mean not infinite temporal duration but
timelessness, then eternal life belongs to
those who live in the present.
Ibid., sect. 6:4311

11 Whereof one cannot speak, thereof one
must be silent.
*(Wovon man nicht sprechen kann, darüber
muss man schweigen.)*
Ibid., sect. 7. Wittgenstein had elaborated in the
book's Preface: 'What can be said at all can be
said clearly, and what we cannot talk about we
must pass over in silence.' KARL POPPER, in his
Conjectures and Refutations (1963), reported
Franz Urbach's rejoinder to this: 'But it is only
here that speaking becomes worthwhile.'

12 You get tragedy where the tree, instead of
bending, breaks.
Journal entry, 1929, publ. in *Culture and Value*
(ed. G. H. von Wright with Heikki Nyman,
1980). 'For a truly religious man nothing is
tragic,' Wittgenstein is recorded as saying in
1930.

13 Philosophy is like trying to open a safe
with a combination lock: each little adjustment of the dials seems to achieve nothing,

only when everything is in place does the door open.

Conversation in 1930, publ. in *Personal Recollections*, ch. 6 (ed. Rush Rhees, 1981)

14 A philosopher who is not taking part in discussions is like a boxer who never goes into the ring.
Ibid.

15 The face is the soul of the body.
Journal entry, 1932–4, publ. in *Culture and Value* (ed. G. H. von Wright with Heikki Nyman, 1980)

16 Resting on your laurels is as dangerous as resting when you are walking in the snow. You doze off and die in your sleep.
Journal entry, 1939–40, publ. ibid.

17 I sit astride life like a bad rider on a horse. I only owe it to the horse's good nature that I am not thrown off at this very moment.
Ibid.

18 Someone who knows too much finds it hard not to lie.
Journal entry, 1947, publ. ibid.

19 Never stay up on the barren heights of cleverness, but come down into the green valleys of silliness.
Journal entry, 1948, publ. ibid.

20 Humour is not a mood but a way of looking at the world. So if it is correct to say that humour was stamped out in Nazi Germany, that does not mean that people were not in good spirits, or anything of that sort, but something much deeper and more important.
Ibid.

21 For a *large* class of cases – though not for all – in which we employ the word 'meaning' it can be defined thus: the meaning of a word is its use in the language.
Philosophical Investigations, pt 1, sect. 43 (1953)

22 Philosophy is a battle against the bewitchment of our intelligence by means of language.
Ibid., pt 1, sect. 109. Wittgenstein argued that most philosophical problems arose from the systematic misuse of language, and could be solved by a new critical method of linguistic analysis.

23 The real discovery is the one which enables me to stop doing philosophy when I want to. – The one that gives philosophy peace, so that it is no longer tormented by questions which bring *itself* into question.
Ibid., pt 1, sect. 133

24 Like everything metaphysical the harmony between thought and reality is to be found in the grammar of the language.
Zettel, sect. 55 (1967)

25 If you do know that *here is one hand*, we'll grant you all the rest.
On Certainty, sect. 1 (ed. G. E. M. Anscombe and G. H. von Wright, 1969). Opening sentence of response to a lecture by the philosopher G. E. Moore which countered Hegelianism on the grounds of common sense. Moore had famously declared, as he raised his hand, 'I *know* this is a hand.'

26 It would strike me as ridiculous to want to doubt the existence of Napoleon; but if someone doubted the existence of the earth 150 years ago, perhaps I should be more willing to listen, for now he is doubting our whole system of evidence.
Ibid., sect. 185

27 Knowledge is in the end based on acknowledgement.
Ibid., sect. 378

(Sir) P. G. Wodehouse (1881–1975)

BRITISH NOVELIST

Pelham Grenville Wodehouse. Called 'English literature's performing flea' by SEAN O'CASEY, *he was the author of bestselling humorous novels which centred on the upper classes. After internment by the Germans in the Second World War, he made a series of radio broadcasts from Berlin which led to accusations of Nazi collusion. He subsequently lived in America, taking US citizenship in 1955.*

1 It is a good rule in life never to apologize. The right sort of people do not want apologies, and the wrong sort take a mean advantage of them.
The Man Upstairs, 'The Man Upstairs' (1914)

2 'What ho!' I said.
'What ho!' said Motty.
'What ho! What ho!'
'What ho! What ho! What ho!'
After that it seemed rather difficult to go on with the conversation.
My Man Jeeves, 'Jeeves and the Unbidden Guest' (1919)

3 In this matter of shimmering into rooms the chappie is rummy to a degree . . . He moves from point to point with as little uproar as a jellyfish.
Bertie Wooster of Jeeves, ibid., 'Jeeves and the Hard-Boiled Egg'.

4 What a queer thing Life is! So unlike anything else, don't you know, if you see what I mean.
Ibid., 'Rallying Round Old George'

5 Chumps always make the best husbands. When you marry, Sally, grab a chump. Tap his forehead first, and if it rings solid, don't hesitate. All the unhappy marriages come from the husbands having brains.

What good are brains to a man? They only unsettle him.

Miss Winch, in *The Adventures of Sally*, ch. 10 (1920)

6 Few things draw two men together more surely than a mutual inability to master golf, coupled with an intense and ever-increasing love for the game.

The Clicking of Cuthbert, ch. 2 (1922)

7 Women have to learn to bear anecdotes from men they love. It is the curse of Eve.

Ibid., ch. 5

8 [He] was a tubby little chap who looked as if he had been poured into his clothes and had forgotten to say 'When!'

Very Good, Jeeves!, 'Jeeves and the Impending Doom' (1930)

9 Into the face of the young man who sat on the terrace of the Hotel Magnifique at Cannes there had crept a look of furtive shame, the shifty, hangdog look which announces that an Englishman is about to talk French.

The Luck of the Bodkins, ch. 1 (1935). Opening words.

10 There is only one cure for grey hair. It was invented by a Frenchman. It is called the guillotine.

The Old Reliable, ch. 1 (1951)

11 You can't stick lighted matches between the toes of an English butler. He would raise his eyebrows and freeze you with a glance. You'd feel as if he had caught you using the wrong fork.

Bill, ibid., ch. 17

12 Has anybody ever seen a dramatic critic in the daytime? Of course not. They come out after dark, up to no good.

Quoted in the *New York Mirror* 27 May 1955

13 She's one of those soppy girls, riddled from head to foot with whimsy. She holds the view that the stars are God's daisy chain, that rabbits are gnomes in attendance on the Fairy Queen, and that every time a fairy blows its wee nose a baby is born, which, as we know, is not the case. She's a drooper.

Bertie Wooster, in *Stiff Upper Lip, Jeeves*, ch. 2 (1963)

14 Marriage is not a process for prolonging the life of love. It merely mummifies the corpse.

Mr Ferris, in *Company for Henry*, ch. 5, sect. 2 (1967)

Terry Wogan (b. 1938)
IRISH BROADCASTER

Associated with the BBC since 1965, he is known for his cosily irreverent humour in his radio shows and for hosting on television the annual Eurovision Song Contest.

1 Television contracts the imagination and radio expands it.

Quoted in the *Observer* 30 December 1984

2 All popular radio is based on repetition and familiarity. It's almost that the listener knows what you're going to say before you say it. . . . If you did it for long enough, you wouldn't have to say anything at all.

Independent on Sunday 15 March 1998

Christa Wolf (b. 1929)
GERMAN NOVELIST

She became well known with the publication of Moscow Novella *(1961) and* The Divided Heaven *(1963). Her best-known book* The Quest for Christa T. *(1968) was originally banned in East Germany.*

1 The ingenuous open heart preserves one's ability to say 'I' to a stranger, until a moment comes when this strange 'I' returns and enters into 'me' again. Then at one blow the heart is captive, one is pre-possessed; that much can be foretold.

The Quest for Christa T., ch. 1 (1968, transl. 1982)

2 *To become oneself, with all one's strength.* Difficult. A bomb, a speech, a rifle shot – and the world can look a different place. And then where is this 'self'?

Ibid., ch. 17

3 The most beautiful thing under the sun is being under the sun.

A Model Childhood, ch. 8 (1976)

Naomi Wolf (b. 1962)
US AUTHOR

Her critique of the stereotypes imposed on women The Beauty Myth *(1990) inspired* FAY WELDON *to hail her as an 'early heroine of Woman's World, Nineties Style'.*

1 'Beauty' is a currency system like the gold standard. Like any economy, it is determined by politics, and in the modern age in the West it is the last, best belief system that keeps male dominance intact.

The Beauty Myth, 'The Beauty Myth' (1990)

2 To ask women to become unnaturally thin is to ask them to relinquish their sexuality.

Ibid., 'Hunger'

3 Pain is real when you get other people to believe in it. If no one believes in it but you, your pain is madness or hysteria or your own unfeminine inadequacy. Women have learned to submit to pain by hearing

authority figures – doctors, priests, psychiatrists – tell us that what we feel is not pain.

Ibid., 'Violence'

Humbert Wolfe (1885–1940)
BRITISH POET AND AUTHOR
His writings include London Sonnets *(1919),* Lampoons *(1925) and* Requiem *(1927) as well as studies of Tennyson, Shelley and George Moore.*

1 *You cannot hope
    to bribe or twist
    (thank God!) the
    British journalist.
    But, seeing what
    the man will do
    unbribed, there's
    no occasion to.*

    The Uncelestial City, bk 1, 'Over the Fire' (1930)

Thomas Wolfe (1900–1938)
US AUTHOR
His small output includes Look Homeward, Angel *(1929), its sequel* Of Time and the River *(1935) and the semi-autobiographical* The Web and the Rock *(1939), published posthumously.*

1 Making the world safe for hypocrisy.

    Luke, in Look Homeward, Angel, pt 3, ch. 36 (1929). Referring to the naval base at Norfolk. See WOODROW WILSON 5 on making the world 'safe for democracy'.

2 If a man has a talent and cannot use it, he has failed. If he has a talent and uses only half of it, he has partly failed. If he has a talent and learns somehow to use the whole of it, he has gloriously succeeded, and won a satisfaction and a triumph few men ever know.

    The Web and the Rock, ch. 29 (1939)

3 It [New York] was a cruel city, but it was a lovely one, a savage city, yet it had such tenderness, a bitter, harsh, and violent catacomb of stone and steel and tunneled rock, slashed savagely with light, and roaring, fighting a constant ceaseless warfare of men and of machinery; and yet it was so sweetly and so delicately pulsed, as full of warmth, of passion, and of love, as it was full of hate.

    Ibid., ch. 30

4 There had been a time on earth when poets had been young and dead and famous – and were men. But now the poet as the tragic child of grandeur and destiny had changed. The child of genius was a woman, now, and the man was gone.

    Ibid. Referring to the poetess Rosalind Bailey.

Tom Wolfe (b. 1931)
US AUTHOR AND JOURNALIST
He was a major figure in the New Journalism with his portrait of 1960s counter-culture, The Electric Kool-Aid Acid Test *(1968), and such essays as* 'Radical Chic and Mau-Mauing the Flak-Catchers' *(1970). His biggest success was his fable of New York in the 1980s,* The Bonfire of the Vanities *(1987, filmed 1990).*

1 His hair has the long jesuschrist look. He is wearing the costume clothes. But most of all, he now has a very tolerant and therefore withering attitude toward all those who are still struggling in the old activist political ways . . . while he, with the help of psychedelic chemicals, is exploring the infinite regions of human consciousness.

    On the hippy stereotype, in The Electric Kool-Aid Acid Test (1968), ch. 26

2 Radical Chic, after all, is only radical in Style; in its heart it is part of Society and its traditions – Politics, like Rock, Pop, and Camp, has its uses.

    Radical Chic and Mau-Mauing the Flak-Catchers (1970). Originally publ. as essay in New York 8 June 1970.

3 All these years, in short, I had assumed that in art, if nowhere else, seeing is believing. Well – how very shortsighted! . . . I had gotten it backward all along. Not 'seeing is believing,' you ninny, but 'believing is seeing,' for *Modern Art has become completely literary: the paintings and other works exist only to illustrate the text.*

    The Painted Word, Introduction (1975)

4 The notion that the public accepts or rejects anything in Modern Art, the notion that the public scorns, ignores, fails to comprehend, allows to wither, crushes the spirit of, or commits any other crime against Art or any individual artist is merely a romantic fiction, a bittersweet Trilby sentiment. The game is completed and the trophies distributed long before the public knows what has happened.

    Ibid., ch. 2

5 We are now in the Me Decade – seeing the upward roll of . . . the third great religious wave in American history.

    Mauve Gloves and Madmen, Clutter and Vine, 'The Me Decade and the Third Great Awakening' (1976)

6 The idea was to prove at every foot of the way up that you were one of the elected and anointed ones who had *the right stuff* and could move higher and higher and even – ultimately, God willing, one day – that you might be able to join that special few at the very top, that elite who had the

capacity to bring tears to men's eyes, the very Brotherhood of the Right Stuff itself.

The Right Stuff, ch. 2 (1979). Of pilots and astronauts on the NASA training programme.

7 A cult is a religion with no political power.

In Our Time, ch. 2, 'Jonestown' (1980)

8 It is very comforting to believe that leaders who do terrible things are, in fact, mad. That way, all we have to do is make sure we don't put psychotics in high places and we've got the problem solved.

Ibid.

9 He [Andy Warhol] was the person who created Attitude. Before Warhol, in artistic circles, there was Ideology – you took a stance against the crassness of American life. Andy Warhol turned that on its head, and created an attitude. And that attitude was 'It's so awful, it's wonderful. It's so tacky, let's wallow in it.'

Quoted in *Rolling Stone* 9 April 1987. Comment made a few days after WARHOL's death.

10 On Wall Street he and a few others – how many? – three hundred, four hundred, five hundred? – had become precisely that ... Masters of the Universe.

The Bonfire of the Vanities, ch. 1 (1987). Referring to bond dealer Sherman McCoy and his colleagues.

11 The phrase pops into his head at that very instant: *social X-rays* ... They keep themselves so thin, they look like X-ray pictures ... You can see lamplight through their bones ... while they're chattering about *interiors* and *landscape gardening* ... and encasing their scrawny shanks in metallic Lycra tubular tights for their Sports Training classes.

Ibid.

12 A liberal is a conservative who has been arrested.

Ibid., ch. 24

13 Pornography was the great vice of the Seventies; plutography – the graphic depiction of the acts of the rich – is the great vice of the Eighties.

Interview in the *Sunday Times* 10 January 1988

14 To a man of sixty ... one of the grimmest reminders of the Reaper's approach comes when his doctors, the people who have attended to his body for decades, begin retiring on him ... or dying on him ... or both.

A Man in Full, ch. 10 (1998)

15 You don't need to worry about what an incalculable luxury literature is. Entire civilizations are founded without any literature at all and without anybody missing it. It's only later on when there's a big enough class of indolent drones to write the stuff and read the stuff that you have literature.

Lewis Gardner, ibid., ch. 28

Kenneth Wolstenholme (1920–2002)

BRITISH SPORTS COMMENTATOR

Having joined the BBC in 1946, he became the channel's leading football commentator during the 1950s and '60s, notably for Match of the Day.

1 They think it's all over – it is now.

BBC television broadcast from Wembley, 30 July 1966. Commentary in closing seconds of World Cup Final, at which England beat West Germany 4–2 in extra time.

Virginia Woolf (1882–1941)

BRITISH NOVELIST, CRITIC AND ESSAYIST

A central figure of the Bloomsbury Group, she founded the Hogarth Press in 1917 with her husband Leonard Woolf. Her ground-breaking writings include To the Lighthouse *(1927),* The Waves *(1931) and* Orlando *(1928).* EDITH SITWELL *considered her 'a beautiful little knitter'. Plagued by mental illness all her life, she committed suicide.*

1 Life is not a series of gig lamps symmetrically arranged; life is a luminous halo, a semi-transparent envelope surrounding us from the beginning of consciousness to the end.

'Modern Fiction', publ. in *The Times Literary Supplement* 10 April 1919 as 'Modern Novels', repr. in *The Common Reader* (1925)

2 The good diarist writes either for himself alone or for a posterity so distant that it can safely hear every secret and justly weigh every motive. For such an audience there is need neither of affectation nor of restraint. Sincerity is what they ask, detail, and volume; skill with the pen comes in conveniently, but brilliance is not necessary; genius is a hindrance even; and should you know your business and do it manfully, posterity will let you off mixing with great men, reporting famous affairs, or having lain with the first ladies in the land.

'Rambling Round Evelyn', publ. in *The Times Literary Supplement* 28 October 1920 as review of *The Early Life and Education of John Evelyn 1620–1641*, repr. ibid.

3 The eyes of others our prisons; their thoughts our cages.

Monday or Tuesday, 'An Unwritten Novel' (1921)

4 But when the self speaks to the self, who is speaking? – the entombed soul, the spirit driven in, in, in to the central catacomb; the self that took the veil and left the world – a coward perhaps, yet somehow beautiful, as it flits with its lantern restlessly up and down the dark corridors.

Ibid.

5 One likes people much better when they're battered down by a prodigious siege of misfortune than when they triumph.

Journal entry, 13 August 1921, publ. in *The Diary of Virginia Woolf*, vol. 1 (ed. Anne O. Bell, 1978)

6 Each had his past shut in him like the leaves of a book known to him by heart; and his friends could only read the title, James Spalding, or Charles Budgeon, and the passengers going the opposite way could read nothing at all – save 'a man with a red moustache', 'a young man in grey smoking a pipe'.

Jacob's Room, ch. 5 (1922). Referring to passengers on an omnibus.

7 It's not catastrophes, murders, deaths, diseases, that age and kill us; it's the way people look and laugh, and run up the steps of omnibuses.

Ibid., ch. 9

8 Never did I read such tosh. As for the first two chapters we will let them pass, but the 3rd 4th 5th 6th – merely the scratching of pimples on the body of the bootboy at Claridges.

Letter to LYTTON STRACHEY, 24 August 1922, publ. in *Letters*, vol. 2 (ed. Nigel Nicolson, 1976). Referring to *Ulysses* by JAMES JOYCE.

9 We are nauseated by the sight of trivial personalities decomposing in the eternity of print.

'The Modern Essay', publ. in *The Times Literary Supplement* 30 November 1922 as 'Modern Essays', repr. in *The Common Reader* (1925). Referring to inferior essayists.

10 A good essay must have this permanent quality about it; it must draw its curtain round us, but it must be a curtain that shuts us in not out.

Ibid.

11 We all indulge in the strange, pleasant process called thinking, but when it comes to saying, even to someone opposite, what we think, then how little we are able to convey! The phantom is through the mind and out of the window before we can lay salt on its tail, or slowly sinking and returning to the profound darkness which it has lit up momentarily with a wandering light.

'Montaigne', publ. in *The Times Literary Supplement* 31 January 1924 as review of *Essays of Montaigne*, repr. in *The Common Reader* (1925)

12 The man who is aware of himself is henceforward independent; and he is never bored, and life is only too short, and he is steeped through and through with a profound yet temperate happiness. He alone lives, while other people, slaves of ceremony, let life slip past them in a kind of dream.

Ibid.

13 Once conform, once do what other people do because they do it, and a lethargy steals over all the finer nerves and faculties of the soul. She becomes all outer show and inward emptiness; dull, callous, and indifferent.

Ibid.

14 If we didn't live venturously, plucking the wild goat by the beard, and trembling over precipices, we should never be depressed, I've no doubt; but already should be faded, fatalistic and aged.

Journal entry, 2 August 1924, publ. in *The Diary of Virginia Woolf*, vol. 2 (ed. Anne O. Bell, 1978)

15 I want the concentration & the romance, & the words all glued together, fused, glowing: have no time to waste any more on prose.

Ibid., 15 August 1924. Referring to poetry.

16 Humour is the first of the gifts to perish in a foreign tongue.

The Common Reader, 'On Not Knowing Greek' (1925)

17 Those comfortably padded lunatic asylums which are known, euphemistically, as the stately homes of England.

Ibid., 'Lady Dorothy Nevill'

18 *Middlemarch*, the magnificent book which with all its imperfections is one of the few English novels for grown-up people.

Ibid., 'George Eliot'

19 The word-coining genius, as if thought plunged into a sea of words and came up dripping.

'Notes on an Elizabethan Play', publ. in *The Times Literary Supplement* 5 March 1925, repr. ibid. Referring to the merits of Elizabethan drama.

20 Really I don't like human nature unless all candied over with art.

Journal entry, 13 May 1926, publ. in *The Diary of Virginia Woolf*, vol. 3 (ed. Anne O. Bell, 1980)

21 A strange thing has happened – while all the other arts were born naked, this [cinema], the youngest, has been born fully-clothed. It can say everything before it has anything to say. It is as if the savage tribe, instead of finding two bars of iron to play with, had found scattering the seashore fiddles, flutes, saxophones, trumpets, grand pianos by Erhard and Bechstein, and had begun with incredible energy, but without knowing a note of music, to hammer and thump upon them all at the same time.

'The Cinema', publ. in the *Nation and Athenaeum* 3 July 1926, repr. in *The Captain's Death Bed* (1950)

22 Arnold Bennett says that the horror of marriage lies in its 'dailiness.' All acuteness of relationship is rubbed away by this. The truth is more like this: life – say 4 days out of 7 – becomes automatic; but on the 5th day a bead of sensation (between husband and wife) forms which is all the fuller and more sensitive because of the automatic customary unconscious days on either side. That is to say the year is marked by moments of great intensity. Hardy's 'moments of vision'. How can a relationship endure for any length of time except under these conditions?

Journal entry, 2 August 1926, publ. in *The Diary of Virginia Woolf*, vol. 3 (ed. Anne O. Bell, 1980)

23 For love . . . has two faces; one white, the other black; two bodies; one smooth, the other hairy. It has two hands, two feet, two tails, two, indeed, of every member and each one is the exact opposite of the other. Yet, so strictly are they joined together that you cannot separate them.

Orlando, ch. 2 (1928)

24 Different though the sexes are, they intermix. In every human being a vacillation from one sex to the other takes place, and often it is only the clothes that keep the male or female likeness, while underneath the sex is the very opposite of what it is above.

Ibid., ch. 4

25 Every secret of a writer's soul, every experience of his life, every quality of his mind is written large in his works.

Ibid.

26 Where the Mind is biggest, the Heart, the Senses, Magnanimity, Charity, Tolerance, Kindliness, and the rest of them scarcely have room to breathe.

Ibid.

27 At 46 one must be a miser; only have time for essentials.

Journal entry, 22 March 1928, publ. in *The Diary of Virginia Woolf*, vol. 3 (ed. Anne O Bell, 1980)

28 The first duty of a lecturer – to hand you after an hour's discourse a nugget of pure truth to wrap up between the pages of your notebooks and keep on the mantelpiece for ever.

A Room of One's Own, ch. 1 (1929). The book was originally a paper read to women students at Cambridge University.

29 A woman must have money and a room of her own if she is to write fiction.

Ibid.

30 One cannot think well, love well, sleep well, if one has not dined well.

Ibid.

31 Why are women . . . so much more interesting to men than men are to women?

Ibid., ch. 2

32 Women have served all these centuries as looking-glasses possessing the magic and delicious power of reflecting the figure of man at twice its natural size.

Ibid.

33 Fiction is like a spider's web, attached ever so lightly perhaps, but still attached to life at all four corners. Often the attachment is scarcely perceptible.

Ibid., ch. 3

34 Publicity in women is detestable. Anonymity runs in their blood. The desire to be veiled still possesses them. They are not even now as concerned about the health of their fame as men are, and, speaking generally, will pass a tombstone or a signpost without feeling an irresistible desire to cut their names on it.

Ibid.

35 Who shall measure the heat and violence of the poet's heart when caught and tangled in a woman's body?

Ibid.

36 The history of men's opposition to women's emancipation is more interesting perhaps than the story of that emancipation itself.

Ibid.

37 It is the nature of the artist to mind excessively what is said about him. Literature is strewn with the wreckage of men who have minded beyond reason the opinions of others.

Ibid.

38 Masterpieces are not single and solitary births; they are the outcome of many years of thinking in common, of thinking by the body of the people, so that the experience of the mass is behind the single voice.

Ibid., ch. 4

39 Some collaboration has to take place in the mind between the woman and the man before the art of creation can be accomplished. Some marriage of opposites has to be consummated. The whole of the mind must lie wide open if we are to get the sense that the writer is communicating his experience with perfect fullness.

Ibid., ch. 6

40 Knew her own mind. But the mind radically commonplace, only its inherited

force, & cumulative sense of power, making it remarkable.

Journal entry, 27 December 1930, publ. in *The Diary of Virginia Woolf*, vol. 3 (ed. Anne O. Bell, 1980). Referring to Queen Victoria.

41 On the outskirts of every agony sits some observant fellow who points.

Bernard, in *The Waves* (1931)

42 Things have dropped from me. I have outlived certain desires; I have lost friends, some by death ... others through sheer inability to cross the street.

Bernard, ibid.

43 Against you I will fling myself, unvanquished and unyielding, O Death!

Bernard, ibid. Final words of the novel, chosen by Leonard Woolf as Virginia's epitaph at her burial-place and former home, Monk's House, Rodmell, Sussex.

44 Now, aged 50, I'm just poised to shoot forth quite free straight & undeflected my bolts whatever they are.

Journal entry, 2 October 1932, publ. in *The Diary of Virginia Woolf*, vol. 4 (ed. Anne O. Bell, 1982)

45 One has to secrete a jelly in which to slip quotations down people's throats – and one always secretes too much jelly.

Letter, 4 July 1938, publ. in *Leave the Letters Till We're Dead: Letters*, vol. 6 (ed. Nigel Nicolson, 1980)

46 We can best help you to prevent war not by repeating your words and following your methods but by finding new words and creating new methods.

Three Guineas (1938)

47 If you insist upon fighting to protect me, or 'our' country, let it be understood soberly and rationally between us that you are fighting to gratify a sex instinct which I can not share; to procure benefits which I have not shared and probably will not share.

Ibid.

48 That great Cathedral space which was childhood.

'A Sketch of the Past', written 1939–40, publ. in *Moments of Being* (ed. Jeanne Schulkind, 1976)

49 There can be no two opinions as to what a highbrow is. He is the man or woman of thoroughbred intelligence who rides his mind at a gallop across country in pursuit of an idea.

The Death of the Moth, 'Middlebrow' (1942)

50 The middlebrow is the man, or woman, of middlebred intelligence who ambles and saunters now on this side of the hedge, now on that, in pursuit of no single object, neither art itself nor life itself, but both mixed indistinguishably, and rather nastily, with money, fame, power, or prestige.

Ibid.

Alexander Woollcott (1887–1943)

US COLUMNIST AND CRITIC

Described by Life *magazine as 'testy as a wasp and much more poisonous', he was a New York theatre critic and a broadcaster in his show* Town Crier *(1929–42).*

1 All the things I really like to do are either immoral, illegal, or fattening.

The Knock at the Stage Door (1933)

Derek Worlock (1920–96)

BRITISH ROMAN CATHOLIC CLERIC

He became Archbishop of Liverpool in 1976 and worked in close cooperation with his Anglican counterpart David Sheppard.

1 I am my brother's keeper, and he's sleeping pretty rough these days.

Observer 16 December 1990. Referring to the homeless.

(Sir) Peregrine Worsthorne

(b. 1923)

BRITISH JOURNALIST

He had a long association with the Daily Telegraph *(1953–89) becoming Assistant Editor from 1961.*

1 The principal purpose of politics [is] the evolution and maintenance of a securely established ruling class with a justified sense of its own honourable superiority.

Quoted in *New Socialist* November 1985, repr. in *We, the Nation*, ch. 3 (1995) by A. J. Davies

Frank Lloyd Wright (1869–1959)

US ARCHITECT

He specialized in geometric forms utilizing modern engineering technology. Among his best-known buildings are the Imperial Hotel in Tokyo (1920, now demolished) and the Guggenheim Museum, New York (1959).

1 The physician can bury his mistakes, but the architect can only advise his client to plant vines – so they should go as far as possible from home to build their first buildings.

The New York Times Magazine 4 October 1953

2 The screech and mechanical uproar of the big city turns the citified head, fills citified ears – as the song of birds, wind in the trees, animal cries, or as the voices and songs of his loved ones once filled his heart. He is sidewalk-happy.

The Living City, pt 1, 'Earth' (1958)

3 All fine architectural values are human values, else not valuable.

Ibid., pt 3, 'Recapitulation'

4 I find it hard to believe that the machine
would go into the creative artist's hand
even were that magic hand in true place. It
has been too far exploited by industrialism
and science at expense to art and true
religion.

Ibid., pt 5, 'Night is But a Shadow Cast by the
Sun'

Allie Wrubel (1905–73)

US COMPOSER

*Active from the 1920s to the '50s, he wrote both
music and lyrics, contributing to many films and
collaborating with* MORT DIXON.

1 *Zip a dee doo dah,*
  Zip a dee ay,
  My, oh my, what a wonderful day.

'Zip a Dee Doo Dah' (song, with music by Ray
Gilbert), in *Song of the South* (film musical,
1946). The song received an Academy Award.

Woodrow Wyatt (1918–97)

BRITISH JOURNALIST AND POLITICIAN

*Baron Wyatt of Weeford. Known as a 'Wodehou-
sian eccentric', he was associated with the Daily
Mirror (1965–73) and Sunday Mirror (1973–83).
He was also a Labour MP (1945–55, 1959–70).*

1 A man falls in love through his eyes, a
woman through her ears.

To the Point, 'The Ears Have It' (1981).Wyatt
elaborated, apropos of women: 'What is said to
them and what they believe about a man's status
is usually more important than the superficiality
of good looks.'

Tammy Wynette (1942–98)

US COUNTRY SINGER

*Originally Virginia Wynette Pugh. From 1966, her
partnership with producer Billy Sherrill, co-writer
of her massive hit 'Stand by Your Man', made her
country music's most successful female singer.*

1 *Our D-I-V-O-R-C-E becomes final today*
  Me and Little Joe will be going away
  I love you both and this will be pure H-E
    double L for me.
  *Oh, I wish that we could stop this D-I-V-O-
    R-C-E.*

'D-I-V-O-R-C-E' (song, 1968, written with
Bobby Braddock and Curly Putman) on the
album *Greatest Hits* (1969)

2 *Sometimes it's hard to be a woman*
  Giving all your love to just one man.

'Stand by Your Man' (song, 1968, written with
Billy Sherrill) on ibid. Opening lines of song.

3 *Stand by your man.*
  Give him two arms to cling to
  And something warm to come to.

Ibid.

Stefan Wyszynski (1901–81)

POLISH ECCLESIASTIC

*He was from 1948 Archbishop of Warsaw and
Gniezno and Primate of Poland, and was
appointed a cardinal in 1952. During the 1970s he
lent his support to opposition movements such as
Solidarity.*

1 The Poles do not know how to hate, thank
God.

Quoted in the *Observer* 8 June 1986

R. J. Yeatman See W. C. SELLAR and R. J. YEATMAN.

William Butler Yeats (1865–1939)
IRISH POET AND PLAYWRIGHT

In the forefront of Ireland's cultural and literary revival, he was the author of plays written for Dublin's Abbey Theatre, which he helped to found in 1904. His poems, later steeped in symbolism and mysticism, include the collections The Wild Swans at Coole *(1919) and* The Tower *(1928). He was a senator of the Irish Free State (1922–8). See also* W. H. AUDEN 17.

1 **In dreams begins responsibility.**
Responsibilities, Epigraph (1914)

2 *I think it better that in times like these*
A poet's mouth be silent, for in truth
We have no gift to set a statesman right.
'On Being Asked for a War Poem', written 1915, publ. in *The Wild Swans at Coole* (1919). Opening lines of poem.

3 *Too long a sacrifice*
Can make a stone of the heart.
O when may it suffice?
'Easter 1916', written 1916, publ. in *Michael Robartes and the Dancer* (1921)

4 *I write it out in a verse –*
MacDonagh and MacBride
And Connolly and Pearse
Now and in time to be,
Wherever green is worn,
Are changed, changed utterly:
A terrible beauty is born.
Ibid. The names are of leaders of the Easter Rising who were executed by the British.

5 *Some burn damp faggots, others may consume*
The entire combustible world in one small room
As though dried straw, and if we turn about
The bare chimney is gone black out
Because the work had finished in that flare.
'In Memory of Major Robert Gregory', st. 11, publ. in *The Wild Swans at Coole* (1919). See HENRY JAMES 3.

6 *I know that I shall meet my fate*
Somewhere among the clouds above;
Those that I fight I do not hate,
Those that I guard I do not love.
'An Irish Airman Foresees His Death', publ. ibid. Opening lines of poem.

7 *My country is Kiltartan Cross;*
My countrymen Kiltartan's poor.
Ibid.

8 *I balanced all, brought all to mind,*
The years to come seemed waste of breath,
A waste of breath the years behind
In balance with this life, this death.
Ibid.

9 *Things fall apart; the centre cannot hold;*
  Mere anarchy is loosed upon the world,
  The blood-dimmed tide is loosed, and
    everywhere
  The ceremony of innocence is drowned;
  The best lack all conviction, while the worst
  Are full of passionate intensity.
'The Second Coming', publ. in *Michael Robartes and the Dancer* (1921)

10 *Now I know*
  That twenty centuries of stony sleep
  Were vexed to nightmare by a rocking
    cradle,
  And what rough beast, its hour come round
    at last,
  Slouches towards Bethlehem to be born?
Ibid. Closing lines of poem.

11 *An intellectual hatred is the worst.*
'A Prayer for My Daughter', publ. ibid.

12 **I agree about Shaw – he is haunted by the mystery he flouts. He is an atheist who trembles in the haunted corridor.**
Letter to George Russell (AE), 1 July 1921, publ. in *The Letters of W. B. Yeats* (ed. Allan Wade, 1954). Yeats expressed ambiguous views towards SHAW in his *Autobiography* (1938): 'We all hated him with the left side of our heads, while admiring him immensely with the right side.'

13 *A shudder in the loins engenders there*
  The broken wall, the burning roof and
    tower
  And Agamemnon dead.
'Leda and the Swan', written 1923, publ. in *The Tower* (1928)

14 **We make out of the quarrel with others, rhetoric, but of the quarrel with ourselves, poetry.**
'Anima Hominis', sect. 5, publ. in *Essays* (1924)

15 *An aged man is but a paltry thing,*
  A tattered coat upon a stick, unless
  Soul clap its hands and sing, and louder
    sing
  For every tatter in its mortal dress.
'Sailing to Byzantium', written 1926, publ. in *The Tower* (1928)

16 **After Stéphane Mallarmé, after Paul Verlaine, after Gustave Moreau, after Puvis de Chavannes, after our own verse, after all our subtle colour and nervous rhythm, after the faint mixed tints of Conder, what more is possible? After us the Savage God.**
Autobiographies, 'The Trembling of the Veil', bk 4, sect. 20 (1926). A. ALVAREZ took from these lines the title for his study on suicide, *The Savage God* (1971).

17 **Englishmen are babes in philosophy and so prefer faction-fighting to the labour of its unfamiliar thought.**
Letter, 24 March 1927, publ. in *The Letters of W. B. Yeats* (ed. Allan Wade, 1954)

18 *Nor dread nor hope attend*
  A dying animal;
  A man awaits his end
  Dreading and hoping all.
'Death', written 1927, publ. in *The Winding Stair and Other Poems* (1933). Opening lines of poem.

19 *The innocent and the beautiful*
  Have no enemy but time.
'In Memory of Eva Gore-Booth and Con Markiewicz', written 1927, publ. ibid.

20 *Swift has sailed into his rest;*
  Savage indignation there
  Cannot lacerate his breast.
  Imitate him if you dare,
  World-besotted traveller; he
  Served human liberty.
'Swift's Epitaph', written 1930, publ. ibid.

21 *The intellect of man is forced to choose*
  Perfection of the life, or of the work,
  And if it take the second must refuse
  A heavenly mansion, raging in the dark.
'The Choice', written 1931, publ. ibid.

22 *Out of Ireland have we come,*
  Great hatred, little room,
  Maimed us at the start.
  I carry from my mother's womb
  A fanatic heart.
'Remorse for Intemperate Speech', written 1931, publ. ibid.

23 *A woman can be proud and stiff*
  When on love intent;
  But love has pitched his mansion in
  The place of excrement;
  For nothing can be sole or whole
  That has not been rent.
'Crazy Jane Talks with the Bishop', publ. in *Words for Music Perhaps* (1932) and ibid.

24 *The ghost of Roger Casement*
  Is beating on the door.
'The Ghost of Roger Casement', publ. in *New Poems* (1938)

25 *You that would judge me, do not judge*
    alone
  This book or that, come to this hallowed
    place
  Where my friends' portraits hang and look
    thereon;
  Ireland's history in their lineaments trace;
  Think where man's glory most begins and
    ends
  And say my glory was I had such friends.
'The Municipal Gallery Re-visited', publ. ibid.

26 *Irish poets, learn your trade,*
  Sing whatever is well made,
  Scorn the sort now growing up
  All out of shape from toe to top.
'Under Ben Bulben', sect. 5, publ. in *Last Poems* (1939)

27 *Cast your mind on other days*
  That we in coming days may be

Still the indomitable Irishry.
Ibid.

28 *Under bare Ben Bulben's head*
In Drumcliff churchyard Yeats is laid.
An ancestor was rector there
Long years ago, a church stands near,
By the road an ancient cross.
No marble, no conventional phrase;
On limestone quarried near the spot
By his command these words are cut:
Cast a cold eye
On life, on death.
Horseman pass by!
Ibid., sect. 6. The last three lines are engraved on Yeats's gravestone at Drumcliff, north of Sligo.

29 Man can embody truth but he cannot know it.
Letter, 4 January 1939, publ. in *The Letters of W. B. Yeats* (ed. Allan Wade, 1954). Written three weeks before his death.

30 You know what the Englishman's idea of compromise is? He says, Some people say there is a God. Some people say there is no God. The truth probably lies somewhere between these two statements.
Quoted by Wilfred Whitten in *John O'London's Weekly* 24 June 1949

31 *Accursed who brings to light of day*
The writings I have cast away.
'Untitled', publ. in *The Variorum Edition of the Poems of W. B. Yeats*, 'Poems Not Included in the Definitive Edition' (ed. Peter Allt and Russell K. Alspach, 1957)

Jack Yellen (1892–1991)
POLISH-BORN US LYRICIST
His songs were used in Broadway revues of the 1920s and musical films. He also co-wrote songs for SOPHIE TUCKER.

1 *Happy days are here again!*
The skies above are clear again.
Let us sing a song of cheer again,
Happy days are here again!
'Happy Days Are Here Again' (song, 1929, with music by Milton Ager)

Boris Yeltsin (b. 1931)
RUSSIAN POLITICIAN AND PRESIDENT
He was elected president of the Russian federation in 1991 and supported GORBACHEV *after the attempted coup two months later. He was re-elected in 1996 but resigned in 1999 after criticism over his handling of the Chechnya conflict and recurring ill health.*

1 Let's not talk about Communism. Communism was just an idea, just pie in the sky.
Remark during a visit to the United States, quoted in the *Independent* 13 September 1989

2 Oh, where is the poet or bard who will compose an ode to Russian rumours?

Thanks to the chronic shortage of truthful (or even false) information, our people live on rumours.
Against the Grain, ch. 9 (1990)

Sergei Yesenin (1895–1925)
RUSSIAN POET
Calling himself the 'last poet of wooden Russia', he was the leading figure of the Russian Imagist group of poets. He was briefly married to ISADORA DUNCAN (1922–3), *and hanged himself after writing a suicide note in his own blood.*

1 *Have you seen it*
Through the steppeland roaring
In misty lakeland rain
With its iron nostril snoring
On iron paws – the train?
'The Colt and the Train', sect. 3, publ. in *Prayers for the Dead* (1920, transl. Peter Tempest)

Yevgeny Yevtushenko (b. 1933)
RUSSIAN POET
A spokesman for the post-Stalinist generation and for greater artistic freedom, he aroused controversy with the poems 'Babii Yar' (1961) and 'Stalin's Heirs' (1962). His later works include Love Poems *(1977) and the novel* Wild Berries *(1982).*

1 *Great twentieth century: sputnik century:*
what an angst is in you, what wide perplexity!
You are a good century and a century of the pit,
cannibal century to the ideas you beget,
century of the angry young men's target.
'The Angries'(1959), repr. in *Collected Translations* (1996) by Edwin Morgan

2 Give me a mystery – just a plain and simple one – a mystery which is diffidence and silence, a slim little, barefoot mystery: give me a mystery – just one!
'Mysteries', st. 10 (1960), repr. in *The Heritage of Russian Verse* (ed. Dimitri Obolensky, 1965)

3 *In my blood there is no Jewish blood.*
In their callous rage,
All anti-Semites must hate me now as a Jew.
For that reason
I am a true Russian.
'Babii Yar' (1961), repr. in *The Poetry of Yevgeny Yevtushenko 1953 to 1965* (1966, transl. George Reavey). Last lines of poem describing the massacre of 96,000 Jews in the Ukraine by the Nazis. The poem, which caused controversy by implying that the Soviet régime was anti-Semitic, was used by Shostokovich as the centrepoint of his Thirteenth Symphony.

4 *In any man who dies there dies with him his first snow and kiss and fight . . .*
Not people die but worlds die in them.
'People', publ. in *Selected Poems* (1962, transl. Robin Milner-Gulland and Peter Levi)

5 *No, Stalin did not die.*
He thinks that death can be fixed.
We removed
him
from the mausoleum.
But how do we remove Stalin
from Stalin's heirs?
'Stalin's Heirs', publ. ibid.

6 Why is it that right-wing bastards always stand shoulder to shoulder in solidarity, while liberals fall out among themselves?
Quoted in the *Observer* 15 December 1991

Anzia Yezierska (c. 1885–1970)
POLISH AUTHOR
After emigrating to the United States, she wrote short story collections, and passionate books about Russian Jewish immigrants such as Salome of the Tenements *(1922).*

1 Without comprehension, the immigrant would forever remain shut out – a stranger in America. Until America can release the heart as well as train the hand of the immigrant, he would forever remain driven back upon himself, corroded by the very richness of the unused gifts within his soul.
Hungry Hearts and Other Stories, pt. 3, 'How I Found America' (1920)

2 Poverty was an ornament on a learned man like a red ribbon on a white horse.
Letter from Boruch Shlomoe Mayer to Anzia Yezierska, in *Red Ribbon on a White Horse*, ch. 9 (1950). Referring to Poland.

Peter York (b. 1950)
BRITISH JOURNALIST
A 'style guru' regularly consulted for his views on social trends, he was the author of Style Wars *(1980) and co-authored* Peter York's The Eighties *(1996). See also* ANN BARR AND PETER YORK.

1 You will not get anyone to *admit* belonging to the Sloanes. Some have even adopted mufti (jeans). But nobody need feel ashamed of being a Sloane Ranger.
'The Sloane Rangers', publ. in *Harpers & Queen* October 1975, repr. in *Style Wars* (1980)

2 If beauty isn't genius it usually signals at least a high level of animal cunning.
'Discontinued Models', publ. in *London Collection Magazine* April 1978, repr. ibid.

3 In the Golden Age, that is the 1970s, the Phoney Wars were . . . style wars. . . . Style became a weapon to forge your own legend. Style started to be accessible in a quite unprecedented way.
Style Wars, 'Style Wars' (1980)

4 NQOCD (not quite our class, darling) is an American joke. You might say 'He's a bit ordinaire . . .'
The Official Sloane Ranger's Handbook, 'The First Social Steps' (1982, written with Ann Barr)

5 Hooray Henries are aged between 18 and 30; main interest, getting drunk together; ambition, if ambitious: to get drunk enough to do some crazy thing which will go down in the Hooray annals as a Historic Act of Hilarity.
Ibid., 'Hooray Henry'

6 One of the less agreeable aspects of the communications age was the message T-shirt. Lacking in charisma? Get a message, get a T-shirt, get a brand. We became a nation of sandwich boards.
Interview in the *Sunday Telegraph* 31 December 1995

7 The eighties are a long story about fun, greed and money. The eighties are what happened when what looked like the majority went out and took what the minority had previously thought of as its own. It was a bloodless revolution.
Peter York's The Eighties, ch. 1 (1996, written with Charles Jennings)

Andrew Young (b. 1932)
US POLITICIAN AND DIPLOMAT
He was a close associate of MARTIN LUTHER KING, *was elected to Congress as a Democrat (1973–7) and was subsequently US representative to the United Nations (1977–9).*

1 Once the Xerox copier was invented, diplomacy died.
Playboy July 1977

2 Moral power is probably best when it is not used. The less you use it the more you have.
Observer 8 September 1979

Neil Young (b. 1945)
CANADIAN ROCK MUSICIAN
A maverick in rock since the 1960s, he played with Buffalo Springfield, as part of Crosby, Stills, Nash and Young, and subsequently with his 'houseband' Crazy Horse.

1 *My my, hey hey*
Rock and roll is here to stay
It's better to burn out
Than to fade away
My my, hey hey.
'My My, Hey Hey (Out of the Blue)' (song, written with Jeff Blackburn) on the album *Rust Never Sleeps* (1979). The words were quoted by KURT COBAIN in his suicide note.

Marguerite Yourcenar (1903–87)

BELGIAN-BORN FRENCH NOVELIST

Originally Marguerite de Crayencour. She is known for her historical novels and for the long prose poem Fires *(1939). In 1980 she became the first woman to be elected to the Académie Française.*

1 Men who care passionately for women attach themselves at least as much to the temple and to the accessories of the cult as to their goddess herself.

Memoirs of Hadrian, 'Varius Multiplex Multi Formis' (1941, transl. 1954)

Darryl Zanuck (1902–79)

US FILM PRODUCER

He was co-founder of Twentieth-Century Pictures in 1933 and became vice-president when it merged with Fox to become Twentieth-Century Fox (1935–52). 'Success in movies boils down to three things,' he asserted, 'stories, stories, stories.'

1 If two men on the same job agree all the time, then one is unnecessary. If they disagree all the time, then both are useless.

Quoted in the *Observer* 23 October 1949

Frank Zappa (1940–93)

US ROCK MUSICIAN

Known for his caustically ironic style, he used a variety of genres to satirize the modern era. Freak Out (1966) was the first of more than fifty albums he recorded, many with his band the Mothers of Invention.

1 Most rock journalism is people who can't write, interviewing people who can't talk, for people who can't read.

Quoted in the *Chicago Tribune* 18 January 1978

2 Music, in performance, is a type of sculpture. The air in the performance is sculpted into something.

The Real Frank Zappa Book, ch. 8 (1989, written with Peter Occhiogrosso)

3 No change in musical style will survive unless it is accompanied by a change in clothing style. Rock is to dress up to.

Ibid., ch. 9

4 The sad thing about the Sixties was the weak-mindedness of the so-called radicals and the way that they managed to get co-opted. I think one of the things that helped that happen was LSD. It's the only chemical known to mankind that will convert a hippy to a yuppie.

Quoted in the *Independent on Sunday* 26 January 1992

Franco Zeffirelli (b. 1923)

ITALIAN THEATRE, OPERA AND FILM DIRECTOR

He is noted for innovative stage productions, and his films are characterized by a visual richness, as in The Taming of the Shrew *(1966) and* Romeo and Juliet *(1968).*

1 I know that theatre people often have a very simplistic view of politics and tend to express very black and white patriotic sentiments but perhaps that is because we know the value of illusion, how it can help strengthen the weak, and stimulate the weary.

Zeffirelli, ch. 12 (1986)

2 It's hard for other people to realize just

how easily we Florentines live with that past in our hearts and minds because it surrounds us in a very real way. To most people, the Renaissance is a few paintings on a gallery wall; to us it is more than an environment – it's an entire culture, a way of life.

Ibid., ch. 14

Zhang Jie (b. 1937)

CHINESE AUTHOR

He is known for his short stories, novellas, such as The Ark *(1984), and novels, including* Only One Sun *(1988).*

1 What do a few lies on TV matter? They can be swallowed, digested and excreted, or follow people when they doze off to sink into oblivion.

Teacher Li, in 'What's Wrong with Him?', publ. in *As Long as Nothing Happens, Nothing Will* (1988)

Fred Zinnemann (1907–97)

AUSTRIAN-BORN US FILM-MAKER

He scored a success with High Noon *in 1952 and won Academy Awards for* From Here to Eternity *(1953) and* A Man for All Seasons *(1966).*

1 Dialogue is a necessary evil.

Interview in the *Independent on Sunday* 31 May 1992

Alexander Zinoviev (b. 1922)

SOVIET PHILOSOPHER

He is famous for Yawning Heights *(1976), a surrealist work which looks forward to a 'great Future' of Soviet society. Later titles include* The Reality of Communism *(1981).*

1 They were right. The Soviet régime is not the embodiment of evil as you think in the West. They have laws and I broke them. I hate tea and they love tea. Who is wrong?

Sunday Times 3 May 1981. Referring to his forced exile from the Soviet Union.

Index

– *C. as distinguished from panic*
Hemingway [20]
– *C. is a power for good*
Compton-Burnett [3]

cowboy
– *last true c. in America* Least
Heat-Moon [3]

cows
– *c. can be eaten* Gandhi, I. [2]
– *facts are like a c.* Sayers [2]

cowslip
– *C. and shad-blow* Crane [1]

crab
– *c. within or the hyaena without*
van der Post [1]

cradle
– *c. to the grave* Churchill, W. [31]
– *c. rocks above an abyss* Nabokov
[7]
– *Instead of rocking the c.*
Robinson, M. [1]

craft
– *In my c. or sullen art* Thomas, D.
[9]

crane
– *Jane, Jane,/Tall as a c.* Sitwell [1]

Cranks
– *C. live by theory* Macaulay [2]

crap
– *it is total c.* Ratner [1]

crash
– *car c. harnesses . . . eroticism*
Ballard [1]

crazy
– *one person who is going c.* Heller
[7]

create
– *Thou didst c. the night* Iqbal [1]
– *Whoever undertakes to c.*
Rosenberg [1]

creation
– *I hold C. in my foot* Hughes, T.
[6]
– *C. is an act of withdrawal*
Smith, Z. [5]

creative
– *impulse to c. work* Horney [1]
– *c. impulse suddenly springs to life*
Klee [6]
– *c. imagination as a fruit machine*
Larkin [5]
– *c. person . . . has to face the fact*
Sarton [2]
– *In the c.process there is the father*
Stanislavsky [1]

creativity
– *Our current obsession with c.*
Huffington [1]
– *C. doesn't flourish* James, P. D.
[4]
– *True c. often starts* Koestler [8]

credulity
– *sin of c.* Muggeridge [10]

credulous
– *Man is a c. animal* Russell, B.
[20]

crème
– *pupils are the c. de la crème*
Spark [3]

cricket
– *far more than a game, this c.*
Cardus [1]

– *c. does not always hurry along*
Cardus [2]
– *C. is . . . a dramatic spectacle*
James [1]
– *quibbling over what 'isn't c.'*
Khan [1]
– *c. is the greatest thing* Pinter [5]

cried
– *when he c. the little children died*
Auden [14]

crime
– *world of c. . . . is a last refuge*
Boorstin [4]
– *C. is terribly revealing* Christie
[3]
– *c. . . . a lefthanded form of
human endeavor* Huston [1]
– *C. is an equal-opportunity
employer* Ice-T [4]
– *original 'c.' of 'niggers'* Walker
[9]
– *c. is due to the repressed desire*
Waugh, E. [5]

crimes
– *C. of which a people is ashamed*
Genet [5]

criminal
– *society gets the kind of c. it
deserves* Kennedy, R. [1]

crises
– *history is nothing but . . . 'c.'*
Ionesco [5]

crisis
– *When is a c. reached?*
Kapuściński [1]
– *can't be a c. next week* Kissinger
[2]
– *easiest period in a c. situation*
Nixon [5]
– *C.? What crisis* Sun [1]
– *exciting to have a real c.* Thatcher
[12]

critic
– *c. is a bundle of biases* Balliet
[2]
– *c. is the only independent source*
Kael [8]
– *proper function of a c.*
Lawrence, D. H. [9]
– *brain of the c. is like a shop* Satie
[1]
– *Any c. is entitled to wrong
judgments* Sontag [4]
– *Give a c. an inch* Steinbeck [11]
– *good drama c. perceives* Tynan
[7]
– *seen a dramatic c. in the daytime*
Wodehouse [12]

critical
– *c. method* de Man [2]

criticism
– *C. should be a casual
conversation* Auden [30]
– *C. prevents art from forgetting*
Ellmann [3]
– *meditative background that is c.*
Kundera [12]
– *c. of the critic himself* Nathan [4]
– *c. merely a preliminary
excitement* Pound [13]
– *Writing c. is to writing fiction*
Updike [19]

– *As far as c. is concerned* Vorster
[1]

criticizes
– *What the public c.* Cocteau [4]

critics
– *what he thinks about c.* Hampton
[6]
– *professional c., make me sick*
Hemingway [3]
– *Around the throne of God . . .
there are no c.* Jarrell [3]
– *When the c. come around* Nolan
[1]
– *C. search for ages for the wrong
word* Ustinov [11]
– *children one's 'mature' c. often
are* Walker [6]

crook
– *Well, I'm not a c.* Nixon [13]

cross
– *husband . . . as a Cross to be
Borne* Smith, S. [1]

crossed out
– *What I have c. o.* De Mille [2]

crosses
– *Are they clinging to their c.?*
Chesterton [9]

crowd
– *c. is a wraparound millipede*
Amis, M. [14]
– *human c. has been the lesson of
my life* Neruda [12]
– *apparition of these faces in the c.*
Pound [5]

crucifixion
– *Every time that I think of the c.*
Weil [23]

crucify
– *They're going to c. me* Lennon
[3]

cruelty
– *Theatre of c.* Artaud [2]
– *C. would be delicious* Shaw, G. B.
[4]

crumpet
– *thinking man's c.* Muir, F. [2]

crusade
– *This c., this war on terrorism*
Bush, George W. [1]
– *Party is a moral c.* Wilson, H. [1]

cry
– *teach them how to c.* Baez [3]

crying
– *C.'s like pissing* Swift [6]

cuckoo
– *hear the pleasant cuckoo, loud
and long* Davies, W. H. [1]

cuckoo clock
– *what did they produce? The c. c.*
Welles [2]

cuddled
– *c. by a complete stranger* Anne
[2]

cult
– *What is a c.* Altman [1]
– *c. of a year ago has dwindled*
Wilson, A. N. [4]
– *c. is a religion with no political
power* Wolfe, Tom [7]

culture
– *C. is only true when . . . critical*
Adorno [3]

fruit tree
– *Fame is but a f. t.* Drake [1]

fruitful
– *'Be f., and multiply'* Allen, W. [1]

fuck
– *zipless f. is absolutely pure* Jong [3]
– *They f. you up, your mum and dad* Larkin [20]

Führer
– *will of the F.* Frank, H. [1]

fun
– *most f. I've ever had* Allen, W. [23]
– *People must not do things for f.* Herbert [1]
– *No f., my babe. No Fun* Pop [1]
– *F.! I think it's disgusting* Westwood [1]

funeral
– *only reason I might go to the f.* Anonymous [14]

funny
– *F. is funny is funny* Connolly, B. [3]
– *only man . . . can be f.* Knox [2]
– *Surely nothing could be that f.* Melly [3]
– *Everything is f.* Rogers, W. [2]
– *f. thing happened to me* Stevenson [11]
– *everything was just being f.* Warhol [7]

fur
– *40 dumb animals to make a f. coat* Political slogans [18]

future
– *f. a . . . suburb of the soul* Ballard [6]
– *I have a Vision of the F.* Betjeman [11]
– *I don't try to describe the f.* Bradbury, R. [1]
– *danger of the f.* Fromm [6]
– *turning away from the f.* Gates [1]
– *f. is already in place* Grass [5]
– *f.'s no calamitous change* Hughes, T. [4]
– *Nobody 'as a f.* Leigh [3]
– *first men of a F.* Lewis, W. [4]
– *When there's no f.* Lydon [3]
– *fixed image of the f.* Mitchell, Juliet [1]
– *better prepared for the f.* Murdoch, I. [22]
– *vision of the f.* Orwell [49]
– *been over into the f.* Steffens [2]
– *F. shock is . . . the premature arrival of the future* Toffler [1]

futures
– *old f. have a way of hanging around* Gibson [2]

fuzzy
– *f. end of the lollipop* Monroe [4]

gadfly
– *be a g. in the conscience* Coggan [1]

gaffe
– *g. is when a politician tells the truth* Kinsley [2]

gag
– *g. that muted those black mouths* Sartre [8]

gain
– *To g. that which is worth having* McAliskey [1]

galaxies
– *all these g. inside of us* Shepard [6]

galleon
– *Stately as a g.* Grenfell [2]

gambler
– *Show me a g.* Puzo [4]

game
– *g. with a lot of waiting* Irving, J. [2]
– *How you played the G.* Rice, G. [1]
– *g. which takes less than three days* Stoppard [12]

games
– *greatest dread of all, the dread of g.* Betjeman [15]

Gandhi
– *G., a seditious Middle Temple lawyer* Churchill, W. [8]

gang
– *with a g. like that* Kerouac [5]

gangster
– *basic creed of the g.* Asbury [1]
– *g. speaks for us* Warshow [1]

gangsterism
– *g. is a very important avenue* Doctorow [5]

garbage
– *chosen the g. disposal unit* Debord [3]

Garbo
– *one sees in G. sober* Tynan [1]

garden
– *in search of my mother's g.* Walker [3]

gardening
– *G. is not a rational act* Atwood [3]

gardens
– *Paradise haunts g.* Jarman [8]

gastronomic
– *complete g. satisfaction* Fisher, M. F. K. [2]

gastronomical
– *G. perfection can be reached* Fisher, M. F. K. [5]

gay
– *condition that is now called g.* Baldwin, J. [11]
– *we must also create a g. life* Foucault [4]
– *g. people . . . get into right-wing politics* Maupin [3]
– *If you don't want people to think you're g.* Michael [1]
– *G. men are guardians of the masculine* Paglia [9]

geezers
– *Old g. don't jump* Barnes, J. [13]

general
– *best service a retired g. can perform* Bradley [1]
– *G. has dedicated himself* Stevenson [19]

General Motors
– *good for G. M.* Wilson, C. E. [1]

general strike
– *G. S. has taught the working classes more* Balfour [2]

generalizations
– *g. work to protect the mind* Nemerov [3]
– *distrust all g. about women* Russell, B. [21]

generation
– *Let us not then speak ill of our g.* Beckett [3]
– *Every g. revolts against its fathers* Mumford [1]
– *energy of a whole g.* Thompson, H. S. [4]
– *Talkin' 'bout my g.* Townshend [1]
– *g. drowned in mortification* Vaneigem [5]

generosity
– *G. is a part of my character* Lever [1]

generous
– *I wish that I'd been more g.* Aitken [3]
– *a g. man defined* Greer [10]
– *g. to a fault* Harris, S. [1]
– *cynic is . . . prematurely disappointed* Harris, S. [2]
– *hoping that the people will be g.* Menzies. [2]

genes
– *go by the name of g.* Dawkins [2]

genetic
– *G. control . . . weapon of the future* Winterson [7]

genetic manipulation
– *g. m. seeks to transform a process* Charles, Prince of Wales [10]

genial
– *more g. human traits are assigned to the underclass* Millett [4]

genital
– *great clot of g. fluid* Pound [12]

genius
– *nature of g. is to provide idiots with ideas* Aragon [3]
– *Almost everybody is born a g.* Bukowski [4]
– *I'm not a g.* Hirst [5]
– *man of g. makes no mistakes* Joyce, J. [19]
– *man of g. has a right* Pound [8]
– *Never confuse a g. with a Saint* Schama [3]
– *takes a lot of time to be a g.* Stein [12]
– *Real g. is nothing else* Weil [14]

genocide
– *G. . . . is an exercise in community building* Gourevitch [1]

gentleman
– *g. doesn't pounce . . . he glides* Crisp [17]
– *Being a g. is the number one priority* Fox [1]
– *g. is something you have to be* Pirandello [1]

genuineness
– *G. only thrives in the dark* Huxley, A. [6]

– My passport's g. Heaney [7]
– G. politics at its worst Patten, C. [1]

grey
– hear him called a g. man Kierans [1]
– No g. hair in my soul Mayakovsky [2]
– only one cure for g. hair Wodehouse [6]

grief
– g. felt so like fear Lewis, C. S. [7]
– g./equal to all these tears! Rich, A. [2]
– To share g. is to double grief Weldon [7]

grievance
– To have a g. is to have a purpose Hoffer [5]

grinning
– just stood there g. Dylan [22]

griot
– when a g. dies Haley, A. [1]

grotesque
– South is . . . called g. O'Connor, F. [3]

grottiness
– concerned with g. Reading [2]

ground
– g. opens up and envelops me Baraka [1]

groups
– G. are an ecological miracle Dury [8]

grow
– Our message: Don't g. up Rubin [2]

growing up
– growing and g. u. are analagous Hornby [2]

grown-ups
– G. never understand anything Saint-Exupéry [12]

grudge
– Even the pawn must hold a g. Dylan [12]

guerrilla
– g. wins if he does not lose Kissinger [1]

guillotine
– You gave the world the g. Jay, A. [1]

guilt
– we find fatally easy the assumption of g. Heilbrun [1]
– G. is never to be doubted Kafka [7]
– G. is . . . the most painful companion Kübler-Ross [1]
– True g. is guilt at the obligation Laing [3]
– one feels most g. about the sins Pritchett [7]
– no such thing as collective g. Waldheim [1]

guilty
– g. man wishes only to be understood de Bernières [1]

Guinness
– G. is good for you Advertising slogans [9]

guitar
– shining/Like a national g. Simon [9]
– You have a blue g. Stevens [7]

Gulf War
– G. W. was like teenage sex Harkin [1]

gun
– man with the spray g. Carson, R. [2]
– happiness is a warm g. Lennon & McCartney [16]
– Is that a g. in your pocket West, M. [2]

guns
– Such a lot of g. Bogart [6]
– They got the g. but we got the numbers Morrison, J. [6]
– monstrous anger of the g. Owen [1]
– inexhaustible anger of the g. Spender, S. [7]
– g. spell money's ultimate reason Spender, S. [8]

gunshot
– g. is the perfect way Kennedy, J. F. [30]

guru
– become a g. by accident Fenton [4]

guy
– pretty nice g., for a girl Mitchum [1]

gypsy
– new and showy g. business García Márquez [1]

habit
– h. is no damn private hell Holiday [5]
– regularity of a h. is . . . in proportion to its absurdity Proust [11]

hackneyed
– h. words in hackneyed songs Gunn [4]

haircut
– I don't advise a h. Robinson, B. [3]

half-truths
– all truths are h. Whitehead [9]

hallucination
– h. is a fact, not an error Russell, B. [1]

hallucinations
– no snake universe h. Ginsberg [9]

halo
– What after all/Is a h. Fry, Christopher [3]

Hamlet
– I am not Prince H. Eliot [5]
– playing H. on a flying trapeze Welles [3]

hammer
– If I had a h. Seeger, P. [1]

hammer-blows
– I feel two h. here García Lorca [6]

hamster
– Freddie Starr ate my h. Sun [4]

hamsters
– children love h. Trollope [1]

hand
– My right h. hasn't seen my left hand Lancaster, B. [1]
– for the sake of a gloved h. waving Osborne [8]
– You should not bite the h. Szasz [7]
– h. that signed the treaty Thomas, D. [3]
– Give a man a free h. West, M. [13]
– If you know that here is one h. Wittgenstein [25]

handbag
– without hitting it with her h. Critchley [2]

hands
– Young h. were made for caresses Gide [2]

hang
– I think we ought to let him h. Ehrlichman [1]

hangover
– the h. became part of the day Fitzgerald, F. S. [17]

hang-ups
– hung up on everybody else's h. Brautigan [1]

happen
– 'Things h.' Neruda [1]

happened
– something h. Green, J. [1]

happening
– Something is h. here Dylan [24]

happiness
– writer has . . . written convincingly about h. Amis, M. [1]
– h. of the common man Beveridge [1]
– recipe for h. Douglas, N. [2]
– H. makes up in height Frost, R. [24]
– something boring about somebody else's h. Huxley, A. [1]
– Here is a possibility of perfect h. Kafka [4]
– perfect h. is unrealizable Levi, P. [2]
– how poor is the language of h. Mandelstam [2]
– lamentable phrase 'the pursuit of h.' Muggeridge [4]
– H. is . . . everyday mode of consciousness Murdoch, I. [7]
– most exciting h. Nash, O. [9]
– if h. forgets you a little bit Prévert [5]
– h. alone is salutary to the body Proust [21]
– h. . . . . is really useful to us in one way Proust [22]
– accursed h. I have dreaded Shaw, G. B. [8]
– H. is a wine of the rarest vintage Smith, L. P. [1]
– never direct people towards h. Solzhenitsyn [4]
– H. is an imaginary condition Szasz [6]

happy
– We all want to be h. Boyd [1]

hound
– *ain't nothin' but a h. dog* Presley [1]
hour
– *Who has matched us with His h.* Brooke [5]
– *this was their finest h.* Churchill, W. [17]
hours
– *golden h. slip by* Barrie [4]
house
– *h. is not a home* Adler [1]
– *serious h. on serious earth* Larkin [8]
– *h. is a machine for living in* Le Corbusier [1]
– *man is a fourteen-room h.* Miller, A. [16]
– *My heart keeps open h.* Roethke [1]
House of Commons
– *Anybody who enjoys being in the H. of C.* Livingstone [3]
House of Lords
– *H. of L. is the British Outer Mongolia* Benn [1]
housewife
– *I hate the word h.* Barr [1]
– *accept the economics of a h.* Chirac [1]
housewives
– *threatened, insecure h.* Friedan [5]
housework
– *no need to do any h.* Crisp [7]
– *h. is the most unproductive* Lenin [10]
– *H. is work directly opposed* Oakley [2]
– *I hate h.* Rivers [1]
– *When it comes to h.* Whitehorn [1]
Houston
– *H., we've had a problem* Lovell, J. [1]
hubris
– *H. is ... the disease of politics* Short, C. [4]
– *We suffer from a h. of the mind* van der Post [2]
Huckleberry Finn
– *book by Mark Twain called H. F.* Hemingway [15]
Hugo
– *H. was a madman* Cocteau [10]
human
– *h. condition is such that pain* Arendt [2]
– *love for h. abilities* Bellow [8]
– *people are only h.* Compton-Burnett [1]
– *every h. being ... is worthy of my respect* Fisher, M. F. K. [6]
– *h. predicament ... a dialogue between lovers* Godard [5]
– *constitutes a real, live h. being* Hesse [1]
– *H. nature ... can endure no restraint* Kafka [14]
– *proper application of the word 'h.'* LaFollette [2]
– *Being h. signifies* Lévi-Strauss [1]

– *H. affairs are not serious* Murdoch, I. [13]
– *An effective h. being is a whole* Rolf [1]
– *h. beings do not have to be prowling wolves* Sinclair, U. [1]
human race
– *wish I loved the h. r.* Raleigh [1]
humanism
– *H. was not wrong in thinking* Weil [10]
humanist
– *h. has four leading characteristics* Forster [20]
humanities
– *h. ... the nursery games of humankind* Bellow [2]
humanity
– *H. is the rich effluvium* Pound [1]
– *serve h. in some function* Spock [1]
– *H. is just a work in progress* Williams, T. [11]
humankind
– *H. can generally be divided* Holub [5]
humble
– *H. people ... don't get very far* Ali [2]
– *I've never had a h. opinion* Baez [4]
humiliated
– *you will always be h.* Auden [53]
humiliation
– *You will find that you survive h.* Eliot [55]
– *Avoiding h. is the core of tragedy* Guare [1]
humiliations
– *suffer more from the h.* Weil [3]
humility
– *H. must always be the portion* Eisenhower [1]
– *H. is not my forte* Halsey [2]
humorists
– *difficulty with h.* Updike [1]
humorous
– *h. man usually has deep pockets of emotion* Rourke [1]
humour
– *my h. is based upon destruction* Bruce [4]
– *own up to a lack of h.* Colby [1]
– *merit in having no sense of h.* Cook, P. [2]
– *H. is ... the most significant activity* De Bono [1]
– *sense of h. gets you much farther* Hanks [4]
– *h. touches the same nerve* Humphries [3]
– *H. ... is to Americans* Keillor [5]
– *H. brings insight and tolerance* Repplier [2]
– *H. does not include sarcasm* Thurber [16]
– *H. is emotional chaos* Thurber [24]
– *h. can be made to alternate* Truffaut [2]
– *H. is not a mood* Wittgenstein [20]

– *H. is the first of the gifts to perish* Woolf [16]
hunchback
– *h. in the park* Thomas, D. [6]
hundred
– *finished in the first h. days* Kennedy, J. F. [8]
– *Letting a h. flowers blossom* Mao Zedong [15]
– *h.'s not enough* Wilder, B. [1]
hunger
– *H. strike is unlike any other ... struggle* Adams, G. [2]
hungry
– *h. mob is a angry mob* Marley [2]
– *h. man is not a free man* Stevenson [4]
hunted
– *most h. person of the modern age* Spencer, C. [3]
hunting
– *Handsome h. man* de la Mare [4]
hurricane
– *h. on the way* Fish [1]
hurting
– *if the policy isn't h., it isn't working* Major [2]
husband
– *Being a h. is a whole-time job* Bennett, Arnold [2]
– *I don't need a h.* Collins, J. [1]
– *My h. and I* Elizabeth II [2]
– *h. is what is left of a lover* Rowland, H. [1]
– *entitled to a middle h.* St. Johns [1]
husbands
– *H. are like fires* Gabor [3]
– *H. should be like kleenex* Lynn, J. [1]
– *H. never become good* Mencken [23]
– *H. are chiefly good as lovers* Monroe [9]
huts
– *like a jumble of h. in a jungle* Capote [7]
hydrocarbons
– *h. released by vegetation* Reagan, R. [9]
hyena
– *integrity of a h.* Thompson, H. S. [1]
hyperbole
– *at every turn we meet h.* Nunn [1]
hypocrisy
– *h. is the vice of vices* Arendt [4]
– *H. is the most ... nerve-racking vice* Maugham [5]
– *Making the world safe for h.* Wolfe, Thomas [1]
hysteria
– *thin whine of h.* Didion [3]

I
– *ability to say 'I' to a stranger* Wolf, C. [1]
Ian
– *trouble with I.* Lehmann [1]
ice-cream
– *emperor of i.* Stevens [3]

icing
– *i. on the pie called Christian civilization* Mencken [16]

id
– *Where i. was* Freud [14]

idea
– *Nothing is more dangerous than an i.* Alain [2]
– *good for an i. to be commonplace* Fitzgerald, P. [1]
– *no i. is so antiquated* Glasgow [2]
– *I had a monumental i.* Goldwyn [5]
– *i. is more important than the object* Hirst [2]
– *better to entertain an i. than to take it home* Jarrell [6]
– *rope around the neck of an i.* O'Casey [1]
– *To love an i. is to love it a little more* Rostand [12]
– *One does not adopt an i.* Sartre [18]
– *in the name of an i.* Tarkovsky [4]

ideal
– *i. has many names* Maugham [7]
– *i., without doubt, varies* Rostand [15]

idealism
– *I. is the noble toga* Huxley, A. [25]

idealist
– *cynic should never marry an i.* Burchill [9]
– *i. walks on tiptoe* Chazal [1]
– *I.: a cynic in the making* Layton [5]
– *i. is one who, on noticing that a rose* Mencken [9]

ideals
– *i. of a nation* Douglas, N. [1]
– *haven't dropped all my i.* Frank, A. [7]

ideas
– *materialism . . . denies the power of i.* Berlin, Isaiah [3]
– *colorless green i.* Chomsky [1]
– *We try not to have i.* Gilbert [1]
– *difficulty lies, not in the new i.* Keynes [14]
– *I. . . . are dangerous for good or evil* Keynes [18]
– *i. of a time are like the clothes* Lewis, W. [3]
– *We try not to have i.* Proesch [1]
– *My i. are a curse* Sexton [7]
– *I. emerge from plays* Shepard [5]
– *I. that enter the mind under fire* Trotsky [6]
– *unpopular i.* Westwood [8]
– *No i. but in things* Williams, W. C. [4]

ideologies
– *Our blight is i.* Jung [11]

ideology
– *If you take away i.* Nelson, R. [1]
– *We must have an i.* Thatcher [5]
– *idleness – I. [is] only a coarse name* Connolly, C. [3]

ignorance
– *I. is an evil weed* Beveridge [3]

– *more dangerous than sincere i.* King, M. L. [4]
– *increase the horizon of i.* Miller, H. [13]
– *our i. must necessarily be infinite* Popper [3]
– *natural i. and . . . artificial ignorance* Pound [32]
– *i. is one's chief asset* Stevens [28]
– *i. is the first requisite of the historian* Strachey [2]
– *our race survived i.* Vizinczey [1]

ignorant
– *sufficient proud and i. people* Flanagan, O. [1]

ill
– *you aren't i.* Ginzburg [1]
– *We are all i.* Trilling [2]

illegal
– *from something i. to something illegal* Pop [3]

illegitimate
– *no i. children* Gladney [1]
– *Oh those i. babies!* Smith, S. [12]

illness
– *I. is the most heeded of doctors* Proust [10]
– *I. is the night-side of life* Sontag [18]
– *Societies need to have one i.* Sontag [22]

illusions
– *I search myself for i.* Larkin [3]
– *It's life i. I recall* Mitchell, Joni [1]

image
– *absurd to make an i.* De Kooning [3]

images
– *we can now manipulate i.* Attenborough [2]
– *to be without i.* Herzog [2]
– *Lords appease us with i.* Morrison, J. [8]
– *life a series of i.* Warhol [16]
– *overdose of i.* Wenders [6]

imagination
– *i. should queen it over the mind* Ellmann [1]
– *i. makes me human* Le Guin [9]
– *failure of the i.* McEwan [12]
– *I., the supreme delight of the immortal* Nabokov [8]
– *Nature uses human i.* Pirandello [5]
– *To regard the i. as metaphysics* Stevens [18]
– *i. is man's power over nature* Stevens [29]

imaginative
– *conceivable i. interest to posterity* Muggeridge [8]

imagine
– *I. there's no heaven* Lennon [10]

imbecility
– *dossier of human i.* Tzara [2]

imitate
– *usually i. each other* Hoffer [3]

imitation
– *I., if it is not forgery* Fenton [6]
– *I. is more interesting* Stein [18]

immigrant
– *i. would forever remain shut* Yezierska [1]
– *immoral – i. to trade on fear* Roddick [1]
– *things I really like to do are . . . i.* Woollcott [1]

immoral
– *deep down . . . we are i.* Borges [3]
– *man is i.* Faulkner [2]

immortality
– *achieve i. through my work* Allen, W. [6]
– *most rigid code of i.* Bradbury, M. [1]
– *Millions long for i.* Ertz [1]
– *I./Is not mere repetition* Ridler [5]

impartial
– *I decline utterly to be i.* Churchill, W. [4]

impatience
– *All human errors are i.* Kafka [2]

imperfection
– *i. is the greatness of man* Fischer [1]

imperialism
– *i. was a bloody sight wiser* Coward [13]
– *world-wide brigandage called i.* Han Suyin [1]
– *I. is capitalism* Lenin [1]

impossible
– *i. takes a little longer* Anonymous [3]
– *Perfect reliance on the i.* Graves [14]
– *If we don't do the i.* Kelly [1]
– *Nothing is i.* Mumford [5]
– *i. that is possible for God* Weil [17]

impotence
– *I. and sodomy are socially O.K.* Waugh, E. [21]

impressionable
– *Give me a girl at an i. age* Spark [4]

impropriety
– *I. is the soul of wit* Maugham [3]

improving
– *you can be certain of i.* Huxley, A. [18]

improvisation
– *I. is too good to leave to chance* Simon [10]

impurities
– *i. are needed* Levi, P. [5]

inch
– *every other i. a gentleman* West, R. [12]

include
– *i. me out* Goldwyn [1]

incorrect
– *our fate to be i.* Walker [2]

independent
– *It's easy to be i.* Jackson, Mahalia [1]
– *learning to be an i. sovereign state* Nkrumah [1]

loser
– *world loves a good l.* Hubbard [5]
losers
– *Why join a bunch of l.* Neil [1]
losing
– *art of l. isn't hard to master* Bishop [5]
lost
– *Nothing is l.* Ridler [3]
– *You are a l. generation* Stein [2]
lottery
– *unhappy L. winner* Parsons, Tony [5]
lounge suit
– *genesis of the modern L. S.* Schumpeter [5]
Louvre
– *L. is like the morgue* Cocteau [6]
love
– *We men have got l. well weighed up* Amis, K. [1]
– *There is l. of course* Anouilh [5]
– *l. one another or die* Auden [24]
– *Women are programmed to l. completely* Bainbridge [6]
– *L. is only what people agree exists* Barnes, J. [11]
– *To fall in l. is to create a religion* Borges [8]
– *And all the little emptiness of l.* Brooke [6]
– *l. and marriage* Cahn [2]
– *Make thy l. sure* Crane [3]
– *L. is the extra effort we make* Crisp [19]
– *Falling in l. again* Dietrich [1]
– *We make l. with anyone* Dietrich [2]
– *true l. is talented* Duffy [2]
– *L.'s a charity ward* Durrell [8]
– *l. . . . when it is reciprocated* Elton [2]
– *path of true l. isn't smooth* Ewart [3]
– *possible to bind together . . . in l.* Freud [11]
– *l. is sufficient unto love* Gibran [1]
– *You may give them your l.* Gibran [2]
– *l. – all the wretched cant of it* Greer [5]
– *perfect l. . . . is not sexual* Greer [14]
– *I wish I were in l. again* Hart [2]
– *L. is everything it's cracked up to be* Jong [15]
– *L. . . . is in fact so unnatural a phenomenon* Joyce, J. [1]
– *Whatever else is unsure . . . mother's l. is not* Joyce, J. [9]
– *All you need is l.* Lennon & McCartney [15]
– *l. you take/Is equal* Lennon & McCartney [17]
– *How alike are the groans of l.* Lowry [3]
– *There's no l. at all* Lydon [2]
– *L.'s boat has been shattered* Mayakovsky [6]
– *There is only l.* McEwan [11]

– *Need we say it was not l.* Millay [6]
– *concept of romantic l.* Millett [3]
– *Falling out of l. is chiefly . . . forgetting* Murdoch, I. [4]
– *No l. is entirely without worth* Murdoch, I. [8]
– *L. evaporates* Oakley [3]
– *never yet the one true l.* O'Brien, E. [5]
– *L. breeds love* Ono [4]
– *no good trying to fool yourself about l.* Osborne [7]
– *make L. not war* Political slogans [11]
– *L. for sale* Porter, C. [1]
– *L. does not consist in gazing* Saint-Exupéry [7]
– *L. means never having to say you're sorry* Segal [1]
– *L. the one you're with* Stills [2]
– *give to the poor people for l.* Teresa [1]
– *If l. is the answer, could you rephrase* Tomlin [3]
– *L. is a stepmother* Tsvetaeva [2]
– *main thing in l.* Tsvetaeva [3]
– *L. is an act of endless forgiveness* Ustinov [3]
– *only been in l. with a beer bottle* Vicious [1]
– *It's true l. because* Viorst [3]
– *That's what passes for l.* Williams, T. [10]
– *l. is a redemptive feature* Winterson [2]
– *'I l. you' is always a quotation* Winterson [3]
– *l. . . . has two faces* Woolf [23]
loved
– *I have never been l.* Pinter [3]
lovely
– *all things l.* de la Mare [2]
lover
– *Scratch a l., and find a foe* Parker, D. [5]
loverly
– *Wouldn't it be l.* Lerner, A. J. [1]
lovers
– *Pity the selfishness of l.* Bowen [5]
– *difficult achievement for true l.* Graves [11]
– *l. who have not played out* O'Brien [6]
loves
– *She l. you* Lennon & McCartney [13]
lower class
– *While there is a l. c.* Debs [2]
loyalty
– *I want l.* Johnson, L. B. [8]
lucid
– *Never be l.* Thomas, D. [1]
Lucifer
– *L.'s greatest work of art* Stockhausen [2]
luck
– *but for the clutch of l.* Durcan [4]
– *worst cynicism: a belief in l.* Oates [1]
lucky
– *Do I feel l.?* Eastwood [1]

Luftwaffe
– *you have to give this much to the L.* Charles, Prince of Wales [4]
lumberjack
– *I'm a l./And I'm OK* Monty Python's Flying Circus [4]
lunatic
– *definition of a l.* Pound [24]
lunatic asylums
– *comfortably padded l. a.* Woolf [17]
lunatics
– *l. have taken charge of the asylum* Rowland, R. [1]
lunch
– *no such thing as a free l.* Anonymous [18]
– *l. is for wimps* Douglas, M. [1]
– *ladies who l.* Sondheim [3]
lust
– *Society drives people crazy with l.* Lahr [1]
– *women being aroused by male l.* Paglia [10]
luxury
– *to get used to l.* Chaplin [3]
– *Every l. was lavished on you* Orton [2]
lying
– *L. increases the creative faculties* Luce [1]
– *L. is like alcoholism* Soderbergh [2]

Macavity
– *M.'s not there* Eliot [40]
Macbeth
– *two pages of M. to translate* Townsend [1]
MacDworkinite
– *M. idea that pornography is violence* Strossen [1]
machine
– *living in the m. age* Allen, F. [5]
– *m. does not isolate man* Saint-Exupéry [4]
– *m. . . . has been too far exploited* Wright [4]
machines
– *M. are worshipped* Russell, B. [5]
machismo
– *tragedy of m.* Greer [9]
mad
– *We all are born m.* Beckett [10]
– *m. about the boy* Coward [10]
– *only people for me are the m. ones* Kerouac [4]
– *We all go a little m. sometimes* Perkins, A. [1]
– *want a few m. people now* Shaw, G. B. [19]
Madeira
– *Have some M.* Flanders & Swann [4]
madhouse
– *England is . . . the European m.* Trotsky [19]
madman
– *difference between a m. and me* Dali [2]

Nicaragua
– *Let N. live* Political slogans [19]
nice
– *Which was n.* Fast Show [6]
– *N. to see you* Forsyth [1]
– *Be n. to people on your way up*
Mizner [1]
nicely
– *That'll do n.* Advertising slogans
[2]
nigger
– *just another n.* Jackson, J. [11]
– *Woman is the n. of the world*
Ono [2]
niggerization
– *N. is the result of oppression*
Kennedy, F. [1]
night
– *n. people are up to no good*
Alvarez [2]
– *n. . . . suppresses idle details*
Borges [9]
– *acquainted with the n.* Frost, R.
[16]
– *Beware thoughts that come in*
the n. Least Heat-Moon [1]
– *It's been a hard day's n.* Lennon
& McCartney [2]
– *N., snow, and sand make up the*
form Neruda [3]
– *N. and day, you are the one*
Porter, C. [2]
– *N., the beloved* Saint-Exupéry
[8]
– *spring, moonless n.* Thomas, D.
[15]
– *something of the n. in him*
Widdecombe [1]
Night Mail
– *This is the N. M. crossing the*
border Auden [4]
nightmare
– *long national n. is over* Ford, G.
[2]
nihilism
– *N. is best done by professionals*
Pop [2]
Nike
– *tomorrow's N. commercial*
Rich, F. [1]
ninety-eight
– *Who wants to be n.* Melly [4]
Nixon
– *only dope worth shooting is*
Richard N. Hoffman, A. [2]
– *person between N. and the White*
House Kennedy, J. F. [3]
– *won't have N. to kick around*
Nixon [6]
– *N. is the kind of politician*
Stevenson [20]
no
– *Just say n.* Reagan, N. [3]
– *In this era of Just Say N. and No*
Means No Roiphe [1]
– *N. No. No.* Thatcher [31]
no one
– *I saw n. o.* Doyle, A. C. [6]
nobility
– *n. of England . . . snored through*
the Sermon on the Mount Bolt
[2]

nobody
– *I always felt I was a n.* Monroe
[10]
nocturnal
– *endless n. processions are*
converging here Wiesel [9]
noise
– *loud n. at one end* Knox [4]
– *culture inebriated by n.* Steiner
[9]
non-belongers
– *we celebrate the n.* Rushdie
[26]
non-combatant
– *no fury like a n.* Montague [3]
non-meeting
– *triumphs of a mysterious n.*
Akhmatova [3]
non-revolutionary
– *One n. weekend is . . . more*
bloody graffito [3]
nonsense
– *n. requires a serious interest in life*
Burgess, G. [2]
– *firm anchor in n.* Galbraith [4]
nonviolence
– *organization of n.* Baez [2]
– *N. is the first article of my faith*
Gandhi, M. [3]
– *Truth and N. are as old as the*
hills Gandhi, M. [4]
– *philosophy of n.* King, M. L. [1]
nonviolent
– *n. theory is practicable* Jackson,
George [2]
– *engage in n. direct action*
King, M. L. [12]
– *'n.' approach to civil rights*
Carmichael [2]
normal
– *n. on the average* Freud [19]
normality
– *n. . . . conquers everything*
Enzensberger [7]
north
– *N., where England tucks its shirt*
Armitage [1]
– *He was my N., my South* Auden
[15]
– *N. will preserve your flesh* Céline
[2]
North Vietnam
– *N. V. cannot defeat or humiliate*
Nixon [10]
Northern Ireland
– *tragedy of N. I.* Holland [1]
nose
– *Some thirty inches from my n.*
Auden [47]
noselessness
– *N. of Man* Chesterton [3]
noses
– *They haven't got no n.*
Chesterton [7]
nostalgia
– *N. excuses everything* Cooper, J.
[1]
– *n. a marketable commodity* Lasch
[1]
– *I don't like n. unless it's mine*
Reed, L. [6]
– *Going on a n. trip* Strummer [1]

nothing
– *N. to be done* Beckett [2]
– *N. happens, nobody comes*
Beckett [7]
– *Never give anything away for n.*
Burroughs, W. [2]
– *I got n., Ma* Dylan [18]
– *whatever you say, you say n.*
Heaney [5]
– *n. to say* Hirst [1]
– *n. deep down inside us* Rorty
[1]
– *N. is the history of the world*
Stoppard [1]
novel
– *final test for a n.* Forster [7]
– *the n. tells a story* Forster [8]
– *Writing a n. is not . . . shopping*
Frame, Janet [4]
– *n. indicates that we are becoming*
Fuentes [2]
– *Knowledge is the n.'s only*
morality Kundera [9]
– *n. is something* Llosa [1]
– *first sentence of every n. should be*
Ondaatje [1]
– *not a n. to be tossed aside lightly*
Parker, D. [24]
– *master of the popular n.* Shaw, I.
[1]
– *never known a n.* Wharton [3]
novelist
– *For a n., a given historic situation*
Kundera [10]
– *not the first duty of the n.*
McEwan [6]
– *n. is . . . more fully at home*
Nabokov [11]
– *N. are . . . last people in the world*
Burgess, A. [9]
– *so are we all n.* Fowles [4]
– *n. keep a distance from journalists*
Greene [22]
novels
– *Writing n. preserves you*
Brookner [4]
– *with bad sentiments that one*
makes good n. Huxley, A. [24]
– *light that radiates from the*
great n. Kundera [11]
– *All great n. . . . are bisexual*
Kundera [18]
– *Good n. are not written by*
orthodoxy-sniffers Orwell [12]
– *in most n. no imagination at all*
Vidal [22]
– *n. are over* Waugh, A. [4]
– *composing unwritten n.* West, R.
[1]
now
– *crackling certainty of N.* Nuttall
[1]
nowadays
– *cause of n. and the end of History*
Sellar & Yeatman [4]
nowhere
– *Everywhere being n.* Heaney [8]
– *He's a real n. man* Lennon &
McCartney [6]
nowness
– *n. of everything is absolutely*
wondrous Potter [8]

NQOCD
– *N. (not quite our class, darling)*
York [4]
nuclear
– *n. destruction of the world* Wiesel
[6]
nuclear bomb
– *protesting against having a n. b.*
Roy [5]
nuclear war
– *If there is a n. w.* Roy [4]
nude
– *In the N., all that is not beautiful*
Bresson [1]
nudes
– *Basically collectors want n.*
Oldenburg [2]
nudge
– *N., nudge, wink, wink* Monty
Python's Flying Circus [2]
nudity
– *N. is a form of dress* Berger [3]
number
– *I am not a n.* McGoohan [1]
numbers
– *n. are the key to both wisdom*
Koestler [7]
nun
– *cult of the household n.* Friday
[4]
nuns
– *he who fucks n.* Strummer &
Jones [3]
nylons
– *Kneeling bags my n.* Wilder, B.
[2]
nymphets
– *propose to designate as 'n.'*
Nabokov [5]
nymphomaniac
– *I'm a raving n.* Madonna [6]

obituary
– *o. column stands fast* Warner
[2]
objection
– *technical o. is the first refuge of a
scoundrel* Broun [3]
objectivity
– *O. . . . is both meaningless and
impossible* Cameron, J. (1911–85)
[3]
objects
– *Inanimate o. are classified*
Baker, R. [1]
obscenity
– *O. is a cleansing process*
Miller, H. [20]
– *violence and o. are left
unadulterated* Nin [3]
– *'o.' . . . means anything that
shocks the magistrate* Russell, B.
[6]
obscurantism
– *O. is the academic theorist's
revenge* Lehman [3]
obscurity
– *O. has another tale to tell*
Rich, A. [3]
observer
– *very meek-spirited creature . . .
the 'O.'* Dunne, J.W. [1]

obsession
– *People have this o.* Jagger, M. [2]
obsolescence
– *Britain . . . is suffering from
galloping o.* Benn [2]
obtrusiveness
– *heroes of o.* Kraus [4]
obvious
– *To spell out the o.* Hoffer [9]
ocean
– *drop in the o.* Teresa [4]
October
– *funny kind of month, O.* Norden
[1]
offal
– *O. is the new black* Townsend [3]
offer
– *o. he can't refuse* Puzo [1]
office
– *impression of being in o.* Lamont
[2]
– *we have had an exciting term
of o.* Morris, D. [2]
official
– *O. dignity tends to increase*
Huxley, A. [15]
Official Secrets Act
– *O. S. A. as a constraint* Ingham
[2]
ogre
– *fantasies about the inner o.*
Warner, M. [3]
oil
– *o. and democracy* Clark, R. [3]
Okie
– *proud to be an O. from Muskogee*
Haggard [1]
old
– *one must learn to grow o.*
Cooper, D. [1]
– *O. age is life's parody* Beauvoir
[8]
– *O. age is an insult* Durrell [7]
– *I grow old.* Eliot [6]
– *o. man in a dry month* Eliot [14]
– *Do they know they're o.* Jennings
[2]
– *being o. is having lighted rooms*
Larkin [23]
– *Let women die o.* Le Guin [4]
– *secret that all o. people share*
Lessing [7]
– *o. will always look cute* McLaren
[1]
– *dance in the o. dame yet* Marquis
[2]
– *o. have rubbed it into the young*
Maugham [8]
– *Growing o. is no more than a bad
habit* Maurois [3]
– *Our generation are the new o.*
Nicholson [4]
– *o. – like children – talk to
themselves* O'Neill [4]
– *Growing o.'s like being . . .
penalized* Powell, A. [4]
– *O. men are dangerous*
Shaw, G. B. [7]
– *o. know what they want*
Smith, L. P. [6]
– *mere process of growing o.
together* Smith, L. P. [10]

old age
– *only thing good for o. a.*
Ayckbourn [1]
– *o. a. is always fifteen years older*
Baruch [2]
– *O.a. isn't so bad* Chevalier [2]
– *value of o. a.* Hardy [3]
– *O. a. is the most unexpected*
Trotsky [20]
old maid
– *being an o. m. is like death*
Ferber [5]
Old Masters
– *they were never wrong,/
The O. M.* Auden [24]
older
– *o. one becomes* Bainbridge [7]
– *I was so much o. then* Dylan [6]
– *O. women are best* Fleming [4]
– *o. you get the stronger the wind*
Nicklaus [1]
omnibus
– *ninety-seven horse power o.*
Flanders & Swann [3]
on
– *go o. and on* Thatcher [20]
one
– *O. realm, one people* Political
slogans [4]
one-party
– *still be a o. state* Reagan, R. [15]
oneself
– *To become o., with all one's
strength* Wolf, C. [2]
oooh-errr
– *O. Viz* [2]
openmindedness
– *O. . . . should be fostered for its
own sake* Rorty [2]
opera
– *o. . . . is one of the strangest
inventions* Clark, K. [2]
operas
– *I have conducted my own o.*
Smyth [2]
opinion
– *whole climate of o.* Auden [16]
– *too high an o. of ourselves*
Carter, A. [9]
– *glowing o. we have of ourselves*
Crisp [11]
– *study of the history of o.* Keynes
[5]
opinions
– *I have o. of my own* Bush,
George W. [4]
– *O. cannot survive* Mann, T. [4]
– *It's not that I don't have o.*
Navon [1]
– *The more o. you have* Wenders
[5]
opponent
– *Never ascribe to an o.* Barrie [2]
– *Never attack an o.* Klein [1]
– *o. cannot be both honest and
intelligent* Orwell [36]
opposites
– *marriage of o. has to be
consummated* Woolf [39]
opposition
– *think of o. as merely perverse*
Tweedie [1]

sterilization
– *s. . . . is one method of birth control* Gandhi, I. [1]

stigma
– *s. . . . will serve to beat a dogma* Guedalla [3]

still
– *be wholly s. and alone* Kafka [6]
– *Happy are those who are s.* Okri [2]

Stock Exchange
– *make a fortune on the S. E.* Mortimer [4]

stocking
– *glimpse of s.* Porter, C. [5]

stolen
– *nothing that happens on s. ground* Smith, Z. [3]

stomach
– *pit of my burning, nauseous s.* Cobain [3]

stone
– *they'll stone you* Dylan [26]

stories
– *precisely the disappointing s.* Frisch [1]
– *s. – in the good sense* Gould [3]
– *all s. . . . end in death* Hemingway [12]
– *We make the oldest s. new* Marcus [1]
– *S. are substitutes for God* Wenders [2]

stormy
– *S. weather* Koestler [1]

story
– *I'll tell you a s.* Fitzgerald, F. S. [26]
– *Every age has its own s.* Morrison, B. [2]

story-teller
– *Death is the sanction of . . . the s.* Benjamin [11]
– *The secret of the s.* Crace [2]

storytellers
– *If a nation loses its s.* Handke [2]

straight
– *I want to be s.* Dury [7]

Strand
never alone with a S. Advertising slogans [32]

stranger
– *You may see a s.* Hammerstein II [7]

strangers
– *S. in the night* Sinatra, F. [3]
– *depended on the kindness of s.* Williams, T. [4]

stream
– *When I heard the word 's.'* Joyce, J. [33]

streets
– *Down these mean s.* Chandler [7]
– *Reclaim the s.* Political slogans [26]

strength
– *s. lined with tenderness* Angelou [3]
– *S. through joy* Political slogans [5]

strife
– *in place of s.* Castle [1]

strike
– *no right to s.* Coolidge [1]
– *push along our little baby s.* Steinbeck [1]

string quartet
– *perfect expression . . . is a s. q.* Tate [1]

striven
To have s. so hard Kissinger [12]

striving
– *salvation is in s. to achieve* Kapuściński [2]

struggle
– *S. is the father of all things* Hitler [9]
– *s. of man against power* Kundera [3]
– *s. is my life* Mandela, N. [1]
– *s. to set oneself free* Marcus [2]
– *s. continues* Saro-Wiwa [1]
living is s. Wilder, T. [1]

stuff
– *Brotherhood of the Right S.* Wolfe, Tom [6]

stupid
– *s. believe that to be truthful is easy* Cather [1]
– *S. is as stupid does* Hanks [1]
– *considered s. . . . is more painful* Levi, P. [8]
– *just a bunch of . . . s. white men* Moore, M. [1]

stupidity
– *no amount of learning can cure s.* Vizinczey [3]

style
– *s. is just the outside of content* Godard [7]
– *Our own epoch is determining . . . its own s.* Le Corbusier [2]
– *S. [is] the hallmark of a temperament* Maurois [5]
– *S. and Structure are the essence* Nabokov [12]
– *This is s.* Neruda [10]
– *cultivated s. would be like a mask* Porter, K. A. [4]
– *s. is eternal* Saint Laurent [1]
– *S. is not something applied* Stevens [20]
– *S. is the ultimate morality of mind* Whitehead [2]
– *Phoney Wars were . . . s. wars* York [3]

subconscious
– *Yanks have colonized our s.* Wenders [1]

subjects
– *order of the great s. of life* Spark [6]

submarine
– *We all live in a yellow s* Lennon & McCartney [8]

suburban
– *Faces, they have, those s. people* Drabble [3]
– *always will have a s. President* Kroker [1]

suburbs
– *s. are incubators of apathy* Connolly, C. [14]

subversives
– *s. are good for the children* Viorst [1]
– *First we kill all the s.* Saint Jean [1]

succeed
– *It is not enough to s.* Vidal [27]

success
– *penalty of s.* Astor [2]
– *got to keep on being a s.* Berlin, Irving [9]
– *A (S.) = X (Work)* Einstein [16]
– *S. is a lousy teacher* Gates [2]
– *S. is more dangerous than failure* Greene [23]
– *idea that s. spoils people* Maugham [10]
– *logic of worldly s.* Merton [2]
– *no point in s.* Otway [1]
– *S. is dangerous* Picasso [16]
– *S. makes life easier* Springsteen [5]
– *one is punished for s.* Warshow [2]

successful
– *cannot bear s. people* John [3]

sucker
– *never give a s.* Fields, W.C. [2]
– *I'll show you a s.* Sinatra, F. [1]

Suez
– *S. Canal was flowing through my drawing room* Eden, C [1]

suffer
– *If we must s.* Ellmann [2]
– *I s. very eloquently* Mitchell, Joni [6]

suffered
– *have s. for things that I am guilty of* Vanzetti [1]

suffering
– *Is s. so very serious?* Colette [2]
– *the marks of s.* Fitzgerald, F. S. [18]
– *will not give up his s.* Gurdjieff [4]
– *Passive/S. makes the world go round* Heaney [10]
– *Human life is reduced to real s.* Hesse [5]
– *s. must become Love* Mansfield [4]
– *not true that s. ennobles the character* Maugham [4]
– *s. of either sex* Mead [4]
– *S. is an aspect of the great Promethean will* Okri [5]
– *day you stop s.* Williams, T. [18]

sugar
– *spoonful of s. helps the medicine* Andrews [1]

suicide
– *If I commit s.* Artaud [1]
– *s. is not worth the trouble* Benjamin [8]
– *prevalence of s.* Ellis, H. [4]
– *s. remains the courageous act* Greene [16]
– *longest s. note in history* Kaufman, Gerald [1]
– *contemplation of s.* Lebowitz [3]
– *s. kills two people* Miller, A. [8]

true
– *t. is inimitable* Bresson [3]
trumpet
– *t. sound like a tin whistle* Bevan [5]
trust
– *people in life you can t.* Slovo [1]
truth
– *t. is often a terrible weapon* Adler, A. [1]
– *t. prevails in the long run* Aldington [3]
– *objective t. is obtainable* Barnes, J. [7]
– *t. has only one face* Bataille [4]
– *person who keeps t. in his hands has lost* Baudrillard [6]
– *Believing T. is staring at the sun* Belloc [9]
– *T. wants to be startled abruptly* Benjamin [5]
– *t. enters our hearts* Duffy [1]
– *t. which we cannot bear* Durrell [5]
– *to make t. laugh* Eco [5]
– *T. is the glue* Ford, G. [3]
– *T. and Non-violence are as old as the hills* Gandhi, M. [4]
– *t. has never been of any real value* Greene [7]
– *t. is not simply what you think it is* Havel [5]
– *every Prophet knows the convulsion of t.* Kerouac [3]
– *ultimate t. is . . . always a falsehood* Koestler [1]
– *T. is a pathless land* Krishnamurti [1]
– *Closest to the t. are those* Mann, G. [1]
– *matter how one comes by the t.* Miller, H. [7]
– *cannot have both t. and . . . civilization* Murdoch, I. [3]
– *T. is sui generis* Murdoch, I. [18]
– *For the t., we are silent* Murray, L. [7]
– *committing ourselves to the t.* Nixon [8]
– *only one t.* O'Connor, F. [1]
– *possession of the 't.' is less important* Orwell [13]
– *When t. is no longer free* Prévert [4]
– *T. is simply a compliment* Rorty [3]
– *unclouded face of t.* Scott, C.P. [1]
– *t. is always something* Sontag [1]
– *t. is balance* Sontag [2]
– *little insane about the t.* Stevens [12]
– *Absolute t. is a very rare . . . commodity* Thompson, H. S. [5]
– *t. is really an ambition* Ustinov [10]
– *frightened of the t.* Wittgenstein [2]
– *Man can embody t.* Yeats [29]
truths
– *t. being in and out of favor* Frost, R. [5]

– *no new t.* McCarthy, M. [8]
– *more t. in twenty-four hours* Vaneigem [3]
truth-telling
– *T. . . . key to responsible citizenship* Hoover, J. E. [1]
T-Shirt
– *Get a message, get a T.* York [6]
tubby
– *Grows t. without exercise* Milne [3]
Tube
– *way people behave on the T.* Swift [1]
tulips
– *T. through the t.* Dubin [1]
tunes
– *t. the chauffeurs . . . can whistle* Beecham [3]
Turgenev
– *I beat Mr T.* Hemingway [24]
turn
– *I'd love to t. you on* Lennon & McCartney [14]
turning
– *lady's not for t.* Thatcher [10]
turnip
– *candle in that great t.* Churchill, W. [42]
TV
– *British T. . . . trivializes the serious* Ballard [7]
– *madness of T. is the madness of human life* Paglia [6]
– *The T. play . . . a 'theatre of the people'* Potter [1]
– *T. isn't fun any more* Street-Porter [2]
– *world works by way of T.* Thomson [1]
– *guilty of misusing T.* Winfrey [3]
twang
– *go t., and you've got music* Vicious [2]
twat
– *dead t.* graffito [12]
twenties
– *the early t.* Fitzgerald, F. S. [16]
twentieth century
– *horror of the T. C.* Mailer [13]
– *filthy t. c.* Rowse [2]
– *Great t. c.* Yevtushenko [1]
twenty-one
– *acute limited excellence at t.* Fitzgerald, F. S. [6]
twilight
– *dreamcrossed t.* Eliot [28]
Twilight Zone
– *area called the T. Z.* Serling [1]
twiminds
– *You have become of twosome t.* Joyce, J. [27]
twinkle
– *our right to t.* Monroe [5]
typewriter
– *sit in front of the t.* Robinson, B. [7]
typing
– *that isn't writing . . . it's t.* Capote [1]
tyrannize
– *t. over his bank balance* Keynes [16]

tyranny
– *Under conditions of t.* Arendt [6]
– *silent in the face of t.* Soyinka [1]

USA
– *God bless the U., so large* Auden [46]
– *turned the U. into a nation of hobbledehoys* Loos [4]
– *Born in the U.* Springsteen [3]
ugliness
– *I seated u. on my knee* Dali [4]
– *u. lasts* Gainsbourg [2]
ukelele
– *my little u.* Formby [1]
– *Little U. In My Hand* Formby [2]
ulcer
– *I am an 8 U. man* Early, S. [1]
Ulster
– *U. says no* Political slogans [21]
ultraliberalism
– *U. today translates into . . . isolationism* Agnew [3]
Ulysses
– *U. . . . is a dogged attempt to cover* Forster [11]
unbearable
– *in victory u.* Churchill, W. [52]
unbelief
– *comprehend me in my u.* Kersh [2]
– *To choose u.* Rushdie [30]
unbloody
– *heads are heroically u.* Nash, O. [3]
unborn
– *cemetery . . . of the u.* John Paul II [3]
unclean
– *This is u.* Reading [1]
unconscious
– *nature of the u.* Clare [1]
– *images of the u.* Jung [21]
– *My u. knows more* Kraus [7]
uncouth
– *Too much Truth/Is u.* Adams, F. P. [2]
under-belly
– *exposure of the u. of the Axis* Churchill, W. [30]
under-class
– *salvation of the u.* Podhoretz [1]
understand
– *The liberals can u. everything* Bruce [6]
– *People who u. your thought* Fulbright [1]
– *desire to u. has a built-in brutality* Høeg [2]
– *What better way to prove that you u.* Rosenberg [5]
– *u. a few words in life* Rostand [3]
understanding
– *sign of the beginning of u.* Kafka [3]
– *Shallow u. from people of good will* King, M. L. [10]
– *more dangerous than sympathetic u.* Picasso [23]
understood
– *I have u. you.* de Gaulle [6]

wrongs
– *Two w.don't make a right* Szasz [11]

xenophobia
– *X. . . . becoming the mass ideology* Hobsbawm [4]
Xerox
– *Once the X. copier was invented* Young, A. [1]
X-ray
– *they look like X. pictures* Wolfe, Tom [11]
XXXX
– *Australians wouldn't give a X.* Saatchi & Saatchi [2]

yabba
– *Y. dabba do!* Hanna [1]
yachtsman
– *y. leaves no tracks* Hughes, Richard [1]
Yale
– *wholesale libel on a Y. prom* Parker, D. [16]
yam
– *I y. what I yam* Popeye [1]
Yanks
– *the Y. are coming* Cohan [1]
years
– *the next thirty y.* Fitzgerald, F. S. [9]
– *waste of breath the y. behind* Yeats [8]
Yeats
– *William Y. is laid to rest* Auden [19]
Yellow Book
– *He rose, and he put down The Y. B.* Betjeman [4]
yes
– *answer Y. to Someone* Hammarskjöld [5]

– *I said y.* Joyce, J. [24]
– *apart from saying 'Y.'* Starr, R. [2]
yesterday
– *I believe in y.* Lennon & McCartney [5]
ying
– *Y. tong iddle I po* Milligan [1]
yobs
– *what one might call y.* Tumim [1]
yoga
– *Y. in Mayfair or Fifth Avenue . . . is a spiritual fake* Jung [12]
yoghurt
– *y. is very good for . . . apotheosis* Ionesco [1]
you
– *It could be y.* Advertising slogans [13]
young
– *y. . . . don't have the patience to make art* Kael [4]
– *We're the y. ones* Richard [1]
– *voices of y. people* Smith, L. P. [7]
– *denunciation of the y. is a necessary* Smith, L. P. [9]
– *as I was y. and easy* Thomas, D. [10]
– *last people with any ideas are y. people* Westwood [10]
yourself
– *trouble with writing a book about y.* Marx, G. [9]
youth
– *Y. would be an ideal state* Asquith, H. [1]
– *Time misspent in y.* Brookner [5]
– *everybody's y. is a dream* Fitzgerald, F. S. [4]
– *Y. itself is a talent* Hoffer [2]
– *y. that must fight* Hoover, H. [3]

– *wine of y. does not always clear* Jung [3]
– *American ideal is y.* Miller, H. [14]
– *Y. possesses the impulse to resist* Mishima [5]
– *Y. is the vilest of all illusions* Montale [5]
– *Y. does not require reasons for living* Ortega y Gasset [9]
– *Y. has no age* Picasso [12]
– *y. is the period of . . . disguises* Pritchett [6]
– *economy has no use or need for y.* Rubin [3]
y-shaped
– *to the grave in a Y. coffin* Orton [5]
yuppies
– *Y. are not defectors from revolt* Baudrillard [5]
– *Y. never gamble* Coupland [3]

zealotry
– *enemy of idealism is z.* Kinnock [3]
Zed
– *Z.'s dead, baby* Tarantino [7]
Zen
– *Z. . . . does not confuse spirituality* Watts [1]
Zionism
– *Z. is not a first name* Oz [1]
zip
– *Z. a dee doo dah* Wrubel [1]
zippers
– *Z. are primal and modern* Robbins, T. [2]
zoo
– *z. cannot but disappoint* Berger [6]